W9-BNX-784

CHAPTER 7
Acquisition and Restructuring Strategies

CHAPTER 8
International Strategy

CHAPTER 9
Corporate Strategy

Spar Aerospace Limited
Spar Aérospatiale Limitée

CHAPTER 10
Corporate Governance

CHAPTER 11
Organizational Structure and Controls

CHAPTER 12
Strategic Leadership

PepsiCo

CHAPTER 13
Corporate Entrepreneurship
and Innovation

Strategic Management

Competitiveness and Globalization

Second Edition

Strategic Management

Competitiveness and Globalization

Second Edition

Michael A. Hitt
Texas A&M University

R. Duane Ireland
Baylor University

Robert E. Hoskisson
Texas A&M University

WEST PUBLISHING COMPANY

I(T)P **An International Thomson Publishing Company**

Minneapolis/St. Paul   New York   Los Angeles   San Francisco

Production Credits
Copyeditor: Lorretta Palagi
Text design: Roz Stendahl, Dapper Design
Cover illustration: Cary Henrie
Composition: Carlisle Communications, Ltd.

WEST'S COMMITMENT TO THE ENVIRONMENT

In 1906, West Publishing Company began recycling materials left over from the production of books. This began a tradition of efficient and responsible use of resources. Today, 100% of our legal bound volumes are printed on acid-free, recycled paper consisting of 50% new fibers. West recycles nearly 27,700,000 pounds of scrap paper annually—the equivalent of 229,300 trees. Since the 1960s, West has devised ways to capture and recycle waste inks, solvents, oils, and vapors created in the printing process. We also recycle plastics of all kinds, wood, glass, corrugated cardboard, and batteries, and have eliminated the use of polystyrene book packaging. We at West are proud of the longevity and the scope of our commitment to the environment.

West pocket parts and advance sheets are printed on recyclable paper and can be collected and recycled with newspapers. Staples do not have to be removed. Bound volumes can be recycled after removing the cover.

 TEXT IS PRINTED ON 10% POST CONSUMER RECYCLED PAPER

COPYRIGHT © 1996 By WEST PUBLISHING COMPANY
610 Opperman Drive
P.O. Box 64526
St. Paul, MN 55164-0526
1-800-328-9352

All rights reserved
Printed in the United States

3 2280 00641 3108

Library of Congress Cataloging-in-Publication Data

Hitt, Michael A.
      Strategic management : competitiveness and globalization : Theory and cases /
    Michael A. Hitt, R. Duane Ireland, Robert E. Hoskisson. -- 2nd ed.
          p.   cm.
      Includes bibliographical references (p.).
      ISBN 0-314-20112-2 (Student Edition) (hard : alk. paper)
      ISBN 0-314-20113-0 (Annotated Instructor's Edition)
      1. Strategic planning--Case studies.   2. Industrial management--Case studies.   I. Ireland, R. Duane.   II. Hoskisson, Robert E.
    III. Title.
    HD30.28.H586   1997
    658.4'012--dc20
                                                            96-43209
                                                              CIP

■ Dedication

To Frankie, Shawn, Angie, and Tamara. Thanks for everything; I love you.

To Mary Ann, Rebecca, and Scott Ireland: My family that continues to shower its husband and father with never-ending love and support.

To Kathy and my children, Dale, Becky, Angela, Joseph, and Matthew, as well as Robyn and Luke Garner for your support. I appreciate all that was sacrificed to allow me the time to co-author this book.

Contents

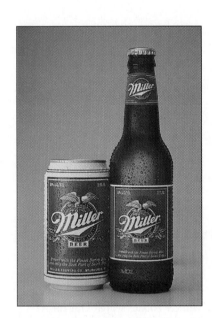

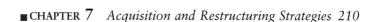

■ **PART III**
STRATEGIC ACTIONS:
STRATEGY
IMPLEMENTATION   307

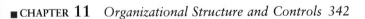

Preface

The second edition of *Strategic Management: Competitiveness and Globalization* presents several new features and revisions that enhance the value of our best-selling first edition of the textbook. For instance, all chapter opening cases and Strategic Focus segments (three per chapter), both of which were popular features of the first edition, are new in this second edition. The content of each chapter has been updated with the latest research and rewritten to ensure that it is presented in a reader-friendly manner. Additionally, a new chapter on cooperative strategies has been developed. Included in this new chapter are discussions of strategic alliances and joint ventures, cooperative relationships that firms are now using frequently to enhance their performance.

Thirty-seven cases are presented in this second edition. Of these cases, 32 are new to this edition. Given the increasing use of the Internet, Internet addresses are provided for each of the companies discussed in the cases (except in a few instances where the organizations do not have information available on the Net). A set of Internet exercises is included at the end of each chapter to make effective use of this informational tool. Finally, an appendix is included that explains how to use the Internet.

Our purpose in preparing this revised edition was to make the book an even better learning mechanism and a highly effective instructional tool, along with providing a complete, accurate, and up-to-date explanation of the strategic management process.

■ Introduction

The strategic management process helps organizations identify *what* they intend to achieve and *how* they will accomplish valued outcomes. The magnitude of this challenge is greater today than it has been historically. A new competitive landscape is developing as a result of the technological revolution and increasing globalization. The technological revolution has placed increased importance on firm innovation and the ability to introduce new goods and services to the marketplace rapidly. The global economy—an economy in which goods and services flow freely among nations—pressures firms continuously to become more competitive. By offering goods or services of value to customers, competitive firms increase the probability of earning above-average returns.

The strategic management process is the focus of this book. Described in Chapter 1, organizations (both for-profit companies and not-for-profit agencies) use the strategic management process to understand competitive forces and to develop competitive advantages systematically and consistently.

This book is intended for use primarily in strategic management and business policy courses. The materials presented in the 13 chapters have been researched thoroughly. Both the academic, scholarly literature and the business, practitioner literature were studied and then integrated to design, write, and revise this book. The academic literature provided the foundation to develop an accurate, yet meaningful description of the strategic management process. The business practitioner literature yielded a rich base of current domestic and global examples that is used to show how the concepts, tools, and techniques of the strategic management process are applied in different types of organizations.

Top-level managers are responsible for effectively developing and using the strategic management process in their organizations. Because they bear this responsibility, the work of top-level managers is considered in greater detail in this book than is the work of middle- and first-level managers.

■ Strategic Management Process

Our treatment of the strategic management process is both *traditional* and *contemporary*. In maintaining tradition, we examine important materials that have historically been a part of understanding strategic management. For example, we thoroughly examine how to analyze a firm's external environment and internal environment as a part of the strategic management process. However, in explaining these important activities, in Chapters 2 and 3, respectively, our treatments are contemporary. In Chapter 3, for example, we emphasize the importance of identifying and determining the value-creating potential of a firm's resources, capabilities, and core competencies. The strategic actions taken as a result of understanding a firm's resources, capabilities, and core competencies have a direct link with the company's ability to establish a sustainable competitive advantage, achieve strategic competitiveness, and earn above-average returns.

Our contemporary treatment of the strategic management process is also exemplified in the chapters on the dynamics of strategic change in the complex global economy. In Chapter 5, for example, we discuss how the dynamics of competition between firms affect the outcomes achieved by individual companies. This chapter's discussion is grounded in the reality that in most industries, the strategic actions taken by a firm are influenced by a series of competitive actions and responses initiated by competitors. Thus, competition in the global economy is fluid, dynamic, and significantly influences a firm's performance. Similarly, in Chapter 7, we address the dynamics of strategic change at the corporate level, specifically addressing the motivation and consequences of mergers, acquisitions, and restructuring divestitures in the global economy.

We also emphasize that the total set of strategic actions known as *strategy formulation* and *strategy implementation* (see Figure 1.1 in Chapter 1) must be integrated carefully if a firm is to achieve strategic competitiveness and earn above-average returns. Thus, a full reading of this book shows that strategic competitiveness is achieved and above-average returns are earned only when firms use implementation tools and actions that are consistent with the nature of different business-level (Chapter 4), corporate-level (Chapter 6), acquisition (Chapter 7), international (Chapter 8), and cooperative (Chapter 9) strategies that firms have chosen.

Contemporary topics and concepts are the foundation for our in-depth analysis of strategic actions firms take to implement their chosen strategies. In Chapter 10, for example, we describe how different corporate governance mechanisms (e.g., boards of directors, institutional owners, executive compensation, etc.) affect strategy implementation. Chapter 11 explains how firms gain a competitive advantage by effectively using structures to implement business-level and corporate-level strategies. The vital contributions of strategic leaders are discussed in Chapter 12. Chapter 13 addresses the important topic of corporate entrepreneurship and innovation through internal corporate venturing, strategic alliances, and external acquisition or venture capital investments. Through integration of the traditional and contemporary topics, readers of this book should be able to fully understand the strategic management process and how to use it successfully in an organizational setting.

A number of contemporary topics and issues are examined in the book as well. These include total quality management (TQM), stakeholder analyses, core competencies, speed of decision making, transnational strategy, strategic refocusing (downsizing, downscoping), and the importance of ethics.

■ Key Features of This Text

To increase the value of this book for readers, several features are included, each of which is described below.

Learning Objectives   Each chapter begins with clearly stated learning objectives. These objectives inform readers of key points they should master from each chapter. To both facilitate and verify learning, students can revisit each chapter's learning objectives by preparing answers to the review questions appearing at the end of each chapter.

Opening Cases   Following the learning objectives, each chapter begins with an opening case. These cases describe current actions taken by well-known companies including Ford Motor Company, AT&T, Texas Instruments, Hitachi, Rubbermaid, Oy Nokia, American Express, PepsiCo, and Procter & Gamble. The purpose of these cases is to demonstrate how a specific firm applies the strategic management concepts that are examined in the chapter. Thus, the opening cases provide a link between the theory and application of the strategic management process in different organizations.

Key Terms   Key terms—those that are critical to understanding the strategic management process—are boldfaced throughout the book. Definitions of these key terms appear in chapter margins as well as in the text.

Strategic Focus Segments   Three Strategic Focus segments are presented in each chapter. As with the opening case, the Strategic Focus segments showcase organizations with which most readers are familiar. These segments provide additional applications of the concepts highlighted in each chapter. Each Strategic Focus describes how a company has applied a particular part of the strategic management process in the pursuit of strategic competitiveness. For instance, Procter & Gamble's successful entry and competition in Chinese markets is explained in a Strategic Focus in Chapter 1, demonstrating the importance of competitiveness in a global economy. The importance of analyzing and adapting to the external environment is shown by the changes Louis Gerstner has made in IBM's strategy as explained in a Strategic Focus in Chapter 2. A Strategic Focus in Chapter 3 describes how The Gap applies its core competencies to a new concept, Old Navy Stores, to achieve a competitive advantage. Time Warner's acquisition of Turner Broadcasting to achieve synergy is explained in a Strategic Focus in Chapter 6. Sony's use of strategic alliances to enter international markets is emphasized in a Chapter 8 Strategic Focus segment. Sematech is one of the more successful research consortia in the United States as discussed in a Strategic Focus in Chapter 9. Finally, the entrepreneurial activity of Chrysler Corporation, the Skunkworks at Rockwell, and the innovative approaches implemented by Brinker International Inc. have all been successful as exemplified in a Chapter 13 Strategic Focus. These examples and others make the concepts in each chapter come alive for the reader and facilitate reality-based learning.

End-of-Chapter Summaries   Each chapter ends with a summary that is related to the learning objectives. These summaries are presented in a bulleted format to highlight concepts, tools, and techniques examined in each chapter.

Review Questions   As mentioned earlier, review questions are largely tied to the learning objectives. As such, students are prompted to focus on the specific learning objectives of each chapter.

Application Discussion Questions   Following the review questions at the end of each chapter is a set of application discussion questions. These questions challenge readers to apply the strategic management process highlighted in the chapter. These questions are intended to stimulate thoughtful classroom discussions and to help students develop critical thinking skills. Lively debates should emerge as students discuss potential applications.

Ethics Questions   While competing in a global economy, firms continuously face ethical challenges and dilemmas. At the end of each chapter, readers are presented with a set of questions about ethical issues that require careful thought and analysis. Preparing answers to these questions helps students confront many of the ethical issues facing those responsible for designing and using effectively a firm's strategic management process. Discussing these difficult issues in class heightens one's awareness of the ethical challenges encountered by modern organizations.

Internet Exercises   The Internet is becoming a popular source of information and a valuable learning tool. As such, a set of Internet exercises, developed by Paul Miesing of the University of Albany, SUNY is included at the end of each chapter. Each set of exercises is designed so the student can use the Internet to apply or further develop concepts presented in the chapter. A general guide to the use of the Internet is presented in the Appendix to the book.

Examples   Besides the opening cases and Strategic Focus segments, the chapters contain many other real-world examples. For instance, AB Volvo's fight for survival by being innovative is discussed in Chapter 13. Chapter 8 explains the international strategy of a number of firms such as Komatsu, Ford, Samsung, and Ispat International, among others. Grounded in descriptions of actual organizations' actions, these examples are used to illustrate key strategic management concepts and to make examining the strategic management process more real and interesting.

Besides the traditional end of book subject and name indices, a company index is provided. This index includes the names of all organizations discussed in the text for easier accessibility.

Strategic Competitiveness and Globalization   The title of this book highlights the importance of strategic competitiveness and globalization to our examination of the strategic management process. The strategic management process is critical to an organization's success. As described in Chapter 1, strategic competitiveness is achieved when a firm develops and exploits a sustained competitive advantage. Attaining such an advantage results in the earning of above-average returns; that is, returns that exceed those an investor could expect from other investments with similar amounts of risk. For example, Rubbermaid developed and sustained a competitive advantage over time because of its significant emphasis on innovation even though it operates in a low-technology industry. Although it has experienced some problems recently because of its pricing strategies, its innovation (introducing sometimes as many as 300 to 400 new products annually) has helped it to remain one of the top firms in the United States in reputation (see Chapters 2 and 3).

Also critical to the approach used in this text is the fact that all firms face increasing global competition. Firms no longer operate in relatively safe domestic markets as U.S. auto firms have discovered. In the past, many companies, including most in the United States, produced large quantities of standardized products. Today, firms typically compete in a global economy that is complex, highly uncertain, and unpredictable. To a greater degree than was the case in a primarily domestic economy, the global economy rewards effective performers, whereas poor performers are forced to restructure significantly to enhance their strategic competitiveness. As noted earlier, increasing globalization and the technological revolution have produced a new competitive landscape. The new competitive landscape presents a challenging and complex environment for firms, but one that also has opportunities.

Success in the new competitive landscape requires specific capabilities, including the abilities to (1) use scarce resources wisely to maintain the lowest possible costs, (2) constantly anticipate frequent changes in customers' preferences, (3) adapt to rapid technological changes, (4) identify, emphasize, and effectively manage what a firm does better than its competitors, (5) continuously structure a firm's operations so objectives can be achieved more efficiently, and (6) successfully manage and gain commitments from a culturally diverse workforce.

The importance of developing and using these capabilities in the new competitive landscape of the twenty-first century should not be underestimated. In the opinion of General Electric's chairman, Jack Welch, firms that cannot sell a top-quality product at the world's lowest price will soon be out of business.[1] Welch's opinion challenges firms to understand the nature of the new competitive landscape and its direct and indirect effects on their operations. In some instances, firms compete directly with global competitors. For companies competing only with domestic competitors (evidence suggests that the number of these firms continues to decline), the effect of globalization is witnessed in terms of competitive standards. Indirectly, then, the competitive landscape forces all companies—even those focused on a domestic market—to compete in terms of the world's highest standards.

Full Four-Color Format   Our presentation and discussion of the strategic management process is facilitated by use of a full four-color format. This format provides the foundation for an interesting and visually appealing treatment of all parts of the strategic management process. Also included is a series of photo-

---

[1] Jack Welch's lessons for success, 1993, *Fortune*, January 25, 86–93.

graphs accompanied by captions integrated with the text material to help students understand the concepts.

Cases The text includes 37 case studies that represent a variety of business and organizational situations and corporate- and business-level strategic issues. For example, there are cases representing manufacturing, service, consumer goods, and industrial goods industries. Furthermore, many of the cases include an international perspective. Also, cases with high technology, entertainment, and utility firms are represented. Some cases focus specifically on social or ethical issues, whereas others emphasize strategic issues of entrepreneurial or small- and medium-sized firms. Finally, a significant number of the cases also provide an effective perspective on the industry examined.

The cases have been reviewed carefully and selected personally by the authors. Our goal was to choose cases that were well written and focused on clear and important strategic management issues. In addition, the cases represent a variety of industries and strategic issues and provide a rich learning experience for those performing case analyses. The cases are multidimensional and, for the readers' convenience, a matrix listing all 37 cases and the dimensions/characteristics of each one is provided following the table of contents. Although most of these cases are concerned with well-known national and multinational companies, several depict the strategic challenges involved in smaller and entrepreneurial firms (e.g., Kitchen Made Pies, The Hue-Man Experience Bookstore). Given the global economy emphasized in this book, more than 50 percent of the cases include an international perspective. Additionally, given that by the year 2000 approximately 50 percent of all businesses will be owned and operated by women, several cases are included that examine firms with women CEOs/owners or entrepreneurs such as Liz Claiborne and Susan's Special Lawns. There are also cases of special interest or topics (e.g., Arizona Public Service Company, The Body Shop, Matsushita Industrial de Baja California, Daimler Benz, and Dow Corning and the Silicone Breast Implant Controversy). Additionally, while most cases focus on profit-oriented companies, we also have cases on nonprofit organizations (e.g., The Greensboro Housing Authority). In summary, the cases represent a wide variety of important and challenging strategic issues and provide an exciting setting for case analyses and presentations.

■ Support Materials

The instructor support package is an innovative response to the growing demand for creative and effective teaching methodologies. The comprehensive set of supplements prepared to accompany this edition of our book is designed to provide an integrated resource package for all faculty adopting this text. The materials used will depend on the faculty member's interest areas, class size, equipment availability, and teaching experience. All supplements not prepared by the authors have been reviewed by them for consistency and accuracy with the text's materials.

■ For the Instructor

Annotated Instructor's Edition An *Annotated Instructor's Edition* has been prepared by Robert D. Nixon of Tulane University. The annotations, based on current events experienced by organizations that are familiar to students, provide a number of suggestions to encourage and facilitate class discussion of important concepts from the book. The annotations also include additional company examples that may be used to enlighten students further about a particular topic. In addition, most chapter opening cases are accompanied by at least one URL so that further information related to the featured company can be researched using the World Wide Web.

Instructor's Manual A comprehensive *Instructor's Manual* has been prepared by Richard A. Menger of St. Mary's University. The instructor's manual provides teaching notes and suggested answers to review questions for each chapter. The teaching notes incorporate boxed discussion summaries or highlights of each opening case, Strategic Focus segment, table, and figure appearing in the text. Teaching suggestions are included to provide strategies for integrating various text features in a lecture format. In addition, a new section on Information Technology for Strategic Management, prepared by Paul Miesing of the University of Albany, SUNY, has been added. This section provides suggestions for incorporating the Internet exercises from each chapter into the course, at least one URL for each Strategic Focus, a Listserv exercise, and a Usenet exercise.

Instructor's Case Notes Samuel M. DeMarie of the University of Nevada at Las Vegas prepared the *Case Notes* that accompany the text. Each note highlights the details of the case within the framework of case analysis presented in the text. The authors have selected cases that represent a myriad of strategy topics and company types. The structure of these case notes allows instructors to organize case discussions along common themes and concepts. For example, each case note details the firm's capabilities and resources, its industry and competitive environment (if applicable), and key factors for success in the industry.

The case notes also feature aspects of the cases that make them unique. Each case is analyzed within its particular time frame, and most include an updating epilogue. Professor DeMarie has also provided summary tables of all the figures and exhibits in each case. Instructors will know the information available to students for preparing a case.

Test Bank The *Test Bank*, prepared by Debora J. Gilliard of Metropolitan State College of Denver, has been thoroughly revised and expanded for this edition. The test bank contains more than 1,000 multiple choice, true/false, and essay questions. Each question has been coded according to Bloom's taxonomy, a widely known testing and measurement device used to classify questions according to level (easy, medium, or hard) and type (application, recall, or comprehension). A text page reference for the answer to each test question has been added to the test bank.

WESTEST™ Computerized Testing Software WESTEST™ allows instructors to create, edit, store, and print exams. The system is menu driven with a desktop format to make the program quick and easy to use. WESTEST™ is available in Macintosh, IBM, and IBM-compatible Windows® and MS-DOS® versions. Instructors can also have tests created and printed by calling West's Call-In-Testing Service.

West's Classroom Management Software West's Classroom Management Software enables instructors to keep track of student performance using a spreadsheet format. This program allows for easy entry of student information (name, ID number, social security number, etc.) and assignment data. The instructor can customize grading parameters by changing grading criteria or determining assignment weighting.

PowerPoint® Presentation Files   Jay Dial of Texas A&M University has developed more than 500 PowerPoint® slides for this text. These slides feature figures from the text, lecture outlines, and innovative adaptations to enhance classroom presentation. These files are available on disk in PowerPoint® 4.0.

Transparency Acetates   The full color transparency acetates include important figures from the text and additional transparencies from the PowerPoint® Presentation Files. Over 75 transparency acetates are included in the set.

Transparency Masters   More than 200 transparency masters are printed from the PowerPoint® Presentation Files and include figures from the text and innovative adaptations to enhance classroom presentation.

West's CD-ROM Product Manager   West's CD-ROM Product Manager provides a simple way to install WESTEST™ microcomputer testing software with the complete test bank, West's Classroom Management Software, and the PowerPoint® Presentation Files for this text. Using this CD-ROM and its installer, you can immediately access and use all of these valuable resources.

Strategic Management Online   Strategic Management Online includes updates to the text and exercises as well as new links and additional Internet exercises. This online service is available to qualified adopters through West's home page on the Internet at http://www.westpub.com/Educate.

Videos   An extensive updated video package is available that includes three to five video segments per chapter. The videos feature real companies and real cases, not company promotions.

Video Guide   A video guide has been developed by Joseph F. Michlitsch of Southern Illinois University at Edwardsville to accompany the video package and provide information on length, alternative points of usage within the text, highlights to address, and some discussion questions to stimulate classroom discussion.

■ For the Student

Office Profit, *SA*   For those adopters who want computer software support for case analysis, we are pleased to offer Office Profit, *SA* Business Analysis Software developed by CFI ProServices, Halcyon Division. The menu-driven Office Profit software is a powerful tool that allows students to calculate any or all of the following:

1. comparison to industry standards;
2. financial ratios;
3. a firm's breakeven point;

4. bankruptcy predictor;
5. cash market value of the firm;
6. cash flow analysis;
7. operating ratio; and
8. operating capital requirements.

The financial data from the following text cases have been loaded on disk for use with the Office Profit software:

Case 2. Arizona Public Service Company and the Electric Utility Industry
Case 3. AT&T: A Strategic Restructuring for the Twenty-First Century
Case 9. Cap Gemni Sogeti
Case 13. Eastman Kodak Company: A New Image
Case 15. Glaxo PLC: Medicine, Management, and Mergers
Case 16. Goodyear: The Gault Years
Case 18. Harley-Davidson, Inc.
Case 19. The Hue-Man Experience Bookstore
Case 23. Liz Claiborne, 1993: Troubled Times for the Woman's Retail Giant
Case 27. Novell: Expanding the Network
Case 29. Polaroid and the Family-Imaging Market

Insights: Readings in Strategic Management, **Second Edition** Prepared by Timothy B. Palmer of Louisiana State University, *Insights* has been revised for this edition and includes multiple selections from academic and popular business periodicals such as the *Academy of Management Executive,* the *Wall Street Journal, Forbes,* and *Fortune.*

Student Note-Taking Guide The *Student Note-Taking Guide,* prepared by Jay Dial of Texas A&M University, addresses the frustration of professors who find that students spend most of their time during lectures frantically copying material from the overheads. The *Student Note-Taking Guide* contains reduced images of the PowerPoint® Presentation Files with space for lecture notes on each page.

■ Acknowledgments

We gratefully acknowledge the help of many people in the development of this edition of our book. The professionalism, guidance, and support provided by Rick Leyh, editor, and his staff, in particular Brent Gordon and Matt Thurber, are gratefully acknowledged. We appreciate the excellent work of Sam DeMarie, Jay Dial, Debora Gilliard, Richard Menger, Joseph F. Michlitsch, Paul Miesing, Robert Nixon, and Timothy Palmer in preparing the supplemental materials accompanying this book. Also, we appreciate the excellent secretarial assistance provided by Wanda Bird. In addition, we owe a debt of gratitude to our colleagues at Texas A&M University and Baylor University. Finally, we gratefully acknowledge the help of many who read and provided feedback on drafts of our chapters for both editions of our book. Their insights enhanced our work. Those who contributed through reviews and evaluations are:

Kendall W. Artz
Baylor University

Kimberly B. Boal
Texas Tech University

Garry D. Bruton
University of Tulsa

Victoria L. Buenger
Vanderbilt University

Lowell Busenitz
University of Houston

Gary R. Carini
Baylor University

Roy A. Cook
Fort Lewis College

James H. Davis
University of Notre Dame

Samuel M. DeMarie
University of Nevada at Las Vegas

Derrick E. Dsouza
University of North Texas

W. Jack Duncan
University of Alabama at Birmingham

Karin Fladmoe-Lindquist
University of Utah

Karen A. Froehlich
North Dakota State University

Debora J. Gilliard
Metropolitan State College of Denver

Ching-Der Horng
National Sun Yat-Sen University

Veronica Horton
Middle Tennessee State University

Sharon G. Johnson
Cedarville College

Anne T. Lawrence
San Jose State University

Franz T. Lohrke
Louisiana State University

Richard A. Menger
St. Mary's University

Joseph F. Michlitsch
Southern Illinois University at Edwardsville

Paul Miesing
University at Albany, SUNY

Douglas D. Moesel
Lehigh University

Benjamin M. Oviatt
Georgia State University

George M. Puia
Indiana State University

Woody Richardson
University of Alabama at Birmingham

Michael V. Russo
University of Oregon

Ronald J. Salazar
Idaho State University

Hugh Sherman
Ohio University

Clayton G. Smith
Oklahoma City University

David C. Snook-Luther
University of Wyoming

Kathleen M. Sutcliffe
University of Michigan

Thomas A. Turk
Chapman University

Margaret A. White
Oklahoma State University

Robert Wiseman
Arizona State University

■ Final Comments

Organizations face exciting and dynamic competitive challenges as the 1990s come to a close and the twenty-first century appears on the horizon. These challenges—and effective responses to them—are explored in this second edition of *Strategic Management: Competitiveness and Globalization*. The strategic management process offers valuable insights for those committed to successfully leading and managing organizations in the 1990s and beyond. We hope you will enjoy the exposure to the strategic management process provided by this book. In addition, we wish you success in your careers and future endeavors.

PART

I Strategic Management Inputs

CHAPTERS

1 Strategic Management and
Strategic Competitiveness

2 The External Environment:
Opportunities, Threats,
Industry Competition, and
Competitor Analysis

3 The Internal Environment:
Resources, Capabilities, and
Core Competencies

1 Strategic Management and Strategic Competitiveness

LEARNING OBJECTIVES

After reading this chapter, you should be able to:

1. Define strategic competitiveness, competitive advantage, and above-average returns.
2. Discuss the challenge of strategic management.
3. Describe the new competitive landscape and how it is being shaped by global and technological changes.
4. Use the industrial organization (I/O) model to explain how firms can earn above-average returns.
5. Use the resource-based model to explain how firms can earn above-average returns.
6. Describe strategic intent and strategic mission and discuss their value to the strategic management process.
7. Define stakeholders and describe the three primary stakeholder groups' ability to influence organizations.
8. Describe the work of strategists.
9. Explain the strategic management process.

Ford 2000: Ford Motor Company's Global Strategy

With vision, self-confidence, and entrepreneurial daring, Alex Trotman, chief executive officer (CEO) of Ford Motor Company, is pushing his firm to design and successfully implement a global strategy. Called Ford 2000, the strategy is bold, complex, and not without risk. It calls for Ford to revolutionize how it designs and manufactures the 70+ cars and trucks it sells in over 200 markets. In some analysts' eyes, if this global strategy works as Trotman expects, he may be able to transform what is generally recognized as a "pretty good automobile company" into the world's best, as measured by quality and profitability.

The core of this strategy is Trotman's vision of a firm capable of manufacturing a variety of cars and trucks through common platforms. To make a larger number of higher quality cars and trucks on a smaller number of common or "universal" platforms, Ford decided to reorganize its design and production processes on a worldwide basis. The company is eliminating its North American and European engineering operations. In their place will be a single setup organized around five vehicle development centers—four in Dearborn, Michigan (the firm's headquarters), and one in Europe. Instead of being regionally oriented, as were the North American and European operations, each new center has a global mission. In the European center, for example, a single basic design of a small car is to be developed. Using the same template, slight modifications of the basic design will be completed for individual markets.

The four Dearborn-based centers also have specific global missions: one to develop large front-wheel-drive cars, including minivans; a second, rear-wheel-drive cars, including Ford Crown Victoria; another, Explorers and pickup trucks; and the fourth, commercial trucks. The similarity across the designs of the cars and trucks allows them to be manufactured through a small number of common platforms. By reducing the duplication of efforts involved with designing unique cars for each market, through volume purchases, lower research and development (R&D) and materials costs, and shorter development times, the company believes it can save between $3 and $4 billion annually.

The scope and complexity of Ford 2000 are revealed by a document called the "Global Cycle Plan." Identified in this plan are all new cars and trucks Ford intends to introduce in every market through 2003 and the resources needed to produce them. This document also shows that Ford 2000 challenges the company to reduce the number of its basic designs or platforms from 24 to 16, while increasing the number of models manufactured from them by 50 percent (all to be accomplished while spending less money). The 1996 Taurus design, for example, was the basis for a new Thunderbird, a six-passenger sedan, several Mercury variations, a new small Lincoln luxury car, and another upmarket car for Europe. Critical to this strategy's success, Ford executives believe, is the involvement and motivation of the company's diverse global workforce.

Source: M. Leach, 1995, Ford Motor, *Value Line*, June 16, 104; A. Taylor III, 1995, Ford's really BIG leap at the future: It's risky, it's worth it, and it may not work, *Fortune*, September 18, 134–144.

■ **Strategic competitiveness** *is achieved when a firm successfully formulates and implements a value-creating strategy.*

The design and implementation of Ford 2000 is one part of Ford Motor Company's ongoing efforts to achieve strategic competitiveness and earn above-average returns. **Strategic competitiveness** is achieved when a firm successfully formulates and implements a value-creating strategy. When a firm implements a value-creating strategy of which other companies are unable to duplicate the benefits or find it too costly to imitate,[1] this firm has a

■ *A sustained* or *sustainable competitive advantage occurs when a firm implements a value-creating strategy of which other companies are unable to duplicate the benefits or find it too costly to imitate.*

sustained or sustainable competitive advantage (hereafter called simply competitive advantage). A firm is assured of a competitive advantage only after others' efforts to duplicate its strategy have ceased or failed.[2] Even if a firm achieves a competitive advantage, it normally can sustain it only for a certain period of time.[3] The speed with which competitors are able to acquire the skills needed to duplicate the benefits of a firm's value-creating strategy determines how long a competitive advantage will last.[4] Understanding how to exploit its competitive advantage is necessary for a firm to earn above-average returns.[5]

By achieving strategic competitiveness and successfully exploiting its competitive advantage, a firm is able to accomplish its primary objective—the earning of above-average returns. **Above-average returns** are returns in excess of what an investor expects to earn from other investments with a similar amount of risk. **Risk** is an investor's uncertainty about the economic gains or losses that will result from a particular investment.[6] Firms that are without a competitive advantage or that are not competing in an attractive industry earn, at best, only average returns. **Average returns** are returns equal to those an investor expects to earn from other investments with a similar amount of risk. In the long run, an inability to earn at least average returns results in failure. Failure occurs because investors will choose to invest in firms that earn at least average returns and will withdraw their investments from firms that earn less.

■ *Above-average returns are returns in excess of what an investor expects to earn from other investments with a similar amount of risk.*

■ *Risk is an investor's uncertainty about the economic gains or losses that will result from a particular investment.*

■ *Average returns are returns equal to those an investor expects to earn from other investments with a similar amount of risk.*

■ *The* **strategic management process** *is the full set of commitments, decisions, and actions required for a firm to achieve strategic competitiveness and earn above-average returns.*

Dynamic in nature, the **strategic management process** (see Figure 1.1) is the full set of commitments, decisions, and actions required for a firm to achieve strategic competitiveness and earn above-average returns.[7] Relevant *strategic inputs,* from analyses of the internal and external environments, are necessary for effective strategy formulation and strategy implementation actions. In turn, effective *strategic actions* are a prerequisite to achieving the desired outcomes of strategic competitiveness and above-average returns. Thus, the strategic management process is used to match the conditions of an ever-changing market and competitive structure with a firm's continuously evolving resources, capabilities, and competencies (the sources of strategic inputs). Effective *strategic actions* that take place in the context of carefully integrated strategy formulation and strategy implementation processes result in desired *strategic outcomes*.[8]

In the remaining chapters of this book, we use the strategic management process to explain what firms should do to achieve strategic competitiveness and earn above-average returns. Through these explanations, it becomes clear why some firms consistently achieve competitive success and others fail to do so.[9] As you will see, the reality of global competition is a critical part of the strategic management process.[10]

Several topics are discussed in this chapter. First, we examine the challenge of strategic management. This brief discussion highlights the fact that the strategic actions taken to achieve and then to maintain strategic competitiveness demand the best of managers, employees, and their organizations on a continuous basis. Second, we describe the new competitive landscape, created primarily by the emergence of a global economy and rapid technological changes. The new competitive landscape establishes the contextual opportunities and threats within which the strategic management process is used by firms striving to meet the competitive challenge raised by demanding global standards.

We next examine two models that suggest conditions organizations should study to gain the strategic inputs needed to select strategic actions in the pursuit

Figure 1.1   The Strategic Management Process

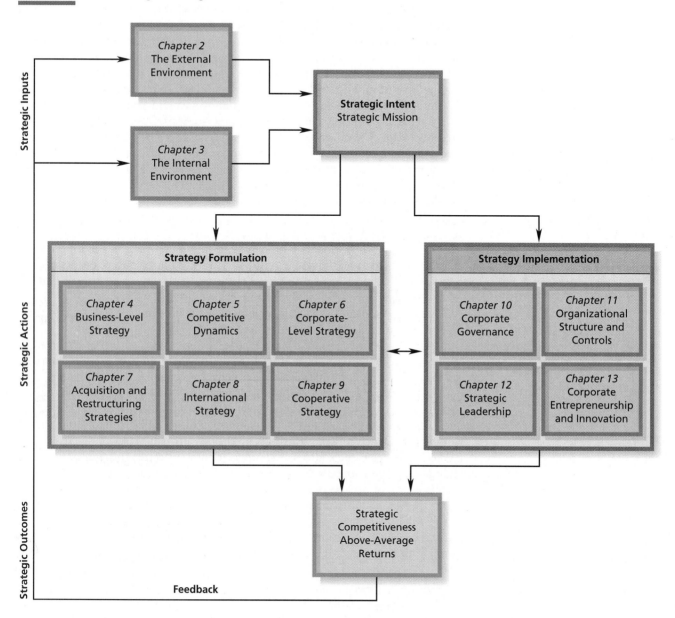

of strategic competitiveness and above-average returns. However, the emphases of these two models differ. The first model (industrial organization) suggests that the *external environment* should be the primary determinant of a firm's strategic actions. The key to this model is locating and competing successfully in an attractive (that is, profitable) industry. The second model (resource based) suggests that the unique resources and capabilities of a firm's internal environment are the critical link to strategic competitiveness. Comprehensive explanations of these two models in this first chapter and the next two show that through combined use of these two models, firms obtain the full set of strategic inputs needed to formulate and implement strategies successfully.

Analyses of its external and internal environments provide a firm with the information it needs to develop its strategic intent and strategic mission (intent and mission are defined later in this chapter). As shown in Figure 1.1, strategic intent and strategic mission influence strategy formulation and implementation actions.

The chapter's discussion then turns to the stakeholders served by organizations. The degree to which stakeholders' needs can be met increases directly with enhancements in a firm's strategic competitiveness and its ability to earn above-average returns. Closing the chapter are introductions to organizational strategists and the elements of the strategic management process.

The Challenge of Strategic Management

The goals of achieving strategic competitiveness and earning above-average returns are challenging—not only for firms as large as Ford Motor Company, but also for those as small as your local dry cleaners. The performance of some companies, of course, more than meets strategic management's challenge. At the end of a recent year, for example, Coca-Cola and General Electric had created more wealth (as measured by market value added) than other U.S. firms (approximately $61 billion in the case of Coca-Cola; roughly $52 billion for GE).[11] The top 10 wealth creators for 1995, including Coca-Cola and GE, are shown in Table 1.1. However, the fact that only 2 of the 25 largest U.S. industrial corporations in 1900 are still competitive today attests to the rigors of business competition and the challenge of strategic management. (The remaining 23 companies have failed, been merged with other firms, or are no longer of significant size relative to competitors.)[12] Moreover, in a recent year, almost 150,000 U.S. businesses either failed or filed for bankruptcy.[13] Results such as these support the view that competitive success is transient.[14] Thomas J. Watson, Jr., formerly IBM's chairman, once cautioned people to remember that "corporations are expendable and that success—at best—is an impermanent achievement which can always slip out of hand."[15]

Successful performance may be transient and impermanent, at least as reflected by *Fortune*'s Most Admired Corporation list. Rubbermaid first appeared on *Fortune*'s list in 1986 when IBM held the number one position for the fourth consecutive year. By 1995, IBM's position had slipped to number 281. Now Rubbermaid is experiencing performance problems and its ranking fell from first in 1995 to third in 1996. It will be interesting to see if the strategic actions Rubbermaid takes in response to its mid-1990s' challenges lead to strategic competitiveness and above-average returns.

What about Ford Motor Company? Will the firm be able to quickly establish the clear and well-defined organizational structure that will be necessary to support implementation of what some view as a radical attempt to produce cars for the global market?[16] And, more generally, will the commitments, decisions, and actions called for by the Ford 2000 global strategy result in strategic competitiveness and above-average returns for Ford Motor Company? The answers to these questions are not obvious, nor are they certain.

The world's second largest motor vehicle producer, Ford has the competitive advantage of being the low-cost U.S. car and truck manufacturer (Toyota, however, is the world leader in factory logistics and production efficiency). CEO

Table 1.1		Top 10 Wealth Creators		
1995	**1994**	**Company**	**Market Value Added**[a] **(Millions)**	**Change from 1994 (%)**
1	2	Coca-Cola	$60,846	13
2	1	General Electric	$52,071	−7
3	3	Wal-Mart Stores	$34,996	−24
4	4	Merck	$31,467	7
5	13	Microsoft	$29,904	59
6	6	Procter & Gamble	$27,830	7
7	5	Philip Morris	$27,338	−5
8	10	Johnson & Johnson	$24,699	21
9	8	AT&T	$22,542	−2
10	16	Motorola	$21,068	32

[a]Market value added is defined as a company's market value minus the capital tied up in the company.

Source: T. P. Pare, 1995, The new champ of wealth creation, *Fortune*, September 18, 131–132.

Trotman's "passion" for his company to succeed in the Asia-Pacific region, where demand for cars and trucks is expected to grow from 12 million to 19 million by the year 2005, is visible evidence for Ford 2000's importance.[17]

Japanese automakers also are committed to the importance of achieving competitive success in Asian and European nations.[18] Furthermore, the partially standardized vehicles produced through Ford's new approach to product development may not meet global customers' needs. General Motors (GM) and Toyota, among others, are also forming global strategies. These competitors' strategies may prove superior to Ford's. GM, for example, decided in the mid-1990s that it had to be either the number one or number two foreign automaker in China to maintain its stature in the global automobile industry. The strategy GM chose to reach this goal called for the company to form significant joint ventures with Chinese firms.[19] Toyota decided to implement an international strategy that is quite different from the one chosen by Ford Motor Company. In a recent annual report, Toyota noted that "Our global strategy used to center on 'world cars,' which we would modify slightly to accommodate demand in different markets. Today, our focus is shifting to models that we develop and manufacture especially for selected regional markets."[20]

Perhaps the most critical concern about Ford Motor Company's global strategy is that the company attempted global integration previously, and failed. Ford spent $6 billion to produce midsize sedans that would appeal to customers in the United States and Europe. Successful in Europe, U.S. shoppers bought few of these cars when they were introduced as the 1995 Ford Contour and Mercury Mystique. Consumers thought the cars' styles were dated. Middle-income families, a primary target customer, considered the cars to be expensive and without adequate passenger space.[21]

If selected through a matching of firm-specific resources, capabilities, and competencies with conditions in the external environment, GM, Ford, and Toyota's different international strategies could all contribute positively to these firms' efforts to achieve strategic competitiveness. Ford's competencies may support the design and implementation of Ford 2000, just as Toyota's competencies may support abandonment of the "world car" concept in favor of the decision to design, manufacture, and distribute cars on a region-by-region basis. The need to match conditions properly between a firm's external and internal environments demonstrates the challenge of strategic management.

In recognition of strategic management's challenge, Andrew Grove, Intel's CEO, observed that only paranoid companies survive and succeed. Such firms know that current success does not guarantee future strategic competitiveness and above-average returns. Accordingly, these companies strive continuously to improve so they can remain competitive. To be strategically competitive and earn above-average returns through implementation of Ford 2000, Ford Motor Company must compete differently than when it was organized regionally. General Motors, Toyota, Intel, and Rubbermaid, too, must compete differently in a world being shaped increasingly by globalization, technological changes, and the information revolution. For all these companies and others that are competing in the new competitive landscape, Andrew Grove believes that a key challenge is to try to do the impossible—namely, to anticipate the unexpected.[22]

The New Competitive Landscape[23]

The fundamental nature of competition in many of the world's industries is changing.[24] The pace of this change is relentless and is increasing. Even determining the boundaries of an industry has become challenging. Consider, for example, how advances in interactive computer networks and telecommunications have blurred the definition of the "television" industry. Because of these advances, the near future will find firms such as ABC, CBS, NBC, and HBO competing not only among themselves but also with AT&T, Microsoft, and Sony. An example of this new form of competition occurred in late 1995 when News Corporation, which owns Fox Broadcasting Company, formed a strategic alliance with Tele-Communications Inc., the largest U.S. cable system. Viewed as a venture that would control a global web of sports TV networks, this alliance was quickly considered to be a major competitor for ESPN and other sources interested in delivering sports events to customers around the world.[25]

Still other characteristics of the new competitive landscape are noteworthy. Conventional sources of competitive advantage such as economies of scale and huge advertising budgets are not as effective in the new competitive landscape. Moreover, the traditional managerial mind-set cannot lead a firm to strategic competitiveness in the new competitive landscape. In its place, managers must adopt a new mind-set—one that values flexibility, speed, innovation, integration, and the challenges that evolve from constantly changing conditions.[26] The conditions of the new competitive landscape result in a perilous business world, one where the investments required to compete on a global scale are enormous and the consequences of failure are severe.

Hypercompetition is a term that is used often to capture the realities of the new competitive landscape (mentioned briefly here, hypercompetitive environments are discussed further in Chapter 5). According to Richard A. D'Aveni, hypercompetition:

> . . . results from the dynamics of strategic maneuvering among global and innovative combatants. It is a condition of rapidly escalating competition based on price-quality positioning, competition to create new know-how and establish first-mover advantage,

competition to protect or invade established product or geographic markets, and competition based on deep pockets and the creation of even deeper pocketed alliances.[27]

Several factors have created hypercompetitive environments and the new competitive landscape. As shown in Figure 1.2, the emergence of a global economy and technology, coupled with rapid technological changes, are the two primary drivers.

■ The Global Economy

■ *A **global economy** is one in which goods, services, people, skills, and ideas move freely across geographic borders.*

A **global economy** is one in which goods, services, people, skills, and ideas move freely across geographic borders. Relatively unfettered by artificial constraints, such as tariffs, the global economy significantly expands and complicates a firm's competitive environment.[28]

Interesting opportunities and challenges are associated with the global economy's emergence. For example, Europe, instead of the United States, is now the world's largest single market. If countries from the former Soviet Union and other Eastern bloc nations are included, the European market has a gross domestic product (GDP) of $5 trillion with 700 million potential customers.[29] In addition, by 2015, China's total GDP will be greater than Japan's, although its per capita output will be much lower.[30] Some believe that the United States, Japan, and Europe are relatively equal contenders in the battle to be the most competitive nation, or group of nations, in the twenty-first century. Achieving this status will allow the "winner's citizens to have the highest standard of living."[31]

To achieve strategic competitiveness in the global economy, a firm must view the world as its marketplace. As explained in the Strategic Focus, P&G believes that it still has tremendous potential to grow internationally where the demand for household products is not as mature as it is in the United States.

A commitment to viewing the world as a company's marketplace creates a sense of direction that can serve the firm well. For example, Whirlpool Corporation, the world's largest manufacturer of major home appliances, intends to

Figure 1.2

The New Competitive Landscape

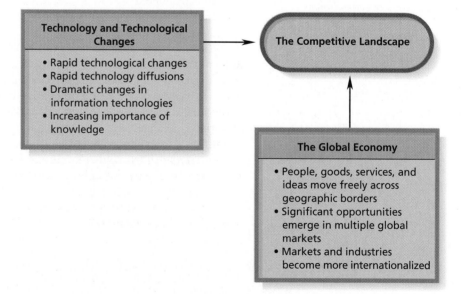

maintain its global leadership position. With production facilities in 12 countries and through its marketing efforts in 120 nations, the company's sales volume outside the United States approached 40 percent in 1994. Recently Whirlpool had investments in three appliance companies in Brazil, one in Canada, a subsidiary in Argentina, and joint ventures in Mexico, India, Taiwan, and China.

Lawrence Bossidy, CEO of AlliedSignal (a manufacturer of aerospace components, automotive parts for original equipment markets, and engineered materials, such as chemicals and plastics), is convinced that globalization is a key to his firm's growth. To achieve his goal of AlliedSignal generating 45 percent of its sales volume outside the United States by 1997, Bossidy is aggressively leading his company into China and India, two markets he believes have great potential.[32]

Large firms such as Whirlpool and AlliedSignal often commit to competition in the global economy quicker than do midsize and small firms. In the recent past, however, the number of U.S. midsize and small firms competing in the global economy has increased. For example, the percentage of U.S. midsize companies competing in markets outside of their home nation increased to 56 percent of the total in 1995.[33]

Overall, as measured by exports, U.S. companies' strategic actions in globalized markets are increasing. U.S. firms' sales are increasing in Japan's high-tech, automobile, consumer goods, and retailing markets. U.S. exports exceeded $800 billion in 1995, an increase of 12 percent over 1994. This total was expected to reach $1 trillion by 1998. In emerging nations, U.S. capital goods exports grew by 25 percent between 1994 and 1995. Although the largest percentage of total U.S. exports still goes to older, more developed markets in Europe, Canada, and Japan, the fastest growing demand for U.S. goods and services is in Asia, excluding Japan. The growth of sales in Asia is expected to average 12 percent annually between 1996 and 2000.[34]

With production facilities in 12 countries, like the one shown here in Mexico, Whirlpool is committed to and involved in the global economy.

■ The March of Globalization

Globalization is the spread of economic innovations around the world and the political and cultural adjustments that accompany this diffusion. Globalization encourages international integration, which has increased substantially during the last generation. In globalized markets and industries, financial capital might be obtained in one national market and used to buy raw materials in another one. Manufacturing equipment bought from a third national market can be used to produce products that are sold in yet a fourth market.[35] Thus, globalization increases the range of opportunities for firms competing in the new competitive landscape.

The internationalization of markets and industries makes it increasingly difficult to think of some firms as domestic companies. For example, in a recent year, Honda Motor Company (1) employed 14,000 people in the United States; (2) sold 660,000 units in the United States, 480,000 (73 percent) of which it produced there; (3) manufactured its automobiles with 75 percent local U.S. content (parts/assemblies manufactured in the United States); (4) purchased $2.9

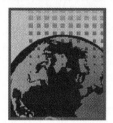

STRATEGIC FOCUS

Procter & Gamble: Competing Successfully in China

One of the most famous consumer products companies in the world, Procter & Gamble (P&G) has long been committed to selling its goods outside the domestic U.S. market. In a recent year, through activities in over 140 countries, P&G generated 52 percent of its sales and 31 percent of net income from its international business operations.

Although it faces competition in China from companies based in different countries including Britain (Unilever Group), Japan (Kao Corporation), Switzerland (Nestle SA), and Germany (Wella AG and Henkel KGAA) as well as from China itself, P&G is dominating the Chinese consumer-goods market. John Pepper, P&G's CEO and a key force in the firm's China strategy, believes that "The potential is enormous for us in China. One out of five people in the world lives there, and we have the kinds of products people use day in and day out." Even competitors admire P&G's accomplishments and potential in China. For example, the manager of Henkel KGAA's China strategy suggests that P&G is out in front in China with the other companies "fighting for second place."

How did this happen? What strategic actions have contributed to P&G's success in this market with vast potential?

Unlike competitors, P&G staked an early claim in China. The firm's aggressive position in China was taken originally to pursue what it saw as a marketplace opportunity. P&G discovered that Chinese shampoos were ineffective treatments for a common malady—dandruff. Spotting the potential to offer a shampoo that was effective in treating dandruff to a nation with large numbers of dark-haired people, P&G introduced Head & Shoulders in China in 1988. Within three years, the firm's antidandruff product was China's best-selling shampoo. Later, P&G introduced Pantene and Rejoice (called Pert in the United States), adding antidandruff formulas to each of these products. As is its customary practice, P&G spent heavily to advertise its shampoos. One indicator of the effectiveness of these efforts is the fact that a market survey firm found that Rejoice ads are more popular than any others appearing on Chinese television.

Determined from the start to hold the number one market position for its products in China, P&G used what one former manager calls "early application of overwhelming force: Salespersons—ground troops—attack secondary cities after an advertising campaign—air cover—clears the way." To this end, P&G has hired thousands of Chinese employees who "work" their local neighborhoods as ground troops. To introduce Tide, for example, the ground troops handed out yellow and orange gift packets of the laundry detergent to their neighbors.

Although losses were suffered early on, P&G earned returns in China during its 1994 and 1995 fiscal years (and expects this level of performance to continue). Moreover, at the end of 1995, P&G was the largest daily-use consumer-products company in China, domestic or foreign. The firm employed over 4,500 workers in eight joint ventures, generating sales of $450 million on its shampoos and detergents in fiscal year 1995. One analyst concluded that P&G is embarking on a "hugely successful invasion" in China.

Source: J. Kahn, 1995, P&G viewed China as a national market and is conquering it, *Wall Street Journal*, September 12, A1, A6.

billion worth of parts from U.S. suppliers; (5) paid $2.5 billion in federal income tax; (6) invested $3 billion in a research and development center in the United States; and (7) exported 40,000 cars from its U.S. facilities to other nations' markets. At the same time, Chrysler Corporation was producing minivans in Canada and LeBarons in Mexico. Similarly, Toyota Motor Corporation continues to reduce its total employment in Japan while expanding its global workforce. Toyota's Kentucky facility is the only place where the company builds its Avalon sedan and Camry Coupe and station wagon. In 1997, this plant became the sole producer of Toyota's new minivan. Beginning in 1998, the firm will build its T100 pickup in the United States.[36]

Given their operations, these firms should not be thought of as Japanese or American. Instead, they can be more accurately classified as global companies striving to achieve strategic competitiveness in the new competitive landscape. Some believe that because of its enormous economic benefits, globalization will not be stopped. It has been predicted, for example, that genuine free trade in manufactured goods among the United States, Europe, and Japan would add 5 to 10 percent to the Triad's annual economic outputs; free trade in the Triad's service sector would boost aggregate output by another 15 to 20 percent. Realizing these potential gains in economic output requires a commitment from the industrialized nations to cooperatively stimulate the higher levels of trade necessary for global growth. Eliminating national laws that impede free trade is an important stimulus to increased trading among nations.[37]

Many businesspeople, from across the globe, are committed to the importance of globalization and the need to eliminate barriers to it. For example, during the latter part of 1995, a group of top U.S. and European executives met to design steps that would remove "... remaining obstacles to trade and investment between the U.S. and the European Union." Additionally, these top-level managers called for negotiations to take place over time to mutually recognize manufacturing, distribution, safety, and environmental standards in specific sectors, including electrical, telecommunications, and computer products.[38]

Global competition has increased performance standards in many dimensions, including those of quality, cost, productivity, production introduction time, and smooth, flowing operations. Moreover, these standards are not static; they are exacting, requiring continuous improvement from a firm and its employees. As they accept the challenges posed by these increasing standards, companies increase their capabilities and individual workers sharpen their skills. Thus, in the new competitive landscape, competitive success will accrue only to those capable of meeting, if not exceeding global standards. This challenge exists for large firms and for small and midsize companies that develop cooperative relationships (e.g., joint ventures) with larger corporations in order to capitalize on international growth opportunities.[39]

The development of newly industrialized countries is changing the global competitive landscape and significantly increasing competition in global markets. As explained in the Strategic Focus, the economic development of Asian countries outside of Japan is increasing the significance of Asian markets. However, firms in the newly industrialized Asian countries such as South Korea are becoming major competitors in global industries. For instance, Samsung has become a market leader in the semiconductor industry taking market share away from Japanese and American firms. With increasing globalization and the spread of information technology, other countries are likely to develop their industrial bases as well. As this occurs, global markets will expand but competition in those markets will also become more intense.

Global markets are attractive strategic options for some companies, but they are not a single source of strategic competitiveness. In fact, for most companies, even for those capable of competing successfully in global markets, it is critical to remain committed to their domestic market. In the words of the director of economic studies at the Brookings Institution, "imported goods are components of a larger share of goods produced and sold in the United States, and

STRATEGIC FOCUS

The Changing Global Competitive Landscape: Emergence of Newly Industrialized Countries

The twenty-first century has been referred to as the "century of Pacific Asia." Undoubtedly, a leader in Pacific Asia has been and continues to be Japan. However, other nations in Asia are developing economic power. Among those are the newly industrialized countries of South Korea, Taiwan, and Singapore. In fact, South Korea has been identified as "Asia's next giant." South Korea is the home of several of the world's largest companies, including Samsung, Lucky-Goldstar, Daewoo, and Hyundai. Having developed from a low-wage economy where firms manufactured low-technology products such as shoes and textiles, Korean firms are now becoming leading producers of high-technology products in global markets. In fact, South Korea is likely to become the first nation to establish itself as an advanced industrial power since the emergence of Japan, making significant investments in the United States and European countries as well.

The emergence of South Korean firms and their economic power is changing the level of competition throughout Asia and, indeed, in global markets. For example, South Korea is currently the world's fifth largest auto manufacturer and the leading producers—Hyundai, Daewoo, and Kia—are making investments to double their manufacturing capacity by 2000. South Korean firms are also playing major competitive roles in the semiconductor, information processing, telecommunications, and nuclear energy industries, among others. With financial and policy support from the South Korean government, many large and small Korean firms deployed deliberate and aggressive technology strategies to develop significant technological capabilities. Creativity and risk-taking values are often emphasized in South Korean firms. These firms are not cautious about undertaking new products or moving into new industries.

South Korean firms evaluate their performance more on their sales and market share than on profitability, which gives rise to their aggressive stance relative to U.S. firms. For example, based on year-end sales estimates for 1992, Hyundai was shown to be the largest company in Korea, and Samsung executives were upset at being number two. As a result, they developed plans for a bold move into passenger-car production to regain the top spot as the largest South Korean firm. This is a risky strategic move, given that there are five other major South Korean automakers and significant foreign competition (e.g., from Japanese and U.S. firms) in the global auto market. Samsung is planning to invest approximately $4.5 billion during the period 1995–1997 to develop its auto manufacturing venture. It also is planning investments of up to $150 million to develop a 100-seat jetliner and $3 billion to build semiconductor manufacturing plants in North America, Europe, and Southeast Asia. In 1995 alone, Samsung invested approximately $9.92 billion in new expansion opportunities. Clearly, Japanese and U.S. firms in the semiconductor industries are extremely concerned about Samsung's emergence as a primary competitor and its expansion plans, such as new plants in Oregon and Texas.

Source: J. Flynn, H. Dawley, D. Woodruff, and G. Edmundson, 1996, Korea's big leap into Europe, *Business Week,* March 18, 52; S. Glain, 1995, Going for growth: Korea's Samsung plans very rapid expansion into autos, other lines, *Wall Street Journal,* March 2, A1, A6; W. J. Holdstein and L. Nakarmi, 1995, Korea, *Business Week,* July 31, 56–63; L. Nakarmi and R. Neff, 1994, Samsung's radical shakeup, *Business Week,* February 28, 74–76; R. L. Tung, 1994, Strategic management thought in East Asia, *Organizational Dynamics,* Spring, 55–65; L. Kim, 1993, National system of industrial innovation: Dynamics of capability building in Korea, in R. R. Nelson (ed.), *National Innovation Systems: A Comparative Analysis* (Oxford, England: Oxford University Press), 375–383; R. P. Kearney, 1991, Managing Mr. Kim, *Across the Board,* April, 40–46; A. H. Amsden, 1989, *Asia's Next Giant* (New York: Oxford University Press).

international trade is likely to grow in significance. Still, the great bulk of the goods and services Americans consume and invest in is entirely domestic."[40] In the new competitive landscape, firms are challenged to develop the optimal level of globalization, a level that results in appropriate concentrations on a company's domestic and global operations.[41]

In many instances then, strategically competitive companies are those that have learned how to apply competitive insights gained locally (or domestically) on a global scale. These companies do not impose homogeneous solutions in a pluralistic world. Instead, they nourish local insights so they can, as appropriate, modify and apply them in different regions around the world.

■ Technology and Technological Changes

There are three categories of technological trends and conditions through which technology is significantly altering the nature of competition.

Increasing Rate of Technological Change and Diffusion

Both the rate of technology changes and the speed at which new technologies become available and are used have increased substantially over the last 15 to 20 years. *Perpetual innovation* is a term used to describe how rapidly and consistently new, information-intensive technologies replace older ones. The shorter product life cycles resulting from these rapid diffusions of new technologies place a competitive premium on being able to quickly introduce new goods and services into the marketplace. In fact, when products become somewhat indistinguishable because of the widespread and rapid diffusion of technologies, speed to market may be the only source of competitive advantage (see Chapter 5).

There are other indicators of rapid technology diffusion. Some evidence suggests that after only 12 to 18 months, companies likely will have gathered information about their competitors' R&D and product decisions. Often, merely a few weeks pass before a new American-made product introduced in U.S. markets is copied, manufactured, and shipped to the United States by one or more companies in Asia.

Once a source of competitive advantage, today's rate of technological diffusion stifles the protection firms possessed previously through their patents. Patents are now thought by many to be an effective way of protecting proprietary technology primarily in the pharmaceutical and chemical industries only. Many firms competing in the electronics industry often do not apply for patents to prevent competitors from gaining access to the technological knowledge included in the patent application.

The Information Age

Dramatic changes in information technology have occurred in recent years. Personal computers, cellular phones, artificial intelligence, virtual reality, and massive databases (e.g., Lexis/Nexis) are a few examples of how information is used differently as a result of technological developments. Intel's Andrew Grove believes that electronic mail (E-mail) systems are the first manifestation of a revolution in the flow and management of information in companies throughout the world. In Grove's view, "The informed use of E-mail has two simple but startling implications: It turns days into minutes, and allows each person to reach hundreds of co-workers with the same effort it takes to reach just one."[42] An important outcome of these changes is that the ability to access and effectively use information has become an important source of competitive advantage in virtually all industries.

Both the pace of change in information technology and its diffusion will continue to increase. It is predicted, for example, that the number of personal computers in use will grow from over 150 million today to 278 million in 2010.

Moreover, the capabilities of PCs (as measured by power and speed) continue to expand. Introduced in late 1995 to business users only, Intel's powerful Pentium Pro microprocessor chip is expected to be included in PCs sold to consumers by 1998. A key advantage of this chip is its ability to complete instructions in an efficient order rather than in the sequence in which they were given.

There are even significant changes occurring in the set of companies manufacturing personal computers. In late 1995, for example, Intel and Sony Corporation joined forces to design a line of home PCs that was available for the 1996 Christmas season. This collective effort called for Intel to build the system's boards; Sony's contribution is to assemble and market the PCs. Both companies expected to reap benefits through this strategic alliance (such complementary alliances are described fully in Chapter 9). With Sony, Intel gets a partner that understands how to compete in mass consumer markets. For its part, Sony gets Intel's computer design skills and more advanced technology.[43] If successful, this alliance could change the competitive dynamics (see Chapter 5) of the computer manufacturing industry.

The declining costs of information technologies and the increased accessibility to them are also evident in the new competitive landscape. The global proliferation of relatively inexpensive computing power and its linkage on a global scale via computer networks combine to increase the speed and diffusion of information technologies. Thus, the competitive potential of information technologies is now available to companies throughout the world rather than only to large firms in Europe, Japan, and North America.[44]

An important electronic pathway through which relatively inexpensive data and information are being distributed is the Internet. Combined, the Internet and World Wide Web create an infrastructure that allows the delivery of information to computers in any location. Access to significant quantities of relatively inexpensive information yields strategic opportunities for a range of industries

Intel's Pentium microprocessor chip. Powerful microprocessing chips, along with the global proliferation of relatively inexpensive computing power and its linkage on a global scale via computer networks, combine to increase the speed and diffusion of information technologies.

and companies. Retailers, for example, use the Internet to provide abundant shopping privileges to customers in multiple locations. The power of this means of information access and application results in an almost astonishing array of strategic implications and possibilities.[45]

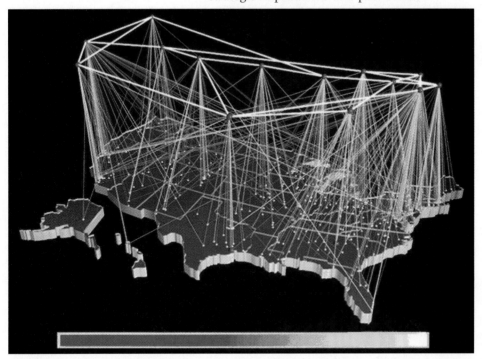

This image represents traffic on the National Science Foundation network (NSFNET), one of the larger networks connected to the Internet. At the time of this book's publication, the Internet had 30 million users located in more than 100 countries, and the number of users was growing at 5 percent per month.

Anticipating and even creating users' future needs for access to and competitive use of information is challenging. The nature of this complex situation in an emerging industry seems to argue against a firm's long-term competitive success. Bill Gates, Microsoft's CEO, observed recently that while his firm may be the most dominant force in the personal computer industry today, "the landscape is changing fast enough that the company's continued role is far from guaranteed." This opinion was offered at a time when Microsoft controlled more than 80 percent of the world market for PC operating systems.[46] Thus, even for companies holding dominant positions such as Microsoft the information age's rapid changes yield an uncertain and ambiguous future.

Increasing Knowledge Intensity

Knowledge (information, intelligence, and expertise) is the basis of technology and its application. In the new competitive landscape, knowledge is a critical organizational resource and is increasingly a valuable source of competitive advantage. Because of this, many companies now strive to transmute the accumulated knowledge of individual employees into a corporate asset. Some argue that the value of intangible assets, including knowledge, is growing as a proportion of total shareholder value.[47] The probability of achieving strategic competitiveness in the new competitive landscape is enhanced for the firm that realizes that its survival depends on the ability to capture intelligence, transform it into usable knowledge, and diffuse it rapidly throughout the company.[48] Companies that accept this challenge shift their focus from obtaining the information to exploiting the information to gain a competitive advantage over rival firms.[49]

Our discussion of conditions in the new competitive landscape shows that firms must be able to adapt quickly to achieve strategic competitiveness and earn above-average returns. The term strategic flexibility describes a firm's ability to do this. **Strategic flexibility** is a set of capabilities firms use to respond to various demands and opportunities that are a part of dynamic and uncertain competitive environments.[50] Firms should develop strategic flexibility in all areas of their

■ *Strategic flexibility is a set of capabilities firms use to respond to various demands and opportunities that are a part of dynamic and uncertain competitive environments.*

operations. Such capabilities in terms of manufacturing allow firms to "switch gears—from, for example, rapid product development to low cost—relatively quickly and with minimum resources."[51]

Headquartered at Miami International Airport, Greenwich Air Services is a company that appears to be strategically flexible. This firm maintains and refurbishes gas turbine engines for companies such as United Parcel Service and Continental Airlines. The environmental opportunity on which Greenwich is capitalizing is that the average commercial airplane is 13+ years old. The engines on these planes require constant maintenance and repair. To prevent cash from being tied up in the inventory, tools, and machines needed for maintenance on their equipment, a number of major airline carriers now contract with firms such as Greenwich to complete this work. Seeing this trend, Greenwich learned how to quickly and effectively service customers' engines at a cost lower than many airlines.[52] Quickly matching its resources with an environmental opportunity demonstrates Greenwich Air Services' strategic flexibility.

Next, we describe two models used by firms to generate the strategic inputs needed to successfully formulate and implement strategies and to maintain strategic flexibility in the process of doing so.

The I/O Model of Above-Average Returns

From the 1960s through the 1980s, the external environment was thought to be the *primary* determinant of strategies firms selected to be successful.[53] The I/O (industrial organization) model explains the dominant influence of the external environment on firms' strategic actions. This model specifies that the industry chosen in which to compete has a stronger influence on a firm's performance than do the choices managers make inside their organizations.[54] Firm performance is believed to be predicted primarily by a range of an industry's properties, including economies of scale, barriers to entry, diversification, product differentiation, and the degree of concentration[55] (these industry characteristics are examined in Chapter 2).

Grounded in the economics discipline, the I/O model has four underlying assumptions. First, the external environment is assumed to impose pressures and constraints that determine the strategies that would result in above-average returns. Second, most firms competing within a particular industry, or within a certain segment of an industry, are assumed to control similar strategically relevant resources and pursue similar strategies in light of those resources. The I/O model's third assumption is that resources used to implement strategies are highly mobile across firms. Because of resource mobility, any resource differences that might develop between firms will be short lived. Fourth, organizational decision makers are assumed to be rational and committed to acting in the firm's best interests as shown by their profit maximizing behaviors.[56]

The I/O model challenges firms to locate the most attractive industry in which to compete. Because most firms are assumed to have similar strategically relevant resources that are mobile across companies, competitiveness generally can be increased only when they find the industry with the highest profit potential and learn how to use their resources to implement the strategy required by the structural characteristics in that industry. The *five forces model of competition* is an analytical tool used to help firms with this task. This model (explained in detail in Chapter 2) encompasses many variables and tries to capture the complexity of competition.[57]

The five forces model suggests that an industry's potential profitability (i.e., its rate of return on invested capital relative to its cost of capital) is a function of interactions among five forces (suppliers, buyers, competitive rivalry among firms currently in the industry, product substitutes, and potential entrants to the industry).[58] Using this tool, a firm is challenged to understand an industry's profit potential and the strategy that should be implemented to establish a defensible competitive position, given the industry's structural characteristics. Typically, this model suggests that firms can earn above-average returns by manufacturing standardized products at costs below those of competitors (a cost leadership strategy) or differentiated products for which customers are willing to pay a price premium (a differentiation strategy). Cost leadership and differentiation strategies are described fully in Chapter 4.

As shown in Figure 1.3, the I/O model suggests that above-average returns are earned when firms implement the strategy dictated by the characteristics of the general, industry, and competitive environments. Companies that develop or acquire the internal skills needed to implement strategies required by the external environment are likely to succeed, while those that do not are likely to fail. As such, above-average returns are determined by external characteristics rather than the firm's unique internal resources and capabilities.

Successful competition in the new competitive landscape mandates that a firm build a unique set of resources and capabilities. However, this should be done within the framework of the dynamics of the industry (or industries) in which a firm competes. In this context, a firm is viewed as a bundle of market activities and a bundle of resources. Market activities are understood through application of the I/O model. The development and effective use of a firm's resources, capabilities, and competencies is understood through application of the resource-based model. Through an effective combination of results gained by using both the I/O and resource-based models, firms dramatically increase the probability of achieving strategic competitiveness and earning above-average returns.

■ The Resource-Based Model of Above-Average Returns

The resource-based model assumes that each organization is a collection of unique resources and capabilities that provides the basis for its strategy and is the *primary* source of its returns. In the new competitive landscape, this model argues that firms are collections of evolving capabilities that are managed dynamically in pursuit of above-average returns.[59] Thus, according to this model, differences in firms' performances across time are driven *primarily* by organizations' unique resources and capabilities rather than by an industry's structural characteristics.[60] This model also assumes that over time, firms acquire different resources and develop unique capabilities. As such, all firms competing within a particular industry may not possess the same strategically relevant resources and capabilities. Another assumption of this model is that resources may not be highly mobile across firms. The differences in resources form the basis of competitive advantage.[61]

Resources are inputs into a firm's production process, such as capital equipment, the skills of individual employees, patents, finance, and talented managers.

■ *Resources are inputs into a firm's production process, such as capital equipment, the skills of individual employees, patents, finance, and talented managers.*

Figure 1.3

The I/O Model of Superior Returns

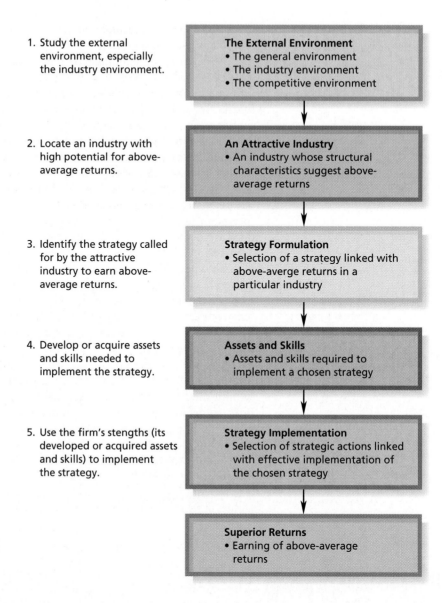

1. Study the external environment, especially the industry environment.

The External Environment
- The general environment
- The industry environment
- The competitive environment

2. Locate an industry with high potential for above-average returns.

An Attractive Industry
- An industry whose structural characteristics suggest above-average returns

3. Identify the strategy called for by the attractive industry to earn above-average returns.

Strategy Formulation
- Selection of a strategy linked with above-averge returns in a particular industry

4. Develop or acquire assets and skills needed to implement the strategy.

Assets and Skills
- Assets and skills required to implement a chosen strategy

5. Use the firm's stengths (its developed or acquired assets and skills) to implement the strategy.

Strategy Implementation
- Selection of strategic actions linked with effective implementation of the chosen strategy

Superior Returns
- Earning of above-average returns

In general, a firm's resources can be classified into three categories: physical, human, and organizational capital.[62] Described fully in Chapter 3, resources are both tangible and intangible in nature.

Individual resources alone may not yield a competitive advantage. For example, a sophisticated piece of manufacturing equipment may become a strategically relevant resource only when its use is integrated effectively with other aspects of a firm's operations (such as marketing and the work of employees). In general, it is through the combination and integration of sets of resources that competitive advantages are formed. A **capability** is the capacity for a set of resources to integratively perform a task or an activity.[63] Through continued use, capabilities become stronger and more difficult for competitors to understand and imitate.[64] As a source of competitive advantage, a capability ". . .

■ *A **capability** is the capacity for a set of resources to integratively perform a task or an activity.*

should be neither so simple that it is highly imitable, nor so complex that it defies internal steering and control."[65]

The resource-based model of competitive advantage is shown in Figure 1.4. In contrast to the I/O model, the resource-based view is grounded in the perspective that a firm's internal environment, in terms of its resources and capabilities, is more critical to the determination of strategic actions than is the external environment. Instead of focusing on the accumulation of resources necessary to implement the strategy dictated by conditions and constraints in the external environment (I/O model), the resource-based view suggests that a firm's unique resources and capabilities provide the basis for a strategy. The strategy chosen should allow the firm to best exploit its core competencies relative to opportunities in the external environment.

Figure 1.4

The Resource-Based Model of Superior Returns

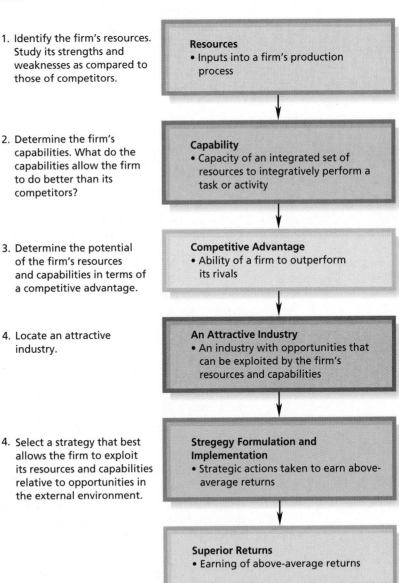

1. Identify the firm's resources. Study its strengths and weaknesses as compared to those of competitors.

Resources
• Inputs into a firm's production process

2. Determine the firm's capabilities. What do the capabilities allow the firm to do better than its competitors?

Capability
• Capacity of an integrated set of resources to integratively perform a task or activity

3. Determine the potential of the firm's resources and capabilities in terms of a competitive advantage.

Competitive Advantage
• Ability of a firm to outperform its rivals

4. Locate an attractive industry.

An Attractive Industry
• An industry with opportunities that can be exploited by the firm's resources and capabilities

4. Select a strategy that best allows the firm to exploit its resources and capabilities relative to opportunities in the external environment.

Stregegy Formulation and Implementation
• Strategic actions taken to earn above-average returns

Superior Returns
• Earning of above-average returns

Not all of a firm's resources and capabilities have the potential to be the basis for competitive advantage. This potential is realized when resources and capabilities are valuable, rare, costly to imitate, and nonsubstitutable.[66] Resources are *valuable* when they allow a firm to exploit opportunities and/or neutralize threats in its external environment; they are *rare* when possessed by few, if any, current and potential competitors; they are *costly to imitate* when other firms either cannot obtain them or are at a cost disadvantage to obtain them compared to the firm that already possesses them; and they are nonsubstitutable when they have no structural equivalents.[67]

When these four criteria are met, resources and capabilities become core competencies. **Core competencies** are resources and capabilities that serve as a source of competitive advantage for a firm over its rivals.[68] Often related to a firm's functional skills (e.g., the marketing function is a core competence at Philip Morris), the development, nurturing, and application of core competencies throughout a firm may be highly related to strategic competitiveness. Thus, the resource-based model argues that core competencies are the basis for a firm's competitive advantage, its strategic competitiveness, and its ability to earn above-average returns.

- *Core competencies* are resources and capabilities that serve as a source of competitive advantage for a firm over its rivals.

Strategic Intent and Strategic Mission

Resulting from analyses of a firm's internal and external environments is the information required to form a strategic intent and develop a strategic mission (see Figure 1.1). Both intent and mission are linked with strategic competitiveness.

Strategic Intent

- *Strategic intent* is the leveraging of a firm's internal resources, capabilities, and core competencies to accomplish the firm's goals in the competitive environment.

Strategic intent is the leveraging of a firm's internal resources, capabilities, and core competencies to accomplish the firm's goals in the competitive environment.[69] Concerned with winning competitive battles and obtaining global leadership, strategic intent implies a significant stretch of an organization's resources, capabilities, and core competencies. For example, when established effectively, a strategic intent can cause people to perform in ways they never imagined would be possible.[70] To achieve what at first may seem to be the unrealistic goal of challenging "Japanese dominance of consumer electronics," Stan Shih, CEO of Acer, a Taiwanese personal computer company, dreams of stretching his firm's manufacturing capability "... to make a slew of new products based on the microprocessor, including digital phones and simple low-priced fax machines."[71] Strategic intent exists when all employees and levels of a firm are committed to the pursuit of a specific (and significant) performance criterion. Some argue that strategic intent provides employees with the only goal worthy of personal effort and commitment—to unseat the best or remain the best, worldwide.[72] Strategic intent has been formed effectively when people believe fervently in their product and industry and when they are focused totally on their firm's ability to outdo its competitors.[73]

The following examples are expressions of strategic intent. Unocal Corporation intends "To become a high-performance multinational energy company— not the biggest, but the *best*." According to Eli Lilly and Company, "It's our strategic intent that customers worldwide view us as their most valued pharma-

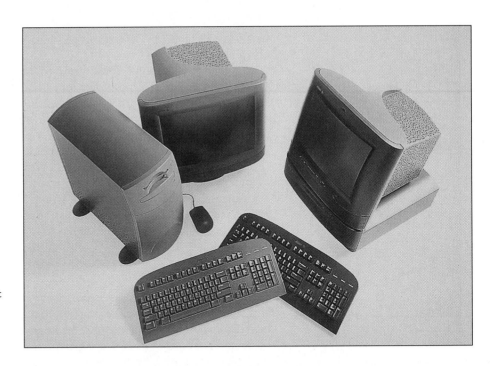

Acer Computer Company's strategic intent includes creating new products based on the microprocessor, including digital phones and simple low-priced fax machines.

ceutical partner." Phillips Petroleum Company seeks "to be the top performer in everything" the company does. Intel intends to become the premier building-block supplier to the computer industry. Microsoft believes that its "holy grail" is to provide the Yellow Pages for an electronic marketplace of on-line information systems. For years, Komatsu's strategic intent was "to catch up with and beat Caterpillar." Canon desires to "beat Xerox" and Honda strives to become a second Ford (a company it identified as a pioneer in the automobile industry). The CEO of Pep Boys does not believe in friendly competition; instead, he wants to dominate the competition and, by doing so, put them out of business. At Procter & Gamble (P&G), employees participate in a program the CEO calls "combat training." The program's intent is to focus on ways P&G can beat the competition. AlliedSignal wants to rank with General Electric and Merck as one of America's premier profitmakers. One way AlliedSignal seeks to achieve this strategic intent is to record six percent annual productivity improvements "forever." Chrysler Corporation's strategic intent is to be the world's premier car and light truck manufacturer by 2000.[74]

Because of its emotional edge, strategic intent may even be described metaphorically. In a recent annual report, Reebok International showed a series of pictures depicting an athlete crossing a high-jump bar. In her own handwriting, the athlete described her commitment to being the best and to winning:

> It's about raising the bar. I can jump higher. I know it. I can see it. I'm stronger, faster, I've learned more. The key is to focus, to concentrate on each basic element that goes into a jump. Jumping is my gift and it's a privilege to improve the gift. When everything works right, when you're focused and relaxed, it's kind of like flying. One thing that keeps you involved in jumping is that you are always trying to clear the next height. Even if you miss, you come away from every jump knowing you can go higher.[75]

The words of this athlete appear to reflect Reebok's intent to focus and concentrate on every part of its business in order to constantly improve its performance and, by doing so, achieve strategic competitiveness and earn above-average returns.

But it is not enough for a firm to know only its own strategic intent. Organizational effectiveness demands that we also identify our competitors' strategic intent. Only when others' intentions are understood can a firm become aware of competitors' resolve, stamina, and inventiveness (traits linked with effective strategic intents).[76] The success of some Japanese companies may be grounded in a keen and deep understanding of the strategic intent of customers, suppliers, partners, and competitors.[77] Worldwide competitors who understand the intentions and stamina of Japanese automobile manufacturers were probably not surprised in 1995 and 1996 when "all of Japan's leading automakers responded to the high yen by transferring more production to cheaper sites overseas, slashing costs and trimming jobs."[78]

■ Strategic Mission

As our discussion shows, strategic intent is *internally focused*. It is concerned with identifying the resources, capabilities, and core competencies on which a firm can base its strategic actions. Strategic intent reflects what a firm is capable of doing as a result of its core competencies and the unique ways they can be used to exploit a competitive advantage.

Strategic mission flows from strategic intent. Externally focused, the **strategic mission** is a statement of a firm's unique purpose and the scope of its operations in product and market terms.[79] A strategic mission provides general descriptions of the products a firm intends to produce and the markets it will serve using its internally based core competencies. The interdependent relationship between strategic intent and strategic mission is shown in Figure 1.5.

An effective strategic mission establishes a firm's individuality and is exciting, inspiring, and relevant to all stakeholders.[80] Together, strategic intent and strategic mission yield the insights required to formulate and implement the firm's strategies.

When a firm is strategically competitive and earning above-average returns, it has the capacity to satisfy its stakeholders' interests. The stakeholder groups a firm serves are examined next.

■ The *strategic mission* is a statement of a firm's unique purpose and the scope of its operations in product and market terms.

Figure 1.5

The Interdependent Relationship Between Strategic Intent and Strategic Mission

Strategic Intent
• Winning competitive battles through deciding how to leverage resources, capabilities, and core competencies

Strategic Mission
• An application of strategic intent in terms of products to be offered and markets to be served

■ Stakeholders

■ *Stakeholders* are the individuals and groups who can affect and are affected by the strategic outcomes achieved and who have enforceable claims on a firm's performance.

An organization is a system of primary stakeholder groups with whom it establishes and manages relationships.[81] **Stakeholders** are the individuals and groups who can affect and are affected by the strategic outcomes achieved and who have enforceable claims on a firm's performance.[82] Claims against an organization's performance are enforced through a stakeholder's ability to withhold participation essential to a firm's survival, competitiveness, and profitability.[83] Stakeholders continue to support an organization when its performance meets or exceeds their expectations.

Thus, organizations have dependency relationships with their stakeholders. However, firms are not equally dependent on all stakeholders at all times; as a consequence, every stakeholder does not have the same level of influence. The more critical and valued a stakeholder's participation is, the greater a firm's dependency on it. Greater dependence, in turn, results in more potential influence for the stakeholder over a firm's commitments, decisions, and actions. In one sense, the challenge strategists face is to either accommodate or find ways to insulate the organization from the demands of stakeholders controlling critical resources.[84]

■ Classification of Stakeholders

The parties involved with a firm's operations can be separated into three groups.[85] As shown in Figure 1.6, these groups are the *capital market stakeholders* (shareholders and the major suppliers of a firm's capital), the *product market stakeholders* (the firm's primary customers, suppliers, host communities, and unions representing the workforce), and the *organizational stakeholders* (all of a firm's employees, including both nonmanagerial and managerial personnel).

Each of these stakeholder groups expects those making strategic decisions in a firm to provide the leadership through which their valued objectives will be accomplished.[86] But these groups' objectives often differ from one another, sometimes placing managers in situations where trade-offs have to be made.

Grounded in laws governing private property and private enterprise, the most obvious stakeholders, at least in U.S. firms, are *shareholders*—those who have invested capital in a firm in the expectation of earning at least an average return on their investments. Shareholders want the return on their investment (and, hence, their wealth) to be maximized. This could be accomplished at the expense of investing in a firm's future. Gains achieved by reducing investment in research and development, for example, could be returned to shareholders (thereby increasing the short-term return on their investments). However, a short-term enhancement of shareholders' wealth can negatively affect the firm's future competitive ability. Sophisticated shareholders, with diversified portfolios, may sell their interests if a firm fails to invest in its future. Those making strategic decisions are responsible for a firm's survival in both the short and the long terms. Accordingly, it is in the interests of neither the organizational stakeholders nor the product market stakeholders for investments in the company to be unduly minimized.

In contrast to shareholders, customers prefer that investors receive a minimum return on their investments. As such, customers could have their interests maximized when the quality and reliability of a firm's products are improved, but without a price increase. High returns to customers might come at the expense of lower returns negotiated with capital market shareholders.

Figure 1.6

The Three Types of
Stakeholders

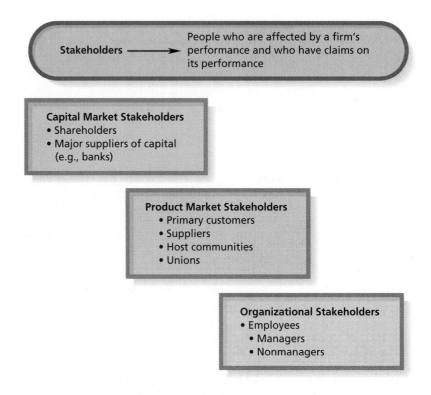

Because of potential conflicts, each firm is challenged to manage its stakeholders. When earning above-average returns, this challenge is lessened substantially. With the capability and flexibility provided by above-average returns, a firm can more easily satisfy all stakeholders simultaneously.

When earning only average returns, however, a firm may find the management of stakeholders to be more difficult. In these situations, trade-offs must be made. With average returns, a firm is unlikely to maximize the interests of all stakeholders. The objective becomes one of at least minimally satisfying each stakeholder. Trade-off decisions are made in light of how dependent the firm is on the support of the stakeholder groups. An example of how stakeholders can demand satisfaction of their claims on a firm's performance is provided in the next subsection. A firm earning below-average returns does not have the capacity to minimally satisfy all stakeholders. The managerial challenge in this case is to make trade-offs that minimize the amount of support lost from stakeholders.

Societal values influence the general weightings allocated among the three stakeholder groups. Although all three groups are served by firms in at least the major industrialized nations, the priorities in their service vary somewhat because of cultural differences. These differences are shown in the following commentary:

> In America . . . shareholders have a comparatively big say in the running of the enterprises they own; workers . . . have much less influence. In many European countries, shareholders have less say and workers more . . . In Japan . . . managers have been left alone to run their companies as they see fit—namely for the benefit of employees and of allied companies, as much as for shareholders.[87]

Thus, it is important that those responsible for managing stakeholder relationships in a country outside their native land use a global mind-set. A **global**

■ *A **global mind-set** is the capacity to appreciate the beliefs, values, behaviors, and business practices of individuals and organizations from a variety of regions and cultures.*

mind-set is the "capacity to appreciate the beliefs, values, behaviors, and business practices of individuals and organizations from a variety of regions and cultures."[88] Use of a global mind-set allows managers to better understand the realities and preferences that are a part of the world region and culture in which they are working.

In the next three subsections, additional information is presented about the stakeholder groups that firms manage.

Capital Market Stakeholders

Both shareholders and lenders expect a firm to preserve and enhance the wealth they have entrusted to it. The returns expected are commensurate with the degree of risk accepted with those investments (i.e., lower returns are expected with low-risk investments; higher returns are expected with high-risk investments).

If lenders become dissatisfied, they can impose stricter covenants on subsequent capital borrowing. Shareholders can reflect their dissatisfaction through several means, including the sale of their stock. When aware of potential or actual dissatisfactions among capital market stakeholders, a firm may respond to their concerns. The firm's response to dissatisfied stakeholders is affected by the nature of its dependency relationship with them (which, as noted earlier, is also influenced by a society's values). The greater and more significant the dependency relationship, the more direct and significant a firm's response will be. Citicorp's actions demonstrate this point. Citicorp was long known as a bank not clearly focused on profitability. In the words of one analyst, "Traditionally, (Citicorp) has been run for growth and for revenue generation and for the fiefdoms of its managers, at all levels. It has not been run for profitability."

Recently Citicorp's capital market stakeholders reacted to this means of operating the organization. Probably because of the importance of the bank's dependency relationship with these stakeholders, its strategists responded aggressively. During a banking conference with Solomon Brothers, Citicorp's chairman announced that one of the bank's key goals had become "to deliver shareholder value, on a sustained basis." In part, Citicorp made this commitment to retain its capital market stakeholders' support.[89] At least in the short run, this additional support for the capital market stakeholders may come at the expense of returns to other stakeholders.

Product Market Stakeholders

Initial observation of customers, suppliers, host communities, and unions representing workers might suggest little commonality among their interests. However, close inspection indicates that all four parties can benefit as firms engage in competitive battles. For example, depending on product and industry characteristics, marketplace competition may result in lower product prices being charged to a firm's customers and higher prices paid to its suppliers (the firm might be willing to pay higher supplier prices to ensure delivery of the types of goods and services linked with competitive success).

As noted in Chapter 4, customers, as stakeholders, demand reliable products at the lowest possible prices. Suppliers seek assured customers willing to pay the highest sustainable prices for the goods and services they receive. Host communities want companies willing to be long-term employers and providers of tax revenues, without placing excessive demands on public support services. Union officials are interested in secure jobs, under ideal working conditions, for employees they represent. Thus, product market stakeholders are generally satisfied when a firm's profit margin yields the lowest acceptable return to capital market stakeholders (i.e., the lowest return lenders and shareholders will accept and still retain their interests in the firm).

All product market stakeholders are important in a competitive business environment. However, in many firms, customers are being emphasized. Jack Welch, CEO of General Electric, is known for his position that satisfied customers are the only source of job security for the firm's organizational stakeholders. At AT&T, one of the company's top-level executives cautions employees to ask why customers (and/or competitors) are not being discussed after the first 15 minutes of any meeting. If they are not being talked about after a second 15-minute period, the executive believes people should leave the meeting.[90]

Rubbermaid recently tried to effectively manage its dependency relationship with Wal-Mart, its largest customer. In essence, the price at which Rubbermaid sells its products to Wal-Mart was at the heart of the issue. Determined to increase its sales and earnings 15 percent annually, Rubbermaid tried to pass along its higher raw materials costs to its customers. Wal-Mart, equally committed to its objective of continuously lowering prices to its customers, balked at Rubbermaid's actions, even refusing at one point to stock a number of Rubbermaid products in its stores.[91] The relationship between satisfaction of customers' needs and strategic competitiveness is examined in detail in Chapter 4.

Organizational Stakeholders

Employees, nonmanagerial and managerial, expect a firm to provide a dynamic, stimulating, and rewarding working environment. These stakeholders are usually satisfied working for a company that is growing and developing their skills, especially the skills required to be effective team members and to meet or exceed global work standards. Workers who learn how to productively use rapidly developing knowledge are thought to be critical to organizational success. In a collective sense, the education and skills of a nation's workforce may be its dominant competitive weapon in a global economy.[92]

In the next section, we describe the people responsible for the design and execution of strategic management processes. Various names are given to these people—top-level managers, executives, strategists, the top management team, and general managers are examples. Throughout this book, these names are used interchangeably. But, in all cases, they describe the work of persons responsible for designing and implementing a successful strategic management process.

As is discussed in Chapter 12, top-level managers can be a source of competitive advantage. The decisions and actions these people make to *combine* resources to create capabilities can also result in a competitive advantage.[93]

■ Organizational Strategists

Small organizations may have a single strategist. In many cases, this person owns the firm and is deeply involved with its daily operations. At the other extreme, large, diversified firms have many top-level managers. In addition to the CEO and other top-level officials (e.g., chief operating officer and chief financial officer), they have managers who are responsible for the performance of individual business units.

Typically, stakeholders have high expectations of top-level managers, particularly the CEO. For example, in the middle of 1993, Leonard Roberts was chosen as Radio Shack's new CEO. Because of his previous successes as chairman and CEO first of Arby's and then Shoney's, Roberts was expected to help Radio Shack complete the sale of its manufacturing businesses, improve its sagging returns margins, and increase its sales.

Based on these expectations, Roberts took bold actions during the first two and one-half years of his tenure at Radio Shack. More branded merchandise was added, the firm chose a new logo, a building plan was initiated that will add 500 stores in the chain by the year 2000, electronics repair and express gift services became a part of the chain's offerings to customers, and all job descriptions were discarded in favor of only two. Eliminating job descriptions was necessary, Roberts believed, to allow the firm to concentrate on its key strength—customer service. In his words, "We now have people who either serve customers or serve someone who does serve the customer."[94]

The early results suggest that Roberts is meeting stakeholders' expectations. During 1995 Radio Shack's returns grew at a double-digit rate, sales increased 9 percent, and the stock price of Radio Shack's parent company, Tandy Corporation, reached an all-time high.[95] The assignment of additional responsibilities to Mr. Roberts in January 1996 is another indicator of his effectiveness. In this new role, Roberts accepted the added responsibility for Tandy Retail Services, a separate unit providing distribution, repair, headquarters, customer service, and manufacturing support for Tandy's Radio Shack, Computer City, and Incredible Universe stores. Combining Radio Shack and Tandy Retail Services and placing them under Mr. Roberts' direction was expected to improve coordination between the two units.[96]

Top-level managers such as Leonard Roberts play critical roles in firms' efforts to achieve desired strategic outcomes. In fact, some believe that every organizational failure is actually a failure of those who hold the final responsibility for the quality and effectiveness of a firm's decisions and actions.[97]

Decisions for which strategists are responsible include how resources will be developed or acquired, at what price they will be obtained, and how they will be used. Managerial decisions also influence how information flows in a company, the strategies a firm chooses to implement, and the scope of its operations. Additionally, how strategists complete their work and their patterns of interactions with others significantly influence the way a firm does business and affect its ability to develop a competitive advantage.

How a firm does business is captured by the concept of organizational culture. Critical to strategic leadership practices and the implementation of strategies, **organizational culture** refers to the complex set of ideologies, symbols, and core values shared throughout the firm and that influences the way it conducts business. Thus, culture is the "social energy that drives—or fails to drive—the organization."[98] Andersen Consulting's core values include the requirement that employees attend company-sponsored training classes in professional attire, an expectation of hard work (up to 80 hours per week), and a willingness to work effectively with others in order to accomplish all tasks that are parts of the company-wide demanding workload.[99] These core values at Andersen Consulting provide a particular type of social energy that drives the firm's efforts. As we discuss in Chapters 2, 12, and 13, organizational culture is a potential source of competitive advantage.[100]

■ *Organizational culture refers to the complex set of ideologies, symbols, and core values shared throughout the firm and that influences the way it conducts business. It is the social energy that drives—or fails to drive—the organization.*

After evaluating available information and alternatives, top-level managers must frequently choose from among similarly attractive alternatives. The most effective strategists have the self-confidence necessary to select the best alternatives, allocate the required level of resources to them, and effectively explain to interested parties why certain alternatives were selected.[101]

When choosing among alternatives, strategists are accountable for treating employees, suppliers, customers, and others with fairness and respect. Preliminary evidence suggests that trust can be a source of competitive advantage, thereby supporting an organizational commitment to treat stakeholders fairly and with respect.[102] Nonetheless, firms cannot succeed without people who, following careful and sometimes difficult analyses, are willing to make tough decisions—the types of decisions that result in strategic competitiveness and above-average returns.[103]

■ The Work of Effective Strategists

Perhaps not surprisingly, hard work, thorough analyses, a willingness to be brutally honest, a penchant for always wanting the firm and its people to accomplish more, and common sense are prerequisites to an individual's success as a strategist.[104] John Sculley, former CEO of Apple Computer, tries to sleep an hour "here and there." In describing the reality of work in the 1990s, Sculley suggested that sleeping through the night is an outmoded remnant of the agrarian and industrial ages. "People don't live that way anymore," Sculley believes. "It's a 24-hour day, not an 8-to-5 day."[105]

In addition to the characteristics mentioned, effective strategists must be able to think clearly and ask many questions. Their strategic effectiveness increases as they find ways for others to also think and inquire about what a firm is doing and why. But, in particular, top-level managers are challenged to "think seriously and deeply . . . about the purposes of the organizations they head or functions they perform, about the strategies, tactics, technologies, systems and people necessary to attain these purposes and about the important questions that always need to be asked."[106] Through this type of thinking, strategists, in concert with others, increase the probability of identifying bold, innovative ideas. When these ideas lead to the development of core competencies—that is, when the ideas result in exploiting resources and capabilities that are valuable, rare, costly to imitate, and nonsubstitutable—they become the foundation for taking advantage of environmental opportunities.

Our discussion highlights the nature of a strategist's work. Instead of simplicity, the work is filled with ambiguous decision situations—situations for which the most effective solutions are not always easily determined. However, the opportunities suggested by this type of work are appealing. These jobs offer exciting chances to dream and to act. The following words, given as advice by his father to Steven J. Ross, the former chairman and co-CEO of Time-Warner, describe the excitement of a strategist's work: "There are three categories of people—the person who goes into the office, puts his feet up on his desk, and dreams for 12 hours; the person who arrives at 5 A.M. and works for 16 hours, never once stopping to dream; and the person who puts his feet up, dreams for one hour, then does something about those dreams."[107] The organizational term used for a dream that challenges and energizes a company is strategic intent.[108]

Strategists have opportunities to dream and to act, and the most effective ones provide a vision (strategic intent) to effectively elicit the help of others in creating a firm's competitive advantage. In the Strategic Focus on Packard Bell, we describe a company where strategists have dreamed and are taking actions to fulfill that dream.

■ The Strategic Management Process

The pursuit of competitiveness is at the heart of strategic management and the choices made when designing and using the strategic management process. Firms are in competition with one another—to gain access to the resources needed to earn above-average returns and to provide superior satisfaction of stakeholders' needs. Effective use of the interdependent parts of the strategic management process results in selecting the direction the firm will pursue and its choices to achieve the desired outcomes of strategic competitiveness and above-average returns.

As suggested by Figure 1.1, the strategic management process is intended to be a rational approach to help a firm respond effectively to the challenges of the new competitive landscape. This process calls for a firm to study its external (Chapter 2) and internal (Chapter 3) environments to identify its marketplace opportunities and threats and determine how to use its core competencies in the pursuit of desired strategic outcomes. With this knowledge, the firm forms its strategic intent so it can leverage its resources, capabilities, and core competencies and win battles in the global economy. Flowing from strategic intent, the strategic mission specifies, in writing, the products a firm intends to produce and the markets it will serve when leveraging its resources, capabilities, and competencies.

A firm's strategic inputs provide the foundation for its strategic actions to formulate and implement strategies. As strategic actions, both formulation and implementation are critical to achieving strategic competitiveness and earning above-average returns.

As suggested by the horizontal arrow linking the two types of strategic actions (see Figure 1.1), formulation and implementation must be integrated simultaneously. When formulating strategies, thought should be given to implementing them. When implementing, effective strategists seek feedback that allows improvement of the selected strategies. Thus, the separation of strategy formulation actions from strategy implementation actions in Figure 1.1 is for discussion purposes only. In reality, these two sets of actions allow the firm to achieve its desired strategic outcomes only when they are carefully integrated.

Figure 1.1 shows the topics we examine to study the interdependent parts of the strategic management process. In Part II of this book, actions related to the formulation of strategies are explained. The first set of actions studied is the formulation of strategies at the business-unit level (Chapter 4). A diversified firm, one competing in multiple product markets and businesses, has a business-level strategy for each distinct product market area. A company competing in a single product market has but one business-level strategy. In all instances, a business-level strategy describes a firm's actions designed to exploit its competitive advantage over rivals. But, as is explained in Chapter 5, business-level strategies are not formulated and implemented in isolation. Competitors respond to and try to anticipate each other's actions. Thus, the dynamics of competition are an important input to the formulation and implementation of all strategies, but especially to business-level strategies.

STRATEGIC FOCUS   Pursuing a Dream at Packard Bell

From October 1994 through March 1995, Packard Bell Electronics sold more personal computers (PCs) in the United States than any other firm. Unlike some of its competitors, Packard Bell sells almost exclusively to consumers through its relationships with retailers such as Best Buy, Wal-Mart, Sears, and Circuit City. A source of competitive advantage, these relationships were developed quietly in the 1980s, a time when other PC manufacturers concentrated on selling their products to firms that in turn sold to businesses. Now that consumers are buying PCs in record numbers, Packard Bell is uniquely positioned to reap the benefits. The company's dominant position with retailing firms (over half of Sears' shelf space for PCs is allocated to Packard Bell's products, for example) is linked to its dramatic sales increases (more than 120 percent from 1993 to 1994).

What accounts for this firm's sales success? A critical component may be the vision or strategic intent established by the company's CEO and the actions taken by his top-level managers (and others in the firm) to achieve it. In the words of Beny Alagem, Packard Bell's CEO, "The vision of the company is to listen to what the consumer wants and to provide an innovative product with the latest technology—to become the voice of the people when it comes to the PC." Moreover, the firm is committed to the position that customers will never be treated like second-class citizens.

Employees throughout Packard Bell also support the firm's vision. How has this been accomplished? In the words of the company's vice president for marketing: "We do not have a rah-rah meeting every morning where we do calisthenics and get injected with the spirit. It is the fact that when you get to the management team that is running all the groups, we all buy into the dream; we all buy into the vision."

However, Packard Bell faces competitive challenges. Hewlett-Packard, for example, has spent considerable time trying to determine what Packard Bell has done to develop its superior relationships with retailers. Facilitating Packard Bell's response to this challenge, and to those yet to come from other competitors, will be the vision shared by the firm's CEO, top-level managers, and employees.

Source: A. L. Sprout, 1995, Packard Bell, *Fortune*, June 12, 82–88.

For the diversified firm, corporate-level strategy (Chapter 6) is concerned with determining the businesses in which the company intends to compete, how resources are to be allocated among those businesses, and how the different units are to be managed. Other topics vital to strategy formulation, particularly in the diversified firm, include the acquisition of other companies and, as appropriate, the restructuring of the firm's portfolio of businesses (Chapter 7) and the selection of an international strategy that is consistent with the firm's resources, capabilities, and core competencies and its external opportunities (Chapter 8). Chapter 9 examines cooperative strategies. Increasingly important in a global economy, firms use these strategies to gain competitive advantage by forming advantageous relationships with other companies.

To examine more direct actions taken to implement strategies successfully, we consider several topics in Part III of this book. First, the different mechanisms used to govern firms are considered (Chapter 10). With demands for improved corporate governance voiced by various stakeholders, organizations are challenged to manage in ways that will result in the satisfaction of stakeholders' interests and the attainment of desired strategic outcomes. Finally, the matters of organizational structure and actions needed to control a firm's operations (Chapter 11), the patterns of strategic leadership appropriate for today's firms and competitive environments (Chapter 12), and the link among corporate entrepreneurship, innovation, and strategic competitiveness (Chapter 13) are addressed.

As noted earlier, competition requires firms to make choices to survive and succeed. Some of these choices are strategic in nature, including those of selecting a firm's strategic intent and strategic mission, determining which strategies to implement to offer a firm's products to customers, choosing an appropriate level of corporate scope, designing governance and organization structures that will properly coordinate a firm's work, and, through strategic leadership, encouraging and nurturing organizational innovation.[109] When made successfully, choices in terms of any one of these sets of actions have the potential to result in a competitive advantage for a firm over its rivals.

Primarily because they are related to how a firm interacts with its stakeholders, almost all strategic decisions have ethical dimensions.[110] Organizational ethics are revealed by an organization's culture; that is to say, a firm's strategic decisions are a product of the core values that are shared by most or all of a company's managers and employees. Especially in the turbulent and often ambiguous new competitive landscape, those making strategic decisions are challenged to recognize that their decisions do affect capital market, product market, and organizational stakeholders differently and to evaluate the ethical implications of their decisions. Relationships between organizational ethics and particular strategic decisions are described in virtually all of the remaining chapters of this book.

As you will discover, the strategic management process examined in this text calls for disciplined approaches to the development of competitive advantages. These approaches are the ones that will be the pathway through which firms are able to achieve strategic competitiveness and earn above-average returns in the latter part of the 1990s and into the twenty-first century. Mastery of this strategic management process will effectively serve readers and the organizations for whom they choose to work.

■ Summary

- Through their actions, firms seek strategic competitiveness and above-average returns. Strategic competitiveness is achieved when a firm has developed and learned how to implement a value-creating strategy successfully. Above-average returns—returns in excess of what investors expect to earn from other investments with similar levels of risk—allow a firm to simultaneously satisfy all of its stakeholders.

- A new competitive landscape—one in which the fundamental nature of competition is changing—has emerged. This landscape challenges those responsible for making effective strategic decisions to adopt a new mind-set, one that is global in nature. Through this mind-set, firms learn how to compete in what are highly turbulent and chaotic environments that produce disorder and a great deal of uncertainty. The

globalization of industries and their markets and rapid and significant technological changes are the two primary realities that have created the new competitive landscape. Globalization—the spread of economic innovations around the world and the political and cultural adjustments that accompany this diffusion—is likely to continue. Globalization also increases the standards of performance companies must meet or exceed to be strategically competitive in the new competitive landscape. Developing the ability to satisfy these global performance standards also helps firms compete effectively in their critical domestic markets.

- There are two major models of what a firm should do to earn above-average returns. The I/O model argues that the external environment is the *primary* determinant of the firm's strategies. Above-average returns are earned when the firm locates an attractive industry and successfully implements the strategy dictated by the characteristics of that industry. The resource-based model assumes that each firm is a collection of unique resources and capabilities that determines a firm's strategy. In this model, above-average returns are earned when the firm uses its valuable, rare, costly to imitate, and nonsubstitutable resources and capabilities (i.e., core competencies) to establish a competitive advantage over its rivals.

- Strategic intent and strategic mission are formed in light of the information and insights gained from studying a firm's internal and external environments. Strategic intent describes how resources, capabilities, and core competencies will be leveraged to achieve desired outcomes in the competitive environment. The strategic mission is an application of strategic intent. The mission is used to specify the product markets and customers a firm intends to serve through the leveraging of its resources, capabilities, and competencies.

- Stakeholders are those who can affect and are affected by a firm's strategic outcomes. Because a firm is dependent on the continuing support of stakeholders (shareholders, customers, suppliers, employees, host communities, etc.), they have enforceable claims on the company's performance. When earning above-average returns, a firm can adequately satisfy all stakeholders' interests. However, when earning only average returns, a firm's strategists must carefully manage all stakeholder groups in order to retain their support. A firm earning below-average returns must minimize the amount of support it loses from dissatisfied stakeholders.

- Organizational strategists are responsible for the design and execution of an effective strategic management process. Today, the most effective of these processes are grounded in ethical intentions and conduct. Strategists themselves, people with opportunities to dream and to act, can be a source of competitive advantage. The strategist's work demands decision trade-offs, often among attractive alternatives. Successful top-level managers work hard, conduct thorough analyses of situations, are brutally and consistently honest, and ask the right questions, of the right people, at the right time.

■ Review Questions

1. What are strategic competitiveness, competitive advantage, and above-average returns? Why are these terms important to those responsible for an organization's performance?

2. What *is* the challenge of strategic management?

3. What are the two factors that have created the new competitive landscape? What meaning does this landscape have for those interested in starting a business firm in the near future?

4. According to the I/O model, what should a firm do to earn above-average returns?

5. What does the resource-based model suggest a firm should do to achieve strategic competitiveness and earn above-average returns?

6. What are the differences between strategic intent and strategic mission? What is the value of the strategic intent and mission for a firm's strategic management process?

7. What are stakeholders? Why can they influence organizations? Do stakeholders always have the same amount of influence over an organization? Why or why not?

8. What words and terms should be used to describe the work of organizational strategists?

9. What are the parts of the strategic management process? How are these parts interrelated?

■ Application Discussion Questions

1. As suggested in the opening case, the outcomes from implementation of Ford 2000 are uncertain. Go to your library to study Ford Motor Company's current performance. Based on your reading, do you judge Ford 2000 to be a success? Why or why not?

2. Choose several firms in your local community with which you are familiar. Describe the new competitive landscape to them and ask for their feedback about how they anticipate the landscape will affect their operations during the next five years.

3. Select an organization (e.g., school, club, church) that is important to you. Describe the organization's stakeholders and the degree of influence you believe each has over the organization.

4. Are you a stakeholder at your university or college? If so, of what stakeholder group, or groups, are you a part?

5. Think of an industry in which you want to work. In your opinion, which of the three primary stakeholder groups is the most powerful in that industry today? Why?

6. Reject or agree with the following statement: "I think managers have little responsibility for the failure of business firms." Justify your view.

7. Do strategic intent and strategic mission have any meaning in your personal life? If so, describe it. Are your current actions being guided by an intent and mission? If not, why not?

■ Ethics Questions

1. Can a firm achieve a competitive advantage and thereby strategic competitiveness without acting ethically? Explain.

2. What are a firm's ethical responsibilities if it earns above-average returns?

3. What are some of the critical ethical challenges to firms competing in the global economy?

4. How should ethical considerations be included in analyses of a firm's internal and external environments?

5. Can ethical issues be integrated into a firm's strategic intent and mission? Explain.

6. What is the relationship between ethics and stakeholders?

7. What is the importance of ethics for organizational strategists?

Internet Exercises

Introduction to Activities

This section in each chapter consists of exercises and specific URLs designed to help you apply your learning through use of the Internet. Each chapter includes Internet exercises and a cohesion case. The Internet is described in the Appendix, which includes a summary of its beginnings and numerous ways to travel around in it. The Internet Exercise materials were developed by Paul Miesing of the State University of New York at Albany. All the information is collected from the Internet and other public sources and documents.

Communications

Much of your class communications may be through electronic mail. To accomplish this, your instructor might set up a Listserv or Newsgroup for your class and you can subscribe to the discussion group. Another possibility is for your instructor to establish a class mailing list, permitting you to post to the entire group by using one simple address. Alternatively, your instructor might decide to form smaller groups for the semester or quarter; you can form your own small teams to work with throughout the course. To help you decide who to work with, send a message to your classmates introducing yourself. Here are some things you might want to include in your initial posting:

- your major,
- outside and personal interests,
- other relevant background information (e.g., home town, current domicile),
- work experience including current job if applicable,
- extracurricular activities, and
- skills you can offer the group (e.g., library research, planning, writing, analytical, etc.).

Chapter Internet Exercises

These exercises require you to find information on the Internet to apply what you have learned in the chapter. Your instructor may want to specify whether you should complete these alone or with your group.

Cohesion Case

You will join a group to develop a strategic plan as you progress through the chapters. Begin by choosing with whom you might want to work for the entire semester or quarter and an industry you are interested in following, perhaps one you worked in or one in which you are interested in working when you graduate. Along with your teammates, you will apply the chapter lessons to one of the companies in that industry.

Chapter 1 Internet Exercise

Read "Strategic Planning," the cover story for the August 26, 1996 issue of *Business Week*:

- http://www.businessweek.com/1996/35/b34901.htm

The sub-title declared: "After a decade of gritty downsizing, Big Thinkers are back in corporate vogue." Can you find additional information that supports or critiques this view? Send your responses to the class via E-mail.

Cohesion Case

Send an E-mail message to your team members suggesting an industry to follow this semester. Next, discuss this industry by using the Internet to find information about several of its stakeholders. You might want to browse discussion groups, or go directly to a company's Home Page. Using E-mail to communicate with your teammates, determine the opportunities available in this industry. What do you think the new competitive landscape is, and how are companies coping with these changes? What strategies are they pursuing? Will any affect the industry? What strategies would be successful? Try to include a vision or mission, environment assessment, and action plan. With your group members, discuss if the plan accurately takes account of the stakeholders you identified.

◼ Notes

1. J. B. Barney, 1994, Commentary: A hierarchy of corporate resources, in P. Shrivastava, A. Huff, and J. Dutton (eds.), *Advances in Strategic Management* 10A, (Greenwich, Conn.: JAI Press), 119.

2. J. B. Barney, 1991, Firm resources and sustained competitive advantage, *Journal of Management* 17: 99–120.

3. D. J. Collis and C. A. Montgomery, 1995, Competing on resources: Strategy in the 1990s, *Harvard Business Review* 73, no. 4: 118–128.

4. R. M. Grant, 1995, *Contemporary Strategy Analysis*, 2nd ed. (Cambridge, Mass.: Blackwell Business), 138–140.

5. R. A. D'Aveni, 1995, Coping with hypercompetition: Utilizing the new 7S's framework, *Academy of Management Executive* IX, no. 3: 54; D. Schendel, 1994, Introduction to the Summer 1994 special issue—Strategy: Search for new paradigms, *Strategic Management Journal* (Special Summer Issue) 15: 3.

6. P. Shrivastava, 1995, Ecocentric management for a risk society, *Academy of Management Review* 20: 119.

7. R. P. Rumelt, D. E. Schendel, and D. J. Teece (eds.), 1994, *Fundamental Issues in Strategy* (Boston: Harvard Business School Press), 527–530; A. D. Meyer, 1991, What is strategy's distinctive competence? *Journal of Management* 17: 821–833.

8. Schendel, Introduction to the Summer 1994 special issue, 1–3.

9. Rumelt, Schendel, and Teece, *Fundamental Issues in Strategy*, 534–547.

10. M. E. Porter, 1994, Toward a dynamic theory of strategy, in R. P. Rumelt, D. E. Schendel, and D. J. Teece (eds.), *Fundamental Issues in Strategy* (Boston: Harvard Business School Press), 423–425.

11. A. B. Fisher, 1995, Creating stockholder wealth, *Fortune*, December 11, 105–106; T. P. Pare, 1995, The new champ of wealth creation, *Fortune*, September 18, 131–132.

12. C. J. Loomis, 1993, Dinosaurs, *Fortune*, May 3, 36–42.

13. *The State of Small Business: A Report of the President*, 1994, Washington, D.C., 41–42.

14. Rumelt, Schendel, and Teece, *Fundamental Issues in Strategy*, 530.

15. Loomis, Dinosaurs, 36.

16. H. Dawley and K. Naughton, 1995, Ford's bumpy odyssey in Europe, *Business Week*, November 20, 47.

17. Associated Press, 1995, Automakers show off vehicles made for Japan, *Dallas Morning News*, October 27, D10.

18. A. Taylor III, 1995, Japan's carmakers have a problem, *Fortune*, November 27, 36.

19. K. Naughton, P. Engardio, K. Kerwin, and D. Roberts, 1995, How GM got the inside track in China, *Business Week*, November 6, 56–57.

20. Toyota, 1995, *Annual Report*, 8.

21. M. Leach, 1995, Ford Motor, *Value Line*, June 16, 104; A. Taylor III, 1995, Ford's really BIG leap at the future: It's risky, it's worth it, and it may not work, *Fortune*, September 18, 134–

144; Ford Motor, 1995, *Standard & Poor's Stock Reports*, August 8, 917.

22. A. S. Grove, 1995, A high-tech CEO updates his views on managing and careers, *Fortune*, September 18, 229–230; S. Sherman, 1993, The secret to Intel's success, *Fortune*, February 8, 14.

23. This section is based largely on information featured in two sources: R. A. Bettis and M. A. Hitt, 1995, The new competitive landscape, *Strategic Management Journal* (Special Summer Issue) 16: 7–19; M. A. Hitt, B. W. Keats, and S. M. DeMarie, 1995, Navigating in the new competitive landscape: Building competitive advantage and strategic flexibility in the 21st century, paper presented at the 1995 Strategic Management Society conference.

24. S. Kotha, 1995, Mass customization: Implementing the emerging paradigm for competitive advantage, *Strategic Management Journal* 16: 21–42.

25. Associated Press, 1995, Fox-TCI to challenge ESPN, *Dallas Morning News*, November 1, D1, D11.

26. C. K. Prahalad, 1995, forward in R. Ashkenas, D. Ulrich, T. Jick, and S. Kerr (eds.), *The Boundaryless Organization: Breaking the Chains of Organizational Structure*, (San Francisco: Jossey-Bass Publishers), xiii-xvii.

27. D'Aveni, Coping with hypercompetition, 46.

28. K. Ohmae, 1995, Letter from Japan, *Harvard Business Review* 73, no. 3: 154–163; P. Gyllenhammar, 1993, The global economy: Who will lead next? *Journal of Accountancy* 175: 61–67.

29. J. C. Madonna, 1992, If it's markets you need, look abroad, *New York Times Forum*, January 5, F13.

30. T. A. Stewart, 1993, The new face of American power, *Fortune*, July 26, 70–86.

31. L. C. Thurow, 1992, Who owns the twenty-first century? *Sloan Management Review* 33, no. 3: 5–17.

32. Whirlpool Corp., 1995, *Standard & Poor Stock Reports*, August 31, 2474; Whirlpool Corp., 1995, *Value Line*, June 16, 135; S. Tully, 1995, So, Mr. Bossidy, we know you can cut. Now show us how to grow, *Fortune*, August 21, 70–80.

33. The big picture, 1995, *Business Week*, November 13, 8.

34. B. Bremner and E. H. Updike, 1995, "Made in America" isn't the kiss of death anymore, *Business Week*, November 13, 62; J. Aley, 1995, New lift for the U.S. export boom, *Fortune*, November 13, 73–78; G. Koretz, 1995, A turnaround in U.S. trade? *Business Week*, November 6, 32.

35. P. Krugman, 1994, Location and competition: Notes on economic geography, in R. P. Rumelt, D. E. Schendel, and D. J. Teece (eds.), *Fundamental Issues in Strategy*, (Boston: Harvard Business School Press), 463–493; W. W. Lewis and M. Harris, 1992, Why globalization must prevail, *McKinsey Quarterly* 2: 114–131.

36. Crain News Service, 1995, Toyota plans to build T100 in U.S., boost plants' autonomy, *Dallas Morning News*, October 28, D39; M. G. Harvey, 1993, "Buy American": Economic concept or economic slogan? *Business Horizons* 36, no. 3: 40–46.

37. Lewis and Harris, Why globalization must prevail, 115; J. Newmith and E. Jaspin, 1993, Japan's patents pending no more, *Waco Tribune-Herald*, January 24, A1, A10.

38. D. White, 1995, End to U.S.-European barriers trade urged, *Dallas Morning News*, November 9, D10.

39. R. M. Kanter, 1995, Thriving locally in the global economy, *Harvard Business Review* 73, no. 5: 151–160; M. E. Porter and C. van der Linde, 1995, Green and competitive: Ending the stalemate, *Harvard Business Review* 73, no. 5: 120–134.

40. H. J. Aaron, 1992, Comments included in a debate called "How real is America's decline?" *Harvard Business Review* 70, no. 5: 172.

41. J. Birkinshaw, A. Morrison, and J. Hulland, 1995, Structural and competitive determinants of a global integration strategy, *Strategic Management Journal* 16: 637–655.

42. Grove, A high-tech CEO, 229.

43. D. Kirkpatrick, 1995, Sony and Intel plan to make a home PC that will take on the industry, *Fortune*, December 11, 27.

44. A. L. Sprout, 1995, The Internet inside your company, *Fortune*, November 27, 161–168.

45. Liberation, courtesy of the Internet, 1995, *Business Week*, December 4, 136; Sprout, The Internet inside your company, 161–168.

46. A. Goldstein, 1995, Microsoft may not always be king of the hill, Gates says, *Dallas Morning News*, November 24, D4.

47. T. A. Stewart, 1995, Mapping corporate brainpower, *Fortune*, October 30, 209–212; T. A. Stewart, 1995, Trying to grasp the intangible, *Fortune*, October 2, 157–161; T. A. Stewart, 1995, The information wars: What you don't know will hurt you, *Fortune*, June 12, 119–121.

48. C. A. Bartlett and S. Ghoshal, 1995, Changing the role of top management: Beyond systems to people, *Harvard Business Review* 73, no. 3: 141.

49. T. A. Stewart, 1995, Getting real about brainpower, *Fortune*, November 27, 201–203.

50. R. Sanchez, 1995, Strategic flexibility in product competition, *Strategic Management Journal* (Special Summer Issue) 16: 135–159.

51. Kotha, Mass customization, 21.

52. E. Schonfeld, 1995, Aging aircraft give maintenance firm a lift, *Fortune*, September 18, 245.

53. Our discussion of the I/O model is informed by the following works: Barney, Firm resources, 99–120; A. A. Lado, N. G. Boyd, and P. Wright, 1992, A competency based model of sustainable competitive advantage: Toward a conceptual integration, *Journal of Management* 18: 77–91; R. M. Grant, 1991, The resource-based theory of competitive advantage: Implications for strategy formulation, *California Management Review* 33 (Spring): 114–135.

54. D. Schendel, 1994, Introduction to competitive organizational behavior: Toward an organizationally-based theory of competitive advantage, *Strategic Management Journal* (Special Winter Issue) 15: 2.

55. A. Seth and H. Thomas, 1994, Theories of the firm: Implications for strategy research, *Journal of Management Studies* 31: 165–191.

56. Seth and Thomas, Theories of the firm, 169–173.

57. Porter, Toward a dynamic theory of strategy, 428.

58. M. E. Porter, 1985, *Competitive Advantage* (New York: Free Press); M. E. Porter, 1980, *Competitive Strategy* (New York: Free Press).

59. J. R. Williams, 1994, Strategy and the search for rents: The evolution of diversity among firms, in R. P. Rumelt, D. E. Schendel, and D. J. Teece (eds.), *Fundamental Issues in Strategy* (Boston: Harvard Business School Press), 229–246.

60. K. Cool and I. Dierickx, 1994, Commentary: Investments in strategic assets: Industry and firm-level perspectives, in P. Shrivastava, A. Huff, and J. Dutton (eds.), *Advances in Strategic Management* 10A (Greenwich, Conn.: JAI Press), 35–44; Rumelt, Schendel, and Teece, *Fundamental Issues in Strategy,* 553; R. Rumelt, 1991, How much does industry matter? *Strategic Management Journal* 12: 167–185.

61. Barney, Commentary, 113–125.

62. Barney, Firm resources; Grant, Resource-based theory; Meyer, What is strategy's distinctive competence?

63. Grant, Resource-based theory, 119–120.

64. Rumelt, Schendel, and Teece, *Fundamental Issues in Strategy,* 31.

65. P. J. H. Schoemaker and R. Amit, 1994, Investment in strategic assets: Industry and firm-level perspectives, in P. Shrivastava, A. Huff, and J. Dutton (eds.), *Advances in Strategic Management* 10A (Greenwich, Conn.: JAI Press), 9.

66. J. B. Barney, 1995, Looking inside for competitive advantage, *Academy of Management Executive* IX, no. 4: 56.

67. Barney, Firm resources.

68. Lado, Boyd, and Wright, A competency based model; Grant, Resource-based theory; M. A. Hitt and R. D. Ireland, 1986, Relationships among corporate level distinctive competencies, diversification strategy, corporate structure, and performance, *Journal of Management Studies* 23: 401–416.

69. G. Hamel and C. K. Prahalad, 1989, Strategic intent, *Harvard Business Review* 67, no. 3: 63–76.

70. G. Hamel and C. K. Prahalad, 1994, *Competing for the Future* (Boston: Harvard Business School Press), 129–136; S. Sherman, 1995, Stretch goals: The dark side of asking for miracles, *Fortune,* November 13, 231–232.

71. L. Kraar, 1995, Acer's edge: PCs to go, *Fortune,* October 30, 190–192.

72. Hamel and Prahalad, Strategic intent, 66.

73. S. Sherman, 1993, The secret to Intel's success, 14.

74. Unocal Corporation, 1994, *Annual Report,* 4; Phillips Petroleum Company, 1994, *Health, Environmental and Safety Report,* 4; Eli Lilly and Company, 1993, *Annual Report to Shareholders,* 1; M. Loeb, 1993, It's time to invest and build, *Fortune,* February 22, 4; S. Sherman, 1993, The new computer revolution, *Fortune,* June 14, 56–84; C. A. Bartlett and S. Ghoshal, 1995, Changing the role of top management: Beyond systems to people, *Harvard Business Review* 73, no. 3: 136–137; A. Taylor III, 1993, How to murder

the competition, *Fortune,* February 22, 87–90; Z. Schiller, 1992, No more Mr. nice guy at P&G—not by a long shot, *Business Week,* February 3, 54–56; S. Tully, 1995, So, Mr. Bossidy, we know you can cut, 73; AlliedSignal, 1995, *Value Line,* August 11, 1357.

75. Reebok, 1992, *Annual Report,* 2–12.

76. Hamel and Prahalad, Strategic intent, 64.

77. M. A. Hitt, D. Park, C. Hardee, and B. B. Tyler, 1995, Understanding strategic intent in the global marketplace, *Academy of Management Executive* IX, no. 2: 12–19.

78. Associated Press, 1995, Let the good times roll, *Dallas Morning News,* October 26, D10.

79. R. D. Ireland and M. A. Hitt, 1992, Mission statements: Importance, challenge, and recommendations for development, *Business Horizons* 35, no. 3: 34–42.

80. A. D. DuBrin and R. D. Ireland, 1993, *Management and Organization,* 2nd ed. (Cincinnati, Ohio: Southwestern), 140.

81. M. B. E. Clarkson, 1995, A stakeholder framework for analyzing and evaluating corporate social performance, *Academy of Management Review* 20: 92–117; T. Donaldson and L. E. Preston, 1995, The stakeholder theory of the corporation: Concepts, evidence, and implications, *Academy of Management Review* 20: 65–91; T. M. Jones, 1995, Instrumental stakeholder theory: A synthesis of ethics and economics, *Academy of Management Review* 20: 404–437.

82. Clarkson, A stakeholder framework; R. E. Freeman, 1984, *Strategic Management: A Stakeholder Approach* (Boston: Pitman), 53–54.

83. G. Donaldson and J. W. Lorsch, 1983, *Decision Making at the Top: The Shaping of Strategic Direction* (New York: Basic Books), 37–40.

84. Rumelt, Schendel, and Teece, *Fundamental Issues in Strategy,* 33.

85. Donaldson and Lorsch, *Decision Making at the Top,* 37.

86. M. J. Polonsky, 1995, Incorporating the natural environment in corporate strategy: A stakeholder approach, *Journal of Business Strategies* 12: 151–168.

87. Donaldson and Preston, The stakeholder theory of the corporation, citing a quote from *The Economist,* 1994, Corporate governance special section, September 11, 52–62.

88. Don't be an ugly-American manager, 1995, *Fortune,* October 16, 225.

89. C. J. Loomis, 1993, The Reed that Citicorp leans on, *Fortune,* July 12, 90–93.

90. D. Kirkpatrick, 1993, Could AT&T rule the world? *Fortune,* May 17, 55–66.

91. L. Smith, Rubbermaid goes thump, *Fortune,* October 2, 89–104.

92. New paths to success, 1995, *Fortune,* June 12, 90–94; T. A. Stewart, 1995, Mapping corporate brainpower, 209–211; S. Lee, 1993, Peter Drucker's fuzzy future, *Fortune,* May 17, 136.

93. D. Lei, M. A. Hitt, and R. Bettis, 1996, Dynamic core competences through meta-learning and strategic context, *Journal of Management* 22: 547–567.

94. D. Olenick, 1995, Back to the future: Radio Shack returns to customer-service roots, *HFN,* September 18, 1.

95. Olenick, Back to the future; Tandy Corp., 1995, *Standard & Poor's Stock Reports,* September 12, 2191; Will new look at Radio Shack help sales? 1995, *Investor's Business Daily,* August 22, A3; T. S. Threlkeld and M. Wrolstad, 1993, Restaurant exec to head Radio Shack, *Dallas Morning News,* July 8, D1, D2.

96. J. Mitchell, 1995, Radio Shack chief named Tandy president, *Dallas Morning News,* December 19, D15.

97. J. O. Moller, 1991, The competitiveness of U.S. industry: A view from the outside, *Business Horizons* 34, no. 6: 27–34.

98. M. A. Hitt and R. E. Hoskisson, 1991, Strategic competitiveness, in L. W. Foster (ed.), *Advances in Applied Business Strategy* (Greenwich, Conn.: JAI Press), 1–36.

99. Bartlett and Ghoshal, Changing the role of top management, 139.

100. K. Weigelt and C. Camerer, 1988, Reputation and corporate strategy, *Strategic Management Journal* 9: 443–454; J. B. Barney, 1986, Organizational culture: Can it be a source of sustained competitive advantage? *Academy of Management Review* 11: 656–665.

101. R. D. Ireland, M. A. Hitt, and J. C. Williams, 1992, Self-confidence and decisiveness: Prerequisites for effective management in the 1990s, *Business Horizons* 35, no. 1: 36–43.

102. R. C. Mayer, J. H. Davis, and F. D. Schoorman, 1995, An integrative model of organizational trust, *Academy of Management Review* 20: 709–734; J. H. Davis, F. D. Schoorman, and R. C. Mayer, 1995, The trusted general manager and firm performance: Empirical evidence of a strategic advantage, paper presented at the Strategic Management Society conference; J. B. Barney and M. H. Hansen, 1994, Trustworthiness as a source of competitive advantage, *Strategic Management Journal* 15: 175–190.

103. G. Belis, 1993, Beware the touchy-feely business book, *Fortune,* June 28, 147; A. E. Pearson, 1988, Tough-minded ways to get innovative, *Harvard Business Review* 66, no. 3: 99–106.

104. J. S. Harris, 1995, Bill Dodson, *Dallas Morning News,* September 3, H1, H2; Tully, So, Mr. Bossidy, we know you can cut, 70–80; K. W. Chilton, M. E. Warren, and M. L. Weidenbaum (eds.), 1990, *American Manufacturing in a Global Market* (Boston: Kluwer Academic Publishers), 72.

105. A. Deutschman, 1993, Odd man out, *Fortune,* July 26, 42.

106. T. Leavitt, 1991, *Thinking About Management* (New York: Free Press), 9.

107. M. Loeb, 1993, Steven J. Ross, 1927–1992, *Fortune,* January 25, 4.

108. Hamel and Prahalad, *Competing for the Future,* 129.

109. Rumelt, Schendel, and Teece, *Fundamental Issues in Strategy,* 9–10.

110. Our discussion of ethics and the strategic management process, both here and in other chapters, is informed by materials appearing in J. S. Harrison and C. H. St. John, 1994, *Strategic Management of Organizations and Stakeholders: Theory and Cases* (St. Paul, Minn.: West Publishing Company).

The External Environment: Opportunities, Threats, Industry Competition, and Competitor Analysis

After reading this chapter, you should be able to:

1. Explain the importance of studying and understanding the external environment.
2. Define the general and industry environments.
3. Discuss the four activities of the external environmental analysis process.
4. Name and describe the six segments of the general environment.
5. Identify the five competitive forces and explain how they determine an industry's profit potential.
6. Define strategic groups and describe how they influence a firm's competitive actions.
7. Describe what firms need to know about their competitors and different methods used to collect competitive intelligence.

Rubbermaid's Struggle to Remain at the Top

Rubbermaid

During the last 10 years, Rubbermaid has been ranked among the top 10 in *Fortune's* most admired companies list. Furthermore, during 1994 and 1995, it was ranked the number one company in corporate America. However, recently, Rubbermaid has begun to experience a number of problems. It is being confronted by several new competitors, trying to placate a number of its retail customers, in particular, Wal-Mart, and trying to achieve its extraordinary financial goals of 15 percent annual growth in revenues and profits. Unfortunately, in recent times, Rubbermaid has not been able to manage these challenges effectively. Thus, its ranking in *Fortune's* most admired companies list fell to number three (still a high ranking) in 1996.

Rubbermaid has experienced major increases in the cost of resin (an important raw material in many of its products) and attempted to pass on these costs with large price increases to its customers. Wal-Mart was particularly angered by the large price increases, because it is a huge customer of Rubbermaid. In response, Wal-Mart refused to stock a number of Rubbermaid products and deleted Rubbermaid's products from its promotional materials provided to customers. Instead, Wal-Mart featured Sterilite, one of Rubbermaid's prominent new competitors, in its promotional materials. Wal-Mart executives were particularly angered when they learned that another Rubbermaid customer was paying lower prices for the same products being purchased by Wal-Mart. Given that Wal-Mart is Rubbermaid's biggest customer, with 2,180 stores and accounting for more than 15 percent of Rubbermaid's total household-product sales, Wal-Mart executives' anger seems well founded.

New, stronger competitors are beginning to take away some of Rubbermaid's market share. Rubbermaid has largely ignored other housewares manufacturers because at one time these competitors had few advantages about which Rubbermaid had to worry. However, several of these rivals have grown and have improved in many product and service areas in the last few years. When Rubbermaid passed on the huge price increases to its customers, its competitors had only small price increases, deciding instead to reduce their profits rather than pass on the full cost of the raw materials. This may have been a major tactical error on Rubbermaid's part. Rubbermaid's sales decreased and its competitors' sales increased. A number of retailers did not believe that they could pass on the higher prices to their consumers and gave more shelf space to Rubbermaid's competitors. Additional Rubbermaid problems include chronic late deliveries to major customers, including Wal-Mart, and lagging development of computer systems that automatically replenish retailers' supplies based on actual sales rather than forecasts. In other words, Rubbermaid has not been servicing its customers as well as its competitors have.

Given these problems, the company's financial targets of 15 percent annual growth in revenues and in profits seem unrealistic. Although these targets have been met in many years in the recent decade, they have not been achieved in the last few years. Furthermore, its goal of doubling in size by the year 2000 would require Rubbermaid to grow from $2.2 billion to $4.4 billion in sales in five years. This also seems unrealistic. Former Rubbermaid managers and external analysts believe that the company has pushed its managers too hard in trying to maintain its significant growth and to achieve these challenging targets. One analyst suggested that "Rubbermaid is a company that has strained so hard it has pulled a muscle." In 1993, sales grew by 8 percent and by 10 percent in 1994. Earnings grew 15 percent in 1993, but only 8 percent in 1994. Thus, Rubbermaid is experiencing some significant problems.

The current CEO, Wolfgang R. Schmitt, is counting on international sales to boost the company's overall growth and meet its short-term and long-term sales and earnings targets. However, outside analysts suggest that Rubbermaid does not have the global exposure and experience to achieve its targets internationally. It had performed so well domestically in the United States that it paid little attention to its international operations. Alternatively, Rubbermaid's long-term prospects in Europe and Asia look positive.

It should be noted that Rubbermaid is a formidable force in its industry and is strong financially. At the end of 1994, it had more than $150 million in cash and marketable assets and only $11 million in debt. Furthermore, it remains a highly innovative company, introducing approximately 400 new products annually. Joint ventures and acquisitions of smaller companies have expanded its annual sales by more than $180 million in 1994 and it intends to become more efficient by cutting its annual costs by $335 million by 1997. Thus, even though it has had significant turnover in its executive ranks in the last few years, there remains significant potential for Rubbermaid to be a high performing company into the twenty-first century.

Source: A. B. Fisher, 1996, Corporate reputations, *Fortune,* March 6, 90–93; L. Smith, 1995, Rubbermaid goes thump, *Fortune,* October 2, 90–104; Z. Schiller, 1995, The revolving door at Rubbermaid, *Business Week,* September 18, 80–83; M.H. Gerstein, 1995, Rubbermaid, *Value Line,* July 21, 970.

Research has shown that the external environment plays a significant role in the growth and profitability of firms,[1] as dramatically shown in the case of Rubbermaid. Rubbermaid's success, increases in sales and profits, and its market share are being eroded by forces in its external environment. In particular, Rubbermaid's problems with customers such as Wal-Mart and significant new competitors have begun to erode its market share and its ability to meet annual targets for growth in profits and sales. To regain its competitive advantages and remain a competitively viable force over the long term, Rubbermaid will have to pay significantly more attention to its external environment, particularly its customers and competitors. This chapter focuses on how firms should analyze and understand their external environment, as shown in Figure 1.1 in Chapter 1.

As noted in the first chapter, the environmental conditions currently facing firms are different from those of past decades. Many companies now compete in global, rather than domestic, markets. Technological changes and the explosion in information gathering and processing capabilities demand more timely and effective competitive actions and responses.[2] The rapid sociological changes occurring in many countries affect labor practices and the nature of products demanded by increasingly diverse consumers. Governmental policies and laws affect where and how firms choose to compete. Firms must be aware of and understand the implications of these environmental realities to compete effectively in the global economy.

In high-performing, strategically competitive organizations, managers seek patterns to help them understand their external environment, which may be different from what they expect.[3] It is vital for decision makers to have a precise and accurate understanding of their company's competitive position. For example, one of the first decisions Louis Gerstner, Jr., made, when chosen as IBM's CEO from outside the firm, was to visit with each member of IBM's senior management team. A key reason for these visits was to learn about each business area's competitive standing in the industry (or industries) in which it competed.[4] Strategic decision makers know that understanding their firm's external environment

Figure 2.1

The External Environment

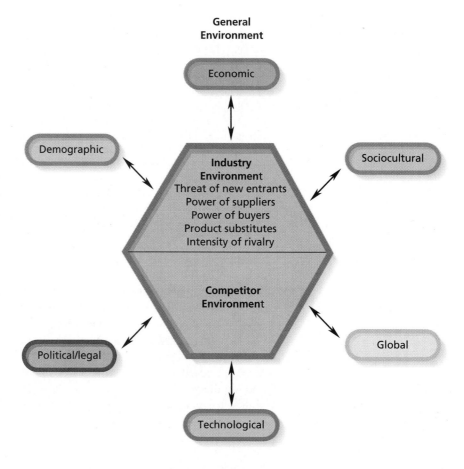

helps to improve a company's competitive position, increase operational efficiency, and win battles in the global economy.[5]

Through a variety of means, firms attempt to understand their external environments by gaining information about competitors, customers, and other stakeholders in the external environment. In particular, firms are attempting to gain information in order to build their own base of knowledge and capabilities.[6] These firms may attempt to imitate the capabilities of able competitors or even successful firms in other industries or build new knowledge and capabilities to develop a competitive advantage. Based on this new information, knowledge, and capabilities, firms may take actions to buffer environmental effects on them or to build relationships with stakeholders in that environment.[7] To build knowledge and firm capabilities and to take actions that buffer or build bridges to external stakeholders, they must effectively analyze their external environment.

In this chapter, we discuss the external environment. Through an integrated understanding of the external and the internal environments, firms gain the information needed to understand the present and predict the future.[8] As shown in Figure 2.1, a firm's external environment has three major components—the general, industry, and competitor environments.

■ The General, Industry, and Competitor Environments

■ *The **general environment** is composed of elements in the broader society that can influence an industry and the firms within it.*

■ *The **industry environment** is the set of factors—the threat of new entrants, suppliers, buyers, product substitutes, and the intensity of rivalry among competitors—that directly influences a firm and its competitive actions and responses.*

The **general environment** is composed of elements in the broader society that can influence an industry and the firms within it.[9] We group these elements into environmental *segments* called the demographic, economic, political/legal, sociocultural, technological, and global segments. Examples of *elements* analyzed in these six segments are shown in Table 2.1. Firms cannot directly control these elements. Instead, the strategic challenge is to understand each segment and its implications so appropriate strategies can be formulated and implemented.

The **industry environment** is the set of factors—the threat of new entrants, suppliers, buyers, product substitutes, and the intensity of rivalry among competitors—that directly influences a firm and its competitive actions and responses. In total, the interactions among these five factors determine an industry's profit potential. The challenge is to locate a position within an industry where a firm can favorably influence these factors or where it can successfully defend against their influence. The greater a firm's capacity to favorably influence its industry environment, the greater the likelihood that it will earn above-average returns.

We also discuss in this chapter how companies gather and interpret information about their competitors. Called *competitor analysis,* a firm's understanding of its current competitors complements the insights provided by study of the general and industry environments. In combination, the results of these three analyses influence the development of a firm's strategic intent, strategic mission, and strategic actions.

Table 2.1 The General Environment: Segments and Elements		
Demographic Segment	■ Population size ■ Age structure ■ Geographic distribution	■ Ethnic mix ■ Income distribution
Economic Segment	■ Inflation rates ■ Interest rates ■ Trade deficits or surpluses ■ Budget deficits or surpluses	■ Personal savings rate ■ Business savings rates ■ Gross domestic product
Political/Legal Segment	■ Antitrust laws ■ Taxation laws ■ Deregulation philosophies	■ Labor training laws ■ Educational philosophies and policies
Sociocultural Segment	■ Women in the workforce ■ Workforce diversity ■ Attitudes about quality of work life	■ Concerns about the environment ■ Shifts in work and career preferences ■ Shifts in preferences regarding product and service characteristics
Technological Segment	■ Product innovations ■ Process innovations ■ Applications of knowledge	■ Focus of private and government-supported R&D expenditures ■ New communication technologies
Global Segment	■ Important political events ■ Critical global markets	■ Newly industrialized countries ■ Different cultural and institutional attributes

Analysis of the general environment is focused on the future; analysis of the industry environment is focused on understanding the factors and conditions influencing a firm's profitability; and analysis of competitors is focused on predicting the dynamics of competitors' actions, responses, and intentions. Although each analysis is discussed separately, a firm's performance improves when the insights from analyses of the general environment, the industry environment, and competitors are integrated.

The process of external environmental analysis is discussed next.

■ External Environmental Analysis

■ **Opportunities** *are conditions in the general environment that may help a company achieve strategic competitiveness.*

■ **Threats** *are conditions in the general environment that may hinder a company's efforts to achieve strategic competitiveness.*

Most firms face external environments that are growing more turbulent, complex, and global, which makes them increasingly difficult to interpret.[10] To cope with what are often ambiguous and incomplete environmental data and to increase their understanding of the general environment, firms engage in a process called external environmental analysis. This process includes four activities—scanning, monitoring, forecasting, and assessing (see Table 2.2)—and should be conducted on a continuous basis.[11]

An important objective of studying the general environment is identification of opportunities and threats. **Opportunities** are conditions in the general environment that may help a company achieve strategic competitiveness. **Threats** are conditions in the general environment that may hinder a company's efforts to achieve strategic competitiveness. In essence, external environmental opportunities represent *possibilities,* while threats are potential *constraints.*

To analyze the general environment, several sources are used. Included among these are a wide variety of printed materials (e.g., trade publications, newspapers, business publications, the results of academic research and of public polls); attendance and participation in trade shows; the content of conversations with suppliers, customers, and employees of public-sector organizations; and even business-related "rumors" provided by many different people.[12] Additional sources of information and data include individuals in "boundary spanning" positions who interact with external constituents such as salespersons, purchasing managers, public relations directors, and human resource managers. Decision makers should verify the validity and reliability of the sources on which their environmental analyses are based.[13]

■ Scanning

Scanning entails the study of all segments in the general environment. Through scanning, firms identify early signals of potential changes in the general environment and detect changes that are already under way.[14] When scanning, analysts typically deal with ambiguous, incomplete, and unconnected information and data. Environmental scanning has been found critically important for effective performance in firms that operate in highly volatile environments.[15]

In the 1990s, analysts in financial institutions are observing several changes in the general environment. First, some government officials and security analysts believe a combination of personal savings, private pensions, and Social Security income may be insufficient to support U.S. baby boomers' (those born between 1947 and 1964) retirement. The first of the baby boomer generation will retire in 2011. These retirements will push the total number of retirees from 25 million in

Table 2.2	Components of the External Analysis
Scanning	▪ Identifying early signals of environmental changes and trends
Monitoring	▪ Detecting meaning through ongoing observations of environmental change and trends
Forecasting	▪ Developing projections of anticipated outcomes based on monitored changes and trends
Assessing	▪ Determining the timing and importance of environmental changes and trends for firms' strategies and their management

1991 to more than 33 million in 2011.[16] Changes in lifestyles and health care systems may result in longer average life spans for the baby boomers. By combining this information with data gleaned from scanning other environmental segments (e.g., the demographic, sociocultural, and political/legal segments), analysts can determine trends to monitor, forecast, and assess. Such analyses might result in an opportunity for financial institutions to serve the baby boomers' retirement needs effectively.

■ Monitoring

When *monitoring*, analysts observe environmental changes to see if, in fact, an important trend is emerging.[17] Critical to successful monitoring is an ability to detect meaning in different environmental events. For example, an emerging trend regarding education might be suggested by changes in federal and state funding for educational institutions, changes in high school graduation requirements, and changes in the content of high school courses. In this instance, analysts should determine whether these different events suggest an educational trend and, if so, whether other information and data should be studied to monitor this trend.

■ Forecasting

Scanning and monitoring are concerned with events in the general environment at a point in time. When *forecasting*, analysts develop feasible projections of what might happen, and how quickly, as a result of the changes and trends detected through scanning and monitoring.[18] For example, analysts might forecast the time that will be required for a new technology to reach the marketplace. Or they might forecast the length of time before different corporate training procedures are required to deal with anticipated changes in the composition of the workforce or how much time will elapse before changes in governmental taxation policies affect consumers' purchasing patterns. A forecast of stagnant sales and a net loss for its fiscal year led AST Research, Inc.'s president and two other top executives to resign from the firm. Therefore, forecasts can lead to unexpected outcomes as well.[19]

■ Assessing

The objective of *assessing* is to determine the timing and significance of the effects of environmental changes and trends on the strategic management of a firm.[20] Through scanning, monitoring, and forecasting, analysts are able to understand the general environment. Going a step further, the intent of assessment is to specify the implications of that understanding for the organization. Without assessment, analysts are left with data that are interesting, but of unknown relevance.

Information in the opening case suggests that Rubbermaid should be carefully scanning, monitoring, forecasting, and assessing its external environment to avoid future problems with its customers and losing market share to emerging competitors. Additionally, these activities are also important to identify the environmental threats and opportunities suggested in the Strategic Focus describing the new visions of Harsco and IBM.

STRATEGIC FOCUS   Creating New Visions with New Opportunities

Harsco Corporation had largely centered its business on defense industry projects. However, it clearly identified an environmental threat to its business from the thawing of the Cold War and reduced expenditures on military hardware for defense purposes. Although Harsco still produces defense products such as self-propelled howitzers and military trucks, its executives have created a new vision. Harsco is now refocusing its primary business activities on the scrap metal and hazardous waste industries. The new vision, and thus new strategic intent, spearheaded by Harsco's relatively new chief executive officer and chairman, Derek Hathaway, is beginning to bear fruit. For example, it sold its unprofitable bus line, thus improving its balance sheet, and has also landed several multi-million dollar service contracts and built metal reclamation plants in the Middle East. By the end of 1994, Hathaway had reduced the firm's total debt by $366 million, down from a high of $428.4 million in 1993.

Harsco's timing was fortuitous, because it benefited from the strong domestic steel production and improving conditions internationally. Harsco's Heckett Multiserve holds 40 percent of the available world market in specialized services for steel producers. Predicted revenue for that division is expected to exceed $650 million by 1997, up from $500 million in 1994.

Similarly, Louis Gerstner, CEO of IBM, has developed a new vision and strategic intent for his firm. Gerstner wants IBM to become the leader in network-centric computing. The driving force for this change is the development of low-cost digital networks that are proliferating across the world. Digital networks use high-speed fiber-optic cables and lightning-fast switches to carry multiple new types of communication (such as teleradiology, distance learning, and electronic business transactions). Thus, Gerstner perceives an opportunity and is attempting to seize it.

Alternatively, Gerstner is also trying to avoid a major environmental threat. IBM had a competitive advantage in the personal computer market at one time. However, it lost its position by ceding technical leadership to Intel and Microsoft. It also ceded marketing leadership to Compaq Computer and multiple other competitors. Rather than compete in this market, Gerstner eliminated a unit that had the charter to create an alternative to Intel-based PCs and used the IBM-Motorola-Apple computer Power PC microprocessor chip. He also pulled IBM from the battle over its OS/2 operating system, which was pitted against Microsoft Windows in desktop computers. The new competitive battle is in networked software, Gerstner believes. That is why he acquired Lotus and its Notes groupware program. Gerstner foresees a future in which networks become the lifeblood of corporations and the primary means of conducting business. He believes that electronic commerce will extend to home shopping and other consumer transactions.

Of course, this new network software will be designed to interface with the Internet and its Worldwide Web, which has created an infrastructure for delivering information to computers virtually across the globe. IBM will have to contend with a new Web-compatible software language, Java, produced by Sun Microsystems and the opportunities for access to new software such as Applets (small bits of software for specific tasks) that will be available through the Internet. This type of software may replace generic software such as Lotus Notes, acquired by IBM. As a result, many firms also perceive the same opportunities.

The Java software that is designed specifically for the Net and is an object-oriented programming tool replaces much of the conventional software. Java can run on any computer or digital device. With the Java virtual machine loaded into a computer, it can run any Java Applet that is available through the network. Obviously, this new software and access to the Internet will make the personal computer even more valuable to a broader number of people.

Thus, there are multiple opportunities with several firms attempting to take advantage of them. In the cases of Harsco and IBM, they have created a new strategic intent, but partially because of new environmental threats encountered in their older existing businesses. In other words, they were forced to look for new opportunities and thus create new strategic intents for their firms.

Source: A. Cortese, J. Verity, K. Rebello, and R. Hof, 1995, The software revolution, *Business Week,* December 4, 78–90; I. Sager, 1995, The view from IBM, *Business Week,* October 30, 142–150; R. Thompson, 1995, Harsco is recharged by scrap metal, hazardous waste, *Wall Street Journal,* October 11, B4.

■ Segments of the General Environment

The general environment is composed of segments (and their individual elements) external to the firm (see Table 2.1). Although the degree of impact varies, these elements affect each industry and its firms. The challenge is to scan, monitor, forecast, and assess those elements in each segment that are of the greatest importance to a firm. Results should include recognition of environmental changes, trends, opportunities, and threats. Opportunities are then matched with a firm's core competencies. When these matches are successful, the firm achieves strategic competitiveness and earns above-average returns.

■ The Demographic Segment

■ *The **demographic segment** is concerned with a population's size, age structure, geographic distribution, ethnic mix, and income distribution.*

The **demographic segment** is concerned with a population's size, age structure, geographic distribution, ethnic mix, and income distribution.[21] As noted previously, executives must analyze the demographics of the global areas potentially relevant to their firms, rather than only those of the domestic population. In the following materials, each demographic element is discussed briefly.

Population Size

Observing the demographic changes in populations highlights the importance of this environmental segment. For example, in some advanced nations, there is negative population growth (discounting the effects of immigration). In some countries, including the United States and several European nations, couples are averaging fewer than two children. Such a birth rate will produce a loss of population over time (even with the population living longer on average).[22] Population loss may require that a country increase immigration to have an adequate labor pool.

In contrast to advanced nations, the rapid growth rate in the populations of some Third World countries is depleting those nations' natural resources and

Businesses must analyze the demographic segment of the global areas potentially relevant to their firms.

reducing citizens' living standards. This rapid growth rate in the populations of some Third World countries may be a major challenge in the 1990s and into the twenty-first century.

Age Structure

In some countries, and certainly in the United States, the population's average age is increasing. Contributing to this change are declining birth rates and increasing life expectancies. Among other outcomes, these changes create additional pressures on health care systems. Beyond this, these trends may suggest numerous opportunities for firms to develop goods and services to meet the needs of an increasingly older population.

It has been projected that some people alive today might live to the age of 200 or more. If such a life span becomes a reality, a host of interesting opportunities and problems will emerge. For example, the impact on individuals' pension plans will be significant and will create potential opportunities and threats for financial institutions.[23]

Geographic Distribution

For several decades, the United States has experienced a population shift from the North and East to the West and South. Similarly, the trend of moving from metropolitan to nonmetropolitan areas continues. Among other effects, these changes have affected local and state governments' tax bases. In turn, the locations of business firms are influenced by the degree of support different taxing agencies offer.

The geographic distribution of populations throughout the world is being affected by the capabilities resulting from advances in communications technology. For example, through computer technologies, people can remain in their homes and communicate with others in remote locations to complete their work. In these instances, people can live where they prefer while being employed by a firm located in an unattractive location. Approximately 25 percent of U.S. employees may work out of their homes by the year 2000.[24]

Partially because of the advances in communication technology, approximately 25 percent of the more than 100 million employed workers in the United States in 1995 were contingency workers. Contingency workers include those who are part time, temporary, and on contract. As a result, these employees are more mobile. It is estimated that the number of contingency workers will continue to grow to as much as 50 percent of the U.S. workforce by the year 2000. This trend exists in other parts of the world as well, including Western Europe, Japan, Latin America, and Canada. Interestingly, the fastest growing segment of contingency workers is in the technical and professional area.[25]

Ethnic Mix

The ethnic mix of countries' populations continues to change. Within the United States, the ethnicity of states, and of cities within the states, varies significantly. For business firms, the challenge is to be aware of and sensitive to these changes. Through careful study, firms can develop and market goods and services intended to satisfy the unique needs and interests of different ethnic groups.

Ethnic mix changes also affect a workforce's composition. In the United States, for example, by the mid-1990s, only 15 percent of the new workers entering the workforce were Caucasian males. The remainder of those entering the workforce during the 1990s were Caucasian, U.S.-born women (42 percent) and immigrants and U.S.-born minorities (43 percent).[26] The Hispanic population is predicted to be the fastest growing segment of the U.S. workforce in the 1990s. By 2000, Hispanics will account for 9.2 percent of the workforce, up from 7.8 percent in 1991. Because a labor force can be critical to competitive success, firms are challenged to work effectively with an increasingly diverse labor force.[27] Diversity in the workforce is also a sociocultural issue.

Advances in communications technologies have allowed people to remain at home and communicate with others to complete their work.

Effective management of a culturally diverse workforce can produce a competitive advantage. For example, heterogeneous work teams have been shown to produce more effective strategic analyses, more creativity and innovation, and higher quality decisions than homogeneous work teams.[28] Because of these potential outcomes, a number of companies promote cultural diversity in their workforce and facilitate effective management of such diversity through specialized management training. Among them are American Express, Northern States Power Company, General Foods, US West, and British Petroleum. For example, all US West employees (more than 60,000) attend a diversity training program.[29]

Income Distribution

Understanding how income is distributed within and across populations informs firms of different groups' purchasing power and discretionary income. Study of income distributions suggests that while living standards have improved over time, there are variances within and between nations.[30] Of interest to firms are the average incomes of households and individuals. These figures yield strategically relevant information.

■ The Economic Segment

Clearly, the health of a nation's economy affects the performance of individual firms and industries. As a result, strategists study the economic environment to identify changes, trends, and their strategic implications.

■ *The economic environment refers to the nature and direction of the economy in which a firm competes or may compete.*

The **economic environment** refers to the nature and direction of the economy in which a firm competes or may compete.[31] As shown in Table 2.1, indicators of an economy's health include inflation rates, interest rates, trade deficits or surpluses, budget deficits or surpluses, personal and business savings rates, and gross domestic product. However, because of the interconnectedness of the global financial community, analysts often must also scan, monitor, forecast, and assess the health of other countries' economies. For example, the economic status of nations with which the United States exchanges many products, such as Japan and Germany, can affect the overall health of the U.S. economy. In this regard, some worry that billions of dollars, yen, and deutsche marks move across national borders without much control by central banks. The delicately balanced global financial system permitting these easy transfers might contribute to an international economic crisis if the balance in the system were lost.[32]

Of course, some of these problems might be eliminated if European countries are able to achieve their goal of a single currency for all of Europe. European countries have set target dates for a European monetary union in which countries will agree on irrevocable exchange rates by 1999 and completely change to a new single currency by 2002. Some speculate that European countries will not be able to meet these target dates nor will they be able to establish a single currency. Alternatively, the single currency may begin with the union of several financially strong nations, such as Germany, Belgium, and France, allowing the others to join later as they are able to meet the requirements. The interrelatedness among different national economies is shown in ways other than currency exchange rates and similarities of their currencies.[33] Agreements to lower or eliminate trade barriers between nations, such as the North American Free Trade Agreement (NAFTA), have potentially significant economic consequences for the nations involved.

Economic issues can also have significant influences on political and legal issues. For example, some argue that the United States cannot afford to cancel favored-nation status for China, even though it has threatened to do so because of perceived human rights concerns. To take such action might have significant negative economic consequences for U.S. firms.

■ The Political/Legal Segment

■ *The political/legal segment is the arena in which organizations and interest groups compete for attention and resources and the body of laws and regulations guiding these interactions.*

The **political/legal segment** is the arena in which organizations and interest groups compete for attention and resources and the body of laws and regulations guiding these interactions.[34] Essentially, this segment represents how organizations try to influence government and how government entities influence them. Constantly changing, this segment (see Table 2.1) influences the nature of competition. Because of this, firms must carefully analyze a new administration's business-related policies and philosophies. Antitrust laws, taxation laws, industries chosen for deregulation, labor training laws, and the degree of commitment to educational institutions are areas where an administration's policies can affect the operations and profitability of industries and individual firms.

Archer-Daniels-Midland (ADM) hedges its bets by contributing to both political parties in presidential and major congressional elections. From 1991 to 1995, ADM contributed more than $800,000 to the Democratic party and more than $1.5 million to the Republican party. One retired congressman suggested that he had not seen anyone more effective in this domain than the CEO of ADM, Dwayne Andreas. The retired congressman noted that Andreas buys futures in Washington by investing in candidates. He takes care of all potential options. Andreas also plays in the international arena. For example, he supported Mikhail Gorbechev and Boris Yeltsin in their leadership roles in Russia. Interestingly, even though ADM provides major campaign contributions, it engages in very little direct lobbying.[35] However, other firms engage in heavy lobbying efforts. Small, rural telephone companies lobby with state legislators and in Congress to maintain subsidies for their operations. They have been particularly successful in maintaining their subsidies to provide service to rural communities. For example, Beehive Telephone Company serves rural communities in Utah and receives direct subsidies from a $1 billion federal fund collected annually from large long-distance carriers. Of course, large phone companies want to eliminate the subsidies to these small firms and to allow more open competition.[36]

Viewpoints regarding government philosophies and policies (federal, state, and local), the most effective means of competition, and the ideal relationship between government and business can vary substantially. In addition to political perspectives, these viewpoints are affected by the nature of the industry in which a firm competes. As the 1990s come to a close, business firms across the globe are confronted by an interesting array of political/legal questions and issues. For example, the debate continues over trade policies. Some believe a nation should erect trade barriers to protect its domestic products. Others argue that free trade across nations serves the best interests of individual countries and their citizens. With the NAFTA and GATT agreements now in place, the trend seems to be toward free trade.

In the United States, frequent debates occur over the appropriate amount of regulation of business. Many want less regulation, while others believe that more regulation is needed to ensure appropriate business practices. Examples of both ends of the spectrum have been observed recently. For example, the Justice Department investigated Microsoft Corporation to determine if it developed its Windows 95 software with the intent of blocking competitive programs that provide users access to the Internet. Some would argue that even if Microsoft wrote Windows 95 with that intent, it is simply an effective competitive action with no unethical or inappropriate practices involved. Alternatively, because of the high market share that Microsoft enjoys with its Windows software, many feel that these actions would be in violation of antitrust regulations.[37] At the other end of the spectrum, the Federal Communications Commission has been liberalizing its control over television networks and program ownership. This loosening of federal government controls over the entertainment industry has allowed the Disney Company to purchase Capital Cities/ABC. This is an interesting acquisition outside of the fact that it involves well-known entertainment industry firms. The acquisition represents a vertical integration for Disney. It provides a means to distribute Disney products and thus is a related diversification move within the same industry (types of diversification are explained in Chapter 6). Certainly, it gives the Disney Company more power within the entertainment industry.[38]

While many U.S. business executives and others decry the regulations under which they have to operate, the U.S. government is actually one of the least intrusive on a global basis. For example, the Venezuelan economy is suffering from too many government economic controls. In 1995, the economy suffered shrinkage for the third consecutive year and the annual inflation rate was 70 percent, one of the world's highest. Since the institution of major government controls, there has been a dramatic reduction in private investment in this country. The savings rate has slumped sharply and the deficit in 1995 was about 10 percent of the country's gross domestic product. One of the problems was the price controls applied to most products sold in Venezuela. In fact, the head of Kellogg Company's operations in Venezuela stated that a few years ago the firm chose Venezuela over Columbia for its regional headquarters. However, this company official now believes that the choice was a poor one. Thus, government leaders struggle to find the appropriate amount of regulation to protect their citizens but to allow business the freedom and flexibility necessary to compete in a global economy and to create economic opportunities within their country.[39] Interestingly, the trend in much of Latin America is toward less government control and freer trade.

■ The Sociocultural Segment

■ *The **sociocultural segment** is concerned with different societies' social attitudes and cultural values.*

The **sociocultural segment** is concerned with different societies' social attitudes and cultural values. Because attitudes and values are a society's cornerstone, they often drive demographic, economic, political/legal, and technological changes. Firms are challenged to understand the meaning of attitudinal and cultural changes across global societies.

As mentioned earlier, a significant workforce trend in many countries concerns diversity. In the United States, for example, 76.3 million women are expected to participate in the labor force by 2011.[40] In addition, a large percentage of new entrants into the workforce will be ethnic minorities. As a result, the workforce will become increasingly diverse.

In the United States, approximately 46 percent of the workforce is composed of women. In Sweden, it's 50 percent, Japan, 41 percent, and Mexico, 37 percent. In the United States, 43 percent of the managerial jobs are held by women. In Sweden, 17 percent are held by women and in Japan, it is only 9.4 percent. In Japan, many women head businesses, but they are self-employed. The same is true in the United States, but approximately 17 percent of all U.S. businesses are headed by women, excluding those who are self-employed. In the United States, women are paid approximately 76 percent of the compensation paid to men. In Sweden, it's 77 percent, in Japan, 61.6 percent, and in Mexico, 68.2 percent. Thus, while women have experienced problems in the U.S. workplace, the barriers to their participation in the workplace in many other countries seem to be greater.[41]

The influx of women and the increasing ethnic and cultural diversity in the workforce yield exciting challenges and significant opportunities. Included among these are the needs to combine the best of both men's and women's leadership styles for a firm's benefit and to identify ways to facilitate all employees' contributions to their firms.[42] For example, some companies now provide training to nurture women's and ethnic minorities' leadership potential. Changes in organizational structure and management practices also may be required to eliminate subtle barriers that may exist. Learning to manage diversity

Many women now choose to start their own business. At the current growth rate, by the year 2000, one-half of U.S. businesses will be owned by women.

■ *The **technological segment** includes the institution and activities involved with creating new knowledge and translating that knowledge into new outputs—products, processes, and materials.*

in the domestic workforce can increase a firm's effectiveness in managing a globally diverse workforce, as it acquires more international operations. The results from these commitments to promote and manage diversity enhance a company's performance.[43]

Many women now choose to start their own businesses, as implied earlier, oftentimes because of frustration in dealing with the *glass ceiling* (a subtle barrier to the advancement of women and ethnic minorities in corporations). In 1982, there were 2.4 million female entrepreneurs in the United States; in 1991, that number exceeded 3 million. In 1994, women owned 7.7 million businesses, more than one third of all U.S. firms. If this rate of start-ups continues, one-half of U.S. businesses will be owned by women by the year 2000. The same trend has been observed in other countries such as Japan.[44]

Another sociocultural phenomenon is occurring in the United States. In effect, there is a move to rewrite the social contract. In an effort to balance the federal budget, welfare and Medicare expenditures may be reduced. Furthermore, other federal expenditures, including business subsidies and possibly even Social Security, will be affected over time. This could have major implications in terms of potential threats and opportunities for businesses. In particular, communities are likely to turn to businesses to provide support for social services that are no longer being provided by the federal government. Only time will tell how these changes will affect society and the operations of business. However, business executives must pay careful attention to these trends.[45]

■ The Technological Segment

Pervasive and diversified in scope, technological changes affect many parts of societies. These effects occur primarily through new products, processes, and materials. The **technological segment** includes the institutions and activities involved with creating new knowledge and translating that knowledge into new outputs—products, processes, and materials.

Given the rapid pace of technological change, it is vital that firms carefully study different elements in the technological segment. For example, research has shown that early adopters of new technology often achieve higher market shares and earn higher returns. Thus, executives must continuously scan the environment to identify potential substitutes for their firm's technology as well as newly emerging technologies from which their firm could benefit. They need to identify the speed with which substitute technologies are likely to emerge and the timing of any major technological changes.[46]

A technology with important implications for business is the Internet, sometimes referred to as the Information Superhighway. The Internet is a global web of more than 25,000 computer networks. Companies such as GE, J.P. Morgan, Merrill Lynch, Motorola, Schlumberger, and Xerox use the Internet. It provides a quick, inexpensive means of global communication (i.e., with strategic alliance partners) and access to information. For example, GE engineers often use the Internet to communicate with their counterparts when doing development work for other companies. The Internet provides access to experts on such topics as chemical engineering and semiconductor manufacturing, to the Library of Congress, and even to satellite photographs. Other information available on the Internet includes Security and Exchange Commission (SEC) filings, Commerce Department data, Census Bureau information, new patent filings, and stock market updates.[47] Therefore, the Internet may be an excellent source of data on a firm's external environment.

A number of firms have benefited from the popularity and use of the Internet. U.S. Robotics is an example of one of those firms. U.S. Robotics makes modems and other communications devices for computers and its sales are booming. In August 1994, its stock was traded at $25.50, but in late July 1995, the price of a share of U.S. Robotics' stock was $141. Modems are important for connecting personal computers to phone lines that help gain access to the Internet. The technology in the manufacture of modems has advanced rapidly. In the not-too-distant past, the standard modem could handle 1,200 bits per second, but in 1995, the standard was 28,800 bits per second. New modems are being developed that now handle 33,600 bits per second and it is envisioned that the next generation of modems will be able to handle 64,000 bits per second, the speed limit of conventional telephone lines.[48]

Another new technology that is gaining rapid popularity is satellite imaging. Several aerospace companies have invested up to one billion dollars in corporate earth-imaging systems. For example, Space Imaging, Inc., a joint venture of Lockheed Martin, E-Systems, Mitsubishi Corporation, and Eastman Kodak Company, is a $500 million venture that will provide images from an advanced satellite to be launched in 1997. Many expect this technology to compete in the global information trade industry and some anticipate that it will create a revolution. There are a number of uses for this technology. For example, Coldwell Banker Corporation is planning to offer real estate shoppers photographs from space of homes, neighborhoods, and traffic patterns. Television networks, such as ABC, will use the technology to provide detailed images of battle zones for evening news broadcasts. Even urban planners may use the technology to update property tax rolls, and other firms may use the technology to plot new phone lines without using crews to study the terrain beforehand.[49]

Alternatively, not all new technologies live up to their promise. For example, a number of the Bell System companies, along with cable companies, promised interactive networks linked into many homes. However, they have experienced multiple technical problems and soaring costs. In a recent pilot test of a new video network by Bell Atlantic, the video and audio portions did not arrive at the same time. Also, because of the significant costs involved in the development and linking of these interactive networks, the number of homes hooked to the networks is much smaller than originally planned. Currently, many of these companies are rethinking their original plans to provide wide access to interactive video networks.[50]

■ The Global Segment

*■ The **global segment** includes relevant new global markets and existing ones that are changing, important international political events, and critical cultural and institutional characteristics of relevant global markets.*

The **global segment** includes relevant new global markets and existing ones that are changing, important international political events, and critical cultural and institutional characteristics of relevant global markets. Although the previous segments should be analyzed in terms of their domestic and global implications, some additional specific global factors should also be analyzed. For example, it is important for firms to analyze the potential impact of significant international political events on their industry and specific operations. Some international political events may present particular threats while others may provide opportunities. An example is the potential peace between Israel and its neighboring Arab countries. With peace, Israel and Arab countries may refocus their efforts on private business activities as opposed to military hardware and software. With peace in the Middle East, Israeli firms are expected to become major competitive forces in high-technology industries. Similarly, peace in Bosnia may provide fewer opportunities for firms that manufacture military hardware but more opportunities for other firms that provide services and goods that may become marketable in Bosnia.

Firms must also attempt to identify critical new global markets and/or those that are changing. It is clear that many global markets are fast becoming borderless and integrated.[51] For example, firms may examine emerging markets such as those in South American countries or markets in newly industrialized countries such as in Asia (e.g., South Korea, Taiwan) for new opportunities. They should also be cognizant of the potential threats from these countries as well.

Newly industrialized countries, such as South Korea, have significant buying power but also have globally competitive firms. Based on significant support and economic planning from the South Korean government, the predominant goal of major South Korean firms is growth. Thus, many South Korean firms place less emphasis on earning net profits and more on attaining major growth goals through their strategic actions. This translates into a major emphasis on market share and sales in many South Korean firms.[52] An example of this is shown by Samsung's new venture into passenger-car production, partially because of executives' concerns at being ranked number two in size to Hyundai. While Samsung is predicted to invest approximately $4.5 billion from 1995 to 1997 to develop its auto manufacturing venture, it also plans to invest up to $150 million in the development of a 100-seat jetliner, $3 billion to build semiconductor manufacturing plants in North America, Europe, and Southeast Asia, and $2 to $3 billion to establish a hypermedia city of offices, shops, entertainment centers, and housing in downtown Seoul by 2000. In 1995 alone, Samsung invested approximately $9.92 billion in expansion opportunities.[53]

Firms must also have a reasonable understanding of the different cultural and institutional attributes of global markets in which they operate or hope to operate. For example, a firm operating in South Korea must understand the value placed on hierarchical order, formality, self-control, and on duty rather than rights. Furthermore, Korean ideology places emphasis on communitarianism, a characteristic of many Asian countries. However, Korea's approach differs from that of Japan and China. In Korea, the focus is on *Inhwa* or harmony based on respect of hierarchical relationships and obedience to authority. Alternatively, the approach in China is focused on *Guanxi* or personal relationships and in Japan on *Wa* or group harmony and social cohesion.[54] The institutional context of Korea suggests a major emphasis on centralized planning by the Korean government. For example, the emphasis placed on growth by many South Korean firms is the result of a policy to promote economic growth in South Korea by the Korean government.[55]

The cultural and institutional contexts in which firms must operate in global markets can be critical. For example, in India there is a current nationalist campaign against multinational firms. This campaign led to the closing of a Kentucky Fried Chicken restaurant in New Delhi in November 1995. Although the official statement was that the KFC outlet was closed for health reasons after an inspection, executives of several U.S. food companies blamed political posturing related to the 1996 general election. KFC was one of the first major fast food giants to open a facility in India. Furthermore, it has been quite successful in Asia with more than 2,200 restaurants operating in that region of the world. Still, even a firm that has been as successful as KFC must carefully and thoroughly analyze the institutional and cultural environments of its global markets.[56]

As explained in the Strategic Focus, China offers potential opportunities but also threats to a number of firms with domestic headquarters outside of China. China's growing economic prowess makes its firms potentially significant competitors, particularly in labor-intensive industries. As a result, firms operating in labor-intensive industries worldwide must view the development of Chinese entrepreneurial operations as an environmental threat. Alternatively, firms that can invest in China may be able to take advantage of the low-cost labor; and, China also offers a huge and growing market for products, as evidenced by the success of Procter & Gamble's products in China. The development of the Chinese economy is one that must be carefully analyzed by firms operating in many industries, regardless of their home country.

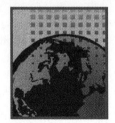

STRATEGIC FOCUS China's Growing Economic Prowess Presents Both Opportunities and Threats to U.S., European, and Other Asian Firms

Nearly 17 years after the world's most populous country launched a campaign to reform its government-controlled economy and open it to free-market enterprise, China has become a major global economic force. For example, with many labor-intensive industries, China has become a global exporting power. China now produces 50 percent of the world's toys and approximately 67 percent of its shoes. Many of the world's bicycles and power tools are also produced in China. Much of its economic prowess is owed to entrepreneurs and small enterprises that now produce more products, employ more workers, and produce more exports than government organizations. In fact, there are now approximately 25 million joint ventures, collectives, shareholding companies, township and village enterprises, and civilian enterprises that are private organizations with a profit orientation and outside of government control.

Interestingly, China is becoming the economic engine for Asia. More than one-third of China's exports come from foreign, primarily Asian, owned manufacturing plants. Of particular prominence are Hong Kong and Taiwanese operations. In 1994 and 1995, China's exports increased annually by 33 percent. As such, it generated a large trade surplus, with a $38 billion surplus in 1995 and an expected surplus of $50 billion in 1996. It is predicted that China's trade surplus with the United States will soon mirror the trade surplus Japan enjoys with the United States.

U.S. firms are investing in China to take advantage of the manufacturing and export opportunities as well as the growing Chinese market due to the increasing wealth of its citizens. Two firms of particular note are Procter & Gamble and Ford. Ford currently has a $40 million investment in Jiangling Motors Company, giving it a 20 percent ownership stake. Ford is hoping that its investment will help it penetrate the large Chinese market. Ford lost the opportunity to join a high-profile $1.1 billion joint venture between General Motors and Shanghai Automotive Industry Corporation developed in 1995. It is uncertain whether its venture with Jiangling will be successful given the massive competition for automobile and truck markets in China. Jiangling is a very small manufacturer in this market and therefore may not have the market power to compete against larger, more formidable competitors.

Alternatively, as noted in Chapter 1, Procter & Gamble has entered the Chinese market with overwhelming success. It sells approximately 50 percent of the shampoo used in China and its nationwide distribution system may be the best in that country. Procter & Gamble owes its success to being an early mover in China and its aggressiveness has paid dividends. It has been successful even though its prices are sometimes 300 percent greater than local brands. Procter & Gamble trains many of its Chinese employees to think like Americans. It recruits the best students from the top 25 universities in China. While Procter & Gamble has a number of formidable competitors, such as Unilever in the Chinese market, one outside observer suggested that China resembles Europe with Procter & Gamble in the leadership role.

Source: J. Kahn, 1995, China swiftly becomes an exporting colossus, straining Western ties, *Wall Street Journal,* November 13, A1, A6; R.L. Simison and J. Kahn, 1995, Ford hopes small investment in China will pay off big, *Wall Street Journal,* November 9, B4; J. Kahn, 1995, P&G viewed China as a national market and is conquering it, *Wall Street Journal,* September 12, A1, A6; M. W. Brauchli, 1995, China's economic role in Asia is burgeoning, *Wall Street Journal,* July 24, A1; J. Kahn, 1995, Spreading capitalism, new entrepreneurs are remaking China, *Wall Street Journal,* July 20, A1, A10.

A key objective of analyzing the general environment is identification of anticipated significant changes and trends among external elements. With a focus on the future, the analysis of the general environment allows firms to identify opportunities and threats. Also critical to a firm's future operations is an understanding of its industry environment and its competitors, which are considered next.

Industry Environment Analysis

■ An **industry** is a group of firms producing products that are close substitutes.

An **industry** is a group of firms producing products that are close substitutes. In the course of competition, these firms influence one another. Typically, industries include a rich mix of competitive strategies that companies use in pursuing strategic competitiveness and above-average returns.[57]

Compared to the general environment, the industry environment has a more direct effect on strategic competitiveness and above-average returns. The intensity of industry competition and an industry's profit potential (as measured by the long-run return on invested capital) are a function of five competitive forces—the threat of new entrants, suppliers, buyers, product substitutes, and the intensity of rivalry among competitors (see Figure 2.2).

Developed by Michael Porter, the five forces model of competition expands the arena for competitive analysis. Historically, when studying the competitive environment, firms concentrated on companies with which they competed directly. But today, competition is viewed as a grouping of alternative ways for customers to obtain the value they desire, rather than being limited to direct competitors. This is particularly important because in recent years industry boundaries have become blurred. For example, telephone communications companies now compete with broadcasters, software manufacturers also provide personal financial services, airlines now sell mutual funds, and automakers sell

Figure 2.2

The Five Forces Model of
Competition

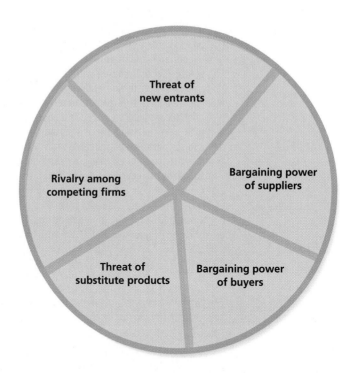

insurance and provide financing.[58] In addition to focusing on customers to define markets rather than specific industry boundaries, one should examine geographic boundaries as well. In fact, research has shown that different geographic markets for the same product can have considerable differences in the competitive conditions.[59]

The five forces model recognizes that suppliers could become a firm's competitor (by integrating forward), as could buyers (by integrating backward). This is graphically illustrated in the pharmaceuticals industry where Merck & Company acquired Medco Containment Services, a mail-order pharmacy and prescription benefits management company. In so doing, Merck integrated forward and became a competitor of other pharmacies and prescription benefits management companies. Perhaps, most importantly, Merck guaranteed a major source of distribution for its products. Shortly after Merck's acquisition, SmithKline Beecham and Eli Lilly announced plans to acquire similar-type companies and forward integrate as well.[60] Additionally, firms choosing to enter a new market and those producing products that are adequate substitutes could become competitors for an existing company.

■ Threat of New Entrants

New entrants to an industry can threaten existing competitors. New entrants bring additional production capacity. Unless product demand is increasing, additional capacity holds consumers' costs down, resulting in less sales revenue and lower returns for all firms in the industry. Often, new entrants have substantial resources and a keen interest in gaining a large market share. As such, new competitors may force existing firms to be more effective and efficient and to learn how to compete on new dimensions (e.g., computer-driven distribution channels). The likelihood that firms will enter an industry is a function of two factors: barriers to entry and the retaliation expected from current industry participants. When firms find entry into a new industry difficult or when firms are at a competitive disadvantage entering a new industry, entry barriers exist.

Barriers to Entry

Existing competitors try to develop barriers to market entry. Alternatively, potential entrants seek markets where the entry barriers are relatively insignificant. The absence of entry barriers increases the probability a new entrant can operate profitably in an industry. There are several potentially significant entry barriers.

Economies of Scale.   As the quantity of a product produced during a given time period increases, the costs of manufacturing each unit declines. These benefits are referred to as *economies of scale*.

Scale economies can be gained through most business functions (e.g., marketing, manufacturing, research and development, and purchasing). New entrants face a dilemma when existing competitors have scale economies. Small-scale entry places them at a cost disadvantage. However, large-scale entry, where the new entrant manufactures large volumes of a product to gain scale economies, risks strong reactions from established competitors.

Although still important in some industries (automobile manufacturing, for example), the competitive realities of the 1990s and the approaching twenty-first century may reduce the significance of scale economies as an entry barrier. Many companies now customize their products for large numbers of small customer groups. Customized products are not manufactured in the volumes necessary to achieve economies of scale. Customization is made possible by new flexible manufacturing systems. In fact, the new manufacturing technology facilitated by advanced computerization has allowed the development of mass customization in some industries. Mass customized products can be individualized to the customer in a very short period of time (e.g., within a day). Mass customization may become the norm in manufacturing products by the end of the 1990s.[61] Companies manufacturing customized products learn how to respond quickly to customers' desires, rather than developing scale economies.

Product Differentiation.   Over time, customers may come to believe that an existing firm's product is unique. This belief can result from service to the customer, effective advertising campaigns, or the firm being the first to market a particular product. Many firms such as Coca-Cola and PepsiCo spend significant amounts of money on advertising to convince potential customers of the distinctiveness of their products. The belief that a firm's product is unique results in loyal customers who have strong brand identification. Typically, new entrants must allocate significant resources over a long period of time to overcome existing customer loyalties. To combat the perception of uniqueness, new entrants frequently offer their products at lower prices. However, this can result in lower profitability or even a loss for the new entrant.

Capital Requirements.   Competing in a new industry requires resources to invest. In addition to physical facilities, capital is needed for inventories, marketing activities, and other critical business functions. Although competing in a new industry may appear attractive, the capital required for successful market entry may not be available.

Switching Costs. *Switching costs* are the one-time costs customers incur when buying from a different supplier. The costs of buying new ancillary equipment and of retraining employees and even the psychic costs of ending a relationship may be incurred in switching to a new supplier. If switching costs are high, a new entrant must offer either a substantially lower price or a much better product to attract buyers. Usually, the more established the relationship, the greater the switching costs.

Access to Distribution Channels.   Over time, industry participants can develop effective means of distributing products. Once developed, firms nurture their relationship with distributors. Such nurturing creates switching costs for distributors. Access to distribution channels can be a strong entry barrier for potential new entrants, particularly in consumer nondurable goods industries (e.g., in grocery stores, shelf space is limited). Thus, new entrants must persuade distributors to carry their products—either in addition to or in place of existing firms' products. Price breaks and cooperative advertising allowances may be used for this purpose. However, their use reduces the new entrant's potential to earn above-average returns.

Cost Disadvantages Independent of Scale.   In some instances, established competitors have cost advantages that new entrants cannot duplicate. Proprietary product technology, favorable access to raw materials, favorable locations, and government subsidies may provide such cost advantages. Successful competition requires new entrants to find ways to reduce the strategic relevance of these factors. For example, the impact of a favorable location can be reduced by offering direct delivery to the buyer (a number of food establishments, with unattractive locations, deliver goods directly to the consumer).

Government Policy.   Through licensing and permit requirements, governments can control entry into an industry. Liquor retailing, banking, and trucking are examples of industries where governments' decisions and actions affect industry entry. Also, governments restrict entrance into some utility industries because of the need to provide quality service to all and the capital requirements necessary to do so.

Expected Retaliation

Decision makers will also anticipate existing competitors' reactions to a new entrant. If retaliation is expected to be swift and vigorous, a decision could be reached against entry. Strong retaliation can be anticipated from firms with a major stake in an industry (e.g., having fixed assets with few, if any, alternative uses), from firms with substantial resources, and when industry growth is slow or constrained. Sometimes, a company will publicly announce its intentions.

The Cable News Network, better known as CNN, has had a monopoly on the broadcast of 24-hour news. However, recently Capital Cities/ABC announced that it will launch a 24-hour news service in 1997, using ABC News correspondents and anchors. Britain's BBC is attempting to start a global news channel and General Electric Company's NBC has been developing a detailed plan for

CNN once had a monopoly in the 24-hour news market. In the next few years, however, other companies will enter the market CNN once dominated.

launching a national news network (with a strong local component). Given that CNN tends to broadcast to an average of 637,000 households at any given time, the market does not seem large enough for this number of competitors. Thus, it will be interesting to see who survives if all of these firms enter the 24-hour news market and to see how CNN, which has had a monopoly for more than 15 years, responds to new competitors.[62]

Firms can avoid entry barriers by searching out market niches that are not being served by the primary competition. Small entrepreneurial firms are generally best suited for searching out and serving these neglected market segments. A number of years ago when Honda entered the U.S. market, it concentrated on small engine motorcycles, a market that firms such as Harley-Davidson ignored. By targeting this neglected market segment, Honda avoided competition. After consolidating its position, however, Honda used its new strength to attack its rivals by introducing larger motorcycles and competing in the broader market.[63] Competitive actions and responses are discussed in more detail in Chapter 5.

■ Bargaining Power of Suppliers

Increasing prices and reducing the quality of products sold are potential means through which suppliers can exert power over firms competing within an industry. If unable to recover cost increases through its pricing structure, a firm's profitability is reduced by the suppliers' actions. A supplier group is powerful when

- it is dominated by a few large companies and is more concentrated than the industry to which it sells;
- satisfactory substitute products are not available to industry firms;
- industry firms are not a significant customer for the supplier group;

- suppliers' goods are critical to buyers' marketplace success;
- the effectiveness of suppliers' products has created high switching costs for industry firms; and
- suppliers are a credible threat to integrate forward into the buyers' industry (e.g., a clothing manufacturer might choose to operate its own retail outlets). Credibility is enhanced when suppliers have substantial resources and provide the industry's firms with a highly differentiated product.

■ Bargaining Power of Buyers

Firms seek to maximize the return on their invested capital. Buyers (customers of the focal industry/firm) prefer to purchase products at the lowest possible price—at which the industry earns the lowest acceptable rate of return on its invested capital. To reduce their costs, buyers bargain for higher quality, greater levels of service, and lower prices. These outcomes can be achieved by encouraging competitive battles among firms in an industry. Customers (buyer groups) are powerful when

- they purchase a large portion of an industry's total output;
- the product being purchased from an industry accounts for a significant portion of the buyers' costs;
- they could switch to another product at little, if any, cost; and
- the industry's products are undifferentiated or standardized, and they pose a credible threat to integrate backward into the sellers' industry.

Relations with customers and the service provided such customers has taken on significant meaning in recent years. For example, one study showed that a firm's value on the stock market increased with improvements in its customer service.[64] Poor relations with customers can also hurt a firm's performance. Without good relations, retail firms may give less shelf space to its products, similar to the action Wal-Mart took against Rubbermaid. In fact, this example is an excellent one where the buyer, Wal-Mart, has significant power over the seller, Rubbermaid. This is exemplified by the fact that Wal-Mart executives openly criticized Rubbermaid for the actions taken, but Rubbermaid only publicly stated positive comments about Wal-Mart. Of course, the differences in power are readily seen in the statistics showing Wal-Mart with $93.6 billion in annual sales compared to Rubbermaid's $2.34 billion in annual sales.[65]

■ Threat of Substitute Products

Substitute products are different goods or services that can perform similar or the same functions as the focal product (functional substitute). Capable of satisfying similar customer needs, but with different characteristics, substitute products place an upper limit on the prices firms can charge. In general, the threat of substitute products is strong when customers face few, if any, switching costs and when the substitute product's price is lower and/or its quality and performance capabilities are equal to or greater than the industry's products. To reduce the attractiveness of substitute products, firms are challenged to differentiate their offerings along dimensions that are highly relevant to customers (e.g., price, product quality, service after the sale, and location).

Because it is available as an alternative or substitute, Nutrasweet places an upper limit on the prices sugar manufacturers can charge. Nutrasweet and sugar perform the same service but with different characteristics. Other product substitutes include fax machines instead of overnight delivery of correspondence, plastic containers instead of glass jars, and paper versus plastic bags.

■ Intensity of Rivalry Among Competitors

In many industries, firms compete actively with one another to achieve strategic competitiveness and earn above-average returns. Competition among rivals is stimulated when one or more firms feel competitive pressure or when they identify an opportunity to improve their market position. Competition among rivals is often based on price, product innovation, and other actions to achieve product differentiation (such as extensive customer service, unique advertising campaigns, and extended product warranties).

Because firms in an industry are mutually dependent, one firm's actions often invite retaliation from competitors. An industry in which this pattern of action and reaction (competitive actions and responses) occurs repeatedly is the deregulated airline industry. Quick reactions to one firm's price cuts are normal in this industry. Similarly, reactions to the introduction of innovative products, such as frequent flyer programs, usually are swift. Originated by American Airlines, virtually all major airlines rapidly developed similar frequent flyer programs. Thus, in the airline industry, as in many industries, firms often *simultaneously* apply two or all three of the principal means of competition (price changes, product/service innovations, and different means of differentiation) used by rivals when trying to gain a favorable marketplace position. Robert Crandall, CEO of American Airlines, stated that the airline "business is intensely, vigorously, bitterly, savagely competitive."[66] The *intensity* of competitive rivalry among firms is a function of several factors, as described in the following subsections.

Numerous or Equally Balanced Competitors

Industries populated by many participants tend to be characterized by intense rivalry. With many participants, often a few firms believe they can take actions without eliciting a response. However, other firms generally notice these actions and choose to respond. Frequent patterns of actions and responses result in intense rivalry.

At the other extreme, industries with only a few firms of equivalent size and power also tend to have high degrees of competitive rivalry. The resource bases of these firms permit vigorous actions and responses. The marketplace battles between Nike and Reebok exemplify an intense rivalry between relatively equivalent competitors. Some have referred to the Nike and Reebok rivalry as war and a battle for hearts, minds, and feet. Nike's revenues surpassed those of Reebok in 1990 and in 1995, Nike had revenues of approximately $4.8 billion versus Reebok's $3.5 billion. One of Reebok's problems has been its poor relations with the Foot Locker, a major sports shoe retailer with over 2,800 outlets and approximately 23 percent of all U.S. athletic shoe sales. Reebok was unwilling to manufacture athletic shoes to be sold under Foot Locker's private brand. However, Nike stepped into that breach and manufactured the shoes for Foot Locker. As a result, in 1995, Foot Locker's Nike sales were approximately

$750 million compared to Reebok's sales of $172 million, in contrast to Nike's $300 million in Foot Locker sales in 1993 and Reebok's $228 million. They also battle for the hearts, minds, and feet of young sports fans by signing promotional contracts with famous athletes. For example, Nike has Michael Jordan under contract and Reebok has Shaquille O'Neal under contract. In 1994, Nike had approximately 29.7 percent of the U.S. market for athletic shoes, while Reebok had 21.3 percent of this market. The battle between these two firms is significant but, currently, Nike is winning the war.[67]

Slow Industry Growth

When a market is growing, firms are challenged to use resources effectively to serve an expanding customer base. In this instance, fewer actions may be taken to attract competitors' customers. The situation changes, however, when market growth either slows or stops. Under these conditions, rivalry becomes much more intense; an increase in one firm's market share usually comes at the expense of competitors' shares.

To protect their market shares, firms engage in intense competitive battles. Such battles introduce market instability, often reducing industry profitability. Parts of the fast food industry are characterized by this situation. In contrast to years past, the market for these products is growing more slowly. To expand market share, many of these companies (e.g., McDonald's, Burger King, and Wendy's) are competing aggressively in terms of pricing strategies, product introductions, and product and service differentiation. These firms also search for new international markets to achieve their growth goals.

High Fixed or Storage Costs

When fixed costs account for a large part of total costs, companies are challenged to utilize most, if not all, of their productive capacity. Operating in this manner allows the costs to be spread across a larger volume of output. Such actions by many firms in an industry can result in excess supply. To reduce inventories, companies typically decrease product prices and offer product rebates as well as other special discounts. These practices often intensify rivalry among competitors. This same phenomenon is observed in industries with high storage costs. Perishable products, for example, rapidly lose their value with the passage of time. When inventories grow, perishable goods producers often use pricing strategies to sell their products quickly.

Lack of Differentiation or Low Switching Costs

Differentiated products engender buyer identification, preferences, and loyalty. Industries with large numbers of companies that have successfully differentiated their products have less rivalry. However, when buyers view products as commodities (i.e., as products with few differentiated features or capabilities), rivalry intensifies. In these instances, buyers' purchasing decisions are based primarily on price and service.

The effect of switching costs is identical to that described for differentiated products. The lower the buyer's switching costs, the easier it is for competitors to attract them (through pricing and service offerings). High switching costs, however, at least partially insulate firms from rivals' efforts to attract their customers.

Capacity Augmented in Large Increments

In some industries, the realities of scale economies dictate that production capacity should be added only on a large scale (e.g., in the manufacture of vinyl chloride and chlorine). Additions of substantial capacity can be disruptive to a balance between supply and demand in the industry. Price cutting is often used to bring demand and supply back into balance. However, achieving balance in this manner has a negative effect on the firms' profitability.

Diverse Competitors

Not all companies seek to accomplish the same goals, nor do they operate with identical cultures. These differences make it difficult to identify an industry's competitive rules. Moreover, with greater firm diversity, it becomes increasingly difficult to pinpoint competing firms' strategic intent. Often firms engage in various competitive actions, in part to see how their competitors will respond. This type of competitive interaction can reduce industry profitability.

High Strategic Stakes

Competitive rivalry becomes more intense when attaining success in a particular industry is critical to a large number of firms. For example, diversified firms' successes in one industry may be important to their effectiveness in other industries in which they compete. This is the case when firms follow a corporate strategy of related diversification (where the separate businesses are often interdependent—this strategy is explained in detail in Chapter 6).

High strategic stakes can also exist in terms of geographic locations. For example, Japanese automobile manufacturers are committed to a significant presence in the U.S. marketplace. Because of the stakes involved, for Japanese and U.S. manufacturers, rivalry in the automobile industry is quite intense.

High Exit Barriers

Sometimes companies continue to compete in an industry even though the returns on their invested capital are low or even negative. Firms making this choice face high exit barriers. *Exit barriers* are economic, strategic, and emotional factors causing companies to remain in an industry even though the profitability of doing so may be in question. Common sources of exit barriers are

- specialized assets (assets with values linked to a particular business or location);
- fixed costs of exit (e.g., labor agreements);
- strategic interrelationships (mutual dependence relationships between one business and other parts of a company's operations, such as shared facilities and access to financial markets);
- emotional barriers (aversion to economically justified business decisions because of fear for one's own career, loyalty to employees, and so forth); and
- government and social restrictions (common outside the United States, restrictions based on government concerns for job losses and regional economic effects).

The higher the exit barriers, the greater the probability that a firm will engage in destabilizing competitive actions (e.g., price cuts, extensive promotions, etc.).

■ Interpreting Industry Analyses

Industry analyses can be challenging and are a product of careful study and interpretation of information and data from multiple sources. A wealth of industry-specific data is available for analyzing an industry. Because of the globalization described in Chapter 1, analysts must include international markets and rivalry in their analyses. In fact, recent research showed that international variables were more important than domestic variables in the determination of competitiveness in some industries. Furthermore, because of the development of global markets, industry structures are no longer bounded by a country's borders; industry structures are often global.[68]

In general, the stronger the competitive forces, the lower the profit potential for firms in an industry. An *unattractive industry* has low entry barriers, suppliers and buyers with strong bargaining positions, strong competitive threats from product substitutes, and intense rivalry among competing firms. These industry attributes make it very difficult for firms to achieve strategic competitiveness and earn above-average returns. Alternatively, an *attractive industry* has high entry barriers, suppliers and buyers with little bargaining power, few competitive threats from product substitutes, and relatively moderate rivalry.[69]

A good example of global rivalry is that between Kimberly-Clark and Procter & Gamble. In 1995, Kimberly-Clark paid $7.36 billion to acquire Scott Paper Company and became the largest manufacturer of tissue products, greatly expanding its presence in Europe. This added strength should help it compete more effectively in the global marketplace with P&G. In 1993 and 1994, Kimberly-Clark had to absorb losses from its European operations, which encountered difficulties in competing against P&G's aggressive promotion of its diapers and other paper products. In the United States, Kimberly-Clark is the dominant manufacturer of diapers with 40 percent of the market, compared to P&G's 36 percent. However, in Europe, P&G has a substantial market share with 68 percent of the British diaper market and up to 55 percent of the French diaper market. The Scott acquisition will accelerate Kimberly-Clark's expansion in Europe, to include the northern countries of Britain, Germany, and the Netherlands, and into southern countries, such as Spain and Italy. Both Kimberly-Clark and Procter & Gamble are investing heavily in corporate R&D in order to develop and market new and more competitive products.[70]

One industry that appears to be attractive, based on multiple characteristics, is that of the microprocessor chip industry. There are multiple barriers to entry such as economies of scale and high capital requirements, the bargaining power of suppliers and buyers (customers) is low, and the threat of substitute products is low. The bargaining power of buyers is low because of a global demand for microchips that is higher than the industry can supply. Even though the growth of the industry is high, there is still a relatively intense rivalry among competitors. Part of this stems from a few major competitors. In particular, Intel is the major U.S. supplier of microchips. NexGen was acquired in 1995 by Advanced Micro Devices, Intel's chief competitor. NexGen has developed a chip that could rival the latest of Intel Corporation's microprocessors. However, Advanced Micro Devices has been able to capture only 8.7 percent of the market, compared to Intel's 85.6 percent. Furthermore, although its sales were up 9 percent, its profits were down 33 percent in 1994. This was due primarily to the relentless price cutting by Intel on its 486 and Pentium chips. Of course, given the economies of scale and market power of Intel, it can do this over the long term without experiencing any major problems. Only time will tell whether the merger of AMD and NexGen will allow the firm to compete effectively with Intel.[71]

■ Strategic Groups

More than 20 years ago, Michael Hunt studied the home appliance industry. He introduced the term *strategic group* to describe competitive patterns observed in that industry. Although he found differences in firms' characteristics and strategies, Hunt also discovered that many firms were following similar strategies. He chose to label the groups following similar strategies strategic groups.[72] Formally, a **strategic group** is "a group of firms in an industry following the same or a similar strategy along the [same] strategic dimensions."[73] Examples of strategic dimensions include the extent of technological leadership, the degree of product quality, pricing policies, the choice of distribution channels, and the degree and type of customer service. Thus, membership in a particular strategic group defines the essential characteristics of a firm's strategy.[74] While the strategies of firms within a group are similar, they are different from the strategies being implemented by firms in other strategic groups.

The notion of strategic groups is popular for analyzing an industry's competitive structure.[75] Contributing to its popularity is the assertion that strategic group analysis is a basic framework that should be used in diagnosing competition, positioning, and the profitability of firms within an industry.[76]

Use of strategic groups for analyzing industry structure requires that dimensions relevant to firms' performance within an industry (e.g., price and image) be selected. Plotting firms in terms of these dimensions helps to identify groups of firms competing in similar ways. For example, Dodge, Chevrolet, and Toyota form a strategic group, as do Mercedes and BMW. The products in each of these groups are similar in price and image (within the group).

There are several implications of strategic groups. First, a firm's major competitors are those within its strategic group. Because firms within a group are selling similar products to the same customers, the competitive rivalry among them can be intense. The more intense the rivalry, the greater the threat to each firm's profitability. Second, the strengths of the five competitive forces differ across strategic groups. As a result, firms within the various strategic groups have different pricing policies. Third, the closer the strategic groups in terms of strategies followed and dimensions emphasized, the greater the likelihood of competitive rivalry between the groups. For example, Nissan and Pontiac are more likely competitors for Dodge than for Mercedes and Porsche. In contrast, strategic groups that differ significantly in terms of strategic dimensions and strategies do not compete directly.

■ The Value of Strategic Group Analysis

Opinions vary about the value of strategic group analysis for understanding industry dynamics and structure. Some argue that there is no convincing evidence that strategic groups exist or that a firm's performance depends on membership in a particular group.[77] Another criticism of strategic groups is that the variances in many firm's product lines make it difficult to capture the nature of a company's outputs through study of a few strategic dimensions. Automobile companies

■ *A **strategic group** is a group of firms in an industry following the same or a similar strategy along the same strategic dimensions.*

manufacture many products with varying attributes. Dodge, for example, manufactures some relatively inexpensive cars with a family orientation. However, the firm also sells the Dodge Viper, a sports car that is expensive and not family oriented.

These criticisms notwithstanding, strategic group analysis yields benefits. It helps in the selection and partial understanding of an industry's structural characteristics, competitive dynamics, evolution, and strategies that historically have allowed companies to be successful within an industry.[78] As is always the case, a tool's strengths and limitations should be known before it is used.

Having an understanding of the general environment, the industry environment, and strategic groups, the final activity in the study of the external environment is competitor analysis.

■ Competitor Analysis

The problems of bribery and other questionable business practices in international markets described in the Strategic Focus are a serious problem for firms from the United States and many other countries as well. It is partially a problem because of different cultural values, but also a problem because of significant global competition for business. The following statements by major firm executives and investors suggest the reality of the new competitive landscape:

> I don't believe in friendly competition. I want to put them out of business.
> —*Mitchell Leibovitz, CEO of Pepboys*

> Major sustainable competitive advantages are almost nonexistent in the field of financial services.
>
> —*Warren Buffett, investor*[79]

STRATEGIC FOCUS   Dirty Competition for Global Business

A secret U.S. Commerce Department study prepared with the help of several U.S. intelligence agencies describes multiple incidences of bribery and other improper inducements used to obtain business by American firms' trading partners. Many of the actions detailed violate international trade agreements, and the cost of such practices to the U.S. economy is potentially huge. The report noted 100 deals, worth a total of $45 billion in 1994, in which international competitors used bribes in an attempt to compete against U.S. firms. In fact, the international competitors won 80 percent of these deals. Many of the firms involved are from major political allies including France, Germany, and Japan.

The United States is more dependent on exports to fuel its economic growth than at any time in the past. Additionally, European countries and Japan are experiencing slow economic growth. As a result, the increased global competition enhances the temptation to seek advantages using ethically questionable tactics. By law, the United States forbids its companies from paying bribes to win international business, regardless of what its international competitors do. During the past eight years, the analysis examined 200 potential international business deals and found that U.S. firms lost about 50 percent of these. The lost business would have meant approximately $25 billion in sales and would have added approximately 500,000 jobs to the U.S. economy. Thus, the losses due to questionable business practices are substantial.

Some U.S. companies have found creative ways to avoid the law. For example, one U.S. firm recently flew officials from a country in which it was seeking business to the United States, housed them in a very nice hotel for a week, and gave them money for shopping. The question is whether this could be considered the same as a bribe. Other companies use middlepersons to negotiate deals. They pay a certain fee to the middle people and they then do what is necessary to obtain the business. As such, no U.S. executives are directly involved in any unethical practices. However, it is common knowledge that the middlepersons often use questionable business practices in order to compete for potential contracts. Sometimes, U.S. firms can use partners in strategic alliances to negotiate deals. Again, while the U.S. executives and firms are not directly involved, they are generally knowledgeable that certain questionable practices are necessary to compete for the business.

Many U.S. executives and firms are placed in a "catch-22" position. Should they compete for international contracts by engaging in questionable business practices or should they simply forego the opportunity for those contracts and allow competitors from other countries to obtain the business? The answer to this question is not easy but is one with which many U.S. executives will have to deal in the coming years.

Source: R.S. Greenberger, 1995, Foreigners use bribes to beat U.S. rivals in many deals, new report concludes, *Wall Street Journal,* November 12, A3; A. Boris, S. Toy, and P. Salz-Trautman, 1995, A world of greased palms, *Business Week,* November 6, 36–38; B. Milbank and M.W. Brauchli, 1995, How U.S. concerns compete in countries where bribes flourish, *Wall Street Journal,* September 29, A1, A14.

As a complement to an analysis of the industry, competitor analysis focuses on each company with which a firm competes directly. Although important in all industry settings, competitor analysis is especially critical for firms facing one or a few powerful competitors.[80] For example, Nike and Reebok are keenly interested in understanding each other's objectives, strategies, assumptions, and capabilities. In successful companies, the process of competitor analysis is used to determine

- what drives the competitor (as shown by its *future objectives*);
- what the competitor is doing and can do (as revealed by its *current strategy*);
- what the competitor believes about itself and the industry (as shown by its *assumptions*); and
- what the competitor's capabilities are (as shown by its *capabilities*).[81]

Information on these four issues helps strategists prepare an anticipated response profile for each competitor (see Figure 2.3). Thus, the results of an effective competitor analysis help a firm understand, interpret, and predict its competitors' actions and initiatives.[82]

Critical to effective competitor analysis is the gathering of needed information and data, referred to as *competitor intelligence.* Analysts are challenged to ethically obtain information and data that inform them about competitors' objectives, strategies, assumptions, and capabilities. Intelligence gathering techniques commonly considered to be both legal and ethical include (1) obtaining publicly available information (e.g., court records, competitors' help-wanted advertisements, annual reports, financial reports of publicly held corporations, and Uniform Commercial Code filings) and (2) attending trade fairs and shows (to obtain competitors' brochures, view their exhibits, and listen to discussions about their products).

Figure 2.3   Competitor Analysis Components

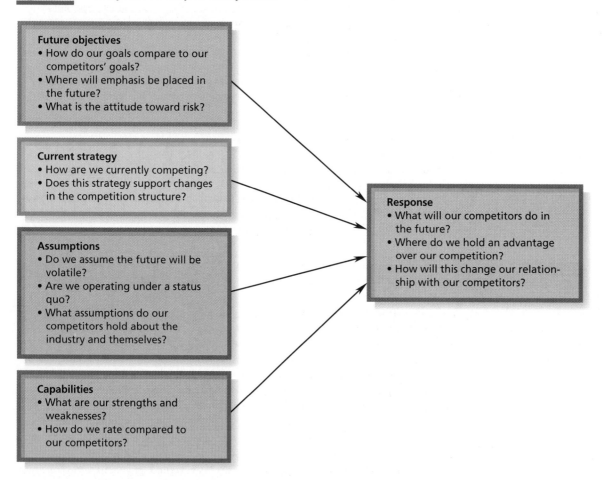

Source: Adapted and reprinted with permission of The Free Press, an imprint of Simon & Schuster from M.E. Porter, 1980, *Competitive Strategy: Techniques for Analyzing Industries and Competitors* (New York: The Free Press). Copyright 1980 by The Free Press.

Interestingly, a report by Deloitte & Touche suggests that 42 percent of major companies do not have a competitor intelligence system. In other words, they do not have a formal process for gathering and analyzing information about competitors. Undoubtedly, many of these firms have informal and less systematic means of gathering information about competitors. For example, 87 percent of these firms obtain information about competitor activities and 82 percent obtain information about changing market structures. Seventy-six percent of the firms also felt that they needed better information on competitor activities and 67 percent felt a need for better information on changing market structures. Nearly all of the firms felt that competitors had used intelligence techniques to gather information on their activities. Thus, firms understand the need for competitor information and gather it, even though in some firms the process may not be systematic.[83]

There is a need to develop a more systematic means of capturing knowledge about a firm's competitive context. In effect, employees have substantial knowledge about their firms and about external constituencies and stakeholders. However, few firms are able to transform this into a firm-wide asset. Firms that are able to do so refer to this as *structural intellectual capital.* Firms such as Monsanto are attempting to link key individuals (e.g., sales representatives) across the globe to share information they obtain about competitors and other important external stakeholders. Some refer to these as *knowledge networks* and linking employees through networks can provide a breadth of knowledge representing a sum of employees' collective experiences and information. Furthermore, the sharing of information helps pass on organizational learning and thus becomes a true organizational asset.[84]

Obtaining competitor information is important, particularly given the statements noted earlier about significant competition and the competitive battlefield. Of course, because of systematic competitor intelligence systems, some firms have trouble maintaining critical secrets about their products, technology, or other operations. Unfortunately, because of the significant competitive pressures in many industries, some adopt questionable business practices as noted in the Strategic Focus. Sometimes, competitors steal information by using insiders (employees of the focal company). A recent study suggested that about 75 percent of the *Fortune* 1000 companies believed that information they desired to remain secret was stolen from them or at least there were attempted thefts within the past five years. Thus, significant pressures can lead to the use of questionable practices to obtain desired information on competitors.[85]

Certain techniques—eavesdropping, trespassing, blackmail, and the theft of drawings, samples, or documents—are unethical and considered to be illegal.[86] While a number of intelligence gathering techniques are legal, decision makers must determine if their use is ethical. In highly competitive environments, employees may feel greater pressure to rely on these techniques. Interestingly, evidence suggests that most businesspeople believe their competitors use questionable intelligence gathering techniques far more frequently than they do.[87] Perhaps an appropriate guideline is to use intelligence gathering techniques that respect the principles of common morality and the right of competitors not to reveal certain information about their products, operations, and strategic intentions.[88]

As with analysis of the general environment, analyses of the industry and competitors should result in the identification of opportunities and threats for the focal firm. A procedure for identification of opportunities and threats is explained in the Introduction to Preparing an Effective Case Analysis (beginning of Part IV).

◼ Summary

- Firms' external environments are often challenging and complex. Because of their effect on performance, firms must develop the skills required to identify opportunities and threats existing in their external environments.

- The external environment has three major parts—the general environment (elements in the broader society that affect industries and their firms), the industry environment (factors—the threat of entry, suppliers, buyers, product substitutes, and the intensity of rivalry among competitors—that influence a firm and its competitive actions and responses), and specific analyses of each major competitor.

- Environmental analyses often must assume a nationless and borderless business environment.

- The external environmental analysis process includes four steps—scanning, monitoring, forecasting, and assessing. Analysis of the external environment leads to the identification of opportunities and threats.

- The general environment includes six segments: demographic, economic, political/legal, sociocultural, technological, and global. For each, the objective is to identify and study the strategic relevance of different changes and trends.

- As compared to the general environment, the industry environment has a more direct effect on a firm's efforts to achieve strategic competitiveness and earn above-average returns.

- The five forces model of an industry includes characteristics that determine the industry's profit potential.

Through study of the five forces, firms select a position in the industry in which they can match their core competencies with an opportunity to achieve strategic competitiveness and earn above-average returns.

- Different strategic groups exist within industries (a strategic group is a collection of firms that follow similar strategies). The competition within each strategic group is more intense than is the competition between strategic groups.

- Competitor analysis informs a firm about the objectives, strategies, assumptions, and capabilities of the firms with which it competes.

- Different techniques are available for gathering the intelligence (information and data) needed to understand competitors' actions and intentions. Analysts must determine the appropriate and ethical techniques for use in their firm.

Review Questions

1. Why is it important for firms to study and understand the external environment?

2. What are the differences between the general environment and the industry environment?

3. What is the environmental analysis process? What do analysts try to learn as they scan, monitor, forecast, and assess?

4. What are the six segments of the general environment? Explain the differences among them.

5. Using information in the chapter, can you justify accepting the following statement: "There are five competitive forces that determine an industry's profit potential." Explain.

6. What is a strategic group? Of what value is the strategic group concept in choosing a firm's strategy?

7. Why do firms seek information about competitors and how is that information best collected?

Application Discussion Questions

1. Given the importance of understanding an external environment, why do some managers, and their firms, fail to do so? Provide an example of a firm that poorly understood its external environment and discuss the implications.

2. Select a firm and describe how you characterize the nature of external environments facing it. As someone who will soon enter the business world, how do you react to these environmental conditions? Why?

3. Describe how it would be possible for one firm to think of a condition in the general environment as an opportunity, whereas a second firm would see that condition as a threat. Provide an example of an environmental characteristic that could be perceived in this way.

4. Choose a firm in your local community. Explain the courses of action you would follow and the materials you would read to understand its industry environment.

5. Select an industry and describe what firms could do to create barriers to entry in this industry.

6. What conditions would cause a firm to retaliate aggressively against a new entrant in the airline industry?

7. Is it possible for an industry to exist with only a single strategic group? If so, how? Please provide an example of such an industry.

■ Ethics Questions

1. How can a firm apply its "code of ethics" in the study of its external environment?

2. What ethical issues, if any, may be relevant in a firm's monitoring of its external environment?

3. For each segment of the general environment, identify an ethical issue to which companies should be sensitive.

4. What is the importance of ethical practices between a firm and its suppliers and distributors? Explain.

5. In an intense rivalry, how can a firm undertake ethical practices and yet maintain its competitiveness? Discuss.

6. While differences in strategies may exist between strategic groups, should commonly accepted ethical values/practices be the same across strategic groups within an industry? Explain.

7. What are the primary ethical issues associated with competitor intelligence practices?

Internet Exercise

Go to the "Internet Bankruptcy Library" to find an example of a firm that failed to properly analyze its external environment:

■ http://bankrupt.com/

How would you characterize the firm's external environment? What would you have done differently? Next, find information on other companies in the same industry by using one of the search engines. What did they do differently to succeed? If you were advising the managers in the bankrupt company, what would you suggest they do to recover?

Cohesion Case

Find some general environmental information pertinent to the industry your group selected. Here are several options:

1. You can access much of the information the federal government collects. To find out about the Freedom of Information Act, go the "Internet Wiretap" (Government Docs—U.S. & World) and enter the directory "Citizen's Guide to using the FOIA":

■ gopher://wiretap.spies.com

2. Examine a recent federal government action by visiting the White House. Go to the Virtual Library and search for the White House documents relevant to your industry:

■ http://www.whitehouse.gov

3. Obtain the business cycle indicators from U.S. Economic Data:

■ http://www.cris.com/~netlink/bci/bci.html

■ Notes

1. S. Kotha and A.P. Nair, 1995, Strategy and environment as determinants of performance: Evidence from the Japanese machine tool industry, *Strategic Management Journal* 16: 497–518.

2. C.J. Fombrun, 1992, *Turning Points: Creating Strategic Change in Organizations* (New York: McGraw-Hill), 13; G. Hamel and C.K. Prahalad, 1989, Strategic intent, *Harvard Business Reveiw* 67, no. 3: 63–76.

3. N.M. Tichy and S. Sherman, 1993, *Control Your Own Destiny, or Someone Else Will* (New York: McGraw-Hill); The post-capitalist executive: An interview with Peter F. Drucker, 1993, *Harvard Business Review* 71, no. 3: 114–122.

4. Lou Gerstner's first 30 days, 1993, *Fortune,* May 31, 57–62.

5. Fombrun, *Turning Points,* 16, 18.

6. U. Zander and B. Kogut, 1995, Knowledge and the speed of the transfer and imitation of organizational capabilities: An empirical test, *Organization Science* 6: 76–92.

7. M.B. Meznar and D. Nigh, 1995, Buffer or bridge? Environmental and organizational determinants of public affairs activities in American firms, *Academy of Management Journal* 38: 975–996.

8. M. Robert, 1993, *Strategy Pure and Simple* (New York: McGraw-Hill), 3.

9. L. Fahey and V.K. Narayanan, 1986, *Macroenvironmental Analysis for Strategic Management* (St. Paul: West Publishing Company), 49–50.

10. M.A. Hitt, B.W. Keats, and S.M. DeMarie, 1995, Navigating in the new competitive landscape: Building competitive advantage and strategic flexibility in the 21st century, Paper presented at the Strategic Management Society Conference.

11. J.F. Preble, 1992, Environmental scanning for strategic control, *Journal of Managerial Issues* 4: 254–268; K. Gronhaug and J.S. Falkenberg, 1989, Exploring strategy perceptions in changing environments, *Journal of Management Studies* 26: 349–359.

12. Fombrun, *Turning Points,* 77; Gronhaug and Falkenberg, Exploring strategy perceptions, 350.

13. L.S. Richman, 1993, Why the economic data mislead us, *Fortune,* March 8, 108–114.

14. Fahey and Narayanan, *Macroenvironmental Analysis,* 37.

15. R.L. Priem, A.M.A. Rasheed, and A.G. Kotulic, 1995, Rationality in strategic decision processes, environmental dynamism and firm performance, *Journal of Management* 21: 913–929.

16. S. Shepard, 1993, Baby boom could bust retirement system, *Waco Tribune Herald,* May 23, A1; How America will change over the next 30 years, 1993, *Fortune,* May 2, 12.

17. Fahey and Narayanan, *Macroenvironmental Analysis,* 39.

18. Ibid., 41.

19. AST president, two executives quit after loss, slow sales forecast, 1995, *Dallas Morning News,* September 12, D7.

20. Fahey and Narayanan, *Macroenvironmental Analysis,* 42.

21. Ibid., 58.

22. E. Cornish, 1990, Issues of the '90s, *Futurist* 24, no. 1: 29–36.

23. Ibid., 35.

24. R.I. Kirkland, 1991, Get ready for a new world of work, *Fortune,* February 11, 136–141.

25. M.N. Martinez, 1995, Contingency workers shed the bad rap, *HR Magazine* 40, no. 4: 16–18; E. Dravo, 1994, How to play the jobs recovery,

Financial World 163, no. 7: 121; J. Fierman, 1994, The contingency work force, *Fortune,* January 24, 30–36; S. Overman, 1993, Temporary services go global, *HR Magazine* 38, no. 8: 72–74.

26. M. McLaughlin, 1989, A change of mind, *New England Business,* April, 42–53.

27. How America will change over the next 30 years, 12; The labor secretary speaks out on training and the two-tier work force, 1993, *Fortune,* March 8, 11.

28. T. Cox and S. Blake, 1991, Managing cultural diversity: Implications for international competitiveness, *Academy of Management Executive* V, no. 3: 45–56.

29. J.P. Fernandez, 1993, *The Diversity Advantage* (New York: Lexington Books).

30. Cornish, Issues of the '90s, 32.

31. Fahey and Narayanan, *Macroenvironmental Analysis,* 105.

32. D. Leebaert, 1990, Top economic trends of the 1990s, *Management Review* 79, no. 1: 21–23; Cornish, Issues of the '90s, 32.

33. R. Norton, 1995, There go those Eurocrats again, *Fortune,* September 18, 51.

34. Fahey and Narayanan, *Macroenvironmental Analysis,* 139, 157.

35. S. Kilman, B. Ingersoll, and J. Abramson, 1995, How Dwayne Andreas rules Archer-Daniels by hedging his bets, *Wall Street Journal,* November 27, A1, A8.

36. D. Pearl, 1995, Despite regulations rural phone subsidies are likely to survive, *Wall Street Journal,* November 11, A1, A12.

37. R. Wells, 1995, Feds want to know if Microsoft is up to something, *Bryan/College Station Eagle,* December 5, A8.

38. K. Harris, 1995, Lights! Camera! Regulation! *Fortune,* September 4, 83–86.

39. M. Moffett, 1995, Venezuela is suffering, its economy strangled by too many controls, *Wall Street Journal,* August 16, A1, A6.

40. How America will change over the next 30 years, 12.

41. P. Thomas, 1995, Success at a huge personal cost: Comparing women around the world, *Wall Street Journal,* July 26, B1.

42. J.B. Roesner, 1991, Ways women lead, *Harvard Business Review* 69, no. 3: 119–125.

43. F.N. Schwartz, 1992, Women as a business imperative, *Harvard Business Review* 70, no. 2: 105–113; C. Torres and M. Bruxelles, 1992, Capitalizing on global diversity, *HR Magazine,* December, 30–33; B. Geber, 1990, Managing diversity, *Training,* July, 23–30.

44. J. Files, 1996, Texas 2nd in women-owned businesses, *Dallas Morning News,* January 30, D5; S.N. Mehta, 1996, Number of women-owned businesses surged 43% in 5 years through 1992, *Wall Street Journal,* January 29, B2; E.H. Buttner, 1993, Female entrepreneurs: How far have they come? *Business Horizons* 36, no. 3: 59–65; A.B. Fisher, 1993, Japanese working women strike back, *Fortune,* May 31, 22; A.L. Dolinsky, 1992, Long term entrepreneurs' patterns: A national study of black and white female entrepreneurs, *Rothman Ink* 13: 3.

45. H. Gleckman, M. Maremont, E. Schine, A.T. Palmer, and J. Hoffman, 1995, Rewriting the social contract, *Business Week,* November 20, 120–134.

46. B.L. Dos Santos and K. Peffers, 1995, Rewards to investors in innovative information technology applications: First movers and early followers in ATMs, *Organization Science* 6: 241–259; S.A. Zahra, S. Nash, and D.J. Bickford, 1995, Transforming technological pioneering into competitive advantage, *Academy of Management Executive IX,* no. 1: 17–31.

47. R. Tetzeli, 1994, The internet and your business, *Fortune,* March 7, 86–96.

48. S. McCartney, 1995, U.S. Robotics dials up dollars in market for modems, *Wall Street Journal,* July 27, B8.

49. J. Cole, 1995, New satellite imaging could soon transform the face of the earth, *Wall Street Journal,* November 30, A1, A5.

50. L. Cauley, 1995, Phone giants discover the interactive path is full of obstacles, *Wall Street Journal,* July 24, A1, A4.

51. J. Birkinshaw, A. Morrison, and J. Hulland, 1995, Structural and competitive determinants of a global integration strategy, *Strategic Management Journal* 16: 637–655.

52. S.M. Lee, S. Yoo, and T.M. Lee, 1991, Korean chaebols: Corporate values and strategies, *Organizational Dynamics,* Spring, 36–50; K.H. Chung, 1989, An overview of Korean management, in K.H. Chung and H.C. Lee (eds.), *Korean Managerial Dynamics* (New York: Praeger Publishers), 1–8.

53. S. Glain, 1995, Going for growth: Korea's Samsung plans very rapid expansion into autos, other lines, *Wall Street Journal,* March 2, A1, A6; L. Nakarmi and R. Neff, 1994, Samsung's radical shakeup, *Business Week,* February 28, 74–76.

54. J.P. Alston, 1989, Wa, guanxi, and inhwa: Managerial principals in Japan, China and Korea, *Business Horizons,* March–April, 26–31.

55. M.A. Hitt, M.T. Dacin, B.B. Tyler, and D. Park, 1997, Understanding the differences in Korean and U.S. executives' strategic orientations, *Strategic Management Journal* 18: in press; S. Yoo and S.M. Lee, 1987, Management style and practice of Korean chaebols, *California Management Review* 29, Summer: 95–110.

56. M. Jordan, 1995, U.S. food firms head for cover in India, *Wall Street Journal,* November 21, A14.

57. R.E. Miles and C.C. Snow, 1986, Network organizations: New concepts for new forms, *California Management Review* 28, no. 2: 62–73; M.E. Porter, 1980, *Competitive Strategy* (New York: Free Press).

58. R.A. Bettis and M.A. Hitt, 1995, The new competitive landscape, *Strategic Management Journal* 16 (Special Summer Issue): 7–19.

59. G.R. Brooks, 1995, Defining market boundaries, *Strategic Management Journal* 16: 535–549.

60. A.M. McGahan, 1994, Industry structure and competitive advantage, *Harvard Business Review* 72, no. 5: 115–124.

61. S. Kotha, 1995, Mass customization: Implementing the emerging paradigm for competitive advantage, *Strategic Management Journal* 16 (Special Summer Issue): 21–42; B. Pine, 1993, *Mass Customization* (Boston: Harvard Business School Press); B. Pine, B. Victor, and A.C. Boynton, 1993, Making mass customization work, *Harvard Business Review* 71, no. 5: 108–119.

62. E. Jensen and J. Lippman, 1995, New competition may mean bad news for CNN, *Wall Street Journal,* December 6, B1, B4.

63. Take on the giants, 1996, *Success,* January/February, 30.

64. P.R. Nayyar, 1995, Stock market reactions to customer service changes, *Strategic Management Journal* 16: 39–53.

65. The *Fortune* 1000 ranked within industries, 1996, *Fortune,* April 29, F1–F60; L. Smith, 1995, Rubbermaid goes thump, *Fortune,* October 2, 90–104.

66. R.A. D'Aveni, 1995, Coping with hypercompetition: Utilizing the new 7S's framework, *Academy of Management Executive IX,* no. 3: 45.

67. K. Labich, 1995, Nike vs. Reebok: A battle for hearts, minds and feet, *Fortune,* September 18, 90–106; J. Pereira, 1995, In Reebok-Nike war, big Woolworth chain is a major battlefield, *Wall Street Journal,* September 22, A1, A5.

68. H.J. Moon and K.C. Lee, 1995, Testing the diamond model: Competitiveness of U.S. software firms, *Journal of International Management* 1: 373–387.

69. Much of the preceding discussion of competitive forces is based on Porter, *Competitive Strategy.*

70. P. Thomas, 1995, Kimberly-Clark and P&G face global warfare, *Wall Street Journal,* July 18, B1, B6.

71. M. Maremont, 1995, Intel won't feel the heat from this fusion, *Business Week,* November 6, 40–41.

72. M.S. Hunt, 1972, Competition in the major home appliance industry, 1960–1970 (doctoral dissertation, Harvard University).

73. Porter, *Competitive Strategy,* 129.

74. R.K. Reger and A.S. Huff, 1993, Strategic groups: A cognitive perspective, *Strategic Management Journal* 14: 103–123; J. McGee and H. Thomas, 1986, Strategic groups: A useful linkage between industry structure and strategic management, *Strategic Management Journal* 7: 141–160.

75. J.B. Barney and R.E. Hoskisson, 1990, Strategic groups: Untested assertions and research proposals, *Managerial and Decision Economics* 11: 198–208.

76. R.M. Grant, 1995, *Contemporary Strategy Analysis,* 2nd ed. (Cambridge, Mass.: Blackwell Publishers), 98.

77. Barney and Hoskisson, Strategic groups, 202.

78. Grant, *Contemporary Strategy Analysis,* 98–99.

79. D'Aveni, Coping with hypercompetition, 45.

80. S. Ghoshal and D.E. Westney, 1991, Organizing competitor analysis systems, *Strategic Management Journal* 12: 17–31.

81. Porter, *Competitive Strategy,* 49.

82. S.A. Zahra and S.S. Shaples, 1993, Blind spots in competitive analysis, *Academy of Management Executive* VII, no. 2: 7–28.

83. U.S. companies slow to develop business intelligence, 1995, *Deloitte & Touche Review,* October 16, 1–2.

84. T.A. Stewart, 1995, Getting real about brain power, *Fortune,* November 27, 201–203; T.A. Stewart, 1995, Mapping corporate brain power, *Fortune,* October 30, 209–211.

85. M. Geyelin, 1995, Why many businesses can't keep their secrets, *Wall Street Journal,* November 20, B1, B3.

86. K.A. Rehbeing, S.A. Morris, R.L. Armacost, and J.C. Hosseini, 1992, The CEO's view of questionable competitor intelligence gathering practices, *Journal of Managerial Issues* 4: 590–603.

87. S.A. Zahra, 1994, Unethical practices in competitive analysis: Patterns, causes and effects, *Journal of Business Ethics* 13: 53–62; W. Cohen and H. Czepiec, 1988, The role of ethics in gathering corporate intelligence, *Journal of Business Ethics* 7: 199–203.

88. J.H. Hallaq and K. Steinhorst, 1994, Business intelligence methods—How ethical?, *Journal of Business Ethics* 13: 787–794; L.S. Paine, 1991, Corporate policy and the ethics of competitor intelligence gathering, *Journal of Business Ethics* 10: 423–436.

3 The Internal Environment: Resources, Capabilities, and Core Competencies

After reading this chapter, you should be able to:

1. Explain the importance of studying and understanding the internal environment.
2. Define value and discuss its importance.
3. Describe the differences between tangible and intangible resources.
4. Define capabilities and discuss how they are developed.
5. Explain how value chain analysis is used to identify and evaluate a firm's resources and capabilities.
6. Define outsourcing and discuss the reasons for its use.
7. Describe four criteria used to determine if a firm's resources and capabilities are core competencies.
8. Discuss the importance of preventing a firm's core competencies from becoming core rigidities.
9. Explain the relationship between a firm's strategic inputs and its strategic actions.

Brand Names As a Source of Competitive Advantage

Some believe that a strong brand name may be the ultimate source of competitive advantage, especially for companies producing and selling either consumer durable products (e.g., automobiles and washing machines) or consumer nondurable products (e.g., foods, household items, and financial services). In fact, 12 of the top 15 companies on *Fortune's* Most Admired list in 1996 sold well-known household brand names. Competitive advantage accrues to a firm when its brand product offers value exceeding that provided by competitors' products.

Coca-Cola is considered to be one of the most valuable and best known brand names in the world. Employees speak in reverent terms about their company's brand. Top-level executives believe that if all of the company's physical assets were simultaneously destroyed, they would be able to immediately borrow $100 billion from financial institutions merely on the strength of the firm's brand name.

In recent years, American Express lost market share to Visa and MasterCard. Nonetheless, American Express remains one of the 10 most recognized brand names in the world. As a result of recent purchases, Warren Buffett, the successful and widely admired chief executive officer (CEO) of Berkshire Hathaway, now owns more than 49 million shares of American Express. The value of Buffett's 10.1 percent ownership position is approximately $2.2 billion. In spite of some performance disappointments, Buffett believes that the American Express brand name remains "synonymous with financial integrity and money substitutes around the world." Representing his employees' view—which is that the brand name is the engine that drives the firm's business decisions and actions—Harvey Golub, the new CEO, is committed to running the company in a way that builds and broadens the American Express brand. Offering an array of credit cards to niche markets around the world is an example of the actions the firm is taking to exploit its brand name.

Brand-name products cost more than their nonbranded counterparts. Companies with a strong brand, such as Coca-Cola, American Express, and Gillette, receive a premium from customers in the form of the price paid for the brand-name product. What do customers receive in return for their payment of a premium? Obviously, the value obtained varies by product. However, in all cases, the value obtained is greater than that gained through the purchase of competitors' products. An image of prestige accrues to the holder of one or more of American Express' cards.

Purchasers of Gillette's razors such as Sensor buy high-quality, innovative products that are produced by sophisticated technology and machinery that the firm designs and manufactures. An indicator of Gillette's commitment to innovation is that 40 percent of the firm's sales every five years come from entirely new products. The fact that in a recent year Gillette earned 69 percent of its profits from the 39 percent of its total sales that were accounted for by blades and razors demonstrates the size of the brand premium the firm earns from its key product line.

Source: B. Morris, 1996, The brand's the thing, *Fortune,* March 4, 72–86; R. M. Grant, 1995, *Contemporary Strategy Analysis: Concepts, Techniques, Applications* 2nd ed. (Cambridge: Blackwell Publishers); L. Grant, 1995, Why Warren Buffett's betting big on American Express, *Fortune,* October 30, 70–84; Gillette Co., 1995, *Standard & Poor's Stock Reports,* October 30, 1010; American Express, 1994, Annual Report.

Coca-Cola, American Express, and Gillette are interested in developing a *sustainable competitive advantage*. A sustainable competitive advantage is achieved when firms implement a value-creating strategy that is grounded in their own unique resources, capabilities, and core competencies (terms defined in Chapter 1). Firms achieve strategic competitiveness and earn above-average returns when their unique core competencies are leveraged effectively to take advantage of opportunities in the external environment.

Over time, the benefits of every firm's value-creating strategy can be duplicated. In other words, all competitive advantages have a limited life.[1] The question of duplication is not *if* it will happen, but *when*. During the 1980s, for example, the competitive advantage of brand names, even for the companies described in the opening case, began to dissipate. Among the factors causing a temporary erosion of the competitive advantage yielded by brand names for some firms was a technological development—the checkout scanner. Studying data available to them from scanners allowed retailers (such as grocery stores) to determine quickly how price promotions on various products affected their sales volume. In the words of one analyst, this new technology ". . . gave retailers tremendous new muscle over the brandmakers, and with all the increased emphasis on discounts and promotions, consumers learned how to bargain."[2]

Effective duplication by competitors may have contributed to Home Depot's recent performance difficulties. "Home Depot isn't such a nimble category killer anymore," says a business writer. Competitors such as Lowe's and Eagle Hardware have built hangar-size warehouses that offer an array of goods similar to that available from Home Depot. Moreover, these competitors' actions have reduced the service gap between them and Home Depot.[3]

In general, the sustainability of a competitive advantage is a function of three factors: (1) the rate of core competence obsolescence due to environmental changes, (2) the availability of substitutes for the core competence, and (3) the imitability of the core competence.[4] The challenge for strategists in all firms—a challenge that can be met through proper use of the strategic management process—is to manage current core competencies effectively while simultaneously developing new ones to use when the competitive advantage derived from application of current ones has been eroded.[5] Only when firms develop a continuous stream of competitive advantages (as explained further in Chapter 5) do they achieve strategic competitiveness, earn above-average returns, and remain ahead of competitors. Intel and Microsoft continuously make investments that are intended to enhance their current sources of competitive advantage and simultaneously spur the creation of new ones.[6] These investments appear to contribute significantly to these firms' ability to achieve and maintain strategic competitiveness.

Firms unable to develop or sustain a competitive advantage eventually fail. For example, more than 2,700 U.S. retail stores closed in 1995. At least another 1,000 retail stores were expected to close their doors by the end of 1996. Table 3.1 lists 12 large U.S. retailers that ceased operations in the early part of 1996, along with descriptions of the causes of their failures.

In Chapter 2, we examined the general environment, the industry environment, and rivalry among competing firms. Armed with knowledge about their firm's environments, managers have a better understanding of the marketplace opportunities and the products necessary to pursue them.

In this chapter, we focus on the firm. Through an analysis of the internal environment, a firm determines *what it can do*—that is, the actions permitted by its unique resources, capabilities, and core competencies. As discussed in Chapter 1, core competencies are a firm's source of competitive advantage. The magnitude of that competitive advantage is a function primarily of its uniqueness

Table 3.1	The Year The Stores Closed Their Doors		
Company (Chains)	How Much Shareholders Lost (In Millions)	Sales 1995 Fiscal Year (In Millions)	What Happened
Caldor	$347	$2,748 Jan. 28	Aggressive expansion by Wal-Mart and Kmart hurt sales. Filed for Chapter 11 in September. Reorganizing.
Bradlees	$125	$1,917 Jan. 28	Rumors of financial trouble caused merchandise shortages and a credit crunch, leading to real financial trouble. Filed for Chapter 11 in June.
Grand Union	$102	$2,392 March 31	Filed for Chapter 11 in January. Emerged in June. But still faces cutthroat competition in the Northeast.
Clothestime (Clothestime, Lingerie Time)	$51	$341 Jan. 28	Women are shopping less and big national chains are slashing prices. Filed for Chapter 11 in December. Reorganizing.
Jamesway	$41	$671 Jan. 28	See Caldor and Bradlees. Filed for Chapter 11 in October after having emerged in January from previous bankruptcy. Now liquidating.
Silo Stores (Subsidiary of Fretter Corp.)	$35	$850 Jan. 31	Operations were unprofitable, with no improvement in sight. Filed for Chapter 11 in December. Liquidating.
Edison Bros. (J. Riggings, Jeans West, Oaktree)	$26	$1,476 Jan. 28	Lenders reluctant to renew or extend financing. "Needed to close a lot of stores quickly." Filed for Chapter 11 in November. Reorganizing.
Rickel Home Centers	Privately held	$640	"Severe downturn in the do-it-yourself marketplace"—and Home Depot got more customers. Filed for Chapter 11 January 10. Reorganizing.
Barney's	Privately held	$300	Overly ambitious expansion and a bitter squabble with Japanese partner Isetan pushed the company into Chapter 11 on January 11. Reorganizing.
Hastings Group (Wallachs, F.R. Tripler, Baskin, Roots)	Privately held	$150	"Extremely difficult conditions in retailing, especially tailored men's clothing. Shortage of capital to spruce up stores." Liquidating.
Petrie Retail (Mary Ann, Stewarts, Petrie)	Privately held	Not disclosed	"The most difficult retail environment in 30 years" created merchandise shortages. Filed for Chapter 11 in October. Reorganizing.
Elder-Beerman Stores (Bee Gee Shoes, Margo's LaMode)	Privately held	Not disclosed	"Mistakes that were made by former management . . . caused profits to decline." Filed Chapter 11 in October. Reorganizing under new CEO.

compared to competitors' competencies.[7] The proper matching of what a firm *can do* with what it *might do* allows the development of strategic intent and a strategic mission and the formulation of strategies. When implemented effectively, a value-creating strategy is the pathway to strategic competitiveness and above-average returns. Outcomes resulting from internal and external environmental analyses are shown in Figure 3.1.

Several topics are examined in this chapter. First, the importance and the challenge of studying a firm's internal environment are addressed. We then discuss the roles that resources, capabilities, and core competencies play in the development of sustainable competitive advantage. Included in these discussions are descriptions of the techniques used to identify and evaluate resources and

Figure 3.1

Outcomes from External and
Internal Environmental Analyses

> By studying the external
> environment, firms identify
> • what they *might* choose
>   to *do*
>
> By studying the internal
> environment, firms
> determine
> • what they *can do*

capabilities and the criteria used to select the firm's core competencies from among its resources and capabilities. While studying these materials, it is important to recall that resources, capabilities, and core competencies are not valuable alone; they have value only because they allow the firm to perform certain activities that result in a competitive advantage.[8]

As shown in Figure 1.1 in Chapter 1, strategic intent and strategic mission, coupled with insights and understandings gained through analyses of the internal and external environments, determine the strategies a firm will select and the actions it will take to implement them successfully. In the final part of the chapter, we briefly describe the relationship between intent and mission and a firm's strategy formulation and implementation actions.

■ The Importance of Internal Analysis

In the new competitive landscape, traditional conditions and factors, such as labor costs, access to financial resources and raw materials, and protected or regulated markets, can still provide competitive advantage, ". . . but to a lesser degree now than in the past."[9] A key reason for this decline is that the advantages created by these sources can be overcome through an international strategy (international strategies are discussed in Chapter 8). As a result, overcapacity is the norm in a host of industries increasing the difficulty of forming competitive advantages. In this challenging competitive environment, few firms are able to make consistently the right strategic decisions. Additionally, less job security for individual employees is an inevitable consequence of operating in this more challenging competitive environment.[10]

The demands of the new competitive landscape make it necessary for top-level managers to rethink the concept of the corporation. Although corporations are difficult to change, earning strategic competitiveness in the 1990s and into the twenty-first century requires development and use of a different managerial mind-set.[11] Most top-level managers recognize the need to change their mind-sets but many hesitate to do so. In the words of a European CEO of a major U.S. company, "It is more reassuring for all of us to stay as we are, even though we know the result will be certain failure. . . than to jump into a new way of working when we cannot be sure it will succeed."[12]

Critical to the managerial mind-set required is the view that a firm is a *bundle* of heterogeneous resources, capabilities, and core competencies that can be used to create an exclusive market position.[13] This view suggests that individual firms possess at least some resources and capabilities that other companies do not have, at least not in the same combination. Resources are the source of capabilities, some of which lead to the development of a firm's core competencies. By using their core competencies, firms are able to perform activities *better* than competitors or that competitors are unable to duplicate. Essentially, the mind-set required in the new competitive landscape ". . . defines a business as an organization that adds value and creates wealth." This is in contrast to managers' traditional mind-set which ". . . has always somehow perceived business as buying cheap and selling dear."[14]

Increasingly, managers are being evaluated in terms of their ability to identify, nurture, and exploit their firm's unique core competencies. By emphasizing competence acquisition and development, organizations learn how to learn—a skill that is linked with the development of competitive advantage. As a process, learning how to learn requires commitment, time, and the active support of top-level executives. In the final analysis, a corporate-wide obsession with the development and use of core competencies may characterize companies able to compete effectively on a global basis in the twenty-first century.[15]

By exploiting their core competencies and meeting the demanding standards of global competition, firms create value for their customers. **Value** entails the performance characteristics and attributes provided by companies in the form of goods or services for which customers are willing to pay. Ultimately, customer value is the source of a firm's potential to earn average or above-average returns. In Chapter 4, we note that value is provided to customers by a product's low cost, by its highly differentiated features, or by a combination of low cost and high differentiation, as compared to competitors' offerings. Core competencies, then, are actually a value-creating system through which a company seeks strategic competitiveness and above-average returns (these relationships are shown in Figure 3.2). In the new competitive landscape, managers need to determine if their firm's core competencies continue to create value for customers.[16]

During the last several decades, the strategic management process was concerned *largely* with understanding the characteristics of the industry in which a firm was competing and, in light of those characteristics, determining how the firm should position itself relative to competitors. The emphasis on industry characteristics and competitive strategy may have understated the role of organizational resources and capabilities in developing competitive advantage. A firm's core competencies, in addition to the results of an analysis of its general, industry, and competitive environments, should drive the selection of strategies. In this regard, core competencies, in combination with product-market positions or tactics, are the most important sources of competitive advantage in the new competitive landscape. Emphasizing core competencies when formulating strategies causes companies to learn how to compete primarily on the basis of firm-specific differences rather than seeking competitive advantage in light of the structural characteristics of their industry(ies).[17]

■ *Value entails the performance characteristics and attributes provided by companies in the form of goods or services for which customers are willing to pay.*

■ The Challenge of Internal Analysis

The decisions managers make in terms of resources, capabilities, and core competencies have a significant influence on a firm's ability to develop competitive advantages and earn above-average returns.[18] Making these decisions—that is, identifying, developing, protecting, and deploying resources, capabilities, and core competencies—may appear to be relatively easy tasks. In fact, however, this work is as challenging and difficult as any other with which managers are involved; and, it is becoming increasingly internationalized and linked with the firm's success.[19]

Figure 3.2

Components of Internal Analysis

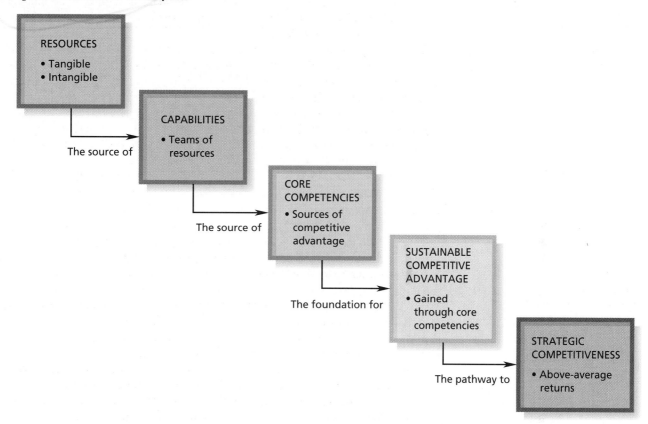

Sometimes, mistakes are made when conducting an internal analysis. Managers might, for example, select resources and capabilities as a firm's core competencies that do not, in fact, yield a competitive advantage. When this occurs, strategists must have the confidence to admit the mistake and take corrective actions. However, firm growth can occur through well-intended errors. Indeed, learning generated by making and correcting mistakes can be important to the creation of new competitive advantages.[20]

To manage the development and use of core competencies, managers must have courage, self-confidence, integrity, the capacity to deal with uncertainty and complexity, and a willingness to hold people accountable for their work.[21] Successful strategists also seek to create an organizational environment in which operating units feel empowered to use the identified core competencies to pursue marketplace opportunities.

Difficult managerial decisions concerning resources, capabilities, and core competencies are characterized by three conditions: uncertainty, complexity, and intraorganizational conflicts (see Figure 3.3).

Managers face *uncertainty* in terms of the emergence of new proprietary technologies, rapidly changing economic and political trends, changes in societal

Figure 3.3

Conditions Affecting
Managerial Decisions About
Resources, Capabilities, and
Core Competencies

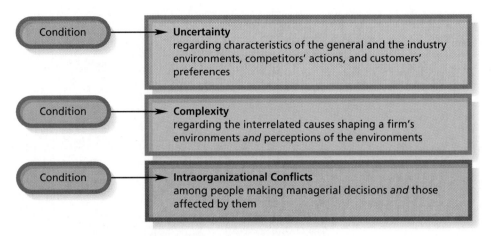

Condition → **Uncertainty**
regarding characteristics of the general and the industry
environments, competitors' actions, and customers'
preferences

Condition → **Complexity**
regarding the interrelated causes shaping a firm's
environments *and* perceptions of the environments

Condition → **Intraorganizational Conflicts**
among people making managerial decisions *and* those
affected by them

Source: Adapted from R. Amit and P. J. H. Schoemaker, 1993, Strategic Assets and Organizational Rent, *Strategic Management Journal* 14:33.

values, and shifts in customer demands. Such environmental uncertainty increases the *complexity* and the range of issues managers examine when studying the internal environment. Managerial biases about how to cope with uncertainty affect decisions about the resources and capabilities that will become the foundation of the firm's competitive advantage. Finally, *intraorganizational conflict* surfaces when decisions are made about core competencies that are to be nurtured and about how the nurturing is to take place.

When making decisions affected by these three conditions, managers should use their judgment. *Judgment* is a capacity for making successful decisions when no obviously correct model or rule is available or when relevant data are unreliable or incomplete.[22] When exercising judgment, the strategist demonstrates a willingness to take intelligent risks in a timely manner. In the new competitive landscape, executive judgment can be a particularly important source of competitive advantage. One reason judgment can result in a competitive advantage is that over time, effective judgment allows a firm to retain the loyalty of stakeholders whose support is linked to above-average returns.[23]

Significant changes in the value-creating potential of a firm's resources and capabilities can occur in a rapidly changing global economy. Because these changes affect a company's power and social structure, inertia or resistance to change may surface. Firms should not deny the changes needed to assure strategic competitiveness; nonetheless, managers sometimes deny the need for organizational and/or personal change. Denial is an unconscious coping mechanism used to block out and not initiate painful changes.[24] Occasionally, an entire industry is accused of being in denial. Some analysts recently cited the automobile manufacturing industry as an example of this. Even in light of saturation in some major markets (such as the United States), stagnating wages, and increasing costs to customers for cars and trucks, it seems that ". . . many in the auto industry are still in denial" about the reality of the situations they face.[25] GE's CEO, Jack Welch, believes that top-level executives must demonstrate unflinching candor when making strategic decisions. Part of this candor demands that decision makers cause their firms and their people to face reality as it is—not as it once was or as they want it to be.[26] Successful strategists have learned that involving many people in decisions about changes reduces denial and intraorganizational conflict.

General Electric CEO Jack Welch believes top-level executives must face reality as it is—not as it once was or as they want it to be—when making strategic decisions.

■ Resources, Capabilities, and Core Competencies

Our attention now turns to a description of resources, capabilities, and core competencies—characteristics that are the foundation of competitive advantage.

■ Resources

Defined in Chapter 1, *resources* are inputs into a firm's production process such as capital equipment, the skills of individual employees, patents, finance, and talented managers. Broad in scope, resources cover a spectrum of individual, social, and organizational phenomena.[27] Individually, resources typically do not yield a competitive advantage. A professional football team may benefit from employing the league's most talented running back. However, it is only when the running back integrates his running style with the blocking schemes of the offensive linemen and the team's offensive strategy that a competitive advantage may develop. Similarly, a firm's production technology, if not protected by patents or other constraints, can be purchased or imitated by competitors. But when that production technology is integrated with other resources to form a capability, a core competence may develop that results in competitive advantage. Thus, a competitive advantage can be created through the *unique bundling of several resources*.[28] In fact, physical assets alone cannot provide a firm with a sustainable competitive advantage.[29]

Some of a firm's resources are tangible; others are intangible. **Tangible resources** are assets that can be seen and quantified. **Intangible resources** range from the intellectual property rights of patents, trademarks, and copyrights to the people-dependent or subjective resources of know-how, networks, organizational culture, and a firm's reputation for its goods or services and the ways it interacts with people (e.g., employees, suppliers, and customers).[30]

Reputation is viewed as an intangible resource that can endow companies with a competitive advantage. Some equate reputation to "what accountants call

■ **Tangible resources** *are assets that can be seen and quantified.*

■ **Intangible resources** *range from the intellectual property rights of patents, trademarks, and copyrights to the people-dependent or subjective resources of know-how, networks, organizational culture, and a firm's reputation for its goods and services and the ways it interacts with people (e.g., employees, suppliers, and customers).*

goodwill and marketers call brand equity."[31] Among other competitive benefits, a positive reputation allows the firm to charge premium prices for its goods or services and to reduce its marketing costs.[32] Boeing is a company whose reputation is a source of competitive advantage. Long known as a manufacturer of some of the world's best airplanes, Boeing's reputation for "superb engineering" contributes to the firm's ability to implement strategies successfully.[33]

The four types of tangible resources are financial, physical, human, and organizational (see Table 3.2). The three types of intangible resources (*technological* and those resulting from the firm's *innovation* and *reputation*) are shown in Table 3.3.

Tangible Resources

As tangible resources, a firm's borrowing capacity and the status of its plant and equipment are visible to all. The value of many tangible resources can be

---

Table 3.2   Tangible Resources

Financial Resources	■ The firm's borrowing capacity
	■ The firm's ability to generate internal funds
Physical Resources	■ Sophistication and location of a firm's plant and equipment
	■ Access to raw materials
Human Resources	■ The training, experience, judgment, intelligence, insights, adaptability, commitment, and loyalty of a firm's individual managers and workers
Organizational Resources	■ The firm's formal reporting structure and its formal planning, controlling, and coordinating systems

Source: Adapted from J.B. Barney, 1992, Firm resources and sustained competitive advantage, *Journal of Management* 17, 101; R.M. Grant, 1991, *Contemporary Strategy Analysis* (Cambridge, England: Blackwell Business), 100–102.

Table 3.3   Intangible Resources

Technological Resources	■ Stock of technology such as patents, trademarks, copyrights, and trade secrets
	■ Knowledge required to apply it successfully
Resources for Innovation	■ Technical employees
	■ Research facilities
Reputation	■ Reputation with customers
	■ Brand name
	■ Perceptions of product quality, durability, and reliability
	■ Reputation with suppliers
	■ For efficient, effective, supportive, and mutually beneficial interactions and relationships

Source: Adapted from R. Hall, 1992, The strategic analysis of intangible resources, *Strategic Management Journal* 13: 136–139; R.M. Grant, 1991, *Contemporary Strategy Analysis* (Cambridge, England: Blackwell Business), 101–104.

established through financial statements. However, financial statements do not account for the value of all of a firm's assets in that they disregard some intangible resources.[34] As such, sources of a firm's competitive advantage often are not reflected on its financial statements.

Managers are challenged to understand fully the strategic value of their firm's tangible and intangible resources. The *strategic value of resources* is indicated by the degree to which they can contribute to the development of capabilities and core competencies and, ultimately, a competitive advantage. For example, as a tangible resource, a distribution facility will be assigned a monetary value on the firm's balance sheet. However, the real value of the facility as a resource is grounded in other factors such as its proximity to raw materials and customers and the manner in which workers integrate their actions internally and with other stakeholders such as suppliers and customers.[35]

As shown in Figure 3.2, resources are the source of a firm's capabilities. Capabilities are the source of a firm's core competencies, which are the basis of competitive advantages. Intangible resources, as compared to tangible resources, are a superior and more potent source of core competencies.[36] In fact, in today's competitive environment, "... the success of a corporation lies more in its intellectual and systems capabilities than in its physical assets. (Moreover), the capacity to manage human intellect—and to convert it into useful products and services—is fast becoming the critical executive skill of the age."[37] Some evidence also suggests that the value of intangible assets is growing as a proportion of a firm's total shareholder value. In a recent 10-year period, for example, one study's results indicate that the relationship between tangible assets (defined as property, plant, and equipment in this study) and total market value for U.S. mining and manufacturing companies declined from 62 to 38 percent.[38]

Intangible Resources

Because they are less visible and more difficult for competitors to understand, purchase, imitate, or substitute, managers prefer to use intangible resources as the foundation for a firm's capabilities and core competencies. In fact, it may be that the more unobservable (that is, intangible) a resource is, the more sustainable will be the competitive advantage based on it.[39]

As noted in the opening case, brand names—an intangible resource that helps to create a firm's reputation—are recognized widely as an important source of competitive advantage for many companies, especially for those manufacturing and selling consumer goods and services. When effective, brand names inform customers of a product's performance characteristics and attributes. When products with strong brand names provide value across time, customers become very loyal by refusing to buy competitors' offerings, including private-label generic products.

When a brand name yields a competitive advantage, companies sometimes strive to find additional ways to exploit it in the marketplace. The new CEO at Century 21 Real Estate, for example, seeks to use his firm's brand name to make his offices a "... virtual home store able to offer and sign up customers for a wide range of discounted home services—all via an agent's lap-top computer"[40] and in the process, to differentiate his firm from other real estate companies. The CEO envisions customers working with Century 21 agents to obtain cable services, appliances, insurance, and mortgages, among other goods and services. The value provided to customers through this use of Century 21's brand name and personnel capabilities is saved time and the purchase of services at dis-

With its vast array of products, Procter & Gamble was the largest advertiser in the United States in 1995, spending a total of $1.51 billion.

counted rates negotiated in advance by Century 21. In essence, a new managerial mind-set was used to find other ways to exploit the competitive advantage of Century 21's brand name. Today, Century 21's managers suggest that their firm ". . . is not about buying and selling homes. . . . It's a marketing and distribution opportunity to the 400,000 to 500,000 people buying homes through us."[41]

One way brand-name products are supported is through advertising. Advertising is considered one of the best ways to build brand equity, as suggested by the fact that spending on advertising has increased during the last several years and was expected to total more than $174 billion in the United States in 1996.[42] Consumer products giant Procter & Gamble was the largest advertiser in the United States in 1995, spending a total of $1.51 billion to advertise Crest toothpaste, Tide detergent, and its other well-known consumer goods (close behind P&G in advertising spending in 1995 were General Motors—$1.5 billion— and Philip Morris—$1.4 billion).[43] In a recent year, the CEO of McCormick & Co., the producer of food flavorings, made a commitment to spend at least $24 million over a three-year period to build brand recognition.[44] To stand out among today's ". . . noisy chorus of competing commercial messages,"[45] some companies with famous brand-name products are returning to slogans used in years past. Examples of these slogans include (1) McDonald's "Two All-Beef Patties," (2) Coca-Cola's "Just For the Taste of It" for Diet Coke, and (3) Ace Hardware's "Ace is the Place" theme song. Supporting these firms' decisions to return to advertising messages of yesterday is some analysts' beliefs that the slogans that first "clicked" with customers are among a company's most potent marketing weapons.

As a source of capabilities, tangible and intangible resources are a critical part of the pathway to the development of competitive advantage (see Figure 3.2). As discussed previously, resources' strategic value is increased when they are integrated or combined. Defined formally in Chapter 1, *capability* is the capacity for a set of resources to integratively perform a task or activity. Capabilities are unique combinations of the firm's information-based tangible resources (see Table 3.2) and/or intangible resources (see Table 3.3) and are what the firm is able to do as a result of teams of resources working together.

■ Capabilities

As just explained, capabilities represent the firm's capacity to deploy resources that have been purposely *integrated* to achieve a desired end state. The glue that binds an organization together, capabilities emerge over time through complex interactions between and among tangible and intangible resources. They are based on developing, carrying, and exchanging information and knowledge through the firm's human capital. Thus, the firm's knowledge base is embedded in and reflected by its capabilities and is a key source of advantage in the new competitive landscape.[46] Because a knowledge base is grounded in organizational actions that may not be explicitly understood by all employees, the firm's capabilities become stronger and more strategically valuable through repetition and practice.

The primary base for the firm's capabilities are the skills and knowledge of its employees. As such, the value of human capital in the development and use of capabilities and, ultimately, core competencies cannot be overstated. Microsoft, for example, believes that its best asset is the "intellectual horsepower" of its employees. To assure continued development of this capability and the core competence that follows, the firm strives continuously to hire people who are more talented than the current set of employees.[47] Table 3.4 lists the guidelines Microsoft follows to upgrade the firm's knowledge base continuously through its recruiting and hiring procedures and practices.

In 1995, Southwest Airlines outperformed all other U.S. carriers, for the fourth year in a row, in terms of on-time performance, baggage handling, and the fewest number of complaints. Southwest's managers attributed the firm's accomplishments to the ". . . commitment and excellence of our more than 21,000 employees who work hard every day. . . ."[48] The views of top-level managers at Microsoft and Southwest Airlines seem to be consistent with those of the head of human resources at Texas Instruments, who believes that "The only nonduplicatable resource (the firm) has is people. That's what's going to make the difference in every organization."[49]

Some believe that the knowledge possessed by the firm's human capital is among the most significant of an organization's capabilities and may ultimately be at the root of all competitive advantages. In the words of a business analyst, "Companies have come to understand that one of the strongest competitive advantages is absolute knowledge."[50] Some even view knowledge as "the sum of everything everybody in (a) company knows that gives (the firm) a competitive edge in the marketplace."[51] Moreover, the *rate* at which firms acquire new knowledge and develop the skills necessary to apply it in the marketplace is a key source of competitive advantage.[52] To facilitate knowledge acquisition, development, and application, some firms (such as Coca-Cola, General Electric, and General Motors) have created a new top management team (this term is discussed in Chapter 12) position—the chief knowledge officer or the chief

Table 3.4   Tips for Nabbing Topnotch Talent
■ Keep senior executives involved in hiring. If they don't care about recruiting, no one else will either.
■ Recruiters should attend meetings of units for which they hire. It helps them keep tabs on hiring needs.
■ When interviewing, teach candidates something in the morning and then ask about it in the afternoon.
■ Written tests yield people who answer the questions correctly, not necessarily those who think creatively.
■ If new hires depart within 12 months, find out why.

Source: E.M. Davies, Wired for hiring: Microsoft's slick recruiting machine, 1996, *Fortune*, February 5, 123–124.

The skills and knowledge of Southwest Airlines' employees allowed it to outperform all other U.S. carriers for the fourth year in a row, in terms of on-time performance, baggage handling, and the fewest number of complaints.

learning officer (CLO). Regardless of the title, the task for these strategists is primarily to help the firm become a learning organization that is open to making the changes required to establish and exploit competitive advantages.

Some evidence suggests that workforces throughout the global economy may lack the skills and knowledge firms require to exploit them as a source of competitive advantage. In high-technology firms, for example, one manager has noted that "high tech is exploding. . . . And the only thing stopping growth from being even stronger is the lack of qualified high-tech professionals."[53] As shown in Table 3.5, a survey of manufacturing executives working in the Southwestern part of the United States revealed that the "lack of adequate workforce skills" is tied with another factor as their top business-related concern. In particular, this concern, which exists across all types of industries, is directed toward the future. "These concerns are not about the existing workforce so much as about the people coming into the workforce."[54] When confronted with a possible shortage of skilled workers, companies desiring to develop their knowledge as source of competitive advantage sometimes scan the global economy to find the required labor skills. For example, a number of firms, including Siemens, Motorola, Hewlett-Packard, and Digital Equipment, have recently employed computer engineers from the city of Bangalore, India. The city's thousands of computer engineers have signalled that Bangalore is an important global source of information technology and workforce capabilities.[55]

The importance of human capital and knowledge to the firm's strategic competitiveness and the need to provide continuous learning opportunities for employees, particularly in light of the forecasted skilled labor force shortages, have been suggested by both business analysts and key government officials. One analyst, for example, believes that in all business organizations (especially those

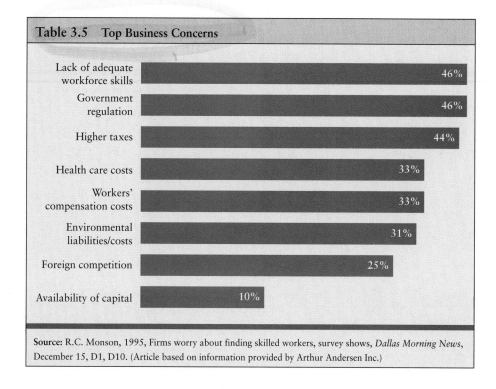

Table 3.5   Top Business Concerns

Concern	Percentage
Lack of adequate workforce skills	46%
Government regulation	46%
Higher taxes	44%
Health care costs	33%
Workers' compensation costs	33%
Environmental liabilities/costs	31%
Foreign competition	25%
Availability of capital	10%

Source: R.C. Monson, 1995, Firms worry about finding skilled workers, survey shows, *Dallas Morning News*, December 15, D1, D10. (Article based on information provided by Arthur Andersen Inc.)

PepsiCo, Inc. 1995

Thirty years ago PepsiCo was created as a company dedicated to aggressive growth.

Since then we've grown a remarkable 15% a year, doubling our business every five years.

Some may think we've come a long way. We think we've just begun.

Determined to grow

PepsiCo's organizational structure is the product of uniquely combining and integrating PepsiCo's resources.

providing services) ". . . learning and productivity grow from the cumulative decision-making experiences of employees in long-term relationships with customers, vendors and fellow employees."[56] The U.S. secretary of labor in the Clinton administration, Robert Reich, proposed that firms must offer continuous training to their workers in order to be competitive. In his words: "Any competitor can come in and use precisely the same machines, the same equipment. The only thing (the firm has) that's unique is the commitment and skills of (its) workforce."[57] It has also been argued that the United States' competitiveness in the global economy and its ability to increase the standard of living of individual citizens is influenced strongly by the degree to which the nation's human capital is nourished and increased.[58]

Capabilities are often developed in specific functional areas (e.g., manufacturing, R&D, marketing, etc.) or in a part (e.g., advertising) of a functional area (marketing). In fact, research results suggest a relationship between distinctive competencies (or capabilities) developed in particular functional areas and the firm's financial performance at both the corporate and business-unit levels.[59] Thus, firms should seek to develop functional area distinctive competencies or capabilities in individual business units and at the corporate level (in the case of diversified firms). Table 3.6 shows a grouping of organizational functions and the capabilities certain companies are thought to possess in terms of all or parts of those functions. These capabilities are core competencies, in that they satisfy the criteria of sustainable competitive advantage (discussed later in the chapter).

PepsiCo, for example, is respected for its organizational structure. The firm's structure, which includes its formal and informal planning, coordinating, and controlling mechanisms, is the product of uniquely combining and integrating

Table 3.6   **Examples of Firm's Capabilities**

Functional Areas	Capabilities	Firm Examples
Distribution	Effective use of logistics management techniques	Wal-Mart
Human resources	Motivating, empowering, and retaining employees	AEROJET
Management information systems	Effective and efficient control of inventories through point-of-purchase data collection methods	Wal-Mart
Marketing	Effective promotion of brand-name products	Gillette
		Ralph Lauren Clothing
		McKinsey & Co.
	Effective customer service	Nordstrom
		Norwest
		Solectron Corporation
		Norrell Corporation
	Innovative merchandising	Crate & Barrel
Management	Effective execution of managerial tasks	Hewlett-Packard
	Ability to envision the future of clothing	The Gap
	Effective organizational structure	PepsiCo
Manufacturing	Design and production skills yielding reliable products	Komatsu
	Product and design quality	The Gap
	Production of technologically sophisticated automobile engines	Mazda
	Miniaturization of components and products	Sony
Research & development	Exceptional technological capability	Corning
	Development of sophisticated engineered elevator control solutions	Motion Control Engineering Inc.
	Rapid transformation of technology into new products and processes	Chaparral Steel
	Deep knowledge of silver-halide materials	Kodak
	Digital technology	Thomson Consumer Electronics

PepsiCo's resources. To improve coordination between its U.S. and foreign snack food operations, the firm recently consolidated the two units into one. Among other benefits, this change in PepsiCo's structure allowed the development of a core corporate leadership team that the firm's CEO believes ". . . will bring even greater firepower to the marketplace."[60]

In the next section, we discuss another framework firms use to identify and evaluate their resources and capabilities. Value chain analysis allows the firm to understand the parts of its operations that create value and those that do not. Understanding these issues is important because the firm earns above-average returns only when the value it creates is greater than the costs incurred to create that value.[61]

■ Value Chain Analysis

The value chain is a template that firms use to understand their cost position and to identify the multiple means that might be used to facilitate the implementation of their business-level strategy.[62] As shown in Figure 3.4, a firm's value chain can

Figure 3.4

The Basic Value Chain

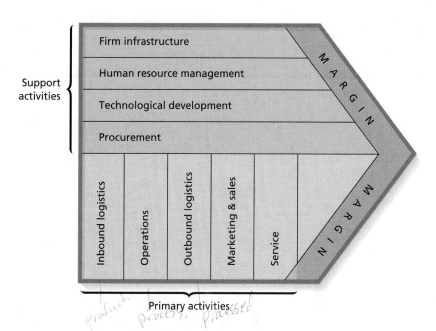

- **Primary activities** *are involved with a product's physical creation, its sale and distribution to buyers, and its service after the sale.*

- **Support activities** *provide the support necessary for the primary activities to take place.*

be segmented into primary and support activities. **Primary activities** are involved with a product's physical creation, its sale and distribution to buyers, and its service after the sale. **Support activities** provide the support necessary for the primary activities to take place. The value chain shows how a product moves from the raw material stage to the final customer. For individual firms, the essential idea of the value chain ". . . is to add as much value as possible as cheaply as possible, and—most important—to capture that value." In a globally competitive economy, ". . . the most valuable links on the chain tend to belong to people who own knowledge—particularly about customers."[63]

Table 3.7 lists the items to be studied to assess the value-creating potential of primary activities. In Table 3.8, the items to consider when studying support activities are shown. As with the analysis of primary activities, the intent in examining these items is to determine areas where the firm has potential to create and capture value. All items included in both tables are to be evaluated with competitors' capabilities in mind. To be a source of competitive advantage, a resource or capability must allow a firm to (1) perform an activity in a manner that is *superior* to competitors' performances or (2) perform a value-creating activity that competitors cannot complete. Only under these conditions does a firm create value for customers and have opportunities to capture that value. Sometimes, this requires firms to reconfigure or recombine parts of the value chain in unique ways. Federal Express (FedEx) changed the nature of the delivery business by reconfiguring both the primary and support activities to create the overnight delivery business, creating value for itself in the process of doing so. The opportunity to purchase automobiles through on-line computer networks is another example of firms' efforts to reconfigure the value chain, especially in terms of primary activities. Companies such as Auto-By-Tel use the capabilities of the Internet to sell cars in cyberspace. Companies providing opportunities for customers to buy cars through electronic shopping networks appear to have reconfigured the value chain in a way that allows them to create and capture value.[64]

Rating a firm's capacities to execute the primary and support activities is challenging. Earlier in the chapter, we noted that identifying and assessing the

Table 3.7   Examining the Value-Creating Potential of Primary Activities

Inbound Logistics

Activities, such as materials handling warehousing, and inventory control, used to receive, store, and disseminate inputs to a product.

Operations

Activities necessary to convert the inputs provided by inbound logistics into final product form. Machining, packaging, assembly, and equipment maintenance are examples of operations activities.

Outbound Logistics

Activities involved with collecting, storing, and physically distributing the final product to customers. Examples of these activities include finished goods warehousing, materials handling, and order processing.

Marketing and Sales

Activities completed to provide means through which customers can purchase products and to induce them to do so. To effectively market and sell products, firms develop advertising and promotional campaigns, select appropriate distribution channels, and select, develop, and support their sales force.

Service

Activities designed to enhance or maintain a product's value. Firms engage in a range of service-related activities, including installation, repair, training, and adjustment.

Each activity should be examined relative to competitors' abilities. Accordingly, firms rate each activity as *superior, equivalent,* or *inferior.*

Source: Adapted with the permission of The Free Press, a division of Simon & Schuster from COMPETITIVE ADVANTAGE: Creating and Sustaining Superior Performance by Michael E. Porter, pp. 39–40, Copyright © 1985 by Michael E. Porter.

value of a firm's resources and capabilities require judgment. Judgment is equally necessary when using value chain analysis. The reason for this is that there is no *obviously* correct model or rule available to help in this process. Moreover, most data available for these evaluations are largely anecdotal, sometimes unreliable, or difficult to interpret.

An effective value chain analysis results in the identification of new ways to perform activities to create value. Because these types of innovations are firm specific—that is, they are grounded in a company's unique way of combining its resources and capabilities—they are difficult for competitors to recognize, understand, and imitate. The greater the time necessary for competitors to understand how a firm is creating and capturing value through its execution of primary and support activities, the more sustainable is the competitive advantage gained by the innovating company.

But what should a firm do with respect to primary and support activities in which its resources and capabilities are not a source of competence and competitive advantage? As discussed next, in these instances, firms should study the possibility of outsourcing the work associated with primary and support activities in which they are unable to create and capture value.

■ Outsourcing

■ *Outsourcing is the purchase of a value-creating activity from an external supplier.*

Outsourcing is the purchase of a value-creating activity from an external supplier. In the view of a consultant, "outsourcing is a strategic concept—a way to add

Table 3.8	Examining the Value-Creating Potential of Support Activities

Procurement

Activities completed to *purchase* the inputs needed to produce a firm's products. Purchased inputs include items fully consumed during the manufacture of products (e.g., raw materials and supplies as well as fixed assets—machinery, laboratory equipment, office equipment, and buildings).

Technological development

Activities completed to improve a firm's product and the processes used to manufacture it. Technology development takes many forms, such as process equipment, design, both basic research and product design, and servicing procedures.

Human Resource Management

Activities involved with recruiting, hiring, training, developing, and compensating all personnel.

Firm Infrastructure

Firm infrastructure includes activities such as general management, planning, finance, accounting, legal support, and governmental relations that are required to support the work of the entire value chain. Through its infrastructure, the firm strives to effectively and consistently identify external opportunities and threats, identify resources and capabilities, and support core competencies.

Each activity should be examined relative to competitors' abilities. Accordingly, firms rate each activity as *superior, equivalent,* or *inferior.*

Source: Adapted with the permission of The Free Press, a division of Simon & Schuster from COMPETITIVE ADVANTAGE: Creating and Sustaining Superior Performance by Michael E. Porter, pp. 40–43, Copyright © 1985 by Michael E. Porter.

value to the business that converts an in-house cost center into a customer-focused service operation."[65] Sometimes, virtually all firms within an industry seek the strategic value that can be captured through effective outsourcing. The automobile manufacturing industry is an example of such an industry. Based on an observation of the outsourcing trend in this industry an analyst concluded that "The whole strategy worldwide now in the auto industry is to get down to your core vehicle-producing operations. . . . That means shedding everything but stamping, powertrains and final assembly. . . and getting rid of everything that doesn't contribute to those areas."[66]

Several statistics demonstrate the increasing scope of outsourcing. For example, U.S. corporations spent more than $38 billion on information technology outsourcing alone in 1995. This amount represented a full 8 percent of total expenditures by U.S. firms on information technology during that year. G2Research predicts that the recent $2 billion ". . . market for voice and data network outsourcing will grow by 22 percent a year through 1999."[67] In fact, approximately 20 percent of the largest U.S. companies use some form of information technology outsourcing.[68] Similar growth rates in outsourcing activities are expected in other fields, including health care, customer service, and human resources. This has been one of the trends that has increased the importance of cooperative strategy (e.g., the more frequent use of strategic alliances, as described in Chapter 9).

Perhaps the major reason outsourcing is being used prominently is that few, if any, firms possess the resources and capabilities required to achieve competitive superiority in all primary and support activities. With respect to technologies, for example, research suggests that few companies can afford to develop internally

Rolls-Royce outsources a number of peripheral items so it can concentrate on its core competencies.

all the technologies that might lead to competitive advantage in the future. By nurturing a few core competencies, the firm increases its probability of developing a competitive advantage. Additionally, by outsourcing activities in which it lacks capabilities, the firm can concentrate fully on those areas in which it can create value.[69]

Rolls-Royce Motor Cars engages in outsourcing. The manufacturer of some of the world's most expensive automobiles (ranging in price from roughly $160,000 to more than $366,000 in 1996), the firm suffered losses during 1991 and 1992. One of the decisions made to reverse this situation was to outsource. Today the company outsources a number of peripheral items such as car bodies and fasteners so it can concentrate "on its core competencies—engines, paint, leather, (and) wood."[70] Recent results suggest that the strategic decision to outsource was appropriate. The company experienced a 10 percent increase in its sales volume between 1994 and 1995, causing the CEO to observe that the firm entered 1996 "in good spirits."[71]

Boeing Co. has decided to expand its outsourcing program. To increase efficiency and eventually save an estimated $600 million annually, the firm has elected to buy more aircraft components and parts from outside suppliers instead of making them. Airplane doors, landing gear components, interiors, and control surfaces are examples of products Boeing decided in the recent past to outsource. However, core products such as engine struts and wings will still be manufactured in house. With these outsourcing decisions, the firm now manufactures approximately 52 percent of the components that make up its airplanes, outside of engines. Of the remaining 48 percent, 34 percent is purchased from American suppliers with 14 percent coming from suppliers in other nations. Although some workers reacted negatively to Boeing's decision to outsource more of its work, the company felt these actions were necessary to help it remain the largest aerospace manufacturer in the world. A review of the firm's choices suggests that no work was being outsourced in which the company's capabilities yielded a core competence that was a source of competitive advantage.[72]

When outsourcing, the firm seeks the greatest value. In other words, a company wants to outsource only to firms possessing a core competence in terms of performing the primary or support activity that is being outsourced. For companies to whom others outsource, being able to create value is the pathway through which they achieve strategic competitiveness and earn above-average returns. Three companies that are able to create and capture value by performing activities that other firms outsource to them are described in the Strategic Focus.

When evaluating resources and capabilities, firms must be careful not to decide to outsource activities in which they can create and capture value. Additionally, companies should not outsource primary and support activities that are used to neutralize environmental threats or complete necessary ongoing organizational tasks. Called a "nonstrategic team of resources" in Figure 3.5, firms must verify that they do not outsource capabilities that are critical to their success, even though the capabilities are not actual sources of competitive advantage.

Another risk that is part of outsourcing concerns the firm's knowledge base. As discussed earlier in the chapter, knowledge continues to increase in importance as a source of competence and competitive advantage for firms in the new competitive landscape. In part, organizations learn through a continuous and integrated sharing of experiences employees have as they perform primary and support activities. One reason for the success of a learning organization is that with continuous and integrated sharing of experiences, it is able to evaluate thoroughly the ongoing validity of the key assumptions it holds about the nature and future of its business operations. Outsourcing activities in which the firm cannot create value can have an unintended consequence of damaging the firm's potential to continuously evaluate its key assumptions, learn, and create new capabilities and core competencies. Therefore, managers should verify that the

Figure 3.5

Core Competence as a Strategic Capability

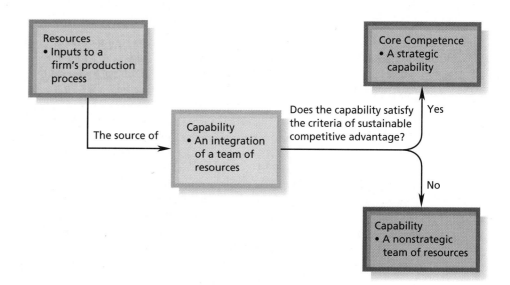

STRATEGIC FOCUS   Creating Value As an Outsourcing Company

A.M. Castle distributes and processes specialty metals. In 1995, more than one-half of the firm's sales came from customers for whom Castle manages their metal inventory. Customers that have outsourced to Castle include Snap-On Tools, Du Pont, and Raytheon. Acting primarily as a raw materials consultant, Castle carefully observes its customers' buying habits, cuts redundancies from its purchasing practices, and delivers metal to them on an as-needed basis. Castle's ability to slash costs provides value to its customers. Competing as a company to which others outsource a support activity has increased Castle's returns. As compared to 1994, the firm's 1995 profits increased 74 percent and the price of its stock doubled.

U.S. Filter offers water-treatment systems and services to a wide array of companies, including automobile and computer chip manufacturers. The firm is exploiting the desire on the part of organizations to outsource all of their water needs to a single company. Through its competencies, U.S. Filter handles on-site water treatment facilities for customers who are charged between $75,000 and $100,000 monthly for the firm's services. In a recent year, third-quarter earnings were 136 percent higher as compared to the previous year on sales that increased only 61 percent.

Canada's Magna International supplies the Big Three U.S. automakers with multiple products including seats, bumpers, fenders, and electronics. By developing and using innovative manufacturing techniques, Magna is able to provide customers with high-quality parts. Recently the firm signed two "systems integrator" contracts, forging even closer links with companies it serves. "Under these pacts, believed to be the first in the industry, Magna will handle much of the design, engineering and development of two planned sport-utility vehicles right from the chalkboard to the assembly line." Although challenged by competitors, Magna still has competitive advantages that allow it to be successful as a firm to which others outsource activities in which they do not have a competitive advantage. The receipt of an award from General Motors in 1995 by a Magna unit for the group's "truly outstanding performance" in quality, service, and price demonstrates the value the firm provides to its customers.

Source: E. Schonfeld, 1996, Open, sesame! *Fortune,* March 4, 207; S. Caminiti, 1995, Outsourcing water, *Fortune,* December 11, 209; M. Heinzl, 1995, Magna International profits on big three outsourcing, *Wall Street Journal,* August 24, B5.

firm does not outsource activities that stimulate the development of new capabilities and competencies.[73]

Occasionally, a firm discovers that areas in which it could perhaps develop a competence can and should be outsourced. For example, many believe that banks should develop a core competence in the area of information technology (IT). However, following careful analysis of its resources and capabilities, managers at Continental Bank concluded that the bank lacked the skills required to develop a core competence in the IT area. As a result, the managers decided to outsource the firm's IT activities so the bank could "focus on its true core competencies—intimate knowledge of customers' needs and relationships with customers."[74]

Armed with knowledge about resources and capabilities, managers are prepared to identify their firm's core competencies. As defined in Chapter 1, *core competencies* are resources and capabilities that serve as a source of competitive advantage for a firm over its rivals. Next, we discuss the fact that not all resources and capabilities are core competencies.

■ Core Competencies

As the source of competitive advantage for a firm, core competencies distinguish a company competitively and reflect its personality. Core competencies emerge over time through an organizational process of accumulating and learning how to deploy different resources and capabilities. As a capacity to take action, core competencies ". . . are the essence of what makes an organization unique in its ability to provide value to customers over a long period of time."[75]

However, not all of a firm's resources and capabilities are strategic assets—that is, assets that have competitive value and the potential to serve as a source of competitive advantage.[76] In fact, some resources and capabilities may result in incompetence because they represent competitive areas in which the firm is weak compared to competitors. Thus, some resources or capabilities may stifle or prevent the development of a core competence. Firms with insufficient financial capital, for example, may be unable to purchase facilities or hire the skilled workers required to manufacture products that yield customer value. In this situation, financial capital (a tangible resource) would be a weakness. Armed with in-depth understandings of their firm's resources and capabilities, strategic managers are challenged to find external environmental opportunities that can be exploited through the firm's capabilities while avoiding competition in areas of weakness.

Managers use four specific criteria to determine which of their firm's resources and capabilities are core competencies. Because they have satisfied the four criteria of sustainable competitive advantage, the capabilities shown in Table 3.6 are core competencies for the firms possessing them. Core competencies differ for every organization, but the realities of the new competitive landscape may demand that every organization seek to develop innovation as a core competence.[77]

How many core competencies are required for the firm to have a competitive advantage? Responses to this question vary. McKinsey & Co. recommends that clients identify three or four competencies around which their strategic actions will be framed.[78] Note the consistency of Rolls-Royce's decisions with this advice. Recall from an earlier discussion that Rolls-Royce has decided to focus on only four competencies—engines, paint, leather, and wood. Trying to support and nurture more than four core competencies prevents the firm from developing the focus it needs to exploit fully its competencies in the marketplace. Moreover, supporting and nurturing more than four competencies dissipates the impact of the firm's available resources. As described in the Strategic Focus, The Gap nurtures a few core competencies that are used consistently to establish competitive advantage in different product markets.

■ Criteria of Sustainable Competitive Advantage

Capabilities that are valuable, rare, costly to imitate, and nonsubstitutable are a source of competitive advantage.[79] Capabilities failing to satisfy these criteria are not core competencies. Thus, as shown in Figure 3.5, every core competence is a capability, but every capability is not a core competence.

A sustained competitive advantage is achieved only when competitors have tried, without success, to duplicate the benefits of a firm's strategy or when competitors lack the confidence to attempt imitation. However, for some period of time, a firm may earn a competitive advantage through the use of capabilities that are, for example, valuable and rare,[80] but are imitable. In such an instance, the length of time a firm can expect to retain its competitive advantage is a function of how quickly competitors can successfully imitate a good, service, or process. It is only through the combination of conditions represented by all four criteria that a firm's capabilities have the potential to create a sustained competitive advantage.

STRATEGIC FOCUS

Old Navy Stores: A New Format for The Gap to Achieve Competitive Advantage?

A specialty retailer, The Gap operates more than 1,600 company outlets under the store names The Gap, GapKids, Banana Republic, and Old Navy. Through the presentation of dressed-down clothes at affordable prices, the firm is thought to have revolutionized the casual-apparel market for women, men, and children. The firm relied on various capabilities to develop competitive advantages in terms of its attention to quality and design and the use of clever advertising slogans and campaigns.

Between 1983 and 1991, sales at The Gap stores increased from $480 million to $2.5 billion. However, by the early 1990s, competitors had learned how to duplicate the benefits of The Gap's value-creating strategies. In commenting about how this happened, the firm's CEO suggested that ". . . there are no secrets in retailing. The minute something new—a store or a look—is created in this industry, it is instantly visible, there for all the world to examine and replicate." Resulting from at least some erosion of its competitive advantage was a decline of 8 percent in 1992's profits (the first decline since 1984).

Evaluation of its resources, capabilities, core competencies, and conditions in the external environment have resulted in several strategic decisions and actions. The firm's employees informed strategic managers that The Gap's clothes were becoming too expensive. While many customers wanted to buy the firm's clothes, only a smaller number of them were able to do so.

To exploit what it saw as an opportunity—to serve customers interested in dressed-down clothes but unable to afford The Gap's goods—the firm decided to use its capabilities and competencies to establish Old Navy stores. In 1996, the target customer for The Gap's new retailing format had an annual income of between $20,000 and $50,000. In contrast to The Gap customer, this individual is more likely to purchase goods and services at strip shopping centers, which is where most Old Navy units are being located. At The Gap, a plain white T-shirt recently cost $10.50; at the same time, a white T-shirt at Old Navy was $7.50. The differences are subtle, yet important. The Gap's shirt has a cotton weight of 180 grams per square meter, whereas Old Navy's shirt has a cotton weight of 165 grams per square meter. The Old Navy shirt can be expected to shrink more as compared to The Gap offering. The Gap's capabilities—those necessary to cleverly advertise products to which attention to design and quality have been devoted—were used to establish and implement the Old Navy concept. In other words, relative to competitors' offerings, Old Navy's goods may offer greater quality and superior product design.

The Old Navy format is not a revolutionary idea. The concept of shopping as theater, with big stores, low prices, loud music, concrete floors, exposed pipes, and whimsical displays is offered by other companies. In addition, J.C. Penney and Sears are courting the lower-price-apparel shoppers with updated stores and clothing lines. Given the similarity across these competing firms, what accounts for analysts' optimism for Old Navy stores? What competitive advantages is The Gap exploiting to implement its value-creating strategy? The words of a retailing analyst seem to answer these questions: "No other retailer combines low prices, quality merchandise, and an absolutely fun atmosphere to shop in the way Old Navy does." Thus, it may be that The Gap is successfully using distinctive competencies—that is, competencies that allow the firm clearly to outperform its rivals—as the foundation for the operation of its various store formats, including Old Navy.

Source: S. Caminiti, 1996, Will Old Navy fill the Gap? *Fortune*, March 18, 59–62.

Valuable

■ *Valuable capabilities are those that help a firm exploit opportunities and/or neutralize threats in its external environment.*

Valuable capabilities are those that help a firm exploit opportunities and/or neutralize threats in its external environment. Valuable capabilities enable a firm to formulate and implement strategies that create value for specific customers.

Sony Corp. has used its valuable capabilities dealing with the designing, manufacturing, and selling of miniaturized electronic technology to exploit a range of marketplace opportunities, including those for portable disc players and easy-to-hold 8mm video cameras.[81]

Rare

■ *Rare capabilities* are those possessed by few, if any, current or potential competitors.

Rare capabilities are those possessed by few, if any, current or potential competitors. A key question managers seek to answer when evaluating this criterion is "How many rival firms possess these valuable capabilities?" Capabilities possessed by many rival firms are ". . . unlikely to be a source of competitive advantage for any one of them. Instead, valuable but common (i.e., not rare) resources and capabilities are sources of competitive parity."[82] Competitive advantage results only when firms develop and exploit capabilities that differ from those they share with competitors.

Costly to Imitate

■ *Costly to imitate capabilities* are those that other firms cannot develop easily.

Costly to imitate capabilities are those that other firms cannot develop easily. Capabilities that are costly to imitate can occur because of one or a combination of three reasons.

First, a firm sometimes is able to develop capabilities because of *unique historical conditions*. "As firms evolve, they pick up skills, abilities, and resources that are unique to them, reflecting their particular path through history."[83] A firm with a unique and valuable organizational culture that emerged in the early stages of the company's history ". . . may have an imperfectly imitable advantage over firms founded in another historical period"[84] —a period of time in which less valuable values and beliefs strongly influence the development of a firm's culture. This may be the case for the consulting firm McKinsey & Co.

McKinsey's culture is thought by competitors, clients, and analysts alike to be a primary source of competitive advantage for the firm. As testimony to the intangibility of culture, even to some of those familiar with it, consider the following description of culture as McKinsey's source of advantage: "It is that culture, unique to McKinsey and eccentric, which sets the firm apart from virtually any other business organization and which often mystifies even those who engage (its) services." The historical foundation for McKinsey's culture was established by Marvin Bower, the company's founding father. In fact, "much of what McKinsey *is* today harks back to the early 1930s" when Bower entered the consulting business. Bower's concept of how his consulting firm would operate was that it should provide advice about effective managerial practices to top-level executives. As guidance for McKinsey's consultants, Bower developed a set of principles. Cited frequently and with intensity, these principles actually define what McKinsey was and is today. As such, they are the backbone of the company's unique, and what some think is an enigmatic, culture. According to Bower's principles, a McKinsey consultant should (1) put the interests of the client ahead of increasing the company's revenues, (2) remain silent about the client's business operations, (3) be truthful and not fear challenging a client's opinion, and (4) perform only work that s/he believes is in the client's best interests and is something McKinsey can do well.[85]

A second condition of being costly to imitate occurs when the link between the firm's competencies and its competitive advantage is *causally ambiguous*. In these instances, competitors are unable to understand clearly how a firm uses its competencies as the foundation for competitive advantage. As a result, competitors are uncertain about the competencies they should develop to duplicate the benefits of a competitor's value-creating strategy. Gordon Forward, CEO of Chaparral Steel, allows competitors to tour his firm's facilities. In Forward's words, competitors can be shown almost "... everything and we will be giving away nothing because they can't take it home with them."[86]

Social complexity is the third reason that capabilities can be costly to imitate. Social complexity means that at least some, and frequently many, of the firm's capabilities are the product of complex social phenomena. Examples of socially complex capabilities include interpersonal relationships, trust and friendships among managers, and a firm's reputation with suppliers and customers. Hewlett-Packard's culture is widely recognized as socially complex and as a source of competitive advantage for the firm. Socially complex capabilities resulting from this culture include the nurturing of innovation across divisional boundaries and the effective use of cross-functional work teams. Recently this culture provided the capability HP needed to develop work processes through which the firm was able to improve operations dramatically in its North American distribution organization. Designed by a cross-functional work team of 35 people from HP and two other companies, the distribution center's new work processes have reduced the number of days required to deliver products to customers from 26 to 8.[87]

Nonsubstitutable

Nonsubstitutable capabilities are those that do not have strategic equivalents. This final requirement for a capability to be a source of competitive advantage "... is that there must be no strategically equivalent valuable resources that are themselves either not rare or imitable. Two valuable firm resources (or two bundles of firm resources) are strategically equivalent when they each can be exploited separately to implement the same strategies."[88] In general the strategic value of capabilities increases the more difficult they are to substitute.[89] The more invisible capabilities are, the more difficult it is for firms to find substitutes and the greater the challenge is to competitors trying to imitate a firm's value-creating strategy. Firm-specific knowledge and trust-based working relationships between managers and nonmanagerial personnel are examples of capabilities that are difficult to identify and for which finding substitutes is challenging.

To summarize this discussion, we reiterate that sustainable competitive advantage results only through the use of capabilities that are valuable, rare, costly to imitate, and nonsubstitutable. Table 3.9 shows the competitive consequences and performance implications resulting from combinations of the four criteria of sustainability. The analysis suggested by this table's contents helps managers determine the strategic value of the firm's capabilities. Resources and capabilities falling into the first row in the table (that is, resources and capabilities that aren't valuable or rare and that are imitable and for which strategic substitutes exist) are ones the firm should *not* emphasize to formulate and implement strategies. However, capabilities yielding competitive parity and either temporary or sustainable competitive advantage will be supported. Large competitors such as Coca-Cola and PepsiCo may have capabilities that can yield only competitive parity. In such cases, the firms will nurture these capabilities while simultaneously emphasizing those that can yield either a temporary or sustainable competitive advantage.

What about The Gap's Old Navy stores? What type of advantage, if any, results from use of some of the firm's capabilities such as product design and

■ *Nonsubstitutable capabilities* are those that do not have strategic equivalents.

Table 3.9   Outcomes from Combinations of the Criteria of Sustainable Competitive Advantage

Is the Resource or Capability Valuable?	Is the Resource or Capability Rare?	Is the Resource or Capability Costly to Imitate?	Is the Resource or Capability Nonsubstitutable?	Competitive Consequences	Performance Implications
No	No	No	No	Competitive disadvantage	Below-average returns
Yes	No	No	Yes/no	Competitive parity	Average returns
Yes	Yes	No	Yes/no	Temporary competitive advantage	Above-average returns/ average returns
Yes	Yes	Yes	Yes	Sustainable competitive advantage	Above-average returns

quality, creative advertising, and store design and layout to develop the Old Navy format? It seems that the capabilities being used in this new retailing format are valuable and rare. However, at least with respect to The Gap's major competitors, these capabilities can be imitated (recall the comments from The Gap's CEO about imitability). Strategic equivalents for these capabilities may or may not exist. Thus, an analysis of these capabilities suggests that The Gap has established a temporary competitive advantage with its Old Navy stores (see Table 3.9). In terms of the performance implications, the firm should earn above-average returns until competitors learn how to duplicate the value Old Navy stores creates through exploitation of The Gap's capabilities in the marketplace.

In the next section, important cautions about core competencies are discussed.

■ Core Competencies—Cautions and Reminders

An attractive attribute of a firm's core competencies is that, unlike physical assets, they tend to become more valuable through additional use. A key reason for this is that they are largely knowledge based. Sharing knowledge across people, jobs, and organizational functions often results in an expansion of that knowledge in competitively relevant ways.[90] At Chaparral Steel, for example, the CEO believes that one of his firm's ". . . core competencies is the rapid realization of new technology into steel products."[91] As a learning organization, Chaparral extends significant efforts to verify that learning is shared across the entire firm. Thus, in a manner that is consistent with the most effective learning organizations, it seems that Chaparral Steel has a ". . . healthy disrespect for the status quo." Resulting from this "disrespect" is a commitment to constant self-examination and experimentation.[92]

Evidence and company experiences show that the value of core competencies, as sources of competitive advantage, should never be taken for granted. Moreover, the ability of any particular core competence to provide competitive advantage on a permanent basis should not be assumed. The reason for these cautions is due to the central dilemma that is associated with the use of core competencies as sources of competitive advantage. This dilemma is that all core capabilities simultaneously have the potential to be core rigidities. All capabilities, then, are both a strength and a weakness. They are strengths because they are the source of competitive advantage and, hence, strategic competitiveness; they are a weakness because if emphasized when they are no longer competitively relevant, they can be the seeds of organizational inertia.[93]

Events occurring in the firm's external environment create conditions through which core competencies can become core rigidities and create inertia. "Often the flip side, the dark side, of core capabilities is revealed due to external events— when new competitors figure out a better way to serve the firm's customers, when new technologies emerge, or when political or social events shift the ground underneath."[94] But, it really isn't changes in the external environment that cause core capabilities to become core rigidities. Rather, it is strategic myopia and inflexibility on the part of a firm's managers that results in core competencies being emphasized to the point that strategic inertia strangles the firm's ability to grow and adapt to environmental changes.[95] The experiences of Sears Roebuck & Co., as described in the Strategic Focus, demonstrate these relationships.

STRATEGIC FOCUS Core Competencies and Core Rigidities at Sears Roebuck & Co.

The retailing environment Sears has faced during the last two decades differs substantially from what it experienced historically. However, as suggested by the following comment from Sam Walton, the founder of Wal-Mart, Sears' managers may have failed to realize that its competitive environment had changed: "One reason Sears fell so far off the pace is that they wouldn't admit for the longest time that Wal-Mart and Kmart were their real competition. They ignored both of us, and we both blew right by them." Instead of reconfiguring its value chain to form new sources of competitive advantage that would allow it to compete effectively in its changed environment, Sears essentially decided to continue emphasizing its existing core competencies. Unfortunately for the firm, its core competencies had become core rigidities.

It wasn't until a new CEO, Arthur Martinez, was appointed in 1993 that Sears began to reshape itself and to develop new core competencies. Acting courageously and demonstrating a willingness to do what he believed had to be done, one analyst observed that the new CEO " . . . came in and immediately made the decisions that had to be made . . . and they resulted in a profitable impact." Among the decisions Martinez implemented quickly were to slash more than 50,000 jobs, close 113 retail stores and eliminate the entire catalog operations. In 1996, Sears decided to sell its 50 percent stock in Prodigy, an on-line network service, because it no longer fit the firm's commitment to focus on its retailing operations. This action followed previous divestitures of Dean Witter, Discover Card, Coldwell Banker real estate, and Allstate insurance. Instead of trying to provide "merchandise and merchandise-related services to the consumer at competitive prices with excellent quality" (which was the previous CEO's mission for the firm), Mr. Martinez observed that "Sears is a moderate-price department store."

Mr. Martinez and Sears' other strategic managers have carefully studied their competitors as well as other retailers to identify and try to understand the core competencies they are using to establish competitive advantages. Wal-Mart's competence with technology and

Appliance section of a Sears store.

logistics is, in Mr. Martinez's view, "a model for anyone." Sears' strategists believe Crate & Barrel's core competence is its brilliant and innovative merchandising. At Nordstrom, the firm's competence to connect with its core customers with a complete inventory of items they value is thought to be a key source of its competitive advantage. Today, Sears is using its capabilities to lauch private brands (e.g., the Canyon River Blues denim collection and its private cosmetics brand known as Circle of Beauty).

Through these actions and others, Sears is striving to develop new sources of competitive advantage. Early results are encouraging—sales per square foot are increasing steadily and the firm's market share has grown. The actions taken at Sears to redeploy some of its resources and capabilities and to eliminate core rigidities while developing new competencies came about because of the bold leadership of the firm's chief strategist, Mr. Martinez. To capture more fully how the firm intended to exploit its competitive advantages in the pursuit of strategic competitiveness in the future, Mr. Martinez and his top management team have mapped out a growth plan that details Sears' intended commitments and strategic actions to the year 2000.

Source: R. Berner and J. Sandberg, 1996, Sears to shed its 50% stake in Prodigy, *Wall Street Journal,* February 22, A3, A4; G. Buck, 1996, Saks veteran hailed as Sears' savior, *Dallas Morning News,* January 21, H1, H5; J.B. Barney, 1995, Looking inside for competitive advantage, *Academy of Management Executive* IX, no. 4: 49–61; D. Leonard-Barton, 1995, *Wellsprings of Knowledge* (Boston: Harvard Business School Press); P. Sellers, 1995, Sears: In with the new out with the old, *Fortune,* October 16, 96–98.

As evidenced by the Strategic Focus, managers operating in the new competitive landscape must remember that core competencies that are allowed to become core rigidities prevent the firm from changing when necessary. Firms that have achieved strategic competitiveness and earned above-average returns for extended periods of time are sometimes hesitant to change what they are doing. However, capabilities are competencies *only* when they are strategically relevant; that is, when their use permits exploitation of opportunities in the external environment. Rapid and significant changes in the global economy prevent firms from permanently exploiting the same competencies. Firms failing to recognize this reality may quickly find themselves at a competitive disadvantage. Thus, executives must seek to strike a balance between nurturing and supporting *existing* core competencies while simultaneously encouraging the type of forthright appraisals that will cause the development of *new* competencies.

■ Strategic Inputs and Strategic Actions

Shown in Figure 1.1 in Chapter 1, the results gained through analyses of the external and internal environments provide the strategic inputs a firm needs to develop its strategic intent and strategic mission. The value of intent and mission is that they describe what a firm seeks to achieve in light of its internal competencies and external opportunities.

To close our discussion of strategic inputs, we offer a few final comments about intent and mission. Defined in Chapter 1, *strategic intent* is the leveraging of a firm's resources, capabilities, and core competencies (hereafter called capabilities for the purpose of this discussion) to accomplish the firm's goals in the competitive environment.[96] Recent evidence suggests that, indeed, successful companies competing in the global economy have learned how to leverage their capabilities to reach challenging goals.[97] Other results suggest that "overextensions" of a firm's resources and capabilities that were ". . . created to challenge the organization characterize the most successful Japanese manufacturing companies."[98] Chaparral Steel's strategic intent may be captured by the following statement ". . . the goal for every hour, the criterion for every person's activity, is crystal clear: make ever more steel—increasingly better than anyone else."[99] The original strategic intent at Netscape, as established by the CEO, was for the firm ". . . to become the fastest-growing software company in history, based on first-year revenues."[100]

Strategic managers are challenged to stimulate the formation of stretch goals for each employee, even when some may not understand the importance of doing so. Individual stretch goals must be consistent with the objective embedded within the firm's strategic intent. When employees are motivated by a well-articulated strategic intent, properly established stretch goals leverage all of a firm's competencies and may create future success—for both individual employees and their firm.[101] Moreover, when handled correctly, pursuing accomplishment of a firm's strategic intent ". . . causes employees to perform in ways they never imagined possible."[102]

Andersen Consulting intends to be the world's foremost full-service consulting firm. This strategic intent may be achieved through effective use of the firm's capabilities and core competencies.

The thoughts of an assistant brand manager at Procter & Gamble's location in Rotterdam, Netherlands, describe positive outcomes from the application of strategic intent. When first exposed to the firm's strategic intent, this employee thought to himself, "You've got to be kidding!" However, after working toward his personal stretch goals that were consistent with the firm's strategic intent, he concluded that ". . . the concept works!" Describing his view about intent, the employee stated that "Even though I might not reach a specific goal, I do get near it, and that is a greater achievement than I would ever have expected."[103]

Andersen Consulting is a firm stretching its capabilities to reach its strategic intent. Viewing itself as the "world's premier business and technology consultancy," the firm intends to become the world's first and foremost full-service consulting emporium, capable of serving clients by rewiring computer systems, recrafting strategies, reeducating employees, and reengineering work processes. Already earning more than 51 percent of its revenues from operations outside the United States, Andersen's work in 46 countries reflects its commitment to remain what some believe is the leading global consulting firm.[104] Capabilities Andersen is using to achieve its strategic intent include its knowledge, skills, and experiences in terms of logistics and operations strategies, total supply chain management processes, and information and technology strategies.[105] Challenging as it should be, this strategic intent may be reached through effective use of Andersen Consulting's capabilities and core competencies.

Strategic intent defines the framework for a firm's strategic mission. The *strategic mission* is a statement of a firm's unique purpose and the scope of its operations in product and market terms.[106] Because it specifies the products a firm will offer in particular markets, and presents a framework within which the firm will work, the strategic mission is an application of strategic intent.[107] In a small private school, for example, the strategic intent is the vigorous pursuit of excellence. The strategic mission flowing from this intent is to serve intellectually gifted or highly motivated students from a six-county region seeking a college preparatory educational experience.

In the case of all firms and organizations, once formulated, the strategic intent and strategic mission are the basis for the development of business-level, corporate-level, acquisitions, restructuring, international, and cooperative strategies (see Chapters 4 and 6 through 9). The first of these strategy types—business-level strategy—is discussed in the next chapter.

■ Summary

- In the new competitive landscape, traditional conditions and factors, including labor costs and effective access to financial resources and raw materials, can still provide a competitive advantage, but to a lesser degree. In this new landscape, the firm's internal environment (that is, its resources, capabilities, and core competencies) may have a stronger influence on the development of competitive advantage and the formulation and implementation of strategies than do the characteristics and conditions of the external environment. But, no competitive advantage lasts forever. Over time, the benefits provided by all competitive advantages can be duplicated. Because of this, firms are challenged to exploit their current competitive advantage while simultaneously using their resources, capabilities, and core competencies to develop advantages that will be relevant in the future.

- Effective management of core competencies requires careful analysis of the firm's resources (inputs to the production process) and capabilities (capacities for teams of resources to perform a task or activity integratively). To complete these analyses successfully, strategic managers must be self-confident, courageous, and willing to hold people accountable for their work.

- Individually, resources are typically not sources of competitive advantage. Capabilities, which result from groupings of both tangible and intangible resources, are more likely to yield an advantage. A key reason for this is that how the firm forms, nurtures, and exploits core competencies that are grounded in capabilities is less visible to competitors and, hence, more difficult to understand and costly to imitate.

- The skills and knowledge of the firm's human capital may be the primary basis for all of its capabilities. Capabilities of this type emerge by developing human capital and sharing information regarding how tangible and intangible resources can be combined in strategically relevant ways.

- Value chain analysis is used to identify and evaluate a firm's resources and capabilities. By studying their primary and support activities, firms better understand their cost structure and the activities in which they can create and capture value.

- In the cases of primary and support activities that must be performed, but for which the firm lacks the resources and capabilities required to create value, outsourcing is considered. Used frequently in the new competitive landscape, outsourcing is the purchase of a value-creating activity from an external supplier. When outsourcing, the firm should outsource only to companies that possess a competitive advantage in terms of the primary or support activity being outsourced. Strategic managers must verify that their firm does not outsource activities in which it can create and capture value. Additionally, firms must avoid outsourcing nonstrategic capabilities that are not a source of competitive advantage, yet are important to the firm's ongoing efforts to develop continuously value-adding knowledge.

- Not all of the firm's capabilities are core competencies. Only capabilities that are valuable, rare, costly to imitate, and nonsubstitutable are sources of competitive advantage and, as such, can be selected as core competencies. Over time, core competencies must be supported and nurtured. However, core competencies cannot be allowed to become core rigidities. Competencies result in competitive advantage over the firm's rivals *only* when they allow the firm to create value by exploiting external environmental opportunities. When this is no longer the case, the firm's attention must be shifted to other capabilities that do satisfy the four criteria of sustainable competitive advantage.

- Strategic intent and strategic mission are grounded in the results obtained through analyses of the firm's external and internal environments. Taken together, the results of environmental analyses and the formation of the firm's strategic intent and mission provide the information needed to formulate and implement an array of strategies, including business-level, corporate-level, acquisition, restructuring, international, and cooperative.

Review Questions

1. Why is it important for firms to study and gain an understanding of their internal environment?

2. What is value? How do firms earn value and why is it important that they be able to do so?

3. What are the differences between tangible and intangible resources? Which of these two categories of resources typically contributes more to the development of competitive advantage, and why?

4. What are capabilities? How are capabilities developed?

5. How is value chain analysis used in organizations? What knowledge can strategic managers gain by using value chain analysis?

6. What is outsourcing? Why is it so valuable to companies competing in the new competitive landscape?

7. What are the four criteria used to determine which of a firm's resources and capabilities are its core competencies? Why is it important for strategic managers to use these criteria?

8. Why is it important for firms to prevent their core competencies from becoming core rigidities?

9. What is the relationship between strategic inputs and strategic actions?

Application Discussion Questions

1. Several companies are discussed in the opening case. Do you purchase goods or services from these firms? If so, which ones? Do you buy these products because of their brand name? For what value are you paying when you buy these products?

2. Select a store in your local community from which you purchase items. Ask one of the store's strategic managers to describe the value the firm provides to its customers. Do you agree with the strategic manager's assessment? Did the manager describe the value you pay for when purchasing goods or services from this store? If not, what might account for the difference in opinions?

3. For an organization or club in which you are a member, prepare a list of what you think are its tangible and intangible resources. Using the categories shown in Tables 3.2 and 3.3, group the resources you identified. Show your list to other members of your organization and ask for their assessment. Did they agree with your groupings? If not, why not?

4. Refer to the third question. Was it easier for you to list the tangible or intangible resources? Why?

5. What competitive advantage does your college or university possess? On what core competencies is this advantage based? What evidence can you provide to support your opinions?

6. Strategic actions being taken by The Gap to achieve strategic competitiveness and earn above-average returns with its Old Navy stores were described in a Strategic Focus. How successful are the Old Navy stores today? Please obtain information from business sources to support your assessment.

Ethics Questions

1. Can an emphasis on developing a competitive advantage result in unethical practices such as the use of questionable techniques to gather information about competitors? If so, do you believe these unethical practices occur frequently? Please provide evidence to support your opinion.

2. Can ethical practices facilitate development of a brand name and a corporate reputation? If so, explain how.

3. What is the difference between exploiting human capital and nurturing human capital to arrive at a competitive advantage? Can exploitation of human capital lead to a competitive advantage? If so, how?

4. Ethically, are strategic managers challenged to use their firm's resources to help train members of their society to reduce the shortage of skilled workers in their country? Why or why not?

5. What, if any, ethical dilemmas are associated with the use of outsourcing? How should strategic managers deal with them?

6. What ethical issues do strategic managers face when they conclude that their firm cannot earn above-average returns if thousands of employees are not laid off?

Internet Exercise

Search for *Fortune's* list of Most Admired companies for various years. These are available by going to *Time's* "Pathfinder" home page:

- http://pathfinder.com/

Then, click on *Fortune.* From there, you can conduct a search for archived articles, including the annual surveys. Select several companies representing different industries. What kinds of images do they convey? Describe both their tangible and intangible resources. How were these resources used to form capabilities that created competitive advantages?

Cohesion Case

Use E-mail to discuss with your team the competitive advantage for the following well-recognized companies mentioned in this Chapter:

- *McKinsey & Co.:* http://www.mckinsey.com/
- *Hewlett-Packard:* http://www.hp.com/
- *Corning:* http://www.corning.com/
- *Kodak:* http://www.kodak.com/
- *Rolls-Royce Motor Cars:* http://www.rolls-royce.com/
- *Boeing Co.:* http://www.boeing.com/

■ Notes

1. R.G. McGrath, I.C. MacMillan, and S. Venkataraman, 1995, Defining and developing competence: A strategic process paradigm, *Strategic Management Journal* 16: 251–275.
2. B. Morris, 1996, The brand's the thing, *Fortune,* March 4, 76.
3. P. Sellers, 1996, Can Home Depot fix its sagging stock? *Fortune,* March 4, 139–146.
4. P.C. Godfrey and C.W.L. Hill, 1995, The problem of unobservables in strategic management research, *Strategic Management Journal* 16: 519–533.
5. D. Leonard-Barton, 1995, *Wellsprings of Knowledge: Building and Sustaining the Sources of Innovation* (Boston: Harvard Business School Press); McGrath, MacMillan, and Venkataraman, Defining and developing competence, 253.
6. H.W. Chesbrough and D.J. Teece, 1996, When is virtual virtuous? *Harvard Business Review* 74, no. 1: 65–73.
7. Godfrey and Hill, The problem of unobservables, 522.
8. M.E. Porter, 1994, Toward a dynamic theory of strategy, in R.P. Rumelt, D.E. Schendel, and D.J. Teece (eds.), *Fundamental Issues in Strategy* (Boston: Harvard Business School Press), 446.
9. J. Pfeffer, 1994, *Competitive Advantage Through People: Unleashing the Power of the Work Force* (Boston: Harvard Business School Press), 6–14.
10. C. Goldsmith, 1996, Netherlands' Fokker seeks protection from creditors, *Wall Street Journal,* January 24, A10; J. Landers, 1996, Job security declines in competitive world, *Dallas Morning News,* February 19, D4; A.J. Slywotzky and D. Morrison, 1996, Insights from a falling Apple, *Wall Street Journal,* January 29, A14.
11. J.B. Barney, 1995, Looking inside for competitive advantage, *Academy of Management Executive* IX, no. 4: 59–60; G. Hamel and C.K. Prahalad, 1993, Strategy as stretch and leverage, *Harvard Business Review* 71, no. 2: 75–84; The future for strategy: An interview with Gary Hamel, 1993, *European Management Journal* 11, no. 2: 150–157; C.K. Prahalad and G. Hamel, 1990, The core competence of the

organization, *Harvard Business Review* 68, no. 3: 79–91.
12. S. Ghoshal and C.A. Bartlett, 1995, Changing the role of top management: Beyond structure to processes, *Harvard Business Review* 73, no. 1: 96.
13. M.A. Peteraf, 1993, The cornerstones of competitive strategy: A resource-based view, *Strategic Management Journal* 14: 179–191; A.A. Lado, N.G. Boyd, and P. Wright, 1992, A competency based model of sustainable advantage: Toward a conceptual integration, *Journal of Management* 18: 77–91.
14. P.F. Drucker, 1995, The information executives truly need, *Harvard Business Review* 73, no. 1: 62.
15. K.Z. Andrews, 1996, Improvement in manufacturing, *Harvard Business Review* 74, no. 2: 12–13; D. Lei, M.A. Hitt, and R. Bettis, 1996, Dynamic core competences through meta-learning and strategic context, *Journal of Management* 22: 247–267; H. Rheem, 1995, The learning organization, *Harvard Business Review* 73, no. 2: 10; G. Hamel and C.K. Prahalad, 1994, *Competing for the Future* (Boston: Harvard Business School Press).
16. Barney, Looking inside for competitive advantage, 51; Porter, Toward a dynamic theory of strategy, 435; R. Normann and R. Ramirez, 1993, From value chain to value constellation: Designing interactive strategy, *Harvard Business Review* 71, no. 4: 65–77.
17. D. J. Collis and C.A. Montgomery, 1995, Competing on resources: Strategy in the 1990s, *Harvard Business Review* 73, no. 4: 118–128; B. Wernerfelt, 1995, The Resource-based view of the firm: Ten years after, *Strategic Management Journal* 16: 171–174; J.B. Barney, 1994, Commentary: A hierarchy of corporate resources, *Advances in Strategic Management* 10A, 113–125; R.P. Rumelt, D.E. Schendel, and D.J. Teece, 1994, Afterword, in R.P. Rumelt, D.E. Schendel, and D.J. Teece (eds.), *Fundamental Issues in Strategy* (Boston: Harvard Business School Press), 533.
18. R.L. Priem and D.A. Harrison, 1994, Exploring strategic judgment: Methods for testing the

assumptions of prescriptive contingency theories, *Strategic Management Journal* 15: 311–324; R. Amit and P.J.H. Schoemaker, 1993, Strategic assets and organizational rent, *Strategic Management Journal* 14: 33–46.
19. C.R. Schwenk, 1995, Strategic decision making, *Journal of Management* 21: 471–493.
20. H.W. Jenkins, 1996, 40,000 job cuts! Where does he get off? *Wall Street Journal,* March 5, A15; McGrath, MacMillan, and Venkataraman, Defining and developing competence, 253.
21. D. Kunde, 1996, Self-control guru, *Dallas Morning News,* February 5, D1, D4; T.A. Stewart, 1996, Looking out for number 1, *Fortune,* January 15, 33–48; M. Loeb, 1993, Making sense of the chaos, *Fortune,* April 5, 6.
22. Five hot ideas for today's economy, 1993, *Fortune,* October 18, 112–121.
23. H.W. Vroman, 1996, The loyalty effect: The hidden force behind growth, profits, and lasting value (book review), *Academy of Management Executive* X, no. 1: 88–90.
24. W. Kiechel, 1993, Facing up to denial, *Fortune,* October 18: 163–165.
25. A. Taylor, III, 1996, It's the slow lane for automakers, *Fortune,* April 1, 59–64.
26. P. Sellers, 1996, What exactly is charisma? *Fortune,* January 15, 68–75.
27. Barney, Looking inside for competitive advantage, 50; A.D. Meyer, 1991, What is strategy's distinctive competence? *Journal of Management* 17: 821–833.
28. McGrath, MacMillan, and Venkataraman, Defining and developing competence, 252; Porter, Toward a dynamic theory of strategy, 445.
29. T. Chi, 1994, Trading in strategic resources: Necessary conditions, transaction cost problems, and choice of exchange structure, *Strategic Management Journal* 15: 271–290; R. Reed and R. DeFilippi, 1990, Causal ambiguity, barriers to imitation, and sustainable competitive advantage, *Academy of Management Review* 15: 88–102.
30. R. Hall, 1991, The contribution of intangible resources to business success, *Journal of General Management* 16, no. 4: 41–52.
31. N.E. Grund, 1996, Reputation: Realizing value from the corporate image, *Academy of Man-*

agement Executive (book review section), X, no. 1: 100.

32. C.J. Fombrun, 1996, *Reputation: Realizing Value from the Corporate Image* (Boston: Harvard Business School Press).

33. A. Taylor, III, 1995, Boeing: Sleepy in Seattle, *Fortune*, August 7, 92–98.

34. T.A. Stewart, 1996, Coins in a knowledge bank, *Fortune*, February 19, 230–233.

35. S. Sherman, 1996, Secrets of HP's 'muddled team,' *Fortune*, March 18: 116–120.

36. McGrath, MacMillan, and Venkataraman, Defining and developing competence, 252; Porter, Toward a dynamic theory of strategy, 445.

37. J.B. Quinn, P. Anderson, and S. Finkelstein, 1996, Making the most of the best, *Harvard Business Review* 74, no. 2: 71–80.

38. T.A. Stewart, 1995, Trying to grasp the intangible, *Fortune*, October 2, 157–161.

39. Godfrey and Hill, The problem of unobservables, 522–523.

40. S. Woolley, 1996, I want my Century 21! *Business Week*, January 15, 72–73.

41. Ibid., 72; K. Blumenthal, 1996, Century 21 dons new garb to face home buyers arriving in Spring, *Wall Street Journal*, January 18, B8.

42. Morris, The brand's the thing, 74.

43. M. Wells, 1996, Ad wars add up to big bucks, *USA Today*, March 12, B4.

44. R. Furchgott, 1995, A full plate for Buzz McCormick, *Business Week*, November 20, 88.

45. S.G. Beatty, 1996, Staid brands put new spin on old jingles, *Wall Street Journal*, January 19, B11.

46. Lei, Hitt, and Bettis, Dynamic core competences; J.B. Quinn, 1994, *The Intelligent Enterprise* (New York: Free Press).

47. E.M. Davies, 1996, Wired for hiring: Microsoft's slick recruiting machine, *Fortune*, February 5, 123–124.

48. Associated Press, 1996, Southwest Airlines earns triple crown award again, *Dallas Morning News*, February 6, D15.

49. D. Kunde, 1996, Utilizing the human resource, *Dallas Morning News*, January 16, D16.

50. D. Kunde, 1996, Corporations thinking ahead with chief knowledge officers, *Dallas Morning News*, January 14, D1.

51. T.A. Stewart, 1991, Brainpower, *Fortune*, June 3, 44.

52. Lei, Hitt, and Bettis, Dynamic core competences.

53. S. Kaufman, 1996, Firm offers essential high-tech component: People, *Dallas Morning News*, January 22, D2.

54. R.C. Monson, 1995, Firms worry about finding skilled workers, survey shows, *Dallas Morning News*, December 15, D10.

55. J. Landers, 1995, New jewel in the crown! *Dallas Morning News*, December 17, H1, H2.

56. F.F. Reichheld, 1996, Solving the productivity puzzle, *Wall Street Journal*, March 2, A14.

57. R. Henkoff, 1993, The labor secretary speaks out on training and the two-tier work force, *Fortune*, March 8, 13.

58. R. Lowenstein, 1996, Why primary voters are so angry, *Wall Street Journal*, February 22, C1.

59. M.A. Hitt and R.D. Ireland, 1986, Relationships among corporate level distinctive competencies,

diversification strategy, corporate structure, and performance, *Journal of Management Studies* 23: 401–416; M.A. Hitt and R.D. Ireland, 1985, Corporate distinctive competence, strategy, industry and performance, *Strategic Management Journal* 6: 273–293; M.A. Hitt, R.D. Ireland, and K.A. Palia, 1982, Industrial firms' grand strategy and functional importance, *Academy of Management Journal* 25: 265–298; M.A. Hitt, R.D Ireland, and G. Stadter, 1982, Functional importance and company performance: Moderating effects of grand strategy and industry type, *Strategic Management Journal* 3: 315–330; C.C. Snow and L.G. Hrebiniak, 1980, Strategy, distinctive competence, and organizational performance, *Administrative Science Quarterly* 25: 317–336.

60. M. Zimmerman, 1996, Frito-Lay gains overseas snack operations, *Dallas Morning News*, March 12, D1.

61. M.E. Porter, 1985, *Competitive Advantage* (New York: Free Press), 33–61.

62. G.G. Dess, A. Gupta, J-F Hennart, and C.W.L. Hill, 1995, Conducting and integrating strategy research at the international, corporate, and business levels: Issues and directions, *Journal of Management* 21: 376; Porter, Toward a dynamic theory of strategy, 437.

63. T.A. Stewart, 1995, The information wars: What you don't know will hurt you, *Fortune*, June 12, 119–121.

64. A. Taylor, III, 1996, How to buy a car on the Internet, *Fortune*, March 4, 164–168.

65. Outsourcing: How industry leaders are reshaping the American corporation, 1996, *Fortune*, Special Advertising Section.

66. T. Box, 1996, Outsourcing to cut jobs in Arlington, *Dallas Morning News*, March 23, F1, F11.

67. Outsourcing, 3.

68. J.W. Verity, 1996, Let's order out for technology, *Business Week*, May 13, 47.

69. Chesbrough and Teece, When is virtual virtuous?, 70; M. Heinzl, 1995, Magna International profits on big three outsourcing, *Wall Street Journal*, August 24, B5.

70. A. Taylor, III, 1993, Shaking up Jaguar, *Fortune*, September 6, 66.

71. Associated Press, 1996, Free-wheeling spenders, *Dallas Morning News*, January 10, D2.

72. J. Haley, 1995, Boeing strategy angers workers, *Daily Herald*, July 14, H2.

73. N.A. Wishart, J.J. Elam, and D. Robey, 1996, Redrawing the portrait of a learning organization: Inside Knight-Ridder, Inc., *Academy of Management Executive* X, no. 1: 7–20; D. Lei and M.A. Hitt, 1995, Strategic restructuring and outsourcing: The effect of mergers and acquisitions and LBOs on building firm skills and capabilities, *Journal of Management* 21: 835–859.

74. R.L. Huber, 1993, How Continental Bank outsourced its 'crown jewels,' *Harvard Business Review* 71, no. 2: 128.

75. D. Leonard-Barton, H.K. Bowen, K.B. Clark, C.A. Holloway, and S.C. Wheelwright, 1994, How to integrate work and deepen expertise, *Harvard Business Review* 72, no. 5: 123.

76. Chi, Trading in strategic resources, 272; Porter, Toward a dynamic theory of strategy, 442.

77. Drucker, The information executives truly need, 60.

78. C. Ames, 1995, Sales soft? Profits flat? It's time to rethink your business, *Fortune*, June 26, 142–146; S. Fatsis, 1993, Bigger is not necessarily better, *Waco Tribune-Herald*, January 17, B1, B6.

79. This section is drawn primarily from two sources: Barney, Looking inside for competitive advantage; J.B. Barney, 1991, Firm resources and sustained competitive advantage; *Journal of Management* 17: 99–120.

80. Barney, Looking inside for competitive advantage, 53.

81. Ibid., 50.

82. Ibid., 52.

83. Ibid., 53.

84. Barney, Firm resources, 108.

85. J. Huey, 1993, How McKinsey does it, *Fortune*, November 1, 56–81.

86. Leonard-Barton, *Wellsprings of Knowledge*, 7.

87. Sherman, Secrets of HP's.

88. Barney, Firm resources, 111.

89. Amit and Schoemaker, Strategic assets, 39.

90. Lei, Hitt, and Bettis, Dynamic core competences; Leonard-Barton, *Wellsprings of Knowledge*, 59–89.

91. Leonard-Barton, *Wellsprings of Knowledge*, 7.

92. Wishart, Elam, and Robey, Redrawing the portrait, 8.

93. M. Hannan and J. Freeman, 1977, The population ecology of organizations, *American Journal of Sociology* 82: 929–964.

94. Leonard-Barton, *Wellsprings of Knowledge*, 30–31.

95. C.A. Bartlett and S. Ghoshal, 1994, Changing the role of top management: Beyond strategy to purpose, *Harvard Business Review* 72, no. 6: 79–88.

96. G. Hamel and C.K. Prahalad, 1989, Strategic intent, *Harvard Business Review* 67, no. 3: 63–76.

97. Chesbrough and Teece, When is virtual virtuous?, 70.

98. Leonard-Barton, *Wellsprings of Knowledge*, 270 (citing the work of Itami and Roehl).

99. Ibid., 8.

100. Sellers, What exactly is charisma, 72.

101. M.S.S. El-Namaki, 1992, Creating a corporate vision, *Long Range Planning* 25, no. 2: 119–121.

102. S. Sherman, 1995, Stretch goals: The dark side of asking for miracles, *Fortune*, November 13, 231–232.

103. H.W. Mentink, 1996, An employee's goals, *Fortune*, February 5, 26.

104. J.A. Byrne, 1995, Hired guns packing high-powered knowhow, *Business Week*, September 18, 92–96.

105. 1996, Andersen Consulting advertisement appearing in *Wall Street Journal*, February 6; R. Henkoff, 1993, Inside Andersen's army of advice, *Fortune*, October 4, 78–86.

106. R.D. Ireland and M.A. Hitt, 1992, Mission statements: Importance, challenge and recommendations for development, *Business Horizons* 35, no. 3: 34–42.

107. C. Marshall, 1996, A sense of mission, *The Strategist* 7, no. 4: 14–16.

PART

II Strategic Actions: Strategy Formulation

CHAPTERS

4 Business-Level Strategy

After reading this chapter, you should be able to:

1. Define strategy and explain business-level strategies.

2. Describe the relationship between customers and business-level strategies.

3. Discuss the issues firms consider when evaluating customers in terms of *who, what,* and *how.*

4. Define the integrated low-cost/differentiation strategy and discuss its increasing importance in the new competitive landscape.

5. Describe the capabilities necessary to develop competitive advantage through the cost leadership, differentiation, focused low-cost, focused differentiation, and the integrated low-cost/differentiation business-level strategies.

6. Explain the risks associated with each of the five business-level strategies.

Achieving Strategic Competitiveness at Callaway Golf Company

For golfers, the greatest thrill may be to take the perfect swing and then watch as one's tee shot travels at least 250 yards in the desired direction. Although seemingly simple, accomplishing this feat is challenging. Indeed, a *Fortune* writer suggests that "anyone who has tried to impel a golf ball forward knows that the task is no harder than doing perfect calligraphy while jogging." Unfortunately, the price of even slight imperfection in one's swing is steep—each millimeter (0.03937 inch) a hit is off the club's center, the penalty incurred is 0.5 percent of the distance. Missing the ball by 10 millimeters from the club's center, which is less than half an inch, results in a loss of 12.5 yards on a 250-yard drive.

Recognizing that committed golfers seek perfection in their games at possibly any cost, Ely Callaway applied new thinking and innovative technology to develop an oversize metal driver called Big Bertha. Immediately successful, this innovator's company serves only the premium golf club market. Callaway Golf Company is known as a leading designer, developer, manufacturer, and marketer of high-quality, premium-priced, innovative golf clubs. Along with Cobra Golf and Taylor Made, Callaway dominates the market for drivers costing a minimum of $200. Recently the market for premium or high-end golf clubs totaled almost $3 billion at wholesale.

As measures of its success, consider Callaway Golf Company's accomplishments during 1994: (1) sales increased 76 percent over 1993 while earnings grew 89 percent, (2) per share earnings grew 82 percent from 1993 to 1994, (3) the Big Bertha drivers were the #1 driver used in all tournaments on all four professional tours in the United States for the year, (4) the firm was the first in more than three decades to hold prominent positions in irons and woods for the premium golf club markets of the world, and (5) export sales exceeded $115 million, a figure greater than the total sales revenues of most of the company's competitors. By the end of 1995, the firm had used its sources of competitive advantage to manufacture and distribute conventional-size metal woods, irons, putters and other golf-related equipment in addition to its metal drivers. Moreover, in 1995, annual sales surpassed $1 billion with expectations of reaching $2 billion in 1996.

Product innovation skills, name recognition, distribution capabilities, and marketing power are the competitive advantages Callaway emphasizes to differentiate itself from competitors and to produce products with unique features for which customers are willing to pay premium prices. Committed to research and development, Callaway integrates technology, ingenuity, and human technique to improve its clubs continuously.

Another innovative product introduced by Callaway was the Great Big Bertha (GBB) driver. This club features the Ruger titanium head and graphite design ultra-lightweight graphite shaft. Even at $500 per club, the GBB achieved rapid marketplace success. In fact, in the latter part of 1995, a shortage of clubheads from the supplier producing this item prevented Callaway from satisfying the demand for the GBB.

Source: G.I.H. Rho, 1995, Callaway Golf Co., *Value Line,* September 1, 1764; B. Saporito, 1995, Can Big Bertha stay in the driver's seat? *Fortune,* June 12, 110–116; Callaway Golf Company, 1995, *Annual Report;* Callaway Golf Company, 1994, *Annual Report.*

C allaway Golf Company serves the needs of golfers willing to pay for exceptional product performance capabilities. The essence of the firm's strategic intent and strategy is suggested by the following statements:

Callaway Golf Company designs, manufactures, and markets high quality, innovative golf clubs. The Company's basic objective is to design and manufacture its clubs in such a way that they are demonstrably superior to, and pleasingly different from, competitors' golf clubs. The Company's golf clubs are sold at premium prices to both average and skilled golfers on the basis of performance, ease of use and appearance.[1]

To achieve strategic competitiveness and earn above-average returns, as Callaway Golf Company has done, a company analyzes its external environment, identifies opportunities in that environment, determines which of its internal resources and capabilities are core competencies, and selects an appropriate strategy to implement.[2] A **strategy** is an integrated and coordinated set of commitments and actions designed to exploit core competencies and gain a competitive advantage. An effectively formulated strategy marshals, integrates, and allocates a firm's resources, capabilities, and competencies so it can cope successfully with its external environment.[3] Such a strategy also rationalizes a firm's strategic intent and strategic mission and what will be done to achieve them.[4] Information about a host of variables, including markets, customers, technology, worldwide finance, and the changing world economy[5] must be collected and analyzed to formulate and implement strategies properly.

Recall from Chapters 1 and 3 that *core competencies* are resources and capabilities that serve as a source of competitive advantage for a firm over its rivals. Strategic competitiveness and the earning of above-average returns hinge on a firm's ability to develop and exploit new core competencies faster than competitors can mimic the competitive advantages yielded by the current ones.[6] When focused on the continuous need to develop new core competencies, firms are able to drive competition in the future as well as the present.[7] Thus, especially in the new competitive landscape, with its continuing globalization and rapid technological changes, only firms with the capacity to improve, innovate, and upgrade their competitive advantages over time can expect to achieve long-term success.[8]

As explained in this chapter, successful firms use their core competencies to satisfy customers' needs. The relationship between appropriate strategic actions and the achievement of strategic competitiveness is increasingly important in today's turbulent and competitive environment.[9] These relationships are shown in Figure 1.1 in Chapter 1. As displayed in that figure, a firm's *strategic inputs* (gained through study of the external and internal environments) are used to select the *strategic actions* (the formulation and implementation of value-creating strategies) that will yield desired *strategic outcomes*.

Callaway Golf Company exemplifies these relationships. Through an examination of the general, industry, and competitor external environments, Ely Callaway saw an opportunity to serve a particular segment of the golf club market by the continuous development of innovative products. The company's strategic intent is to provide customers with products that are "demonstrably superior and pleasingly different."[10] Flowing from this intent is the strategic mission of offering these innovative products to customers willing to pay premium prices. Focused differentiation is the business-level strategy (this strategy is defined and discussed later in the chapter) the firm chose to implement to achieve the desired outcomes of strategic competitiveness and above-average returns.

The initial environmental opportunity pursued by Callaway Golf Company was identified through careful study. However, opportunities to continue implementing a chosen business-level strategy also surface somewhat unexpectedly for already established firms. For example, Anheuser-Busch Cos.' recent attempt to

■ *A **strategy** is an integrated and coordinated set of commitments and actions designed to exploit core competencies and gain a competitive advantage.*

sell the Eagle Snacks unit so it could refocus on its world-leading beer business provided an opportunity for Frito-Lay (a division of PepsiCo) to expand its already dominant share of the salty snack market.[11] Similarly, in light of major competitors' financial woes (identified through study of the firm's industry environment), Luby's Cafeterias decided to aggressively build additional units in one of its key Southwest locations. Because of its superior financial position (a source of competitive advantage), Luby's CEO concluded that "The stagnation of our competitors from the standpoint of expansion has allowed us a unique opportunity to continue to expand . . . ."[12]

At a broader level, companies committed to the importance of competing successfully in the global economy constantly study developments in the world's markets to identify emerging opportunities to exploit their competitive advantages. The breakup of the former Soviet Union in 1991, for example, has resulted in numerous commercial opportunities, especially for consumer goods companies. To succeed in the Russian consumer revolution, companies are advised to ". . . quickly seize opportunities to position themselves, and then prepare for keener competition."[13]

Hewlett-Packard (HP) is an example of a company that may be positioned effectively to capitalize on developing competitive opportunities in the Russian market. HP has conducted business in Russia for more than two decades. However, sales of its computer equipment in this market were minimal (only $16 million in 1992, for example). Things changed for HP with the beginning of Russian economic reforms. The establishment of thousands of new banks, securities exchanges, and trading companies created significant demand for computer equipment. In a position to satisfy this demand, HP's 1995 sales volume in Russia reached approximately $200 million. By the end of 1995, the Russian PC market had grown to the point that it "was half the size of Canada's and a quarter the size of Japan's."[14] HP hoped to continue capitalizing on its favorable market position to further increase its sales in Russia.

Rapid development of Poland is also yielding opportunities that are somewhat unexpected for many types of companies. Some observers of the Polish business environment feel that Poland "is emerging as Europe's star performer" following a difficult beginning. Reasons for this emergence include a commitment among Polish firms to benchmark their operations against the world's best performers and the restructuring of state-owned corporations. Foreign investment in Poland is on the rise "because foreign companies see the potential of Poland's domestic market and its attractiveness as a supply base for both West and East." Employing more than 6,600 people in Poland, PepsiCo already operates three divisions in this growing economy: soft drinks and bottling, fast-food restaurants, and snack foods and chocolates. Korea's Daewoo Motor Co. selected Poland as its center for automobile production in Europe. In addition, "a number of French and German retail chains have also been quietly positioning themselves to supply Poland's rising middle class."[15]

Business-level strategy, the focus of this chapter, is an integrated and coordinated set of commitments and actions designed to provide value to customers and gain a competitive advantage by exploiting core competencies in specific, individual product markets.[16]

Customers are the foundation of successful business-level strategies. In the words of one CEO, "When you get people focused on customers, it has a very remarkable effect" on the firm's performance outcomes.[17] Because of their

■ *A **business-level strategy** is an integrated and coordinated set of commitments and actions designed to provide value to customers and gain a competitive advantage by exploiting core competencies in specific, individual product markets.*

strategic importance, we begin this chapter with a discussion of customers. Three issues are considered in this analysis. Each firm determines (1) *who* it will serve, (2) *what* needs target customers have that it will satisfy, and (3) *how* those needs will be satisfied through implementation of a chosen strategy. For Callaway Golf Company, *who* the firm serves is both average and skilled golfers; the *what* (or customer need) Callaway serves is for high-quality premium golf clubs; and *how* these needs are satisfied is through use of the firm's competitive advantages of product innovation skills, name recognition, distribution capabilities, and marketing power.

Following the discussion on customers, we describe four generic business-level strategies. These strategies are called *generic* because they can be implemented in both manufacturing and service industries.[18] Our analysis of the generic strategies includes descriptions of how each one allows a firm to address the five competitive forces discussed in Chapter 2. In addition, we use the value chain (see Chapter 3) to show examples of primary and support activities necessary to implement each generic strategy successfully. Risks associated with each generic strategy are also presented in this chapter. Organizational structures and controls required for the successful implementation of business-level strategies are explained in Chapter 11.

A fifth business-level strategy that both manufacturing and service firms are implementing more frequently is considered in the chapter's final section. Some believe that this integrated strategy (a combination of attributes of the cost leadership and differentiation strategies) is essential to establishing and exploiting competitive advantages in the global economy.[19]

■ Customers: Who, What, and How

Organizations must satisfy some group of customers' needs to be successful. *Needs* refer to the benefits and features of a good or service that customers want to purchase.[20] A basic need of all customers is to buy products that provide value.

A key reason that firms must be able to satisfy customers' needs is that in the final analysis, returns earned from relationships with customers are the lifeblood of all organizations.[21] The challenge of identifying and determining how to satisfy the needs of what some business analysts believe are increasingly sophisticated, knowledgeable, and fickle customers is difficult.[22] Moreover, it is only through *total* satisfaction of their needs that customers develop the type of firm-specific loyalty companies seek. The belief of the president and chief operating officer (COO) of the Ritz-Carlton® Hotel Company describes the relationship between total need satisfaction and customer loyalty: "Unless you have 100 percent customer satisfaction—and I don't mean that they are just satisfied, I mean that they are excited about what you are doing—you have to improve."[23] Although difficult to earn, the estimate that "raising customer retention rates by five percentage points increases the value of an average customer by 25 percent to 100 percent"[24] is another indicator of the value of loyal customers.

Strategically competitive organizations in the latter part of the 1990s and into the twenty-first century will (1) think continuously about who their customers are, (2) maintain close and frequent contacts with their customers, (3) determine

The Ritz-Carlton Hotel Company stresses total satisfaction of customers' needs to develop firm-specific loyalty.

how to use their core competencies in ways that competitors cannot imitate, and (4) design their strategies to allow them to satisfy customers' current, anticipated, and even unanticipated needs.[25] The chairman of AlliedSignal, a manufacturer of aerospace equipment, automobile parts, and a range of engineered materials, observes that there is a near unanimous opinion in his firm that its businesses should be run primarily by customer-oriented processes[26] such as the four mentioned here.

■ Who: Determining the Customers to Serve

Customers can be divided into groups based on differences in their needs. Almost any identifiable human or organizational characteristic can be used to subdivide a large potential market into segments that differ from one another in terms of that characteristic.[27] Common characteristics on which customers' needs vary include (1) demographic variables (e.g., age, gender, income, occupation, education, race, nationality, and social class), (2) geographic segmentation (e.g., regions, countries, states, counties, cities, and towns), (3) lifestyle choices (lifestyle refers to a set of values or tastes exhibited by a group of customers, especially as they are reflected in consumption patterns[28]), (4) individual personality traits, (5) consumption patterns (e.g., usage rate and brand loyalty), (6) industry structural characteristics, and (7) organizational size.[29]

Recent experiences at Kmart demonstrate the importance of continuously focusing on the needs of a firm's target customer group. Kmart's core U.S. customer is over 55 years of age with an average income of under $20,000 and no children at home. Wal-Mart's average customer is under 44 and has an annual income of slightly under $40,000. These data suggest that compared to competitor Wal-Mart, Kmart's core customer seeks to purchase discounted products. Recent surveys also show that only 19 percent of Kmart shoppers are loyal to the chain. In comparison, 46 percent of Wal-Mart's customers are considered to be loyal (recall our earlier discussion about the positive effects of customer loyalty). One reason for this difference in customer loyalty percentages may be Kmart's apparent inability to effectively serve its core customers. In late 1995, for example, Kmart concluded that it had "stockpiled goods better suited for a department store than a discounter." Describing this matter, the firm's CEO admitted that "There are literally hundreds of items that don't fit" Kmart's core customer. Following study of the company's recent status, an analyst concluded that relatively little progress has been made to solve Kmart's core merchandising problems.[30]

Increasing Segmentation of Markets

In the new competitive landscape, many firms have become adept at identifying precise differences among customers' needs. Armed with these understandings, companies segment customers into *competitively relevant groups*—groups of customers with unique needs. As shown by the following statement, General Motors believes that four of its automobile product groups serve the unique needs of four competitively relevant groups: "The Chevy is squarely aimed at people shopping for a low price. The Pontiac targets performance enthusiasts. The Olds is for upscale buyers who might normally shop for import sport sedans, and the Buick will appeal to older buyers who want premium cars with conservative styling and room for six riders."[31]

In the United States, estimates are that at least 62 distinct classes of citizens exist, each with its own beliefs, aspirations, tastes, and needs. Some believe that, if anything, the trend toward fragmentation into smaller classes and subgroups is accelerating in the United States and throughout the world's markets.[32] Accompanying this growth are significant opportunities for companies to serve customers' specialized needs through use of their competitive advantages.

U.S. teenagers represent a large but competitively relevant group whose purchasing power continues to expand (some of the spending patterns of this group are shown in Table 4.1). Teenagers are the target customer at Gadzooks, a successful specialty retailer of clothing and accessories.[33] Just because individuals are 15 years old, says a Gadzooks store manager, doesn't mean they don't deserve good service.[34] J.C. Penney Co. uses its competitive advantage of private

---

Table 4.1 Spending Patterns of United States' Teenagers

- They eat a lot, spending an average of $2,648.36 a year on food. As a group that is $64.48 billion a year, not including what parents purchase on weekly shopping trips to the supermarket.

- They read little. They spend an average of $13.82 a year on books for a total of $120.7 million.

- They like music, spending an average of $17.40 on compact disks and $12.96 on cassette tapes a year. Annual tab: $195.4 million on CDs and $129.6 million on tapes.

- Teens fork over an average of $62.10 a year of their own money for jeans or about $1 billion as a group.

- Teens spend an average of $95.35 of their own money each year for sneakers and athletic shoes. That represents about $1.4 billion a year.

Source: Simmons Market Research Bureau Inc. as reported in M. Halkias, 1995, To buy for—at least today, *Dallas Morning News*, October 14, F1, F2.

brands to design, manufacture, and sell its Arizona jeans.[35] Launched in 1989, this brand is targeted to and driven by teens. In only five years, sales from the brand's tops, jeans, and jackets exceeded $500 million. In discussing reasons for the Arizona brand's success, a Penney's spokeswoman observed that teenagers identify with the brand, "... and even have given the brand their own pet name. They're calling it Zonez—with a 'z' at the end."[36]

Sophisticated information processing technologies allow firms such as Gadzooks and J.C. Penney to identify unique customer needs. With an understanding of different customer groups' needs, firms are able to mass customize their product offerings. **Mass customization** is a set of actions companies use to give all customers—regardless of how many there are—whatever they want.[37]

■ *Mass customization is a set of actions companies use to give all customers— regardless of how many there are—whatever they want.*

■ What: Determining the Customer Needs to Satisfy

As a firm decides who it will serve, it must simultaneously identify the needs of the chosen customer group that its goods or services can satisfy. Top-level managers play a critical role in efforts to recognize and understand customers' needs. Their capacity to gain valuable insights from listening to and studying customers influences product, technology, and distribution decisions.

At Staples, a $2 billion office-supply retailer, top-level managers spend significant amounts of their time analyzing reports about their customers' buying habits and solving customer problems. Spending executive time in this manner sends a strong signal to all employees that "Staples cares deeply, very deeply, about (understanding and) pleasing customers."[38] Because of this, Staples posted the best total return to investors for 1994 among specialist retailers. Thus, in strategically competitive firms, such as Staples, customer contact is a key responsibility for top-level managers and also for marketing and sales personnel.[39]

As described in the Strategic Focus about Casual Fridays, customers' needs sometimes change. Effective firms use their core competencies to satisfy newly emerging customer needs.

An additional competitive advantage accrues to firms capable of anticipating and then satisfying needs that were unknown to target customers. Firms able to do this provide customers with unexpected value—that is, a product performance capability or characteristic they did not request, yet do value.[40] Moreover, anticipating customers' needs yields opportunities for firms to shape their industry's future and gain an early competitive advantage (an early competitive advantage is called a *first mover advantage* and is discussed in Chapter 5). For example, Sprint, a diversified telecommunications company, believes that it "set the standard in long distance with its fiber optic network." In terms of the future, the firm also believes that "by joining with our cable partners in a revolutionary venture, we will be setting the standard once again. We're creating the blueprint that other communications companies will have to follow: a new kind of company that delivers the entire interconnected world of globe-spanning voice, video and data—all from a single source."[41]

■ How: Determining Core Competencies Necessary to Satisfy Customers' Needs

Firms use their core competencies to implement value-creating strategies and satisfy customers' needs. One of the strategic imperatives at IBM is to more

STRATEGIC FOCUS Casual Fridays: A Change in Corporate Dress Codes

Relaxed corporate dress codes are creating different clothing needs for women and men. The fact that an estimated 75 percent of *Fortune* 500 companies have some sort of casual dress policy demonstrates the broad appeal and acceptance of this clothing trend. In 1995, even IBM "axed its stringent dress code in favor of the casual look altogether."

Partly because of these changes, the middle part of the 1990s saw rather dramatic declines in the sales of men's suits and dress shirts with a simultaneous increase in the sales of casual apparel (including items such as knit sport shirts, sweaters, and shorts). Between 1994 and 1995, for example, suit and suit separates sales declined 27.3 percent while sales of sportcoats and blazers increased 21.6 percent. Sometimes called Casual Fridays and Friday Wear, this trend toward occasionally wearing less formal garments when working is, in some analysts' opinions, boosting the sagging fortunes of the U.S. menswear industry. Men appear to want casual clothing that "offers an appropriate look for the office that lies somewhere between a suit and jeans."

In recognition of this trend, which may be the most important movement in men's apparel in more than a decade, some manufacturers, retailers, and advertisers are responding aggressively. For example, footwear manufacturer Cole-Haan and *GQ* magazine combined efforts to launch a program called "Brave New Work." This program provides retail clothiers and customers with a video and brochure about casual clothes. Upscale merchandiser Neiman Marcus offers a free video (called "Feel Free—The Art of Casual Dressing") to customers featuring tips describing what women and men should do to dress casually. In some of its catalogs, Spiegel suggests that because they are more frequently in charge of deciding what type of clothing to wear to the office and when to wear it, women should "take charge" of this opportunity to create a different and unique wardrobe.

Haggar Clothing Co. is strongly committed to serving businesspeople's needs for casual clothing. This commitment is a product of a careful analysis which suggested that there was an opportunity for the company to use its core competencies "to create a whole category of clothing."

One example of Haggar's efforts to exploit this opportunity is the firm's development of a line of clothing called City Casuals. To advertise this line, Haggar introduced a 12-page document that details the specifics of "The Casual Philosophy" and provides information about Haggar's City Casuals products. Additionally, the firm offers a toll-free line (1-800-HAGGAR) for employers interested in establishing a corporate casual dress code. In response to an inquiry, prospective corporate clients receive a workbook to help them design, implement, and monitor a casual dress code. Haggar suggests that those wearing its City Casuals products are able to successfully satisfy their need to dress down (dressing down is defined as "the idea of wearing more casual clothes than tradition dictates, especially at the office").

Source: C. Y. Coleman, 1996, Apparel firms plan blitz to lure shoppers, *Wall Street Journal,* January 29, B8; L. Castaneda, 1995, Dressing down, *Dallas Morning News,* October 21, F1, F2; Haggar Clothing Co., 1995, *The Guy's Guide.*

quickly convert the firm's technological competence into commercial products that customers value. Honda's motorcycle, car, lawn mower, and generator businesses are all based on the company's core competence in engines and power trains. At Canon, core competencies in optics, imaging, and microprocessor controls provide the foundation to satisfy customer needs in a range of product markets including copiers, laser printers, cameras, and image scanners.[42]

Next, we discuss the business-level strategies firms implement in the pursuit of strategic competitiveness and above-average returns.

■ Types of Business-Level Strategy

Business-level strategies are concerned with a firm's industry position relative to competitors.[43] Companies that have established favorable industry positions are better able to cope with the five forces of competition (see Chapter 2). Thus, favorably positioned firms may have a competitive advantage over their industry rivals.

Originally, it was determined that firms choose from among four generic business-level strategies to establish and exploit a competitive advantage within a particular competitive scope: *cost leadership, differentiation, focused low cost,* and *focused differentiation* (see Figure 4.1). A fifth generic business-level strategy, the integrated low-cost/differentiation strategy, has evolved through firms' efforts to find the most effective ways to exploit their competitive advantages.

When selecting a business-level strategy, firms evaluate two types of competitive advantage: "lower cost than rivals, or the ability to differentiate and command a premium price that exceeds the extra cost of doing so."[44] Competitive advantage is achieved within some scope. Scope has several dimensions, including the group of product and customer segments served and the array of geographic markets in which a firm competes. Competitive advantage is sought by competing in many customer segments when implementing either the cost leadership or the differentiation strategy. In contrast, through implementation of focus strategies, firms seek either a cost advantage or a differentiation advantage in a *narrow competitive scope* or *segment*. With focus strategies, the firm "selects a segment or group of segments in the industry and tailors its strategy to serving them to the exclusion of others."[45]

None of the five business-level strategies is inherently or universally superior to the others.[46] The effectiveness of each strategy is contingent on the opportunities and threats in a firm's external environment *and* the possibilities permitted by the firm's unique resources, capabilities, and core competencies.

Figure 4.1

Four Generic Strategies

Source: Adapted with the permission of The Free Press, a division of Simon & Schuster from COMPETITIVE ADVANTAGE: Creating and Sustaining Superior Performance by Michael E. Porter, Fig. 1-3, 12. Copyright © 1985 by Michael E. Porter.

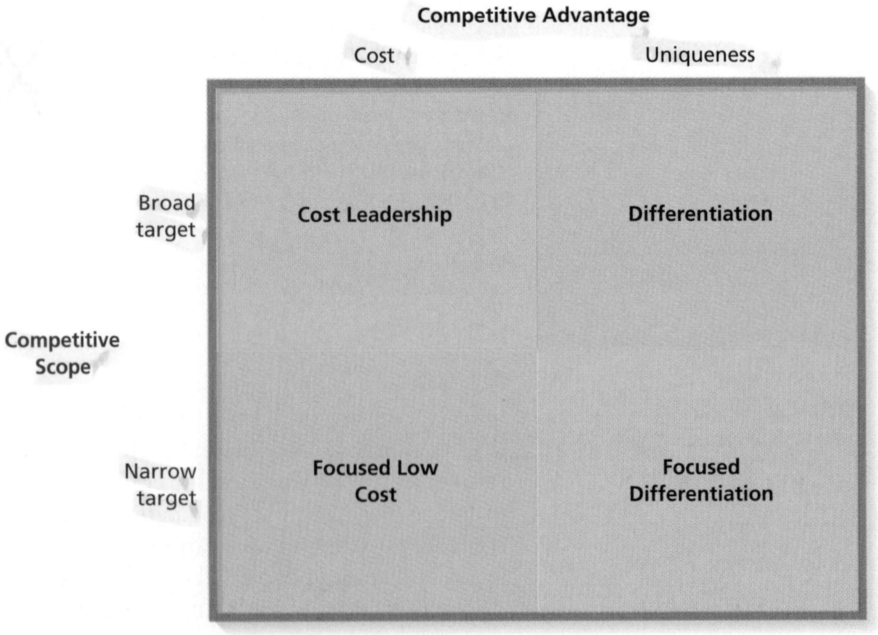

■ Cost Leadership Strategy

■ *A cost leadership strategy* is an
integrated set of actions designed to
produce products at the lowest cost,
relative to competitors, with features that
are acceptable to customers.

■ *A differentiation strategy* is an
integrated set of actions designed to
produce products that customers perceive
as being different in ways that are
important to them.

A **cost leadership strategy** is an integrated set of actions designed to produce products at the lowest cost, relative to competitors, with features that are acceptable to customers. A **differentiation strategy** is an integrated set of actions designed to produce products that customers perceive as being different in ways that are important to them.[47] The differentiation strategy calls for firms to sell nonstandardized products to customers with unique needs. The cost leadership strategy should achieve low cost relative to competitors while not ignoring means of differentiation that customers value. Alternatively, the differentiation strategy should consistently upgrade a product's differentiated features that customers value without ignoring costs to customers.

Firms seeking competitive advantage by implementing the cost leadership strategy often sell no-frills, standardized products to the most typical customers in the industry. In the new competitive landscape, it is increasingly difficult for firms implementing this type of strategy to differentiate between product features that are standard and those providing benefits that exceed the price the company's target customers are willing to pay.[48]

Successful implementation of the cost leadership strategy requires a consistent focus on driving costs lower, relative to competitors' costs. Firms often drive their costs lower through investments in efficient-scale facilities, tight cost and overhead control, and cost minimizations in such areas as service, sales force, and R&D. For example, Unifi Inc., one of the world's largest texturizers of filament polyester and nylon fiber, makes significant investments in its manufacturing technologies to drive its costs lower in an environment of upward pressure on prices of raw materials and packaging supplies. Already one of the most efficient producers in its industry, the firm opened a new plant in September 1996. This facility is expected to increase the firm's technological lead over its competitors and further reduce its production costs.[49]

Emerson Electric Co., a U.S. manufacturer that has earned above-average returns during both favorable and unfavorable economic climates, bases its operations on several principles—continuous cost reduction, use of state-of-the-art equipment, and open communications. The firm's adherence to these principles has resulted in impressive outcomes: "Adjusted for inflation, Emerson Electric's revenues have barely increased in the past half-dozen years. Yet in that period its earnings, cash flow and dividends per share have all increased by about 50 percent."[50]

As described in Chapter 3, a firm's value chain determines which parts of its operations create value and which do not. Primary and support activities that allow a firm to create value through a cost leadership strategy are shown in Figure 4.2. Companies that cannot link the activities included in this figure lack the resources and capabilities (and hence the core competencies) required to implement the cost leadership strategy successfully.

When implementing the cost leadership strategy, firms must be careful not to ignore completely sources of differentiation (e.g., innovative designs, service after the sale, product quality, etc.) that customers value. Emerson Electric Co. implements what it calls a best-cost producer strategy—"achieving the lowest cost consistent with quality."[51] Thus, the firm's products provide customers with a level of quality that at least meets, and often exceeds, their expectations relative to the purchase price.

Figure 4.2   **Examples of Value-Creating Activities Associated with the Cost Leadership Strategy**

	Inbound Logistics	Operations	Outbound Logistics	Marketing and Sales	Service
Firm Infrastructure	Cost-effective management information systems.	Relatively few managerial layers in order to reduce overhead costs.	Simplified planning practices to reduce planning costs.		
Human Resource Management	Consistent policies to reduce turnover costs.		Intense and effective training programs to improve worker efficiency and effectiveness.		
Technology Development	Easy-to-use manufacturing technologies.		Investments in technologies in order to reduce costs associated with a firm's manufacturing processes.		
Procurement	Systems and procedures to find the lowest cost (with acceptable quality) products to purchase as raw materials.		Frequent evaluation processes to monitor suppliers' performances.		
	Highly efficient systems to link suppliers' products with the firm's production processes.	Use of economies of scale to reduce production costs. Construction of efficient-scale production facilities.	A delivery schedule that reduces costs. Selection of low-cost transportation carriers.	A small, highly trained sales force. Products priced so as to generate significant sales volume.	Efficient and proper product installations in order to reduce the frequency and severity of recalls.

(Diagram shows value chain with MARGIN along the right-side arrows)

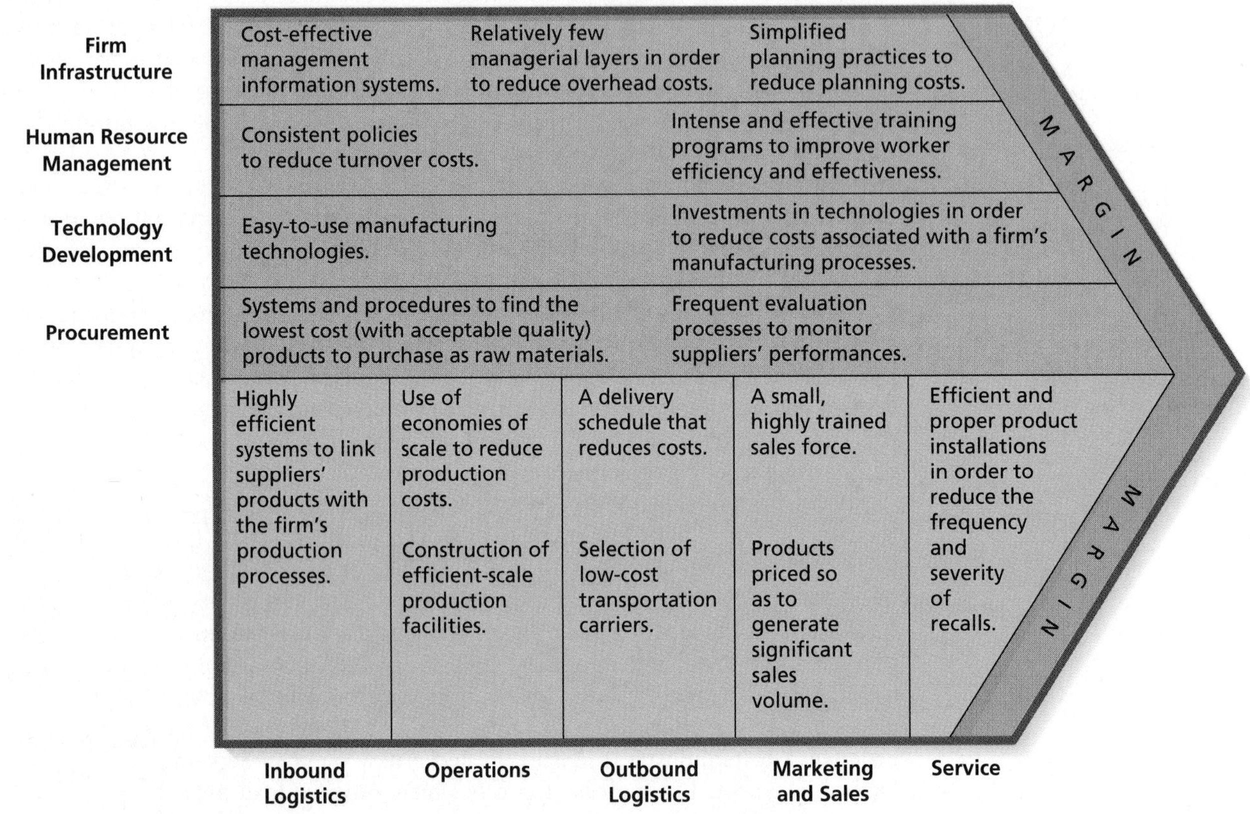

Source: Adapted with the permission of The Free Press, a division of Simon & Schuster from COMPETITIVE ADVANTAGE: Creating and Sustaining Superior Performance by Michael E. Porter. Copyright © 1985 by Michael E. Porter.

Recently some worldwide travelers expressed dissatisfaction with the value they received from budget-priced hotels. In the words of one customer in response to her stay in a budget-priced Paris hotel, "Budget to me means clean, comfortable service for a good rate. But what I ended up getting was mediocre for a high price."[52] This feedback shows that customers evaluate a cost leader's product in terms of its cost, relative to the benefits its features provide.

As explained next, effective implementation of a cost leadership strategy allows a firm to earn above-average returns in spite of the presence of strong competitive forces.

Rivalry with Existing Competitors

Having the low-cost position serves as a valuable defense against rivals. Because of the cost leader's advantageous cost position, rivals hesitate to compete on the basis of price. However, if rivals do challenge the firm to compete on the basis of price, the low-cost firm can still earn at least average returns after its competitors have lost theirs through competitive rivalry.[53]

Bargaining Power of Buyers (Customers)

Powerful customers can force the low-cost leader to reduce its prices. However, price will not be driven below the level at which the next-most-efficient industry competitor can earn average returns. Although powerful customers could force the low-cost leader to reduce prices even below this level, they probably would not choose to do so. Still lower prices would prevent the next-most-efficient competitor from earning average returns, resulting in its exit from the market and leaving the low-cost leader in a stronger position. Customers lose their power, and pay higher prices, when forced to buy from a firm operating in an industry without rivals.

Occasionally, a firm's bargaining power allows it to transfer increased costs to customers. In 1995, for example, Unifi incurred substantially higher costs for raw materials and packaging products. But, because it is a dominant supplier in many of its markets (up to a 70 percent share in some), Unifi was able to pass through higher costs to customers.[54]

Bargaining Power of Suppliers

A firm in the low-cost position operates with margins greater than those of its competitors. Recently, for example, Emerson Electric Co. earned a net profit margin of 9 cents per sales dollar, a figure " . . . that's far higher than the industry average."[55] Moreover, analysts' expectations are that the firm's margins should continue to expand, especially in light of its efforts aimed at productivity gains and lower payroll costs (gained partly by directing production to low-wage regions).[56]

Among other benefits, higher margins relative to competitors make it possible for the low-cost firm to absorb price increases from suppliers. When an industry is faced with substantial increases in the cost of its supplies, the low-cost leader may be the only one able to pay the higher prices and continue to earn either average or above-average returns. Alternatively, powerful low-cost leaders may be able to force suppliers to hold down their prices, reducing their margins in the process.

Potential Entrants

Through continuous efforts to reduce costs to levels below those of competitors, low-cost leaders become very efficient. Because they enhance profit margins, ever-improving levels of efficiency serve as a significant entry barrier to an industry for potential entrants. New entrants must be willing to accept no better than average returns until they gain the experience required to approach the efficiency of the low-cost leader. To earn even average returns, new entrants must have the competencies required to match the cost levels of other competitors.

The low-cost leader's low profit margins (relative to the margins earned by firms implementing the differentiation strategy) make it necessary for the firm to sell large volumes of its product to earn above-average returns. At Acer, the firm's CEO notes that the margins on his company's products, including its personal computers, are "shell-thin." "But sell enough of them," he believes, "and a formula emerges: Low margins and high turnover can be a recipe for success."[57] However, firms striving to be the low-cost leader must avoid pricing their products at a level that precludes them from earning above-average returns and encourages new industry entrants. Another computer manufacturer, Packard Bell (recall our discussion of this firm's strategic intent in a Strategic Focus in Chapter 1), is sometimes thought to price its products too low in efforts to gain volume. "A favorite with first-time PC buyers seeking the latest multimedia features at rock-bottom prices," Packard Bell is challenged to sell its products at prices that permit the earning of at least average returns.[58]

Product Substitutes

As compared to its industry rivals, the low-cost leader holds an attractive position in terms of product substitutes. When faced with the possibility of a substitute, the low-cost leader has more flexibility than its competitors. To retain customers, the low-cost leader can reduce its product's price. With still lower prices and features of acceptable quality, the low-cost leader increases the probability that customers will prefer its product, rather than a substitute.

■ Competitive Risks of the Cost Leadership Strategy

The cost leadership strategy is not without risks. One risk is that the low-cost leader's manufacturing equipment could become obsolete because of competitors' technological innovations. These innovations may allow rivals to produce at costs lower than those of the original cost leader.

A second risk is too much focus. Because of their focus on continuously driving costs lower, firms implementing a cost leadership strategy sometimes fail to detect significant changes in customers' needs or in competitors' efforts to differentiate what has traditionally been an undifferentiated, commodity-like product.

Before Orville Redenbacher and Charles Bowman launched Orville Redenbacher's Gourmet Popping Corn, for example, popcorn was thought to be a humble, commodity-like product. Convinced that people would pay more for high-quality popcorn, Orville Redenbacher developed a popcorn hybrid that produced fuller popping corn. He also perfected harvesting and packaging techniques that minimized kernel damage. In a tribute to Mr. Redenbacher, who died recently at the age of 88, the executive director of The Popcorn Institute observed that "He pioneered the gourmet popcorn niche. He promoted it very effectively and helped bring popcorn to a new level of acceptance."[59]

A final risk of the cost leadership strategy concerns imitation. Competitors sometimes learn how to imitate the low-cost leader's strategy successfully. When this occurs, the low-cost leader is challenged to find ways to increase the value provided by its good or service. Usually, value is increased by selling the current product at an even lower price or by adding features customers' value while maintaining price.

■ Differentiation Strategy

With the differentiation strategy, the *unique* attributes and characteristics of a firm's product (other than cost) provide value to customers. Because a differentiated product satisfies customers' unique needs, firms implementing the differentiation strategy charge premium prices. To do this successfully, a "firm must truly be unique at something or be perceived as unique."[60] It is the ability to sell its differentiated product at a price that exceeds what was spent to create it that allows the firm to outperform its rivals and earn above-average returns.

Rather than costs, the focus of the differentiation strategy is on continuously investing in and developing features that differentiate products in ways that customers value. Overall, a firm using the differentiation strategy seeks to be different from its competitors along as many dimensions as possible. The less similarity between a firm's goods or services and those of competitors, the more buffered the firm is from rivals' actions. Commonly recognized differentiated products include Toyota's Lexus ("the relentless pursuit of perfection"), Ralph Lauren's and Tommy Hilfiger's clothing lines (image), Caterpillar (a heavy equipment manufacturing firm committed to providing rapid delivery of spare parts to any location in the world), Maytag appliances (product reliability), McKinsey & Co. (the highest priced and most prestigious consulting firm in the world), and Rolex watches (prestige and image).

A product can be differentiated in an almost endless number of ways. Unusual features, responsive customer service, rapid product innovations and technological leadership, perceived prestige and status, different tastes, and engineering design and performance are examples of approaches to differentiation. In fact, virtually anything a firm can do to create real or perceived value for customers is a basis for differentiation. The challenge is to determine which features create value for the customer.

A leading manufacturer of integrated circuits, Intel seeks to differentiate its microprocessor chips. Intended to meet the needs of current and future sophisticated software applications, speed is a primary feature on which Intel's chips are differentiated. Market share is one indicator of the success achieved by Intel through implementation of its strategy. At the end of 1995, Intel's chips powered 80 percent of all personal computers. With annual sales of approximately $16 billion in 1995, some analysts predicted the firm would earn as much as $50 billion in sales by 2000.

To maintain and enhance its chips' differentiated features, Intel allocates significant financial resources to research and development and capital improvements. The firm's 1995 capital budget of $3.5 billion exceeded capital expenditures in 1994 by 45 percent. The objective sought through this increase was to convert more rapidly to the new process technologies Intel is using to manufacture higher speed microprocessors. The firm also intends to build plants in Israel, Ireland, and Malaysia. These facilities are scheduled to open in 1998. Overall, Intel spent approximately $17 billion on research and development and new plants in the decade that ended in 1995.[61]

Intel's efforts to continuously differentiate its microprocessor chips are necessary, especially in light of strategic actions taken by competitors. In late 1995, Cyrix Corp. unveiled a chip that some analysts called "the first real challenge" to Intel's leadership in microprocessor performance. At the same time, Advanced Micro Devices (AMD) and Nexgen merged their operations. This merger, some believe, will create a company that has the potential to be a formidable competitor for Intel.[62]

The introduction of turbocharged Pentium chips (150-megahertz and 166-megahertz versions) in early 1996 was an immediate competitive action that Intel took in response to the possible challenges from competitors such as Cyrix Corp. and the firm created through the merger of AMD and Nexgen. Some analysts suggested that this rapid introduction of faster chips was clear evidence of Intel's commitment to maintaining its position as the dominant provider of superior microprocessor chips.[63]

Figure 4.3   **Examples of Value-Creating Activities Associated with the Differentiation Strategy**

Firm Infrastructure	Highly developed information systems to better understand customers' purchasing preferences.	A company-wide emphasis on the importance of producing high-quality products.		
Human Resource Management	Compensation programs intended to encourage worker creativity and productivity.	Somewhat extensive use of subjective rather than objective performance measures.	Superior personnel training.	
Technology Development	Strong capability in basic research.	Investments in technologies that will allow the firm to produce highly differentiated products.		
Procurement	Systems and procedures used to find the highest quality raw materials.	Purchase of highest quality replacement parts.		
	Superior handling of incoming raw materials so as to minimize damage and improve the quality of the final product.	Consistent manufacturing of attractive products. Rapid responses to customers' unique manufacturing specifications.	Accurate and responsive order-processing procedures. Rapid and timely product deliveries to customers.	Extensive granting of credit buying arrangements for customers. Extensive personal relationships with buyers and suppliers.	Extensive buyer training to assure high-quality product installations. Complete field stockings of replacement parts.
	Inbound Logistics	**Operations**	**Outbound Logistics**	**Marketing and Sales**	**Service**

Source: Adapted with the permission of The Free Press, a division of Simon & Schuster from COMPETITIVE ADVANTAGE: Creating and Sustaining Superior Performance by Michael E. Porter, Fig 4-1, 122. Copyright © 1985 by Michael E. Porter.

A firm's value chain can also be used to determine if it can link the activities required to create value through implementation of the differentiation strategy. Examples of primary and support activities that are used commonly to differentiate a good or service are shown in Figure 4.3. Companies without the core competencies needed to link these activities cannot expect to implement the differentiation strategy successfully.

As explained next, successful implementation of the differentiation strategy allows a firm to earn above-average returns in spite of the presence of strong competitive forces.

Rivalry with Existing Competitors

Customers tend to be loyal purchasers of products that are differentiated in ways meaningful to them. As their loyalty to a brand increases, their sensitivity to price increases lessens. This relationship between brand loyalty and price sensitivity insulates a firm from competitive rivalry. Thus, McKinsey & Co. is insulated from its competitors, even on the basis of price, as long as it continues to satisfy the differentiated needs of what appears to be a loyal customer group. The same outcome is true for Tommy Hilfiger, as long as its "classic preppy . . . with a twist" clothes[64] continue to satisfy the needs of "America's multicultural society" for garments with unique features.[65]

Bargaining Power of Buyers (Customers)

The *uniqueness* of differentiated goods or services insulates the firm from competitive rivalry and reduces customers' sensitivity to price increases. Based on a combination of unique materials and brand image, Ralph Lauren's clothes satisfy certain customers' unique needs better than do competitors' offerings. A key reason that some buyers are willing to pay a premium price for this firm's clothing items is that for them, other products do not offer a comparable combination of features and cost. The lack of perceived acceptable alternatives increases the firm's power relative to its customers.

Bargaining Power of Suppliers

Because a firm implementing the differentiation strategy charges a premium price for its products, suppliers must provide it with high-quality parts. However, the high margins the firm earns when selling effectively differentiated products partially insulate it from the influence of suppliers. Higher supplier costs can be paid through these margins. Alternatively, because of buyers' relative insensitivity to price increases, the differentiated firm might choose to pass the additional cost of supplies on to the customer by raising the price of its unique product.

Potential Entrants

Customer loyalty and the need to overcome the uniqueness of a differentiated product are substantial entry barriers faced by potential entrants. Entering an industry under these conditions typically demands significant investments of resources and a willingness to be patient while seeking the loyalty of customers.

Product Substitutes

Firms selling brand-name goods and services to loyal customers are positioned effectively against product substitutes. In contrast, companies without brand loyalty are more subject to their customers switching either to products that offer differentiated features that serve the same function as the current product, particularly if the substitute has a lower price, or to products that offer more features that perform more attractive functions.

As our discussion shows, firms can gain competitive advantage through successful implementation of the differentiation strategy. Nonetheless, several risks are associated with this strategy.

■ Competitive Risks of the Differentiation Strategy

One risk of the differentiation strategy is that customers might decide that the price differential between the differentiator's and the low-cost leader's product is too significant. In this instance, a firm may be providing differentiated features that exceed customers' needs. When this happens, the firm is vulnerable to competitors that are able to offer customers a combination of features and price that is more consistent with their needs.

Another risk of the differentiation strategy is that a firm's means of differentiation no longer provide value for which customers are willing to pay. Upscale retailer Bloomingdale's discovered that its focus on "glitz" as a means of differentiation no longer provided value to at least some of its customers, especially those shopping in the store's new locations. A review of the firm's situation resulted in one analyst concluding that "The mystique of the store hasn't been transferable" from New York City. Moreover, the analyst felt that the stores were "either too avant-garde or too humdrum. And in many cases, their prices were too high." In response to its situation, Bloomingdale's decided to emphasize comfort—a means of differentiation the firm thought would provide customer value—rather than glitz. Among other actions taken to focus on comfort was renovation of the chain's stores to provide customers with user-friendly designs.[66]

A third risk of the differentiation strategy is that learning can narrow customers' perceptions of the value of a firm's differentiated features. The value of the IBM name on personal computers was a differentiated feature for which some customers were willing to pay a premium price as the product emerged. However, as customers familiarized themselves with the standard features and as a host of PC clones entered the market, IBM brand loyalty began to fail. Clones offered customers features similar to those of the IBM product at a substantially lower price, reducing the attractiveness of IBM's product.

■ Focus Strategies

In contrast to the cost leadership and differentiation strategies, a company implementing a focus strategy seeks to use its core competencies to serve the needs of a certain industry segment (e.g., a particular buyer group, segment of the product line, or geographic market).[67] A **focus strategy** is an integrated set of actions designed to produce products that serve the needs of a particular competitive segment. Although the breadth of target is clearly a matter of degree, the essence of the focus strategy "is the exploitation of a narrow target's differences from the balance of the industry."[68] Through successful implementation of a focus strategy, a company can gain a competitive advantage in its chosen target segments even though it does not possess an industry-wide competitive advantage.[69]

> ■ *A **focus strategy** is an integrated set of actions designed to produce products that serve the needs of a particular competitive segment.*

The foundation of focus strategies is that a firm can serve a particular segment of an industry more effectively or efficiently than can industry-wide competitors. Success with a focus strategy rests on a firm's ability either to find segments where unique needs are so specialized that broad-based competitors choose not to serve them or locate a segment being served poorly by the broad-based competitors.[70]

Value can be provided to customers through two types of focus strategies: focused low cost and focused differentiation.

Focused Low-Cost Strategy

Using a double-drive-through format, Rally's Hamburgers Inc. implements the focused low-cost strategy. At the end of a recent year, Rally's had approximately 500 restaurants operating in 20 U.S. states.[71] These restaurants have limited menus and no indoor seating. According to the firm's CEO, Rally's serves "the little-spare-time-or-cash crowd that McDonald's and Burger King have all but

In its stores outside of New York, Bloomingdale's decided to emphasize comfort, a means of differentiation, to provide customer value.

abandoned." Concentrating on the value-adding dimensions of price and speed, the firm recently sold and delivered to customers in 45 seconds a "fully-dressed burger, a 16-ounce soft drink and a good-sized fries for $1.97."[72]

Family Dollar operates a chain of more than 2,400 self-service, retail discount stores in 37 states. This firm's narrow competitive scope is geographic in nature. Although it has units throughout the United States, most of them are in states that are east of the Rocky Mountains (states with significant concentrations of stores include Georgia, Tennessee, Alabama, and Texas). Additionally, its relatively small stores (the typical store averages between 6,000 and 8,000 square feet) are located mostly in rural areas and small towns with populations under 50,000. The average price of a Family Dollar item is $5; most goods are priced under $17.99.[73]

As noted in the Strategic Focus, a focused differentiation strategy can be quite successful. Both Fingerhut and Polar Electro provide goods and/or services that are differentiated from their competitors and are focused on a particular market niche. Fingerhut, for example, targets low- and moderate-income families who represent good credit risks. Alternatively, Polar Electro targets athletes, weight watchers, and individuals suffering from stress. Thus, Polar Electro focuses on a fitness and wellness market niche. Although neither of these two firms has been subjected to product forgeries, firms using a differentiation strategy suffer from this potentially serious concern. Forgeries are a significant problem for firms with products that can be easily imitated in type but are differentiated on the basis of quality and brand reputation. Firms with positive brand reputations in the apparel industry are particularly vulnerable. In the following section, we explain the focused differentiation strategy in more detail.

Focused Differentiation Strategy

Other firms (such as Callaway Golf Company, the firm described in the chapter's opening case) implement the focused differentiation strategy. The number of

STRATEGIC FOCUS

Successful Focus on a Market Niche: Watch Out for Pirates

Some firms have been highly successful by focusing on a particular market niche. For instance, Fingerhut is second only to J.C. Penney Company in consumer catalog marketing in the United States. In its catalogs, Fingerhut sells many different products, ranging from toy telephones that can be bought for $20 to big-screen TVs that sell for $2,000. However, Fingerhut clearly focuses on the low- and moderate-income U.S. households. Furthermore, it differentiates its services from competitors by extending credit to these individuals, many of whom would find it difficult to obtain credit from other sources. In fact, some argue that Fingerhut's real business is in extending credit at rates up to 24 percent per year.

Fingerhut is able to extend such credit because it compiles an extensive database on active and potential customers. In fact, its database contains more than 500 pieces of information on 50 million plus active and potential customers. It attempts to focus on the best credit risks among the low- and moderate-income households. To take further advantage of its successful focused differentiation strategy, Fingerhut launched its co-branded Visa and Mastercard. Its goal is to reach one million accounts, which it almost achieved in 1996. One analyst suggested that Fingerhut's core competence is an intense knowledge of its customers.

Similarly, Finnish entrepreneur Seppo Saynajakangas operates his firm Polar Electro OY using a focused differentiation strategy. The firm began with a new product invented by Seppo that operated as a heart rate monitor for use by athletes. Today, the monitors are marketed to athletes, weight watchers, and stress sufferers. Furthermore, Polar has offices in Britain, the United States, Holland, Germany, Switzerland, and Hong Kong. During the last 10 years, sales have grown by 50 to 60 percent per year. In all, the heart rate monitor is sold in 40 different countries and the firm has $125 million in total annual sales. Focused on the market niche described above, Polar Electro has approximately 80 percent of the U.S. market. The firm also is developing other related electronic products such as a blood pressure monitor. The focus is on products for fitness and wellness.

One of the primary risks of a focused differentiation strategy is that a competitor will develop a similar product for the same market niche. Unfortunately, these firms face other problems, too. For example, a phenomenon creating significant problems for a number of firms in recent times is that of product forgery. Forgeries of successful products are often sold on the black market. The forgeries are cheap imitations that use the logo of the branded product. The problem is estimated to be significant, with annual losses due to product forgeries being approximately $200 billion per year in the United States alone. The problem can be even more significant in that not only do the branded products lose sales, but their reputations can be tarnished because of the poor-quality forgeries, particularly when the customers are unaware that they are buying a forgery. While Fingerhut may not have to worry about this concern, Polar Electro could experience these problems. However, forgeries are more likely to occur in products that are more easily imitated such as apparel where the differentiation is seen in terms of quality and brand reputation.

Source: S. Chandler, 1996, Data is power. Just ask Fingerhut, *Business Week,* June 3, 69; T. Stein, 1996, The world's greatest entrepreneurs: Their powerful strategies for creating success, *Success,* June 36–37; D. Stipp, 1996, Farewell, my logo, *Fortune,* May 27, 128–140.

ways products can be differentiated to serve the unique needs of particular competitive segments is virtually endless. Consider the following example.

Located in strip shopping centers that are accessible to the public, Sally Beauty Supply stores stock more than 4,000 hair, skin, and nail care products and salon equipment. Some of the chain's sales are to the general public. However, the majority of its business is selling to professional hair and nail stylists. Because of its target customer, Sally Beauty Supply competes mainly with wholesalers rather than retailers. The key to the firm's success appears to be its ability to locate and offer new and "hot" products to a group of professionals that is interested in purchasing and using cutting-edge products. One analyst has suggested that the firm has "found a niche that others haven't tried to exploit."[74]

Focusing on the after-market (sales made to customers after their purchase of the original product), Custom Chrome distributes more than 10,500 engine parts (many of which it designs internally) and accessories that are for only one product segment—Harley-Davidson motorcycles. A global competitor, the firm groups its products into 16 categories and sells them in the United States, Europe, and Japan. Selling under different brand names, including RevTech, C.C. Rider, Dyno Power, Tour Ease, and Premium, Custom Chrome can supply parts for Harley models built as long ago as 1936. The primary way the firm earns the higher margins necessary to continue differentiating its unique products is shown in the following comments: "Custom Chrome offers a large number of proprietary products, which it designs and engineers and for which it typically owns the manufacturing tooling. The proprietary products are not widely available from any other source, allowing the company to obtain higher margins than may be available on products for which it acts only as a distributor."[75] A final example of a company implementing the focused differentiation strategy is described in the Strategic Focus dealing with the Hummer.

Firms must be able to complete various primary and support activities in a competitively superior manner to achieve strategic competitiveness and earn above-average returns when implementing a focus strategy. The activities that must be completed to implement the focused low-cost and the focused differentiation strategies are virtually identical to those shown in Figures 4.2 and 4.3, respectively. Similarly, the manners in which the two focus strategies allow a firm to deal successfully with the five competitive forces parallel those described with respect to the cost leadership and the differentiation strategies. The only difference is that the competitive scope changes from industry wide to a narrow competitive segment of the industry. Thus, a review of Figures 4.2 and 4.3 and the text regarding the five competitive forces yields a description of the relationship between each of the two focus strategies and competitive advantage.

■ Competitive Risks of Focus Strategies

When implementing either type of focus strategy, a firm faces the same general risks as does the company pursuing the cost leadership or the differentiation strategy on an industry-wide basis. However, focus strategies have three additional risks beyond these general ones. First, a competitor may be able to focus on a more narrowly defined competitive segment and "outfocus" the focuser. For example, a firm might decide that it can better serve the specialized needs of one or the other of Sally Beauty Supply's two key customer groups—professional hair stylists and nail stylists. Second, a firm competing on an industry-wide basis may decide that the market segment being served by the focus-strategy firm is attractive and worthy of competitive pursuit. The third risk of a focus strategy is that the needs of customers within a narrow competitive segment may become more similar to those of customers as a whole. When this occurs, the advantages of a focus strategy are either reduced or eliminated.

STRATEGIC FOCUS

Is It a Truck or a Jeep? Neither: It's a Hummer!

"The Hummer is not like any other car or truck on the road. It is an attitude and almost a way of life."

This statement may capture the essence of the customer need that AM General, a private company in South Bend, Indiana, seeks to satisfy with its highly differentiated product. At prices ranging from $44,000 for a stripped-down pickup to $80,000 for the largest fully equipped wagon with many accessories (such as carpets and CD players), Hummers are targeted to a narrow competitive segment of the automobile and truck markets. Identified by some as a toy for the rich, the company's records indicate that the typical customer earns between $200,000 and $300,000 annually. Most customers already have two or three other cars when they decide to purchase a Hummer. While physicians like the Hummer, lawyers seem to prefer Range Rovers. Popular on both the U.S. west and east coasts, Hummers do not sell well in America's heartland. A descendant of both the old Kaiser-Jeep Corp. and Willys Motors, the Hummer was designed initially for the military. Its intended purpose was to transport troops across any type of terrain. Since production started in 1983, AM General has sold more than 110,000 vehicles to the military.

After the Gulf War ended in 1991, Arnold Schwarzenegger called AM General to express his desire to buy a Hummer. The firm had already decided that logging and mining companies would be a new target customer group; however, it was not certain that there was sufficient demand from individuals. Input from "The Arnold," coupled with its own market research, convinced AM General that a narrow customer group would be interested in buying its highly differentiated product. Beginning in 1992, after the company added the equipment that allowed the Hummer to meet federal safety and environmental standards, Arnold Schwarzenegger was able to buy the first of his five Hummers. (Apparently, the Hummer had no difficulty satisfying the federal safety standards. In fact, according to the firm's principal engineer, "in crash-barrier tests, the Hummer broke the barrier").

How do customers use their Hummers? Many take trips (with friends who also own a Hummer) to remote, demanding areas. One satisfied owner says that he likes the "mechanics and geometry of getting out of difficult situations." In these situations, he believes, "there's an aspect of danger" that requires the driver to think carefully about how to cope with what has been encountered.

Popular though it may be with a narrow competitive segment, the Hummer will likely not become a product that is targeted industry wide. In fact, "for all the electrifying response the truck gets from its civilian owners and despite the growing popularity of four-wheel-drive vehicles, the Hummer will probably remain an oddity in the automobile business."

Source: B. Woolley, 1996, Humdinger!, *Dallas Morning News,* January 18, C1, C2; B. O'Reilly, 1995, What's a Hummer? Aah: Thought you'd never ask, *Fortune,* October 2, 146–155.

Next, we describe a business-level strategy that is being used more prominently in the new competitive landscape. A key reason for this is the requirements of global competition.

■ Integrated Low-Cost/Differentiation Strategy

Particularly in global markets, a firm's ability to blend the low-cost and the differentiation approaches may be critical to sustaining competitive advantages.[76]

Compared to firms relying on one dominant generic strategy for their success, a company capable of successfully implementing an integrated low-cost/differentiation strategy should be better positioned to adapt quickly to environmental changes, learn new skills and technologies more quickly, and effectively leverage its core competencies across business units and product lines.

A growing body of evidence supports the relationship between implementation of an integrated strategy and the earning of above-average returns.[77] Some time ago, for example, a researcher found that the most successful firms competing in low-profit potential industries were able to effectively combine the low-cost and differentiation strategies.[78] In a more recent comprehensive study, it was discovered that "businesses which combined multiple forms of competitive advantage outperformed businesses which only were identified with a single form."[79] Other research found that the highest performing companies in the Korean electronics industry were those combining both the differentiation and cost leadership strategies, suggesting the viability of the integrated strategy in different nations.[80]

A key reason firms capable of successfully implementing the integrated strategy earn above-average returns is that the benefits of this strategy are additive: "differentiation leads to premium prices at the same time that cost leadership implies lower costs."[81] Thus, the integrated strategy allows firms to gain competitive advantage by offering two types of value to customers—some differentiated features (but often fewer than those provided by the product-differentiated firm) and relatively low cost (but not as low as the products of the low-cost leader).

Mabuchi Motor, a Japanese company, implements the integrated low-cost/differentiation strategy. This firm manufactures the small electric motors that power compact disk players, toy airplanes, and car windows. Mabuchi's focus is singular and consistent. The firm's objective is to produce "high-quality products at low prices, but in limited variety." Approximately 99 percent of revenues are earned from the sales of motors. Costs are kept low by the firm's decision to design and manufacture a limited variety of its products. The company produces 4.9 million motors daily, but fills 55 percent of its orders with just 10 different models. These products are differentiated through the firm's "obsession" with its miniature devices. At a modern technical center, Mabuchi scientists constantly research ways to differentiate their firm's products from competitors' offerings, seeking ways to make their motors "lighter, quieter, hardier and cheaper." Indicators of Mabuchi's strategic competitiveness include control of more than one-half of the world's market for small motors and routine double-digit operating margins.[82]

Toyota Motor Company also implements the integrated low-cost/differentiation strategy. Often, Toyota focuses on actions it believes simultaneously reduce costs and improve the differentiated features of its products. (The firm believes that its "competitive edge in quality is the cornerstone of its business.") For example, Toyota feels that by following its methods of operations, each employee "becomes an expert in identifying waste and in discovering ways to eliminate it. Waste, by our definition, is any expenditure of time, energy, or material that does not add perceptible value for the customer. Eliminating waste means continuously raising quality as well as productivity, since squandering resources on less-than-perfect products is the worst waste of all."[83] To further reduce costs, Toyota is committed to ensuring that every plant purchases parts and materials from the world's most competitive suppliers and that all waste from its sales operations is eliminated. Significant commitments to research and development activities allow Toyota to upgrade continuously its products' differentiated features.

As suggested by these company-specific descriptions, firms must be strategically flexible to implement successfully the integrated low-cost/differentiation strategy. Discussed next are three approaches to organizational work that can increase the strategic flexibility that is associated with implementation of this strategy.

Flexible Manufacturing Systems

Made possible largely as a result of the increasing capabilities of modern information technologies, flexible manufacturing systems increase the "flexibilities of human, physical and information resources"[84] that are integrated to create differentiated products at low costs. A *flexible manufacturing system* (FMS) is a computer-controlled process used to produce a variety of products in moderate, flexible quantities with a minimum of manual intervention.[85]

The goal of FMS is to eliminate the low-cost versus product-variety trade-off inherent in traditional manufacturing technologies. The flexibility provided by an FMS allows a plant to "change nimbly from making one product to making another."[86] When used properly, an FMS can help a firm become more flexible in response to changes in its customers' needs, while retaining low-cost advantages and consistent product quality. Because an FMS reduces the lot size needed to manufacture a product efficiently, a firm's capacity to serve the unique needs of a narrow competitive scope is increased. Thus, FMS technology is a significant technological advance that allows firms to produce a large variety of products at a low cost.

Effective use of an FMS is linked with a firm's ability to understand constraints these systems may create (in terms of materials handling and the flow of supporting resources in scheduling, for example) and to design an effective mix of machines, computer systems, and people.[87] As a result, this type of manufacturing technology facilitates the implementation of complex competitive strategies such as the integrated low-cost/differentiation strategy that lead to strategic competitiveness in global markets.[88]

Incorporated into firms' processes somewhat slowly at first, the number of companies anticipating their use of FMSs in the near future is substantial. For example, among U.S. firms with more than 10,000 employees, "68 percent of electrical equipment manufacturers, 78 percent of machinery producers, 93 percent of automobile makers, and 100 percent of aerospace companies expect to have some form of FMS by the year 2000."[89] Although these expressed intentions are impressive, it is interesting to note that according to a researcher's results, "the bulk of the major firms in Japan, Western Europe and the United States will have begun using FMS by (2000), but the percentage will still be higher in Japan than in the United States or Western Europe."[90] Contributing to the slower rate of adoption of FMSs in the United States is the reality that U.S. firms, as compared to European and especially Japanese companies, tend to require higher rates of return to justify investments in these systems.[91] Moreover, evidence to date suggests that Japanese manufacturing firms have derived greater benefits from investments in FMSs as compared to their U.S. counterparts. The cause of this outcome may be that FMSs are managed less effectively in U.S. firms.[92]

Information Networks Across Firms

New information networks linking manufacturers with their suppliers, distributors, and customers are another technological development that increases a firm's strategic flexibility and responsiveness.[93] Recent changes in a range of information technologies facilitated the development of competitively valuable information networks. Examples of these technologies include CADD (computer-assisted design and development) systems, CIM (computer-integrated manufacturing) systems, and EDI (electronic data integration). Ford Motor Co., Allen Bradley, Hitachi, Motorola, and Boeing are but a few of the many companies using information networks to coordinate the development, production, distribution, and marketing of their products. Among many benefits, these computer-based information links substantially reduce the time needed to design and test new products and allow a firm to compete on the basis of fast delivery (a differentiated feature) and low cost.

Total Quality Management Systems

Although difficult to implement,[94] many firms have established total quality management (TQM) systems (also see Chapter 5). Important objectives sought through use of TQM systems include increases in the quality of a firm's product and the productivity levels of the entire organization.[95] Enhanced quality focuses customers' attention on improvements in product performance, feature utility, and reliability. This allows a firm to achieve differentiation and ultimately higher prices and market share. An emphasis on quality in production techniques lowers manufacturing and service costs through savings in rework, scrap, and warranty expenses. These savings can result in a competitive advantage for a firm over its rivals. Thus, TQM programs integrate aspects of the differentiation and cost leadership strategies.

Four key assumptions are the foundation of TQM systems. The first assumption is that "the costs of poor quality (such as inspection, rework, lost customers and so on) are far greater than the costs of developing processes that produce high-quality products and services."[96] The second assumption is that employees naturally care about their work and will take initiatives to improve it. However, these initiatives are taken only when the firm provides employees with the tools and training they need to improve quality and when managers pay attention to their ideas. The third assumption is that "organizations are systems of highly interdependent parts."[97] Problems encountered in such systems often cross traditional functional (e.g., marketing, manufacturing, finance, etc.) lines. Solving interdependent problems requires integrated decision processes with participation from all affected functional areas. The fourth assumption is that the responsibility for an effective TQM system rests squarely on the shoulders of upper-level managers. These people must openly and totally support use of a TQM system and accept the responsibility for an organizational design that allows employees to work effectively.

As with the other business-level strategies, there are risks associated with use of the integrated low-cost/differentiation strategy.

■ Competitive Risks of the Integrated Low-Cost/Differentiation Strategy

The potential of the integrated strategy, in terms of above-average returns, is significant. However, this potential comes with substantial risk. Selecting a business-level strategy calls for firms to make choices about how they intend to compete. Achieving the low-cost position in an industry, or a segment of an industry (e.g., a focus strategy), demands that the firm be able to reduce its costs consistently relative to competitors. Use of the differentiation strategy, with either an industry-wide or a focused competitive scope (see Figure 4.1), results in above-average returns only when the firm provides customers with differentiated products they value and for which they are willing to pay a premium price.

The firm failing to establish a leadership position in its chosen competitive scope, as the low-cost producer or as a differentiator, risks becoming *"stuck-in-the-middle."*[98] Kmart is a firm whose strategic actions may have caused it to become *stuck in the middle.* Following study of the firm's recent performance difficulties, an analyst concluded that Kmart tried to compete with Wal-Mart (below) and Sears (above), and at the same time run its boutiques (Builders Square, Waldenbooks, OfficeMax, Borders bookstores, and Sports Authority). Instead of achieving competitive success, Kmart lost ground in all markets through these strategic actions.[99]

Being stuck in the middle prevents firms from dealing successfully with the five competitive forces and from earning above-average returns. Indeed, some research results show that the lowest performing businesses are those lacking a distinguishable competitive advantage. Not having a clear and identifiable competitive advantage results from a firm being stuck in the middle.[100] Such firms can earn average returns only when an industry's structure is highly favorable or when the firm is competing against others that are in the same position.[101]

Midsize accounting firms (those with as many as 50 partners and 300 employees) appear to be stuck in the middle. These companies lack the size and resources to offer the wide array of services available from the Big Six giants; at the same time, their overhead rates prevent them from matching the low prices charged by small accounting firms and solo practitioners. Thus, these firms' services seem to be too expensive to compete with the low-cost small firms and too undifferentiated to provide the value offered by the large, differentiated accounting firms. In an accounting firm consultant's opinion, these conditions suggest that by the year 2000, middle size accounting firms may be "as extinct as the dodo."[102]

Evidence also suggests that some firms competing in the coffee-bar business may be stuck in the middle. Industry leader Starbucks continues to expand rapidly, with intentions to grow from approximately 700 stores in the United States and Canada at the end of 1995 to 2,000 units by 2000. In addition, the firm has introduced larger units in select markets. With 50 or more seats rather than the standard seating capacity of 20 to 25, these larger Starbucks locations permit expanded menus and live entertainment.[103] Starbucks' "shotgun strategy of getting bars open in a hurry" contributes to the Specialty Coffee Association of America's prediction that the number of coffee bars will double between 1996 and 2000. This explosive growth is expected to result in an

To avoid being one of the stuck-in-the-middle businesses, Starbucks Coffee intends to grow from approximately 700 stores in the United States and Canada at the end of 1995 to 2,000 units by the year 2000.

industry shakeout. Michael Bergman, CEO of Second Cup, another coffee-bar business, believes that as a result of events occurring in this industry, "You will have the strong, big players and the small, well-run chains that really understand their particular customer. The victims are going to be marginal players in the middle."[104]

To avoid being stuck in the middle, some industry competitors are taking actions. Timothy's World Coffee operates the bulk of its 28 U.S. stores in the "brutally competitive New York City market." To differentiate itself and to serve the needs of a narrow customer group, the firm established Timothy's World-News Cafe. At these locations, customers can buy coffee as well as purchase and read their favorite magazines while in the store. Chock Full O'Nuts is expanding its Quikava coffee chain as the foundation to a focused differentiation strategy to avoid becoming stuck in the middle. Each Quikava unit is a tiny, double-drive-through that sells coffee, road-ready sandwiches and baked goods.[105]

Once a firm has selected its business-level strategy, it must both anticipate and be prepared to respond to competitors' actions and responses. The dynamics of competition that occur as firms implement their strategies are examined in the next chapter. While these dynamics take place with respect to all types of strategies (see Chapters 6 through 9), the majority of competitive actions and competitive responses are initiated in efforts to implement successfully a firm's business-level strategy.

■ Summary

- A business-level strategy is an integrated and coordinated set of commitments and actions designed to provide value to customers and gain a competitive advantage by exploiting core competencies in specific, individual product markets. Five business-level strategies are examined in this chapter. Strategic competitiveness is enhanced when a firm is able to develop and exploit new core competencies faster than competitors can mimic the competitive advantages yielded by its current competencies.

- Customers are the foundation of successful business-level strategies. When considering customers, firms simultaneously examine three issues: *who, what,* and *how.* Respectively, these issues cause the firm to determine the customer groups it will serve, the needs those customers have that it seeks to satisfy, and the core competencies it possesses that can be used to satisfy customers' needs. The increasing segmentation of markets occurring throughout the world creates multiple opportunities for firms to identify unique customer needs.

- Firms seeking competitive advantage through the cost leadership strategy often produce no-frills, standard-ized products for an industry's typical customer. Above-average returns are earned when firms continuously drive their costs lower than those of their competitors while providing customers with products that have low prices and acceptable levels of differentiated features.

- Competitive risks associated with the cost leadership strategy include (1) a loss of competitive advantage to newer technologies, (2) a failure to detect changes in customers' needs, and (3) the ability of competitors to imitate the low-cost leader's competitive advantage through their own unique strategic actions.

- Through implementation of the differentiation strategy, firms provide customers with products that have different (and valued) features. Because of their uniqueness, differentiated products are sold at a premium price. Products can be differentiated along any dimension that is valued by some group of customers. Firms using this strategy seek to differentiate their products from competitors' goods or services along as many dimensions as possible. The less similarity with competitors' products, the more buffered a firm is from competition with its rivals.

- Risks associated with the differentiation strategy include (1) a customer group's decision that the differences between the differentiated product and the low-cost leader's product are no longer worth a premium price, (2) the inability of a differentiated product to create the type of value for which customers are willing to pay a premium price, and (3) the ability of competitors to provide customers with products that have features similar to those associated with the differentiated product, but at a lower cost.

- Through the low-cost and the differentiated focus strategies, firms serve the needs of a narrow competitive segment (e.g., buyer group, product segment, or geographic area). This strategy is successful when firms have the core competencies required to provide value to a narrow competitive segment that exceeds the value available from firms serving customers on an industry-wide basis.

- The competitive risks of focus strategies include (1) a competitor's ability to use its core competencies to "outfocus" the focuser by serving an even more narrowly defined competitive segment, (2) decisions by industry-wide competitors to serve a customer group's specialized needs that the focuser has been serving, and (3) a reduction in differences of the needs between customers in a narrow competitive segment and the industry-wide market.

- Firms using the integrated low-cost/differentiation strategy strive to provide customers with relatively low-cost products that have some valued differentiated features. The primary risk of this strategy is that a firm might produce products that do not offer sufficient value—in terms of either low cost or differentiation. When this occurs, the company is "stuck in the middle." Firms stuck in the middle compete at a disadvantage.

Review Questions

1. What is a strategy and what are business-level strategies?

2. What is the relationship between a firm's customers and its business-level strategy? Why is this relationship important?

3. When studying customers in terms of *who, what,* and *how,* what questions are firms trying to answer?

4. What is the integrated low-cost/differentiation strategy? Why is this strategy becoming more important to firms?

5. How is competitive advantage achieved through successful implementation of the cost leadership strategy? The differentiation strategy? The focused low-cost strategy? The focused differentiation strategy? The integrated low-cost/differentiation strategy?

6. What are the risks associated with selecting and implementing each of the five strategies mentioned in question 5?

Application Discussion Questions

1. You are a customer of your university or college. What actions does your school take to understand *what* your needs are? Be prepared to discuss your views.

2. Choose a firm in your local community that is of interest to you. Based on interactions with this company, which business-level strategy do you believe the firm is implementing? What evidence can you provide to support your belief?

3. Assume that you have decided to establish and operate a restaurant in your local community. *Who* are the customers you would serve? *What* needs do these customers have that

you could satisfy with your restaurant? *How* would you satisfy those needs? Be prepared to discuss your responses.

4. What business-level strategy is your school implementing? What core competencies are being used to implement this strategy?

5. Assume you overheard the following comment: "It is impossible for a firm to produce a low-cost, highly differentiated product." Accept or reject this statement and be prepared to defend your position.

Ethics Questions

1. Can a commitment to ethical conduct on issues such as the environment, commitment to product quality, and fulfilling contractual agreements affect competitive advantage? If so, how?

2. Is there more incentive for differentiators or low-cost leaders to pursue stronger ethical conduct? Think of an example to support your answer.

3. Can an overemphasis on low-cost leadership or differentiation lead to ethical problems (such as poor product design and manufacturing) that create costly problems (e.g., product liability lawsuits)?

4. Reexamine the assumptions about effective TQM systems presented in this chapter. Do these assumptions urge top-level managers to maintain higher ethical standards? If so, how?

5. A brand image is one way a firm can differentiate its good or service. However, many questions are now being raised about the effect brand images have on consumer behavior. For example, considerable concern has arisen about brand images that are managed by tobacco firms and their effect on teenage smoking habits. Should firms be concerned about how they form and use brand images? Why or why not?

Internet Exercise

Read about several types of businesses in one of the on-line business periodicals (e.g., *Business Week, Fortune*). What type of business-level strategies are they pursuing? Next, visit the home pages of these companies using one of the search engines listed in the Appendix. Based on their product offerings, how are they positioning themselves? Based on their slogans, what image are they conveying? What customer groups are they trying to attract? You can find demographic information about this group from the Census Bureau at:

■ http://www.census.gov

Cohesion Case

For your team's industry, select several specific products on which to focus. Find similar offerings on the Internet. A good starting point to find products is "The Commercial Sites Index" at:

■ http://www.directory.net/

Based on the product positions, what business-level strategy do you recommend for your own group? Is it possible for your team to offer a product that is both low cost and highly differentiated?

■ Notes

1. Callaway Golf Company, 1995, *Annual Report,* 1.

2. D.J. Collis and C.A. Montgomery, 1995, Competing on resources: Strategy in the 1990s, *Harvard Business Review* 73, no. 4: 118–128; J.T. Mahoney and J.R. Pandian, 1992, The resource-based view within the conversation of strategic management, *Strategic Management Journal* 13: 363–380.

3. A. Seth and H. Thomas, 1994, Theories of the firm: Implications for strategy research, *Journal of Management Studies* 31: 167.

4. R.R. Nelson, 1994, Why do firms differ, and how does it matter? in R.P. Rumelt, D.E. Schendel, and D.J. Teece (eds.), *Fundamental Issues in Strategy* (Boston: Harvard Business School Press), 247–269.

5. P. F. Drucker, 1995, The information executives truly need, *Harvard Business Review* 73, no. 1: 54–63.

6. R.A. Bettis and M.A. Hitt, 1995, The new competitive landscape, *Strategic Management Journal* (Special Issue, Summer) 16: 7–19; D. Leonard-Barton, 1995, *Wellsprings of Knowledge* (Boston: Harvard Business School Press); G. Hamel and C.K. Prahalad, 1989, Strategic intent, *Harvard Business Review* 67, no. 3: 63–76.

7. N. Tichy and C. DeRose, 1995, Roger Enrico's master class, *Fortune,* November 27, 105–106; G. Hamel and C.K. Prahalad, 1994, *Competing for the Future* (Boston: Harvard Business School Press).

8. D. Lei, M.A. Hitt, and R. Bettis, 1996, Dynamic core competences through meta-learning and strategic context, *Journal of Management* 22: 549–569; M.E. Porter, 1994, Toward a dynamic theory of strategy, in R.P. Rumelt, D.E. Schendel, and D.J. Teece (eds.), *Fundamental Issues in Strategy* (Boston: Harvard Business School Press), 423–461.

9. R.H. Hayes and G.P. Pisano, 1994, Beyond world-class: The new manufacturing strategy, *Harvard Business Review* 72, no. 1: 77–86.

10. Callaway Golf Company, *Annual Report,* 2.

11. M. Zimmerman, 1995, Frito-Lay stands to gain from rival's exit, *Dallas Morning News,* October 26, D1, D10.

12. M. Zimmerman, 1995, Luby's adds units as rivals face troubles, *Dallas Morning News,* November 6, D1, D4.

13. J. Jenk, C.H. Michel, and V. Margotin-Roze, 1995, The Russian consumer revolution, *The McKinsey Quarterly,* no. 2: 35–46.

14. P. Klebnikov, 1995, A world to conquer, *Forbes,* December 4, 256–257.

15. K.L. Miller, F.J. Comes, and P. Simpson, 1995, Poland: Rising star of Europe, *Business Week,* December 4, 64–70.

16. G.G. Dess, A. Gupta, J. F. Hennart, and C.W.L. Hill, 1995, Conducting and integrating strategy research at the international, corporate, and business levels: Issues and directions, *Journal of Management* 21: 357–393; M.A. Peteraf, 1993, The cornerstones of competitive advantage: A resource based view, *Strategic Management Journal* 14: 179–191.

17. B. Saporito, 1993, How to revive a fading firm, *Fortune,* March 22, 80.

18. M.E. Porter, 1980, *Competitive Strategy* (New York: Free Press).

19. Lei, Hitt, and Bettis, Dynamic core competences.

20. A.J. Slywotzky, 1996, *Value Migration* (Boston: Harvard Business School Press), 13.

21. A.W.H. Grant and L.A. Schlesinger, 1995, Realize your customers' full profit potential, *Harvard Business Review* 73, no. 5: 59–72.

22. F.F. Reichheld, 1996, Learning from customer defections, *Harvard Business Review* 74, no. 2: 57–69; M. Hammer, 1996, Who's to blame for all the layoffs? *Wall Street Journal,* January 22, A14; Slywotzky, *Value Migration,* 207–227; T.O. Jones and W.E. Sasser, Jr., 1995, Why satisfied customers defect, *Harvard Business Review* 73, no. 6: 88–99.

23. Jones and Sasser, Why satisfied customers defect, 99.

24. T.A. Stewart, 1995, After all you've done for your customers, why are they still not happy? *Fortune,* December 11, 182.

25. Slywotzky, *Value Migration,* 13; R. McKenna, 1995, Real-time marketing, *Harvard Business*

Review 73, no. 4: 87–95; S.E. Prokesch, 1995, Competing on customer service: An interview with British Airways' Sir Colin Marshall, *Harvard Business Review* 73, no. 6: 101–112; S.F. Wiggins, 1995, New ways to create lifetime bonds with your customers, *Fortune,* October 30, 115; Hamel and Prahalad, *Competing for the Future,* 73–105.

26. A master class in radical change, 1993, *Fortune,* December 13, 82–90.

27. T.C. Kinnear, K.L. Bernhardt, and K.A. Krentler, 1995, *Principles of Marketing,* 4th ed. (New York: Harper Collins Publishers), 149–150.

28. Ibid., 153.

29. Ibid., 149–161; D.F. Abell, 1980, *Defining the Business: The Starting Point of Strategic Planning* (Englewood Cliffs, N.J.: Prentice-Hall).

30. P. Sellers, 1996, Kmart is down for the count, *Fortune,* January 15, 102–103; B. Vlasic and K. Naughton, 1995, Kmart: Who's in charge here? *Business Week,* December 4, 104, 108.

31. Associated Press, 1996, Automakers rolling out new models, *Dallas Morning News,* January 4, D2.

32. Wiggins, New ways to create; K. Labich, 1994, Class in America, *Fortune,* February 7, 114–126.

33. Strong holiday sales enable Gadzooks to expand, 1996, *Dallas Morning News,* January 4, D11.

34. M. Halkias, 1995, To buy for—at least today, *Dallas Morning News,* October 14, F1, F2.

35. M. Moukheiber, 1993, Our competitive advantage, *Forbes,* April 12, 59–60.

36. Halkias, To buy for, F2.

37. Wiggins, New ways to create.

38. R. Jacob, 1995, How one red hot retailer wins customer loyalty, *Fortune,* July 10, 72–79.

39. R. McKenna, Real-time marketing; F.J. Gouillart and F.D. Sturdivant, 1994, Spend a day in the life of your customers, *Harvard Business Review* 72, no. 1: 116–125; B. Dumaine, 1993, The new non-manager managers, *Fortune,* February 22, 80–84.

40. The future for strategy: An interview with Gary Hamel, 1993, *European Management Journal* 14: 179–191.

41. Sprint, 1994, *1994 Annual Report to Shareholders,* 1.

42. IBM, 1994, *Annual Report,* 4–5; D. Kirkpatrick, 1993, Gerstner's new vision for IBM, *Fortune,* November 15, 119–126; C.K. Prahalad and G. Hamel, 1990, The core competence of the corporation, *Harvard Business Review* 68, no. 3: 79–91.

43. M.E. Porter, 1985, *Competitive Advantage* (New York: Free Press), 26.

44. Porter, Toward a dynamic theory, 434.

45. Porter, *Competitive Advantage,* 15.

46. P.M. Wright, D.L. Smart, and G.C. McMahan, 1995, Matches between human resources and strategy among NCAA basketball teams, *Academy of Management Journal* 38: 1052–1074; Porter, Toward a dynamic theory, 434.

47. Porter, *Competitive Strategy,* 35–40.

48. J.C. Anderson and J.A. Narus, 1995, Capturing the value of supplementary services, *Harvard Business Review* 73, no. 1: 75–83.

49. C. Sirois, 1995, Unifi, Inc., *Value Line,* August 25, 1640; Unifi, Inc., 1995, *Standard & Poor's Stock Reports,* September 21, 227OU.

50. S. Lubove, 1994, It ain't broke, but fix it anyway, *Forbes,* August 1, 56–60.

51. Ibid., 56.

52. J. Simmons, 1995, Budget hotels aren't bargains abroad, *Wall Street Journal,* November 17, B1, B4.

53. Porter, *Competitive Strategy,* 36.

54. Sirois, Unifi, Inc., 1640.

55. Lubove, It ain't broke, 57.

56. P.M. Seligman, 1995, Emerson Electric, *Value Line,* 1006.

57. L. Kraar, 1995, Acer's edge: PCs to go, *Fortune,* October 30, 192.

58. *Los Angeles Times,* 1995, Intel filing suggests trouble at PC maker Packard Bell, *Dallas Morning News,* November 28, D6.

59. T. Zorn, 1995, Orville Redenbacher leaves premium legacy, *Dallas Morning News,* September 24, H5.

60. Porter, *Competitive Advantage,* 14.

61. Associated Press, 1995, Intel to build 3 chip plants overseas, *Dallas Morning News,* F1, F2; B. Schlender, 1995, Why Andy Grove can't stop, *Fortune,* July 10, 88–98; E.B. Swort, 1995, Intel, *Value Line,* July 28, 1062.

62. A. Goldstein, 1995, Cyrix to introduce 6th-generation chip, *Dallas Morning News,* October 6, D1, D10; C. Ortiz, 1995, Intel's 6th-generation Pentium hits stores, *Waco Tribune Herald,* November 1, C4; Wire Reports, 1995, Chipmakers Advanced Micro, Nexgen merge, *Dallas Morning News,* F1, F10.

63. D. Takahashi, 1996, Intel to introduce turbocharged Pentium chip, *Dallas Morning News,* January 4, D2.

64. It's Tommy's world, 1996, *Vanity Fair,* February, 110.

65. F. Rice, 1995, Hilfiger's bipartisan fashions are hot, *Fortune,* October 30, 32.

66. S. Chandler and A.T. Palmer, 1995, Bloomie's tries losing the attitude, *Business Week,* November 13, 52.

67. Porter, *Competitive Strategy,* 38.

68. Porter, *Competitive Advantage,* 15.

69. Ibid., 15.

70. Ibid., 15–16.

71. Rally's Hamburgers Inc., 1995, *Wall Street Journal,* December 6, B8.

72. N.J. Perry, 1992, Hit'em where they used to be, *Fortune,* October 19, 112–113.

73. B.L. Mook, 1995, Family Dollar, *Value Line,* August 25, 1648; Family Dollar Stores, 1995, *Standard & Poor's Stock Reports,* August 25, 859.

74. M. Halkias, 1995, Blush is on at Sally Beauty, *Dallas Morning News,* October 23, D1, D4.

75. Custom Chrome, 1995, *Standard & Poor's Stock Reports,* March 29, 3652C; Custom Chrome, 1995, *Value Line,* November 24,

5058; J. Labate, 1993, Custom Chrome, *Fortune,* May 31, 99.

76. Lei, Hitt, and Bettis, Dynamic core competences.

77. Insights presented in this section are drawn primarily from Dess, Gupta, Hennart and Hill, Conducting and integrating strategy research, 376–379.

78. W.K. Hall, 1980, Survival strategies in a hostile environment, *Harvard Business Review* 58, no. 5: 75–87.

79. Dess, Gupta, Hennart, and Hill, Conducting and integrating strategy research, 377.

80. L. Kim and Y. Lim, 1988, Environment, generic strategies, and performance in a rapidly developing country: A taxonomic approach, *Academy of Management Journal* 31: 802–827.

81. Porter, *Competitive Advantage,* 18.

82. R. Henkoff, 1995, New management secrets from Japan—really, *Fortune,* November 27, 135–146.

83. Toyota, 1995, *Annual Report,* 4.

84. R. Sanchez, 1995, Strategic flexibility in product competition, *Strategic Management Journal* 16 (Special Issue, Summer): 140.

85. Ibid., 141; E.E. Adam, Jr., and R. Ebert, 1992, *Production and Operations Management,* 5th ed. (Englewood Cliffs, N.J.: Prentice-Hall).

86. D.M. Upton, 1995, What really makes factories flexible? *Harvard Business Review* 73, no. 4: 74–84.

87. S.W. Flanders and W.J. Davis, 1995, Scheduling a flexible manufacturing system with tooling constraints: An actual case study, *Interfaces* 25, no. 2: 42–54; Upton, What really makes factories flexible?

88. D. Lei, M.A. Hitt, and J.D. Goldhar, 1996, Advanced manufacturing technology, organization design and strategic flexibility, *Organization Studies* 17: 501–523.

89. E. Mansfield, 1993, The diffusion of flexible manufacturing systems in Japan, Europe and the United States, *Management Science* 39: 149–159 as quoted in Sanchez, Strategic flexibility in product competition, 141.

90. Mansfield, The diffusion of flexible manufacturing systems, 153–154.

91. Ibid., 158.

92. R. Garud and S. Kotha, 1994, Using the brain as a metaphor to model flexible production systems, *Academy of Management Review* 19: 671–698.

93. Sanchez, Strategic flexibility in product competition, 140–141.

94. R.K. Reger, L.T. Gustafson, S.M. DeMarie, and J.V. Mullane, 1994, Reframing the organization: Why implementing total quality is easier said than done, *Academy of Management Review* 19: 565–584.

95. R.E. Cole (ed.), 1995, *The Death and Life of the American Quality Movement* (New York: Oxford University Press).

96. J.R. Hackman and R. Wageman, 1995, Total quality management: Empirical, conceptual, and practical issues, *Administrative Science Quarterly* 40: 310.

97. Ibid., 311.

98. Porter, *Competitive Advantage*, 16.

99. Associated Press, 1995, Wall Street lenders growing impatient with Kmart efforts, *Dallas Morning News*, November 14, D4; M.J. Rindos, 1995, Kmart Corp., *Value Line*, August 25, 1653; B. Saporito, 1994, Bloody new year for retailers, *Fortune*, February 7, 16, 20.

100. A. Miller and G.G. Dess, 1993, Assessing Porter's (1980) model in terms of its generalizability, accuracy and simplicity, *Journal of Management Studies* 30: 553–585.

101. Porter, *Competitive Advantage*, 17.

102. L. Berton, 1995, Midsize accountants lose clients to firms both large and small, *Wall Street Journal*, November 15, A1, A4.

103. Something's brewing, 1996, *Entrepreneur*, January 22.

104. S. Caminiti, 1995, Coffee chains are getting the jitters, *Fortune*, November 27, 42, 44.

105. Ibid., 42, 44.

CHAPTER
5 Competitive Dynamics

After reading this chapter, you should be able to:

1. Define the conditions for undertaking competitive actions.
2. Identify and explain factors affecting the probability that a competitor will initiate a response to competitive actions.
3. Describe first, second, and late movers and the advantages and disadvantages of each.
4. Understand the factors that contribute to the likelihood of a response to a competitive action.
5. Explain the effects of firm size, speed of strategic decision making and implementation, innovation, and quality on a firm's ability to take competitive action.
6. Understand three basic market situations as outcomes of competitive dynamics.
7. Discuss the types of competitive actions most relevant for each of the three stages of an industry evolution.

Competitive Dynamics Among Breakfast Cereal Producers

GENERAL MILLS

In the new competitive landscape that companies face in the late 1990s and into the twenty-first century, one small mistake can lead to reductions in market share and earnings. General Mills encountered difficulties in its breakfast cereals market. General Mills, Inc., has been in a continuous competitive battle with the Kellogg Corporation and Post (Kraft Foods, owned by Philip Morris) in this large market. Besides the continual price competition as well as frequent new product developments, General Mills also had other difficulties. For example, some of its grains used to make cereals was contaminated by a contractor using an illegal pesticide. This crisis evolved at the same time a new marketing plan was in early crucial stages of development. Its star brands in breakfast cereals, Cheerios and Wheaties, also have experienced difficulties due to increased competition in recent years.

General Mills was not as innovative as it had been previously. In past years, expanding on its Cheerios brand, it had created many new products such as Honey-Nut, Apple-Cinnamon, and Multi-Grain Cheerios. One recent product, a premium-priced cereal, Fingos, was not a hit with consumers. Fingos was designed to be eaten dry, right out of the box, but consumers did not respond well to it. To combat increased competition, its Betty Crocker brand introduced two new cereals with baked-goods flavors, Cinnamon Streusal and Dutch Apple.

General Mills and Kellogg have been competing by deploying grocery-store promotions emphasizing buy-one-get-one-free deals that were increasing sales volume but at the expense of earnings. The intent was to increase market share and earnings over time. In 1995, however, the new president of General Mills, Steven W. Sanger, signaled a truce and cut back on the two-for-one promotional deals. This tactical action was risky because it was unilateral; one that he hoped the other big players, Kellogg and Post, would follow. Although Kellogg halted the costly promotions, Post did not because Post managers saw a chance to regain lost market share. With brands such as Shredded Wheat and Grape-Nuts, Post not only recovered lost market share, it gained—mostly at the expense of General Mills, which lost market share.

At the same time, the private-label firms that had lost significant market share in previous years due to the competition from General Mills and Kelloggs were now becoming competitively stronger. Ralcorp Holdings, Inc., a recent Ralston Purina Company spin-off, which dominates the private-label store brands, has been making clones of top brands. For instance, Tasteeos, Fruit Rings, and Ralcorp Corn Flakes are direct imitations of General Mills Cheerios, and Kellogg's Fruit Loops and Corn Flakes brands. In the past, private-label cereal makers have lacked the skill in quality, packaging, and marketing clout to compete with firms like Kellogg and General Mills. However, in 1994, private-label cereal sales grew an average of eight percent, while branded cereals grew at a meager three percent. Ralcorp has recently created Nutty Nuggets (a copy of Post Grape-Nuts) and Apple Dapples (a copy of Kellogg Apple Jacks) and they have done well relative to their counterparts. Further plans for imitations of Shredded Wheat, Trix, and a dozen other cereals that lack store brand counterparts are planned.

Ralcorp's new CEO, Richard Pearce, began investing in new plant technology, to help the firm copy leading brands more effectively. Furthermore, its packaging was improved in quality. Some believe that private-label cereal brands have not come close to their potential, because they also provide retailers with better profit margins. For example, Fred Meyer, Inc., a large retailer, recently voted a 20 percent increase in shelf space to private-label cereal, giving most of it to in-store brands and promoting them heavily. Some analysts believe that the large firms are not worried because the private-label firms only have 11 or 12 percent of the market. Moreover, branded product manufacturers are exercising their muscle. For example, in April 1996, Kraft's Post announced a reduction of 20 percent on its cereal price while reducing use of costly coupons. This follows earlier actions by General Mills and Kelloggs to selectively reduce prices and deemphasize coupons. As a result Ralcorp's stock price declined by almost eight percent because analysts believe that the private-label clone cereals (e.g., Ralcorp's Nutty Nuggets versus Post's Grapenuts) will lose market share. As a result of such actions, the price gap between the branded and private label cereals has decreased from $1.05 in 1993 to $.95 in 1995. Ralcorp's performance continued to suffer from the price war; thus, it sold its primary name brand cereal line, Chex, to General Mills in 1996.

In the final analysis, making competitive mistakes can be extremely costly even for such a savvy player as General Mills with strong brand equity. Firms can no longer take lightly either their competitors or more generic private-label producers. A continual focus on promotion, new product development, and increasing use of sophisticated technology to improve packaging and distribution are essential in the new competitive landscape as these examples indicate.

Source: R. Gibson, 1996, General Mills to buy Ralcorp's Chex, other branded cereals for $570 million, *Wall Street Journal,* August 15, B8; R. Gibson, 1996, Can Betty Crocker heat up General Mills' cereal sales, *Wall Street Journal,* July 19, B1, B10; T. Carvell, 1996, Cereal Wars: A tale of bran, oats and air, *Fortune,* May 13, 30; K. Holland, 1996, Cereal Killer, *Business Week,* April 29, 50; R. Gibson, 1996, Cereal prices are cut by Philip Morris's Post, *Wall Street Journal,* April 16, A2; J. A. Quelch and D. Harding, 1996, Brand versus private labels: Fighting to win, *Harvard Business Review,* 74, no. 1, 99–109; G. Burns, 1995, Has General Mills had its Wheaties?, *Business Week,* May 8, 68–69; G. Burns, 1995, A Fruit Loop by another name: Ralcorp's private-label cereals are gobbling market share, *Business Week,* June 26, 72, 76.

The breakfast cereal industry features the type of competitive landscape that will exist in many industries during the latter part of the 1990s and into the twenty-first century. Among other traits, this new landscape is more volatile and unpredictable. In many industries, including breakfast cereals, heavy emphasis is being placed on international markets. For instance, Kellogg's substantial investment in marketing and promotion in India is intended to foster a demand for ready-to-eat cereals among the middle class.[1]

A changed competitive landscape requires firms to compete differently to achieve strategic competitiveness and earn above-average returns. For instance, current successes through improved quality and quicker design have already led to changes in the nature of auto industry competition. New car sales are slowing because higher quality cars are lasting longer.[2] Longer lasting cars and new automobile sticker shock have led to more intense competition among used-car retailers. The used-car business was estimated to be a $100 billion dollar business in 1995. National used-car retailers such as CarMax (a subsidiary of Circuit City), Autonation (originally formed by the CEO of Blockbuster Entertainment), and CarChoice are building 1,000-vehicle superstores. This is important to new-car dealers because used-car dealers have higher profit margins than new-car dealers— 11.6 compared to 6.6 percent. Although new-car manufacturers are expected to be a continuing force in the U.S. economy, their dominance may be questioned.

Several reasons account for the changes taking place in many industries' competitive landscapes (discussed in Chapter 1).[3] First, in most industries, emphasis on a single domestic market is now decreasing, whereas emphasis on international and global markets is increasing. For example, foreign auto manufacturers made up 19 percent of North American production in 1995 compared to 4 percent in 1985. During the decade, Japanese and German automakers have opened about as much capacity as GM, Ford, and Chrysler have closed.[4] As firms diversify internationally, their view of competition expands to multiple markets. Second, significant advances in communications technology allow more effective coordination across operations in multiple markets and faster decision making and competitive responses. Third, new technology and innovations, particularly in the information technology and computer industries, have changed competitive landscapes in ways that facilitate small and medium-sized businesses' efforts to compete more effectively. This also facilitates more emphasis on imitation as demonstrated by Ralcorp's private-label imitations of dominant breakfast cereal brands.[5] Finally, the increasing number of agreements to allow free trade across country borders (such as the 1993 North American Free Trade Agreement, NAFTA) is facilitating a growing cross-border focus. The changing competitive landscape even has former competitors cooperating in such areas as new technology development and forming strategic alliances to compete against other competitors (as discussed in Chapter 9).[6]

This chapter focuses on competitive dynamics. The essence of this important topic is that a firm's strategies and their implementation (see Figure 1.1) are dynamic in nature. Actions taken by one firm often elicit responses from competitors. These responses, in turn, typically result in responses from the firm that acted originally as illustrated by the opening case on breakfast cereals. The series of competitive actions and competitive responses among firms competing within a particular industry creates **competitive dynamics.** Such dynamic competitive interaction often shapes the competitive position of firms undertaking the business-level strategies described in the previous chapter and to some extent, corporate strategies (product diversification, international diversification, and cooperative strategies) described in later chapters.

To discuss the part of the strategic management process called competitive dynamics, we introduce a model (see later discussion of Figure 5.1) of competitive dynamics and the remainder of the chapter describes it. After the overall model is introduced, we examine the factors that lead to competitive attack and potential response. This is followed by a discussion of the incentives of market leadership (first-mover advantages) and its disadvantages. We also discuss the advantages and disadvantages of followership (second or late movers). Once competitive action is taken, a number of factors help determine the potential response. These factors are discussed next. We then examine firms' capabilities for attack and response, including firm size, speed of decision making, innovation, and product and process quality. Following these descriptions is a discussion of three different types of market competition (defined later as slow cycle, standard cycle, and fast cycle) that result from competitive interaction. In particular, we explore the nature of rivalry and propose strategies for competition in fast-cycle markets where competitive rivalry has escalated to an intense level and where the new competitive landscape is probably the most evident. This discussion examines the strategy of competitive disruption, in which firms capitalize on temporary compared to sustained competitive advantage by cannibalizing their past new product entry to introduce the next product or process innovation. Finally, we describe competitive rivalry outcomes as industries move through the emerging, growth, and maturity stages.

- *Competitive dynamics* results from a series of competitive actions and competitive responses among firms competing within a particular industry.

- *Competitive rivalry* exists when two or more firms jockey with one another in the pursuit of an advantageous market position.

■ Model of Competitive Dynamics and Rivalry

Over time, firms competing in an industry are involved with a number of competitive actions and competitive responses. **Competitive rivalry** exists when two or more firms jockey with one another in the pursuit of an advantageous market position. Competitive rivalry takes place between and among firms because one or more competitors feel pressure or see opportunities to improve their market position. In most industries, a firm's competitive actions have observable effects on its competitors and may cause responses designed to counter the action.[7]

As the example of competitive actions and competitive responses among General Mills, Kellogg, Post, and Ralcorp demonstrates, firms are mutually interdependent with their competitors.[8] **Mutual interdependence** among firms means that strategic competitiveness and above-average returns result only when companies recognize that their strategies are not implemented in isolation from their competitors' actions and responses. Over time, General Mills, along with its competitors, will engage in a series of competitive actions and responses in efforts to establish sustainable competitive advantages. Thus, because it affects strategic competitiveness and returns, firms are concerned about the pattern of competitive dynamics and the rivalry it creates.[9]

Figure 5.1 illustrates a summary model of interfirm rivalry and the likelihood of attack and response. As can be seen from the model, competitor analysis begins with analyzing competitor awareness and motivation to attack and respond to competitive action. *Awareness* refers to whether or not the attacking or responding firm is aware of the competitive market characteristics such as the market commonality and the resource similarity of a potential attacker or respondent (these terms are defined in a subsequent section). Managers may have "blind spots" in their industry and competitor analyses due to underestimation or an inability to analyze these factors. This lack of awareness may lead to such things as industry overcapacity and excessive competition.[10] *Motivation* relates to the incentives a firm has to attack and respond if attacked. A firm may perceive advantages to moving first, given the potential for interaction.

As Figure 5.1 suggests, both market commonality and resource similarity mediate the awareness and motivation to undertake actions and responses. The likelihood of action and response will result in the competitive outcomes. These outcomes, however, will be moderated by a firm's ability to undertake strategic actions and responses. Furthermore, Figure 5.1 illustrates that feedback from the nature of rivalry will also influence the nature of a competitor's view of the previous exchange and may change the nature of awareness and motivation.

■ Market Commonality

Many firms, for example, those in the airlines, chemical, pharmaceutical, breakfast cereals, and electronics industries compete in the same multiple markets. In the brewery industry, for instance, many beer producers compete in the same regional markets.[11] Regional competition is also evident in international markets through "triad" competition or the necessity for multinational corporations to have businesses in Asia (traditionally Japan), Europe, and North America.[12] When multimarket overlap exists between firms, this presents opportunities for **multipoint competition,** a situation in which firms compete against each other simultaneously in several product or geographic markets.[13] In the airline industry for instance, there are opportunities for multipoint competition. The three largest U.S. airlines, United, American, and Delta, have substantial market overlap and therefore substantial awareness and motivation to respond to competitive actions. However, research has shown that such commonality reduces the likelihood of competitive interaction in the industry.[14] Because these three airlines operate in many common markets, competitive peace will reign until one firm makes a competitive move, then the competitive response will be swift.[15] Multipoint competition can also be seen in the introductory example on

■ *Mutual interdependence among firms means that strategic competitiveness and above-average returns result only when companies recognize that their strategies are not implemented in isolation from their competitors' actions and responses.*

■ *Multipoint competition occurs when firms compete against each other simultaneously in several product or geographic markets.*

Figure 5.1   A Summary Model of Interfirm Rivalry: The Likelihood of Attack and Response

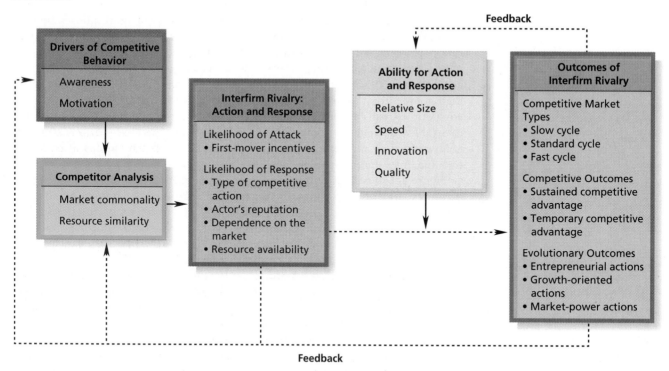

Source: Adapted from M. J. Chen, 1996, Competitor analysis and interfirm rivalry: Toward a theoretical integration, *Academy of Management Review* 21: 100–134.

breakfast cereals. The two dominant competitors, Kellogg and General Mills, responded to each other's signals of peace, which, in effect, reduced rivalry. However, Ralcorp, the private-label firm, and Post did not choose to follow General Mills' lead to pursue more diplomacy in the competitive situation. Besides their market commonality, this may also be explained by the perceived similarity of their internal resources.

■ Resource Similarity

The intensity of competitive rivalry often is based on a potential response and is of great concern for an attacker. An attacker may not be motivated to target a rival that seems likely to retaliate. This is especially true for firms with strategic resources similar to those of a potential attacker.[16] Resource dissimilarity likely plays a vital role in a competitor's motivation to attack or respond. Although the degree of market commonality is quite visible to the strategists of both firms, strategic resources, because of their possible indeterminable nature (due to, for example, causal ambiguity and social complexity as described in Chapter 3), tend to be much less identifiable. For example, probably because of resource similarity, Kellogg and General Mills were able to establish a level of competitive peace. However, Post, not having the same level of resource similarity and not being as dependent on the breakfast cereal market, was prepared to attack and did so at the expense of General Mills when it experienced difficulties. Furthermore, the resource dissimilarity of Ralcorp, a private-label firm, allowed it to capture market share from name brand competitors.

Likewise, Citrus World, a little known farmer's cooperative, started to market its own brand of pasteurized orange juice because of resource dissimilarity between itself and diversified giants, Seagram Co., owner of Tropicana, and Coca-Cola Co. with its Minute Maid line. Although Citrus World was an improbable player in the $3 billion juice market, it overtook Coke's Minute Maid brand to take the second place market share position in pasteurized orange juice. Now both Seagram and Coke are planning large advertising campaigns to counter the incursion by Citrus World. Although Coke and Seagram are likely to win the battle because of their size, Citrus World was able to make progress because the resource dissimilarity between Citrus World and these larger firms' diversification created a lack of awareness of Citrus World's significant market incursion.[17]

Likelihood Of Attack

■ *A competitive action is a significant competitive move taken by a firm that is designed to gain a competitive advantage in a market.*

Although awareness and motivation to respond are largely derived from competitor analysis of market commonality and resource similarity, there are strong incentives to be the first mover in a competitive battle if the attacking firm believes it has potential to win. A **competitive action** is a significant competitive move taken by a firm that is designed to gain a competitive advantage in a market. Some competitive actions are large and significant; others are small and designed to help fine-tune or implement a strategy. The first mover in a competitive interaction may be able to gain above-average returns while competitors consider potential countermoves. Furthermore, the first mover may be able to deter counterattack if given enough time. Therefore, there are significant incentives to be a first mover and the order of each competitive action and response influences an industry's competitive dynamics. Of greatest importance are first movers, second movers, and late movers.

First-, Second-, and Late-Movers

■ *A first mover is a firm that takes an initial competitive action.*

A **first mover** is a firm that takes an initial competitive action. The concept of first movers has been influenced by Joseph Schumpeter, an economist. In particular, he believed that firms achieve competitive advantage through entrepreneurial discovery and innovative competitive action.[18] Through these competitive actions, first movers hope to gain a sustainable competitive advantage by taking pioneering actions.

Several competitive advantages can accrue to the firm that is first to initiate a competitive action. Successful actions allow a firm to earn above-average returns until other competitors are able to respond effectively. In addition, first movers have the opportunity to gain customer loyalty, thereby making it difficult for responding firms to capture customers. For instance, Harley-Davidson has been able to maintain a competitive lead in large motorcycles due to intense customer loyalty, even though it has had significant management and product quality difficulties to overcome.[19]

The advantages, and the length of time a firm receives them, vary by type of competitive action and industry. First-mover advantages also vary based on the ease with which competitors can imitate the action.[20] The more difficult and costly an action is to imitate, the longer a firm may receive the benefits of being a first mover. When core competencies are the foundation of a competitive action, first-mover advantages tend to last for a longer period of time. Core competence-based competitive actions have a high probability of resulting in a sustained competitive advantage.

However, potential disadvantages may result from being the first firm to initiate a competitive action. Chief among these is the degree of risk taken by first movers. Risk is high because it is not easy to predict the amount of success a particular competitive action will produce prior to its initiation.[21] Oftentimes, first movers have high development costs. Second movers can avoid these costs through reverse engineering (taking apart a new product and then reassembling it to learn how it works). Another potential disadvantage of being a first mover may exist if the market in which the firm is competing is dynamic and uncertain. In other words, the extent and range of marketplace competition heighten the potential risk. In fact, in a highly uncertain market, it may be more appropriate to be a second or late mover.

A **second mover** is a firm that responds to a first mover's competitive action, often through imitation or a move designed to counter the effects of the action. When the second mover responds quickly to a first mover's competitive action, it may earn some of the first-mover advantages without experiencing the potential disadvantages. For example, a fast second mover may gain some of the returns and obtain a portion of the initial customers and thereby customer loyalty, while avoiding some of the risks encountered by the first mover. The firm taking a second action as a competitive response to the first mover can do so after evaluating customers' reactions to the first mover's action.[22] To be a successful first or fast second mover, a company must be able to analyze its markets and identify critical strategic issues.[23]

In some instances, it may not be possible to move quickly in response to a first mover's action. For example, if the first mover introduces a sophisticated new product and competitors have not undertaken similar research and development, considerable time may be required to respond effectively. Therefore, there are some risks involved in being a follower, as opposed to a leader, in the market. However, there are no blueprints for first-mover success. Followers may be able to respond without significant market development costs by learning from a first mover's successes and mistakes. Thus, the actions and outcomes of the first firm to initiate a competitive action may provide a more effective blueprint for second and late movers.[24] Table 5.1 provides a list of classic cases where imitators were able to overcome the pioneers' early entries.

The competitive dynamics in the athletic shoe business provide an interesting case in point. The athletic shoe business was created in 1920 by Adi Dassler, the founder of Adidas, the German athletic shoe firm. Adidas reigned for years as the first mover in this business, but Nike and Reebok have overtaken the $12 billion market leadership. Although Robert Louis-Dreyfus brought the company back from the brink of bankruptcy in 1992, Adidas holds only 5 percent of the U.S. market and 10 percent of the global market share.[25] Nike was the clear winner in the recent battle with 37 percent of the U.S. market share and Reebok with 20 percent. In 1994, Nike held 30 to Reebok's 21 percent. Reebok's stock market performance has been so poor that Reebok's CEO was criticized by large institutional shareholders.[26]

■ *A second mover is a firm that responds to a first mover's competitive action, often through imitation or a move designed to counter the effects of the action.*

Table 5.1   Cases Where Second/Late Movers Surpassed First Movers

Product	First Movers	Second/Late Movers	Comments
35mm cameras	Leica (1925) Contrax (1932) Exacta (1936)	Canon (1934) Nikon (1946) Nikon SLR (1959)	The German pioneers were the technology and market leader for decades until the Japanese copied their technology, improved on it, and lowered prices. The pioneers then failed to react and ended up as incidental players.
Ballpoint pens	Reynolds (1945) Eversharp (1946)	Parker "Jotter" (1954) Bic (1960)	The pioneers disappeared when the fad first ended in the late 1940s. Parker entered eight years later. Bic entered last and sold pens as cheap disposables.
Caffeine-free soft drinks	Canada Dry's "Sport" (1967) Royal Crown's RC100 (1980)	Pepsi Free (1982) Caffeine-free Coke, Tab (1983)	The pioneers had a three-year head start on Coke and Pepsi but could not hope to match the distribution and promotional advantages of the giants.
CAT scanners (computed axial Tomography)	EMI (1972)	Pfizer (1974) Technicare (1975) GE (1976) Johnson & Johnson (1978)	The pioneers had no experience in the medical equipment industry. Imitators ignored its patents and drove the pioneer out of business with marketing, distribution, and financial advantages, as well as extensive industry experience.
Commercial jet aircraft	deHavilland Comet 1 (1952)	Boeing 707 (1954) Douglas DC-8 (1955)	The British pioneer rushed to market with a jet that crashed frequently. Boeing followed with safer, larger, and more powerful jets unsullied by tragic crashes.
Diet soft drinks	Kirsch's No-Cal (1952) Royal Crown's Diet Rite Cola (1962)	Pepsi's Patio Cola (1963) Coke's Tab (1963) Diet Pepsi (1964) Diet Coke (1982)	The pioneers could not match the distribution advantages of Coke and Pepsi. Nor did they have the money needed for massive promotional campaigns.
Dry beer	Asahi (1987)	Kirin, Sapporo, and Suntory in Japan (1988) Michelob Dry (1988) Bud Dry (1989)	The Japanese pioneer could not match Anheuser-Busch's financial, marketing, and distribution advantages in the U.S. market.
Light beer	Rheingold's Gablinger's (1966) Meister Brau Lite (1967)	Miller Lite (1975) Natural Light (1977) Coors Light (1978) Bud Light (1982)	The pioneers entered nine years before Miller and sixteen years before Bud Light, but financial problems drove both out of business. Marketing and distribution determined the outcome. Costly legal battles were commonplace.
MRI (magnetic resonance imaging)	Fonar (1978)	Johnson & Johnson's Technicare (1981) General Electric (1982)	The tiny pioneer faced the huge medical equipment suppliers, which easily expanded into the MRI arena. The pioneer could not hope to match their tremendous market power.
Operating systems personal computers	CP/M (1974)	MS-DOS (1981) Microsoft Windows (1985)	The pioneer created the early standard but did not upgrade for the IBM-PC. Microsoft bought an imitative upgrade and became the new standard. Windows entered later and borrowed heavily from predecessors, then emerged as the leading interface.
Personal computers	MITS Altair 8800 (1975) Apple II (1977) Radio Shack (1977)	IBM-PC (1981) Compaq (1982) Dell (1984) Gateway (1985)	The pioneers created computers for hobbyists, but when the market turned to business uses, IBM entered and quickly dominated, using its reputation and its marketing and distribution skills. The second movers then copied IBM's standard and sold at lower prices.
Pocket calculators	Bowmar (1971)	Texas Instruments (1972)	The pioneer assembled calculators using TI's integrated circuits. TI controlled Bowmar's costs, which rose as calculator prices fell. Vertical integration was the key.

Source: S. P. Schnaars, 1994, *Managing Imitation Strategies: How Later Entrants Seize Markets from Pioneers* (New York: The Free Press).

Nike's ascendancy has come through creative market promotions that used athletic stars such as Michael Jordan. Furthermore, Nike's airsole product technology has created a solid product innovation to complement its marketing creativity. Also, it has developed a strong network of low-cost manufacturing contractors in emerging countries, especially in Korea, Taiwan, and China.[27]

Reebok's strength came through promotion of women's athletic shoes. Reebok also followed Nike's lead in men's athletic shoes by signing Shaquille O'Neal, an NBA basketball star, to a marketing contract to sell its new product. However, it has not been as successful in copying Nike's other advantages and Nike has started to move more strongly into the women's shoe business, Reebok's area of traditional strength.[28] Finally, a new innovation has been announced by Puma AG, another German firm which was a leader, along with Adidas, in the 1970s. Puma is the first firm to begin shipping a foamless athletic shoe, beating to market its larger rivals, Nike, Reebok, and Adidas. The Puma shoe, called the "Concept," costs less and is said to last for 600 miles of wear, which is twice as long as current athletic shoes. However, the other leaders are planning their own new introductions.[29]

Reebok has not been successful in competing against Nike, possibly because it was a late mover in the men's athletic shoe business. A **late mover** is a firm that responds to a competitive action, but only after considerable time has elapsed after the first mover's action and the second mover's response. Although some type of competitive response may be more effective than no response, late movers tend to be poorer performers and often are weak competitors. Although Reebok is stronger than Adidas and Puma currently, its recent problems relative to Nike are significant.

■ *A **late mover** is a firm that responds to a competitive action, but only after considerable time has elapsed after the first mover's action and the second mover's response.*

Nike and Reebok have used athletic stars such as Michael Jordan and Shaquille O'Neal to sell their products.

■ Likelihood of Response

■ *A **competitive response** is a move taken to counter the effects of an action by a competitor.*

■ *A **strategic action** represents a significant commitment of specific and distinctive organization resources; it is difficult to implement and to reverse.*

■ *A **tactical action** is taken to fine-tune a strategy; it involves fewer and more general organizational resources and is relatively easy to implement and reverse.*

Once firms take competitive action, the success of the particular action will often be determined by the likelihood and nature of response. A **competitive response** is a move taken to counter the effects of an action by a competitor. Firms considering offensive action need to be cognizant of the potential response from competition. An offensive action may escalate rivalry to a point where action becomes self-defeating and an alternative strategy may be necessary. A *de-escalation strategy* is an attempt to reduce overly heated competition that has become self-defeating. General Mills, in effect, attempted a de-escalation strategy because competition became self-defeating when it tried to reduce its discount strategy. Although Kellogg responded positively, the other firms, Post and Ralcorp, did not. As Figure 5.1 shows, the probability of a competitor response to a competitive action is based on the type of action, the reputation of the competitor taking the action, the competitor's dependence on the market, and competitor resource availability.

■ Type of Competitive Action

The two types of competitive actions are strategic and tactical. A **strategic action** represents a significant commitment of specific and distinctive organizational resources; it is difficult to implement and to reverse. The introduction of an innovative product to a market exemplifies a strategic action. A **tactical action** is taken to fine-tune a strategy; it involves fewer and more general organizational resources and is relatively easy to implement and reverse. A price increase in a particular market (e.g., in airfares) is an example of a tactical action. This action involves few organizational resources (e.g., communicating new prices/changing prices on products), its implementation is relatively easy, and it can be reversed (through a price reduction, for example) in a relatively short period of time.

Responses to a strategic action, as compared to a tactical action, are more difficult because they require more organizational resources and are more time consuming. As compared to strategic actions, tactical actions usually have more immediate effects. The announcement of a price increase in a price-sensitive market such as airlines could have immediate effects on competitors. As such, it is not uncommon to find airlines responding quickly to a competitor's price change, particularly if the announced change represents a price decrease, because without a response other airlines may lose market share.[30] This is often true in low-cost goods and services markets. Cash flow is critical in the airline industry, and consumers are price sensitive because there is relatively little differentiation in the services provided.

Not all competitive actions will elicit or require a response from competitors. On the whole, there are more competitive responses to tactical than to strategic actions.[31] It is usually easier to respond to tactical than to strategic actions and sometimes more necessary, at least in the short term. The tactical action of General Mills to reduce or eliminate its deep discounts through coupons was easier to respond to than a strategic action by a competitor to duplicate one of its products through a new private-label product introduction.[32] General Mills' Cheerios cereal has been duplicated by Ralcorp's Tasteeos. In response, General Mills created a number of new brands: Honey-Nut, Apple-Cinnamon, and Multi-Grain Cheerios.[33]

■ Actor's Reputation

An action (either strategic or tactical) taken by a market leader is likely to serve as a catalyst to a larger number of and faster responses from competitors and to a higher probability of imitation of the action. In other words, firms are more likely to imitate the actions of a competitor that is a market leader. Firms also often react quickly to imitate successful competitor actions. An example is the personal computer market, where IBM quickly dominated the market as a second mover, but was also imitated by Compaq, Dell, and Gateway (see Table 5.1). Alternatively, firms that have a history as strategic players that take risky, complex, and unpredictable actions are less likely to solicit responses to and imitation of their actions.[34] Finally, firms that are known to be price predators (frequently cutting prices to hurt competitors and obtain market share, only to raise prices later) also do not elicit a large number of responses or imitation. In fact, there is less imitation and a much slower response to price predators than to either of the other two types of firms (market leader and strategic player).[35]

■ Dependence on the Market

Firms with a high dependency on a market in which a competitive action is taken are more likely to respond to that action. For example, firms with a large amount of total sales from one industry are more likely to respond to a particular competitive action taken in their primary industry than is a firm with businesses in multiple industries (e.g., a conglomerate). Thus, if the type of action taken has a major effect on them, they are likely to respond, regardless of whether it is a strategic or a tactical action. Of course, a strategic action tends to require more time to respond effectively, assuming it had not been anticipated and a strategic response had not been planned. Swift action can be anticipated with tactical actions in these cases.

For instance, the announced breakup of AT&T into three separate business units—telecommunications services, telecommunications equipment, and computer equipment (as described in introductory example in Chapter 6)—will force each separate company to be more rivalrous. AT&T, as a long-distance company, will not be able to depend on support from its profitable equipment arm to subsidize the losses associated with its computer business.[36] As such, it will likely respond more swiftly to competitive actions because it is now more focused on the telecommunications service business. General Mills is also more focused now because it spun off its restaurant business.[37] Because it is more dependent on its cereal business, it is more likely to respond to competitive actions. Kmart lost the race to Wal-Mart to lead in discount stores partly because of its lack of focus and emphasis on acquisitions in other retail concepts. Kmart did not respond effectively when Wal-Mart attacked.[38]

■ Competitor Resource Availability

A competitive response to a strategic or tactical action also requires organizational resources. Firms with fewer resources are more likely to respond to tactical actions than to strategic ones because responses to tactical actions require fewer resources and are easier to implement. In addition, firm resources may dictate the type of response. For example, neither MCI nor British Telecommunications (BT) was in a position to respond individually to AT&T's strategic action to offer global telecommunications services. They could not act alone because they did not have the resources necessary to mount a formidable challenge to a firm as large as AT&T. Although MCI and BT are large ($10 billion and $25 billion annual revenues, respectively), AT&T is huge by comparison ($65 billion annual revenues) and has significantly more resources to implement a global telecommunications service. Therefore, MCI and British Telecommunications formed a strategic alliance that allowed them to combine their resources and mount a substantive challenge to AT&T in the global telecommunications market. Moreover, the pooling of their resources may allow each partner to take other strategic actions, either alone or in concert.[39] However, AT&T, since its breakup into three businesses, may now have to attack through an alliance because it will be much smaller. This is especially true in light of the announced merger between local Bell operators, SBC (formerly Southwestern Bell), and Pacific Telesis and between Nynex and Bell Atlantic.[40]

Small firms probably cannot compete effectively with any of these firms in the global telecommunications market. Other companies (both large and small) have applied for licenses for international telephone service in the British market. It is unlikely, however, that many will be able to compete successfully against AT&T and the alliance of MCI and British Telecommunications. Although it is not a small firm, relative to the resources available to AT&T and to the alliance between MCI and British Telecommunications, Sprint is small.[41] It is possible that AT&T, MCI, and BT may earn above-average returns at the expense of Sprint and other smaller competitors with fewer resources. Competitors may wish to respond to the competitive actions taken by AT&T, MCI, and BT; however, their inability to muster adequate resources may preclude them from doing so.[42] The intensity of the competitive rivalry of the long-distance markets is likely to increase considerably as regional Bell operating companies, cable companies, and others enter this market with the implementation of deregulation through the end of the 1990s.[43]

Firms' Abilities to Take Action and Respond

As indicated earlier, resource availability and ability to respond affect the probability of a company's response to a competing firm's competitive actions. Firms' abilities therefore moderate the relationship between interfirm rivalry and the competitive outcomes (see Figure 5.1). There are four general firm abilities to take action and influence competitive interaction within a market or industry: (1) relative firm size within a market or industry, (2) the speed at which competitive actions and responses are made, (3) the extent of innovation by firms in the market or industry, and (4) product quality. These factors are illustrated in the Strategic Focus on Morgan Stanley's emerging market strategy.

■ Relative Firm Size

The *size* of a firm can have two important, but opposite, effects on an industry's competitive dynamics. First, the larger a firm, the greater its market power. Of course, the extent of any firm's market power is relative to the power of its competitors. The Strategic Focus shows that Morgan Stanley has taken great risks by moving into emerging markets, but it may be overtaken by a second mover such as Merrill Lynch, a larger competitor. In the U.S. auto industry, all competitors are large; however, no firm has relative and critical power over the others. Nonetheless, it is difficult for small firms to enter the market, because the sheer size of the larger firms creates substantial entry barriers to the industry. As Table 5.1 shows, many innovative pioneers were overtaken by larger second movers.

STRATEGIC FOCUS   Morgan Stanley's Emerging Market Strategy

Headquartered in the United States, Morgan Stanley Trust Company is one of the most trusted and largest investment banks in the world. Morgan Stanley is trying to establish first-mover competitive advantage in emerging markets. For instance, in India, where the phone infrastructure is very unreliable, the Bombay Stock Exchange is often a mountain of paper. Even though the infrastructure to support an investment bank is poor in India, Morgan Stanley is the largest American investment bank there. Since 1992, Morgan Stanley has invested more than $25 million and recruited 62 employees and plans to hire another 150 by 1998. It hopes to capitalize on the expansion in the Indian economy as India's government establishes its reforms. Pradip Darooka, a Morgan Stanley manager, suggests "the advantage of being first is you can help shape things and events."

Although there are advantages to being first in the market, there are significant risks. A firm such as Morgan Stanley, which has a strong reputation for innovation and quality, may lose its good reputation if it leads investors into trouble in risky emerging markets. However, Morgan Stanley's managers feel that not to invest is an even bigger risk. The firm is investing in an information system that will allow emerging market information to be controlled through desktop personal computers and on-line databases derived from data in 65 countries (to improve transaction quality).

Of course, Morgan Stanley is not alone in waging this battle in emerging markets. Its many U.S. rivals such as Merrill Lynch, Goldman Sachs, and J. P. Morgan and many other foreign banks and brokers too numerous to mention are also pursuing these emerging markets. For instance, C.S. First Boston has a significant lead in Russia. Merrill Lynch has been able to bring to the market more large privatizations than Morgan Stanley. However, Morgan Stanley is still perceived to be the premier emerging markets investment bank among clients and rivals. It is viewed to be the broadest in scope and the most daring to move into new places with a larger commitment.

Because it has been a pioneer, it has also been an architect of modern financial market innovation in countries such as India and China. Morgan Stanley acts as a link to world financial markets for clearing trades in Bombay. It is also helping to build the first Chinese investment bank and was the first pioneer of emerging market country funds and thereby brought more long-term capital into developing markets.

One of its problems may be its relative size. Merrill Lynch is a much bigger competitor. In emerging market assets, Morgan Stanley ranks fourth after Templeton, Fidelity, and Capital Guardian with $5.2 billion. Morgan Stanley also faces tough competition with commercial banks that have investment banking arms such as J. P. Morgan and C. S. First Boston.

Substantial hazards and risks are associated with this emerging markets strategy. Having a number of diverse employees and offices around the world may create problems, especially during periods of high levels of business growth and in new employees. Some new hires may make significant mistakes that will affect Morgan's reputation. It may try to move too fast as it did in India. It oversold a fund and when the fund dropped rather than increased in price, its reputation was negatively affected as clients were disappointed. This can be a severe problem when the asset management portfolio is 1.25 percent of the capitalization of the Bombay market and represents about 7 percent of trading volume.

As can be seen, Morgan Stanley's strategy of being a first mover in emerging markets, while trying to sustain these moves through its size, reputation, quality, and innovation, as well as trying to deal with the competitive dynamics in its industry creates a complex and often risky situation. The benefits of such risks, however, may be high returns. Only time will tell whether this strategy will produce strategic competitiveness and above-average returns.

Source: A. Gaghavan, 1996, Morgan Stanley had record net in quarter, exceeding estimates, *Wall Street Journal,* March 28, B3; L. N. Spiro, S. Moshavi, M. Shari, I. Katz, H. Dawley, G. Smith, and D. Lindorff, 1996, Global gamble: Morgan Stanley is charging into the third world, *Business Week,* February 12, 63–72; M. Carroll, 1995, Morgan Stanley's global gamble, *Institutional Investor,* March, 40–44; H. Sender, 1994, New pioneers: Morgan Stanley is banking on China, *Far Eastern Economic Review,* November 3, 55.

Another example of market power is shown by the problems that A&W (owned by Cadbury Schweppes PLC) faces in its central focus, root beer. Its larger rivals—Coca-Cola and PepsiCo—have been competing in the root beer market. Coca-Cola bought the second largest market share leader (behind A&W), Barq. The next largest competitor, Mug brand, is owned by PepsiCo. Many believe that A&W's new products will fail, not because customers will deem them unattractive, but because of the potential responses by the firm's larger and more powerful competitors (e.g., Pepsi and Coke).[44] Citrus World has made significant advances in pasteurized orange juice against Coke and Seagram. However, these larger firms are preparing an overwhelming response.[45]

As firms grow larger, they often implement complicated structures and bureaucratic rules that inhibit their competitive abilities. In particular, these structures and rules stifle a firm's innovativeness. Without innovation, it is difficult for a firm to be a first mover and to respond quickly to competitors' actions. Innovation allowed Citrus World to increase market share against the Tropicana and Minute Maid brands of Seagram and Coke. Even when a competitor takes a strategic action that could affect a large firm, a significant amount of time may be required for that firm to develop and implement an effective competitive response. The content of the response is important, but its timing could be more critical.

Problems created by firm size are demonstrated by events—both historical and current—in the computer industry. Although the giant in the industry, IBM, was highly successful, it did not invent or first introduce the microcomputer, which is the primary basis of the industry today. It took entrepreneurial ventures, such as Apple Computer, Dell Computer, and Compaq, to introduce the innovations in goods and services that revolutionized the industry. Small firms often do this by fostering what Joseph Schumpeter referred to as creative destruction.[46] As Steven Jobs and his partner Steve Wozniak revolutionized the computer industry, Michael Dell, who was in high school when Apple introduced its computers, revolutionized the way computers were produced and distributed. Small businesses, often stronger in lower technology industries (because of lower required capital investments), have become a force for change in high-technology industries.[47]

A quote attributed to Herbert Kelleher, co-founder and CEO of Southwest Airlines, best describes the approach needed by large firms. In Kelleher's words, "Think and act big and we'll get smaller. Think and act small and we'll get bigger."[48] This suggests that large firms should use their size to build market power, but that they must think and act like a small firm (e.g., move quickly and be innovative) in order to achieve strategic competitiveness and earn above-average returns over the long run. This is the approach Morgan Stanley is using in emerging markets. Firms such as Thermo Electron, 3M, GTE, and Xerox are trying to overcome the liabilities of size by creating and supporting entrepreneurship in their respective organizations.[49]

■ Speed of Competitive Actions and Competitive Responses

Our world is one in which time and speed are important. We go to fast food restaurants and use microwave ovens. We regularly use e-mail, overnight express mail (public and private), and fax machines. The same is true with competition. The speed with which a firm can initiate competitive actions and competitive responses may determine its success. In the global economy, speed in developing a new product and moving it to the marketplace is becoming critical to a firm's efforts to establish a sustainable competitive advantage and earn above-average returns.[50] The speed of the first mover allows a firm to maximize the window between competitive action and response. A fast second mover tries to minimize the advantage of the first mover's window of opportunity. Puma AG is hoping that its speed to market with the "Concept" shoe will help it recover some lost market share.[51] Puma's competitors are hurrying to introduce their new shoes with longer lasting soles to reduce Puma's potential advantage.

Under the leadership of a new CEO, AST Research, Inc., a personal computer manufacturer, is trying to come back from significant losses in 1994 and 1995. AST's problems started because it kept missing product-launch dates as its engineers tried to get more and more features into its new product offerings.[52] It spent considerable time designing motherboards and even keyboard controller chips itself, whereas rivals such as Packard Bell were buying the newest technology from suppliers such as Intel. Rivals were coming out with their new products much sooner than AST. One of the new CEO's first changes was to suggest that "Being first is more important than being best." Although this may not always be true because a firm also must have variety and flexibility in its ability to respond,[53] speed is very important among personal computer rivals as the AST example illustrates.

Speed to the marketplace is one of the problems U.S. automobile manufacturers have experienced in competing with Japanese firms. Some time ago, Japanese auto companies were able to design a new product and introduce it to the market within three years. In comparison, U.S. firms required between five and eight years to complete these activities. This time differential made it possible for Japanese firms to design and move to the market two or three new automobiles in the same time it took a U.S. automaker to do one.

The competitive actions initiated by Chrysler to design and introduce the Neon into the global marketplace were partly in response to the successful actions taken some time ago by its Japanese competitors. Chrysler is using its experiences with the Neon and other models to eliminate speed-based competitive advantages enjoyed by its Japanese competitors. Chrysler's improvement was accomplished through cross-functional teams described more fully in Chapter 13.[54] Eliminating this advantage is important because in a global economy firms must think in terms of speed to market in order to earn above-average returns.[55]

In a global economy, time is a critical source of competitive advantage. However, managing for speed requires more than attempting to have employees work faster. Essentially, it requires working smarter, using different types of organizational structures, and having the time required for completion as a primary work-related goal.[56] Research has shown that the pace of strategic decision making may be affected by an executive's cognitive ability, use of intuition, tolerance for risk, and propensity to act.[57] Executives who use intuition and have a greater tolerance for risk are predisposed to make faster strategic decisions than do those without such characteristics. It is also known that decisions are likely to occur faster in centralized organizations because they will not have to go through as many levels or get approval from as many people. More formalized and bureaucratic organizations, however, may find it difficult to make fast strategic decisions[58] because they require more layers of approval.

Jack Welch, chairman and CEO of General Electric, states that speed is the ability sought by all of today's organizations.[59] He suggests that companies are striving to develop products faster, speed up production cycles in moving them to the market, and improve response time to customers. In Welch's opinion, having faster communications and moving with agility are critical to competitive success.

■ Innovation

A third general factor, innovation, has long been known in some industries, such as pharmaceuticals and computers, to have a strong influence on firm performance.[60] The strategic importance of innovation is explored further in Chapter 13. In today's global economy, research suggests that innovation (both product innovation and process innovation) is becoming linked with above-average returns in a growing number of industries. One study, for example, found that companies with the highest performance also invested the most in research and development. In 1960, U.S. firms held more than two-thirds of the world market in 10 of the top 15 major industries. By 1970, the United States continued to dominate 9 of those 15 industries. However, by 1980, U.S. domination was limited to only 3 of the 15 industries. The study found that this was due largely to changes in innovation. Firms from other countries were more innovative than U.S. firms in many of the industries.[61] In fact, a contributing factor to the productivity and technology problems experienced by U.S. firms has been managers' unwillingness to bear the costs and risks of long-term development of product and process innovations.[62]

An integral part of developing and sustaining a competitive advantage is to deny competitors access to proprietary technology. Thus, firms need to innovate to be market leaders and then deny access to the technology in order to sustain the competitive advantage created.[63] However, as explained in the Strategic Focus, Sun Microsystems was able to build a competitive advantage and sustain it for a considerable period of time by sharing its technology with others in the industry. The key is continous innovation.

Innovation can be a great equalizer for small firms competing against large firms as discussed in Chapter 13. Ironically, small firms often need the resource availability of large firms to commercialize innovations. Sun Microsystems has used larger firms to help it commercialize its innovations as its recent experience with Java software indicates. As the case illustrates, the advantage of size may be decreasing as the opportunities for joint ventures and strategic alliances, availability of venture capital, and increased licensing opportunities have become more prevalent.

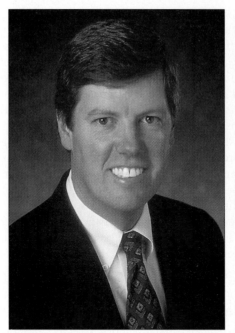

Sun Microsystems CEO Scott McNealy was able to build a competitve advantage and sustain it for a considerable period of time by sharing Sun's technology with others in the industry, such as Microsoft's CEO Bill Gates.

Our discussion of factors influencing an industry's competitive dynamics suggests that large firms with significant market power that act like small firms—making strategic decisions and implementing them with speed—and that are innovative are strong competitors and are likely to earn above-average returns. No matter how large, fast, and innovative organizations are, product quality also affects an industry's competitive dynamics and influences firms' ability to achieve strategic competitiveness in domestic and global markets.

■ Quality

Product quality has become a universal theme in the global economy and continues to shape the competitive dynamics in many industries.[64] Today product quality is important in all industry settings and is a necessary, but not sufficient, condition to successful strategy implementation. Without quality goods or services, strategic competitiveness cannot be achieved. Quality alone, however, does not guarantee that a firm will achieve strategic competitiveness or earn above-average returns. In the words of the president of the National Center for Manufacturing Sciences, a nonprofit research consortium, "Quality used to be a competitive issue out there, but now it's just the basic denominator to being in the market."[65]

In the global economy, ISO 9000 (International Organization for Standardization) standards are rapidly becoming important in establishing the quality level as a basic requirement of effective competition in worldwide markets.[66] As observed recently by the vice president and general manager of Caterpillar's engine division, "Today, having ISO 9000 is a competitive advantage. Tomorrow, it will be the ante to the global poker game."[67]

Detailed in a slender paperback volume and available from the American National Standards Institute, among other sources, ISO 9000 standards do not tell firms how to design and manufacture their products (either goods or services)

STRATEGIC FOCUS

Sun Microsystems Competes Through Innovation

Sun Microsystems operated as an open system with regard to its workstation products. It was able to gain market share and transform the market with its unique strategy. In 1983, Sun held approximately 15 percent of the workstation market; Apollo, a competing firm, commanded approximately 43 percent of the market. However, Sun Microsystems' unique open-system strategy of sharing technology allowed it to gain market share equal to almost 30 percent by 1989. In contrast, Apollo's market share decreased markedly during this time period (to under 15 percent). Others in the industry, such as Hewlett Packard (HP) and Digital Equipment Co. (DEC), achieved marginal gains in market share. Sun's revenues increased by almost $1.8 billion during this time; Apollo's revenues increased by only $300 million.

Essentially, the strategy Sun implemented between 1983 and 1989 called for sharing its technology with rivals to build a consensus on industry standards and a network of systems in support of customers' needs. With this strategy, Sun avoided investing large amounts of dollars in R&D to develop products for specific market segments. Because Sun allowed competitors to develop unique products that were compatible with its own workstations, it did not have to invest heavily in its own R&D.

In contrast to Sun Microsystems' competitive actions and strategy, some competitors, including IBM and DEC, chose not to share their technology with others, preferring instead to develop noncompatible systems. Although this was a positive short-term strategy, eventually the Sun strategy began to erode IBM's and DEC's shares of the workstation market. Sun's strategy of sharing technology and allowing a consensus to develop on standards transformed the workstation segment of the computer industry, providing valued products to customers in the process. Sun's strategy allowed the firm to achieve strategic competitiveness during the 1980s.

By 1992, Sun held a 38.3 percent share of the workstation market. In comparison, HP had a 17.1 percent share, DEC had a 12.1 percent share, and IBM had a 7.3 percent share (HP, IBM, and DEC were Sun's major competitors). Sun's revenues reached $3.5 billion in the same year. But these positive indicators did not mask the fact that Sun faced serious competitive challenges. Its returns have fallen, and there is potential competition from personal computer makers, such as Compaq, on the horizon. With the new operating systems and powerful microprocessors that have been developed recently, Sun's technological edge in workstations may be deteriorating.

In 1995, however, Sun's fortunes took off again as Scott McNealy, the CEO, persuaded the top firms in the computing industry that Java, Sun's Internet software should be the basic programming language for internet operating systems. Besides Netscape, Oracle, and IBM, the software giant Microsoft also found reason to make a deal. The flexibility of Java to run on any hardware or operating system, including Windows and Windows 95, encouraged Microsoft to obtain a license with Sun. Java changes the computer from a single operating system to a network environment. Therefore, even though Sun was beginning to lose market share in its core business, workstations, due to pressure from HP, IBM, DEC, and Silicon Graphics, its stock price more than doubled in 1995.

Source R. D. Hof, K. Rebello, and P. Burrows, 1996, Scott McNealy's rising sun, *Business Week,* January 22, 66–73; M. Chase, 1993, Sun Microsystems juggles new strategies and old rivals, *Wall Street Journal,* May 19, B2; R. Garud and A. Kumaraswamy, 1993, Changing competitive dynamics in network industries: An exploration of Sun Microsystems' open systems strategy, *Strategic Management Journal* 14: 351–369.

more effectively and efficiently. But the standards do "provide a framework for showing customers how [a firm committed to quality management practices] tests products, trains [its] employees, keeps records, and fixes defects."[68] ISO 9000 standards are formally described as "the refinement of all the most practical and generally applicable principles of quality systems and the culmination of agreement between the world's most advanced authorities on these standards as the basis of a new era of quality management."[69] Firms earning an ISO-based certificate (certificates are awarded by one of many independent auditors) have demonstrated that their factory, office, or laboratory has satisfied the quality management requirements determined by the ISO.

■ **Quality** *involves meeting or exceeding customer expectations in the goods and/or services offered.*

Quality involves meeting or exceeding customer expectations in the goods and/or services offered.[70] The quality dimensions of goods and services are shown in Table 5.2. As a competitive dimension, quality is as important in the service sector, as the Morgan Stanley example illustrates, as it is in the manufacturing sector.[71]

Quality begins at the top of the organization. Top management must create values for quality that permeate the entire organization.[72] These values should be built into strategies that reflect long-term commitments to customers, stockholders, and other important stakeholders.[73] In so doing, a process of total quality management pervades the firm in all activities and processes.

Quality and total quality management are closely associated with the philosophies and teachings of W. Edward Deming (and, to a lesser extent, Armand Feigenbaum and Joseph Juran).[74] Simple, yet powerful, in its value, these individuals' contributions to the practice of management is based on the understanding that it costs less to make quality products than defect-ridden ones.

■ **Total quality management** *is a total company-wide effort that includes all employees, suppliers, and customers, and that seeks continuously to improve the quality of products and processes to meet the needs and expectations of customers.*

Total quality management (TQM) is a "total, company-wide effort that includes all employees, suppliers, and customers, and that seeks continuously to improve the quality of products and processes to meet the needs and expectations of customers."[75] Actually a philosophy about how to manage, TQM "combines the teachings of Deming and Juran on statistical process control and group problem-solving processes with Japanese values concerned with quality and continuous improvement."[76] Statistical process control (SPC) is a technique used to upgrade continually the quality of the goods or services a firm produces. SPC

Table 5.2   Product and Service Quality Dimensions

Product Quality Dimensions	*Service Quality Dimensions*
1. *Performance*—Operating characteristics	1. *Timeliness*—Performed in promised time period
2. *Features*—Important special characteristics	2. *Courtesy*—Performed cheerfully
3. *Flexibility*—Meeting operating specifications over some time period	3. *Consistency*—All customers have similar experiences each time
4. *Durability*—Amount of use before performance deteriorates	4. *Convenience*—Accessible to customers
5. *Conformance*—Match with preestablished standards	5. *Completeness*—Fully serviced, as required
6. *Serviceability*—Ease and speed of repair or normal service	6. *Accuracy*—Performed correctly each time
7. *Aesthetics*—How a product looks and feels	
8. *Perceived quality*—Subjective assessment of characteristics (product image)	

Source: Adapted from J.W. Dean, Jr., and J.R. Evans, 1994, *Total Quality: Management, Organization and Society* (St. Paul, Minn.: West Publishing Company); H.V. Roberts and B.F. Sergesketter, 1993, *Quality Is Personal* (New York: The Free Press); D. Garvin, 1988, *Managed Quality: The Strategic and Competitive Edge* (New York: The Free Press).

benefits the firm through the detection and elimination of variations in processes used to manufacture a good or service.[77]

Although there are skeptics, when applied properly, the principles of total quality management can help firms achieve strategic competitiveness and earn above-average returns.[78] Three principal goals sought when practicing total quality management are boosting customer satisfaction, reducing product introduction time, and cutting costs. As discussed in this chapter, achievement of these goals can be expected to have a positive effect on a firm's performance. To reach these goals, firms must provide their employees and leaders with effective TQM training.[79]

Ironically, Deming's and Juran's ideas on quality and continuous improvement were adapted and implemented by Japanese firms long before many U.S. firms acknowledged their importance. For this reason, a host of Japanese firms developed a competitive advantage in product quality that has been difficult for U.S. firms to overcome.[80] Deming's 14 points for managing and achieving quality (see Table 5.3) have become a watchword in many businesses globally.

Embedded within Deming's 14 points for management is the importance of striving continuously to improve how a firm operates and the quality of its goods or services. In fact, Deming did not support use of the TQM term, arguing that he did not know what total quality was and that it is impossible for firms to reach a goal of "total quality." The pursuit of quality improvements, Deming believed, should be a never-ending process.

Newer methods of TQM use benchmarking and emphasize organizational learning.[81] Benchmarking facilitates TQM by developing information on the best practices of other organizations and industries. This information is often used to establish goals for the firm's own TQM efforts. Benchmarking provides a process from which a firm can learn from the outcomes of other firms.[82] Because of the importance of product (both goods and service) quality in achieving competitive parity or a competitive advantage, many firms in the United States and around the world are emphasizing total quality management and integrating it with their strategies.

As our discussions have indicated, relationships between each of the four general abilities (size, speed, innovation, and quality) influence a firm's competitive actions and outcomes. Those responsible for selecting a firm's strategy should understand these relationships and anticipate that competitors will take competitive actions and competitive responses designed to exploit the positive relationships depicted in Figure 5.2. In the next section, we describe the different outcomes of competitive dynamics.

■ Outcomes of Interfirm Rivalry

Figure 5.1 illustrates potential outcomes of interfirm rivalry. In some competitive environments, sustainable competitive advantage may be more likely. As discussed in Chapter 3, one of the key determinants of sustainability is whether a firm's products are costly to imitate. A sustainability framework, therefore, might focus on different market types where product imitability is largely or partially shielded.[83] All major markets have seen their foreign rivals make inroads into what had been their domestic markets. However, even with strong rivalry and increasing potential for imitability, some markets have been shielded from such

Table 5.3   Deming's 14 Points for Management

1. Create and publish to all employees a statement of the aims and purposes of the company or other organization. The management must demonstrate constantly their commitment to this statement.

2. Learn the new philosophy, top management and everybody.

3. Understand the purpose of inspection, for improvement of processes and reduction of costs.

4. End the practice of awarding business on the basis of price tag alone.

5. Improve constantly and forever the system of production and service.

6. Institute training.

7. Teach and institute leadership.

8. Drive out fear. Create trust. Create a climate for innovation.

9. Optimize toward the aims and purposes of the company the efforts of teams, groups, staff areas.

10. Eliminate exhortations for the workforce.

11. (a) Eliminate numerical quotas for production. Instead, learn and institute methods for improvement. (b) Eliminate management by objective. Instead, learn the capabilities of processes and how to improve them.

12. Remove barriers that rob people of pride of workmanship.

13. Encourage education and self-improvement for everyone.

14. Take action to accomplish the transformation.

Source: Reprinted from *Out of the Crisis* by W. Edwards Deming by permission of MIT and The W. Edwards Deming Institute. Published by MIT, Center for Advanced Engineering Study, Cambridge, MA 02139. Copyright © 1986 by W. Edwards Deming.

competition. These markets are described as slow-cycle or sheltered markets. In other markets, product imitability is moderate. As such, they are labeled standard-cycle markets, often described as oligopolistic. In still other markets, firms are in rapid, dynamic, and often entrepreneurial environments where changes are identified as fast cycle.

■ Competitive Market Outcomes

■ *Products in **slow-cycle markets** reflect strongly shielded resource positions where competitive pressures do not readily penetrate a firm's sources of strategic competitiveness.*

Products in **slow-cycle markets** reflect strongly shielded resource positions where competitive pressures do not readily penetrate the firm's sources of strategic competitiveness. This is often characterized in economics as a monopoly position. A firm that has a unique set of product attributes or an effective product design may dominate its market for decades as did IBM with large mainframe computers. This type of competitive position can be established even in markets where there is significant technological change, such as Microsoft's position with difficult to imitate, complex software systems. Drug manufacturers often have established such a position legally under patent laws. Shielded advantages may be geographic, therefore, the opening of huge emerging markets in Eastern Europe, Russia, China, and India offers strong motivation for firms to pursue such opportunities.

Although the idea of a monopoly, which has a single seller, restricted output, and high prices, is not likely to be attained in the United States due to government policy restrictions, subtle and more complex variations are possible with a local monopoly approach. This is what Wal-Mart did in its early years. It established a local monopoly in rural areas in the southwest United States, especially when coupled with an efficient distribution systems. Many airlines also seek to establish a shielded advantage by the innovation of hub control at

Figure 5.2

Effects of Firm Size, Speed of Decision Making/Actions, Innovation, and Quality on Sustainability of Competitive Actions and Outcomes

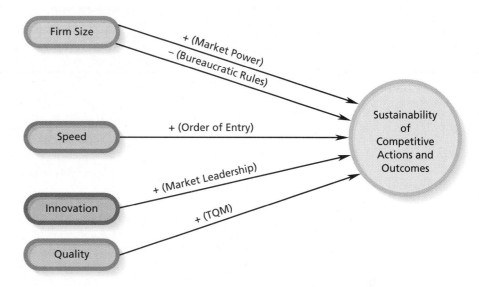

*Plus and minus signs indicate effects on performance.

airports. Examples include USAir's dominance at Pittsburgh and Delta's hubs in Atlanta and Salt Lake City.

Effective product designs may be able to dominate their markets for many years. For example, the McIlhenny family of Louisiana has dominated the hot sauce industry for 125 years with a single product unchanged since its inception: Tabasco sauce.[84] These firms may be closely associated with the main idea of the resource-based view of the firm, because their resources and capabilities are difficult to imitate. The sustainability of competitive action associated with a slow-cycle market is depicted in Figure 5.3.

Standard-cycle markets may be more closely associated with the industrial organization economics approach following Porter's five force model on competitive strategy. In these organizations, strategy and organization are designed to serve high-volume or mass markets. The focus is on coordination and market control as in automobile and appliance industries.[85] These organizations, even though they may be able to sustain world-class products for decades (e.g., Kellogg, Coca-Cola), may experience severe competitive pressures as illustrated by the introductory case about breakfast cereals. However, extended dominance and, in fact, world leadership is possible through continuing capital investment and superior learning as is the case with Coca-Cola. This contrasts with protected markets because there is not such a high rate of ongoing investment into the production of Tabasco sauce. Although it may be difficult to enter standard-cycle markets because of the competitive intensity, if successful and if duplicated by competitors, more intense competitive pressures can be brought to bear. More intense competition may be similar to that found in fast-cycle markets.[86]

In **fast-cycle markets,** such as cellular telephones and DRAM computer chips, it does not appear that a first-mover advantage yields sustained competitive advantage. One way to examine the intensity of dynamics in these industries is to study the long-run pricing patterns of some products. For instance, in 1988, the cost per megabyte of DRAM computer chips was $378. Three years later, the

■ *Products in **standard-cycle markets** reflect moderately shielded resource positions where competitive interaction penetrates a firm's sources of strategic competitiveness but with improvement of its capabilities, the firm may be able to sustain a competitive advantage.*

■ *In **fast-cycle markets,** a competitive advantage cannot be sustained; firms attempt to gain temporary competitive advantages by strategically disrupting the market.*

Figure 5.3

Gradual Erosion of a Sustained
Competitive Advantage

Source: Adapted from I.C. MacMillan, 1988,
Controlling competitive dynamics by taking
strategic initiative, *Academy of Management
Executive* II, no. 2: 111–118.

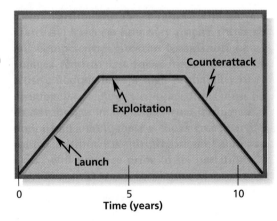

market price for a one-megabyte chip had dropped to $35.[87] When cellular
phones were introduced, they were priced at around $3,500, but five years later
the price dropped below $100 and now cellular phone equipment is often given
away if you subscribe to a cellular system service. Perpetual innovation and
shorter product cycles dominate this market class. Standard-cycle markets are
scale oriented, whereas fast-cycle markets are idea driven.

■ Competing in Fast-Cycle Markets

To this point in the chapter, the focus has been on trying to obtain a sustained
competitive advantage. Sustained competitive advantage is possible in slow- and
standard-cycle markets. Figure 5.3 focuses on this type of competitive advantage.
Usually there is an entrepreneurial launch stage of the strategy, a period of
exploitation, and, ultimately, a period of counterattack where the competitive
advantage erodes. In fast-cycle markets, a sustained competitive advantage may
be a goal that creates inertia and exposes one to aggressive global competitors.
Even though GM and IBM have economies of scale, huge advertising budgets,
the best distribution systems in their industry, cutting edge R&D, and deep
pockets, many of their advantages have been eroded by global competitors in
Europe, Japan, and now Korea.

A new competitive advantage paradigm is emerging where a firm seizes the
initiative through a small series of steps as illustrated in Figure 5.4. As you can
see from this figure, the idea is to create a counterattack before the advantage is
eroded. This actually leads to cannibalizing your own products through the next
stage of product evolution and entry.[88] Thus, the focus of this new paradigm is
competitive disruption.[89] In this competitive approach, one can escalate competition in an arena such as price and quality only so far, then the dominant
competitor should seek to jump to another level of competition such as speed and
know-how or innovation. This is the approach that Komatsu took in competing
with Caterpillar. It first developed strong quality products that were competitively priced. As Caterpillar responded in a similar fashion, Komatsu, in turn,
improved the products in new niches and it attacked in emerging markets where
Caterpillar was not strong. This approach requires the four basic aspects
described in Table 5.4. This form of strategy is illustrated in the Strategic Focus
on Hewlett Packard, Tandem Computers, Intel, and BMW.

Figure 5.4

Obtaining Temporary Advantages to Create Sustained Advantage

Source: Adapted from I. C. MacMillan, 1988, Controlling competitive dynamics by taking strategic initiative, *Academy of Management Executive* II, no. 2: 111–118.

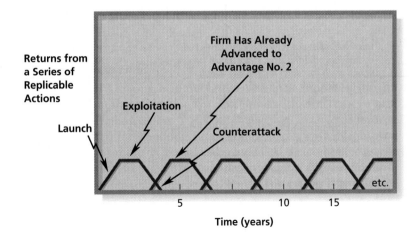

Table 5.4	Strategic Steps for Seizing the Initiative in Fast-Cycle Markets
1. Disrupting the status quo.	Competitors disrupt the status quo by identifying new opportunities to serve the customer and by shifting the rules of competition. These moves end the old pattern of competitive interaction between rivals. This requires speed and variety in approach.
2. Create temporary advantage.	Disruption creates temporary advantages. These advantages are based on better knowledge of customers, technology, and the future. They are derived from customer orientation and employee empowerment throughout the entire organization. These advantages are short lived and eroded by fierce competition.
3. Seizing the initiative.	By moving aggressively into new areas of competition, acting to create a new advantage or undermine a competitor's old advantage, the company seizes the initiative. This throws the opponent off balance and puts it at a disadvantage for awhile. The opponent is forced to play catch up, reacting rather than shaping the future with its own actions to seize the initiative. The initiator is proactive, whereas competitors are forced to be reactive.
4. Sustaining the momentum.	Several actions in a row are taken to seize the initiative and create momentum. The company continues to develop new advantages and does not wait for competitors to undermine them before launching the next initiative. This succession of actions sustains the momentum. Continually offering new initiatives is the only source of sustainable competitive advantage in fast-cycle environments.

Source: Adapted from R.A. D'Aveni, 1995, Coping with hypercompetition: Utilizing the new 7's framework, *Academy of Management Executive* IX, no. 3: 45–60.

As several examples in the Strategic Focus illustrate, many firms are seeking to disrupt their own markets through a cannibalistic approach before the old product has matured or completed its life cycle and before competitive counterattack begins. This approach seems to match quite readily the fast-cycle market discussed earlier. In earlier frameworks studied in past chapters, the dominant issue is to fit the characteristics of the strategy with the demands of the competitive environment. In fast-cycle markets, however, strategic flexibility becomes more important than fit with the environment. The dominant aspect of this strategy therefore becomes flexibility. The new competitive landscape requires firms to respond quickly to technological change and market opportunities by offering more new products, broader product lines, and product upgrades more rapidly.[90]

STRATEGIC FOCUS   Cannibalism Is a Virtue

NEC Corporation, the large Japanese computer firm, provided a challenge for Hewlett Packard's (HP's) dominance in the computer printer market. The Japanese undercut prices in 1993 with new, better designed models. While successful in the past, the approach failed in printers. HP launched an improved color version and slashed prices simultaneously on its black-and-white model by more than 40 percent in six months. NEC withdrew its entry, because it was overpriced and not competitive enough after about four months on the market. HP was also able to block Canon's ink-jet printer business. HP had a better understanding of computers and American customers and got its product to market faster.

HP engineers adopted Japanese tactics by creating an abundance of patents to protect HP's design and frustrate rivals as it continually sought to improve the ink-jet technology. Ink-jet technology, introduced in 1988, improved on dot matrix technology in both quality and color performance. At that time, Epson held the lead in low-price printers. While Epson had low-cost manufacturing, HP responded by demanding that stores put ink-jet printers alongside Epson's. It also tripled its warranty to three years and redesigned the printers with manufacturing costs in mind. In 1992, dot matrix printers were under assault with falling sales, while ink-jet sales soared. Therefore, HP was able to surprise and provide simultaneous improvements in product quality and reductions in price. When a rival, Canon, was trying to get back in the market with a color ink-jet printer, HP cut the price of its own version, even before its rival's product reached the market. Although these strategies cannibalized their old products (color for black-and-white), they allowed HP to maintain dominance and continue market share growth.

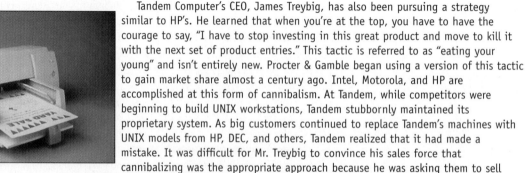

Tandem Computer's CEO, James Treybig, has also been pursuing a strategy similar to HP's. He learned that when you're at the top, you have to have the courage to say, "I have to stop investing in this great product and move to kill it with the next set of product entries." This tactic is referred to as "eating your young" and isn't entirely new. Procter & Gamble began using a version of this tactic to gain market share almost a century ago. Intel, Motorola, and HP are accomplished at this form of cannibalism. At Tandem, while competitors were beginning to build UNIX workstations, Tandem stubbornly maintained its proprietary system. As big customers continued to replace Tandem's machines with UNIX models from HP, DEC, and others, Tandem realized that it had made a mistake. It was difficult for Mr. Treybig to convince his sales force that cannibalizing was the appropriate approach because he was asking them to sell twice the number of computers for lower commissions and pay. But he indicated to them that if they didn't take this approach, Tandem would ultimately go out of business. Now as

Tandem begins to launch a new high-end product, it simultaneously cuts prices on its old low-end product. This strategy has worked well: Tandem recorded above-average returns in 1994.

Intel has been using the strategy of product cannibalism for years to deal with competitors such as Cyrix and Advanced Micro Devices (AMD). Intel moved somewhat prematurely from each of its new entries to the next in its 86 family of chips (286, 386, and 486). It changed the family name as it sought to establish brand equity with its next entry through the Pentium label. Now it is moving to a new chip called the P6 as it continues its strategy of market disruption and product cannibalism.

Even a traditional firm such as BMW has been using new methods to turn around its falling sales and competition with upstart Japanese models such as Acura, Infinity, and Lexus. BMW cut prices on its high-end lines and also provided a new marketing strategy focusing on quality, safety, and social responsibility. It simultaneously sought to revitalize its dealership network to focus on providing customer service and benefits. BMW defined new roles for dealers and established an active bonus payment system based on customer satisfaction, rather than sales volume. Furthermore, it eliminated concern about commitment to the U.S. market by developing a large-scale manufacturing operation in South Carolina. Although sales decreased from 1986 through 1991, from the years 1992 to 1994, there was a 58 percent increase in sales growth with unit sales at 84,500 in 1994. BMW executives established a goal for 100,000 vehicles in 1997.

Source R. Dolan, 1995, Marketing turnarounds, *European Management Journal* 13: 239–244; R. D. Hof, 1995, Intel: Far beyond the Pentium, *Business Week,* February 20, 88–90; J. E. Rigdon, 1994, Cannibalism is a virtue in computer business, Tandem's CEO learns, *Wall Street Journal,* August 24, A1, A4; S. K. Yoder, 1994, How HP used tactics of the Japanese to beat them at their game, *Wall Street Journal,* August 8, A1.

■ Competitive Dynamics and Industry Evolution Outcomes

Because industries and markets evolve over time, so do the competitive dynamics between firms in the industry. We have examined how firms interact in a short span of time using an action–reaction framework, but we have not yet examined how competitive interaction evolves over longer periods of time. Three general stages of industry evolution are relevant to our study of competitive dynamics: emerging entrepreneurial, larger growth-oriented, and mature firms. These are shown in Figure 5.5.

Firms entering emerging industries attempt to establish a niche or an initial form of beginning dominance within an industry. Competitive rivalry for the loyalty of customers is serious. In these industries, depending on the types of products, firms often attempt to establish product quality, technology, and/or advantageous relationships with suppliers in order to develop a competitive advantage in the pursuit of strategic competitiveness. These firms are striving to build their reputation. As a result, a variety of different competitive strategies may be employed in such an industry. Such diversity can be beneficial to many of the firms in the industry. The diversity of competitive strategies may avoid direct competition and help firms gain dominance in market niches.[91] Although speed is important in new emerging industries, access to capital is often the critical issue. Therefore, it is not uncommon to have strategic alliances develop between a new firm entering the market and a more established firm that wishes to gain a foothold in the new industry.[92]

These firms often rely on top management to develop market opportunities. Stephen Jobs and Bill Gates were able to foresee the future possibilities of the microcomputer and the standardized microcomputer operating system. Their vision of an uncertain environment gave rise to both Apple Computer and

Figure 5.5

An Action-Based Model of the Industry Life Cycle

Source: Adapted from C. Grimm and K.G. Smith, 1997, *Industry Rivalry and Coordination* (St. Paul, MN: West Publishing Co.).

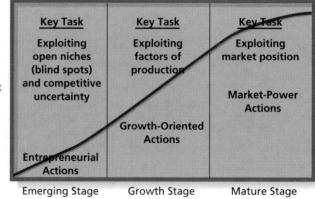

Microsoft. Thus, firms in the emerging stage take *entrepreneurial actions* which focus on entrepreneurial discovery in uncertain environments.

Growth-oriented firms are the survivors from the emerging industry stage. In the growth stage, *growth-oriented actions* are emphasized, which tend to create product standardization as consumer demand creates a mass market with growth potential. Thus, many of these firms are more established, but no less competitive. In fact, as the industry begins to mature, the variety of strategies being implemented tends to decrease.[93] As such, entrepreneurial actions are still taking place but there is more emphasis on growth-oriented actions. Oftentimes, groups of firms will follow a similar strategy and thus become directly competitive. However, the rivalry between groups may be more indirect.[94] In industries where there is considerable within-strategic-group rivalry and competitive rivalry between firms in separate strategic groups, firms frequently earn below-average returns.[95]

Some of these industries may also be fragmented. Fragmented markets, such as fast food restaurants, tend to offer standardized facilities and products, but decentralized decision making to the local units. The standardization allows for low-cost competition. The primary value added comes from services provided. These markets offer a prime opportunity for franchising because of the ability to standardize facilities, operations, and products.

In nonfragmented industries, the speed of new product development and introduction to the marketplace becomes an important competitive weapon. Consumers tend to be more sophisticated and expect not only quality products, but also product designs that meet their needs. Firms that can move new products that better meet consumers' needs to the market more quickly than competitors are likely to gain a competitive advantage.

In mature industries, there are usually fewer surviving competitors. Those that do survive tend to be larger with dominant market share positions. Therefore, firms in the mature stage emphasize *market-power actions* which focus the firm's attention on offering product lines that are profitable and producing those products in an efficient manner. New product innovation or entrepreneurial actions continue but are greatly deemphasized. Process innovations are emphasized more because they maintain dominance through cost efficiencies and the quality of the product manufactured and provided to customers.[96] Finally, firms in industries in the mature stage frequently seek international expansion or an increasing emphasis on their international operations and sales, a move that often extends a product's life. Thus, growth-oriented actions also continue even though the primary emphasis is on market-power actions.

In summary, once mature firms have a dominant market share, they seek to exploit their market power and extensive resources and capabilities in an attempt to maintain dominance. In a study examining the 1950–1972 period, market leaders Kellogg, General Mills, General Foods, and Quaker Oats introduced more than 80 new brands without significant product innovation in an attempt to fill all niches and deter entry.[97] This strategy was very successful until the private-label producers grew powerful enough to counter this strategy, as the introductory case illustrates.

This chapter concludes our emphasis on business-level strategy, although some business-level issues are discussed in future Chapters (e.g., Chapters 8, 9 and 11). The next chapter begins our discussion of corporate-level strategy.

■ Summary

- Competitive rivalry entails actions and responses to competitive actions taken by other firms. Competitive attack and response are more likely when awareness, motivation, and abilities to attack or respond are present.

- Market commonality, as determined by multimarket contact in such industries as airlines, is likely to lead to a dampening of potential attack. However, if an offensive action is taken, a response is more likely in the presence of market commonality.

- Awareness of competitors' ability to attack or respond is facilitated by resource similarity among competitors. Those with similar resources are more likely to attack and respond than are those with fewer resources.

- First movers can gain a competitive advantage and customer loyalty by being the first in the market. First movers also take more risks. However, first movers often are higher performers. Second movers, particularly those that are larger and faster, can also gain a competitive advantage and/or earn at least average returns because they imitate, but do not take some of the risks that first movers do. The longer the time required to respond, the higher the probability that the first mover will enjoy strong performance gains. Late movers (those that respond a long time after the original action was taken) tend to be lower performers and much less effective.

- The probability of a response by a competitor to a competitive action is based partially on the extent to which the competitor is dependent on the particular market in which the action was taken. In addition, the probability of response is based on the type of action, the reputation of the firm taking the strategic action (the expectation of success), and the resources available to the competitor contemplating response.

- The two types of competitive actions are strategic and tactical. Strategic actions are more long term in nature, require many specific resources, and are difficult to reverse. Alternatively, tactical actions tend to be more short term in orientation, require fewer and more general resources, and can be more easily reversed. More tactical, rather than strategic, actions are taken and more responses are made to tactical than to strategic actions. It is easier to respond to a tactical action, partly because it requires fewer resources. In addition, a tactical action is likely to have a shorter term effect than a strategic action. Responses to strategic actions are more difficult, require more resources, and require a longer-term investment.

- When competitors are highly dependent on a market in which competitive actions are taken, there is a high probability that they will respond to such actions. However, firms that are more diversified across markets are less likely to respond to a particular action that affects only one of the markets in which they compete.

- The highest probability of a response comes when an action is taken by a market leader. Furthermore, when an action is taken by a market leader, it is more likely that a competitor will imitate the action taken.

Alternatively, if the firm has a reputation as a strategic player (a firm that takes more complex and risky actions), there is a lower probability of response. A price predator is also less likely to elicit a response from competitors.

- Those with more resources are more likely to respond to strategic actions than are those with fewer resources. Furthermore, the probability of response is determined not only by the amount of resources, but by the ability to use those resources in taking competitive action.

- Abilities needed to engage in competitive actions and responses include the relative size of the acting and responding firms, the function of speed in the market or industry, the importance of innovation in competitive moves, and product quality.

- Large firms often have strong market power. Alternatively, as firms grow larger, they often institute bureaucratic rules, procedures, and structures. These have the effect of reducing the probability that a firm will take actions and respond to others' actions. In addition, they reduce the speed with which a firm may be able to implement an action or respond to competitors' actions.

- Speed is becoming increasingly important in many industries in order to gain and hold a competitive advantage. In fact, many large firms must act like small firms (flexible and agile) to be competitive. This may require that they decentralize many responsibilities and decisions and that they create cross-functional teams in order to speed multiple processes (e.g., the innovation process).

- Both product and process innovation are becoming more important in the competitive posture of many industries. Some research has shown that firms that invest more in R&D and that are more innovative tend to have higher performance in multiple industries. Product innovation tends to be more important in emerging and growth industries. However, mature industries may emphasize process innovation.

- Product quality has become critical in order to maintain competitive parity in most industries. Total quality management must be infused throughout the organization by top management and integrated with firm strategies. Benchmarking is used to help make comparative judgments about quality relative to other firms' best practices.

- There are three basic market outcomes from interfirm rivalry. Slow-cycle markets allow a firm to establish competitive advantage in a near monopoly situation. Until recently, many utility firms were in this position. Standard-cycle markets allow market situations where sustainability is possible. Firms that have multimarket contact may dampen competition somewhat. Fast-cycle markets create a situation where only temporary competitive advantage is possible such as in the electronics and pharmaceutical industries.

- In fast-cycle markets, a new paradigm of competitive action may be necessary, competitive disruption. This usually involves cannibalization of a previous product entry through decreasing prices, while establishing the new innovative product at the high end of the market, with increased product performance at a premium price.

- Industry evolution is important in determining the type of competition and the type of competitive actions that are emphasized. For example, firms in an emerging stage attempt to establish a reputation and develop a market niche in technology or quality of products provided. The main task is to establish an entrepreneurial action, usually in an uncertain environment. In growth firms, special emphasis may be placed on innovation to increase economies of scale. Speed of competitive actions taken is also important. The key task is to pursue growth-oriented actions by exploiting factors of production to increase dominance. In mature industries with fewer competitors, special emphasis is placed on market-power actions designed to defend the most profitable product lines and processes in order to produce and distribute those products with the greatest efficiency (lowest cost). However, entrepreneurial, growth-oriented, and market-power actions are taken at all stages, although the emphasis is different at each stage.

■ Review Questions

1. What two factors contribute to awareness, motivation, and ability in competitor analysis?

2. What are the advantages and disadvantages of being a first, second, or late mover?

3. On what four factors is the likelihood of a response to a competitive action based?

4. What is the likelihood of response to a tactical action, a strategic action, and actions taken by market leaders? Explain why.

5. What are the advantages and the disadvantages of size regarding strategic actions and responses thereto?

6. Why is speed important in many industries? What can firms do to increase the speed at which they make and implement strategic decisions?

7. In what types of industries is innovation important for competitive advantage? Explain the importance of different types of innovation (product and process) for success in different industries.

8. Describe three types of markets and the nature of rivalry in each.

9. How does industry evolution affect interfirm rivalry? Identify three stages of industry evolution, and briefly explain the types of competitive actions emphasized in those stages.

Application Discussion Questions

1. Read the popular business press (e.g., *Business Week, Fortune*) and identify a strategic action and a tactical action taken by firms approximately two years ago. Next, read the popular business press to see if, and how, competitors responded to those actions. Explain the actions and the responses, linking your findings to the discussion in this chapter.

2. Why would a firm regularly choose to be a second-mover? Likewise, why would a firm purposefully be a late mover?

3. Explain how Sun Microsystems' strategic actions affected its primary competitors (e.g., IBM, DEC, HP, Silicon Graphics).

4. Choose a large firm and examine the popular business press to identify how its size, speed of actions, level of innovation, and quality of goods or services have affected its competitive position in its industry. Explain your findings.

5. Identify a firm in a fast-cycle market and trace why its strategy was successful or unsuccessful over several strategic actions.

Ethics Questions

1. In your opinion, are some industries known for ethical practices, while others are not? If so, name industries thought to be ethical and those that are evaluated less favorably in terms of ethics. How might the competitive actions and competitive responses differ between an "ethical" and an "unethical" industry?

2. When engaging in competitive rivalry, firms jockey for a market position that is advantageous, relative to competitors. However, in this jockeying, what kind of competitor intelligence gathering approaches are ethical?

3. A second mover is a firm that responds to a first mover's competitive actions, often through imitation. Is there anything unethical about how a second mover engages in competition? Why or why not?

4. Standards for competitive rivalry differ in countries throughout the world. What should firms do to cope with these differences?

5. Is it possible that total quality management practices could result in firms operating more ethically than before such practices were implemented? If this is possible, what might account for an increase in the ethical behavior of a firm when using TQM principles?

6. What ethical issues are involved in fast-cycle markets?

Internet Exercise

Read about several businesses in one of the on-line business periodicals (e.g., *Business Week, Fortune*). Then, gather additional information from The Society of Competitive Intelligence Professionals at:

■ http://www.scip.org/

Based on your findings, can you explain the competitive actions and responses taken? How important are size, speed, innovation, and quality for the firms you selected?

Cohesion Case

Gather business intelligence about two of the major companies in your group's industry by examining the checklists, strategies, and software at the "Intelligence Competitive Engine":

■ http://www.icemfg.com/icemfg/

Send an E-mail message to your group recommending one of the firms for further analysis. Justify your selection.

■ Notes

1. S. Dubey, 1994, Kelloggs invites India's middle class to breakfast of ready-to-eat cereals, *Wall Street Journal,* August 29, B3.
2. A. Taylor III, 1996, It's the slow lane for automakers, *Fortune,* April 1, 59–64.
3. R. Bettis and M. A. Hitt, 1995, The new competitive landscape, *Strategic Management Journal* 16 (Special Issue, Summer), 7–19.
4. Taylor, It's the slow lane for automakers, 60.
5. J.A. Quelch and D. Harding, 1996, Brand versus private equity labels: Fighting to win, *Harvard Business Review* 74, no. 1: 99–109; S. P. Schnaars, 1994, *Managing Imitation Strategies: How Later Entrants Seize Markets from Pioneers* (New York: The Free Press).
6. J. Stiles, 1995, Collaboration for competitive advantage: The changing world of alliances and partnerships, *Long Range Planning* 28: 109–112.
7. M. E. Porter, 1980, *Competitive Strategy* (New York: Free Press), 17.
8. Ibid.
9. C. Grimm and K.G. Smith, 1997, *Industry Rivalry and Coordination,* (St. Paul, MN: West Publishing Co.); M. Chen and D. Miller, 1994, Competitive attack, retaliation and performance: An expectancy-valence framework, *Strategic Management Journal* 15: 85–102.
10. G. P. Hodgkinson and G. Johnson, 1994, Exploring the mental models of competitive strategists: The case for a processual approach, *Journal of Management Studies* 31: 525–551; J. F. Porac and H. Thomas, 1994, Cognitive categorization and subjective rivalry among retailers in a small city, *Journal of Applied Psychology* 79: 54–66; E. J. Zajac and M. H. Bazerman, 1991, Blind spots in industry and competitor analysis: Implications of interfirm "mis" perception to strategic decisions, *Academy of Management Review* 16: 37–46; J. F. Porac and H. Thomas, 1990, Taxonomic mental models in competitor definition, *Academy of Management Review* 15: 224–240.
11. G. P. Carroll and A. Swaminathan, 1992, The organizational ecology of strategic groups in the American brewing industry from 1975–1988, *Industrial and Corporate Change* 1: 65–97.
12. K. Ohmae, 1985, *Triad Power* (New York: The Free Press).
13. f. i. smith and R. L. Wilson, 1995, The predictive validity of the Karnani and Wernerfelt model of multipoint competition, *Strategic Management Journal* 6: 43–160; A. Karnani and B. Wernerfelt, 1985, Multipoint competition, *Strategic Management Journal* 6: 87–96.
14. J. Gimeno and C. Y. Woo, 1996, Hypercompetition in multimarket environment: The role of strategic similarity and multimarket contact in competitive de-escalation, *Organization Science* 7: in press; W. N. Evans and I. N. Kessides, 1994, Living by the "golden rule": Multimarket contact in the U.S. airline industry, *Quarterly Journal of Economics* 109: 341–366.
15. M. J. Chen, 1996, Competitor analysis and interfirm rivalry: Toward a theoretical integration, *Academy of Management Review* 21: 100–134.
16. M. A. Peteraf, 1993, Intraindustry structure and response toward rivals, *Journal of Managerial and Decision Economics* 14: 519–528.
17. Y. Ono, 1996. A pulp tale: Juice co-op squeezes big rival, *Wall Street Journal,* January 30, B1, B2.
18. J. Barney, 1986, Types of competition and the theory of strategy: Toward an integrative framework, *Academy of Management Review* 11: 791–800.
19. R. A. Melcher, 1996, Tune-up time for Harley: It must soothe impatient customers and fight imitators, *Business Week,* April 8, 90, 94.
20. S. P. Schnaars, 1982, Managing imitation strategies: How later entrants seize markets from pioneers, in R. R. Nelson and S. G. Winter (eds.), *An Evolutionary Theory of Economic Change* (Cambridge: Harvard University Press).
21. M. B. Lieberman and D. B. Montgomery, 1988, First-mover advantages, *Strategic Management Journal* 9: 41–58.
22. K.G. Smith, C.M. Grimm, and M.J. Gannon, 1992, *Dynamics of Competitive Strategy* (Newberry Park, Calif.: Sage).
23. A. Ginsberg and N. Venkatraman, 1992, Investing in new information technology: The role of competitive posture and issue diagnosis, *Strategic Management Journal* 13 (Special Issue): 37–53.
24. Smith, Grimm, and Gannon, *Dynamics of Competitive Strategy.*
25. J. Levine, 1996, Adidas flies again, *Forbes,* March 25, 44–45.
26. G. Smith, 1996, Reebok is tripping over its own laces, *Business Week,* February 26, 62–66; S. Pulliam and J. Pereira, 1995, Reebok CEO faces criticism by institutional holders, *Wall Street Journal,* September 14, C1, C2.
27. K. Labich, 1995, Nike vs. Reebok: A battle for hearts, minds and feet, *Fortune,* September 18, 90–106.
28. D. Fischer, 1995, Global hopscotch: Reebok jumps from one Asian site to another in search of low-cost labor, *U.S. News & World Report,* June 5, 43–45; R. Sandomir, 1995, Nike enlists female athlete for a new line of footwear, *New York Times,* March 30, D9.
29. J. Pereira, 1996, Puma beats rivals by shipping sneakers with the next technology, *Wall Street Journal,* January 11, B4.
30. K. Labich, 1994, Air wars over Asia, *Fortune,* April 4, 93–98.
31. Smith, Grimm, and Gannon, *Dynamics of Competitive Strategy.*
32. T. Triplett, 1994, Cereal makers await reaction to General Mills coupon decision, *Marketing News,* May 9, 1–2.
33. G. Burns, 1995, Has General Mills had its Wheaties?, *Business Week,* May 8, 68–69.
34. Smith, Grimm, and Gannon, *Dynamics of Competitive Strategy.*
35. Ibid.
36. J. J. Keller, 1995, Divide to conquer, *Wall Street Journal,* September 21, A1.
37. R. Gibson, 1995, General Mills gets in shape for turnaround, *Wall Street Journal,* September 26, B1; L. Richards, 1995, General Mills gathers rewards of change: Cereal takes center stage after restaurant spinoff, *Advertising Age,* July 10, 4.
38. C. Duff and B. Ortega, 1995, How Wal-Mart outdid once-touted Kmart in the discount store race, *Wall Street Journal,* March 24, A1.
39. J. J. Keller and M. L. Carnevale, 1993, MCI-BT tie is seen setting off a battle in communications, *Wall Street Journal,* June 3, A1, A6.
40. L. Cauley and S. Lipin, 1996, Bell Atlantic and Nynex make it official, *Wall Street Journal,* April 23, A4; L. Cauley, 1996, Cellular-phone spinoff market start of slide leading to PacTel deal, *Wall Street Journal,* April 2, A1, A8; J. J. Keller and G. Naik, 1996, PacTel-SBC merger is likely to ring in an era of alliances among baby bells, *Wall Street Journal,* April 2, B1, B4; S. Lipin and D. Kansas, 1996, Two ex-Bell siblings to combine, *Wall Street Journal,* April 2, A3.
41. J. J. Keller, 1993, Sprint hangs back as its rivals forge global alliances, *Wall Street Journal,* June 4, B4.
42. K. G. Smith, C. M. Grimm, M. J. Gannon, and M. J. Chen, 1991, Organizational information-processing, competitive responses and performance in the U.S. domestic airline industry, *Academy of Management Journal* 34: 60–85.
43. M. Lewyn, 1996, Showtime for the watch dog: Now the FCC must set the rules for reform, *Business Week,* April 8, 86–87; G. Naik, 1996, Bell companies ready a charge into long-distance, *Wall Street Journal,* February 5, B4.
44. R. Frank, 1995, Root beer, bit player, may yet be a star, *Wall Street Journal,* November 20, B1, B4.
45. Ono, A pulp tale.
46. J. A. Schumpeter, 1961, *Theory of Economic Development* (New York: Oxford University Press).
47. H. Gleckman, 1993, Meet the giant-killers, *Business Week,* (Special Issue), 68–73.
48. R. A. Melcher, 1993, How Goliaths can act like Davids, *Business Week,* (Special Issue), 193.
49. Harvard Business Review Perspectives, 1995, How can big companies keep the entrepreneurial spirit alive? *Harvard Business Review* 73, no. 6: 183–192.
50. S. L. Brown and K. M. Eisenhardt, 1995, Product development: Past research, present findings, and future directions, *Academy of Management Review* 20: 343–378; K. M. Eisenhardt and B. N. Tabrizi, 1995, Accelerating adaptive processes: Product innovation in the global computer industry, *Administrative Science Quarterly* 40: 84–110.

51. Pereira, Puma beats rivals by shipping sneakers with the next technology.

52. L. Armstrong, 1996, Savior from down under?, *Business Week,* January 15, 85–86.

53. R. R. Nayyar and K. A. Bantel, 1994, Competitive agility: A source of competitive advantage based on speed and variety, *Advances in Strategic Management* 10A, 193–222.

54. P. S. Adler, 1995, Interdepartmental interdependence and coordination: The case of the design/manufacturing interface, *Organization Science* 6: 147–167.

55. J. T. Vessey, 1991, The new competitors: They think in terms of "speed to market," *Academy of Management Executive* V, no. 2: 23–33.

56. Nayyar and Bantel, Competitive agility.

57. S. Wally and J. R. Baum, 1994, Personal and structural determinants of the pace of strategic decision-making, *Academy of Management Journal* 37: 932–956.

58. Ibid.

59. T. Smart and J. H. Dobrzynski, 1993, Jack Welch on the art of thinking small, *Business Week,* (Special Enterprise Issue), 212–216.

60. S. C. Wheelwright and K. B. Clark, 1995, *Leading Product Development* (New York: The Free Press).

61. L. G. Franko, 1989, Global corporate competition: Who's winning, who's losing, and the R&D factor as one reason why, *Strategic Management Journal* 10: 449–474.

62. R. E. Hoskisson and M. A. Hitt, 1994, *Downscoping: How to Tame the Diversified Firm* (New York: Oxford University Press).

63. P. Ghemawat, 1986, Sustainable advantage, *Harvard Business Review* 64, no. 5: 53–58.

64. J. W. Dean, Jr., and D. E. Bowen, 1994, Management theory and total quality: Improving research and practice through theory development. *Academy of Management Review* 19: 392–419.

65. J. Aley, 1994, Manufacturers grade themselves, *Fortune,* March 21, 26.

66. F. Havard, 1994, BS ISO 9000 certification, in D. Lock (ed.), *Handbook of Quality Management,* (Brookfield, Vt.: Gower Publishing), 219–228.

67. R. Henkoff, 1993, The hot new seal of quality, *Fortune,* June 28, 117.

68. Ibid., 116.

69. B. Rothery, 1993, *ISO 9000,* 2nd ed. (Brookfield, Vt.: Gower Press), 19.

70. J. W. Dean, Jr., and J. R. Evans, 1994, *Total Quality: Management, Organization and Society* (St. Paul: West Publishing Company).

71. T. F. Rienzo, 1993, Planning Deming management for service organizations, *Business Horizons* 36, no. 3: 19–29.

72. S. Chatterjee and M. Yilmaz, 1993, Quality confusion: Too many gurus, not enough disciples, *Business Horizons* 36, no. 3: 15–18.

73. Dean and Evans, *Total Quality.*

74. W. S. Sherman and M. A. Hitt, 1996, Creating corporate value: Integrating quality and innovation programs, in D. Fedor and S. Ghosh (eds.), *Advances in the Management of Organizational Quality* (Greenwich, Conn.: JAI Press), 221–244.

75. Dean and Evans, *Total Quality,* 12.

76. E. E. Lawler III, 1994, Total quality management and employee involvement: Are they compatible? *Academy of Management Executive* VIII, no. 1: 68.

77. E. Adam, Jr., and R. J. Ebert, 1992, *Production and Operations Management,* 5th ed. (Englewood Cliffs, N.J.: Prentice-Hall), 634–641.

78. R. Jacob, 1993, TQM: More than a dying fad, *Fortune,* October 18, 66–72; R. Krishnan, A. B. Shani, and G. R. Baer, 1993, In search of quality improvement: Problems of design and implementation, *Academy of Management Executive* VII, no. 4: 7–20.

79. R. Blackburn and B. Rosen, 1993, Total quality and human resources management: Lessons learned from Baldridge award-winning companies, *Academy of Management Executive* VII, no. 3: 49–66.

80. H. V. Roberts and B. F. Sergesketter, 1993, *Quality Is Personal* (New York: The Free Press).

81. S. B. Sitkin, K. M. Sutcliffe, and R. G. Schroeder, 1994, Distinguishing control from learning in total quality management: A contingency perspective, *Academy of Management Review* 19: 537–564.

82. J. R. Hackman and R. Wageman, 1995, Total quality management: Empirical, conceptualization and practical issues, *Administrative Science Quarterly* 40, 309–342.

83. J. R. Williams, 1992, How sustainable is your competitive advantage? *California Management Review* 34 (Spring): 29–51.

84. J. H. Perser, 1993, McIlhenny Company used shrewd marketing to keep Tabasco a hot export product, *Traffic World,* April 5, 15–16.

85. A. D. Chandler, 1990, The enduring logic of industrial success, *Harvard Business Review* 68, no. 2: 130–140.

86. J. L. Bower and T. M. Hout, 1988, Fast-cycle capability for competitive power, *Harvard Business Review* 66, no. 6: 110–118.

87. Williams, How sustainable is your competitive advantage?

88. K. R. Conner, 1995, Obtaining strategic advantage from being imitated: When can encouraging "clones" pay? *Management Science* 41: 209–225; K. R. Conner, 1988, Strategies for product cannibalism, *Strategic Management Journal* 9 (Special Issue, Summer), 9–26.

89. R. A. D'Aveni, 1995, Coping with hypercompetition: Utilizing the new 7'S framework, *Academy of Management Executive* IX, no. 3: 45–60.

90. R. Sanchez, 1995, Strategic flexibility in product competition, *Strategic Management Journal,* 16 (Special Issue, Summer), 135–159.

91. M.A. Hitt, B. B. Tyler, C. Hardee, and D. Park, 1994, Understanding strategic intent in the global marketplace, *Academy of Management Executive* IX, no. 2: 12–19.

92. G. Miles, C. Snow, and M. P. Sharfman, 1993, Industry variety and performance, *Strategic Management Journal* 14: 163–177.

93. D. Lei, 1989, Strategies for global competition, *Long-Range Planning* 22: 102–109.

94. Miles, Snow, and Sharfman, Industry variety.

95. K. Cool and I. Dierickx, 1993, Rivalry, strategic groups and firm profitability, *Strategic Management Journal* 14: 47–59.

96. D. M. Schroeder, 1990, A dynamic perspective on the impact of process innovation upon competitive strategies, *Strategic Management Journal* 11: 25–41.

97. R. Schmalensee, 1978, Entry deterrence in the ready-to-eat breakfast cereal industry, *Bell Journal of Economics* IX: 305–328.

6 Corporate-Level Strategy

LEARNING OBJECTIVES

After reading this chapter, you should be able to:

1. Define corporate-level strategy and discuss its importance to the diversified firm.
2. Describe the advantages and disadvantages of single-business and dominant-business strategies.
3. Explain three primary reasons why firms move from single-business and dominant-business strategies to more diversified strategies.
4. Describe how related-diversified firms use activity sharing and the transfer of core competencies to create value.
5. Discuss the two ways an unrelated diversification strategy can create value.
6. Discuss the incentives and resources that encourage diversification.
7. Describe motives that can encourage managers to further diversify a firm.
8. Explain the business portfolio matrix technique as a means to evaluate the success of diversification strategies.

The Downscoping of AT&T

The largest corporate breakup in history was the involuntary divestiture by AT&T of its seven regional Bell companies. This set of divestitures was required by the federal government. However, since this large restructuring in 1984, AT&T has been growing and diversifying. During the term of current CEO Robert E. Allen, AT&T has made two very large acquisitions. In 1991, it paid $7.4 billion to take over NCR, largely against the wishes of NCR's top management. In 1994, AT&T paid $12.6 billion for McCaw Cellular Communications, Inc. The intent of these two acquisitions was to help AT&T meld itself into an enormous technology and communications power.

Unfortunately, these acquisitions and AT&T's other attempts to diversify into related areas have not produced the synergy and market power desired. As a result, its performance has suffered in recent years. Thus, in September 1995, AT&T announced that it was going to restructure into three separate independent companies. CEO Allen stated "we reached a time when the advantage of integration was outweighed by the disadvantage of complexity."

This is the largest voluntary breakup in U.S. corporate history. Of major importance to AT&T is the spin off its Global Information Solutions computer business, which is the loss-plagued legacy of the NCR acquisition. Its equipment business, Lucent Technologies, formerly known as Western Electric, will also be spun off into a separate company. The assets of Bell Labs will largely remain with the equipment business.

Clearly, the move by AT&T into the computer business and the acquisition of NCR to bolster this business have not succeeded. In fact, it is reported that AT&T has lost approximately $8 billion in this business since its inception. The takeover of NCR was hostile and opposed by NCR management. Thus, AT&T experienced considerable problems integrating the former AT&T computer business with that of NCR.

This breakup also allows AT&T management to avoid some of its internal conflict between the units (as opposed to cooperation and synergy). For example, increasing competition in the local and long-distance markets sometimes placed the services group in conflict with key customers of AT&T's equipment business. Within the last several years, one of AT&T's divisions had to back off of its aggressive competitive stances to allow the equipment business to close some big sales with competitors in the communications business. By separating these businesses into independent companies, this conflict should be largely avoided.

AT&T was also facing a rapidly changing external environment. One AT&T executive suggested that its industry was changing at the speed of light. As a result, many feel that AT&T will face severe competitive challenges during the next several years from the regional Bell companies and other telecommunications service providers. This competition is likely to be enhanced by the new U.S. legislation deregulating the telecommunications industries. AT&T executives felt the need to refocus on its core business and to ensure that it was "lean and mean" in preparation for the forthcoming competitive battles. A result of this restructuring into three independent companies was the elimination of approximately 40,000 jobs. In total, the changes may reduce AT&T's employment by 16 percent, to slightly more than 250,000.

Thus, AT&T's downscoping (refocusing on the firm's core business through spinoffs of two related but noncore businesses) is partially the result of poor strategic decisions in the past (e.g., acquisition of NCR) and a changing and highly competitive industry (e.g., deregulation and new competition). Some predict that the computer business may not survive, but expectations are that both of the other two companies will, with AT&T's core service business doing quite well with this new change. It should allow AT&T managers to focus their efforts on ensuring competitive goods and services for its market, and to increase its market power during the next several years.

Source: J. J. Keller, 1996, AT&T will eliminate 40,000 jobs and take a charge of $4 billion, *Wall Street Journal,* January 3, A3; E. Ramstad, 1996, AT&T to cut 40,000 jobs: Cost savings, breakup, new competition cited, *Houston Chronicle,*

January 3, B1, B2; C. Arnst, L. N. Spiro, and P. Burrows, 1995, Divide and conquer? *Business Week,* October 2, 56–57; J. J. Keller, 1995, High anxiety: AT&T breakup jolts managers, *Wall Street Journal,* November 21, B1, B10; J. J. Keller, 1995, Why AT&T takeover of NCR hasn't been a real bell ringer, *Wall Street Journal,* September 19, A1, A5; B. Kirkpatrick, 1995, AT&T has the plan: Is Mandl the man? *Fortune,* October 16, 84–90.

A s indicated in the opening case, AT&T has changed its corporate-level strategy. It had been following a strategy of related diversification with the hopes of achieving synergy among its various related businesses. Unfortunately, some of those businesses were not performing as well as intended (e.g., Global Information Solutions) and the top-level executives were unable to achieve the synergy expected among its major businesses of telecommunications services, electronic equipment, and computers.[1] In fact, rather than achieving synergy among the businesses, the outcomes sought and strategic actions of the businesses sometimes conflicted. For example, some of the largest competitors of AT&T in the telecommunications services industry were also customers of the network systems business that sold equipment to large telephone companies. Some of AT&T's competitors in the telecommunications services industry were concerned about buying equipment from an AT&T business because they were providing resources that might be used by AT&T to compete against them. Thus, at times AT&T's telecommunications service business had to change its strategic actions in order to help the equipment sales of the network systems business.[2]

Perhaps the major reason, however, for the change in AT&T's corporate-level strategy relates to its unproductive venture into the computer industry. In particular, AT&T's hostile acquisition of NCR did not produce the expected positive returns. AT&T's computer business was not performing well prior to the acquisition of NCR, and the attempted integration of NCR into this business did not produce a performance turnaround. Rather, significant problems arose during the integration of NCR with AT&T's computer business, which hampered performance of this division.[3] As a result, AT&T decided to create three independent businesses thereby refocusing top corporate executives on its telecommunications business. Many feel that AT&T's breakup spells trouble for its competitors. Rather than facing a confusing group of businesses, each of which has significant internal problems, they now must deal with a potentially highly focused and powerful competitor.[4] Thus, AT&T has reversed its prior strategy of product diversification, downscoped, and refocused on its core business.

In Chapters 4 and 5, our discussions focused on the selection and use of business-level strategies.[5] Our discussions of different business-level strategies (Chapter 4) and the competitive dynamics associated with their use (Chapter 5) were focused primarily on firms competing in a single industry or product market.

When a firm chooses to diversify its operations beyond a single industry and to operate businesses in several industries, it is pursuing a corporate-level strategy of diversification. A diversified company, then, has two levels of strategy: a business-level (or competitive) strategy and a corporate-level (or company-wide) strategy.[6] In diversified firms, each business unit chooses a business-level strategy to implement to achieve strategic competitiveness and earn above-average returns. But diversified firms must also choose a strategy that is concerned with the selection and management of its businesses. Defined formally, a **corporate-level strategy** is action taken to gain a competitive advantage through the

■ *A **corporate-level strategy** is action taken to gain a competitive advantage through the selection and management of a mix of businesses competing in several industries or product markets.*

selection and management of a mix of businesses competing in several industries or product markets. In essence, a corporate-level strategy is what makes "the corporate whole add up to more than the sum of its business unit parts."[7] Corporate-level strategy is concerned with two key questions: what businesses the firm should be in and how the corporate office should manage its group of businesses.[8] In the current complex global environment, top-level managers should view their firm's businesses as a portfolio of core competencies when seeking answers to these critical questions.[9]

Relating back to Figure 1.1 in Chapter 1, our focus herein is on the formulation of corporate-level strategy. The corporate-level strategy should evolve from the firm's strategic intent and mission. Also, as with business-level strategies, corporate-level strategies are expected to help the firm earn above-average returns (create value).[10] However, some have suggested that few corporate-level strategies actually create value.[11] In the final analysis, the value of a corporate-level strategy "must be that the businesses in the portfolio are worth more under the management of the company in question than they would be under any other ownership."[12] When managed effectively, then, corporate-level strategies enhance a firm's strategic competitiveness and contribute to its ability to earn above-average returns.[13] In the latter part of the 1990s and into the twenty-first century, corporate-level strategies will be managed in a global business environment characterized by high degrees of risk, complexity, uncertainty, and ambiguity.[14]

A primary approach to corporate-level strategy is diversification, which requires corporate-level executives to craft a multibusiness strategy. One reason for the use of a diversification strategy is that managers of diversified firms possess unique, general management skills that can be used to develop multibusiness strategies and enhance a firm's strategic competitiveness.[15] The prevailing theory of diversification suggests that firms should diversify when they have excess resources, capabilities, and core competencies that have multiple uses.[16] Multibusiness strategies often encompass many different industry environments, and, as discussed in Chapter 11, these strategies require unique organizational structures.

This chapter begins by addressing the history of diversification. Included in this discussion are descriptions of the advantages and disadvantages of single-business and dominant-business strategies. We next describe different levels of diversification (from low to high) and reasons firms pursue a corporate-level strategy of diversification. Two types of diversification strategy—related and unrelated—are then examined.

Large diversified firms often compete against each other in several markets. This is called *multipoint competition.* For instance, RJR Nabisco competes against Philip Morris in both cigarettes and consumer foods. Vertical integration strategies designed to exploit market share and gain power over competitors are also explored. To help understand strategic allocations of resources among a firm's portfolio of businesses, a technique for evaluating diversification strategies, the portfolio matrix, is discussed. We selected this particular matrix for analysis because it is the most widely known.

Of course, there are alternatives to diversification. These options entail long-term contracts, such as strategic alliances and franchising, discussed in Chapter 9, and expanding into new geographic markets such as international diversification, discussed in Chapter 8.

History of Diversification

In 1950, only 38.1 percent of the *Fortune* 500 U.S. industrial companies generated more than 25 percent of their revenues from diversified activities. By 1974, this figure had risen to 63 percent. In 1950, then, more than 60 percent of the largest *Fortune* 500 industrial companies were either single-business or dominant-business firms; by 1974, this had dropped to 37 percent.[17]

Beginning in the late 1970s, and especially through the middle part of the 1980s, a significant trend toward refocusing and divestiture of business units unrelated to core business activities took place in many firms. In fact, approximately 50 percent of the *Fortune* 500 companies refocused on their core businesses from 1981–1987.[18] As a result, by 1988, the percentage of single- or dominant-business firms on the *Fortune* 500 list of industrial companies had increased to 53 percent.[19] Although many diversified firms have become more focused, this is somewhat masked because extensive market and international diversification (compared to product diversification) has occurred that is not included in these statistics. As Chapter 8's discussion reveals, international strategy has been increasing in importance and has led to greater financial performance relative to product diversification.[20]

The trend toward product diversification of business organizations has been most significant among U.S. firms. Nonetheless, large business organizations in Europe, Asia, and other parts of the industrialized world have also implemented diversification strategies. In the United Kingdom, the number of single- or dominant-business firms fell from 60 percent in 1960 to 37 percent in 1980. A similar, yet less dramatic trend toward more diversification occurred in Japan. Among the largest Japanese firms, 60 percent were dominant- or single-business firms in 1958, although this percentage fell only to 53 percent in 1973.

These trends toward more diversification, which have been partially reversed due to restructuring (see Chapter 7),[21] indicate that learning has taken place regarding corporate diversification strategies. The main lesson learned is that firms performing well in their dominant business may not want to diversify. Moreover, firms that diversify should do so cautiously, choosing to focus on a relatively few, rather than many, businesses.[22] However, there are risks to limited diversification, as Iverson Technology discovered.

Iverson Technology Corporation was a small defense contractor that began to grow rapidly with the defense buildup in the 1980s. In fact, this firm was listed among the top growth companies in the United States during this time. Its peak annual sales revenue was $60 million. Unfortunately, with the move of the former Soviet Union and Eastern Europe to more democratic and less military governments, the large buildup in the U.S. defense industry came to an end. By 1994, annual sales at Iverson were below $1 million and its losses in recent years were greater than $30 million. Thus, the continued focus on defense industry equipment, particularly anti-eavesdropping equipment for government computers, was a problem for Iverson's survival. Currently, Iverson is attempting to diversify into the manufacture and marketing of athletic shoes with customized college and other types of logos. Only time will tell whether Iverson will be able to survive.[23]

Other companies not only survive but flourish by focusing on single or highly related businesses. Two prominent examples include Wal-Mart and Coca-Cola. In fact, the chief financial officer for the Coca-Cola Company, James Chestnut, explained that focusing on one business allowed the company to create greater efficiency. Another example of an effective focused firm is that of Mabuchi Motor, a midsize but highly successful Japanese firm. Ninety-nine percent of its annual revenues comes from the sale of motors. The focus on motors allows company scientists to continuously examine ways to improve the motors, such as making them lighter, quieter, more enduring, and cheaper.[24]

■ Levels of Diversification

Diversified firms vary according to the level of diversification and connection between and among their businesses. Figure 6.1 lists and defines five categories of businesses according to increasing levels of diversification. Besides single- and dominant-business categories, more fully diversified firms are classified into related and unrelated categories. A firm is related through its diversification when there are several links between business units. For example, units share products or services, technologies, and/or distribution channels. The more links among businesses, the more "constrained" the relatedness of diversification. Unrelatedness refers to a lack of direct links between businesses.

■ Low Levels of Diversification

A firm pursuing a low level of diversification focuses its efforts on a single or a dominant business. The Wm. Wrigley Jr. Co. is an example of a firm with little diversification. Its primary focus is on the chewing gum market.[25] A firm is

---

Figure 6.1

Levels and Types of Diversification

Source: Adapted from R. P. Rumelt, 1974, *Strategy, Structure and Economic Performance* (Boston: Harvard Business School).

Low Levels of Diversification

Single business:	More than 95% of revenues comes from a single business.	
Dominant business:	Between 70% and 95% of revenues comes from a single business.	

Moderate to High Levels of Diversification

Related constrained:	Less than 70% of revenues comes from the dominant business, and all businesses share product, technological, and distribution linkages.	
Related linked: (mixed related and unrelated)	Less than 70% of revenues comes from the dominant business, and there are only limited links between businesses.	

Very High Levels of Diversification

Unrelated:	Less than 70% of revenues comes from the dominant business, and there are no common links between businesses.	

classified as a single business when revenues generated by the dominant business are greater than 95 percent of the total sales.[26] Dominant businesses are firms that generate between 70 percent and 95 percent of their total sales within a single category. Because of the sales it generates from breakfast cereals, Kellogg is an example of a dominant business firm. Often dominant business firms have some level of vertical integration. Many firms (such as Texaco) started as single businesses and evolved to use a dominant-business strategy involving vertical integration.

■ Moderate and High Levels of Diversification

When a firm earns more than 30 percent of its sales volume outside a dominant business, and when its businesses are related to each other in some manner, the company is classified as a related-diversified firm. With more direct links between the businesses, the firm is defined as related constrained. Examples of related-constrained firms include Campbell Soup Co., Procter & Gamble, Xerox, and Merck & Co. If there are only a few links between businesses, the firm is defined as a mixed related and unrelated business, or a related-linked firm (see Figure 6.1). Johnson and Johnson, Westinghouse, General Electric, and Schlumberger are examples of related-linked firms. Related-constrained firms share a number of resources and activities between businesses. However, related-linked firms have less sharing of actual resources and assets and relatively more transfers of knowledge and competencies between businesses. Highly diversified firms, which have no relationships between businesses, are called unrelated-diversified firms. There are more unrelated-diversified firms in the United States than in other (e.g., European or Asian) countries although this could change in the future with continued restructuring throughout the world. Firms that have pursued unrelated diversification in past years include Tenneco, Textron, ITT, TRW, and Hanson PLC (a British firm).

Consistent with a global trend of refocusing, at least some firms pursuing a strategy of unrelated diversification are now concentrating on fewer lines of business. Hanson PLC, an unrelated diversified firm, has recently decided to streamline its operations. In so doing, it either sold off or spun off a number of its operating businesses and decided to separate the firm into four independent companies. For example, it spun off 34 operating companies into a new business named U.S. Industries, Inc. These changes allow Hanson to concentrate on its core holdings and to eliminate $1.4 billion of debt. Thus, Hanson PLC has taken an action similar to that of AT&T described in the opening case.[27]

The Time Warner acquisition of Turner Broadcasting is designed to create a highly related (related-constrained) entertainment giant. Many potential synergies are possible between these two businesses, but significant management attention will be required to achieve them. In particular, the two firms must be effectively integrated and the managers of the separate businesses must be encouraged strongly to cooperate and coordinate their efforts where feasible. This will not be an easy task for Time Warner CEO Gerald Levin because the firm has not been able to achieve the expected synergies in the merger between Time, Inc., and Warner Communications that created the current media giant, Time Warner. Likely, Mr. Levin was interested in acquiring Turner Broadcasting because of the potential economies of scope and the market power that could be achieved by integrating the two businesses (see the Strategic Focus).

STRATEGIC FOCUS

The Marriage of Time Warner and Turner Broadcasting: Will It Create Positive Synergy?

In 1995, Turner Broadcasting agreed to be acquired by Time Warner for approximately $8.5 billion to create a news and entertainment empire. Undoubtedly, a number of potential synergies can be gained from this new marriage. For example, Turner's Newline films can be distributed through Warner Bros. and Warner's new cartoons can be displayed on Turner's cartoon network. Also, reruns of Warner's programs such as *Lois and Clark,* can be played on TNT. Furthermore, the merger integrates some of the entertainment industry's prized assets. For example, it will reunite the Warner Bros. film library. In 1985, Turner Broadcasting acquired the rights to Warner Bros. films made prior to 1948. As a result, the acquisition looks like a marriage made in heaven.

However, there are potential problems in this new highly related (related-constrained) firm. For example, part of the reason for the new acquisition may have been the pressure felt by Gerald Levin, CEO of Time Warner, from his shareholders and board of directors. During the year prior to the acquisition, Mr. Levin was under increasing pressure from shareholders and the board to take actions that would improve the firm's stock price. Although the historic merger between Time, Inc., and Warner Communications in 1989 was intended to create an entertainment giant, there have been continued problems integrating those two major sets of assets to achieve the synergy and performance gains expected.

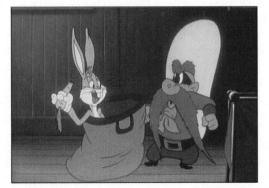

Even during the negotiations with Turner Broadcasting, problems were encountered. For example, John Malone, CEO of Telecommunications, Inc., a major cable firm, owned 21 percent of Turner Broadcasting's stock. Mr. Malone negotiated to obtain favorable terms in carrying Time Warner and Turner products on his firm's cable systems.

In addition to these concerns, Time Warner's debt level was high prior to the Turner Broadcasting and other recent acquisitions. After the acquisitions, it had a huge $19 billion debt. Furthermore, internal conflicts between managers prevented synergy between units and there was some concern that integrating Ted Turner into the management structure at Time Warner may be difficult.

Thus, although there seemed to be ample opportunities for synergy in this highly related strategic move, capturing that synergy may be difficult. Levin believes that restructuring the firm into three major units—entertainment, news and information, and telecommunications—will create the synergy that has eluded the current Time Warner businesses. He expects a different kind of teamwork to emerge in the restructured firm. Furthermore, Levin has reworked the executive pay incentives to encourage managers to not only help improve overall firm performance, but also to reward teamwork in addition to divisional performance. Thus, significant effort is necessary to help highly related firms achieve the synergies available among their multiple businesses.

Source: G. Fabrikant, 1995, A possible hitch is seen as talks on Turner slow, *New York Times,* September 6, B4, D6; M. Oneal, 1995, The unlikely mogul, *Business Week,* December 11, 86–96; M. Oneal, K. Rebello, and R. Grover, 1995, If Time-Warner divides itself, can it conquer? *Business Week,* February 20, 37; E. Shapiro and L. Landro, 1995, Frustrated investors ratchet up pressure on Time-Warner chief, *Wall Street Journal,* April 21, A1, A12; A. Sharpe and E. Shapiro, 1995, Time-Warner offers $8 billion in stock for Turner empire, *Wall Street Journal,* August 30, A1, A4.

■ Reasons for Diversification

Firms implement a diversification strategy as their corporate-level strategy for many reasons. A partial list of these is shown in Table 6.1. These reasons are discussed throughout the remainder of this chapter in relationship to specific diversification strategies.

Most firms implement a diversification strategy to enhance the strategic competitiveness of the entire company. When this is accomplished, the total value

Table 6.1   Motives, Incentives, and Resources for Diversification

Motives to Enhance Strategic Competitiveness
- Economies of scope (related diversification)
  - Sharing activities
  - Transferring core competencies
- Market power (related diversification)
  - Blocking competitors through multipoint competition
  - Vertical integration
- Financial economies (unrelated diversification)
  - Efficient internal capital allocation
  - Business restructuring

Incentives and Resources with Neutral Effects on Strategic Competitiveness
- Antitrust regulation
- Tax laws
- Low performance
- Uncertain future cash flows
- Firm risk reduction
- Tangible resources
- Intangible resources

Managerial Motives (Value Reduction)
- Diversifying managerial employment risk
- Increasing managerial compensation

of the firm is increased. Value is created through either related diversification or unrelated diversification when those strategies allow a company's business units to increase revenues and/or reduce costs while implementing their business-level strategies. Another reason for diversification is to gain market power relative to competitors, as suggested in the Time Warner and Turner Broadcasting merger.

Other reasons for implementing diversification may not enhance strategic competitiveness; in fact, diversification could have neutral effects or actually increase costs or reduce a firm's revenues. These reasons include diversification (1) to neutralize a competitor's market power (e.g., to neutralize the advantage of another firm by acquiring a distribution outlet similar to those of the competitors) or (2) to expand a firm's portfolio in order to reduce managerial employment risk (e.g., if a single business fails, a top-level manager remains employed in a diversified firm). Because diversification can increase firm size and thus managerial compensation, managers may have motives to diversify a firm. This type of diversification may reduce the firm's value.

- ***Economies of scope*** *are cost savings attributed to transferring the capabilities and competencies developed in one business to a new business without significant additional costs.*

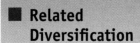

■ Related Diversification

Firms that have selected related diversification as their corporate-level strategy seek to exploit economies of scope between business units. Available to firms operating in multiple industries or product markets,[28] **economies of scope** are cost savings attributed to transferring the capabilities and competencies developed in one business to a new business without significant additional costs.

Firms seek to create value from economies of scope through two basic kinds of operational economies: sharing activities and transferring core competencies. The difference between sharing activities and transferring competencies is based on how separate resources are used jointly to create economies of scope. Tangible resources, such as plant and equipment or other business-unit physical assets, often must be shared to create economies of scope. Less tangible resources, such as sales forces, also can be shared. However, when know-how is transferred between separate activities and there is no physical or tangible resource involved, a core competence has been transferred as opposed to sharing activities.

■ Sharing Activities

Activity sharing is quite common, especially among related-constrained firms. At Procter & Gamble, a paper towels business and a baby diapers business both use paper products as a primary input to the manufacturing process. Having a joint paper production plant that produces inputs for both divisions is an example of a shared activity. In addition, these businesses are likely to share distribution sales networks because they both produce consumer products.

In Chapter 3, primary and support value chain activities were discussed. In general, primary activities, such as inbound logistics, operations, and outbound logistics, might have multiple shared activities. Through efficient sharing of these activities, firms may be able to create core competencies. In terms of inbound logistics, the business units may share common inventory delivery systems, warehousing facilities, and quality assurance practices. Operations might share common assembly facilities, quality control systems, or maintenance operations. With respect to outbound logistics, two business units might share a common sales force and sales service desk. Support activities could include the sharing of procurement and technology development efforts. For example, Otis Elevator has a number of different businesses, all of which are combined through the firm's electrical engine utilization technology. Today many large automobile firms use the standard platform around which many of their vehicles are designed, thus saving costs on engineering design.[29]

Although activity sharing may reduce costs through economies of scope, the savings must overcome other costs that are created by such sharing. Because separate business units are required to coordinate thoroughly their activities to achieve sharing, overcoming the costs of coordination can be formidable. Business-unit leaders may also have to compromise their separate business-unit strategies to accommodate the coordination of shared activities. This is often not a simple problem because in the United States, relative to other countries, division managers usually have an individualistic ethic. That is, individual business-unit managers seek to control their own strategic destiny. For example, Michael Fuchs, manager of Warner Music Group, Inc., was asked to resign by Gerald Levin, CEO of Time Warner, because of an inability to work cooperatively with Warner Bros., Inc., studio co-CEOs Robert Daily and Terry Semel. Under the new structure Levin created, Daily and Semel control both music and film and TV businesses.[30]

Sharing activities requires sharing business-unit strategic control. Moreover, one business-unit manager may feel that another business-unit manager is receiving more benefit from the activity sharing. Such a perception could create conflicts between division managers. Activity sharing is also risky because business-unit ties create links between outcomes. If demand for the product of one business is reduced, there may not be sufficient revenues to cover the fixed costs of running the joint plant. Shared activities create interrelationships that affect the ability of both businesses to achieve strategic competitiveness. Activity sharing may be ineffective if these costs are not taken into consideration.

The costs of activity sharing notwithstanding, research has shown that the sharing of activities and resources across businesses within a firm can increase the firm's value. For example, recent research examining acquisitions of firms in the same industry (referred to as horizontal acquisitions) such as in the banking industry, has found that sharing resources and activities (thereby creating economies of scope) contributed to postacquisition performance increases and higher returns to shareholders.[31] Additionally, research showed that firms selling off related units where resource sharing is a possible source of economies of scope produced lower returns than selling off businesses unrelated to the firm's core business.[32] Still other research found that firms with more related units had lower risk.[33] These results suggest that gaining economies of scope by sharing activities and resources across businesses within a firm may be important to reduce risk and gain positive returns from diversification efforts.

■ Transferring of Core Competencies

Over time, a strategically competitive firm's intangible resources, such as know-how, become the foundation for competitively valuable capabilities and core competencies. Marketing expertise is an example of a core competence that could

The marketing competence transferred from Philip Morris to Miller Brewing resulted in the introduction of improved marketing practices to the brewing industry.

be used this way. Because the expense of developing such a competence has already been incurred, and because competencies based on intangible resources are less visible and more difficult for competitors to understand and imitate, transferring these types of competencies from an original business unit to another one may reduce costs and enhance an entire firm's strategic competitiveness.[34] A key reason Philip Morris decided to acquire Miller Brewing Company was that it believed a competitive advantage could be achieved by transferring its marketing core competence to Miller.

As a cigarette company, Philip Morris developed a particular expertise in marketing. When Philip Morris purchased Miller Brewing, the beer industry had efficient operations. However, no firm in the industry had established marketing competence as a source of competitive advantage. The marketing competence transferred from Philip Morris to Miller resulted in the introduction of improved marketing practices to the brewing industry. These practices, especially in terms of advertising, proved to be the source of competitive advantage that allowed Miller Brewing to earn above-average returns for a period of time. In fact, several years passed before Anheuser-Busch, the largest firm in the brewing industry, developed the capabilities required to duplicate the benefits of Miller's strategy. A strong competitive response from Anheuser-Busch was predictable, however, in that beer is the firm's core business as discussed in a later Strategic Focus.

Some firms discover that they either are unable to transfer competencies or they transfer competencies that do not help a business unit establish a competitive advantage. One way managers facilitate the transfer of competencies is to move key people into new management positions. Philip Morris accomplished competence transfer to Miller Brewing in this way. However, a business-unit manager of an older division may be reluctant to transfer key people who have accumulated the knowledge and experience necessary to transfer the competencies. Thus, managers with the ability to facilitate the transfer of a core competence may come at a premium or may not want to transfer, and the top-level managers from the transferring division may not want them to be transferred to a new division to fulfill a diversification objective.

Some related-diversified firms use their core competencies to establish competitive advantages in markets that are new to them. For instance, AT&T sought to create a joint business in communications and computers because many office products will require their combined application in the future. To implement this part of its corporate-level diversification strategy, AT&T purchased NCR Corp. Furthermore, Bell Labs continued to provide shared research and development activities for all of AT&T's diverse communications and computer businesses. As noted in the opening case, however, AT&T was not successful in transferring competence across these businesses. As such, positive synergy was not created and the computer and communications businesses were separated.

■ Market Power

■ *Market power* exists when a firm is able to sell its products above the existing competitive level or reduce the costs of its primary and support activities below the competitive level, or both.

Related diversification can also be used to gain market power. **Market power** exists when a firm is able to sell its products above the existing competitive level or reduce the costs of its primary and support activities below the competitive level, or both.[35]

One approach to gaining market power through diversification is multipoint competition. *Multipoint competition* exists when two or more diversified firms compete in the same product areas or geographic markets.[36] For example, when Philip Morris moved into foods by buying General Foods and Kraft, RJR's competitive response was the acquisition of another foods company, Nabisco. The competitive rivalry between these two companies is an example of multipoint competition.

If these firms compete head to head in each market, multipoint competition will not create potential gains; instead, it will generate excessive competitive activity. However, over time, if these firms refrain from competition and in effect realize mutual forbearance, this may be classified as a form of related diversification that creates value for each firm through less competitive activity (see discussion in Chapter 5). *Mutual forbearance* is a relationship between two or more firms in which excessive competition leads to a situation where all firms in the competitive set see that such competition is self-destructive and, without formal agreement, cease the self-destructive competitive actions and responses.

Walt Disney and Time Warner operate in similar businesses—theme parks, movie and television production, and broadcasting activities. Disney has spent considerable amounts of money advertising its theme parks in Time Warner magazines. Time Warner, however, began an aggressive advertising campaign aimed at taking Disney's theme park customers. Disney retaliated by canceling its advertising in Time Warner's publications. Time Warner responded by canceling corporate meetings in Florida at a Disney resort. Disney responded by canceling Time Warner advertisements of its theme parks on a Los Angeles television station owned by Disney.[37] This illustrates the potential negative side of multipoint competition. Disney's actions represent a counterattack mode, argued to be a prominent strategic action when multipoint competition exists.[38] However, counterattacks are not common where multipoint competition exists because the threat of a counterattack may prevent strategic actions from being taken or, more likely, firms may retract their strategic actions with the threat of counterattack.[39]

Another approach to creating value by gaining market power is the strategy of vertical integration. **Vertical integration** exists when a company is producing its own inputs (backward integration) or owns its own source of distribution of outputs (forward integration). It is also possible to have partial vertical integration where some inputs and outputs are sold by company units, while other inputs and outputs are produced or sold by outside firms.

A company pursuing vertical integration is usually motivated to strengthen its position in its core business by gaining market power over competitors. This is done through savings on operations costs, avoidance of market costs, better control to establish quality, and, possibly, protection of technology. The Time Warner diversification move of acquiring Turner Broadcasting Company represents an attempt to increase market power, partially by vertical integration. As described in the Strategic Focus, businesses within each of the major companies will act as suppliers and distributors to each other. For example, Warner Communications will help distribute some of Turner's classic movies. Alternatively, Warner cartoons will be shown on the Turner cartoon network.

Vertical integration can also enable a company to protect product quality. The opening of McDonald's first restaurant in Moscow provides a good example. To protect product quality, McDonald's vertically integrated backward. This strategy allowed the company to prepare its products in the same way it does in locations throughout the world. Ownership of its input and output sources protects the firm's core technology from information diffusion to other competitors through buyer and supplier sources. Vertical integration therefore is a way to protect core technology from imitation.

Of course, there are limits to vertical integration. For example, an outside supplier may produce the product at a lower cost. As a result, internal transactions from vertical integration may be expensive and reduce profitability. Also, bureaucratic costs are incurred when implementing this strategy. Because it can require that substantial sums of capital be invested in specific technologies, vertical integration may be problematic when technology changes quickly. Changes in demand also create capacity balance and coordination problems. If one division is building a part, but realization of state-of-the-art economies of scale requires the division to build it at a scale beyond the capacity of the internal buyer to absorb demand, this would compel sales outside the company. However, if demand slackens, an overcapacity would result, because the internal users cannot absorb total demand. This problem led General Motors to make many unnecessary expansions and contractions in employment.

Japanese firms, instead, have developed a network of suppliers. Often Japanese firms have more than one supplier for each part.[40] Alternatively, care must be taken in outsourcing key activities to external suppliers and partners. Overdependence on external suppliers and partners can weaken a firm and make

■ *Vertical integration* exists when a company is producing its own inputs (backward integration) or owns its own source of distribution of outputs (forward integration).

In the early 1990s, Walt Disney and Time Warner operated in a counterattack mode. This mode is a frequently used strategic action when multipoint competition exists.

it vulnerable to future competitive attacks.[41] For example, strategic alliances may end and a firm may not have the internal capabilities to continue in the market without the partner. These concerns are explored further in Chapter 9. Thus, firms must carefully balance the need for control over key activities with the efficiency of having them completed by external parties. In summary, although vertical integration can create value and contribute to strategic competitiveness, especially in gaining market power over competitors, it is not without risks and costs.

■ Unrelated Diversification

■ *Financial economies* *are cost savings* *realized through improved allocations of* *financial resources based on investments* *inside or outside the firm.*

An unrelated diversification strategy can create value through two types of financial economies. **Financial economies** are cost savings realized through improved allocations of financial resources based on investments inside or outside the firm.[42]

The first type of financial economy involves efficient internal capital allocations. This type also seeks to reduce risks among the firm's business units. This can be achieved, for example, through development of a portfolio of businesses with different risk profiles, thereby reducing business risk for the total corporation. A second approach of financial economies is concerned with purchasing other corporations and restructuring their assets. This approach allows a firm to buy and sell businesses in the external market with the intent of increasing its total value.

■ Efficient Internal Capital Market Allocation

Capital allocation is usually distributed efficiently in a market economy by capital markets. Efficient distribution of capital is induced because investors seek to purchase shares of firm equity (ownership) that have high future cash-flow values. Capital is allocated not only through equity, but also through debt, where shareholders and debtholders seek to improve the value of their investment by investing in businesses with high growth prospects. In large diversified firms, however, the corporate office distributes capital to divisions to create value for the overall company. Such an approach may provide potential gains from internal capital market allocation, relative to the external capital market.[43] The corporate office, through managing a particular set of businesses, may have access to more detailed and accurate information as well as actual business and performance prospects.

Compared to corporate office personnel, investors would have relatively limited access to internal information and can only estimate actual divisional performance and future business prospects. Although businesses seeking capital must provide information to capital providers (e.g., banks, insurance firms), firms with internal capital markets may have at least two informational advantages. First, information provided to capital markets through annual reports and other sources may not include negative information, but rather only positive prospects and outcomes. External sources of capital have limited ability to know *specifically* what is taking place inside large organizations. Although owners have access to information, they have no guarantee of full and complete disclosure.[44]

Second, although a firm must disseminate information, this information becomes available to potential competitors simultaneously. With insights gained by studying this information, competitors might attempt to duplicate a firm's competitive advantage. Without having to reveal internal information, a firm may protect its competitive advantage through an internal capital market.

If intervention from outside the firm is required to make corrections, only significant changes are possible, such as forcing the firm into bankruptcy or changing the dominant leadership coalition (e.g., the top-management team described in Chapter 12). Alternatively, in an internal capital market, the corporate office may choose to adjust managerial incentives or suggest strategic changes in the division to make fine-tuned corrections. Thus, capital allocation can be adjusted according to more specific criteria than is possible with external market allocation. The external capital market may fail to allocate resources adequately to high-potential investments, compared to corporate office investments, because it has less accurate information. The head office of a diversified company can more effectively perform such tasks as disciplining underperforming management teams and allocating resources.[45]

Some firms are more effective at allocating these financial resources to unrelated businesses than others. For example, industry observers, stock market analysts, and critics are concerned about the Seagram Company's acquisition of entertainment giant MCA, Inc., from Matsushita Electric Industrial Company. Seagram's core business focuses on the beverage market, specifically, alcoholic beverages. In recent times, Seagram's acquired a partially related business, Tropicana Beverages, that markets fruit juices and fruit-flavored drinks. Unfortunately, its product line extensions into fruit-flavored drinks were not successful and Tropicana has performed poorly. Furthermore, Seagram's foray into the unrelated entertainment business is not being perceived positively by external analysts. While Seagram executives evaluated other acquisitions in the food industry, it decided to buy into an unrelated industry. Beverage industry analysts argue that the beverage and entertainment industries move at different speeds and are concerned that Seagram's management will be absorbed in managing the movie and record business. Furthermore, Seagram's core business has recently undergone a major change in management, thereby creating some chaos in that business as well. Thus, its stock has not performed well. Only time will tell whether Seagram will be able to more effectively allocate resources and manage these diverse, unrelated businesses to improve overall corporate performance.[46]

A firm can also reduce its overall risk by allocating resources among a set of diversified businesses. However, such risk reduction strategies may not be valuable to all firms' stakeholders. Shareholders and debtholders have lower cost ways of reducing their risk through diversification of their own investment portfolios. Successful implementation of an unrelated diversification strategy requires that a firm incur fewer costs to reduce an individual investor's risks as compared to the costs that investor would experience to diversify his or her own portfolio.[47]

The Dover Corporation and MacAndrews & Forbes Holdings, Inc., discussed in the Strategic Focus, exemplify the unrelated conglomerate firm. In both cases, these firms rely largely, or at least partially, on efficient allocation of financial resources across businesses within the firm. Efficient allocation of financial resources is clearly the value-added contribution made by the corporate office of the Dover Corporation. Although allocation of financial resources is important in MacAndrews & Forbes, the CEO also is actively involved in the operations of many of the businesses. Thus, there may be other value-producing activities at MacAndrews & Forbes. Still, the primary function of the corporate office at

STRATEGIC FOCUS

Different Methods for Successfully Managing Unrelated Businesses

Two companies, the Dover Corporation and MacAndrews & Forbes Holdings, Inc., represent the traditional unrelated conglomerate. Both are successful firms that are managed in quite different ways. The Dover Corporation has 54 different companies operating in more than 70 diverse business markets, including elevators, garbage trucks, valves, and welding torches. Alternatively, MacAndrews & Forbes has 60,000 employees working in such companies as Revlon, Marvel Comics, Coleman Camping Equipment, New World Communications (television and production company), and Consolidated Cigar. These are multibillion dollar companies that also have produced excellent returns.

The Dover Corporation attempts to acquire companies that are small but highly successful, operating in specific market niches where they do not have major competitors. Oftentimes, these companies have a share of the market in their niches that is between 30 and 50+ percent. They not only dominate their markets but maintain high profit margins as well. For example, Dover regularly achieves a return on equity between 15 and 20 percent.

Dover also provides maximum autonomy to the managers of its separate businesses. It encourages the heads of these businesses to manage them as if they were owners, and to be aggressive and opportunistic. Dover's CEO, Thomas Reece, notes that all but 45 of the more than 22,000 employees of Dover companies are engaged in activities directly related to manufacturing and marketing the products. Dover has a very small corporate staff. As such, Dover corporate management does not attempt to achieve synergies among its various businesses. Thus, the goal of Dover top management is to achieve financial synergy, allocating resources to the appropriate businesses where they will achieve the highest returns on their investment.

In contrast to Dover, Ronald Perelman, CEO and owner of MacAndrews & Forbes Holdings, Inc., is a hands-on manager. In fact, he and others would argue that the businesses owned by MacAndrews & Forbes are flourishing at least in part because Perelman spends a lot of time overseeing their operations. For example, he is credited with a turnaround of the Revlon Company, changing its market focus from major department stores to mass marketing. Perelman often invites the executives of the MacAndrews & Forbes companies to the corporate offices for breakfast when they are in New York and he receives daily or weekly information on each company, getting heavily involved in the operational details.

While this may seem difficult, he also attempts to hire managers of these businesses that have a good operational knowledge of the industry. For example, he hired former NBC executive Fran Tartikoff and a producer of action TV shows, Steven J. Cannell, to oversee New World Communications and produce hit shows for the networks and syndication.

Perelman also has developed an effective structure that yields tax, financial, and other management benefits. For example, when Perelman bought First Gibraltar Savings and Loan, he got a $5.1 billion grant-in-aid from the U.S. government and approximately $900 million in tax breaks, which have been used to offset the earnings of other MacAndrews & Forbes companies thereby reducing its tax costs. While First Gibraltar has been sold (but MacAndrews & Forbes maintained the tax breaks), it also bought First Nationwide Bank from the Ford Motor Company. Perelman installed Gerald Ford, the former CEO of Gibraltar, as head of the First Nationwide Bank business.

Overall, Perelman limits his holding company debt to 20 percent of the equity value of all of his businesses. Because his companies grow at approximately 20 percent annually, he estimates his debt costs are only about 10 percent. While Perelman's approach to managing an unrelated conglomerate is unconventional and quite different from the more typical approach used by the Dover Corporation, it is nonetheless successful and has helped Perelman amass a $5 billion empire.

Source: L. N. Spiro and R. Grover, 1995, The operator: An inside look at Ron Perelman's $5 billion empire, *Business Week*, August 21, 54–60; P. L. Zweig, 1995, Who says the conglomerate is dead? *Business Week*, January 23, 92–93; G. Steinmetz and R. T. King, Jr., 1994, Perelman wins bidding for Ford's struggling thrift, *Wall Street Journal*, April 15, B4; J. Mendes, 1992, Motivate and get out of the way, *Fortune*, December 14, 94–98.

MacAndrews & Forbes is one of efficiently allocating and managing the financial resources of the firm. Therefore, in both cases, financial economies are critical to earning above-average returns.

■ Restructuring

Another alternative, similar to the internal capital market approach, focuses exclusively on buying and selling other firm assets in the external market. It is similar to the real estate business, where profits are earned by buying assets low, restructuring them, and selling them as high as possible. The restructuring approach usually entails buying the firm, selling off assets such as corporate headquarters, and terminating corporate staff members.

Selling underperforming divisions and placing the remaining divisions under the discipline of rigorous financial controls are other often used restructuring actions. Rigorous controls require divisions to follow strict budgets and account regularly for cash inflows and outflows to corporate headquarters. A firm pursuing this approach may have to use hostile takeovers or tender offers. Hostile takeovers have the potential to increase the resistance of the target firm's top-level managers. In these cases, corporate-level managers often are dismissed, while division managers are retained.

Implementing an unrelated diversification strategy requires an understanding of significant trade-offs. First, success usually requires a focus on mature, low-technology businesses. Otherwise, resource allocation decisions become too complex because the uncertainty of demand for high-technology products requires information-processing capacities beyond the smaller corporate staffs of unrelated-restructuring firms. Service businesses are also difficult to buy and sell in this way because of their client or sales orientation. Sales staffs of service businesses are more mobile than those of manufacturing-oriented businesses and may seek jobs with a competitor, taking their clients with them. This is true in professional service businesses such as accounting, law, advertising and investment banking. As such, these businesses probably would not create value if acquired by an unrelated-restructuring firm.

■ Diversification: Incentives and Resources

The economic reasons given in the last section summarize the conditions under which diversification strategies increase a firm's value. However, diversification is often undertaken with the expectation that doing so will prevent a firm from reducing its value. Thus, there are reasons to diversify that are value neutral. As we explain next, several incentives may lead a firm to pursue further diversification.[48]

■ Incentives to Diversify

Incentives provide reasons to diversify; they come from both the external environment and a firm's internal environment. The term *incentive* implies that managers have some choice whether to pursue the incentive or not. Incentives external to the firm include antitrust regulation and tax laws. Internal firm incentives include low performance, uncertain future cash flows, and overall firm risk reduction.

Antitrust Regulation and Tax Laws

Government antitrust policies and tax laws provided incentives for U.S. firms to diversify in the 1960s and 1970s. Applications of antitrust laws regarding mergers that create increased market power (vertical and horizontal integration) were stringent in the 1960s and 1970s.[49] As a result, many of the mergers during this time were unrelated—that is, they involved companies pursuing different lines of business. Thus, the merger wave of the 1960s was "conglomerate" in character. Merger activity leading to conglomerate diversification was encouraged primarily by the Celler-Kefauver Act (which discouraged horizontal and vertical mergers). For example, in the 1973–1977 period, 79.1 percent of all mergers were conglomerate.[50]

The mergers of the 1980s, however, were different. Antitrust enforcement ebbed, permitting more and larger horizontal mergers (acquisition of the same line of business, such as a merger between two oil firms).[51] In addition, investment bankers became more freewheeling in the kinds of mergers they would try to facilitate; as a consequence, hostile takeovers increased to unprecedented numbers.[52] The conglomerates or highly diversified firms of the 1960s and 1970s became more "focused" in the 1980s and 1990s as merger constraints were relaxed and restructuring implemented.[53]

Tax effects on diversification stem not only from individual tax rates, but also from corporate tax changes. Some companies (especially mature companies) may have activities that generate more cash than they can reinvest profitably. Michael Jensen (a prominent financial economist) believes that such *free cash flows* (liquid financial assets for which investments in current businesses are no longer economically viable) should be redistributed to shareholders in the form of dividends.[54] However, in the 1960s and 1970s, dividends were taxed more heavily than ordinary personal income. As a result, in the pre-1980s, shareholders preferred that companies retain these funds for use in buying and building companies in high-performance industries. If the stock value appreciated over the long term, shareholders might receive a better return for these funds than through dividends because they would be taxed more lightly under capital gains rules.

In 1986, however, the top ordinary individual income tax rate was reduced from 50 percent to 28 percent, and the special capital gains tax was changed, causing capital gains to be treated as ordinary income. These changes suggested that shareholders would no longer encourage firms to retain funds for purposes of diversification. Moreover, the elimination of personal interest deductions, as well as the lower attractiveness of retained earnings to shareholders, has prompted the use of more leverage by firms (interest expense is tax deductible for firms). These tax law changes also influenced an increase in divestitures of unrelated business units after 1984. Thus, individual tax rates for capital gains and dividends may have created a shareholder incentive for increased diversification before 1986, but an incentive for reduced diversification after 1986, unless funded by debt (which is tax deductible).

Regarding corporate taxation, acquisitions typically increase a firm's depreciable asset allowances. Increased depreciation (non–cash-flow expense) produces lower taxable income, thereby providing additional incentive for acquisitions. Before 1986, acquisitions may have been the most attractive means for securing tax benefits.[55] The tax incentives are particularly important because acquisitions represent the primary means of firm diversification. However, the

1986 Tax Reform Act reduced some of the corporate tax advantages of diversification.[56] Over the years, then, government policy has provided incentives for both increased and reduced levels of diversification. In addition to these external incentives, there are incentives internal to the firm that increase the likelihood that diversification will be pursued.

Low Performance

It has been proposed that "high performance eliminates the need for greater diversification,"[57] as in the example of the Wm. Wrigley Jr. Co. Conversely, low performance may provide an incentive for diversification. Often firms plagued by poor performance seek to take higher risks.[58] Interestingly, though, some researchers have found that low returns are related to greater levels of diversification.[59] Poor performance may lead to increased diversification, especially if resources exist to pursue additional diversification. Continued poor returns following additional diversification, however, may slow the pace of diversification and even lead to divestitures. Thus, an overall curvilinear relationship, as illustrated in Figure 6.2, may exist between diversification and performance.

Germany's Daimler-Benz provides an example of poor performance fueled by diversification. Under its former CEO, Edzard Reuter, Daimler-Benz diversified to become a manufacturer of jets, helicopters, trains, and electronics in addition to its core automotive and truck businesses. Unfortunately, these diversification efforts produced net losses over time. In 1993 and in 1995, Daimler-Benz had substantial net losses, largely attributed to the new businesses added in previous years. Its core business, Mercedes-Benz Automotive and Truck Division, continued to be profitable during this time period. The CEO following Reuter, Juergen Schrempp, has been placed under increasing pressure to reverse the diversification strategy begun by Reuter. He is expected to reduce significantly the size of the Daimler-Benz aerospace business and close the Daimler-Benz Industrie business by selling off parts and transferring selected operations to other divisions. These actions are critical to stem the severe losses experienced in 1995.[60]

Figure 6.2

The Curvilinear Relationship Between Diversification and Performance

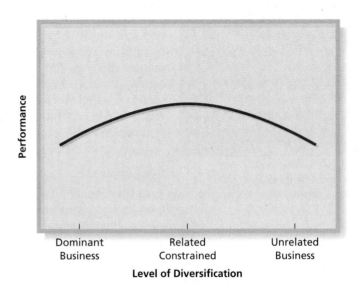

In contrast to Daimler-Benz, Anheuser-Busch companies, (see Strategic Focus) achieved an overall positive net return. However, a number of its diversified businesses were producing net losses or only marginal returns. Unfortunately, Daimler-Benz's diversification efforts produced net losses for the corporation, whereas Anheuser-Busch's earned positive returns overall (due largely to the performance of its core business). In both cases, however, the corporations decided to divest or downsize the problem businesses and to refocus on their profitable core businesses (see Chapter 7 for more discussion of restructuring.)

Uncertain Future Cash Flows

As a firm's product line matures and/or is threatened, diversification may be perceived as an important defensive strategy. Firms in mature or maturing industries sometimes find it necessary to diversify to survive over the long term.[61] Certainly, this has been one of the dominant reasons for diversification among railroad firms during the 1960s and 1970s. Railroads diversified primarily because the trucking industry was perceived to have significant negative effects on the demand for rail transportation. However, uncertainty can be derived from both supply and demand sources.

Diversification because of uncertainty also pertains to firms in industries where foreign competitors with lower average costs have penetrated domestic markets. The diversification in the steel industry in the 1970s exemplifies this type of supply-side uncertainty as an incentive. To reduce its dependence on steel, U.S. Steel bought Marathon Oil and Texas Oil and Gas. This competitive action was taken because international integrated steel makers (such as Nippon Steel) were able to produce steel at a lower cost due to lower labor costs and newer, more efficient production facilities. After these acquisitions, U.S. Steel was renamed USX to signal that it was more than a steel manufacturer.

The U.S. defense industry has significantly downsized in recent years and many of the firms in this industry have diversified in order to survive. Major defense industry diversification is exemplified by firms such as General Dynamics and Grumman. In fact, General Dynamics diversified into businesses in other industries and sold all of its defense industry businesses. Earlier, we described how Iverson Technology was trying to survive by diversifying into athletic shoes because demand for its anti-eavesdropping equipment had dissolved. Thus, demand uncertainties about expected future cash flows affected defense firm diversification strategies.[62] Although diversification may increase shareholder wealth in selected instances, the evidence indicates generally that it can reduce the uncertainty of future cash flows, but often at the expense of profitability.

Demand uncertainties about expected future cash flows have affected defense firms' diversification strategies.

■ **Synergy** exists when the value created by business units working together exceeds the value those same units create when working independently.

Firm Risk Reduction

Because diversified firms pursuing economies of scope often have investments that are too inflexible to realize synergy between business units, several potential problems exist. **Synergy** exists when the value created by business units working together exceeds the value those same units create when working independently. For example, as a firm increases its relatedness between business units, it increases its risk of corporate failure because synergy produces joint interdepen-

STRATEGIC FOCUS

The Extinction of Cardinals and Eagle

Anheuser-Busch Companies is a powerful manufacturer and marketer in the U.S. beer industry. In fact, the firm controls approximately 45 percent of this market. Additionally, Anheuser-Busch is profitable, but primarily because of the dominant brewery business. A number of years ago, it began a diversification effort that started with the acquisition of the St. Louis Cardinals baseball team. Later, it started the Eagle snacks business and acquired Campbell Taggart. These businesses were related and many thought they should be a great success operating under the Anheuser-Busch umbrella. Baseball, beer, and snack foods are often highly linked in the mind of the consumer. Furthermore, Anheuser-Busch's knowledge of yeast from its brewing operations could be applied in the Campbell Taggart bakery business as well. As a result, there seemed to be strong potential synergies among these diversified businesses.

However, in 1995, Anheuser-Busch announced that it was putting the St. Louis Cardinals and the Eagle snacks business up for sale and spinning off the Campbell Taggart bakery business. In so doing, Anheuser-Busch would be downscoping and refocusing top management efforts on its brewery business. Anheuser-Busch was never able to parlay the strong potential relationships into synergy between the related businesses. As a result, the Eagle snacks business continued to lose money, the St. Louis Cardinals experienced net losses in recent times, and the Campbell Taggart bakery business achieved only minor net profits. These businesses were draining much of the Anheuser-Busch executives' time and effort and producing few, if any, returns. Thus, poor performance of the diversified businesses has led to their divestiture.

In 1996, Anheuser-Busch announced that it was going to close the Eagle snacks business. It was unable to find a buyer who would pay an appropriate price for the assets. Anheuser-Busch was unwilling to continue the operation of the business even though it could not sell the assets. The Eagle snacks business had been able to build only a 6.5 percent market share in 16 years of operation. This compares to the Frito-Lay market share of approximately 50 percent in 1995. Unfortunately, Anheuser-Busch was unable to overcome logistical problems in the distribution differences between beer and snack foods. The same problem existed with the Campbell Taggart products. To build appropriate market share and deal with the problems of these businesses required a substantial capital investment. Conversely, Anheuser-Busch has identified major opportunities for expansion of its beer market internationally. Thus, top executives would prefer to use the capital investments to expand Anheuser-Busch brewery operations internationally rather than to invest in the ongoing operations of the food businesses. This is a logical decision because the brewery business is producing significant positive returns and there are substantial opportunities in international markets. In fact, the sales and earnings from its current small base of international sales have continued to grow at approximately 20 percent annually. Thus, Anheuser-Busch executives have concluded that its product diversification efforts have been unsuccessful.

Source: R. A. Melchor and G. Burns, 1996, How Eagle became extinct, *Business Week,* March 4, 68–69; R. Gibson, 1995, Anheuser-Busch will sell snacks unit, Cardinals and the club's home stadium, *Wall Street Journal,* October 26, A3, A5; M. Quint, 1995, Cardinals and snack unit are put on block by Busch, *New York Times,* October 26, D2.

dence between business units and the firm's flexibility of response is constrained. This threat may force two basic decisions.

First, the firm may reduce the level of technological change by operating in more certain environments. This may make the firm risk averse and, thus, uninterested in pursuing new product lines that have potential, but are not proven. Alternatively, the firm may constrain the level of activity sharing and forego the benefits of synergy. Either or both decisions may lead to further diversification. The former would lead to related diversification into industries where more certainty exists. The latter result may produce further, but unrelated, diversification.[63]

◼ Resources and Diversification

Although incentives to diversify may exist, a firm must possess the resources required to make diversification economically feasible. As mentioned earlier, tangible, intangible, and financial resources may facilitate diversification. Resources vary in their utility for value creation, however, because of differences in rarity and mobility; that is, some resources are easier for competitors to duplicate because they are not rare, valuable, costly to imitate, and nonsubstitutable. For instance, free cash flows may be used to diversify the firm. Because financial resources such as free cash flows are more flexible and common, they are less likely to create value as compared to other types of resources.[64] The diversification mentioned earlier for steel firms was facilitated significantly by the presence of free cash flows. This is also likely true of the diversification efforts by Anheuser-Busch. Anheuser-Busch was a very profitable company and significant cash flows were created from the success of the brewery business. These resources were then used to purchase the St. Louis Cardinals, to invest almost $400 million in the development and operation of the Eagle snack food business, and to acquire the Campbell Taggart bakery business. However, the use of these resources did not produce significant positive returns for Anheuser-Busch.

Tangible firm resources usually include the plant and equipment necessary to produce a product. Such assets may be less flexible. Any excess capacity of these resources (plant and equipment) often can be used only for very closely related products, especially those requiring highly similar manufacturing technologies. Excess capacity of other tangible resources, such as a sales force, can be used to diversify more easily. Again, excess capacity in a sales force would be more effective with related diversification because it may be utilized to sell similar products. The sales force would be more knowledgeable about related product characteristics, customers, and distribution channels. Tangible resources may create resource interrelationships in production, marketing, procurement, and technology, defined earlier as activity sharing. The intent of Time Warner is to use intangible resources to create synergy between its businesses and those of Turner Broadcasting. Clearly, the distribution of each firm's separate products can be facilitated by some of the other firm's businesses, as described earlier. As noted previously, these synergies are not necessarily easy to achieve, even with tangible resources available. There were fewer tangible resources available for synergy among the diversified businesses within Anheuser-Busch than within the merged firm of Time Warner and Turner Broadcasting.

Intangible resources would, of course, be more flexible than actual tangible physical assets in facilitating diversification. Although the sharing of tangible resources may induce diversification, intangible resources could encourage even more diversification. Clearly, there were some potential intangible resource synergies that could be achieved by Anheuser-Busch. For example, Anheuser-Busch's knowledge of yeast products may have been useful in the use of yeast within Campbell Taggart. However, this did not produce significant positive synergies between the brewery and bakery businesses as hoped by Anheuser-Busch executives. Apparently, there was little sharing of tangible or intangible resources, thus no value was created.

■ Extent of Diversification

If a firm has incentives and resources to diversify, the extent of diversification will be greater than if it just has incentives or resources alone.[65] The more flexible, the more likely the resources will be used for unrelated diversification; the less flexible, the more likely the resources will be used for related diversification. Thus, flexible resources (e.g., free cash flow) are likely to lead to relatively greater levels of diversification. Also, because related diversification requires more information processing to manage links between businesses, more unrelated units can be managed by a small corporate office.[66]

■ Managerial Motives to Diversify

Managerial motives for diversification may exist independent of incentives and resources. These motives include managerial risk reduction and a desire for increased compensation.[67] For instance, diversification may reduce top-level managers' *employment risk* (risk of job loss or income reduction). That is, corporate executives may diversify a firm in order to diversify their employment risk, as long as profitability does not suffer excessively.[68] Diversification also provides an additional benefit to managers that shareholders do not enjoy. Diversification and firm size are highly correlated and, as size increases, so does executive compensation.[69] Large firms are more complex and harder to manage and, thus, managers of larger firms are compensated more highly.[70] As a result, diversification provides an avenue for increased compensation and therefore may serve as a motive for managers to engage in greater diversification. Governance mechanisms, such as the board of directors, ownership monitoring, executive compensation, and the market for corporate control may limit managerial tendencies to overdiversify. These governance mechanisms are discussed in more detail in Chapter 10.

Governance mechanisms may not be strong and, in some instances, managers may diversify the firm to the point that it fails to earn even average returns.[71] Resources employed to pursue such diversification are most likely to include financial assets (e.g., free cash flows), but may also involve intangible assets. Thus, this type of diversification is not likely to lead to improved performance. The loss of adequate internal governance may result in poor relative performance, thereby triggering a threat of takeover. Although external controls, such as the threat of takeover, may create improved efficiency by replacing ineffective managerial teams, managers may avoid takeovers through defensive tactics (golden parachutes, poison pills, etc.). Therefore, an external governance threat, although having a restraining influence on managers, does not provide flawless control of managerial motives for diversification.[72]

Most of the large, publicly held firms are profitable because managers are positive agents and many of their strategic actions (e.g., diversification moves) contribute to this success. As mentioned, governance devices are designed to deal with exceptions to the norms of achieving strategic competitiveness and increasing shareholder wealth in the process. It is overly pessimistic to assume that managers will usually act in their own self-interest as opposed to their firm's interest.[73]

Managers may also be held in check by concerns for their reputation in the labor market. If reputation facilitates power, a poor reputation may also reduce power. Likewise, a market for managerial talent may constrain managerial abuse of power to pursue inappropriate diversification.[74] In addition, some diversified firms also provide policing of other diversified firms. These large, highly diversified firms seek out poorly managed diversified firms for acquisition to restructure the target firm's asset base. Knowing that their firms could be acquired if not managed successfully, managers are encouraged to find ways to achieve strategic competitiveness.

In summary, although managers may be motivated to increase diversification, governance mechanisms are in place to discourage such action merely for managerial gain. However, this governance is imperfect and may not always produce the intended consequences. Even when governance mechanisms cause managers to correct a problem of overdiversification, these moves are not without trade-offs. For instance, spinoff firms may not realize productivity gains, although it is in the best interest of the divesting firm.[75] As such, the assumption that managers need disciplining may not be entirely correct, and sometimes governance may create consequences that are worse than those resulting from overdiversification.[76] Therefore, the diversification level of firms must be based on optimal levels indicated by market and strategic characteristics (resources) peculiar to each firm. Optimality may be judged by the factors discussed in this chapter: resources, incentives, and managerial motives.

Because there are many incentives to diversify, a number of firms have diversified too much. AT&T and Anheuser-Busch were not highly diversified. In both cases, their diversification would be classified as related constrained and there were opportunities for synergies among the businesses. However, neither of these corporations was able to achieve the appropriate synergies to offset the costs of diversification. In both cases, these firms were overdiversified. Firms are overdiversified when the operation of diversified businesses reduces rather than improves overall firm returns. Thus, the diversification was not manageable for the top executives in these firms. Some have argued that firms should stay focused on their core business. Any diversification efforts that detract from this emphasis may be problematic.[77]

Some have argued that a dominant logic develops over time within a firm. As such, managers steeped in this dominant logic find it difficult to manage businesses that do not fit well with such logic.[78] This may have been the case with both AT&T and Anheuser-Busch. For example, the management of the computer business may not have fit well with the dominant logic developed in AT&T to manage its core telecommunications business. Similarly, the management of a baseball team or firms operating in the food industry may not have fit well with the dominant logic developed in the management of Anheuser-Busch's brewery business. Thus, firms do not have to be highly diversified into unrelated businesses to be overdiversified.

As shown in Figure 6.3, diversification level is based partly on how the interaction of resources and incentives affects the adoption of particular diversification strategies. As indicated earlier, the greater the incentives and the more flexible the resources, the higher the level of expected diversification. Financial

Figure 6.3

Summary Model of the Relationship Between Firm Performance and Diversification

Source: R. E. Hoskisson and M.A. Hitt, 1990, Antecedents and performance outcomes of diversification: A review and critique of theoretical perspectives, *Journal of Management* 16: 498.

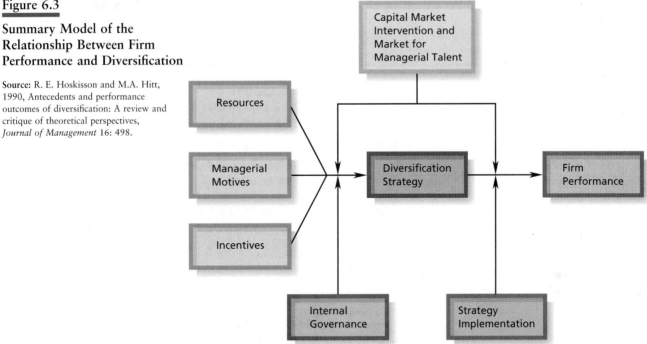

resources (the most flexible) should have a stronger relationship to the extent of diversification than either tangible or intangible resources. Tangible resources (the most inflexible) would be useful primarily for related diversification.

The model suggests that implementation issues are important to whether diversification creates value or not (see Chapter 11). It also suggests that governance mechanisms are important to the level and type of diversification implemented (see Chapter 10).

■ Techniques for Analyzing Diversified Companies' Portfolios

Once a firm has a set of diversified businesses, three issues confront corporate-level strategic decision makers. First, the attractiveness of the current group of businesses (in terms of their ability to create value) must be determined. Second, assuming the current set of businesses is attractive, an estimate of each unit's future potential must be developed. Finally, if these answers are not satisfactory, top-level managers must decide which businesses to divest and which ones to develop in order to maximize the firm's strategic competitiveness.

There are several techniques managers can use to manage portfolios by seeking to answer these three basic questions. The most famous portfolio matrix is a four-square grid devised by the Boston Consulting Group (BCG), a leading management consulting firm (see Figure 6.4). The matrix is composed of two different dimensions: relative industry growth rate and relative market share position. The relative industry growth rate dimension suggests future attractiveness of the business. The relative market share dimension represents current attractiveness and market and future staying power. *Relative market share* is the

Figure 6.4

Growth-Share Business
Portfolio Matrix

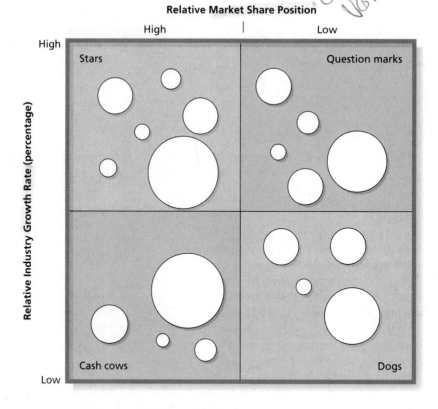

Relative Market Share Position

ratio of a business's market share to the market share held by the most significant, comparable rival firms in the industry. This dimension is measured in unit volume, not dollars. The standard ratio between high and low relative market share is 1. Businesses with a ratio above 1 are in a strong position relative to rivals. Firms trailing rivals in market share have a ratio below 1.0. The original BCG matrix arbitrarily placed the dividing line between high- and low-growth industry rates at around twice the original GNP growth rate. However, individual users can raise or lower the desired growth rate to suit their preferences.

Next, we discuss the strategic meaning of each quadrant shown in Figure 6.4.

■ The Four Matrix Quadrants

Stars

Star businesses have high growth with relatively high market share positions. Although they require large cash investments to expand production facilities, they have strong future prospects for stable growth because of their strong market positions. However, these businesses often require substantial capital investment beyond what they can generate on their own and may require significant amounts of cash infusions from corporate headquarters.

Cash Cows

Cash cow businesses generate substantial surpluses over what is needed for reinvestment and growth. These businesses, having relatively high market share

■ *Star businesses have high growth with relatively high market share.*

■ *Cash cow businesses generate substantial surpluses over what is needed for reinvestment and growth. They have relatively high market share and an industry leadership position.*

and an industry leadership position, are usually mature and have sales volumes and reputations that earn substantial returns. Because the industry growth rate is slow and the business is mature, the cash requirements to sustain market position are not as great. As a consequence, these businesses generate extra cash that may be allocated to other businesses (e.g., stars).

Question Marks

■ *Question mark businesses have high growth, but low relative market share.*

Businesses falling within the **question mark** quadrant have high growth, but low relative market share. These fast-growing businesses may require large infusions of cash to maintain pace with the market's growth rate. However, the question mark label is applied because there is a question as to whether the parent corporation will decide this business is a cash drain or a worthwhile investment because of the amount of cash necessary to fund market share growth, which may not lead to market leadership.

Dogs

■ *Dogs are businesses that trail market share leaders in slow-growth industries and thus may be considered to have dim prospects for growth.*

Dogs are businesses that trail market share leaders in slow-growth industries and thus may be considered to have dim prospects for growth. The logic is to divest businesses with poor prospects because they may not be able to defend their positions relative to market share leaders.

■ Pitfalls of Matrix Techniques

There are two disaster sequences in the BCG matrix that highlight misallocation of resources. First, a star's position may erode, so that, over time, it loses relative market share and its industry growth rate slows. Ultimately, a star business experiencing these realities becomes a dog. Second, a cash cow may lose market leadership and become a dog. Also, overinvestment and underinvestment may occur. Overinvesting in a safe cash cow or underinvesting in a question mark can be a mistake, resulting in negative outcomes.

The BCG matrix and other similar matrices have been criticized because of their lack of emphasis on strategic considerations and their use of historical data (regarding industry growth rates and market share positions).[79] Heavy reliance on these matrices has produced poor performance.[80] If an unrelated diversified firm is using such a matrix, it may overinvest in new growth businesses, given the logic of the BCG matrix. The high-performing, unrelated firms often buy and sell strong cash cows.

The example in Figure 6.4 illustrates a balanced portfolio. A balanced portfolio contains businesses in each quadrant. The logic of portfolio matrices draws attention to the cash flow and investment characteristics of various types of businesses and has implications for resource allocations among businesses. Given the logic of the BCG matrix, to pursue a balanced portfolio would be a mistake for an unrelated firm because this would force it to invest in uncertain growth businesses. This strategy goes against the nature of the successful unrelated strategy, which usually requires investment in low-growth, mature businesses.

A firm pursuing a related diversification strategy needs to focus on industries where there is a strategic fit with its core competencies. Because the BCG and other matrices emphasize cash flow for resource allocation, they create separation between divisions and do not account for strategic interconnectedness.

These matrices have fallen out of favor, because they do not take into consideration the nature of unrelated strategies or the underlying nature of related strategies. Moreover, firms following the proposed guidelines usually underinvest in innovation.[81]

Because of these problems, fewer firms now use portfolio matrices as a decision tool when selecting corporate-level strategies. Experience has shown that adhering strictly to the guidelines of portfolio matrices is unlikely to help a firm develop core competencies and, in turn, sustainable competitive advantages. In fact, strict adherence to the guidelines might even result in a competitive disadvantage. Portfolio guidelines are well known throughout the executive community. Because of this, their use signals competitively relevant information to competitors. One senior executive, for example, stated that "We're glad to find a competitor managing by the portfolio concept—we can almost predict how much share we'll have to take away to put the business on the CEO's sell list."[82] On a positive note, these matrices can assist top-level managers to determine the *attractiveness* of the businesses currently in their firm's portfolio.

■ Summary

■ Pursuing a single- or dominant-business corporate-level strategy may be preferable to a more diversified-business strategy, unless a corporation can develop economies of scope or financial economies between businesses, or obtain market power through additional levels of diversification. These economies and market power are the main sources of value creation for firm diversification.

■ The primary reasons a firm pursues increased diversification are value creation through economies of scope, financial economies, or market power; actions because of government policy, performance problems, or uncertainties about future cash flow; and managerial motivations (e.g., to increase their compensation).

■ Managerial motives to diversify can lead to overdiversification. However, managers can also be good stewards of the firm's assets.

■ The level of firm diversification is a function of the incentives, firm resources and the managerial motives to diversify.

■ Related diversification can create value by sharing activities or transferring core competencies.

■ Activity sharing usually involves sharing tangible resources between businesses. Core competence transfer involves transferring the core competencies developed in one business to another business. It also may involve transferring competencies between the corporate office and a business unit.

■ Activity sharing is usually associated with related-constrained diversification. Activity sharing is costly to implement and coordinate, may create unequal benefits for the divisions involved in sharing, and may lead to fewer risk-taking behaviors.

■ Successful unrelated diversification is accomplished by efficiently allocating resources or restructuring a target firm's assets and placing them under rigorous financial controls.

■ The BCG matrix is a technique used to evaluate diversification strategies. However, such techniques have fallen out of favor recently and do not facilitate strategic specialization in related or unrelated businesses.

■ Review Questions

1. What is corporate-level strategy? Why is it important to the diversified firm?

2. Identify the advantages and disadvantages of single- and dominant-business strategies as compared to firms with higher levels of diversification.

3. What are three reasons why firms choose to move from either a single- or a dominant-business position to a more diversified position?

4. How do firms share activities and transfer core competencies to obtain economies of scope, while pursuing a related diversification strategy?

5. Describe the two ways to obtain financial economies when pursuing an unrelated diversification strategy.

6. What incentives and resources encourage diversification in firms?

7. What motives might encourage managers to engage a firm in more diversification?

8. Discuss the problems of portfolio matrices such as the BCG matrix.

■ Application Discussion Questions

1. This chapter suggests that there is a curvilinear relationship between diversification and performance. How can this relationship be modified so that the negative relationship between performance and diversification is reduced and the downward curve has less slope or begins at a higher level of diversification?

2. The *Fortune* 500 industrial firms are very large, and many of them have significant product diversification. Are these large firms overdiversified currently and experiencing lower performance than they should? Explain.

3. What is the primary reason for overdiversification, industrial policies, such as taxes and antitrust regulation, or because managers pursue self-interest, increased compensation, and reduced risk of job loss? Why?

4. Discuss the situations when portfolio analysis techniques might be applicable. When might they harm corporate performance?

5. One rationale for pursuing related diversification is to obtain market power. In the United States, too much

market power, however, may result in a challenge by the Justice Department (because it may be perceived as anticompetitive). Under what situations might related diversification be considered unfair competition?

6. AT&T is the subject of this chapter's opening case. What is the status of AT&T currently? How are the three separate businesses created currently performing? Given the information you have acquired, what recommendations do you have for AT&T's CEO and why?

7. Assume you have received two job offers—one from a dominant-business firm and one from an unrelated-diversified firm (the beginning salaries are virtually identical). Which offer would you accept and why?

8. By the year 2010, do you believe large firms will be more or less diversified than they are today? Why? Will the trends regarding diversification be identical in Europe, the United States, and Japan? Explain.

■ Ethics Questions

1. Assume you overheard the following statement: "Those managing an unrelated-diversified firm face far more difficult ethical challenges than do those managing a dominant-business firm." Based on your reading of this chapter, do you accept or reject this statement? Why?

2. Is it ethical for managers to diversify a firm rather than return excess earnings to shareholders? Provide reasoning in support of your answer.

3. What unethical practices might occur when a firm restructures its operations? Explain.

4. Is it harder to ethically manage a "dog" business unit as compared to a "star" unit? If so, why? What advice would you offer to someone asked to manage a diversified firm's most unattractive business unit?

5. Do you believe ethical managers are unaffected by the managerial motives to diversify discussed in this chapter? If so, why? In addition, do you believe ethical managers should help their peers learn how to avoid making diversification decisions on the basis of the managerial motives to diversify? Why or why not?

Internet Exercises

Use one of the search engines in the Appendix to find a company that is diversifying. Then, find information about the motives, resources, and performance of the company at the American Stock Exchange, NASDAQ, or the SEC's Edgar database (see the Appendix for URLs).

Cohesion Case

At this point, your group might have selected a company to study and know what different businesses it has. Use E-mail to discuss with your team members the business portfolio the selected firm should have (you could add or delete businesses). What type of diversification does the firm currently have and what type will it be after the changes you recommend?

▓ Notes

1. C. R. Arnst, L. N. Spiro, and P. Burrows, 1995, Divide and conquer? *Business Week,* October 2, 56–57.

2. D. Kirkpatrick, 1995, AT&T has the plan, is Mandl the man? *Fortune,* October 16, 84–90.

3. J. J. Keller, 1995, Why AT&T takeover of NCR hasn't been a real bell ringer, *Wall Street Journal,* September 19, A1, A5.

4. Arnst, Spiro, and Burrows, Divide and conquer?

5. M. E. Porter, 1980, *Competitive Strategy* (New York: The Free Press), xvi.

6. M.E. Porter, 1987, From competitive advantage to corporate strategy, *Harvard Business Review* 65, no. 3: 43–59.

7. Ibid., 43.

8. C. A. Montgomery, 1994, Corporate diversification, *Journal of Economic Perspectives* 8: 163–78; Porter, From competitive advantage to corporate strategy, 43–59.

9. D. Lei, M. A. Hitt, and R. Bettis, 1996, Dynamic core competences through meta-learning and strategic context, *Journal of Management* 22: 547–567; J. Robins and M. F. Wiersema, 1995, A resource-based approach to the multibusiness firm, *Strategic Management Journal* 16: 277–299; C. K. Prahalad and G. Hamel, 1990, The core competence of the corporation, *Harvard Business Review* 68, no. 3: 79–91.

10. B. C. Reimann, 1987, *Managing for Value: A Guide to Value-Based Strategic Management* (Oxford, Ohio: The Planning Forum), 50.

11. C. C. Markides and P. J. Williamson, 1996, Corporate diversification and organizational structure: A resourced-based view, *Academy of Management Journal* 39: 340–367; M. Goold and K. Luchs, 1993, Why diversify? Four decades of management thinking, *Academy of Management Executive* VII, no. 3: 7–25.

12. A. Campbell, M. Goold, and M. Alexander, 1995, Corporate strategy: The question for parenting advantage, *Harvard Business Review* 73, no. 2: 120–132; Goold and Luchs, Why diversify?, 22.

13. A. A. Lado, N. G. Boyd, and P. Wright, 1992, A competency based model of sustainable competitive advantage: Toward a conceptual integration, *Journal of Management* 18: 77–91.

14. M. A. Hitt, B. W. Keats, and S. M. DeMarie, 1995, Navigating in the new competitive landscape: Building competitive advantage and strategic flexibility in the 21st century, paper presented at the Strategic Management Society conference; N. A. Nichols, 1994, Scientific management at Merck: An interview with CFO Judy Lewent, *Harvard Business Review* 72, no. 1: 88–99.

15. Campbell, Goold, and Alexander, Corporate strategy; Goold and Luchs, Why diversify?, 8.

16. D. Collis and C. A. Montgomery, 1995, Competing on resources: Strategy in the 1990s, *Harvard Business Review* 73, no. 4: 118–128; M. A. Peteraf, 1993, The cornerstones of competitive advantage: A resource-based view, *Strategic Management Journal* 14: 179–191.

17. R. P. Rumelt, 1974, *Strategy, Structure and Economic Performance* (Cambridge, Mass.: Harvard University Press).

18. C. C. Markides, 1995, Diversification, restructuring and economic performance, *Strategic Management Journal* 16: 101–118.

19. R. E. Hoskisson, M. A. Hitt, R. A. Johnson, and D. S. Moesel, 1993, Construct validity of an objective (entropy) categorical measure of diversification strategy, *Strategic Management Journal* 14: 215–235.

20. M. A. Hitt, R. E. Hoskisson, and H. Kim, 1996, International diversification: Effects on innovation and firm performance in product diversified firms, working paper, Texas A&M University; M. A. Hitt, R. E. Hoskisson, and R. D. Ireland, 1994, A mid-range theory of the interactive effects of international and product diversification on innovation and performance, *Journal of Management* 20: 297–326.

21. R. Comment and G. A. Jarrell, 1995, Corporate focus and stock returns, *Journal of Financial Economics* 37: 67–87; R. E. Hoskisson, R. A. Johnson, and D. D. Moesel, 1994, Corporate divestiture intensity in restructuring firms: Effects of governance, strategy and performance, *Academy of Management Journal* 37: 1207–1251; A. Bhide, 1990, Reversing corporate diversification, *Journal of Applied Corporate Finance* 3: 70–81.

22. W. M. Bulkeley, 1994, Conglomerates make a surprising comeback—with a '90s twist, *Wall Street Journal,* March 1, A1, A6.

23. A. Barrett, 1995, Beating swords into plimsolls, *Business Week,* July 3, 56–57.

24. N. Byrnes, P. C. Judge, K. Kelly, and D. Greising, 1995, Companies that live alone—and like it, *Business Week,* October 30, 136–138; R. Henkoff, 1995, New management secrets from Japan—really, *Fortune,* November 27, 135–146.

25. *Value Line,* 1994, Edition 10 (February 18): 1494.

26. Rumelt, *Strategy, Structure, and Economic Performance;* L. Wrigley, 1970, Divisional autonomy and diversification (Ph.D. dissertation, Harvard Business School).

27. L. L. Brownlee and J. R. Dorfman, 1995, Birth of U.S. industries isn't without complications, *Wall Street Journal,* May 18, B4.

28. M. E. Porter, 1985, *Competitive Advantage* (New York: The Free Press), 328.

29. A. Taylor III, 1994, Will success spoil Chrysler? *Fortune,* January 10, 88–92.

30. M. Oneal, 1995, The unlikely mogul, *Business Week,* December 11, 86–96.

31. T. H. Brush, 1996, Predicted change in operational synergy and post-acquisition performance of acquired businesses, *Strategic Management Journal* 17: 1–24; H. Zhang, 1995, Wealth effects of U.S. bank takeovers, *Applied Financial Economics* 5: 329–336.

32. D. D. Bergh, 1995, Size and relatedness of units sold: An agency theory and resource-based perspective, *Strategic Management Journal* 16: 221–239.

33. M. Lubatkin and S. Chatterjee, 1994, Extending modern portfolio theory into the domain of corporate diversification: Does it apply? *Academy of Management Journal* 37: 109–136.

34. N. Argyres, 1996, Capabilities, technological diversification and divisionalization, *Strategic Management Journal* 17: 395–410; R. M. Grant, 1991, The resource-based theory of competitive advantage: Implications for strategy formulation, *California Management Review* (Spring): 114–135.

35. W. G. Shepherd, 1986, On the core concepts of industrial economics, in H. W. deJong and W. G. Shepherd (eds.), *Mainstreams in Industrial Organization* (Boston: Kluwer Publications).

36. K. Hughes and C. Oughton, 1993, Diversification, multi-market contact and profitability, *Economica* 60: 203–224.

37. L. Landro, P. M. Reilly, and R. Turney, 1993, Disney relationship with Time Warner is a strained one, *Wall Street Journal,* April 14, A1, A9.

38. A. Karnani and B. Wernerfelt, 1985, Multipoint competition, *Strategic Management Journal* 6: 87–96.

39. f. i. smith and R. L. Wilson, 1995, The predictive validity of the Karnani and Wernerfelt model of multipoint competition, *Strategic Management Journal* 16: 143–160.

40. J. Richardson, 1993, Parallel sourcing and supplier performance in the Japanese automobile industry, *Strategic Management Journal* 14: 339–350.

41. D. Lei and M. A. Hitt, 1995, Strategic restructuring and outsourcing: The effect of mergers and acquisitions and LBOs on building firm skills and capabilities, *Journal of Management* 21: 835–860.

42. C. W. L. Hill, 1994, Diversification and economic performance: Bringing structure and cor-

porate management back into the picture, in R. P. Rumelt, D. E. Schendel, and D. J. Teece (eds.), *Fundamental Issues in Strategy* (Boston: Harvard Business School Press), 297–321.

43. O. E. Williamson, 1975, *Markets and Hierarchies: Analysis and Antitrust Implications* (New York: Macmillan Free Press).

44. R. Kochhar and M. A. Hitt, 1996, Linking corporate strategy to capital structure: Diversification strategy, type and source of financing, working paper, Texas A&M University.

45. P. Taylor and J. Lowe, 1995, A note on corporate strategy and capital structure, *Strategic Management Journal* 16: 411–414.

46. S. L. Hwang, 1995, As Seagram goes Hollywood, a crowd frets over drinks, *Wall Street Journal*, April 11, B4.

47. R. Amit and J. Livnat, 1988, A concept of conglomerate diversification, *Journal of Management* 14: 593–604.

48. M. A. Fox and R.T. Hamilton, 1994, Ownership and diversification: Agency theory or stewardship theory, *Journal of Management Studies* 31: 69–81; R. E. Hoskisson and M. A. Hitt, 1990, Antecedents and performance outcomes of diversification: A review and critique of theoretical perspectives, *Journal of Management* 16: 461–509.

49. D. L. Smart and M. A. Hitt, 1996, A test of the agency theory perspective of corporate restructuring, working paper, Texas A&M University.

50. R. M. Scherer and D. Ross, 1990, *Industrial Market Structure and Economic Performance* (Boston: Houghton Mifflin).

51. A. Shleifer and R. W. Vishny, 1994, Takeovers in the 1960s and the 1980s: Evidence and implications, in R. P. Rumelt, D. E. Schendel, and D. J. Teece (eds.), *Fundamental Issues in Strategy* (Boston: Harvard Business School Press), 403–422.

52. D. J. Ravenscraft and R. M. Scherer, 1987, *Mergers, Sell-Offs and Economic Efficiency* (Washington, D.C.: Brookings Institution), 22.

53. P. L. Zweig, J. P. Kline, S. A. Forest, and K. Gudridge, 1995, The case against mergers, *Business Week*, October 30, 122–130; J. R. Williams, B. L. Paez, and L. Sanders, 1988, Conglomerates revisited, *Strategic Management Journal* 9: 403–414.

54. M. C. Jensen, 1986, Agency costs of free cash flow, corporate finance, and takeovers, *American Economic Review* 76: 323–329.

55. R. Gilson, M. Scholes, and M. Wolfson, 1988, Taxation and the dynamics of corporate control: The uncertain case for tax motivated acquisitions, in J. C. Coffee, L. Lowenstein, and S.

Rose-Ackerman (eds.), *Knights, Raiders, and Targets: The Impact of the Hostile Takeover* (New York: Oxford University Press), 271–299.

56. C. Steindel, 1986, Tax reform and the merger and acquisition market: The repeal of the general utilities, *Federal Reserve Bank of New York Quarterly Review* 11, no. 3: 31–35.

57. Rumelt, *Strategy, Structure and Economic Performance,* 125.

58. E. H. Bowman, 1982, Risk seeking by troubled firms, *Sloan Management Review* 23: 33–42.

59. Y. Chang and H. Thomas, 1989, The impact of diversification strategy on risk-return performance, *Strategic Management Journal* 10: 271–284; R. M. Grant, A. P. Jammine, and H. Thomas, 1988, Diversity, diversification, and profitability among British manufacturing companies, 1972–1984, *Academy of Management Journal* 31: 771–801.

60. J. Templeman, 1995, The shocks for Daimler's new driver, *Business Week,* August 21, 38–39.

61. C. G. Smith and A. C. Cooper, 1988, Established companies diversifying into young industries: A comparison of firms with different levels of performance, *Strategic Management Journal* 9: 111–121.

62. J. Dial and K. J. Murphy, 1995, Incentives, downsizing, and value creation at General Dynamics, *Journal of Financial Economics* 37: 261–314.

63. N. M. Kay and A. Diamantopoulos, 1987, Uncertainty and synergy: Towards a formal model of corporate strategy, *Managerial and Decision Economics* 8: 121–130.

64. Jensen, Agency costs.

65. Hoskisson and Hitt, Antecedents and Performance Outcomes of diversification.

66. C.W.L. Hill and R.E. Hoskisson, 1987, Strategy and Structure in the Multiproduct Firm, *Academy of Management Review* 12: 331–341.

67. S. Finkelstein and D. C. Hambrick, 1996, *Strategic Leadership: Top Executives and Their Effects on Organizations* (St. Paul, Minn.: West Publishing Company).

68. D. L. May, 1995, Do managerial motives influence firm risk reduction strategies?, *Journal of Finance* 50: 1291–1308; Y. Amihud and B. Lev, 1981, Risk reduction as a managerial motive for conglomerate mergers, *Bell Journal of Economics* 12: 605–617.

69. H. Tosi and L. Gomez-Mejia, 1989, The decoupling of CEO pay and performance: An agency theory perspective, *Administrative Science Quarterly* 34: 169–189.

70. S. Finkelstein and R.A. D'Aveni, 1994, CEO duality as a double-edged sword: How boards of directors balance entrenchment avoidance and unity of command, *Academy of Management Journal* 37: 1070–1108.

71. R. E. Hoskisson and T. Turk, 1990, Corporate restructuring: Governance and control limits of the internal market, *Academy of Management Review* 15: 459–477.

72. J. K. Seward and J. P. Walsh, 1996, The governance and control of voluntary corporate spin offs, *Strategic Management Journal* 17: 25–39; J. P. Walsh and J. K. Seward, 1990, On the efficiency of internal and external corporate control mechanisms, *Academy of Management Review* 15: 421–458.

73. Finkelstein and D'Aveni, CEO duality as a double-edged sword.

74. E. F. Fama, 1980, Agency problems and the theory of the firm, *Journal of Political Economy* 88: 288–307.

75. R. A. Johnson, 1996, Antecedents and outcomes of corporate refocusing, *Journal of Management* 22: 439–483; C. Y. Woo, G. E. Willard, and U. S. Dallenbach, 1992, Spin-off performance: A case of overstated expectations, *Strategic Management Journal* 13: 433–448.

76. H. Kim and R. E. Hoskisson, 1996, Japanese governance systems: A critical review, in S. B. Prasad (ed.), *Advances in International Comparative Management* (Greenwich, Conn.: JAI Press), in press.

77. A. Y. Illinitch and C. P. Zeithaml, 1995, Operationalizing and testing Galbraith's center of gravity theory, *Strategic Management Journal* 16: 401–410.

78. R. A. Bettis and C. K. Prahalad, 1995, The dominant logic: Retrospective and extension, *Strategic Management Journal* 16: 5–14.

79. S. F. Slater and T. J. Zwirlein, 1992, Shareholder value and investment strategy using the general portfolio model, *Journal of Management* 18: 717–732.

80. R. G. Hamermesh, 1986, *Making Strategy Work* (New York: John Wiley and Sons).

81. R. E. Hoskisson, M. A. Hitt, and C. W. L. Hill, 1991, Managerial risk taking in diversified firms: An evolutionary perspective, *Organization Science* 2: 296–313.

82. G. Hamel and C. K. Prahalad, 1989, Strategic intent, *Harvard Business Review* 67, no. 3: 63–76.

7 Acquisition and Restructuring Strategies

LEARNING OBJECTIVES

After reading this chapter, you should be able to:

1. Describe why acquisitions have been a popular strategy.
2. List and explain the reasons why firms make acquisitions.
3. Describe seven problems that work against developing a competitive advantage when making acquisitions.
4. Name and describe the attributes of acquisitions that help make them successful.
5. Define restructuring and distinguish among its common forms.
6. Describe how a firm can achieve succcessful outcomes from a restructuring strategy.

Mega-Media Acquisitions

abc

In anticipation of a telecommunications bill that was moving through Congress which would allow networks to own more stations, and eventually create several new digital channels, Michael Eisner, Disney's CEO, decided to acquire Capital Cities/ABC, Inc. The deal nearly doubled the size of Disney's assets and included a number of complementarities. Disney's prior international investments had not been performing well, whereas Capital Cities has a number of successful investments in European media companies. For instance, ESPN has a healthy presence abroad, particularly in Asia. Therefore, the Disney Channel, along with ESPN, will provide Disney with two opportunities for entry in foreign markets. Domestically, Capital Cities will give Disney more opportunity to distribute its products through the networks owned by Capital Cities/ABC. Of course, buying the number one network at its cyclical peak, when advertising sales are at all-time record levels, can be expensive.

Shortly after the $19.3 billion Disney acquisition of Capital Cities was announced July 31, 1995, another media deal was revealed. Westinghouse Electric Corporation announced its long-anticipated agreement to acquire CBS, Inc., for $5.4 billion. With this purchase, Michael H. Jordan, the Westinghouse chairman, signaled that broadcasting would become the cornerstone of Westinghouse's corporate-level strategy. Westinghouse has long been a large, highly diversified conglomerate. Much of its interest in pursuing diversification is driven by the downturn in its current largest business, electronic defense systems. To finance the acquisition, Westinghouse will likely borrow $4 billion and have to sell another $2 billion in assets. It could consider selling its Thermo-King refrigerator-equipment business as well as its Knoll furniture unit. Although CBS had been having performance difficulties before the announcement, Westinghouse will try to transform CBS's business and run it more efficiently. The most significant problem facing Westinghouse will be the heavy debt load it will carry to pay for the CBS assets.

A little over a month after these deals were announced, on September 22, 1995, Time Warner announced an acquisition of Turner Broadcasting. Time Warner already owned 18 percent of Turner and indicated that it would buy the remaining 82 percent. However, there were several stumbling blocks to the deal. TCI Communications controlled 21 percent of Turner stock and held veto power over the deal. Furthermore, U S West, a regional Bell Telephone company that owns a $2.5 billion stake in Time Warner's film and cable businesses, tried to block the acquisition through a court action. As a result of the deal, Ted Turner would become vice chairman of Time Warner and Gerald M. Levin of Time Warner would remain chairman. This deal would have projected revenues of $19.8 billion and the combined company would be larger than the Walt Disney and Company's $19.3 billion in revenues after its planned acquisition of Capital Cities/ABC, Inc.

Some potential synergies of the Time Warner/Turner deal include the ability of CNN and Time Magazine to share news gathering resources. Time Warner/Turner would control a huge amount of programming that could be distributed by its vast cable network. Noncable businesses such as regional telephone companies may find it difficult or costly to buy programming from its new, bigger rival. Although there are potential synergies and market power advantages to the combination, they will only be realized through effective implementation.

Although the acquisition would make 60 percent of Time Warner's cash flow come from programming and 40 percent from cable, which is considered positive in the industry, it's not clear how well the two firms can integrate their operations. Each of the CEOs has a large ego and has had entrepreneurial operating control of their separate businesses. Therefore, this acquisition as well as the others discussed above illustrate both the potential returns and the potential risks of engaging in acquisitions.

Source: B. Gruley, 1995, Time Warner, Turner facing scrutiny on deal, *Wall Street Journal*, September 21, A20; E. Jensen, 1995, "What's up, dock?" "Vertical integration," *Wall Street Journal*, October 16, B1; M.J. Mandel, C. Farrell, and C. Yang, 1995, Land of the giants: Today's merger wave is different from '80s mania. The overriding goal: Market dominance, *Business Week*, September 11, 34–35; 1995, Time-Warner to acquire Turner Broadcasting, *Houston Chronicle*, September 23, A1; M. Oneal, S. Baker, and R. Grover, 1995, Disney's kingdom: As seismic shifts shake the media biz, Eisner lands on top—for now, *Business Week*, August 14, 30–35; A. Sharpe and E. Shapiro, 1995, Time-Warner offers over $8 billion in stock for Turner empire, *Wall Street Journal*, August 30, A1, A4.

C hapter 6 examined corporate-level strategy and, in particular, discussed types and levels of product diversification that can build core competencies. The dominant means for fashioning a diversification strategy is through acquisitions. Although acquisitions have been a popular strategy among U.S. firms for many years, the decade of the 1980s was labeled by some as "merger mania." In fact, depending on whether only whole-firm acquisitions or partial (ownership) acquisitions are included, the number of acquisitions completed in the United States during the 1980s varies from slightly over 31,000 to as many as 55,000. The total value of these acquisitions exceeded $1.3 trillion, with 1988 representing the peak year with $246.9 billion invested in acquisitions.[1] This investment in acquisitions is even more significant because it accounted for almost 40 percent of U.S. firms' 1988 capital expenditures.[2] However, this total amount of acquisition was topped in 1995 with 383 transactions valued at more than $100 million with record U.S. volume of more than $450 billion. Furthermore, global or cross-border mergers and acquisitions increased 17 percent to $229 billion in 1995.[3]

With the large amount of acquisition activity evidenced in the 1980s and 1990s and the substantial capital investment required to support this activity, one would expect such activity to be driven by strong positive returns to shareholders of the acquiring firms. However, the outcomes do not fully support this expectation. For example, research has shown that *shareholders of acquired firms* often earn above-average returns from the acquisition, but that *shareholders of acquiring firms* are less likely to gain such returns. In fact, the average returns earned by shareholders of acquiring firms was close to zero.[4] The significant negative returns earned from some acquisition activity and the overdiversification of some firms (see Chapter 6) have produced a need for restructuring strategies. Restructuring involves acquiring and divesting businesses or assets to position a firm's operations strategically and develop effective core competencies.[5] Furthermore, many firms including AT&T, ITT, Hanson PLC, 3M, Melville, W. R. Grace, Sprint, Tenneco, Sears, Roebuck, and General Motors have been spinning off or breaking up their diversified portfolios to create greater returns for shareholders. Often these firms reduce employment levels in corporate headquarters where highly integrated corporate structures exist.[6] For instance, in the breakup of AT&T (see introductory case in Chapter 6), up to 40,000 are slated to lose their jobs.

The purpose of this chapter is to explore the reasons for acquisitions and the potential problems firms encounter in attempting to achieve strategic competitiveness through an acquisition strategy (see Figure 1.1). As the opening case illustrates, many of these large media acquisitions have the potential to create market dominance for the firms involved. However, realizing returns from that potential may be very difficult. The critics claim that the Time Warner acquisition of Turner has already lowered returns.[7] As such, we also examine the primary reasons for the lack of strategic competitiveness among acquiring firms, along with the attributes of acquisitions that create competitive advantage. Thereafter, we explore the phenomenon of restructuring, the reasons for its use, and the restructuring alternatives that create strategic competitiveness. Finally, we explain how a few unique firms are able to create a competitive advantage through unrelated diversification. These firms may obtain a core competence of continually acquiring other firms, restructuring them, and retaining certain firm assets, while divesting others.

■ Mergers and Acquisitions

A **merger** is a transaction in which two firms agree to integrate their operations on a relatively coequal basis because they have resources and capabilities that together may create a stronger competitive advantage. Alternatively, an **acquisition** is a transaction in which one firm buys controlling or 100 percent interest in another firm with the intent of more effectively using a core competence by making the acquired firm a subsidiary business within its portfolio. Usually, the management of the acquired firm reports to the management of the acquiring firm. Most mergers represent friendly agreements between the two firms whereas acquisitions include unfriendly takeovers. A **takeover** is an acquisition in which the target firm did not solicit the bid of the acquiring firm. Only a small minority of these transactions are mergers; most are acquisitions. Therefore, the primary focus in this chapter is on acquisitions.

■ *A **merger** is a transaction in which two firms agree to integrate their operations on a relatively coequal basis because they have resources and capabilities that together may create a stronger competitive advantage.*

■ *An **acquisition** is a transaction in which one firm buys controlling or 100 percent interest in another firm with the intent of more effectively using a core competence by making the acquired firm a subsidiary business within its portfolio.*

■ *A **takeover** is an acquisition in which the target firm did not solicit the bid of the acquiring firm.*

■ Reasons for Acquisitions

Firms follow an acquisition strategy and/or make selected acquisitions for several potential reasons.[8] Among them are achieving a competitive advantage through greater market power, overcoming barriers to entry, increasing the speed of market entry, the significant costs involved in developing new products, avoiding the risks of new product development, achieving diversification (either related or unrelated), and, finally, avoiding competition.[9] These reasons are described more fully in the following sections.

Increased Market Power

A primary reason for acquisitions is to achieve greater market power. Many firms may have core competencies, but lack the size to exercise their resources and capabilities. Market power usually is derived from the size of the firm and the firm's resources and capabilities to compete in the marketplace. Therefore, most acquisitions designed to achieve greater market power entail buying a competitor, supplier or distributor, or a business in a highly related industry to allow exercise of a core competence and gain competitive advantage in the acquiring firm's primary market. Acquisition of a competing firm is referred to as a *horizontal acquisition*. A *vertical acquisition* refers to a firm acquiring a supplier or distributor of its good or service. Acquisition of a firm in a highly related industry is referred to as a *related acquisition*. All three of these acquisition types are illustrated in the Strategic Focus on acquisitions in the pharmaceutical industry.

The opportunity to make horizontal and vertical acquisitions was enhanced by changes in the interpretation and enforcement of U.S. antitrust laws in the early

1980s (see Chapter 10).[10] Prior to that time, very few acquisitions of direct competitors were allowed by the U.S. government. Of course, this action by the federal government represented a major impetus to an acquisition strategy. Firms that gain greater market share and/or have more resources for gaining competitive advantage have more power to use against competitors in their markets.

As suggested in the Strategic Focus, market power dominance was probably the driving force behind many mergers in the drug industry such as Merck's vertical acquisition of Medco Containment Services, Inc., a drug distribution company. Other pharmaceutical companies such as Eli Lilly and SmithKline Beecham PLC have made similar vertical acquisitions to ensure distribution of their drug product lines by managing prescription plans.[11] Sandoz AG's acquisition of Gerber Products Company, however, was a related acquisition. Many of these pharmaceutical mergers—vertical, horizontal, and related—are directed at increased market power because managed-care and potential regulatory changes in the health care industry challenged the traditional power of pharmaceutical firms. The trade-off for pharmaceutical firms, however, is that they will likely reduce spending on R&D and new product development as they invest money in acquisitions and the transaction costs associated with them.[12]

The Time Warner/Turner transaction represented a related acquisition designed to create synergy that would afford greater market power in domestic and global markets. For example, Time Warner may be better able to compete with Disney after its acquisition of Capital Cities/ABC, although Time Warner has had difficulty integrating past acquisitions.[13] Also, with increased market power, these merged firms are likely to receive increased scrutiny from Federal regulators.[14] Often, increased size allows a firm to not only compete at home but also abroad. Such size allows better control of distribution channels and guaranteed access to markets.

Slow growth in domestic power consumption and increased competition from deregulation have spurred many horizontal acquisitions in electric utilities. Peco Energy has made a $3.8 billion offer for its neighbor PP&L Resources, and Union Electric and Scipsco merged in a $1.2 billion transaction.[15] These deals as well as many others in the electric utilities industry will consolidate the acquiring firm's market power.

STRATEGIC FOCUS   Acquirers in the Pharmaceutical Industry Seek Market Power

Market power, among other reasons, has increased the number of acquisitions in the pharmaceutical industry. Firms have been using all three types of acquisitions strategies: horizontal, vertical, and related. First, we consider a number of horizontal acquisitions. Glaxo PLC and Wellcome PLC (both U.K. firms) announced that they would merge early in 1995. They have a huge stable of drug lines and significant and varied research opportunities. They have been combining their manufacturing and distribution operations to reduce costs of distribution and technological development. However, through reorganization, a number of individuals have lost their jobs at different locations throughout the world. Similarly, American Home Product's hostile takeover of American Cyanamid in August 1994 brought together two complementary product lines and a number of opportunities to reduce redundant costs.

—Continued

—Continued

Because size is becoming increasingly important in the pharmaceutical industry, Upjohn proposed a cross-border merger with Pharmacia to create a merger of equals financed by a tax-free stock swap. Pharmacia would get a U.S. sales network and Upjohn would receive a needed source of new drugs.

Other pharmaceutical companies have been seeking control over the prices they might charge for drugs through vertical acquisitions. Merck bought Medco Containment in 1993 for $6.6 billion. Similarly, Eli Lilly bought PCS Health Systems for $4.1 billion in 1994. SmithKline Beecham PLC also acquired Diversification Pharmaceutical Services for $2.3 billion. These deals put these two companies in the middle of the pharmacy benefits business, which helps insurance companies and other health care plan sponsors manage drug costs. In their new role as managers of drug cost containment systems, it is easier for the drug makers to get their products into distribution through the fast-growing managed-care market. Analysts have suggested that Merck's earnings will increase from 16 percent in 1995 to 19 percent in 1996, largely due to increased sales and margins associated with the Medco deal.

Other pharmaceuticals have been seeking to make related acquisitions. Sandoz AG, a Swiss pharmaceutical company, acquired Gerber Products Company, the baby-food maker for $3.7 billion in 1994, and now appears to be looking for other food holdings to acquire. The Gerber acquisition will allow it to get over-the-counter drugs into distribution more quickly. Johnson & Johnson, however, has taken a different tack. It launched a $1.6 billion hostile takeover bid for Cordis Corporation. Cordis, a Miami-based medical-devices producer sought to thwart the uninvited bid, but ultimately agreed at a higher price, $1.8 billion. Johnson & Johnson felt that Cordis' new high-pressure balloon to open arteries fits with Johnson & Johnson's stent, which props open blocked coronary arteries and would give it more name recognition and thus more market power in this product line. Also, the medical equipment business is related to Johnson & Johnson's over-the-counter and prescription pharmaceutical products.

Other pharmaceuticals are also making related acquisitions among biotech firms. Many of the Swiss pharmaceutical firms, Roche Holding, Ciba-Geigy, and Sandoz, have infused $7 billion into biotechnology companies. Although much of the more recent activity has been in strategic alliances (see Chapter 9), substantial investments were made in acquisitions. The first such acquisition was by Roche when it bought 60 percent of Genentech for $2.1 billion in 1990. Ciba-Geigy bought a 50 percent interest in Chiron Corp. in 1995 for $2.1 billion. The Swiss firms and others have used acquisitions because they lack a strong biotech sector in Europe. Although the biotechnology industry is closely related to the pharmaceuticals industry, the basic scientific approach for producing drugs using biotechnology is significantly different from standard approaches in pharmaceutical companies.

Source: N. Bray, 1995, Glaxo Wellcome to cut or relocate 1,000 jobs in U.S., *Wall Street Journal,* July 26, B5; R.T. King, Jr., 1995, Pharmaceutical giants are eagerly shopping biotech bargain bin, *Wall Street Journal,* April 19, A1, A10; R.T. King, Jr., and S.D. Moore, 1995, Basel's drug giants are placing huge bets on U.S. biotech firms, *Wall Street Journal,* November 29, A1, A5; K. Naughton and H. Dawley, 1995, Upjohn finally makes it to the big leagues, *Business Week,* September 4, 35; M. Studer, 1995, Sandoz AG is foraging for additional food holdings, *Wall Street Journal,* February 21, B4; E. Tanouye, 1995, Big drug makers regain control over their prices, *Wall Street Journal,* July 12, B6; E. Tanouye and S. Lipin, 1995, Cordis agrees to be acquired by J&J in a stockswap valued at $1.8 billion, *Wall Street Journal,* November 7, B6; J. Wyatt, 1995, Drugs stocks—where M&A pays off, *Forbes,* October 30, 222.

Overcome Entry Barriers

Barriers to entry (introduced in Chapter 2) represent factors associated with the market and/or firms currently operating in the market that make it more expensive and difficult for a new firm to enter that market. For example, it may be difficult to develop a new venture in a market because large and established competitors may already occupy the market niche of interest. Such an entry may require substantial investments in a large manufacturing facility and substantial advertising and promotion to produce adequate sales for the manufacturer to achieve economies of scale and offer products at a competitive price. Market entry also requires the firm to have an efficient distribution system and outlets to reach the consumer. If consumers have loyalty to existing brands already in the market, even these actions may not be adequate to produce a successful new venture. In this case, a firm may find it easier to enter the market by acquiring an established company. Although the acquisition can be costly, the acquiring firm can achieve immediate access to the market and can do so with an established product that may have consumer loyalty. In fact, the higher the barriers to entry are, the more likely it is that acquisitions will be used to enter a particular market.

The merger of Scott Paper and Kimberly-Clark Corporation in 1995 not only increased their market power as discussed earlier, but it allowed Kimberly-Clark to overcome entry barriers in Europe. Kimberly-Clark sought the merger partially because Scott Paper had strength in Europe that Kimberly lacked.[16] The Disney/Capital Cities/ABC merger will strengthen Disney's media offerings in both Europe and Asia. Capital/ABC had stronger foreign operations in these geographic areas than did Disney. Many hospitals are being acquired by large chains such as Columbia/HCA. This allows the individual hospitals to enjoy increased name recognition, possibly enhancing their reputation, and to participate in shared cost reduction programs.[17]

Utilities have also been making a number of foreign acquisitions to overcome barriers to entry. For example, Texas Utilities agreed to acquire for $1.55 billion Eastern Energy Ltd., a government-owned electric utility in the state of Victoria, Australia. Eastern's market includes the metropolitan area of Melbourne, Australia's second largest city. Texas Utilities and other electric utilities are using acquisitions to overcome government regulatory barriers both domestically and internationally.[18]

Cost of New Product Development

Oftentimes, the development of new products internally and the start-up of new ventures can be quite costly and require significant time to develop the products and achieve a profitable return. For example, new ventures require an average of 8 years to achieve profitability and 12 years to generate adequate cash flows.[19] In addition, it has been estimated that almost 88 percent of innovations fail to achieve adequate returns on investment.[20] Furthermore, about 60 percent of innovations are effectively imitated within 4 years after patents are obtained. Therefore, internal development is often perceived by managers as entailing high risk.[21] The basic problem is that the costs of developing and bringing a new product to market can be substantial.[22] As a result, managers may prefer other means of market entry that are much quicker and less risky. This is becoming an important strategy in the pharmaceutical industry as the Strategic Focus segment suggests. Acquiring an established firm, although sometimes costly, is less risky than a new venture because there is a track record on which that firm can be evaluated. Furthermore, an acquisition offers immediate access to the market with an established sales volume and customer base.[23] Alternatively, new ventures often have to build their sales volume over time, working hard to develop a relationship with customers. One of the reasons Johnson and Johnson acquired Cordis (see the Strategic Focus on acquisitions in the pharmaceutical industry) was to more fully establish its name among doctors and hospitals who were worrying about the cost of its stent device to open clogged arteries. Cordis also provides devices that facilitate the opening of clogged arteries. This builds credibility for Johnson and Johnson's stent device and may result in reduced R&D and distribution costs.[24] Therefore, acquisition of an established firm provides a significant presence in the market and can provide profitability in the short term. Thus, reduced cost compared to new product development can be one reason why acquisitions have been a popular strategy.

Increased Speed to Market

Firms can increase their speed to market by pursuing an acquisition rather than new product development.[25] To enter the popular U.S. market for sports utility vehicles, BMW acquired 80 percent of Rover Cars from parent British Aerospace PLC for $1.2 billion. With the deal, BMW could immediately have three sports utility vehicles to sell, ranging in price from $50,000 to below $30,000.

Even more promising for BMW is the fact that the Discovery, introduced in 1994, could upstage Daimler-Benz AG (the parent of Mercedes-Benz), which is not expected to sell its first sports utility vehicle in the United States until 1997. Mercedes-Benz is currently building a $300 million plant in Tuscaloosa, Alabama, to produce its sports utility vehicles. Helmut Panke, CEO of BMW, said, "We are on the fast track into this segment" through this acquisition. In the short-term, BMW is the leader and Mercedes has higher risks but only time will tell which one will be the winner in the market.[26]

With the significant changes in telecommunications regulations, as a result of the bill passed by Congress in 1996, many firms are merging quickly to take advantage of perceived market entry opportunities. Bell Atlantic signaled a potential acquisition of Nynex. This $22 billion combination would quickly catapult these two Baby Bells into a size position second only to AT&T with $27 billion in revenues. Two weeks prior to the Bell Atlantic/Nynex announcement, SBC Communications and Pacific Telesis Group, Baby Bells headquartered in Texas and California, respectively, signaled a similar $16.7 billion marriage with $21 billion in sales (SBC is acquiring Pacific Telesis).[27] These acquisitions provide opportunities to rapidly become significant competitors in long-distance services. Because this is a significant strategic action, AT&T as well as other telecommunications firms will likely respond.

Banks and insurance firms are experiencing freer regulatory environments as well as an increased

To enter the popular U.S. sports utility vehicle market, Mercedes-Benz is currently building a $300 million plant in Tuscaloosa, Alabama.

pace of technological change and, as the Strategic Focus illustrates, have been pursuing acquisitions to manage these changes.

There has been a record number of bank mergers and acquisitions recently and an increasing number in the insurance industry as well. These are representative of attempts to reduce costs available through technological change and increase market power in the banking and insurance industry rapidly as regulations have been relaxed to allow entry into new markets.

Lower Risk Compared to Developing New Products

As noted in the BMW-Rover example mentioned earlier, internally developed new ventures can be quite risky, as Mercedes-Benz may experience. New ventures have high failure rates and take longer to achieve adequate cash flows and profitability. Alternatively, acquisitions provide outcomes that are more certain and can be estimated more accurately. This is because the target firms (e.g., Rover) have a track record that can be carefully analyzed, and forecasts of future revenues and costs can be based on historical records.[28] No such records exist for newly developed products such as Johnson & Johnson's coronary stent innovation.

It has been suggested that acquisitions have become a common means of avoiding risky internal ventures (and therefore risky R&D investments). In fact, acquisition may become a substitute for innovation.[29] Firms also may use acquisitions to avoid internal ventures because of constraints on their resources and capabilities requires decisions on whether to invest their scarce resources in developing new products or in making acquisitions. Of course, acquisitions are not riskless ventures. The risks of making an acquisition are discussed later in the chapter.

Increased Diversification

A firm may find it easier to develop new products and new ventures within its current market because its managers better understand the products and the market. However, it is often more difficult for a firm to develop new products that are quite different from its existing set of products and to enter new markets because its managers may have less understanding of such markets. Thus, it is uncommon for a firm to develop new products and ventures internally as a means of diversifying its product line.[30] Instead, a firm usually opts to diversify through acquisition.

In addition, as mentioned earlier, until the early 1980s, the U.S. government did not favor horizontal acquisitions and often precluded them through the enforcement of antitrust laws. However, as noted in Chapter 6, changes in the interpretation and enforcement of such laws led to a substantial number of horizontal acquisitions within the same market and acquisitions of firms in related businesses. Therefore, acquisitions have become a popular means of expanding market share and/or moving into related markets (and thus achieving related diversification) as well as making unrelated diversification moves.

Avoiding Excessive Competition

Firms sometimes use acquisitions to move into related and unrelated markets to decrease dependence on markets with substantial competitive pressure, frequently from foreign firms. In the 1980s, U.S. firms in many industries experienced problems maintaining their competitiveness in markets where Japanese, German, and other foreign firms had a strong presence. This is probably best

STRATEGIC FOCUS

Insurance Companies and Banks Make Acquisitions to Save Costs and Increase Market Power

Although banking and insurance seem to be quite stodgy businesses, the increase in value of banks and insurance companies has outpaced technology firms in the early part of the 1990s. While Chase Manhattan traded at $10 per share in 1990, in 1996, it was trading for over $60. Wells Fargo went from around $40 to over $240. In 1995, Citicorp climbed 75 percent in value. Similar values have been obtained in the insurance industry. Eighty-six acquisitions, valued at over $14 billion, had taken place in the insurance industry by December 1995, according to Morgan Stanley & Co. Life insurance stocks as a group gained 36 percent in 1995, and property and casualty insurers were up 32 percent, outperforming the overall stock market's gain.

As banks made acquisitions after 1989, the number of total banks fell 21 percent from 12,713 to approximately 10,000 by the end of 1995. GE Capital, with over $160 billion in assets, spent $2 billion plus in 1994 and 1995 buying insurance businesses. If GE Capital were a bank, it would be the fourth largest bank in the country behind Chemical-Chase (see discussion later), Citicorp, and Bank Americorp. Many of the acquisitions are driven by cost savings. USAA uses an automated voice response system to field inquiries about banking, investing, and insurance. By selling direct through centralized communication systems, as do USAA and Geico Corp. (a large insurance provider), significant cost savings are realized.

The largest bank merger between Chemical Banking Corp. and Chase Manhattan Corp., a $10 billion transaction, when completed, will create the largest U.S. bank. The combined companies expect to save $1 billion in costs from consolidated operations. Significant savings will also result from technological changes being implemented in the banking industry through the increased use of ATMs and the expected use of on-line banking through the Internet. Also, the overlap in operations will allow the integrated bank to close scores of its nearly 600 branches.

The combined bank would dominate a number of businesses including global custody or servicing large firm debt, where Chase is among the leaders, retail banking in New York, middle-market banking, and syndicated lending, where Chemical is number one. Chase is also a leader in origination of mortgages for wealthy individuals as well as in foreign-exchange trading. In syndicated lending, Chemical is the leading bank with a 26 percent market share. Chase's 8 percent market share would add to this and would allow the combined bank to dominate corporate lending. Chemical Bank already has expertise in managing the integration process because it learned from its acquisition of Manufacturers Hanover in 1991. That acquisition was also driven by potential expense reductions.

Whereas some banks such as Chemical and Chase are pursuing mergers and acquisitions for cost reasons, others are pursuing geographical niches. First Chicago Corp.'s acquisition of NBD Corp. gives it the largest market share in Illinois as well as two neighboring states. Likewise, the marriage between First Union and First Fidelity, to be headquartered in Charlotte, North Carolina, will produce the strongest East Coast retail bank, but will not generate as much cost savings as others. Similarly, NationsBank has bought BankSouth Corp. for $1.6 billion. Although the price was 2.4 times book value, a very high price, the deal will give NationsBank a commanding lead in the booming Atlanta market in the Southeast. Others are now examining the opportunity to buy Barnett Banks in Jacksonville, Florida. Barnett is the last major independent bank in Florida. However, the price of Barnett Banks had already been driven up 37 percent by September 1995. The price at that time was at $5.6 billion of market capitalization, but could climb to $8 billion.

The banking merger and acquisition wave could also take off in other countries such as the United Kingdom. Lloyds Bank PLC, in fact, has tried to negotiate a merger with TSB

Group PLC. If the transaction is effected, it could set off a round of banking marriages in Britain and Europe like the wave under way in the United States. In response to the negotiations, TSB shares jumped 29 percent on the London Stock Exchange.

Therefore, although substantial cost savings result, the price of insurance and banking assets is escalating significantly. Although the cost savings and regional market power may be worth the price, there is no guarantee that the integration of two firms with potentially different cultures will produce an efficient system.

Source: C. T. Greer, 1995, Look where the smart money is going now, *Forbes,* December 4, 160–163; N. Bray, 1995, Lloyds Bank and TSB plan merger, *Wall Street Journal,* October 10, A3; N. Deogun, 1995, With BankSouth gone, what's left to buy in Southeast?, *Wall Street Journal,* September 6, B4; J.S. Hirsch, 1995, Biggest banks get bigger by narrowing focus to financial, geographical niches, *Wall Street Journal,* August 29, B1, B6; K. Holland and J. Meehan, 1995, The next feeding frenzy will feature smaller fish, *Business Week,* September 11, 38–39.

exemplified by the U.S. automobile market. At the start of the 1980s, General Motors had approximately a 50 percent share of the U.S. automobile market. However, by the early 1990s, General Motors' share of the U.S. automobile market fell to near 30 percent. Much of the lost market share went to Japanese and German and later South Korean firms. During the mid-1980s, General Motors acquired Electronic Data Systems (EDS) and Hughes Aerospace possibly to avoid competition with the Japanese. Now, U.S. firms are becoming more competitive and GM has spun off EDS, its computer services business.

U.S. Steel's mergers with Marathon Oil and Texas Oil and Gas were, in part, an attempt to avoid competition with imported steel from Japan. The Japanese do not have a strong industrial sector in petroleum and natural gas. Therefore, many U.S. firms attempted to spread their risks and diversify into other industries because of significant foreign competition. This has not been an effective strategy because it did not help U.S. firms gain strategic competitiveness or earn above-average returns, although, in some cases, it prevented below-average returns.

The Japanese have been much less active in acquisitions than have U.S. firms, and many of the earlier acquisitions in Japan, such as the merger to create Nippon Steel, were designed primarily to increase the market power of firms within Japanese markets.[31] However, as Sony's acquisition of CBS Records and Bridgestone's acquisition of Firestone Tire and Rubber Co. illustrate, the Japanese became important players in the international market for acquisitions in the 1980s. The increase in Japanese acquisitions at this time was partly motivated by the lower value of the dollar relative to the yen; as the yen appreciates in value relative to the dollar, U.S. assets can be bought with yen that are worth more dollars.

There were multiple reasons for these acquisitions. In both the Sony and the Bridgestone cases, the acquisitions provided the acquiring firms with significant footholds in the market. Sony's acquisition of CBS Records and Columbia Pictures provided vertical integration and outlets for some of Sony's new technology and products. For instance, Sony's new president, Noboyuki Idei, has refused to sell Sony's entertainment division (previously CBS Records and Columbia Pictures) in order to help standardize the digital video disk (DVD) format on which Sony and other consumer electronic producers have temporarily agreed.[32] After the final standard emerges, Sony's entertainment unit will provide the firm with an important distribution presence to market its products. (Matsushita, on the other hand, sold its film producer, MCA, to Seagram's and took a significant charge on its earnings because of competitive pressure.) Also, these acquisitions helped both Sony and Bridgestone overcome significant barriers to entry in U.S. markets, were completed rapidly, and seemed to entail less risk because of the known markets and past performance of each firm.

The Bridgestone acquisition of Firestone Tire and Rubber Co. was a horizontal acquisition. Therefore, while it did not represent product diversification, it did represent international diversification, an important topic covered in Chapter 8. Alternatively, Sony's acquisitions of CBS Records and Columbia Pictures represented related diversification moves. As such, neither seemed to entail significant risk because of potential increased capabilities for market power and synergies from these acquisitions. These and other primary reasons for making acquisitions are summarized in Figure 7.1.

Although advantages can be gained from acquisitions, potentially significant problems can also accrue. Sometimes, these problems may equal or exceed the benefits gained. As a result, the average returns on acquisitions have varied closely around zero, as noted earlier in this chapter. Next, we examine some of these potential problems.

Figure 7.1   Reasons for Acquisitions and Problems in Achieving Success

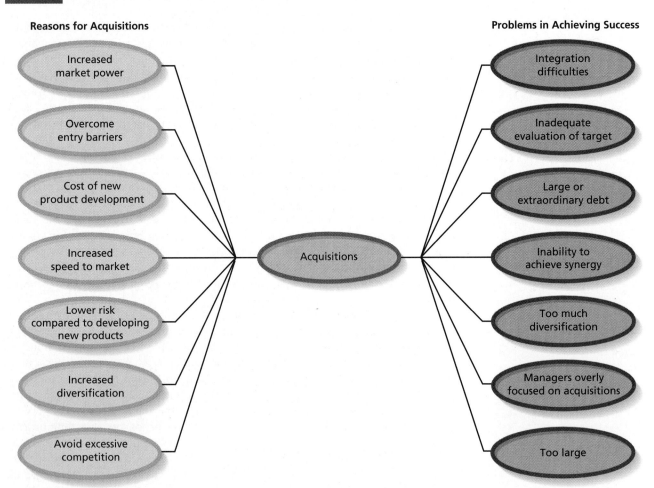

■ Problems in Achieving Acquisition Success

Among the potential problems of an acquisition strategy are difficulties integrating the acquired firm into the acquiring firm, inadequate analysis of target firm and managerial hubris, the large or extraordinary debt assumed to complete the acquisition, an inability to achieve synergy (no complementarities), too much diversification, managers who are overly focused on acquisitions, and acquiring firms that become too large.[33] These problems are also shown in Figure 7.1.

Integration Difficulties

Integrating two companies after an acquisition can be quite difficult.[34] Among the problems that can arise are melding two disparate corporate cultures,[35] linking different financial and control systems, building effective working relationships (particularly when management styles differ), and resolving problems regarding the status of acquired firm executives.[36]

The problem of melding different corporate cultures is exemplified by Merrill Lynch & Company's acquisition of British brokerage Smith Newcourt PLC. Clashes between the two firms' cultures emerged shortly after the acquisition and prompted some high-profile departures of key people including Merrill's head of strategy and Smith's head of research. In the European Research Center, Merrill had 20 analysts who focused mostly on Pan-European business sectors. Smith had 100 analysts who focused on U.K. sectors or individual countries on the continent. Furthermore, their styles and attitudes were significantly different. Merrill's approach kept analysts in their own offices and working in small groups of two or three. In contrast, Smith's analysts shared an open floor with their firm's traders, keeping in close contact and feeding them a constant flow of information. When the two teams were moved together, a competitive mentality emerged. In some ways, the Merrill executives may have been indecisive and wasted time trying to accommodate their new colleagues. However, pursuing too hard a line may have led to even further turnover of top people from both firms.[37] These issues often are not discussed in the negotiations.[38] The new deal between Turner and Time Warner may be even more difficult to integrate than the Merrill/Smith merger because of the strong personalities involved, Ted Turner and Gerald Levin.[39]

Robert Frankenberg, the CEO of Novell, Inc., which at one point was the second largest personal computer software company next to Microsoft, took over for Raymond Noorda. However, Novell became smaller when Frankenberg divested WordPerfect software and other application programming assets. Frankenberg found it necessary to sell WordPerfect for $124 million, compared to a purchase price of $855 million, in part, due to fierce competition from Microsoft. However, there was an extraordinary clash between the staffs of Novell and WordPerfect that crippled the acquisition and compounded management errors. Thus, the culture clash added significantly to the decreased value in the company and further necessitated selling WordPerfect. As the next section discusses, Novell may also have paid too much for WordPerfect.[40]

Inadequate Evaluation of Target

Another potential problem is that a firm may pay too much for the target. If a firm does not thoroughly analyze the target and does not develop adequate knowledge of its market value, too much money may be offered to acquire it. In addition, current shareholders in the target firm must be enticed to sell their stock. To do so, they often require a premium over the current stock price. The bank acquisitions are requiring significant premiums. These premiums frequently are between 40 and 60 percent. However, as the Strategic Focus indicates, many of these mergers and acquisitions have resulted in decreasing bank costs. Furthermore, the seemingly large premiums paid for banks pale in comparison to what Federated Department Stores recently paid for Broadway Department Stores. Federated paid a huge premium of $8 per share for a stock that was selling for less than $2 per share in a $1.6 billion transaction. In fact, between 1994 and 1996, Federated made two huge acquisitions of R.H. Macy's and Company (centered in New York City) with 123 department stores and Broadway Stores (based in Los Angeles) with 82 stores.

Allen Questrom, CEO of Federated Department Stores, now presides over 444 department stores from coast to coast. Its flagship stores are Bloomingdale's and Macy's, mostly in the Northeast, plus Rich's in the Southeast, Burdine's in Florida, Lazereth in Ohio, and Bon Marche in the Northwest. These takeovers placed Federated ahead of May Department Stores, making it the largest department store company in the United States. However, in making the deal, long-term debt increased to $5.5 billion, 60 percent of total capital.

The biggest potential problem is the acquisition of Broadway. Questrom indicated that he "couldn't resist the once-in-a-lifetime chance to buy Broadway's prime real estate locations in potentially lucrative urban markets like San Francisco, Los Angeles, and San Diego." However, critics suggest that Questrom's ego may have clouded his judgment. Some analysts argued that hubris (an overvalued view of one's managerial skills) may have been a factor in overpaying for the Broadway stores.[41] In fact, managerial hubris has been blamed for overpayment and inadequate rational evaluation of many targets.[42] Raymond Noorda may have also been influenced by hubris when he was CEO of Novell Corporation before Robert Frankenberg. Noorda completed the failed acquisition of WordPerfect. Ex-employees indicate that Noorda may have been overly obsessed with William Gates, Microsoft's chairman, causing Noorda to jump at the chance to acquire WordPerfect and Borland International's Quattro Pro spreadsheet software.[43]

Large or Extraordinary Debt

Many of the acquisitions completed in the 1980s and 1990s were financed with significant debt. In fact, the 1980s produced an innovation called *junk bonds*.[44] Junk bonds represented a new financing option in which risky acquisitions were financed with money (debt) that provided a high return to the lenders (often referred to as the bondholders). Some of the interest rates on junk bonds were as high as 18 and 20 percent because they are unsecured (not tied to specific assets as collateral) and thus are risky. Furthermore, firms were encouraged to take on significant debt because it was believed to positively discipline managerial actions. Some well-known finance scholars argued that debt disciplines managers not to misuse funds and, therefore, executives were often encouraged to utilize significant leverage to complete large acquisitions.[45] However, there are dramatic and unfortunate examples of the significant costs entailed in financing acquisitions. The debt assumed by Westinghouse to buy CBS, as the opening case indicates, is significant and may become problematic. As mentioned, Federated Department Stores has taken on substantial debt to buy Macy's and Broadway.

The debt and other transaction expenses have resulted in a $62 million loss on Federated's 1995 $43 billion annual sales. A study by Stern Stewart, a consulting firm that tracks market value created in the last decade, indicated that Federated had destroyed $2.6 billion in capital. This performance ranked close to the bottom of the 1,000 firms tracked in the study.[46] A great deal of the increased number and dollar value of bankruptcies has been attributed to the use of excess leverage, the cost of such debt, and the reduced managerial flexibility resulting from high leverage.[47]

Some of the use of leverage was fueled by the sale of junk bonds, described earlier, and by the notion that the use of high levels of debt constrains managers from taking opportunistic actions in their own interest and forces them to act more in shareholders' interests.[48] Although this is an accurate characterization of the effects of debt, it fails to recognize the potential trade-offs that firms may have to make when large amounts of debt are used, particularly when the costs of debt are high. Obviously, resources are finite, and when payments for interest and principal on the debt are high, those dollars cannot be invested in other opportunities. A substantial amount of evidence suggests that when a firm has significant debt, managers forego investments that are likely to have long-term payoffs. These investments may include research and development and capital equipment. In both cases, these types of investments appear to be important for long-term firm competitiveness.[49]

Therefore, we conclude that the use of debt has both positive and negative effects. On the one hand, leverage can be a positive force in the development of a firm, allowing it to take advantage of attractive expansion opportunities. However, the use of too much leverage (e.g., extraordinary debt) can lead to negative outcomes, such as postponing or eliminating investments necessary to maintain strategic competitiveness. As such, many acquisitions in the 1990s are using more equity offerings instead of debt.[50] For instance, the merger between Pharmacia and Upjohn, mentioned in the Strategic Focus on the pharmaceutical industry mergers, used a tax-free stock swap to accomplish the transaction.

Inability to Achieve Synergy

Another significant problem in achieving success with acquisitions is assessing the potential synergy involved and/or the benefits of such synergy. To achieve a competitive advantage through an acquisition, a firm must realize private synergy and core competence that cannot be imitated easily by competitors. Private synergy refers to the benefit from merging the acquiring and target firms that is due to a unique resource or a capability (set of resources) that is complementary between the two firms and not available among other potential bidders for that target firm.[51] Unfortunately, private synergy that is not easily imitated by competitors is uncommon. Perhaps this is one of the primary reasons that acquisitions rarely provide significant positive returns to acquiring firms' shareholders.

Early in 1996, Anheuser-Busch, the largest brewer in the United States, admitted defeat in two of its acquired businesses, snack foods and bread. It bought Eagle Snacks in 1979 because it saw that it could not only distribute beer but also salty snacks on regular beer routes to taverns and supermarkets. Anheuser also bought Campbell Taggart, a bakery unit. In doing so, Anheuser felt that because one of beer's main ingredients is yeast, it could also use this expertise in bread making. Furthermore, it could use its distribution process and network associated with its other products. Eagle boosted quality and began expanding from peanuts and pretzels to potato and tortilla chips. This created a significant strategic response from Frito-Lay. Frito launched an array of new products and upgraded its distribution while cutting costs. Frito's market share jumped to around 50 percent from 40, while Anheuser's never topped 6 percent and poor returns were realized year after year. As competition increased in Anheuser's main market, beer, these added businesses were distractions and diverted top manager's attention. This led to delays in new brand rollouts and the need to rebuild beer momentum. Instead of focusing on product diversification as it did earlier, Anheuser-Busch is now focusing on international markets where synergies are more likely to be realized in their dominant beer market.[52]

Quaker Oats similarly overestimated the synergy among Snapple, Gatorade, and Quaker's other beverage lines in its acquisition of Snapple for $1.7 billion. After paying a premium price and divesting its pet food business to focus on iced tea and fruit drink beverages, Quaker found that managing Snapple was different from managing Gatorade, even though the potential fit seemed clear. Snapple's distribution system was different from Gatorade's. At the same time, Coca-Cola and PepsiCo targeted both beverages for aggressive competitive action. For example, Coca-Cola pushed Fruitopia against Snapple and Powerade against Gatorade.[53] As a result, Quaker's overall performance suffered significantly and analysts were suggesting that Quaker paid too high a price for Snapple.[54]

Too Much Diversification

An outcome of the trend toward acquisitions over the 1960s, 1970s, and 1980s was that firms often became overdiversified. Research suggests that the long-term performance of many acquisitions is not positive. It is not uncommon for prior acquisitions to be divested several years thereafter, primarily because of poor performance.[55] As noted earlier, acquisition has been used as a primary means of diversifying a firm's product line. When a firm becomes overdiversified, it is difficult to manage effectively. The level at which a firm becomes overdiversified differs for each firm. This is because each firm's type of diversification and managerial expertise determine when a firm reaches a point of diversification that is too complex and unmanageable. Because related diversification requires more information processing than unrelated diversification, overdiversification is reached with fewer business units than with unrelated diversification.[56] When overdiversification occurs, firm performance usually suffers.[57]

In addition, high diversification often is accompanied by other attributes that can produce lower long-term performance. For example, when a firm becomes more diversified, top-level executives often emphasize financial controls over strategic controls in the evaluation of divisional performance.[58] Defined and explained more extensively in Chapters 11 and 12, strategic control in the diversified firm refers to top executive understanding of business unit strategy and operations, whereas financial control refers to objective evaluation (e.g., ROI) criteria of business unit performance. The change in emphasis comes about because the top executives do not have adequate knowledge of the various businesses to evaluate effectively the strategies and strategic actions taken by division general managers. As a result, the division general managers become short-term oriented because strategic controls do not balance the risk that is shifted to them. Oftentimes, their compensation is tied to the achievement of certain financial outcomes. As a result, they may reduce long-term investments (e.g., R&D, capital investment) that entail some risk in order to boost short-term profits.[59] When they do so, long-term performance may suffer.

Too much diversification through acquisition creates significant problems for the management of the firm. Top-level managers may not effectively manage each of the businesses and maintain strategic competitiveness. Over time, this may result in lower innovation in those businesses.[60]

Firms following an acquisition strategy may begin to use acquisitions as a substitute for innovation. They become locked into a self-reinforcing cycle. They make several acquisitions that produce less innovation over time. As they encounter significantly stronger competition and lose their competitive advantage in certain markets, they may seek to acquire firms in other markets. This reinforces the cycle. As a result, if firms use acquisitions as a substitute for innovation, they are eventually likely to encounter performance problems.[61]

Managers Overly Focused on Acquisitions

An active acquisition strategy often requires much managerial time and energy. For example, the process of making acquisitions requires extensive preparation and sometimes lengthy negotiations. Searches for viable acquisition candidates must be conducted that involve extensive data gathering and analyses. Although executives are rarely involved in the data gathering and analyses, they must review the results and select the best candidate from the alternatives. After selecting the acquisition candidate, an effective acquisition strategy must be formulated and implemented. Negotiations with target firm representatives can consume considerable time, particularly if the acquisition is an unfriendly takeover. Therefore, because the process involves much time and energy, executives may become overly focused on the process. Such focused energy can divert managerial attention from other important matters within the firm, particularly those that are long term and require significant time and attention.[62] Furthermore, these negotiations often do not consider potential postmerger integration problems.[63]

Target firm executives also may spend substantial amounts of time and energy on the acquisition. In fact, operations in target firms being pursued for acquisition have been described as being in a state of virtual suspended animation.[64] While day-to-day operations continue, albeit sometimes at a slower pace, most target firm executives are unwilling to make long-term commitments. Long-term decisions are frequently postponed until the negotiation process has been completed. Therefore, the acquisition process can create a short-term perspective and greater risk aversion among top-level executives in the target firm.[65]

Besides creating a short-term perspective and greater risk aversion among top-level managers, acquisitions and change of ownership can foster neglect of the firm's core business. For instance, in the 1980s and early 1990s, car rental companies neglected their core business because of many changes of ownership through acquisitions. Since its start-up in the 1940s, Avis has been owned by 12 different parents, including ITT Corp., Beatrice Companies, and Wesray Capital Corporation. In 1990, GM owned a small stake in Avis and in National Car Rental System, which is also now independent. Ford controlled Budget and part of Hertz. Chrysler owned Snappy, Dollar, and Thrifty rental car companies. In the early 1990s, the car rental companies were receiving so many incentives to take new cars from the Detroit Big Three that they made more money buying and selling cars than they did in the rental business. However, between 1992 and 1996, the cash incentives to rental car companies dried up. During this period, many of the rental car companies lost the focus of their business, did not update technology and reservation systems, ended up with too many cars, and did not have consistent brand identities. For instance, Alamo pioneered the off-airport rental plaza but now is in more airport locations. To improve performance, they must refocus on their core business, car rentals. Hopefully, the employee ownership programs at Avis and National will help facilitate an improved focus on their core business.[66]

Additionally, it is not unusual for significant layoffs to occur after acquisitions, particularly in the acquired business. For example, the combined Chase and Chemical bank plans to layoff about 12,000 employees. Given the large amount of turnover in the executive ranks of acquired firms, it is not surprising that many executives are reluctant to make major decisions for fear that they may be evaluated negatively by acquiring firm executives and laid off after the acquisition is completed.[67] This loss of managerial personnel can be problematic. In addition to losing significant managerial experience and expertise, those championing new products may leave and, therefore, the development and transfer of those new products to the market may be postponed or eliminated.[68]

Too Large

Most acquisitions create a larger firm. In theory, increased size should help the firm gain economies of scale and therefore develop more efficient operations. This would be true, for example, in research and development operations and, thus, larger firms should over time produce greater amounts of innovation. However, it has been found that increases in size create efficiencies only when the acquiring firm is not too large. After reaching some level of size, the problems created by large size outweigh the benefits gained from increased size. For example, larger firms can become unwieldy to manage. If too many levels of managers exist, approval for the development and implementation of innovations can become lengthy and burdensome. Furthermore, to manage the larger size, firms often use more bureaucratic controls. **Bureaucratic controls** are formalized supervisory and behavioral rules and policies that are designed to ensure consistency of decisions and actions across different units. Although these more formalized rules and policies can be beneficial to the organization, they sometimes produce more rigid and standardized behavior among managers.

It is not uncommon for the acquiring firm to adopt and implement centralized controls within the acquired firm in order to facilitate integration. This reduces flexibility and, in the long run, may produce less innovation and less creative decision making, thus harming long-term firm performance.[69]

The preceding discussion provides reasons to pursue acquisitions and delineates the problems in realizing success. Next, we summarize the characteristics of effective acquisitions.

■ *Bureaucratic controls are formalized supervisory and behavioral rules and policies that are designed to ensure consistency of decisions and actions across different units.*

■ Effective Acquisitions

As noted, the evidence suggests that acquisition strategies rarely produce positive returns for the acquiring firm's shareholders. However, an acquisition strategy can have positive outcomes. Some of the specific attributes of acquisitions are more likely than others to produce positive outcomes and therefore may require the careful attention of top executives considering an acquisitions strategy.

Recent research identified some potentially important attributes of successful and unsuccessful acquisitions.[70] The research indicated that successful acquisitions entailed target firms that had complementary assets or resources for the acquiring firm. As a result, when the acquired firm was integrated into the acquiring firm, positive synergy and capability were created. In fact, the integration of the two firms frequently produced unique resources, a requirement to build strategic competitiveness, as described earlier.[71] Thus, the acquisitions were generally highly related to the acquiring firm's businesses. In fact, the acquiring firm maintained its focus on core businesses and leveraged those core businesses with the complementary assets and resources from the acquired firm. Oftentimes targets were selected and "groomed" by establishing a working relationship sometime prior to the acquisition (e.g., through strategic alliances).[72]

In addition, friendly acquisitions normally facilitate integration of the two firms. The two parties work together to find ways to integrate their firms and achieve positive synergy. In hostile takeovers, animosity often results between the two top management teams, which can permeate the new joint organization. As a result, more key personnel in the acquired firm may be lost, and those who remain may resist the changes necessary to integrate the two firms and create synergy.[73] However, with effort, cultural clashes can be overcome and fewer key managers and employees will become discouraged and leave.[74] Thus, successful acquisitions tend to be friendly, although there are exceptions.

Research suggests that successful acquirers often conduct a deliberate and careful selection of target firms and also consider the ensuing negotiations. In addition, the acquiring and frequently the target firms have considerable financial slack in the form of cash and/or debt capacity. A significant attribute is that the merged firm continues to maintain a low or moderate debt position, even if a substantial amount of leverage is used to finance the acquisition. Where substantial debt is used to finance the acquisition, it is quickly reduced by selling off assets from the acquired firm. Often the assets sold are not complementary to the acquiring firm's businesses or are performing poorly. Also, the acquiring firm may sell its own lower performing businesses after making an acquisition. In this way, high debt and debt costs are avoided. Therefore, the debt cost does not prevent long-term investments such as R&D, and managerial discretion in the use of cash flow is relatively flexible.

Another characteristic of firms that launch successful acquisitions is that they emphasize innovation and continue to invest in R&D as part of their overall strategy. As a result, they maintain a high managerial commitment to innovation. This is clearly evidenced in the case of Johnson & Johnson that has made a number of acquisitions over the years. Nonetheless, it continues to focus on creating internal innovation as well. Although the firm recently developed a new R&D lab, it has continued to make excellent acquisitions that are complementary to its various product lines such as the Cordis acquisition, which aligns with Johnson & Johnson's coronary stent.[75] Johnson & Johnson also maintains its manufacturing skills and improves the operations of its acquired firms.[76]

The final two characteristics of successful acquisitions are flexibility and adaptation skills. When both the acquiring and the target firms have experience in managing change, they will be more skilled at adapting their capabilities to new environments. As a result, they are more adept at integrating the two organizations, which is particularly important when disparate cultures are encountered. Adaptation skills allow the two firms to integrate more quickly, efficiently, and effectively the two firms' assets. As a result, the merged firm begins to produce the positive synergy and capabilities envisioned more quickly.

Table 7.1   Atttributes of Successful Acquisitions

Attributes	Results
1. Acquired firm has assets and/or resources that are complementary to the acquiring firm's core business	High probability of positive synergy and competitive advantage by maintaining strengths
2. Friendly acquisition	Faster and more effective integration; possibly lower premiums
3. Careful and deliberate selection of target firms and conduct of negotiations	Acquire firms with strongest complementarities and avoid overpayment
4. Financial slack (cash and/or favorable debt position)	Financing (debt or equity) easier to obtain and less costly
5. Merged firm maintains low-to-moderate debt position	Lower financing cost, lower risk (e.g., of bankruptcy and avoids trade-offs associated with high debt)
6. Has experience with change and is flexible and adaptable	Faster and more effective integration; facilitates achievement of synergy
7. Sustained and consistent emphasis on R&D and innovation	Maintain long-term competitive advantage in markets

The attributes of a successful acquisition and their results are summarized in Table 7.1. Although some acquisitions have been successful, the majority of acquisitions completed during the last three decades have not been highly successful. Because of their lack of success and the growth of some firms to unmanageable sizes with too much diversity, a number of firms, in the United States and internationally, have begun to restructure.

■ Restructuring

■ *Restructuring refers to changes in the composition of a firm's set of businesses and/or financial structure.*

A significant wave of restructuring began in the late 1980s and increased in the 1990s that changed the composition of many U.S. and international firms. Although restructuring was a common strategy among many U.S. firms during this period, it has spread internationally to countries such as Japan, Germany, and South Korea (see Strategic Focus on international restructuring). **Restructuring** refers to changes in the composition of a firm's set of businesses and/or financial structure.[77] Much restructuring has entailed downsizing and the divestiture of businesses.[78] During this restructuring, a significant reduction in the number of acquisitions occurred, as firms attempted to "get their houses in order." The primary impetus for restructuring was poor performance, along with correction of overdiversification.[79] For example, Sears, Roebuck and Co. has gone through a painful downsizing and divestiture of a number of its diversified businesses. These changes were quite difficult not only for the firm, but sometimes for the communities in which it operated. The closing of Sears' catalog business and 113 retail stores in 1993 meant the loss of jobs for 50,000 employees. This is not the end of the story, however. A number of others with ties to Sears and/or to the communities in which it closed operations also lost business and their jobs, because of the substantial multiplier effect.[80] However,

Sears was more successful in spinning off its Allstate insurance business in 1995. The spinoff provided an advantage to Sears (it received an injection of capital to improve its retail focus) and Allstate, free of Sears' retail culture, expected improved returns without significant employee layoffs.[81]

Although restructuring has been a worldwide phenomenon, some of the most significant restructuring has taken place in U.S. firms. Next, we examine some common means of restructuring—downsizing, downscoping, and leveraged buyouts.

STRATEGIC FOCUS

Corporate Restructuring in Germany, Japan, and South Korea

Restructuring of German firms has been quite difficult. First, German banks, which own substantial stock in German firms and are often the largest shareholders, may protect management from market pressures. Another hurdle is German labor arrangements, called *codetermination laws.* Labor representatives sit on German boards and have a strong voice in human resource matters that might prevent restructuring. However, Ulrich Hartmann, the chief executive of Veba AG, is trying to change this by getting firms to focus on shareholder value. Veba is Germany's fourth largest company in terms of revenue. Additionally, Juergen Dormann at Hoechst AG and Juergen Schrempp at Daimler-Benz AG are embracing the idea of shareholder value creation. The rules are changing because capital markets are globalizing and all firms must begin to play by the same rules. Veba became one of the first German companies to report earnings according to methods requested by security analysts. Operations that failed to measure up were either sold or closed. In the process, Veba's profits rose 40 percent in 1995.

Daimler-Benz AG has restructured its aerospace unit (DASA), which has faced chronic problems of poor performance due to the aerospace and defense cutbacks. The restructuring, known as project Dolores (for dollar low rescue), had been planned for a long time and the 9,000 jobs announced for cutback were far lower than the 15,000 feared by union personnel. Schrempp has cut the number of businesses Daimler is in from 38 in 1994 to 28 and hopes to cut that to 25 by the end of 1996. Siemens, another German firm, has also been making layoffs and selling noncore businesses. With the restructuring, Siemens hopes to be in a better position to compete with General Electric and Asea Brown Boveri, both large firms operating in markets similar to Siemens'.

Japanese firms have also been undergoing substantial restructuring. Although some firms have been reducing their level of diversification (as Matsushita did through its sale of MCA to Seagram's), most firms are adjusting to worldwide competition by putting more operations overseas. For instance, in 1986, 3 percent of Japanese firms' total manufacturing output was done overseas. In 1995, that figure had increased to 9 percent. As a result, domestic vehicle production is below the 1985 amount in millions of units. Therefore, imports are rising as domestic production in key industries, such as television manufacturing and motor vehicle production, is declining. U.S. companies are also helping to increase the productivity of Japan's distribution system. If something is 10 percent cheaper overseas, Japanese companies stay with domestic suppliers. However, if it is 40 percent cheaper, the domestic suppliers move overseas to a new source. Historically, Japanese firms have been reticent to move production overseas. U.S. productivity is increasingly helping to facilitate this change. In 1993, U.S. transportation and communication workers were being paid 35 percent less than their Japanese counterparts and Japanese factory workers produced 85 percent as much as U.S. workers.

—Continued

—Continued

Similar pressures have been put on South Korean *chaebols* as these large Korean conglomerates meet global competition. Samsung was being pressured by the government to reduce its level of diversification. In response, Samsung engineered its businesses to allow it to compete more strongly in world markets. Furthermore, Korean firms are moving more production overseas to take advantage of sourcing supplies locally to increase productivity. These *chaebols* likely will transform themselves into significant global corporations and more focused businesses that will be competitive against U.S., Japanese, and European multinationals.

Source: H. Banks, 1996, A tough deadline: Juergen Schrempp at Daimler-Benz has a lot of restructuring yet to do, *Forbes,* April 22, 165–174; G. Steinmetz, 1996, Satisfying shareholders is a hot new concept at some German firms, *Wall Street Journal,* March 6, A1, A6; C. Ju Choi, 1995, Samsung: Re-engineering Korean style, *Long Range Planning,* 28 August, 74–80; C. Goldsmith, 1995, Daimler-Benz' DASA to cut 9,000 jobs, *Wall Street Journal,* October 24, A18; T.R. King and J. Lippmann, 1995, Matsushita aims to move quickly in sale of MCA, *Wall Street Journal,* April 3, A3; K.L. Miller, 1995, Siemens shapes up, *Business Week,* May 1, 52–53; L. Nakarmi, 1995, A flying leap toward the 21st century? Pressure from competitors and Seoul may transform the Chaebol, *Business Week,* March 20, 78–79.

■ Downsizing

■ *Downsizing is a reduction in the number of employees, and sometimes in the number of operating units, but it may or may not change the composition of businesses in the corporation's portfolio.*

One of the most common means of making changes among U.S. firms is that of downsizing. **Downsizing** is a reduction in the number of employees, and sometimes in the number of operating units, but it may or may not change the composition of businesses in the corporation's portfolio. The late 1980s and 1990s evidenced the loss of thousands of jobs in private and public organizations throughout the United States. This includes workforce reductions of up to 40,000 employees at AT&T. There have also been significant workforce reductions at General Motors, IBM, Kodak, Procter & Gamble, TRW, Unisys, and Xerox, among many others. In fact, one study estimates that 85 percent of the *Fortune* 1000 firms have done some downsizing.[82] The intent of these downsizings was to become "lean and mean."[83] However, results of a survey published in the *Wall Street Journal* suggest that many of the firms that downsized did not meet their goals. Eighty-nine percent of the firms surveyed suggested that the downsizing had a goal of reducing expenses, but only 46 percent achieved this goal. Another 71 percent suggested that their goal was to improve productivity, but only 22 percent of the respondents said that they met their goal for increasing productivity. Finally, 67 percent stated a goal of increasing competitive advantage, but only 19 percent noted that this goal was achieved.[84] These results have been confirmed in a study sponsored by the American Management Association and by other studies as well.[85]

However, when overcapacity exists, as in the defense industry, downsizing can produce above-average returns as it did for General Dynamics as the first mover to reduce the overcapacity.[86] Thus, although downsizing can be successful, it has not generally been as successful as intended. Furthermore, it has other unintended and potentially negative consequences. For instance, it is often problematic because corporations do not have total control over which employees stay and which seek new positions elsewhere. Often the best employees take advantage of separation payments during layoffs because they have other employment options. Research has shown that downsizing improves shareholder wealth when it is done for strategic purposes as in the General Dynamics case.[87] This has also been confirmed in other studies where the term *rightsizing* is used to mean that when downsizing is necessary make sure that cuts are not done too deeply so that the firm's human capital changes do not affect strategic competitiveness.[88]

■ Downscoping

■ *Downscoping refers to divestiture, spinoffs, or some other means of eliminating businesses that are unrelated to a firm's core businesses.*

Other firms have downscoped and met more success.[89] **Downscoping** refers to divestiture, spinoffs, or some other means of eliminating businesses that are unrelated to a firm's core businesses. This is often referred to as strategically refocusing on the firm's core businesses. A firm that downscopes often also downsizes.[90] However, it does not eliminate key employees from its primary businesses, which could lead to loss of core competence. The firm reduces its size by reducing the diversity of businesses in its portfolio. When accomplished, the top management team can more effectively manage the firm. This is because the firm becomes less diversified, and the top management team can better understand and manage the remaining businesses, primarily the core businesses and other related businesses.[91] Strategic leadership exercised by the top management team is the focus of Chapter 12.

A number of very large spinoffs have been undertaken in recent times. EDS was successfully spunoff from General Motors. The EDS spinoff created the largest independent computer services company. EDS has grown with the outsourcing of computer systems. However, it is now designing software and selecting hardware and training clients to use the software and hardware. EDS also operates one of the world's top six management consulting practices.[92] 3M also spun off its data storage and imaging systems business and divided the remaining companies into two business sectors, industrial and consumer and life sciences. As part of the restructuring, it eliminated 5,000 jobs or about 6 percent of its workforce. It also discontinued its audio tape and videotape businesses.[93] Besides these businesses, Melville Corporation, Tenneco, H&R Block, Viacom, and others have spun off significant businesses. Usually, the firms, both the parent and the spinoff firm, increase shareholder value and accounting performance.[94]

ITT downscoped its operations by splitting into four businesses in 1995 and shareholders received a share in each business. This was done after CEO Rand Araskog had already sold 250 businesses beginning in 1992. Since 1992, ITT has been performing better than the S&P 500 in regard to investor returns. It appears that Araskog, however, has continued using an acquisition strategy subsequent to the ITT breakup. He is apparently pursuing a "new style" conglomerate in hotels and entertainment, the business he chose to run himself. How this new entity will evolve remains to be seen.[95]

■ Leveraged Buyouts

■ *A leveraged buyout is a restructuring action whereby the managers of the firm and/or an external party buys all of the assets of the business, largely financed with debt, and takes the firm private.*

Although downscoping is a prominent and generally successful restructuring strategy, another restructuring strategy, leveraged buyouts, has received significant attention in the popular press. A **leveraged buyout** (LBO) is a restructuring action whereby the managers of the firm and/or an external party buys all of the assets of the business, largely financed with debt, and takes the firm private. The firm is bought by a few owners often in partnership associations such as Kolberg, Kravis and Roberts (KKR), primarily by obtaining significant amounts of debt, and the stock is no longer traded publicly. This form of restructuring was predicted by a prominent finance scholar to be the corporate form of the future.[96] Oftentimes the new owners of the LBO firm also sell a significant number of assets after the purchase and, in so doing, downscope the firm.[97] Some of these assets are sold to help reduce the significant debt costs. In addition, it is frequently the intent of the new owners to increase the efficiency of the firm and sell it within a period of five to eight years. It is interesting to note, however, that recent research suggests that increased efficiency does not come from pressures of debt. Researchers have found that managerial ownership creates more effective incentives in the buyout than debt.[98] This is supported by anecdotal evidence at Clayton, Dubilier & Rice, Inc., a firm that facilitates leveraged buyouts.[99] This firm reports that managers who received ownership incentives help implement performance improvements. It is the equity incentive rather than the fear of not making debt payments that creates improvement.

The three types of leveraged buyouts are (1) management buyouts (MBO), (2) employee buyouts (EBO), and (3) an LBO in which another firm or partnership such as KKR buys the whole firm, as opposed to a part of the firm, and takes it private. MBOs have been found to lead to downscoping, increased strategic focus, and improved performance.[100] As part of CBS, Fender Musical Instruments was a poor performer. In 1981, William Schultz was brought in to fix it, but ended up putting together an MBO in 1985. Fender's independence proved Schultz's strategy to be correct. It began with $11 in debt for every $1 in equity, but the brand name was strong. In 1995, Fender's sales were $300 million with nearly 50 percent of the guitar market share. Recent evaluation has seen the equity of Schultz's group grow to more than $100 million compared to an initial investment of $500,000.[101]

Improvements at United Airlines are attributed to the employee buyout of the company. At United, there has been a more cooperative spirit, with gains in market share and the firm's returns.

Improvements at UAL (parent of United Airlines) and Avis Rent-A-Car are attributed to EBOs at these firms. However, the UAL arrangement appears to be working better than the situation at Avis. At UAL there has been more of a cooperative spirit with gains in market share and above-average returns.[102] However, at Avis and other EBOs, difficulties have arisen between management and employees. Furthermore, few employee owners have been requested to sit on boards.[103] These problems are very similar to the problems of the employee buyouts experienced in Russia. Needed restructuring is hard to accomplish because employees resist due to job security fears.[104] When change is needed, more problems usually occur between managers and employees.

Whole-firm LBOs, on the other hand, see improvements through downsizing and retrenchment. This approach was illustrated through a buyout at Dr Pepper by Forsmann Little, a leverage buyout specialist like KKR. Dr Pepper was successful enough to receive a new infusion of capital through an initial public offering. It subsequently was bought out by Cadbury Schweppes PLC.[105]

While LBOs have been hailed as a significant innovation in the financial restructuring of firms, there are potentially negative trade-offs. First, the large debt increases the financial risk of the firm, as evidenced by the number of LBO firms that have had to file for bankruptcy in the 1990s. Several were mentioned earlier in the chapter in our discussion of problems with debt. In addition, Northwest Airlines bordered on bankruptcy in 1993, the primary result of a $4 billion LBO a few years earlier. The firm had significant problems in its cash flow during the recession and was unable to repay the debt costs required in its agreement to obtain the debt financing.

The intent of owners to increase the efficiency of the LBO firm and sell it within five to eight years sometimes creates a short-term and risk-averse managerial focus. As a result, many of these firms fail to invest in R&D or take other major actions designed to maintain or improve the core competence of the firm.[106]

Research has shown that LBOs are most successful with mature businesses that have been relatively inefficient and do not require large investments in R&D or other actions to maintain strategic competitiveness.[107] In these cases, improvements in operating efficiency may improve the performance of the firm, and the short-term orientation is less of a problem because R&D is less necessary in mature product industries to maintain strategic competitiveness. Often, however, improvements in efficiency are short term, around three years.[108]

■ Restructuring Outcomes

The restructuring alternatives, along with typical short- and long-term outcomes, are presented in Figure 7.2. As shown in the figure, the most successful restructuring actions are those that help top management regain strategic control of the firm's operations. Thus, downscoping has been the most successful because it refocuses the firm on its core business(es). Executives can control the strategic actions of the businesses because they are fewer, are less diverse, and deal with operations with which top management is more knowledgeable. However, some firms are able to manage highly diversified businesses successfully, as discussed in Chapter 6. Although this is usual, we briefly review how they are able to do so.

We have suggested that most unrelated diversification strategies are unsuccessful and require firms to restructure and downscope in pursuit of higher

Figure 7.2   Restructuring and Outcomes

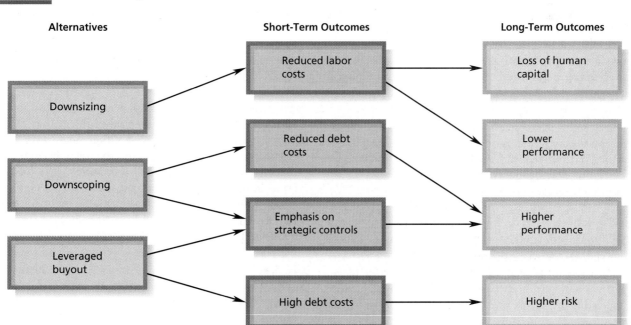

performance. However, some firms may actually become more unrelated because they divest related businesses. In addition, some firms that initiate restructuring by divesting unrelated businesses continue to be unrelated diversified businesses or are classified as conglomerates. This is partly because they may continue to make acquisitions of other unrelated businesses. In other words, they are restructuring their portfolio of businesses, but not with the purpose of changing their overall level of diversification.[109] It has been shown that under some circumstances, unrelated acquisitions can produce higher performance for shareholders.[110]

Jack Welch of General Electric has been very successful in restructuring GE's portfolio of businesses and building shareholder wealth. GE is reported to have built $52 billion of market value added or the difference between the cash that investors have put into a business over its lifetime and the amount they could get out of it today by selling their shares. GE has done this through divesting and acquiring businesses and emphasizing human capital development.[111] Significant downsizing was also involved, especially through the 1980s. GE still has a very diverse set of businesses ranging from the lighting unit to jet engines, but GE continues to restructure them to create shareholder value. It also manages its annual earnings reports well through balancing restructuring charges in some businesses with improvements in others.[112] GE Capital represents a conglomerate within a conglomerate and continues to make acquisitions in financial services. However, this unit has outperformed the other manufacturing-oriented businesses. Again, this has been accomplished through strong negotiations in acquisitions and continual restructuring of acquired units.[113]

■ Summary

- Acquisition has been a popular strategy for many years, but the number and the size of acquisitions increased greatly during the 1980s and 1990s. The popularity of acquisitions was facilitated by a change in the interpretation of U.S. antitrust laws and innovations in the financing of large acquisitions (i.e., junk bonds).

- Firms might make acquisitions for several reasons. Among these are increasing their market power, overcoming barriers to entry, avoiding the costs involved in developing new products internally and bringing them to market, increasing the speed at which the firm can enter a new business, reducing the risk of entering a new business, diversifying the firm more easily, and avoiding severe competition, often from foreign firms.

- Acquisitions produce their share of problems for the acquiring firm as well. It is often difficult to achieve effective integration between the acquiring and the acquired firms. Firms sometimes inadequately evaluate the target firm because of the bidding process. In

addition, firms can overestimate the potential capabilities and synergy that can be created between the acquiring and the acquired firms. The costs of acquisition can be significant. These include the costs of obtaining financing and arranging for the acquisition of another firm. When a firm takes on large or extraordinary levels of debt to complete an acquisition, problems can arise as in the potential problem that Federated Department Stores faces. Other firms have been unsuccessful because the acquiring firm became too diversified. Managers have also become overly focused on making acquisitions, which may lead to inappropriate managerial oversight over other firm operations. Finally, a firm may become too large in size through acquisition, which makes the firm more difficult to manage.

- However, acquisitions can be successful. Successful acquisitions often require deliberate and careful selection of the target and firm negotiations. In addition, both the acquiring and the target firms in successful mergers frequently have considerable slack in the form of cash and/or debt capacity. Successful acquiring firms often maintain a low or moderate debt position. Even if significant leverage is used to finance the acquisition, the firm quickly reduces the debt and debt costs by selling off portions of the acquired firm or some of its own lower performing businesses. Successful acquisitions involve firms with complementary assets/resources, and those complementary resources are used to leverage the core competence of the joint firm. Related to this point, friendly acquisitions often lead to more success. Acquisitions also tend to be more successful when both the acquiring and the target firms have experience in adapting to change and therefore are better able to achieve effective integration. Finally, many of the successful acquiring firms maintain an emphasis on innovation and R&D as a part of their overall strategy.

- In the late 1980s and 1990s, restructuring became a common and important strategic action. Oftentimes this restructuring is undertaken to downsize the firm. The approach requires employee layoffs and also seeks to reduce the number of hierarchical levels in an organization. Although it does reduce formal behavioral controls, it is problematic because corporations do not have total control of which employees stay and which seek new positions elsewhere. Therefore, a firm may lose many high-performing employees.

- Another approach to restructuring is downscoping. The goal of downscoping is to reduce the level of a firm's diversification. This form of restructuring is often accomplished by divesting unrelated businesses, whereby the firm's top executives can strategically refocus on the firm's core business. It is often accompanied by downsizing as well. This approach has been more successful than downsizing alone.

- Another popular form of restructuring is known as the leveraged buyout (LBO). In a leveraged buyout, the management or an external party buys 100 percent of the firm's stock, largely financed with debt, and takes the firm private. The three types of LBOs are management buyouts (MBOs), employee buyouts (EBOs), and whole-firm LBOs. MBOs have functioned best because they provide clear incentives for managers. EBOs provide the potential for improved cooperation, but power struggles can occur between managers and workers if significant change is required. In general, LBOs have met with mixed success. Oftentimes, the intent is to improve the firm's efficiency and performance and to sell the firm (or take it public) within five to eight years after the leveraged buyout. Many LBO firms have been successful because of improved incentives for managers, but in recent years some have experienced performance problems, primarily because of the high debt and debt costs.

- The primary goal of corporate restructuring, in most cases, is to gain or regain strategic control of the firm. Downscoping and strategic refocusing on core businesses reduce the pressure for processing information to manage a wider diversity of businesses and allow the top executives to control the businesses by evaluating strategic actions, as opposed to placing an emphasis on financial outcomes. This generally produces higher performance and achieves strategic competitiveness over the long term.

- Although most restructuring is designed to reduce the level of diversification, some firms may restructure and remain highly diversified. A few of these firms such as General Electric are able to do so and perform quite well. Generally, they can do so if they continually restructure to improve results. In addition, if they can acquire underperforming businesses and turn around their performance, they may be able to enhance the value of those firms and either maintain or resell them at a profit.

■ Review Questions

1. Why have acquisitions been a popular strategy?

2. For what reasons might firms follow an acquisition strategy?

3. What problems might be encountered by firms following an acquisition strategy?

4. What are some of the approaches that firms employ to complete an acquisition strategy successfully?

5. What are the common forms of restructuring and their goals?

6. How can a firm successfully implement a restructuring strategy?

■ Application Discussion Questions

1. Given the evidence that the shareholders of many acquiring firms gain little or nothing in value from acquisitions, why do so many firms follow such a strategy?

2. Of the reasons for following an acquisition strategy described in the chapter, which are positive, and which are more negative and likely to create performance problems over the long term?

3. After reading popular press accounts of large acquisitions, choose a recent one and detail the important characteristics of the acquiring and the acquired firms. Based on these characteristics and other information, do you think this acquisition will succeed in achieving high performance? Explain why or why not.

4. Search popular press accounts to find an acquisition that has the attributes necessary for success. Why do you feel this acquisition has a high probability of success over the long term?

5. What is meant by the term *synergy?* Explain how the merger of two separate businesses can create synergy. How can firms create private synergy that cannot be easily imitated by other companies?

6. How can top executives in a firm determine the most appropriate level of diversification and thereby avoid becoming overdiversified? How can they determine the appropriate level of debt/leverage to utilize?

7. Why have LBOs not become the organization of the future, as proposed by a prominent finance scholar? Why have MBOs been more successful than EBOs?

8. In comparing acquiring a business with developing a new product/business internally, what are the advantages and disadvantages of each?

■ Ethics Questions

1. If there is a relationship between the size of the firm and a top executive's compensation, is there an inducement for top executives to engage in mergers and acquisitions in order to increase their compensation? What is the board of directors role in maintaining the integrity of the compensation system?

2. When a manager seeks to restructure (acquire or divest firm assets), are there incentives to do it in a way that builds the manager's power relative to shareholders or other stakeholders such as employees, rather than the firm's power relative to the market in order to achieve strategic competitiveness? Could this motive be related to the lack of success among acquiring firms?

3. If shareholders increase their wealth through a downsizing, does this come at the expense of employees who have invested a considerable portion of their life in the firm or at the expense of whole communities dependent on employment from the downsizing firm?

4. Do "corporate raiders" always target firms that are performing poorly and thus have a rational reason for pursuing the restructuring due to mismanagement, or is there also an incentive to pursue firms that have resources to "buy off" hostile suitors ("green mail")?

5. When a leveraged buyout is attempted, shareholders often increase their wealth (e.g., stock price increases), but debtholders may find their investment at risk because bond ratings are often downgraded. Are there any ethical issues associated with the transfer of wealth from debtholders to shareholders?

6. Should a manager reveal information about planned new products before the LBO that might bring personal gain (e.g., the manager becomes an owner through the LBO) rather than gain to public shareholders, once the firm is private?

 # Internet Exercise

The LBO Home Page has a "List of Companies Purchased by LBO":

■ http://www.iagi.net/~tt/lbo.html

Select three of these companies and determine how they have performed. If they remain private, you might have to use one of the search engines in the Appendix. Sometimes the LBO goes public again. If this is the case, find stockholder returns at the American Stock Exchange, NASDAQ, or the SEC's Edgar database (see the Appendix for URLs).

Cohesion Case

Examine "M&A Online, Inc." to find companies for sale that might fit your firm's portfolio of businesses:

■ http://www.maol.com/maol/

Discuss with your team how your firm might go about targeting a firm and integrating it into your organization. What characteristics are necessary to attain important synergies?

■ Notes

1. M. A. Hitt, R. E. Hoskisson, R. D. Ireland, and J. S. Harrison, 1991, Effects of acquisitions on R&D inputs and outputs, *Academy of Management Journal* 34: 693–706; M. Sikora, 1990, The M&A bonanza of the '80s and its legacy, *Mergers and Acquisitions,* March/April, 90–95; J. F. Weston and K. S. Chung, 1990, Takeovers and corporate restructuring: An overview, *Business Economics* 25, no. 2: 6–11.

2. L. Weiner, 1989, No slowdown in mergers foreseen, *American Banker* 154, no. 222: 8.

3. G. Koretz, 1996, All the world's an M&A stage, *Business Week,* February 12, 26; S. Lipin, 1996, Merger action heats up after first-quarter dip, *Wall Street Journal,* April 8, A1, A9.

4. M. C. Jensen, 1988, Takeovers: Their causes and consequences, *Journal of Economic Perspectives* 1, no. 2: 21–48.

5. D. Lei and M. A. Hitt, 1995, Strategic restructuring and outsourcing: The effect of mergers and acquisitions and LBOs on building firm skills and capabilities, *Journal of Management* 21: 835–860.

6. J. S. Lublin, 1995, Spinoffs may establish new companies but they often spell the end of jobs, *Wall Street Journal,* November 21, B1, B8.

7. P. L. Zweig, J. P. Kline, K. Gudridge, and S. A. Forest, 1995, The case against mergers, *Business Week,* October 30, 122–130.

8. P. C. Haspeslagh and D. B. Jemison, 1991, *Managing Acquisitions: Creating Value Through Corporate Renewal* (New York: The Free Press).

9. D. K. Datta, G. E. Pinches, and V. K. Narayanan, 1992, Factors influencing wealth creation from mergers and acquisitions: A meta-analysis, *Strategic Management Journal* 13: 67–84; G. F. Davis and S. K. Stout, 1992, Organization theory and the market for corporate control: A dynamic analysis of the characteristics of large takeover targets, 1980–1990, *Administrative Science Quarterly* 37: 605–633; W. B. Carper, 1990, Corporate acquisitions and shareholder wealth: A review and exploratory analysis, *Journal of Management* 16: 807–823.

10. A. Shleifer and R. W. Vishny, 1991, Takeovers in the '60s and the '80s: Evidence and implications, *Strategic Management Journal* 12 (Special Issue, Winter): 51–59.

11. J. Wyatt, 1995, Drug stocks—where M&A pays off, *Fortune,* October 30, 222.

12. E. Tanouye and G. Anders, 1995, Drug industry takeovers mean more cost-cutting, less research spending, *Wall Street Journal,* February 1, B1, B4.

13. Time-Warner chairman facing a daunting task, 1995, *Dallas Morning News,* September 25, D3.

14. J. Weber, 1995, Not the best prescription for growth, *Business Week,* October 30, 124–125.

15. M. J. Mandel, C. Farrell, and C. Yang, 1995, Land of the giants: Today's merger wave is different from '80s mania. The overriding goal: Market dominance, *Business Week,* September 11, 34–35.

16. S. Lipin and P. Thomas, 1995, Kimberly-Clark, Scott in talks to merge firms in stock swap, *Wall Street Journal,* June 23, A3, A4; Mandel, Farrell, and Yang, Land of the giants.

17. D. Dranove and M. Shanley, 1995. Cost reductions or reputation enhancement as motives for mergers: The logic of multi-hospital systems, *Strategic Management Journal* 16: 55–74.

18. G. Jones, 1995, Texas Utilities buys Australian firm, *Dallas Morning News,* November 6, D1, D4.

19. R. Biggadike, 1979, The risky business of diversification, *Harvard Business Review* 57, no. 3: 103–111.

20. E. Mansfield, 1969, *Industrial Research and Technological Innovation* (New York: Norton).

21. L. H. Clark, Jr., and A. L. Malabre, Jr., 1988, Slow rise in outlays for research imperils U.S. competitive edge, *Wall Street Journal,* November 16, A1, A5; E. Mansfield, M. Schwartz, and S. Wagner, 1981, Imitation costs and patents: An empirical study, *Economic Journal* 91: 907–918.

22. J. K. Shank and V. Govindarajan, 1992, Strategic cost analysis of technological investments, *Sloan Management Review* 34 (Fall): 39–51.

23. M. A. Hitt, R. E. Hoskisson, R. A. Johnson, and D. D. Moesel, 1996, The market for corporate control and firm innovation, *Academy of Management Journal,* in press.

24. E. Tanouye and S. Lipin, 1995, Cordis agrees to be acquired by J&J in a stockswap valued at $1.8 billion, *Wall Street Journal,* November 7, B6; R. Winslow, 1995, Going for flow: Simple device to prop clogged arteries open changes coronary care: Johnson & Johnson's 'stent' is a hit, but the cost is worrying hospitals, *Wall Street Journal,* October A1, A8.

25. K. F. McCardle and S. Viswanathan, 1994, The direct entry versus takeover decision and stock price performance around takeovers, *Journal of Business* 67: 1–43.

26. A. Taylor III, 1996, Speed! Power! Status! Mercedes and BMW race ahead with a new generation of cars to lust for, *Fortune,* June 10, 47–58; A. Choi, R. L. Hudson, and O. Saris, 1994, BMW to buy 80 percent of Rover Cars, *Wall Street Journal,* February 1, A3, A6.

27. L. Cauley and S. Lipin, 1996, Bell Atlantic and Nynex revive talks on $22 billion-plus merger, *Wall Street Journal,* April 17, A3, A6.

28. M. A. Hitt, R. E. Hoskisson, and R. D. Ireland, 1990, Mergers and acquisitions and managerial commitment to innovation in M-form firms, *Strategic Management Journal* 11 (Special Issue): 29–47.

29. Hitt et al., The market for corporate control and innovation; J. Constable, 1986, Diversification as a factor in U.K. industrial strategy, *Long Range Planning* 19: 52–60.

30. Hitt et al., Effects of acquisitions; Hitt, Hoskisson, and Ireland, Mergers and acquisitions.

31. W. C. Kester, 1991, *Japanese Takeovers: The Global Contest for Corporate Control* (Boston: Harvard Business School Press), 94–95.

32. P. Newcomb, 1996, Video games, *Forbes,* May 6, 45.

33. M. A. Hitt, J. S. Harrison, R. D. Ireland, and A. Best, 1995, Learning how to dance with the Tasmanian devil: Understanding acquisition success and failure, paper presented at the Strategic Management Society conference; Zweig, Kline, Gudridge, and Forest, The case against mergers.

34. D. K. Datta, 1991, Organizational fit and acquisition performance: Effects of post-acquisition integration, *Strategic Management Journal* 12: 281–297; J. Kitching, 1967, Why do mergers miscarry? *Harvard Business Review* 45, no. 6: 84–101.

35. H. Aaron, 1994, A poisoning of the atmosphere, *Wall Street Journal,* August 29, A10; P. M. Elsass and J. F. Veiga, 1994, Acculturation in acquired organizations: A force field perspective, *Human Relations* 47: 453–471.

36. A. F. Buono and J. L. Bowditch, 1989, *The Human Side of Mergers and Acquisitions* (San Francisco: Jossey-Bass).

37. N. Bray, 1996, Merrill's British marriage spawns spats: Different cultures spark tensions after Smith deal, *Wall Street Journal,* April 19, A9.

38. D. B. Jemison and S. B. Sitkin, 1986, Corporate acquisitions: A process perspective, *Academy of Management Review* 11: 145–163.

39. L. Landro, 1995, Giants talk synergy but few make it work, *Wall Street Journal,* September 25, B1, B6.

40. R. Tamburri and D. Clark 1996, Technology: Corel to acquire Novell's WordPerfect for $124 million in cash and stock, *Wall Street Journal,* February 1, B5; D. Clark, 1996, Software firm fights to remake business after ill-fated merger, *Wall Street Journal,* January 12, A1, A6.

41. L. Grant, 1996, Miracle or mirage on 34th Street? *Fortune,* February 5, 84–90.

42. R. Roll, 1986, The hubris hypothesis of corporate takeovers, *Journal of Business* 59: 197–216.

43. Clark, Software firm fights.

44. G. Yago, 1991, *Junk Bonds: How High Yield Securities Restructured Corporate America* (New York: Oxford University Press), 146–148.

45. M. C. Jensen, 1987, A helping hand for entrenched managers, *Wall Street Journal,* November 4, A6; M. C. Jensen, 1986, Agency costs of free cash flow, corporate finance, and takeovers, *American Economic Review* 76: 323–329.

46. Grant, Miracle or mirage on 34th Street?, 85.

47. M. A. Hitt and D. L. Smart, 1994, Debt: A disciplining force for managers or a debilitating force for organizations? *Journal of Management Inquiry* 3: 144–152.

48. M. C. Jensen, 1989, Is leverage an invitation to bankruptcy? On the contrary—it keeps shaky

firms out of court, *Wall Street Journal,* February 1, A14; Jensen, A helping hand.

49. B. H. Hall, 1990, The impact of corporate restructuring on industrial research and development, in M. N. Baily and C. Winston (eds.), *Brookings Papers on Economic Activity* 3: 85–135; B. Baysinger and R. E. Hoskisson 1989, Diversification strategy and R&D intensity in multi-product firms, *Academy of Management Journal* 32: 310–332.

50. L. Grant, 1993, Corporate connections: Mergers are on the rise, but unlike deals of the 80s they aren't debt laden, *U.S. News & World Report,* August 2, 46–49.

51. Hitt et al., Effects of acquisitions; J. B. Barney, Returns to bidding firms in mergers and acquisitions: Reconsidering the relatedness hypothesis, *Strategic Management Journal* 9 (Special Issue): 71–78.

52. R. Gibson, 1996, Anheuser-Busch plans to spin off baking unit, ending costly foray, *Wall Street Journal,* February 29, B3; R. A. Melcher and G. Burns, 1996, How Eagle became extinct: Anheuser saw synergies in beer and snacks, *Business Week,* March 4, 68–69.

53. Bottling success, 1996, *Dallas Morning News,* April 6, F2.

54. Z. Moukheiber, 1996, He who laughs last, *Forbes,* January 1, 42–43; R. Gibson, 1995, At Quaker Oats, Snapple is leaving a bad aftertaste, *Wall Street Journal,* August 7, B4.

55. M. E. Porter, 1987, From competitive advantage to corporate strategy, *Harvard Business Review* 65, no. 3: 43–59; D. J. Ravenscraft and R. M. Scherer, 1987, *Mergers, Sell Offs and Economic Efficiency* (Washington, D.C.: Brookings Institute).

56. C. W. L. Hill and R. E. Hoskisson, 1987, Strategy and structure in the multiproduct firm, *Academy of Management Review* 12: 331–341.

57. R. A. Johnson, R. E. Hoskisson, and M. A. Hitt, 1993, Board of director involvement in restructuring: The effects of board versus managerial controls and characteristics, *Strategic Management Journal* 14 (Special Issue): 33–50; C. C. Markides, 1992, Consequences of corporate refocusing: Ex ante evidence, *Academy of Management Journal* 35: 398–412.

58. Hill and Hoskisson, Strategy and structure.

59. Hitt, Hoskisson, and Ireland, Mergers and acquisitions.

60. Hitt et al., The market for corporate control and innovation.

61. Hitt, Hoskisson, and Ireland, Mergers and acquisitions.

62. Ibid.

63. Jemison and Sitkin, Corporate acquisitions.

64. Hitt et al., Effects of acquisitions.

65. R. E. Hoskisson, M. A. Hitt, and R. D. Ireland, 1994, The effects of acquisitions and restructuring (strategic refocusing) strategies on innovation, in G. von Krogh, A. Sinatra, and H. Singh (eds.), *Managing Corporate Acquisitions* (London: Macmillan Press), 144–169.

66. L. Miller and G. Stern, 1996, Car rental companies neglect core business, often skid into

losses, *Wall Street Journal,* February 15, A1, A8.

67. J. P. Walsh, 1988, Top management team turnover following mergers and acquisitions, *Strategic Management Journal* 9: 173–183.

68. M. A. Hitt, R. E. Hoskisson, R. D. Ireland and J. Harrison, 1991, Are acquisitions a poison pill for innovation?, *Academy of Management Executive* V, no. 4, 22–34.

69. Hitt, Hoskisson, and Ireland, Mergers and acquisitions.

70. Hitt et al., Learning how to dance with the Tasmanian devil.

71. J. S. Harrison, M. A. Hitt, R. E. Hoskisson, and R. D. Ireland, 1991, Synergies and post acquisition performance: Differences versus similarities in resource allocations, *Journal of Management* 17: 173–190; Barney, 1988, Returns to bidding firms.

72. M. A. Lubatkin and P. J. Lane, 1996, Psst. . . The merger mavens still have it wrong! *Academy of Management Executive* X, no. 1: 21–39.

73. J. P. Walsh, 1989, Doing a deal: Merger and acquisition negotiations and their impact upon target company top management turnover, *Strategic Management Journal* 10: 307–322.

74. L. S. Lublin, 1995, Strategies for preventing post-takeover defections, *Wall Street Journal,* April 28, B1, B8.

75. Tanouye and Lipin, Cordis agrees to be acquired by J&J.

76. G. P. Pisano and S. C. Wheelwright, 1995, The new logic of R & D, *Harvard Business Review* 73, no. 5: 93–105.

77. J. E. Bethel and J. Liebeskind 1993, The effects of ownership structure on corporate restructuring, *Strategic Management Journal* 14 (Special Issue): 15–31.

78. E. Bowman and H. Singh, 1990, Overview of corporate restructuring: Trends and consequences, in L. Rock and R. H. Rock (eds.), *Corporate Restructuring* (New York: McGraw-Hill).

79. R. E. Hoskisson, R. A. Johnson, and D. D. Moesel, 1994, Divestment intensity of restructuring firms: Effects of governance, strategy and performance, *Academy of Management Journal* 37: 1207–1251.

80. J. Valente and C. Duff, 1993, Trickle down pain: Demise of the catalog hurts small businesses that counted on Sears, *Wall Street Journal,* March 2, A1, A6.

81. J. R. Laing, 1995, In better hands, freed from Sears and a culture of complacency, Allstate is on the rise, *Barron's,* August 15, 25–29; G. A. Patterson, 1995, As Sears prepares to spin off stake in insurer, some investors say there's a bargain to be had, *Wall Street Journal,* February 3, C2.

82. W. McKinley, C. M. Sanchez, and A. G. Schick, 1995, Organizational downsizing: Constraining, cloning, learning, *Academy of Management Executive* IX, no. 3: 32–44.

83. R. E. Hoskisson and M. A. Hitt, 1994, *Downscoping: How to Tame the Diversified Firm* (New York: Oxford University Press).

84. A. Bennet, 1991, Downsizing doesn't necessarily bring an upswing in corporate profitability, *Wall Street Journal,* June 4, B1, B4.

85. K. S. Cameron, S. J. Freeman, and A. K. Mishra, 1991, Best practices in white-collar downsizing: Managing contradictions, *Academy of Management Executive* V, no. 3: 57–73.

86. J. Dial and K. J. Murphy, 1995, Incentives, downsizing and value creation at General Dynamics, *Journal of Financial Economics* 37: 261–314.

87. D. L. Worrell, W. M. Davidson, and V. M. Sharma, 1991, Layoff announcements and stockholder wealth, *Academy of Management Journal* 34: 662–678.

88. M. A. Hitt, B. W. Keats, H. F. Harback, and R. D. Nixon, 1994, Rightsizing: Building and maintaining strategic leadership and long-term competitiveness, *Organizational Dynamics* 23 (Autumn), 18–32; J. S. Lublin, 1994, Don't stop cutting staff, study suggests, *Wall Street Journal,* September 27, B1.

89. Hoskisson and Hitt, *Downscoping.*

90. J. Kose, H. P. Lang, and J. Nitter, 1992, The voluntary restructuring of large firms in response to performance decline, *Journal of Finance* 47: 891–917; J. S. Luldin, 1995, Spin offs may establish new companies, but they often spell the end of jobs, *Wall Street Journal,* November 21, B1, B8.

91. Johnson, Hoskisson, and Hitt, Board of directors involvement; R. E. Hoskisson and M. A. Hitt, 1990, Antecedents and performance outcomes of diversification: A review and critique of theoretical perspectives, *Journal of Management* 16: 461–509.

92. N. Templin, 1996, Under Alberthal, EDS is out of limelight but triples revenue, *Wall Street Journal,* February 21, A1, A6.

93. T. D. Schellhardt, 1995, Minnesota Mining to spin off units, take major charge and cut 5,000 jobs, *Wall Street Journal,* November 15, A3, A14.

94. R. A. Johnson, 1996, Antecedents and outcomes of corporate refocusing, *Journal of Management* 22: 439–483.

95. S. N. Chakravarty and S. Lubove, 1996, Plenty of glitter, but where's the gold? *Forbes,* March 25, 106–111.

96. M. C. Jensen, 1989, Eclipse of the public corporation, *Harvard Business Review* 67, no. 5: 61–74.

97. M. F. Wiersema and J. P. Liebeskind, 1995, The effects of leveraged buyouts on corporate growth and diversification in large firms, *Strategic Management Journal* 16: 447–460.

98. P. H. Phan and C. W. L. Hill, 1995, Organizational restructuring and economic performance in leveraged buyouts: An ex-post study, *Academy of Management Journal* 38: 704–739.

99. W. C. Kester and T. A. Luehrman, 1995, Rehabilitating the leveraged buyout, *Harvard Business Review* 73, no. 3: 119–130.

100. A. Seth and J. Easterwood, 1995, Strategic redirection in large management buyouts: The evi-

dence from post-buyout restructuring activity, *Strategic Management Journal* 14: 251–274.

101. M. Matzer, 1996, Playing solo, *Forbes,* March 25, 80–81.

102. S. Chandler, 1996, United we own, *Business Week,* March 18, 96–100.

103. A. Bernstein, 1996, Why ESOP deals have slowed to a crawl, *Business Week,* March 18, 101–102.

104. I. Filatochev, R. E. Hoskisson, T. Buck, and M. Wright, 1996, Corporate restructuring in Russian privatizations: Implications for US investors, *California Management Review* 38, no. 2: 87–105.

105. B. Ortega, 1995, Cadbury seeking a new king of pop to oversee no. 3 soft-drink business, *Wall Street Journal,* January 30, B2.

106. W. F. Long and D. J. Ravenscraft, 1993, LBOs, debt, and R&D intensity, *Strategic Management Journal* 14 (Special Issue): 119–135.

107. J. S. Harrison, 1994, LBOs slash R&D: So what?, *Academy of Management Executive* VIII, no. 2: 83–84.

108. Phan and Hill, Organizational restructuring and economic performance in leveraged buyouts.

109. R. E. Hoskisson and R. A. Johnson, 1992, Corporate restructuring and strategic change: The effect on diversification strategy and R&D intensity, *Strategic Management Journal* 13: 625–634.

110. W. B. Lee and E. S. Cooperman, 1989, Conglomerates in the 1980s: A performance appraisal, *Financial Management* 18, no. 2: 45–54; J. R. Williams, B. L. Paez, and L. Sanders, 1988, Conglomerates revisited, *Strategic Management Journal* 9: 403–414.

111. B. Morris, 1995, Roberto Goizueta and Jack Welch: The wealth builders, *Fortune,* December 11, 80–94.

112. R. Smith, S. Lipin, and A. K. Naj, 1994, How General Electric damps fluctuations in its annual earnings, *Wall Street Journal,* November 3, A1, A11.

113. S. Lipin and R. Smith, 1994, A brutal negotiator, GE Capital's Wendt builds a conglomerate, *Wall Street Journal,* November 2, A1, A10.

CHAPTER

8 International Strategy

After reading this chapter, you should be able to:

1. Explain traditional and emerging motives for firms to pursue international diversification.

2. Explore the four factors that lead to a basis for international business-level strategies.

3. Name and define generic international business-level strategies.

4. Define the three international corporate-level strategies: multidomestic, global, and transnational.

5. Discuss the environmental trends affecting international strategy.

6. Name and describe the five alternative modes for entering international markets.

7. Explain the effects of international diversification on firm returns and innovation.

8. Name and describe two major risks of international diversification.

9. Explain why the positive outcomes from international expansion are limited.

Russia and China: Opportunities and Risks

Lukoil

Firms such as Lukoil, Rosneft, and Yukos are unheard of in most places. However, these are 3 of the 13 oil companies that were privatized in Russia in the early 1990s. These newly-created private entities faced challenges of ancient equipment, badly managed fields, and underperforming refineries along with distant subsidiaries that had operated independently. However, it is clear that these companies produced a lot of crude oil. For example, Lukoil's daily output in 1995 was 1.07 million barrels, whereas Exxon's comparison figure was 1.73 million. Six of the major oil companies each had reserves greater than the 8.6 million barrels held by Royal Dutch–Shell Group, the world's largest private oil company outside of Russia. Although the Russian numbers may be overstated, the country's massive fields probably contain more than 100 million barrels, which is greater than Iraq's but less than Saudi Arabia's 250 million barrels. Ownership of these oil companies is quite varied. For instance, Surgutneftegaz, Russia's third largest oil producer, is 40 percent owned by the company's pension fund. On the other hand, Yukos, the second largest producer, is 78 percent owned by a Moscow banking and investment group, Menatep.

Even though ownership is varied, each company's control usually emphasizes a top-down mentality. This is partially due to the fact that the most senior executives in the oil firms came from top positions in the former Soviet Union. Alexander Putilov, chief of Rosneft, held a high rank in the Soviet ministry of oil. Vaget Alekperov, Lukoil's chairman, was acting minister of oil when the Soviet Union disintegrated. Sergei Muravlenko, head of Yukos, led a powerful subsidiary in Siberia. Yukos' vice president, Viktor Ivanenco, is a former head of the KGB. Ivanenco indicates that when the subsidiaries don't listen, he talks to them. They are afraid of him because of his former position.

None of this stops the companies from attracting Western partners. Amoco is a partner with Yukos and plans to spend $29 billion developing fields in western Siberia. Probably the most ambitious is Lukoil. It has signed a 10-year agreement with Arco to spend $3 billion on development projects throughout the former Soviet Union. Yuri Shafranik, Russia's minister of fuels and energy, is one of Lukoil's big shareholders. Mr. Alekperov, therefore, has no difficulty making his way through the corridors of power in Moscow. Furthermore, he is the son of an oil worker in Baku and has contacts in the capitol of Azerbaijan in the south.

China is also seeking to revitalize its state sector. By policy, China has chosen to develop the highly populated cities along the Yangtze River. At the mouth of the Yangtze, Shanghai has nearly 15 million residents. Along the river, up to Chongqing, live approximately 180 million inhabitants. This is the world's third longest river and one of its oldest commercial waterways. In the past five years, the Yangtze corridor has produced a quarter of the 10 percent economic growth in China. Average incomes in this area are surging approximately 20 percent a year with households surpassing $1,500-a-year levels. This is similar to the original foreign investment center in Guangdong, situated close to Hong Kong. Shanghai is emerging as a financial center and beginning to focus on services. Chongqing is an emerging industrial center with many money-losing state factories. As income levels improve downriver, Shanghai companies are starting to source further upriver where income levels are lower.

The Chinese privatization process has been significantly different than that of Russia. Ostensibly, there is no privatization, but rather decentralization of power and ownership to the ministries and the provinces. In China, larger public enterprises (ministries) have been forced to give power over their local business operations to the provinces. Also, China merges small public factories that remain a drain on the state into larger enterprises. In a merger in China, no one is fired because of the state ownership. However, some provinces have sold off entire state factories to foreign investors. The central government worries it is getting a poor deal as foreign entrepreneurs collude with local officials to buy factories at steep discounts. Despite the official propaganda by the government that privatization isn't allowed, provincial officials, under whose control most state factories fall, remain pragmatic. State assets are regularly transferred to joint ventures controlled by foreigners. Accordingly, factory sales are very common.

Despite the progress toward privatized economies, both the Russian and Chinese approaches have advantages and disadvantages. In China, the state officially still owns most businesses, although it has delegated management of the main assets to the provinces. In Russia, on the other hand, a huge privatization program resulted in approximately 75 percent of the state-owned enterprises being privatized in a voucher, or "giveaway," program. However, Russia is now experiencing a backlash in that many private citizens are blaming economic woes on the privatization process. A significant threat has arisen: Many state industries, including the 13 oil firms, may be renationalized because they represent a significant amount of foreign investment and income to reduce the trade balance. Alternatively, China had a $35 billion trade surplus with the United States in 1995, a $14 billion surplus with Japan, and the surplus with Europe has doubled to more than $13 billion. Therefore, the potential for China as well as Russia to be significant economic powerhouses is easily observable. As a result, these emerging markets contain significant opportunities but also significant risks for firms considering entry into the market and seeking to produce products in these countries.

Source: J. Barnathan, S. Crock, and B. Einhorn, 1996, Rethinking China, *Business Week,* March 4, 57–58; J. Barnathan, D. Roberts, A. Borrus, and K. Kerwin, 1996, A chill wind blows from Beijing: To keep control, its leaders are cooling risky reforms, *Business Week,* January 15, 44–45; I . Filatotchev, R.E. Hoskisson, T. Buck, and M. Wright, 1996, Corporate restructuring in Russian privatizations: Implications for U.S. investors, *California Management Review* 38, no. 2: 87–105; S. Liesman, 1996, Looking back: Some Russian officials are moving to reverse business privatization, *Wall Street Journal,* March 20, A1, A6; A. Reifenberg and M. Banerjee, 1996, Crude enigma: Despite iffy finances, Russian oil companies draw Western dollars, *Wall Street Journal,* March 29, A1, A4; C. Rosett, 1996, Russian communists target privatizers, *Wall Street Journal,* February 13, A11; C.S. Smith, 1996, Industrial form: China is revitalizing state sector, starting at the factory level, *Wall Street Journal,* March 26, A1, A12; M.W. Brauchli, 1995, River of dreams: The mighty Yangtze seizes a major role in China's economy, *Wall Street Journal,* December 13, A1, A5.

I n the 1980s, the dramatic success of Japanese firms and products in the United States and other international markets provided a powerful jolt to U.S. managers and awakened them to the importance of international competition and global markets. In the 1990s, Russia and China represent potential major international market opportunities for firms from many countries, including the United States, Japan, Korea, and European nations. They also represent formidable competitors, particularly China in low-technology manufacturing industries. As the opening case indicates, China currently has a large trade surplus with the United States, Japan, and Europe. Therefore, the international arena affords many potential opportunities, but also a number of potential threats. This chapter focuses not only on the opportunities to develop capabilities and core competencies through diversifying into international markets, but also on the problems and complexities of managing such operations.[1]

In this chapter, as illustrated in Figure 1.1 in chapter 1, we discuss the importance of international strategy as a source of strategic competitiveness and above-average returns. The chapter focuses first on the incentives to internationalize. Once a firm decides to go international, it must select its strategy and choose a mode of entry. For instance, it may enter international markets by exporting from domestic-based operations, licensing, forming joint ventures with international partners, acquiring a foreign-based firm, or establishing a new subsidiary. Such international diversification can extend product life cycles, provide incentives for more innovation, and produce above-average returns.

Figure 8.1   Opportunities and Outcomes of International Strategy

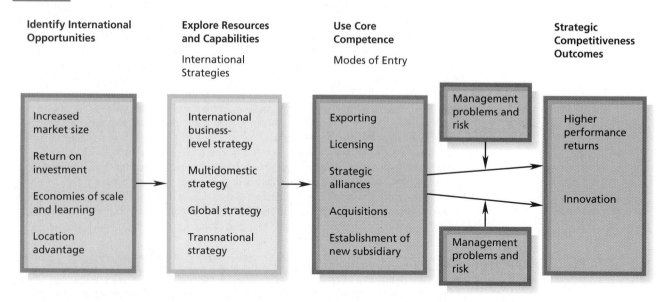

However, this is tempered by political and economic risks and the problems of managing a complex international firm with operations in multiple countries. Figure 8.1 provides an overview of these choices and outcomes. The relationships among international opportunities, exploration of resources and capabilities that result in strategies, and ultimate modes of entry based on core competencies are explored in this chapter.

◼ Identifying International Opportunities: The Incentive to Pursue an International Strategy

◼ An **international strategy** refers to the selling of products in markets outside the firm's domestic market.

An **international strategy** refers to the selling of products in markets outside the firm's domestic market. One of the primary reasons for implementing an international strategy (as opposed to a strategy focused on the domestic market) is that international markets yield potential new opportunities. Raymond Vernon captured the classic rationale for international diversification.[2] He suggested that typically a firm discovers an innovation in its home country market, especially in advanced economies such as that found in the United States. However, some demand for the product may develop in other countries and, thus, exports are provided by domestic operations. Increased demand in foreign countries justifies direct foreign investment in production capacity abroad, especially as foreign competitors also organize to meet increasing demand. As the product becomes standardized, the firm may rationalize its operations by moving production to a region where manufacturing costs are low. Vernon, therefore, suggests that firms pursue international diversification to extend a product's life cycle.

Another traditional motive for firms to become multinational is to secure key resources. Key supplies of raw material, especially minerals and energy, are important in some industries. For instance, aluminum producers need a supply of bauxite, tire firms need rubber, and oil companies scour the world to find new petroleum reserves.

Others seek to secure access to low-cost factors of production. Clothing, electronics, watchmaking, and many other industries have moved portions of their operations to foreign locations in pursuit of lower cost labor or capital (possibly government subsidized). Many international firms such as Daimler-Benz have moved into the United States because wages are lower in the United States than Germany. In fact, in 1995 German companies doubled their rate of direct investments abroad.[3] Britain has manufacturing costs that are 40 percent lower than Germany, prompting Siemens to locate a new $1.7 billion semiconductor plant there. Additionally, many local governments are offering subsidies and incentives. For example, Alabama outbid North and South Carolina for the first U.S. Mercedes-Benz car plant.[4] The state provided land and training wages for new workers and made commitments that government and utilities would buy large quantities of the four-wheel-drive recreational vehicles the plant will produce.

Although these traditional motives continue to exist, as the Mercedes example illustrates, other emerging motivations have been driving international expansion (see Chapter 1). For instance, pressure has increased for global integration of operations, mostly driven by more universal product demand. As nations industrialize, demand for commodity products appears to become more similar.[5] This nationless or borderless demand for products may be due to lifestyle similarities in developed nations. Also, increases in global communication media facilitate the ability of people in different countries to visualize and model lifestyles in disparate cultures.[6]

In some industries, technology is driving globalization because economies of scale necessary to reduce costs to the lowest level often require efficient scale investment greater than that needed to meet domestic market demand. There is also pressure for cost reductions in purchasing from the lowest cost global suppliers. For instance, R&D expertise for a new emerging business start-up may not be found in the domestic market.[7]

Many of the mouse devices connected to personal computers are made by Logitech. Logitech was founded in 1982 by a Swiss and two Italians who had aspirations to form a global venture. The venture had dual headquarters both in California and Switzerland. The R&D and manufacturing originally were split between California and Switzerland. However, additional operations were soon established in Taiwan and Ireland. These locations provided unique workforce skills to make the new global venture function effectively.

New large-scale markets, such as Russia, China, and India, also provide a strong incentive because of potential demand. And, because of currency fluctuations, firms may desire to have their operations distributed across many countries to reduce the risk of currency devaluation in one country.[8] However, the risk evidenced in Russia and China in the opening case underscores the need to manage not only currency risk but political risk as well.

On the other hand, there has been increased pressure for local country or regional responsiveness, especially where products require customization because of cultural differences.[9] Most products require local repair and service. This localization may even affect industries that are seen as needing more global economies of scale such as white goods (e.g., refrigerators and other appliances).[10] For large products, such as heavy earthmoving equipment, transportation costs become significant. Employment contracts and labor forces differ significantly. It is more difficult to negotiate employee layoffs in Europe than in the United States because of employment contract differences. Often host governments demand joint ownership, which allows the entering firm to avoid tariffs. Also, host governments often require a high percentage of local procurement, manufacturing, and R&D. These issues increase the need for local investment and responsiveness compared to seeking global economies of scale.

Given the traditional and emerging motivations for expanding into international markets, firms may achieve four basic opportunities through international diversification: increased market size; greater returns on major capital investments and/or investments in new product and process developments; greater economies of scale, scope, and/or experience; and/or a competitive advantage through location (e.g., access to low-cost labor, critical resources, or customers).

■ Increased Market Size

Firms can expand the size of their potential market, sometimes dramatically, by moving into international markets. Moving into international competitive arenas is a particularly attractive strategy to firms with domestic markets that are limited in growth opportunities. For example, the soft drink industry in the United States is saturated. Most changes in market share for any single firm must come at the expense of competitors' share. As a result, there is fierce competition to maintain—and increase—market share. The two major soft drink manufacturers, Coca-Cola and PepsiCo, moved into international markets several years ago because of the limited growth opportunities in the U.S. PepsiCo moved into the Soviet Union many years ago, and later Coca-Cola moved into China. Originally each obtained an exclusive franchise in those countries. However, recently these two potentially huge markets are beginning to open to other competitors. Although Pepsi had an early lead in Russia, Coke has been able to achieve competitive parity, not only in Russia but throughout Eastern Europe.[11] However, PepsiCo is fighting back in countries where Coke is not strong.[12] Additionally, the cola wars are heating up in China and India.[12] As a result, the potential market for the two firms is substantial and many other firms are attempting to exploit these huge emerging markets.

■ Return on Investment

Large markets may be crucial for earning a return on significant investments, such as plant and capital equipment and/or R&D. Therefore, most R&D-intensive industries are international. For example, the aerospace industry requires heavy investments in order to develop new aircraft. To recoup this investment, aerospace firms may need to sell the new aircraft in both the domestic and international markets. The Chinese market for aircraft is experiencing significant growth. Passenger traffic is growing by approximately 25 percent per year. As a result, Chinese airlines are ordering significant numbers of aircraft. Boeing has contracted for large orders of small planes, but is facing competition from Airbus and McDonnell Douglas.[13] China is expected to purchase $40 billion worth of commercial jets from U.S. and Western European firms during the next 20 years. China will rank second to Japan as the largest export market for Boeing, Airbus, and McDonnell Douglas.[14] In fact, Boeing has been realigning its production to accommodate more joint ventures with China and fewer with Japan.[15]

In addition to the need for a large market to recoup heavy investment in R&D, the pace of new technology development is increasing. As a result, new product obsolescence occurs more rapidly. Therefore, investments need to be recouped more quickly before a product is made obsolete by a newer one. In addition to rapid obsolescence, abilities to develop new technologies are expanding, and because of different patent laws across country borders, competitor imitation is more likely. In fact, through reverse engineering, competitors are able to take apart a competitive product, learn the new technology, and develop a similar product that imitates the new technology (see Chapters 5 and 13). Because of competitors' abilities to do this relatively quickly, the need to recoup new product development costs rapidly is increasing. Therefore, the larger markets provided by international expansion are particularly attractive in many industries (e.g., computer hardware) because they expand the opportunity to recoup large capital investment and large-scale R&D expenditures.[16]

■ Economies of Scale and Learning

When firms expand their markets, they may be able to enjoy economies of scale, particularly in their manufacturing operations. Thus, to the extent that firms are able to standardize products across country borders and use the same or similar production facilities, coordinating critical resource functions, they are likely to achieve more optimal economic scale.[17] This is the goal of many firms in Europe as the common market continues to evolve.

Firms may also be able to exploit core competencies across international markets. This allows resource and knowledge sharing between units across country borders.[18] It generates synergy and helps the firm produce higher quality goods or services at lower cost.

■ Location Advantages

Firms may locate facilities in other countries in order to lower the basic costs of the goods and/or services provided.[19] For example, they may have easier access to lower cost labor, energy, and other natural resources. Other location advantages include access to critical supplies/resources and to customers.

Motorola has entered the Chinese market in a significant way. In 1992, Motorola built a makeshift plant in the northern port city of Tianjin to manufacture paging devices for Chinese and export markets. In 1993, Motorola sold 10,000 units in China. Demand for pagers in China has increased dramatically from 1 million in 1991 to 4 million in 1993. However, in 1996, Motorola planned the largest manufacturing venture in China by any U.S. firm. In 1993, it completed a $120 million first-phase plan to make pagers, simple integrated circuits, and cellular phones. Currently it plans to build a second plant to manufacture automotive electronics, advanced microprocessors, and walkie-talkie systems.[20] In 1995, Motorola announced plans to build a $720 million plant to fabricate chip components of its equipment. It has even formed a joint venture with Ericsson (a Swedish telecommunications MNC) to create a cellular telephone system network. Motorola's location commitment is indicative of the potential significance of the Chinese market.[21]

We have explored why international strategies may be important and some of their advantages. Next, we describe the types and content of international strategies that might be formulated.

■ International Strategies

An international strategy may be one of two basic types, business or corporate level. At the business level, firms follow generic strategy types: low cost, differentiation, focused low cost, focused differentiation, or integrated low cost/differentiation. At the corporate level, firms can formulate three types: multidomestic, global, or transnational (a combination of multidomestic and global). However, to create competitive advantage, each of these strategies must realize a core competence based on difficult to duplicate resources and capabilities.[22]

■ International Business-Level Strategy

Each business must develop a competitive strategy focused on its own domestic market. We discussed business-level generic strategies in Chapter 4 and competitive dynamics in Chapter 5. However, international business-level strategies have some unique features. In pursuing an international business-level strategy, the home country of operation is often the most important source of competitive advantage. The resources and capabilities established in the home country often allow the firm to pursue the strategy beyond the national boundary. Michael Porter developed a model that describes the factors contributing to the advantage of firms in a dominant global industry and associated with a specific country or regional environment.[23] His model is illustrated in Figure 8.2.

The first dimension in the model, *factors of production,* refers to the inputs necessary to compete in any industry, such as labor, land, natural resources, capital, and infrastructure (e.g., highway, postal, and communication systems). Of course, there are basic (e.g., natural and labor resources) and advanced (e.g., digital communication systems and highly educated workforces) factors. There are also generalized (highway systems, supply of debt capital) and specialized factors (skilled personnel in a specific industry, such as a port that specializes in handling bulk chemicals). If a country has both advanced and specialized

Figure 8.2

Determinants of National Advantage

Source: Adapted and reprinted with the permission of The Free Press, an imprint of Simon & Schuster from *The Competitive Advantage of Nations* by Michael E. Porter, p. 72. Copyright © by Michael E. Porter.

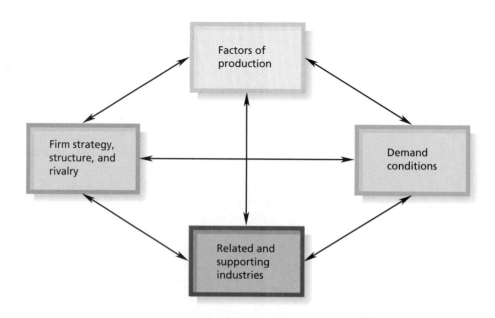

production factors, it is likely that this will serve an industry well in spawning strong home-country competitors that can become successful global competitors. Ironically, countries often develop advanced and specialized factor capabilities because they lack critical basic resources. Some Asian countries, such as Korea, lack abundant natural resources, but the strong work ethic, large numbers of engineers, and the systems of large firms have created an expertise in manufacturing. Germany developed a strong chemical industry, partially because Hoechst and BASF spent years developing a synthetic indigo dye to reduce their dependence on imports. This was not the case in Britain because large supplies of natural indigo were available in the colonies.[24]

The second dimension, *demand conditions,* is characterized by the nature and size of the buyers' needs in the home market for the industry's goods or services. The sheer size of a sales segment could produce the demand necessary to create scale-efficient facilities. This efficiency could also lead to domination of the industry in other countries. However, specialized demand may also create opportunities beyond national boundaries. For example, Swiss firms have long led the world in tunneling equipment, because of the need to tunnel through mountains for rail and highway passage. Japanese firms have created a niche market for compact, quiet air conditioner units. Small, but quiet units are required in Japan because homes are often small and packed together tightly. Under these conditions, large, noisy units would be unacceptable.[25]

Related and supporting industries are the third dimension in the model. Italy has become the leader in the shoe industry because of related and supporting industries. The leather supplies necessary to build shoes are furnished by a well-established industry in leather processing. Also, many people travel to Italy to purchase leather goods. Thus, there is support in distribution. In addition, supporting industries in leather-working machinery and design services contribute to the success of the shoe industry. In fact, the design services industry supports many related industries, such as ski boots, fashion apparel, and furniture. In Japan, cameras and copiers have been related industries. In Denmark, the dairy products industry is related to an industry focused on food enzymes.

Firm strategy, structure, and rivalry, the final country dimension, also foster the growth of certain industries. The pattern of firm strategy, structure, and rivalry among firms varies greatly from nation to nation. Earlier, much attention was placed on examining U.S. enterprise managers; more recently, the Japanese have been scrutinized and emulated. In Germany, because of the excellent technical training system, there is a strong inclination toward methodological product and process improvement. In Japan, unusual cooperative and competitive systems have facilitated cross-functional management of complex assembly operations. In Italy, the national pride of its designers has spawned strong industries in sports cars, fashion apparel, and furniture. In the United States, competition among computer manufacturers and software producers has favored the development of these industries.

The four basic dimensions of the "diamond" model shown in Figure 8.2 emphasize the environmental or structural attributes of a national economy that may contribute to national advantage. One could therefore conclude that chance or luck has led to the competitive advantage of individual firms in these industries. To a degree this is true, but government policy also has contributed to the success and failure of firms and industries. This is certainly the case in Japan, where the Ministry of International Trade and Investment (MITI) has contributed significantly to the corporate strategies followed. However, each firm must create its own success. Not all firms have survived to become global competitors, given the same country factors that spawned the successful firms. Therefore, the actual strategic choices managers make may be the most compelling reason for success or failure. The factors illustrated in Figure 8.2, therefore, are likely to lead to firm competitive advantages only when an appropriate strategy is applied, taking advantage of distinct country factors. We therefore reiterate examples of the low-cost, differentiation, focused low-cost, focused differentiation, and integrated low-cost/differentiation generic strategies discussed in Chapter 4, but also pursued in international markets.

International Low-Cost Strategy

The international low-cost strategy is likely to develop in a country with a large demand. Usually the operations of such an industry are centralized in a home country, and obtaining economies of scale is the primary goal. Outsourcing of low value-added operations may take place, but high value-added operations are retained in the home country. As such, products are often exported from the home country.

However, there are risks associated with this strategy. Often, they are related to the underlying factors supporting the strategy. In the late 1970s, Korea was the dominant manufacturer in the sport shoe industry. In the 1980s, the Korean conglomerate HS Corporation had a plant employing 9,000, and Kukje Corporation had the largest shoe factory in the world, with 24 lines and 20,000 employees. In Pusan, the Korean shoe hub, these and other Korean firms manufactured sport shoes for Nike, Reebok, and other well-known brands. In 1990, there were approximately 130,000 shoe workers in 302 factories, but by 1993, there were just over 80,000 workers in 244 factories, most employing fewer than 100 people. Of course, the large corporations, even the Korean ones, are still in the shoe business. However, their manufacturing takes place in China and Indonesia where the wages are $40 versus the current $800 per month in Pusan. The industry has moved from the United States to Taiwan and from Korea to China and Indonesia. However, the Koreans have built a level of expertise and have moved to manufacturing specialty shoes, such as high-technology hiking boots. They also have strong supporting industries, such as petrochemicals (synthetic fabrics) and leather tanneries. However, their strategy must change to differentiation because they can no longer compete on wage differentials with other Asian countries.[26]

International Differentiation Strategy

A country with advanced and specialized factor endowments is likely to develop an international differentiation strategy. Germany has a number of world-class chemical firms. The differentiation strategy followed by many of these firms to develop specialized chemicals was possible because of the factor conditions surrounding the development of this industry. The Kaiser Wilhelm (later Max Planck) Institutes and university chemistry programs were superior in research and produced the best chemistry education in the world. Also, Germany's emphasis on vocational education fostered strong apprenticeship programs for workers.[27]

The Japanese capabilities in consumer electronics have given them an advantage in memory chips and integrated circuits, the basic components in this industry. However, differentiation by Sharp Corporation, a Japanese electronics firm, has given it the lead in liquid crystal displays (LCDs), which are used with laptop computers and camcorders.[28] Alternatively, the United States is the leader in logic chips, the main components of computers, telecommunications equipment, and defense electronics. Intel is the world's leading producer of computer logic chips, and its products are differentiated worldwide by the slogan "Intel inside."[29]

International Focus Strategies

Many firms have remained focused on small market niches and yet have pursued international focus strategies.[30] The ceramic tile industry in Italy contains a number of medium and small fragmented firms that produce approximately 50 percent of the world's tile.[31] These tile firms, clustered in the Sassuolo area of Italy, have formed a number of different focus strategies. Firms such as Marazzi, Iris, Cisa-Cerdisa, and Flor Gres invest heavily in technology to improve product quality, aesthetics, and productivity. These firms have close relationships with equipment manufacturers. They tend to emphasize the focused low-cost strategy, while maintaining a quality image. Another group, including Piemme and Atlas Concorde, attempts to compete more on image and design. It invests heavily in advertising and showroom expositions. Because they try to appeal to selected customer tastes, they emphasize the focused differentiation strategy.[32]

International Integrated Low-Cost/Differentiation Strategy

The integrated strategy has become more popular because of flexible manufacturing systems, improved information networks within and across firms, and total quality management systems (see Chapter 4). Because of the wide diversity of markets and competitors, following an integrated strategy may be the most effective in global markets.[33] Therefore, competing in global markets requires sophisticated and effective management. Komatsu illustrates a classic case where this strategy was well executed. Komatsu was able to gain on a strong competitor, Caterpillar, by pursuing the integrated low-cost/differentiation strategy. Caterpillar had a very strong brand image in world markets, but Komatsu was able to overcome this differentiation advantage by improving its image and reducing its costs. It was initially able to do this because of lower labor costs and steel prices. Furthermore, in the 1970s, the dollar was strong, and this allowed a successful export strategy. Although Komatsu has remained very competitive, it faces critical challenges today due to a resurging Caterpillar and a stronger yen.[34]

■ International Corporate-Level Strategy

The business-level strategies previously discussed depend, to a degree, on the type of international corporate strategy the firm is following. Some corporate strategies give individual country units the authority to develop their own strategies; other corporate strategies require that country business-level strategies be compromised because of dictates from the home office to accomplish standardization of products and sharing of resources across countries. International corporate-level strategy is distinguished from international business-level strategy by the scope of the operations in both product and geographic diversification. International corporate-level strategy is required when the level of product complexity increases to multiple industries and multiple countries or regions.[35] Corporate strategy is guided by headquarters, rather than by business or country managers.

Multidomestic Strategy

■ *A **multidomestic strategy** is one in which strategic and operating decisions are decentralized to the strategic business unit in each country in order to tailor products to the local market.*

A **multidomestic strategy** is one in which strategic and operating decisions are decentralized to the strategic business unit in each country in order to tailor products to the local market.[36] A multidomestic strategy focuses on competition within each country. It assumes that the markets differ and therefore are segmented by country boundaries. In other words, consumer needs and desires, industry conditions (e.g., number and type of competitors), political and legal structures, and social norms vary by country. Multidomestic strategies allow for the customization of products to meet the specific needs and preferences of local customers. Therefore, they should be able to maximize competitive response to the idiosyncratic requirements of each market. However, multidomestic strategies do not allow for the achievement of economies of scale and thus can be more costly. As a result, firms employing a multidomestic strategy decentralize strategic and operating decisions to the strategic business units operating in each country. The multidomestic strategy has been more prominent among European multinational firms because of the varieties of cultures and markets found in Europe.

Global Strategy

■ *A **global strategy** is one in which standardized products are offered across country markets and competitive strategy is dictated by the home office.*

Alternatively, a global strategy assumes more standardization of products across country markets.[37] As a result, competitive strategy is centralized and controlled by the home office. The strategic business units operating in each country are assumed to be interdependent, and the home office attempts to achieve integration across these businesses. Therefore, a **global strategy** is one in which standardized products are offered across country markets and competitive strategy is dictated by the home office. Thus, a global strategy emphasizes economies of scale and offers greater opportunities to utilize innovations developed at the home office or in one country in other markets. However, a global strategy often lacks responsiveness to local markets and is difficult to manage because of the need to coordinate strategies and operating decisions across country borders. Therefore, achieving efficient operations with a global strategy requires the sharing of resources and an emphasis on coordination and cooperation across country boundaries. This requires more centralization and central headquarters control. The Japanese have often pursued this strategy with success.[38]

Transnational Strategy

■ *A **transnational strategy** is a corporate strategy that seeks to achieve both global efficiency and local responsiveness.*

A **transnational strategy** is a corporate strategy that seeks to achieve both global efficiency and local responsiveness. Realizing the diverse goals of the transnational strategy is difficult because one goal requires close global coordination, while the other requires local flexibility. Thus, "flexible coordination" is required to implement the transnational strategy.[39] It requires building a shared vision and individual commitment through an integrated network. In reality, it is difficult to achieve a pure transnational strategy because of the conflicting goals. As the Strategic Focus segment suggests, Citicorp has sought to build the appropriate structure and culture to overcome the difficulties of managing the conflicting

Figure 8.3

International Corporate Strategies

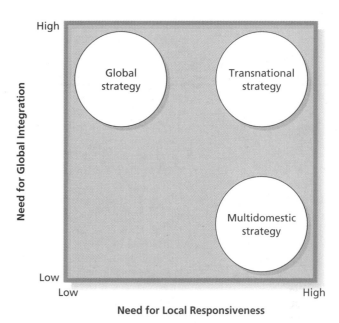

Citicorp's transnational strategy now has the company operating in 98 countries, such as Saudi Arabia and Hong Kong, with two more countries to be added soon.

requirements. Citicorp is finding that it is difficult also for competitors to duplicate its strategy. It is hoping that its global strategy will thereby yield above-average returns. The three international corporate strategies are depicted in Figure 8.3.

STRATEGIC FOCUS

The Evolution of Citicorp Toward a Transnational Strategy

In 1991, John S. Reed, CEO of Citicorp, was experiencing difficulty. Citicorp lost $457 million in 1991 and its stock price fell to a low of $8.50 per share in December of that year. During this period, a large number of real estate loans went bad and Reed was called on to resign. However, by April 1996, the stock sold for $81 per share and the company was viewed as savvy because in December 1995, it had bought back its own stock at $66 per share.

During those difficult years, when operating returns were poor, Citibank continued to invest in emerging markets. It now operates in 98 countries with 2 more soon to be added.

—Continued

—Continued

Citicorp, in those earlier years, was almost forced to divest its credit card business. However, in 1995, this business provided $1.2 billion in profits, about one-third of Citicorp's total. Once the Chemical-Chase merger is complete (see Strategic Focus segment in Chapter 7), Citicorp will no longer be the largest bank in the United States. However, Citibank, Citicorp's worldwide consumer brand name, is an asset in worldwide competition. It will seek to establish its brand name in financial services in the same manner as Coca-Cola and McDonald's have in their respective markets.

Citibank has been building its global brand through its branches around the world. Four hundred thirty-nine of 1,203 branches operate outside the United States. In every country that will accept it, the Citicard looks the same and has two big blue arrows as prominent signals of the brand. In the Asia/Pacific area, Citibank pushes the Citigold account and requires its customers to have at least $100,000 in either investments or cash deposited at the bank. In return, customers get special services such as a daily sweep of cash deposits into money market funds. In each of its local markets, Citibank has global competition such as Chase and J.P. Morgan, as well as local banks. In credit cards, Citibank also faces American Express, which may be the only other global brand in financial services.

Behind the brand the company is working on an ambitious $700 million database called the Relationship Banking System (RBS). RBS will allow Citibank consumer customers, by use of their Citicards or home computers, to keep tabs on all of their financial products at Citibank. Citibank also expects to use this service to build a relationship not only with present customers but also with the children of customers. Therefore, they plan to obtain household information and when it is time for a young child to enter college, the system will send a mailing to the parents that Citibank is ready to make a student loan or offer a low-interest credit card for the transitioning child. The global part of this strategy would fit into all markets and provide efficiency that supports the global brand. This may lead to a virtual banking system done totally with a person's personal computer.

Historically, Citibank was highly decentralized. Each branch had its own branch manager and enjoyed independence to develop local consumer loyalty. From the outset, the bank operated through autonomous affiliates responsible for all activities within each country. Also, each country unit was evaluated based on local profitability. A central bank in each country maintained tight centralized financial and credit controls. Citibank's depositor geographic-based (multidomestic) strategy lasted into the 1980s. However, a major impetus for change came from its European subsidiaries. The movement toward a global strategy first took place on a regional basis. In Europe, regional management was reduced by cutting staff and closing branches in more costly locations. However, rather than altering the focus on local product and customer service that was emphasized in the decentralized structure, it tried to maintain a strong local customer focus. As the organization grew, it developed regional links between banks to support the local activities. Thus, its informal, specialized cross-border units sought to support national affiliates rather than replacing them. By the late 1980s, a new concept had emerged: "The Unique European Bank," which had a common vision for all corporate banking activities in Europe. The vision entailed a focus on geography (assessing local country customers), products (preparing product strategies and delivery systems), and customer or industry units (coordinating relations with important customer groups across borders). This approach was very different from the bank's traditional multidomestic, geography-based strategy.

In the early 1990s, Citibank underwent a global reorganization in which it created global activity centers for institutional and investment banks by dividing the world into three central areas (Japan, Europe, and North America), with another branch for emerging markets. Over time, these units were reorganized so that at least two layers of management were removed. Ultimately in Europe, this left 25 activity centers. Additionally, the focus on cross-border market opportunities increased. By 1994, Citibank's European corporate strategy closely resembled a multinational corporation network-based strategy (a transnational strategy). The bank's strategy incorporated centralized service products and functional support through centers of excellence. Each region had targeted products and specific customer markets. Resources were reallocated across these specialized operating units. However, the units shared much information through a strong information system that delivers the needed coordination. Because the managers of each node in the network (the centers of excellence) facilitated coordination, their roles were more that of area managers. They focused on local issues but coordinated across borders to facilitate more global efficiency. Thus, much of the above-average returns, at least in the international part of the business, is because of successful evolution toward a transnational strategy.

Source: C.J. Loomis, 1996, Citicorp: John Reed's second act, *Fortune,* April 29, 89–98; T.W. Malnight, 1996, The transition from decentralized to network-based MNC structures: An evolutionary perspective, *Journal of International Business Studies* 27: 43–65; P.L. O'Brien, 1995, Citicorp plans stock buyback of $3 billion, *Wall Street Journal,* June 21, A3; M. Schifrin, 1995, The wizard of Citi, *Forbes,* March 13, 44–46.

As can be seen in the Strategic Focus, Citicorp has been pursuing a transnational strategy. However, as the earlier history indicates, it initiated an international emphasis by implementing a multidomestic strategy. But, to pursue its global brand strategy, it was necessary to switch to a transnational strategy. This would allow it to maintain the historical emphasis on meeting local customer tastes and government requirements while creating global efficiencies. Furthermore, it is seeking to create geographic centers of excellence and implement a network organization that can share product and service innovations across borders (network organizations are discussed in Chapter 11).

■ Environmental Trends

Although the transnational strategy is difficult to implement, emphasis on the need for global efficiency is increasing as more industries begin to experience global competition as well as an increased emphasis on local requirements. As the Citicorp example illustrates, global goods and services often require some customization to meet government regulations within particular countries or to fit customer tastes and preferences. In addition, most multinational firms desire to achieve some coordination and sharing of resources across country markets to hold down costs. Furthermore, some products and industries may be better suited for standardization across country borders than others. Citicorp is seeking to standardize through its emphasis on a global brand. As a result, most large multinational firms with diverse products may employ a partial multidomestic strategy with certain product lines and global strategies with others.

These trends are also exemplified by international automobile manufacturers. Ford, for example, has reorganized to foster more global transfer of knowledge between its previously independent units in Europe and the United States.[40] Ford's Mondeo, the first newly designed auto from this reorganization, has 75 percent common parts. However, the U.S. version is slightly longer and has more chrome than the European model. The interiors of the two automobiles also differ slightly. Before the "world car" comes out in 1998, its current models, the new Ford Fiesta (Ford's number one seller in Europe) and Escort are likely to receive only minor design changes until after the reorganization is complete.[41]

Ford's original plan was to coordinate the design of the Escort between the North American and the European divisions. However, the problems of coordinating that design were so great that two distinct models were developed. When the Escort was finally introduced to both markets, the North American and the European versions shared only one part, a water pump seal. Therefore, achieving global integration to produce a world product that is acceptable to consumers in multiple international markets is no easy task.

■ Regionalization

Regionalization in world markets is becoming more common. Location can affect a firm's strategic competitiveness.[42] Firms must decide whether to compete in all (or many) world markets or to focus on a particular region(s). The advantage of attempting to compete in all markets relates to the economies that can be achieved because of the combined market size. However, if the firm is competing in industries where the international markets differ greatly (e.g., it must employ a multidomestic strategy), it may wish to narrow its focus to a particular region of the world. In so doing, it can better understand the cultures, legal and social norms, and other factors important for effective competition in those markets. Therefore, a firm may focus on Far East markets, rather than attempting to compete in the Middle East, Europe, and the Far East. It may choose a region of the world where the markets are more similar and thus some coordination and sharing of resources would be possible. In this way, the firm may be able not only to understand the markets better, but also to achieve some economies, even though it may have to employ a multidomestic strategy.

Regional strategies may be promoted by countries that develop trade agreements to increase the economic power of a region. For example, the European Community (EC) and the Organization of American States (OAS, South America) are collections of countries that developed trade agreements to promote the flow of trade across country boundaries within the region. For example, many European firms have been acquiring and integrating their businesses in Europe to better rationalize pan-European brands as the EC creates more unity in European markets. The North American Free Trade Agreement (NAFTA), signed by the United States, Canada, and Mexico, is designed to facilitate free trade

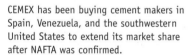

CEMEX has been buying cement makers in Spain, Venezuela, and the southwestern United States to extend its market share after NAFTA was confirmed.

across country borders in North America and may be expanded to include other countries in South America, such as Argentina, Brazil, and Chile.[43] These agreements loosen restrictions on international strategies within a region and provide greater opportunity to realize the advantages of international strategies. NAFTA does not exist for the sole purpose of U.S. businesses going north and south. Bernardo Dominguez, a Mexican businessman, arranged to purchase Westin Hotels Group in North America, South America, and Europe for $708 million from Aoki Corp. of Japan.[44] Also, Cementos de Mexico (CEMEX), the largest cement company in Mexico, has been buying cement makers in Spain and Venezuela as well as in the southwestern United States to extend its market share after the NAFTA agreement was confirmed. Anticipating entry by foreign competitors into Mexico, CEMEX is readying itself to compete globally, especially in emerging markets. For instance, it is stepping up exports to Asia. It received orders for 2 million tons of cement in 1995 from Taiwan, Thailand, and Indonesia.[45]

After firms decide on their international strategies and whether to employ them in regional or world markets, they must decide how to accomplish such international expansion. Therefore, the next section discusses how to enter new international markets.

■ Choice of International Entry Mode

International expansion is accomplished through exporting, licensing, strategic alliances, acquisitions, and establishing new wholly owned subsidiaries. These means of entering international markets and their characteristics are depicted in Table 8.1. Each has its advantages and disadvantages as described in the following subsections.

■ Exporting

Many industrial firms initially begin international expansion by exporting their goods or services to other countries.[46] Exporting does not require the cost of establishing operations in the host countries, but exporters must establish some means of marketing and distributing their products. In so doing, exporting firms must develop contractual arrangements with host country firms. Its disadvantages

Table 8.1 Global Market Entry: Choice of Entry Mode	
Type of Entry	**Characteristics**
Exporting	High cost, low control
Licensing	Low cost, low risk, little control, low returns
Strategic alliances	Shared costs, shared resources, shared risks, problems of integration (e.g., two corporate cultures)
Acquisition	Quick access to new market, high cost, complex negotiations, problems of merging with domestic operations
New wholly owned subsidiary	Complex, often costly, time consuming, high risk, maximum control, potential above-average returns

include the often high costs of transportation and possible tariffs placed on incoming goods. Furthermore, the exporter has less control over the marketing and distribution of its products in the host country and must pay the distributor and/or allow the distributor to add to the price to recoup its costs and make a profit. As a result, it may be difficult to market a competitive product through exporting or to provide a product that is customized to each international market through exporting. Historically, many Japanese firms have been successful at doing this. However, more recently, larger Japanese firms are engaging in significant foreign direct investment.[47]

■ Licensing

A licensing arrangement allows a foreign firm to purchase the right to manufacture and sell the firm's products within a host country or set of countries.[48] The licenser is normally paid a royalty on each unit produced and sold. The licensee takes the risks and makes the monetary investments in facilities for manufacturing, marketing, and distributing the goods or services. As a result, licensing is possibly the least costly form of international expansion.

Tetra Pak, a privately held packaging maker headquartered in Lund, Sweden, used an intensive licensing strategy to create a worldwide $7.8 billion operation in 130 countries. It facilitates manufacture of squishy, brick-shaped drink cartons made from paper laminated with plastic and aluminum. As a result, the Rausing family, which controls Tetra Laval Group, Tetra Pak's parent, has amassed an $8 billion fortune primarily by selling these little cartons. Some have suggested that the innovation of their carton has "revolutionized the beverage industry globally."[49] Tetra Pak's strategy is to license its machines in each country in which it operates and then, as part of the contract, obligate the licensee to buy the packaging material from Tetra Pak. Through this strategy, Tetra Pak has half the noncarbonated drink package market in Europe and almost 40 percent in Japan.

Licensing is also a way to expand returns based on previous innovations. For instance, Sony and Philips codesigned the audio CD. In 1994, makers of CDs and CD-ROM players and disks generated $50 billion in revenues. Sony and Philips collected 5 cents for every CD sold.[50] As the Sony–Philips example demonstrates, many firms can stand on the shoulders of their past innovations. Continual focus on research and patent licensing allows a firm to gain strong returns from its innovations for many years in the future.[51]

Of course, licensing has its disadvantages. For example, this approach to international expansion provides the firm very little control over the manufacture and marketing of its products in other countries. In addition, licensing provides the least potential returns because returns must be shared between the licenser and the licensee. It is also the least costly and therefore the least risky (the firm does not have to make major capital investments in a foreign country). However, the international firm may learn the technology and, after the license expires, produce and sell a similar competitive product. Komatsu, for example, first licensed much of its technology from U.S. companies International Harvester, Bucyrus-Erie, and Cummins Engine to enter the earthmoving equipment business to compete against Caterpillar. It subsequently dropped these licenses and developed its own products using the technology it gained from the U.S. companies.[52]

Apple Computer experienced severe difficulties in 1995 and 1996. Michael Spindler resigned from his CEO position in the firm. Much of the difficulty was blamed on the lack of licensing to establish Apple's state-of-the-art technology as a standard. Although there was talk of developing licensing agreements with other firms as far back as 1985, to establish the Macintosh operating system as the standard and spawn a clone industry to increase the market share of the Macintosh platform, every time top management considered this alternative, it was scuttled. For instance, in 1992, when Apple came close to outsourcing its production of low-end Macintosh computers to Taiwan's Acer, Inc., Apple negotiators left the discussions when Apple executives decided that the firm could do it alone. Not licensing its technology allowed a successful version of Windows to enter the market in 1990. Apple was concerned about licensing its technology for fear that it would lose its technology leadership if it had an agreement with one of the larger producers such as Hewlett-Packard or IBM. However, perhaps too late, it has agreed with Motorola to do what it most likely should have done many years previously: license its low-end production to build market share for its leading edge operating systems and software.[53] Motorola plans to build and sell the Apple clones in China. It is also negotiating with IBM to develop a similar license. IBM may be trying to increase sales of its PowerPC chips through such a venture.[54] Therefore, licensing can be an important strategy in world markets, if used properly. Apple had the opportunity to establish a worldwide standard. It was very successful in Japan and the United States, but the lack of early key licensing agreements may have led to the difficulties experienced by Apple.

■ Strategic Alliances

Strategic alliances have enjoyed popularity in recent years as a primary means of international expansion. As explained in the Strategic Focus describing some of Sony Corp.'s strategic actions, strategic alliances allow firms to share the risks and the resources required to enter international markets. In addition, most strategic alliances are with a host country firm that has knowledge of the competitive conditions, legal and social norms, and cultural idiosyncrasies that should help the firm manufacture and market a competitive product. Alternatively, the host firm may find access to technology and new products attractive. Therefore, each partner in an alliance brings knowledge and/or resources to the partnership. Strategic alliances are discussed in more depth in Chapter 9.

STRATEGIC FOCUS   Sony Uses Strategic Alliances As an International Entry Mode

Sony has used many modes of entry strategies over the years with both extraordinary success and extraordinary failure. Sony produced the transistor radio, the Trinitron TV, the Walkman, the camcorder, and the CD player. These, of course, represent the extraordinary success facilitated by Akio Morita as the leader of Sony for many years. Morita also set in motion a significant strategy in multimedia through Sony's $3.4 billion acquisition of Columbia and Tristar Film Studios in 1989. In 1994, Sony wrote off $2.7 billion from Sony Pictures

—Continued

—Continued

Entertainment, Inc., its combined movie and music operations. The synergy between Sony's electronics business and its entertainment operations did not produce the expected significant success. However, Sony is refusing to give up on its entertainment division as did Matsushita, which sold MCA Studios to Seagram in 1995.

Noboyuki Idei is the new president of Sony. Under Idei, the primary strategic actions apparently will focus on the convergence of audio, video, computers, and communication. Currently, Sony executives view the personal computer (PC) as the initial driving force to launch new high-tech electronic consumer products. They feel that PC users will be the first to test the new potential products. They are equally intent on creating new types of digital products and tapping into the Internet. For example, Sony might develop Internet-ready televisions with wide-screens and high resolution. They have also thought about multimedia eyeglasses that can project television images and data onto eyeglass lenses that allow users to watch movies or read E-mail. On-line stereo music may be available for downloading off the Internet onto a smaller version of the PC. These smaller PCs might lead to personal digital assistants that will allow the user to browse the Worldwide Web for less than $500.

Many of these products are likely to be developed through strategic alliances. However, if Sony is able to create technology through strategic alliances similar to the CD technology it created with Philips, it may be able to collect royalties off its license agreements.

The next future challenge in consumer electronics may be production and distribution of the digital video disk (DVD). These new disks are expected to do for movie pictures what the CD did for sound. It will make it possible to play digitized images on TV screens. However, Sony faces the very real prospect of a replay of its Betamax versus VHS fiasco in the format of video cassette players. Sony lost to Matsushita, which established the VHS format. Matsushita accomplished this through joint ventures with other firms rather than trying to do it alone. Currently, Sony and Philips have teamed together to create their version of the DVD. However, Toshiba and Time Warner have a different format that will hold more information than the Sony–Philips format. Furthermore, with Time Warner's connections in Hollywood, the Toshiba–Time Warner alliance was prodding studio executives to form a council to set performance criteria and standards. The key player in the format battle was again Matsushita. Sony found that Matsushita would participate in the new potential Toshiba–Time Warner product. Sony sought to produce a truce in the battle. A common format was arrived at in the fall of 1995. New products that use the DVD technology to play the new disks were expected to be on the market in 1996.

Over the years, Sony has used all of the various market entry approaches to establish its global strategy. It has done substantial exporting of radios and Walkman players. It has licensed its technology to garner significant revenues from its CD and CD-ROM format through its joint venture with Philips. It has made acquisitions in the entertainment industry through which it hopes to establish its format and garner greater returns when each CD or DVD disk is sold. However, at this point it is critical that Sony use alliances with other firms to ensure that it is a significant player in each format that is launched. The outcome of the DVD cooperative agreements is likely to determine, to a large extent, Sony's potential returns in the near future.

Source: P. Coy and R. Grover, 1995, It's Noboyuki Idei's Sony now, *Business Week,* December 18, 39; D.P. Hamilton, 1995, Sony picks insider, tapping crisis-management skills, *Wall Street Journal,* March 23, A8; A. Pollack, 1995, New Sony president hopes to fill missing links in U.S., *New York Times,* March 29, D6; B.R. Schlender, 1995, Sony on the brink, *Fortune,* June 12, 60–78; B.R. Schlender, 1995, Sony's new president: Here's the plan, *Fortune,* April 17, 18–19; J.A. Trachtenberg, 1995, Sony president rules out buying American network, *Wall Street Journal,* November 21, B6.

■ Acquisitions

Cross-border acquisitions have been increasing significantly with free trade in global markets.[55] They have also been increasing among Japanese and German firms because the value of the dollar has fallen relative to their home countries' currencies.[56] As explained in Chapter 7, acquisitions can provide quick access to a new market. In fact, acquisitions may provide the fastest and often the largest initial international expansion of any of the alternatives. This was the case with BMW's acquisition of Rover Cars in order to enter the sport utility vehicle market. Therefore, international acquisitions have become a popular mode of entering international markets. They are not without their costs, however. International acquisitions carry some of the same disadvantages that exist for domestic acquisitions, as discussed in Chapter 7. In addition, they can be expensive and often require debt financing (which also carries an extra cost). International negotiations for acquisitions can be exceedingly complex—generally more complicated than in domestic acquisitions. Dealing with the legal and regulatory requirements in the foreign host country of the target firm and obtaining appropriate information for effective negotiation of the agreement frequently present significant problems. Finally, the problems of merging the new firm into the acquiring firm often are more complex than for domestic acquisitions. The acquiring firm must deal not only with different corporate cultures, but also with potentially different social cultures and practices. Therefore, while international acquisitions have been popular because of the rapid access to new markets they provide, they also carry with them important costs and multiple risks.

Interestingly, Japanese acquisitions of firms in other countries grew from less than 50 in 1981 to almost 450 in 1989. However, Japan ranked only fifth in the number of U.S. firms acquired during this period. Firms from the United Kingdom, Canada, West Germany, and France (listed in order of the number of acquisitions) acquired more U.S. firms than did Japanese firms during the 1980s.[57] However, Japan was the leading percentage leader in foreign direct investment in the United States through 1992.[58] Since then, Japanese acquisitions have slowed due to the recession in Japan. Furthermore, foreign firms have been making some acquisitions in Japan such as Ford's deeper investment in Mazda.[59]

Ford Motor Company, along with other owners, recently installed a Ford manager, Henry D.G. Wallace, as the new president of Mazda Motor Corporation. Earlier, Mazda, with its renown prowess in engineering, taught Ford how to build better small cars and manage production systems. Mazda provided Ford with basic technology and design for popular models such as the Probe and Escort. However, the strong yen has crippled Mazda, given its export-dependent strategy. Mazda did not have as much direct foreign investment as the other major firms such as Toyota and Nissan. This change in leadership came about because Ford's ownership stake was increased to 33 percent from 25 percent.[60]

John Labatt was recently acquired by Interbrew. This is an example of foreign entry into the North American market by a powerful European brewer headquartered in Belgium. John Labatt, the Canadian brewer, lost its independence because of a shareholder revolt regarding Labatt's international strategy. Labatt's distribution system gave Interbrew the opportunity to enter the North American market including the United States, Canada, and Mexico. The acquisition will also give Interbrew the opportunity to bring its brands to the United States as well. Furthermore, Labatt can gain entry into Europe through Interbrew's network. Thus, in the acquisition of John Labatt, Interbrew has been able to establish a strong market position in a short period of time.[61]

■ New, Wholly Owned Subsidiary

■ *A greenfield venture is one in which a new, wholly owned subsidiary is established.*

The establishment of a new, wholly owned subsidiary is referred to as a **greenfield venture.** This is often a complex and potentially costly process. This alternative has the advantage of providing maximum control for the firm and, therefore, if successful, has the most potential to provide above-average returns. However, because of the costs involved in establishing a new business operation in a new country, the risks are also great. The firm may have to acquire the knowledge and expertise of the existing market by hiring host country nationals, possibly from competitive firms, and/or consultants (which can be costly). It maintains control over the technology, marketing, and distribution of its products through this process. Alternatively, it must build new manufacturing facilities, establish distribution networks, and learn and implement appropriate marketing strategies to compete in the new market.

The establishment of a new, wholly owned subsidiary in a host country, such as the Mercedes-Benz plant in Alabama, can be a lengthy process and more time consuming than the alternative modes of entering international markets. Therefore, the firm must choose between the importance of protecting its technology and controlling its manufacturing and marketing versus the costs of establishing the new operation. Oftentimes, firms will choose this alternative only after expanding into markets through other alternatives, such as exporting and forming strategic alliances. In addition, this means of international market entry may be attractive in high-technology industries where the protection and control of a technological competence are critical to gaining and/or maintaining a competitive advantage in global markets.

■ Dynamics of Mode of Entry

Choice of mode of entry is determined by a number of factors.[62] However, initial market entry will often be through export because this requires no foreign manufacturing expertise and investment only in distribution. Licensing can also facilitate the product improvement necessary to enter foreign markets, as in the Komatsu example. Strategic alliances have been popular because they allow partnering with an experienced player already in the targeted market. Strategic alliances also reduce risk through the sharing of costs. These modes therefore are best for early market development tactics.

However, to secure a stronger presence, acquisitions or greenfield ventures may be required. The Philips acquisition by Whirlpool has allowed Whirlpool to challenge Electrolux and Siemens in the European appliance market.[63] Merck has gained a significant presence in Japan's pharmaceutical market through its acquisition of Banyu.[64] Alternatively, many Japanese automobile manufacturers, such as Honda, Nissan, and Toyota, have gained presence in the United States through a greenfield venture in addition to joint ventures. Both acquisitions and greenfield ventures are likely to come at later stages in the development of an international diversification strategy. Many consider these approaches more risky, as Disney recently found with its Euro-Disney operation.

Euro-Disney found that there were cultural differences in Europe that were not encountered in its successful U.S. and Japanese operations. Just because a number of visitors come from Europe each year to visit Disney World in Florida did not mean that a Disney operation would be successful in Europe. The troubled resort was losing $1 million a day. Its park entry prices, emphasis on American culture, and lack of European ethnic and convenience foods in its restaurants contributed to the alienation of European tour operators.[65] Therefore, considerable time passed before the Euro-Disney park produced a return on investment.[66]

As indicated earlier, there are multiple means of entering new markets, and firms may employ some or all of these alternatives in sequential fashion or use different modes with different products or market types.

■ Strategic Competitiveness Outcomes

Once the strategy and mode of entry have been established, firms need to be concerned about overall success. However, international expansion can be risky and may not result in a competitive advantage. Thus, the following strategic competitiveness issues are discussed, as suggested in Figure 8.1.

■ International Diversification and Returns

The primary international corporate-level strategy may be referred to as international diversification. In Chapter 6, we discussed the corporate-level strategy of product diversification, in which a firm engages in the manufacture and sale of multiple diverse products. In contrast, **international diversification** is the manufacture and sale of a firm's product lines across country boundaries (in multiple international markets).

■ *International diversification is the manufacture and sale of a firm's product lines across country boundaries (in multiple international markets).*

As noted earlier, multiple reasons exist for firms to diversify internationally. Because of its potential advantages, international diversification should be positively related to firm returns. Research has shown that as international diversification increases, firm returns increase, whereas domestic product diversification is often negatively related to firm returns.[67] There are many reasons for the positive effects of international diversification, such as the potential economies of scale and experience, location advantages, increased market size, and potential to stabilize returns. The stabilization of returns helps reduce a firm's overall risk.[68]

The Japanese automobile firms, despite the difficulties encountered because of a recession in their domestic economy, have continued to pursue international diversification as illustrated in the Strategic Focus segment.

STRATEGIC FOCUS   Japanese Automobile Manufacturers' Use of International Diversification

In 1995, the large U.S. auto firms shipped 163,553 cars from U.S. and Canadian plants for sale in the United States, whereas Japanese firms shipped 167,000 from the United States and Canada. Of course, if trucks, minivans, and sport utility vehicles are counted, the U.S. firms were way ahead. However, Japan did not make these types of vehicles for export to the United States in 1995. But, many Japanese trucks and minivans from U.S. plants will be exported.

In early 1995, Nissan's financial performance (and those of other Japanese automakers) was suffering greatly from a rising yen, falling sales, and the possibility of a significant trade war with the United States. Nissan dropped the age for retirement by almost a third and some 1,600 employees accepted early retirement offers. In 1996, Nissan emerged from the

—*Continued*

—Continued

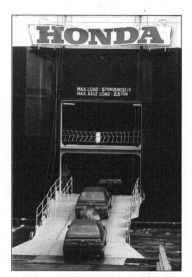

Honda has emerged as one of the largest exporters of North American cars.

depths. The yen softened dramatically, the Japanese economy was growing, and Nissan expected to show a profit after three years of losses. Not only Nissan but Toyota, Mitsubishi Motors, and Honda were increasing the global competitiveness. In fact, all 11 vehicle manufacturers in Japan have managed to survive without widely predicted mergers. Many of the second-tier players averted greater difficulties by becoming more deeply involved with larger players and focusing on narrower market segments. Mazda Motor Corporation, for example, has narrowed its product range and has survived only through the auspices of Ford Motor Company. In fact, Mazda's top manager was recently replaced by an American manager. This situation may have resulted because Mazda was the least internationally diversified auto company of the larger Japanese auto firms.

As the dollar rises (and the yen declines), the upward pressure on Japanese car prices in the United States eases, allowing Japanese firms to offer big discounts and win back lost market share. Nissan reported that its annualized operating profits rose roughly $74 million each time the dollar's value increases by one yen. Theoretically, Toyota reckoned that it would gain $160 million in annualized profit with a one yen rise in the dollar's value. Furthermore, the sharp depreciation of the yen since summer 1995 helped boost the broader Japanese economy. As such, Japanese are spending more on new cars. However, while Japanese exports were sliding before the recent rise in the yen, there was a significant increase in overseas investment in production facilities to take advantage of the depreciated yen. Although this caused the downturn in the Japanese economy, it lead to increased investment in overseas production facilities.

As such, the Japanese auto firms, through their international diversification strategy, are well positioned to compete globally in all international markets. Furthermore, Japanese companies have continued to make great strides in speeding up and improving their manufacturing cycles. Additionally, although the United States is beginning to penetrate the Japanese market more fully, many of the imports coming to Japan come from Japanese plants abroad. For instance, Toyota and Honda have emerged as the largest exporters of North American cars, about half of which are headed for Japan. Moreover, Japanese firms are helping U.S. firms to sell in Japan. For instance, Toyota is marketing approximately 20,000 Chevrolet Cavaliers annually in Japan for General Motors. Ford hopes to sell 200,000 cars in Japan annually, half made in Japan by Mazda. In total, General Motors is aiming for 100,000 units in Japan, including its German Opels. Although the Japanese firms have focused on market share in the past, they are now in competitive shape to improve their potential returns. Although the problems of too much manufacturing capacity in Japan as well as low white-collar productivity will continue to present challenges to the Japanese firms, with higher earnings, they are likely to have time and money to deal effectively with them.

Source: M. Kanabayashi, 1996, Strong dollar boosts Japan's auto firms, *Wall Street Journal,* April 15, C1; K. Naughton and A. Borrus, 1996, America's number one car exporter is . . . Japan? *Business Week,* February 26, 113; A. Taylor III, 1996, It's the slow lane for automakers, *Fortune,* April 1, 60–64; J. Updike, L. Armstrong, K. Kerwin, K. Naughton, and D. Woodruff, 1996, Japan turns a corner: Car makers come on strong around the globe, *Business Week,* February 26, 108–112; H. Cooper and V. Reitman, 1995, Averting a trade war, U.S. and Japan reach agreement on autos, *Wall Street Journal,* June 29, A1, A8; N. Weinberg, 1995, Toyota loves GM, *Forbes,* December 18, 262–266.

Firms in the Japanese automobile industry have found that international diversification may allow a firm to better exploit its core competencies. Therefore, the sharing of knowledge resources can produce synergy among the operations in different countries/international markets as it has among Japanese automakers.[69] On the other hand, firm returns may affect international diversification. For example, poor returns in a domestic market may encourage a firm to expand internationally in order to enhance its profit potential. In addition, internationally diversified firms may, in turn, have access to more flexible labor markets, as the Japanese do in the U.S., and benefit from global scanning for competition and market opportunities.[70] As a result, multinational firms with efficient and competitive operations are more likely to produce above-average returns for their investors and better products for their customers than are solely domestic firms.[71] However, as explained later, international diversification can be carried too far.

■ International Diversification and Innovation

In Chapter 1, we noted that the development of new technology is at the heart of strategic competitiveness. Michael Porter stated that a nation's competitiveness depends on the capacity of its industry to innovate and suggested that firms achieve competitive advantage in international markets through innovation. Competitors eventually and inevitably outperform firms that fail to innovate and improve their operations and products. Therefore, the only way to sustain a competitive advantage is to upgrade it continually.[72]

International diversification provides the potential for firms to achieve greater returns on their innovations (through larger and/or more numerous markets) and thus lowers the often substantial risks of R&D investments. Therefore, international diversification provides incentives for firms to innovate. In addition, international diversification may be necessary to generate the resources required to sustain a large-scale R&D operation. An environment of rapid technological obsolescence makes it difficult to invest in new technology and the capital-intensive operations required to take advantage of it. Firms operating solely in domestic markets may find such investments difficult because of the length of time required to recoup the original investment. Furthermore, if the time is extended, it may not be possible to recover the investment before the technology becomes obsolete.[73] As a result, international diversification improves the firm's ability to appropriate additional and necessary returns from innovation before competitors can overcome the initial competitive advantage created by the innovation.

Therefore, the relationship among international diversification, innovation, and returns is complex. Some level of performance is necessary to provide the resources to generate international diversification. International diversification provides incentives and resources to invest in research and development. Research and development, if done appropriately, should enhance the returns of the firm, which, in turn, provides more resources for continued international diversification and investment in R&D.

Because of the potential positive effects of international diversification on performance and innovation, some have argued that such diversification may even enhance returns in product diversified firms. International diversification would increase market potential in each of the product lines. However, the complexity of managing a product diversified and internationally diversified firm is significant. Therefore, it is likely that international diversification can enhance the returns of a firm that is highly product diversified, but only when it is well managed.

This is exemplified by the goals and international diversification efforts of Korean chaebols, Korea's large diversified firms. For example, because of rising wages in Korea, saturated markets in the United States, and a desire to be a global competitor, Korean firms are investing billions in Europe in sophisticated products such as cars and electronics.[74] LG Electronics is spending upwards of $1.5 billion to build a semiconductor and consumer electronics factory in Britain. Samsung inaugurated a $700 million plant for microwave ovens and personal computer monitors also in the United Kingdom. Daewoo Corp., has bought several Eastern European car plants and plans to spend $3 billion upgrading them.[75] Hyundai Corp. is considering a $1.3 billion semiconductor plant in Europe and is scouting Romania for a car-assembly site. Until recently, Koreans put their capital in the faster growing Asian and the U.S. markets. However, they realized that the only other market that could absorb their more expensive products was Western Europe. Although not true across Europe, O.S. Kong of LG Electronics found "in certain parts of northern England, labor costs are lower than they are in Korea." Furthermore, Korean firms hope to improve their technology through acquisition and licensing within Europe. The Korean car makers have had some initial success. In the first nine months of sales, Daewoo sold 60,000 vehicles. It wants to sell 300,000 annually by the year 2000. Although it may not reach this goal, it has made an excellent start. Thus, the Europeans will have to learn to compete and cooperate with these dynamic Asian firms. However, it remains to be seen whether these large diversified firms will manage the complexity well in a new area of the world. Furthermore, much of the investment is also going into risky emerging markets such as Eastern Europe.[76]

■ Complexity of Managing Multinational Firms

Although many potential benefits can be realized by implementing an international strategy, problems and complexities can also arise. For example, multiple risks are involved when operating in several different countries. Firms can become only so large and diverse before becoming unmanageable or the costs of managing them exceed their benefits. Other complexities include the highly competitive nature of global markets, multiple cultural environments, potentially rapid shifts in the value of different currencies, and the possible instability of some national governments.

■ Risks in an International Environment

International diversification carries with it multiple risks. International expansion is difficult to implement and manage after implementation because of these risks. Primary among these are the political and economic risks. Specific examples of political and economic risks are shown in Figure 8.4.

■ Political Risks

■ *Political risks are related to instability in national governments and to war, civil or international.*

Political risks are related to instability in national governments and to war, civil or international. Instability in a national government creates multiple problems. Among these are economic risks and the uncertainty created in terms of government regulation, many legal authorities, and potential nationalization of private assets. For example, foreign firms that are investing in Russia may have concerns about the stability of the national government and what might happen to their investments/assets in Russia should there be a major change in government. As politics have potentially shifted back toward the Communist position, noted in the opening case, these risks have been intensified.[77] Different concerns

Figure 8.4

Risks in the International Environment

Source: N. Banerjee, 1996, Russia's many regions work to attract funds from foreign investors, *Wall Street Journal,* April 30, A1, A8; P. Engardio and D. Roberts, 1996, Rethinking China, *Business Week,* March 4, 57–64; R.S. Greenberger, 1996, U.S. sharply attacks China over intellectual property, *Wall Street Journal,* May 1, A3, A4; A.D. Marcus, 1996, Israel seems to target Lebanon economy, *Wall Street Journal,* April 17, A16; C. Rosett, 1996, Russian Communists target privatizers, *Wall Street Journal,* February 13, A11; P. Stein, 1996, Hong Kong feels heavy hand of China, *Wall Street Journal,* April 17, A16; J. Templeman, 1996, The economy that fell to earth, *Business Week,* January 15, 46.

exist for foreign firms investing in China. They are less worried about the potential for major changes in China's national government than about the uncertainty of China's regulation of foreign business investments in that country. Tensions between Hong Kong, Taiwan, and China create concern about investment in the region. Taiwan is the second largest investor in China behind Hong Kong. Much of the tension is political: Taiwan and Hong Kong have been a laboratory in which capitalism was tested against socialism in China.[78]

Uncertainties are exemplified by events and actions such as tensions in the Middle East. For example, Lebanon's burgeoning economy, which had rebounded after a devastating civil war, suffered a reversal after Muslim guerrillas and the Israeli military increased the fighting in Lebanon. A $100 million Eurobond offering directed at reconstruction projects in Lebanon was postponed due to the escalation.[79] Civil war in Bosnia (formerly part of Yugoslavia), the Persian Gulf War, frequent coups in African countries, tensions between North and South Korea and between China and Taiwan, and internal strife in Ireland have created significant economic uncertainty for the countries and neighboring regions.

■ Economic Risks

Economic risks are interdependent with political risks, as noted earlier. However, there are other economic risks associated with international diversification. Chief among these are the differences and fluctuations in the value of different currencies. For example, with U.S. firms, the value of the dollar relative to other

Political risks and wars, such as in Sarajevo, pose difficulties for multinational corporations seeking to internationally diversify their operations.

currencies determines the value of their international assets and earnings. An increase in the value of the dollar can reduce the value of U.S. multinational firms international assets and earnings in other countries. Furthermore, the value of different currencies can, at times, dramatically affect a firm's competitiveness in global markets because of its effect on the prices of goods manufactured in different countries.[80] For example, an increase in the value of the dollar can harm U.S. firms' exports to international markets because of the price differential of the products.

Another economic risk is the different inflation rates across country borders. The U.S. inflation rate over the last several years has been less than 5 percent annually. As such, the United States and many of the Western industrialized countries enjoy low inflation rates relative to many countries throughout the world. There have been many countries, including South American and Eastern European countries, that have experienced annual inflation rates of several hundred percent. Of course, the inflation rate is interdependent with the value of the currency because high inflation rates lower the value of the currency relative to the currencies in other countries with lower inflation rates. Chile is an anomaly in Latin America because while it had an 8 percent growth rate, inflation hit a 35-year low of 8.2 percent in 1995. It has a strong peso, pegged to the dollar, supported by a 25 percent savings rate, eight straight budget surpluses, and $14.5 billion in foreign currency reserves. Although it has been stymied temporarily from gaining entry into NAFTA, it will try to negotiate its own trade agreement with Canada. It already has a trade agreement with Mexico. As the Chile example illustrates, effective political action can reduce perceived political and economic risks and facilitate an improved economic outlook.[81]

■ Limits to International Expansion: Management Problems

Research has shown that there are positive returns to early international diversification, but they tend to level off and become negative as the diversification increases past some point.[82] There are multiple reasons for the limits to the positive effects of international diversification. For example, greater geographic dispersion across country borders increases the costs of coordination between units and the distribution of products. Also, different government regulations and trade laws across countries create significant barriers to coordination.

The problems experienced in international diversification are shown by the recent difficulties of the U.K.'s Ispat International Ltd.[83] Ispat has become one of the world's 10 largest steel makers by buying and trying to turn around previously state-owned steel mills. It has bought such privatized steel mills at a good price in Mexico, Indonesia, Ireland, Germany, Trinidad, and Tobago. It seeks to turn around each mill by cutting costs and installing newer technology to increase returns. However, in its most recent $1 billion investment in Karmet, a privatized steel mill in Kazakstan, in the southern part of the former Soviet Union near China, it has experienced difficulties. It is a very important test case in that of the 126 large state enterprises slated for privatization, it was the only deal completed in Kazakstan. Although approximately 9,000 small businesses have been privatized in Kazakstan, these have been mostly small stores and state farms. While the region desperately needs foreign capital, the market for steel in the area has dried up. Prior to the acquisition, Karmet's annual production was at half capacity. Ispat was able to buy the plant after another deal for its acquisition failed.

After the acquisition, Ispat moved to cut a third of Karmet's 38,000-person workforce. Malay Mukherjee, Ispat's current manager, said, "There must be 10 layers of management here. Everyone has got his assistant and his assistant and his assistant." He also indicated that Ispat was going to emphasize natural attrition, but it was currently firing 100 people a week for coming to work drunk and others for allegedly cheating the company by getting paid for two jobs but working only one. Although this has created ire among some workers, Ispat, at least, has been paying its workforce, which was not the case prior to the acquisition. It has provided $11 million for back pay, $31 million in supplier debts, and $75 million to begin to rebuild the decaying plant. Furthermore, it has pledged to invest another $450 million over the next four years and an additional $550 million for new technology and maintenance.

Ispat has also embarked on an ambitious training program to teach about managing in the new capitalistic environment and becoming customer oriented.[84] It has been hunting for customers in China, Iran, Iraq, Turkey, and Afghanistan because further expansion creates expensive transportation difficulties. However, doing business in Russia is difficult and expensive. For example, to order supplies, an agreement must be established for review by the Russian customs agency. Each subsequent order represents an amendment to the original agreement. Translating contracts into both Russian and English can be a frustrating experience. Nevertheless, they still have to train employees to be more productive and customer oriented, and they have to deal with the Russian government bureaucracy. Russians also expect the company to be a social service agency because prior to privatization all social needs (housing, medical, and social welfare) were handled by company officials. Also, when Ispat took over the plant, the KGB office had to be removed. The KGB office had been in the plant since the 1940s when Stalin built the mill as a work camp. Mukherjee said it took two months of negotiation to get the KGB operatives out of their electronically sophisticated corner office. Therefore, because of the plant and human capital investments as well as cultural change necessary, it remains to be seen whether this will be a long-term profitable venture.

Trade barriers, logistical costs, cultural diversity, and other differences by country (e.g., access to raw materials, different employee skill levels) greatly complicate the implementation of international diversification.[85] As the Ispat example illustrates, institutional and cultural factors often represent strong barriers to the transfer of a firm's competitive advantages from one country to another. Marketing programs often have to be redesigned and new distribution networks established when firms expand into new countries. In addition, they may encounter different labor costs and capital charges. Therefore, it is difficult to effectively implement, manage, and control international operations.[86]

Scholars have argued that it is necessary for most internationally diversified firms to establish a global integration of international operations and at the same time allow local operations the autonomy to respond to local markets. This is extremely difficult because it requires firms to be managed as if they are simultaneously centralized and decentralized.[87] Although some mixed structures might be able to facilitate partial centralization and decentralization, no structure is available that allows both needs (global integration and coordination and local business autonomy) to be completely satisfied simultaneously. (See Chapter 11 for additional discussion of this issue.)[88]

The amount of international diversification that can be managed will vary by firm and the abilities of the managers. The problems of central coordination and integration are reduced if the firm diversifies into more friendly countries that have similar cultures. In so doing, there are fewer trade barriers, a better understanding of the laws and customs, and the product is easier to adapt for local markets. For example, U.S. firms may find it less difficult to expand their operations into Canada and Western European countries (e.g., Great Britain, France) than into Asian countries (e.g., Japan, Korea).[89]

■ Other Management Problems

One critical concern is that the global marketplace is highly competitive. Firms accustomed to a highly competitive domestic market experience more complexities in international markets. That is caused not only by the number of competitors encountered, but also by the differences of those competitors. A U.S. firm expanding operations into a European country may encounter competitors not only from Great Britain, Germany, France, and Spain, but also from countries outside of Europe, such as Hong Kong, Japan, Korea, Taiwan, Canada, and possibly even South America. Firms from each of these countries may enjoy different strategic advantages. Some may have low labor costs, others may have easy access to financing and low capital costs, and still others may have access to new high technology. Finally, attempting to understand the strategic intent of a competitor is more complex because of the different cultures and mind-sets.[90]

Another problem focuses on the relationships between the host government and the multinational corporation. For example, while Japanese firms face few trade barriers in competing in U.S. markets, U.S. firms often encounter many barriers to selling their products and operating in Japanese markets.[91] These regulations have traditionally kept the yen high relative to the dollar by keeping out imports and reducing the value of Japanese exports. This increases the price of Japanese products abroad. As noted earlier, the problem has been reversing itself somewhat, but much more remains to be done to reduce entry barriers. However, to overcome entry barriers many firms, such as Toyota and General Motors, are turning to strategic alliances.

The nature of managerial complexity not only in international markets, but in domestic ones as well, has led managers to seek help in meeting this challenge. The next chapter focuses on how firms are cooperating with each other to meet some of their management challenges.

■ Summary

- International diversification is increasing not only because of traditional motivations, but also for emerging reasons. Traditional motives include extending the product life cycle, securing key resources, and having access to low-cost labor. Emerging motivations focus on increased pressure for global integration as the demand for commodity products becomes borderless, and yet pressure for local country responsiveness is increasing.

- An international strategy usually attempts to capitalize on four important opportunities: potential increased market size; opportunity to earn a return on large investments, such as plant and capital equipment and/or research and development; economies of scale and learning; and, potential location advantages.

- International business-level strategies are similar to the generic business strategy types: international low cost, international differentiation, international focus, and international integrated low cost/differentiation. However, each of these strategies is usually grounded in some home country advantage, as Porter's diamond model suggests. The diamond model emphasizes four determinants: factors of production, demand conditions, related and supporting industries, and patterns of firm strategy, structure, and rivalry.

- International corporate-level strategies are classified into three types. A multidomestic strategy focuses on competition within each country in which the firm operates. Firms employing a multidomestic strategy decentralize strategic and operating decisions to the strategic business units operating in each country so each can tailor its goods and services to the local market. A global strategy assumes more standardization of products across country boundaries. Therefore, competitive strategy is centralized and controlled by the home office. A transnational strategy seeks to combine aspects of both multidomestic and global strategies in order to emphasize both local responsiveness and global integration and coordination. The strategy is difficult to implement, requiring an integrated network and a culture of individual commitment.

- Although the transnational strategy is difficult to implement, environmental trends are causing all multinational firms to consider the needs for both global efficiencies and local responsiveness. Most large multinational firms, particularly those with many diverse products, may use a multidomestic strategy with some product lines and a global strategy with others.

- Some firms decide to compete only in certain regions of the world, as opposed to viewing all markets in the world as potential opportunities. Competing in regional markets allows firms and managers to focus their learning on specific markets, cultures, location resources, etc.

- Firms may enter international markets in one of several different ways, including exporting, licensing, forming strategic alliances, making acquisitions, and establishing new, wholly owned subsidiaries, often referred to as greenfield ventures. Most firms begin with exporting and/or licensing because of their lower costs and risks, but later may expand to strategic alliances and acquisitions. The most expensive and risky means of entering a new international market is through the establishment of a new, wholly owned subsidiary. Alternatively, it provides the advantages of maximum control for the firm and, if successful, potentially the greatest returns as well.

- International diversification facilitates innovation in the firm. It provides a bigger market to gain more and faster returns from investments in innovation. In addition, international diversification may generate the resources necessary to sustain a large-scale R&D program.

- In general, international diversification is related to above-average returns. However, this assumes effective implementation of international diversification and management of international operations. International diversification provides greater economies of scope and learning. These, along with the greater innovation, help produce above-average returns.

- Several risks are involved with managing multinational operations. Among these are political risks (e.g., instability of national governments) and economic risks (e.g., currency value fluctuations).

- There are also limits to the ability to manage international expansion effectively. International diversification increases coordination and distribution costs, and management problems are exacerbated by trade barriers, logistical costs, and cultural diversity, among other factors.

- Additionally, international markets are highly competitive and firms must maintain an effective working relationship with the host government.

Review Questions

1. What are the traditional and emerging motives that are causing firms to expand internationally?

2. What four factors are a basis for international business-level strategies?

3. What are the generic international business-level strategies? How do they differ from each other?

4. What are the differences among the following corporate-level international strategies: multidomestic, global, and transnational?

5. What environmental trends are affecting international strategy?

6. What five modes of international expansion are available, and what is the normal sequence of their use?

7. What is the relationship between international diversification and innovation? How does international diversification affect innovation? What is the effect of international diversification on firm returns?

8. What are the risks involved in expanding internationally and managing multinational firms?

9. What are the factors that create limits to the positive outcomes of international expansion?

Application Discussion Questions

1. Given the advantages of international diversification, why do some firms choose not to expand internationally?

2. How do firms choose among the alternative modes for expanding internationally and moving into new markets (e.g., forming a strategic alliance versus establishing a wholly owned subsidiary)?

3. Does international diversification affect innovation similarly in all industries? Why or why not?

4. What is an example of political risk in expanding operations into China or Russia?

5. Why do some firms gain competitive advantages in international markets? Explain.

6. Why is it important to understand the strategic intent of strategic alliance partners and competitors in international markets?

7. What are the challenges in pursuing the transnational strategy? Explain.

Ethics Questions

1. As firms attempt to internationalize, there may be a temptation to locate where product liability laws are lax to test new products. Are there examples where this motivation is the driving force behind international expansion?

2. Regulation and laws regarding the sale and distribution of tobacco products are stringent in the U.S. market. Undertake a study of selected U.S. tobacco firms to see if sales are increasing in foreign markets compared to

domestic markets. In what countries are sales increasing and why?

3. Some firms may outsource production to foreign countries. Although the presumed rationale for such outsourcing is to reduce labor costs, examine the liberality of labor laws (for instance, the strictness of child labor laws) and laws on environmental protection in another country.

4. Are there markets that the U.S. government protects through subsidy and tariff? If so, which ones and why?

5. Should the United States seek to impose trade sanctions on other countries such as China because of human rights violations?

6. Latin America has been experiencing a significant change in both political orientation and economic development. Describe these changes. What strategies should foreign international businesses implement, if any, to influence government policy in these countries? Is there a chance these political changes will reverse? How would business strategy change if Latin American politics reverses its current course?

Internet Exercise

Look at the "Big Emerging Markets" compiled by the National Trade Data Bank at:

- http://www.stat-usa.gov/itabems.html

Select three countries and compare their political risk, demographics, and other noneconomic factors. What makes one market attractive to enter and another unattractive?

Cohesion Case

Go to the U.S. Department of Commerce's International Trade Administration at:

- http://www.ita.doc.gov/

Find information about a region to which your group is interested in exporting. Can you determine how companies are expanding into that area? Is there any information available on innovation or technology transfer? What are the strategic and economic advantages of the region you have chosen? Decide on an appropriate mode for a firm to enter a market in the region.

Notes

1. C.A. Bartlett and S. Ghoshal, 1991, Global strategic management: Impact on the new frontiers of strategy research, *Strategic Management Journal* 12: 5–16.
2. R. Vernon, 1966, International investment and international trade in the product cycle, *Quarterly Journal of Economics* 80: 190–207.
3. J. Templeman, 1996, Germany: The economy that fell to earth, *Business Week*, January 15, 46.
4. D. Woodruff and K.L. Miller, 1995, Mercedes' maverick in Alabama, *Business Week*, September 11, 64–65; E. S. Browning and H. Cooper, 1993, States bidding war over Mercedes plant made for costly chase, *Wall Street Journal*, September 24, A1, A6.
5. N. J. Adler, R. Doktor, and S. G. Redding, 1986, From the Atlantic to the Pacific century: Cross-cultural management review, *Journal of Management* 12: 295–318.
6. K. Sera, 1992, Corporate globalization: A new trend, *Academy of Management Executive* VI, no. 1: 89–96.
7. B.J. Oviatt and P.P. McDougall, 1995, Global start-ups: Entrepreneurs on a worldwide stage, *Academy of Management Executive* IX, no. 2: 30–44.
8. K.A. Froot and G. Stein, 1991, Exchange rates and foreign direct investment: An imperfect markets approach, *Quarterly Journal of Economics* 106: 1191–1217; J.J. Choi, 1989, Diversification, exchange risk and corporate international investment, *Journal of International Business Studies* 20: 145–155; J. Atherton and D.C.L. Yap, 1979, Risk reduction by international diversification, *Managerial Finance* 5: 18–28.
9. S. Schneider and A. DeMeyer, 1991, Interpreting and responding to strategic issues: The impact of national culture, *Strategic Management Journal* 12: 307–320.
10. C. Baden-Fuller and J. Stopford, 1991, Globalization frustrated: The case of white goods, *Strategic Management Journal* 12: 493–507.
11. E. Beck, 1995, Where West faced East, colas now at war: Coke is ahead in Eastern Europe; Pepsi fires back, *Wall Street Journal*, September 7, A10.
12. S. Dubey, 1994, Pepsi fights for India's beverage business: Battle with Coke heats up for potentially huge market, *Wall Street Journal*, June 3, B3; G.G. Marcial, 1994, Two reasons why Coke is it: China and Russia, *Business Week*, March 7, 106.
13. J. Cole, 1995, Airbus attempts to persuade Air China to rethink pact to buy Boeing planes, *Wall Street Journal*, August 22, B16.
14. J. Barnathan and D. G. Yang, 1993, Look up in the sky: A swarm of Chinese airplanes, *Business Week*, May 17, 60.
15. Dropping Japan for China, 1995, *The Economist*, September 9, 66.
16. M. Kotabe, 1990, The relationship between offshore sourcing and innovativeness of U.S. multinational firms: An empirical investigation, *Journal of International Business Studies* 21: 623–638.
17. A.J. Venables, 1995, Economic integration and the location of firms, *The American Economic Review* 85: 296–300; S. J. Kobrin, 1991, An empirical analysis of the determinants of global integration, *Strategic Management Journal* 12 (Special Issue): 17–37.
18. A. DeMeyer, 1993, Internationalizing R&D improves a firm's technical learning, *Research-Technology Management* 36, (July/August): 42–49; B. Kogut and U. Zander, 1993, Knowledge of the firm and the evolutionary theory of the multinational corporation, *Journal of International Business Studies* 24: 625–645.
19. J.Y. Murray, M. Kotabe, and A.R. Wildt, 1995, Strategic and financial performance implications of global sourcing strategy: A contingency analysis, *Journal of International Business Studies* 26, no. 1: 181–202; A.D. MacCormack, L.J. Newman III, and D.B. Rosenfield, 1994, The new dynamics of global manufacturing site location, *Sloan Management Review* 35, Summer: 69–80; P.M. Swamidass and M. Kotabe, 1993, Component sourcing strategies of multinationals: An empirical study of European and Japanese multinationals, *Journal of International Business Studies* 24: 81–99.
20. P. Engardio, 1993, Motorola in China: A great leap forward, *Business Week*, May 17, 58–59.
21. C.S. Craig, 1995, Motorola, Ericsson to link Chinese cellular systems, *Wall Street Journal*, October 23, A15; C.S. Craig, 1995, Motorola is planning major investment of $720 million on

chip plant in China, *Wall Street Journal,* September 25, A8.

22. K. Fladmoe-Linquist and S. Tallman, 1994, Resource-based strategy and competitive advantage among multinationals, *Advances in Strategic Management* 10A (Greenwich, Conn.: JAI Press), 45–72.

23. M.E. Porter, 1990, *The Competitive Advantage of Nations* (New York: The Free Press).

24. Ibid., 84.

25. Ibid., 89.

26. S. Gain, 1993, Korea is overthrown as sneaker champ, *Wall Street Journal,* October 7, A14.

27. Porter, *The Competitive Advantage,* 133.

28. J. Friedland, 1994, Sharp's edge: Prowess in LCD screens puts it ahead of Sony, *Far Eastern Economic Review,* July 28, 74–76.

29. R.A. Shaffer, 1995, Intel as conquistador, *Forbes,* February 27, 130.

30. Oviatt and McDougall, Global start-ups; B. Mascarenhas, 1986, International strategies of non-dominant firms, *Journal of International Business Studies* 17, no. 1: 1–26.

31. Porter, *The Competitive Advantage,* 210–225.

32. M.J. Enright and P. Tenti, 1990, How the diamond works: The Italian ceramic tile industry, *Harvard Business Review* 68, no. 2: 90–91.

33. D. Lei, M.A. Hitt, and J.D. Goldhar, 1996, Advanced manufacturing technology: The impact on organization design and strategic flexibility, *Organization Studies* 17: 501–523.

34. A.L. Cowan, 1994, Caterpillar: Worldwide watch for opportunities, *New York Times,* January 3, C4; D.F. Abell, 1993, *Managing with Strategies: Mastering the Present and Pre-Empting the Future* (New York: The Free Press), 210–214.

35. M.A. Hitt, R.E. Hoskisson, and R.D. Ireland, 1994, A mid-range theory of the interactive effects of international and product diversification on innovation and performance, *Journal of Management* 20: 297–326.

36. S. Ghoshal, 1987, Global strategy: An organizing framework, *Strategic Management Journal* 8: 425–440.

37. Ibid.

38. J.K. Johaansson and G.S. Yip, 1994, Exploiting globalization potential: U.S. and Japanese strategies, *Strategic Management Journal* 15: 579–601.

39. C.A. Bartlett and S. Ghoshal, 1989, *Managing Across Borders: The Transnational Solution* (Boston: Harvard Business School Press).

40. A. Taylor III, 1995, Ford's really big leap at the future: It's risky, it's worth it, and it may not work, *Fortune,* September 18, 134–136; J.B. Treece, 1995, Ford: Alex Trotman's daring global strategy, *Business Week,* April 3, 94–97.

41. H. Dawley, 1995, Ford's bumpy odyssey in Europe, *Business Week,* November 20, 47.

42. A. Saxenian, 1994, *Regional Advantage: Culture and Competition in Silicon Valley and Route 128* (Cambridge, Mass.: Harvard University Press).

43. J.I. Martinez, J.A. Quelch, and J. Ganitsky, 1992, Don't forget Latin America, *Sloan Management Review,* 33 (Winter): 78–92.

44. P.B. Carroll, 1994, Buyer of Westin deal may represent new breed of Mexican businessman, *Wall Street Journal,* March 1, A15.

45. G. Smith and J. Person, 1996, CEMEX: Solid as Mexico sinks, *Business Week,* February 27, 58–59.

46. G.M. Naidu and V.K. Prasad, 1994, Predictors of export strategy and performance of small- and medium-sized firms, *Journal of Business Research* 31: 107–115; S.C. Jain, 1989, *Export Strategy* (New York: Quorum Books).

47. R. Grosse and L.J. Trevino, 1996, Foreign direct investment in the United States: An analysis by country of origin, *Journal of International Business Studies* 27: 139–155.

48. J. Clegg, 1990, The determinants of aggregate international licensing behavior: Evidence from five countries, *Management International Review* 30, no. 3: 231–251.

49. D. Milbank, 1994, Risky strategies prove profitable for Swedish company, *Wall Street Journal,* July 1, B4.

50. B. Schlender, 1995, Sony on the brink, *Fortune,* June 12, 66.

51. J.R. Green and S. Scotchmer, 1995, On the division of profit in sequential innovation, *The Rand Journal of Economics* 26: 20–33; S. Scotchmer, 1991, Standing on the shoulders of giants: Cumulative research in the patent law, *Journal of Economic Perspectives* 5: 29–41.

52. C.A. Barlett and S. Rangan, 1992, Komatsu limited, in C.A. Bartlett and S. Ghoshal (eds.), *Transnational Management: Text, Cases and Readings in Cross-Border Management* (Homewood, Ill.: Irwin), 311–326.

53. K. Rebello and P. Burrows, 1996, The fall of an American icon, *Business Week,* February 5, 34–42.

54. B. Ziegler, 1996, IBM is close to licensing Apple system, *Wall Street Journal,* April 10, B7.

55. R.J. Kish and G.M. Vasconcellos, 1993, An empirical analysis of factors affecting cross-border acquisitions: U.S.–Japan, *Management International Review* 33, no. 3: 227–245.

56. S. Lipin, 1995, Acquisition bargains rise on dollar's fall, *Wall Street Journal,* March 8, C1.

57. M. Mason, 1992, United States direct investment in Japan: Trends and prospects, *California Management Review* 35, no. 1: 98–115; W. C. Kester, 1991, *Japanese Takeovers: The Global Contest for Corporate Control* (Boston: Harvard Business School Press).

58. Grosse and Trevino, Foreign direct investment.

59. N. E. Benes, 1995, Glimmers of hope for the inbound acquisition in Japan, *Mergers & Acquisitions* 30 (July–August): 25–30; L. Armstrong, 1994, Look who's stuck in the slow lane, *Business Week,* March 28, 28–29.

60. B. Reitman, 1996, Japan is aghast as foreigner takes the wheel at Mazda, *Wall Street Journal,* April 15, A11.

61. W.C. Symonds and L. Bernier, 1995, A Belgian brewer's plans come to a head, *Business Week,* June 19, 56.

62. W.C. Kim and P. Hwang, 1992, Global strategy and multinationals' entry mode choice, *Journal of International Business Studies* 23: 29–53.

63. Z. Schiller, 1988, Whirlpool plots the invasion of Europe, *Business Week,* September 5, 70.

64. L. Smith, 1985, Merck has an ache in Japan, *Fortune,* March 18, 42–44.

65. P. Gumbel, 1994, Euro Disney calls in Mary Poppins to tidy up the mess at resort in France, *Wall Street Journal,* February 22, A17.

66. J. Tagliabue, 1995, Step right up, monsieur!, *New York Times,* August 25, D1.

67. R. Buhner, 1987, Assessing international diversification of West German corporations, *Strategic Management Journal* 8: 25–37.

68. J. M. Geringer, P. W. Beamish, and R. C. daCosta, 1989, Diversification strategy and internationalization: Implications for MNE performance, *Strategic Management Journal* 10: 109–119; R. E. Caves, 1982, *Multinational Enterprise and Economic Analysis* (Cambridge, Mass.: Cambridge University Press); A. M. Rugman, 1979, *International Diversification and the Multinational Enterprise* (Lexington, Mass.: Lexington Books).

69. G. Hamel, 1991, Competition for competence and interpartner learning within international strategic alliances, *Strategic Management Journal* 12: 83–103.

70. Kobrin, An empirical analysis.

71. M. Kotabe, 1989, Hollowing-out of U.S. multinationals and their global competitiveness, *Journal of Business Research* 19: 1–15.

72. Porter, *The Competitive Advantage.*

73. Kotabe, The relationship.

74. J. Flynn, H. Dawley, D. Woodruff, and G. Edmundson, 1996, Korea's big leap into Europe, *Business Week,* March 18, 52.

75. L. Kraar, 1996, Daewoo's daring dive into Europe, *Fortune,* May 13, 145–152.

76. M. Sehuman, 1996, Korea speeds its global expansion as life grows tougher in home markets, *Wall Street Journal,* May 14, A13.

77. N. Banerjee, 1996, Russia's many regions work to attract funds from foreign investors, *Wall Street Journal,* April 30, A1, A8.

78. A. Tanzer, 1996, How Taiwan is invading China, *Forbes,* April 8, 86–91.

79. A.D. Marcus, 1996, Israel seems to target Lebanon economy, *Wall Street Journal,* April 17, A16.

80. A. K. Sundaram and J. S. Black, 1992, The environment and internal organization of multinational enterprises, *Academy of Management Review* 17: 729–757.

81. More smooth sailing in Santiago, 1996, *Business Week,* January 15, 24.

82. S. Tallman and J. Li, 1996, Effects of international diversity and product diversity on the performance of multinational firms, *Academy of Management Journal* 39: 179–196; Hitt, Hoskisson, and Ireland, The interactive effects; Geringer, Beamish, and daCosta, Diversification strategy.

83. K. Pope, 1996, A steelmaker built up by buying cheap mills finally meets its match, *Wall Street Journal,* May 2, A1, A6.

84. S.M. Puffer, 1994, Understanding the bear: A portrait of Russian business leaders, *Academy of Management Executive* VIII, no. 1: 41–54.

85. Porter, *The Competitive Advantage*.

86. B. Kogut, 1985, Designing global strategies: Comparative and competitive value added change (Part I), *Sloan Management Review* 26 (Summer): 15–28.

87. C. A. Bartlett and S. Ghoshal, 1988, Organizing for a worldwide effectiveness: The transnational solution, *California Management Review* 30: 54–74; C. A. Bartlett and S. Ghoshal, 1987, Managing across borders: New strategic requirements, *Sloan Management Review* 28: 7–17.

88. C. K. Prahalad and Y. L. Doz, 1987, *The Multinational Mission: Balancing Local Demands and Global Vision* (New York: The Free Press).

89. C. Horng, 1991, Cultural variability: Managing headquarters-subsidiary relations (Ph.D. dissertation, Texas A&M University).

90. M.A. Hitt, B.B. Tyler, and C. Hardee, 1996, Understanding strategic intent in the global marketplace, *Academy of Management Executive* IX, no. 2: 12–19.

91. D.P. Hamilton, M. Williams, and N. Shirouzu, 1995, Japan's big problem: Freeing its economy from over regulation, *Wall Street Journal,* April 25, A1, A6.

CHAPTER
9 Cooperative Strategy

After reading this chapter, you should be able to:

1. Identify and define different types of cooperative strategy.

2. Explain the rationales for a cooperative strategy in three types of competitive situations: slow-cycle, standard-cycle, and fast-cycle markets.

3. Understand competitive advantages and disadvantages and competitive dynamics of cooperative strategies at the business level.

4. Describe uses of cooperative strategies at the corporate level.

5. Identify appropriate applications of cooperative strategies when pursuing international strategies.

6. Distinguish the competitive risks of cooperative strategies.

7. Understand the nature of trust as a strategic asset in forming cooperative strategies.

8. Describe the two basic management approaches for managing strategic alliances.

Strange Bedfellows: The Art of Partnering

The number of strategic alliances has increased dramatically in the last 10 years. Interestingly, alliances between competitors are becoming increasingly common. For example, Texas Instruments and Hitachi began conducting joint research in 1988 and incrementally expanded their relationship. During the early part of their relationship, managers from the two firms had to bridge their cultural differences. For example, there were significant differences in their decision-making processes. Texas Instruments (TI) used a common American approach in which the managers would have a meeting to discuss the issue, then spend time brainstorming, followed by a decision. Hitachi executives, on the other hand, more commonly held informal discussions and came to a decision prior to the meeting used to ratify the final decision. However, over time, the two companies have learned to work together effectively. For example, Hitachi and TI developed a joint venture to produce memory chips. Although it took almost six months of negotiations to agree on the venture, they decided that the new venture would sell its chips to both companies at the same price and Hitachi and TI would then be free to sell the chips in competition with each other. TI's executives suggest that it intends to provide better services for its customers to differentiate itself from Hitachi.

Two U.S.-based competitors, Nucor Corporation and USX Corporation, formed an alliance to take advantage of each firm's unique competencies. USX researchers developed the idea for a revolutionary new steel-making process that eliminates the use of blast furnaces and coke batteries. They estimated that this new process would reduce the cost of steel production by 20 to 25 percent. Nucor brings to the team expertise on how to construct these new types of plants. Currently, the firms are jointly studying the feasibility of the process. If it is found to be feasible, they will build a new manufacturing plant.

Silicon Graphics is attempting to become the dominant player in visual computing by defining the standards for new applications of 3-D technology. However, it is attempting to build its competitive position through the development of a network of strategic alliances. Currently, it has formed a network of alliances involving 13 different businesses, including AT&T Network Systems, Time Warner Entertainment, and Nintendo of America. It is competing with firms such as Sun Microsystems and Hewlett-Packard; the network of strategic alliances created by Silicon Graphics provides unique and valuable competencies that allow it to be an effective competitor against such strong firms. Sun and HP also have alliances that strengthen their competitive position against Silicon Graphics and other firms.

Not all alliances are successful, however. For example, the alliance between AT&T and Pacific Bell has generated considerable conflict between the two firms. Part of the conflict is derived from direct competition between the two firms as AT&T enters the local phone service market and Pacific Bell moves into the long-distance market. Pacific Bell buys approximately 50 percent of its equipment from AT&T. Recently, Pacific Bell sought approval from the California Public Utilities Commission to provide schools with high-speed data transmission lines (which would use significant amounts of AT&T equipment and software). However, AT&T representatives argued that the commission should reject Pacific Bell's proposal. AT&T fought the proposal because Pacific Bell would use these lines to compete against it. Pacific Bell's managers were angry about the AT&T action and threatened to reduce their firm's purchases of AT&T equipment.

There is an art to managing alliances and partnering effectively. Stan Meresman, chief financial officer (CFO) of Silicon Graphics, suggests that alliance participants must remain flexible enough to evolve with their partner relationships. They have to change as the dynamics of competition change. In fact, the Silicon Graphics CFO argues that the difficult job begins after the alliance has been negotiated and structured. Silicon Graphics' strategic alliances network, built largely by CEO Edward McCracken, has been quite successful.

Source: R. Myers, 1995, The art of partnering: How Silicon Graphics grapples with more than a dozen strategic alliances, *CFO,* December, 28–32; N. Templin, 1995, Strange bedfellows: More and more firms enter joint ventures with big competitors, *Wall Street Journal,* November 1, A1, A12; J. Holusha, 1994, U.S. Steel and Nucor join on production technology, *New York Times,* October 13, D1, D2.

Cooperative strategies have become increasingly popular since the mid 1980s. For example, the number of petitions to the U.S. Justice Department for clearance of joint ventures increased by 423 percent during the period 1986-1995. Some have referred to this new trend as "coopetition" in that major competitors are now forming cooperative alliances to fend off other competition, oftentimes from foreign firms. These alliances help firms obtain new technology rapidly and reduce the investment necessary to develop and introduce new products, to enter new markets, or to survive in their existing ones.[1] Also, cooperative strategies such as strategic alliances help firms overcome managerial limits to growth.[2] An increasing number of small and medium-sized companies, like Silicon Graphics, have been engaging in cooperative strategies. One survey of small companies by Coopers and Lybrand found that such companies participating in alliances increased their revenues faster than those not involved in them. Furthermore, while 37 percent of the small businesses were involved in some form of alliance, 50 percent noted their intention to establish an alliance in the near future.[3] Alliances have become even more popular in international markets (between firms with headquarters in different countries) in recent years.[4] The Texas Instruments–Hitachi strategic alliance described in the opening case exemplifies this popularity.

Although strategic alliances can serve a number of purposes and many are successful, such as the TI–Hitachi alliance seems to be, the opening case also suggests that alliances can be difficult to manage. In fact, the failure rates of alliances are notably high. For example, a recent study on the airline industry found that less than 30 percent of the alliances between international carriers have been successful.[5] As we will learn in this chapter, firms must be careful when selecting partners for alliances. They need to understand their potential partner's strategic intent and should attempt to develop trust among the partners to facilitate more effective operation of the alliance.[6] Because of the high failure rate associated with alliances (a prominent cooperative strategy), top executives must develop a good understanding of the appropriate cooperative strategy to use and how to best implement it.

To this point in the book, we have focused on competition among firms. The previous chapters facilitate understanding of competitive advantage and strategic competitiveness through strong positions against external challenges, maximizing of core competencies, and minimizing of weaknesses. This chapter focuses on gaining competitive advantage through cooperation with other firms. As with other strategies, cooperative strategies are embedded in a competitive context. Thus, this chapter explores how firms cooperate to compete.[7]

■ Types of Cooperative Strategies

■ *Strategic alliances* are partnerships between firms whereby their resources, capabilities, and core competencies are combined to pursue mutual interests to develop, manufacture, or distribute goods or services.

■ *Joint ventures* occur when an independent firm is created by at least two other firms.

■ An *equity strategic alliance* is a strategic alliance in which the partners do not own equal equity.

■ A *nonequity strategic alliance* is an alliance in which a contract license is given to supply, produce, or distribute a firm's goods or services without equity sharing.

A primary cooperative strategy is strategic alliances. **Strategic alliances** are partnerships between firms whereby their resources, capabilities, and core competencies are combined to pursue mutual interests to develop, manufacture, or distribute goods or services. Strategic alliances are explicit forms of relationships between firms. They come in three basic types. The first type is **joint ventures,** in which an independent firm is created by at least two other firms. For instance, Dow Corning and Owens Corning were joint ventures created by Corning, Inc. (formerly Corning Glass) with Dow Chemical Corporation and Owens Corporation, respectively. In these joint ventures, often each partner owns 50 percent of the equity. A second type of strategic alliance in which the partners do not own equal equity is called an **equity strategic alliance** (the partners own different percentages of equity in the venture such as 60 and 40 percent). Telmex (Mexico's dominant telephone company) is an equity strategic alliance with SBC Communications (formerly Southwestern Bell), Alcatel (a French telecommunications firm), and Grupo Carso (a Mexican conglomerate) as partners. This partnership was formed when the nationalized Mexican telephone exchange was privatized. Although some government ownership remains, the privatization allowed this equity strategic alliance to be formed. In this equity strategic alliance, SBC owns 24.5 percent, Alcatel 24.5 percent, and Grupo Carso 51 percent. Other significant equity strategic alliances have been formed by Ford Motor Company and Mazda Motor Corporation and by Chrysler Corporation and Mitsubishi Motors.

Finally, **nonequity strategic alliances** are alliances in which a contract license is given to supply, produce, or distribute a firm's goods or services without equity sharing. For instance, Power Computing Corporation was given a license by Apple Computer to produce its Macintosh line of computers. Stephen Kahng, Power Computing's CEO, has a history of producing clones through such

Telmex, Mexico's dominant telephone company, has formed an equity strategic alliance with three partners.

agreements. He previously produced IBM-style clones for Daewoo Corporation during the 1980s.[8] Apple's goal was to encourage more users of its Macintosh computers so as to compete with the Windows 95 operating system introduced in the summer of 1995. Some analysts worry that the cloning of the Macintosh may happen too late to have much effect because Microsoft's Windows 95 operating system emulates much of what Apple's simplified system offers to consumers. Besides licensing agreements, other types of cooperative contractual arrangements include distribution agreements, supply contracts, and marketing agreements between potential competitors (such as flight code sharing arrangements between airlines), all representing nonequity strategic alliances.

Although this chapter focuses primarily on the explicit forms of strategic alliances as noted above, there are other types of more implicit cooperative arrangements. One is called tacit collusion. **Tacit collusion** exists when several firms in an industry tacitly cooperate to reduce industry output below the potential competitive level and thereby increase prices above the competitive level. Most strategic alliances, however, exist not to reduce industry output, but to increase learning, facilitate growth, or increase returns and strategic competitiveness.[9]

Of course, cooperative agreements may also be explicitly collusive, which is illegal in the United States unless regulated by the government as was the case in the telecommunications industries until recent deregulation. Mutual forbearance (another term for tacit collusion) is tacit recognition of interdependence, but it has the same effect as explicit collusion in that it reduces output and increases prices (defined and explained in Chapter 6).

The remainder of the chapter examines strategic alliances (a primary cooperative strategy) in depth. We first discuss strategic alliances at the business-unit level, followed by the corporate and international levels. Additionally, we examine network strategies where the cooperative relations among firms produce multiple alliances with the partnering firms. Strategies among multiple alliance partnerships are usually different than those with partners forming primarily dyadic relations (between two firms). The major risks of pursuing the various types of alliances are considered. Finally, we discuss the importance of trust as a strategic asset to foster cooperative strategies that create competitive advantage and endure over time.

■ Reasons for Alliances

A number of different rationales are used for participating in strategic alliances and other forms of cooperation.[10] The reasons for cooperation differ based on three types of basic market situations: slow-cycle, standard-cycle, and fast-cycle.[11] These three market situations were introduced in Chapter 5. As noted earlier, *slow-cycle* markets refer to markets that are sheltered or near monopolies such as railroads and, historically, telecommunications companies and utilities. Often, these companies cooperate to develop standards (e.g., to regulate air or train traffic), but they can also collude to reduce competition so the government usually provides significant regulation to avoid consumer price discrimination. *Standard-cycle* market cooperation can result from firms trying to avoid overcapacity rather than increasing their opportunities. As such, these cooperative arrangements are often focused on obtaining market power. *Fast-cycle* markets

■ *Tacit collusion exists when several firms in an industry tacitly cooperate to reduce industry output below the potential competitive level and thereby increase prices above the competitive level.*

are dynamic and entrepreneurial and new goods or services are imitated quickly. In these markets, cooperative strategy is used to increase the speed of product development or market entry as well as to gain strategic competitiveness. The reasons for strategic alliances in each of these markets are listed in Table 9.1.

Firms in slow-cycle markets often seek entry into restricted markets or to establish franchises in new markets. In fact, many firms in slow-cycle markets seek cooperative strategic alliances in emerging markets (often restricted). In emerging markets in Eastern Europe, Russia, Latin America, India, China, and elsewhere, utility firms from developed countries are strongly motivated to form strategic alliances with local partners. For example, as deregulation occurs in the United States, U.S. telecommunications firms have the opportunity to share in establishing a near-monopoly franchise in these emerging markets. Firms operating in emerging markets desire these alliances because they need the expertise and technological know-how that can be provided by firms from developed countries. France's Alcatel has established a strong market position through joint ventures with local partners in Mexico and China.[12] This approach has been used by utility firms participating in energy, electricity, and gas pipeline projects such as the one in India arranged by Enron Corporation.

Cooperation, however, may be difficult to establish in slow-cycle markets. Near monopolies usually seek to be self-sustaining rather than maintained jointly by partners. On the other hand, deregulation and privatization (e.g., in Russia) create opportunities for establishing monopoly franchises in emerging market countries, and slow-cycle market firms often seek to take advantage of these opportunities.

In standard-cycle markets, which are often large and economies of scale oriented, such as the automobile, earthmoving and construction equipment, and

Table 9.1 Reasons for Strategic Alliances by Market Type	
Market	**Reason**
Slow Cycle	■ Gain access to a restricted market
	■ Establish franchise in a new market
	■ Maintain market stability (e.g., establishing standards)
Standard Cycle	■ Gain market power (reduce industry overcapacity)
	■ Gain access to complementary resources
	■ Overcome trade barriers
	■ Meet competitive challenge by other competitors
	■ Pool resources for very large capital projects
	■ Learn new business techniques
Fast Cycle	■ Speed up new goods or service entry
	■ Speed up new market entry
	■ Maintain market leadership
	■ Form an industry technology standard
	■ Share risky R&D expenses
	■ Overcome uncertainty

commercial aerospace markets, alliances are more likely between partners with complementary resources, capabilities, and core competencies (see Table 9.1). In these markets where economies of scale are important for competitive advantage or parity, large international alliances are useful because national markets may be too small to support the scale-efficient nature of the businesses. Therefore, the increasing globalization of markets presents opportunities to combine resources, capabilities, and competencies. This is a primary reason for alliances between automobile firms such as Ford and Mazda.

Firms also may cooperate in standard-cycle markets to reduce industry overcapacity and pool resources to meet capital needs. Mergers can help to overcome overcapacity, such as in the defense industry. Mergers (e.g., between Martin Marietta and Lockheed to form Lockheed Martin) exemplify such an approach. However, mergers are not forms of cooperative strategy. The European alliances in aerospace, for instance Airbus Industrie, have been designed to help the partners become more competitive with U.S. aerospace firms. Because most aerospace projects require huge capital outlays, pooling resources is often a rational step. Also, when a firm has a project that requires significant R&D investment, as in a new casting approach for a steel mill, it may be necessary to seek a partner to share in these outlays.[13] Finally, firms in standard-cycle markets also may form alliances to overcome trade barriers and to learn new business techniques.

Fast-cycle markets, in which product cycles are shortened such as among electronics firms, also create incentives for cooperation. Cooperation can allow faster development, manufacture, and distribution of a new product. Furthermore, cooperation can lead to the development of standard products in a high-technology market. For instance, Sematech, a cooperative strategic alliance among multiple electronic and semiconductor firms, was quite important in establishing the adoption of the UNIX standard operating system for workstation computer producers.[14]

Uncertainty is also a rationale for increased cooperation among fast-cycle market firms. As on-line electronic services compete, their future remains uncertain. Microsoft signed a partnership agreement with GE's NBC to produce an array of programming as Microsoft launched its on-line service. This agreement undercuts similar arrangements with America Online and Prodigy, originally a joint venture between IBM and Sears, Roebuck & Co. Perhaps this is why Sears put its 50 percent share of Prodigy up for sale (recently sold to International Wireless Inc.). The Microsoft–GE alliance did not include GE's own on-line service, GEnie Information Services.[15] This example suggests the uncertain and competitive nature of fast-cycle markets. Alliances between firms in fast-cycle markets also may be formed to share risky R&D investments, to maintain market leadership, and to develop an industry technology standard.

Microsoft probably has several reasons for forming alliances with firms such as NBC and DreamWorks SKG, but these alliances clearly help the firm hedge against the uncertainty of fast-cycle and high-technology markets. The uncertainty present in these firms' industries relates to the increasing knowledge requirements and the range of products required to survive and maintain at least competitive parity.[16] Furthermore, the alliances between Microsoft and DreamWorks SKG and Compaq and Fisher-Price (see Strategic Focus) take advantage of each firm's unique capabilities and competencies that are complementary to one another. Both of these alliances show much promise.

STRATEGIC FOCUS

From Dream Alliances in Hollywood to Compu-Toys

Two new alliances exemplify partnerships in fast-cycle markets. The first, between Microsoft and DreamWorks SKG (a movie studio formed by Steven Spielberg, Jeffrey Katzenberg, and David Geffen), is called DreamWorks Interactive. The purpose of this strategic alliance is to team Microsoft's technology with the creative talent from DreamWorks SKG to develop interactive entertainment, specifically adventure-based games and children's stories. The alliance will also attempt to exploit any new technology developed in products such as computers, video game machines, electronic networks, and interactive television. The alliance has access to all of Microsoft's research and development. For example, it owns a large amount of the current digital technology for making movies. This is partly because in June, 1994, it acquired Soft Image, a company that develops special effects software for Hollywood features. Furthermore, Microsoft has launched its new on-line service called Microsoft Network, which will provide the opportunity to test market new video products produced by the partnership.

Interestingly, Compaq Computer Corporation and Fisher-Price Toy Company have also launched a strategic alliance that will focus on the development of new compu-toys. The primary goal of this alliance is to develop computer attachments such as oversized keyboards and car-like controls that make personal computers accessible to children under the age of seven.

One of the first products from the alliance is named the Wonder Tools Cruiser, a toy that provides a throttle, steering wheel, and horn to navigate adventure programs on the PC. A second product is a special keyboard geared to children's small hands. Toys 'R' Us executives are excited about this new line of products aimed at children.

Fisher-Price Toy Company's and Compaq Computer Corporation's alliance focuses on the development of new compu-toys.

The electronic learning toy market is lucrative and growing at approximately 28 percent annually. It also changes rapidly with short product life cycles. Compaq and Fisher-Price believe that their alliance will help them maintain a competitive advantage. Compaq is now searching for other alliance partners to focus on products for teenagers, working single mothers, and senior citizens.

Source: G. McWilliams, 1996, Babes in cyberland, *Business Week*, January 15, 38; M. Berniker, 1995, Dream date: Microsoft and DreamWorks SKG, *Telemedia Week*, March 27, 42, 47; R. Brandt and R. Grover, 1995, Hollywood's digital Godzilla, *Business Week*, April 3, 49; M. Krantz, 1995, Dream team adds players, *Media Week*, March 27, 9, 12.

■ Business-Level Cooperative Strategies

In this section we explain four types of business-level cooperative strategies: complementary strategies, competition reduction strategies, competition response strategies, and uncertainty reduction strategies. Following our discussion of these four general types of business-level cooperative strategies is an assessment of the potential competitive advantages associated with each one. Each of the four types is shown in Figure 9.1.

■ Complementary Alliances

■ *A **complementary strategic alliance** is a partnership designed to take advantage of market opportunities by combining partner firm assets in complementary ways to create new value.*

Complementary strategic alliances are partnerships designed to take advantage of market opportunities by combining partner firm assets in complementary ways to create new value.[17] As Figure 9.2 illustrates, there are two types of complementary strategic alliances, vertical and horizontal. The vertical chain alliances include distribution alliances, supplier alliances, and outsourcing alliances (different stages in

Figure 9.1

Types of Business- and Corporate-Level Strategic Alliances

Business Level ⟶

Complementary Alliances
Competition Reduction Alliances
Competition Response Alliances
Uncertainty Reduction Alliances

Corporate Level ⟶

Diversifying Alliances
Synergistic Alliances
Franchising

Figure 9.2   Vertical and Horizontal Complementary Strategic Alliances

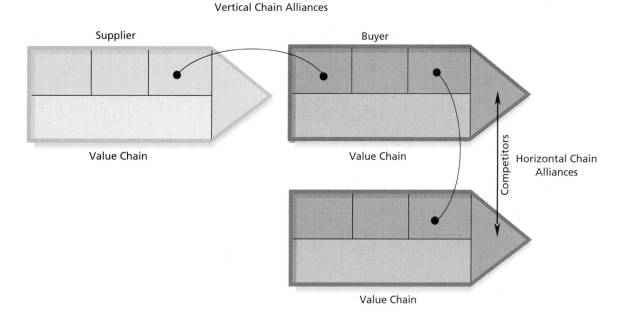

value chain). Benetton and Marks and Spencer are successful clothing firms that use alliances for suppliers and distributors of their products. TI's recently developed notebook computer provides an example. TI's products have garnered industry awards for their innovative qualities. However, it only held 2.7 percent of the notebook market in early 1995. It has not been successful in selling its strong product offering to those who could really use it, *Fortune* 1000 executives. Instead of placing its products with dealers that cater to big corporation buyers, TI decided to use small retailers and computer superstores. Recognizing this problem, TI has negotiated distribution agreements with Intelligent Electronics, Inc., and Intex Information Services. Both have strong contacts among the *Fortune* 1000 firms.

TI hopes that these new partnerships will facilitate distribution of its notebook computers to the appropriate market.[18]

U.S. firms have experimented with supply partnerships that do not entail ownership, although traditionally large U.S. firms have preferred to own suppliers (vertical integration). This has been especially true in the U.S. automobile industry. Comparatively, Japanese auto manufacturers also use supply partnerships in a larger system of cooperation and competition between partner suppliers.[19] Performance of supply partnerships suggests that they provide an effective substitute for vertical integration (ownership of supply source).[20] Just-in-time inventory systems for the suppliers and distributors require significant amounts of cooperation between partnering firms. Such systems can reduce costs for both parties and increase the solidarity of the relationship between manufacturers and their suppliers and distributors.

Outsourcing (discussed in Chapter 3) has been an important means of reducing costs and the basis for an increasing number of strategic alliances. For instance, many large firms such as Xerox, Delta Air Lines, and Kodak have outsourced their information technology (IT) function.[21] Sears, Ameritech, Lucent Technologies (an AT&T spinoff), and J.P. Morgan have announced that they are outsourcing data and computer support as well.[22] As such, a growing number of traditional consulting firms have added this function because of their ability to manage IT efficiently. For example, in addition to EDS, Andersen Consulting has been increasingly performing outsourced IT operations along with IT consulting. Magna International has been increasing its revenues by performing outsourced manufacturing and design work for the big three U.S. automakers.[23] Although Magna faces increased competition, it possesses the capabilities to not only manufacture goods effectively, but also to design high value-added goods. In fact, Magna can perform initial design, engineering, and development of whole vehicles and thus could become a strong supplier. However, such significant outsourcing might concern traditional automakers, because it would give suppliers more power and increase automakers' costs. Also, as Chapter 3 indicates, outsourcing can harm the development and maintenance of a firm's core competence. A firm needs to ensure that critical functions (critical resources and capabilities) are not outsourced in order to maintain its core competencies.[24]

Horizontal complementary strategic alliances (partners at same stage in value chain) are often used to increase the strategic competitiveness of the partners involved. Horizontal chain alliances usually focus on long-term product and service technology development.[25] For instance, complementary alliances discussed in the Strategic Focus case between Compaq and Fisher-Price in new compu-toys and between Microsoft and DreamWorks SKG in interactive entertainment are examples of the horizontal type focused on new product development.

In addition, many competitors form joint marketing agreements (horizontal chain alliances). Some of these agreements not only reduce costs but increase revenues and market power. European airlines have formed many joint marketing agreements inside and outside of Europe. For example, Lufthansa and Scandinavian Airlines have outlined a strategic alliance in Europe and extended their reach internationally.[26] Similarly, Delta has extended its agreements with SwissAir, Sabena World, and Austrian Airlines in Europe.[27] Such partnerships can increase market power substantially and reduce competition. Because of this, there have been calls to regulate the international airline links and route allocations.[28]

■ Competition Reduction Strategies

In the heat of rivalry, many firms may seek to avoid destructive or excessive competition. One means of avoiding such competition is tacit collusion or mutual forbearance. This may be accomplished in some markets through cartels such as OPEC that seek to manage the price and output of companies in a specific industry (e.g., oil companies in member countries). Japan's economy entails a number of entrenched cartels and significant collusion. Even though economic and political forces have been working against cartels and collusion, approximately 50 percent of the manufacturing industries in Japan engage in forms of price fixing. Because some cartels date to the 1600s, such anticompetitive activity in Japan is accepted and tolerated. Thus, it has been difficult to change cartels and collusive practices. Although the situation is complex, Eastman Kodak argues that cartels and collusion have given Japanese competitors excessive returns against which it is difficult for international firms to compete.[29]

Reduction of competition also can be accomplished through industry trade organizations or government policy designed to reduce excessive competition.[30] For example, some firms follow pricing rules that have developed without direct coordination among competitors. Sometimes firms use direct collusion; consider the recent ADM example where managers were accused of trying to fix prices on farm commodities with other competitors.[31]

■ Competition Response Strategies

As Chapter 5 suggests, some firms enter into strategic alliances to respond to major strategic actions by industry competitors. This is illustrated by the response to AT&T's expansion of long-distance service to international markets by the formation of a joint venture between BT (British Telecommunications) and MCI Communications Corp. As competition for telecommunications services in emerging markets has mushroomed, alliance formation in these areas has increased. Many firms have recently formed alliances in Mexico, for example. When MCI formed an alliance in Mexico with Grupo Financiero Banamex in January 1994, it was followed by other strategic alliances among competitors to battle for this emerging market. Specifically, AT&T and Grupo Alpha and Sprint and Texmex formed partnerships in November and December 1994, respectively.[32]

Bell South, Ameritech, SBC Communications, and Disney formed a joint venture to develop, market, and deliver video programming to consumers as the interactive telecommunications and media market develops.[33] This venture was largely in response to a venture announced earlier between Michael Ovitz, chairman of Creative Artists Agency at the time, and Bell Atlantic Corp., Nynex Corp., and Pacific Telesis Group. Michael Ovitz has since moved to Disney. The telecommunication companies will now have to sort out the nature of these two agreements in an environment of deregulation.

■ Uncertainty Reduction Strategies

Strategic alliances also can be used to hedge against risk and uncertainty.[34] For instance, the recent changes in regulation of the telecommunications industry have led to a significant number of alliances. For example, longtime competitors

AT&T and MCI Communications Corp. are exploring an alliance to build local telephone markets in the United States. Their goal is to share their facilities and bypass the networks of the Bell companies and other local carriers (e.g., GTE). Thus, this is an important strategic action to compete in the local phone market.[35] On-line services are signing agreements to allow users access to the Internet because of its greatly expanded acceptance and popularity. However, significant uncertainty exists with this technology. Therefore, many of the on-line service firms are establishing alliances with other firms to ensure they will have a relationship with strong firms in areas where competitive advantage may ultimately exist. Exemplifying this uncertainty, Prodigy, a joint venture between IBM and Sears, Roebuck & Co., was placed for sale in 1996. Its sales had been lagging other competitive on-line services even though the parent firms had provided more than $1 billion in capital. In May, 1996, the sale of Prodigy to International Wireless Inc. was announced.[36]

■ Assessment of Competitive Advantage

Although all alliances are undertaken for strategic purposes, it does not mean that they will realize complementary assets, achieve strategic competitiveness, and earn above-average returns. For instance, alliances to reduce competition are more likely to achieve competitive parity than competitive advantage. Therefore, such alliances are likely to result in average returns. Alliances that are formed by firms lagging their competitors with the purpose of improving firm capabilities also are likely to achieve no more than competitive parity.

Complementary alliances, however, are more likely than others to create competitive advantage, achieve strategic competitiveness, and earn above-average returns. When potential synergy between two firms is realized, there is usually a cost saving advantage or creation of new capabilities or both, which enhances performance. Furthermore, when a firm is able to enter a market quicker through alliance activities than it could otherwise, it may gain at least a short-term competitive advantage. Many supplier and distributor agreements are of this nature.

Uncertainty reduction strategies, however, are likely to realize only average returns, because they attempt to buffer uncertainty and rely, to some degree, on luck. This type of alliance increases the number of options a firm has and thus increases its flexibility. As such, these alliances are important because without them, a firm may experience below-average returns. For example, earlier entrants into the market have established relationships with key firms and thus may create stronger barriers to the entry of new competitors.

■ *Corporate-level cooperative strategies are strategic alliances designed to facilitate product and market diversification.*

■ *Diversifying strategic alliances allow a firm to expand into new product or market areas without an acquisition.*

■ Corporate-Level Cooperative Strategies

Strategic alliances designed to facilitate product and market diversification (see Chapter 6) are called **corporate-level cooperative strategies**. The three types of corporate-level cooperative strategies are diversifying, synergistic, and franchising. **Diversifying strategic alliances** allow a firm to expand into new product or market areas without an acquisition. Large diversified firms generally seek growth through mergers and acquisitions, as explained in Chapters 6 and 7. However, two firms that do not want to merge can still achieve growth by forming a strategic alliance.

South Korea's Samsung Group is a large conglomerate (referred to in Korea as a *chaebol*) that uses strategic alliances to expand into new markets. For instance, Samsung is investing $4.5 billion to develop cars with Nissan. The first models are expected to roll off the assembly line by 1998. Samsung Aerospace Ltd. is also heading a strategic alliance with the Chinese government and aerospace contractors to develop a 100-seat jetliner by the end of the decade. Additionally, Samsung is negotiating with Boeing and Airbus Industrie of Europe to buy three 100- to 200-seat commercial jetliners. Some speculate that it is trying to create a domestic airline that would compete with Korean Air and Asiana Airlines. Samsung is also a part owner of DreamWorks SKG. Additionally, the conglomerate has had discussions with Disney about a possible multimedia alliance.[37]

In some ways, joint ventures have some similar strategic characteristics to mergers and acquisitions. In the United States, legal restrictions can constrain the ability of firms to make major acquisitions. Historically, the U.S. government has tried to prevent horizontal acquisitions that created excessive market power. Such acquisitions may be prohibited because they are viewed as fostering explicit collusion. Acquisitions lack the flexibility that strategic alliances allow. As mentioned earlier, strategic alliances are similar to financial options that create flexibility and reduce risk when moving into uncertain markets.[38] Large diversified firms may adopt diversifying strategic alliances to increase flexibility and reduce their risk. Firms also may use a strategic alliance as an experimental step prior to acquisition.[39] If the alliance proves successful, the firm can then acquire its alliance partner.

If potential business partners have unique resources or capabilities that are not easily imitated by competitors, strategic alliances may be more efficient than acquisitions. These characteristics may be lost in the acquisition process. To buy them on the open market may be very expensive because of their unique qualities and value.[40]

Additionally, some firms are using alliances as a preliminary step to ease the difficulty of other forms of restructuring.[41] For instance, Daimler-Benz Aerospace (DASA) has had significant performance problems, given the downturn of the defense industry. DASA and Thomson CSF, a French missile component and armament sales firm, have formed a joint venture to be known as TDA. This alliance, along with others, will allow DASA and Thomson to circumvent local politics in both countries. It will provide more flexibility to consolidate operations and alleviate excess capacity in the defense and aerospace industries.[42]

■ *Synergistic strategic alliances create joint economies of scope between two or more firms.*

Synergistic strategic alliances create joint economies of scope between two or more firms. They are similar to horizontal strategic alliances at the business level, but they create synergy across multiple functions or multiple businesses between partner firms. Two firms might, for example, create joint research and manufacturing facilities that they both use to their advantage and thus attain economies of scope without a merger. Sony Corporation shares its know-how through strategic alliances with multiple small firms. A key reason Sony forms these strategic alliances is to acquire commercially useful economies of scope without incurring the costs of acquisitions.[43]

■ *Franchising is an alternative to diversification that may be considered a cooperative strategy based on contracting.*

Franchising is another alternative to diversification that may be considered a cooperative strategy based on contracting.[44] Franchising provides an alternative to vertical integration and has been a popular strategy.[45] It allows relatively strong centralized control without significant capital investment. Approximately one-third of all retail sales in the United States and Canada are made through franchised outlets.[46] Firms often diversify because focus on a single business is risky (i.e., potential for loss of demand for goods and services without counterbalancing demand from other markets). Service firms may diversify some of their business and financial risk by creating franchises. Many hotels and fast food restaurants (e.g., Hilton Hotels and McDonald's) use this cooperative alternative to diversify into new markets. Real estate firms, such as Century 21, also create nationwide chains through franchising. Examples of other firms that pursue franchising include Charles Schwab in financial services, HCA/Columbia in hospitals, and Service Corporation International in mortuaries. Franchising reduces financial risk because franchisers invest their own capital to expand the service. Due to their capital investment, franchisers are motivated to perform well by perpetuating the quality, standards, and reputation of the original business. As such, franchising may provide growth at less risk than diversification. Of course, the franchising firm loses some control, but the franchise contract usually provides performance and quality auditing. The three types of corporate strategic alliances—diversifying alliances, synergistic alliances, and franchising—are depicted in Figure 9.1.

■ Motives for Corporate-Level Cooperative Strategies

Because corporate-level cooperative strategies involve not only motives for obtaining competitive advantage but also for reducing risk, assessment of the effects of these motives is essential (for a related discussion, see motives for diversification in Chapter 6). Managers have incentives to increase sales when performance is low as well as to increase their salaries by expanding the size of the business. Alliances can help managers achieve both of these objectives similar to diversification. For example, they can expand the size of the business and thus increase their compensation. Therefore, unless a corporation has strong corporate governance to guard against managers using strategic alliances inappropriately (see Chapter 10 regarding governance mechanisms), alliances may be used for purposes that do not enhance a firm's strategic competitiveness. In addition, managers may use the intricacy of alliance networks to enrich their position in the firm. Alliances may be built on current CEO contacts and relationships. Furthermore, the current CEO may be one of only a few who effectively understands the complex web of relationships existing in a corporate network of alliance partners.

Alternatively, the capability to manage a large number of strategic alliances may exist in very few firms and may be difficult for competitors to imitate. In this light, managing a cooperative network may result in another competitive advantage for the firm.

Although networks of alliances can be used to diversify the firm, to create competitive advantage, and possibly to enrich managers' positions, the cost and difficulty of managing them should not be underestimated. Monitoring these relationships and maintaining cordial and trusting relations require time and effort. Such costs need to be considered before entering into numerous strategic alliances.[47]

As suggested in the Strategic Focus, the network of alliances established by Ciba Geigy seemed to have significant potential to help the firm achieve industry leadership. Alternatively, the risk and complexity involved in the alliances and their management indicated that Ciba had to cover many tangible and intangible costs as well.

STRATEGIC FOCUS   Multiple R&D Alliances to Create Biotech Innovations Also Carry Significant Risk

Oftentimes, partners in biotechnology R&D alliances eventually become competitors. One firm, Ciba Geigy, a large Swiss pharmaceutical manufacturer that recently merged with Sandoz AG to form a new company, Novartis AG, has formed multiple alliances with companies that are or may become their competitors. In 1994, Ciba bought a 49.9 percent stake in Chiron, a large U.S. biotechnology firm, with the purpose of forming a "unique global biotechnology partnership." In 1995, Ciba and Chiron formed a cooperative venture with New York University combining Ciba's financial resources, Chiron's cutting-edge technology, and New York University's expertise in mapping genes. Additionally, Ciba developed a cooperative agreement with Medarex, Inc., which developed a new class of monoclonal antibodies that provides a promising treatment for cancer and AIDS. Alliances with these smaller biotechnology companies were intended to be helpful to Ciba, a much larger pharmaceutical firm, because the smaller research-oriented companies have more flexibility in developing innovations and applying them to various diseases. Alternatively, Ciba had significant expertise in developing and commercializing experimental new drugs.

Interestingly, Ciba had developed a strategic plan in 1993 that identified potential alliance partners. Three of those potential partners identified in the plan were Medarex, New York University, and Chiron. Thus, Ciba strategically targeted alliance partners and successfully implemented its plans for those strategic alliances.

Ciba also developed links with other firms such as Myriad Genetics, Inc., and made venture capital investments and established university collaborations with specific research programs in Europe. In 1994, Ciba and DuPont expanded their fluorocarbon joint venture, established in 1989, to enter the paper and fire-fighting foam markets. This expansion was expected to double the annual sales of this venture to $50 million within five to seven years. Thus, Ciba used strategic alliances to navigate in the $200 billion a year global pharmaceutical market and to hedge against risk in this market by expanding into other related markets. Its recent merger with Sandoz AG is also intended to give the firm more power in the global pharmaceutical market.

Source: S.D. Moore, 1996, Sandoz, Ciba fill 300 executive posts for merged firm, *Wall Street Journal,* May 8, B2; S.D. Moore, 1995, Ciba's alliance with Chiron is an open relationship, *Wall Street Journal,* June 21, B4; Ciba confirms its interest in Chiron, 1994, *Chemical & Industry,* December 5, 932; M. Coeyman, 1994, DuPont and Ciba expand joint venture, *Chemicalweek,* March 16, 8.

■ International Cooperative Strategies

In general, multinational corporations have achieved higher performance than firms operating domestically.[48] Also, as domestic economies have grown more global, the importance of international cooperative strategies has increased.[49] Often, firms that develop distinct resources and capabilities in their home markets may be able to leverage them by making direct investments in international markets as opposed to licensing or exporting their products.[50] Cooperative strategies (e.g., international strategic alliances) are a common mode for making such investments in international markets.

Firms can create more corporate flexibility and extend or leverage their core competencies in new geographic regions by developing international strategic alliances.[51] However, such alliances are more complex and risky than domestic ones. For example, there is a higher failure rate for international joint ventures than for international greenfield ventures (establishing a wholly-owned subsidiary).[52] Although strategic alliances allow partner firms to share risks, and thus are less risky for each individual partner than a greenfield venture, they are difficult to manage. The need to coordinate and cooperate to share skills and knowledge requires significant processing of information on the part of managers of all partners.[53] Where significant demands are placed on partners' managers to achieve effective cooperation, there is less alliance success. Thus, while international cooperative strategies can have significant positive outcomes, care must be taken when choosing the particular partners, managers, and ventures to better ensure their success.[54]

As indicated in Chapter 8, some countries regard local ownership as an important national policy objective. In general, western governments, though nervous about foreign ownership in some industries, are less concerned than many other governments. India, on the other hand, strongly prefers to license local companies as opposed to foreign ownership and joint ventures with a local firm or wholly foreign-owned subsidiaries. Another example is South Korea, whose government increased the ceiling on foreign investment in South Korean firms from 15 to 18 percent in 1996.[55] Accordingly, in some countries, managers may not have the full range of entry mode choices discussed in Chapter 8. Investment by foreign firms may only be allowed through cooperative agreements such as a joint venture. This is often true in newly industrialized and developing countries with emerging markets. Joint ventures can be helpful to foreign partners because the local partner can provide information about local markets, capital sources, and management skills.

As trade agreements have proliferated globally, the rules of competition have changed and, therefore, cooperative strategies have likewise changed. More than 100 countries are signatories to the World Trade Organization (WTO) and the International Monetary Fund (IMF). However, with other treaties, such as the North American Free Trade Agreement (NAFTA), only two or three countries are involved. Accordingly, the strategies have also changed to adjust to these agreements. In the European Union, for instance, firms have increased their direct control over subsidiaries and use Pan-European strategies rather than individual country strategies. In other words, these firms establish a strategy for all of their operations in Europe as opposed to a different strategy for each European country. However, in general, the trade agreements spawned more cooperative ventures between partners from those countries that were a party to the agreement. These trade agreements promote freer trade and therefore increase the opportunity for more foreign direct investment, at least from firms headquartered in countries covered by the agreement. This trend is occurring in the European union and in North America and also in Asia through the Asia-Pacific Economic Cooperation Forum (APEC).

As mentioned earlier, joint ventures are more prominent in emerging markets. For instance, international joint ventures represent 52 percent of the value of new manufacturing ventures in China.[56] Additionally, since 1985, alliances between U.S. and international firms have been growing at a 27 percent annual rate across all industries.[57] This growth occurs even though many alliances are eventually replaced by mergers or acquisitions.[58]

■ Strategic Intent of Partner

With the increased number of international cooperative strategies comes a greater variance in the partner's strategic intent. For example, some may intend to learn a partner's technology and use it later to become a competitor. Thus, it is important to assess potential partners' strategic intent in forming cooperative relationships.[59]

Emerging economies, such as Russia's, have a distinct need for foreign investment and technology transfer. Approximately 75 percent of the Russian economy has been privatized. However, there was no large influx of capital associated with this privatization. The Russian process was intended more to establish private property rights. Thus, the nature of the Russian economy is changing and there is a dire need for new investment,[60] but the Russians are wary of foreign investment in their country. They are quite sensitive about the strategic intent of foreign partners who want to establish cooperative agreements and operations in their country.

On the other hand, some countries and firms within those countries have distinct needs for the transfer of technology to facilitate their economic development. Oftentimes, firms in these countries, especially in Asia, have an organizational culture that promotes and facilitates learning. These firms then have the strategic intent in cooperative arrangements of learning from their partner(s).

If a firm does not understand its partners' strategic intent and its country's social norms and culture, cooperation may be difficult to achieve and the alliance may fail. For instance, in 1984, General Motors and Daewoo Motor Company signed an agreement to jointly build a factory to produce the Pontiac LeMans subcompact automobile. Each firm had a different strategy for the venture. Daewoo officials wanted to expand rapidly and hence had growth as its major objective, whereas General Motors executives wanted to focus on building better automobiles with net profit as its major objective. Furthermore, each used different accounting methods, such that Daewoo reported a profit for the venture of $13.6 million in 1991, whereas General Motors reported a loss for the same period of $1.3 million. The partners obviously did not understand each other's intent before or during the alliance, and the venture failed.[61] Komatsu used joint ventures to overcome technological barriers to growth in the earthmoving equipment industry and targeted the market share of the dominant player,

Emerging economies, such as Russia's, have a distinct need for foreign investment and technology transfer.

Caterpillar, as its primary competitor. Firms that have different strategic intents may realize a loss of the competitive advantage of their core competence if their alliance partner learns it; therefore, technology and knowledge transfer must be carefully controlled.[62]

■ Network Strategies

■ *A **network strategy** involves a group of interrelated firms that work for the common good of all.*

To this point, the focus has been on the cooperative relations between two (or a very few) firms, such as joint ventures or contractual arrangements. However, networks are an important complement to other forms of cooperative strategy. A **network strategy** involves a group of interrelated firms that work for the common good of all. The relationships may be formal or informal. Examples of such networks include Japanese keiretsus and U.S. R&D consortia.

In the 1950s, the emphasis was on bigger and stronger firms as product diversification grew popular and larger firms expanded into new product and geographic markets. Similarly, in the multinational and matrix organizations of the 1970s, a combination of functional and divisional structures was used to create large firms of enormous strength and complexity. More recently, however, a newer type of strategy known as a network has emerged. The structural characteristics of a network organization are discussed in Chapter 11. Herein, we outline the strategic approach of these networks. There are three types of networks: stable, dynamic, and internal.[63]

Stable networks often appear in mature industries with largely predictable market cycles and demand. In Japan, these relationships usually include some shared ownership among the network firms as part of a keiretsu.[64] Among U.S. firms ties have grown stronger and, thus, stable relationships are more common. For example, in the athletic footwear and apparel business, Nike has long established relationships with a network of suppliers and distributors throughout the world.

Dynamic networks often emerge in industries where rapid technological innovations are introduced, frequently because of short product life cycles. Apple Computer employed a dynamic network. Apple was the first to market a personal digital assistant, its innovative Newton. Although the product was developed by Apple, Newtons are manufactured almost entirely by Sharp Corporation. It is also involved in an alliance with Motorola and IBM to develop a new microprocessor. Apple provided its partners, suppliers, dealers, and consultants with access to its internal electronic mail system, which greatly reduced the boundaries across these organizations.[65] Unfortunately, Apple's network of alliances has not proven very successful.

Internal networks can also be implemented to facilitate firm operations. For example, the global electric products firm, Asea Brown Boveri (ABB), buys and sells many products across many country boundaries using an internal network for coordination. Benetton, serving as a chief broker among many independent specialist suppliers and distributors, has an external network similar to ABB's internal network.[66]

■ ***Strategic center** refers to the firm that manages a network.*

Each of these network types has a focal **strategic center** or firm that manages the network. The main bank is the strategic center in horizontal Japanese keiretsus that entail loosely coupled, diverse businesses. The primary relationship among these diverse businesses is common ownership and arrangements with the same bank or set of banks. In vertical keiretsus, such as Toyota and Nissan automobile manufacturers, a dominant firm manages a supplier network. Firms like Nike, Nintendo, Benetton, Apple, Sun Microsystems, and IKEA (a Swedish furniture maker) are strategic centers associated with network structures. These companies are not "virtual firms" where all central competence is outsourced;[67] instead, they have capabilities and core competencies that allow them to decentralize to other companies important activities that create value when these companies are better able to perform such activities.[68] Virtual companies go beyond alliances and must depend totally on their network to sustain performance. Thus, while a virtual company is the ultimate form of network and can be powerful, it also is vulnerable to its network partners. If the partners do not perform well, the virtual company may fail.[69]

■ R&D Consortia and Other Network Strategies

R&D consortia represent a form of a network strategy where there is strong need for cooperation among firms (often direct competitors) in an industry. The U.S. National Cooperative Research Act of 1984 allowed the formation of joint venture and research consortia among domestic competitors fostering the development and realization of R&D objectives for industrial progress. These network organizations have been in existence for some time in Japan, Korea, and more recently in the European Union.[70] For example, the Japanese government's industrial policy and the Japanese Machine Tool Building Association (a trade association) have fostered the successful development of the machine tool industry in Japan.[71] The Japanese machine tool industry accounted for less than 1 percent of world production in 1955, but accounted for 28 percent of world output in 1991. In contrast, the American share of world machine tool production declined from about 40 percent in 1955 to 6.6 percent in 1991.

In high-technology industries, where there is significant uncertainty, coalitions among firms are likely to form to develop an industry technological standard, thereby reducing consumer uncertainty. The videotape VHS Alliance, coordinated by Matsushita to sponsor video recorder standards and the Technical Work Station Alliance created in 1988 to develop and sponsor the UNIX operating system standards are two examples of this phenomenon.[72] Such alliances may be developed by a sponsoring firm that offers a technology license at a low cost to induce other firms to adopt its technology. In these cases, there is an incentive to make the consortium as large as possible so that there is broad acceptance of the standard across firms using the technology. However, these firms still often compete with one another. Participating firms are concerned with potential disproportionate gains by rival firms. This is most likely when alternative standards are being proposed. The firms proposing a standard try to make it as functionally equivalent to their pre-alliance technology as possible. Interestingly, the alliance partners frequently compete in similar market segments. This is illustrated by the nine computer companies that participated in two different alliances sponsoring competing UNIX operating systems standards in 1988.[73] Therefore, R&D consortia tend to develop naturally as competition evolves.

As explained in the Strategic Focus, Sematech is one of the successful examples of a major research consortium headquartered in the United States. Its predecessor, Microelectronics Computer Cooperation (MCC), was not as successful in transferring R&D technology products to the marketplace as Sematech. MCC's top management concluded that its main value was in the collaboration and shared technology generated by the industry cooperation. Sematech accomplished the same outcomes as MCC and more.[74] The cooperation among industry competitors has probably generated multiple intangible benefits as well. However, although there are multiple potential benefits from the use of cooperative strategies, there continues to be some significant competitive risks.

STRATEGIC FOCUS   Sematech: A Victim of Its Own Success?

Sematech, a U.S. research consortium, was founded in 1987 by 14 firms that accounted for 80 percent of the semiconductor manufacturing industry and by the U.S. government. The 14 firms initially agreed to provide financial and human resource support for five years; member companies worked to provide $100 million annually and the U.S. government agreed to provide another $100 million. In its first five years of operation, Sematech spent $990 million. Its goal was to help the U.S. semiconductor industry regain its competitiveness by increasing the number of usable chips that could be manufactured from each wafer of silicon and make each chip capable of being more productive.

Sematech was the outgrowth of significant problems in the U.S. semiconductor industry. For example, in 1986, Japan bypassed the United States to become the world's number one supplier of semiconductors. Sematech was considered critical for protection of U.S. economic and national security. Other reasons for U.S. government and private industry cooperation include the observation that Japan had used similar forms of cooperation between government and business to develop highly competitive firms operating in diverse markets from automobiles to video cassette recorders. Thus, Sematech was partially an outgrowth of attempts to imitate the Japanese model of cooperation.

Because the U.S. semidconductor industry has rebounded and is currently very strong, several have argued that Sematech has accomplished its goals. The question now is whether it should remain in existence and, if so, what its focus should be in the future. Federal government funding has been reduced considerably and likely will disappear in the near future. Alternatively, some people feel that Sematech is more a model of where the world is headed than where it has been. In other words, it represents a model of cooperation among domestic industry members. Thus, it is a model of cooperative strategy.

In the future, some see a more global role for Sematech. Others suggest that the only constant at Sematech is change, similar to the semiconductor industry that it serves. Sematech focuses on research in precompetitive technologies. The researchers develop next-generation standards for manufacturing in the industry and bridge the boundaries between the manufacturing industries and the equipment makers used to manufacture semiconductors. Currently, Sematech's corporate members include 10 of the largest semiconductor manufacturers in the United States. These companies invest in Sematech to hedge their risks for operating in this industry. As noted by one industry analyst, "With the required investment to build a new semiconductor plant being approximately $1–2 billion, a $10 million investment to remain a member of the consortium is small when placed in context." Thus, most industry observers believe that Sematech has been a success and will continue to operate as a cooperative effort among major semiconductor industry competitors.

Source: L.D. Browning, J.M. Beyer, and J.C. Shetler, 1995, Building cooperation in a competitive industry: Sematech and the semiconductor industry, *Academy of Management Journal* 38: 113–151; A. Goldstein, 1995, Sematech's mid-life crisis, *Dallas Morning News*, November 13, D1, D7; P. Grindly, D.C. Mowery, and B. Silverman, 1994, Sematech and collaborative research: Lessons in the design of high-technology consortia, *Journal of Policy Analysis and Management* 13: 723–758.

■ Competitive Risks with Cooperative Strategies

Even as firms attempt to cooperate, they are also competing, often with some of the same firms. As such, there are significant risks with a cooperative strategy. These risks include such actions or outcomes as poor contract development, misrepresentation of partner firms' competencies, failure of partners to make complementary resources available, being held hostage through specific investments associated only with the alliance or the partner, and misunderstanding of a partner's strategic intent.

While there are incentives to cooperate in strategic alliances, there are also incentives to act opportunistically in alliances. If a poor contract is developed, the partnership is likely to dissolve in time. The strategic intent of the parties forming an alliance should be identified and incorporated in the contract to guard against potential cheating.

Some partnerships may dissolve because firms misrepresent their potential competencies to partners. Such misrepresentation is more likely when a partner brings intangible resources such as "knowledge of local conditions." Some partnerships may fail because partners refuse to allow their complementary resources to be available to the venturing firm. Contractual arrangements can sometimes discourage this form of adverse behavior.

Once a firm makes an investment, in a joint venture for example, those assets may be held hostage by the local partner if foreign countries do not have laws protecting them. With the Russian government increasingly interested in rationalizing enterprises after the privatization process, many foreign partner firms have been concerned about being able to recoup their investments and earn returns from their ventures. For example, Seattle-based Radio Page formed a joint venture with the Moscow Public Telephone Network and another Russian company in 1992. Together, they built a system of telephone pagers in the Moscow region, with Radio Page getting a 51 percent stake. "At first, the partners worked well together," said Radio Page president, Lawrence P. Childs.

Seattle-based Radio Page accepted competitive risks, including the possibility that the partners misunderstood each other's strategic intent, when it formed a cooperative joint venture with the Moscow Public Telephone Network.

Figure 9.3   Managing Competitive Risks in Cooperative Strategies

Revenues hit $5 million a year and the venture was expected to earn a profit of $1 million in 1995. However, in mid-1995, the venture started to unravel as the Russian partners sought control. They asked the Russian government to threaten to revoke access to the critical radio frequencies if they didn't get their way.[75]

In addition to the moral hazards (potential cheating by partner firms), there are other risks. One of those risks is having the ability to form and manage a joint venture effectively. Prior experience may not be adequate for collaborative strategies to endure. Another risk is having the ability to collaborate. Alternatively, it may be difficult to identify trustworthy partners with which to collaborate.

Substitutes for alliances include mergers and acquisitions or internal development of new products. To the extent that there are reasonable substitutes (e.g., acquisitions) and cooperative strategies are risky, such strategies may lose their attractiveness. The increasing number of strategic alliance suggests that they are easily imitated by competitors. Many firms form alliances with other firms because their competitors have done so. The different risks and means of managing them in strategic alliances are shown in Figure 9.3.

Trustworthiness As a Strategic Asset

A component critical to the success of alliances is trust between partners. The fact that there are incentives to pursue cooperative strategies does not mean that partnering firms have the capability to manage such cooperative relationships and maintain them. Corning, over time, has developed a strong reputation for collaborative venturing. Because of Corning's reputation, potential partners know that a strategic alliance formed with Corning is likely to be successful. It has a reputation for being trustworthy.[76] If a firm takes advantage of other firms in cooperative relationships, it will develop a reputation that will prevent future cooperative opportunities; the firm will be considered untrustworthy by potential partners.[77] Trustworthiness is a strategic asset in cooperative relations but it is uncommon in firms. Because all aspects of a cooperative relationship cannot be specified in a contract, trustworthiness is an important attribute.[78] As mentioned, horizontal strategic alliances have been found to be successful in developing and bringing new products to the market.[79] However, because this form of cooperation occurs between competitors, trust is critical to the success of the alliance. Over time, collaborators gain knowledge about the reliability of partner firms as well as knowledge about partner capabilities.[80]

Frito-Lay, Inc. and Sara Lee Corp. formed a new strategic alliance to produce a product line of sweet snack items for sale in convenience stores, vending machines, and supermarkets. Frito-Lay, a unit of PepsiCo, has approximately $5 billion in annual sales and controls more than 50 percent of the U.S. market for salty snacks such as pretzels and potato chips. Sara Lee is an $18 billion consumer products firm that has other food businesses such as Jimmy Dean and Hillshire Farm as well as consumer businesses such as Playtex, Hanes, and L'Eggs. While not competitors, both Sara Lee and Frito-Lay have strong reputations in the food business. The products from the new alliance will be made in Sara Lee bakeries and marketed under the brand name BreakAways carrying the Sara Lee logo. However, the products will be distributed by Frito-Lay, which has one of the best distribution systems in the food industry. This new product line will provide both firms their first entry into the $914 million a year snack cake market. Some analysts have estimated that the joint venture could eventually generate as much as $500 million in annual sales. While each firm brings distinct and important capabilities to the alliance, the need to work together closely will require a significant degree of trust. For example, the new snacks will be produced in Sara Lee bakeries but with help from Frito-Lay technical teams. The manufacture and distribution of these goods will require careful coordination between the two parent firms. The alliance will have to fend off a powerful competitor who also just entered the market, Nabisco. Thus, time will tell whether this alliance between two highly successful snack food producers and marketers will lead to the success predicted.[81]

■ Strategic Approaches to Managing Alliances

Two basic approaches to managing assets and liabilities are associated with cooperative strategies (Figure 9.3).[82] One approach, based on minimizing alliance costs, requires that firms develop capabilities to create effective partner contracts and capabilities to monitor such contracts. The other approach, focused on maximizing value-creation opportunities, requires trustworthy partners with complementary assets and emphasizes trusting relationships. The first approach may produce successful joint ventures, but it is costly to write protective contracts and to develop effective monitoring systems. Furthermore, protective contracts and monitoring systems shield parts of the organization from both participating partners. Although monitoring systems can largely prevent opportunism and cheating among partner firms, they also preclude spontaneous opportunities that might develop between cooperating partners. Thus, they may preclude both firms from realizing the full potential from the venture. If trust can be used as a strategic asset in choosing partners, monitoring costs will be lower and opportunities between collaborating firms can be maximized. It is important, then, for firms to consider both the assets and liabilities of monitoring systems that will be used to manage the alliance.[83] In summary, trust is not required for cooperation between two parties, but without it, monitoring costs will be higher. Furthermore, trust will increase risk-taking behavior between partners to take advantage of opportunities.[84] Trust has distinct advantages, but it also has increased liabilities associated with the risks of cooperative strategies.

Interestingly, if lasting peace is achieved in the Middle East, there is an expectation of significant new strategic alliances being formed in the Israel–Jordan–Palestine region. Several joint projects are currently being planned. A number of international firms are also entering the region. For example, Sprint Corp. has announced a deal to launch Internet and e-mail services in Jordan. Amoco is working with AGIP from Italy on a $300 million pipeline to bring Egyptian natural gas to the Israel–Jordan–Palestine region. A number of other major cross-border strategic alliances are in the planning stages. However, major political differences still have to be resolved and trust among the parties must be developed. It is the last element that may be the most difficult to achieve.[85]

Our focus in the next major section of the book is the strategic actions taken to implement formulated strategies. The first topic examined is corporate governance. How firms align managers' interests with those of the shareholders and control their operations affect their strategic competitiveness.

■ Summary

- Strategic alliances are partnerships between firms whereby resources, capabilities, and core competencies are combined to pursue mutual interests. Usually, firms' complementary assets are combined in strategic alliances. Strategic alliances have three basic varieties: joint ventures, equity strategic alliances, and nonequity strategic alliances.

- Other types of cooperative strategies are usually implicit rather than explicit. These include mutual forbearance or tacit collusion, in which firms in an industry tacitly cooperate to reduce industry output below the potential competitive output level and thereby raise prices above the competitive level. Firms might also explicitly collude, which is an illegal practice. However, firms may be allowed to collude if supervised by government regulations such as in electric and telecommunications utilities.

- Cooperative strategies are often used at the business-unit level. We identified four types of business-level strategic alliances. Complementary strategic alliances are firm partnerships created to take advantage of market opportunities that combine assets between partner firms in ways that create value. Often, complementary alliances are vertically organized in a way to facilitate supply or distribution. Outsourcing strategies are also of this type when complementarities are possible. Highly visible examples of outsourcing are shown in large firms such as Xerox, Delta Air Lines, and Kodak, which have outsourced their information technology functions.

- Horizontal complementary strategic alliances facilitate business-level strategies. These alliances include marketing agreements and joint product development between competitors and other complementary firms (e.g., domestic and international airlines).

- Competition reduction and response alliances are formed to respond to competitive interactions between firms. Competition reduction alliances are proposed to avoid excessive competition. Competition response alliances are used to respond to competitors' actions such as the alliance between British Telecommunications and MCI in response to global strategic positioning by AT&T in long-distance services.

- Uncertainty also fosters the use of strategic alliances. Strategic alliances can be used to hedge against risks if there is significant uncertainty about performance or new technologies.

- All business-level strategic alliances may not achieve strategic competitiveness and above-average returns. Complementary alliances are most likely to create strategic competitiveness, whereas competition reduction and competitive response alliances are more likely to achieve competitive parity. Uncertainty reduction alliances may prevent a firm from experiencing below-average returns.

- Strategic alliances also can be used at the corporate level. Corporate-level diversifying strategic alliances reduce risk but, at the same time, can be highly complex. Strategic alliances may also help to avoid government prohibitions against horizontal mergers. Furthermore, strategic alliances may be used as an experimental step before acquisition.

- Corporate-level synergistic alliances create economies of scope between two firms. Such alliances facilitate achievement of synergy across multiple businesses and functions at the corporate level.

- Franchising is an additional corporate-level cooperative strategy that provides an alternative to diversification. Firms following a franchising strategy can diversify their risk associated with a single business (even those in many markets) without adding new products. McDonald's has used this strategy extensively.

- A number of international cooperative strategies exist. Many firms pursue cooperative international strategies because some countries regard local ownership as an important national policy objective. Furthermore, the new trade agreements (e.g., World Trade Organization, NAFTA, etc.) have facilitated an increased number of cooperative ventures as firms are allowed to participate in more foreign investments. This is especially true in emerging markets where foreign partners are often essential. International strategic alliances can be risky. One of the most serious errors managers make in forming foreign ventures is not understanding the strategic intent of the partner.

- Adding to the number of cooperative strategies is the network organization. Network organizations are associations of firms with formal or informal relationships that work for the common good of all. These networks can be one of three types: stable, dynamic, or internal.

- Stable networks appear in mature industries with predictable cycles and market demands. Japanese horizontal keiretsus are a central example of this type of network.

- Dynamic networks produce rapid technological innovations, where short product life cycles are prominent and shifts in consumer tastes alter frequently. Often, these networks are formed to create more stability and facilitate adoption of a new industry technology standard such as the VHS format in video recorders.

- Internal networks occur in firms that have established a network across countries that facilitates coordination between headquarters and subsidiary organizations. ABB and Benetton are examples of firms with significant internal networks.

- R&D consortia represent an additional type of network strategy. This type of network organization has been used by governments in Japan, Korea, and the European union to foster a strategic objective—garnering a larger market share of production.

- A number of competitive risks are associated with cooperative strategies. Often, if a contract is not developed appropriately or if a potential partner firm misrepresents its competencies or fails to make available promised complementary resources, failure is likely. Furthermore, a firm may be held hostage through asset-specific investments made in conjunction with a partner. As such, the partner may exploit the other partner's assets.

- Trust is an important asset in many strategic alliances. Firms recognize other firms who have a reputation for trustworthiness in cooperative strategic relations. This suggests that firms pursuing cooperative relations may have two competing objective functions, one fostering strong governance and contract development capabilities and another focusing on selecting trustworthy partners where complementary assets exist.

■ Review Questions

1. What are the three types of cooperative strategies?

2. What are the different rationales for cooperative strategies in slow-cycle, standard-cycle, and fast-cycle markets?

3. What are the advantages and disadvantages of the four different types of cooperative strategies at the business level?

4. How are cooperative strategies used at the corporate level of strategic analysis? When would these strategy types be used and what are the potential problems associated with each one?

5. How are cooperative strategies applied in international operations?

6. What are the four competitive risks of engaging in cooperative strategies?

7. Why is trust important in cooperative strategies?

8. Describe how the cost minimization approach is different from the opportunity maximization approach to managing strategic alliances.

■ Application Discussion Questions

1. Select an issue of the *Wall Street Journal* and identify all of the articles that focus on cooperative strategies. Classify the particular type of cooperative strategy and identify the strategic objective of the cooperative venture for each.

2. Find two articles describing a cooperative strategy, one where trust is being used as a strategic asset and another where contracts and monitoring are being emphasized. Examine the differences between the management approaches and describe advantages and disadvantages of each approach.

3. Choose a *Fortune* 500 firm that has a significant need to outsource some aspect of its business such as its informa-tion technology function. Describe the potential outsourc-ing opportunities available and explain the approach you would use to achieve the outsourcing objective.

4. Find an example of a research consortia and examine its organization and strategic approaches. Provide an alterna-tive strategy using the network organization that you think would be equivalent in performance.

5. How can corporate-level cooperative strategies help achieve a boundaryless organization? Describe the advantages and disadvantages to such an organization.

■ Ethics Questions

1. Think about the idea of asset-specific investment and hos-tage taking in cooperative relations. Is hostage taking, as described in the chapter, a central problem in strategic alliances or is it more a problem in vertical relationships between firms (e.g., suppliers, distributors)? Please explain.

2. "A contract is necessary because most firms cannot be trusted to act ethically in a cooperative venture such as a strategic alliance." Please explain whether you think this statement is true or false.

3. Ventures in foreign countries without strong contract law are more risky because managers are subject to bribery and lack of commitment once assets have been invested in the country. How can managers deal with these problems?

4. Monopoly firms are regulated in the United States. How-ever, a monopoly enterprise is often considered unethical if it seeks to enter an emerging country. Please explain why.

5. Firms with a reputation for ethical behavior in strategic alliances are likely to have more legitimate venture oppor-tunities than firms without this reputation for good charac-ter. How do firms develop such positive reputations?

Internet Exercise

Select one of the business periodicals on the Internet (see the Appendix, "General Locations for Business"). Conduct a keyword search for companies using one of the topics in this chapter (e.g., alli-ances, consortia, networks, outsourcing, partnerships, etc.). Classify the strategies used by the companies you find. Can you explain the reasons for different approaches?

Cohesion Case

At this point, you might want to join another team or pool group resources. One way to do this is to combine your findings with those of another team. To explore this option, send a message to several other classmates (not on your team) offering to combine your cohesion case with theirs. What must each side give up, and what do you expect in return? Is it possible to combine (e.g., merge) the actual firms each team has selected and studied to date? Is it preferable to form an alliance between the teams? What are the advantages and disadvantages of doing so?

■ Notes

1. N. Templin, 1995, Strange bedfellows: More and more firms enter joint ventures with big competi-tors, *Wall Street Journal*, November 1, A1, A12.

2. S.A. Shane, 1996, Hybrid organizational ar-rangements and their implications for firm growth and survival: A study of new franchisers, *Academy of Management Journal* 39: 216–234.

3. R. Myers, 1995, The art of partnering: How Silicon Graphics grapples with more than a dozen strategic alliances, *CFO*, December, 31.

4. C. Handy, 1992, Balancing corporate power: A new federalist paper, *Harvard Business Review* 70, no. 6: 59–72; R.M. Kanter, 1989, *When Giants Learn to Dance* (London: Simon and Schuster).

5. Airline alliances: Flying in formation, 1995, *The Economist,* July 22, 59.

6. R.C. Hill and D. Hellriegel, 1994, Critical contingencies in joint venture management: Some lessons from managers, *Organization Science* 5: 594–607; B. Gomes-Casseres, 1987, Joint venture instability: Is it a problem? *Columbia Journal of World Business* 22, no. 2: 97–102.

7. J. Gimeno and C.Y. Woo, 1997, The embeddedness of competitive and cooperative behavior in the extended interdependence of firms, in J.A.C. Baum and J.E. Dutton (eds.), *Advances in Strategic Management* (Greenwich, Conn.: JAI Press), Vol. 13, in press; B. Gomes-Casseres, 1994, Group versus group: How alliance networks compete, *Harvard Business Review* 72, no. 4: 62–74.

8. J. Karlton, 1995, King Kahng: Master of cheap clones may hold key to fate of Apple Computers, *Wall Street Journal,* April 14, A1, A4.

9. B. Kogut, 1988, Joint ventures: Theoretical and empirical perspectives, *Strategic Management Journal* 9: 319–332.

10. F.J. Contractor and P. Lorange, 1988, Why should firms cooperate? The strategic and economic bases for cooperative strategy, in F.J. Contractor and P. Lorange (eds.), *Cooperative Strategies in International Business* (Lexington, Mass.: Lexington Books).

11. E.E. Bailey and W. Shan, 1995, Sustainable competitive advantage through alliances, in E. Bowman and B. Kogut (eds.), *Redesigning the Firm* (New York: Oxford University Press); J.R. Williams, 1992, How sustainable is your competitive advantage? *California Management Review* 34, no. 2: 29–51.

12. J. Kahn, 1996, Alcatel's local call paying off in China, *Wall Street Journal,* January 15, A8.

13. Harvard Business School, 1989, *Technology Collaboration in Europe,* Boston, Mass.: HBS Cases Services Harvard Business School, Case 9-389-130.

14. R. Axelrod, W. Mitchell, R.E. Thomas, D.S. Bennett, and E. Bruderer, 1995, Coalition formation in standard-setting alliances, *Management Science* 41: 1493–1508.

15. R. Berner and J. Sandberg, 1996, Sears to shed its 50% stake in Prodigy, *Wall Street Journal,* February 22, A3, A4; G. Pascal and P. Zachary, 1995, NBC agrees to produce programming for new Microsoft electronic network, *Wall Street Journal,* May 17, B6.

16. R.M. Grant and C. Baden-Fuller, 1995, A knowledge-based theory of inter-firm collaboration, *Academy of Management Best Papers Proceedings,* August, 17–21.

17. R. Johnston and P. Lawrence, 1988, Beyond vertical integration—The rise of the value adding partnership, *Harvard Business Review* 66, no. 4: 94–101.

18. S. McCartney, 1995, TI's notebook computers have competitors worried: But Dallas firm needs more marketing power, broader product line, *Wall Street Journal,* January 11, B6.

19. X. Martin, W. Mitchell, and A. Swaminathan, 1995, Recreating and extending Japanese automobile buyer-supplier links in North America, *Strategic Management Journal* 16: 589–619; J.

Dyer and W.S. Ouchi, 1993, Japanese style partnerships: Giving companies a competitive edge, *Sloan Management Review* 35, no. 1: 51–63; B. Asanuma, 1989, Manufacturer-supplier relationships in Japan and the concept of relation-specific skill, *Journal of the Japanese and International Economies* 3: 1–30.

20. J.H. Dyer, 1996, Specialized supplier networks as a source of competitive advantage: Evidence from the auto industry, *Strategic Management Journal* 17: 271–291; J.T. Mahoney, 1992, The choice of organizational form: Vertical financial ownership versus other methods of vertical integration, *Strategic Management Journal* 13: 559–584.

21. L. Willcocks and C.J. Choi, 1995, Cooperative partnership and "total" IT outsourcing: From contractual obligation to strategic alliance? *European Management Journal* 13, no. 1: 67–78.

22. J.W. Verity, 1996, Let's order out for technology, *Business Week,* May 13, 47.

23. M. Heinzl, 1995, Magna International profits on big three outsourcing, *Wall Street Journal,* August 24, B5.

24. R.A. Bettis, S.P. Bradley, and G. Hamel, 1992, Outsourcing and industrial decline, *Academy of Management Executive* VI, no. 1: 7–22.

25. M. Kotabe and K.S. Swan, 1995, The role of strategic alliances in high technology new product development, *Strategic Management Journal* 16: 621–636.

26. B. Coleman, 1995, Lufthansa and Scandinavian Airlines unveil plans for a strategic alliance, *Wall Street Journal,* May 12, A9.

27. E. McDowell, 1995, Delta seeks to expand its tie with three airlines in Europe, *New York Times,* September 9, 34.

28. M. Brannigan, 1995, Airlines' 'code sharing' helps them, hinders travelers, *Wall Street Journal,* October 13, B1; T.H. Oum and A.J. Taylor, 1995, Emerging patterns in intercontinental air linkages and implications for international route allocation policy, *Transportation Journal* 34 (Summer): 5–27.

29. D.P. Hamilton and N. Shirouzu, 1995, Japan's business cartels are starting to erode, but change is slow, *Wall Street Journal,* December 4, A1, A6.

30. R. Brahm, 1995, National targeting policies, high technology industries, and excessive competition, *Strategic Management Journal* 16 (Special Issue): 71–92.

31. H.S. Bryne, 1995, Damage control at ADM, *Barrons,* October 23, 14.

32. C. Torres, 1996, Mexican phone competition heats up, *Wall Street Journal,* April 23, A15.

33. L. Cauley, 1995, Three Baby Bells near pact to set up video program venture with Disney, *Wall Street Journal,* January 16, A3.

34. B. Kogut, 1991, Joint ventures and the option to expand and acquire, *Management Science* 37: 19–33.

35. J.J. Keller, 1996, AT&T and MCI explore local alliances, *Wall Street Journal,* February 12, A3.

36. Management, telecom firm buy Prodigy, 1996, *Dallas Morning News,* May 13, D5; B. Ziegler and J. Sandberg, 1996, IBM, Sears exploring

selling Prodigy on-line service, *Wall Street Journal,* January 15, A3, A4.

37. S. Glain, 1995, Korea's Samsung plans very rapid expansion into autos, other lines, *Wall Street Journal,* March 2, A1, A11.

38. H. Ingham and S. Thompson, 1994, Wholly-owned versus collaborative ventures in diversifying financial services, *Strategic Management Journal* 15: 325–334.

39. M.A. Hitt, J.S. Harrison, R.D. Ireland, and A. Best, 1995, Learning to dance with the Tasmanian devil: Understanding acquisition success and failure, paper presented at the Strategic Management Society conference; B. Kogut, 1991, Joint venture formation and the option to expand and acquire, *Management Science* 37: 19–33.

40. J.B. Barney, 1988, Returns to bidding firms in mergers and acquisitions: Reconsidering the relatedness hypothesis, *Strategic Management Journal* 9 (Special Issue): 71–78.

41. A. Nanda and P.J. Williamson, 1995, Use joint ventures to ease the pain of restructuring, *Harvard Business Review* 73, no. 6: 119–128.

42. C. Covault, 1995, German, French firms merge armaments units, *Aviation Week & Space Technology,* January 30, 25.

43. U. Gupta, 1991, Sony adopts strategy to broaden ties with small firms, *Wall Street Journal,* February 28, B2.

44. Shane, Hybrid organizational arrangements.

45. R. Martin and R. Justis, 1993, Franchising, liquidity constraints and entry, *Applied Economics* 25: 1269–1277; S.W. Norton, 1988, Franchising, brand name capital, and the entrepreneurial capacity problem, *Strategic Management Journal* 9 (Special Issue): 105–114.

46. G.F. Mathewson and R.H. Winter, 1985, The economies of franchise contracts, *Journal of Law and Economics* 28: 503–526.

47. J.E. McGee, M.J. Dowling, and W.L. Megginson, 1995, Cooperative strategy and new venture performance: The role of business strategy and management experience, *Strategic Management Journal* 16: 565–580; C. Hampden-Turner, 1991, The boundaries of business: The cross-cultural quagmire, *Harvard Business Review* 69, no. 5: 94–96.

48. R. Morck and B. Yeung, 1991, Why investors value multinationality, *Journal of Business* 64, no. 2: 165–187.

49. L.K. Mytelka, 1991, *Strategic Partnerships and the World Economy* (London: Pinter Publishers).

50. Contractor and Lorange, Why should firms cooperate?

51. J. Hagedoorn, 1995, A note on international market leaders and networks of strategic technology partnering, *Strategic Management Journal* 16: 241–250.

52. J. Li, 1995, Foreign entry and survival: Effects of strategic choices on performance in international markets, *Strategic Management Journal* 16: 333–351.

53. R. Madhavan and J.E. Prescott, 1995, Market value impact of joint ventures: The effect of industry information-processing load, *Academy of Management Journal* 38: 900–915.

54. J.M. Geringer, 1991, Measuring performance of international joint ventures, *Journal of International Business Studies* 22, no. 2: 249–263; J.M. Geringer and L. Hebert, 1989, Control and performance of international joint ventures, *Journal of International Business Studies* 20, no. 2: 235–254.

55. M. Schuman, 1996, South Korea raises limit to 18% on foreign investment in firms, *Wall Street Journal,* February 27, A12.

56. *The Bulletin of the Ministry of Foreign Trade and Economic Cooperation of the People's Republic of China,* 1995, issues no. 1 and no. 2.

57. J. Bleeke and W. Ernst, 1992, The way to win in cross-border alliances, *Harvard Business Review* 70, no. 6: 475–481.

58. G. Pisano, 1990, The R&D boundaries of the firm: An empirical analysis, *Administrative Science Quarterly* 35: 153–176.

59. M.A. Hitt, B. Tyler, C. Hardee, and D. Park, 1995, Understanding strategic intent in the global marketplace, *Academy of Management Executive* IX, no. 2: 12–19.

60. I. Filatochev, R.E. Hoskisson, T. Buck, and M. Wright, 1996, Corporate restructuring in Russian privatizations: Implications for U.S. investors, *California Management Review* 38, no. 2: 87–105.

61. Hitt et al., Understanding strategic intent in the global marketplace; D. Darlin and J.B. White, 1992, Failed marriage: GM venture in Korea nears end, betraying firms' fond hopes, *Wall Street Journal,* January 16, A1, A12.

62. G. Hamel, 1991, Competition for competence and interpartner learning with international strategic alliances, *Strategic Management Journal* 12: 83–103.

63. R. Miles and C.C. Snow, 1994, *Fit, Failure and the Hall of Fame: How Companies Succeed or Fail* (New York: The Free Press).

64. M.L. Gerlach, 1992, *Alliance Capitalism: The Social Organization of Japanese Business* (Berkeley: University of California Press).

65. H. Bahrami, 1992, The emerging flexible organization: Perspectives from Silicon Valley, *California Management Review* 34, no. 3: 33–52.

66. J. Levine, 1996, Bennetton has ambitions beyond sweaters, *Forbes,* March 11, 58–60.

67. W. Davidow and M. Malone, 1992, *A Virtual Corporation: Structuring and Revitalizing the Corporation of the 21st Century* (New York: Harper Business).

68. G. Lorenzoni and C. Baden-Fuller, 1995, Creating a strategic center to manage a web of partners, *California Management Review* 37, no. 3: 146–163.

69. H.W. Chesbrough and D.J. Teece, 1996, When is virtual virtuous? Organizing for innovation, *Harvard Business Review* 74, no. 1: 65–73.

70. R. Brahm, National targeting policies.

71. S. Kotha and A. Nair, 1995, Strategy and environment as determinants of performance: Evidence from the Japanese machine tool industry, *Strategic Management Journal* 16: 497–518.

72. G. Saloner, 1990, Economic issues in computer interface standardization, *Economic Innovation and New Technology* 1: 135–156.

73. Axelrod et al., Coalition formation in standard-setting alliances.

74. L.D. Browning, J.M. Beyer, and J.C. Shetler, 1995, Building cooperation in a competitive industry: Sematech and the semiconductor industry, *Academy of Management Journal* 38: 113–151.

75. P. Galuszka and S. Chandler, 1995, A plague of disjointed ventures: Many partnerships from the Gorbachev era are at odds, *Business Week,* May 1, 55.

76. J.B. Barney and M.H. Hansen, 1994, Trustworthiness: Can it be a source of competitive advantage? *Strategic Management Journal* 15 (Special Issue): 175–203.

77. C.W.L. Hill, 1990, Cooperation, opportunism, and the invisible hand: Implications for transaction cost theory, *Academy of Management Review* 15: 500–513.

78. J. Bleeke and D. Ernst, 1995, Is your strategic alliance really a sale? *Harvard Business Review* 73, no. 1: 97–105.

79. Kotabe and Swan, The role of strategic alliances.

80. R. Gulati, 1996, Social structure and alliance formation patterns: A longitudinal analysis, *Administrative Science Quarterly* 40: 619–652.

81. M. Zimmerman, 1996, A BreakAway success? *Dallas Morning News,* January 8, D1, D4.

82. M. Hansen and R.E. Hoskisson, 1996, Managing strategic alliances: Opportunism minimization versus opportunity maximization, working paper, Texas A&M University; K.G. Provan and J.B. Gassenheimer, 1994, Supplier commitment in relational contract exchanges with buyers: A study of interorganizational dependence and exercised power, *Journal of Management Studies* 31: 55–68.

83. A. Parke, 1993, Strategic alliance structuring a game theoretic and transaction cost examination of interfirm cooperation, *Academy of Management Journal* 36: 794–829.

84. R.C. Mayer, J.H. Davis, and F.D. Schoorman, 1995, An integrative model of organizational trust, *Academy of Management Review* 20: 709–734.

85. J. Rossant and S. Reed, 1995, All roads may soon lead to the triangle, *Business Week,* November 13, 119.

PART

III Strategic Actions: Strategy Implementation

CHAPTERS

10 Corporate Governance

11 Organizational Structure and Controls

12 Strategic Leadership

13 Corporate Entrepreneurship and Innovation

10 Corporate Governance

After reading this chapter, you should be able to:

1. Define corporate governance and explain why it is used to monitor and control managers' strategic decisions.

2. Explain how ownership came to be separated from managerial control in the modern corporation.

3. Define an agency relationship and managerial opportunism and describe their strategic and organizational implications.

4. Explain how four internal corporate governance mechanisms—ownership concentration, board of directors, executive compensation, and the multidivisional (M-form) structure—are used to monitor and control managerial decisions.

5. Discuss trends among the three types of compensation executives receive and their effects on strategic decisions.

6. Describe how the external corporate governance mechanism—the market for corporate control—acts as a restraint on top-level managers' strategic decisions.

7. Discuss the use of corporate governance in Germany and Japan.

8. Describe how corporate governance mechanisms can foster ethical strategic decisions and behaviors on the part of top-level executives.

The Effect of Corporate Governance Mechanisms on Firms' Strategic Competitiveness

Spar Aerospace Limited
Spar Aérospatiale Limitée

Corporations are governed through interactions among their stakeholders. Collectively, these interactions determine and control the direction a company pursues and the performance outcomes it achieves. Parties with important governance roles include top-level managers, especially the CEO, the board of directors, and particularly for U.S. firms, the shareholders who actually own the corporation.

T. Boone Pickens, founder and former CEO of Mesa Petroleum, is credited with creating a focus on the argument that actions taken by a firm's upper-level managers should always be intended to increase shareholders' wealth. In this regard, Pickens argued strongly that the primary job of a CEO is to make strategic decisions that will maximize shareholder wealth. In today's highly competitive environments, CEOs failing to serve shareholders' best interests may lose their jobs. In a similar manner, a primary role of a firm's board members is to establish controls and incentives that will result in top-level managerial decisions that maximize a company's value and the wealth of its shareholders. Additionally, a board of directors should continuously evaluate a CEO's vision to assess the degree to which that vision, if achieved, would result in the desired outcome of maximizing shareholder wealth. As an image of the firm's future, a CEO's vision helps to control corporate actions.

The vision established by Westinghouse Electric's new CEO, Michael Jordan, is to move the firm out of low-growth enterprises and into broadcasting—a business area Jordan believes is more promising. Among the strategic decisions Jordan has made to reach this vision are those of selling Westinghouse's defense electronics unit to Northrop Grumman for $3.5 billion and the purchase of CBS for $5.4 billion in cash. Some analysts have concluded that if Jordan's vision for Westinghouse becomes a reality, more value would be created for the firm's shareholders than had been created in many of the years prior to his service as CEO. Westinghouse Electric's board of directors bears the responsibility of establishing controls and incentives for top-level executives—including Michael Jordan—that will result in a continuation of decisions that are in shareholders' best interests.

The world leader in space robotics for approximately 30 years, Spar Aerospace Ltd. developed the world famous Canadarm robotic arm for the U.S. space shuttle program. Among other current projects, this Canadian firm is designing and manufacturing robotics for the U.S. Department of Energy in the area of environmental clean-up and is developing the next-generation space robotics as Canada's contribution to the international space station Alpha. In spite of the promise of these projects and the firm's storied past, Spar Aerospace is not without serious problems.

Accustomed to bidding on government contracts, Spar is Canada's largest space contractor and is viewed as a symbol of Canadian technical and engineering achievement. Because of the slowdown in aerospace and defense markets that occurred on a worldwide basis in the late 1980s, Spar decided to diversify into communications and software. To date, the results of these diversification efforts have fallen short of expectations. In 1996, Colin Watson, the firm's new CEO, informed shareholders of an unexpected first quarter loss. Some analysts viewed this loss as an indication that Spar had yet to adapt to the realities of competition in the communications and software markets. Other analysts blamed Spar's previous president and board of directors for the firm's current problems. One analyst suggested that "Most of the difficulties at Spar can be laid squarely at the feet of the departing CEO . . . and the ineffectiveness of Spar's board of directors."

New CEO Watson and the firm's board of directors are working together to cope successfully with Spar's competitive challenges. In the exercise of corporate governance, cooperative efforts between a board of directors and a firm's CEO can ultimately contribute to a competitive advantage. Among other actions, the acceptance by the CEO of a board's legal responsibilities and the power required to fulfill them and the willingness of a CEO to work cooperatively with the firm's board of directors increase the probability that a company will be governed effectively—that is, that the firm will be controlled in ways that result in the maximization of shareholders' wealth.

Source: S. De Santis, 1996, In reaching to diversify, Spar Aerospace loses its grip, *Wall Street Journal,* June 26, B4; M. Kessel, 1996, Boardroom teamwork, *Wall Street Journal,* June 24, A22; K. Labich, 1996, Maybe Jordan does know what he's doing at Westinghouse, *Fortune,* July 22, 20–21; J. Nocera, 1996, T. Boone Pickens gets the boot at Mesa, *Fortune,* July 22, 21–22; Dick Jenrette's gentlemanly advice for handling a crisis, 1996, *Fortune,* July 22, 98; Spar Aerospace Ltd., 1996, Netscape, http://www.ocri.ca/op-com/spar.html, June 28.

■ *Corporate governance is a relationship among stakeholders that is used to determine and control the strategic direction and performance of organizations.*

Increasingly important as a part of the strategic management process,[1] corporate governance is the focus of this chapter. **Corporate governance** is a relationship among stakeholders that is used to determine and control the strategic direction and performance of organizations.[2] At its core, corporate governance is concerned with identifying ways to ensure that strategic decisions are made effectively.[3] Additionally, governance can be thought of as a means used in corporations to establish order between parties (the firm's owners and its top-level managers) whose interests may be in conflict.[4] In modern corporations, especially those in the United States and the United Kingdom, a primary objective of corporate governance is to ensure that the interests of top-level managers are aligned with the interests of shareholders. Corporate governance involves oversight in areas where owners, managers, and members of boards of directors may have conflicts of interest. These areas include the election of directors, general supervision of CEO pay and more focused supervision of director pay, and the corporation's overall structure and strategic direction.[5]

Effective governance of the modern organization is of interest to shareholder activists, businesspeople, business writers, and academic scholars. One reason for this interest is the belief held by some that corporate governance mechanisms have failed to adequately monitor and control top-level managers' strategic decisions.[6] Although perhaps more frequently associated with firms in the United States and the United Kingdom, this perspective is causing changes in governance mechanisms in corporations throughout the world, especially with respect to efforts intended to improve the performance of boards of directors.[7] This attention and interest, however, are understandable for a second and more positive reason; namely, evidence suggests that a well-functioning corporate governance and control system can result in a competitive advantage for individual firms.[8] For example, with respect to one governance mechanism—the board of directors—it has been suggested that the board of directors' role is rapidly evolving into a major strategic force in U.S. business firms.[9] Thus, in this first chapter describing strategic actions used to implement formulated strategies, we describe monitoring and controlling mechanisms that, when used properly, ensure occurrence of the type of top-level managerial decisions and actions that contribute to the firm's strategic competitiveness and its ability to earn above-average returns.

Effective corporate governance is also of interest to nations. As stated by a researcher, "Every country wants the firms that operate within its borders to flourish and grow in such ways as to provide employment, wealth, and satisfaction, not only to improve standards of living materially but also to

Table 10.1   Corporate Governance Mechanisms
Internal Governance Mechanisms
Ownership Concentration ■ Relative amounts of stock owned by individual shareholders and institutional investors *Board of Directors* ■ Individuals responsible for representing the firm's owners by monitoring top-level managers' strategic decisions *Executive Compensation* ■ Use of salary, bonuses, and long-term incentives to align managers' interests with shareholders' interests *Multidivisional Structure* ■ Creation of individual business divisions to monitor closely top-level managers' strategic decisions
External Governance Mechanism
Market for Corporate Control ■ The purchase of a firm that is underperforming relative to industry rivals in order to improve its strategic competitiveness

enhance social cohesion. These aspirations cannot be met unless those firms are competitive internationally in a sustained way, and it is this medium- and long-term perspective that makes good corporate governance so vital."[10] Thus, in many individual corporations, shareholders are striving to hold top-level managers more accountable for their decisions and the results generated by them. As with individual firms, nations that govern their corporations effectively may gain a competitive advantage over their country rivals.[11]

In a range of countries, but especially in the United States and the United Kingdom, the fundamental goal of business organizations is to maximize shareholder value.[12] Traditionally, shareholders are treated as the firm's key stakeholder because they are the company's legal owners. The firm's owners expect top-level managers and others influencing the corporation's actions (e.g., the board of directors) to make decisions that will result in the maximization of the company's value and, hence, of their own wealth.[13]

In this chapter's first section, we describe the relationship that is the foundation on which the modern corporation is built. For the most part, this relationship provides an understanding of how U.S. firms operate. The majority of this chapter is then devoted to an explanation of various mechanisms owners use to govern managers and ensure that they comply with their responsibility to maximize shareholder value.[14]

Four internal governance mechanisms and a single external one are used in the modern corporation (see Table 10.1). The four internal governance mechanisms examined here are (1) ownership concentration, as represented by types of shareholders and their different incentives to monitor managers, (2) the board of directors, (3) executive compensation, and (4) the multidivisional (M-form) organizational structure. (As explained in Chapter 11, in addition to governing managers' decisions, the M-Form structure is the one required to implement successfully different types of related and unrelated corporate-level diversification strategies.)

We next consider the market for corporate control, an external corporate governance mechanism. Essentially, the market for corporate control is a set of potential owners seeking to "raid" undervalued firms and earn above-average returns on their investments by replacing ineffective top-level management teams.[15] The chapter's focus then shifts to the issue of international corporate governance. We briefly describe governance approaches used in German and Japanese firms whose traditional governance structures are being affected by the realities of competing in the global economy. In part, this discussion suggests the possibility that the structures used to govern global companies that have their home base in many different countries, including Germany, Japan, the United Kingdom, and the United States, are becoming more, rather than less, similar to each other. Closing our analysis of corporate governance is a consideration of the need for these control mechanisms to encourage and support ethical behavior in organizations.

Before we begin, we need to highlight two matters related to corporate governance. First, research results suggest that the mechanisms explained in this chapter have the potential to influence positively the governance of the modern corporation.[16] This evidence is important, because the development of the modern corporation has placed significant responsibility and authority in the hands of top-level managers. The most effective of these managers hold themselves accountable for their firm's performance and respond positively to the demands of the corporate governance mechanisms explained in this chapter.[17] Second, it is the appropriate use of a variety of mechanisms that results in the effective governance of a corporation. The firm's owners should not expect any single mechanism to govern the company effectively across time. It is through the proper use of several mechanisms—appropriate to the firm's situation—that owners are able to govern the corporation in ways that maximize strategic competitiveness and increase the financial value of their firm.[18]

■ Separation of Ownership and Managerial Control

Historically, U.S. firms were managed by their founder–owners and their descendants. In these cases, corporate ownership and control resided in the same person(s). As firms grew larger, " ... the managerial revolution led to a separation of ownership and control in most large corporations, where control of the firm shifted from entrepreneurs to professional managers while ownership became dispersed among thousands of unorganized stockholders who were removed from the day-to-day management of the firm."[19] These changes created the modern public corporation, which is based on the efficient separation of ownership and managerial control. A basic legal premise supporting this efficient separation is that the primary objective of a firm's activities should be to increase the corporation's profit and the gains of the corporation's owners, that is, the shareholders.[20]

Through the separation of ownership and managerial control, shareholders purchase stock, which entitles them to income (residual returns) from firm operations after expenses have been paid. This right, however, requires that they also take risk—risk that the firm's expenses may exceed its revenues. To manage this investment risk, shareholders seek to maintain a diversified portfolio by investing in several companies to balance their overall risk.

In small firms, managers often are the owners, so there is no separation between ownership and managerial control. However, as firms grow and become more complex, owners/managers contract with managerial specialists. These specialists are hired to oversee decision making in the owner's firm and are compensated on the basis of their decision-making skills. Managers, then, operate a corporation through use of their decision-making skills and are viewed as agents of the firm's owners.[21] In terms of the strategic management process (see Figure 1-1 in Chapter 1), managers are expected to form a firm's strategic intent and strategic mission and then formulate and implement the strategies that realize them. Thus, in the modern public corporation, top-level managers, especially the CEO, have primary responsibility for initiating and implementing an array of strategic decisions.

Shareholders can diversify their risk by owning shares in several firms. As owners diversify their investments over a number of corporations, their risk declines (the poor performance or failure of any one firm in which they invest has less overall effect). Shareholders thus specialize in managing their investment risk. As noted earlier, managers specialize in decision making. Without management specialization in decision making and owner specialization in risk bearing, a firm probably would be limited by the abilities of its owners to manage and make effective strategic decisions. Therefore, the separation and specialization of ownership (risk bearing) and managerial control (decision making) is economically efficient.

■ Agency Relationships

■ *An **agency relationship** exists when one or more persons (the principal or principals) hire another person or persons (the agent or agents) as decision-making specialists to perform a service.*

The separation between owners and managers creates an agency relationship. An **agency relationship** exists when one or more persons (the principal or principals) hire another person or persons (the agent or agents) as decision-making specialists to perform a service.[22] Thus, an agency relationship exists when one delegates decision-making responsibility to a second party for compensation[23] (see Figure 10.1). In addition to shareholders and top-level managers, other examples of agency relationships include consultants and clients and insured and insurer. Moreover, within organizations, an agency relationship exists between managers and their employees as well as between top-level executives and the firm's owners.[24] In the modern corporation, managers must understand the link between this relationship and the firm's effectiveness.[25] Although the agency relationship between managers and their employees is important, this chapter focuses on the agency relationship between the firm's owners (the principals) and top-level managers (the principals' agents).

The separation between ownership and managerial control, however, can result in agency problems. Research evidence in the strategic management and finance literatures documents a variety of agency problems in the modern corporation.[26] These problems surface because the potential exists for divergence between the interests of the principal and the agent in the agency relationship. The lack of direct control of large publicly traded corporations by shareholders is another reason an agency problem may develop.

An agency problem exists when an agent makes decisions that result in the pursuit of goals that conflict with the principals' goals. Thus, when ownership and control are separated, a relationship is formed that *potentially* allows

Figure 10.1

An Agency Relationship

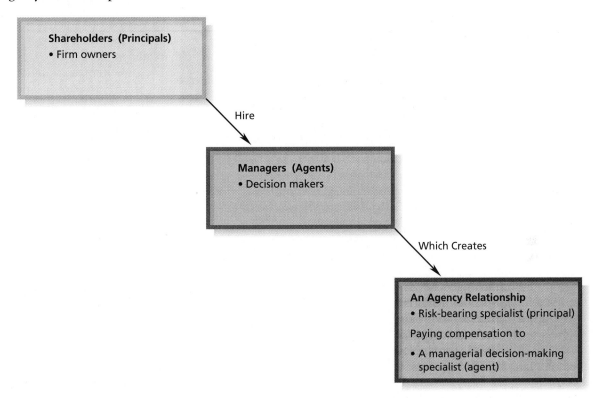

Shareholders (Principals)
• Firm owners

Hire

Managers (Agents)
• Decision makers

Which Creates

An Agency Relationship
• Risk-bearing specialist (principal)

Paying compensation to

• A managerial decision-making
  specialist (agent)

■ *Managerial opportunism is the se[ ]*
of self-interest with guile.

livergent interests (between principals and agents) to surface,[27] which can lead
o managerial opportunism. **Managerial opportunism** is the seeking of self-
nterest with guile (cunning, deceit).[28] Opportunism is both an attitude (e.g., an
.nclination or proclivity) and a set of behaviors (i.e., specific acts of self-interest
seeking with guile).[29] Not all agents act opportunistically. The inclination and
proclivity to engage in opportunistic behaviors vary among individuals and
across cultures.[30] The problem for principals, however, is that it is impossible
before observing results to know with certainty which agents will or will not
engage in opportunistic behavior. Because a top-level manager's reputation is an
imperfect guide to future behavior, and because opportunistic behavior cannot
be observed until it has taken place, principals establish governance and control
mechanisms on the basis of their perception that some agents might act
opportunistically.[31]

Thus, the principals' delegation of decision-making responsibilities to agents
creates the *opportunity* for conflicts of interest to surface. Top-level managers,
for example, may make strategic decisions that maximize their personal welfare
and minimize their personal risk.[32] Decisions such as these prevent the maximization of shareholder wealth. Decisions regarding product diversification demonstrate these possibilities.

■ Product Diversification As an Example of an Agency Problem

As explained in Chapter 6, corporate-level strategies involving product diversification can enhance the firm's strategic competitiveness and increase its returns. Product diversification leading to these results serves the interests of both shareholders and top-level managers. However, because product diversification can provide two benefits to managers that shareholders do not enjoy, top-level executives sometimes prefer more product diversification than do shareholders.[33]

The first managerial benefit occurs because of the positive relationships between diversification and firm size and between firm size and executive compensation. Thus, increased product diversification provides an opportunity for higher compensation for top-level managers through growth in firm size.[34]

The second managerial benefit is that product diversification and the resulting diversification of the firm's portfolio of businesses can reduce top-level managers' employment risk.[35] *Managerial employment risk* is the risk of job loss, loss of compensation, and loss of managerial reputation. These risks are reduced with increased diversification because the firm and its upper-level managers are less vulnerable to the reduction in demand associated with a single or a limited number of product lines or businesses. Furthermore, the firm may have free cash flows over which top-level managers have discretion. *Free cash flows* are resources generated after investment in all projects that have positive net present values within the firm's current product lines.[36] Managers may decide to use these funds to invest in products that are not associated with the current lines of business where they anticipate positive returns, even if the investments increase the firm's level of diversification. The managerial decision to consume free cash flows to increase the firm's diversification inefficiently is an example of self-serving and opportunistic managerial behavior. In contrast to managers, shareholders may prefer that free cash flows be returned as dividends so they will have control over reinvestment decisions.[37]

Curve *S* in Figure 10.2 depicts shareholders' optimal level of diversification. Owners seek the level of diversification that reduces the risk of the firm's total failure while simultaneously increasing the company's value through the development of economies of scale and scope (see Chapter 6). Of the four corporate-level diversification strategies shown in Figure 10.2, shareholders might prefer the diversified position noted by point *A* on curve *S*—a position that is located between the dominant business and related-constrained diversification strategies. Of course, the optimum level of diversification sought by owners varies from firm to firm. Factors that affect shareholders' preferences include the firm's primary industry, the intensity of rivalry among competitors in that industry, and the top management team's experience with implementing diversification strategies.

As with principals, upper-level executives—as agents—seek what they perceive to be an optimal level of diversification. Declining performance resulting from too much product diversification increases the probability that the firm will be acquired through the market for corporate control. Once acquired, the employment risk for the acquired firm's top-level managers increases substantially. Furthermore, a manager's employment opportunities in the external managerial labor market (discussed in Chapter 12) are affected negatively by a firm's poor performance. Therefore, top-level managers prefer diversification, but not to a point that increases their employment risk and reduces their employment opportunities.

Figure 10.2

Manager and Shareholder Risk and Diversification

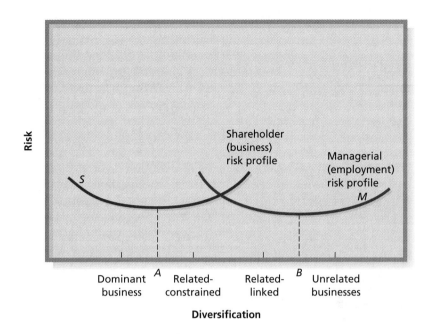

Curve *M* (in Figure 10.2) shows that executives prefer higher levels of product diversification as compared to shareholders. Top-level managers might prefer the level of diversification shown by point B on curve M. In general, shareholders prefer riskier strategies with more focused diversification, whereas top-level managers prefer more diversification in order to maximize firm size and executive compensation and reduce employment risk. As this example of product diversification as a potential agency problem suggests, principals incur costs to control their agents' behaviors.

■ Agency Costs and Governance Mechanisms

The potential conflict illustrated in Figure 10.2, coupled with the fact that principals do not know which managers might act opportunistically, demonstrates why principals establish governance mechanisms. But, establishing and using the governance mechanisms discussed in this chapter is not without costs. **Agency costs** are the sum of incentive, monitoring, and enforcement costs, and any residual loss incurred by principals because it is impossible to use governance mechanisms to guarantee total compliance by the agent.[38]

In general, managerial interests prevail when governance mechanisms are weak. For example, the firm's level of diversification will move closer to curve *M* in Figure 10.2 when governance mechanisms permit significant autonomy to managers making strategic decisions. However, if managerial autonomy is controlled by the board of directors, or if other strong governance mechanisms are used, the firm's diversification level will approach that desired by shareholders (see curve *S*).

In the following sections, we explain the effects of various means of governance on managerial decisions to formulate and implement the firm's different strategies, especially corporate-level diversification strategies. We focus on this

■ *Agency costs are the sum of incentive, monitoring, and enforcement costs, and any residual loss incurred by principals because it is impossible to use governance mechanisms to guarantee total compliance by the agent.*

■ *Ownership concentration is defined by both the number of large-block shareholders and the total percentage of shares they own.*

strategy type because the relationship between principals and agents, developed through the use of governance mechanisms, is observed easily. Moreover, this relationship is critical in diversified firms. The failure to govern strategic decisions properly in companies implementing diversification strategies often results in significant negative effects on the firm's performance as measured by strategic competitiveness and financial returns.[39]

■ Ownership Concentration

■ *Large-block shareholders are investors who typically own at least five percent of the corporation's issued shares.*

Ownership concentration is defined by both the number of large-block shareholders and the total percentage of shares they own. **Large-block shareholders** are investors who typically own at least five percent of the corporation's issued shares. Ownership concentration as a governance mechanism has been researched extensively.[40] One reason for this level of interest and analysis is that large-block shareholders are increasingly active in their demands that corporations adopt effective governance mechanisms to control the decisions of their managerial agents.[41]

In general, *diffuse ownership* (a large number of shareholders with small holdings and no large-block shareholders) produces weak monitoring of managerial decisions. Among other problems, diffuse ownership makes it difficult for owners to coordinate their actions effectively.[42] An outcome of weak monitoring might be diversification of the firm's product lines beyond the shareholders' optimum level. Higher levels of monitoring could encourage managers to avoid levels of diversification that exceed shareholders' preferences. Such monitoring could also disallow excessive compensation paid to managers by holding down diversification and thereby the size of the firm. In fact, research evidence shows that ownership concentration is associated with lower levels of firm diversification.[43] Thus, with high degrees of ownership concentration, the probability is greater that managers' strategic decisions will be intended to maximize shareholder value.[44]

Typically, shareholders monitor managerial decisions and firm actions through the board of directors. Shareholders elect members to their firm's board. Elected members are expected to oversee managerial agents and to ensure that the corporation is operated in ways that will maximize shareholders' wealth.

■ The Growing Influence of Institutional Owners As Large-Block Shareholders

A classic work published in the 1930s argued that the "modern" corporation had become characterized by a separation of ownership and control.[45] This change occurred as firm growth prevented founders–owners from maintaining their dual positions as owners and managers of their corporations. More recently, another shift has occurred. Ownership of many modern corporations is now concentrated in the hands of institutional investors rather than individual shareholders.[46]

■ *Institutional owners are financial institutions such as stock mutual funds and pension funds that control large-block shareholder positions.*

Large-block ownership of a corporation's stock by individuals has decreased in recent years; however, concentration of ownership positions by institutional owners has increased substantially over the same time period. **Institutional owners** are financial institutions such as stock mutual funds and pension funds that control large-block shareholder positions. Because of their prominent ownership positions, institutional owners, as large-block shareholders, are a powerful governance mechanism.[47] Institutions of these types now own more than 50 percent of the stock in large U.S. corporations. In the top 1,000 corporations, they own an average of 55.8 percent of the stock.[48] Pension funds alone are expected to control at least one-half of corporate equity by 2000.[49] Thus, as these ownership percentages suggest, institutional owners have both the size and incentive to discipline ineffective top-level managers and are able to influence significantly the firm's choice of strategies and overall strategic decisions.[50]

Research evidence indicates that institutional and large-block shareholders are becoming more active in efforts to influence a corporation's strategic decisions.[51] Initially, the focus seemed to be on the accountability of CEOs for a corporation's performance. For example, Paul Fireman, CEO of Reebok International Ltd., was criticized by some institutional investors, including Chieftain Capital Management (which owns 6 percent of Reebok's outstanding shares) and GEICO (which owns 4.9 percent of the firm's stock). Some of these investors wrote letters to Reebok's board and to Fireman complaining of mistakes that they believed had led to three years of flat operating profits and a lagging share price of the firm's stock.[52] To deal with these concerns, Fireman met with shareholders and analysts to detail his intended strategic initiatives to improve Reebok's performance.

After focusing on CEOs' performances, contributing to the ouster of a number of them in the process of doing so, shareholder activists and institutional investors are targeting what they perceive as ineffective boards of directors. A senior vice president at Campbell Soup Co. believes that the trend toward higher accountability for a board of directors is unstoppable.[53] For instance, some institutional investors, angered over AT&T CEO Robert Allen's pay increase while the firm was in the process of laying off tens of thousands of employees, withheld their support (during the firm's annual meeting) for the reelection of members of AT&T's board of directors. A relatively unusual action, this lack of support was seen by some analysts as a rare public slap by investor groups.[54]

The largest public employee pension fund in the United States, with a portfolio approximating $98.5 billion that is invested in more than 1,200 companies, CalPERS (California Public Employees' Retirement System) is recognized as an active institutional owner.[55] The firm's actions have earned it a reputation for bullying some U.S. companies into adopting its recommendations.[56] CalPERS provides retirement and health coverage to more than one million current and retired public employees.[57]

CalPERS is generally thought to act aggressively to promote decisions and actions that it believes will enhance shareholder value in companies in which it invests. To pressure boards of directors to make what it believes are needed changes, CalPERS annually issues a target list of companies in which it owns stock that it believes are underachieving. This list is based on corporations' relative rates of shareholder return, their degree of responsiveness to CalPERS inquiries, labor practices, and the percentage of shares owned by CalPERS.[58] Once published, CalPERS usually demands meetings with top-level managers from companies included on the list and is known to flex its muscle to oust directors when its requests are denied.[59] According to CalPERS officials, the intent of these sessions is to persuade corporate boards to force management and strategic changes inside the targeted company. Based on inputs from this institutional investor, some believe that top-level executives at various companies, including GM, IBM, and Kodak, have lost their jobs.[60]

CalPERS is the largest public employee pension fund in the United States.

However, public pension funds such as CalPERS also must achieve strategic success through their operations. In fact, research results suggest that the activism of large public pension funds such as CalPERS has not been universally successful. These findings indicate that activists' proposals to top-level managers that are not focused on firm performance issues can have a negative effect on the company's efforts to earn above-average returns. Thus, questions exist regarding the practices of shareholder activists and the long-term performance effects of their actions on targeted firms.[61]

In the recent past, complaints have been expressed about what some perceive to be poor performances by a number of the largest U.S. pension funds, including CalPERS. These complaints, and the reasons for them, are described in the Strategic Focus on the governance of public funds as large institutional investors.

STRATEGIC FOCUS   The Governance of Public Pension Funds

With what has been labeled as almost brutal efficiency, some public pension funds, as large institutional investors, challenge top-level executives at companies in which they invest. These challenges have led to departures of CEOs, cost reductions, and changes in the strategic directions pursued by targeted corporations. In fact, CalPERS historically has been proud of its intolerance of poor corporate performance.

As is the case for companies in which they have taken ownership positions, institutional investors, too, must perform in ways that maximize shareholders' value. In the recent past, some public pension funds have been criticized for what some perceive to be poor financial performance. State employees, retirees, taxpayers, and politicians are wondering why their public fund investments are not providing returns equivalent to the mutual funds they see advertised.

Those responsible for large public pension fund performances are taking decisive actions to address concerns articulated by key stakeholders. For example, legislators in Texas forced the director of the state's $48 billion teacher pension system into early retirement. Additionally, these elected officials commissioned an external group to study the system's poor performance, high costs, and meager payments.

One of the first major actions taken by Christopher Burnham as treasurer of Connecticut was the firing of 41 money managers employed by the state's pension system. To further overhaul Connecticut's $12.6 billion system, the treasurer reduced the system's administrative staff from 54 people to 14. The decision to place most of the state's pension money into indexed portfolios, recreations of the major stock market indexes that require little managerial control, made it feasible for Burnham to eliminate a large number of positions. In Oregon, three high-level fund managers were fired for their faltering investment performances.

Concerns about the mediocre performance of its real estate investments have been expressed to CalPERS' top-level managers. In response, an internal review of its more than $4 billion real estate investment was launched. However, by mid-1996, this review had lasted for nearly two years but failed to result in definitive recommendations for corrective action. During the time period of the internal review, CalPERS' real estate investments slipped in value by $1 billion.

Outside consultants were also retained by CalPERS to evaluate the performance of its real estate positions. One of the three reports submitted by these consultants to CalPERS' real estate committee classified the pension fund's two primary outside real estate managers, Equitable Real Estate Investment Management and LaSalle Advisors, and two smaller advisors as well, as candidates for "termination." Officials from both Equitable and LaSalle disagreed with the conclusions reached regarding their performance for CalPERS. In fact, these two companies suggested that their results for CalPERS exceeded industry averages.

A large portion of the criticism of CalPERS focused on the length of time the pension fund took to review the performance of an underperforming unit. Some argued, for example, that CalPERS' laborious review of its own real-estate managers was in contrast to the swift manner in which the firm often takes actions against poorly performing executives at the companies in which it invests. One reason for the delay appeared to be different views about appropriate courses of action. Within both the real estate investment committee and CalPERS' board of directors, there seemed to be an even split regarding support for Equitable and LaSalle. An observer of this situation suggested that the split was between the "old guard" and the relative newcomers to CalPERS' board.

Source: M. Pacelle, 1996, Performance tables turned for CalPERS, *Wall Street Journal*, May 20, C1, C21; A. Schultz and K. Fitzsimmons, 1996, Public-pension funds are on a hot seat, *Wall Street Journal*, March 5, C1, C9; CalPERS statement of governance principles, 1996, Netscape, http:/www.wp.com/corpgov/persgov.html, June 10.

As shown in the Strategic Focus, institutional investors also have stakeholders who expect their firms to achieve strategic competitiveness and earn at least average or, better yet, above-average returns. Guiding CalPERS' actions and decisions regarding an evaluation of the performance of its real estate investments could be the requirements included in its Statement of Governance Principles. In this statement, the board of directors, as a governance mechanism, is charged with the overriding goal of protecting fund assets and ensuring that CalPERS is governed and managed appropriately.[62] Therefore, even institutional investors need to be governed to ensure effective management of their assets.

■ Shareholder Activism: How Much Is Possible?

The U.S. Securities and Exchange Commission has issued rulings that support shareholder involvement and control of managerial decisions. One such action is the easing of the rule regarding communications among shareholders. Historically, shareholders could communicate among themselves only through what had proved to be a cumbersome and expensive filing process. Because of the commission's new ruling, shareholders can now meet to discuss a corporation's strategic direction following a simple notification to the SEC of the intended meeting. If a consensus on an issue exists, shareholders can vote as a block. For example, the 20 largest shareholders of Philip Morris own approximately 25 percent of the firm's stock. Coalescing around a position and voting as a block would send a powerful message to Philip Morris' top-level managers and its board of directors. This voting capability has been referred to as *shareholder empowerment.*

Others argue that even greater latitude should be extended to those managing the funds of large institutional investor groups. Allowing these individuals to hold positions on the board of directors of corporations in which their firm has significant investments might allow fund managers to better represent the interests of those they serve.[63] If a possibility such as this were to become a reality, institutional investors may be able to influence corporations' strategic decisions more effectively. Additionally, this capability would foster disciplining of poor performing or dissident top-level managers when needed.

The type of shareholder and board of director activism we have described sometimes provokes reactions from top-level managers. Unintended and not always anticipated, these reactions require still further attention by those monitoring the decisions being made by the firm's agents. A reaction articulated by a corporation's CEO demonstrates this issue.

When asked to evaluate results achieved through shareholder activism, one CEO suggested that at least some of the actions requested by shareholder activists exceed the roles specified by the separation of ownership and managerial control. When this occurs, the CEO argues, owners and directors begin to micromanage the corporation, which is not their job.[64] Faced with this situation, executives may reduce their managerial employment risk. Implementing strategies with greater diversification, as explained earlier, is one path top-level managers can pursue to achieve this objective.

Thus, executives may protect themselves against employment risks when institutional investors have major investments in their firm. Moreover, they may seek protection from a possible acquisition. Evidence suggests that the number of executives receiving such protection is increasing. In mid-1996, 57 percent of U.S. public companies offered severance packages to top-level executives in case a firm changes hands. The percentage of firms engaging in these practices in 1987 was only 35 percent.[65] A golden parachute, a type of managerial protection that pays a guaranteed salary for a specified period of time in the event of a takeover and the loss of one's job, is sought by many top-level managers, particularly the CEO.[66] A more recently developed protection is called the golden goodbye. A golden goodbye provides automatic payments to top-level executives if their contracts are not renewed, regardless of the reason for nonrenewal. Michael Ovitz, president of Walt Disney Co., has a five-year contract that includes a $10 million golden goodbye. This money is payable to Ovitz if Disney decides not to renew his contract or if the two parties can't agree on a successor agreement. In theory, the golden goodbye arrangement protects top-level managers working at corporations whose long-term prospects are uncertain.[67]

In general, though, the degree to which institutional investors can monitor actively the decisions being made in all of the companies in which they are invested is questionable. CalPERS, for instance, targets 12 companies at a time. The New York Teachers Retirement Fund, another activist institutional investor, focuses on 25 of the 1,300 plus companies in its portfolio. Given limited resources, even large-block shareholders tend to concentrate on corporations in which they have significant investments. Thus, although shareholder activism has increased, institutional investors face barriers to the exercise of governance.[68]

Next, we examine boards of directors—another governance mechanism used to control managerial decisions and verify that owners' and managers' interests are aligned.

■ Boards of Directors

■ The **board of directors** *is a group of elected individuals whose primary responsibility is to act in the owners' interests by formally monitoring and controlling the corporation's top-level executives.*

As we have described, the practices of large institutional investors have resulted in an increase in ownership concentration in U.S. firms. Nonetheless, diffuse ownership still describes the status of most U.S. firms.[69] Because of diffuse shareholdings, monitoring and control of managers by individual shareholders is limited in large U.S. corporations. Furthermore, large financial institutions are prevented from directly owning firms and from having representatives on boards of directors. These conditions highlight the importance of the board of directors for corporate governance. Our analysis of the board of directors shows that, although they are imperfect, there is a respected body of thought and research supporting the view that boards of directors can influence positively both managers and the companies they serve.[70]

The **board of directors** is a group of elected individuals whose primary responsibility is to act in the owners' interests by formally monitoring and controlling the corporation's top-level executives.[71] This responsibility is a product of the American legal system, which " . . . confers broad powers on corporate boards to direct the affairs of the organization, punish and reward managers, and protect the rights and interests of shareholders."[72] Thus, an appropriately structured and effective board of directors protects owners from managerial opportunism.

Generally, board members (often called directors) are classified in one of three groups (see Table 10.2). *Insiders* are active top-level managers in the corporation. Insiders are appointed to the board because they are a source of information about the firm's day-to-day operations.[73] *Related outsiders* have some relationship with the firm—contractual or otherwise—that may create questions about their independence. However, these individuals are not involved with the corporation's day-to-day activities. *Outsiders* are individuals appointed to the board to provide independent counsel to the firm. Outside directors may hold top-level managerial positions in another company and may have been appointed to the board prior the beginning of the current CEO's tenure.[74]

Some argue that many boards are not effectively fulfilling their primary fiduciary duty to protect shareholders. Among other possibilities, it may be that boards are a managerial tool—a tool that largely rubber stamps managers'

A primary responsibility of the board of directors is to protect the owners from managerial opportunism.

Table 10.2   Classifications of Board of Directors' Members
Insiders
■ The firm's CEO and other top-level managers
Related outsiders
■ Individuals not involved with the firm's day-to-day operations, but who have a relationship with the company
Outsiders
■ Individuals who are independent of the firm—in terms of day-to-day operations and other relationships

self-serving initiatives.[75] In general, those critical of boards as a governance mechanism believe that inside managers dominate boards and exploit their personal ties with them. A widely accepted view is that a board with a significant percentage of its membership from the firm's top-level executives tends to result in relatively weak monitoring and control of managerial decisions.[76] Board critics advocate reforms to ensure that independent outside directors represent a significant majority of the total board's membership.[77] However, determination of the most appropriate role of outside directors in a firm's strategic decision-making process is debated by practitioners and academics.[78]

Because of external pressures, board reforms have been initiated. To date, these reforms have generally called for an increase in the number of outside directors, relative to insiders, serving on a corporation's board. For example, in 1984, the New York Stock Exchange started requiring that listed firms have board audit committees composed solely of outside directors.[79] As a result of external pressures, more boards of large corporations are now dominated by outsiders. But, with fewer insiders and related outsiders on a firm's board, legitimate managerial concerns may not be adequately represented. Thus, there are potential strategic implications associated with the movement toward having corporate boards dominated by outsiders.

Outsiders do not have contact with the firm's day-to-day operations. This lack of contact precludes easy access to the rich information about managers and their skills that is required to evaluate managerial decisions and initiatives effectively. Rich and valuable information may be obtained through frequent interactions with insiders during board meetings. Inside directors possess such information by virtue of their organizational positions. Thus, boards with a critical mass of insiders can be informed more effectively about intended strategic initiatives—both in terms of the reasons for them and the outcomes expected through their accomplishment.[80] Without this type of information, outsider-dominated boards may emphasize financial, as opposed to strategic, evaluations. Such evaluations shift risk to top-level managers, who, in turn, may make decisions to maximize their interests and reduce their employment risk. Reductions in R&D investments, additional diversification of the firm, and pursuit of greater levels of compensation are examples of decisions managers could make to achieve these objectives.

■ Enhancing the Effectiveness of the Board of Directors As a Governance Mechanism

Our discussion has suggested that the board of directors is an important source of control and governance in the modern corporation. Because of this importance, and as a result of increased scrutiny from shareholders, particularly large institutional investors, the performances of individual board members and of entire boards are being evaluated more formally and with great intensity.[81] For individual board members, some believe that directors increase the probability of fulfilling their responsibilities effectively when they are honest and are willing to act with prudence and integrity for the good of the entire firm and are committed to reaching independent judgments on an informed basis rather than rubber-stamping management proposals.[82]

Given demands for greater accountability and improved performance, many boards of directors have initiated voluntary changes. Among these changes are (1) increases in the diversity of board members' backgrounds (e.g., a greater number of directors are being selected from public service, academic, and scientific settings; the percentage of boards with ethnic minorities has increased; and more U.S. boards now have members from different countries), (2) the strengthening of internal management and accounting control systems, and (3) the establishment and consistent use of formal processes to evaluate the board's performance. The product of changes such as these should be enhancements in the effectiveness of the board of directors as a means of control.

Next, we discuss a highly visible corporate governance mechanism—executive compensation. A reading of the business press shows that the compensation of top-level managers, and especially of CEOs, generates a great deal of interest and strongly held opinions. What factors account for this level of visibility and interest? In response to the issues suggested by this question, two researchers observed that while "widespread interest in CEO pay can be traced to a natural curiosity about extremes and excesses . . . it also stems from a more substantive reason. Namely, to observe CEO pay is to observe in an indirect but very tangible way the fundamental governance processes in large corporations. Who has power? What are the bases of power? How and when do owners and managers exert their relative preferences? How vigilant are boards? Who is taking advantage of whom?"[83]

Executive Compensation

■ *Executive compensation is a governance mechanism that seeks to align managers' and owners' interests through salary, bonuses, and long-term incentive compensation such as stock options.*

The purpose of executive compensation is to improve the alignment of management and shareholder interests.[84] The board of directors is responsible for determining the extent to which the firm's executive compensation structure provides incentives to top-level managers to act in the owners' best interests.[85]

Executive compensation is a governance mechanism that seeks to align managers' and owners' interests through salary, bonuses, and long-term incentive compensation such as stock options. Stock options are a mechanism used to link executives' performance to the performance of their company's stock.[86] Increasingly, long-term incentive plans are becoming a critical part of compensation plans in U.S. firms.[87] At Baxter International, for example, more than 70 senior-level managers were extended an opportunity to take out personal loans from a bank in order to buy up to several times their annual compensation in the company's common stock.[88] This decision is supported by the conviction of many board directors that linking more of top-level managers' overall compensation to the corporation's financial performance is a superior way to align managers' and owners' interests.

Effectively using executive compensation as a governance mechanism is particularly challenging in firms implementing international strategies. For example, preliminary evidence suggests that the interests of multinational corporations' owners are served best when there is less uniformity among the firm's foreign subsidiaries' compensation plans rather than more.[89] Developing an array of unique compensation plans requires additional monitoring and increases the firm's agency costs.

■ A Complicated Governance Mechanism

For several reasons, executive compensation, especially long-term incentive compensation, is complicated. First, the strategic decisions made by top-level managers are typically complex and nonroutine; as such, direct supervision of executives is inappropriate for judging the quality of their decisions. Because of this, there is a tendency to link the compensation of top-level managers to measurable outcomes such as financial performance. Second, executives' decisions often affect the firm's financial outcomes over extended periods of time, making it difficult to assess the effect of current decisions on the corporation's performance. In fact, strategic decisions are more likely to have long-term, rather than short-term, effects on a company's strategic outcomes. Third, a number of variables intervene between top-level managerial decisions and behavior and firm performance. Unpredictable economic, social, or legal changes (see Chapter 2) make it difficult before implementation to discern the effects of strategic decisions. Thus, although performance-based compensation may provide incentives to managers to make decisions that best serve shareholders' interests, such compensation plans alone are imperfect in their ability to monitor and control managers.

Although incentive compensation plans may increase firm value in line with shareholder expectations, they are subject to managerial manipulation. For instance, annual bonuses may provide incentives to pursue short-run objectives at the expense of the firm's long-term interests. Supporting this conclusion, some research has found that bonuses based on annual performance were negatively related to investments in R&D, which may affect the firm's long-term strategic competitiveness.[90] Although long-term performance-based incentives may reduce the temptation to underinvest in the short run, they increase executive exposure to risks associated with uncontrollable events, such as market fluctuations and industry decline.[91] The longer the focus of incentive compensation, the greater the long-term risks borne by top-level managers.

■ The Effectiveness of Executive Compensation

In recent times, many stakeholders, including shareholders, have been angered by the compensation received by some top-level managers, especially CEOs. However, CEOs may have a different perspective. George Fisher, chairman and CEO of Eastman Kodak, stated that "We all should be compensated based on competitive issues. If you want a world-class shortstop, you pay. The good news is that many CEOs are getting well-compensated for really good performances."[92] Indeed, it is the rare CEO who does not sincerely believe that she or he has earned a reward.[93] Thus, some executives argue that they are being rewarded for effectively making critical decisions that affect their firm's performance in the highly competitive global economy.[94]

The level and intensity of the dissatisfaction with executive compensation appears to be influenced by layoffs announced by a host of corporations—in the

United States and across the world.[95] In 1996, some of those critical of executive compensation as a means of corporate governance cited the experiences of AT&T's workers and CEO. During the year in which AT&T decided to lay off perhaps as many as 40,000 employees, CEO Robert E. Allen received $16.2 million in salary and stock payouts. However, as an indication of the complexity of achieving strategic competitiveness in the global economy, AT&T expected to hire as many as 15,000 new employees during 1996 while laying off thousands of others in order to restructure the businesses in its diversified portfolio.[96]

In general, it may be that organizational employees, a key stakeholder, are feeling disenfranchised, discouraged, and angry in a time period of significant downsizings, stagnant wages, and ever more burdensome workloads for layoff survivors.[97] Contributing to these feelings is the fact that during 1995, the average salary and bonus for CEOs increased by 18 percent. This increase compares to an average gain of 4.2 percent for white-collar professionals and of 1 percent for factory employees during the same year. Moreover, the spread between the pay of the typical worker and CEOs concerns employees. The 1960s' 30-to-1 ratio between a worker's pay and that of the CEO grew to more than 100-to-1 by the end of 1995.[98]

Among several challenges facing board directors striving to use executive compensation to align managers' interests with shareholders' interests is the determination of what represents "fair" compensation for top-level managers. As guidance for making this decision, board directors should remember that the most important criterion to consider is shareholder wealth creation. This is necessary because the economic principles on which executive compensation is based are concerned not with fairness but with productivity.[99] The situation at Green Tree Financial Corp. demonstrates the effectiveness of linking an executive's compensation with her or his performance.

At Green Tree Financial Corp., the CEO received a $65.1 million bonus during 1995. However, Lawrence M. Coss, the firm's CEO, was not granted a raise at the same time. Based in St. Paul, Minnesota, this company finances manufactured housing and home improvement loans. A company spokesperson suggested that Green Tree had been one of the best performing stocks on the New York Stock Exchange during 1995 and the previous four years. For example, a $100 investment in the firm in 1990 had a value of $2,065 at the end of 1995. As a result of the creation of wealth for shareholders, " . . . Green Tree isn't getting gripes from stockholders about Mr. Coss' compensation," said John Dolphin, Green Tree's vice president for investor relations. Dolphin further noted that Coss' contract is entirely performance based and that shareholders are thrilled with his work and the corporation's financial performance.[100] Somewhat similarly, GE's CEO Jack Welch saw his salary and bonus increase 22.3 percent between 1994 and 1995. Welch was also awarded 320,000 stock-appreciation rights valued at a potential $12.9 million at the close of the firm's 1995 fiscal year. GE's compensation committee observed that Welch's compensation was appropriate in light of the corporation's financial performance and the CEO's decisive management of both operational and strategic issues.[101] The amount of shareholder wealth created at GE during Welch's tenure as CEO (see Chapter 1) appears to support the compensation committee's position.

As with each mechanism examined in this chapter, executive compensation is an imperfect means of corporate governance. The dissatisfaction with executive compensation being expressed by shareholders and other stakeholders as well may have surfaced because of the mechanism's imperfection and/or ineffective use. It is possible that members of corporations' boards of directors have not been effective in their use of this governance mechanism. If executive compensation plans are not aligning top-level managers' interests with the interests of other stakeholders, especially those of shareholders, appropriate changes must be made.

Thus, the activist positions concerning executive compensation taken by institutional investors and individual shareholders have been effective. Input from these stakeholders should result in modifications to executive compensation that will improve its value as a means of corporate governance.

A company's organizational structure also influences the alignment of principals' and agents' interests. As indicated in the next section, structure can be an especially valuable governance mechanism in diversified firms.

The Multidivisional Structure

Oliver Williamson argues that organizational structure, particularly the multidivisional (M-form) structure, serves as a governance mechanism. The M-form's governance service is a function of its ability to control managerial opportunism.[102] The corporate office that is a part of the M-form structure, along with the firm's board of directors, closely monitors the strategic decisions of managers responsible for the performance of the different business units or divisions that are a part of the diversified corporation's operations. Active monitoring of an individual unit's performance suggests a keen managerial interest in making decisions that will maximize shareholders' wealth. Williamson believes that the M-form structure brings forth a greater managerial interest in wealth maximization than do other organizational structures such as the variations of the functional structure (another type of structure that is discussed in Chapter 11).

To improve his firm's financial performance, Domenico Cempella, CEO of the Italian flag carrier Alitalia SpA, announced a restructuring plan that calls for use of the M-form structure. To provide managerial incentives and controls so Alitalia could better compete in what was to become a deregulated European market after 1998, the CEO intended to split the company into two separate, highly competitive carriers—one for long routes and one for medium and short routes—as well as other operating divisions.[103] Recently GE, another corporation using a multidivisional organizational structure, allocated $200 million to a program (called Six Sigma, which refers in statistical terms to a very high level of quality) that was designed to sharply improve the quality of the firm's vast array of products. At the time of the announced allocation, GE generated approximately 35,000 defects per million products. The objective of the program was to reduce defects to less than 4 per million. To align the interests of division managers with those of the CEO and the program being implemented to enhance shareholder wealth, CEO Jack Welch decided that GE would weight 40 percent of bonus compensation on the intensity of managers' efforts and progress being made toward achieving Six Sigma quality.[104]

While the M-form may limit division managers' opportunistic behaviors, it may not limit corporate-level managers' self-serving actions. For example, research evidence suggests that diversified firms organized through the M-form structure are likely to implement corporate-level strategies that cause them to become even more diversified.[105] In fact, one of the potential problems with the divisionalization that is a part of the M-form structure is that it will be used too aggressively.[106] As discussed in Chapters 6 and 11, beyond some point, diversification serves managers' interests more than it serves shareholders' interests.

In addition, a depth-for-breadth trade-off often occurs in an extensively diversified firm with an M-form structure. Because of the diversification of product lines (breadth of businesses), top-level executives do not have adequate information to evaluate the strategic decisions and actions of divisional managers. To complete their evaluations, they must wait to observe the financial results achieved by individual business units. In the interim period, however, managers are able to act opportunistically.[107]

Where internal controls are limited because of extensive diversification, the external market for corporate control and the external managerial labor market may be the primary controls on managers' decisions and actions, such as pursuing acquisitions to increase the size of their firm and their compensation. Because external markets lack access to relevant information inside the firm, they tend to be less efficient than internal governance mechanisms for monitoring top-level managers' decisions and performance. Therefore, in diversified firms, corporate executives' decisions can be controlled effectively only when other strong internal governance mechanisms (e.g., the board of directors) are used in combination with the M-form structure. When used as a single governance mechanism, the M-form structure may actually facilitate overdiversification and inappropriately high compensation for corporate executives.[108]

■ Market for Corporate Control

■ *The **market for corporate control** is composed of individuals and firms that buy ownership positions in (or take over) potentially undervalued corporations so they can form new divisions in established diversified companies or merge two previously separate firms.*

The market for corporate control is an external governance mechanism that becomes active when a firm's internal controls fail.[109] The **market for corporate control** is composed of individuals and firms that buy ownership positions in (or take over) potentially undervalued corporations so they can form new divisions in established diversified companies or merge two previously separate firms. Because they are assumed to be the party responsible for formulating and implementing the strategy that led to poor performance, the top management team of the purchased corporation is usually replaced. Thus, when operating effectively, the market for corporate control ensures that managerial incompetence is disciplined.[110] This governance mechanism should be activated by a firm's poor performance relative to industry competitors. A firm's poor performance, often demonstrated by the earning of below-average returns, is an indicator that internal governance mechanisms have failed—that is, their use did not result in managerial decisions that maximized shareholder value.

Mark Boyar is a participant in the market for corporate control. Known by various terms, including value investor and corporate raider, individuals such as Boyar purchase shares of underperforming corporations' stock. Through his ownership position, Boyar pressures firms to maximize shareholder value by breaking up assets or selling out. He was among the first to pressure Sears Roebuck, Hilton Hotels, and U.S. Shoe. Partly because of Boyar's demands, Sears spun off some units, Hilton Hotels split up, and U.S. Shoe agreed to be acquired by Luxottica.

Recently Boyar targeted Pier 1 Imports, the largest retailer in the United States of imported home furnishings and related items. Pier 1 operates more than 645 stores in 47 U.S. states and in locations in Britain, Canada, and Mexico. According to Boyar, between 1988 and 1994, Pier 1's stock trailed its industry competitors and the Standard & Poor's 500-stock index. Based on the performance of this firm relative to industry rivals, Boyar concluded that Pier 1 should earn higher returns on sales, and that the stock deserved a higher price. Following his purchase of some 350,000 shares in what he perceived to be a poorly managed and underperforming corporation, Boyar informed Pier 1's chairman in a letter that he was among the frustrated shareholders hoping that management would begin to make decisions that were in the best interests of shareholders. At the time of his purchase, the price of Pier 1's stock was approximately $10 per share. By confronting top-level managers and stimulating what he believed would be more appropriate strategic decisions, Boyar thought the stock would sell at $20 per share within two years of his investment.[111]

■ Managerial Defense Tactics

Historically, the increased use of the market for corporate control has created an enhancement of the sophistication and variety of managerial defense tactics that are used to reduce the influence of this governance mechanism. Among other outcomes, "Takeover defenses affect the likelihood and costs of mounting an outside bid for the firm protecting incumbent management while reducing shareholders' chances of introducing a more efficient management."[112] Mark Boyar, for example, argued that a factor discouraging additional investment in Pier 1 was the takeover defenses that had been established to thwart takeover bids.[113] Some defense tactics require the type of asset restructuring that results from divesting one or more divisions in the diversified firm's portfolio of businesses. Others necessitate only financial structure changes such as repurchasing shares of the firm's outstanding stock. Some tactics (e.g., a change in the state of incorporation) require shareholder approval, but the greenmail tactic (wherein money is used to repurchase stock from a corporate raider to avoid the takeover of the firm) does not.

A potential problem with the market for corporate control is that it may not be totally efficient. A study of several of the most active corporate raiders in the 1980s showed that approximately 50 percent of their takeover attempts targeted firms with above-average performance in their industry—corporations that were neither undervalued nor poorly managed.[114] The targeting of high-performance businesses may lead to acquisitions at premium prices and to decisions by target firm managers to establish what may prove to be costly takeover defense tactics in order to protect their corporate positions.

Thus, the market for corporate control is not flawless. An important reason is that it lacks the precision possible with internal governance mechanisms. Nonetheless, the fear of acquisition and influence by corporate raiders is an effective constraint on the managerial growth motive.[115] The market for corporate control has been responsible for significant changes in many firms' strategies and has, when used appropriately, served the best interests of corporations' owners—the shareholders.

Next, we address the topic of international corporate governance primarily through a description of governance structures used in Germany and Japan.

■ International Corporate Governance

Comparisons of corporate governance structures used in other economic systems with the one used in the United Kingdom and the United States are interesting. In this section, we describe the governance structures used in Germany and Japan.

Among other points, our brief discussion of the governance of German and Japanese corporations shows that the nature of corporate governance in these two nations is being affected by the realities of the global economy and the competitive challenges that are a part of it.[116] Thus, while the stability associated with German and Japanese governance structures has been viewed historically as an asset, some believe that it may now be a burden.[117]

We chose to examine Germany and Japan here because of their prominent positions in the global economy. However, the nature and complexity of the global economy demands that firms use the strategic management process to study the governance structures of nations throughout the world.

■ Corporate Governance in Germany

In many private German firms, the owner and manager are still the same individual. In these instances, there is no agency problem. Even in publicly traded corporations, there is often a dominant shareholder.

Historically, banks have been at the center of the German corporate governance structure. As lenders, banks become major shareholders when companies they had financed earlier sought funding on the stock market or defaulted on loans. Although stakes are usually under 10 percent, there is no legal limit on how much of a firm's stock banks can hold (except that a single ownership position cannot exceed 15 percent of the bank's capital). Today, various types of specialized institutions—savings banks, mortgage banks, savings and loan associations, leasing firms, and insurance companies—are also important sources of corporate funds.

Through their own shareholdings and by casting proxy votes for individual shareholders who retain their shares with the banks, three banks in particular—Deutsche, Dresdner, and Commerzbank—exercise significant power. Individual shareholders can tell the banks how to vote their ownership position; however, they generally elect not to do so. A combination of their own holdings with their proxies results in majority positions for these three banks in many German companies. These banks, as well as others, monitor and control managers both as lenders and as shareholders by electing representatives to supervisory boards.

German firms with more than 2,000 employees are required to have a two-tier board structure. Through this structure, the supervision of management is separated from other duties normally assigned to a board of directors, especially the nomination of new board members. Thus, Germany's two-tiered system places the responsibility to monitor and control managerial (or supervisory) decisions and actions in the hands of a separate group. "One of the reasons underlying this division is that the stronger management is the less safe it is to assume that its interests coincide with those of the owners of the business. The application of this principle is to place all the functions of direction and management in the hands of the management board—the Vorstand—except appointment to the Vorstand itself, which is the responsibility of the supervisory tier—the Aufsichtsrat."[118]

A combination of their own holdings with their proxies results in majority shareholder positions for Commerzbank in many German companies.

Employees, union members, and shareholders appoint members to the Aufsichtsrat.

As implied by our discussion of the importance of banks in Germany's corporate governance structure, private shareholders do not have major ownership positions in their country's firms. One reason for this is grounded in the historical continental European belief that the control of large corporations is too important an asset to be left only to the discretion of public shareholders.[119] Identically, large institutional investors such as pension funds and insurance companies are relatively insignificant owners of corporate stock. Thus, at least historically, top-level managers in German corporations generally have not been dedicated to the proposition that their decisions and actions should result in maximization of shareholder value. However, as explained in the Strategic Focus, this lack of emphasis on shareholder value is changing in some German firms.

STRATEGIC FOCUS   Seeking to Satisfy Shareholders' Interests at Veba AG

Some have argued that the German public is accustomed to a fabled "German model" of management—a model that advocates capitalism with a human face. Resulting from this model was a virtual lack of concern for maximizing stockholder value. In fact, a top-level manager at Daimler-Benz AG, Juergen Schrempp, was interrupted recently during an interview to be informed of Daimler's opening stock price for that day. Commenting about this event, Schrempp noted that "A year ago, no one in the company knew what the stock price was." Daimler now keeps stockholders in mind with everything it does. This has resulted from an increased emphasis on global capital markets that require more accountability. For instance, Daimler's stock was recently listed on the New York Stock Exchange.

At Veba AG, a diversified industrial giant that builds shopping malls, runs a cable-television system, and is Germany's largest operator of gasoline stations, CEO Ulrich Hartmann has taken actions that are quite different from those observed normally in German firms. To create value for shareholders, he has laid off thousands of workers, fired longtime managers, and closed divisions that date back to Veba's origins. Contributing to Hartmann's actions, and those of like-minded top-level managers at other German corporations, is the conviction that individual capital markets no longer exist. To compete effectively in the global capital market, argues Hartmann, firms must play by the same rules, seeking to increase shareholders' wealth in the process. Moreover, Hartmann, and other company officials, did not want Veba AG to be purchased through actions taken in the global market for corporate control. The possibility of a takeover was expressed prominently in a 1991 report prepared by the British brokerage firm S.G. Warburg. Based on its analysis, Warburg concluded that Veba was worth twice its then-current market capitalization and was easily the most undervalued company in Germany. If actions were not taken to boost its stock price, the Warburg report cautioned, Veba was quite vulnerable to a takeover.

One of the first actions Hartmann took to better serve shareholders, and to prevent the firm from becoming a target in the market for corporate control, was to update investor relations efforts. In addition to providing more financial details in the firm's annual report, Hartmann made personal visits to shareholders in Canada, the United States, and Great Britain. These visits were used to detail actions Veba was taking in order to boost its stock price and to increase shareholders' wealth. Commitments explained to key investors included those of using accounting methods requested by security analysts to report company earnings and the establishment of internal control methods that would allow Veba to assess accurately its progress toward improved financial performance.

Veba's portfolio of businesses was evaluated and changed. Founded originally in 1848 as a coal trader, the firm's Raab Karcher division exited from the coal-trading part of its then-current business areas. At Veba's chemicals operations, Huels, a new aggressive top management team reduced the workforce by 12,000, closed its tire-rubber business, and sold its synthetic-rubber operation.

To date, Veba's efforts appear to be successful. In 1995, profits increased 40 percent to two billion marks. The firm's stock price has doubled since 1991 and has consistently outperformed the German market. Because 43 percent of Veba's shares are in foreign hands, the primary beneficiaries of the company's financial accomplishments have been international investors.

Source: G. Steinmetz, 1996, Satisfying shareholders is a hot new concept at some German firms, *Wall Street Journal,* March 6, A1, A6.

■ Corporate Governance in Japan

Attitudes toward corporate governance in Japan are affected by the concepts of obligation, family, and consensus. In Japan, obligation does not result from broad general principles; rather, it is a product of specific causes or events. In this context, an obligation " . . . may be to return a service for one rendered or it may derive from a more general relationship, for example, to one's family or old alumni, or one's company (or Ministry), or the country. This sense of particular obligation is common elsewhere but it feels stronger in Japan."[120] As part of a company family, individuals are members of a unit that envelops their lives to an unusual degree. Families command the attention and allegiance of parties from the top to bottom in corporations. Moreover, keiretsus (described later) are more than an economic concept—they, too, are families. Consensus, the most important influence on the Japanese corporate governance structure, calls for the expenditure of significant amounts of energy to win the hearts and minds of people when possible as opposed to proceeding by edict of top-level managers. Consensus is highly valued, even when a firm's commitment to it results in a slow and cumbersome decision-making process.

As in Germany, banks play a more important role in financing and monitoring large public firms in Japan. Among the Japanese banks holding stock in a firm, the bank owning the largest share of stocks and largest amount of debt, the main bank, has the closest relationship with the company's top-level managers. The main bank not only provides financial advice to the firm, but also is responsible for closely monitoring managerial agents. Thus, Japan has a bank-based financial and corporate governance structure while the United States has a market-based financial and governance structure.

Aside from lending money (debt), a Japanese bank can hold up to 5 percent of a firm's total stock; a group of related financial institutions can hold up to 40 percent. In many cases, main bank relationships are part of a keiretsu. A keiretsu is a group of firms tied together by cross-shareholdings. Thus, firms in a keiretsu develop interrelationships and are interdependent. A keiretsu firm usually owns less than 2 percent of any other member firm; however, each company typically has a stake of that size in every firm in the keiretsu. As a result, somewhere between 30 percent and 90 percent of a firm is owned by other members of the keiretsu.[121] Thus, a keiretsu is a system of relationship investments. Other characteristics of Japan's corporate governance structure include (1) powerful government intervention (the Japanese Ministry of Finance maintains strong regulatory control of all of Japan's businesses), (2) close relationships between corporations and government sectors, (3) passive and stable shareholders—individuals and groups who exercise little monitoring and control of managerial agents, and (4) the virtual absence of an external market for corporate control, although mergers are common.

As is the case in Germany and the United States, Japan's corporate governance structure is changing. For example, because of their continuing development as economic organizations, although still important, the role of banks in the monitoring and control of managerial behavior and firm outcomes is less significant than it had been previously.[122] As with German firms, the availability of global capital increases the sources of funds for Japanese corporations. Additionally, the business arrangements resulting from keiretsus and relationships between companies and government agencies are being studied. Some observers of Japan's corporate governance structure suggest that significant competition from global rivals and the strong yen are among factors stimulating efforts to study governance practices that may not be as effective as they have been historically.[123]

As our explanation of governance structures suggests, it is possible that the new competitive landscape (see Chapters 1 and 5) and the global economy that is a critical part of it will foster the creation of a relatively uniform governance structure that will be used by firms throughout the world.[124] As markets shrink, customer demands become more similar, and shareholders become the focus of managerial agents' efforts in an increasing number of companies. This is especially true of German and Japanese systems that are becoming more shareholder oriented. In turn, however, U.S. firms are becoming increasingly tied to financial institutions with higher debt levels and increased institutional investor activism. Thus, regardless of their national origin, the structures used to govern corporations operating in different countries will likely tend to become more similar than is the case today.

In this chapter's final section, we discuss the need for governance mechanisms to support ethical behaviors.

■ Governance Mechanisms and Ethical Behavior

The governance mechanisms described in this chapter are designed to ensure that the agents of the firm's owners—that is, the corporation's top-level managers—make strategic decisions that best serve the interests of the entire group of stakeholders that was described in Chapter 1. In the United States at least, shareholders are recognized as a company's most significant stakeholder. As such, the focus of governance mechanisms is on the control of managerial decisions to increase the probability that shareholders' interests will be served. But product market stakeholders (e.g., customers, suppliers, and host communities) and organizational stakeholders (e.g., managerial and nonmanagerial employees) are important as well. In this regard, at least the minimal interests or needs of all stakeholders must be satisfied by outcomes achieved through the firm's actions. Without satisfaction of at least minimal interests, stakeholders will decide to withdraw their support or contribution to one firm and provide it to another (e.g., customers will purchase products from a supplier offering an acceptable substitute).

John Smale, an outside member of General Motors' board of directors, believes that all large capitalist enterprises must be concerned with goals in addition to serving shareholders. In Smale's opinion, "A corporation is a human, living enterprise. It's not just a bunch of assets. The obligation of management is to perpetuate the corporation, and that precedes their obligation to shareholders."[125] The argument then, is that the firm's strategic competitiveness is enhanced when its governance mechanisms are designed and implemented in ways that take into consideration the interests of all stakeholders.

Although subject to debate, some believe that ethically responsible companies design and use governance mechanisms that are intended to serve all stakeholders' interests. However, there is a more critical relationship between ethical behavior and corporate governance mechanisms.

Evidence demonstrates that all companies are vulnerable to a display of unethical behaviors by their employees, including, of course, top-level managers. For example, in April 1996, a federal grand jury indicted the CEO of Mid-American Waste System Inc. on bribery charges. The indictment alleged that the CEO approved bribes to be paid to members of the Gary, Ind., city council. The bribes were thought to be efforts to influence voting on a lucrative municipal-landfill contract. The CEO, who resigned his position after announcement of the indictment, expressed "surprise" upon learning of the charges against him. He also stated that he looked forward to being "vindicated by a jury." A business writer suggested that the indictment painted a picture of a cozy confluence of interests between Mid-American and a few local politicians.[126]

The charges concerned with alleged decisions and actions at Mid-American Waste System Inc. were adjudicated through the U.S. judicial system. Nonetheless, these alleged behaviors—behaviors that are unethical—are an example of those that corporate governance mechanisms should prevent. The decisions and actions of a corporation's board of directors can be an effective deterrent to unethical behaviors. In fact, some believe that the most effective boards participate actively in setting boundaries for business ethics and values.[127] Once formulated, the board's expectations related to ethical decisions and actions by all of the firm's stakeholders must be communicated clearly to top-level managers. Moreover, these managers should be made to understand that the board will hold them fully accountable for the development and support of an organizational culture that results in only ethical decisions and behaviors.

Events at another company show the positive role CEOs can play in demanding the exercise of only ethical behaviors. Shortly after becoming CEO at Par Pharmaceuticals, Kenneth Sawyer discovered that unethical and unlawful decisions had been made previously at the firm. For example, Quad Pharmaceuticals was one of the most profitable units of Par. However, the audit ordered by Sawyer revealed that managers had submitted false drug test data to the U.S. Food and Drug Administration (FDA). The audit results led to indictments of three managers of the Par unit. Sawyer also found that false data had been submitted to the FDA. Two managers, the head of R&D and the head of production, pleaded guilty to conspiracy to obstruct FDA's regulatory functions.

Obviously, Par Pharmaceuticals' internal governance mechanisms had failed. The board of directors failed in its role of monitoring top-level managers. The compensation system for top-level executives did not elicit managerial decisions that were in the shareholders' best interests. To cope with the firm's difficulties and to prevent a reoccurrence of unethical behavior, Sawyer initiated several courses of action. He voluntarily withdrew drugs from the market until he could ensure that proper testing had been completed. He implemented a number of strict drug testing policies to guide future efforts. He hired new executives and tried to repair the firm's corporate image. While engaged in these decisions and actions, Sawyer endured death threats to himself and his family.[128]

Fortunately, the unethical behaviors that occurred at Par Pharmaceuticals and alleged at Mid-American Waste System Inc. are extreme examples of what can transpire when governance mechanisms fail to align the interests of the firm's principals and agents. Nonetheless, these events emphasize the importance of effective corporate governance. It is only when the proper controls of governance mechanisms are in place that strategies are formulated and implemented in ways that result in strategic competitiveness and above-average returns.

As this chapter's discussion suggests, corporate governance mechanisms are a vital, yet imperfect, part of firms' efforts to implement strategies successfully. Described in the Strategic Focus are several contemporary corporate governance issues. While these issues are important, a consensus about their individual resolutions does not exist. Nonetheless, these are issues that either directly or indirectly affect the use of the governance mechanisms examined in this chapter.

STRATEGIC FOCUS Contemporary Corporate Governance Issues

Deloitte & Touche LLP and the National Association of Corporate Directors (NACD) recently brought 13 corporate governance leaders together to examine issues of concern to board directors and other stakeholders. Representing three countries, the group included prominent board directors, top-level managers, shareholder activists, academic scholars studying governance, and a leading business journalist. Among the issues examined by the assembled group were (1) director certification and accreditation, (2) separation of the CEO and chairperson roles, (3) assessment of the proper role of a board of directors "lead person," and (4) evaluation of the board's role in strategic decision making and CEO succession.

Director Certification and Accreditation. Some believe that requiring directors to participate in formal education programs prior to beginning active service on the board would increase the profile of directors to the level of a profession. Moreover, certifying an individual's knowledge about a firm's business and the processes it follows to monitor and control its operations might enhance an individual's ability to substantively evaluate proposed managerial initiatives. Courses being offered in various companies at a minimum provide incoming directors with the legal and financial basics relevant to operating the company they will serve. Voluntary accreditation is taking hold in Australia and may soon appear in the United Kingdom and United States.

Separation of the CEO and Chairperson Roles. In the view of some of the roundtable participants, separating the CEO and chairperson roles helps companies avoid undue concentrations of power. This separation is thought to be especially appropriate if one assumes that top-level managers' will engage in opportunistic behavior. There is a growing interest in the United States to separate the roles, although the evidence to date about the effects of such separation on the firm's financial performance is not definitive. In Australia, the roles are separated in 76 percent of all companies.

The Lead Director's Role. As the occupant of a key position, the person chosen as the lead director for the board typically chairs a key committee. Among other responsibilities, the lead director should verify that important governance-related questions are asked and answered appropriately by the right people.

The Board's Role in Strategy and Succession.   Participants split over this issue. Some argued that the board should be more involved in the formulation of the corporation's strategies. The perspective was that for directors to have ownership of a strategy, they needed to be a part of its formation. Urging caution, others suggested that directors should only evaluate the assumptions behind top-level managers' intended strategies. Without an in-depth knowledge of the firm's executives, these participants suggested, directors lacked the input required to make valid strategic decisions. In terms of CEO succession, however, all roundtable members voiced support for a strong and active board role.

Given their diverse backgrounds and experience, the lack of complete agreement among the 13 people identified as corporate governance leaders regarding the array of issues they evaluated is not surprising. Nonetheless, the following statement captures summaries of the general conclusions reached by the participants: "Although Roundtable members did not agree on all corporate governance issues, they collectively foresee an increase in continuing education for directors, a clearer separation of the roles of CEO and chairman (even when held by the same individual), more and stronger ways to ensure board independence (through the lead director's efforts) . . . and a greater role for directors in strategy and succession."

Source: Deloitte & Touche LLP and National Association of Corporate Directors, 1996, *Corporate Governance Roundtable* (Washington, D.C.: National Association of Corporate Directors).

■ Summary

- Corporate governance is a relationship among stakeholders that is used to determine the firm's direction and control its performance. How firms monitor and control top-level managers' decisions and actions, as called for by governance mechanisms, affects the implementation of strategies. Effective governance—governance that aligns managers' interests with shareholders' interests—can result in a competitive advantage for the firm.

- In the modern corporation, there are four internal governance mechanisms—ownership concentration, board of directors, executive compensation, and the multidivisional structure—and one external—the market for corporate control.

- Ownership is separated from control in the modern corporation. Owners (i.e., principals) hire managers (i.e., agents) to make decisions that will maximize the value of their firm. As risk specialists, owners diversify their risk by investing in an array of corporations. As decision-making specialists, top-level managers are expected by owners to make decisions that will result in the earning of above-average returns. Thus, modern corporations are characterized by an agency relationship—a relationship that is created when one party (the firm's owners) hires and pays another party (top-level managers) because of their decision-making skills.

- Separation of ownership and control creates an agency problem. This type of problem exists when an agent pursues goals that are in conflict with the principals' goals. In efforts to control the effects of these problems, principals establish and use governance mechanisms.

- An internal governance mechanism, ownership concentration, is defined by the number of large-block shareholders and the percentage of shares they own. With significant ownership percentages such as those held by large mutual funds and pension funds, institutional investors often are able to influence top-level managers' strategic decisions and actions. Thus, unlike diffuse ownership, which tends to bring about relatively weak monitoring and control of managerial decisions, concentrated ownership results in more active and effective monitoring of top-level managers.

- An increasingly powerful force in corporate America, institutional owners are actively using their positions of concentrated ownership in individual companies to force managers and boards of directors to make decisions that maximize a firm's value. These owners (e.g., CalPERS) have caused executives in prominent companies to lose their jobs because of their failure to serve shareholders' interests effectively.

- In the United States and the United Kingdom, the board of directors, composed of insiders, related outsiders, and outsiders, is a governance mechanism shareholders expect to represent their collective interests, especially because ownership is diffuse. The percentage of outside directors on most boards now exceeds the percentage of insider directors. This relative percent of outsiders would seem appropriate, in that these individuals are expected to be more independent of a firm's top-level managers than are those selected from inside the firm.

- A highly visible and often criticized governance mechanism is executive compensation. Through the use of salary, bonuses, and long-term incentives, this mechanism is intended to strengthen the alignment of managers' and shareholders' interests. A strong emphasis on executive incentives has widened the gap between the pay of the typical worker and CEOs. A firm's board of directors has the responsibility of determining the degree to which executive compensation is succeeding as a governance mechanism and to initiate all appropriate corrective actions when required.

- As a governance mechanism, the multidivisional (M-form) structure is intended to reduce managerial opportunism and to align principals' and agents' interests as a result. By creating independent business divisions in the diversified firm, the M-form makes it possible for the corporate office to monitor and control managerial decisions in the individual divisions. However, at the corporate level, the M-form may actually stimulate managerial opportunism. The results of this possibility can be seen when top-level executives overdiversify their firms.

- In general, evidence suggests that shareholders and board directors have become more vigilant in their control of managerial decisions. Nonetheless, these mechanisms are insufficient to govern the diversification of many large companies. As such, the market for corporate control is an important governance mechanism. Although it, too, is imperfect, the market for corporate control has been effective in causing corporations to downscope and reduce their degree of inefficient diversification.

- Corporate governance structures used in Germany and Japan differ from each other and from the one used in the United States. Historically, the U.S. governance structure has focused on maximizing shareholder value. In Germany, employees, as a stakeholder group, have a more prominent role in governance than is the case in the United States. Until recently, Japanese shareholders played virtually no role in the monitoring and control of top-level managers. However, these systems are becoming more similar.

- Effective governance mechanisms ensure that the interests of all stakeholders are served. Thus, long-term strategic success results when firms are governed in ways that permit at least minimal satisfaction of capital market stakeholders (e.g., shareholders), product market stakeholders (e.g., customers and suppliers), and organizational stakeholders (managerial and nonmanagerial employees). Moreover, effective governance causes the establishment and consistent use of ethical behavior as the firm formulates and implements its strategies.

■ Review Questions

1. What is corporate governance? What factors account for the considerable amount of attention corporate governance receives from several parties, including shareholder activists, business press writers, and academic scholars? Why are governance mechanisms used to control managerial decisions?

2. What does it mean to say that ownership is separated from control in the modern corporation? What brought about this separation?

3. What is an agency relationship? What is managerial opportunism? What assumptions do owners of modern corporations make about managerial agents? What are the strategic implications of these assumptions?

4. How are four internal governance mechanisms—ownership concentration, boards of directors, executive compensation, and the multidivisional (M-form) structure—used to align the interests of managerial agents with those of the firm's owners?

5. What trends exist in terms of executive compensation? What is the effect of increased use of long-term incentives on executives' strategic decisions?

6. What is the market for corporate control? What conditions generally cause this external governance mechanism to become active? How does this mechanism constrain top-level managers' decisions?

7. What is the nature of corporate governance mechanisms used in Germany and Japan?

8. How can corporate governance mechanisms foster ethical strategic decisions and behaviors on the part of managerial agents?

Application Discussion Questions

1. The roles and responsibilities of top-level managers and members of a corporation's board of directors are different. Traditionally, executives have been responsible for determining the firm's strategic direction and implementing strategies to achieve it, whereas the board has been responsible for monitoring and controlling managerial decisions and actions. Some argue that boards should become more involved with the formulation of a firm's strategies. In your opinion, how would the board's increased involvement in the selection of strategies affect a firm's strategic competitiveness? What evidence can you offer to support your position?

2. Do you believe that large U.S. firms have been overgoverned by some corporate governance mechanisms and undergoverned by others? Provide an example of a business firm to support your belief.

3. How can corporate governance mechanisms create conditions that allow top-level managers to develop a competitive advantage and focus on long-term performance? Search the business press to find an example of a firm in which this occurred and prepare a description of it.

4. Some believe that the market for corporate control is not an effective governance mechanism. If this is an accurate view, what factors might account for the ineffectiveness of this method of monitoring and controlling managerial decisions?

5. Assume that you overheard the following comments: "As a top-level manager, the only agency relationship I am concerned about is the one between myself and the firm's owners. I think that it would be a waste of my time and energy to worry about any other agency relationship." How would you respond to this person? Do you accept or reject this view? Be prepared to support your position.

Ethics Questions

1. As explained in this chapter, the use of corporate governance mechanisms should establish order between parties whose interests may be in conflict. Do firm owners have any ethical responsibilities to managers when using governance mechanisms to establish order? If so, what are they?

2. Is it ethical for a firm owner to assume that agents (managers hired to make decisions that are in the owner's best interests) are averse to work and risk? Why or why not?

3. What are the responsibilities of the board of directors to stakeholders other than shareholders?

4. What ethical issues are involved with executive compensation? How can we determine if top-level executives are paid too much?

5. Is it ethical for firms involved in the market for corporate control to target companies performing at levels exceeding the industry average? Why or why not?

6. What ethical issues, if any, do top-level managers face when asking their firm to provide them with either a golden parachute or a golden goodbye?

7. How can governance mechanisms be designed to ensure against managerial opportunism, ineffectiveness, and unethical behaviors?

Internet Exercises

Search for CEO compensation data from Time Warner's numerous business magazines at:

- http://pathfinder.com/welcome/

Select several companies that represent a wide range of CEO compensation. Then, examine the 10-K and other financial reports for these companies at the SEC's Edgar database:

- http://www.sec.gov/edgarhp.htm

Compare these two sets of data for each of the companies (CEO compensation and the firm's financial results). Do the financial results explain the disparity of compensation? Might the industry or competitive dynamics be the reason for these differences? Can you find background information about the CEOs?

Cohesion Case

Select outside "directors" for your firm. Decide on a governance scheme for your organization including the compensation for your teammates and the newly appointed outside directors. Does either group prefer receiving stock options to salary or a cash bonus? How involved do you want each group to be? How will you balance financial incentives with ethical considerations?

■ Notes

1. R.D. Kosnik and S. Chatterjee, 1997, *Corporate Governance* (St. Paul: West Publishing Company).

2. R.A.G. Monks and N. Minow, 1995, *Corporate Governance* (Cambridge, Mass.: Blackwell Business), 1; J. Charkham, 1994, *Keeping Good Company: A Study of Corporate Governance in Five Countries* (New York: Oxford University Press), 1.

3. J. Pound, 1995, The promise of the governed corporation, *Harvard Business Review* 73, no. 2: 90.

4. O.E. Williamson, 1996, Economic organization: The case for candor, *Academy of Management Review* 21: 48–57.

5. R.A.G. Monks, 1993, Relationship investing, Netscape, http://www.lens-inc.com/Academic/papers/colum.html, June 10.

6. Kosnik and Chatterjee, *Corporate Governance*; R. Lowenstein, Corporate governance's sorry history, 1996, *Wall Street Journal,* April 18, C1.

7. The invisible hand, 1994, *The Economist,* October 8, 81.

8. J.K. Seward and J.P. Walsh, 1996, The governance and control of voluntary corporate spin-offs, *Strategic Management Journal* 17: 25–39.

9. M. Weidenbaum, 1994, The evolving corporate board, *Contemporary Issues Series* 65 (St. Louis: Center for the Study of American Business, Washington University), 1.

10. Charkham, *Keeping Good Company,* 1.

11. A survey of corporate governance, 1994, *The Economist,* January 29, 12–36.

12. Cadbury Committee, 1992, *Report of the Cadbury Committee on the Financial Aspects of Corporate Governance* (London: Gee).

13. T.E. Copeland, 1994, Why value value? *McKinsey Quarterly* 1994, no. 4: 97–109.

14. Parts of this discussion are based on Chapters 3 and 6 from R.E. Hoskisson and M.A. Hitt, 1994, *Downscoping: How to Tame the Diversified Firm* (New York: Oxford University Press).

15. J.P. Walsh and R. Kosnik, 1993, Corporate raiders and their disciplinary role in the market for corporate control, *Academy of Management Journal* 36: 671–700.

16. R. Chaganti and F. Damanpour, 1991, Institutional ownership, capital structure, and firm performance, *Strategic Management Journal* 12: 479–491.

17. Charkham, *Keeping Good Company,* 2.

18. K.J. Rediker and A. Seth, 1995, Boards of directors and substitution effects of alternative governance mechanisms, *Strategic Management Journal* 16: 85–99.

19. G.F. Davis and T.A. Thompson, 1994, A social movement perspective on corporate control, *Administrative Science Quarterly* 39: 141–173.

20. M.A. Eisenberg, 1989, The structure of corporation law, *Columbia Law Review* 89, no. 7: 1461 as cited in Monks and Minow, *Corporate Governance,* 7.

21. E.F. Fama and M.C. Jensen, 1983, Separation of ownership and control, *Journal of Law and Economics* 26: 301–343; E.F. Fama, 1980,

Agency problems and the theory of the firm, *Journal of Political Economy* 88: 288–307.

22. P.C. Godfrey and C.W.L. Hill, 1995, The problem of unobservables in strategic management research, *Strategic Management Journal* 16: 519–533; M. Jensen and W. Meckling, 1976, Theory of the firm: Managerial behavior, agency costs, and ownership structure, *Journal of Financial Economics* 11: 305–360.

23. E.J. Zajac, 1990, CEO selection, succession, compensation, and firm performance: A theoretical integration and empirical analysis, *Strategic Management Journal* 11: 217–230.

24. T.M. Welbourne and L.R. Gomez Mejia, 1995, Gainsharing: A critical review and a future research agenda, *Journal of Management* 21: 577.

25. T.H. Hammond, 1994, Structure, strategy, and the agenda of the firm, in R.P. Rumelt, D.E. Schendel, and D.J. Teece (eds.) *Fundamental Issues in Strategy* (Boston: Harvard Business School Press), 97–154.

26. P. Wright, S.P. Ferris, A. Sarin, and V. Awasthi, 1996, Impact of corporate insider, blockholder, and institutional equity ownership on firm risk taking, *Academy of Management Journal* 39: 441–463.

27. P.B. Firstenberg and B.G. Malkiel, 1994, The twenty-first century boardroom: Who will be in charge? *Sloan Management Review,* Fall, 27–35, as cited in C.M. Daily, 1996, Governance patterns in bankruptcy reorganizations, *Strategic Management Journal* 17: 355–375.

28. O.E. Williamson, 1996, *The Mechanisms of Governance* (New York: Oxford University Press), 6; O.E. Williamson, 1993, Opportunism and its critics, *Managerial and Decision Economics* 14: 97–107.

29. S. Ghoshal and P. Moran, 1996, Bad for practice: A critique of the transaction cost theory, *Academy of Management Review* 21: 13–47.

30. Williamson, Economic organization, 50.

31. Godfrey and Hill, The problem of unobservables, 521; C.W.L. Hill, 1990, Cooperation, opportunism, and the invisible hand, *Academy of Management Review* 15: 500–513.

32. S. Finkelstein and R.A. D'Aveni, 1994, CEO duality as a double-edged sword: How boards of directors balance entrenchment avoidance and unity of command, *Academy of Management Journal* 37: 1079–1108.

33. R.E. Hoskisson and T.A. Turk, 1990, Corporate restructuring: Governance and control limits of the internal market, *Academy of Management Review* 15: 459–477.

34. Rediker and Seth, Boards of directors and substitution effects; S. Finkelstein and D.C. Hambrick, 1989, Chief executive compensation: A study of the intersection of markets and political processes, *Strategic Management Journal* 16: 221–239.

35. Hoskisson and Turk, Corporate restructuring.

36. M.S. Jensen, 1986, Agency costs of free cash flow, corporate finance, and takeovers, *American Economic Review* 76: 323–329.

37. C.W.L. Hill and S.A. Snell, 1988, External control, corporate strategy, and firm perfor-

mance in research intensive industries, *Strategic Management Journal* 9: 577–590.

38. Welbourne and Gomez Mejia, Gainsharing, 578, who based their definition on E.A. Dyl, 1988, Corporate control and management compensation: Evidence on the agency problem, *Managerial and Decision Economics* 9, no. 1: 21–25 and J. Barney and W. Ouchi (eds.), 1986, *Organizational Economics* (San Francisco: Jossey-Bass).

39. R. Comment and G. Jarrel, 1995, Corporate focus and stock returns, *Journal of Financial Economics* 37: 67–87.

40. A. Shleifer and R.W. Vishny, 1986, Large shareholders and corporate control, *Journal of Political Economy* 94: 461–488.

41. M.P. Smith, 1996, Shareholder activism by institutional investors: Evidence from CalPERS, *Journal of Finance* 51: 227–252.

42. Hoskisson and Turk, Corporate restructuring.

43. R.E. Hoskisson, R.A. Johnson, and D.D. Moesel, 1994, Corporate divestiture intensity in restructuring firms: Effects of governance, strategy, and performance, *Academy of Management Journal* 37: 1207–1251.

44. Hill and Snell, External control.

45. A. Berle and G. Means, 1932, *The Modern Corporation and Private Property* (New York: Macmillan).

46. Smith, Shareholder activism; Davis and Thompson, A social movement, 141.

47. J.D. Bogert, 1996, Explaining variance in the performance of long-term corporate blockholders, *Strategic Management Journal* 17: 243–249.

48. R. Amen, 1996, Most companies tell it like it is, *Wall Street Journal,* March 2, A16.

49. C.M. Dailey, 1996, Governance patterns in bankruptcy reorganizations, *Strategic Management Journal* 17: 355–375.

50. Hoskisson and Hitt, *Downscoping;* Hoskisson et al., Corporate divestiture intensity.

51. Smith, Shareholder activism.

52. S. Pulliam and J. Pereira, 1995, Reebok CEO Fireman faces criticism by institutional holders, *Wall Street Journal,* August 14, C1, C2.

53. J.S. Lublin, 1995, Irate shareholders target ineffective board members, *Wall Street Journal,* November 6, B1, B8.

54. Associated Press, 1996, AT&T board to get slap from big investor groups, *Dallas Morning News,* April 17, D2.

55. M. Pacelle, 1996, Performance tables turned for CalPERS, *Wall Street Journal,* May 20, C1, C21.

56. M.R. Sesit, 1996, CalPERS voice may be heard outside U.S., *Wall Street Journal,* March 19, C1, C17.

57. CalPERS announces results of governance survey, 1996, Netscape, http://www.slb.com/shar/CalPERS/press.html, June 4.

58. E. Schine, 1995, This gadfly is really buzzing, *Business Week,* February 13, 48–49.

59. CalPERS highlights retailers in its list of underperformers, 1996, *Wall Street Journal,* February 7, C18.

60. CalPERS economic underperformers list, 1996, Netscape, http://www.hoovers/com/lists/calpers.html, June 4.

61. Smith, Shareholder activism.

62. CalPERS statement of governance principles, 1996, Netscape, http://www.wp.com/corpgov/persgov.html, June 10.

63. M.J. Roe, 1993, Mutual funds in the board room, *Journal of Applied Corporate Finance 5,* no. 4: 56–61.

64. S. Mieher, 1993, Weak force: Shareholder activism, despite hoopla, leaves most CEOs unscathed, *Wall Street Journal,* May 24, A1.

65. Bloomberg Business News, 1996, More companies add severance package for execs., survey says, *Dallas Morning News,* July 6, F3.

66. C. Sundaramurthy, 1996, Corporate governance within the context of antitakeover provisions, *Strategic Management Journal* 17: 377–394; P. Mallette and K.L. Fowler, 1992, Effects of board composition and stock ownership on the adoption of "poison pills," *Academy of Management Journal* 35: 1010–1035.

67. Not getting a contract renewed, 1996, *Wall Street Journal,* May 2, A1.

68. B.S. Black, 1992, Agents watching agents: The promise of institutional investors voice, *UCLA Law Review* 39: 871–893.

69. Rediker and Seth, Boards of directors, 85.

70. Daily and Schwenk, Chief executive officers, 189.

71. Seward and Walsh, The governance and control, 28.

72. P. Mallete and R.L. Hogler, 1995, Board composition, stock ownership, and the exemption of directors from liability, *Journal of Management* 21: 861–878.

73. B.D. Baysinger and R.E. Hoskisson, 1990, The composition of boards of directors and strategic control: Effects on corporate strategy, *Academy of Management Review* 15: 72–87.

74. Seward and Walsh, The governance and control, 29; C.M. Daily, 1995, The relationship between board composition and leadership structure and bankruptcy reorganization outcomes, *Journal of Management* 21: 1041–1056; J. Wade, C.A. O'Reilly, and I. Chandratat, 1990, Golden parachutes: CEOs and the exercise of social influence, *Administrative Science Quarterly* 35: 587–603.

75. J.D. Westphal and E.J. Zajac, 1995, Who shall govern? CEO/board power, demographic similarity, and new director selection, *Administrative Science Quarterly* 40: 60–83.

76. R.P. Beatty and E.J. Zajac, 1994, Managerial incentives, monitoring, and risk bearing: A study of executive compensation, ownership, and board structure in initial public offerings, *Administrative Science Quarterly* 39: 313–335.

77. M. Eisenberg, 1986, *The Structure of the Corporation* (Boston: Little, Brown and Co.).

78. W.Q. Judge, Jr., and G.H. Dobbins, 1995, Antecedents and effects of outside directors' awareness of CEO decision style, *Journal of Management* 21: 43–64.

79. I.F. Kesner, 1988, Director characteristics in committee membership: An investigation of type, occupation, tenure and gender, *Academy of Management Journal* 31: 66–84.

80. S. Zahra, 1997, Governance, ownership and corporate entrepreneurship among the *Fortune* 500: The moderating impact of industry technological opportunity, *Academy of Management Journal* 40: in press.

81. D. Kunde, 1995, Dallas boards of directors smaller, paid less than average, *Dallas Morning News,* October 20, D11.

82. H. Kaback, 1996, A director's guide to board behavior, *Wall Street Journal,* April 1, A14.

83. D.C. Hambrick and S. Finkelstein, 1995, The effects of ownership structure on conditions at the top: The case of CEO pay raises, *Strategic Management Journal* 16: 175.

84. V.R. Loucks, Jr., 1995, An equity cure for managers, *Wall Street Journal,* September 26, A19.

85. S. Werner and H.L. Tosi, 1995, Other people's money: The effects of ownership on compensation strategy and managerial pay, *Academy of Management Journal* 38: 1672–1691.

86. I. Kristol, 1996, What is a CEO worth? *Wall Street Journal,* June 5, A14.

87. L. Wines, 1996, Compensation plans that support strategy, *Journal of Business Strategy* 17, no. 4: 17–20.

88. Loucks, Jr., An equity cure, A19.

89. K. Roth and S. O'Donnell, 1996, Foreign subsidiary compensation: An agency theory perspective, *Academy of Management Journal* 39: 678–703.

90. R.E. Hoskisson, M.A. Hitt, and C.W.L. Hill, 1993, Managerial incentives and investment in R&D in large multiproduct firms, *Organization Science* 4: 325–341.

91. K.A. Merchant, 1989, *Rewarding Results: Motivating Profit Center Managers* (Boston: Harvard Business School Press); J. Eaton and H. Rosen, 1983, Agency, delayed compensation, and the structure of executive remuneration, *Journal of Finance* 38: 1489–1505.

92. C. Duff, 1996, Top executives ponder high pay, decide they're worth every cent, *Wall Street Journal,* May 15, B1.

93. Kristol, What is a CEO worth?

94. L. Uchitelle, 1996, Performance pay made 1995 bonus year for executives, *Houston Chronicle,* March 30, C3.

95. R.E. Yates, 1995, Restless in the ranks, *Dallas Morning News,* October 12, D1, D10.

96. Associated Press, 1996, Downsized firms start adding staff, *Dallas Morning News,* May 29, D2.

97. Special Report, 1996, How high can CEO pay go? *Business Week,* April 22, 100–121.

98. Uchitelle, Performance pay.

99. D. Machan, 1996, The last article you will ever have to read on executive pay? No way! *Forbes,* May 20, 176–234.

100. Associated Press, 1996, Low-profile exec gets high-profile bonus, *Dallas Morning News,* April 11, D2.

101. GE chief's salary, bonus rose 22.3% to $5.32 million in '95, 1996, *Wall Street Journal,* March 13, B5.

102. O.E. Williamson, 1985, *The Economic Institutions of Capitalism: Firms, Markets and Relational Contracting* (New York: Macmillan Free Press).

103. New CEO presents plan for restructuring airline, 1996, *Wall Street Journal,* May 17, B8.

104. W.M. Carley, 1996, GE implements $200 million program to slash number of defects per product, *Wall Street Journal,* April 25, A4.

105. B.W. Keats and M.A. Hitt, 1988, A causal model of linkages among environmental dimensions, macro organizational characteristics, and performance, *Academy of Management Journal* 31: 570–598.

106. O.E. Williamson, 1994, Strategizing, economizing, and economic organization, in R.P. Rumelt, D.E. Schendel, and D.J. Teece (eds.), *Fundamental Issues in Strategy* (Boston: Harvard Business School Press), 380.

107. R.E. Hoskisson and M.A. Hitt, 1988, Strategic control and relative R&D investment in large multiproduct firms, *Strategic Management Journal* 9: 605–621.

108. M.A. Hitt, R.E. Hoskisson, and R.D. Ireland, 1990, Mergers and acquisitions and managerial commitment to innovation in M-form firms, *Strategic Management Journal* 11 (Special Issue): 29–47.

109. Walsh and Kosnik, Corporate raiders.

110. Mallette and Hogler, Board composition, 864.

111. G.G. Marcial, 1995, A stiff broom goes after Pier 1, *Business Week,* October 23, 106.

112. Sundaramurthy, Corporate governance, 377.

113. Marcial, A stiff broom.

114. Walsh and Kosnik, Corporate raiders.

115. S. Johnston, 1995, Managerial dominance of Japan's major corporations, *Journal of Management* 21: 191–209.

116. Our discussion of corporate governance structures in Germany and Japan is drawn from Monks and Minow, *Corporate Governance,* 271–299; Charkham, *Keeping Good Company,* 6–118; A survey of corporate governance, 12–36.

117. H. Kim and R.E. Hoskisson, 1996, Japanese governance systems: A critical review, in B. Prasad (ed.), *Advances in International Comparative Management* (Greenwich, CT: JAI Press), in press.

118. Charkham, *Keeping Good Company,* 17.

119. B. Riley, 1996, French leave for shareholders, *Financial Times,* June 23, XX.

120. Charkham, *Keeping Good Company,* 70.

121. A survey of corporate governance, 16.

122. Williamson, The Mechanisms, 320.

123. D.P. Hamilton and N. Shirouau, 1996, Japan's business cartels are starting to erode, but change is slow, *Wall Street Journal,* December 4, A1, A6.

124. M.E. Porter, 1992, Capital disadvantages: America's failing capital investment system, *Harvard Business Review* 70, no. 5: 65–82.

125. A. Taylor, III, 1996, GM: Why they might break up America's biggest company, *Fortune,* April 29, 84.

126. J.P. Miller, 1996, Mid-American Waste System CEO quits after indictment on bribery charges, *Wall Street Journal,* April 17, B5.

127. R.F. Felton, A. Hudnut, and V. Witt, 1995, Building a stronger board, *McKinsey Quarterly* 1995, no. 2: 169.

128. R. Stodgill, 1994, Red ink, wiretaps and death threats, *Business Week,* February 21, 80–82.

11 Organizational Structure and Controls

After reading this chapter, you should be able to:

1. Explain the importance of integrating strategy implementation and strategy formulation.
2. Describe the dominant path of evolution from strategy to structure to strategy again.
3. Identify and describe the organizational structures used to implement different business-level strategies.
4. Discuss organizational structures used to implement different corporate-level strategies.
5. Identify and distinguish among the organizational structures used to implement three international strategies.
6. Describe organizational structures used to implement cooperative strategies.

Troubled Times at Oy Nokia

Finland's Oy Nokia quickly "came out of nowhere" to become the world's second largest mobile phone manufacturer behind Motorola Inc. Continuing increases in its sales, earnings, and stock prices at first seemed to suggest that this Finnish company could do no wrong. Results from the firm's 1995 operations, however, differed dramatically from the highly positive outcomes achieved in the early 1990s. Compared to 1994, for example, Nokia's net income declined 43 percent, to 2.23 billion Finish markkaa, while sales grew, to 36.81 billion markkaa. First quarter 1996 results were also discouraging: Nokia reported a pretax profit of 399 million markkaa, down from 1995 first quarter profits of 1.35 billion markkaa.

Several factors contributed to what Nokia executives believed would be a temporary performance setback. CEO Jormal Ollila cited the decline of approximately 40 percent in 1995 in U.S. mobile phone prices. Although less challenging, the price decline of about 20 percent in Europe and Asia during the same year also affected the firm's profit margins. Ollila observed that while Nokia was able to maintain its world market share in 1995, this was accomplished ". . . at the expense of low pricing." Ollila's belief that worldwide revenue from Nokia's network equipment sales would grow between 30 and 45 percent in 1996, coupled with an anticipated increase in revenues from mobile phone sales of up to 40 percent, was the foundation for his expectation that 1996's performance, and those of subsequent years, would improve over 1995's.

Nokia's color television business also affected the firm's performance. Never a consistent, positive contributor to growth and profitability, Nokia took a one-time charge of 2.3 billion markkaa in 1995 to cover the costs of withdrawing from the color television business market.

Additional causes for the difficulties Nokia has encountered recently have been suggested. One cause noted by analysts was the firm's relative lack of extensive international experience. Its relative inexperience in international markets may have contributed to the firm's lack of complete success in efforts to predict the 1995 decline in the demand for mobile phones in the United States. Compounding this problem was the company's inability to predict accurately which of its products would be the most popular in the key U.S. market, which resulted in a glut of unwanted goods and shortages of high-demand items, particularly digital products. One analyst noted that at the end of 1995, Nokia had a large inventory of expensive parts at a time when prices on mobile-phone handsets were falling. According to some estimates, the average selling price of some mobile phones in the United States during this time was below the cost of their manufacture. This relationship between production costs and selling prices places a premium on accurate predictions of product demand.

As this discussion suggests, a number of factors contributed to Nokia's recent performance problems. Of particular importance, the firm may not have had the appropriate organizational structure or controls required to achieve success in the global marketplace. In the words of one analyst, "What you have here is a (once) small company that has operated in a localized environment and suddenly projected itself into a global market. . . . They just ran out of control." The firm may have grown faster than did its capabilities to control that growth. For example, fixed costs in the mobile phone division grew 10 percent faster than the business itself, causing a decline in the division's operating profit. Moreover, the firm's continuing logistic and supply problems were still unresolved by mid-1996.

When growth occurs rapidly in a large diversified firm such as Nokia, top-level managers sometimes rely on financial controls rather than strategic controls (which are described later in this chapter). The danger of relying on financial controls, Ollila believes, is that executives often read reports based on financial criteria rather than understanding their firm's future. In other words, a company that grows rapidly sometimes exceeds the immediate strategic control capabilities of top-level managers to guide it effectively. To overcome its performance difficulties, Nokia may require a different organizational structure as well as different corporate- and business-level controls. By continuing his efforts to restructure Nokia so it can focus on telecommunications and to implement new strategies and controls, Ollila seeks to find ways to constantly provide goods and services with better features to customers at increasingly lower prices.

Source: R. Jacob, 1996, Nokia fumbles, but don't count it out, *Fortune,* February 19, 86–88; S.D. Moore and R.T. King, Jr., 1996, Finland's Nokia posts big loss for 4th period, *Wall Street Journal,* February 29, B8; K. Pope, 1996, Troubles at phone giant Nokia offer a sobering lesson on runaway growth, *Wall Street Journal,* March 12, A15; T. Parker-Pope, 1996, Finland's Nokia reports 70% decline in earnings, sending stock down 6%, *Wall Street Journal,* May 10, A6.

As the Oy Nokia example suggests, formulated strategies may fail to result in the strategic competitiveness and above-average returns firms seek. This failure sometimes occurs because the wrong strategy was formulated. In other words, the top-level managers responsible for formulating strategies are not infallible; mistakes are made. The failure to understand the effects of an industry's structural characteristics, coupled with an inability to identify the firm's actual sources of competitive advantage, might, for example, result in the formulation of a cost leadership business-level strategy when a differentiation strategy should have been formulated. Similar types of mistakes can occur when formulating corporate-level, acquisition, restructuring, international, and cooperative strategies.

Even properly formulated strategies, however, do not always yield desired outcomes. This type of failure occurs when formulated strategies are implemented poorly. Recently Wal-Mart's strategy implementation effectiveness has been questioned. Some believe that the firm's almost legendary ability to implement strategies in ways that result in a competitive advantage is slipping.[1]

As explained in Chapter 12, a formulated strategy will not be implemented effectively by individuals lacking either the motivation and/or required skills.[2] James March, a prominent management scholar, observes that for decisions to have effects, they must be implemented properly. March further notes that the study of organizations has repeatedly examined the way strategies are executed, modified, and elaborated by those who implement them.[3]

In the previous chapter, we described mechanisms companies use to govern their operations and to align various parties' interests, especially the interests of top-level executives, with those of the firm's owners. Governance mechanisms can influence a company's ability to implement formulated strategies successfully and thereby facilitate competitive advantage. In this chapter, our focus is on the organizational structures and controls used to implement the strategies discussed previously (e.g., business-level, Chapter 4; corporate-level, Chapter 6; international, Chapter 8; and cooperative, Chapter 9). Moreover, as the Oy Nokia example suggests, the proper use of organizational structure and accompanying controls improves firm value.[4]

We also note in this chapter that proper matches between strategy and structure can result in a competitive advantage. For example, it may be that what makes 3M's competitive advantage sustainable "... is its unique blend of practices, values, autonomous structures, funding processes, rewards, and selection and development of product champions."[5] On the other hand, ineffective strategy/structure matches may result in firm rigidity and failure, given the complexity and need for rapid changes in the new competitive landscape. Thus, effective strategic leaders (see Chapter 12) seek to develop an organizational structure and accompanying controls that are superior to those of their competitors.[6] Using competitively superior structures and controls explains in part why some firms survive and succeed while others do not.[7] As with the other parts of the strategic management process, top-level managers bear the final responsibility to make choices about organizational structures that will enhance firm performance.[8]

Selecting the organizational structure and controls that result in effective implementation of chosen strategies is a fundamental challenge for managers, especially top-level managers. A key reason is that in the global economy, firms must be flexible, innovative, and creative to exploit their core competencies in the pursuit of marketplace opportunities.[9] However, firms simultaneously require a certain degree of stability in their structures so day-to-day tasks can be completed efficiently. Accessible and reliable information is required for executives to reach decisions regarding the selection of a structure that can provide the desired levels of flexibility and stability.[10] By helping executives improve their decision making, useful information contributes to the formation and use of effective structures and controls.[11]

Firms may use several organizational structures before an effective one is found. For example, during an 18-month period, employees at Digital Equipment Corporation (DEC) felt that their firm was in an era of perpetual reorganization. New CEO Robert Palmer first formed nine customer-focused units that were designed to concentrate on specific industries. "A year later, when that plan proved unsuccessful, he reorganized the company into 'strategic business units,' diminishing the role of the industry groups. Four months after that, in April 1994, when the company was hit with a quarterly loss three times as large as expected, Mr. Palmer pushed through yet another reorganization—now abolishing the industry groups and forming five independent business units around product lines. . . . "[12] Because they consume significant managerial energy, frequent structural changes, such as those that occurred at DEC, are undesirable. Moreover, such changes may be symptomatic of problems with the firm's formulated strategies.

To examine organizational structure and controls, this chapter first describes a pattern of growth and accompanying changes in organizational structure experienced by strategically competitive firms. This pattern is one in which structural change follows strategic growth and success. In turn, structural adjustments can affect future formulations of strategies.

The chapter's second major section discusses organizational structures and controls that are used to implement different business-level strategies. The dominant structures and control characteristics that contribute to the effective implementation of each of the business-level strategies described in Chapter 4 are explained in this part of the chapter.

Corporate-level strategy implementation is then described. The transition from the functional to the multidivisional structure is highlighted in this section. This major structural innovation took place in several firms during the 1920s, including DuPont. In fact, noted business historian Alfred Chandler cites DuPont as the innovator in both the strategy of diversification and the multidivisional structure.[13] Specific variations of the multidivisional structure are discussed in terms of their relationship with effective implementation of related and unrelated diversification strategies.

Next, we describe structures that are used to implement different international strategies. Because of the increasing globalization of many industries, the number of firms implementing international strategies continues to grow. As noted in previous chapters, the trend toward globalization is significant and pervasive.[14] In the words of Joe Gorman, CEO of TRW, a large diversified firm with operations in defense, auto parts, and data, "There's no question in my mind that a great transformational change is occurring. It's a change from regional economies and industries to truly global ones."[15] Almost identically, a business historian believes that the "global restructuring of industries and work (that is occurring today) is the most significant economic change in 100 years."[16] To examine the use of structure to implement international strategies effectively, we first describe the structure and control characteristics of the multidomestic strategy. This section is followed by a similar discussion of the global strategy. The transnational strategy is examined next, along with the variations in structure that are required to implement it. In the chapter's final two sections, we discuss the use of organizational structures to implement cooperative strategies and a few issues concerning organizational forms that should be of interest to those responsible for effective use of a firm's strategic management process.

■ Evolutionary Patterns of Strategy and Organizational Structure

■ *Organizational structure is a firm's formal role configuration, procedures, governance and control mechanisms, and authority and decision-making processes.*

All firms require some form of organizational structure to implement their strategies. In this section, we describe how organizational structures have evolved in response to managerial and organizational needs.

Principally, structures are changed when they no longer provide the coordination, control, and direction managers and organizations require to implement strategies successfully.[17] A structure's ineffectiveness typically results from increases in a firm's revenues and levels of diversification. In particular, the formulation of strategies involving greater levels of diversification (see Chapter 6) demands structural change to match the strategy. Some structures become elaborate while others become focused on financial rather than strategic control.

Organizational structure is a firm's formal role configuration, procedures, governance and control mechanisms, and authority and decision-making processes.[18] Through structure, managers largely determine *what* a firm does and *how* it completes that work, given its chosen strategies.[19] Strategic competitiveness can be attained only when the firm's selected structure is congruent with its formulated strategy.[20] As such, a strategy's potential to create value is reached only when the firm configures itself in ways that allow the strategy to be implemented effectively. Thus, as firms evolve and change their strategies, new structural arrangements are required. Additionally, existing structures influence the future selection of strategies. Accordingly, the two key strategic actions of strategy formulation and strategy implementation continuously interact to influence managerial choices about strategy and structure. At KPMG Peat Marwick, for example, the chairman is committed to simultaneous study of the interdependent influence of the firm's domestic and global organizational structures and strategies on decisions being made about KPMG's future strategic directions.[21]

Figure 11.1 shows the growth pattern many firms experience. This pattern results in changes in the relationships between the firm's formulated strategies and the organizational structures used to support and facilitate their implementation.

Figure 11.1

Strategy and Structure Growth Pattern

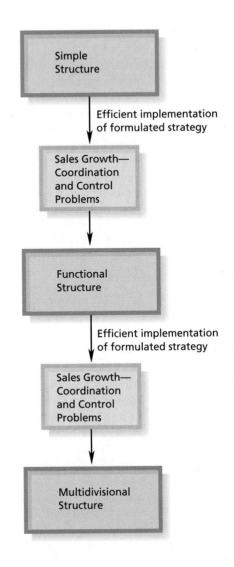

■ Simple Structure

■ *A **simple structure** is an organizational form in which the owner-manager makes all major decisions directly and monitors all activities, while the staff serves as an extension of the manager's supervisory authority.*

A **simple structure** is an organizational form in which the owner-manager makes all major decisions directly and monitors all activities, while the staff serves as an extension of the manager's supervisory authority. This structure involves little specialization of tasks, few rules, and limited formalization. Although important, information systems are relatively unsophisticated, and owner-managers participate directly in the firm's day-to-day operations. Typically, this structure is used by firms offering a single product line in a single geographic market. Because of the small organization size, the simple structure is used frequently in firms implementing either the focused low-cost or focused differentiation strategy. Restaurants, repair businesses, and other specialized enterprises are examples of firms whose limited complexity calls for the use of the simple structure. In this structure, communication is frequent and direct, and new products tend to be introduced to the market quickly, which can result in a competitive advantage.

Because of these characteristics, few of the coordination problems that are common in larger organizations exist.

However, as the firm grows larger and more complex, managerial and structural challenges emerge. For example, the amount of competitively relevant information requiring analysis increases substantially. These more complicated information processing needs place significant pressures on the simple structure and the owner-manager. Commonly, owner-managers lack the organizational skills and experiences required to manage effectively the specialized and complex tasks involved with multiple organizational functions.

■ Functional Structure

■ *The **functional structure** consists of a chief executive officer and limited corporate staff, with functional line managers in dominant organizational areas such as production, accounting, marketing, R&D, engineering, and human resources.*

To coordinate more complex organizational functions, firms abandon the simple structure in favor of the functional structure. The functional structure is used by larger firms implementing one of the business-level strategies and by firms with low levels of diversification (for instance, by companies implementing either the single- or dominant-business corporate-level strategy). The **functional structure** consists of a chief executive officer and limited corporate staff, with functional line managers in dominant organizational areas such as production, accounting, marketing, R&D, engineering, and human resources. This structure allows for functional specialization, thereby facilitating knowledge sharing and idea development.[22] Because the differences in orientation among organizational functions can impede communication and coordination, the central task of the CEO is to integrate the decisions and actions of individual business functions for the benefit of the entire corporation.[23] This organizational form also facilitates career paths and professional development in specialized functional areas.

An unintended negative consequence of the functional structure is the tendency for functional-area managers to focus on local versus overall company strategic issues. Such emphases cause specialized managers to lose sight of the firm's overall strategic intent and strategic mission. When this situation emerges, the multidivisional structure often is implemented to overcome this difficulty.

Another condition that encourages a change from the functional to the multidivisional structure is greater diversification. Strategic success often leads to growth and diversification. Deciding to offer the same products in different markets (market diversification) and/or choosing to offer additional products (product diversification) creates control problems. The multidivisional structure provides the controls required to deal effectively with additional levels of diversification. In fact, the firm's returns may suffer when increased diversification is not accompanied by a change to the multidivisional structure.

■ Multidivisional Structure

The chief executive's limited ability to process increasing quantities of strategic information, the focus of functional managers on local issues, and increased diversification are primary causes of the decision to change from the functional to the multidivisional (M-form) structure. According to Alfred Chandler, "The M-form came into being when senior managers operating through existing centralized, functionally departmentalized ... structures realized they had neither the time nor the necessary information to coordinate and monitor day-to-

■ *The **multidivisional (M-form) structure** is composed of operating divisions where each division represents a separate business or profit center and the top corporate officer delegates responsibility for day-to-day operations and business-unit strategy to division managers.*

day operations, or to devise and implement long-term plans for the various product lines. The administrative overload had become simply too great."[24]

The **multidivisional (M-form) structure** is composed of operating divisions where each division represents a separate business or profit center and the top corporate officer delegates responsibilities for day-to-day operations and business-unit strategy to division managers. Because the diversified corporation is the dominant form of business firm in the industrialized world, the M-form is being used in most of the corporations competing in the global economy.[25] However, only effectively designed M-forms enhance a firm's performance. Thus, for all companies, and perhaps especially for diversified firms, performance is a function of the goodness of fit between strategy and structure.[26]

Chandler's examination of the strategies and structures of large American firms documented the M-form's development.[27] Chandler viewed the M-form as an innovative response to coordination and control problems that surfaced during the 1920s in the functional structures being used by large firms such as DuPont and General Motors.[28] Among other benefits, the M-form allowed firms to greatly expand their operations.[29]

Use of the Multidivisional Structure at DuPont and General Motors

Chandler's studies showed that firms such as DuPont began to record significant revenue growth through the manufacture and distribution of diversified products while using the functional structure. However, functional departments such as sales and production found it difficult to coordinate the conflicting priorities of the firm's new and different products and markets. Moreover, the functional structures being used allocated costs to organizational functions rather than to individual businesses and products. This allocation method made it virtually impossible for top-level managers to determine the contributions of separate product lines to the firm's return on its investments. Even more damaging for large firms trying to implement newly formulated diversification strategies through use of a functional structure that was appropriate for small companies and for those needing proprietary expertise and scale[30] was the increasing allocation of top-level managers' time and energies to short-term administrative problems. Focusing their efforts on these issues caused executives to neglect the long-term strategic issues that were their primary responsibility.

To cope with similar problems, General Motors CEO Alfred Sloan, Jr., proposed a reorganization. Sloan conceptualized separate divisions, each representing a distinct business, that would be self-contained and have its own functional hierarchy. Implemented in 1925, Sloan's structure delegated day-to-day operating responsibilities to division managers. The small staff at the corporate level was responsible for determining the firm's long-term strategic direction and for exercising overall financial control of semiautonomous divisions. Each division was to make its own business-level strategic decisions. However, because its focus was on the outcomes achieved by the entire corporation rather than the performance of separate units, decisions made by division heads could be superseded by the corporate office. Sloan's structural innovation had three important outcomes: "(1) it enabled corporate officers to more accurately monitor the performance of each business, which simplified the problem of control; (2) it facilitated comparisons between divisions, which improved the resource allocation process; and (3) it stimulated managers of poor performing divisions to look for ways of improving performance."[31]

The Use of Internal Controls in the Multidivisional Structure

The M-form structure holds top-level managers responsible for formulating and implementing overall corporate strategies; that is, they are responsible for the corporate-level, acquisition and restructuring, international, and cooperative strategies that we examined in Chapters 6 through 9.

Strategic and financial controls are the two major types of internal controls used to support implementation of strategies in larger firms. Properly designed organizational controls provide clear insights to employees regarding behaviors that enhance the firm's competitiveness and overall performance.[32] Effective implementation of diversification strategies results when firms appropriately use both types of controls. For example, when Ford Motor Company increased its ownership in Mazda Motor Corp. to a controlling interest of approximately 33 percent, top-level managers acknowledged the need to use strategic controls when evaluating the performance of all Ford units. Simultaneously, however, the appointment of Ford executive Henry D. G. Wallace as Mazda's new president (Wallace was the first foreigner to head a Japanese automaker) was a partial signal of the need for financial controls to manage Mazda's extensive product line and base of supplier costs.[33]

Strategic control entails the use of long-term and strategically relevant criteria by corporate-level managers to evaluate the performance of division managers and their units. Strategic control emphasizes largely subjective judgments and may involve intuitive evaluation criteria. Corporate-level managers rely on strategic control to gain an operational understanding of the strategies being implemented in the firm's separate divisions or business units. Because strategic control allows a corporate-level evaluation of the full array of strategic actions—those concerned with both the formulation and implementation of a business-unit strategy—corporate-level managers must have a deep understanding of a division's or business unit's operations and markets.[34] The use of strategic controls also demands rich information exchanges between corporate and divisional managers. These exchanges take place through both formal and informal (i.e., unplanned) face-to-face meetings.[35] As diversification increases, strategic control can be strained.[36] Sometimes, this strain results in a commitment to reduce the firm's level of diversification. For example, the strategic decisions made by top-level managers at Anheuser-Busch to either sell or spin off its Eagle Snacks and Campbell-Taggart Inc. units, as well as the St. Louis Cardinals baseball team, may have resulted from the difficulties top-level managers encountered when trying to use strategic controls. These divestitures were an attempt to end a costly foray into foods so the world's largest brewer could stick to what it knows best, making beer.[37]

Financial control entails objective criteria (e.g., return on investment) that corporate-level managers use to evaluate the returns being earned by individual business units and the managers responsible for their performance. An emphasis on financial control requires divisional performance to be largely independent of other divisions. As such, when the firm chooses to implement a strategy calling for interdependence among the firm's different businesses, such as the related-constrained corporate-level strategy, the ability of financial control to add value to strategy implementation efforts is reduced.[38]

Next, we discuss the organizational structures and controls that are used to implement different business-level strategies.

■ *Strategic control entails the use of long-term and strategically relevant criteria by corporate-level managers to evaluate the performance of division managers and their units.*

The appointment of a Ford executive, Henry Wallace, as Mazda's new president was a partial signal of the need for financial controls to manage Mazda's extensive product line and base of supplier costs.

■ *Financial control entails objective criteria (e.g., return on investment) that corporate-level managers use to evaluate the returns being earned by individual business units and the managers responsible for their performance.*

Implementing Business-Level Strategies: Organizational Structure and Controls

As discussed in Chapter 4, business-level strategies establish a particular type of competitive advantage (typically either low cost or differentiation) in a particular competitive scope (either an entire industry or a narrow segment of it). Effective implementation of the cost leadership, differentiation, and integrated low-cost/ differentiation strategies occurs when certain modifications are made to the characteristics of the functional structure based on the unique attributes of the individual business-level strategies.

Using the Functional Structure to Implement the Cost Leadership Strategy

The structural characteristics of specialization, centralization, and formalization play important roles in the successful implementation of the cost leadership strategy. *Specialization* refers to the type and numbers of job specialties that are required to perform the firm's work.[39] For the cost leadership strategy, managers divide the firm's work into homogeneous subgroups. The basis for these subgroups is usually functional areas, products being produced, or clients served. By dividing and grouping work tasks into specialties, firms reduce their costs through the efficiencies achieved by employees specializing in a particular and often narrow set of activities.

Centralization is the degree to which decision-making authority is retained at higher managerial levels. Today, the trend in organizations is toward decentralization—the movement of decision-making authority down to people in the firm who have the most direct and frequent contact with customers. However, to coordinate activities carefully across organizational functions, the structure used to implement the cost leadership strategy calls for centralization. Thus, when designing this particular type of functional structure, managers strive to push some decision-making authority lower in the organization while remaining focused on the more general need for activities to be coordinated and integrated through the efforts of a centralized staff.

Because the cost leadership strategy is often chosen by firms producing relatively standardized products in large quantities, formalization is necessary. *Formalization* is the degree to which formal rules and procedures govern organizational activities.[40] To foster more efficient operations, R&D efforts emphasize improvements in the manufacturing process.

As summarized in Figure 11.2, successful implementation of the cost leadership strategy requires an organizational structure featuring strong task specialization, centralization of decision-making authority, and formalization of work rules and procedures. This type of functional structure encourages the emergence of a low-cost culture—a culture in which all employees seek to find ways to drive their firm's or unit's costs lower than rivals' costs. Using highly specialized work tasks, low-cost leader Southwest Airlines strives continuously to increase the efficiency of its production and distribution systems. For example, Southwest was one of the first carriers to sell tickets on the Internet. Beginning in mid-1996, customers could book reservations and buy tickets on the firm's World Wide Web site. A travel industry consultant concluded that Southwest's simple fares and schedule make it easy to sell travel directly to consumers on the Internet.[41]

Figure 11.2   Functional Structure for Implementation of a Cost Leadership Strategy

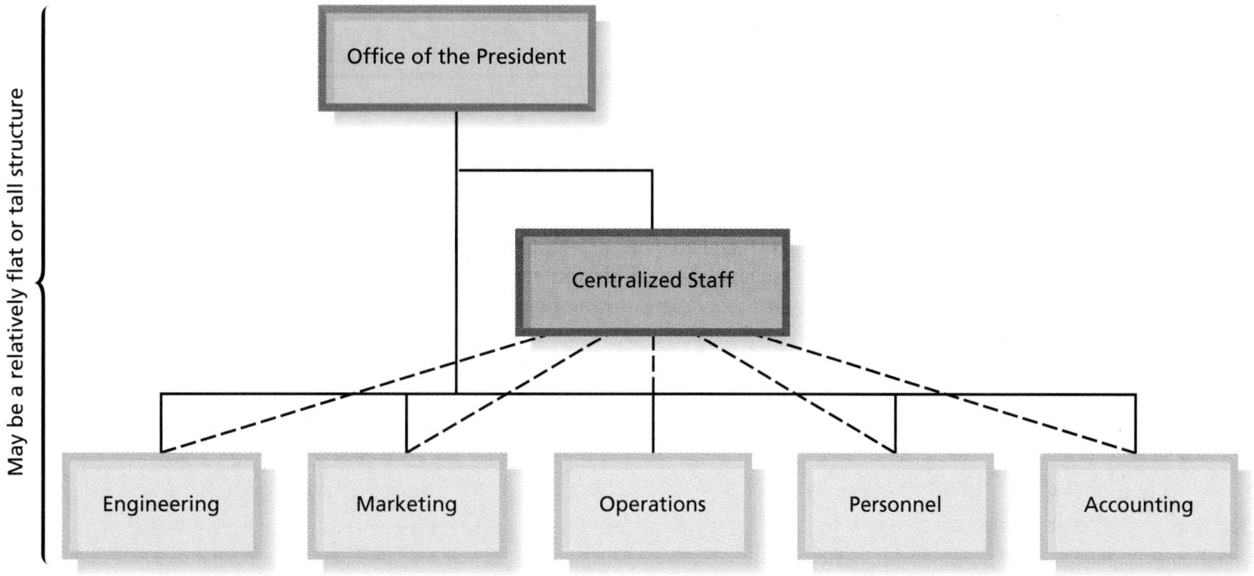

Notes:
• Operations is the main function
• Process engineering is emphasized rather than new product R&D
• Relatively large centralized staff coordinates functions
• Formalized procedures allow for emergence of a low-cost culture
• Overall structure is mechanical; job roles are very structured

■ Using the Functional Structure to Implement the Differentiation Strategy

Successful implementation of the differentiation strategy occurs when a functional structure is used in which decision-making authority is decentralized. Unlike the cost leadership strategy, where coordination and integration of organizational functions' activities occurs through centralization of decision-making authority, the functional structure used to implement the differentiation strategy demands that people throughout the firm learn how to coordinate and integrate their activities effectively. This is the expectation at Nordstrom, the successful retailer. This firm's structure calls for individual stores to employ buyers who specialize in purchasing products that will satisfy the unique tastes of customers in different geographic locales.[42]

The marketing and R&D functions are often emphasized in the differentiation strategy's functional structure. For example, in mid-1996, Apple Computer's next-generation software, dubbed Copland, was thought to be crucial to the firm's turnaround efforts. Given its importance, R&D was being heavily emphasized at Apple.[43] As with Apple's Copland software, the emphasis on R&D in firms implementing the differentiation strategy typically is focused on those activities required to develop new products. Centralized staffs make certain that the efforts of those working in these two critical functions are integrated

Figure 11.3   Functional Structure for Implementation of a Differentiation Strategy

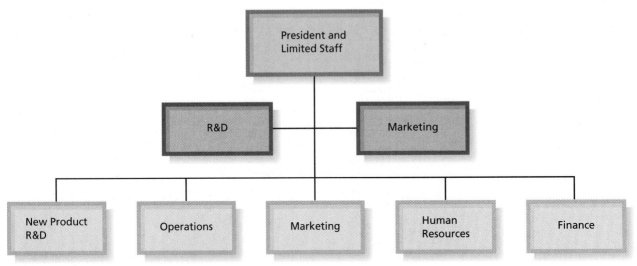

Notes:
- Marketing is the main function for keeping track of new product ideas
- New product R&D is emphasized
- Most functions are decentralized, but R&D and marketing may have centralized staffs that work closely with each other
- Formalization is limited so that new product ideas can emerge easily and change is more readily accomplished
- Overall structure is organic; job roles are less structured

successfully. To properly control new product development, a centralized research facility may be established. Also, to maintain efficiency, the manufacturing facility may be partially centralized. This allows integration of new products quickly while maintaining the highest possible efficiency.[44] Alternatively, many firms use decentralized cross-functional teams composed of representatives from marketing, R&D, and manufacturing to integrate these functions for new product design, manufacturing, and introduction to the marketplace.

Finally, to capitalize on emerging trends in key markets, the firm implementing the differentiation strategy often makes rapid changes based on ambiguous and incomplete information. Such rapid changes demand that the firm use a relatively flat organizational structure to group its work activities (in a relatively flat structure, workers are likely to have a number of tasks included in their job descriptions). The implementation of the differentiation strategy is affected negatively when the firm has extensive centralization and formalization, especially in a rapidly changing environment. Thus, the overall organizational structure needs to be flexible and job roles less structured. Additional characteristics of the form of the functional structure used to implement the differentiation strategy are shown in Figure 11.3.

■ Using the Functional Structure to Implement the Integrated Low-Cost/Differentiation Strategy

To implement the integrated low-cost/differentiation strategy, companies seek to provide value that differs from that offered by the low cost and the differentiated firm—low cost, relative to the cost of the differentiated firm's product, and valuable differentiated features, relative to the features offered by the low-cost firm's product.

Now being formulated more frequently, especially by global firms, the integrated low-cost/differentiation strategy is difficult to implement. The primary reason for this is that the strategic and tactical actions required to implement the low-cost and the differentiation strategies are not the same. For example, to achieve the low-cost position, relative to rivals, emphasis is placed on production and manufacturing process engineering, with infrequent product changes. In contrast, to achieve a differentiated position, marketing and new product R&D are emphasized. But, as explained earlier, the structural characteristics used to emphasize new product development differ from those needed to emphasize process engineering.

As noted in Chapter 4, being "stuck-in-the-middle" is a risk associated with the integrated strategy. Disappointing performance results reported recently by National Semiconductor Corp. may be partly attributable to ineffective implementation of the integrated strategy. Some of the firm's senior-level executives, for example, believe ". . . that on one hand, the company has focused on commodity-chip markets, relying on its traditional manufacturing skills to keep costs low enough to generate profit in a low-margin business. At the same time, (the firm) has been trying to move toward the cutting edge with innovative chips that use proprietary technology and carry a premium price." Study of these actions caused an analyst to suggest that "It is difficult to reconcile cost-cutting and risky innovation within a single company, as National's recent efforts to do so are showing." An organizational structure featuring three chief operating officers who were jointly running the company may have prevented successful implementation of the firm's integrated low-cost/differentiation strategy.[45] Awkward at best, this structural arrangement is inconsistent with the assignment of CEO-level responsibilities to a single individual as called for by the functional structure. To improve National Semiconductor's performance, the unusual management structure has been eliminated. The firm now has a single CEO who was selected from the external managerial labor market (a topic that is discussed in Chapter 12).

National Semiconductor's experiences suggest that a functional structure is appropriate for implementing the integrated low-cost/differentiation strategy. To implement this strategy successfully at National Semiconductor and in other companies as well, managers are challenged to form an organizational structure that allows the development of differentiated product features while costs, relative to rivals' costs, are reduced. Often the functional structure has to be supplemented by horizontal coordination, such as cross functional teams and a strong organizational culture to implement this strategy effectively.

■ Using the Simple Structure to Implement Focused Strategies

As noted earlier, many focus strategies—strategies through which a firm concentrates on serving the unique needs of a narrow part or scope of the industry—are implemented most effectively through the simple structure. At some point, however, the increased sales revenues resulting from success necessitate changing from a simple to a functional structure. The challenge for managers is to recognize when a structural change is required to coordinate and control effectively the firm's increasingly complex operations.

Regional or "cult" brand colas, such as Moxie, Big Red, and Sun-drop, serve a narrow group of customers with individualized tastes for soft drinks.

The intent of companies manufacturing regional soft drinks is to serve the needs of a narrow group of customers better than do giants Coca-Cola and PepsiCo. People targeted by the regional manufacturers are those with individualized tastes for soft drinks. To describe these firms and their products, an analyst noted that ". . . obscure soft drinks like Cheerwine are thriving in local markets across the country. These regional or 'cult' brands—with down-home names like Moxie, Big Red, Sun-drop and Kickapoo Joy Juice—grew up in mostly rural areas. Many eschew marketing, relying on the appeal of long histories, local pride and wild formulas, including one derived from a Russian cake-icing recipe and another that sprang from a failed pharmaceutical experiment."[46] Revolving around flexible production functions, these manufacturers have low levels of specialization and formalization. Additionally, as demonstrated by the nature of their marketing efforts, the regional soft drink companies centralize few of the decisions about the activities of different organizational functions.

■ Movement to the Multidivisional Structure

The above-average returns gained through successful implementation of a business-level strategy often result in diversification of the firm's operations. This diversification can take the form of offering different products (product diversification) and/or offering the same or additional products in other markets (market diversification). As explained in Chapter 6, increased product and/or market diversification demands that firms formulate a corporate-level strategy as well as business-level strategies for individual units or divisions (see Figure 6.1 to review the different corporate-level strategies and their respective levels of diversification). With greater diversification, the simple and functional structures must be discarded in favor of the more complex, yet increasingly necessary multidivisional structure.

■ Implementing Corporate-Level Strategies: Organizational Structure and Controls

■ *The **cooperative form** (of the multidivisional structure) is an organizational structure that uses many integration devices and horizontal human resource practices to foster cooperation and integration among the firm's divisions.*

Effective use of the multidivisional structure helps firms implement their corporate-level strategy (diversification). In this section, we describe three M-form variations (see Figure 11.4) that are required to implement the related-constrained, related-linked, and unrelated diversification strategies.

■ Using the Cooperative Form to Implement the Related-Constrained Strategy

To implement the related-constrained strategy, firms use the cooperative form of the multidivisional structure. The **cooperative form** is an organizational structure that uses many integration devices and horizontal human resource practices to foster cooperation and integration among the firm's divisions. The cooperative form (see Figure 11.5) emphasizes horizontal links and relationships more than two other variations of the multidivisional structure described later in the chapter. Cooperation among divisions that are formed around either products or served markets is necessary to realize economies of scope and to facilitate the transferring of skills.[47] Increasingly, it is important for these links to allow and support the sharing of a range of strategic assets, including employees' "know-how" as well as tangible assets such as facilities and methods of operations.[48]

To facilitate cooperation among divisions that are either vertically integrated or related through the sharing of strategic assets, some organizational functions (e.g., human resource management, R&D, and marketing) are centralized at the corporate level. Work completed in these centralized functions is managed by the firm's central administrative, or headquarters, office. When the central office's efforts allow exploitation of commonalties among the firm's divisions in ways that yield a cost or differentiation advantage (or both) in the divisions as compared to undiversified rivals, the cooperative form of the multidivisional structure is a source of competitive advantage for the diversified firm.[49]

Besides centralization, a number of structural integration links are used to foster cooperation among divisions in firms implementing the related-constrained diversification strategy. Direct contact between division managers is frequent to encourage and support cooperation and the sharing of strategic assets. Sometimes, liaison roles are established in each division to reduce the amount of time

Figure 11.4

Three Variations of the Multidivisional Structure

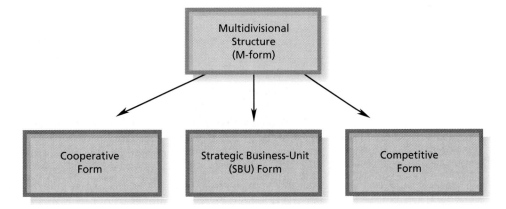

Figure 11.5   Cooperative Form of the Multidivisional Structure for Implementation of a
Related-Constrained Strategy

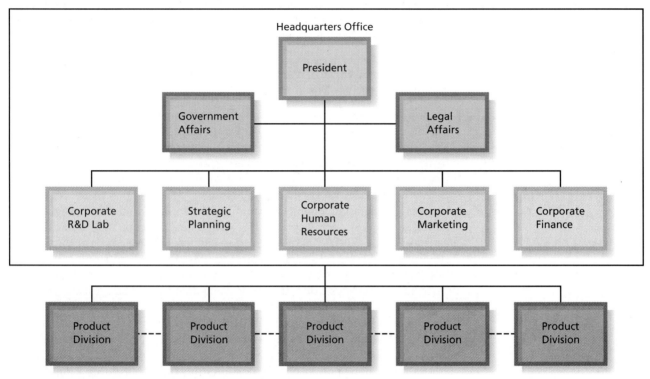

Notes:
• Structural integration devices create tight links among all divisions
• Corporate office emphasizes centralized strategic planning, human resources, and marketing to foster cooperation
  between divisions
• R&D is likely to be centralized
• Rewards are subjective and tend to emphasize overall corporate performance in addition to divisional performance
• Culture emphasizes cooperative sharing

division managers spend facilitating the integration and coordination of their
units' work. Temporary teams or task forces may also be formed around projects
and may require the efforts of many people from separate divisions to achieve
desired levels of divisional coordination. Formal integration departments might
be formed in firms requiring the work of temporary teams or task forces on a
continuous basis. Ultimately, a matrix organization evolves in firms implementing the related-constrained strategy. A *matrix organization* is an organizational
structure in which there is a dual structure combining both functional specialization and business product or project specialization.[50] Although complicated,
effective matrix structures can lead to improved coordination among the firm's
various divisions.[51]

As implied by the horizontal procedures used for coordination that we described earlier, information processing must increase dramatically to implement
the related-constrained diversification strategy successfully. But, because cooperation among divisions implies a loss of managerial autonomy, division managers
may not readily commit themselves to the type of integrative information

processing activities demanded by this organizational structure. Moreover, coordination among divisions sometimes results in an unequal flow of positive outcomes to divisional managers. In other words, when managerial rewards are based at least in part on the performance of individual divisions, the manager of the division able to derive the greatest marketplace benefit from the sharing of the firm's strategic assets might be viewed as receiving relative gains at others' expense. In these instances, performance evaluations are emphasized to facilitate sharing of strategic assets. Additionally, using reward systems that emphasize overall company performance besides outcomes achieved by individual divisions is a method that helps overcome problems associated with the cooperative form.

When there are fewer and/or less constrained links among the firm's divisions, the related-linked diversification strategy should be implemented. As explained next, this strategy can be implemented successfully through use of the SBU form of the multidivisional structure.

■ Using the SBU Form to Implement the Related-Linked Strategy

The **strategic business unit (SBU) form** (of the multidivisional structure) consists of at least three levels, with the top level being corporate headquarters; the next level, SBU groups; and the final level with divisions grouped by relatedness (either product or geographic market) within each SBU (see Figure 11.6). The firm's business portfolio is organized into those related to one another within a SBU group and those unrelated in other SBU groups. Thus, divisions within groups are related, but groups are largely unrelated to each other. Within the SBU structure, divisions with similar products or technologies are organized to achieve synergy. Each SBU is a profit center that is controlled by the firm's headquarters office. An important benefit of this structural form is that individual division makers, within their strategic business unit, look to SBU executives rather than headquarters personnel for strategic guidance.

Scotts Co. uses the SBU form of the multidivisional structure. A producer and marketer of products for do-it-yourself lawn care, professional turf care, and horticulture, the firm seeks $1 billion in sales revenues by 2000 (revenues were $606 million in 1994).[52] Recently Scotts revamped its organizational structure to facilitate accomplishment of its sales revenues goal and the profitability managers believe will be associated with achieving it. Scotts is now organized into four main business units: consumer lawn, for its mainstay fertilizers and other home products; consumer garden, primarily consisting of Stern's Miracle-Gro Products Inc., acquired in 1995; professional, which includes commercial applications such as golf courses; and, international.[53] As explained in the Strategic Focus, Unisys Corp. also uses the SBU form of the multidivisional structure. A primary reason the firm eliminated its previous structure in favor of a new one was to foster better and more direct relationships with customers who have specialized needs.

The organizational structure for large diversified firms such as Scotts Co. and Unisys Corp. can be complex. This complexity is a reflection of the size and diversity of a diversified firm's operations. Consider the case of General Electric. Implementing the related-linked corporate-level strategy, this firm's structure calls for integration among divisions within SBUs, but independence between the SBUs. In mid-1996, General Electric's SBU form of the multidivisional structure featured 14 major businesses (or strategic business units). GE Power Systems is

■ *The strategic business unit (SBU) form (of the multidivisional structure) consists of at least three levels, with the top level being corporate headquarters; the next level, SBU groups; and the final level with divisions grouped by relatedness (either product or geographic market) within each SBU.*

Figure 11.6   SBU Form of the Multidivisional Structure for Implementation of a Related-Linked Strategy

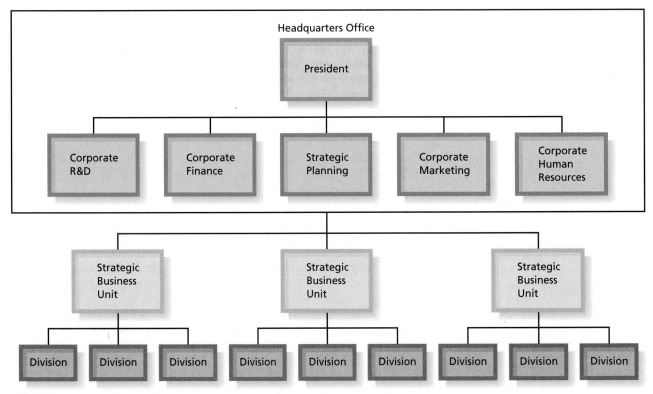

Notes:
• Structural integration among divisions within SBUs, but independence among SBUs
• Strategic planning may be the most prominent function in headquarters to manage the strategic planning approval process of SBUs for the president
• Each SBU may have its own budget for staff to foster integration
• Corporate headquarters staff serve as consultants to SBUs and divisions, rather than having direct input to product strategy as in the cooperative form

one of these 14 major businesses (others include GE Aircraft Engines, GE Appliances, GE Capital Services, and GE Medical Systems). The GE Power Systems product and service portfolio (or SBU) serves those who are supplying the world's need for reliable, highly efficient electricity.[54] Gas Turbines is one of at least 15 divisions within the Power Systems portfolio. Other divisions with which Gas Turbines is integrated to varying degrees include Steam Turbines, Hydro Turbines and Generators, Boiling Water Reactor Services, and Advanced Nuclear Reactor Systems. Featuring the broadest line of gas turbines in the industry today, GE is the acknowledged world leader with more than 5,000 units installed and more than 4,600 combustion turbines operating successfully around the globe.[55]

Recently, however, the Power Systems unit encountered competitive challenges. An observer of this situation suggested that GE, once the undisputed leader in power technology and quality, may be losing its edge. To deal with this matter, GE Chairman Jack Welch made a top-level management change, installing

Robert Nardelli as the head of Power Systems. In a further modification to the firm's management structure, Nardelli simultaneously became a GE senior vice president. Following an initial assessment of what should be done in the Power Systems business, Nardelli suggested that engineering *must* be faster, more efficient, more productive, and *get it right the first time.*[56] As this example demonstrates, changes in the personnel holding key positions within an organization's structure are sometimes required to ensure effective implementation of formulated strategies.

STRATEGIC FOCUS   Organizational Structure and Unisys Corp.'s Intended Future

A global company seeking to transform business and government through information management, Unisys Corp. has changed its organizational structure a number of times in recent years. In fact, over a seven-year period ending in 1995, the firm completed five restructurings. During this time, Unisys cut its payroll and facilities by half as it faced a downturn in its traditional mainframe business and as it derived more revenue from lower-profit computer consulting and services. These structural changes, combined with reformulations of Unisys' corporate-level strategies, have created a substantially different company. As noted by CEO James Unruh in the company's 1995 *Annual Report,* "Four years ago, Unisys was primarily a mainframe and defense electronics company in a mature industry. Today, we provide not only a full portfolio of leading-edge client/server technologies, but also the services needed by clients to apply and support information technology for a business advantage."

In late 1995, Unisys adopted the SBU form of the multidivisional structure to implement the related-linked diversification strategy. This structure was chosen following an extensive review of key business execution issues. By realigning its operations into the SBU form, Unisys sought to improve its profitability by reducing the firm's cost base and becoming more focused and competitive in the markets it serves.

Three highly focused global business groups (or strategic business units) comprise Unisys' new structure: information services, computer systems, and global customer services. Through this structure, the firm intends to work with organizations to help them gain competitive advantages by exploiting the benefits that accrue when information is managed effectively and in competitively relevant ways. The information services group provides high-level services and market sector expertise to help clients reengineer their business processes and use information for a tangible business benefit. The computer systems business group provides hardware and software technologies used by clients and by systems integrators, software developers, and other sales partners as the building blocks of advanced information management solutions. Finally, the global customer services group provides network integration, desktop services, and other support services to help clients maximize the availability and effectiveness of their distributed computing systems.

Unisys discarded the matrix organizational structure in favor of the SBU form of the multidivisional structure. The key reason for this structural change was the top management team's belief that the matrix form had outlived its usefulness. Under the matrix form, Unisys' service and technology businesses shared common resources to market and support their products. However, the businesses' growth created coordination and control problems that the matrix form failed to handle effectively and efficiently. "Our newer service businesses had grown and gained momentum. Our core technology business had its own market

—Continued

—Continued

opportunities to pursue. We needed to eliminate the time, cost, and bureaucracy involved in coordinating different businesses with different strategies. We needed to better serve the needs of our customer base and build that base by attracting new clients . . . . In short, we needed to streamline and simplify our operations."

The SBU form allows Unisys to simplify its operations and to focus on particular needs of specific clients. To support commitments to the requirements of unique and individual customers, each business group has its own sales and marketing force. The managers in charge of each group are responsible for revenue growth and the unit's profitability. Two clear mandates for each of the three units are to become more global in scope and to focus continuously on satisfying the firm's 50,000 plus customers.

Changing to this new organizational structure was expected to yield annualized cost savings of more than $500 million by the end of 1996 and $600 million by the end of 1997. As such, this structural change was thought to enhance both competitiveness and the firm's returns.

Source: B. Ziegler, 1996, Unisys holders reject proposal for a break-up, *Wall Street Journal*, April 26, B5; B. Ziegler, 1996, Unisys reports $13.4 million loss, wider than analysts' estimates, *Wall Street Journal*, April 25, B4; Unisys Corp., 1995, *Annual Report*.

■ Using the Competitive Form to Implement the Unrelated Diversification Strategy

Firms implementing the unrelated diversification strategy seek to create value through efficient internal capital allocations or by restructuring, buying, and selling businesses.[57] The competitive form of the multidivisional structure is used to implement the unrelated diversification strategy. The **competitive form** is an organizational structure in which controls are used that emphasize competition between separate (usually unrelated) divisions for corporate capital. To realize benefits from efficient resource allocations, divisions must have separate, identifiable profit performance and must be held accountable for such performance. In fact, the internal capital market requires organizational arrangements that emphasize *competition* rather than *cooperation* between divisions.[58]

To emphasize competitiveness among divisions, the headquarters office maintains an arms-length relationship and does not intervene in divisional affairs except to audit operations and to discipline managers whose divisions perform poorly. In this situation, the headquarters office sets rate-of-return targets and monitors the outcomes of divisional performance. It allocates cash flow on a competitive basis, rather than automatically returning cash to the division that produced it. The competitive form of the multidivisional structure is illustrated in Figure 11.7.

In summary, our discussion describes three major forms of the multidivisional structure and the relationship of the individual forms with particular corporate-level strategies. Table 11.1 shows the characteristics of these structures. As shown in the table, differences are seen in the degree of centralization, the focus of performance appraisal, the horizontal structures (integrating mechanisms), and the incentive compensation schemes necessary to implement the three corporate-level strategies of related-constrained, related-linked, and unrelated diversification successfully. The most centralized and most costly organizational form is the cooperative structure. The least centralized, with the lowest bureaucratic costs, is the competitive structure. The SBU structure requires partial centralization and involves some of the mechanisms necessary to implement the relatedness between divisions. Also, the divisional incentive compensation awards are allocated

■ The **competitive form** (of the multidivisional structure) is an organizational structure in which controls are used that emphasize competition between separate (usually unrelated) divisions for corporate capital.

Figure 11.7   Competitive Form of the Multidivisional Structure for Implementation of an Unrelated Strategy

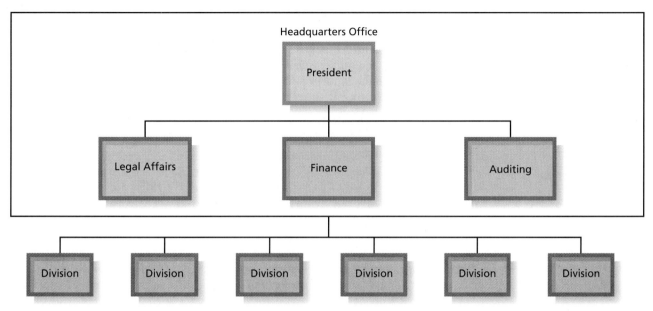

Notes:
- Corporate headquarters has a small staff
- Finance and auditing are the most prominent functions in the headquarters to manage cash flow and ensure accuracy of performance data coming from divisions
- Legal affairs function becomes important when acquiring and divesting assets
- Divisions are independent and separate for financial evaluation purposes
- Divisions retain strategic control, but cash is managed by corporate office
- Divisions compete for corporate resources

Table 11.1   Attributes of the Structures Necessary to Implement the Related-Constrained, Related-Linked, and Unrelated Diversification Strategies

Structural Characteristics	Overall Structural Form		
	Cooperative M-form (Related-Constrained Strategy[a])	*SBU M-form (Related-Linked Strategy[a])*	*Competitive M-form (Unrelated Diversification Strategy[a])*
Centralization of operation	Centralized at corporate office	Partially centralized (in SBUs)	Decentralized to division
Use of integrating mechanisms	Extensive	Moderate	Nonexistent
Divisional performance appraisal	Emphasizes subjective criteria	Uses a mixture of subjective and objective criteria	Emphasizes objective (financial or ROI) criteria
Divisional incentive compensation	Linked to overall corporate performance	Mixed linkage to corporate, SBU and divisional performance	Linked to divisional performance

[a]Strategy implemented with structural form.

according to both SBU and corporate performance. In the competitive structure, the most important criterion is divisional performance.

Earlier in the chapter, we indicated that, once formed, an organizational structure can influence the firm's efforts to implement its current strategy and the selection of future strategies. Using the multidivisional structure as the foundation for the discussion, we present an explanation in the next section that exemplifies the relationship between structure and strategy.

■ The Effect of Structure on Strategy

As explained earlier, the M-form is a structural innovation intended to help managers deal with the coordination and control problems created by increasing product and market variety. Once established, however, the M-form structure has the potential to positively influence the firm's diversification strategy.[59] Strong and appropriate incentives, ones that encourage managers to pursue additional marketplace opportunities, coupled with improved accountability and superior internal resource allocations from the corporate office, may stimulate additional diversification. Furthermore, these additional levels of diversification can result in greater returns on the firm's investments.[60] Eventually, however, there is a tendency for the M-form to encourage inefficient levels of diversification. Following a comprehensive review of research evidence, some researchers noted that there is a growing body of evidence which suggests that adoption of the M-form structure (facilitates) the pursuit of inefficient diversification.[61] Again, this cause/effect relationship—that is, the influence of the M-form on a firm's pursuit of additional diversification—is not inherently negative. The complicating factor is that at some point, the additional amounts of diversification stimulated by the M-form become inefficient. Inefficient diversification reduces the firm's strategic competitiveness and its returns.

STRATEGIC FOCUS   Changing of Diversification Strategies and Organizational Structures in Large Diversified Firms

Because of disappointing performance outcomes, a number of firms implementing the unrelated diversification strategy are changing to either the related-constrained or related-linked strategy. Thus, top-level managers in some highly diversified firms are deciding to reduce the diversified scope of their firms' operations. A key reason for this strategic decision is that only a few firms have been able to earn above-average returns by implementing the unrelated diversification strategy. To implement successfully a newly chosen corporate-level strategy—a strategy featuring more relatedness across units—firms that have decided to become less diversified should also change their organizational structure to either the cooperative form (for the related-constrained strategy) or the SBU form (for the related-linked strategy) of the multidivisional structure.

Until recently, the unrelated diversification strategy had been the corporate-level strategy of choice at Tenneco Inc. The firm decided in 1996 to shed its energy and shipbuilding divisions. This announcement followed previous divestitures of Tenneco's remaining stakes in farm and construction equipment maker Case Corp. and the elimination of its Albright & Wilson chemicals business through a public offering in the United Kingdom. After completing its divestitures and spinoffs, Tenneco was left with packaging and automotive divisions. Everything from plastics and cartons to shock absorbers and exhaust systems are manufactured by these divisions. Objectives sought through these divestitures were for the firm to be able to avoid businesses that are vulnerable to economic ups and downs and for it to be able to concentrate on auto parts and packaging—businesses the firm's top-level managers believe are more stable and profitable. Observation of these decisions and actions caused one analyst to conclude that Tenneco is transforming itself from the prototypical unrelated diversified firm that once had six operating units into a tightly focused industrial products and global manufacturing business. With more than 100 manufacturing locations, the rising star of Tenneco, Tenneco Packaging, supplies a variety of innovative packaging solutions to dozens of industries in virtually every corner of the world. To support this change in strategy, Tenneco may require use of the cooperative form of the multidivisional structure.

American Home Products Corp. (AHP) also is becoming less diversified. In mid-1996, the firm announced its intention to sell its food businesses. Although this unit of AHP featured a number of venerable brands such as Chef Boyardee and Jiffy Pop popcorn, its performance was lackluster. Selling this unit will allow the firm to concentrate on its more profitable health care and agricultural businesses. Previously, to reduce its diversification and thus sharpen its focus, AHP sold unrelated businesses in oral health, home products, and candy. Proceeds from the sale of these assets, as well as those anticipated from the sale of the food businesses, are to be reinvested in AHP's higher margin operations. Estimates suggest that the operating profit margins for prescription drugs are about twice that of foods. To fully concentrate its energies and resources on its remaining businesses, AHP may decide to change to either the SBU or cooperative form of the multidivisional structure.

As part of the continuing effort to reduce its reliance on financial services and to become less diversified, Textron, Inc., sold its Paul Revere Corp. insurance unit to Provident Cos. Inc. A diversified manufacturer of planes and helicopters, golf carts, and automotive interiors and a provider of consumer loans, Textron's top-level managers intended to use approximately one-half of the assets obtained by selling Paul Revere to search aggressively for acquisitions in manufacturing. Although profitable, the returns earned from Paul Revere could not be used to support the firm's other units. Textron's chief financial officer noted that earnings had always been reinvested in Paul Revere because it's a regulated insurance company and the money has to stay in the company. Thus, this divestiture reduces Textron's diversification and supports growth in its key businesses. However, the total level of diversification remaining at Textron may still require the implementation support provided by the competitive form of the multidivisional structure.

Source: Associated Press, 1996, Tenneco to split off shipbuilding, *Dallas Morning News,* March 22, D2; C. Bukro, 1996, Tenneco to spin off shipyard, gas units, *Chicago Tribune,* March 22, F2; W.M. Bulkeley, 1996, Textron to seed takeovers with sale of unit, *Wall Street Journal,* April 30, B4; P. Fritsch, 1996, Tenneco Inc. plans to shed energy, shipbuilding units, *Wall Street Journal,* March 12, A2, A4; S. Lipin, 1996, Provident nears accord with Textron to buy Paul Revere unit for $1.2 billion, *Wall Street Journal,* March 29, A3, A17; E. Tanouye, 1996, American Home puts its food unit up for sale in move to reduce debt, 1996, *Wall Street Journal,* May 7, A3; Healthcare and Pharmaceuticals Companies, 1996, Netscape, http://www.ida.ie/moreheal.htm, May 12; Tenneco Packaging, 1996, Netscape, http://www.tennecopackaging.com/pack01.htm, May 14.

Other theory and research suggests that once the M-form influences the pursuit of more diversification that yields inefficient strategic outcomes, the relationship between structure and strategy may reverse in direction.[62] In other words, firms that become inefficiently diversified implement strategies that result in less (and more efficient) levels of diversification. One researcher found, for example, that half of the diversified acquisitions made by unrelated diversified firms were later divested.[63] Another discovered that a decrease in the diversified scope of M-form firms was associated with an improvement in shareholder wealth. This finding, too, suggests that these firms' diversification had become inefficient.[64] Examples of firms that have recently changed their diversification strategies in efforts to pursue more efficient diversification are presented in the Strategic Focus. In all likelihood, these firms will also change their organizational structures to provide the controls needed to implement less-diversified strategies successfully.

Our discussion now turns to an explanation of organizational structures used to implement the three international strategies explained in Chapter 8.

Implementing International Strategies: Organizational Structure and Controls

Increasingly, a firm's ability to achieve strategic competitiveness is a function of its competitive success in the global marketplace.[65] Although important for many firms, competing successfully in global markets is perhaps especially critical for large companies. General Motors CEO Jack Smith, for example, intends for his company to expand sales outside the United States, Canada, and Mexico to 4.5 million vehicles by 2006. Critical to accomplishing this objective will be a successful implementation of GM's international strategy. Included as parts of this strategy are plans to make an inexpensive family car in Poland, start making Chevrolet Blazers in Russia, finish a plant in Argentina for Chevy Corsicas by 1997, construct a plant in Southeast Asia and build another one to make midsize Buick sedans in China.[66] Supporting implementation of GM's international and domestic strategies are newly formed organizational structures that are designed to integrate effectively the work of engineers, manufacturing, and marketing personnel.[67] As explained in this section of the chapter, international strategies such as those chosen by GM's top-level executives cannot be implemented successfully without use of the proper organizational structure.[68]

Using the Worldwide Geographic Area Structure to Implement the Multidomestic Strategy

The *multidomestic strategy* is a strategy in which strategic and operating decisions are decentralized to business units in each country to facilitate tailoring of products to local markets. Through this strategy, Campbell Soup Co. customizes its products to local tastes. For example, the firm's cream of pumpkin soup is Australia's largest selling canned soup. In Hong Kong, Campbell sells watercress-and-duck-gizzard soup.[69] Firms implementing the multidomestic strategy often attempt to isolate themselves from global competitive forces by establishing protected market positions or by competing in industry segments that are most affected by differences among local countries. The worldwide geographic area structure (see Figure 11.8) is used to implement the multidomestic strategy. The **worldwide geographic area structure** is an organizational form in which national interests dominate and that facilitates managers' efforts to satisfy local or cultural differences.

One of the world's leading diversified telecommunications companies, SBC Communications Inc., realigned its businesses into three segments—regional, national, and international. The result of this realignment was the creation of a worldwide geographic area structure. By selecting this organizational form, SBC demonstrated its desire to create more local market areas that the firm's top-level managers believe will result in a sharper emphasis on accountability in terms of satisfying customers' unique sales and service needs in different geographic areas.[70]

■ The *worldwide geographic area structure* is an organizational form in which national interests dominate and that facilitates managers' efforts to satisfy local or cultural differences.

Figure 11.8

Worldwide Geographic Area Structure for Implementation of a Multidomestic Strategy

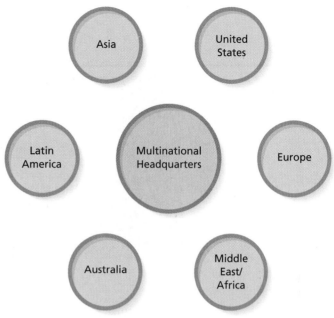

Notes:
- Blue shaded perimeter circles indicate decentralization of operations
- Emphasis is on differentiation by local demand to fit an area or country culture
- Corporate headquarters coordinates financial resources among independent subsidiaries
- The organization is like a decentralized federation

Recently, Coca-Cola shed the management structure it had been using to implement the firm's strategy with its core soft drink business. Previously, soft drinks had been divided into two units— North America and International. "But given that some of (the firm's) individual operating groups outside of North America now generate income equal to that of our entire Company in the mid-1980s, bundling those units under the title of "International" had become artificial and impractical." Today, Coca-Cola's worldwide soft drink operations are divided into five groups, with North America but one of the five newly formed units. Forming this worldwide geographic area structure will likely enhance the firm's ability to manage its soft drink business globally.[71]

Because implementing the multidomestic strategy requires little coordination between different country markets, there is no need for integrating mechanisms among divisions in the worldwide geographic area structure. As such, formalization is low and coordination among units in a firm's worldwide geographic area structure is often informal. Because each European country has a distinct culture, the multidomestic strategy and the associated worldwide geographic structure were a natural outgrowth of the multicultural marketplace. This type of structure often was developed originally by friends and family members of the main business who were sent as expatriates into foreign countries to develop the independent country subsidiary. The relationship to corporate headquarters by divisions took place through informal communication among "family members."[72]

Using a worldwide geographic area structure, Campbell Soup Company tailors its products to local markets.

The primary disadvantage of the multidomestic strategy and worldwide geographic area structure combination is the inability to create global efficiency. As the emphasis on lower cost products has increased in international markets, the need to pursue worldwide economies of scale and scope has increased. These changes have fostered use of the global strategy.

■ Using the Worldwide Product Divisional Structure to Implement the Global Strategy

The *global strategy* is a strategy in which standardized products are offered across country markets and where competitive strategy is dictated by the firm's home office. International scale and scope economies are sought and emphasized when implementing this international strategy. Because of the important relationship between scale and scope economies and successful implementation of the global strategy, some activities of the firm's organizational functions are sourced to the most effective worldwide providers.

The worldwide product divisional structure (see Figure 11.9) is used to implement the global strategy. The **worldwide product divisional structure** is an organizational form in which decision-making authority is centralized in the worldwide division headquarters to coordinate and integrate decisions and actions among disparate divisional business units.[73] This form is the organizational structure of choice for rapidly growing firms seeking to manage their diversified product lines effectively.[74] Integrating mechanisms also create effective coordination through mutual adjustments in personal interactions. Such integrating mechanisms include direct contact between managers, liaison roles between departments, temporary task forces or permanent teams, and integrating roles. As managers participate in cross-country transfers, they are socialized in the philosophy of managing an integrated strategy through a worldwide product divisional structure. A shared vision of the firm's strategy and structure is developed through standardized policies and procedures (formalization) that facilitate implementation of this organizational form.

■ *The worldwide product divisional structure is an organizational form in which decision-making authority is centralized in the worldwide division headquarters to coordinate and integrate decisions and actions among disparate divisional business units.*

Figure 11.9

Worldwide Product Divisional
Structure for Implementation of
a Global Strategy

Notes:
- Red shaded headquarters circle indicates centralization to coordinate information flow among worldwide products
- Corporate headquarters uses many intercoordination devices to facilitate global economies of scale and scope
- Corporate headquarters also allocates financial resources in a cooperative way
- The organization is like a centralized federation

Two primary disadvantages of the global strategy and its accompanying worldwide product divisional structure are the difficulty involved with coordinating decisions and actions across country borders and the inability to respond quickly and effectively to local needs and preferences. Recently, for example, Federal Express was reported to have encountered difficulties with its expansion into Asia, an area of international growth the company believed had significant potential. One problem the firm experienced concerned attempts to establish hub systems. The hub system is vital to FedEx's ability to achieve required levels of coordination across country borders. As an analyst noted, "The hub system is critical; it positions Federal Express to simultaneously pursue two massive markets—trans-Pacific and intra-Asian—at lower costs. The same planes that carry freight to the hub destined for the U.S. and Japan can also provide regular overnight delivery between cities on the continent."[75]

■ Using the Combination Structure to Implement the Transnational Strategy

The *transnational strategy* is an international strategy through which the firm seeks to provide the local responsiveness that is the focus of the multidomestic strategy *and* to achieve the global efficiency that is the focus of the global strategy. To become the world's leading accounting and consulting firm, KPMG seeks to implement the transnational strategy. To develop groups of local office franchises and eventually transfer them into national firms, KPMG's organizational structure features six regions—Europe, North America, Latin America, Asia, the Middle East, and Africa. This aspect of the firm's structure allows it to provide services that are responsive to the expectations of culturally distinct clients who are parts of the 131 countries included in the six regions. However, to simultaneously gain the benefits of the global part of the transnational strategy, KPMG wants to be able to transform all these national firms into one global practice.[76] Use of the combination structure should facilitate KPMG's efforts to implement the transnational strategy. The **combination structure** is an organizational form with characteristics and structural mechanisms that result in an emphasis on both geographic and product structures.

■ The **combination structure** is an organizational form with characteristics and structural mechanisms that result in an emphasis on both geographic and product structures.

Recently Unilever Group was reorganized into a combination structure. To deal with performance challenges, the firm's operations were divided into 14 new business groups. Some of these groups are framed around emerging markets; others are framed around the company's European food and drink businesses.[77] Thus, this structure has the multidomestic strategy's geographic area focus and the global strategy's product focus. Unilever's top-level managers believe that this new organizational structure will speed decision making and enhance the firm's ability to respond flexibly to conditions that are emerging throughout world markets.

The fits between the multidomestic strategy and the worldwide geographic area structure and the global strategy and the worldwide product divisional structure are apparent. However, when the firm seeks to implement both the multidomestic and global strategies simultaneously through a combination structure, the appropriate integrating mechanisms for the two structures are less obvious. The structure used to implement the transnational strategy must be simultaneously centralized and decentralized, integrated and nonintegrated, and formalized and nonformalized. These seemingly opposing structural characteristics must be managed by a structure that is capable of encouraging all employees to understand the effects of cultural diversity on a firm's operations. Moreover, the combination structure should allow the firm to learn how to gain competitive benefits in local economies by adapting capabilities and core competencies that often have been developed and nurtured in less culturally diverse competitive environments.

In the next section, we focus on implementation of the dominant forms of the cooperative strategies that were discussed in Chapter 9.

■ Implementing Cooperative Strategies: Organizational Structure and Controls

Increasingly, companies develop multiple rather than single joint ventures or strategic alliances to implement cooperative strategies. Furthermore, the global marketplace accommodates many interconnected relationships among firms. Resulting from these relationships are networks of firms competing through an array of cooperative arrangements or alliances.[78] When managed effectively, cooperative arrangements can contribute positively to each partner's ability to achieve strategic competitiveness and earn above-average returns.

To facilitate the effectiveness of a *strategic network*—a grouping of organizations that has been formed to create value through participation in an array of cooperative arrangements such as a strategic alliance—a strategic center firm may be necessary. A *strategic center firm* facilitates management of a strategic network. Through its management, the central firm creates incentives that reduce

Figure 11.10

A Strategic Network

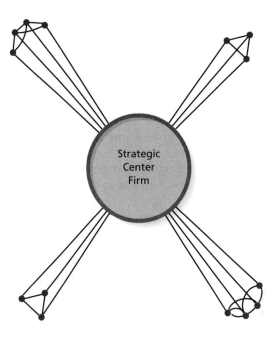

the probability of any company taking actions that could harm its network partners, and it identifies actions that increase the opportunity for each firm to achieve competitive success through its participation in the network. Illustrated in Figure 11.10, the strategic center firm is vital to the ability of companies to create value and increase their strategic competitiveness. The four critical aspects of the strategic center firm's function are:

Strategic outsourcing: The strategic center firm outsources and partners with more firms than do the other network members. Nonetheless, the strategic center firm requires partners to be more than contractors. Partners are expected to solve problems and to initiate competitive courses of action that can be pursued by the network.

Capability: The strategic center firm has core competencies that are not shared with all network partners. To increase the network's effectiveness, the central firm attempts to develop each partner's core competencies and provides incentives for network firms to share their capabilities and competencies with partners.

Technology: The strategic center firm manages the development and sharing of technology-based ideas among network partners.

Race to learn: The strategic center firm emphasizes to partners that the principal dimension of competition in competitive environments is between value chains and networks of value chains. As a result, a strategic network is as strong as its weakest value chain link. As a value chain link, a strategic network seeks to develop a competitive advantage in a primary or support activity (see Chapter 3). The need for each firm to be strong for the benefit of the entire network encourages positive rivalry among partners to learn rapidly and effectively.[79] The most effective strategic center firms learn how to manage learning processes occurring among network members.

The dominant problem in single venture cooperative arrangements is the lack of ability to control innovation and learning. However, a well-managed strategic network can overcome this problem. Therefore, as explained in the following discussions, the managerial role of the strategic center firm is critical to the successful implementation of business-level, corporate-level, and international cooperative strategies.

■ Implementing Business-Level Cooperative Strategies

As noted in Chapter 9, there are two types of complementary assets at the business level—vertical and horizontal. Vertical complementary strategic alliances are formed more frequently than horizontal alliances. Focused on buyer–supplier relationships, vertical strategic networks usually have a clear strategic center firm. Japanese vertical keiretsus such as those developed by Toyota Motor Company are structured this way. Acting as the strategic center firm, Toyota fashioned its lean production system around a network of supplier firms.

A strategic network of vertical relationships in Japan such as the network between Toyota and its suppliers often includes the following implementation issues. First, the strategic center firm encourages subcontractors to modernize their facilities and provides them with technical and financial assistance if necessary. Second, it reduces its transaction costs by promoting longer term contracts with subcontractors so that supplying partners increase their long-term productivity, rather than continually negotiating short-term contracts based on unit pricing. Third, it provides engineers in upstream companies (suppliers) better communication with contractees. Thus, the contractees and center firms become more interdependent and less independent.[80]

The lean production system pioneered by Toyota has been diffused throughout the Japanese and U.S. automobile industries. However, no automobile producer is able to duplicate the effectiveness and efficiency Toyota derives from use of this manufacturing system.[81] A key factor accounting for Toyota's ability to derive a competitive advantage from this system is the cost to imitate the structural form used to support its application. In other words, Toyota's largely proprietary actions as the strategic center firm in the strategic network it created are ones that competitors are unable to duplicate.

In vertical complementary strategic alliances such as the one between Toyota and its suppliers, the company that should function as the strategic center firm is obvious. However, as shown by the following examples, this is not the case with horizontal complementary strategic alliances.

A recently formed jet engine joint venture between rivals General Electric and United Technologies Corp.'s Pratt and Whitney unit promises significant returns for both firms.[82] However, other cooperative arrangements between jet engine manufacturers have not yielded anticipated results. Previously, for example, GE and Rolls-Royce's jet engine division formed a joint venture to manufacture engines for Boeing's 777 commercial jet. Bitter disputes between the partners led to this venture's break up. Similarly, an earlier venture among Pratt, Rolls-Royce, and other small contractors to build smaller jet engines failed. A problem common to all of these ventures was the difficulty of selecting the strategic center firm. The distrust that had formed among the joint venture companies through years of aggressive competition prevented agreements regarding the firm that should function as the strategic center of a network.

It is also difficult to identify strategic center firms with respect to horizontal cooperative arrangements among airline companies. For instance, British Airways (BA) and American Airlines are seeking to establish a horizontal complementary strategic alliance. However, BA has formed a similar alliance with USAir, a company in which BA has a 25 percent ownership stake. This ownership position poses questions about which firm should function as the strategic center in any strategic network that might eventually form between these airlines. Delta Air Lines is strengthening its horizontal agreement with Swiss Air and is forming agreements with Austrian Airlines and Sabena World Airlines to enhance its competitive position in Europe. Still to be resolved, however, is the issue of which company should serve as the strategic center in this expanding strategic network. Thus, because the dominant strategic center firm is evident, vertical complementary strategic alliances tend to be far more stable than horizontal complementary strategic alliances.

■ Implementing Corporate-Level Cooperative Strategies

Corporate-level cooperative strategy partnerships should also select a strategic center firm to operate the network of alliances effectively. However, it is more difficult to choose a strategic center firm in some types of corporate-level cooperative strategies. It is easier, for example, for a strategic center firm to emerge in a centralized franchise network than in a decentralized set of diversified strategic alliances. This situation is demonstrated by McDonald's Corp.

McDonald's has formed a centralized strategic network in which its corporate office serves as the strategic center for its franchisees. Recently, McDonald's decided that the firm should use its core competencies to better serve the adult market. Long a favorite of children, many adolescents' parents do not share their sons' and daughters' excitement about eating at McDonald's. Developed through the strategic center's centralized R&D function, a new product, aimed at adults, was introduced in mid-1996. Called the Arch Deluxe, this food item was pitched as "the burger with a grownup taste." The Arch Deluxe comes in a potato-flour bun, consists of a quarter pound of seasoned beef dressed with lettuce, tomato, cheese, onion, and a sauce of Dijon and stone-ground mustards and mayonnaise. Because market research showed that bacon is among the most popular dressings on burgers, peppered bacon is optional. Supported by a substantial marketing effort, the Arch Deluxe was "part of a broader effort by McDonald's to convince adults that its restaurants are the place to eat even if they aren't accompanied by a child."[83] Initial reactions from franchisees to the strategic center's efforts were positive. Following a sampling of the Arch Deluxe and study of the strategic center's advertising campaigns for it, a Seattle-area franchisee observed that "Strategically, I think we're headed in the right direction."[84]

Unlike McDonald's, Corning's corporate-level cooperative strategy has resulted in implementation of a system of diversified strategic alliances. This has required Corning to implement a decentralized network of joint ventures and strategic alliances in which it is more difficult to form a strategic center firm among network partners. Over time, Corning has focused on intangible resources, such as a reliable reputation for being a trustworthy and committed partner, to develop competitively successful strategic networks. In these situations, the strategic network has loose connections between joint ventures or multiple centers, although Corning is typically the principal center. However, the joint ventures are less dependent on the strategic center firm and, as such, require less managerial attention from it.[85]

■ Implementing International Cooperative Strategies

Competing in multiple countries increases dramatically the complexity associated with attempts to manage successfully strategic networks formed through international cooperative strategies. A key reason for this increased complexity is the differences among countries' regulatory environments. These differences are especially apparent in regulated industries such as telecommunications and air travel. For example, country-specific regulatory environments may partially explain the difficulty of establishing international airline alliances. Many airlines are wholly or partially owned by their home country's government.[86] Relinquishing control of a national asset is a difficult decision to reach for some country officials. These types of conditions stifle the establishment of a strategic center firm that is vital to the success of international strategic networks.

As shown in Figure 11.11, many large, multinational firms form distributed strategic networks with multiple regional strategic centers to manage their array of cooperative arrangements with partner firms.[87] These distributed strategic networks are illustrated by several large multinational firms. Swedish firms such as Ericsson (telecommunications exchange equipment) and Electrolux (white goods, washing machines) have strategic centers located in countries throughout the world instead of only in Sweden where they are headquartered.[88] Ericsson, for example, is active in more than 100 countries and employs over 85,000. Divided into five business areas (public telecommunications, radio communications, business networks, components, and microwave systems), the firm has cooperative agreements with companies throughout the world.

Similarly, Citibank established strategic centers (called centers of excellence) throughout Europe and the world as it adopted a partially centralized form of

Figure 11.11

A Distributed Strategic Network

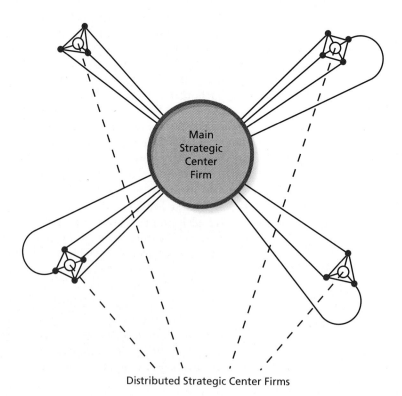

Distributed Strategic Center Firms

network management with its wholly owned subsidiaries and strategic network partners. Although Citibank has relinquished some control in the process, it has competed successfully in international markets through use of this structural form to implement its international cooperative strategy.[89] A world leader in electrical engineering, ABB is involved with a significant number of distributed strategic networks. Organized into four key business segments (power generation, power transmission and distribution, industrial and building systems, and financial services), ABB Asea Brown Boveri Group features 1,000 companies and 36 separate business areas. With a new, global 11-member board of directors representing seven nationalities, ABB considers itself a truly global company—one without a single country home. The firm has formed strategic networks in its key world areas of the Americas, Europe (including the former Soviet Union), Middle East and North Africa, sub-Sahara Africa, and Asia Pacific.[90]

■ Contemporary Organizational Structures: A Cautionary Note

Contemporary organizational structures such as those used to implement international cooperative strategies emerge typically in response to social and technological advances.[91] However, the redesign of organizations throughout the society—indeed globally—necessarily entails losses as well as gains.[92] With new organizational forms, many workers become deskilled—that is, their abilities are not sufficient to perform successfully in a new structure that often demands constant innovation and adaptation. The learning organization that is a part of new organizational forms requires that each worker become a self-motivated, continuous learner. At least in the short run, a number of employees lack the level of confidence necessary to participate actively in organizationally-sponsored learning experiences. Moreover, the flatter organizational structures that accompany contemporary structures can seem intrusive as a result of their demand for more intense and personal interactions with internal and external stakeholders. Combined, these conditions may create stress for many.

These realities do not call for managers to abandon efforts to adopt organizational structures that have the greatest probability of facilitating successful

STRATEGIC FOCUS

The Use of a "Honeycomb" Organizational Structure at AES Corporation

AES Corp. is an independent U.S. power producer operating plants in various countries including Ireland, Argentina, the United States, and the United Kingdom. Historically, AES' sales revenues have grown an average of 23 percent annually. Profits in 1995 reached $100 million, up sixfold since 1990. These performance results demonstrate AES' strategic competitiveness and ability to earn above-average returns.

Thought by some to be a "maverick," AES sells electricity to public utilities and steam to firms in different industries. Founded approximately 15 years ago by current CEO Dennis Bakke and chairman Roger Sant, this firm has "zealously shunned corporate convention" regarding organizational structure. Work tasks have not been grouped into common organizational functions such as purchasing, finance, human resources, and manufacturing. Instead, these functions are the responsibility of individual plant managers who in turn form volunteer teams to complete the tasks involved with different organizational functions. Individuals accepting

—Continued

—Continued

membership on a team simultaneously commit to gaining the knowledge required to complete the team's task successfully. Bakke contends that centralization of organizational functions prevents the majority of workers from feeling accountable and fails to encourage them to think about critical issues. In this regard, Bakke argues that "As soon as you have a specialist who's very good, then everyone else quits thinking. (And), the better that person is, the worse it is for the organization. The information goes through the specialist, so all the education is to the person who knows the most." Because AES believes this method of assigning work responsibilities creates beehive-like frenzy and appears to lack order, it calls the organizational structure a "honeycomb." Formally, this structure has only four layers: workers, plant managers, division managers, and corporate officers. The company's top-level managers believe that the honeycomb structure supports a free-wheeling organization—an organization that defiantly snubs many of the checks and controls that typify large corporations.

Supporting the use of this organizational structure are the firm's core values. Bakke and Sant believe that spreading responsibility for the firm's work tasks and its success across the entire workforce encourages individual workers to support the core values of integrity, fairness, social responsibility, and fun. And, these values are taken seriously. In the late 1980s, for example, the firm's empowered employees determined how much carbon dioxide one of its plants would produce over its useful life. To compensate for the anticipated damage to the environment, employees chose to support the planting of thousands of trees in Guatemala. The cost of this decision and commitment to the social responsibility core value was $2 million, an amount equal to the company's annual profit at the time.

Perhaps unique to AES, the "fun" core value is operationalized to mean that employees should be intellectually excited about their work. Additionally, the flexibility embedded within the firm's structure supports innovative efforts. Sant states that "It's the struggle, and even the failures that go with it, that makes work fun." Through its highly decentralized structure, AES has given authority to plant technicians to budget for and purchase supplies ranging from mops to turbines. Furthermore, "engineers are delegated the authority to arrange financings for new plants and sometimes even to negotiate multimillion-dollar contracts. And before plant employees are hired, ad hoc teams of a dozen or more workers, from pipe fitters to accountants, evaluate applicants, including their ability to fit the AES mold." Although sometimes challenged by other stakeholders, including investors and market analysts, to form and use a more conventional organizational structure, Bakke and Sant remain committed to what they believe is both the promise and ability of AES' honeycomb structure to support implementation of the firm's strategies.

Source: A. Markels, 1995, A power producer is intent on giving power to its people, *Wall Street Journal,* July 3, A1, A12.

implementation of the firm's strategies. The challenge for those responsible for effective use of the strategic management process depicted in Figure 1.1 of Chapter 1 is to respond to various issues associated with the development and use of new organizational structures in ways that will enhance the productivity of individuals and the firm. As explained in the next chapter, this responsibility belongs to strategic leaders. Described in this chapter's last Strategic Focus are actions taken by one firm's strategic leaders to enhance individual and company performance through the use of an innovative organizational structure.

■ Summary

- Organizational structure is a formal configuration that largely determines *what* a firm will do and *how* the firm will complete its work. Different structures are required to implement different strategies. A firm's performance increases when strategy and structure are matched properly.

- Business-level strategies are usually implemented through the functional structure. The cost leadership strategy requires a centralized functional structure—one in which manufacturing efficiency and process engineering are emphasized. The differentiation strategy's functional structure decentralizes implementation-related decisions, especially those concerned with marketing, to those involved with individual organizational functions. Focus strategies, used in small firms, require a simple structure until such time that a firm begins to compete in multiple markets and/or sells multiple products.

- The evolution from the functional structure to the three types of the multidivisional structure (M-form) occurred from the 1920s to the early 1970s. The cooperative M-form, used to implement the related-constrained corporate-level strategy, has a centralized corporate office and extensive integrating mechanisms. Divisional incentives are linked to overall corporate performance. The related-linked SBU M-form structure establishes separate profit centers within the diversified firm. Each profit center may have divisions offering similar products, but the profit centers are unrelated to each other. The competitive M-form structure, used to implement the unrelated diversification strategy, is highly decentralized, integrating mechanisms are nonexistent, and objective financial criteria are used to evaluate each unit's performance.

- Initially, an organizational structure is chosen in light of support required to implement a firm's strategy. Once established, however, structure influences strat-

egy. This is observed most prominently in the M-form structure's ability to stimulate additional diversification in the diversified firm.

- The multidomestic strategy, implemented through the worldwide geographic area structure, emphasizes decentralization and locates all functional activities in the country or geographic area. The worldwide product divisional structure is used to implement the global strategy. This structure is centralized to coordinate and integrate functions' activities to gain global economies of scope and scale. Decision-making authority is centralized in the firm's worldwide division headquarters. The transnational strategy—a strategy through which the firm seeks the local responsiveness of the multidomestic strategy *and* the global efficiency of the global strategy—is implemented through the combination structure. Because it must be simultaneously centralized and decentralized, integrated and nonintegrated, and formalized and nonformalized, the combination structure is difficult to organize and manage successfully.

- Increasingly important to competitive success, cooperative strategies are implemented through organizational structures framed around strategic networks.

■ Review Questions

1. Why is it important that the strategic actions of strategy implementation and strategy formulation be integrated carefully?

2. What is the meaning of the following statement? "In organizations, there is a consistent path of structure following strategy and then strategy following structure."

3. What organizational structures are used to implement the cost leadership, differentiation, integrated low-cost/differentiation, and focus business-level strategies?

4. What organizational structures are used to implement the related-constrained, related-linked, and unrelated corporate-level diversification strategies?

5. What organizational structures should be used to implement the multidomestic, global, and transnational international strategies?

6. What is a strategic network? What is a strategic center firm? What roles do they play in organizational structures used to implement cooperative strategies?

■ Application Discussion Questions

1. Why do firms experience evolutionary cycles where there is a fit between strategy and structure punctuated with periods in which strategy and structured are reshaped? Provide examples of prominent U.S. firms that have experienced this pattern.

2. Oy Nokia is the subject firm of this chapter's opening case. Has this firm regained its ability to achieve strategic competitiveness and earn above-average returns? If so, what accounts for these more positive results? If not, what conditions seem to be preventing the firm from regaining its strategic momentum? Use materials from business periodicals to support your answers.

3. Select an organization (for example, an employer, a social club, or a nonprofit agency) in which you currently hold membership. What is this organization's structure? Do you believe this organization is using the structure that is appropriate, given its strategy? If not, what structure should be used?

4. Examine the popular business press to find a firm using the multidivisional structure. Which form of the multidivisional structure is the firm using? What is there about the firm that makes it appropriate for the M-form to be in use?

5. Through reading of the business press, locate one firm implementing the global strategy and one implementing the multidomestic strategy. What organizational structure is being

used in each firm? Are these structures allowing each firm's strategy to be implemented successfully? Why or why not?

6. Identify a businessperson in your local community. Provide definitions to the person of strategic and financial controls.

Ask that the businessperson describe to you the use of each type of control in his or her business. In which type of control does the businessperson have the greatest confidence, and why?

Ethics Questions

1. When a firm changes from the functional structure to the multidivisional structure, what responsibilities do you believe it has to current employees?

2. Are there ethical issues associated with the use of strategic controls? With the use of financial controls? If so, what are they?

3. Are there ethical issues involved in implementing the cooperative and competitive M-form structures? If so, what are they? As a top-level manager, how would you deal with them?

4. Global and multidomestic strategies call for different competitive approaches. What ethical concerns might surface when firms attempt to market standardized products globally or when they develop different products/approaches for each local market?

5. What ethical issues are associated with the view that the "redesign of organizations throughout the society—indeed globally—necessarily entails losses as well as gains?"

Internet Exercise

Examine one of the newspaper or magazine home pages listed in the Appendix to find a firm that is restructuring. What strategy is it pursuing? How has it performed? What else might explain its changes?

Cohesion Case

Use one of the structures discussed in the chapter to organize your company. Then ask each of your team members to take responsibility for one of the organizational elements. What will each specialize in and how will the team be integrated? Can you devise a new organizational form? Please explain.

Notes

1. P. Sellers, 1996, Can Wal-Mart get back the magic? *Fortune*, April 29, 130–136.
2. T.A. Stewart, 1996, Why value statements don't work, *Fortune*, June 10, 137–138.
3. J.G. March, 1994, *A Primer on Decision Making: How Decisions Happen* (New York: The Free Press), 168.
4. K.E. Weick, 1995, *Sensemaking in Organizations* (Thousand Oaks, Calif.: Sage Publications).
5. J.R. Galbraith, 1995, *Designing Organizations* (San Francisco: Jossey-Bass Publishers), 6.
6. Ibid., 1.
7. F.F. Suarez and J.M. Utterback, 1995, Dominant designs and the survival of firms, *Strategic Management Journal* 16: 415–430.
8. R.H. Hall, 1996, *Organizations: Structures, Processes, and Outcomes* (6th ed.) (Englewood Cliffs, N.J.: Prentice Hall), 106–107.
9. R. Simons, 1995, Control in an age of empowerment, *Harvard Business Review* 73, no. 2: 80–88.
10. D.E. Leidner and J.J. Elam, 1995, The impact of executive information systems on organizational design, intelligence, and decision making, *Organization Science* 6: 645–664.
11. M.P. Mangaliso, 1995, The strategic usefulness of management information as perceived by middle managers, *Journal of Management* 21: 231–250.
12. A. Choi, 1996, Digital's new attitude toward old enemies puts it back in game, *Wall Street Journal*, April 9, A1, A16.
13. A.D. Chandler, Jr., 1990, *Scale and Scope: The Dynamics of Industrial Capitalism* (Cambridge:

The Belknap Press of Harvard University Press), 182–183.
14. F.R. Bleakley, 1996, The future of the global marketplace, *Wall Street Journal*, May 15, A13.
15. G.P. Zachary, 1995, Behind stocks' surge is an economy in which big U.S. firms thrive, *Wall Street Journal*, November 22, A1, A3.
16. Ibid., A1.
17. S. Singhal, 1994, *Senior Management—The Dynamics of Effectiveness* (New Delhi: Sage Publications), 48.
18. Ibid., 48; Galbraith, *Designing Organizations*, 13; R.R. Nelson, 1994, Why do firms differ, and how does it matter? in R.P. Rumelt, D.E. Schendel, and D.J. Teece (eds.), *Fundamental Issues in Strategy* (Boston: Harvard Business School Press), 259.
19. Nelson, Why do firms, 259.
20. C.W.L. Hill, 1994, Diversification and economic performance: Bringing structure and corporate management back into the picture, in R.P. Rumelt, D.E. Schendel, and D.J. Teece (eds.), *Fundamental Issues in Strategy* (Boston: Harvard Business School Press), 297–321.
21. L. Berton, 1996, Peat Marwick is facing turmoil among staff, tricky financial issues, *Wall Street Journal*, May 17, A1, A8.
22. Galbraith, *Designing Organizations*, 25.
23. P. Lawrence and J.W. Lorsch, 1967, *Organization and Environment* (Boston: Harvard Business School Press).

24. A.D. Chandler, 1994, The functions of the HQ unit in the multibusiness firm, in R.P. Rumelt, D.E. Schendel, and D.J. Teece (eds.), *Fundamental Issues in Strategy* (Boston: Harvard Business School Press), 327.
25. J.M. Liedtka, 1996, Collaboration across lines of business for competitive advantage, *Academy of Management Executive X*, no. 2: 20–37; R.P. Rumelt, D.E. Schendel, and D.J. Teece, 1994, *Fundamental Issues in Strategy* (Boston: Harvard Business School Press), 44; R.E. Hoskisson, C.W.L. Hill, and H. Kim, 1993, The multidivisional structure: Organizational fossil or source of value? *Journal of Management* 19: 269–298.
26. G.G. Dess, A. Gupta, J.F. Hennart, and C.W.L. Hill, 1995, Conducting and integrating strategy research at the international, corporate, and business levels: Issues and directions, *Journal of Management* 21: 357–393.
27. A.D. Chandler, 1962, *Strategy and Structure: Chapters in the History of the American Industrial Enterprise* (Cambridge: The MIT Press).
28. O.E. Williamson, 1994, Strategizing, economizing, and economic organization, in R.P. Rumelt, D.E. Schendel, and D.J. Teece (eds)., *Fundamental Issues in Strategy* (Boston: Harvard Business School Press), 361–401.
29. S. Ghoshal and C.A. Bartlett, 1995, Changing the role of top management: Beyond structure to processes, *Harvard Business Review* 73, no. 1: 87–88.
30. Galbraith, *Designing Organizations*, 27.

31. Hoskisson, Hill, and Kim, The multidivisional structure, 273.

32. C.M. Farkas and S. Wetlaufer, 1996, The ways chief executive officers lead, *Harvard Business Review* 74, no. 3: 110–122.

33. Associated Press, 1996, Trouble-shooter aims to galvanize Mazda, Ford, *Dallas Morning News,* April 13, F2; V. Reitman, 1996, Japan is aghast as foreigner takes the wheel at Mazda, *Wall Street Journal,* April 15, A11.

34. M.A. Hitt, R.E. Hoskisson, R.A. Johnson, and D.D. Moesel, 1996, The market for corporate control and firm innovation, *Academy of Management Journal* 39: in press.

35. Ibid.; R.E. Hoskisson, M.A. Hitt, and R.D. Ireland, 1994, The effects of acquisitions and restructuring (strategic refocusing) strategies on innovation, in G. von Krogh, A. Sinatra, and H. Singh (eds.), *Managing Corporate Acquisitions* (London: Macmillan Press), 144–169.

36. R.E. Hoskisson and M.A. Hitt, 1988, Strategic control and relative R&D investment in large multiproduct firms, *Strategic Management Journal* 9: 605–621.

37. R. Gibson, 1996, Anheuser-Busch plans to spin off baking unit, ending costly foray, *Wall Street Journal,* February 29, B3.

38. M.A. Hitt, R.E. Hoskisson, and R.D. Ireland, 1990, Mergers and acquisitions and managerial commitment to innovation in M-form firms, *Strategic Management Journal* 11 (Special Issue): 29–47.

39. Hall, *Organizations,* 13.

40. Ibid., 64–75.

41. T. Maxon, 1996, Southwest to let surfers use Net to arrange flights, *Dallas Morning News,* April 30, D1.

42. M. Halkias, 1996, Changing the retail landscape, *Dallas Morning News,* March 17, H1, H2.

43. P. Burrows and K. Rebello, 1996, Apple: Tick, tock. Tick, tock, *Business Week,* April 29, 36–37.

44. V. Govindarajan, 1988, A contingency approach to strategy implementation at the business-unit level: Integrating administrative mechanisms with strategy, *Academy of Management Journal* 31: 828–853.

45. P.B. Carroll, 1996, National Semi resets agenda with new CEO, *Wall Street Journal,* May 6, A3, A8.

46. R. Frank, 1996, Moxie, Big Red, other cult drinks thrive on being hometown heroes, *Wall Street Journal,* May 6, B1, B5.

47. C.C. Markides and P.J. Williamson, 1996, Corporate diversification and organizational structure: A resource-based view, *Academy of Management Journal* 39: 340–367; C.W.L. Hill, M.A. Hitt, and R.E. Hoskisson, 1992, Cooperative versus competitive structures in related and unrelated diversified firms, *Organization Science* 3: 501–521.

48. J. Robins and M.F. Wiersema, 1995, A resource-based approach to the multibusiness firm: Empirical analysis of portfolio interrelationships and corporate financial performance, *Strategic Management Journal* 16: 277–299.

49. Markides and Williamson, Corporate diversification, 342.

50. J.R. Galbraith and R.K. Kazanjian, 1986, *Strategy Implementation: Structure, Systems and Process* (St. Paul, Minn.: West Publishing Company).

51. Hall, *Organizations,* 186; March, *A Primer,* 117–118.

52. Master Entrepreneur Award, 1996, Netscape, http://www.sddt.com, May 12.

53. M. Murray, 1996, Massive restructuring at Scotts to include cuts in spending, staff, *Wall Street Journal,* April 3, B4.

54. GE Power Systems: What We Offer, 1996, Netscape, http://www.ge.com/powersystems/ps2.htm, May 13.

55. GE Power Generation Equipment and Systems: GE Gas Turbines, 1996, Netscape, http://www.ge.com/powergeneration/pg6.htm, May 13.

56. W.M. Carley, 1996, GE taps trains chief in effort to shore up troubled energy unit, *Wall Street Journal,* May 6, A1, A6.

57. R.E. Hoskisson and M.A. Hitt, 1990, Antecedents and performance outcomes of diversification: A review and critique of theoretical perspectives, *Journal of Management* 16: 461–509.

58. C.W.L. Hill, M.A. Hitt, and R.E. Hoskisson, 1992, Cooperative versus competitive structures in related and unrelated diversified firms, *Organization Science* 3: 501–521.

59. Williamson, Strategizing, economizing, 373.

60. B.W. Keats and M.A. Hitt, 1988, A causal model of linkages among environmental dimensions, macro organizational characteristics, and performance, *Academy of Management Journal* 31: 570–598.

61. Hoskisson, Hill, and Kim, The multidivisional structure, 276.

62. R.E. Hoskisson, R.A. Johnson, and D.D. Moesel, 1994, Corporate divestiture intensity: Effects of governance strategy and performance, *Academy of Management Journal* 37: 1207–1251; R.E. Hoskisson and T. Turk, 1990, Corporate restructuring, governance and control limits of the internal capital market, *Academy of Management Review* 15: 459–471.

63. M.E. Porter, 1987, From competitive advantage to corporate strategy, *Harvard Business Review* 65, no. 3: 43–59.

64. C.C. Markides, 1992, Consequences of corporate refocusing: Ex ante evidence, *Academy of Management Journal* 35: 398–412.

65. M.A. Hitt, R.E. Hoskisson, and R.D. Ireland, 1994, A mid-range theory of the interactive effects of international and product diversification on innovation and performance, *Journal of Management* 20: 297–326.

66. Wire Reports, 1996, GM to focus on global sales market, *Dallas Morning News,* May 25, F1, F3.

67. K. Naughton and K. Kerwin, 1995, At GM, two heads may be worse than one, *Business Week,* August 14, 46.

68. M.A. Hitt, M.T. Dacin, B.B. Tyler, and D. Park, 1997, Understanding the differences in Korean and U.S. executives' strategic orientations, *Strategic Management Journal* 18: in press; Y.L. Doz and C.K. Prahalad, 1994, Managing DMNCs: A search for a new paradigm, in R.P. Rumelt, D.E. Schendel, and D.J. Teece (eds.), *Fundamental Issues in Strategy* (Boston: Harvard Business School Press), 495–526.

69. L. Grant, 1996, Stirring it up at Campbell, *Fortune,* May 13, 80–86.

70. Winning in a new era of communications, 1995, SBC Communications Inc. *Annual Report,* 7, 13.

71. G. Collins, 1996, Coke changes its recipe for administration, *Austin American-Statesman,* January 13, C1, C2; Our Company, 1995, Coca-Cola *Annual Report,* 3.

72. C.A. Bartlett and S. Ghoshal, 1989, *Managing Across Borders: The Transnational Solution* (Boston: Harvard Business School Press).

73. Bartlett and Ghosal, *Managing Across Borders.*

74. Galbraith, *Designing Organizations,* 30–34.

75. D.A. Blackmon, 1996, Fedex swings from confidence abroad to a tightrope, *Wall Street Journal,* March 15, B4.

76. J. Madonna, 1996, Why I'm going global, *Inside KPMG,* April, 1996, 1–4; KPMG International: Global mission, 1996, Netscape, http://www.kpmg.com/mission/html, May 15.

77. C. Rohwedder, 1996, Unilever reorganizes its management as a first step in broad restructuring, *Wall Street Journal,* March 14, A11.

78. B. Gomes-Casseres, 1994, Group versus group: How alliance networks compete, *Harvard Business Review* 72, no. 4: 62–74.

79. G. Lorenzoni and C. Baden-Fuller, 1995, Creating a strategic center to manage a web of partners, *California Management Review* 37, no. 3: 146–163.

80. T. Nishiguchi, 1994, *Strategic Industrial Sourcing: The Japanese Advantage* (New York: Oxford University Press).

81. W.M. Fruin, 1992, *The Japanese Enterprise System* (New York: Oxford University Press).

82. W.M. Carley, 1996, GE–Pratt venture, like others before it, faces hurdles, *Wall Street Journal,* May 10, B3.

83. The Washington Post, 1996, Ronald McDonald seeks bigger bite of grown-up market, *Dallas Morning News,* May 9, D2.

84. R. Gibson, 1996, McDonald's plays catch-up with BLT burger, *Wall Street Journal,* May 2, B1.

85. J.R. Houghton, 1990, Corning cultivates joint ventures that endure, *Planning Review* 18, no. 5: 15–17; C. Mitchell, 1988, Partnerships are a way of life at Corning, *Wall Street Journal,* July 12, 6.

86. A.Q. Nomani, 1996, U.S. moves to allow Delta, American to form close links to foreign rivals, *Wall Street Journal,* May 22, A2, A4.

87. G.G. Dess, A.M.A. Rasheed, K.J. McLaughlin, and R.L. Priem, 1995, The new corporate architecture, *Academy of Management Executive* IX, no. 3: 7–20.

88. M. Forsgren and J. Johanson, 1991, Managing internationalization in business networks, in M. Forsgren and J. Johanson (eds.) *Managing Internationalization in Business Networks* (Philadelphia: Gordon and Breach), 1–30.

89. T.W. Malnight, 1996, The transition from decentralized to network-based MNC structures: An evolutionary perspective, *Journal of International Business Studies* 27: 43–65.

90. ABB History, 1996, Netscape, http://www.abb.ch/abbgroup/brief/history.htm, May 27; ABB Group home page, http://www.abb.com/, May 27.

91. Chandler, *Scale and Scope.*

92. B. Victor and C. Stephens, 1994, The dark side of the new organizational forms: An editorial essay, *Organization Science* 5: 479–482.

CHAPTER
12 Strategic Leadership

After reading this chapter, you should be able to:

1. Define strategic leadership and describe the importance of top-level managers as an organizational resource.

2. Define top management teams and explain their effects on the firm's performance and its ability to innovate and make appropriate strategic changes.

3. Describe the internal and external managerial labor markets and their effects on the development and implementation of firm strategy.

4. Discuss the value of strategic leadership for determining the firm's strategic direction.

5. Explain the role of strategic leaders in exploiting and maintaining core competencies.

6. Describe the importance of strategic leaders in developing a firm's human capital.

7. Define organizational culture and explain the importance of what must be done to sustain an effective culture.

8. Describe what strategic leaders can do to establish and emphasize ethical practices in their firms.

9. Discuss the importance and use of organizational controls.

Strategic Leadership at Compaq Computer

COMPAQ

Known as a serious, reserved, and slightly dispassionate CEO who is oriented to perfectionism, Eckhard Pfeiffer sometimes drives up to 100 miles per hour in his black Porsche convertible while going to work. The culture Pfeiffer has developed at Compaq seems to parallel that desire to drive fast. In fact, it has been suggested that under Pfeiffer's leadership, ". . . Compaq has proved itself a master of what may be the most critical task of business in the Nineties: doing everything fast." The firm's intentions and goals and work procedures indicate that Compaq's entrepreneurial culture thrives on speed.

Compaq has been successful during Pfeiffer's tenure as the firm's CEO. From the time of his 1991 appointment as the company's key strategic leader through 1995, Compaq's annual revenues grew from $3.3 billion to $14.8 billion. Additionally, sales in the first quarter of 1996 increased by 46 percent over sales for the same time period in 1995. In 1993, Pfeiffer established a strategic intent that challenged the firm to stretch its resources and capabilities to reach what some thought was an unattainable goal. Ranked third in 1993 sales, Pfeiffer said that he wanted Compaq to be the leading PC manufacturer in the world by 1996. This goal was reached in 1994. Based on this success, the CEO has framed another set of goals that may be even more challenging than the set in 1993. Pfeiffer now ". . . wants Compaq to own at least twice as much share as its nearest competitor in every market it enters. He wants Compaq to become one of the top three computer companies in the world. Today it's fifth, behind IBM, Fujitsu, Hewlett-Packard, and NEC. Finally, he wants $30 billion in yearly sales by 2000."

Pictured as a highly competent, relentlessly competitive strategic leader, Pfeiffer has made change a way of life at Compaq. Resulting from the CEO's commitment to strategic change is a culture that ensures change is desirable. In fact, employees never assume that what led to success in one time period or one market will lead to success a second time. Because environments change quickly, Compaq's employees believe strongly in bringing innovative products to the marketplace rapidly.

Recently Pfeiffer and his top management team decided to change Compaq's strategy. Historically a PC company, the firm began to apply its competencies to the PC server market. Servers are the workhorse computing systems which enable files to be shared, communications to take place, and other applications to be used among networks of PCs. The industry's most profitable segment, Compaq dominates the server market, recently holding a 36 percent share. IBM held the second position at 14 percent. Now, Compaq intends to be a systems company as well as a PC and server company. Compaq's brand name and its distribution channel are two competencies being used to implement the firm's strategy for network products.

Compaq also intends to be a major player in consumer markets. A member of Compaq's top management team believes that the firm will miss a dramatic long-term market opportunity if it fails to establish a presence in the consumer market. Over the long term, Compaq wants to sell consumers content, software, and services. Across all of its products, the firm intends to provide value to customers in the form of performance, quality, and affordability.

Although he works long hours (65 to 70 hours per week), Pfeiffer drives the company no harder than he drives himself. Never satisfied, he does not like to lose, but this tenacious CEO emanates reassuring calm among his employees. Members of the top management team consider these qualities to be a tremendous asset and find them helpful in an environment of strategic change.

Source: D. Kirkpatrick, 1996, Fast times at Compaq, *Fortune,* April 1, 121–128; N. Templin, 1996, Compaq plans to slice Apple's share in dominating school-computer market, *Wall Street Journal,* February 21, B2; N. Templin, 1996, Compaq reduces prices sharply on network goods, *Wall Street Journal,* March 26, B6.

The example of Eckhard Pfeiffer's leadership as the CEO of Compaq Computer emphasizes the importance and outcomes of effective strategic leadership, the focus of this chapter. It is through effective strategic leadership that firms are able to use the strategic management process successfully (see Figure 1.1). Thus, as strategic leaders, top-level managers must guide the firm in ways that result in the formation of strategic intent and strategic mission. Moreover, strategic leaders are then challenged to facilitate the development of appropriate strategic actions and determine how to implement them, culminating in strategic competitiveness and above-average returns[1] (see Figure 12.1).

This chapter begins with a definition of strategic leadership and its importance as a potential source of competitive advantage. Next, we examine top management teams and their effects on the firm's innovation, strategic change, and performance. Following this discussion is an analysis of the internal and external managerial labor markets from which firms select their strategic leaders. Closing the chapter are descriptions of the six key components of effective strategic leadership: determining strategic direction, exploiting and maintaining core competencies, developing human capital, sustaining an effective organizational culture, emphasizing ethical practices, and establishing balanced organizational control systems.

There is an evident consistency between many of the strategic leadership components just mentioned and the actions taken by Eckhard Pfeiffer as Compaq Computer's CEO. By providing the vision for strategic intent, Pfeiffer has determined the firm's strategic direction. Existing core competencies (e.g., brand name and distribution channels) are being used to implement the firm's new strategies. Efforts are taken to develop and support the firm's human capital and to maintain what seems to be an effective organizational culture. This evidence suggests that Compaq Computer's CEO is an effective strategic leader.

■ Strategic Leadership

■ *Strategic leadership* entails the ability to anticipate, envision, maintain flexibility, and empower others to create strategic change as necessary.

Strategic leadership entails the ability to anticipate, envision, maintain flexibility, and empower others to create strategic change as necessary. It is multifunctional in nature, involves managing through others, connotes the management of an entire enterprise rather than a subunit, and helps organizations cope with change that seems to be increasing exponentially in today's new competitive landscape.[2] Because of the complexity and global nature of this new landscape, strategic leaders must learn how to influence human behavior effectively in an environment of uncertainty. By word and/or personal example and through their ability to dream pragmatically, effective strategic leaders meaningfully influence the behaviors, thoughts, and feelings of those with whom they work.[3]

The ability to manage human capital may be the most critical of the strategic leader's skills.[4] In the opinion of a well-known leadership observer, the key to competitive advantage in the 1990s and beyond ". . . will be the capacity of top leadership to create the social architecture capable of generating intellectual capital. . . . By intellectual capital, I mean know-how, expertise, brainpower, innovation (and) ideas."[5] Competent strategic leaders also establish the context

Figure 12.1

Strategic Leadership and the Strategic Management Process

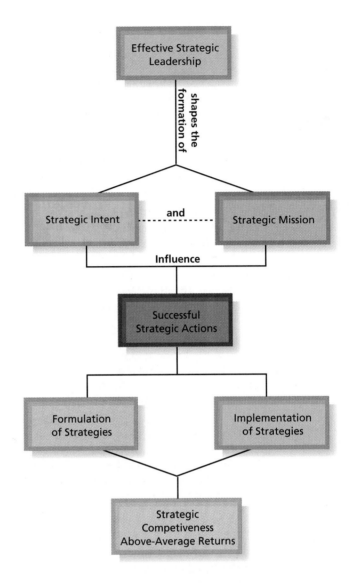

A *managerial frame of reference* is the set of assumptions, premises, and accepted wisdom that bounds—or *frames*—a manager's understanding of the firm, the industry(ies) in which it competes, and the core competencies it uses in the pursuit of strategic competitiveness.

through which stakeholders (e.g., employees, customers, and suppliers) are able to perform at peak efficiency.[6]

To be effective strategic leaders in the twenty-first century, many managers working in nations throughout the world are challenged to change their frames of reference so they will be better able to deal with the rapid and complex changes occurring in the global economy. A **managerial frame of reference** is the set of assumptions, premises, and accepted wisdom that bounds—or *frames*—a manager's understanding of the firm, the industry(ies) in which it competes, and the core competencies it uses in the pursuit of strategic competitiveness. A frame of reference is the foundation on which a manager's mind-set is built (see Chapter 3).

The firm's ability to achieve strategic competitiveness and earn above-average returns is compromised when strategic leaders fail to respond appropriately and quickly to mind-set-related changes that are mandated by an increasingly complex and globalized competitive landscape. Two researchers, for example, suggest that a firm's "long-term competitiveness depends on managers' willingness to challenge continually their managerial frames" and that global competition is more than product versus product or company versus company—it is also a case of "mindset versus mindset, managerial frame versus managerial frame."[7] Competing on the basis of mind-set demands that strategic leaders learn how to deal with diverse and cognitively complex competitive situations. Being able to complete successfully assignments that are challenging, yet directly linked to achieving strategic competitiveness early and frequently in one's career appears to improve managers' abilities to make appropriate changes to their mind-sets.[8]

Effective strategic leaders are willing to make candid, courageous, yet pragmatic, decisions—decisions that may be difficult, yet necessary in light of internal and external conditions facing the firm.[9] A manager at Briggs & Stratton, for example, suggested that his employer is thriving because the firm's leaders are willing to make tough decisions that aren't always popular.[10] Effective strategic leaders solicit corrective feedback from their peers, superiors, and employees about the value of their difficult decisions. Often, this feedback is sought through face-to-face communications. The unwillingness to accept feedback may be a key reason talented executives fail, highlighting the need for strategic leaders to solicit feedback consistently from those affected by their decisions.[11]

The primary responsibility for effective strategic leadership rests at the top—in particular, with the firm's CEO. In addition to CEOs, other commonly recognized strategic leaders include members of the firm's board of directors, top management teams, and division general managers. Regardless of title and organizational function, strategic leaders have substantial decision-making responsibilities—responsibilities that cannot be delegated.[12]

Strategic leadership is an extremely complex, but critical, form of leadership. Strategies cannot be formulated and implemented to achieve above-average returns without effective strategic leaders. Because it is a requirement of strategic success, and because organizations may be poorly led and overmanaged, firms competing in the new competitive landscape are challenged to develop effective strategic leaders.[13] Wayne Calloway, PepsiCo's former CEO, has suggested that ". . . most of the companies that are in life-or-death battles got into that kind of trouble because they didn't pay enough attention to developing their leaders."[14]

Managers As an Organizational Resource

As the introductory discussion suggests, top-level managers are an important resource for firms seeking to effectively formulate and implement strategies. A key reason for this is that the strategic decisions made by top managers influence how the firm is designed and whether performance outcomes will be achieved. Thus, a critical element of organizational success is having a top management team that has superior managerial skills.[15]

Often based on perceptions, managers use their discretion (or latitude of action) when making strategic decisions, including those concerned with the effective implementation of strategies.[16] Managerial discretion differs significantly across industries. The primary factors that determine the amount of a manager's (especially a top-level manager's) decision discretion include (1) external environmental sources (e.g., industry structure, rate of market growth in the firm's primary industry, and the degree to which products can be

Figure 12.2

Factors Affecting
Managerial Discretion

Source: Adapted from S. Finkelstein and D. C.
Hambrick, 1996, *Strategic Leadership: Top
Executives and Their Effects on Organizations*
(St. Paul, Minn: West Publishing Co.).

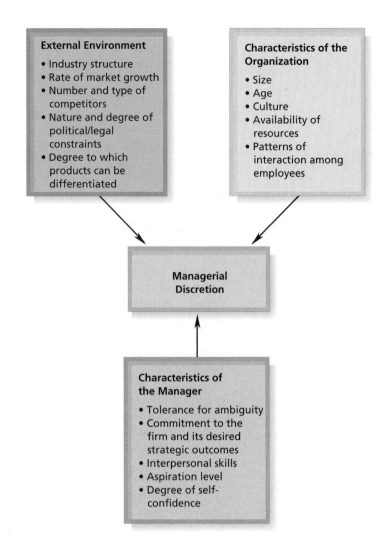

External Environment

- Industry structure
- Rate of market growth
- Number and type of competitors
- Nature and degree of political/legal constraints
- Degree to which products can be differentiated

Characteristics of the Organization

- Size
- Age
- Culture
- Availability of resources
- Patterns of interaction among employees

Managerial Discretion

Characteristics of the Manager

- Tolerance for ambiguity
- Commitment to the firm and its desired strategic outcomes
- Interpersonal skills
- Aspiration level
- Degree of self-confidence

differentiated), (2) characteristics of the organization (e.g., size, age, resource availability, and culture) and (3) characteristics of the manager (e.g., commitment to the firm and its strategic outcomes, tolerance for ambiguity, skills to work with different people, and aspiration level) (see Figure 12.2). Because strategic leaders' decisions are intended to help the firm gain a competitive advantage, the way in which managers exercise discretion when determining appropriate strategic actions is critical to the firm's success.[17]

In addition to determining new strategic initiatives, top-level managers also develop the appropriate organizational structure and reward systems of the firm. In Chapter 11, we described how organizational structure and reward systems affect strategic actions taken to implement different types of strategies. Furthermore, top-level managers have a major impact on a firm's culture. Evidence suggests that managers' values are critical in shaping a firm's base cultural values.[18] As this discussion shows, top-level managers have an important effect on organizational activities and performance.[19] The significance of this effect should not be underestimated.

The degree to which top-level managers influence a firm's performance is observed by financial markets. For example, William Fields' sudden resignation as the chief of Wal-Mart's main discount store business in 1996 to become the head of Viacom Inc.'s Blockbuster Entertainment unit resulted immediately in a four percent loss in the value of Wal-Mart's stock and an identical percentage increase in the value of Viacom's stock. The market's reaction may have been due in part to Fields' broad experience with Wal-Mart during his 25 years with the company and some observers' beliefs that Fields would one day be the giant discounter's CEO. Called a major hiring coup for Viacom, analysts credit Fields with playing a critical role in building Wal-Mart into the largest retailer in the United States.[20] Thus, a strategic leader's experience and judgment, and the quality of the decisions based on them, is oftentimes of keen interest to various stakeholders, including current and potential shareholders.[21]

The effects of some strategic leaders' decisions and performances on their firms' outcomes and strategic competitiveness are described next. As this discussion shows, the decisions and actions of some, but not all, strategic leaders result in their becoming a source of competitive advantage for their firm. Consistent with the criteria of sustainability discussed in Chapter 3, strategic leaders can be a source of competitive advantage only when their work is valuable, rare, costly to imitate, and nonsubstitutable.

STRATEGIC FOCUS   Some Strategic Leaders Do It Right and Others Do Not

As CEO of Greyhound Lines Inc., Craig Lentzsch is credited with making a series of strategic and operational decisions that dramatically improved the firm's performance. Known for his understanding of the technical side of the bus industry, Lentzsch joined the firm when it was on the brink of financial collapse. Confident in his strategic leadership abilities, Greyhound's new CEO took immediate and decisive actions to turn the company around. To better serve customers, changes were made regarding how the firm sold tickets for seats on its buses. Previously, the "airline reservation" model was used—people phoned ahead of time to reserve a seat. A key problem with this was that more than 80 percent of those making a reservation became no-shows. An analysis of the firm's customers revealed that approximately 75 percent of them buy tickets with cash about three hours before a scheduled departure. Thus, the firm's core customer group had little interest in making reservations days or weeks ahead of time. Today, Greyhound has no reservation system in place. Instead, under Lentzsch's leadership, the firm guarantees a person a seat on a bus if she or he shows up at a terminal within a reasonable period of time before a scheduled departure.

In light of customer demographics, Lentzsch also decided that the firm's pricing structure had to be changed. Lentzsch observed that "My biggest competitors are not airlines, or Amtrak, or cars, it's affordability. It's customers not having enough money in their pockets to take a trip." Thus, Greyhound has reduced its prices significantly. For example, the one-way fare from Los Angeles to Portland, Oregon, dropped from $269 in 1994 to $139 in 1996.

Because of the results gained through these decisions, and others made by Lentzsch and members of his top management team—including rebuilding the firm's package express business and expanding bus fleets and routes—the firm's financial performance continues to improve. Greyhound's operating income in 1995 was $9.4 million. Compared to 1994's loss of $65.5 million, this financial performance was a significant improvement and Greyhound expected to earn a profit in 1996.

—Continued

—Continued

Unlike Craig Lentzsch, J. Kermit Campbell was not a source of competitive advantage as a CEO. In fact, Campbell's short-lived tenure as the CEO of Herman Miller, the furniture maker widely admired as an innovator and as a model of effective human resource practices, did not result in an enhancement of the firm's strategic competitiveness. Serious troubles apparently started for Campbell when he refused advice, from the firm's chief financial officer, that the company ". . . desperately needed to control expenses." Although Campbell eventually saw the need to reign in costs, his decision to do so, and the actions resulting from it, were too little, too late. Through downsizing that started only at the end of fiscal year 1995, almost 200 people left Herman Miller. Year-end results, though, were discouraging. While 1995 sales increased 13.6 percent over 1994, profits declined nearly 90 percent during the same time period. The firm simultaneously announced its disappointing 1995 results and the departure of Kermit Campbell as its CEO. This example and that of Greyhound Corp. demonstrate the significant impact a CEO's decisions and actions can have on a firm's ability to formulate and implement effective strategies.

Source: B. Deener, 1996, The Greyhound turnaround, *Dallas Morning News*, January 14, H1, H2; W. Zellner, 1996, Leave the driving to Lentzsch, *Business Week*, March 18, 66, 69; J. M. Meachem, 1995, Broken furniture at Herman Miller, 1995, *Fortune*, August 7, 32.

Effective strategic leaders focus their work on the key issues that ultimately shape the firm's ability to earn above-average returns. For example, Helmut Maucher at Nestlé and Michael Dell, Dell Computer, focus their energies on determining how their companies can be market leaders and then structure their organizations to support this focus.[22] Obviously, Craig Lentzsch of Greyhound was able to do this but J. Kermit Campbell of Herman Miller was not, as explained in the Strategic Focus.

Many actions are taken by CEOs to gain the desired results, including those of delegating day-to-day operations to others so they can ask "big picture" questions of their managers, suppliers, shareholders, and customers. The most effective strategic leaders also travel to other companies to study successful work processes and they build time into their schedules to think. One of the most important issues effective strategic leaders think about is the source of their firm's competitive advantage. "At companies like Motorola, Ogilvy & Mather, and Cooper Industries, the CEO and (the) top staff identify the particular expertise that is their competitive advantage and then focus their energies on guaranteeing that that expertise moves up, down, and among operating units."[23] Finding ways to release employees' brainpower influences the degree to which the firm's expertise is applied throughout the company in a competitively relevant fashion.[24]

■ Top Management Teams

■ *The top management team is composed of the key managers who are responsible for formulating and implementing the organization's strategies.*

The **top management team** is composed of the key managers who are responsible for formulating and implementing the organization's strategies. Typically, the top management team includes the officers of the corporation as defined by the title of vice president and above and/or service as a member of the board of directors.[25] The quality of the strategic decisions made by a top management team affects the firm's ability to innovate and engage in effective strategic change.[26]

Top Management Team, Firm Performance, and Strategic Change

The job of top-level executives is complex and requires a broad knowledge of firm operations, as well as the three key parts of the firm's external environment.

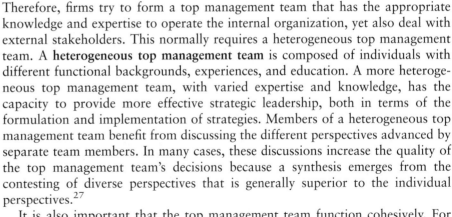

*■ A **heterogeneous top management team** is composed of individuals with different functional backgrounds, experiences, and education.*

Therefore, firms try to form a top management team that has the appropriate knowledge and expertise to operate the internal organization, yet also deal with external stakeholders. This normally requires a heterogeneous top management team. A **heterogeneous top management team** is composed of individuals with different functional backgrounds, experiences, and education. A more heterogeneous top management team, with varied expertise and knowledge, has the capacity to provide more effective strategic leadership, both in terms of the formulation and implementation of strategies. Members of a heterogeneous top management team benefit from discussing the different perspectives advanced by separate team members. In many cases, these discussions increase the quality of the top management team's decisions because a synthesis emerges from the contesting of diverse perspectives that is generally superior to the individual perspectives.[27]

It is also important that the top management team function cohesively. For example, some believe that an apparent inability to work effectively as a top management team negatively affected efforts to engineer a strategic turnaround at Cable & Wireless PLC, an international telephone company competing in more than 50 countries.[28] In general, the more heterogeneous and larger the top management team is, the harder it is for the team to implement strategies effectively.[29] Having substantive expertise on the top management team in the functions and businesses that are core to the firm is also important. In a high-technology industry, it may be critical for a firm to have R&D knowledge and expertise included on the top management team, particularly when growth strategies are being implemented.[30]

The characteristics of top management teams are related to firm innovation and strategic change. For example, more heterogeneous top management teams are associated positively with innovation. In addition, top management team heterogeneity has been discovered to be related positively to strategic change. Thus, firms that need to change their strategies are more likely to do so if they have top management teams with diverse backgrounds and expertise. A top management team with various areas of expertise is more likely to identify environmental changes (opportunities and threats) or changes within the firm that require a different strategic direction.[31] This fact may explain CEO Louis Gerstner's decision to change IBM's top management team. Relying more extensively on hiring from outside the company, Gerstner chose top-level managers that he believed had the skills required to help IBM better exploit the firm's core competencies.[32]

CEO and Top Management Team Power

As suggested in Chapter 10, the board of directors is an important mechanism for monitoring a firm's strategic direction and for representing the interests of stakeholders, especially those of stockholders. In fact, higher performance normally is achieved when the board of directors is involved more directly in shaping a firm's strategic direction.[33]

However, boards of directors may find it difficult to direct the strategic actions of powerful CEOs and top management teams. It is not uncommon for a powerful CEO to appoint a number of outside board members. In addition, the inside board members are also members of the top management team and report to the CEO. Therefore, the CEO may have significant control over the board's actions. "A central question is whether boards are an effective management

When IBM required a different strategic direction, CEO Louis Gerstner decided to change IBM's top management team, and focused on hiring from outside the company.

control mechanism . . . or whether they are a 'management tool,' . . . a rubber stamp for management initiatives, . . . and often surrender to management their major domain of decision-making authority, which includes the right to hire, fire, and compensate top management."[34]

CEOs and top management team members can also achieve power in other ways. Holding the titles of chairperson of the board *and* chief executive officer usually gives a CEO more power than the one who is not simultaneously serving as chairman of the firm's board.[35] Although the practice of CEO duality (CEO duality exists when the CEO and the chairperson of the board are the same person) has become more common in U.S. businesses, it ". . . has recently come under heavy criticism—duality has been blamed for poor performance and slow response to change in firms such as General Motors, Digital Equipment Corporation, and Goodyear Tire and Rubber."[36] Although it varies by industry setting, duality occurs most commonly in the largest firms. Moreover, because of increased shareholder activism, CEO duality is also coming under increased scrutiny and attack in European firms. Historically, an independent board leadership structure—a structure in which the CEO and chairperson of the board positions are not held by a single person—was believed to enhance a board's ability to monitor top-level managers' decisions and actions, particularly in terms of the firm's financial performance.[37] However, stewardship theory suggests that CEO duality facilitates effective decisions and actions by the person serving as both CEO and chairperson of the board. In these instances, the increased effectiveness gained through CEO duality accrues from the individual who wants to perform effectively and desires to be the best possible steward of the firm's assets. Because of this person's positive orientations and actions, extra governance and the coordination costs resulting from an independent board leadership structure would be unnecessary.[38]

To date, the question of the impact of duality on the firm's strategic outcomes is unresolved. In a recent study of the relationship between duality and firm performance, researchers found that (1) the stock market is indifferent to changes in a company's duality status, (2) changes in a company's duality status has a negligible effect on its financial performance, and (3) "there is only weak evidence that duality status affects long-term performance, after controlling for other factors that might impact that performance."[39] Thus, it may be that, in general, the potential for managerial abuse created through CEO duality is unrealized in many firms.

Top management team members, including CEOs, that have longer tenure—on the team and in the organization—have an increased ability to influence board decisions.[40] Moreover, long tenure is known to restrict the breadth of an executive's knowledge base. With the limited perspective associated with a restricted knowledge base, long-tenured top-level managers typically develop fewer alternatives to evaluate when making strategic decisions.[41] A net result of long tenure and a restricted knowledge base is an executive ability to forestall or avoid board involvement in strategic decisions. However, managers of long tenure also are better able to exercise strategic controls, thereby forstalling board of directors' involvement. The exercise of strategic control generally produces higher performance eliminating the need for the board to intervene.[42]

In the final analysis, boards of directors are challenged to develop an effective relationship with the firm's top management team. The relative degrees of power to be held by the board and top management team members should be examined in light of an individual firm's situation. For example, the abundance of resources in a firm's external environment and the volatility of that environment may affect the ideal balance of power between boards and top management teams.[43] Through the development of effective working relationships, boards, CEOs and other top management team members are able to serve the best interests of the firm's stakeholders.

Managerial Labor Market

The choice of top-level managers, especially CEOs, is a critical organizational decision with important implications for firm effectiveness.[44] Moreover, selection of new members for a top management team represents an opportunity for the firm to adapt to changes occurring in its external environment (that is, in its general, industry, and competitive environments—see Chapter 2).

Successful companies develop screening systems to identify those with managerial and strategic leadership potential. The most effective of these systems evaluates people within the firm and gains valuable information about the capabilities of other firms' managers, particularly their strategic leaders. Screening systems are vital, in that just because a person shares the firm's values ". . . doesn't mean he or she is leadership material."[45] For current managers, training and development programs are provided to preselect and attempt to shape the skills of people who may become tomorrow's leaders. (PepsiCo's strategic leadership training program is described in a later Strategic Focus.)

There are two types of managerial labor markets—internal and external—from which organizations select managers and strategic leaders. An **internal managerial labor market** consists of the opportunities for managerial positions within a firm. An **external managerial labor market** is the collection of career opportunities for managers in organizations outside of the one for which they work currently. Given this chapter's topic of strategic leadership, our discussion of managerial labor markets focuses on their use to select CEOs.

Several benefits are thought to accrue to a firm when the internal labor market is used to select a new CEO. Because of their experience with the firm and the industry environment in which it competes, insiders are familiar with company products, markets, technologies, and standard operating procedures. Additionally, internal hiring results in less turnover among existing personnel, many of whom possess valuable firm-specific knowledge.

It is not unusual for employees to have a strong preference for use of the internal managerial labor market to select top management team members and the CEO. For example, the initial reaction among employees to the choice of outsider Ronald Zarrella as the head of all of General Motors' marketing efforts was negative. With previous executive experience at Playtex and Bausch & Lomb, employees felt that Zarrella lacked the skills and background to understand the intricacies of selling cars. However, after a relatively brief time in his new position, his style and decisions earned him the respect and acceptance of many, including Jack Smith, GM's internally appointed CEO.[46]

The selection of insiders to fill top-level management positions reflects a desire for continuity and a continuing commitment to the firm's current strategic intent, strategic mission, and chosen strategies. Because of the potential importance and

■ An **internal managerial labor market** consists of the opportunities for managerial positions within a firm.

■ An **external managerial labor market** is the collection of career opportunities for managers in organizations outside of the one for which they work currently.

Employees questioned the choice of Ron Zarrella as General Motors' head of marketing efforts. However, his style and decisions quickly earned him respect and acceptance.

perceived desirability of organizational continuity, internal candidates tend to be valued over external candidates[47] when selecting a firm's CEO and other top-level managers. In fact, outside succession to the CEO position "is an extraordinary event for business firms (and) is usually seen as a stark indicator that the board of directors wants change."[48]

Valid reasons exist, however, for a firm to select an outsider as its new CEO. For example, research evidence suggests that executives who have spent their entire career with a particular firm prior to their selection as its CEO may become "stale in the saddle."[49] Long tenure with a firm seems to reduce the number of innovative ideas top-level managers are able to develop to cope with conditions facing their firm. Given the importance of innovation for firm success in the new competitive landscape (see Chapter 13), an inability to innovate and/or to create conditions that stimulate innovation throughout the firm is a liability for strategic leaders. In contrast to insiders, CEOs selected from outside the firm may have broader, less limiting perspectives. As such, they usually encourage innovation and strategic change. However, CEOs selected from outside the firm and even the firm's industry are sometimes disadvantaged by a lack of firm-specific knowledge and industry experience. For example, although credited with strategic leadership success at ConAgra Inc., Charles Harper's tenure as CEO of RJR Nabisco Holdings Corp. disappointed many stakeholders, including board members, employees, and financial investors. Among reasons cited for Harper's inability to boost RJR's struggling stock price was his lack of experience running a cigarette company.[50]

Figure 12.3 shows how the composition of the top management team and CEO succession (managerial labor market) may interact to affect strategy. For example, when the top management team is homogeneous (e.g., members have similar functional experiences and educational backgrounds) and a new CEO is selected from inside the firm, the current strategy is unlikely to change. On the other hand, when a new CEO is selected from outside the firm and the top management team is heterogeneous, there is a high probability of a change in strategy. When the new CEO is from inside the firm, the strategy may not change, but with a heterogeneous top management team, innovation is likely to continue. An external CEO succession with a homogeneous team creates a more ambiguous situation.

Figure 12.3

Effects of CEO Succession and Top Management Team Composition on Strategy

	Managerial Labor Market: CEO Succession	
	Internal CEO succession	External CEO succession
Top Management Team Composition Homogeneous	Stable strategy	Ambiguous: possible change in top management team and strategy
Heterogeneous	Stable strategy with innovation	Strategic change

Figure 12.4 Exercise of Effective Strategic Leadership

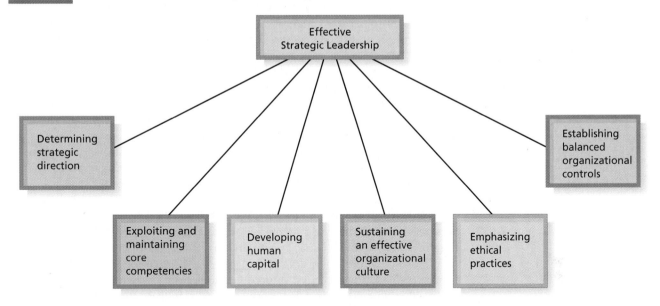

As noted earlier, the type of strategic leadership that results in successful implementation of strategies is exemplified by several key actions. The six most critical of these are shown in Figure 12.4. The remainder of this chapter is devoted to explaining each action. Note that many of these actions interact with each other. For example, developing human capital through executive training contributes to establishing a strategic direction, fostering an effective culture, exploiting core competencies, using effective organizational control systems, and establishing ethical practices.

■ Determining Strategic Direction

■ *Determining the strategic direction of the firm refers to the development of a long-term vision of a firm's strategic intent.*

Determining the strategic direction of the firm refers to the development of a long-term vision of a firm's strategic intent. A long-term vision of strategic intent normally entails a view of the firm at least 5 to 10 years in the future. A philosophy with goals, a long-term vision is the ideal image and character the firm seeks.[51] For example, Texaco Inc.'s vision is to be a company that is widely admired, profitable, and competitive. Because of its vision, Texaco is committed ". . . to quality, teamwork, leadership, technological excellence and customer service, as well as to corporate responsibility, respect for the individual, high ethical standards, open communication and fully competitive stockholder return."[52] The ideal long-term vision motivates employees to stretch beyond their expectations of accomplishment. As such, it serves as a guide to many aspects of the firm's strategy implementation process, including those of motivation, leadership, empowerment, and organizational design. For firms competing in many different industries, evidence suggests that the most effective long-term vision is one that has been accepted by those affected by it.[53]

Rockwell International Corporation recently developed what the firm calls a "newly defined corporate vision." This vision calls for Rockwell to become "The world's best diversified high-technology company." To achieve this vision, the firm will implement "four primary action strategies": (1) create the world's most successful customers, (2) aggressively pursue global growth, (3) execute leading-edge practices, and (4) contribute to the well-being of its communities.

This specification of the company's strategic direction—in the form of a new corporate vision—was stimulated by rapidly changing environmental conditions. Rockwell's strategic leaders believed that these environmental changes offered both challenges and opportunities. The challenges and opportunities for businesses provided motivation to devote considerable time and effort to the clear definition of a vision.

Rockwell's new corporate vision and primary action strategies were distilled from recommendations developed by thousands of the firm's employees. On a worldwide basis, employees are now determining actions needed to achieve the firm's vision. In this regard, employees at each Rockwell facility are challenged to determine what they need to do to become the best. Helping the firm's units reach these decisions is the work of the 23 vision implementation groups and teams that have been formed. These groups and teams are identifying the strengths and weaknesses of units in order to develop suggestions about the changes that should be made for each unit to become the best.[54]

To determine the firm's long-term vision, managers must take a sufficient amount of time to think about its framing. Areas requiring executive thought include an analysis of the firm's external and internal environments and its current performance levels. Most top-level managers ask people with a range of skills to help them analyze various aspects of the firm's operations. Macroeconomists, for example, through their study of trends in the global economy, often provide competitive insights to strategic leaders.[55] The process Rockwell International Corporation used to form a new corporate vision is one that involved the efforts of many people.

As explained in the Strategic Focus, some, but not all, top-level managers are thought to be charismatic strategic leaders. Although charisma is perceived as helpful, it is not a requirement for strategic leadership success. A key reason for this is that noncharismatic people often have other skills and traits—intelligence, vision, ambition, and toughness, for example—that provide benefits similar to those gained when one is thought to be charismatic. In certain situations, charismatic CEOs might facilitate better performance.

STRATEGIC FOCUS   Charisma: Strategic Leaders Who Have It, and Strategic Leaders Who Don't

Properly thought of as a relationship between a leader and subordinates rather than as a separate personality trait, charisma is associated with some well-known strategic leaders, but not with others. Jack Welch, General Electric's CEO, combines outrageous self-confidence, high-strung passion for ideas he unabashedly borrows, and unforgiving candor and appears to have charisma. Charlotte Beers, CEO at Ogilvy & Mather Worldwide, is unpredictable and difficult to work for. But humor, charm, and ingenuity helped her turn the ad giant around and Tony O'Reilly, H. J. Heinz's CEO, is a charming, pretentious Renaissance man. Extra-

Charisma is an attribute associated with Charlotte Beers and Tony O'Reilly.

curricular activities—he owns newspapers in his native Ireland—divert his attention. But, his star power enchants Heinz investors.

Other strategic leaders, however, are not perceived as charismatic. Michael Jordan, Westinghouse's CEO, seems not to have charisma. CBS execs thought that no CEO was less charismatic than their own Larry Tisch. Then, Westinghouse bought the company. Other CEOs who are typically not described as charismatic include Wal-Mart's David Glass. Though a fierce competitor, this earnest boss stands no chance in a personality contest with the larger-than-life Sam Walton. To inspire associates, Glass wisely milks the late founder's legacy. General Motors' Jack Smith is as charismatic as his name. He eschews TV cameras and the press. A pragmatic consensus builder, he accumulates power by giving it away. He has made GM shine even though he doesn't.

Perhaps to the disappointment of top-level managers interested in learning how to become charismatic, charisma is difficult to define and describe. Basically, it is a quality that we know only when we encounter it. Recognizing and studying the abilities that appear to be associated with charismatic people, however, can help managers become better strategic leaders. The most important of these abilities include those that allow people to (1) simplify and exaggerate—by using symbols, analogies, metaphors, and stories, charismatic leaders are skilled at reducing complex ideas to simple, yet powerful messages; (2) romanticize risk—charismatic leaders seek to be involved with projects and tasks that when completed successfully, allow them and their firm to perform at levels previously unattained; (3) defy the status quo—willing to fight convention, leaders with charisma seek out innovative ways for the firm to achieve high levels of success; (4) step into another's shoes—able to see and feel events and conditions from another person's perspective, charismatic leaders often are able to make each individual with whom they come into contact feel extremely important, and (5) spar and rile—challenging and prodding, charismatic leaders test people's courage, commitment, and intellect in efforts to motivate all individuals to accomplish a strategic intent that they may have thought impossible.

Not all strategic leaders can be charismatic, nor is it vital that they become so. Recall, for example, that even though he is not viewed as being charismatic, Jack Smith, GM's CEO, is considered to be an effective strategic leader. It is possible, however, that actions dedicated to enhancing one's skills (as discussed earlier) contribute positively to strategic leaders' efforts to help their firm reach its desired strategic outcomes.

Source: S. Finkelstein and D. C. Hambrick, 1996, *Strategic Leadership: Top Executives and Their Effects on Organizations* (St. Paul, Minn.: West Publishing Company), 69-72; P. Sellers, 1996, What exactly is charisma? *Fortune*, January 15, 68-75.

A charismatic CEO may help gain employees' commitment to a new vision and strategic direction. For all firms, it is important not to lose sight of the strengths of the organization when making strategic changes required by a new strategic direction. Achieving this objective demands the balancing of a firm's short-term needs with its long-term survival and growth. This suggests the necessity of emphasizing and maintaining core competencies.

■ Exploiting and Maintaining Core Competencies

Examined in Chapters 1 and 3, core competencies are resources and capabilities that serve as a source of competitive advantage for a firm over its rivals. Typically, core competencies relate to an organization's functional skills, such as manufacturing, finance, marketing, and research and development. As shown by the following descriptions, firms develop and exploit core competencies in many different functional areas while implementing their strategy. Strategic leaders must verify that the firm's competencies are emphasized in strategy implementation efforts. Recall, as described in the opening case, that several existing core competencies—including those of brand name and distribution channels—are being emphasized to implement Compaq Computer's new strategies to compete in the server and systems markets.

AEROJET, a manufacturer of propulsion systems and chemical products, is known for its core competence in the human resource function. In particular, AEROJET has been recognized as a firm that is able to motivate and retain its employees. Using more than 144 active work teams to design and complete tasks, empowered employees are a way of life at AEROJET. These cross-functional work teams facilitate the use of specialized knowledge in a team environment. In commenting about the firm's core competence, a top-level manager observed that "Our culture focuses on the power of the employee to make change and have ownership in the process."[56] Hewlett-Packard and Intel are thought to have core competencies in terms of competitive agility (an ability to act in a variety of competitively relevant ways) and competitive speed (an ability to act quickly when facing environmental and competitive pressures).[57] Retailer Nordstrom Inc.'s customer service is a core competence, although some analysts believe the firm's ability to select unique combinations of quality merchandise is an equally valuable core competence. Recently Nordstrom decided to use these competencies to launch a men's catalog. Addressing an emerging trend, this catalog emphasizes casual clothing, furnishings, and shoes. Product lines represented in Nordstrom's presentation to men include its own brand, Cole-Haan, Hickey Freeman, Nautica, Polo Sport, and Timberland.[58] Each of the core competencies we have described briefly serves as a source of a firm's competitive advantage over its rivals.

In many large firms, and certainly in diversified ones, core competencies are effectively exploited when they are developed and applied across different organizational units (see Chapter 6). This is demonstrated by Philip Morris applying its marketing and promotion competencies across multiple businesses. Its well-known rejuvenation of Miller Beer by applying its marketing expertise is considered a classic example. Additionally, Whirlpool has well known competencies that can be emphasized to create value across country borders.[59] In fact, some argue that the development, nurturing, and application of core competencies within multinational firms facilitates management of the complex relationships across businesses operating in different international markets.[60] Core competencies, however, cannot be developed or exploited effectively without appropriate human capital.

■ Developing Human Capital

■ *Human capital refers to the knowledge and skills of the firm's entire workforce.*

Human capital refers to the knowledge and skills of the firm's entire workforce. In other words, employees are viewed as a capital resource. Much of the development of U.S. industry can be attributed to the effectiveness of human capital. One-third of the growth in the U.S. gross national product from 1948 to 1982 was attributed to increases in the education level of the workforce. Fifty percent of this growth resulted from technical innovations and knowledge that also are based strongly on education. Only 15 percent of the growth of gross national product during this time was attributed to investment in capital equipment.[61] Outcomes such as these support the position, as discussed in Chapter 3, that "... as the dynamics of competition accelerate, people are perhaps the only truly sustainable source of competitive advantage."[62] In turn, the effective development and management of the firm's human capital—that is, of all of the firm's managerial and nonmanagerial personnel—may be the primary determinant of a firm's ability to formulate and implement strategies successfully.[63]

For individuals, active participation in company-sponsored programs to develop their abilities is highly desirable, in that being able to upgrade one's skills continuously leads to more job and economic security.[64] Increasingly, part of the development required to be selected as a strategic leader is an international experience. As a business analyst noted, "With nearly every industry targeting fast-growing foreign markets, more companies are requiring foreign experience for top management positions."[65] Thus, companies committed to the importance of competing successfully in the global economy provide opportunities for their future strategic leaders to work in locations other than their home nation.

Through participation in effective training and development programs, the probability increases that a manager will be a successful strategic leader. Among other outcomes, strategic leadership development programs help build skills and inculcate core values and a systematic view of the organization. Because development programs socialize and help inculcate a common set of core values, they promote the firm's strategic vision and organizational cohesion. Furthermore, they help strategic leaders improve skills that are critical to completing other tasks that are associated with effective strategic leadership (e.g., determining the firm's strategic direction, exploiting and maintaining core competencies, and developing an organizational culture that supports ethical practices). As described in the Strategic Focus, PepsiCo's CEO, Roger Enrico, helped to design a program that is intended to develop and train the firm's future strategic leaders.

The efforts at PepsiCo demonstrate an emphasis on developing strategic leaders so that they in turn can develop human capital in their areas of responsibility. This is an important challenge, given that most strategic leaders need to enhance their ability to develop employees.[66] When human capital investments are successful, the result is a workforce capable of learning continuously. Being able to learn continuously and to leverage the firm's expanding

STRATEGIC FOCUS

The Development and Training of Strategic Leaders at PepsiCo

Roger Enrico's recent selection as PepsiCo's CEO and chairman was expected to bring changes to the firm and to competitive practices in the beverage industry. Based on his previous turnarounds as the top strategic leader of PepsiCo's three major business units—beverages, restaurants, and snacks—Enrico had long been regarded as a probable successor to Wayne Calloway, the firm's former CEO and chairman.

In 1991, then-CEO Calloway exerted a major influence on PepsiCo's approach to the training and development of strategic leaders. Having discovered that PepsiCo's division presidents were spending no more than one-half of funds earmarked for leadership development, Calloway openly criticized his colleagues. In Calloway's opinion, not using these funds resulted in a missed opportunity to build the company's future. To deal with this issue, Calloway asked the firm's director of executive development (Paul Russell) to develop a world-class executive development program.

Critical to completing this assignment were the outcomes of Russell's extensive interviews with Roger Enrico. During these discussions, Enrico offered observations about his leadership experiences as a long-term member of PepsiCo's top management team. The 50-page document developed through these interviews became the foundation for PepsiCo's program called "Executive Leadership: Building the Business." This program begins with a five-day, off-site seminar led by Enrico. For the next 90 days, participants apply what they learned in the seminar while completing their regular jobs, remaining in close contact with Enrico in the process of doing so. The program concludes with a three-day workshop in which participants discuss their experiences and what they have learned over the previous three months. Because only nine people enroll in each program, they have ready access to Enrico.

Intended to train PepsiCo's future strategic leaders, this program is built around Enrico's five leadership tenets: (1) *Think in different terms*—effective strategic leaders work continuously on ideas that will drive competition in the future, not the present. Moreover, as soon as people are committed to implementing a newly developed idea, successful leaders begin working on the next one (2) *Develop a point of view*—strategic leaders must have a point of view on leadership, growing their business and creating change that they can teach to others (3) *Take it on the road*—effective strategic leaders are learners; they are open to new ideas and feedback and are willing to admit their mistakes (4) *Pull it all together*—successful strategic leadership demands that people fully understand the leader's goals and imperatives (5) *Make it happen*—effective strategic leaders are able to create an emotionally engaging process through which employees are willing to take risks and to learn from their experiences. To date, the evidence suggests that successful completion of this program enhances the skills of PepsiCo's future strategic leaders.

Source: R. Frank, 1996, Enrico to lead new generation at top of Pepsi, *Wall Street Journal,* February 23, B1, B5; R. Frank, 1996, Excitement brews in beverage industry as Enrico's rise at PepsiCo stirs market, *Wall Street Journal,* February 26, B8; M. Zimmerman, 1996, Enrico to lead PepsiCo, *Dallas Morning News,* February 23, D1, D3; N. Tichy and C. DeRose, 1995, Roger Enrico's master class, *Fortune,* November 27, 105–106.

knowledge base is linked with strategic success in the new competitive landscape.[67] At Johnson & Johnson, for example, the CEO stated, when asked to name what accounts for the firm's competitive success, that his company is ". . . not in the product business. (It) is in the knowledge business."[68]

It is important to continue the development of the firm's future strategic leaders, as described in the Strategic Focus on PepsiCo. Programs that gain outstanding results in the training of future strategic leaders become a competitive advantage for a firm. General Electric's system of training and development of future strategic leaders is comprehensive and thought to be among the best.[69] As such, this training system may be a source of competitive advantage for the firm.

As discussed in Chapter 7, millions of managers, strategic leaders, and nonmanagerial personnel have lost jobs in recent years through the restructuring and downsizing in many companies. In the mid-1980s, IBM employed 405,000 loyal workers; today, the firm employs around 225,000. During the 1990s, Sears shed 50,000 people; in 1996, AT&T announced its intended layoffs of up to 40,000 employees. The view of AT&T's CEO, Robert Allen, about his firm's intended job reductions, captures the sentiment of many strategic leaders facing this reality: "My company had to make the necessary, even painful changes today or forfeit the future."[70] Almost identically, Robert Eaton, Chrysler Corp.'s CEO, believes that "Downsizing and layoffs are part of the price of becoming more competitive. The price for not doing it, however, is much higher in both economic and human terms."[71]

It is important to note that company restructurings and the resulting job reductions are not just an American phenomenon. For example, the 1996-announced merger between Ciba-Geigy AG and Sandoz AG, which created the world's second largest drug maker with a broad array of products, was expected to result in losses of 10,000 of the combined firm's 134,000 workforce. The losses were to cut across employees—"managers, salespeople and researchers will be just as vulnerable as factory workers, (with locations) in the United States (a likely) major target."[72]

Regardless of the cause, layoffs can result in a significant loss of knowledge that is possessed by a firm's human capital. It is also not uncommon for restructuring firms to reduce their expenditures/investments in training and development programs. However, restructuring may be an important time to increase investment in such development. These firms have less slack and cannot absorb as many errors; moreover, many employees may be placed into positions without all of the skills or knowledge necessary to perform required tasks effectively.[73] In the final analysis, a view of employees as a resource to be maximized rather than a cost to be minimized facilitates successful implementation of a firm's strategies. The effectiveness of implementation processes also increases when strategic leaders approach layoffs in a manner that employees believe is fair and equitable.[74]

As described next, human capital is an important part of the firm's ability to develop and sustain an effective organizational culture.

Sustaining an Effective Organizational Culture

An *organizational culture* consists of a complex set of ideologies, symbols, and core values that is shared throughout the firm and influences the way it conducts business. Evidence suggests that a firm can develop core competencies both in terms of the capabilities it possesses and the way the capabilities are used to produce strategic actions. In other words, because it influences how the firm conducts its business and helps regulate and control employee behavior, organizational culture can be a source of competitive advantage.[75] Thus, shaping the context within which the firm formulates and implements its strategies—that is, shaping the organizational culture—is a central task of strategic leaders.[76]

Hewlett-Packard provides an example of the potential power of culture. The core values of this firm's culture are grounded in the basic belief that ". . . men and women want to do a good job, a creative job, and that if they are provided the proper environment, they will do so."[77] Bear Stearns Co.'s culture, too, is a competitive advantage. Thought of as an anomaly on Wall Street, Bear Stearns has followed a path that differs from the one chosen by its major competitors, electing not to become highly structured, multilayered, and broadly diversified in the process of doing so. Instead, ". . . 'the Bear' retains the feeling of an informal, old-fashioned partnership run by partners who take a visceral interest in their trading positions. Its culture stresses entrepreneurship, thriftiness, and performance." This culture has contributed to the firm's historical ability to simultaneously mine opportunities and sidestep disasters.[78] An effective organizational culture encourages and supports an entrepreneurial orientation.

■ Entrepreneurial Orientation

Encouragement (or discouragement) of the pursuit of entrepreneurial opportunities, especially in large firms, is often affected by organizational culture.[79] At AlliedSignal, culture is used to encourage employees to develop an entrepreneurial orientation leading to the pursuit of new business opportunities outside the United States. In fact, CEO Lawrence Bossidy wants the percentage of the firm's sales revenues earned overseas to increase from 38 to 45 percent by 1997.[80] Pursuit of opportunities such as these must be rewarded and the penalty for failure minimized. At Bear Stearns, for example, rich rewards accrue to employees who excel in the culture's virtues of entrepreneurship, thriftiness, and performance.[81]

Successful outcomes derived through employees' pursuit of entrepreneurial opportunities are a major source of growth and innovation for firms competing in today's complex, globalized environment. Innovation, and the culture that nurtures it, may account for Magna International Inc.'s ability to earn above-average returns. A manufacturer of a range of products, including air bags, seating systems, mirrors, and bumpers, Magna has grown at a compound rate of 21 percent annually for a decade. Some analysts believe that "Magna's great strength is the entrepreneurial culture that (CEO Frank) Stronach has created. By offering employees huge financial incentives, Stronach has made profit-oriented innovation one of Magna's key products."[82]

Five dimensions are thought to characterize a firm's entrepreneurial orientation (EO).[83] In combination, these dimensions influence the activities a firm uses in efforts to be innovative and to launch new ventures. Discussed in Chapter 13, one of the key ways new ventures are launched in large firms is through internal corporate entrepreneurship. Particularly for firms seeking first-mover advantages (see Chapter 5), an entrepreneurial orientation among employees is critical.

Autonomy is the first of an EO's five dimensions. Autonomy is an active part of a firm's culture when employees are able to take actions that are free of stifling organizational constraints. Generally, autonomy allows individuals and groups to be self-directed in the pursuit of entrepreneurial opportunities. The second dimension, *innovativeness,* "reflects a firm's tendency to engage in and support new ideas, novelty, experimentation, and creative processes that may result in new products, services, or technological processes."[84] Cultures with a tendency toward innovativeness encourage employees to think beyond existing knowledge, technologies, and parameters in efforts to find creative ways to add value. *Risk taking* reflects a willingness by employees and their firm to accept risks in the pursuit of marketplace opportunities. These risks can include assuming significant levels of debt and allocating large amounts of other resources (e.g., people) to risky projects. Often, these risks are accepted to seize marketplace opportunities that can substantially increase the firm's strategic competitiveness and its returns. The fourth EO dimension, *proactiveness*, describes a firm's ability to be a market leader rather than a follower. Proactive organizational cultures constantly use processes to anticipate future market needs and to satisfy them before competitors learn how to do so. Finally, *competitive aggressiveness* is a firm's propensity to take actions that allow it to outperform its rivals consistently and substantially. Thus, the key dimensions that characterize an EO include acting autonomously, a willingness to innovate and take risks, and a tendency to be aggressive toward competitors and proactive relative to marketplace opportunities.[85]

■ Changing Organizational Culture and Reengineering

Changing organizational culture is more difficult than maintaining it. But effective strategic leadership also involves recognizing the need to change the organizational culture. Incremental changes to the firm's culture typically are used to implement strategies more effectively; more significant and sometimes even radical changes to organizational culture are designed to support the selection of strategies that differ from the ones the firm has implemented historically. Regardless of the reasons for change, shaping and reinforcing of a new culture requires effective communication and problem solving, along with the selection of the right people (those who have the values managers wish to infuse throughout the organization), effective performance appraisals (establishing goals and measuring individual performance toward those goals that fit with the new core values), and appropriate reward systems (rewarding the desired behaviors that reflect the new core values).[86]

Evidence suggests that cultural changes succeed only when they are supported actively by the firm's CEO, other key top management team members, and middle-level managers.[87] In fact, for large-scale changes to organizational culture, approximately one-third of middle-level managers should be effective change agents. These change agents ". . . have a nice balance of capabilities: They are technically skilled people who are also very capable in personal relationships. They're an odd combination. On the one hand, they're tough decision-makers who are highly disciplined about performance results. But they also know how to get lots of people energized and aligned in the same direction."[88]

One catalyst for change in organizational culture, particularly for critical changes, is the selection of new top management team members from outside the corporation. Company founder and CEO Michael Dell of Dell Computer Corp., who pioneered the direct marketing of computers to customers, recently recruited executives from companies such as Motorola, Hewlett-Packard, and Apple Computer to deal with problems the firm encountered in late 1993 and early 1994. Interestingly, Dell is 10 years younger than the next youngest member of the newly formed top management team.[89]

A key member of Dell's new team is Mort Topfer, a former Motorola executive. As vice chairman, Topfer has changed Dell Computer's organizational culture. Prior to his arrival, relatively few control systems were in place. For example, the company lacked a clear understanding of the ". . . relationships between costs and revenues and profits and losses within the different lines of business."[90] Relying on discipline and planning, Topfer designed a number of strategic and financial control systems that affect both the selection and implementation of Dell Computer's strategies. Michael Dell believes that Topfer's contributions have helped his firm change from a relatively undisciplined organizational culture to one that is more focused on sustained performance and market momentum.[91] Working together effectively, Dell Computer Corp.'s top management team has collectively accepted the responsibility for running the firm successfully and for initiating required changes to its organizational culture.[92]

Business reengineering is the fundamental rethinking and radical redesign of business processes to achieve dramatic improvements in performance in such areas as cost, quality, service, and speed.[93] It is a technique used by companies to survive and succeed in the new competitive landscape. Business reengineering is of significant benefit to strategic leaders seeking ways to implement chosen strategies more effectively and perhaps change the organization's culture in the process of doing so. By focusing on the activities necessary to transform materials into a good or service that is valuable to customers, business reengineering challenges firms to find ways to increase dramatically the effectiveness and efficiency of their organizational culture. For a differentiation business-level strategy (see Chapter 4), reengineering efforts are directed at finding ways to more sharply and meaningfully differentiate the firm's products from competitors' offerings. Similarly, firms implementing a cost leadership business-level strategy (see Chapter 4) use business reengineering to drive their costs lower than competitors.

The benefits of reengineering are attained through the efforts of dedicated employees. Business reengineering success is maximized when employees believe that (1) every job in the company is essential and important, (2) all employees must create value through their work, (3) constant learning is a vital part of every person's job, (4) teamwork is essential to implementation success, and (5) problems are solved only when teams accept the responsibility for their solution.[94] These beliefs and commitments appear to exist at Phillips Petroleum Company. In commenting about why the firm's performance improved, CEO Wayne Allen suggested that improvement ". . . often comes down to our employees finding better ways to do their jobs. One change is that we're working more in teams, and we're finding this approach to be successful. In almost any effort, teamwork leads to better results."[95]

■ Emphasizing Ethical Practices

The effectiveness of strategy implementation processes increases when they are grounded in ethical practices. Ethical companies encourage and enable people at all organizational levels to exercise ethical judgment. To properly influence employee judgment and behavior, ethical practices must shape the firm's decision-making process and be an integral part of an organization's culture. Once accepted, ethical practices serve as a moral filter through which potential courses of action are evaluated.[96]

Surveys conducted by the Center for Business Ethics at Bentley College provide an interesting snapshot of corporate actions that promote ethical practices. The center administered a survey in the mid-1980s and again at the end of the decade, with feedback from 244 major corporations. Results showed that at the end of the decade more corporations were focusing on promoting ethical practices than was the case in the mid-1980s. A more recent survey found that 93 percent of the firms were taking active steps to incorporate ethical values into their daily operations. This has been accomplished by developing codes of ethics, implementing ethics training programs for managers and employees, and developing ethics committees. An overwhelming percentage of the responding firms (96 percent) felt that they had made satisfactory progress toward achieving their goals. However, only 18 percent of the respondents felt significant public pressure to develop ethical policies and practices. Fifty-seven percent of the respondents felt no or very little such pressure. Thus, managers are cognizant of the importance of ethical practices and are implementing them without feeling pressure from external sources (e.g., customers, government agencies, etc.).[97] Promoting ethical practices is good business sense for many reasons, not the least of which is that it promotes a positive reputation with stakeholders.

The results of the survey suggest that a number of firms have instituted training programs in ethics and have developed codes of ethics. Nonetheless, potential problems remain. For example, some have questioned the potential exploitation of management buyouts (often in the form of leveraged buyouts, described in Chapter 7), because of the concern for managerial opportunism.

Managerial opportunism occurs when managers take actions that are in their own best interests, but not in the firm's best interests. In other words, managers take advantage of their positions and therefore make decisions that benefit them to the detriment of the owners (shareholders).[98] An implicit assumption of the agency model described in Chapter 10's discussion of corporate governance is that top-level managers may act as opportunistic agents who will capitalize on every chance to maximize personal welfare at the expense of shareholders. Individual opportunism is well documented by Wall Street insider trading scandals and other actions taken by those who financed large leveraged buyouts and acquisitions.[99] Other potential problems that have been documented include questionable hiring practices and a willingness to commit fraud by understating write-offs that reduce corporate returns.[100] It is possible, too, that very high CEO compensation is a sign of opportunism being pursued by those in the upper echelons of management.[101]

Another set of studies sheds light on these issues. Research examining managers' ethical values and beliefs in the mid-1980s and again in the early 1990s showed little change. At both times, managers emphasized utilitarian goals, that is, the achievement of economic gains for the organization's stakeholders. In fact, the earlier survey found that one of the primary reasons managers emphasized ethical practices was to achieve greater profits. Some argue that the managerial and organizational gains are mutually beneficial. In other words, firms that establish and maintain ethical practices are more likely to achieve strategic competitiveness and earn above-average returns. A key reason for this is that a reputation for ethical practices attracts loyal customers.[102]

However, recent evidence suggests that at least some individuals from different groups—including top-level executives and business students—may be willing to commit either illegal actions (e.g., fraud) or actions that many think are unethical. In one study, researchers found that 47 percent of upper-level executives, 41 percent of controllers, and 76 percent of graduate-level business students expressed a willingness to commit fraud (as measured by a subject's willingness to misrepresent his/her company's financial statements). Moreover, these researchers discovered that 87 percent of the managers made at least one fraudulent decision out of a total of seven situations requiring a decision. Another interesting finding from this work is that the more an individual valued a comfortable life and/or pleasure, and the less he or she valued self-respect, the greater was the probability that a fraudulent decision would be made.[103]

Events alleged to have occurred in one company seem to support the need for organizations to have an ethical culture. A suit filed by a former high-level executive claims that "by using suspect methods to boost revenue and reduce costs . . . management was able to meet aggressive corporate targets. . . ." In response to the suit, the firm publicly announced that: "The case is absolutely without merit. We deny each and every allegation made by the plaintiff. We will aggressively defend our position and fully expect to prevail."[104] The outcome of this matter is to be determined. Nonetheless, the possibility that fraudulent reporting methods were used highlights the need for top-level managers to develop and support ethical organizations—ones in which the consistent use of ethical practices is enforced.

Another study's results appear to have important implications for organizations and those who manage them.[105] The study found that although cheating was observed, there was reluctance to report it. An unwillingness to report wrongdoing calls for the development of comprehensive organizational control systems to assure that individuals' behaviors are consistent with the firm's needs and expectations.

Thus, these studies' findings seem to support the need for firms to employ ethical strategic leaders—ones who include ethical practices as part of their long-term vision for the firm, who desire to do the right thing, and for whom honesty, trust, and integrity are important.[106] Strategic leaders who consistently display these qualities inspire employees as they work with others to develop and support an organizational culture in which ethical practices are the expected behavioral norms. For instance, Stan Shih, CEO of Acer Computer, states that for his firm's employees, there is no alternative to dealing honestly with people. Shih's belief that human nature is basically good may be the driving force behind his forthright and ethical practices.[107]

As our discussion suggests, strategic leaders are challenged to take actions that increase the probability that an ethical culture will exist in their organization. When these efforts are successful, the practices associated with an ethical culture become institutionalized in the firm; that is, they become the set of behavioral commitments and actions accepted by most of the firm's employees and other stakeholders with whom employees interact. Actions that strategic leaders can take to develop an ethical organizational culture include (1) establishing and communicating specific goals to describe the firm's ethical standards (e.g., developing and disseminating a code of conduct), (2) continuously revising and updating the code of conduct, based on inputs from people throughout the firm and from other stakeholders (e.g., customers and suppliers), (3) disseminating the code of conduct to all stakeholders to inform them of the firm's ethical standards and practices, (4) developing and implementing methods and procedures to use in achieving the firm's ethical standards (e.g., use of internal auditing practices that are consistent with the standards), (5) creating and using explicit reward systems that recognize acts of courage (e.g., rewarding those who use proper channels and procedures to report observed wrongdoings), and (6) creating a work environment in which all people are treated with dignity.[108] The effectiveness of these actions increases when they are taken simultaneously; the six major actions support one another. A failure to develop and engage in all six actions reduces the likelihood that the firm can establish an ethical culture. Moreover, when strategic leaders engage successfully in these actions they serve as moral role models—for the firm's employees and other stakeholders.

Organizational control systems can help to foster ethical practices and other areas important for the exercise of strategic leadership.

Establishing Balanced Organizational Controls

Organizational controls have long been viewed as an important part of strategy implementation processes. Controls are necessary to help ensure that firms achieve their desired outcomes of strategic competitiveness and above-average returns.[109] Defined as the ". . . formal, information-based . . . procedures used by managers to maintain or alter patterns in organizational activities," controls help strategic leaders build credibility, demonstrate the value of strategies to the firm's stakeholders, and promote and support strategic change.[110] Most critically, controls provide the parameters within which strategies are to be implemented as well as corrective actions to be taken when implementation-related adjustments are required. In this chapter, we focus on two organizational controls—strategic and financial—that were introduced in Chapter 11. Our discussion of organizational controls in this chapter emphasizes strategic and financial controls because strategic leaders are responsible for their development and effective use.

Although critical to the firm's success, evidence suggests that organizational controls are imperfect. "Consider the spate of control failures that have made headlines in the past several years: Kidder, Peabody & Company lost $350 million when a trader allegedly booked fictitious profits; Sears, Roebuck and Co. took a $60 million charge against earnings after admitting that it recommended unnecessary repairs to customers in its automobile service business; (and) Standard Chartered Bank was banned from trading on the Hong Kong stock market after being implicated in an improper share support scheme."[111] Control failures such as these have a negative effect on the firm's reputation and divert managerial attention from actions necessary to use the strategic management process effectively.

As explained in Chapter 11, financial controls are often emphasized in large corporations. Financial controls focus on short-term financial outcomes, as opposed to the strategic actions employed. In contrast, strategic control focuses on the *content* of strategic actions, rather than their *outcomes*. Because there are multiple effects on financial outcomes, some strategic actions can be correct, but result in poor financial outcomes (caused by recessionary economic problems, unexpected domestic or foreign government actions, and natural disasters, etc.). Therefore, an emphasis on financial control often produces more short-term and risk-averse managerial decisions. Alternatively, strategic controls encourage lower level managers to make decisions that incorporate moderate and acceptable levels of risk.

Successful strategic leaders balance strategic control and financial control (they do not eliminate financial control) with the intent of achieving more positive long-term returns.[112] In fact, most corporate restructuring action is designed to refocus the firm on its core businesses, thereby allowing top-level executives to reestablish strategic control of their separate business units.[113]

Effective use of strategic control by top-level managers is integrated frequently with appropriate autonomy for the various subunits so that they can better gain competitive advantage in their respective markets. Strategic control can be used to promote the sharing of both tangible and intangible resources among interdependent businesses within a firm's portfolio. In addition, the autonomy provided allows the flexibility necessary to take advantage of specific marketplace opportunities. As a result, strategic leadership promotes the simultaneous use of strategic control and autonomy.[114]

Interestingly, the new CEO of Time Warner's Home Box Office has indicated that both financial and strategic controls are necessary for his firm to be successful. Challenged to keep HBO as a "must-have" for its almost 21 million subscribers, Jeffrey Bewkes is committed to finding ways for his firm to continue offering programs that viewers cannot find anywhere else. To accomplish this goal, Bewkes decided to increase HBO's 1996 programming budget by 10 percent over the previous year's allocation. Among the strategic controls used by Bewkes are frequent interactions with the firm's "creative" executives and personnel and a commitment to support and nurture HBO's efforts to expand internationally (into Latin America and China, as examples). Because Bewkes "... came up on the financial side at HBO," he is knowledgeable about the financial controls required for the firm to reach its shorter range performance goals.[115] Therefore, Bewkes has achieved an effective balance between strategic and financial controls. However, he emphasizes strategic controls when a significant strategic decision is to be made.

As our discussion suggests, organizational controls establish an integrated set of analyses and actions that reinforce one another. Through effective use of strategic controls, strategic leaders increase the probability that their firm will gain the benefits of carefully formulated strategies, but not at the expense of the financial control that is a critical part of the strategy implementation process. Effective organizational controls provide an underlying logic for strategic leadership, focus attention on critical strategic issues, support a competitive culture, and provide a forum that builds commitment to strategic intent.

■ Summary

- Effective strategic leadership is required to use the strategic management process successfully, including the strategic actions associated with the implementation of strategies. Strategic leadership entails the ability to anticipate, envision, maintain flexibility, and empower others to create strategic change.

- Top-level managers are an important resource that is required for the firm to develop and exploit competitive advantages. In addition, strategic leaders can be a

source of competitive advantage. Top executives exercise discretion in making critical strategic decisions.

- The top management team is composed of key managers who formulate and implement strategies. Generally, they are officers of the corporation and/or members of the board of directors.

- There is a relationship among top management team characteristics, firm strategy, and performance. For example, a top management team that has significant marketing and R&D knowledge often enhances the firm's effectiveness as the team steers the firm toward implementation of growth strategies. Overall, most top management teams are more effective when they have diverse and heterogeneous skills.

- When boards of directors are involved in shaping strategic direction, firms generally improve their strategic competitiveness. Alternatively, boards may be less involved in strategic decisions, about strategy formulation and strategy implementation, when CEOs have more power. CEOs obtain power when they appoint people to the board and when they simultaneously serve the firm as its CEO and board chair.

- Strategic leaders are selected from either the internal or the external managerial labor market. Because of their effect on firm performance, the selection of strategic leaders from these markets has implications for a firm's effectiveness. Valid reasons exist to use both labor markets when selecting strategic leaders and managers with the potential to become strategic leaders. The internal market is used in the majority of cases to select the firm's CEO. Outsiders often are selected to initiate needed change.

- Effective strategic leadership has six components: determining the firm's strategic direction, exploiting and maintaining core competencies, developing human capital, sustaining an effective organizational culture, emphasizing ethical practices, and establishing balanced organizational controls.

- Often requiring a significant amount of thinking and time to form, determining strategic direction refers to the development of a long-term vision of the firm's previously framed strategic intent. A charismatic leader can help achieve strategic intent.

- Strategic leaders must verify that their firm exploits its core competencies, used to create and deliver products that create value for customers, to implement strategies. In diversified and large firms, in particular, core competencies are exploited effectively when they are shared across units and products.

- A critical element of strategic leadership and effective strategy implementation processes is the ability to develop the firm's human capital. Effective strategic leaders and firms view human capital as a resource to be maximized rather than as a cost to be minimized. Resulting from this perspective is the use of programs intended to train current and future strategic leaders so they will have the skills needed to nurture and develop the rest of the firm's human capital.

- Shaping the firm's culture is a central task of effective strategic leadership. In the new competitive landscape, an appropriate organizational culture encourages the development of an entrepreneurial orientation among employees and an ability to change the culture as necessary. Reengineering can facilitate this process.

- In ethical organizations, employees are enabled and encouraged to exercise ethical judgment and to display only ethical practices. Ethical practices can be promoted through several actions, including those of setting specific goals to describe the firm's ethical standards, using a code of conduct, rewarding ethical behaviors, and creating a work environment in which all people are treated with dignity.

- The final component of effective strategic leadership is the development and use of effective organizational controls. It is through organizational controls that strategic leaders provide the direction the firm requires to flexibly, yet appropriately use its core competencies in the pursuit of marketplace opportunities. Best results are obtained when there is a balance between strategic and financial controls.

■ Review Questions

1. What is strategic leadership? In what ways are top-level managers considered important resources for an organization?

2. What is a top management team and how does it affect a firm's performance and its abilities to innovate and make appropriate strategic changes?

3. What are the differences between the internal and external managerial labor markets? What are the effects of each labor market type on the formulation and implementation of firm strategy?

4. How does strategic leadership affect determination of the firm's strategic direction?

5. Why is it important for strategic leaders to make certain that their firm exploits its core competencies in the pursuit of strategic competitiveness and above-average returns?

6. What is the importance of human capital and its development for strategic competitiveness?

7. What is organizational culture? What must strategic leaders do to sustain an effective organizational culture?

8. As a strategic leader, what actions could you take to establish and emphasize ethical practices in your firm?

9. What are organizational controls? Why are strategic controls and financial controls, two types of organizational controls, an important part of the strategic management process?

Application Discussion Questions

1. Choose a CEO of a prominent firm you believe exemplifies the positive aspects of strategic leadership. What actions does this CEO take that demonstrate effective strategic leadership? What are the effects of these actions on the firm's performance?

2. Select a CEO of a prominent firm you believe does not exemplify the positive aspects of strategic leadership. What actions does this CEO take that are inconsistent with effective strategic leadership? How have these ineffective actions affected the firm's performance?

3. What are managerial resources? What is the relationship between managerial resources and a firm's strategic competitiveness?

4. By examining popular press articles, select an organization that has recently gone through a significant strategic change. While reading these articles, collect as much information as you can about the organization's top management team. Does your analysis suggest that there is a relationship between the top management team's characteristics and the type of change the organization experienced? If so, what is the nature and outcome of that relationship?

5. Through a reading of popular press articles, identify two new CEOs—one chosen from the internal managerial labor market and one from the external labor market. Based on your reading, why do you think these individuals were chosen? What do they bring to the job and what strategy do you think they will implement in the future?

6. In light of your reading of this chapter and popular press accounts, select a CEO you feel has exhibited vision. Has the CEO's vision been realized? If so, what have the effects been of its realization? If it has not been realized, why not?

7. Identify a firm in which you believe strategic leaders have emphasized and developed human capital. What do you believe are the effects of this emphasis and development on the firm's performance?

8. Select an organization you think has a unique organizational culture. What characteristics of that culture make it unique? Has the culture had a significant effect on the organization's performance? If so, what is that effect?

9. Why is the strategic control exercised by a firm's strategic leaders important for long-term competitiveness? How do strategic controls differ from financial controls?

Ethics Questions

1. As discussed in this chapter, effective strategic leadership occasionally requires managers to make difficult decisions. In your opinion, is it ethical for managers to make these types of decisions without being willing to receive feedback from employees about the effects of those decisions? Be prepared to justify your response.

2. As an employee with less than one year of experience in a firm, what actions would you pursue if you encountered unethical practices by a strategic leader?

3. In your opinion, are firms obligated ethically to promote from within, rather than relying on the external labor market to select strategic leaders? What reasoning supports your position?

4. What are the ethical issues involved, if any, with the firm's ability to develop and exploit a core competence in the manufacture of goods that may be harmful to consumers (e.g., cigarettes)? Be prepared to discuss the reasons for your response.

5. As a strategic leader, would you feel ethically responsible to develop your firm's human capital? Why or why not? Do you believe your position is consistent with the majority or minority of today's strategic leaders?

6. Select an organization, social group, or volunteer agency in which you hold membership that you believe has an ethical culture. What factors caused this culture to be ethical? Are there events that could occur that would cause this culture to become less ethical? If so, what are they?

Internet Exercises

Go to Hoover's at:

http://www.hoovers.com/

Select several corporations from the "Corporate Directory" and review the CEO's message at each. Compare their visions and values. Are the differences due to the industry or the CEO? Do you find any to be inspiring? What do they reveal about the organization or its leader?

Chapter Internet Exercise

You have visited numerous corporate Home Pages during the semester. Go back to several and review the CEO message at each or other information from an executive. Compare their visions and values. Are the differences due to the industry or the CEO? Do you find any inspiring? What do they reveal about the organization or its leader?

Cohesion Case

Send an E-mail message to your teammates that discusses what you have learned in this class that will help you manage in the future. Based on the members' learning, select an individual to be the strategic leader of your team. As a group, decide on that person's responsibilities to complete the cohesion case project.

▇ Notes

1. D. Lei, M. A. Hitt, and R. Bettis, 1996, Dynamic core competencies through meta-learning and strategic context, *Journal of Management* 22: 547–567; A. A. Lado, N. G. Boyd, and P. Wright, 1992, A competency based model of sustainable competitive advantage: Toward a conceptual integration, *Journal of Management* 18: 77–91.
2. S. Finkelstein and D. C. Hambrick, 1996, *Strategic Leadership: Top Executives and Their Effects on Organizations* (St. Paul, Minn.: West Publishing Company), 2; R. D. Ireland, M. A. Hitt, and D. L. Sexton, 1996, Cooperative networks: The key to strategic innovation and competitive success in dynamic entrepreneurial firms, paper presented at the Strategic Management Society conference; The top managers of 1995, 1996, *Fortune,* January 8, 50–60; J. P. Kotter, 1995, Leading change: Why transformation efforts fail, *Harvard Business Review* 73, no. 2: 59–67; D. C. Hambrick, 1989, Guest editor's introduction: Putting top managers back in the strategy picture, *Strategic Management Journal* 10: 5–16.
3. H. Gardner, 1995, *Leading Minds: An Anatomy of Leadership* (New York: Basic Books); S. Sherman, 1995, How tomorrow's best leaders are learning their stuff, *Fortune,* November 27, 90–102.
4. J. B. Quinn, P. Anderson, and S. Finkelstein, 1996, Managing professional intellect: Making the most of the best, *Harvard Business Review* 74, no. 2: 71–80.
5. M. Loeb, 1994, Where leaders come from, *Fortune,* September 19, 241–242.
6. M. F. R. Kets de Vries, 1995, *Life and Death in the Executive Fast Lane* (San Francisco: Jossey-Bass).
7. G. Hamel and C. K. Prahalad, 1993, Strategy as stretch and leverage, *Harvard Business Review* 71, no. 2: 75–84.
8. Sherman, How tomorrow's best, 99; R. Calori, G. Johnson, and P. Sarnin, 1994, CEOs' cognitive maps and the scope of the organization, *Strategic Management Journal* 15: 437–457.
9. L. Kraar, 1995, Acer's edge: PCs to go, *Fortune,* October 30, 187–204; Loeb, Where leaders come from, 241; N. Nohria and J. D. Berkley, 1994, Whatever happened to the take-charge manager? *Harvard Business Review* 72, no. 1: 128–137.
10. J. Treffer, 1994, Post-heroic leadership—a comment, *Fortune,* April 4, 45–46.
11. Sherman, How tomorrow's best, 102; D. L. Bradford and A. R. Cohen, 1994, Post-heroic leadership—a comment, *Fortune,* March 21, 29.
12. Finkelstein and Hambrick, *Strategic Leadership,* 2; J. Hagel, III, 1993, The CEO as chief performance officer, *McKinsey Quarterly* 1993, no. 4: 16–28.
13. J. P. Kotter, 1990, What leaders really do, *Harvard Business Review* 68, no. 3: 103–111.
14. Sherman, How tomorrow's best, 102.
15. M. A. Hitt, B. W. Keats, H. F. Harback, and R. D. Nixon, 1994, Rightsizing: Building and maintaining strategic leadership and long-term competitiveness, *Organizational Dynamics* 23: 18–32; R. L. Priem and D. A. Harrison, 1994, Exploring strategic judgment: Methods for testing the assumptions of prescriptive contingency theories, *Strategic Management Journal* 15: 311–324.
16. M. J. Waller, G. P. Huber, and W. H. Glick, 1995, Functional background as a determinant of executives' selective perception, *Academy of Management Journal* 38: 943–974; N. Rajagopalan, A. M. Rasheed, and D. K. Datta, 1993, Strategic decision processes: Critical review and future directions, *Journal of Management* 19: 349–384.
17. Finkelstein and Hambrick, *Strategic Leadership,* 26–34; D. C. Hambrick and E. Abrahamson, 1995, Assessing managerial discretion across industries: A multimethod approach, *Academy of Management Journal* 38: 1427–1441; D. C. Hambrick and S. Finkelstein, 1987, Managerial discretion: A bridge between polar views of organizational outcomes, in B. Staw and L. L. Cummings (eds.), *Research in Organizational Behavior* (Greenwich, Conn.: JAI Press), 369–406.
18. R. C. Mayer, J. H. Davis, and F. D. Schoorman, 1995, An integrative model of organizational trust, *Academy of Management Review* 20: 709–734.
19. N. Rajagopalan and D. K. Datta, 1996, CEO characteristics: Does industry matter? *Academy of Management Journal* 39: 197–215.
20. Associated Press, 1996, Wal-Mart, Inc. stock dips as executive joins Blockbuster, *Dallas Morning News,* March 30, F2; E. Shapiro and S. Pulliam, 1996, Viacom to name Wal-Mart's heir apparent, William Fields, to head Blockbuster Video, *Wall Street Journal,* March 29, C2.
21. A. C. Amason, 1996, Distinguishing the effects of functional and dysfunctional conflict on strategic decision making: Resolving a paradox for top management teams, *Academy of Management Journal* 39: 123–148; Priem and Harrison, Exploring strategic judgment, 311.
22. C. M. Farkas and P. De Backer, 1996, There are only five ways to lead, *Fortune,* January 15, 109–112.
23. Ibid., 110.
24. Loeb, Where leaders come from, 242.
25. J. G. Michel and D. C. Hambrick, 1992, Diversification posture and top management team characteristics, *Academy of Management Journal* 35: 9–37.
26. Amason, Distinguishing the effects, 123; K. G. Smith, D. A. Smith, J. D. Olian, H. P. Sims, Jr., D. P. O'Bannon, and J. A. Scully, 1994, Top management team demography and process: The role of social integration and communication, *Administrative Science Quarterly* 39: 412–438.
27. Amason, Distinguishing the effects, 127.
28. K. Pope, 1995, Cable & Wireless, hurt by tougher rivals, is losing phone wars, *Wall Street Journal,* September 27, A1, A3.

29. Finkelstein and Hambrick, *Strategic Leadership,* 148.

30. D. K. Datta and J. P. Guthrie, 1994, Executive succession: Organizational antecedents of CEO characteristics, *Strategic Management Journal* 15: 569–577; M. A. Hitt and R. D. Ireland, 1986, Relationships among corporate-level distinctive competencies, diversification strategy, corporate structure, and performance, *Journal of Management Studies* 23: 401–416; M. A. Hitt and R. D. Ireland, 1985, Corporate distinctive competence, strategy, industry, and performance, *Strategic Management Journal* 6: 273–293.

31. M. F. Wiersema and K. Bantel, 1992, Top management team demography and corporate strategic change, *Academy of Management Journal* 35: 91–121; K. Bantel and S. Jackson, 1989, Top management and innovations in banking: Does the composition of the top team make a difference? *Strategic Management Journal* 10: 107–124.

32. I. Sager and A. Cortese, 1995, At IBM, the great shrink-down may be over, *Business Week,* September 25, 58.

33. W. Q. Judge, Jr., and C. P. Zeithaml, 1992, Institutional and strategic choice perspectives on board involvement in the strategic decision process, *Academy of Management Journal* 35: 766–794; J. A. Pearce II and S. A. Zahra, 1991, The relative power of CEOs and boards of directors: Associations with corporate performance, *Strategic Management Journal* 12: 135–154.

34. J. D. Westphal and E. J. Zajac, 1995, Who shall govern? CEO/board power, demographic similarity, and new director selection, *Administrative Science Quarterly* 40: 60.

35. Ibid., 66; E. J. Zajac and J. D. Westphal, 1995, Accounting for the explanations of CEO compensation: Substance and symbolism, *Administrative Science Quarterly* 40: 283–308.

36. B. K. Boyd, 1995, CEO duality and firm performance: A contingency model, *Strategic Management Journal* 16: 301.

37. C. M. Daily and D. R. Dalton, 1995, CEO and director turnover in failing firms: An illusion of change? *Strategic Management Journal* 16: 393–400.

38. L. Donaldson and J. H. Davis, 1991, Stewardship theory or agency theory: CEO governance and shareholder returns, *Australian Journal of Management* 16: 49–64.

39. B. R. Baliga and R. C. Moyer, 1996, CEO duality and firm performance: What's the fuss? *Strategic Management Journal* 17: 41–53.

40. Zajac and Westphal, Accounting for the explanations, 292; A. K. Buchholtz and B. A. Ribbens, 1994, Role of chief executive officers in takeover resistance: Effects of CEO incentives and individual characteristics, *Academy of Management Journal* 37: 554–579; C. Hill and P. Phan, 1991, CEO tenure as a determinant of CEO pay, *Academy of Management Journal* 34: 707–717.

41. Rajagopalan and Datta, CEO characteristics, 201.

42. R. A. Johnson, R. E. Hoskisson and M. A. Hitt, 1993, Board involvement in restructuring: The effect of board versus managerial controls and characteristics, *Strategic Management Journal,* 14 (Special Issue): 33–50.

43. B. K. Boyd, 1995, CEO duality and firm performance: A contingency model, *Strategic Management Journal* 16: 301–312.

44. Ibid.

45. Sherman, How tomorrow's best, 92.

46. D. Woodruff and M. Maremont, 1995, GM learns to love an outsider, *Business Week,* July 3, 32.

47. Datta and Guthrie, Executive succession, 570.

48. Finkelstein and Hambrick, *Strategic Leadership,* 180–181.

49. D. Miller, 1991, Stale in the saddle: CEO tenure and the match between organization and environment, *Management Science* 37: 34–52.

50. S. L. Hwang, 1995, RJR's CEO Harper quits his position, *Wall Street Journal,* December 6, A3, A4.

51. J. E. Ettlie, 1996, Review of *The Perpetual Enterprise Machine: Seven Keys to Corporate Renewal Through Successful Product and Process Development,* E. Bowman (ed.) (New York: Oxford University Press), appearing in *Academy of Management Journal* 21: 294–298; Hitt et al., Rightsizing, 20.

52. Texaco Inc., 1995, *Annual Report,* 22.

53. Kraar, Acer's edge, 188; L. Larwood, C. M. Falbe, M. P. Kriger, and P. Miesing, 1995, Structure and meaning of organizational vision, *Academy of Management Journal* 39: 740–769.

54. Rockwell International Corporation, 1995, Its time to change your perception of Rockwell, *Annual Report,* 2–5.

55. Farkas and De Backer, There are only five ways, 109; B. Wysocki, Jr., 1995, As firms downsize, business economists find jobs dwindling, *Wall Street Journal,* October 9, A1, A8.

56. J. Bowles, 1996, The enterprise awards for best business practices, *Fortune,* March 4 (special advertising section).

57. P. R. Nayyar and K. A. Bantel, 1994, Competitive agility: A source of competitive advantage based on speed and variety, in P. Shrivastava, A. Huff, and J. Dutton (eds.), *Advances in Strategic Management* 10A, (Greenwich, Conn.: JAI Press), 193–222.

58. P. Lane, 1995, Nordstrom targeting men with 2nd catalog, *The Seattle Times,* September 20, D1; J. E. Meyers-Sharp, 1995, Nordstrom offers service and quality, *The Indianapolis Star,* September 7, D12.

59. R. F. Maruca, 1994, The right way to go global: An interview with Whirlpool CEO David Whitwam, *Harvard Business Review* 72, no. 2: 136.

60. Lei, Hitt, and Bettis, Dynamic core competences.

61. B. Nussbaum, 1988, Needed: Human capital, *Business Week,* September 19, 100–102.

62. S. A. Snell and M. A. Youndt, 1995, Human resource management and firm performance: Testing a contingency model of executive controls, *Journal of Management* 21: 711–737.

63. Snell and Youndt, Human resource, 711; K. Chilton, 1994, *The Global Challenge of American Manufacturers* (St. Louis, Mo.: Washington University, Center for the Study of American

Business); J. Pfeffer, 1994, *Competitive Advantage Through People* (Boston: Harvard Business School Press), 4.

64. H. W. Jenkins, Jr., 1996, What price job security? *Wall Street Journal,* March 26, A19.

65. J. S. Lublin, 1996, An overseas stint can be a ticket to the top, *Wall Street Journal,* January 29, B1, B2.

66. Sherman, How tomorrow's best, 90.

67. Snell and Youndt, Human resource, 731.

68. H. Rudnitsky, 1996, One hundred sixty companies for the price of one, *Forbes,* February 26, 56–62.

69. L. Grant, 1995, GE: The envelope, please, *Fortune,* June 26, 89–90.

70. J. Nocera, 1996, Living with layoffs, *Fortune,* April 1, 69–71.

71. *New York Times,* 1996, Chrysler CEO calls downsizing the price of competitiveness, *Dallas Morning News,* March 19, D8.

72. Associated Press, 1996, Swiss merger threatens drug companies in U.S., *Dallas Morning News,* March 8, D1, D10.

73. M. A. Hitt, R. E. Hoskisson, J. S. Harrison, and B. Summers, 1994, Human capital and strategic competitiveness in the 1990s, *Journal of Management Development* 13, no. 1: 35–46; C. R. Greer and T. C. Ireland, 1992, Organizational and financial correlates of a contrarian human resource investment strategy, *Academy of Management Journal* 35: 956–984.

74. C. L. Martin, C. K. Parsons, and N. Bennett, 1995, The influence of employee involvement program membership during downsizing: Attitudes toward the employer and the union, *Journal of Management* 21: 879–890.

75. C. M. Fiol, 1991, Managing culture as a competitive resource: An identity-based view of sustainable competitive advantage, *Journal of Management* 17: 191–211; J. B. Barney, 1986, Organizational culture: Can it be a source of sustained competitive advantage? *Academy of Management Review* 11: 656–665.

76. S. Ghoshal and C. A. Bartlett, 1994, Linking organizational context and managerial action: The dimensions of quality of management, *Strategic Management Journal* 15: 91–112.

77. Sherman, How tomorrow's best, 102.

78. L. N. Spiro and P. Engardio, 1995, Can Bear Stearns trade up? *Business Week,* November 27, 98–100.

79. S. G. Scott and R. A. Bruce, 1994, Determinants of innovative behavior: A path model of individual innovation in the workplace, *Academy of Management Journal* 37: 580–607.

80. S. Tully, 1995, So, Mr. Bossidy, we know you can cut. Now show us how to grow, *Fortune,* August 21, 70–80.

81. Spiro and Engardio, Can Bear Stearns trade up?, 98.

82. W. C. Symonds and E. Frey, 1995, Frank Stronach's secret? Call it empower steering, *Business Week,* May 1, 63–65.

83. G. T. Lumpkin and G. G. Dess, 1996, Clarifying the entrepreneurial orientation construct and linking it to performance, *Academy of Management Review* 21: 135–172.

84. Ibid., 142.

85. Ibid., 137.

86. Hitt and Keats, Strategic leadership.

87. C. Hall, 1996, Getting results with less time, more profits, *Dallas Morning News,* February 25, H1, H2.

88. S. Sherman, 1995, Wanted: Company change agents, *Fortune,* December 11, 197–198.

89. R. Jacob, 1995, The resurrection of Michael Dell, *Fortune,* September 18, 117.

90. Ibid., 118.

91. A. Goldstein, 1995, Dell powers up, *Dallas Morning News,* September 19, D1, D4.

92. T. M. Hout and J. C. Carter, 1995, Getting it done: New roles for senior executives, *Harvard Business Review* 73, no. 6: 133–145.

93. M. Hammer and J. Champy, 1995, *Reengineering the Corporation* (New York: Harper Collins).

94. Ibid.

95. Phillips Petroleum Company, 1995, *Annual Report,* 8.

96. J. M. Lozano, 1996, Ethics and management: A controversial issue, *Journal of Business Ethics* 15: 227–236; J. Mitchell, 1996, Professor leads attack on big business, *Dallas Morning News,* March 17, H6; J. Milton-Smith, 1995, Ethics as excellence: A strategic management perspective, *Journal of Business Ethics* 14: 683–693.

97. Center for Business Ethics, 1992, Instilling ethical values in large corporations, *Journal of Business Ethics* 11: 863–867.

98. C. W. L. Hill, 1990, Cooperation, opportunism, and the invisible hand: Implications for transaction cost theory, *Academy of Management Review* 15: 500–513.

99. M. Zey, 1993, *Banking on Fraud* (New York: Aldine De Gruyter).

100. D. Blalock, 1996, Study shows many execs are quick to write off ethics, *Wall Street Journal,* March 26, C1, C3; A. P. Brief, J. M. Dukerich, P. R. Brown, and J. F. Brett, 1996, What's wrong with the Treadway Commission Report? Experimental analysis of the effects of personal values and codes of conduct on fraudulent financial reporting, *Journal of Business Ethics* 15: 183–198; G. Miles, 1993, In search of ethical profits: Insights from strategic management, *Journal of Business Ethics* 12: 219–225.

101. Zajac and Westphal, Accounting for the explanations of CEO compensation.

102. S. R. Premeaux and R. W. Mondy, 1993, Linking management behavior to ethical philosophy, *Journal of Business Ethics* 12: 219–225.

103. Brief et al., What's wrong?.

104. A. Pasztor and L. Bannon, 1996, Former executive claims Mattel inflated sales and used questionable accounting, *Wall Street Journal,* April 3, A6.

105. B. K. Burton and J. P. Near, 1995, Estimating the incidence of wrongdoing and whistle-blowing: Results of a study using randomized response technique, *Journal of Business Ethics* 14: 17–30.

106. Milton-Smith, Ethics as excellence, 685.

107. Kraar, Acer's edge, 198.

108. Brief et al., What's wrong? 194; P. E. Murphy, 1995, Corporate ethics statements: Current status and future prospects, *Journal of Business Ethics* 14: 727–740.

109. L. J. Kirsch, 1996, The management of complex tasks in organizations: Controlling the systems development process, *Organization Science* 7: 1–21.

110. R. Simons, 1994, How new top managers use control systems as levers of strategic renewal, *Strategic Management Journal* 15: 170–171.

111. R. Simons, 1995, Control in an age of empowerment, *Harvard Business Review* 73, no. 2: 80.

112. M. A. Hitt, R. E. Hoskisson, and R. D. Ireland, 1990, Mergers and acquisitions and managerial commitment to innovation in M-form firms, *Strategic Management Journal* 11 (Special Issue): 29–47.

113. R. E. Hoskisson and M. A. Hitt, 1994, *Downscoping: How to Tame the Diversified Firm* (New York: Oxford University Press); R. E. Hoskisson and R. A. Johnson, 1992, Corporate restructuring and strategic change: The effect on diversification strategy and R&D intensity, *Strategic Management Journal* 13: 625–634.

114. Hitt and Keats, Strategic leadership.

115. E. Shaprio, 1996, New HBO honcho must hone pay network's creative edge, *Wall Street Journal,* March 19, B1, B6.

13 Corporate Entrepreneurship and Innovation

After reading this chapter, you should be able to:

1. Describe three strategic approaches used to produce and manage innovation.

2. Discuss the two sources of internal corporate venturing: autonomous strategic behavior and induced strategic behavior.

3. Define three types of innovation.

4. Discuss how the capability to manage cross-functional teams can facilitate implementation of internal corporate ventures and innovation efforts.

5. Explain how strategic alliances can be used to produce innovation.

6. Discuss how a firm can create value by acquiring another company to gain access to its innovations or innovative capabilities.

7. Explain how large firms use venture capital to increase the effectiveness of their innovation efforts.

8. Describe the resources, capabilities, and core competencies of small versus large firms in producing innovation.

Entrepreneurship Is Creating the Future

PepsiCo

According to Peter Drucker, entrepreneurs should consider what exists as obsolete and create the future. Both large and small firms must engage in entrepreneurship to achieve strategic competitiveness and earn above-average returns. Thus, firms must be innovative and introduce new products and processes to gain and maintain competitive advantages. For example, the president of PepsiCo, Craig Weatherup, suggests that it takes a significant amount of innovation and energy to keep his company growing. PepsiCo owns some of the world's leading brand names such as Pepsi, Frito-Lay, Taco Bell, KFC, and Pizza Hut. Fortunately, for PepsiCo, there are many people in the world who eat, drink, and snack and whose needs the company can attempt to fulfill.

More than 50 percent of Frito-Lay's business growth comes from new products.

According to Steve Reinemund, CEO of Frito-Lay, more than 50 percent of his business' growth comes from new products. In fact, he suggested that Frito-Lay's double-digit growth could not be obtained with old products for the consumer. He stated that "if it gets tired, it doesn't sell." In fact, PepsiCo's chairman suggested that "someone once said that insanity is doing the same thing and expecting different results." Frito-Lay is following the philosophy that innovative new products are necessary, which led to new product introductions in 1996. For example, it introduced Texas Grill in 1996, a strip-shaped corn chip that is less oily than the standard Fritos and has grill marks. It comes in honey barbeque and fajita flavors. A new product line called 3-D's has been test marketed. The product is a hollow triangle of puffed corn or potato with nacho cheese and ranch flavors. It is introducing a new line of flavored pretzels and baked low-fat potato chips. Frito-Lay has also developed a number of new products, including single-serve crackers, aimed at convenience store customers. As a testament to Frito-Lay's innovation, it has approximately 50 percent of the domestic U.S. snack chip market. Its innovation and market power in domestic markets and expansion to global markets in recent times led Anheuser-Busch to exit the snack food business.

The toy industry should take heed of the results achieved by PepsiCo businesses such as Frito-Lay. Although the toy industry was built on creative ideas, few of the large toy companies have been innovative in the last several years. Some argue that the industry is suffering from a chronic shortage of creativity. Most new products being introduced are updated versions of old reliable products. In fact, many of the toy makers are using the profits from these old toy staples to buy other toy businesses (someone else's old toy staples). For example, Mattel tried to acquire Hasbro but the executives at Hasbro rebuffed Mattel's offer. One of Mattel's leading products is the Barbie doll, which is 37 years old. Hasbro's featured attraction is a Star Wars action figure that is now more than 20 years old. The strategy of remaking and updating older but reliable toys has been derived largely from observing many new products fail. Restyling and promoting older established toys is a relatively dependable, low-risk strategy. For example, Mattel gained $1.4 billion in sales from the Barbie doll and its product line extensions in 1995.

However, this incremental innovation strategy may lead to missed opportunities. The lack of innovation by U.S. toy companies allowed Japanese companies to become the market leaders in video games. Companies such as Sega Enterprises, Inc., and Nintendo Company have major shares of the $6 billion annual market for video games.

The large toy companies also need to watch out for small innovative companies. Todd McFarlane was a comic book artist who decided to branch out on his own. In 1992, he and several other artists formed Image Comics, now the third largest publisher of comic books. The character created by McFarlane, Spawn, was initiated in 1992 and the first issue sold 1.7 million copies (an industry record). As a result of its success, large toy companies such as Mattel and Hasbro have attempted to license the Spawn characters for toys. Because they would not give McFarlane the control he desired, he decided to start his own toy company. He founded Todd Toys in January 1994 and began shipping Spawn action figures to retailers in the United States and Canada in September of that year. His firm sold out its entire production run of figures, play sets, and vehicles in that year. In 1995, the company branched into video and CD-ROM games and began offering other characters from the Image Comics stable. Thus, McFarlane, an entrepreneur, has created a major competitor in the comic book industry and a new and growing competitor in the toy business. He has done so by offering new innovative products that existing firms in the industry were unable or unwilling to offer.

Source: J. Pereira, 1996, Toy business focuses more on marketing and less on new ideas, *Wall Street Journal,* February 29, A1, A4; M. Warshaw, 1996, Renegades, *Success,* January/February, 32–40; M. Zimmerman, 1995, The PepsiCo challenge: Finding new products key to company's growth goals, *Dallas Morning News,* September 5, D1, D4; M. Zimmerman, 1995, Frito-Lay, Inc. puts growth on snack menu, *Dallas Morning News,* August 28, D1, D4.

The opening case illustrates the importance of entrepreneurship and innovation to large and small businesses alike. As noted in the case, the introduction of new products is very important to all of PepsiCo's separate businesses. For example, Frito-Lay has maintained its market leadership through the continuous introduction of new products. It introduced a number of new products in 1996 and has a number of others planned for the future. The importance of entrepreneurship and innovation is also shown in the discussion of the toy industry. Mattel and Hasbro are leaders in the toy industry but have not been very innovative in recent years. They have major products that sell well but each of their major product lines is more than 20 years old. As such, the U.S. toy companies lost out on a major opportunity in the video games market. Furthermore, the ability of a small entrepreneurial firm like Todd Toys to move into the industry with success against much larger and more powerful companies such as Mattel and Hasbro shows that innovation is a critical element in this industry. Mattel and Hasbro may not remain as powerful in this industry if they continue to rely on old products rather than introduce new, creative toys.[1]

Relating back to Figure 1–1 in Chapter 1, our focus herein is on a critical element for implementing strategy—producing and managing innovation. (Innovation may also provide feedback for the formulation of new strategies; see the feedback loop in Figure 1–1.) As noted in Chapter 1, the current competitive landscape requires most firms to be entrepreneurial and innovative. Also, innovation is a direct requirement of specific strategies such as differentiation (product innovation) and cost leadership (process innovation). Additionally, innovation is an important capability associated with competitive dynamics (see Chapter 5). This chapter examines the resources and skills required to produce and manage innovation. Although this chapter emphasizes innovation in large companies, evidence shows that they are not the sole generators of product and process innovations. Many small and medium-sized firms are also effective innovators, as demonstrated by Todd Toys. Moreover, large companies often develop relationships and alliances with smaller firms to help them produce innovations. Because of the importance of their innovative abilities, the chapter's final section addresses the different capabilities of small firms that produce and manage innovation.

■ Innovation and Corporate Entrepreneurship

Some evidence suggests that effective innovation results in a sustainable competitive advantage. More specifically, innovations that are (1) difficult for competitors to imitate, (2) able to provide significant value to customers, (3) timely, and (4) capable of being exploited commercially through existing capabilities and core competencies help firms develop competitive advantages.[2] Because of the link between the development of competitive advantages and the earning of above-average returns, many companies, especially those active in the global marketplace, are interested in producing innovations and effectively managing the innovation process.

■ Need for Innovation and Entrepreneurship

The technological revolution and greater competition in international markets have increased the competitive importance of innovation.[3] Research has shown that firms competing in global industries that invest more in innovation also achieve the highest returns.[4] In fact, investors often react positively to new product introductions, thereby increasing the price of a firm's stock. Thus, entrepreneurship is an essential feature of high-performance firms.[5] William R. Howell, chairman of the J.C. Penney Company, noted that you can never "rest on your laurels. Rather, you have to try to stay ahead of the curve, since competitors tend to pick up on your successes."[6]

■ Entrepreneurship and Innovation Defined

Entrepreneurs seek to create the future. To do so, they must take risks and be aggressive, proactive, and innovative.[7] Furthermore, they must identify anomalies in markets or opportunities where no current market exists.[8]

Corporate entrepreneurship includes the commitments, mind-sets, and actions firms take to develop and manage innovations. Formally, **corporate entrepreneurship** is the set of capabilities possessed by a firm to produce or acquire new goods or services and manage the innovation process.[9] Corporate entrepreneurship is based on effective product design and successful commercialization. Because it is a set of capabilities that results in the effective *and* efficient design and manufacture of products, corporate entrepreneurship can be a basis for strategic competitiveness.

In U.S. companies, the role of corporate entrepreneurship in both effectiveness and efficiency has been recognized only somewhat recently. After World War II, for example, U.S. manufacturers sought to satisfy worldwide demand for their goods and services by focusing on mass-production techniques that allowed them to produce products in large quantities. This focus resulted in an opportunity for other producers (e.g., those in Japan and what was then West Germany) to use a different set of strategic actions.[10] The focus of U.S. firms on quantity allowed inefficiencies, which the Japanese and the Germans exploited commercially with high levels of product quality. By the 1970s, Japanese manufacturers were more competitive than their U.S. rivals as a result of the development and use of a host of product, process, and managerial innovations. Workers in Japanese factories, for example, exercised a degree of responsibility not allowed in U.S. factories. In Japanese factories, the activities of everyone—from top-level managers to line workers to suppliers—were combined into a tightly integrated whole. Firms committed to these methods set their sights on perfection: "continually declining costs, zero defects, zero inventories, and endless product variety."[11] However, more has been learned about operating a manufacturing enterprise in the 1980s

■ *Corporate entrepreneurship* is the set of capabilities possessed by a firm to produce or acquire new goods or services and manage the innovation process.

and 1990s than in all of the rest of the century. Regional dominance is a thing of the past. Global markets and competition dominate the new competitive landscape. Thus, innovations in manufacturing and service companies alike have become necessary for survival in a highly competitive world.[12]

Joseph Schumpeter's classic work on management of the innovation process suggests that firms engage in three types of innovative activity.[13] **Invention** is the act of creating or developing a new product or process idea. **Innovation** is the process of creating a commercial product from invention. Finally, **imitation** is adoption of the innovation by similar firms. Imitation usually leads to product or process standardization. In the United States in particular, the most critical of these activities has been innovation. Many firms are able to create ideas that lead to invention. However, commercializing those inventions through innovation has, at times, proved to be difficult.

Strategic leaders, managers, and entrepreneurs all have roles that are critical to effective corporate entrepreneurship.[14] Especially with regard to corporate entrepreneurship, the strategic leader's role is to inspire an organization's members to work together in the pursuit of meaningful outcomes. Leaders and their words assume symbolic value to inspire organizational members to accomplish a firm's strategic intent and strategic mission. Lee Iacocca, for example, facilitated the return of Chrysler Corp. to profitability. During the firm's darkest days, Iacocca provided strong leadership and a sense of urgency about the actions the firm had to take to survive.[15] Of course, Chrysler's turnaround was a team effort, but without Iacocca's inspiration, it is likely that the firm would have been forced to file for bankruptcy.[16] The example of Chrysler shows that even troubled firms in hostile environments can change their past behaviors by adopting policies that foster innovation. In fact, corporate entrepreneurship that produces innovation can provide a platform on which industry leadership can be built.[17]

Middle- and lower-level managers are promoters and caretakers of organizational efficiency. Their work is especially important once a product idea has been commercialized and the organization necessary to support and promote it has been formed.[18] At Chrysler, the work of managers was instrumental in creating the turnaround Iacocca had inspired. In particular, these managers became more flexible and labored intensively to eliminate the barriers between workers and themselves that had developed over many years.[19]

Entrepreneurs are people who are the first to see an economic opportunity and seek to take advantage of it. Often, entrepreneurs' commercial insights are not initially shared by others, forcing them to live with the social burden of not being accepted until the economic value of their insights is confirmed. Inside large organizations, entrepreneurial activities have been labeled "intrapreneurship."[20]

The most effective entrepreneurs and intrapreneurs are often those who work against existing product standards by behaving as if they do not exist. This mind-set seems to facilitate creativity and innovation. However, within large organizations, effective corporate entrepreneurship can be difficult to establish and support. In large organizations, people engaged in entrepreneurial practices must fully understand the corporate culture and mind-set (see Chapter 1) that drive the firm's innovation process and the attributes of the structure, controls, and reward systems within which organizational work is completed.

Chrysler has changed considerably from its days in the early 1980s when it was close to bankruptcy. As noted in the Strategic Focus, it is now considered one

In Japanese factories, the activities of managers to line workers to suppliers are combined into a tightly integrated whole.

■ *Invention* is the act of creating or developing a new product or process idea.

■ *Innovation* is the process of creating a commercial product from invention.

■ *Imitation* is adoption of the innovation by similar firms.

of the most innovative of the U.S. automobile companies. The new Prowler and Dodge Viper autos provide smartly styled vehicles for specialized market niches. Similarly, Rockwell International continues to apply corporate entrepreneurship to produce innovative new products. Through innovation, Rockwell became a dominant force in the modem market and now hopes to do so in wireless communications. Its innovative five-chip package may well make it a leader in the wireless market as well. Brinker International has a reputation as an entrepreneurial firm that has introduced several new successful restaurant concepts. Among those is Chili's Grill and Bar and the Macaroni Grill. The new concept, Eatzi's, is the first restaurant of its kind. If it is as successful as its predecessors at Brinker, this firm may become one of the top restaurant chains in the world. Finally, the new product, bacon pizza, introduced by Taco Bell provides another example of the emphasis on innovation within PepsiCo businesses. Thus, we can conclude that corporate entrepreneurship is alive and well and, at least in some firms, leads to strategic competitiveness.

While innovativeness in Japanese firms has received some attention during the last two decades, U.S. firms continue to be perceived as the most innovative. However, corporate entrepreneurship and innovation are not limited to the United States and Japan.

STRATEGIC FOCUS

Creating New Products and Services with Corporate Entrepreneurship

■ *A skunkworks research project is the name often given to autonomous research teams charged with developing highly unique ideas.*

Although Chrysler almost went bankrupt in the early 1980s, it has become one of the more innovative U.S. automobile companies in the 1990s. In 1992, it produced a flashy new vehicle, the Dodge Viper, aimed at a specialized market niche. In 1996, it announced another new niche-type vehicle, the Prowler. The Prowler is a retro-styled roadster intended to retail for about $35,000. Chrysler developed this car for a minor investment (in automobile terms) of only $75 million. Approximately 40 percent of the Prowler's parts are borrowed from other Chrysler cars, and Chrysler required its suppliers to work as a team and to absorb a large amount of the engineering and tooling costs. This bold, new vehicle is intended to help reshape Plymouth's stodgy image. One analyst suggested that Chrysler was lapping the competition in innovativeness.

At Rockwell International, a central focus is wireless communication. Based on a **skunkworks research project,** at the end of 1995, Rockwell announced a five-chip package that forms the basis of a new 900-megahertz digital cordless phone. It will have to compete against strong industry leaders such as Toshiba and Motorola. However, executives at Rockwell are confident that it will succeed in the wireless communications market as it did against Intel in the modem business. Essentially, Rockwell eliminated Intel as a competitor in the modem market. One analyst suggests that Rockwell has done an amazing job of staying ahead of the market. By the year 2000, Rockwell executives predict that approximately one-third of its expected $1.7 billion sales in chips will come from wireless products.

Innovation is also highly important in retail and service markets. For example, Brinker International, Inc., the parent company of Chili's Grill and Bar and other successful restaurant chains, has opened its newest concept in restaurants, called Eatzi's. This new retail concept has a supermarket casual dining theme and combines the convenience of prepared meals with freshly prepared menu choices in a traditional restaurant. The motto of Eatzi's is "meals for the taking." Eatzi's target customers are those who want to eat at home but don't want to prepare a meal. Furthermore, these target customers don't want fast food or take-out pizza. Meals heated at home but not prepared there now compose 42 percent of all meals eaten. These types of meals have surpassed home-prepared meals (39 percent). During the last 10 years, take-out meals have increased 12 percentage points to 47 percent of all meals eaten. Eatzi's offers approximately 400 items, including breads, entrees, vegetables, and desserts prepared fresh daily. Additionally, the restaurant will sell multiple other supplemental items such as fruit, sodas, condiments, wine, and flowers. This is a new approach to the restaurant/take-out food market. To the customer, Eatzi's may appear to be more like a market than a restaurant. Only time will tell whether this new concept will succeed, but Brinker International has been highly successful in introducing new types of restaurants to the consuming public.

Another new product in the restaurant market is Taco Bell's bacon pizza. It is a combination of Italian and Mexican style food. The bacon pizza is composed of a flour tortilla and a crispy shell, covered with refried beans, pizza sauce, cheese, and bacon. The intent is to appeal to its main customers, 18 to 34 year olds. Taco Bell executives suggested that the recent introduction of this product has met with tremendous consumer appeal and success. Taco Bell has been innovative in introducing the value menu in the 1980s and the reduced-fat Border-Lites items in the 1990s. Thus, Taco Bell is another example of an innovative PepsiCo business.

Source: B. Vlasic, 1996, That daring old company and its jaunty jalopy, *Business Week,* January 15, 31; L. Armstrong, 1995, At Rockwell the word is wireless, *Business Week,* November 13, 87–88; J.D. Opdyke, 1995, Dallas eatery aims to cash in on taking out, *Wall Street Journal,* November 22, B1; Taco Bell weighs in new pizza, 1995, *Dallas Morning News,* December 28, D1.

■ Cross-Cultural Comparisons of Entrepreneurship

In the late 1970s, Chinese economic reforms allowed more autonomy to market forces and legalized private entrepreneurship. As such, many Chinese people have more disposable income, are better informed and have more personal freedom than at any time since 1949 when the Communists took control of the country. The outcomes are primarily the result of the reforms unleashing the entrepreneurial spirit of the Chinese people. In fact, considerable entrepreneurship is currently being exhibited in the People's Republic of China.[21] However, some significant tension has arisen between the need for individualism to promote entrepreneurship and the more traditional Chinese cultural characteristic of collectivism. Individualism, a dominant characteristic in U.S. society, is important to exhibit the creativity needed for entrepreneurial behavior. Furthermore, research has shown that entrepreneurship declines as collectivism is emphasized. However, the same research shows that exceptionally high levels of individualism can be dysfunctional for entrepreneurship as well. Thus, a balance is needed between individual initiative and the spirit of cooperation and group ownership of innovation. For firms to achieve corporate entrepreneurship, they must provide appropriate autonomy and incentives for individual initiative to surface, but also promote cooperation and group ownership of an innovation if it is to be implemented successfully. Thus, corporate entrepreneurship often requires teams of people with unique skills and resources.[22]

The importance of balancing individualism and collectivism for entrepreneurship is perhaps best exemplified by the success of Asian entrepreneurs in North America. Some have argued that the success of those of Chinese origin in North America was due to their industriousness, perseverance, frugality, and emphasis on family. Research shows, however, that there are other traits that promote their success. In North America, these individuals are allowed the autonomy necessary to exhibit creativity and entrepreneurial behavior. However, their cultural background emphasizes collectivism, which helps them promote cooperation and group ownership of innovation. Additionally, many of the immigrants from Asia, particularly Hong Kong and Taiwan, came to North America with appropriate capital and significant incentive to succeed.[23]

Similarly, Korean immigrants have achieved significant success in entrepreneurial ventures. Interestingly, in their case, success has been attributed to their human capital endowments (high education) and financial capital investments (affluence prior to entrepreneurial activity). Research has shown that individuals with the necessary financial capital and high education are the most likely to succeed in entrepreneurial endeavors. Thus, when these characteristics are combined with a balance between the cultural attributes of individualism and collectivism, the probability for success in entrepreneurial ventures is substantively greater.[24]

We now understand the importance of innovation and corporate entrepreneurship as well as some of the factors that contribute to them. The next section examines the internal corporate venturing process.

■ Internal Corporate Venturing

■ *Internal corporate venturing is the set of activities used to create inventions and innovations within a single organization.*

■ *Autonomous strategic behavior is a bottom-up process in which product champions pursue new product ideas, often through a political process, whereby they develop and coordinate the commercialization of a new good or service until it achieves marketplace success.*

■ *A product champion is a member of an organization who has an entrepreneurial vision of a new good or service and seeks to create support for its commercialization.*

Composed of two processes, **internal corporate venturing** is the set of activities used to create inventions and innovations within a single organization.[25] Internal corporate venturing's two processes are shown in Figure 13.1. The first internal corporate venturing process involves a bottom-up approach to the creation of product and process innovations. **Autonomous strategic behavior** is a bottom-up process in which product champions pursue new product ideas, often through a political process, whereby they develop and coordinate the commercialization of a new good or service until it achieves marketplace success. A **product champion** is a member of an organization who has an entrepreneurial vision of a new good or service and seeks to create support for its commercialization. Autonomous strategic behavior is based on a firm's wellsprings of knowledge and resources that provide the sources of a firm's innovation. Thus, a firm's capabilities and competencies are the basis for new products and processes.[26]

The autonomous strategic behavior of a product champion sometimes alters a firm's strategic intent and mission and thereby its corporate- or business-level strategy. For example, Sears' original catalog (mail-order) business ultimately became dominated by its retail strategy through experiments with retailing outlets at its catalog warehouses.[27] To support its commitment to innovation, Hewlett-Packard encourages its workers to serve as product champions. The firm's employees are challenged continuously to strive for innovativeness, speed, and efficiency. Product champions are also encouraged at Rubbermaid. Rubbermaid's CEO has challenged the firm's employees to innovate in ways that would allow the company to enter a new product category every 12 to 18 months and earn 33 percent of sales from products introduced within the past five years. While Rubbermaid has experienced some performance problems in recent years as noted in Chapter 2, it remains among the top 10 most admired firms in America and continues to be highly innovative. For example, Rubbermaid regularly introduces 300 to 400 new products to the market each year.[28] Across time, the products Hewlett-Packard and Rubbermaid introduce modify the implementation of some of the firms' business-level strategies.

Changing the concept of corporate-level strategy through autonomous strategic behavior, as was the case with Sears, Roebuck and Co., results when product

Figure 13.1

Model of Internal Corporate Venturing

Source: Adapted from R.A. Burgelman, 1983, A model of the interactions of strategic behavior, corporate context, and the concept of strategy, *Academy of Management Review* 8: 65.

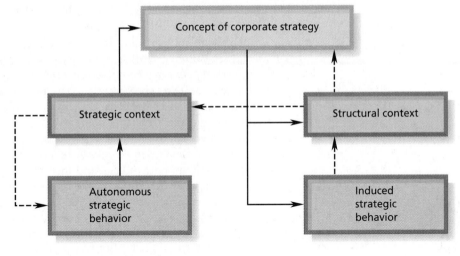

■ *Induced strategic behavior is a top-down process whereby the current strategy and structure foster product innovations that are associated closely with the current strategy and structure.*

■ *A skunkworks research project is the name often given to autonomous research teams charged with developing highly unique ideas.*

championing takes place within strategic and structural contexts (see Figure 13–1). The strategic context refers to the process used to arrive at strategic decisions (often requiring political processes to gain acceptance). At Sears, the original strategic context favored the mail-order business. Considerable amounts of product championing by a range of people ultimately led to the change in the firm's concept of its corporate strategy. The structural context refers to the hierarchical structure and reward system used to support the implementation of a corporate-level strategy. The structural context associated with Sears' commitment to the mail-order business also was a barrier to the emergence of a focus on a new retail strategy.

Induced strategic behavior is a top-down process whereby the current strategy and structure foster product innovations that are associated closely with the current strategy and structure. In this situation, the strategy in place is filtered through a matching structural hierarchy.

Outcomes achieved primarily through induced strategic behaviors are shown in Rockwell's decision to enter the wireless communication market as described in the Strategic Focus. Clearly, top executives made the decision to direct a **skunkworks research project** to develop new microprocessor chips that will serve as a basis for new digital cordless phones. Skunkworks is the name often given to autonomous research teams charged with developing highly unique ideas.

Another example of induced strategic behavior is shown by Sony's decision to enter the home personal computer market.[29] In fact, the CEO of Sony, Nobuyuki Idei, believes that if the firm is able to combine its audiovisual know-how with computer networks, it can initiate an entirely new industry. Sony has engaged Intel Corporation to help it develop and enter the personal computer business. Sony intends to develop PCs that also include audio and video functions. For example, Sony executives intend to market PCs with Trinitron monitors and digital video disk players.

Sony already has some expertise in the manufacture of computers. It has manufactured computer workstations and a small line of PCs for Dell and Apple. Sony is confident that it can use its brand recognition and electronics expertise to carve out a niche in the growing but competitive personal computer market.[30]

Sony is attempting to integrate digital technologies into multiple new products in addition to personal computers, including high-resolution television and multimedia eyeglasses. In fact, Nobuyuki Idei's strategic intent for Sony is to become a "digital dream kid." Thus, the vision of the firm's new CEO is to integrate digital technologies into multiple new products.[31]

Although Sony has the vision and technical experience to accomplish its goals, large firms often encounter difficulties when striving to pursue internal corporate ventures effectively. The induced processes can dominate and create strategic and structural contexts that become barriers to change. Effective internal corporate venturing processes are established only when both internal political processes and strategic and structural contexts allow a new strategic mission to emerge.

AB Volvo has to obtain a larger share of the global automobile market if it is to survive. As such, top-level Volvo executives have developed aggressive plans to invest heavily in new models and increase car production capacity and sales 30 percent by the year 2000. However, one analyst suggests that Volvo has not effectively managed its investments in new product development and that such overspending is one of the firm's current problems. In fact, Volvo engineers have a reputation for spending too much money to develop new model automobiles such as the 850 series. The 850 series is a large boxy automobile that sells mainly on Volvo's reputation for building sturdy vehicles that will survive major crashes. However, Volvo is in a fight for its life and must manage its new product development investments wisely if it is to be successful in the highly competitive global automobile market.[32]

The difficulties involved with developing effective internal corporate venturing processes provide incentives for large firms to seek innovation from strategic alliances (see Chapter 9) and external acquisitions rather than through internal venturing. New small firms, without a long corporate strategic history, may be better at initiating strategic change. Small firms, however, often lack the resources, capabilities, and core competencies necessary to commercialize a large volume of innovation-based projects. This point is discussed in greater detail later in the chapter. Nonetheless, with an appropriate culture, large firms can be entrepreneurial by encouraging new ideas through rewards and support for visible intrapreneurs.[33]

Several recent products developed and introduced to the market by large firms serve as examples of innovation. Two examples come from the automobile industry. General Motors has introduced to the market its new electric car called

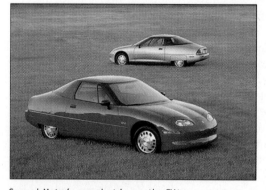

General Motor's new electric car, the EV1, provides an example of innovation.

the EV1. It is a part of the Saturn line of General Motors automobiles. The EV1 will be available for lease rather than purchase in order to insulate drivers from resale value worries. The intent is to treat these drivers as members of an exclusive club and ensure that they are satisfied customers. The electric car has a range of 70 to 90 miles without recharging. Thus, there are still limits to its ability to serve all customers' automobile needs. GM also intends to introduce an electric truck in 1997.[34] Like GM, Ford also has introduced a new automobile concept: a smog-eating technology. The technology allows automobiles to consume ground-level ozone, the main air pollutant produced by automobiles. The new system is expected to remove approximately 80 percent of the ozone from the air the automobile encounters. Although this product is only being test marketed, if it proves to be successful, automobiles with this technology could be particularly attractive in markets with heavy air pollution problems (e.g., around large cities).[35]

As described in the Strategic Focus, Microsoft is one of the most innovative companies in the world. One of the reasons it has been so innovative is its effective use and management of teams to develop new software. Similarly, other

STRATEGIC FOCUS   The Power of Teams

Microsoft was developed by a team composed of Bill Gates and Paul Allen. Microsoft continues the team concept today in its quest to be one of the most innovative corporations in the world. According to one analyst, Microsoft presents an interesting balance among strategy, culture, and process. The firm provides incentives to employees to be creative by allowing them to pursue pet projects but balances that freedom with critical time deadlines to produce. It uses a process called "sync and stabilize." This process starts with a product team organized around a software concept that Microsoft is developing. The team is responsible for defining this software concept and preparing a detailed report that defines how the user interface will work. Programmers are free to set their own hours and to pursue their ideas for new features as long as the project is completed within the assigned time. The policy seems to be effective in part because of significant peer pressure within the team and the firm. If a project deadline is not met, individuals and teams have to answer to their peers. Microsoft's culture is antibureaucratic and emphasizes responsiveness to market demands. For example, it requires programmers to develop software products on the same type of computer used by the customers. Microsoft's primary strengths are hiring smart people, managing complex software projects, and inspiring creativity.

Other companies also use teams to develop and implement new product or process innovations. For example, United Airlines has used teams to develop and implement ISO-9000 quality guidelines in its operations and services processes. Likewise, Mercedes-Benz is using a team of executives and engineers to design and implement its new manufacturing facility designed to produce a sport utility vehicle in Alabama. Andreas Renschler, the Mercedes executive heading this project, is known as a deft manager, creative problem-solver, and effective idea generator. Renschler and team have to overcome problems of simultaneously implementing a new product, manufacturing process, and workforce. To ensure the best operating techniques, Renschler has hired managers from multiple other companies such as Chrysler, Ford, Mitsubishi, and Sony. Their varied backgrounds spark lengthy debates on the team but bring different dimensions that should help in designing and implementing more effectively a successful manufacturing process. Use of such a team is a new concept for Mercedes-Benz. However, top executives have decided to use a similar free-wheeling team to design the new micro-compact car being developed in an alliance with Swatch parent SMH Corp.

Source: United Airlines bases its success on technology, innovation and team management, 1995, *Plating & Surface Finishing*, September, 14–18; E. Williams, 1995, "Secrets" looks behind mask at Microsoft, *Dallas Morning News*, November 26, B5; D. Woodruff and K.L. Miller, 1995, Mercedes' maverick in Alabama, *Business Week*, September 11, 64–65.

companies such as United Airlines and Mercedes-Benz are using the team concept to develop and implement new product and process technologies. In fact, the use of the team concept to design and implement a new manufacturing facility to produce a new product at Mercedes-Benz is the first application of teams within that company. Moreover, it is now using a team concept to develop a new compact automobile. Thus, teams can facilitate innovation in firms and represent a wave for the future.

■ Implementing Internal Corporate Ventures

The creation and commercialization of a new good or service is a complex process. The design and transfer of technology from engineering to manufacturing and ultimately to distribution and to the marketplace are critical. The design stage entails a high degree of integration among the various functions involved in the innovation process—from engineering to manufacturing and ultimately to market distribution. Initial design efforts that do not consider down-line aspects in the production process (manufacturing, testing, marketing, service, etc.) may result in high product costs and low product quality. Such cross-functional integration facilitates reciprocal information flows among the functions responsible for development, design, and implementation. Developing a capability to innovate rapidly using team processes, as Microsoft has done, helps large firms overcome the difficulties they encounter when trying to be entrepreneurial. These matters are discussed in greater detail in the next subsection.

■ Implementing Product Development Teams and Facilitating Cross-Functional Integration

The importance of cross-functional integration has been recognized for some time, but it has not been practiced widely in industry until recently. However, because of an emerging emphasis on horizontal organization, firms are becoming more skilled at cross-functional integration. **Horizontal organization** refers to changes in organizational processes where managing across functional units becomes more critical than managing up and down functional hierarchies.[36] Therefore, instead of being built around vertical hierarchical functions or departments, the organization is built around core horizontal processes similar to the teams used by Chrysler, Microsoft, Mercedes-Benz, and United Airlines.

Evidence suggests that a key benefit that can be gained through successful application of horizontal organizational processes is effective utilization of sophisticated manufacturing technologies [e.g., the computer-aided design and manufacturing (CAD/CAM) system].[37] Thus, cross-functional integration can facilitate a firm's efforts to establish a competitive advantage.

■ Barriers to Integration

Barriers may exist that can stifle attempts to integrate functions effectively within an organization. For example, an emphasis on functional specialization may affect cross-functional integration. Such specialization creates distancing of divergent functions and characteristically different roles for engineering, manufacturing, and marketing. Functional departments have been found to be differentiated along four dimensions: time orientation, interpersonal orientation, goal orientation, and formality of structure.[38] Individuals from different functional departments that have different orientations understand separate aspects of product development in different ways. As such, they place emphasis on separate design characteristics and issues. For example, a design engineer may place strong importance on characteristics that make a product functional and workable. Alternatively, a person from the marketing function may place extreme importance on product characteristics that satisfy customer needs. These types of characteristics may overlap or they may differ. These different orientations can create barriers to effective communication across functions.[39] Although functional specialization may be damaging to the horizontal relationships necessary for implementing innovation, such specialization has an important purpose in creating an efficient organization. Therefore, eliminating such task specialization to overcome barriers to cross-functional integration may do more harm than good to the organization.

Another barrier to integration can be organizational politics. In some organizations, considerable political activity may center around resource allocations to the different functions. If different functions have to compete aggressively with each other to obtain adequate or needed resources, it can lead to conflict between

■ *Horizontal organization* *refers to changes in organizational processes where managing across functional units becomes more critical than managing up and down functional hierarchies.*

the functions. Of course, dysfunctional conflict between functions creates a barrier to their integration.[40] Methods must be found through which cross-functional integration can be promoted without excessive concurrent political conflict and without concurrently changing the basic structural characteristics necessary for task specialization and efficiency.

■ Facilitating Integration

Firms can use four methods to achieve effective cross-functional integration.[41] The first of these methods utilizes *shared values*. Shared values, when linked clearly with a firm's strategic intent and mission, reduce political conflict and become the glue that promotes coupling among functional units. Hewlett-Packard has remained an accomplished technological leader because it has established the "HP way." In essence, the HP way refers to the firm's esteemed organizational culture that promotes unity and internal innovation.

Leadership is a second method of achieving cross-functional integration. Effective strategic leaders remind organizational members continuously of the value that product innovations create for the company (see Chapter 12). In the most desirable situations, this value-creating potential becomes the basis for the integration and management of functional department activities. At General Electric, Jack Welch frequently highlights the importance of integrated work, among both business units and different functions. To frame this message consistently, Welch has been instrumental in establishing and operating a managerial training center that focuses on these relationships among all levels of the company's management structure.

A third method of achieving cross-functional integration is concerned with *goals and budgets*. This method calls for firms to formulate goals and allocate the budgetary resources necessary to accomplish them. These goals are specific targets for the integrated design and production of new goods and services. Chrysler Corp.'s reorganization to focus on platform teams, for example, effectively reinforced in employees' minds the importance of team processes.

A fourth means of facilitating cross-functional integration is an *effective communication system*. This may be achieved by developing a horizontal organization and emphasizing the use of cross-functional teams. More is often required, however, to overcome the barriers to integration noted earlier.[42] Shared values, effective leadership, appropriate resources to accomplish team tasks, and

Companies use four methods to achieve cross-functional integration.

an information system that facilitates communications between team members and different functions contribute to an effective communication system within teams.[43] A network information system can facilitate communication among geographically dispersed team members, even those located in different countries. Because of the growing popularity of horizontal organizational structures, in particular cross-functional teams that may be geographically dispersed across international borders, firms such as IBM are emphasizing network-centered computing. According to Louis Gerstner, CEO of IBM, network-centered computing "will change the way we do business, the way we teach our children, how we communicate, how we interact as individuals."[44]

■ Appropriating (Extracting) Value from Innovation

Cross-functional integration, when implemented properly, may also facilitate reduced time to market, improve product quality, and create value for customers. For firms competing globally, increasing attention is being paid to the amount of time required to transfer products from the lab to the consumer.[45] A firm can gain a competitive advantage if it is able to develop a product idea and transfer it to the market sooner than competitors, especially in high-tech environments such as biotechnology.[46] If the product has wide consumer appeal, the first mover has an advantage.[47] Although there is inherent risk in being a pioneer, a first mover may be able to establish a dominant position from which to build future market share and earn above-average returns (see discussion in Chapter 5). Research evidence suggests that firms with long development cycles typically are outperformed by companies with short ones.[48] Although shorter time-to-market cycles can help firms appropriate value from their innovations, poor design can lead to expensive recalls, higher production costs, low product performance, and product liability exposure.

As noted in the Strategic Focus, speed has become a major factor on which firms compete.[49] In fact, Kim Sheridan, chairman of Avalon Software, Inc., stated that "it's not the big companies that eat the small; it's the fast that eat the slow."[50] A recent study showed that the competitive clock continues to tick while a firm delays adopting a new generation of technology. The sooner a firm innovates, the better it performs.[51] There is no single means of increasing a firm's speed. Clearly, integrating new technology into a firm's operations can increase the speed with which it accomplishes tasks. Many firms are attempting to accelerate product development and integration through cross-functional teams.[52]

Because product design teams often are composed of many different players, each of whom possesses critical knowledge and skills, cross-functional integration may reduce uncertainty and facilitate the successful introduction of innovative goods or services. In fact, the simultaneous evaluation of multiple alternatives, as is often the case with cross-functional teams, increases decision speed.[53] Hewlett-Packard, for example, is divided into global, cross-functional teams that are capable of making decisions quickly to deal with rapidly changing market conditions. However, it is essential that design teams be managed effectively. If implementation is not effective in a complex situation, uncertainty may be increased.

In summary, the model presented in Figure 13.2 shows how value may be appropriated from internal innovation processes. As our discussion has indicated, the internal innovation process must be managed to facilitate cross-functional integration to appropriate the greatest amount of value from product design and commercialization efforts. Effective management of internal innovation processes can reduce both the time required to introduce innovations into

STRATEGIC FOCUS   Speed and More Speed to Survive

The old adage that time is money was never more appropriate than today. Speed is one of the primary factors on which firms compete. Because of the emphasis on speed, firms try to reduce the time required for most work, including design, development, and introduction of new products. These firms also change their manufacturing processes, means of processing orders and jobs, and also improve their quality. But time is of the essence.

Perhaps the importance of time is best seen in the development and introduction of new products. In general, Japanese automakers require 26 to 30 months to take the concept of an automobile to production. In contrast, U.S. automakers require between 29 and 46 months to do the same thing. Interestingly, Toyota recently developed a new compact minivan called the Ipsum in only 19 months—about half the time required by most U.S. automakers to do the same thing.

Mazda is the world leader, averaging approximately 21 months to introduce a new product, whereas General Motors is the laggard requiring an average of 46 months. The acknowledged leader of speed in the U.S. auto industry is Chrysler Corporation, requiring 29 months on average to get a new vehicle concept into production. The goal of Chrysler and Ford is to reduce this time to 24 months, whereas GM's goal is to reduce it to 38 months.

Outside of the auto industry, Gillette Company is now introducing new products in a two-year cycle, down from its previous average of three years. In fact, it introduced 20 new products in 1994. Similarly, Bell Helicopter has reduced its product development time from 24 to 12 months. This helped it win a new $113 million Army contract for helicopter trainers.

Interestingly, one recent study found that firms that took less time to innovate performed better than their competitors. However, although speed is extremely important in many industries, overemphasis on speed may encourage firms to introduce new products before they are fully tested. For example, IBM had to recall its Warp version of the OS/2 software for PCs after rushing it to market. This particular version had a flaw in it that potentially could destroy data. However, given the emphasis on speed and increasing global competition, firms must be concerned about speed in all that they do in order to survive.

Source: M.W. Lawless and P.C. Anderson, 1996, Generational, technological change: The effects of innovation and local rivalry on performance, *Academy of Management Journal* 39: in press; K.M. Eisenhardt and B.N. Tabrizi, 1995, Accelerating adaptive processes: Product innovation in the global computer industry, *Administrative Science Quarterly* 40: 84–110; V. Reitman and R.L. Simison, 1995, Japanese car makers speed up car making, *Wall Street Journal,* December 29, B10; W.M. Bulkeley, 1994, The latest big thing at many companies is speed, speed, speed, *Wall Street Journal,* December 23, A1, A5.

the marketplace and the degree of decision uncertainty associated with the design of an innovative product and the demand for it.[54]

■ Strategic Alliances: Cooperating to Produce and Manage Innovation

It is difficult for most firms to possess all the knowledge required to compete successfully in their product areas over the long term. Thus, internal innovation may contribute to the development of a sustainable competitive advantage when a firm possesses the capabilities and core competencies required to innovate effectively and efficiently. But because the stock of human knowledge is large and increasing at an accelerated pace, many firms, regardless of their size, cannot keep up to date on this vast pool of knowledge. Complicating this matter is the fact that the knowledge base confronting today's organizations is not only vast, but also increasingly more specialized. As such, the knowledge needed to commercialize goods and services is frequently embedded within different corporations and countries that have the ability to create specialized products.

Figure 13.2 Appropriating Value from Internal Firm Innovation

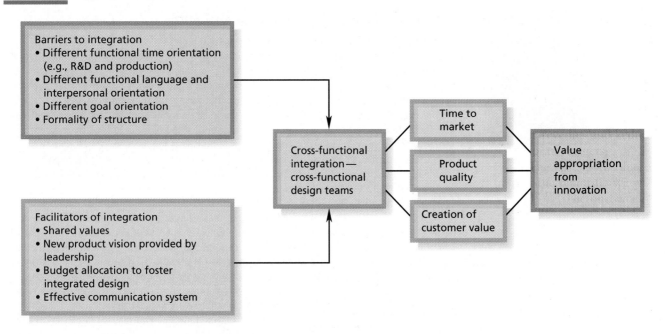

Source: Adapted from M.A. Hitt, R.E. Hoskisson, and R.D. Nixon, 1993, A mid-range theory of interfunctional integration, its antecedents and outcomes, *Journal of Engineering and Technology Management* 10: 161–185.

In Chapter 9, we discussed why and how firms use strategic alliances (*strategic alliances* are partnerships between firms whereby resources, capabilities, and core competencies are combined to pursue common interests and goals)[55] to gain either competitive parity or competitive advantage relative to rivals. Moreover, one of the specific reasons to enter into a strategic alliance is to introduce innovative goods or services. Strategic alliances are often used to innovate by sharing two or more firms' knowledge and skill bases.[56]

The dreams of many biotechnology firms of becoming the next Merck are being scaled back. Most of these firms are small and many have experienced failures of new drugs, a significant problem because of their lack of resources. Thus, survival is of key concern. To avoid failure and to obtain the needed resources to continue biotechnology research, many of these companies are seeking strategic alliances with larger resource-rich firms. Over a 12-month period between July 1994 and June 1995, biotechnology companies entered into 246 alliances with larger pharmaceutical firms. It is expensive and quite risky for new startup firms to operate independently in this industry. The average cost of developing a new drug is approximately $300 million and only 10 percent of the experimental drugs used in human trials are further developed and brought to the market.

Centocor, Inc., represents this new breed of biotechnology firm. In the early 1990s, the company had a huge sales force and approximately 1,600 employees at its peak. This number of employees was needed to market a new anti-infective drug, Centoxin, that many believed would be a blockbuster. However, the Food and Drug Administration rejected the drug in 1992 and the company's fortunes fell dramatically (stock price went from $60 to $5). Centocor has formed a strategic alliance with Eli Lilly and Company and Glaxo Wellcome PLC to market Realpro (an anticlotting drug) and Panorex (a colon and rectal cancer drug), respectively. It now employs approximately 500 people. Perhaps the new attitude is best explained by ChromaXome president, Michael Dickman, who stated, "We'd rather have a piece of 100 drug products than have one product all our own and take the chance that it might fail."[57]

Similarly, the large pharmaceutical firms are eagerly shopping for opportunities to team with biotechnology firms (see Strategic Focus section in Chapter 9). Some of them are using the small biotechnology companies to perform the early-stage research. As such, they can reduce their in-house research costs and some of the risks as well. Forming an alliance with these firms enables the pharmaceutical firms to convert some of their fixed research costs to variable costs and to diversify their risk. Thus, the pharmaceutical firms are attempting to reduce their risk and some of their fixed costs without reducing the probability of discovering and marketing new blockbuster drugs.[58]

In a more general sense, some argue that strategic alliances can be dangerous. Supporting this argument is the contention that they allow partner firms to gain knowledge and resources that make them stronger competitors,[59] which, if true, could ultimately lower profitability for an industry's leading firms. Thus, organizations are challenged to evaluate carefully all the risks associated with strategic alliances that might be formed in the pursuit of strategic competitiveness and above-average returns.

Across time, strategic alliances can slowly reduce the skills of a partner that does not understand the inherent risks. Collaboration within alliances can lead to competition, both in learning new skills and in refining new capabilities and core competencies that can be used to design and produce other innovative products and processes.

Japanese corporations, for example, appear to be expert in learning new technologies through strategic alliances. This skill has been instrumental in helping these firms learn how to compete in markets where they were locked out previously. For instance, all electronics products sold under the Eastman Kodak, General Electric, RCA, Zenith, and Westinghouse brand names are made by their foreign alliance partners and imported into the United States.[60]

As our discussion has suggested, alliances can lead to a company's dependence on partners through outsourcing to obtain low-cost components and inexpensive assembly. Often manufacturing skills and knowledge related to upgrading precision manufacturing and testing are lost, whereas such skills are gained by the competitors to which the firm is outsourcing.[61] Ultimately, then, a firm may lose its core competence by participating in alliances if it is not careful.

In summary, building successful strategic alliances requires focusing on knowledge, identifying core competencies, and developing strong human resources to manage these core competencies. Expecting to gain financial benefits in the short run may lead to unintended consequences in the long run. Firms may view their collaboration with other firms as an indirect form of competition for knowledge.[62]

■ Buying Innovation: Acquisitions and Venture Capital

In this section, we focus on the third approach firms use to produce and manage innovation. The intent of this approach is to acquire innovation, and innovative capabilities, from outside the organization. For example, in addition to strategic alliances, some pharmaceutical firms are acquiring small biotechnology companies with promising new drugs. Ciba-Geigy Ltd. bought a 50 percent interest in Chiron Corp. for $2.1 billion. Also, Glaxo PLC bought Affymax NV in a contest against three other bidders. The pharmaceutical firms are buying biotechnology firms not only for their promising new drugs but also their research techniques using gene-based analysis and computerization. Some time-honored techniques for creating drugs are becoming obsolete. Thus, they are attempting to buy innovation and the skills to create more innovation.[63]

As approaches to producing and managing innovation, both strategic alliances and acquisitions appear to be increasing in popularity. One reason is that the innovation prowess of other countries is growing at a rapid pace. A number of indicators suggest that Japanese firms, for instance, have progressed during the post-war period from borrowing, magnifying, and successfully commercializing foreign technologies to operating at the technological frontier, especially in process innovation. The National Science Foundation recently reported that Japanese firms accounted for the largest single share of foreign-origin patents.[64] Japanese companies are becoming skilled at transferring technologies from Japan into their global R&D networks. One way for companies from the world's other nations to gain competitive parity or perhaps competitive advantage when facing this situation is to gain access to Japanese technology by acquiring companies that have such technology.

■ Acquisitions

Acquiring other firms as a method of producing and managing innovation is becoming more common and may be used as a substitute for internally developed innovation.[65] A key risk of this method is that a firm may substitute the ability to buy innovations for the ability to produce innovations internally. Recent research supports this suggested trade-off and its negative effect on the processes a firm uses to produce innovations internally.[66]

Figure 13.3 shows that firms gaining access to innovations through the acquisition of other companies risk reductions in both R&D inputs (as measured by investments in R&D) and R&D outputs (as measured by the number of patents). Evidence in Figure 13.3 suggests that the R&D-to-sales ratio drops after acquisitions have been completed and that the patent-to-sales ratio drops significantly after companies have been involved with large acquisitions. Further research shows that firms engaging in acquisitions introduce fewer new products to the market.[67] These relationships indicate that firms substitute acquisitions for their internal innovation process. This may result because firms lose strategic control and emphasize financial control of original, and especially of acquired, business units.[68] Although reduced innovation may not always result, managers in acquiring firms should be aware of this potential outcome.

■ Venture Capital

Another approach used to acquire innovations involves venture capital. Some firms choose to establish their own venture capital divisions. These divisions carefully evaluate other companies to identify those with innovations or innovative capabilities that could help the firm develop a sustainable competitive advantage. In other instances, firms decide to serve as an internal source of capital for innovative product ideas that can be spun off as independent or affiliate firms.

Historically, the venture capital business has been associated primarily with independent venture capital firms. However, both domestic and foreign corporations have discovered that investing in venture capital adds a new dimension to their corporate development strategies and can produce an attractive return on their

Figure 13.3 Evidence of R&D Inputs (Expenditures) and Outputs (Number of Patents) per Dollar of Sales Before and After Large Acquisitions

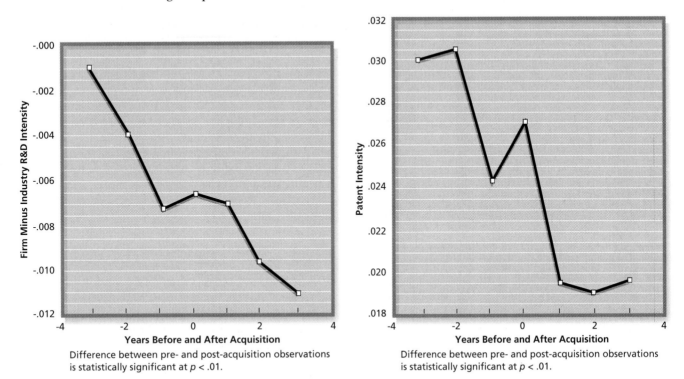

Difference between pre- and post-acquisition observations is statistically significant at $p < .01$.

Difference between pre- and post-acquisition observations is statistically significant at $p < .01$.

Source: M.A. Hitt, R.E. Hoskisson, R.D. Ireland, and J.S. Harrison, 1991, Are acquisitions a poison pill for innovation? *Academy of Management Executive V,* no. 4: 24–25.

investments.[69] The strategic benefits to a corporation include the ability to invest early and observe what happens to the new venture. This may lead to subsequent acquisitions, technology licensing, product marketing rights, and possibly the development of international opportunities. Large firms often view venture capital as a window on future technological development. Participation by corporations can take many forms, but usually begins with investment in several venture capital funds as a limited partner and evolves into direct investments in new business ventures. Many firms begin this strategy by forming a venture development division.

Disdain of large corporations by outside entrepreneurs can be a potential pitfall. Entrepreneurs may be wary of large corporations that seek to dominate fledgling companies. The syndication of venture funds to reduce risk may also be a factor limiting potential gains from venture capital investments. Other large firms may become part of the syndication and reduce the potential returns for the large corporate partner (through sharing of knowledge).[70] With corporate restructuring and downsizing continuing, executives seem willing to try more entrepreneurial ventures. Venture capital is apparently one way to participate and may be less risky than internal development.[71]

Interestingly, a number of small innovative companies are seeking capital through initial public offerings (IPOs). For example, in 1974, $0.1 billion was invested in initial public offerings. By 1995, however, the amount invested in IPOs had grown to $29 billion. In 1995, companies such as Pixar Animation Studios, controlled by Steven Jobs, one of the original entrepreneurs who started Apple, went public in an initial offering. It was to be priced between $12 and $14 a share, but it opened at $22 and closed at $39 a share on the day it went public. In fact, Jobs' 80 percent ownership stake was worth $1.1 billion at the end of that day. Another startup firm, Netscape Communications Corp., manufacturer of software for navigating the Internet, went public at $28 a share in August 1995 and by December of that year, its stock price was $171 per share. In particular, successful first-generation high-technology entrepreneurs are funding a new generation of innovators. One analyst suggested that money and ideas are combining at a faster rate, creating new products that in turn replenish the IPO capital available.[72]

Up to this point, the focus of our discussion has been on corporate entrepreneurship in large firms. However, small firms may even be better at producing revolutionary innovations. Although large firms often possess the significant financial resources and organizational capabilities necessary to more fully exploit innovative product opportunities, small firms may have more flexibility to produce innovations.

■ Entrepreneurship and the Small Firm

Research suggests that small firms, based in the United States and other nations throughout the world, are awarded a large number of U.S. patents.[73] Although 80 percent of the world's R&D activities in developing nations is concentrated in firms with 10,000 or more employees, these same large firms account for under half of the world's technological activity, as measured by U.S. patenting. These facts show that while large firms are very important in technological advancement, small firms and private individuals account for more than their share of the innovative activity and technological progress. There has been a significant shift toward self-employment and entrepreneurial ventures in the United States.[74] Small entrepreneurial firms have become an important part of the mainstream economy and business activity in the United States.[75]

Younger people are turning to entrepreneurial activities. For example, in 1994, 272,000 twenty to twenty-four year olds in the United States were self-employed. This amount is up 10 percent over the number in 1993. The largest percentage of Americans starting new businesses come from the 25- to 34-year-old age group.[76] Although the types of businesses started represent many different industries, high-technology industries provide special opportunities. For example, in January 1994, Vannevar New Media was started by several young entrepreneurs to provide Internet services. Anna Grace, one of the four partners in the venture and 24 at the time the business was started, suggested that "we're really inventing this industry as we go."[77]

Others like Ludmila Rusakova and Jannifer Kramer, immigrants from Russia, are successful entrepreneurs of a service firm. Their firm, called MasterWord Services, offers translations of documents into as many as 40 different languages. Rusakova, who is 26 and president of the firm, has nine full-time employees and 30 contractors and the firm has revenues of approximately $2 million. Its customers include major oil and gas corporations, engineering companies, and law firms and it provides services on call 24 hours a day. Currently, Rusakova is building contacts with thousands of interpreters around the world that can be hired to help on projects as needed.[78]

Even in some of the areas where large firms are effective innovators, individual entrepreneurs and small firms still make significant contributions. This relationship is demonstrated by the interactions between small and large firms operating in the electronics industry (especially among firms located in the Silicon Valley in the United States). For instance, the semiconductor industry benefited significantly by the development of new technology-based firms. Most of these firms were spinoffs created by former employees of large firms.[79] The complementarity of small and large firms in innovation is exemplified by the integration of biotechnology and pharmaceutical firms to produce innovative drugs as discussed earlier.

The balance of power between large and small companies appears to be shifting. In the United States, small and midsize companies have been responsible for nearly all of the new jobs created since 1987.[80] The Davids have what the Goliaths so desperately want: agility, resourcefulness, and flexibility. Computers and communications technologies have been great equalizers, giving individual entrepreneurs and small firms an enhanced ability to mobilize resources, hire qualified individuals, and market their goods and services (e.g., on the Internet).[81] Small firms have created most of the new jobs in the U.S. economy in the 1990s because of (1) the flexibility provided by desktop computers, (2) networks of small firms that have the ability to communicate with each other, (3) vast computerized information databases, and (4) computer-controlled machine tools that help small companies provide quality equal to that of large manufacturers.[82]

Although small firms do not have large safety nets and benefits for employees, there is a certain excitement in working for such firms. Employees feel a clear sense of purpose. Lines of communication are short and direct; often the boss walks around the facility several times a day. Employees are dedicated and care and are given serious responsibility. They are trained in numerous jobs and typically are rewarded in ways that encourage their allegiance to their employer.[83]

Interestingly, new entrepreneurial firms have tended to perform better and have a higher survival rate than franchised startup firms. Franchised firms often receive considerable support from the larger businesses from which they are franchised but also must adhere to many of the larger firm's corporate policies and procedures. As such, franchises have less flexibility and are less innovative. Research has shown that over a three-year period, the average net loss for retailing franchising was a $4,000+, whereas cohort independent entrepreneurial retailing firms had an average net income for the same three-year period of more than $14,000. Similarly, franchise firms had a 45 percent failure rate, whereas young entrepreneurial independent retail firms had a slightly less than 24 percent failure rate for the same time period.[84]

Additionally, entrepreneurs who founded firms are significantly more innovative in their decisions than owners who did not initially establish the firm. These findings suggest that entrepreneurs who operate independent companies are likely to be more innovative and more successful than nonentrepreneurs, particularly those connected to larger firms and operating under their policies and procedures, like franchises.[85] One example of entrepreneurial success is provided by Centana Cycles, started 20 years ago by Bill and Jan McCready. It started as a small bike shop and now it is known as the premier tandem bike manufacturer in the United States. The firm sells approximately 2,000 two-seater bicycles annually. The firm does not provide old-fashioned tandem bicycles; instead, it employs sophisticated engineering to deliver the same handling as fancy single bicycles. It produces high-quality custom bicycles for its buyers. Currently, Centana is close to $3 million in sales annually. Centana markets its bikes on the Internet through a Worldwide Web page.[86]

Successfully innovating and commercializing a new product idea outside large corporations is not an easy task. Putting together the funding, marketing plan, and production facilities, along with completing the regulatory paperwork, is a challenge for entrepreneurs seeking to start their own private company. Nonetheless, small new technology-based firms have fostered the growth of many industries, including semiconductors, CAD, and biotechnology. These examples illustrate the importance of entrepreneurs and small firms in the development of new products and the diffusion of innovation.

What can large firms do to act small and be innovative? First, many firms, through restructuring as described in Chapter 7, are being organized into more manageable units.[87] Accompanying these restructurings, firms are reengineering to reduce organizational processes to the essential functions, share risks with partners, and listen more fully and effectively to customers. Second, large companies are trying to make themselves attractive places to work and are also seeking to bind employee interests to those of the company. This is accomplished through arrangements such as self-managed teams and customer-satisfaction bonuses. For example, Herbert Kelleher, CEO of Southwest Airlines, has sought to keep a small-firm culture by using traditional profit-sharing plans and a buddy system linking longtime and new employees.

Many large firms have handled decreasing competitiveness by laying off tens of thousands of employees. But downsizing has not realized the gains anticipated. Although head-count cuts happen fast and the stock market sometimes reacts favorably, research indicates that 50 percent or more of the firms end up worse after their downsizing.[88] Much to large firms' chagrin, massive layoffs can sometimes merely erode morale. Divestitures and spinoffs have produced much more favorable results.[89] In the long run, large firms must practice a delicate balancing act that allows autonomy at the lowest levels, while maintaining the advantages of size.

Several large companies have been able to overcome the problems noted and act more like small firms. As such, they have continued to be high-growth and high-return businesses. These firms are listed in Table 13.1, ranked in order of size. They are included in the ranking because of their ability to introduce better products than their competitors, attack and gain significant shares of new markets, and maintain a reasonable level of costs and bureaucratic controls. As shown in Table 13.1, most of these 10 firms are very well known to the public. The list includes such well-known firms as Wal-Mart, Hewlett-Packard, Motorola, and Southwest Airlines. Others may be less well known but no less important for the characteristics noted earlier. Included among these are VF, U.S. Healthcare, and Nucor. Obviously, Microsoft, Home Depot, and Intel have been high-growth firms during the last several years. In fact, they have the highest growth in sales among all on the list.[90]

Obviously, other large firms are also known for their innovative abilities. Among those are Thermo Electron and Xerox. During the last 12 years, for example, Thermo Electron has developed and spun off 12 new businesses. Thermo Electron spins off these businesses as independent companies but maintains a substantive equity position in them. Xerox has developed an innovative corporate approach to venture capital called Xerox Technology Ventures. The intent of this operation is to help commercialize new leading-edge technology. Since 1989, Xerox Technology Ventures has supported 12 start-ups and eight of those are generating at least $2 million annually in revenues. Another new venture, Advanced Workstation Products, Inc., was sold by Xerox Technology Ventures to Xerox for $15 million yielding a 375 percent return on the investment. Thus, the Xerox Technology Ventures operation provides evi-

Table 13.1   Top Large Entrepreneurial Firms Ranked by Total Size (Annual Sales)

1. Wal-Mart
2. Hewlett-Packard
3. Motorola
4. Intel
5. Home Depot
6. Microsoft
7. VF
8. U.S. Healthcare
9. Southwest Airlines
10. Nucor

Source: Based on data from W. Zellner, R. D. Hof, R. Brandt, S. Baker, and D. Greising, 1995, Go-go goliaths: These giants keep on expanding—just like scrappy startups, *Business Week*, February 13, 64–70.

dence that large corporations can be involved successfully in venture capital investments. These start-ups come from proposals developed by Xerox entrepreneurs. Approximately 100 Xerox engineers and scientists have applied since the beginning of Xerox Technology Ventures. The new venture operation eliminates many of the negative features of the large corporation in order to promote and support new entrepreneurial ideas.[91]

Thus, large and small firms alike can be innovative. Oftentimes, cooperative efforts between large and small firms may produce the best opportunity to commercialize innovations. The small firms can develop the innovation and the large firms can best get it to the market. This type of cooperative endeavor may be a key link to the ability of both large and small firms to achieve strategic competitiveness and earn above-average returns.[92]

■ Summary

- Three basic strategic approaches are used to produce and manage innovation. The first approach is called internal corporate venturing. This approach emphasizes the development of autonomous strategic behavior wherein product champions pursue new product ideas and executives help them manage the strategic context to commercialize the new products within a larger firm. Induced strategic behavior is a top-down process wherein incremental product changes and adjustments are made to the original product. This is a process driven by the organization's current corporate strategy, structure, and reward and control systems.

- The innovation process has three stages. Invention is the act of creating and developing a new product idea. The next stage, innovation, is the process of commercializing products from invention. Ultimately, other firms in the industry imitate the new product and diffuse the innovation. Imitation results in product standardization and market acceptance.

- In the past, internal innovation was done serially. Now, more parallel innovation is done through cross-functional teams. Facilitated by cross-functional teams, cross-functional integration can reduce the time a firm needs to introduce innovative products into the marketplace, improve product quality, and ultimately help a firm create value for its targeted customer. When innovations decrease the time to market (speed is a critical competitive factor) and create product quality and customer value, it is likely that a firm will be able to appropriate (or extract) value from the innovation process.

- A second approach used to produce and manage innovation is to obtain innovation through strategic alliances. Because knowledge is exploding and is often located in specialized firms, the only way a firm may

be able to obtain the knowledge necessary to create new products is through strategic alliances and/or joint ventures.

- The third basic approach for large firms to produce and manage innovation is to acquire it. Innovation can be acquired either through direct acquisition or through indirect investment. An example of indirect investment is the formation of a wholly owned venture capital division and/or the use of private placement of venture capital. Buying innovation, however, may be risky and detrimental to a firm's internal innovation process.

- The best way to succeed with a wholly owned venture capital operation is to consider the venture capital as an investment and only secondarily as a strategy to acquire innovation. Alternatively, a firm may seek to invest venture capital directly in small firms or to spin off firms into a network of affiliate companies.

- Small firms are particularly well suited for fostering innovation that does not require large amounts of capital (as semiconductors and chemicals do). Small firms have therefore become a vibrant part of industrialized nations, accounting for more job creation than large firms during the last decade. Where there are low-cost ways to invent, for example, through mechanical inventions, small firms are likely to have a higher innovation rate than large firms.

- Large firms are needed to foster innovation due to capital requirements. Small firms are often found to be better at creating specialty products and diffusing the innovation through spinoffs from large corporations. Large firms are seeking ways to think and act smaller in order to become more entrepreneurial. Often, however, the best way for both small and large firms to solve technological problems is to cooperate and collaborate.

■ Review Questions

1. What are three strategic approaches firms use to produce and manage innovation?

2. What are the two processes used to engage in internal corporate venturing known as autonomous strategic behavior and induced strategic behavior?

3. What are three types of innovation developed in organizations?

4. Some believe that when managed successfully, cross-functional teams facilitate the implementation of internal corporate ventures and a firm's innovation efforts. How should cross-functional teams be managed to achieve these desirable outcomes?

5. Some firms use strategic alliances to contract for innovation. What are the actions taken to use strategic alliances for this purpose?

6. How can a firm create value when it acquires another company to gain access to its innovations and/or its ability to produce innovations?

7. How do large firms use venture capital to create innovations and to identify new product opportunities?

8. What are the differences in the resources, capabilities, and core competencies of large and small firms to produce and manage innovation?

■ Application Discussion Questions

1. In the 1980s and 1990s, the number of acquisitions has accelerated. The number of dollars being spent as venture capital also increased. Discuss whether or not you think there is a relationship between the wave of acquisitions and the increase in venture capital funding.

2. In your opinion, is the term *corporate entrepreneurship* an oxymoron? In other words, is it a contradiction of terms? If so, why?

3. Discuss the reasons for using cross-functional teams as a popular approach to develop new product designs.

4. How would you suggest that developing countries with a tradition of centralized bureaucracy, such as China and Russia, begin to compete in a global economy that emphasizes product innovation? What should be emphasized in these countries to make firms and their countries more competitive on a global basis? Should they encourage

entrepreneurial firms (as is the case in Taiwan)? Should they encourage large firms (as is the case in South Korea)? Should both types of firms be emphasized? Be prepared to justify your views.

5. The restructuring movement (e.g., acquisitions, divestitures, and downsizing) of the 1980s and 1990s has apparently made U.S. firms more *productive* (as measured by traditional output-per-employee ratios). But, in your opinion, are U.S. firms more innovative due to the restructuring and downsizing activity? Why or why not?

6. Are strategic alliances a way to increase existing technological capacity, or are strategic alliances used more by firms that are behind technologically and trying to catch up? In other words, are strategic alliances a tool of firms that have a technological advantage, or are they a tool of technologically disadvantaged companies? Please explain.

■ Ethics Questions

1. Is it ethical for a company to purchase another firm in order to gain ownership of its innovative products? Why or why not?

2. Entrepreneurs are sometimes more effective when they work against existing product standards. How do entrepreneurs know when their new products might harm consumers? Should government agencies or trade associations establish guidelines to assist entrepreneurs on this issue? If so, what might some of those guidelines be?

3. Are there any ethical concerns surrounding the use of an internal venturing process to produce and manage innovation? Why or why not?

4. When participating in a strategic alliance, partner firms may legitimately seek to gain knowledge from each other. At what point does it become unethical for a firm to gain additional and competitively relevant knowledge from a strategic alliance partner? Is this point different when partnering with a domestic firm as opposed to a foreign firm? If so, why?

5. Small firms often have innovative products. When is it appropriate for a large firm to buy a small firm for its new products and new product ideas?

Internet Exercises

Here are the home pages for several exemplary innovative organizations:

- *3M*: http://www.3m.com/
- *Bellcore*: http://www.bellcore.com/

- *Microelectronics and Computer Technology Corporation*: http://www.mcc.com/
- *Motorola*: http://www.mot.com/

- *Southwest Airlines*: http://www.iflyswa.com/
- *Xerox*: http://www.parc.xerox.com/

Name other innovative companies. To what extent are these companies utilizing alliances, cross-functional teams, and speed of new product introduction? Or, do you think they are successful because of their size and other advantages unavailable to smaller firms?

Cohesion Case

The Defense Technical Information Center provides a directory of "Cooperative Programs for Reinvestment" (CPR) at:

- http://www.dtic.dla.mil/cpr

Find innovations in the public domain you can transfer for your own purposes.

Finally, you can also find small business development aids, services, and a lot of information on federal programs to assist small businesses from the Small Business Administration, which also has a long, well-organized list of links to other valuable servers:

- http://www.sba.gov/

▓ Notes

1. J. Pereira, 1996, Toy business focuses more on marketing and less on new ideas, *Wall Street Journal*, February 29, A1, A4; M. Warshaw, 1996, Renegades, *Success*, January/February, 32–40.

2. C. A. Lengnick-Hall, 1992, Innovation and competitive advantage: What we know and what we need to learn, *Journal of Management* 18: 399–429.

3. R.A. Bettis and M.A. Hitt, 1995, The new competitive landscape, *Strategic Management Journal* 16 (Special Issue): 7–19; M.A. Hitt, B.W. Keats, and S.M. DeMarie, 1995, Navigating in the new competitive landscape: Building competitive advantage and strategic flexibility in the 21st century, paper presented at the Strategic Management Society conference.

4. R. Price, 1996, Technology and strategic advantage, *California Management Review* 38, no.3: 38–56; L.G. Franko, 1989, Global corporate competition: Who's winning, who's losing and the R&D factor as one reason why, *Strategic Management Journal* 10: 449–474.

5. G.T. Lumpkin and G.G. Dess, 1996, Clarifying the entrepreneurial orientation construct and linking it to performance, *Academy of Management Review* 21: 135–172; K.M. Kelm, V.K. Narayanan, and G.E. Pinches, 1995, Shareholder value creation during R&D innovation and commercialization stages, *Academy of Management Journal* 38: 770–786.

6. B.C. Reimann, 1995, Leading strategic change: Innovation, value, growth, *Planning Review* 23 (September/October): 6–9.

7. Lumpkin and Dess, Clarifying the entrepreneurial orientation construct.

8. R.C. Solomon, 1995, Marketing heidegger: Entrepreneurship and corporate practices, *Inquiry* 38: 75–81.

9. J.M. Stopford and C.W.F. Baden-Fuller, 1994, Creating corporate entrepreneurship, *Strategic Management Journal* 15: 521–536.

10. C. Farrell, 1993, A wellspring of innovation: Factories have changed relentlessly from 18th century mills to today's worker-empowered auto plants, *Fortune* (Special Bonus Issue): 62.

11. J.P. Womack, D.T. Jones, and D. Roos, 1990, *The Machine That Changed the World* (New York: Rawson Associates), 14.

12. R.J. Schonberger, 1996, *World Class Manufacturing: The Next Decade* (New York: The Free Press).

13. J. Schumpeter, 1934, *The Theory of Economic Development* (Cambridge: Harvard University Press).

14. B. Czarniawska-Joerges and R. Wolff, 1991, Leaders, managers, entrepreneurs on and off the organizational stage, *Organization Studies* 12: 529–546.

15. A. Taylor III, 1994, Iacocca's minivan, *Fortune*, May 30, 56–66.

16. B. M. Bass, 1984, Leadership: Good, better, best, *Organization Dynamics* 12: 26–40.

17. Stopford and Baden-Fuller, Creating corporate entrepreneurship.

18. J. P. Kotter, 1990, *A Force for Change* (New York: The Free Press); H. Mintzberg, 1971, Managerial work: Analysis from observation, *Management Science* 18, no. 2: 97–110.

19. Taylor, Iacocca's minivan.

20. J. Pinchot, 1985, *Intrapreneuring* (New York: Harper and Row).

21. F.N. Pieke, 1995, Bureaucracy, friends and money: The growth of capital socialism in China, *Comparative Studies in Society and History* 37: 494–518.

22. M.H. Morris, D.L. Davis, and J.W. Allen, 1994, Fostering corporate entrepreneurship: Cross-cultural comparisons of the importance of individualism versus collectivism, *Journal of International Business Studies* 25: 65–89.

23. P.S. Li, 1993, Chinese investment and business in Canada: Ethnic entrepreneurship reconsidered, *Pacific Affairs* 66: 219–243.

24. T. Bates, 1994, An analysis of Korean-immigrant-owned small-business start-ups with comparisons to African-American and non-minority-owned firms, *Urban Affairs Quarterly* 30: 227–248.

25. R.A. Burgelman, 1983, A model of the interaction of strategic behavior, corporate context, and the concept of strategy, *Academy of Management Review* 8: 61–70.

26. D. Leonard-Barton, 1995, *Wellsprings of Knowledge: Building and Sustaining the Sources of Innovation* (Boston: Harvard Business School Press).

27. A.D. Chandler, 1962, *Strategy and Structure: Chapters in the History of Industrial Enterprise* (Cambridge: The MIT Press), 233–236.

28. L. Smith, 1995, Rubbermaid goes thump, *Fortune*, October 2, 91–104; Z. Schiller, 1995, The revolving door at Rubbermaid, *Business Week*, September 18, 80–83.

29. S. Brull, 1996, Nobuyuki Idei's big idea, *Business Week*, February 12, 90.

30. J.A. Trachtenberg and B. Ziegler, 1995, Sony is close to U.S. debut for home PCs, *Wall Street Journal*, November 13, A3.

31. P. Coy and R. Grover, 1995, It's Nobuyuki Idei's Sony now, *Business Week*, December 18, 39.

32. S.D. Moore, 1996, To stay independent, Volvo may need a plant in U.S., *Wall Street Journal*, January 11, B4.

33. A.K. Bryor and E.M. Shays, 1993, Growing the business with intrapreneurs, *Business Quarterly* (Spring): 43–50; D.F. Kuratko, K.V. Montagno, and J.S. Hornsby, 1990, Developing an intrapreneurial assessment instrument for an effective corporate entrepreneurial environment, *Strategic Management Journal* 11 (Special Issue): 49–58; H.B. Sykes and Z. Block, 1989, Corporate venturing obstacles: Sources and solutions, *Journal of Business Venturing* 4: 159–167; R.S. Schuler, 1986, Fostering and facilitating entrepreneurship in organization: Implications for organization structure and human resource management practices, *Human Resource Management* 25: 607–629; R.M. Kanter, 1985, Supporting innovation and venture development in established companies, *Journal of Business Venturing* 1: 47–60; W. Souder, 1981, Encouraging entrepreneurship in large corporations, *Research Management* (May): 18–22.

34. R. Blumenstein, 1996, GM to lease, rather than sell, electric cars, *Wall Street Journal*, February 15, A3.

35. T. Box, 1995, Ford unveils smog-eating technology, *Dallas Morning News*, December 2, F1, F2.

36. J.A. Byrne, 1993, The horizontal corporation: It's about managing across, not up and down, *Business Week*, December 20, 76–81.

37. J.E. Ettlie, 1988, *Taking Charge of Manufacturing* (San Francisco: Jossey-Bass).

38. A.C. Amason, 1996, Distinguishing the effects of functional and dysfunctional conflict on strategic decision making: Resolving a paradox for top management teams, *Academy of Management Journal* 39: 123–148; P.R. Lawrence and J.W. Lorsch, 1969, *Organization and Environment* (Homewood, Ill.: Richard D. Irwin).

39. D. Dougherty, 1992, Interpretive barriers to successful product innovation in large firms, *Organization Science* 3: 179–202; D. Dougherty, 1990, Understanding new markets for new

products, *Strategic Management Journal* 11 (Special Issue): 59–78.

40. M.A. Hitt, R.D. Nixon, R.E. Hoskisson, and R. Kochhar, 1996, The birth, life and death of a cross-functional new product design team, paper presented at the Academy of Management meetings, August, Cincinnati, Ohio.

41. J.D. Orton and K.E. Weick, 1990, Loosely coupled systems: A reconsideration, *Academy of Management Review* 15: 203–223.

42. S.L. Brown and K.M. Eisenhardt, 1995, Product development: Past research, present findings and future directions, *Academy of Management Review* 20: 343–378.

43. A. Barua, C.H.S. Lee, and A.B. Whinston, 1995, Incentives and computing systems for team-based organizations, *Organization Science* 6: 487–504.

44. I. Sager, 1995, The view from IBM, *Business Week,* October 30, 142–150; IBM says it's ready for networking era, 1995, *Dallas Morning News,* November 14, D4.

45. K.M. Eisenhardt, 1989, Making fast strategic decisions in high-velocity environments, *Academy of Management Journal* 32: 543–576.

46. W.Q. Judge and A. Miller, 1991, Antecedents and outcomes of decision speed in different environmental contexts, *Academy of Management Journal* 34: 449–463.

47. M.B. Lieberman and D.B. Montgomery, 1988, First-mover advantages, *Strategic Management Journal* 9 (Special Issue): 41–58.

48. W. Davidson, 1988, Technology, environments and organizational choice, paper presented at the conference on Managing the High-Tech Firm, Graduate School of Business, University of Colorado.

49. M.J. Chen and D.C. Hambrick, 1995, Speed, stealth and selective attack: How small firms differ from large firms in competitive behavior, *Academy of Management Journal* 38: 453–482.

50. W.M. Bulkeley, 1994, The latest big thing at many companies is speed, speed, speed, *Wall Street Journal,* December 23, A1, A5.

51. M.W. Lawless and P.C. Anderson, 1996, Generational technological change: The effects of innovation and local rivalry on performance, *Academy of Management Journal* 39: in press; U. Zander and B. Kogut, 1995, Knowledge and the speed of the transfer and imitation of organizational capabilities: An empirical test, *Organization Science* 6: 76–92.

52. K.M. Eisenhardt and B.N. Tabrizi, 1995, Accelerating adaptive processes: Product innovation in the global computer industry, *Administrative Science Quarterly* 40: 84–110.

53. Judge and Miller, Antecedents and outcomes.

54. M.A. Hitt, R.E. Hoskisson, and R.D. Nixon, 1993, A mid-range theory of interfunctional integration, its antecedents and outcomes, *Journal of Engineering Technology Management* 10: 161–185.

55. J.E. Forrest, 1992, Management aspects of strategic partnering, *Journal of General Management* 17, no. 4: 25–40; B. Borys and D.B. Jemison, 1989, Hybrid arrangements as strategic alliances: Theoretical issues in organizational

combinations, *Academy of Management Review* 14: 234–249.

56. J.L. Badaracco, Jr., 1991, *The Knowledge Link: How Firms Compete Through Strategic Alliances* (Boston: Harvard University School Press).

57. R. Langreth, 1995, Biotech companies abandon go-it-alone approach, *Wall Street Journal,* November 21, B4.

58. R.T. King, Jr., 1995, Pharmaceutical giants are eagerly shopping biotech bargain bin, *Wall Street Journal,* April 19, A1, A10.

59. G. Hamel, 1991, Competition for competence and interpartner learning within international strategic alliances, *Strategic Management Journal* 12: 83–103.

60. C.K. Prahalad and G. Hamel, 1990, The core competence of the corporation, *Harvard Business Review* 68, no. 3: 79–93.

61. D. Lei and M.A. Hitt, 1995, Strategic restructuring and outsourcing: The effect of mergers and acquisitions and LBOs on building firm skills and capabilities, *Journal of Management* 21: 835–860.

62. Hamel, Competition for competence.

63. King, Pharmaceutical giants are eagerly shopping.

64. D.C. Mowery and D.J. Teece, 1993, Japan's growing capabilities in industrial technology: Implications for U.S. managers and policy makers, *California Management Review* 35, no. 2: 9–34.

65. M.A. Hitt, R.E. Hoskisson, R.A. Johnson, and D.D. Moesel, 1996, The market for corporate control and firm innovation, *Academy of Management Journal* 39: in press.

66. M.A. Hitt, R.E. Hoskisson, R.D. Ireland, and J.S. Harrison, 1991, Effects of acquisitions on R&D inputs and outputs, *Academy of Management Journal* 34: 693–706.

67. Hitt et al., The market for corporate control and firm innovation.

68. M.A. Hitt, J.S. Harrison, R.D. Ireland, and A. Best, 1995, Learning to dance with a Tasmanian devil: Understanding acquisition success and failure, paper presented at the Strategic Management Society Conference; M.A. Hitt, R.E. Hoskisson, and R.D. Ireland, 1990, Mergers and acquisitions and managerial commitment to innovation in M-form firms, *Strategic Management Journal* 11 (Special Issue): 29–47.

69. T.E. Winters and D.L. Murfin, 1988, Venture capital investing for corporate development objectives, *Journal of Business Venturing* 3: 207–222.

70. G.F. Hardymon, M.J. DeNino, and M.S. Salter, 1983, When corporate venture capital doesn't work, *Harvard Business Review* 61, no. 3: 114–120.

71. U. Gupta, 1993, Venture capital investment soars, reversing four-year slide, *Wall Street Journal,* June 1, B2.

72. C. Farrell, K. Rebello, R.D. Hoff, and M. Maremont, 1995, The boom in IPOs, *Business Week,* December 18, 64–72; America's IPO edge, 1995, *Business Week,* December 18, 106.

73. P. Patel and K. Pavitt, 1992, Large firms in the production of the world's technology: An important case of non-globalization, in O. Granstrand, L. Hakanson, and S. Sjolander (eds.), *Technology Management and International Business: Internationalization of R&D and Technology* (New York: John Wiley & Sons), 53–74.

74. B. O'Reilly, 1994, The new face of small business, *Fortune,* May 2, 82–88.

75. Farrell et al., The boom in IPOs.

76. S.N. Mehta, 1995, Young entrepreneurs turn age to advantage, *Wall Street Journal,* September 1, B1.

77. C. Boisseau, 1996, Young entrepreneurs finding themselves in good company, *Houston Chronicle,* March 26, C1, C6.

78. Ibid, C6.

79. R. Rothwell, 1984, The role of small firms in the emergence of new technologies, *International Journal of Management Science* 12, no. 1: 19–29.

80. J.A. Byrne, 1993, Enterprise: Introduction, *Business Week* (Special Bonus Issue): 12.

81. G. McWilliams, 1995, Small fry go on-line, *Business Week,* November 20, 158–164.

82. P. Coy, 1993, Start with some high-tech magic, *Business Week* (Special Bonus Issue): 24–28.

83. C. Burck, 1993, The real world of the entrepreneur, *Fortune,* April 5, 62–81.

84. T. Bates, 1995, Analysis of survival rates among franchise and independent small business startups, *Journal of Small Business Management* 33: 26–36.

85. J.S. Walsh and P.H. Anderson, 1995, Owner-manager adaptations/innovation preference and employment performance: A comparison of founders and non-founders in the Irish small firm sector, *Journal of Small Business Management* 33: 1–8.

86. N.R. Brooks, 1996, Two-wheelers for two, *Dallas Morning News,* February 26, D1, D4.

87. R.A. Melcher, 1993, How Goliaths can act like Davids, *Business Week* (Special Bonus Issue): 192–201.

88. M.A. Hitt, B.W. Keats, H.F. Harback, and R.D. Nixon, 1994, Rightsizing: Building and maintaining strategic leadership and long-term competitiveness, *Organizational Dynamics* 23, no. 2: 18–32.

89. R.E. Hoskisson and M.A. Hitt, 1994, *Downscoping: Taming the Diversified Firm* (New York: Oxford University Press).

90. W. Zellner, R.D. Hof, R. Brandt, S. Baker, and D. Greising, 1995, Go-go Goliaths: These giants keep on expanding-just like scrappy start-ups, *Business Week,* February 13, 64–70.

91. How can big companies keep the entrepreneurial spirit alive?, 1995, *Harvard Business Review* 73, no. 6, 183–192; S. Kaufman, 1993, Xerox proves a big company can think small, *San Jose Mercury News,* November 29, E1, E2

92. Hitt, Keats, and DeMarie, Navigating in the new competitive landscape.

Cases

■ INTRODUCTION Preparing an Effective Case Analysis

In most strategic management courses, cases are used extensively as a teaching tool. A key reason for this is that cases allow opportunities to identify and solve organizational problems through use of the strategic management process. Thus, through analyzing cases and presenting the results, students learn how to effectively use the tools, techniques, and concepts that combine to form the strategic management process.

The cases that follow involve actual companies. Presented within them are problems and situations that managers must analyze and resolve. As you will see, a strategic management case can focus on an entire industry, a single organization, or a business unit of a large, diversified firm. The strategic management issues facing not-for-profit organizations also can be examined through the case analysis method.

Basically, the case analysis method calls for a careful diagnosis of an organization's current conditions (internal and external) so that appropriate strategic actions can be recommended. Appropriate actions not only allow a firm to survive in the long run, but also describe how it can develop and use core competencies to create sustainable competitive advantages and earn superior profits. The case method has a rich heritage as a pedagogical approach to the study and understanding of managerial effectiveness.[1]

Critical to successful use of the case method is your *preparation*—that is, the preparation of the student or case analyst. Without careful study and analysis, you will lack the insights required to participate fully in the discussion of a firm's situation and the strategic actions that are appropriate.

Instructors adopt different approaches in their use of the case method. Some require their students to use a specific analytical procedure to examine an organization; others provide less structure, expecting students to learn by developing their own unique analytical method. Still other instructors believe that a moderately structured framework should be used to analyze a firm's situation and make appropriate recommendations. The specific approach you take will be determined by your professor. The approach we are presenting to you here is a moderately structured framework.

Discussion of the case method is divided into four sections. First, it is important for you to understand why cases are used and what skills you can expect to learn through successful use of the case method. Second, a process-oriented framework is provided that can help you analyze cases and effectively discuss the results of your work. Using this framework in a classroom setting yields valuable experiences that can, in turn, help you successfully complete assignments received from your employer. Third, we describe briefly what you can expect to occur during in-class discussions of cases. As this description shows, the relationship and interactions between instructors and students during case discussions are different than they are during lectures. Finally, a moderately structured framework is offered for effective completion of in-depth oral and written presentations. Written and oral communication skills also are attributes valued highly in many organizational settings; hence, their development today can serve you well in the future.

Using the Case Method

The case method is based on a philosophy that combines knowledge acquisition with significant student involvement. In the words of Alfred North Whitehead, this philosophy "rejects the doctrine that students had first learned passively, and then, having learned should apply knowledge."[2] The case method, instead, is based on principles elaborated by John Dewey:

> Only by wrestling with the conditions of this problem at hand, seeking and finding his own way out, does [the student] think. . . . If he cannot devise his own solution (not, of course, in isolation, but in correspondence with the teacher and other pupils) and find his own way out he will not learn, not even if he can recite some correct answer with a hundred percent accuracy.[3]

The case method brings reality into the classroom. When developed and presented effectively, with rich and interesting detail, cases keep conceptual discussions grounded in reality. Experience shows that simple fictional accounts of situations and collections of actual organizational data and articles from public sources are not as effective for learning as are fully developed cases. A comprehensive case presents you with a partial clinical study of a real-life situation that faced practicing managers. A case presented in narrative form provides motivation for involvement with and analysis of a specific situation. By framing alternative strategic actions and by confronting the complexity and ambiguity of the practical world, case analysis provides extraordinary power for your involvement with a personal learning experience. Some of the potential consequences of using the case method are summarized in Table 1.

As Table 1 suggests, the case method can help you develop your analytical and judgment skills. Case analysis also helps you learn how to ask the right questions—that is, the questions that drive to the core of the strategic issues included

Table 1   Consequences of Student Involvement with the Case Method
1. Case analysis requires students to practice important managerial skills—diagnosing, making decisions, observing, listening, and persuading—while preparing for a case discussion.
2. Cases require students to relate analysis and action, to develop realistic and concrete actions despite the complexity and partial knowledge characterizing the situation being studied.
3. Students must confront the *intractability of reality*—complete with absence of needed information, an imbalance between needs and available resources, and conflicts among competing objectives.
4. Students develop a general managerial point of view—where responsibility is sensitive to action in a diverse environmental context.

Source: C. C. Lundberg and C. Enz, 1993, A framework for student case preparation, *Case Research Journal* 13 (Summer): 134.

within a case. Students aspiring to be managers can improve their ability to identify underlying problems, rather than focusing on superficial symptoms, through development of the skills required to ask probing, yet appropriate, questions.

The particular set of cases your instructor chooses to present to you and your classmates can expose you to a wide variety of organizations and managerial situations. This approach vicariously broadens your experience base and provides insights into many types of managerial situations, tasks, and responsibilities. Such indirect experience can help you make a more informed career decision about the industry and managerial situation you believe will prove to be challenging and satisfying. Finally, experience in analyzing cases definitely enhances your problem-solving skills.

Furthermore, when your instructor requires oral and written presentations, your communication skills will be honed through use of the case method. Of course, these added skills depend on your preparation as well as your instructor's facilitation of learning. However, the primary responsibility for learning is yours. The quality of case discussion is generally acknowledged to require, at a minimum, a thorough mastery of case facts and some independent analysis of them. The case method therefore first requires that you read and think carefully about each case. Additional comments about the preparation you should complete to successfully discuss a case appear in the next section.

Student Preparation for Case Discussion

If you are inexperienced with the case method, you may need to alter your study habits. A lecture-oriented course may not require you to do intensive preparation for *each* class period. In such a course, you have the latitude to work through assigned readings and review lecture notes according to your own schedule. However, an assigned case requires significant and conscientious *preparation before class*. Without it, you will be unable to contribute meaningfully to in-class discussion. Therefore, careful reading and thinking about case facts, as well as reasoned analyses and the development of alternative solutions to case problems, are essential. Recommended alternatives should flow logically from core problems identified through study of the case. Table 2 shows a set of steps that can help you develop familiarity with a case, identify problems, and propose strategic actions that increase the probability that a firm will achieve strategic competitiveness and earn superior profits.

Gaining Familiarity

The first step of an effective case analysis process calls for you to become familiar with the facts featured in the case and the focal firm's situation. Initially, you should become familiar with the focal firm's general situation (e.g., who, what, how, where, and when). Thorough familiarization demands appreciation of the nuances as well as the major issues in the case.

Gaining familiarity with a situation requires you to study several situational levels, including interactions between and among individuals within groups, business units, the corporate office, the local community, and the society at large. Recognizing relationships within and among levels facilitates a more thorough understanding of the specific case situation.

It is also important that you evaluate information on a continuum of certainty. Information that is verifiable by several sources and judged along similar

Table 2	An Effective Case Analysis Process
Step 1: *Gaining Familiarity*	a. In general—determine who, what, how, where, and when (the critical facts of the case). b. In detail—identify the places, persons, activities, and contexts of the situation. c. Recognize the degree of certainty/uncertainty of acquired information.
Step 2: *Recognizing Symptoms*	a. List all indicators (including stated "problems") that something is not as expected or as desired. b. Ensure that symptoms are not assumed to be the problem (symptoms should lead to identification of the problem).
Step 3: *Identifying Goals*	a. Identify critical statements by major parties (e.g., people, groups, the work unit, etc.). b. List all goals of the major parties that exist or can be reasonably inferred.
Step 4: *Conducting the Analysis*	a. Decide which ideas, models, and theories seem useful. b. Apply these conceptual tools to the situation. c. As new information is revealed, cycle back to substeps a and b.
Step 5: *Making the Diagnosis*	a. Identify predicaments (goal inconsistencies). b. Identify problems (discrepancies between goals and performance). c. Prioritize predicaments/problems regarding timing, importance, etc.
Step 6: *Doing the Action Planning*	a. Specify and prioritize the criteria used to choose action alternatives. b. Discover or invent feasible action alternatives. c. Examine the probable consequences of action alternatives. d. Select a course of action. e. Design an implementation plan/schedule. f. Create a plan for assessing the action to be implemented.

Source: C. C. Lundberg and C. Enz. 1993, A framework for student case preparation, *Case Research Journal* 13 (Summer): 144.

dimensions can be classified as a *fact*. Information representing someone's perceptual judgment of a particular situation is referred to as an *inference*. Information gleaned from a situation that is not verifiable is classified as *speculation*. Finally, information that is independent of verifiable sources and arises through individual or group discussion is an *assumption*. Obviously, case analysts and organizational decision makers prefer having access to facts over inferences, speculations, and assumptions.

Personal feelings, judgments, and opinions evolve when you are analyzing a case. It is important to be aware of your own feelings about the case and to evaluate the accuracy of perceived "facts" to ensure that the objectivity of your work is maximized.

■ Recognizing Symptoms

Recognition of symptoms is the second step of an effective case analysis process. A **symptom** is an indication that something is not as you or someone else thinks

■ *A **symptom** is an indication that something is not as you or someone else thinks it should be.*

■ *True problems* *are the conditions or situations requiring solution before an organization's, unit's, or individual's performance can improve.*

it should be. You may be tempted to correct the symptoms instead of searching for true problems. **True problems** are the conditions or situations requiring solution before an organization's, unit's, or individual's performance can improve. Identifying and listing symptoms early in the case analysis process tends to reduce the temptation to label symptoms as problems. The focus of your analysis should be on the *actual causes* of a problem, rather than on its symptoms. It is important therefore to remember that symptoms are indicators of problems; subsequent work facilitates discovery of critical causes of problems that your case recommendations must address.

■ Identifying Goals

The third step of effective case analysis calls for you to identify the goals of the major organizations, units, and/or individuals in a case. As appropriate, you should also identify each firm's strategic intent and strategic mission. Typically, these direction-setting statements (goals, strategic intents, and strategic missions) are derived from comments of the central characters in the organization, business unit or, top management team described in the case and/or from public documents (e.g., an annual report).

Completing this step successfully sometimes can be difficult. Nonetheless, the outcomes you attain from this step are essential to an effective case analysis because identifying goals, intent, and mission helps you to clarify the major problems featured in a case and to evaluate alternative solutions to those problems. Direction-setting statements are not always stated publicly or prepared in written format. When this occurs, you must infer goals from other available factual data and information.

■ Conducting the Analysis

The fourth step of effective case analysis is concerned with acquiring a systematic understanding of a situation. Occasionally cases are analyzed in a less-than-thorough manner. Such analyses may be a product of a busy schedule or the difficulty and complexity of the issues described in a particular case. Sometimes you will face pressures on your limited amounts of time and may believe that you can understand the situation described in a case without systematic *analysis* of all the facts. However, experience shows that familiarity with a case's facts is a necessary, but insufficient, step to the development of effective solutions—solutions that can enhance a firm's strategic competitiveness. In fact, a less-than-thorough analysis typically results in an emphasis on symptoms, rather than problems and their causes. To analyze a case effectively, then, you should be skeptical of quick or easy approaches and answers.

A systematic analysis helps you understand a situation and to determine what can work and probably what will not work. Key linkages and underlying causal networks based on the history of the firm become apparent. In this way, you can separate causal networks from symptoms.

Also, because the quality of a case analysis depends on applying appropriate conceptual tools (such as those presented in this book), it is important that you consider which ideas, models, and theories seem to be useful for evaluating and solving individual and unique situations. As you consider facts and symptoms, a useful theory may become apparent. Of course, having familiarity with conceptual models may be important in the effective analysis of a situation. Successful students and successful organizational strategists add to their intellectual tool kits on a continual basis.

■ Making the Diagnosis

■ *Diagnosis is the process of identifying and clarifying the roots of the problems by comparing goals to facts.*

■ *Predicaments are situations in which goals do not fit with known facts.*

The fifth step of effective case analysis—**diagnosis**—is the process of identifying and clarifying the roots of the problems by comparing goals to facts. In this step, it is useful to search for predicaments. **Predicaments** are situations in which goals do not fit with known facts. When you evaluate the actual performance of an organization, business unit, or individual, you may identify over- or under achievement (relative to established goals). Of course, single-problem situations are rare. Accordingly, you should recognize that the case situations you study probably will be complex in nature.

Effective diagnosis requires you to determine the problems affecting longer-term performance and those requiring immediate handling. Understanding these issues will aid your efforts to prioritize problems and predicaments, given available resources and existing constraints.

■ Doing the Action Planning

■ *Action planning is the process of identifying appropriate alternative actions.*

The final step of an effective case analysis process is called action planning. **Action planning** is the process of identifying appropriate alternative actions. Important in the action planning step is selection of the criteria you will use to evaluate the identified alternatives. You may derive these criteria from the analyses; typically, they are related to key strategic situations facing the focal organization. Furthermore, it is important that you prioritize these criteria to ensure a rational and effective evaluation of alternative courses of action.

Typically managers "satisfice" when selecting courses of actions; that is, they find *acceptable* courses of action that meet most of the chosen evaluation criteria. A rule of thumb that has proved valuable to strategic decision makers is to select an alternative that leaves other plausible alternatives available if the one selected fails.

Once you have selected the best alternative, you must specify an implementation plan. Developing an implementation plan serves as a reality check on the feasibility of your alternatives. Thus, it is important that you give thoughtful consideration to all issues associated with the implementation of the selected alternatives.

■ What to Expect From In-Class Case Discussions

Classroom discussions of cases differ significantly from lectures. The case method calls for instructors to guide the discussion, encourage student participation, and solicit alternative views. When alternative views are not forthcoming, instructors typically adopt one view so students can be challenged to respond thoughtfully to it. Often students' work is evaluated in terms of both the quantity and the quality of their contributions to in-class case discussions. Students benefit by having their views judged against those of their peers and by responding to challenges by other class members and/or the instructor.

During case discussions, instructors listen, question, and probe to extend the analysis of case issues. In the course of these actions, peers or the instructor may challenge an individual's views and the validity of alternative perspectives that have been expressed. These challenges are offered in a constructive manner; their intent is to help students develop their analytical and communication skills. Commonly instructors encourage students to be innovative and original in the development and presentation of their ideas. Over the course of an individual discussion, students can develop a more complex view of the case, benefiting from the diverse inputs of their peers and instructor. Among other benefits, experience with multiple case discussions should help students increase their knowledge of the advantages and disadvantages of group decision-making processes.

Comments that contribute to the discussion are valued by student peers as well as the instructor. To offer *relevant* contributions, you are encouraged to use independent thought and, through discussions with your peers outside of class, to refine your thinking. We also encourage you to avoid using "I think," "I believe," and "I feel" to discuss your inputs to a case analysis process. Instead, consider using a less emotion laden phrase, such as "My analysis shows. . . ." This highlights the logical nature of the approach you have taken to complete the six steps of an effective case analysis process.

When preparing for an in-class case discussion, you should plan to use the case data to explain your assessment of the situation. Assume that the case facts are known to your peers and instructor. In addition, it is good practice to prepare notes before class discussions and use them as you explain your view. Effective notes signal to classmates and the instructor that you are prepared to engage in a thorough discussion of a case. Moreover, thorough notes eliminate the need for you to memorize the facts and figures needed to discuss a case successfully.

The case analysis process we described above can help you prepare effectively to discuss a case during class meetings. Adherence to this process results in consideration of the issues required to identify a focal firm's problems and to propose strategic actions through which the firm can increase the probability it will achieve strategic competitiveness.

In some instances, your instructor may ask you to prepare either an oral or a written analysis of a particular case. Typically such an assignment demands even more thorough study and analysis of the case contents. At your instructor's discretion, oral and written analyses may be completed by individuals or by groups of two or more people. The information and insights gained through completing the six steps shown in Table 2 often are of value in the development of an oral or a written analysis. However, when preparing an oral or written presentation, you must consider the overall framework in which your information and inputs will be presented. Such a framework is the focus of the next section.

Preparing an Oral/Written Case Presentation

Experience shows that two types of thinking are necessary to develop an effective oral or written presentation (see Figure 1). The upper part of the model in Figure 1 outlines the *analysis* of case preparation.

In the analysis stage, you should first analyze the general external environmental issues affecting the firm. Next your environmental analysis should focus on the particular industry (or industries, in the case of a diversified company) in

Figure 1

Types of Thinking in Case
Preparation: Analysis and
Synthesis

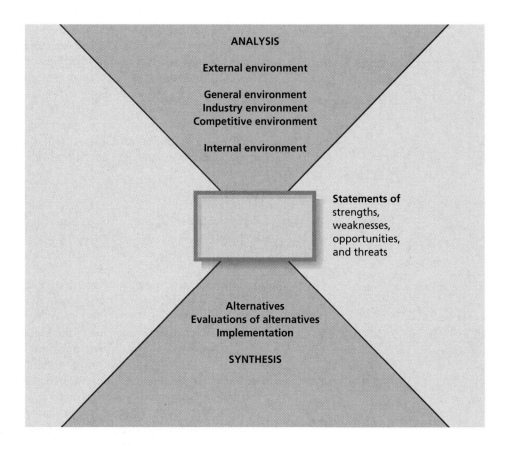

which a firm operates. Finally, you should examine the competitive environment of the focal firm. Through study of the three levels of the external environment, you will be able to identify a firm's opportunities and threats. Following the external environmental analysis is the analysis of the firm's internal environment. This analysis results in the identification of the firm's strengths and weaknesses.

As noted in Figure 1, you must then change the focus from analysis to *synthesis*. Specifically, you must *synthesize* information gained from your analysis of the firm's internal and external environments. Synthesizing information allows you to generate alternatives that can resolve the significant problems or challenges facing the focal firm. Once you identify a best alternative, from an evaluation based on predetermined criteria and goals, you must explore implementation actions.

Table 3 outlines the sections that should be included in either an oral or a written presentation: introduction (strategic profile and purpose), situation analysis, statements of strengths/weaknesses and opportunities/threats, strategy formulation, and implementation. These sections, which can be completed only through use of the two types of thinking featured in Figure 1, are described in the following discussion. Familiarity with the contents of your book's 12 chapters is helpful because the general outline for an oral or a written presentation shown in Table 3 is based on an understanding of the strategic management process detailed in those chapters.

Table 3   General Outline for an Oral or a Written Presentation
I. Strategic Profile and Case Analysis Purpose
II. Situation Analysis
A. General environmental analysis
B. Industry analysis
C. Competitive environmental analysis
D. Internal analysis
III. Identification of Environmental Opportunities and Threats and Firm Strengths and Weaknesses (SWOT Analysis)
IV. Strategy Formulation
A. Strategic alternatives
B. Alternative evaluation
C. Alternative choice
V. Strategic Alternative Implementation
A. Action items
B. Action plan

◼ Strategic Profile and Case Analysis Purpose

The strategic profile should state briefly the critical facts from the case that have affected the historical strategic direction and performance of the focal firm. The case facts should not be restated in the profile; rather, these comments should show how the critical facts lead to a particular focus for your analysis. This primary focus should be emphasized in this section's conclusion. In addition, this section should state important assumptions about case facts on which the analyses may be based.

◼ Situation Analysis

As shown in Table 3, a general starting place for completing a situation analysis is the general environment.

General Environmental Analysis

First, your analysis of the general environment should consider the *effects of globalization* on the focal firm and its industry. Following that evaluation, you should analyze general environmental trends. Table 4 lists a number of general environmental trends that, when studied, should yield valuable insights. Many of these issues are explained more fully in Chapter 2. These trends need to be evaluated for their impact on the focal firm's strategy and on the industry (or industries) in which it competes in the pursuit of strategic competitiveness.

Industry Analysis

Once you analyze the general environmental trends, you should study their effect on the focal industry. Often the same environmental trend may have a significantly different impact on separate industries. Furthermore, the same trend may affect firms within the same industry differently. For instance, with deregulation of the airline industry, older, established airlines had a significant decrease in

Table 4	Sample General Environmental Categories
Technology	■ Information technology continues to become cheaper and have more practical applications. ■ Database technology allows organization of complex data and distribution of information. ■ Telecommunications technology and networks increasingly provide fast transmission of all sources of data, including voice, written communications, and video information.
Demographic Trends	■ Computerized design and manufacturing technologies continue to facilitate quality and flexibility. ■ Regional changes in population due to migration ■ Changing ethnic composition of the population ■ Aging of the population ■ Aging of the "baby boom" generation
Economic Trends	■ Interest rates ■ Inflation rates ■ Savings rates ■ Trade deficits ■ Budget deficits ■ Exchange rates
Political/Legal Environment	■ Anti-trust enforcement ■ Tax policy changes ■ Environmental protection laws ■ Extent of regulation/deregulation ■ Developing countries privatizing state monopolies ■ State-owned industries
Sociocultural Environment	■ Women in the work force ■ Awareness of health and fitness issues ■ Concern for the environment ■ Concern for customers
Global Environment	■ Currency exchange rates ■ Free trade agreements ■ Trade deficits

profitability, while many smaller airlines, with lower cost structures and greater flexibility, were able to aggressively enter new markets.

Porter's five force model is a useful tool for analyzing the specific industry (see Chapter 2). Careful study of how the five competitive forces (i.e., supplier power, buyer power, potential entrants, substitute products, and rivalry among competitors) affect firm strategy is important. These forces may create threats or opportunities relative to the specific business-level strategies (i.e., differentiation, low cost, focus) being implemented. Often a strategic group's analysis reveals how different environmental trends are affecting industry competitors. Strategic group analysis is useful for understanding the industry's competitive structure and the profit possibilities within those structures.

Competitive Environmental Analysis

Firms also need to analyze each of their primary competitors. This analysis should identify competitors' current strategies, strategic intent, strategic mission, capabilities, core competencies, and a competitive response profile. This information is useful to the focal firm in formulating an appropriate strategy and in predicting competitors' probable responses. Sources that can be used to gather information about an industry and companies with whom the focal firm competes are listed in Appendix I. Included in this list is a wide range of publications, such as periodicals, newspapers, bibliographies, directories of companies, industry ratios, forecasts, rankings/ratings, and other valuable statistics.

Internal Analysis

Assessing a firm's strengths and weaknesses through a value chain analysis facilitates moving from the external environment to the internal environment. Analysis of the primary and support activities of the value chain provides opportunities to understand how external environmental trends affect the specific activities of a firm. Such analysis helps highlight strengths and weaknesses (see Chapter 3 for an explanation of the value chain).

For purposes of preparing an oral or a written presentation, it is important to note that **strengths** are internal resources and capabilities that have the potential to be core competencies. **Weaknesses,** on the other hand, are internal resources and capabilities that have the potential to place a firm at a competitive disadvantage relative to its rivals. Thus, some of a firm's resources and capabilities are strengths; others are weaknesses.

When evaluating the internal characteristics of the firm, your analysis of the functional activities emphasized is critical. For instance, if the strategy of the firm is primarily technology driven, it is important to evaluate the firm's R&D activities. If the strategy is market driven, marketing functional activities are of paramount importance. If a firm has financial difficulties, critical financial ratios would require careful evaluation. In fact, because of the importance of financial health, most cases require financial analyses. Appendix II lists and operationally defines several common financial ratios. Included are tables describing profitability, liquidity, leverage, activity, and shareholders' return ratios. Other firm characteristics that should be examined to study the internal environment effectively include leadership, organizational culture, structure, and control systems.

■ Identification of Environmental Opportunities and Threats and Firm Strengths and Weaknesses (SWOT Analysis)

The outcome of the situation analysis is the identification of a firm's strengths and weaknesses and its environmental threats and opportunities. The next step requires that you analyze the strengths and weaknesses and the opportunities and threats for configurations that benefit or do not benefit the firm in its efforts to achieve strategic competitiveness. Case analysts, and organizational strategists as well, seek to match a firm's strengths with its external environmental opportunities. In addition, strengths are chosen to prevent any serious environmental threat from impacting negatively on the firm's performance. The key objective of conducting a SWOT analysis is to determine how to position the firm so it can take advantage of opportunities, while simultaneously avoiding or minimizing environmental threats. Results from a SWOT analysis yield valuable insights into the selection of strategies a firm should implement to achieve strategic competitiveness.

The *analysis* of a case should not be overemphasized relative to the *synthesis* of results gained from your analytical efforts. There may be a temptation to spend most of your oral or written case analysis on results from the analysis. It is important, however, that you make an equal effort to develop and evaluate alternatives and to design implementation of the chosen strategy.

■ *Strengths* are internal resources and capabilities that have the potential to be core competencies.

■ *Weaknesses* are internal resources and capabilities that have the potential to place a firm at a competitive disadvantage relative to its rivals.

■ Strategy Formulation—Strategic Alternatives, Alternative Evaluation, and Alternative Choice

Developing alternatives is often one of the most difficult steps in preparing an oral or a written presentation. Development of three to four alternative strategies is common (see Chapter 4 for business-level strategy alternatives and Chapter 6 for corporate-level strategy alternatives). Each alternative should be feasible (i.e., it should match the firm's strengths, capabilities, and especially core competencies), and feasibility should be demonstrated. In addition, you should show how each alternative takes advantage of the environmental opportunity or avoids/buffers against environmental threats. Developing carefully thought out alternatives requires synthesis of your analyses' results and creates greater credibility in oral and written case presentations.

Once you develop strong alternatives, you must evaluate the set to choose the best one. Your choice should be defensible and provide benefits over the other alternatives. Thus, it is important that both alternative development and evaluation of alternatives be thorough. The choice of the best alternative should be explained and defended.

■ Strategic Alternative Implementation—Action Items and Action Plan

After selecting the most appropriate strategy (that is, the strategy with the highest probability of enhancing a firm's strategic competitiveness), you must consider effective implementation. Effective synthesis is important to ensure that you have considered and evaluated all critical implementation issues. Issues you might consider include the structural changes necessary to implement the new strategy. In addition, leadership changes and new controls or incentives may be necessary to implement strategic actions. The implementation actions you recommend should be explicit and thoroughly explained. Occasionally, careful evaluation of implementation actions may show the strategy to be less favorable than you thought originally. A strategy is only as good as the firm's ability to implement it effectively. Therefore, effort to determine effective implementation is important.

■ Process Issues

You should make sure that your presentation (either oral or written) has logical consistency throughout. For example, if your presentation identifies one purpose, but your analysis focuses on issues that differ from the stated purpose, your logical inconsistency will be apparent. Likewise, your alternatives should flow from the configuration of strengths, weaknesses, opportunities, and threats you identified by the internal and external analyses.

Thoroughness and clarity also are critical to an effective presentation. Thoroughness is represented by the comprehensiveness of the analysis and alternative generation. Furthermore, clarity in the results of the analyses, selection of the best alternative strategy, and design of implementation actions are important. For example, your statement of the strengths and weaknesses should flow clearly and logically from the internal analyses presented.

Presentations (oral or written) that show logical consistency, thoroughness, and clarity of purpose, effective analyses, and feasible recommendations (strategy and implementation) are more effective and will receive more positive evaluations. Furthermore, developing the skills necessary to make such presentations will enhance your future job performance and career success.

■ Appendix I   ■ Sources for Industry and Competitor Analyses

Abstracts and Indexes

Periodicals	*ABI/Inform*
	Business Periodicals Index
	InfoTrac (CD-ROM computer multidiscipline index)
	Investext (CD-ROM)
	Predicasts F&S Index United States
	Predicasts Overview of Markets and Technology (PROMT)
	Predicasts R&S Index Europe
	Predicasts R&S Index International
	Public Affairs Information Service Bulletin (PAIS)
	Reader's Guide to Periodical Literature
Newspapers	*NewsBank*
	Business NewsBank
	New York Times Index
	Wall Street Journal Index
	Wall Street Journal/Barron's Index
	Washington Post Index

Bibliographies

Encyclopedia of Business Information Sources
Handbook of Business Information

Directories

Companies—General	*America's Corporate Families and International Affiliates*
	Hoover's Handbook of American Business
	Hoover's Handbook of World Business
	Million Dollar Directory
	Standard & Poor's Corporation Records
	Standard & Poor's Register of Corporations, Directors, and Executives
	Ward's Business Directory
Companies—International	*America's Corporate Families and International Affiliates*
	Business Asia
	Business China
	Business Eastern Europe
	Business Europe
	Business International
	Business International Money Report
	Business Latin America
	Directory of American Firms Operating in Foreign Countries
	Directory of Foreign Firms Operating in the United States
	Hoover's Handbook of World Business
	International Directory of Company Histories
	Moody's Manuals, International (2 volumes)
	Who Owns Whom
Companies—Manufacturers	*Manufacturing USA: Industry Analyses, Statistics, and Leading Companies*
	Thomas Register of American Manufacturers
	U.S. Office of Management and Budget, Executive Office of the President, *Standard Industrial Classification Manual*
	U.S. Manufacturer's Directory

Companies—Private	*Million Dollar Directory*
	Ward's Directory
Companies—Public	Annual Reports and 10-K Reports
	Disclosure (corporate reports)
	Q-File
	Moody's Manuals:
	Moody's Bank and Finance Manual
	Moody's Industrial Manual
	Moody's International Manual
	Moody's Municipal and Government Manual
	Moody's OTC Industrial Manual
	Moody's OTC Unlisted Manual
	Moody's Public Utility Manual
	Moody's Transportation Manual
	Standard & Poor's Corporation, *Standard Corporation Descriptions:*
	Standard & Poor's Handbook
	Standard & Poor's Industry Surveys
	Standard & Poor's Investment Advisory Service
	Standard & Poor's Outlook
	Standard & Poor's Statistical Service
Companies—Subsidiaries and Affiliates	*America's Corporate Families and International Affiliates*
	Ward's Directory
	Who Owns Whom
	Moody's Industry Review
	Standard & Poor's Analyst's Handbook
	Standard & Poor's Industry Report Service
	Standard & Poor's Industry Surveys (2 volumes)
	U.S. Department of Commerce, *U.S. Industrial Outlook*

Industry Ratios

Dun & Bradstreet, *Industry Norms and Key Business Ratios*
Robert Morris Associates Annual Statement Studies
Troy Almanac of Business and Industrial Financial Ratios

Industry Forecasts

International Trade Administration, *U.S. Industrial Outlook Predicasts Forecasts*

Rankings & Ratings

Annual Report on American Industry in *Forbes*
Business Rankings and Salaries
Business One Irwin Business and Investment Almanac
Corporate and Industry Research Reports (CIRR)
Dun's Business Rankings
Moody's Industrial Review
Rating Guide to Franchises
Standard & Poor's Industry Report Service
Value Line Investment Survey
Ward's Business Directory

Statistics

American Statistics Index (ASI) Bureau of the Census, U.S. Department of Commerce, *Economic Census Publications*
Bureau of the Census, U.S. Department of Commerce, *Statistical Abstract of the United States*
Bureau of Economic Analysis, U.S. Department of Commerce, *Survey of Current Business*
Internal Revenue Service, U.S. Treasury Department, *Statistics of Income: Corporation Income Tax Returns*
Statistical Reference Index (SRI)

■ Appendix II   ■ Financial Analysis in Case Studies

Table A–1 Profitability Ratios

Ratio	Formula	What it Shows
1. Return on total assets	$\dfrac{\text{Profits after taxes}}{\text{Total assets}}$ or $\dfrac{\text{Profits after taxes + interest}}{\text{Total assets}}$	The net return on total investment of the firm or The return on both creditors' and shareholders' investments
2. Return on stockholders' equity (or return on net worth)	$\dfrac{\text{Profits after taxes}}{\text{Total stockholders' equity}}$	How profitably the company is utilizing shareholders' funds
3. Return on common equity	$\dfrac{\text{Profit after taxes} - \text{preferred stock dividends}}{\text{Total stockholders' equity} - \text{par value of preferred stock}}$	The net return to common stockholders
4. Operating profit margin (or return on sales)	$\dfrac{\text{Profits before taxes and before interest}}{\text{Sales}}$	The firm's profitability from regular operations
5. Net profit margin (or net return on sales)	$\dfrac{\text{Profits after taxes}}{\text{Sales}}$	The firm's net profit as a percentage of total sales

Table A–2 Liquidity Ratios

Ratio	Formula	What it Shows
1. Current ratio	$\dfrac{\text{Current assets}}{\text{Current liabilities}}$	The firm's ability to meet its current financial liabilities
2. Quick ratio (or acid-test ratio)	$\dfrac{\text{Current assets} - \text{inventory}}{\text{Current liabilities}}$	The firm's ability to pay off short-term obligations without relying on sales of inventory
3. Inventory to net working capital	$\dfrac{\text{Inventory}}{\text{Current assets} - \text{current liabilities}}$	The extent to which the firm's working capital is tied up in inventory

Table A–3   Leverage Ratios

Ratio	Formula	What it Shows
1. Debt-to-assets	$\dfrac{\text{Total debt}}{\text{Total assets}}$	Total borrowed funds as a percentage of total assets
2. Debt-to-equity	$\dfrac{\text{Total debt}}{\text{Total shareholders' equity}}$	Borrowed funds versus the funds provided by shareholders
3. Long-term debt-to-equity	$\dfrac{\text{Long-term debt}}{\text{Total shareholders' equity}}$	Leverage used by the firm
4. Times-interest-earned (or coverage ratio)	$\dfrac{\text{Profits before interest and taxes}}{\text{Total interest charges}}$	The firm's ability to meet all interest payments
5. Fixed charge coverage	$\dfrac{\text{Profits before taxes and interest} + \text{lease obligations}}{\text{Total interest charges} + \text{lease obligations}}$	The firm's ability to meet all fixed-charge obligations including lease payments

Table A–4   Activity Ratios

Ratio	Formula	What it Shows
1. Inventory turnover	$\dfrac{\text{Sales}}{\text{Inventory of finished goods}}$	The effectiveness of the firm in employing inventory
2. Fixed assets turnover	$\dfrac{\text{Sales}}{\text{Fixed assets}}$	The effectiveness of the firm in utilizing plant and equipment
3. Total assets turnover	$\dfrac{\text{Sales}}{\text{Total assets}}$	The effectiveness of the firm in utilizing total assets
4. Accounts receivable turnover	$\dfrac{\text{Annual credit sales}}{\text{Accounts receivable}}$	How many times the total receivables has been collected during the accounting period
5. Average collection period	$\dfrac{\text{Accounts receivable}}{\text{Average daily sales}}$	The average length of time the firm waits to collect payments after sales

Table A–5   Shareholders' Return Ratios

Ratio	Formula	What it Shows
1. Dividend yield on common stock	$\dfrac{\text{Annual dividends per share}}{\text{Current market price per share}}$	A measure of return to common stockholders in the form of dividends.
2. Price-earnings ratio	$\dfrac{\text{Current market price per share}}{\text{After-tax earnings per share}}$	An indication of market perception of the firm, usually, the faster-growing or less risky firms tend to have higher PE ratios than the slower-growing or more risky firms.
3. Dividend payout ratio	$\dfrac{\text{Annual dividends per share}}{\text{After-tax earnings per share}}$	An indication of dividends paid out as a percentage of profits
4. Cash flow per share	$\dfrac{\text{After-tax profits} + \text{depreciation}}{\text{Number of common shares outstanding}}$	A measure of total cash per share available for use by the firm.

■ Notes

1. C. Christensen, 1989, *Teaching and the Case Method* (Boston: Harvard Business School Publishing Division); C. C. Lundberg, 1993, Introduction to the case method, in C. M. Vance (ed.), *Mastering Management Education* (Newbury Park, Calif.: Sage).

2. C. C. Lundberg and C. Enz, 1993, A framework for student case preparation, *Case Research Journal* 13 (Summer): 133.

3. J. Soltis, 1971, John Dewey, in L. E. Deighton (ed.), *Encyclopedia of Education* (New York: Macmillan and Free Press).

Apple Computer

Jerry Culver
Tom Schipper
James Wylie

■ http://www.apple.com/

■ Apple 1996

During 1995, while Silicon Valley experienced record sales and profits, Apple was losing out. While worldwide sales of PCs increased 25 percent, Apple's total sales increased by only 12 percent and Apple's U.S. sales increased by only 4 percent.[1] Apple's already declining worldwide market position was further pressured by Microsoft's summer, multimedia blitzkrieg release of Windows 95. With Windows 95, Microsoft offered an operating system that matched the Macintosh in terms of ease of use and look. As Apple's woes became apparent, a management standoff came about during a board meeting in October, 1995 that resulted in the departure of Joseph Graziano and Dan Eilers, two well-respected senior executives with long tenures at Apple. Since then, many other top management executives have resigned.

Facing pressure from less-than-satisfactory sales and market penetration from Windows 95, Apple tried to pursue significant Christmas sales and regain some of its lost ground. Although sales had been plagued by a backlog due to a shortage in parts, Apple hoped to solve its manufacturing problems in time for Christmas. However, it underestimated the demand for high-end Power Macintoshes and instead shipped out tens of thousands of the low-end Performas with prices discounted up to 50 percent. Instead of increasing market share as intended and salvaging the last quarter, Apple ended up with $80 million dollars worth of inventory, a larger backlog on its Power Macintoshes, and a loss in the fourth quarter of 1995.[2]

In January, 1996, Apple announced a $69 million dollar loss for the fourth quarter and an impending layoff of 1,300 employees—roughly 8 percent of the company's workforce. More losses are expected in the second quarter of 1996 due to a $125 million dollar restructuring charge.[3] Further complicating Apple's situation, Moody's lowered Apple's bond rating and a major mutual fund sold most of its Apple holdings.[4]

Chairman Mike Markkula and CEO Michael Spindler were well aware of the poor financial results, and knew that they would be pressed at the upcoming shareholders meeting for explanations. New York money manager Orin McCluskey

---

This case was prepared under the direction of Professor Robert E. Hoskisson. It was written for the purpose of stimulating class discussion and is not intended to convey any judgment on the strategic decision making of the firm.

was one of the shareholders present. McCluskey declared, "You have misman-aged assets, you have wasted a valuable franchise, and you have brought a great company to its knees. Mr. Spindler, it is time to go."[5]

Jordan Mattson, a 32-year-old Apple employee who had been watching the meeting on a screen nearby, listened as CEO Spindler listed the company's assets: technology, loyal customers, and a significant brand name. When it was time for Q&A, Mattson said, "Mr. Spindler, I was looking at the list of Apple's most valuable assets you put up on the screen. You mentioned technology, customers, and the brand name, but employees are not there. Does the executive management team and the board consider the employees an asset of Apple Computer?"[6] Employees all over the Apple campus cheered in concentrated exasperation. During recent months, stock options had been withheld, departments were reorganized, and corporate indecision seemed to be the norm. Mr. Spindler scrambled for an answer, claiming it was a mistake and that he had meant to include the employees in his list of company assets.

Following the shareholders meeting were rumors, later confirmed, that Apple was holding talks with Sun Microsystems over a potential buyout deal. A union between Sun and Apple looked promising. There could certainly be synergies between Sun and Apple. Sun was a leading producer of workstations and Internet servers. Apple computers' multimedia capabilities made them the preferred choice as client computers and content creators on the Internet. There were also serious concerns, however, such as a potential culture clash. Apple's culture was relaxed and nonconforming while Sun's was all business. However, later reports were that the Sun Microsystems' offer for Apple was too low and talks were stalling.

Apple faced some daunting prospects despite its strong customer loyalty in niche markets, such as high-end publishing, education, and graphics applications, if the Sun talks fell through. These prospects included dissatisfaction from most of its stakeholders, the loss of its technological edge, the lack of a clear direction, problems in its marketing and distribution, and manufacturing operations. Perhaps most important is Apple's future identity: Will Apple go it alone or seek a buyer? Chairman Markkula, "the king maker," and Apple have many chal-lenges to address. Has Apple's leadership failed? Is Apple's business model a failure or is it a matter of execution? If it is a failure, should Apple switch to the Microsoft operating system/Intel chip standard? Is cloning part of the solution? Can Apple regain its status as a first mover and, if so, how?

■ Company Profile

Apple Computer, Inc., develops, manufactures, licenses, and markets products, technologies, and services globally for business, education, consumer, scientific and engineering, and government customers.[7]

Apple markets products for enhancing knowledge and ability, and communi-cating in new ways. Apple Computer, Inc., is a recognized pioneer in the information industry, although its relative lead has eroded in recent years. The company's success has been based on its innovative and easy-to-use personal computers, servers, peripherals, software, personal digital assistants, and com-munications products.[8]

■ Overview of Apple's History

Apple's origin dates back to 1976 when Steven P. Jobs and Stephen G. Wozniak set up shop in Cupertino, California. Jobs was a college drop out and Wozniak was a Hewlett-Packard engineer. Both men quit their jobs to devote their time to developing Apple.[9]

The money to buy and assemble the first 50 Apple I computer circuit boards was in part supplied through the sale of a Volkswagen van and a programmable calculator. Jobs and Wozniak's original plans to sell only circuit boards changed following a larger than expected first order. About 200 Apple I computers were sold, without a monitor, keyboard, or casing. The choice of the company name was "reminiscent of the time Jobs spent on an Oregon farm."[10] The company name and "user-friendly" design set the Apple computer apart from the computers and computer companies of the time.[11]

Seeing the potential of the business, Jobs convinced several successful industry figures to join Apple. When it incorporated in January 1977, A.C. "Mike" Markkula joined the company as an equal partner, president, and CEO. He has remained a key figure in Apple's strategy.

From its modest beginnings, Apple grew rapidly using financing from supportive investors, creative and dedicated employees, and innovative products.[12] Apple had sold over 130,000 Apple IIs by the end of 1980. Revenues grew from $7.8 million in 1978 to $117 million in 1980.[13] Also in 1980, Apple went public at $22 per share. All 4.6 million shares were bought within minutes.[14] Competition in the desktop computer market steadily intensified, especially with IBM's entry into the personal computer arena in 1981.

In 1983, Apple took a large step toward becoming recognized as a legitimate player in the computer industry by recruiting Pepsi-Cola president John Sculley. Sculley replaced Markkula as Apple's chief executive officer. In that same year Apple introduced Lisa®. Lisa was not a financial success, because of its high price tag, but it established a radical new direction in personal computing and set the industry standard for software based on a graphical user interface. The much-anticipated Macintosh®, introduced on January 24, 1984, improved on the technology developed from the Lisa program. Macintosh set a new standard for ease of use in the industry with its icons, pull-down menus, windows, and a mouse pointing device.[15]

In 1985, after a highly publicized legal dispute with Sculley and Apple's board of directors, Jobs left to form NeXt, with some former Apple personnel.[16] Despite this key change in management, Apple remained successful. The Macintosh recovered from slow initial sales and began to increase in popularity. Between 1986 and 1990, Apple's profits increased dramatically. New Mac computers competed well against the newest IBM offerings in terms of processing speed. Additionally, Apple's computers offered superior software and a better variety of peripherals, such as laser printers. These capabilities provided Apple with some key competitive advantages and enabled the company to gain market share while earning high margins.

Recent Competitive Difficulties

Microsoft's position as the leading operating system provider was firmly established by a 1992 court ruling. In the 1992 ruling, Apple lost its lawsuit against

Microsoft and Hewlett-Packard for infringement of Apple's copyrighted "look and feel" of the Macintosh user interface.[17] In 1993, Michael Spindler assumed the position of CEO. Sculley was forced out and A. C. Markkula moved back to the position of chairman.

Apple's initial decision to be the only manufacturer of both its hardware and operating system resulted in high sales volume and superb return on equity. By 1990, Apple had $1 billion in cash and sales of $5.5 billion. Its return on equity reached 32 percent, one of the highest in the industry. However, at this time its market share stabilized near 10 percent. Microsoft's Windows began gaining advantages and moved into the lead as the dominant supplier in the operating system market. In attempting to increase its market share, Apple decreased profit margins from a high of over 50 percent down to 25.8 percent in fiscal 1995.[18]

Manufacturing and distribution problems have recently reduced Apple's market share. In 1994, Apple released its PowerMac®. Its unanticipated popularity led to chronic shortages and missed sales opportunities, as well as negative publicity. Also in 1994, Apple finally agreed to allow outside firms to license its products. This strategic move was due to continuing erosion of market share caused by rapidly expanding personal computer cloning using Microsoft's operating system. Power Computing, Pioneer Electronic Corp., and Radius were among the firms first licensed to build Macintosh-compatible machines.[19] However, the numbers of Apple clones never became significant. This was in part due to Apple licensing primarily to small companies with limited distribution. As a result, the amount of software written for the Mac did not increase dramatically either.

The release of Windows 95 and its associated marketing blitz have left Apple's future viability in question. Mutual fund giant Fidelity Investments sold three-quarters of its almost 11 percent stake in Apple at the end of 1995, another indicator of lost confidence in the company.[20] Although Apple has been developing its own next-generation operating system—*Copland*—it is not expected to be ready for release before 1997. *Copland* is expected to offer better performance than Microsoft's Windows 95, but Apple may lose any potential benefits from this system if it further delays its release. Windows 95 will have gained significant market share and have even more software written for its operating system, to the detriment of Apple.

Pressures from Windows 95's rapid market penetration have led to speculation of an early release of a partially finished *Copland* that could include upgrades as they become available. This strategy would allow Apple to get its new operating system out sooner, but might lead to considerable consumer disappointment and lower than expected sales of the system.

■ Leadership and Corporate Culture

All Apple CEOs have had two things in common: They have all gotten in big trouble and Markkula has come in and helped to repair the strategic damage. Initial leadership came from Steve Jobs, the man whose technical vision allowed Apple to do the two things that have revolutionized the computer industry: make personal computers popular, and define the standard for the computer-user interface for ease of use. It was Steve Jobs who had the vision to recognize the marketing potential of the ideas that gave Apple its initial success and created the foundations for the corporate culture that remains today. Under Jobs, a culture formed that was ideal for creativity and a far cry from the stuffy, blue suits at

IBM. The mindset at Apple was not based on the precept of profits, but something greater: changing the world. This mindset and Jobs' lack of managerial discipline created an atmosphere legendary for its long working hours (people worked long hours, but kept whatever schedule they wanted), lack of dress codes, acts such as a pirate flag being hoisted at the Apple campus, and a continual supply of free fruit juice in the office refrigerator—a combination that resulted in unbridled creativity. Other examples of the leadership behavior Jobs used to nurture innovation were the purchase of a state-of-the-art stereo system, which was frequently played late into the night, and several luxury items (i.e., a BMW motorcycle and a Bosendorfer piano) intended to inspire the Mac development team. Although Jobs was the driver behind the Mac—pushing the development team to the limit and protecting the team from corporate meddling and compromising—he also tended to be arrogant and to fly off the handle. He was able to encourage creativity and had great technical vision during Apple's early development. However, Jobs was perceived by some to be the wrong leader to manage a larger, more stable company.[21]

Recognizing his own inability to lead a large company, Jobs recruited John Sculley (who was at the time Pepsi Cola's president) to be Apple's new CEO and lend stability. With Sculley at the helm, Apple developed and implemented an extremely expensive, brilliant, and daring marketing campaign to introduce the Macintosh (never equaled again until Microsoft's recent, lavish release of Windows 95). The centerpiece of the campaign was a Super Bowl ad that presented Apple as the liberator of intellectual tyranny, and its product, Macintosh, as a computer for everyone. Although the Mac's initial high sales were followed by a sluggish period, eventually the Mac's potential began to be realized. This potential was unlocked by software companies like Aldus, the developer of PageMaker—the application that revolutionized desktop publishing. The Mac eventually became a big hit with consumers and provided Apple with 53 percent profit margins.[22]

However, during the Mac's period of woes, the company's divided views over the direction it should take became embodied in a clash between Jobs and Sculley. As Jobs' ego got the best of him, he made an all-or-nothing ploy to wrestle control of the company from Sculley. However, Sculley was highly skilled in boardroom politics and when the board took a vote, Markkula backed Sculley; Sculley was in and Jobs was out.[23]

Although things looked grim at Apple with a layoff of 20% of its workforce and low sales, some advents in technology and software development changed the tide of Apple's fortune and made the initial part of Sculley's tenure a success.[24] As new chips increased the Mac's memory and processing power and new products like Aldus' PageMaker and the laser printer came out, the potential of the Mac was finally recognized. The combination of products like these thrust the Macintosh into the forefront of what came to be known as desktop publishing. As success came, so did the perks Apple became famous for: thousands of T-shirts given away for every occasion (they were considered the company's mood rings), lavish cafeteria food at subsidized prices, free Japanese-style neck massages, big parties, and luxurious retreats.[25] However, time would prove that in spite of the initial success, Sculley did not have the technical vision or insight to keep Apple at the vanguard of the personal computer industry.[26]

Sculley's leadership at Apple was marred by strategic mistakes, a lack of innovation, and indecision. In 1985, Apple made perhaps the costliest mistake in its history. Apple allowed Microsoft to copy the Mac's operating system's look and feel for an indefinite term. Although it would take Microsoft 10 years to come close to the Mac's operating system, Apple's lack of a significant upgrade on the Mac OS allowed Microsoft to catch up and jeopardize the future viability of Apple. Also, even though the strategic ramifications were not evident until about 1990, already in 1985, people at Apple had realized that as others copied Apple's graphical user interface, their advantage would erode. Eventually Apple would be isolated against the personal computer industry.

Experts recommended that Apple seize the moment, license its operating system, and cannibalize its own profits to become the industry standard. Although consideration was given to the recommendations, attachment to the philosophy of software/hardware integration and the high profits being yielded from the arrangement kept the executive staff and the board from acting. Although several plans were made to deal with the situation, no alternative seemed plausible without destroying the company's bottom line. The board of directors, composed mostly of investors who lacked computer industry experience (only two, including Markkula, had that experience), felt that the bottom line was more important than perceived threats caused by shifts in the computer industry.[27]

As pressure mounted for Apple to reestablish itself as a market leader, Sculley put himself in charge of R&D to more closely control new product lines. The result was the much publicized and technically flawed Newton—a digital personal assistant. The resulting flop and Sculley's aloofness (Markkula believed that Sculley was spending too much time with Hollywood celebrities and with President and Mrs. Clinton) led the board to unseat Sculley and replace him with Michael "Diesel" Spindler. Spindler had been in charge of Apple's European operations before being selected for the chief operations officer position by Markkula.[28]

Spindler, unlike Sculley, had the technical background, but was not an inspirational leader. Spindler oversaw a smooth transition to the Power Macintosh product line which was the result of an alliance with Motorola and IBM to produce PowerPC chips that could run Microsoft or Mac operating systems. During Sculley's tenure, Spindler helped prepare a plan to move Apple into a partnership in which Apple would determine the course of the relationship. A result of this plan was secret talks with IBM in 1994 to sell Apple. However, when IBM offered $40 per share, Apple counteroffered $60 per share, and IBM balked.[29] There were subsequent discussions of a buyout, but these were no longer met with interest by Louis V. Gerstner, Jr., IBM's CEO. On the public side, arguments broke out over the PowerPC chip's design. Apple had secretly hoped that IBM would clone its operating system, but IBM became disinterested as demand for its mainframe products surged. IBM, with the acquisition of Lotus, became more focused on the corporate network market and less interested in the PC market.[30]

Although the PowerMac platform had potential, many opportunities were missed. During the transition to the PowerMac product line, Apple's share prices went from $23 to $42 each.[31] However, a series of mistakes occurred that brought Apple to where it is today. Although the initial demand for the PowerMacs was high, Spindler targeted very conservative growth levels. This error and a series of forecasting problems created considerable unmet demand for Apple products. Even as Apple acknowledged the need to allow mass cloning, it proceeded cautiously and was hampered by the same shortage of parts that affected the company as a whole due to the proprietary nature of its hardware. Apple's mistakes shrank its market share and caused its profits to dwindle. But most critically, Apple's employees became demoralized. The situation was further complicated by Spindler's stern demeanor and unease in the public eye. The combination of Spindler's leadership style, and a series of marketing mistakes and reorganizations led to many executives leaving the company. Seventeen of the firm's top executives left between February 1995 and January 1996, and many others remain unsettled.[32] The market also did not respond well to Spindler's constant concern with golden parachutes for himself and his staff. Spindler, like his predecessors, was unable to curb the consensus mind-set that permeates Apple.[33]

Markkula, "the king maker/breaker," has always placed his firm support behind Spindler, but how much longer that will continue is being questioned. Markkula, a retiree from Intel in his thirties, had initially supported Jobs and Wozniak with the finances necessary to start Apple in exchange for a one-third stake.[34] Markkula was also the deciding vote between Sculley and Jobs— although he voted for Sculley, he did not do so until calling 35 different Apple managers to check up on Sculley.[35] Markkula was also central in the surprise dismissal of Sculley eight years later. The word on Markkula and his role at Apple can be encapsulated by Tim Bajarin (an industry consultant): "Nothing gets done at Apple without Markkula's consent."[36] Markkula is widely respected throughout the industry and is somewhat of a tinkerer. When not dealing with Apple's latest crisis, Markkula is usually overseeing a home electronics concern he owns.[37] However, in 1995, Markkula sold 30 percent of his stake in Apple.[38]

■ Geographic Business Units

To facilitate quicker decision making and better responsiveness to its markets, Apple has embarked on an overall effort to reorganize its marketing strategy by shifting from a global scale to a more responsive regional orientation.

Apple Americas

Apple Americas is a newly-defined geographic business unit that includes the United States, Canada, and Latin America. Until 1995, this unit did not include Canada, which was part of the Pacific group. In the United States, Apple's market share and its sales to corporate customers have been rapidly declining.[39] As mentioned previously, Apple has refocused its marketing and distribution in an effort to increase its performance in the American markets.

Apple Europe

Apple's operations in Europe were viewed as critical for maintaining its international growth. However, through early 1995, the European division suffered from declining market share. In March 1995, Marco Landi, a 52-year-old Italian, was recruited from Texas Instruments to lead the European division. Since taking the helm, Landi has overhauled the headquarters, replaced 7 of his 12 direct subordinates, restructured the marketing orientation from a country orientation to a regional focus, and brought in many more business controls. The results have been a slowing of the loss of market share, a fourth quarter 1995 jump in sales of 18 percent (resulting in a tripling in the annual profits), a 20 percent cut in overall costs, reduction in delivery time, and a much more disciplined atmosphere. Many of these concepts are being adopted at Apple's other business units. Landi is also credited with ensuring that every Apple shipped to Europe has a highly visible "Internet-ready" sticker applied to the box. Before Landi took over operations, there was no effort to capitalize on the multimedia readiness that makes Apple the preferred choice for Internet access.[40]

Apple Japan/Asia

Apple had a strong presence in the Japanese market during the middle 1990s. The reason for this strength was the importance of Apple's graphical capabilities in dealing with the written language symbols found in the Asian markets. In addition, operating systems in Japan remained fragmented and no dominant standard had been accepted. However, rather than try to establish itself as the standard, Apple has continued with its strategy of producing high-premium, proprietary systems. While the Microsoft standard gained strength, Apple limited its own growth with significant mistakes. Symantec, one of Apple's largest independent software developers, was not informed of changes in the Mac OS being released in Japan. This oversight resulted in over $1 million in lost sales due to software that was not compatible.[41] Also, even with a 50 percent increase in sales over the 1995 holidays, low margins resulting from price wars in the Japanese market left Apple in the red.[42] Apple is also seeking a presence in China, but it is not a market that is expected to mature for quite some time.

■ Apple's Customers

Entering 1995, Apple's sales, marketing, and customer solutions were supervised on a global level. Dan Eilers was made the senior vice president of marketing and put in charge of reorganizing these functions in order to stem the erosion of Apple's market share. The end result was a market segmentation strategy that consolidates the marketing functions within the three geographic business units. The expected benefits are "swifter decision making, better coordination of sales and marketing programs, and greater cost efficiencies for the company."[43] As part of the reorganization, responsibility for the functions was also shifted to the major geographic business units, each of whose heads will report directly to the CEO. Eilers effectively reorganized himself out of a job and was offered no position with similar authority; hence, that probably is why he left the company in October, 1995.

The company is focused primarily on delivering quality products to three broad customer segments: home/individual, business/government, and education. These markets collectively account for about 80 percent of Apple's business.

1. *Home:* Apple is the leader in home computer unit sales. In the early 1990s, the home-market segment accounted for 31 percent of personal computer unit sales and 23 percent of revenues.[44] According to research published in 1994 by Dataquest, Apple Macintosh personal computers held 13.9 percent of the worldwide home computer market, and an even stronger 18.7 percent in the U.S. home market. The sales in the home computer segment were projected to be the largest single market for U.S. producers in 1995.[45]

2. *Business:* Apple is the third largest personal computer vendor to business and government in the world, according to research by Dataquest. Apple's

revenues from business and government account for 45 percent of total revenues. Apple leads one of the fastest growing parts of the business market—business communication and publishing, which Apple estimates accounted for 25 percent of net sales in 1994. Apple also attempts to lead in one promising segment of the business market—mobile computing. Apple's PowerBook Duo® computer and PowerBook® bolster Apple's presence in the business and government markets.

3. *Education:* The education market represented 9 percent of personal computer unit purchases and 7 percent of revenues. According to Dataquest, Apple holds a 28 percent share of the worldwide education market. According to Field Research Corp, Apple holds a 63 percent share of the installed K–12 education market in the United States. Quality Education Data also claims Apple has earned a 63 percent share of the installed base of computers in K–12 public schools in the United States.

Apple has invested more than $20 million into Apple Classrooms of Tomorrow (ACOT), a joint research and development arrangement with public schools, universities and research agencies. The company has also awarded over $27 million in grants to more than 500 institutions across America during the past two decades.

In January 1996, Apple attempted to reassure the public that it was still firmly in the lead in education markets. Full-page ads appeared in the *New York Times* and *Wall Street Journal,* reminding the public that 56 million people are currently using Macintoshes and that the Mac is the No. 1 computer on college campuses. It is also the machine used for at least 40 percent of authoring activities of Internet sites.

Apple estimates that sales to education contribute 25 percent of its net sales. This area has always been viewed as critical for establishing high recognition and familiarity among potential personal computer customers. Microsoft's growing position in education segments puts greater pressure on Apple to get younger users to become loyal to Apple computers. The lifetime patronage and value of such customers is important to Apple's ongoing success.

Additionally, Apple products have significant advantages for creators of entertainment content. Beginning with the integration of sound in the very first Macintosh, Apple continues to offer entertainment products and services such as the QuickTime Music Tool Kit I, Apple Interactive Music Track, and QuickTime VR (virtual reality) for people who want to create and enjoy movies, music videos, special effects, CD-ROMs, and interactive music.

■ Products, Services, and Solutions

Apple produces a full line of computer hardware, software and services including personal computers, servers, peripherals, applications software, online services, personal digital assistants, and networking and communication products that integrate Macintosh systems into different computing environments.

Hardware

Apple offers two distinct lines of computers. The first line is the continuation of its original Macintosh product and includes the Macintosh Classic, Macintosh II, Quadra series, Macintosh Performa, and PowerBook portables. These computers

Exhibit 1

Growth in Native Applications
for PowerPC Processor-Based
Products

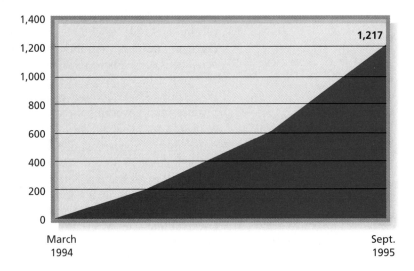

are manufactured solely by Apple and use Motorola 68000 series processors. In 1996, the installed base of Macintosh computers exceeded 16 million.

In March 1994, Apple began its second line of computers when it introduced the first Power Macintosh and began an important transition to integrate RISC technology into its entry-level, portable, and high-end desktop systems. The Power Macintosh is based on the PowerPC™ RISC microprocessor developed in alliance with IBM and Motorola.

Apple sold 1.4 million PowerMac computers and upgrades the first year and more than 1200 native applications are available from independent software developers (see Exhibit 1). Apple also offers a range of high-performance, large-storage PowerPC-based workgroup servers. In November 1994, Apple, IBM, and Motorola agreed to create a common hardware reference platform based on the PowerPC microprocessor, and designed to run multiple operating systems. The platform will be openly licensed and available for other companies to manufacture and can operate Windows, Windows NT, UNIX, and Mac OS.

Mac OS

The Macintosh operating system (Mac OS) is an acknowledged industry leader in ease of use, plug and play compatibility, and support for sophisticated graphics and productivity. The latest release of Mac OS is System 7.5. In the coming years, the Mac OS will feature a new user interface that conforms even more to the way people work, improved speech-to-text and text-to-speech technologies, and "agents" that can anticipate users' needs and learn from their work habits. Apple's cross-platform component software technology is designed to let users customize their computer work environment. In addition, Apple will offer new products based on QuickTime® multimedia technology software, and Quick-Draw™ GX graphics technology. In 1994, Apple announced plans to license the Mac OS to other personal computer vendors in order to expand the market for the platform, give customers the benefit of more choices and sources, and offer developers a larger installed base of users.

In February, 1996, three licensing arrangements were created. Motorola licensed the Mac OS; Toy Biz, Inc., licensed the Apple logo for a new line of electronic learning aids for preschool students; and a joint venture company was formed in the United Kingdom with Acorn Group, a leading education technology provider.

Newton

In 1992, Apple developed this pocket-sized portable computer. Newton was to provide a solid lead in the multimedia era. Sales of the Newton never reached forecasted levels. However, Newton is experiencing renewed interest. Although the Newton was initially criticized for its lack of functionality, refinements and new-found uses have injected some much needed vitality back into the product. The Newton now has much better accuracy in reading both cursive and printing and can also double as a Filofax/address book, an Internet terminal, as well as an E-mail/fax machine. The Newton is still expensive at $500, but it is getting great reviews from the computer press. China and Japan, both of which use Kanji, the Chinese characters with over 10,000 different variations, have found the Newton useful for recognizing Kanji characters.[46]

Networking and Communications

In addition to offering a range of networking and communications products, in 1996 Apple announced its alliance with VERSIT, a global cross-industry initiative with Apple, AT&T, IBM, and Siemens that will improve the interoperability between computers and communications platforms. By leveraging these standards, Apple plans to make the Macintosh a universal platform for telephone, PBX system, and computer networks.

■ Operations

Until the 1990s, Apple had historically based its manufacturing policy on high-end, high gross margin products. This was considered vital to finance the large R&D expenses of developing both hardware and software products. However, Joe Graziano, Apple's recently departed CFO, stated that "we have no choice. We must bring down our expense structure, raise our productivity, and fundamentally alter the way we do business."[47]

Apple began a systematic reorganization intended not just to reduce costs in the short term, but to change the basic cost structures of the company for long-term success. New, low-end products were developed to gain market share and reduce both development time and costs.

In the past, Apple performed most manufacturing-related functions in-house. Under the new system, items/services that can be bought from outside sources will be, rather than being developed by Apple. The manufacturing facilities were expanded to accommodate the greater variety of products being developed and the larger volumes intended to further reduce costs.

Apple's next step in reorganizing was to move away from focusing operations at the main campus in California. It currently has manufacturing facilities located in Sacramento, California; Fountain, Colorado; Cork, Ireland; and Singapore.

■ Cloning

When cloning began in 1985, an interesting contest emerged with regard to how Apple and Microsoft approached cloning. Microsoft adopted cloning as its model, whereas Apple shunned it in favor of proprietary hardware/software development. Apple's board members and executives scoffed at giving up their $2,000-per-machine profits in exchange for $50 per machine for loading its operating system onto machines made by cloners. Consequently, its sales have not kept up with the industry's growth, its market share has remained small, and its gross margins have gone from above 50 percent to below 20 percent.[48] As the validity of the Microsoft business model proved itself (over 80 percent in both market share and gross margins), there has been talk at Apple about cloning its own computers. However, not until 1994 did Spindler take action in that direction.

Even as Apple has taken steps toward cloning, it has done so cautiously. Considerable difficulty has arisen in developing a network of firms to clone the Apple products. A critical barrier to expanding the base of Apple clones is the amount of proprietary components involved in cloning an Apple product. This has led to problems finding a cloner that can produce inexpensive units with the same degree of seamlessness between hardware and software as Apple. Once identified and/or licensed, the cloners face the same parts shortages Apple has been experiencing. The logistical problem has prevented Apple from licensing to large-scale cloners such as Gateway 2000. Even when the reversal in the noncloning policy was announced, Apple was slow in identifying potential suitors; and many analysts believed that Apple was doing so because it was afraid of being outsold by the cloners. As of the beginning of 1996, cloning represented a negligible share of Apple computer sales.

■ Joint Ventures

As the Microsoft and Intel standard became dominant in the early 1990s, a strategic alliance was formed between Apple and IBM in 1991. The result has been several joint ventures plagued with problems stemming from clashing cultures to divergent agendas. The strategy was to create a three-pronged alliance. The first prong, Taligent, was a software venture between IBM and Apple, later joined by Hewlett-Packard, to develop new object-oriented technologies. Although some promising new object technology was developed, none of it gained widespread acceptance in the industry. In December 1995, Taligent was taken over by IBM, with Apple and H-P retaining licensing rights.[49]

Another venture, Kaleida, was created in the area of multimedia software with the intention of developing software that could be run on any personal computer, game player, or TV. However, Kaleida has been plagued by the overlap between its interests and those of its parent companies, which would sometimes deadlock over issues of proprietary technology. Although it was successful in creating a universal software layer for multimedia devices and a technologically sound language called ScriptX, the former has not been adopted widely and the latter has been hampered by the parent companies' disavowal to allow Kaleida Labs to interact with independent software developers in order to market products. In November 1995, this joint venture also folded, in this case within Apple (although IBM retains licensing rights).[50]

Additionally, the PowerPC alliance between IBM, Apple, and Motorola, was designed as a chip design venture. Even though IBM and Motorola have not enjoyed widespread success with the new PowerPC chips, Apple has converted almost all of its new product lines to the PowerPC chip design. This alliance is still in effect, but IBM has abandoned most of its efforts to adopt it as the standard for its OS/2 operating system.[51]

■ Markets and Competition

The computer industry is in a constant state of flux. One of the largest changes began in 1981, when IBM entered the market with an "open" system. At the time, each producer had its own hardware standards with little compatibility, but the IBM system enabled companies to build a computer to a set of standardized specifications. After the majority of incompatible systems were eliminated from the market, IBM's and Apple's systems were the industry leaders.

The change to standardized computer systems resulting from the spread of IBM clones had the effect of making the computer industry a commodity market with price rather than differentiation as the primary basis of competition. In many cases, clones of new or improved products were being developed even before the original product reached market. Of the proprietary systems competing against IBM, only Apple survived (see Exhibits 2 and 3). This benefited Apple by helping it maintain its differentiation and earn higher profit margins. In addition, Apple was the only producer of an operating system for its processors and had great control over the market for software that could be used on its machines. On the other hand, remaining the only proprietary producer of its systems forced Apple to compete on processor, computer, and operating system levels while its competitors could focus on any one of these areas. This permitted those making IBM clones to gain from economies of scale, reduced R&D, and quicker to-market introductions of their products, as well as broader brand recognition.

Because of the large number of computer product suppliers now competing against Apple, through mostly commodity pricing strategies, it must focus on achieving a series of incremental market advantages. Repeated breakthroughs and innovations could provide the long-term dominance, which is increasingly difficult to achieve by limited long-term sustained advantages. This strategy of continual market disruption offers a niche provider advantages that allow it to compete successfully against larger firms.

Exhibit 2
_____

Pre-1985 PC Industry

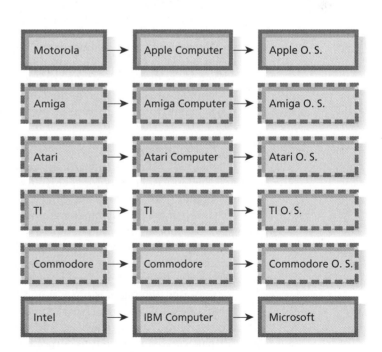

Exhibit 3

Present PC Industry

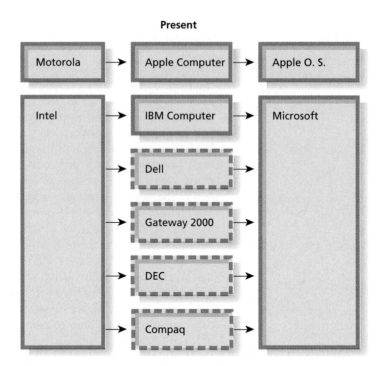

Processors

Apple is indirectly in competition with Intel and to a lesser extent Cyrix and Advanced Micro Devices (AMD). Realistically, Apple is also facing competition from "all" producers of technology and from some of those firms who have yet to enter the market with unknown products. Apple is closely involved in the design of its processors, but contracts out the production to Motorola for production of its 68000-based processors and to IBM for its PowerPC processors. This enables Apple to focus on software and marketing, which it considers to be core competencies. In addition, the support from Motorola and IBM has been beneficial in the development of the processors. Both companies have made many advances in the use of semiconductors and chip manufacture. However, the low number of suppliers gives the company no alternative when one of the suppliers is unable to meet demand or increases costs of the processors.

Computers

The computer manufacturing industry is a highly competitive environment. Apple faces competitors ranging from IBM and Compaq to little known local brands. While companies have sought, with varying degrees of success, to differentiate their computers, most of the IBM compatible computers are seen as a commodity item and competition is based largely on price.

This price competition is particularly damaging to Apple at this point because the firm has recently lost its edge in cost of computer ownership. Until 1996, despite higher initial costs, Macs were less costly to own when considering end-user training, customer support, and software expenses. Despite rising costs of operation and ownership, Apple systems were still rated the highest in terms of reliability, customer service, and customer satisfaction. The cost of ownership is particularly important to corporate customers and may be part of the reason U S

West, Deloitte & Touche, and EDS recently decided to move away from Apple machines and systems.[52]

Apple has been particularly strong in certain segments of the computer market. In the U.S. educational market Apple maintained its long-term advantage and captured 58 percent of the market in the 1995–96 school year, up from 46 percent in 1994–95.[53] Much of this gain was due to high sales of the low-end PowerPCs and was attributed to low prices and the ability to run both Apple and Microsoft based software.

A second stronghold for Apple is the multimedia market. In 1994, Apple held 22.9 percent of this rapidly growing market. Apple gained this advantage by being one of the first computer companies to offer multimedia systems and by continuing to support the development of this technology.[54]

■ Operating Systems

The final major area that Apple competes in is operating systems. Here Apple had competed with DOS and later with Windows. Apple's Macintosh operating system was unique in its visual interface when it was first introduced. However, by 1996 Windows competed directly with it.

Key to Apple's competitiveness in operating systems is that it is offering a complete package of processor, computer, and operating system. In contrast, most competitors produce only one of the three, and default to the Intel/IBM/Microsoft format. Because Apple is the only company making an operating system for its computers, the firm controls this market as long as it can continue to sell the computers to run the systems.

However, Apple faces problems in that increasingly, software developers are focusing on the IBM-compatible market, creating software for it before transferring it over to the Apple system. As a result, most software is available for PC clones sooner, influencing customers to buy PCs rather than Apple computers.

■ New Technologies

Since its inception, innovation has been key to Apple's success. Apple currently has a series of leading-edge products and technologies. These could determine the company's future. It is critical for Apple to convince other firms to adopt its standards and products.

The first and most important product is the pending release of the next-generation operating system, *Copland*. Although *Copland* is not expected to look all that different on the screen, it is supposed to revolutionize the way users organize and keep track of their files and documents. The secret behind this new improved capability is the inclusion of a relational database engine that can scan and analyze any type of text, file, document, drawing, or picture and sort it on demand with any parameters the user wants to use. For example, the computer could be told to find anything that mentions the holocaust, Primo Levi, and Italy, but not his suicide (you could also specify within a certain time span). *Copland* would then create a folder (i.e., put it into its pertinent place within the hard drive) that would contain icons representing all the relevant documents—users would not have to remember their file names in order to retrieve them. *Copland* is projected to be able to do the same with information flowing into the computer from the Internet or a private network. Plans include the licensing of *Copland*. The crucial element for Apple here is time (see Exhibit 4).[55]

Exhibit 4   Apple's Promised and Actual Release Dates

	Promised	Actual or Projected
System 7.5	October 1994	October 1994
System 7.5.2 for PCI	May 1995	May 1995
System 8 (Copland)—Alpha	September 1995	December 1995
Copland—Beta	End of 1995	1st Quarter 1996
Copland to ship	Mid-1996	1st Quarter 1997

Source: B. Picarille, 1995, Copland may miss '95 Boat, *Computerworld*, November 6, 45.

Apple also has major plans for a new product, Pippin, a computer/CD-ROM game machine/Internet terminal/TV box. Pippin is part of an effort to enter the future of home electronics. The new product will be bundled with Internet services and the ability to play on line with other Pippin players. Pippin is expected to sell for around $650, which is much less than the $1,500 a family might have to spend to attain the same capabilities from combinations of products by other companies, but without the need to buy all the computing power of a desktop computer. Pippin also marks the first time Apple is following the Microsoft business model of being solely a software company—it is licensing the product to Bandai, a Japanese company famous for its Mighty Morphin Power Ranger action figures. Plans are to release Pippin in both the Japanese and American markets during the first half of 1996.[56]

Apple also hopes to be an important player in digital video disks (DVDs), the next generation in CDs that can hold expansive amounts of digital data. Digital data can include anything from audio to computer code to video. DVD is expected to make video conventional on computers. David Nagel, Apple's R&D chief, says, "Apple is moving into the consumer electronics space. We think DVD can be the bridge to take us there."[57]

In addition to new products, Apple will introduce a series of new services that will be created from the merging of computers, telecommunications, and entertainment. Legislation is about to be enacted that will allow the deregulation of the telecommunications industry and enable the conglomeration of communications, content, and personal computing. Already there have been mergers between Disney and Capital Cities (ABC), and Time Warner and Turner Broadcasting. This trend will only increase as the new rules become more clear. As these industries merge, new services such as interactive TV and the bundling of services ranging from long-distance phone service to unlimited Internet access will become commonplace. Technology will play a big role in determining possibilities and feasibility.

■ Major Competitors

Intel

Although Apple actually relies on Motorola and IBM to produce its processors, competition at this level is key to Apple's success. When it first began to make the computers on a large scale, Apple picked Motorola as its chip manufacturer.

Similarly, Intel became a major competitor in the computer industry when IBM contracted with it to design and produce processors for its personal computers. Starting with the 8086 chip, Intel has built a line of processors first for IBM and later for the majority of IBM-compatible machines. By 1993 it had 74 percent of the worldwide microprocessor market, compared to Motorola's 8 percent.[58]

Intel is known as a powerful engineering company and has developed one of the best known names in the computer industry. They are driven not only by competition with Apple, but by competition with Cyrix and AMD for the IBM-compatible market.

Competition on the processor level became more complex with the recent addition of IBM as a supplier for Apple's PowerPC processors.

IBM (and Compatibles)

The major competition Apple faces on the computer system level is IBM and the many IBM compatibles. This collection of compatibles has resulted from the key difference in IBM's strategy as opposed to Apple's. Rather than fiercely defending its patents, IBM created an open system and freely gave out its specifications. This enabled many companies to create peripherals and upgrades for IBM's hardware, and also expanded the market greatly as other computer makers copied the IBM set standard.

Microsoft

Microsoft has established itself as the software standard for IBM compatibles with its DOS and Windows operating systems. In addition, it is a major producer of software for these systems. This makes it Apple's major competitor on the software level. While Apple for a long time had the advantage in areas such as graphical user interfaces (GUIs), Microsoft's Windows has closed this gap and continues to improve with new releases.

The August, 1995, release of Windows 95 was carried out with unprecedented fanfare. The marketing campaign Microsoft has jointly developed with original equipment manufacturers (OEMs) and retailers is predicted to be in the $700 million to $1 billion range—arguably the largest ever. The hoopla surrounding *the event* included a light show at the Empire State Building, submarine rides in Poland, local midnight madness sales, and TV ads featuring the Rolling Stones.[59] Although Microsoft delayed the release of Windows 95 for almost two years, giving Apple time to come out with a parallel release, the product finally came out and has put much pressure on Apple since it goes far toward eliminating many perceptions of the advantage that the Macintosh system may have had in ease of use. Although corporate customers have been slow to adopt the new operating system because of fears of bugs, there have been high sales in the home users' market and focused efforts to penetrate the education market, one of Apple's mainstays.

Although the education market is not the most lucrative and it is one of Apple's mainstays, there are reasons for Microsoft's attempts to penetrate it. From the beginning Apple has had a strong market presence in the education market; its marketing function was developed to provide strong support at all levels and for differing needs. The theory behind providing strong support for education is that if somebody uses an Apple as a child, they will want to use one as an adult. Albeit a long-term strategy, Microsoft sees the value of such a strategy and is attempting to invade Apple's turf by developing its own education-specific support programs. Although there is strong built-in loyalty for Apple, Microsoft is providing similar programs and focusing on the PTA boards, where many parents will see the value of their children using the same computers they see in their workplaces. Furthermore, Microsoft is already getting the upper hand in the area of software development.[60]

A key part of the desktop battle that Apple is losing to Windows 95 is software development.[61] Without the software, a desktop computer is useless to most consumers. Although advents in hardware allow increased power, it is advances in the software that allow end users to make use of this increased power. As software developers see Windows products take a commanding 90 percent worldwide market share, it is not difficult to see which platform takes priority in the development schedule.

Apple's response to the release of Windows 95 was timid because of a wait-and-see attitude, and because it could not hope to match it. The ads that Apple released following the release of Windows 95 focused on Microsoft's history for flawed products. Although it had plenty of time to anticipate and plan for the release of Microsoft's Windows 95, Apple's own next-generation operating system, code named *Copland,* has been plagued by setbacks. It is currently not planned to be released until sometime in 1997.

■ Financial Analysis

Apple's historical financial data provide some insight into its current situation. Income, ROE, and ROA have fluctuated greatly with no obvious trend despite continual sales growth. These fluctuations are a result of Apple's continual price cutting in attempts to maintain market share. While these attempts have been somewhat successful in the past, Apple's current margins do not leave it much room to continue this strategy and no longer provide the funds required for the research and development needed to compete on a technological basis (see Exhibits 5 through 9).

■ Apple Faces Many Challenges

How Apple can manage its present problems and position itself for the future is at the crux of its very existence. Apple must determine if it would be better served to remain independent or to find a potential suitor. If a suitor is desired, what criteria should Apple apply in determining the suitor's attractiveness? Any consideration of a merger with a buyer would also have to entail the effect it would have on the portion of Apple's brand equity that stems from its corporate culture. If Apple decides to remain independent, how could it do so in the face of shrinking margins, erosion of market share, and industry isolation?

If Apple decides it can succeed on its own, it must discover solutions to the problems that it faces now. Apple's recent performance has shaken confidence in all the major stakeholder groups. Apple's leadership must find a way to restore the different stakeholder groups' confidence. Also imperative is the need to eliminate the "group think" syndrome that has afflicted Apple at the top. Can the board of directors play a role in this solution? Perhaps more importantly, can

Exhibit 5   Apple Historical Financial Data

	1995	1994	1993	1992	1991	1990	1989	1988
Income								
(Dollars in millions, except per-share amounts)								
Net Sales	$11,062	$9,189	$7,977	$7,087	$6,309	$5,558	$5,284	$4,072
Cost and Expenses								
Cost of Goods Sold	$8,204	$6,846	$5,249	$3,991	$3,314	$2,606	$2,695	$1,991
Research and Development	$614	$564	$665	$602	$583	$478	$420	$273
Selling, General and Administrative	$1,583	$1,384	$1,632	$1,687	$1,740	$1,729	$1,535	$1,188
Net Income	$424	$310	$87	$530	$310	$475	$454	$400
Earnings Per Share	$3.45	$2.61	$.073	$4.47	$2.62	$4.12	$3.60	$3.26
Outstanding Shares (thousands)	123,047	118,735	119,125	118,479	118,386	115,358	126,270	122,768
Cash Flows								
Cash and Cash Equivalents, Beginning of Period	$1,203	$676	$498	$604	$375	$438	$372	
Cash from Operations	−$240	$737	−$661	$884	$129	$964	$507	
Cash from Investment Activities	−$402	−$2	$493	−$913	$58	−$574	−$403	
Cash from Financing Activities	$195	−$208	$346	−$77	$42	−$454	−$38	
Total Cash Generated (used)	−$447	$527	$178	−$106	$229	−$64	$66	
Cash and Cash Equivalents, End of Period	$756	$1,203	$676	$498	$604	$375	$438	
Balance Sheet								
Current Assets	$5,224	$4,476	$4,338	$3,558	$2,864	$2,403	$2,294	$1,783
Total Assets	$6,231	$5,303	$5,171	$4,224	$3,494	$2,976	$2,744	$2,082
Liabilities								
Current Liabilities	$2,325	$1,944	$2,508	$1,425	$1,217	$1,027	$895	$827
Long-Term Debt	$303	$305	$7	$0	$0	$0	$0	$0
Stockholders' Equity	$2,901	$2,383	$2,026	$2,187	$1,767	$1,447	$1,486	$1,003
Employees	17,615							
Ratios								
ROA	6.80%	5.85%	1.68%	12.55%	8.87%	15.96%	16.55%	19.21%
ROE	14.62%	13.01%	4.29%	24.23%	17.54%	32.83%	30.55%	39.88%
Gross Margin	25.84%	25.50%	34.20%	43.69%	47.47%	53.11%	49.00%	51.11%

Source: U.S. Securities & Exchange Commission, form 10-K, Apple Computer, Inc., 1988–1995.

Apple's corporate culture be managed? Apple's corporate culture is a source of creativity, resiliency, and brand equity. Any plans to reshape the corporate culture must be balanced carefully against these. If changes are desirable, what should they be and why? Apple also faces a series of marketing problems stemming from mistakes in the accuracy of its forecasting and problems with its operations. How might these areas be improved and does cloning play a part in the solution?

Apple's decision to follow a proprietary hardware/software business model has left it vulnerable to its dependency on suppliers and competing against the industry on a vertical basis. Is Apple's business model a failure or is it a matter of execution? Is the Microsoft/Intel model of business better? As Windows 95 has

Exhibit 6   Competitor Information (Dollars in Millions)

	Intel		IBM			Microsoft	
	1994	*1993*	*1994*	*1993*	*1995*	*1994*	*1993*
Net Sales	$15,521	$8,782	$64,052	$62,716	$5,937	$4,649	$3,753
Costs and Expenses							
Cost of Goods Sold	$5,576	$3,252	$38,768	$38,568	$877	$763	$633
Research and Development	$1,111	$970	$4,363	$5,558	$860	$610	$470
Selling, General, and Administrative	$1,447	$1,168	$15,916	$18,282	$2,162	$1,550	$1,324
Net Income	$2,288	$2,295	$3,021	−$8,101	$1,453	$1,146	$953
Total Assets	$13,816	$11,344	$81,091	$81,113	$7,210	$5,363	$3,805
Long-Term Debt	$392	$426	$12,548	$15,245	$0	$0	$0
Stockholders' Equity	$9,267	$7,500	$23,413	$19,738	$5,738	$4,450	$3,242
Employees	32,600		219,839		17,801		
ROA	16.56%	20.23%	3.73%	−9.99%	20.15%	21.37%	25.05%
ROE	24.69%	30.60%	12.90%	−41.04%	25.32%	25.75%	29.40%
Gross Margin	51.60%	62.97%	39.47%	38.50%	85.23%	83.59%	83.13%

Source: U.S. Securities & Exchange Commission, form 10-K, for Intel, IBM, Microsoft, 1993–1995.

Exhibit 7   Wall Street Journal 1996 Shareholder Scoreboard: Computers & Information

Company Name	1 Year Return	Surplus/Deficit Relative to Industry	3 Year Avg. Return	S/D Rel. to Industry	5 Year Avg. Return	S/D Rel. to Industry
3Com Corp.	80.9	40.5	84.6	62.6	87.7	59.9
Adaptec Inc.	73.5	33.2	46.6	24.6	77.7	49.9
EMC Corp/MA	−30.1	−70.5	37.3	15.2	63.1	35.2
Dell Computer Corp	68.9	28.5	13	−9.1	41.2	13.3
Hewlett-Packard Co	69.4	29	35.4	13.3	41	13.1
Sun Microsystems Inc.	157	116.7	39.5	17.4	33.7	5.8
Silicon Graphics Inc.	−11.4	−51.8	24.5	2.4	32.6	4.7
Diebold Inc.	37.6	−2.8	30.1	8	32.4	4.5
Seagate Technology	97.9	57.5	34.3	12.2	32.2	4.4
Komag Inc.	76.6	36.2	38.1	16	31.2	3.3
General Motors CI E	37.1	−3.3	18	−4.1	23.5	−4.4
Compaq Computer Corp	21.5	−18.9	43.5	21.4	20.6	−7.2
Unisys Corp	−36.2	−76.6	−18.4	−40.5	17.1	−10.8
Digital Equipment	92.9	52.5	23.9	1.8	3.2	−24.7
Storage Technology Cp	−17.7	−58	4.8	−17.3	2.1	−25.7
Int'l Business Machines Corp	25.7	−14.7	24.3	2.2	−1	−28.9
Tandem Computers Inc.	−38	−78.3	−10.9	−33	−1.8	−29.6
Conner Peripherals Inc.	121.1	80.7	0.4	−21.7	−2.3	−30.2
Apple Computer Inc.	−17.3	−57.7	−17.9	−39.9	−4.7	−32.6
Read-Rite Corp.	25.3	−15.1	−9.4	−31.5	N.A.	N.A.
Gateway 2000	13.3	−27.1	N.A.	N.A.	N.A.	N.A.
Peer Average	**40.4**		**22.1**		**27.9**	

Source: 1996, Shareholder Scoreboard, *Wall Street Journal*, February 29, Shareholder Scoreboard Section. Reprinted with permission of *Wall Street Journal*, ©1996 Dow Jones & Company, Inc. All Rights Reserved Worldwide.

Exhibit 8

Apple Computer's Market Share

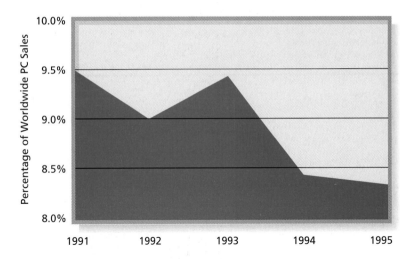

Exhibit 9

Apple Computer's Gross
Margins

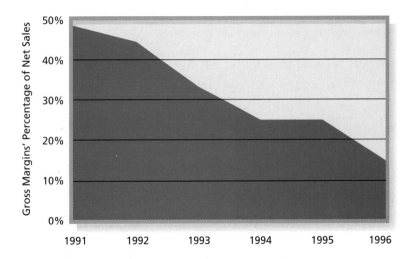

bridged consumers' perceptions of a technological gap, how can Apple regain its technological edge and impress this on consumers? If Apple is successful in correcting its present woes, what kind of changes should it implement to ensure future competitiveness? Should Apple attempt to regain its position as a first mover, and if so, how? In the future, should Apple focus on its strong markets or attempt to regain mainstream acceptance?

■ Notes

1. P. Burrows, 1996, Why fewer buyers are bobbing for Apples, *Business Week,* February 5, 38.
2. B. Schlender, 1995, Paradise lost: Apple's quest for life after death, *Fortune,* February 19, 64–74.
3. J. Carlton and J. E. Rigdon, 1996, Core business: After an Apple buyout, Sun could be mighty in Internet computers, *Wall Street Journal,* January 24, A1.
4. Ibid.
5. J. Goodell, 1996, The rise and fall of Apple Inc.: Part II, *Rolling Stone,* April 18, 59–63, 85–88.
6. Ibid.
7. U.S. Securities and Exchange Commission, Form 10-K, Apple Computer, Inc., 1995.
8. Ibid.
9. Apple Computer, Inc., 1996. G. Hoover, A. Campbell, and P. J. Spain (eds.), *Hoover's Handbook of American Business* (Austin, Tex.: Reference Press), 166.
10. Ibid.
11. Ibid.
12. N. M. Scarborough and T. W. Zimmerer, 1991, *Effective Small Business Management* (3rd ed.) (Columbus, Ohio: Merrill Publishing Company), 256–257.
13. Anon., Apple Computer, Inc.

14. J. Goodell, 1996, The rise and fall of Apple Inc., Part I, *Rolling Stone,* April 4, 51–57, 72–73.
15. Apple home page, March 1996.
16. Goodell, The rise and fall of Apple Inc.: Part II.
17. Anon., Apple Computer, Inc.
18. U.S. Securities and Exchange Commission, Form 10-K.
19. Apple Computer, Inc., 1996.
20. Ibid.
21. Goodell, 1996, The rise and fall of Apple Inc.
22. Goodell, 1996, The rise and fall of Apple Inc.: Part II.
23. Goodell, 1996, The rise and fall of Apple Inc.
24. Ibid.
25. Goodell, 1996, The rise and fall of Apple Inc.: Part II.
26. Ibid.
27. Ibid.
28. P. Burrows, K. Rebello, and I. Sager, 1996, The fall of an American icon, *Business Week,* February 5, 34–42.
29. Ibid.
30. Ibid.
31. Ibid.
32. Ibid.
33. Ibid.
34. J. Goodell, 1996, The rise and fall of Apple Inc.
35. P. Burrows and K. Rebello, 1995, Kingmaker and breaker: Will chairman Mike Markkula shake up Apple again?, *Business Week,* October 9, 40.
36. J. Carlton and D. Clark, 1996, Apple's fate lies in hands of Markkula, *Wall Street Journal,* January 26, A2.
37. Ibid.
38. Burrows and Rebello, Kingmaker and breaker.
39. Anon., 1995, Apple Computer, Inc. forms Apple North American division; James Buckley named president, *PR Newswire Association,* Financial Section, October 12.
40. G. Edmonson, 1995, A blueprint from Europe?, *Business Week,* February 5, 42.
41. Carlton and Rigdon, Core business.
42. Schlender, Paradise lost.
43. Apple to consolidate sales and marketing to accelerate successful market share strategy, *PR Newswire,* November 2, 1995.
44. D. B. Yoffie, J. Cohn, and D. Levy, 1992, Apple Computer 1992, Harvard Business Case 9–792–081, 5.
45. Ibid.
46. N. Huthseeing, 1996, The mother of development, *Forbes,* January 22, 88.
47. Goodell, The rise and fall of Apple Inc.
48. U.S. Securities and Exchange Commission, Form 10-K, Apple Computer, Inc., 1995.
49. B. Ziegler, 1995, Technology: Apple and H-P are leaving Taligent to IBM, *Wall Street Journal,* December 20, B2.
50. Ibid.
51. Ibid.
52. C. Levin and M. Perenson, 1995, Pay now—or you'll pay later, *PC Magazine,* May 16, 30.
53. Apple holds school market, despite decline, 1995; *New York Times,* September 11, C5.
54. Anon., 1995, Apple top worldwide multimedia PC vendor 3/14/95; Apple computer has 22.9% of multimedia personal computer market, *Newsbytes News Network,* March 14.
55. Schlender, Paradise lost.
56. Ibid.
57. Ibid.
58. Intel market share rises, 1994, *New York Times,* February 21, C4.
59. Advertisement, 1995, *Advertising Age,* August 28, 33.
60. Popular MS technology nights help parents and kids this year in 30 metropolitan areas discover the joy of learning with computers, 1995, *PR Newswire Association,* August.
61. Goodell, The rise and fall of Apple Inc.

■ CASE 2 Arizona Public Service Company and the Electric Utility Industry

Barbara W. Keats
Arizona State University

Samuel M. DeMarie
University of Nevada Las Vegas

■ http://www.epri.com/

Arizona Public Service Company, and its CEO Mark De Michele, are facing the challenges of responding to a rapidly changing environment. They have chosen to look for innovative ways to address the problems associated with large-scale organizational change. The following case study highlights the recent experiences of this company and its employees.

■ Industry Environment

The electric utility industry is composed of companies that generate, transmit, and distribute electrical power. Organizations must add real value in each of these areas of operation to be successful. With few exceptions, companies in this industry operate as regulated monopolies within governmentally determined territorial boundaries. Three primary sources of electrical power generation are used by utilities in the United States: fossil fuels (such as coal and oil), water, and nuclear reaction. A utility company may use either a single source or multiple sources for power generation.

As members of a regulated industry, utility companies have historically based their customer rate structure on a "cost-plus" basis. When costs rose, they went before their particular regulatory board with a "rate case" to justify and receive approval for a rate increase. These were generally approved, and the higher costs were then passed on to customers. Utilities have two very distinct classes of customers—residential and industrial or commercial—each with a unique rate structure (typically industrial and commercial customers pay lower rates per kilowatt hour than residential customers, based on volume discounts and economies of scale).

A number of changes have occurred during the last decade. This formerly regulated (monopoly-based) industry has become increasingly deregulated and more market driven (i.e., competitive). Thus, many electric utilities are anticipating experiences similar to those encountered by other organizations in previously regulated, now deregulated, industries (such as airlines, financial services, and telecommunications).

The most critical issue that these changes present to utility companies is the need to transform themselves from rate-driven monopolies into strategically driven competitive organizations. Those that do not perceive this critical challenge, or fail to respond adequately, risk losing both market share and profits. Six main forces are reshaping this industry:

1. *The emergence of independent power producers:* These are small companies that are not regulated. They typically have lower costs of overhead and capital investment than those borne by large utilities. This allows them to generate and deliver electrical power to both current and potential customers of existing utilities (including bids to entire municipalities) at greatly reduced rates. They may also offer more attractive rate/service packages. Independent power producers achieve competitive advantage by building generation capabilities designed to serve the specific needs of a narrow group of very large customers such as manufacturing facilities, mines, industrial parks, or universities, while the larger, regulated utilities are mandated to serve a broad range of customers.

2. *Wheeling:* This is a process whereby a large company with transmission "lines" already in place may be forced to allow the use of those lines by independent producers or other electric utilities (just as AT&T has had to allow access to its long-distance lines by other companies).

3. *Changing relationships with regulatory agencies:* In recent years, these relationships have become more adversarial, or at least more challenging. This may be attributed to the emergence of more effective consumer advocacy groups, as well as more challenging economic conditions in general.

4. *The emergence of more (and more varied) customer classes:* Increasingly, customer groups are demanding different configurations of price and service options. A major consideration is the ability to present a desirable "package" to new business customers considering relocation to the respective territory. (New business customers are an increasing source of competition given the forces listed here because they use more power and have more alternative sources of energy available to them than homeowners.)

5. *Cogeneration:* This is the ability of some businesses to generate a portion of their own power internally (using natural gas, for example), and the obligation on the part of the utility company to both buy back any excess power generated and maintain the capacity to supply power if the private source becomes incapacitated or insufficient for any reason. This is a "double" threat because every megawatt of business lost means a utility's fixed costs have to be recovered from a smaller customer base, which in turn increases the pressure to raise prices to the remaining customers.

6. *Environmentalism:* Utilities face pressures from a number of sources related to environmental issues. For example, there are governmental pressures to reduce emissions of compounds such as sulphur dioxide and carbon dioxide. In addition, public concerns have been voiced over issues such as

(1) the safety of nuclear generators and disposal of the waste they produce, (2) "stray voltage," and (3) increased environmental stewardship in general. Industry members are searching for cost-effective responses to these issues.

These forces are requiring utility companies to recognize the need for strategic management, strategic planning, cost management, and a customer/driven (rather than rate-driven) approach to their operations. Thus, members of this industry are being forced to reexamine their organizational structures and control systems. This case is concerned with one organization's attempt to cope with these emerging forces and their anticipated impact on its future. Arizona Public Service Company (APS) is the largest investor-owned utility in Arizona. Operating as a regulated utility, APS is accountable to the Arizona Corporation Commission, a body of elected officials that hears and decides utility rate cases in the state of Arizona.

Historical Overview

The operation of utility companies (both gas and electric) in the state of Arizona dates back to 1886. Since that time, a number of mergers and divestitures have occurred among these companies. For the purposes of this case, the largest and most important of the mergers occurred in 1952. It was this merger that resulted in the establishment of the company that is known today as Arizona Public Service Company. APS is based in the city of Phoenix and provides electric service to 11 of the state's 15 counties. Within the state of Arizona, there are many variations in climate and terrain. Thus, APS must provide service and maintain facilities in locales ranging from large, well-developed metropolitan areas to rugged desert or steep mountains. Its primary source of power is fossil fuels, but APS is also the managing partner in a nuclear generating plant.

Pinnacle West Holding Company

In 1985, APS became part of the holding company Pinnacle West Capital Corporation. APS is the largest "component" within that holding company. Until 1989, Pinnacle West's holdings included APS, Merabank (purchased in 1986 for $422 million, and at the time the state's second largest financial institution), SunCor Development Company (a real estate development firm), Malapai Resources Company (uranium mining), and El Dorado Investment Company (a venture capital firm). In late 1989, Pinnacle West, in the throes of the savings and loan crisis, paid the federal government $450 million to take Merabank off its hands. Merabank was later acquired by Bank of America Arizona.

During the next few years, Pinnacle West also divested Malapai Resources, reducing its portfolio to include only APS, SunCor, and El Dorado. APS accounts for 98 percent of the combined revenues, and has been the only consistently profitable subsidiary. Despite this consistency, during the five-year period from the fourth quarter of 1988 through the third quarter of 1993, Pinnacle West lost a total of $438 million. This apparent paradox was the result of (1) operating losses at the other subsidiaries, (2) losses incurred by the divestiture of Merabank and Malapai, and (3) a $407 million write-off in 1991 for costs associated with the nuclear generating plant, which regulators ruled could not be recovered via increased rates to customers. As a result, Pinnacle West paid no dividends to common stock shareholders between December 1989 and December 1993, at which time it announced a dividend of 20 cents per share (its last dividend in 1989 was 40 cents per share). Given these factors and its position as the largest component of the holding company, APS remains the principal focus of Pinnacle West.

Past Management Philosophy at APS

From 1952 to 1988, the top management of APS remained in the hands of a relatively small group of people who had been promoted from within the company ranks. During this period the company was consistently profitable. These positive financial results were due in large part to the fact that the company operated in a protected, stable industry environment, and had a rapidly growing customer base. As a result, there was little incentive for the management team to be particularly innovative, or to keep abreast of, or implement, leading-edge management practices. The management style was predominantly control oriented, and did not acknowledge the need to deal with human resource issues. In the words of one top executive, the public image of the company at that time was that it was "arrogant, expensive, out of touch, and shareholder rather than customer driven."

Until 1990, as was common among members of regulated industries, APS had not articulated anything resembling what might be called a mission, vision, strategy, or strategic plan. Capacity was the primary focus, and the company was consistently driven by preparing for the next rate case to put before the Arizona Corporation Commission (ACC). That is, as costs rose, the company merely assumed that they would pass those increases along to the consumer by going before the ACC, making their case, and receiving a rate increase approval. In 1991, the ACC granted APS a rate increase (an average of 5.2 percent), but included the condition that APS was not to seek another increase for at least two years.

Complying with this provision in the 1991–1993 time period became more challenging than had been anticipated, however. This was due in large part to APS's involvement with the operation and maintenance of the Palo Verde Nuclear Generating Station, a nuclear power plant. Palo Verde is owned by a consortium of seven utilities, including APS, which acts as the managing partner. APS's role as the managing partner means that all difficulties, public relations, and sanctions from the Nuclear Regulatory Commission (NRC) are APS's responsibility. Thus, despite its dispersed ownership, Palo Verde's impact on APS is quite large. To provide some perspective on this impact, the following section discusses its history and operations.

Palo Verde Nuclear Generating Station

In the late 1960s and early 1970s, APS faced a growing population in both residential and industrial/commercial customers, as well as sharply increasing costs associated with the use of fossil fuels to produce electricity. In response to these factors, the company turned to the possibility of using nuclear power generation, as did many other utilities. At the time, it was considered to be a relatively safe and clean source of power. Planning for a facility began in 1972. In

1974, a consortium of seven southwestern utilities (including APS), collectively known as the Arizona Nuclear Power Project, filed a construction permit with the NRC. The result was the Palo Verde Nuclear Generating Station. APS was designated the managing partner, and was the largest owner with a 29.1 percent stake.

The Palo Verde plans were subjected to comprehensive reviews by the NRC for coverage of safety, environmental, financial, and legal requirements. The construction permit was granted in May 1976, and construction began the next month. The personnel recruited for this project were drawn primarily from the ranks of those who had been involved in the construction of naval nuclear submarines. From the very beginning, this project was held at "arm's length" by APS's top management. Isolated in the Arizona desert, more than an hour's drive from the western boundaries of Phoenix, Palo Verde employees developed their own culture and ways of thinking and doing things. It was a militaristic culture, focused primarily on construction, with little concern for organizational issues, particularly strategic management and intraorganizational development. To make matters worse, top management at APS did little to integrate this operation into the larger organization. Thus, nothing interfered with the proliferation of this local, isolated culture. Palo Verde employees developed a sense of distance from (and, at times, resentment of) top management and company headquarters.

Palo Verde consists of three main operating units. The construction of the three units took more than 10 years to complete (1976–1988). By the time the first unit began to generate electrical power, the project had been strongly affected by inflation-driven construction costs and increasing interest rates. The actual costs at time of completion far exceeded initial estimates. The total dollar costs, including construction, start-up, and preoperational costs for the three units, the associated water reclamation facility, and all common facilities (but excluding financing charges handled by each co-owner, which were substantial), were nearly $6 billion (exceeding the original budget projections by more than $4 billion).

The project encountered a number of other difficulties. For example, in March 1989, all three units began experiencing a variety of equipment failures that would, in combination with subsequent regulatory action, take them out of service. Two of the units remained off line for the rest of the year. APS had to obtain approval from the NRC before restarting each unit. The outages contributed to a reduced ROE for 1989 of 9.4 percent, well below the 12.5 percent authorized by the ACC.

As noted earlier, in 1991 Pinnacle West took a $407 million write-off for Palo Verde costs. Regulators ruled that these costs could not be recovered from ratepayers. They were judged to be outside of the scope of previous rate hearings and determined to be excessive. This forced APS, as "managing partner," to absorb these costs, which resulted in a reported net loss for 1991 (see Exhibits 1, 2, and 3). In 1993, unit 2 was "down" from the time of a steam tube rupture in March until September of that year. Unit 3 output was reduced at the same time, as a precaution. Furthermore, the general public was becoming increasingly disenchanted with nuclear power as a source of electrical generation (for example, a plant built in Shoreham, Long Island, New York was built but never put into service), and the issue of waste disposal became problematic for all companies involved in such activities, including APS. To address NRC issues, and the host of other concerns, William Conway, a 21-year veteran of the commercial nuclear industry was hired in May 1989 to direct Palo Verde activities. Conway,

Exhibit 1 Arizona Public Service Company Statements of Income (Summarized)					
	Year Ended December 31, (thousands of dollars)				
	1994	1993	1992	1991	1990
Net Operating Revenues	$1,626,168	$1,602,413	$1,587,582	$1,515,289	$1,508,325
Fuel Expenses (Total)	$300,689	$300,546	$287,201	$327,207	$289,048
Operating Revenues Less Fuel Expenses	$1,325,479	$1,301,867	$1,300,381	$1,188,082	$1,219,277
Other Operating Expenses:					
Operations	$292,292	$282,660	$270,838	$286,187	$298,533
Maintenance	$119,629	$118,556	$119,674	$115,569	$109,814
Depreciation	$236,108	$222,610	$219,118	$217,198	$211,727
Taxes	$309,017	$305,553	$298,493	$239,892	$239,315
Total	$957,046	$929,379	$908,123	$858,846	$859,389
Operating Income	$368,433	$372,488	$392,258	$329,236	$359,888
Other Income (Deductions)	$44,510	$54,220	$48,801	$(324,922)	$56,713
Interest Expenses	$169,457	$176,322	$194,254	$226,983	$236,589
Net Income (Loss)	$243,486	$250,386	$246,805	$(222,669)	$180,012
Preferred Stock Dividend Requirements	$25,274	$30,840	$32,452	$33,404	$31,060
Earnings Available for Common Stock	$218,212	$219,546	$214,353	$(256,073)	$148,952

in turn, hired 13 executive or senior managers with nuclear industry experience. Conway served in this capacity until he retired in July 1993.

Major Organizational Change: The Impact of New Leadership

Mark De Michele was hired by APS in 1978, originally in the area of public relations. He became chief operating officer in 1982. However, given the nature of the board, and the existing management philosophy, De Michele's input was not sought or desired in any area other than day-to-day operations. This situation existed until 1988, when De Michele was appointed president and chief executive officer.

One of the first issues De Michele decided to tackle in this new role was one he had recognized for some time, but could do little about, his realization that the organization was "grossly overstaffed." In fact, according to his calculations, APS was last in the industry in terms of its customer-to-employee ratio. In his words, "People had been added as a response to immediate and often short-term problem situations, then just stayed around" (after all, past management philosophy assumed that increased costs could always be absorbed by the ratepayers).

There were other immediate issues facing De Michele in his new role. First, there was direct pressure from the ACC to abandon the notion that recovery of

Exhibit 2   Arizona Public Service Company Balance Sheets (Summarized)

	Year Ended December 31, (thousands of dollars)				
	1994	*1993*	*1992*	*1991*	*1990*
Assets					
Current Assets:					
Cash and Equivalents	$6,532	$7,557	$1,152	$139,085	$10,720
Accounts Receivable (Net)	$128,543	$121,267	$152,156	$118,191	$137,948
Accrued Utility Revenues	$55,432	$60,356	$51,517	$44,462	$46,466
Materials and Supplies	$89,864	$96,174	$95,978	$107,225	$101,440
Fossil Fuel	$35,735	$34,220	$36,668	$30,515	$27,810
Other	$104,267	$75,877	$6,037	$9,832	$9,520
Total	$420,373	$395,451	$343,508	$449,310	$333,904
Deferred Debits:					
Deferred Income Taxes	$576,163	$614,411	$223,417	$267,289	$149,118
Palo Verde Cost Deferrals	$464,522	$479,746	$494,169	$510,193	$624,526
Unamortized Debt Costs	$78,615	$81,146	$69,816	$43,518	$45,479
Other	$184,515	$185,258	$100,738	$75,944	$71,583
Total	$1,303,815	$1,360,561	$888,140	$896,944	$890,706
Utility Plants:					
Electric Plants	$4,352,810	$4,342,741	$4,359,528	$4,276,612	$4,886,824
Construction Work in Progress	$224,312	$197,556	$162,168	$197,643	$209,266
Nuclear Fuel (Net)	$46,951	$60,953	$61,603	$67,472	$81,980
Total	$4,624,073	$4,601,250	$4,583,299	$4,541,727	$5,178,070
Total Assets	$6,348,261	$6,357,262	$5,814,947	$5,887,981	$6,402,680
Liabilities					
Current Liabilities:	$131,500	$148,000	$195,000	$———	$159,000
Notes Payable	$3,428	$3,179	$94,217	$299,550	$173,366
Current Maturities of L-T Debt	$110,854	$81,772	$82,062	$79,905	$74,288
Accounts Payable	$134,582	$158,022	$148,309	$145,124	$154,572
Accrued Taxes and Interest	$50,487	$60,737	$75,089	$91,180	$34,297
Other	$430,851	$451,710	$594,677	$615,759	$595,523
Total					
Deferred Credits and Other:					
Deferred Taxes	$1,579,178	$1,541,003	$1,054,260	$1,020,839	$1,046,965
Other	$316,719	$325,783	$242,661	$236,718	$235,115
Total Liabilities	$2,326,748	$2,318,496	$1,891,598	$1,873,316	$1,877,603
Capitalization					
Common Stock	$1,217,465	$1,215,843	$1,216,491	$1,217,489	$1,212,523
Retained Earnings	$353,655	$307,098	$259,899	$215,974	$647,587
Preferred Stock	$268,561	$391,171	$394,196	$395,839	$361,014
Long Term Debt (Less Current)	$2,181,832	$2,124,654	$2,052,763	$2,185,363	$2,303,953
Total Capitalization	$4,021,513	$4,038,766	$3,923,349	$4,014,665	$4,525,077
Total Liab. & Capitalization	$6,348,261	$6,357,262	$5,814,947	$5,887,981	$6,402,680

Exhibit 3

Arizona Public Service Co. Gross Revenues

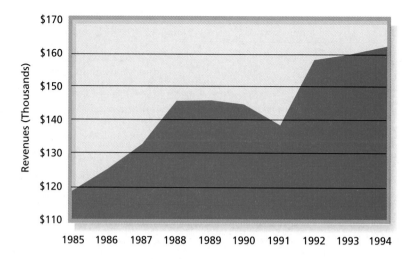

cost escalation would continue to be granted automatically through favorable rate cases. Second, there were indirect pressures from the financial markets due to the deteriorating perception among investors of the viability of APS's parent holding company (Pinnacle West), which threatened its debt rating. Finally, the workforce was deeply demoralized due to the large amount of negative publicity APS was receiving about the questionable investments of Pinnacle West, the poor financial and operating results of Palo Verde, and the high rates that APS charged its residential customers.

Employees were very aware of the unfavorable external perceptions of the company. In fact, interviews with some long-term APS employees in late 1993 echoed the words of the executive mentioned earlier regarding the public's perception of the company. They recalled that in the early 1980s, the company had such a poor public image that members of the organization were almost ashamed to admit they worked for APS.

When he became president and CEO in 1988, De Michele developed several projections to assess both the current and most likely future industry and company scenarios. He concluded that despite the high rates already being charged to customers, unless some major change was enacted relatively quickly, APS would need to seek a substantial rate increase (of approximately 36 percent) in order to recoup the projected cost increases. The political climate made the probability of receiving approval of a rate increase of this magnitude highly unlikely.

De Michele was developing a vision for the company. However, he was constrained by the "officer" group (shown in Exhibit 4) as to the manner in which he could approach the overriding issue that the organization was over-staffed. He decided that the organization needed to undergo a major downsizing. His initial target figure for reduction was 3,000 employees from the total of 9,000. This number was chosen to bring APS to the level of staffing that benchmarking studies of other utilities suggested as appropriate. De Michele determined that the layoffs would be distributed evenly across each major segment of the company, with the exception of Palo Verde (discussed later). However, in response to the pressure from the officer group the number was revised to 1,500 *positions* (some of which were not currently filled); thus, the outcome was a reduction of 1,200 *people*.

Exhibit 4   Arizona Public Service Company Organization Chart, 1987

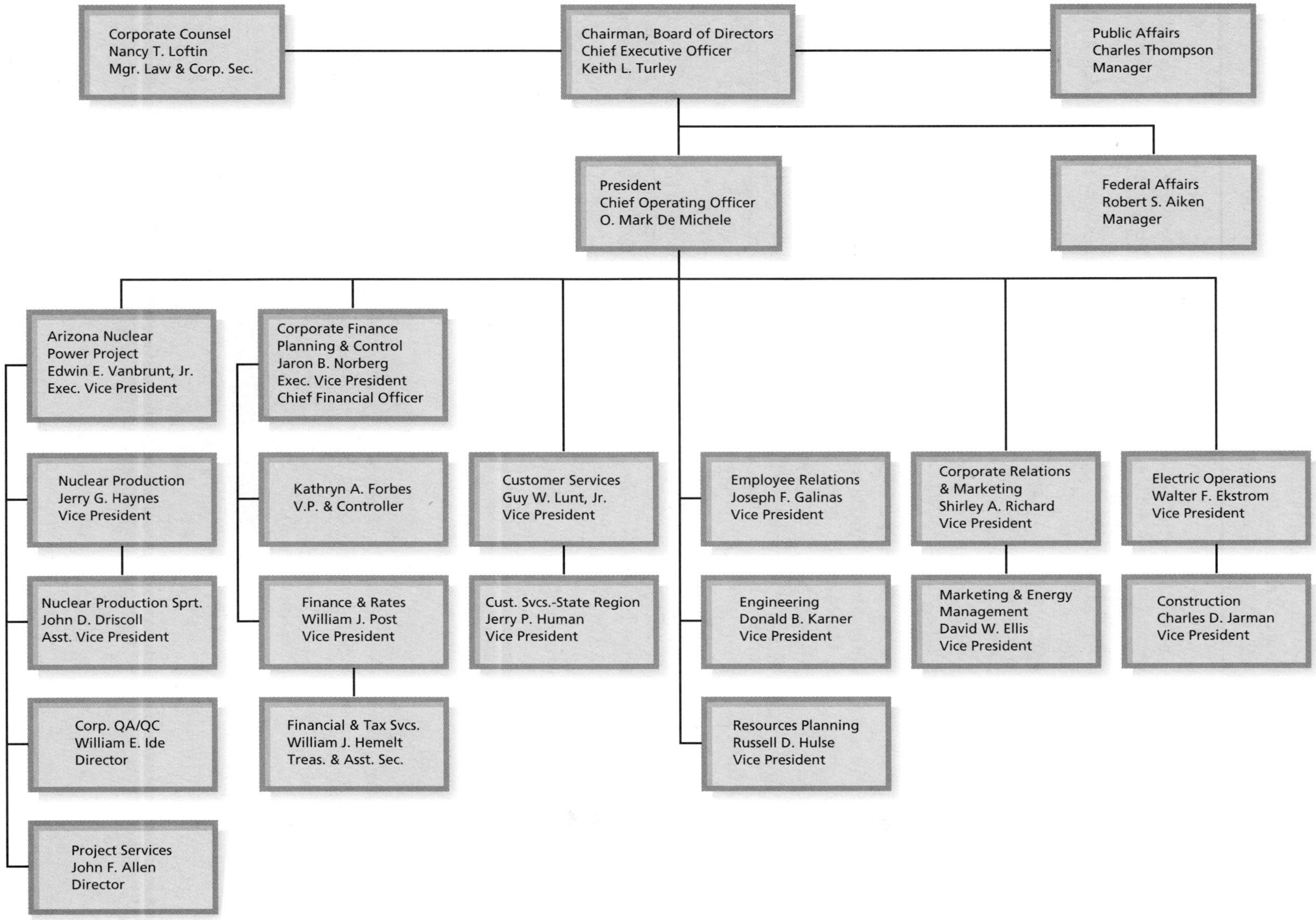

Public Affairs
Charles Thompson
Manager

Federal Affairs
Robert S. Aiken
Manager

Chairman, Board of Directors
Chief Executive Officer
Keith L. Turley

President
Chief Operating Officer
O. Mark De Michele

Corporate Counsel
Nancy T. Loftin
Mgr. Law & Corp. Sec.

Electric Operations
Walter F. Ekstrom
Vice President

Construction
Charles D. Jarman
Vice President

Corporate Relations
& Marketing
Shirley A. Richard
Vice President

Marketing & Energy
Management
David W. Ellis
Vice President

Employee Relations
Joseph F. Galinas
Vice President

Engineering
Donald B. Karner
Vice President

Resources Planning
Russell D. Hulse
Vice President

Customer Services
Guy W. Lunt, Jr.
Vice President

Cust. Svcs.-State Region
Jerry P. Human
Vice President

Corporate Finance
Planning & Control
Jaron B. Norberg
Exec. Vice President
Chief Financial Officer

Kathryn A. Forbes
V.P. & Controller

Finance & Rates
William J. Post
Vice President

Financial & Tax Svcs.
William J. Hemelt
Treas. & Asst. Sec.

Arizona Nuclear
Power Project
Edwin E. Vanbrunt, Jr.
Exec. Vice President

Nuclear Production
Jerry G. Haynes
Vice President

Nuclear Production Sprt.
John D. Driscoll
Asst. Vice President

Corp. QA/QC
William E. Ide
Director

Project Services
John F. Allen
Director

■ The First Major Downsizing

APS had just experienced what appeared to be one of its best years ever (1987) in terms of revenues (see Exhibit 5). However, cash flow was very poor, a fact that was not obvious to many people in the company. This is not difficult to understand given the existing industry context. In a cost-plus, rate-based culture, it would be assumed that any shortfall would be made up via the next rate case hearing. Thus, for De Michele, the immediate goals of the downsizing process were to improve the company's financial performance and decrease the likelihood of the need for another rate case.

Procedurally, the layoff in 1988 began as a one-third reduction in force "across the board." There was no differentiation among the areas of the company with regard to some cuts being "deeper" than others, with one exception—Palo Verde—where the number of employees was not reduced. According to De Michele, the reasoning for the latter was based primarily on timing. As early as 1987, the plant was experiencing operating problems that made compliance with NRC regulations difficult, and De Michele felt APS did not have sufficient time and information to undertake a general reduction in force at Palo Verde. He wanted to avoid any appearance of compromising safety in the pursuit of efficiency.

De Michele's goals for this process were primarily financial (the expected result of salary savings from the layoffs). However, the actual outcomes were well below what De Michele had anticipated, primarily due to the limitations imposed by the officer group (see Exhibit 6). Furthermore, part of the plan had been to offer an optional early retirement package, and the number of employees who accepted the offer far exceeded projections. As a result, many members of the organization, including some of the remaining top-level managers, felt that the company lost some of its most valuable employees, those who might have provided critical input in determining the future direction of the company.

According to De Michele, one of the most important lessons learned from the 1988 downsizing was "how not to do it." In organizational terms, there was no real restructuring, so the "survivors" were left in an environment where they were expected to do more with less. Culturally, there was no real change—the

Exhibit 5

Arizona Public Service Co. Net Profits

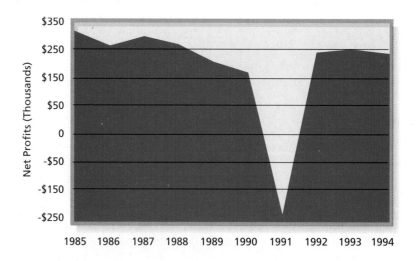

Exhibit 6

Arizona Public Service Co.
Number of Employees

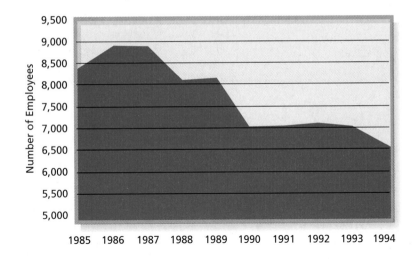

organization retained a rate-based mentality, and morale plummeted even further. He realized that a major restructuring was needed. Drawing on the outcomes of his first layoff attempt, he developed employee/management teams, encouraged greater interfacing among departments, and focused on department consolidation. He felt very strongly that the demoralized workforce needed to be brought into the downsizing process—to see it as something of which they were a part, rather than experiencing change as something that was being done *to* them. In making the case to the organization, De Michele met individually with large numbers of employees to bring the point home in a very personal way that, without radical change among the members of the organization in how they thought about and conducted their operations, their organization might not survive the impact from the changes occurring in their industry.

He believed that the organization's culture needed to play a key role. In response to that belief, he developed a target for the employees to make APS one of the "Top Five" utility companies in the United States by 1995. Thus, "Top 5 by '95" was issued as a rallying focus for the organization, although the set of specific goals attached to it was not developed until several months later (see Exhibit 7). At the time, it was primarily an attempt to create a sense of purpose, urgency, and shared vision among organization members.

In the fall of 1989, Pacificorp (a Northwestern utility) attempted a takeover of APS, claiming that the merger could save $500 million, particularly through the sharing of periodic excess capacity. Pacificorp used an extensive advertising campaign that focused on APS's high rates and inefficient operations to try to generate public support for the takeover. This action was perceived by APS's employees and top management as an external threat, and served to galvanize them into a sense of community. It created a sense of urgency around the case for collective action that De Michele had been articulating and provided immediate external validation of his message. In addition, as noted by De Michele, it forced him to "wake up" and step up his vision for the future. It became clear that enactment of this vision depended on continued difficult decisions—including the need for another round of reductions in force.

Exhibit 7   APS Top 5 by '95 Goals

By 1995 APS will:

Be one of the top five investor-owned electric utilities in America in terms of cost management, customer service, power plant performance, nuclear and industrial safety, and environmental performance.

Have significantly improved our price competitiveness.

Have improved our competitive marketplace position.

Be recognized as the premier corporate citizen in Arizona.

Succeed through employee commitment to continuous improvement with emphasis on team-work, workplace innovation, and corporate culture change.

Accomplish this through strategic community involvement, high-impact employee volunteer efforts, and innovative environmental and educational programs.

Source: Adapted from the APS 1994 Corporate Strategic Plan.

The Second Major Downsizing

Anticipating the need for a second major layoff in early 1990, De Michele established job review committees to evaluate every existing position in the company. The committees tried to assess the value of each position to the overall organization and the particular qualifications required to perform each job effectively. They rewrote job descriptions to include not only technical skills and competencies, but personal characteristics such as flexibility and adaptability. The output from these committees was used to develop a new organizational structure that reflected 1,150 fewer positions and eliminated two officers (see Exhibit 8).

In the implementation of this new structure, De Michele chose a high-risk position that he believed mirrored the need to communicate the case for radical rethinking and redefinition of the organization. He essentially "fired" everyone in the organization. All employees, including himself (to convey that no one would be "spared"), were required to reapply for the redefined jobs. In the attempt to enhance morale, and keep the employees involved, De Michele emphasized communication, especially with respect to which jobs had been filled, which remained open, and so on. In De Michele's view, the outcomes of this second major downsizing were, on balance, positive. Unfortunately, the goals of this reduction in force were still primarily financial (and mostly short term). The company now had 1,150 fewer employees, and had effectively lowered its cost structure. In fact, in November 1993, APS announced that it would not seek another rate case hearing in the foreseeable future—although top management did not define the meaning of this term explicitly—despite the expiration of the two-year moratorium.

Yet, De Michele soon realized that the company was still "doing what it had always done," only with fewer people. Despite the restructuring, APS was still operating as a rate-driven monopoly. He recognized the need to focus on the future—to look to the year 2000 and beyond and develop a picture of the organization that would make sense then. His picture included increased cooperation among the elements of the organization and bringing the organization members into an understanding of the nature of a truly competitive environment,

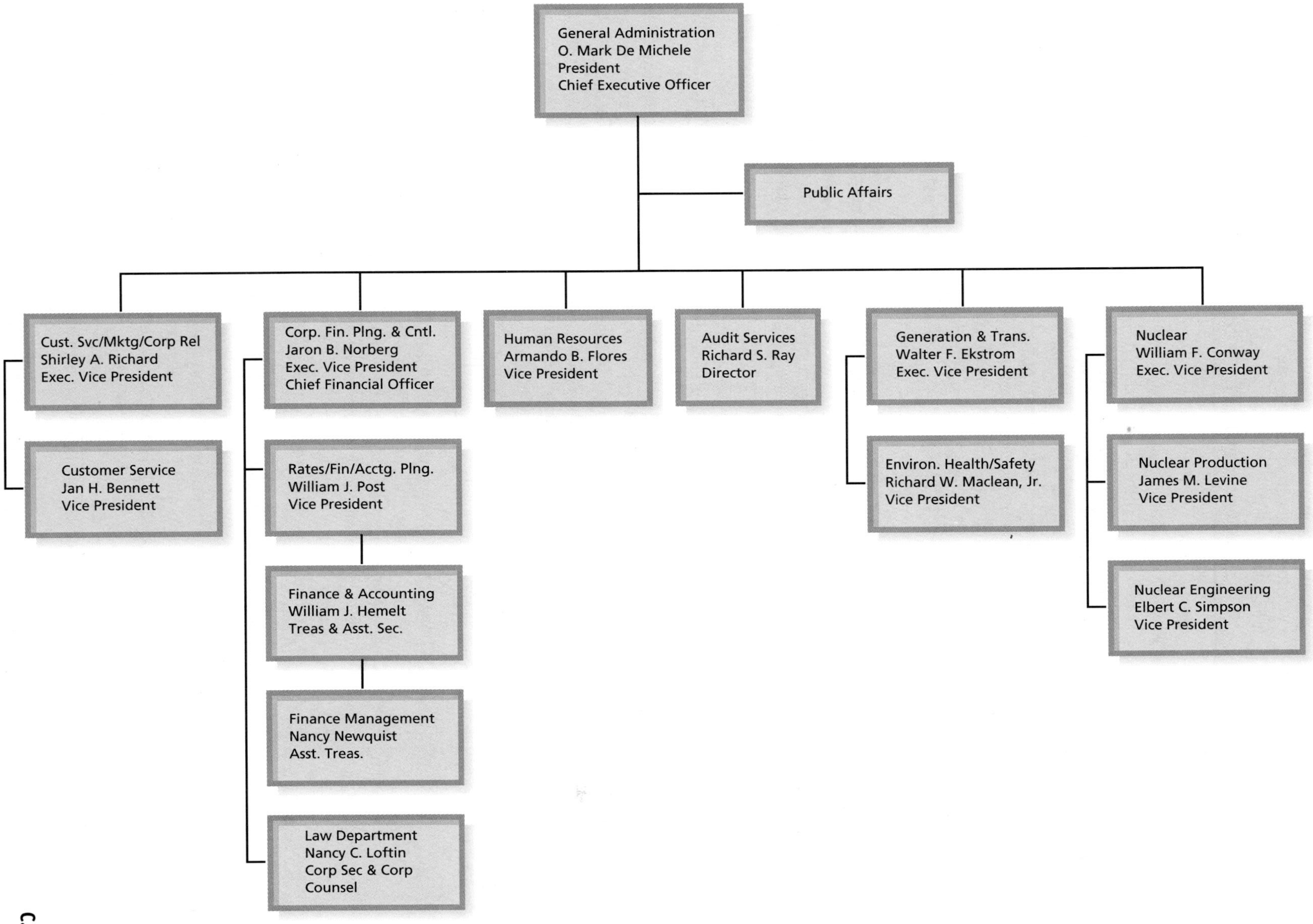

Exhibit 8   Arizona Public Service Company Organization Chart, 1993

which he could see looming clearly on the horizon. De Michele realized the potential force for change that a well-managed organizational culture could provide.

The existing theme of "Top 5 by '95" (which was later codified into a set of goals) seemed to him to provide the perfect medium to focus energy on the future rather than on the past and current distress (see Exhibit 7). Unfortunately, however, he also discovered that there was some perception that "Top 5 by '95" might be too difficult, and that it was being forced on the organization. To some extent, this was true; it had been singularly his idea. In a meeting with the newly downsized management team, the concern was that if the target was in fact too difficult, and was not met, morale would be even more devastated. The employees were still adjusting psychologically to the loss of 1,150 coworkers, and many were questioning their own job security. The top management team needed to find a way to improve morale and focus the employees' attention on the future. They eventually agreed that "Top 5 by '95" could fulfill this need.

In a way, De Michele was working to peel away the old culture, build an entirely new one, and use it to create a base for real strategic change. There was not a clear vision of what the required strategy would be at this time, just a recognition that the company needed to prepare itself to operate in the highly competitive environment it would eventually face. However, there was some feeling among the management team that they lacked the knowledge and expertise to take "giant steps" in this area. Based on their feedback, and his belief that culture could be the key ingredient in the process of enacting true strategic change, De Michele brought in a consultant, Wayne Widdis, to assist in the process of developing a strategic plan, building a new culture, and developing a clear mission statement.

A principal outcome of the discussions between Widdis and the officer group was the creation of a special team to spearhead a program known as the "Strategic Cultural Change Initiative." De Michele selected a high-visibility, creative, and energetic individual, Scott Jacobson, to lead this team. The team's initial action was the implementation of a process Widdis referred to as "Focus," intended to bring about an enhanced sense of cultural identity among organizational members.

The Focus program involved taking cross-functional teams of APS employees through a week-long marathon simulation experience to assist them in gaining awareness of what it meant to function in a more competitive strategic environment. At the end of the week, the teams were required to present to a top management team (headed by Mark De Michele) a proposed project, anchored in this new strategic thinking mode, that they (the teams) believed would significantly improve operations at APS. The top management team would then vote immediately either to accept or not accept the proposed project.

An immediate response was deemed appropriate to show both the strength of management's commitment to the new vision and to convey the sense of urgency in the need for immediate action. Those projects that were accepted were assigned an executive vice president to serve as the project's sponsor, which implied a responsibility to ensure implementation and accountability.

The original intent was to start with a few sessions, specifically designed for employees involved with customer service. However, the enormously successful experiences and employee excitement that resulted from these first few sessions led De Michele to believe the process would be valuable for all organization members. The excitement reflected the fact that for the first time many employees felt truly empowered. Not only were they being challenged to improve APS, but to assume ownership of their projects, present their proposals directly to the top management team, and receive immediate feedback. The Focus experience proved to be a powerful motivator of employees. Management soon realized that Focus could be used as an effective tool to create a new strategically oriented culture, the type of culture that they were convinced was required to meet both the near- and far-term competitive challenges that lay ahead.

The Focus program resulted in APS employees learning new ways of thinking about the organization and its environment. Furthermore, the organization began to experience some real successes. The Focus projects lowered costs, improved customer service, and reduced bureaucracy in the organization. These significant improvements to APS became noticeable to a number of their most important external constituencies, including customers and members of the industry. In fact, in 1992, APS was the recipient of the Edison Award, the most prestigious award in the industry based on overall excellence. The award is given annually to the electric utility that contributes the most to growth and development of the industry. APS was specifically cited for its "transformation from a traditional rate-driven utility to a customer-focused company." It is considered a great honor by those in the industry to win this award.

These initial successes inspired De Michele and the top managers to look beyond "Top 5 by '95" and give serious consideration to their ability to develop and give impetus to longer term goals. They used input from the Focus sessions to help generate these new goals that were labeled "Mission 2000" and "Vision 2000" (see Exhibit 9). Clearly, the Focus program, and the successes that seemed attributable to that experience, was perceived as very positive. However, De Michele realized that the new goals would require changes that would be far more radical and encompassing than anything the organization had attempted before.

Exhibit 9   APS 2000

APS Vision 2000
We will compete for our future with our price, service, and growth.

APS Mission 2000
To succeed as a competitive energy services business, we must deliver value to our customers, employees and shareholders.

Specifically we will:

- Provide reliable, hassle-free, competitively-priced service.
- Aggressively reduce our average cost in cents/kWh.
- Grow our business.
- Create an agile and competitive-ready company.
- Build brand loyalty in the market.

By integrating bold strategic actions and relentless financial discipline, we will thrive in an uncertain, but promising future.

Source: Adapted from the APS 1996 Corporate Strategic Plan.

Top management decided that a two-pronged "plan of attack" would be required. First, the company would need to prepare employees psychologically and emotionally to cope with the coming changes. This program became known as "Breakthrough Leadership." Second, they would need to redesign work processes from the bottom up throughout the entire organization. This program was to be based on the concept of "reengineering." Reengineering is defined by Michael Hammer and James Champy, authors of the book *Reengineering the Corporation* (1993), as "the fundamental rethinking and radical redesign of business processes to achieve dramatic improvements in critical, contemporary measures of performance, such as cost, quality, service, and speed." This kind of redesign effort would be far more radical than that attempted in 1990. The previous restructuring had focused almost exclusively on eliminating duplication of effort and inefficiencies within the current structure and work processes. Reengineering, on the other hand, requires that the current structure be discarded and a new one focused on work *processes* be created.

■ "Breakthrough Leadership"

More confident now in the ability to create real, substantive change in the organization, De Michele undertook these bold steps in the cultural change process via the enactment of "Breakthrough Leadership" and "Reengineering." The emerging evidence from those who had participated in Focus indicated that belief systems and organizational culture could be reshaped. If so, De Michele reasoned, organization members could begin to stretch that belief system into a meaningful long-term vision.

Groups of about 80 people each were selected to participate in a program that included reading new, leading-edge books on management and corporate culture. Participants were chosen on the basis of their perceived ability to model appropriate leadership behavior to their peers and subordinates. The officer group, De Michele, and Widdis developed indicators of critical leadership characteristics. They were carefully crafted to reflect the mission, goals and values that had been articulated to the organization members (see Exhibit 10 for APS's list of leadership principles).

Participants were selected from all functional areas and levels of the organization, and organized into teams of 10 members. Each team was assigned one of the selected books to read, and through discussion distill its critical ideas prior to the start of their week-long Breakthrough Leadership program. During the program each team presented what was learned from the book and how these learnings could be applied to improving the management of APS. The second major phase of each Breakthrough Leadership program focused on learning and integrating the concepts of reengineering (the second major change initiative) and identifying their potential effects on the organization's culture. The culmination of the week was a full-day session devoted to a collective sharing of all these learnings by the teams in the presence of top management, and making a case for how they would help APS achieve its long-term goals (see Exhibit 10). The intent of this program was to create a cadre of individuals (who became known as cultural change warriors) who were charged with modeling the desired behaviors and belief systems back in the context of the organization.

Exhibit 10   APS Leadership Principles

Leadership must be concerned about what we will need in the future combined with an intense focus on high-level performance. Our management team is committed to the following leadership principles. APS leaders:

Communicate, clarify, support, reinforce, and model our mission.

Spend most of their time with their employees, focusing on their performance and results.

Do not allow organizational or personal boundaries to get in the way and do strategically empower others to act within the framework of our vision and targets.

Make strategic decisions quickly, openly, and based on our values, mission, critical success indicators, and strategic priorities.

Acknowledge mistakes and make necessary adjustments.

Demonstrate behaviors consistent with a high-performing culture.

Demand results from themselves and others and eliminate habitual activities that get in our way.

Value a high level of business competency.

Embrace and relish the concept of continuous strategic change.

Demonstrate enormous energy and have the ability to energize others.

Model the behaviors and commitment to the cultural diversity strategy.

Our future will be determined by our sustained vision, these leadership principles and our will to apply them.

Source: Adapted from the APS 1994 Corporate Strategic Plan.

■ The Reengineering Process

The Breakthrough Leadership program might be compared to a strategy formulation process, designed to create a new way of understanding what it means to be a competitive, strategically driven organization. The second major effort, the reengineering process, was undertaken to address the issues of efficiency and effectiveness through redesigning the organizational structure, similar to a strategy implementation process. In this context the actual organizational process began by identifying reengineering teams in two major segments of the organization—Palo Verde and the Transmission & Distribution operations. These two areas were selected to be first due to their relatively clear definition of *current* structure and process and the relatively short-term projected initial cost saving estimates (in excess of 30 percent). These would provide a basis for reasonably visible "wins" in a relatively short time frame.

The teams were asked to start with a "blank sheet of paper" and totally recreate these areas of the company with the idea of simplifying work processes. The reengineering teams completed their plans for the new organizational design in these two areas and began implementation in 1994. However, top management was so impressed by these new designs that they decided to expand the reengineering efforts to include essentially the entire organization. In their enthusiasm, they may have set overly ambitious goals in an effort to challenge and "stretch" employees. However, they believed that reengineering, grounded in the new culture, belief systems, and behaviors, would encourage the needed shift from a rate-based to a strategically driven company. Additionally, reengineering was seen as a tool to maintain continuous improvement and not simply as a one-time event.

■ Initial Results

Despite some projects falling short of these ambitious goals, reengineering and breakthrough leadership have produced impressive results. APS's total costs per kilowatt hour dropped from 9.32 cents in December 1993 to 8.05 cents in October 1995, a 14 percent reduction. During this same period, the workforce also was reduced by 10 percent (see Exhibit 7).

Most significantly, in May 1994 APS implemented a 2.2 percent rate *reduction,* the first in its long history, followed by a second reduction announcement in December 1995 of 3.3 percent to be effective in July 1996. The second announcement also stated that the company plans to implement additional rate cuts in 1997, 1998, and 1999 contingent on their continued effectiveness at managing costs, and "at a minimum APS commits to no price increases through the end of the decade."

Although these accomplishments are impressive, the company still faces significant challenges. APS's future success depends on its continued ability both to reduce costs and generate new sources of revenues. The management of APS seems convinced that the way to achieve these goals is through employee development, and plans several new programs in the future designed to help employees reach their full potential.

■ CASE 3 # AT&T: A Strategic Restructuring for the Twenty-First Century

Elif Caglar
Carlos Garcia
Anuj Kumar
Andreas Treuer
Kyriakos Parpounas

We have changed our strategy. For 100 years AT&T has focused on integration. But we have determined that AT&T shareholders would be better off by separation.

—Robert Allen, CEO

■ http://www.att.com/

On September 20, 1995, at a New York press conference, AT&T made public its decision to break up its businesses. The company's CEO, Robert Allen, along with six collaborators, had been considering the strategic move for several months, but was surprisingly able to keep it from any media exposure. Determining that the potential businesses combined were not achieving the desired goals, the decision was made to separate the company's core business, the telecommunication services, from its other activities. Emerging from one of the largest voluntary corporate breakups in U.S. history, AT&T will now focus on communications services, while the other two businesses, communications equipment and computer systems, will be spun off. In the process, the PC business will be folded and the finance arm, AT&T Capital Corporation, will be sold off.

The decision is a complete reversal for a company that has pursued a policy of expansion throughout its history. In the last five years alone, AT&T has completed two major acquisitions: NCR Corporation, the computer manufacturer for $7 billion, and McCaw Cellular for $12 billion.

Concentrating only on consumer and business communications, AT&T apparently hopes to become leaner and meaner, and position itself to better compete in

Case prepared under the direction of Professor Robert E. Hoskisson for class discussion purposes only.

this rapidly changing industry. An important issue underlying the divestitures and refocusing is the shifting regulatory landscape and the likelihood that AT&T and the local service providers, the Bell operating companies (BOCs), will soon be competing in each other's core businesses. According to Allen, AT&T would have taken the same action regardless of the outcome of the telecommunications legislation. However, analysts say the move signals AT&T's intentions to go all out against the BOCs.[1]

Beginning sometime in early 1996, pending regulatory approval, AT&T will be broken into the following three publicly traded companies:

- *AT&T Corporation,* offering consumer and business communications services, wireless services, Universal Card services, and including AT&T Solutions, as well as the new AT&T laboratories;
- *Network Systems Group,* focusing on equipment manufacturing, multimedia products, and including Bell Labs; and
- *Global Information Solutions,* focusing on the computer business, information systems consulting, and retail computers and banking (ATMs).

Although AT&T shareholders (2.4 million)[2] will be offered shares in all three companies, the major managerial focus will be on AT&T Corporation, specifically on its communication services, and on improving the AT&T brand name. Allen will become president of the new AT&T Corporation after the completion of the breakup. This new company will likely operate in a more hostile and aggressive telecommunications environment and, despite the intention to become more nimble, it will face some of the following new challenges as a result of the breakup:

- How will losing the equipment business affect AT&T's future potential?
- How will the loss of the Bell Labs influence the company?
- How well will the company be able to manage the change, avoiding employee demotivation?
- What kind of strategies will the telecommunications company pursue in the process of entering new markets and expanding into new technologies? Will the resources left with the telecommunications company be enough to fuel the expansion into the international telecommunications arena?
- Will the smaller AT&T be able to lobby and affect the telecommunications regulations in the future as effectively as it did in the past?

■ Company Background

AT&T was incorporated as American Telephone and Telegraph Company by American Bell Telephone Company (formally known as National Bell Telephone Company) on March 3, 1885, in New York. The purpose of this company was to construct, finance, and operate Bell's long-distance telephone system.

In March, 1900, AT&T became the parent company to the Bell System. Since then, AT&T has been the dominant leader of the telecommunication industry, in spite of the constant battle against antitrust government regulations and pressure. In the first half of the century, AT&T was *the* industry, with virtually no competition.

Competition began for AT&T during the 1950s and 1960s with companies such as Hush-a-Phone Company and Microwave Communications Inc. (MCI). At the time, AT&T's actions were clearly monopolistic. AT&T restricted the use of its network to AT&T operating companies (the regional BOCs). Although the company was involved in costly antitrust litigation at various times throughout these years, it was able to grow profitably both domestically and globally. It was also able to lever its success through its R&D division, Bell Laboratories. The Bell Labs had been providing scientific and technological research and development to AT&T since its creation in 1925. They have housed the world's best recognized scientists, and have produced prominent innovations such as sound motion pictures (1926), the transistor (1947), the laser (1958), the communications satellite (1962), and the cellular telephone (1978).[3]

The Telecommunications Industry

As of 1995, the U.S. telecommunications industry serves more than 90 million households and 25 million businesses nationwide. There are more than 2,000 companies employing about 875,000 persons that serve these markets as both regulated common carriers and unregulated private network providers.

Regulations

This industry has been highly regulated since its inception in 1877. Although most of the changes in the industry today are driven by technological and strategic change, regulations still play an important role in shaping the industry. Telecommunication companies are still engaged in vast lobbying efforts and committing significant amounts of capital to influence the relevant regulatory processes and the prevailing regulations in ways that best serve their interests.

Regulation of the telecommunications industry has been entrusted primarily to the Federal Communications Commission (FCC), an entity created by the Federal Communication Act of 1934. Initially, the Bell System (Bell) held the essential patents and, hence, enjoyed a complete monopoly. Federal government concern for this monopoly power was as old as Bell itself. Three major consent decrees between the government and Bell were agreed on between 1914 and 1982:

1. *The 1914 decree:* The 1914 decree was the result of increasing government concern with Bell monopolizing some of the long-distance services. In its "Kingsbury Commitment," Bell agreed to refrain from acquiring competing independent telephone companies. In 1921, Congress passed the Willis-Graham Act, which overrode the Kingsbury Commitment and gave the Interstate Commerce Commission authority to accept telephone company mergers.[4]

2. *The 1956 decree:* In 1949 the government filed a second antitrust action, this time alleging that Bell had attempted to monopolize telecommunications equipment and services through its practices of acquiring and licensing patents. The case was settled in 1956 by a consent decree in which the company agreed to grant nonexclusive licenses for all existing and future Bell System patents. Western Electric, Bell's equipment manufacturing branch,

would thereafter manufacture only equipment used in providing telephone service. Bell would stay out of any business "other than furnishing of common carrier communications services," though it would be allowed to supply services of any kind to the federal government.[5]

3. *The 1982 decree:* On November 20, 1974, the government filed its third antitrust action against the Bell System. The complaint alleged an unlawful combination among various Bell entities resulting in the monopoly of both long-distance service and telecommunication equipment manufacturing. Hence, the government wanted to break up AT&T to reduce its monopolistic power.

AT&T fought against its breakup through lobbying and negotiations efforts. The argument for AT&T was that opening the market to competition would hurt rather than benefit the consumers. Given AT&T's asset base and resources, including the lines network in place, no other company would be able to compete with them and survive. The first-round approval of the modified decree was issued on August 24, 1982. Following extensive negotiations, a transfer of assets was completed on the stroke of midnight, December 31, 1983, and the Bell Telephone Operating Companies (BOCs) were reorganized into seven regional companies. The stock of each of these newly formed companies was spun off to AT&T shareholders.

The decree had four basic provisions:

- It required AT&T to divest its local BOCs.
- It required the BOCs to provide equal interconnections to long-distance carriers and information providers and barred certain acts defined as discriminatory.
- It prohibited BOCs from engaging in competitive long-distance, information services, equipment businesses, or indeed any other competitive businesses at all.
- It freed AT&T from the restrictions of the 1956 decree.[6]

At the time of the consent decree, AT&T's revenues of $35 billion accounted for about 90 percent of all long-distance revenues (even though the FCC had introduced limited competition in the earlier years). The decree opened the regulatory doors for numerous competitors to enter the market or expand. The FCC decided to regulate AT&T significantly in order to promote healthy competition, which would benefit consumers. Hence AT&T, definitely the dominant company in the industry, was subject to price-cap regulations. In some business markets where the FCC determined that AT&T lacked market power, its services were subject to less stringent regulation under which its prices were presumed lawful and did not need to be justified by cost support materials.[7]

■ Competition

Long-Distance Service

The 1984 consent decree became an important milestone that allowed the competitive nature of the telecommunications industry to emerge. By 1993, 480 companies, plus a number of others that provide operator services, were competing in the U.S. long-distance market, limiting AT&T's market share to only 60 percent. In 1995, AT&T's share declined to about 58 percent. Long-distance service is now provided by AT&T, MCI, Sprint, WilTel, Metromedia Communications, Litel Telecommunications, Allnet, and more than 475 other small carriers. AT&T's largest competitors are MCI and Sprint, which together hold a significant 28 percent of the market.[8] As competition grew, AT&T found itself in a difficult position. AT&T was no longer the dominant player of the past, and felt that it was constrained by the 1984 regulations (see Appendix D for market share changes by year).

Local Telephone Service

Before the consent decree, local telephone services were provided by about 1,325 local telephone companies (telcos), including 22 Bell system exchanges, as well as telcos owned by GTE, Sprint, and other independent local telephone companies. These local telephone services, which were monopolized by the seven BOCs after the 1984 decree, were also becoming increasingly competitive. In response to these pressures, the BOCs stepped up a campaign to obtain authority to enter the long-distance and telecommunications equipment manufacturing businesses. The BOCs had won a number of important regulatory freedoms in the past few years, which enabled them to enter new markets as aggressive competitors to AT&T (see Appendix B for a list of local phone companies). On the other hand, there were signs that some states would open up their local exchange service market for competition, including long-distance competitors.

Cable Services

At the same time, another source of competition was about to enter the telecommunications services arena. The cable companies, already having a cable connection with the customers, started pushing for regulatory changes that would allow them to offer telecommunication services. The cable companies felt that if regulations allowed local and long-distance providers to enter their traditional market, they should also be allowed to enter telecommunication markets to promote real and unrestricted competition. As the regulatory climate became more open to such changes, the cable companies' argument started to gain momentum.

Wireless Services

With the advent of newer technology, the telecommunications industry has become increasingly fragmented into different segments. The 1990s have been characterized by record-breaking growth in most wireless service segments, including cellular, paging, and specialized mobile radio. This thriving market, which is considered to have enormous growth potential through the year 2000 and beyond, is gaining momentum from a series of legislative and regulatory developments that encourage emerging wireless technologies. Largely driven by declining equipment costs, the cellular industry has begun to attract users from the consumer market at a higher rate than business users. Not surprisingly, most companies are pursuing this market. Six of the seven regional BOCs joined GTE and eight other companies to form MobiLink, a cellular consortium covering 80 percent of the U.S. population and marketing under a common brand name. In

March 1993, Sprint merged with Centel Cellular, and formed Sprint Cellular, which added a new dimension to Sprint's telecommunications service offerings. AT&T pursued the wireless market by acquiring McCaw Cellular, the largest wireless services provider in the United States.[9]

Within the wireless market, Personal Communication Services (PCS) constituted another emerging front of competition. Described as another form of cellular telecommunication, PCS promises a single mobile phone number which extends cellular use to larger areas but, in addition, lets one transmit video images or check e-mail from anywhere in the country through lightweight devices. The main competitor AT&T faces in the emerging PCS industry is from Wireless Co. LP., an alliance formed by Sprint, Telecommunications Inc., Cox Enterprises Inc., and Comcast Corp. The PCS strategy of Sprint's alliance with cable TV companies relies on the marketing synergy between wireless service and local phone lines so that customers receive one-stop shopping for services such as digitized data, films, TV shows, and magazine and newspaper articles transmitted on the Sprint network.[10]

Cyberspace Services

The Clinton Administration has expressed its commitment to promote the development of the "information superhighway," which is expected to require a minimum investment of $300 billion. Although the government admitted that it cannot spare that kind of resources at this point in time, the major players in the telecommunications industry have the resources and know-how to pursue such an investment. According to Peter Huber, a senior fellow at the Manhattan Institute, "Vice President Gore doesn't have $300 billion to spend on the information superhighway. These guys [telecommunication companies] do. Set them free and they will."[11]

The trend among telecommunications companies has been to increase their resources invested on the Internet, and to try to take advantage of the nature of the Internet system as a communication medium and enhance and improve the potential services they can offer to customers.

International Arena

In the last few years, a global telecommunications market has developed, in part due to the increased importance of international trade and investment in the world economy, and spurred by the liberalization of telecommunications sectors in many countries. According to estimates, international telecommunications in the next 10 years will become a $3 trillion industry. As a result, most of the major U.S. telecommunication companies are pursuing international growth. The seven regional BOCs are pursuing their expansion by building and operating dual cable television and telephone networks in different countries. In 1993, Sprint acquired access to a foreign telecommunications service market by forging an alliance with Canada's largest reseller, Call-Net Enterprises, acquiring a 25 percent stake in the company. Another major alliance was British Telecom's (BT) acquisition of 20 percent of MCI. BT also established a joint venture with MCI to market products and services around the world. Besides joining forces with the world's third largest telecommunications company, MCI received $4.3 billion from BT's investment. It is possible that MCI will use much of the money to secure a presence in the U.S. local exchange market, cable TV companies, multimedia or software projects, and PCS and other projects. This alliance is expected to be the most formidable competitor for AT&T in the international arena, because of the combined size and resources of the two companies. Appendix C contains a list of international phone companies and their efficiency ratings.[12]

Regulatory Uncertainty

After the breakup of AT&T in 1983, regulators realized that competition was viable and indeed a better option than the previous monopoly. Looking at how the rates for long-distance calls went down after the major deregulation, as well as the wealth of new services offered by the competitors in their efforts to gain a competitive advantage, the government decided to allow market forces to determine prices and services.[13]

The general consensus in Washington was that the regulations would have to be rewritten. According to a telecommunications analyst: "Both the 1984 Cable Act [which bars telephone companies from going head-to-head with local cable operators], and the 1984 Decree are about as dated as a rotary phone. Does anyone really believe that consumers would be hurt by adding more competitors to the long-distance and local cable marketplace?"[14]

The debate among lawmakers is whether a new set of regulations will serve the interests of the consumers. Many analysts and telecommunication professionals believe that the time has come to remove all regulatory restrictions and free up the market completely. They believe that a sensible government policy would discourage regulators from micromanaging everything and let the parties concentrate on creating full-service broadband networks. According to Phil Quigley, chairman and CEO of Pacific Telesis (a BOC): "it's time to let the regional Bell companies become full service providers, offering local and long distance service as well as interactive video. It's time to let cable companies offer telephone service. And it's time to let long distance companies into the local telephone market."[15]

All the players in the industry were lobbying to reform the regulations in ways that would best serve their interests. However, some perceived the local BOCs to have an advantage when Republicans gained the majority in the U.S. Congress in 1994. Long-distance companies have not enjoyed particularly smooth communication with Republicans. As a result, changes in the regulations are expected to favor the local BOCs. BOCs are expected to be able to enter the long-distance market without first having to show that their local phone systems face widespread competition. They will be able to get into long distance, buying access from AT&T or its rivals wholesale, before long-distance companies have a real choice to buy local access.[16] However, Republicans are also generally in favor of deregulation. Therefore, this is a very speculative assertion. Nonetheless, specific, though uncertain, expectations on the outcome of the pending regulations can be found in Exhibit 1.

Despite the analysts' expectations about the new regulations, it is still uncertain whether they will allow long-distance carriers to compete and offer local telephone services, and whether they will allow local service companies (BOCs) to compete and offer long-distance services. It is also unclear how the new regulation will address the concerns and arguments of the cable companies.

Exhibit 1   Industry Analysts' Expectations for Pending Bill

Republican leaders are seeking the following changes in the way a House telecommunications bill would let the regional Bells into the long-distance market:

- Before selling long-distance, Bells would have to have local competition, but the competitor would not have to match the Bell network in price, features, and geographic reach.
- Bells could apply for long-distance entry after 6 months instead of 18 months.
- Bells could merge their long-distance and local operations in 18 months instead of three years.
- The wholesale rates Bells charge a local phone competitor for access to its network of lines and switches would be based on the Bells' costs, instead of what is economically feasible for the competitor.
- Smaller companies would be allowed to market long-distance services jointly with local service they bought from the Bells. But the four largest long-distance companies would still be barred from such joint marketing.

Source: *Politics and policy; Long-distance companies can't get through to Congress in telecommunications bill debate,* The Wall Street Journal, July 24, 1995, A14.

■ AT&T Since 1984

Beginning in 1984, AT&T had to adapt from defining the industry to being a player in the new competitive environment. The trends in the industry forced AT&T to revise its strategy and to adapt to the evolving technology and regulations.

■ Change in Strategy

Given the increased competition and the regulatory turbulence in telecommunications, AT&T decided to change its vision to help maintain a dominant position in the market and foster growth. As such, the company pursued acquisitions and alliances as a means of growth and expansion. According to the company, "we make an acquisition when that seems the most effective way to take advantage of a particular market opportunity to further our growth goals. We also look for partnerships—whether equity investments, joint ventures, or other alliances that complement our own strength." (see Exhibits 2 and 3 and Appendix I).[17]

The champion behind this corporate strategy at AT&T was Robert Allen. He became president in 1986 as part of the restructuring of the company after the 1984 divestiture. In 1988 he became chairman. Under his leadership, AT&T pursued an aggressive program of growth through alliances and acquisitions. At the same time AT&T has sought to transform itself from a rigid, hierarchical service company to one that was more market oriented and open to input from all levels of the system.

The acquisition strategy is illustrated in the following select list of the largest corporate transactions undertaken by the company:

- In 1986, AT&T's 50 percent interest in Bell Telephone Laboratories was transferred to a separate company known as AT&T Technologies. This transaction amounted to $538 million. AT&T Technologies was involved mainly in the manufacture and sale of telecommunications equipment for consumers and businesses. The stated purpose of this transaction was to win

Exhibit 2   AT&T's Most Important Joint Ventures and Equity Investments

- *AG Communication Systems Corporation:* AT&T has a joint venture with GTE in Phoenix, Arizona, to develop Integrated Services Digital Network (ISDN) and other technologies for GTE switching systems. AT&T owns 49 percent.

- *APT Italia:* AT&T Network Systems International is a 51 percent owner of this company that manufacturers and markets dedicated network transmission systems for Italy and export.

- *Atesia:* A joint venture with Italy's Italcable and STET, Atesia provides telemarketing services to Italian companies and public entities.

- *AT&T Italtel Network Systems S.A./N.V.:* This joint export company of AT&T Network Systems International and Italtel markets telecommunications products for businesses.

- *AT&T JENS:* AT&T owns 60 percent of this joint venture with 22 major Japanese firms to provide value-added network services in Japan.

- *AT&T Network Systems Espana:* This joint venture of AT&T Network Systems International and Amper develops, markets, and manufactures 5ESS digital switching systems and transmission equipment for the Spanish market.

- *AT&T Network System International B.V.:* Based in the Netherlands, this joint venture company with Italy's STET (20 percent) and Spain's/Telefonica de Espana SA (6 percent) is AT&T's holding and management company for marketing, development, manufacturing, and sales of all network communication products, primarily for public telecommunications in Europe, the middle East, Africa, and selected countries.

- *AT&T of St. Petersburg:* AT&T Network Systems International owns 68 percent of this joint venture with Dalnya Sviaz (DALS), a Russian telecommunications company. Initially this venture will market and sell AT&T digital transmission equipment in Russia.

- *AT&T of Shanghai Ltd.:* AT&T Networks Systems International holds 50 percent of this venture with Shanghai Optical Fiber Communications Engineering and Shanghai Telecommunications Equipment Factory. It manufactures, sells, and services digital transmission equipment for public and private network customers in China.

- *AT&T Software Japan, Ltd.:* AT&T is the majority owner, with Industrial Bank of Japan and Software Research Associates, of this company that offers UNIX and fault-tolerant software applications.

- *AT&T Taiwan Telecommunications Co., Ltd.:* This joint venture with the Directorate General of Telecommunications of Taiwan, the Bank of Communications, United Fiber Optic Communications Inc., and the Yao Hua Glass Company manufactures the 5ESS switch for use in Taiwan.

- *Audi Electronique:* In Canada, this venture, of which AT&T owns half, sells AT&T's products for the small business market.

- *Business Communications Europe:* With 20 percent owner Italtel Telematica, this venture markets, sells and services AT&T Italtel products including the Definity communications system, in Europe.

- *Call Interactive:* AT&T partners with American Express' First Data Corporation to offer interactive marketing and entertainment services through this Omaha, Nebraska, company.

- *Compagnie Industrial Ruinite S.p.A. (CIR):* AT&T owns 17 percent of this Italian holding company involved in information technology and other industries.

- *Goldstar Fiber Optics Co., Ltd:* This joint venture with the Lucky Goldstar Group of the Republic of Korea manufactures fiber-optic cable for Korea and a selected export market.

- *Hutchison AT&T Network Services:* This joint venture with Hutchison Telecommunications Ltd. provides value-added networking services in Hong Kong and the Pacific region.

- *Jamaica Digiport International, Ltd.:* This joint venture with Cable and Wireless Ltd. and Telecommunications of Jamaica provides telecommunications services to and from free-trade zones in Jamaica.

- *Lycom A/S:* AT&T owns 51 percent of this joint venture with Nortic Cable and Wire Works to make and market optical fiber for sale primarily is Scandinavia.

- *Transporte Digital De Information (TDI):* This Venezuelan company, owned equally by AT&T and COMSAT Investments, Inc., provides multinational companies with digital private line service within Venezuela and between that country and other locations around the world.

- *Ukraine:* A joint venture—of which AT&T owns 39 percent, PPT Telecom of the Netherlands owns 10 percent, and Ukraine State Committee of Communications owns 51 percent—will modernize and operate that country's international and domestic long-distance communications networks.

- *Western Electric Saudi Arabia, Ltd.:* With A.S. Bugshan Brothers, AT&T provides installation, operation, and maintenance services in Saudi Arabia, Jordan, Dubai, and Sudan.

Exhibit 3   AT&T Organizations

- *Actuarial Sciences Associates, Inc.,* is a wholly owned AT&T subsidiary that advises corporations in designing and maintaining employee benefit programs of all types, including benefit planning and analysis for mergers and divestitures, and analysis of insurance products used to finance or provide benefits.

- The *AT&T Foundation,* the company's principal vehicle for corporate philanthropy, makes grants in support of education, health care, and cultural organization.

- *AT&T Tridom* is a wholly owned subsidiary that designs, manufactures, and services very small aperture terminals (small satellite earth stations) used in private communications networks that link a hub and multiple remote sites.

- *Sandia National Laboratories,* is an engineering and science lab operated by AT&T since 1949 for the U.S. Department of Energy. Sandia research and development plays a vital role in nuclear conflict deterrence, energy environment, economic competitiveness, and other areas of importance to national security.

- *UNIX System Laboratories, Inc.,* is an AT&T subsidiary that provides computer vendors with the UNIX operating system and related software based on open standards for computing and communications.

---

back the telephone equipment market share lost during the upheaval of the 1983 divestiture.[18]

- In March 1989, the company, through AT&T Capital Corporation, acquired Eaton Financial Corporation. This was part of AT&T's business plan to buy into other financial businesses that would extend its portfolio beyond equipment financing.[19]

- The same month (March 1989), AT&T acquired all of Paradyne Corporation's common equity for about $250 million. Paradyne then merged with one of AT&T's divisions to form AT&T Paradyne. This acquisition was aimed at strengthening AT&T's data networking strategy.[20]

- In the second quarter of 1989, AT&T acquired a 20 percent stake in Italtel in exchange for a 20 percent stake in AT&T Network Systems International B.V. plus $135 million in cash. Italtel Societa Italiana Telecomunicazioni S.p.A., Italy's state-owned telephone company allowed AT&T to gain access to additional overseas markets in the globalizing telecommunications industry.[21]

- In October 1989, AT&T purchased Istel Ltd, a British systems integrator and network service provider, for approximately $285 million. This transaction was part of a country-by-country strategy to penetrate the European market with AT&T client–server systems, computers, network hardware, terminals, and peripherals.[22]

- In 1991, through a hostile takeover, AT&T became the new owner of NCR for $7.5 billion. With NCR in its portfolio, AT&T sought to gain an edge over both long-distance companies and computer vendors. At the time, no single competitor had AT&T's combination of fiber optics, semiconductors, and software technology.[23]

- In September 1994, AT&T closed the purchase of McCaw Cellular Communications Inc. for $12.7 billion, which provided access to the wireless market.[24]

Of the preceding list of corporate transactions, the acquisition of NCR was not only a major step for AT&T to grow in size, but also a milestone to a more diversified AT&T. AT&T pursued this acquisition to improve the synergy of operations achieved by merging the telecommunication and the computer businesses.[25] With 53 percent of its revenue generated from outside the United States, NCR also provided AT&T an increased international presence. The experience of NCR in retail, banking, point-of-sale, and other markets would add new market opportunities and product strategies for AT&T.[26]

The newly created division was named AT&T Global Information Solutions (GIS). The results of this marriage were far below AT&T's expectations. Despite the company's continuous restructuring efforts, by 1995 AT&T's computer business had lost millions. According to Jack B. Grubman, an analyst at Salomon Brothers Inc., "Scale is everything in the computer industry . . . AT&T has never had it."[27]

After the NCR purchase, the company made its next move toward global networking by acquiring McCaw Cellular Communications Inc. in 1994. AT&T believes, "wireless technologies enable true anytime, anywhere communications via voice, data, images and messages. Multimedia adds an extra dimension by engaging several of our senses at once. Wireless communications is central to our networking strategy. That's why we initiated a merger with McCaw Cellular, America's top cellular service provider. We want to be a leader in shaping the trends that will influence lifestyles in the 21st Century."[28]

McCaw's acquisition enabled the company to enter the wireless market that was growing 25 to 30 percent annually.[29] It also gave an edge to the company in the provision of a nationwide service. Entry into the wireless market, however, required significant integration, setting the standards to make the technology work, developing microprocessors on which it runs, and using the marketing and distribution channels to allow service on both wired and wireless platforms. On the other hand, a potential advantage of the cellular business for AT&T was the possibility of establishing a direct link to customers, thus bypassing the access fees the company had to pay to the local phone service providers, mainly the Baby Bells.[30]

■ An International AT&T

After the 1984 divestiture, AT&T faced a new reality in the U.S. market, where numerous competitors were eroding its dominance and market share. Realizing that there was only limited growth potential in this market, AT&T changed its strategy and redefined itself as a global company.[31] AT&T claimed to be just a small fish in the huge pond of the $3 trillion telecommunication industry.[32]

At the time of the divestiture AT&T had fewer than 100 employees outside the United States. Its new goal was to increase dramatically the portion of the firm's revenues coming from international activities. In 1995 AT&T did business in more than 130 countries and had about 55,000 employees outside the United States. Most AT&T business units are involved in marketing and sales abroad, with AT&T's international division coordinating AT&T's global interests. In meeting the service needs of multinational companies around the world, and in taking advantage of tremendous openings in several markets around the world (China, former Eastern bloc countries), AT&T preferred to partner with local telecommunications operators where and whenever possible. AT&T has rapidly expanded its international marketing capability through joint ventures, alliances, and other equity investments.[33] Because AT&T established numerous subsidiary companies and offices throughout the world, it implemented an international organizational structure, along regional lines, to complement the functional groups and to promote sharing and accountability between regional units and functional groups. All of AT&T's non-U.S. businesses are represented in three regional units: Asia/Pacific, with headquarters in Hong Kong; Europe/Middle East/Africa, with headquarters in Brussels; and Caribbean/Latin America, with headquarters in Florida.

AT&T has been gaining market share in Europe and China as deregulation there has been opening up markets for telecommunications equipment. In 1992 AT&T was finally allowed back in the Chinese market from which it had been banned in 1979. With expected additions of 15 million telephone lines by 1995, the Chinese market is a big opportunity for AT&T's equipment division. In 1992, AT&T also joined the Ukrainian government to own and modernize large portions of the Ukrainian telephone network. This was the first time AT&T built, owned, and operated a long-distance network outside the United States.[34] Despite these efforts, analysts still complain that the company's alliances thus far are nebulous and have yet to produce meaningful revenue, whereas other alliances are more visibly successful, such as MCI's alliance with British Telecom, which is already producing $1 billion in yearly revenue for MCI.[35]

■ The Business of AT&T

> *We are dedicated to being the world's best at bringing people together—giving them access to each other and to the information and services they want—anytime, anywhere.*
>
> —AT&T Mission Statement

AT&T considered itself a global company that provided communications services and products, as well as network equipment and computer systems to businesses, consumers, telecommunications service providers, and government agencies.

At a corporate level, AT&T's business units were the basic building blocks of the company. Corporate organizations and operating divisions, such as finance, network services, and R&D, support the business units. The business units formed five groups—Communication Products, Communication Services, Network Systems, NCR (GIS), and Financial Services—supported by group executives (see Exhibit 4). A Management Executive Committee led the development and implementation of AT&T's vision, mission, and strategic intent, while an Operations Committee had responsibility for execution of policies and strategies established by the Management Executive Committee.

■ Consequences of Strategic Change

AT&T's growth strategy, implemented since the consent decree, resulted in the dispersal of scarce resources among growing but sometimes unprofitable businesses. This caused some limitation in the company's profitability, and led to doubts about the effectiveness of the "growth by acquisitions" and diversification

Exhibit 4 AT&T Businesses	
	Purpose and Operations
Communication Services	
Consumer Services	Reaches out to customers around the world with a number of long-distance and customer assistance services.
AT&T Universal Card Services Corp.	Markets a consumer credit card in cooperation with the Universal Bank of Columbus, Georgia, for general purchases and long-distance calling.
Business Communications Services	Markets some 75 U.S. and international long-distance services for business customers.
AT&T EasyLink Services	Develops and markets global electronic messaging services for business customers worldwide.
AT&T American Transtech	Provides telephone marketing, direct mail, market research, and database management services and administrative support for employee benefit plans.
Communications Products	
AT&T Consumer Products	Designs, manufactures, leases, and sells personal communications products and services for the home and very small businesses in the U.S. and worldwide.
Business Communications Systems	Offers products and customer service to business customers who have more than 80 phone lines.
General Business Systems	Offers products, systems, and customer service generally to small and emerging businesses.
AT&T Paradyne	Offers data communications equipment, such as modems and multiplexes, to large and small business customers.
AT&T Ventures Corp.	Establishes new businesses based on applications of AT&T technology that address markets outside the scope of existing business units.
Federal Systems Advanced Technologies	Supports the federal government's military and civilian need for specially designed systems.
GIS (NCR)	
NCR Corp.	Develops, produces, markets, and supports enterprise-wide information systems and services for worldwide markets.
Financial Services	
AT&T Capital Corporation	Provides leasing and financing services for AT&T products and systems and for non–AT&T products, including transportation, office, computer, and manufacturing equipment.
Network Systems	
AT&T Network Systems	Leading worldwide manufacturer and marketer of network telecommunications products.
Switching Systems	Manufactures and markets telecommunications switches.
Transmission Systems	Designs, manufactures, and markets transmission equipment.
Operations Systems	Develops and markets software and hardware for telecommunications systems and networks.
Network Cable Systems	Leading worldwide supplier of fiber-optic and copper cables for communications providers and users worldwide.
Network Wireless Systems	Manufactures and markets radio and switching systems for wireless phone networks.
AT&T Microelectronics	Designs and manufactures advanced electronic and photonic components and power systems for AT&T and other high-tech firms worldwide.

Source: AT&T Fact Book.

strategy. "We found ourselves always concerned about coordination and even reluctant to act sometimes for fear we would hurt the other parts of AT&T," according to Allen.[36] He also indicated:

> the complexity of trying to manage these different businesses began to overwhelm the advantage of [AT&T's] integration strategy. The world has changed, the market has changed. Conflicts have arisen, and each of [AT&T's] businesses has to react more quickly.[37]

> Even at a personal level, the champion behind these strategic changes, Allen, said "I was probably as frustrated as I'd ever been trying to coordinate across our various businesses."[38]

These sentiments provided grounds for a change in AT&T's strategy; one that would help it unleash the true potential of each one of its business units individually. In particular, the long-distance service, the company's cash cow, would have fewer constraints on its growth.

AT&T's profitable long-distance service business had to support GIS's lack-luster performance with its resources. In the first six months of 1995 alone, GIS lost $332 million.[39] This loss appeared despite continuous restructuring efforts and the layoff of 10,000 employees by GIS. Had this loss not taken place, AT&T's earnings would have been 25 percent greater for the first half of 1995.[40]

Furthermore, the success of AT&T's equipment business was perceived to be hindered, because its long-distance competitors were not willing to purchase equipment from AT&T's equipment division, since they would be helping their long-distance competitor grow (refer to Appendices J and K).[41] This was of particular concern in international markets where just the potential threat of AT&T's entry hindered AT&T's other businesses from developing (see Appendices E, F, G, and H for financial data).

As a reaction to these consequences, AT&T's market value was undervalued, mainly because "Investors couldn't understand the strategy of the combined companies."[42]

The 1995 Breakup

On September 20, 1995, AT&T announced its breakup into three separate entities and took the business world by surprise.

According to AT&T, changes in customer needs, technology, and public policy are radically transforming the global information industry, and AT&T is at the intersection of all that change and of all the opportunity it creates. Accordingly, AT&T executives believe this restructuring will ensure that each of AT&T's businesses can seize those opportunities, and that they can follow the best path to creating value for their customers and shareowners without bumping into another AT&T unit along the way.

> AT&T's restructuring is about size, it's about focus, speed and enormous opportunity.
>
> —Robert Allen, CEO

Beginning in 1996 AT&T will likely consist of:

- A phone company that provides long-distance and cellular service, AT&T Services, with estimated revenues of $53.3 billion in 1996. The projected CEO of the largest international phone company in the world, which currently holds close to 60 percent of the U.S. long-distance market share, will be Alex J. Mandl, 51, who is currently CEO of AT&T's Communications Service Group.

- An equipment company that makes switches and phone lines, AT&T Network Equipment, with estimated revenues of $24.5 billion in 1996. The second largest telecom equipment maker in the world, with 40 percent operating margins, will be headed by Henry B. Schacht, 60, former CEO of Cummings Engine Company, Inc.
- A computer company formed from the NCR acquisition, AT&T Global Information Systems, with estimated revenues of $8.3 billion in 1996. This troubled unit of the old AT&T will be headed by Richard A. McGinn, 49, currently CEO of AT&T's Network System Group.[43]

Robert Allen, the present CEO and chairman of AT&T, will become the president of AT&T Corporation after he completes the reengineering of the company.

The communications services and the communications systems companies created by this action will both be powerhouses within their industries. The third company, Global Information Solutions—or GIS, is in the midst of a difficult turnaround. As GIS returns to profitability, AT&T will seek to launch it as a healthy, independent computer company. AT&T also plans to sell off the remaining interests in its leasing and financing company, AT&T Capital Corporation. (AT&T had sold about 14 percent of its interest in AT&T Capital Corporation to the public several years ago.) In 1995, the Capital Corporation had some $8 billion in assets. AT&T could use the proceeds of the sale to retire part of its debt to ensure that the new companies start life with the capital flexibility they need to take advantage of opportunities within their markets.[44] AT&T plans to split its famed research center in two—prompting many observers to fret that Bell Labs may soon become a neglected relic of the golden age of corporate research. The majority of Bell Labs' 26,000 employees will be shifted to the new phone equipment company, based in the AT&T Network System division, and will retain the Bell Labs name. After this split the funding for Bell Labs will rely highly on the performance of the equipment unit, which supplies the vast majority of the Labs' annual budget.[45]

The new communications services company will be built around the Communications Services Group, AT&T Wireless Services, AT&T Universal Card Services, and the newly formed AT&T Solutions organization. AT&T Solutions does consulting and systems integration. The communication services company will seek to keep the "AT&T" brand name and expand its meaning to include a wide range of new on-line information services, as well as electronic commerce. However, this company may also have to develop its own research facilities.

The new systems and technology company will consist of the Network Systems Group, the Multimedia Products Group, and Bell Laboratories. The power and reputation of Bell Laboratories will make this new systems and technology company a formidable global competitor.

The new information systems company will continue to offer customers personal computers as part of its total solutions approach, but will no longer develop and manufacture its Globalyst™ line of personal computers. It plans to restructure and focus on the three transaction-intensive industries where it has a commanding position—retailing, financial services, and communications.

Although some headline writers might call this breakup "Divestiture II," AT&T believes it is much more than that. "Divestiture was thrust upon us. We undertake this restructuring by our own choice. It's a step that anticipates the direction our industry is taking and gets us ahead of the curve. This restructuring will make AT&T's businesses more valuable to our shareowners. It will make our businesses even more responsive to their customers. And it will enable our employees to focus even more sharply on the growth opportunities in their individual markets."[46]

"This restructuring will allow us to take energy that we have been spending in coordinating complex strategies across our businesses and turn it into creating new offers for our customers. Each of our shareowners' businesses will now be free to follow its individual path to creating greater value without worrying about bumping into another AT&T unit along the way. Finally, this restructuring will give shareowners a more focused investment in each of three high-growth industries. It will allow them to evaluate each independent company on its own merits."[47]

AT&T is looking to gain the following benefits from its restructuring:

- Each new business will have a sharper focus on its individual market and clearer strategic intent.
- The restructuring will eliminate strategic conflict between businesses (e.g., simultaneously selling to and competing with service providers). This will not only remove complications of sales to existing markets (e.g., the regional BOCs), it will open new markets (e.g., competitors of AT&T's current service and equipment businesses).
- It will accelerate decision making by greatly simplifying AT&T's corporate structure.
- It will give each business unit financial flexibility appropriate to its market and opportunities (e.g., capital structure and cost structure).

■ Challenges Facing the New AT&T Corporation

Because they operated in so many different areas of the market, the different divisions of AT&T were constrained because of conflicting interests. For example, the telecommunications service company was constrained by buying its hardware and software and operating in different markets without hurting the other parts of the company. The equipment division was also facing a problem for equipment sales, because most of AT&T's long-distance competitors refused to buy equipment from them. At the same time, the local telephone service providers started delaying or canceling their equipment orders to AT&T due to the fear of feeding a potential competitor. AT&T now expects to be able to focus more on its telecommunication services, without being distracted by equipment making and computers.

This move could significantly change the competitive landscape for many telephone companies and suppliers giving AT&T the opportunity to act in the telephone service business without taking responsibility for implications at the equipment and computer business. AT&T now expects to have more room to maneuver in a new arena set up by expected changes in legislation. At the same time, however, AT&T is going to be a smaller company and, hence, might not be as effective in its lobbying efforts as it was in the past.

In the international arena, the breakup will give the units more freedom. There are companies which chose not to buy AT&T equipment because they were competitors on the service side. The breakup will make them a more flexible and formidable competitor on the hardware side. On the other hand, AT&T will not be able to leverage the advantages of entering new markets with its equipment or computer division, establishing its reputation, and using this as a stepping stone to offer its telecommunications services in these markets.

To realize the benefits of the restructuring, AT&T has to overcome a lot of new challenges, resulting from the breakup's reality. The new telecommunication services company will be stripped of some of its most successful sister divisions. On the one hand, the company will be freed up to better utilize its resources and seize an advantage in the telecommunication market, but on the other hand the company will have fewer resources to do so.

For instance, AT&T will no longer have its successful equipment unit, which provided a comfortable cushion for financial losses in other divisions. In addition, it will no longer have an internal supplier that put AT&T's needs first. Now AT&T will also have to shop for its equipment in competitive markets, like its competitors do. Despite company announcements stating that there will still be cooperation between the new independent companies, each company will now have to focus on better serving the interests of its own shareholders, rather than serving AT&T's needs as a priority.

AT&T is also losing its research and development facilities, the world famous Bell Labs, which have served the company for more than seven decades. AT&T will now be forced to develop its own research competence in the future. Will AT&T be able to develop its research facilities fast enough or purchase innovation that will allow it to keep it ahead of competition in new telecommunication service developments?

AT&T will restructure its workforce as well as its finances. As many as 40,000 jobs are expected to be cut by the time the breakup takes effect late in 1996. A lot of the cuts are expected to take place in AT&T's corporate staff of 28,000 workers. More than one competitor is looking forward to the possibility of uncertainty among AT&T employees and executives as they compete for contracts while the spin-off is completed. Managing the change related to such a major restructuring and downsizing will be a monumental challenge for AT&T.

The company will be smaller both in terms of resources and human capital. Given that the communication services is a $750 billion global market, growing at a rate of 7 percent per year,[48] will this trimmed-down AT&T be able to seize the opportunities it identifies in order to compete as effectively with its resource base prior to the breakup? How will this affect the formulation of AT&T's future corporate strategies? Will this initiate a reversal of their "growth by acquisition" strategy?

At the same time, the international telecommunications industry is expected to present significant opportunities for the telecommunication companies. Over the next 10 years, this is expected to be a $3 trillion industry. In the past, AT&T has pursued a global strategy aiming to take advantage of the openings in the international arena. As this industry is getting larger, and competitors join forces and combine resources through strategic alliances to take better advantage of the opportunities, will the smaller size of AT&T constrain its ability to compete?

Another major challenge will be facing the results of the changes in the regulatory environment. How will AT&T react to possible further deregulation of the industry? How will it behave in a more competitive environment?

Moreover, will the smaller AT&T have the resources to lobby effectively, and the corporate clout to influence the policy making process and outcomes?

These as well as other challenging questions face the top executives of AT&T as they confront the future after the breakup.

■ Notes

1. John Mulqueen and Margie Semilof, 1995, New era dawns for AT&T—Again. *Communications-Week.* September 25, no. 576: 177.
2. AT&T, 1993, *Annual Report.*
3. AT&T fact book, AT&T Corporate Public Relations.
4. M. K. Kellog, P. W. Huber, and J. Thorne, 1992, *Federal Telecommunications Law* (Canada: Little, Brown & Company Limited).
5. Ibid., 28.
6. Ibid., 28.
7. U.S. Industrial Outlook 1994, Telecommunications Services.
8. Ibid.
9. Ibid.
10. Naik Gautam and Daniel Pearl, 1995, Wireless sale winners include AT&T, Sprint: 'Personal communications Services' auction ends: bids topped $7 billion, *Wall Street Journal,* March 14, A3.
11. Toward a free market in telecommunications, *Wall Street Journal,* April 19, 1994, A20.
12. U.S. Industrial Outlook 1994, Telecommunications Services.
13. Ibid.
14. Toward a free market in telecommunications, A20.
15. Ibid.
16. Daniel Pearl, 1995, Long-distance companies can't get through to congress in telecommunica-

tions bill debate, *Wall Street Journal,* July 24, A14.
17. AT&T, 1993, *Annual Report.*
18. Bart Ziegler and Naik Gautam, 1995, Bell labs is facing a mundane future under breakup plan, *Wall Street Journal,* September 22, A10.
19. Nathaniel Gilbert, 1991, AT&T capital finds a winner, *Financier,* 15, no. 8: 43–44.
20. Ibid.
21. The strategic alliance of AT&T and Italtel, *Mergers & Acquisitions,* January–February, 1990, 24, no. 4: 70–71.
22. Ibid.
23. Cindy Skrzycki, 1991, NCR Corp. agrees to AT&T merger, *Washington Post,* May 7, C1.
24. Andrew Kupfer, 1994, AT&T's $12 billion cellular dream, *Fortune,* December 12, 100.
25. Skrzycki, NCR Corp. agrees to AT&T merger, C1.
26. *Business Marketing,* November, 1993, 23.
27. AT&T, 1993, *Annual Report.*
28. John J. Keller, 1995, AT&T begins slicing computer unit, *Wall Street Journal,* September 15, A3.
29. Ida Picker, 1995, The M&A Masters, *Institutional Investor,* 27, no. 86: 165–166.
30. Naik Gautam, 1995, Cutting the cord: No big deal? PCS is coming and there may be a lot less to it than you've been led to believe, *Wall Street Journal,* March 20, R16.

31. AT&T, 1993, *Annual Report.*
32. AT&T's Internet home page: www.att.com.
33. AT&T, 1993, *Annual Report.*
34. John Mintz, 1992, AT&T Ukraine agree on phone giant joint venture, *Washington Post,* January 15, F1.
35. John J. Keller, 1995, Divide to conquer, *Wall Street Journal,* September 21, A1.
36. David Kirkpatrick, 1995, Is Mandl the man?, *Fortune,* October 16, 85.
37. Keller, Divide to conquer, A1.
38. Kirkpatrick, Is Mandl the man?, 85.
39. Mulqueen and Semilof, New era dawns for AT&T, 177.
40. Allan Sloan and Johnnie L. Roberts, 1995, Big deals, big talk, *Newsweek,* October 2.
41. Keller, Divide to conquer, A1.
42. Ibid.
43. Catherine Arnst, Leah Spiro Nathans, and Peter Burrows, 1995, Divide and conquer?, *Business Week,* October 2, 56–57.
44. AT&T's Internet home page: www.att.com.
45. Ziegler and Gautam, Bell labs is facing a mundane future, A10.
46. AT&T's Internet home page: www.att.com.
47. Ibid.
48. Ibid.

Appendix A Trends and Forecasts: Telecommunications Services[a]											
Forecasts (in millions of dollars except as noted) Percent Change (1989–1994)											
Item	*1989*	*1990*	*1991*	*1992*	*1993E*	*1994F*	*89–90*	*90–91*	*91–92*	*92–93*	*93–94*
Operating revenues											
Domestic	143,086	146,147	153,942	160,480	168,975	180,700	2.1	5.3	4.2	5.3	6.9
International	4,892	5,752	7,158	8,720	10,375	12,400	15.5	24.4	21.8	19.0	19.5
Operating revenues (1987$)											
Domestic	140,349	143,803	151,473	157,441	165,321	175,864	2.5	5.3	3.9	5.0	6.4
Total employment (000)	900.5	925.5	914.8	895.0	883.6	876.4	2.8	−1.2	−2.2	−1.3	−0.8
Production workers (000)	646.3	666.6	670.9	671.2	668.1	671.5	3.1	0.6	0.0	−0.5	0.5

E, Estimate; F, Forecast.
[a]Includes AT&T, BOCs, cellular, independents, mobile radio, VANs, telex, and telegraph.
Source: U.S. Department of Commerce.

Appendix B   Largest Local Telephone Companies by Access Lines, 1992

Company	Lines
Bell Atlantic Corp.	18,181,000
Bell South Corp.	18,109,000
Ameritech Corp.	17,001,000
GTE Corp.	16,191,000
NYNEX	15,698,088
Pacific Telesis Group	14,551,000
U S West Communications	13,344,975
Southwest Bell Corp.	12,609,033
Sprint Corp.	4,241,443
Southern New England Telephone Co.	1,902,100

Source: United States Telephone Association.

Appendix C   Telecom Carrier Efficiency, 1993

Company	Revenue* (Per Employee in Thousands of Dollars)
MCI	383
Sprint	216
AT&T	213
Hong Kong Telecom	200
NTT (Japan)	196
RBOCs (USA)	168
TELMEX (Mexico)	165
Cable & Wireless (UK)	163
GTE	149
TEF (Spain)	147
Bell (Canada)	143
STET (Italy)	136
Telecom New Zealand	123
British Telecom	120
Telephonica de Argentina	101
Telephonos de Chile	97
Telekom Malaysia	51

*Estimate.
Source: Merrill Lynch.

Appendix D   Total Toll Service Revenues

(in millions of dollars except as noted)

Company	1984	1985	1986	1987	1988	1989	1990	1991	1992
Total All Carriers	51,156	54,815	57,486	58,519	62,600	66,024	66,792	69,375	
Total local exchange companies	12,401	12,185	12,873	13,736	15,113	14,840	14,690	14,115	
Bell operating companies	9,037	9,026	9,599	10,268	10,668	10,549	10,578	10,066	
Other local exchange companies	3,364	3,159	3,274	3,468	4,445	4,291	4,112	4,049	
Total Long Distance Carriers	38,755	42,630	44,595	44,783	47,486	51,184	52,102	55,260	59,372
AT&T Communications	34,935	36,770	36,514	35,219	35,407	34,549	33,880	34,384	35,495
MCI Telecommunications	1,761	2,331	3,372	3,938	4,886	6,171	7,392	8,266	9,719
(Telecom[a] USA)	105	201	291	396	524		713		
US Sprint			1,141	2,592	3,405	4,320	5,041	5,378	5,655
(GTE Sprint[b])	1,052	1,122	779						
(US Telecom)		387	212						
LDDS Communications, Inc.[c]						110	154	263	801
(Advanced Telecomm. Corp)	72	86	124	162	178	326	342	356	
Cable & Wireless		146	171	180	218	275	359	406	495
Wiltel, Inc.						300	376	405	494
Allnet		309	450	395	394	334	326	347	376
(Lexitel[d])		127							
Metromedia Communic. Corp						127	381	369	369
(ITT Communications Services[e])	161	241	282	287	379	404			
ALASCOM	255	271	267	262	272	278	259	338	333
Litel Telecommun. Corp						197	215	208	243
RCI Long Distance, Inc.						104	142	155	168
International Telecharge, Inc.						275	230	181	159
Comsystems Network Services							130	131	135
Telesphere Network, Inc.						192	293	308	
(National Telephone Services, Inc.[f])						150			
Others	414	639	992	1,352	1,823	2,359	2,582	3,765	4,927
Long-Distance Carriers' Share (%)									
AT&T Communications	90.1	86.3	81.9	78.6	74.6	67.5	65.0	62.2	59.8
MCI Communications	4.5	5.5	7.6	8.8	10.3	12.1	14.2	15.0	16.4
US Sprint	2.7	2.6	4.3	5.8	7.2	8.4	9.7	9.7	9.5
Others	2.6	5.6	6.3	6.8	8.0	12.0	11.1	13.1	14.3

Source: Federal Communications Commission; Industry Analysis Division
[a]-MCI Telecommunications and Telecom USA merged during 1989.
[b]-In July 1986, GTE Sprint and US Telecom merged into US Sprint. Effective February 26 1992, the company's name became Sprint Communications.
[c]-LDDS Communications, Inc., and Advanced Telecommunications Corp. merged during 1992.
[d]-Allnet and Lexitel merged at the end of 1985.
[e]-Metromedia Communications Corp. and ITT Communications Corp. merged during 1988.
[f]-Telesphere Network, Inc., and National Telephone Services, Inc., merged during 1989. In 1991, Telesphere Network, Inc., went into bankruptcy.

Appendix E Balance Sheets

Fiscal Year Ending	12/31/94	12/31/93	12/31/92	12/31/91
Annual Assets (000$)				
Cash	1,208,000	671,000	1,310,000	2,148,000
Receivables	28,623,000	23,664,000	19,609,000	16,526,000
Inventories	3,633,000	3,222,000	2,659,000	3,125,000
Other current assets	4,147,000	2,811,000	2,936,000	2,814,000
Total current assets	37,611,000	30,368,000	26,514,000	24,613,000
Prop, plant, & equip	22,035,000	21,015,000	19,358,000	18,689,000
Net prop & equip	22,035,000	21,015,000	19,358,000	18,689,000
Invest & adv to subs	2,708,000	3,060,000	864,000	976,000
Other non-cur assets	4,513,000	3,815,000	3,643,000	3,180,000
Deferred charges	8,402,000	7,570,000	3,480,000	3,084,000
Deposits & oth asset	3,993,000	3,565,000	3,329,000	2,813,000
Total Assets	79,262,000	69,393,000	57,188,000	53,355,000
Annual Liabilities (000$)				
Accounts payable	6,011,000	4,853,000	5,045,000	4,989,000
Current long-term debt	13,666,000	11,063,000	7,600,000	7,053,000
Accrued expenses	4,105,000	3,802,000	3,336,000	3,259,000
Other current liab	7,148,000	6,336,000	5,405,000	5,690,000
Total current liab	30,930,000	26,054,000	21,386,000	20,991,000
Deferred charges/inc	4,921,000	2,764,000	5,191,000	4,333,000
Long-term debt	11,358,000	11,802,000	8,604,000	8,484,000
Other long-term liab	13,039,000	13,446,000	2,634,000	2,902,000
Total liabilities	60,248,000	54,066,000	37,815,000	36,710,000
Minority int (liab)	1,093,000	648,000	452,000	417,000
Preferred stock	NA	1,305,000	NA	NA
Common stock net	1,569,000	1,547,000	1,340,000	1,309,000
Capital surplus	15,825,000	14,324,000	11,425,000	10,624,000
Retained earnings	687,000	−2,110,000	6,498,000	4,599,000
Other equities	−160,000	−387,000	−342,000	−304,000
Shareholder equity	17,921,000	14,679,000	18,921,000	16,228,000
Total liab & net worth	79,262,000	69,393,000	57,188,000	53,355,000

Appendix F Income Statements

Fiscal Year Ending	12/31/94	12/31/93	12/31/92	12/31/91
Annual Income (000$)				
Net sales	75,094,000	69,351,000	66,647,000	63,089,000
Cost of goods	44,317,000	41,635,000	40,391,000	38,825,000
Gross profit	30,777,000	27,716,000	26,256,000	24,264,000
R & D expenditures	3,110,000	3,111,000	2,924,000	3,114,000
Sell gen & admin exp	19,637,000	18,037,000	16,704,000	19,792,000
Inc bef dep & amort	8,030,000	6,568,000	6,628,000	1,358,000
Non-operating inc	236,000	467,000	163,000	251,000
Interest expense	748,000	1,032,000	1,153,000	726,000
Income before tax	7,518,000	6,003,000	5,638,000	883,000
Prov for inc taxes	2,808,000	2,301,000	2,196,000	361,000
Net inc bef ex items	4,710,000	3,702,000	3,442,000	522,000
Ex items & disc ops	NA	−9,608,000	NA	NA
Net income	4,710,000	−5,906,000	3,442,000	522,000
Outstanding shares	1,569,006	1,352,398	1,339,831	1,309,352

Appendix G   Selected Annual Financial Ratios

Fiscal Year Ending	12/31/94	12/31/93	12/31/92
Quick ratio	0.96	0.93	0.98
Current ratio	1.22	1.17	1.24
Sales/cash	62.16	103.35	50.88
SG&A/sales	0.26	0.26	0.25
Receivables turnover	2.62	2.93	3.4
Receivables days sales	137.22	122.84	105.92
Inventories turnover	20.67	21.52	25.06
Inventories days sales	17.42	16.73	14.36
Net sales/working capital	11.24	16.08	13
Net sales/plant & equipment	3.41	3.3	3.44
Net sales/current assets	2	2.28	2.51
Net sales/total assets	0.95	1	1.17
Net sales/employees	246614	224655	213134
Total liab/total assets	0.76	0.78	0.66
Total liab/invested capital	2.06	2.04	1.37
Total liab/common equity	3.58	4.25	2.05
Times interest earned	11.05	6.82	5.89
Current debt/equity	0.76	0.75	0.4
Long-term debt/equity	0.63	0.8	0.45
Total debt/equity	1.4	1.56	0.86
Total assets/equity	4.42	4.73	3.02
Pretax inc/net sales	0.1	0.09	0.08
Pretax inc/total assets	0.09	0.09	0.1
Pretax inc/invested capital	0.26	0.23	0.2
Pretax inc/common equity	0.45	0.47	0.31
Net income/net sales	0.06	−0.09	0.05
Net income/total assets	0.06	−0.09	0.06
Net income/invested capital	0.16	−0.22	0.13
Net income/common equity	0.28	−0.46	0.19

Appendix H   Eight-Year Summary of Selected Financial Data[a]

(Dollars in Millions, Except Per Share Amounts)

Results	1991[b]	1990	1989	1988[c]	1987	1986[d]	1985	1984
Results of Operations								
Total revenues	63,089	62,191	61,100	61,756	60,530	61,906	63,130	60,318
Total cost	61,731	56,695	56,076	64,031	56,249	60,907	59,561	57,494
Net income (loss)	522	3,104	3,109	(1,230)	2,463	476	1,872	1,713
Earnings (loss) per common share	0.40	2.42	2.40	(0.94)	1.82	0.29	1.31	1.23
Dividends declared per common share	1.32	1.32	1.20	1.20	1.20	1.20	1.20	1.20
Assets and Capital								
Total assets	53,355	48,322	42,187	39,869	44,014	43,617	44,683	43,418
Common shareowners' equity	16,228	15,883	14,723	13,705	16,617	15,946	16,951	15,839
Net capital expenditures	3,860	4,018	3,951	4,288	3,805	3,904	4,295	3,685
Other Information								
Return on average common equity	3.1%	19.7%	21.8%	(7.2%)	15.0%	2.2%	10.7%	10.5%
Stock price per common share	39.125	30.125	45.50	28.75	27.00	25.00	25.00	19.50
Employees	317,100	328,900	339,500	364,700	365,000	378,900	399,600	427,200

Source: AT&T Fact Book
[b] 1991 data reflect $4.5 billion of business restructuring and other charges.
[c] 1988 data reflect a $6.7 billion charge due to accelerated digitalization of the long-distance network.
[d] 1986 data reflect $3.2 billion charges for business restructuring, an accounting change and other items.

Appendix I   AT&T's Agreement and Alliances

- With *British Telecom, France Telecom,* and *Kokusai Denshin Denwa* of Japan, AT&T offers a variety of voice, data, and private line services to business customers.
- *Mitsubishi:* AT&T Microelectronics and Mitsubishi have cooperative agreements in the following areas: the manufacture of static random access memory (SRAM) chips, the packaging of integrated circuits at AT&T's Thailand plant, and the development of high-performance gallium arsenide chips.
- *NEC:* AT&T is cooperating with NEC in Japan on a wide range of semiconductor products and technologies.
- *Olivetti:* This Italian company is marketing AT&T smart card technology in Italy.
- *Sematech:* AT&T is a member of this consortium, which is a Department of Defense/industry partnership focused on developing world-leading semiconductor manufacturing technology.
- *Toshiba:* This Japanese company is a distributor of AT&T's Datakit VCS systems and the System 75 PBX.
- *X/OPEN:* NCR is a member participant of this London industry consortium dedicated to furthering open systems and applications software portability.
- With *Zenith,* AT&T is codeveloping an all-digital high-definition television system using AT&T microchips and video compression research and Zenith's television technology.

Appendix J

Equipment Vendor Revenues, 1992

Source: International Telecommunications Union, adapted from company reports.

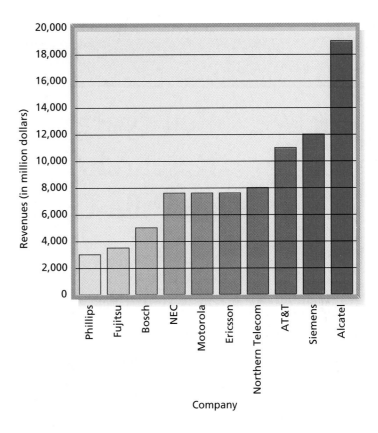

Appendix K

US Transmission Equipment Market Leaders, 1992

Source: Datapro Research Group & Northern Business Information.

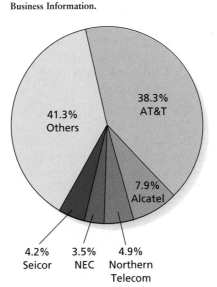

Projected Wireless Distribution, 1998

Source: Personal Communications Industry Association.

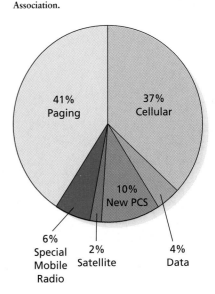

Bell Northern Research/Northern Telecom and the Cable TV Industry

Norman McGuinnes
Keith Dawson
Bell Northern Research

■ http://www.nortel.com
■ http://www.commscope.com/Cable TV.html

In late 1991 a small technical team at Northern Telecom's R&D arm in Ottawa, Bell Northern Research Ltd. (BNR), was coming to the end of its task. The team had been funded for a year to explore development possibilities for a new market for Northern Telecom—the cable TV industry in the United States.

Keith Dawson, technology manager at BNR, now had to write a report outlining the situation and suggesting the best course of action. Much hinged on whether the cable TV industry began to switch from analog to digital transmission technologies. Should that happen, Northern Telecom, with its expertise in digital products, could be poised to become a strong competitor in the emerging market. Any action by Northern, however, had to consider how technology was changing both the cable TV and the telephone industry. New opportunities were opening up for each and the boundaries between the two industries were becoming less distinct. Northern had to assess how both industries were likely to change and how rapidly; it had to decide how much development effort to exert, and what kinds of systems and products to emphasize.

■ BNR and Northern Telecom

Northern Telecom Ltd. was a large Canadian manufacturer of telecommunications equipment with sales in 1990 of $6.7 billion. Its recent acquisition of STC in the United Kingdom added another $1.6 billion sales. AT&T of the United States and Alcatel of France were the largest manufacturers in the industry, each having telecommunications equipment sales greater than $12 billion. Sales and R&D spending levels for the top six manufacturers in the industry are shown in

Norman McGuinnes, Ph.D., and Keith Dawson, Bell Northern Research, prepared this case solely to provide material for class discussion. The case is not intended to illustrate either effective or ineffective handling of a managerial situation. Certain names and other identifying information may have been disguised to protect confidentiality.
Copyright © 1994, The University of Western Ontario

Exhibit 1	Largest Telecommunication Equipment Suppliers		
Company	Home Country	Telecommunication Sales[a] US $ Billions 1990	R&D (% of sales) 1990
A T & T	United States	12.4	12.4
Alcatel	France	13.7	8.4
Siemens	Germany	8.3	11.0
Northern Telecom	Canada	6.7	11.4
Ericsson	Sweden	6.6	10.4
NEC	Japan	6.5	8.4

[a]Equipment sales only.

Source: Northern Telecom data. The size ordering of the companies may change depending on the exchange rate in any given year.

Exhibit 1. All were global in scope and were full-line suppliers of equipment to the telephone industry. They offered everything from complex transmission and switching equipment to simple telephones.

BNR had grown to be the largest R&D operation in Canada, employing 6,800 employees, 4,500 of whom were located in Ottawa. The remainder worked at various sites in the United States, Europe, and Japan. BNR was 70 percent owned by Northern Telecom. The remaining 30 percent was owned by Bell Canada, the largest telephone operating system in Canada. BNR, Northern Telecom, and Bell Canada, therefore, worked very closely together.

▪ Products

New technologies had greatly changed the telephone industry and were still doing so. Much of Northern Telecom's success had been achieved by being first with one of those technologies, digital switching. Northern made its Digital World announcement in 1976. The DMS, Northern's first digital, local-office, class 5 switch, was an enormously costly R&D project that was by no means assured of either technical or market success.[1] Digital presented a major change to the analog systems of the telephone companies and was accompanied by all the uncertainties that characterize any technical discontinuity.

Digital technology, however, offered major advantages. It greatly improved signal quality because digital repeaters regenerated attenuated signals exactly. Analog amplifiers, in contrast, added distortion and noise. The DMS also integrated the carrier system and network termination equipment into the switch itself in a way that resulted in large savings for the telephone companies. Over the longer term, the DMS offered further benefits because the cost of digital was expected to decline relative to analog electronics, and the functional features of digital systems were predicted to expand.

[1] Central office switches linked telephone networks and routed calls to their destinations. They ranged in capacity from a few thousand telephone lines to hundreds of thousands. Different classes of switches were used for different applications on a network. Class 5 switches, used for local switching, were the most common type. Switches accounted for about 40 percent of the total investment in a typical telephone system.

In the 1970s, the telephone companies began to use another new technology, fiber optic transmission, which used laser-generated light beams to transmit information over glass fiber cables. By 1991 they had upgraded about 50 percent of their trunk lines. Cable TV operators began fiber trials in 1977 but had only started to use fibers extensively in the last three to four years. Fiber has a virtually unlimited bandwidth. Potentially, the amount of information (and number of channels) it could carry was immense. In practice, however, the bandwidth of a fiber system was limited by the transmission format used and by the optoelectronic devices on the system.

Fiber provided other important benefits in addition to wider bandwidth. It reduced transmission losses, so signals could be carried much longer distances before being amplified. Fewer amplifiers improved reliability and reduced maintenance costs by as much as 80 percent. (Amplifiers were one of the major sources of trouble on systems.) The cost of fiber and related components was declining rapidly and was expected to match the steadily rising cost of copper within the next decade.

Northern began manufacturing fiber in 1977 and made a major Fibre World product line announcement in 1989. It continued to spend heavily on fiber optic R&D in 1991.

On the horizon in 1991 was the possibility of a new form of wireless telephone called personal communication services (PCS). It was being widely discussed in the industry and was expected to create a very large new market. PCS featured extremely light, wallet-sized phones that could be carried anywhere, giving subscribers greater mobility and flexibility. Subscribers would be given a lifetime number that would remain the same wherever they lived or traveled. However, many technical and standards issues had to be resolved before PCS could become a practical option.

■ Markets

Northern Telecom benefited greatly from the deregulation of the U.S. market in 1984. Although Northern, with its digital advantage, had already penetrated the market, its share was small. Prior to deregulation, AT&T controlled about 80 percent of the equipment market through its ownership of 22 of the telephone operating systems. Following its agreement with the Justice Department, AT&T divested its ownership and the telephone systems were reorganized into seven independent and regulated Regional Bell Operating Companies (RBOCs) to serve local calling needs. The existing long distance system remained under AT&T's control, but was opened up to competition. AT&T also retained its manufacturing arm (Western Electric) and its R&D (Bell Labs), which was acknowledged to be one of the foremost R&D establishments in the world. The RBOCs each had their own R&D labs as well as a common standards-setting and planning group called Bellcore.

With established contacts and a market base, Northern was well positioned to exploit its digital leadership. It was able to convince the RBOCs that the cost-effective DMS made it possible for them to switch to digital much sooner than AT&T had been telling them. By 1990, Northern had gained a 42 percent share of the U.S. central office switch market, which was second to AT&T. Siemens was a distant third. As a result, the U.S. market accounted for 58.2 percent of Northern Telecom's sales in 1990. Canada made up 35.8 percent and

6 percent was sold in other parts of the world. The North American market was still the largest in the world, but was saturating. Markets elsewhere were growing faster and becoming increasingly important.

The Project to Investigate Digital Applications for Cable

The project Keith Dawson worked on had been initiated and vigorously championed by Jack Terry, a very senior and respected engineer who had been one of the key figures in successfully designing the original DMS switch. Cable companies were seriously discussing the possibility of switching to digital. Terry believed they would be driven to do so in order to service emerging entertainment and communication markets. He wanted Northern Telecom to take a leading position, or at least to be early enough to influence whatever industry standards developed, in what he predicted would be a very large new market.

Jack Terry sought funding for the project from funds available for small exploratory projects. These were funds BNR set aside to support leading-edge projects that explored new technologies and architectures. Most exploratory projects were proposed by middle managers in BNR who had spotted opportunities that seemed promising. Competition was intense for the funds, because engineers liked the challenge and career opportunities such projects presented. Many, if not most, of the projects were funded for one year only and had to compete again each year to continue. It was not unusual for a project that may have been under way for three years to be suddenly halted in favor of other options.

BNR management responded quickly to Jack Terry's proposal. Within two weeks, funds were provided to finance a team of five engineers to explore basic technical issues. Keith Dawson was the only business development person on the team. During the project, another 10 to 15 engineers, with differing technical skills, provided substantial help on a voluntary basis.

Cable Industry Operations and Programming

During the project, Keith Dawson collected information on the cable industry to assess the directions it was likely to take in the future. Most of the information came from books, published reports, cable industry trade news items, and interviews with cable TV executives. Because the project focused only on the large U.S. market, little Canadian information was collected. The following sections on the cable industry summarize these data.

Community Antenna Systems (CATV), using a large central antenna, originated in the early days of television when many smaller and remote communities could not receive television broadcast signals with simple home antennas. By the late 1960s CATV systems had spread to most communities where broadcast signals were not easily received, including parts of major cities where signal reflections and shadowing by large buildings were a problem.

It was the advent of satellite transmission in the mid-1970s, however, that created the present-day cable TV industry. Satellite transmission gave birth to a wide range of new channels that bypassed and competed with the traditional broadcast networks. The role of the CATV operators expanded accordingly as

Exhibit 2   Growth of the Cable TV Industry

Year	Basic Subscribers Number (000s)	Basic Subscribers % Growth	% of TV Households	Pay TV % of Basic	Number of Systems	% Growth in Number of Systems
1975	9,197		13.0		3,506	
1976	10,788	17.3	15.1	23.6	3,681	5.0
1977	12,168	12.8	16.6	22.3	3,832	4.1
1978	13,392	10.1	17.9	25.3	3,875	1.1
1979	14,814	10.6	19.4	35.0	4,150	7.1
1980	17,671	19.3	22.6	41.3	4,225	1.8
1981	23,219	31.4	28.3	50.6	4,375	3.6
1982	29,341	26.4	35.0	68.6	4,825	10.3
1983	34,114	16.3	40.5	76.4	5,600	16.1
1984	37,291	9.3	43.7	84.2	6,200	10.7
1985	39,872	6.9	46.2	87.5	6,600	6.5
1986	42,237	5.9	48.1	83.5	7,500	13.6
1987	44,971	6.5	50.5	80.8	7,900	5.3
1988	48,637	8.2	53.8	81.6	8,500	7.6
1989	52,564	8.1	57.1	85.0	9,050	6.5
1990	54,871	4.4	59.0	83.3	9,575	5.8
1991	56,073	2.2	60.3	80.2	10,704	11.8

Source: National Cable Television Association Cable Television Association.

they added the new channels to their offerings. Most of the new channels operated in specialized niches such as news, sports, religion, music, or movies. There were also channels for weather, home shopping, comedy, education, and those that catered to specialized regional interests. By 1990, the Cable Facts Book listed over 100 such channels, including 10 pay-TV and 10 pay-per-view services.

This explosion of new channels created a rapid growth in demand for cable services, as seen in Exhibit 2. It also pressured the cable companies to provide more channels (Exhibit 3). By 1991, the industry served 56 million subscribers, which constituted 60 percent of the homes with television. About 90 percent of these received more than 30 channels. The coax cables of the industry passed about 95 percent of the households in the country. As a result the viewing share of the basic cable networks rose from 9 to 21 percent between 1984 and 1990. Over the same period, the viewing share of the broadcast affiliates of the three traditional networks declined from 69 percent to 55 percent.[2]

To receive a satellite channel, a cable operator needed to install the receiving antenna and other headend equipment and pay a fee to the satellite program provider. There were three principal categories of programming, with a different fee structure for each:

---

[2] Source of data in this paragraph: National Cable Television Association, *Cable Television Developments*, 1991.

Exhibit 3	Channel Capacity of Cable Systems in 1990	
Number of Channels	% of Total Systems	% of Total Subscribers
54 and over	8.41	24.02
30–53	50.42	65.34
20–29	14.25	7.29
13–19	2.94	0.37
6–12	11.25	1.31
5 or less	0.33	0.016
Not Available	12.40	1.66
Total	100.0%	100.0%

Source: Cable and TV Fact Book.

Basic Programming

This category included all the channels cable subscribers received by paying their basic monthly cable fee, which averaged $17.58 in 1990. The cable operators in turn paid a monthly fee to receive each satellite channel, commonly around $0.20 per subscriber. The basic package also included the signals of the major broadcast networks, which were essentially free to the cable operator who also carried the advertising associated with them. However, the satellite networks and the cable operators also sold advertising time in competition with the networks. Between 1987 and 1991 these revenues grew from $1.2 to $3 billion.

Pay Channels

For an additional monthly fee, which averaged $10.38 in 1990, subscribers could receive a pay channel using a decoder. There were only a small number of these channels and they all offered movies as their chief programming fare. Typically, the cable system would pay 50 percent of the subscriber monthly fee to the satellite network. The satellite system in turn would pay half of what it received to the owners of the program rights.

To offer a full schedule, a pay channel needed to show about 300 movies per year. Although 80 percent of basic subscribers subscribed to at least one pay channel, a continuing problem for the cable systems was what was referred to as "churn." Pay subscribers had a tendency to drop their subscription to one channel and switch to another, according to the kinds of movies being shown. Subscribers complained about too much repetition of the same movies on the pay channels, and not enough difference between one pay channel and another. The market share of subscribers for the main pay channels and their ownership is shown in Exhibit 4.

Pay-per-View (PPV) Channels

Pay-per-view channels, a recent addition to the TV scene, required subscribers to pay for each program they viewed. To view a program, subscribers phoned in

Exhibit 4   Pay Channel Share of Subscribers—1989

Channel	% Share of Subscribers[a]	Channel Owned By
Home Box Office (HBO)	45.7%	Time Warner
Cinemax	17.7	Time Warner
Showtime	17.7	2 MSOs[b]
Disney Channel	11.6	Disney
Movie Channel	7.3	Time Warner

[a]Share of total subscribers (37.2 million) to all 5 channels. **Source:** Market Share Reporter.

[b]The term MSO, or multiple system operator, designates a cable system organization that owns and operates more than one cable system. Some of the MSOs were very large organizations.

their order and the fee would be added to their credit card or monthly cable service charge. On a few systems, subscribers could place their PPV order using the set-top converter. The PPV fee depended on the demand for the program, but for movies was generally in the same range as the charge for rental of a VCR movie. Orders had to be phoned in well ahead, because the telephone lines could become overly busy close to program time. Once placed, orders could not be cancelled.

To offer PPV channels, the cable system had to use subscriber decoder boxes that were addressable by the system. In 1991, there were 17 million subscribers on systems that could address decoder boxes. This number was expected to grow with PPV coverage of the 1992 Olympics. In preparation for that event, TCI, the last of the top 10 MSOs (multiple system operators) without addressability, had announced it would be providing that feature to all of its 6.5 million subscribers spread over 500 separate systems. The company estimated that if only 8 percent of its customers signed up for the Olympics, it would yield $50 million revenues within a year. TCI felt that was very attractive when compared to the four to five years it took to gain revenues of $80 million from winning a new franchise.

So far, PPV had been successful only with major athletic events such as heavyweight boxing championships. Among the movies and other programs offered, only those with a strong erotic content, such as the Playboy at Night channel, had been profitable. Estimated cable industry revenues for PPV in 1990 were $395 million, of which major events accounted for $295 million.

Cable operators blamed their lack of success with PPV on the satellite program providers. They needed to get the hit movies sooner, they said, before the video stores had saturated the market. For that to happen, however, the way in which new movies were put on the market would have to change. The distribution of movies was tightly controlled by the studios owning the rights. About 300 to 400 movies were produced per year; only 25 to 50 of those would become major box office successes. To maximize returns, the movie studios normally launched a movie first through theatres, accompanied by an intensive domestic and international promotional campaign. When theatre box office revenues slowed, distribution began to video stores. Video store rentals had been growing fast and there were speculations they might already exceed theatre revenues. After a good run, for six weeks or so, at the video store market, the movie would be made available to PPV, then to the pay channels, and finally to the major broadcasters and basic networks. Occasionally, someone from Holly-wood would make futuristic comments about the day when PPV would get the movies first. There were no signs that it was likely to happen in the near term.

For their part, the PPV satellite systems blamed the cable operators for poor marketing and promotion of PPV. The cable companies were not accustomed to promoting programs to build an audience. What little marketing they did was aimed more at attracting and retaining subscribers and building good relations in the community.

Cable Industry Regulation and Structure

The cable industry operated in a regulated environment where the Federal Communications Commission (FCC) had ultimate control over standards and other matters. An early concern of the regulators was to keep the cable industry out of the control of both the telephone companies and the large broadcast networks. Thus, the FCC prohibited both groups from owning cable systems in their own operating areas.

Initially, the FCC also regulated the subscriber fees charged by the cable systems. A major objective of the Cable Communications Policy Act of 1984, however, was to decentralize much of the control of the cable industry to the municipal level and to give the cable operators more freedom in setting their own fee structure. Control of cable systems at the local level was exercised through franchises granted by municipalities for 5- to 15-year terms. The trend was toward shorter terms to make the cable systems more accountable. Obtaining a franchise was a lengthy, competitive process whereby cable companies would negotiate and submit tenders detailing items such as the number of channels to be offered, signal quality, planned system extensions and improvements, and the franchise fee they would pay. Typically, the franchise fee was around three percent of revenues, but it sometimes went as high as five percent. Municipalities could also require the cable company to provide channels and TV studios for use by local organizations such as government, community groups, and educational organizations.

If the cable franchisee lived up to the terms of the agreement, the act provided some legal protection so that the franchise could not be taken away without good reason at renewal time. However, competitive bidding for franchises on renewal was quite common and the winner of the franchise was usually required to implement major upgrades to deal with demands of the municipality. Common subscriber complaints related to the poor quality of the video signal, the number of system outages experienced, and the number and types of channels offered. In one of the larger systems in New York City, a system upgrade under way in 1991 was going to make 150 channels available and presumably some new services. About 40 of these channels were intended for PPV but there was uncertainty as to where the programming would be found to fill them.

Recent court rulings had determined that local franchises could no longer be offered on an exclusive basis. As a result, in 1991 about 50 cities had competing cable systems, twice as many as in 1989. In these competitive situations a second system would "overbuild" the first by simply installing its cables along the same

Exhibit 5   Cable Fees and Revenues

| Year | Monthly Rates | | Annual Revenues ($ Millions) | | |
	Basic	Pay	Basic	Pay	Total[a]
1980	$7.85	$8.80	$1,615	$765	$2,549
1981	8.14	9.03	2,061	1,317	3,656
1982	8.46	9.56	2,530	2,020	4,984
1983	8.76	9.84	3,048	2,747	6,424
1984	9.20	10.08	3,545	3,370	7,774
1985	10.24	10.42	4,145	3,727	8,938
1986	11.09	10.31	4,891	3,895	10,166
1987	13.27	10.15	6,014	4,106	11,761
1988	14.45	10.18	7,343	4,491	13,619
1989	15.97	10.21	8,670	4,890	15,757
1990	17.58	10.38	10,047	5,146	17,874

[a]Also includes revenue from sources such as advertising, expanded basic, PPV, installation charges, second sets, etc.

Source: National Cable Television Association, *Cable Television Developments,* 1991.

poles and routes as the first system. Where overbuilding occurred, intense competition emerged between the rivals, in advertising, free service giveaways, and door-to-door selling.

The subscriber fees charged by the cable operators were essentially deregulated by the act (except in rural areas) on the grounds that cable TV was not a natural monopoly. It was argued that consumers had a choice of whether or not to subscribe and that a sufficient number of other sources of competitive entertainment existed to keep fees down. Fees had risen, however, and had provoked demands for tighter regulatory control. The recent pattern of fees and revenues is shown in Exhibit 5.

Cries for more controls were also prompted by the size of some of the cable operators and the monopoly power they were thought to have acquired. During the 1980s a great deal of acquisition activity had taken place whereby larger systems had bought up the smaller ones. By the late 1980s, systems were selling for around $2,500 per subscriber. This was considerably higher than the average system's undepreciated book value of plant and equipment of about $465 per subscriber. Some MSOs concentrated on acquisitions in particular regions. Others claimed to have a semblance of national coverage. However, the systems owned by an MSO were usually not geographically adjacent and were not run as a single big system from a signal distribution standpoint. Information on the percent of subscribers served by MSO's is given in Exhibit 6.

The MSOs gained important benefits from consolidation. Larger size made it easier and more economical for them to raise the large amount of funds needed for system upgrades and expansions. A MSO also had greater bargaining power in dealing with satellite program providers and could offer more to attract potential advertising revenue. Additional scale economies were derived in areas

Exhibit 6	Percent of Total Basic Subscribers Served by MSOs			
Rank	MSO	No. of Basic Subscribers	% of Total Basic Subs.	Cumulative %
1.	Tele-Communications Inc. (TCI)	7,861,570	14.3	14.3
2.	Time Warner	6,590,000	12.0	26.3
3.	United Artists Cable Systems	2,839,500	5.2	31.5
4.	Continental Cablevision Inc.	2,764,000	5.0	36.5
5.	Comcast Cable Communications	1,661,300	3.0	39.6
6.	Cox Cable Communications	1,639,000	3.0	42.6
7.	Storer Communications Cable Div.	1,614,600	2.9	45.5
8.	Jones Intercable	1,611,500	2.9	48.4
9.	Cablevision Systems Corporation	1,593,800	2.9	51.3
10.	Newhouse Broadcasting	1,259,600	2.3	53.6
Total of Rankings				
1–10		29,434,870	53.6	53.6
11–20		8,905,500	16.2	69.9
21–30		4,457,100	8.1	78.0
31–40		2,858,400	5.2	83.2
41–50		1,898,500	3.5	86.7

Source: National Cable Television Association, *Cable Television Developments*, 1991.

such as administration, dealing with regulatory bodies, and franchise negotiations. As a result, the larger MSOs attained cash flows of 50 percent or more of revenues, as compared to the industry average in 1988 of 45 percent. However, the industry debt ratio was 72.45 percent and earnings were only 1.4 percent of sales. Capital investment by the cable industry in 1988 was around $4 billion, of which approximately $1.6 billion was spent on new construction.[3]

Most of the larger MSOs had diversified into other areas of the entertainment and information industry. Ownership positions in satellite delivery systems, cellular telephone systems, and in the development of programs in Hollywood and elsewhere were not uncommon. A few had expanded into England and Europe. The Time Warner MSO, for instance, was part of a huge global entertainment conglomerate that included revenues from publishing enterprises ($2.93 billion), music recording ($2.93 billion), film production ($2.90 billion), pay movie channels ($1.3 billion), and cable systems and basic programming satellite channels ($1.75 billion). The highest operating income as a percentage of sales, 43.9 percent, was derived from cable systems; next highest was music recording at 19 percent.[4]

[3] Source of most data in this paragraph: Bruce L. Egan and Douglas A. Conn, 1990, Capital budgeting alternatives for residential broadband networks, in Stuart N. Brotman (ed.), *Telephone Company and Cable Competition* (Norwood, Mass.: Artech House).
[4] Source: "Time Warner", 1991, *Business Week*, July 22, 70–74.

Competition in the Cable TV Industry

Except for a small amount of overbuilding activity, cable systems had not had much direct competition for video access to cable households. One mode of existing competition that could become more important was DBS (direct broadcast satellites) where viewers received signals directly from the satellite using their own receiving dish. Although widely used in Japan and in Europe, DBS was not popular in the United States except where cable was not available. Where cable was well established, it was less expensive than DBS. However, new digital technology promised to make DBS competitive with cable subscriber fees. A new company, owned by MSOs, had already started to launch a satellite system that would transmit 80 scrambled channels which viewers could receive with a small economical dish and a descrambler. An earlier attempt by another company had been abandoned because of the difficulty of getting programming. Critics of DBS noted that it would be unable to carry enough channels to provide anticipated new services such as VOD (video on demand).

Other potentially powerful competitors were the local telephone operating companies, which included the RBOCs. The seven RBOCs, with about 77 percent of the access lines, were very large and had individual revenues in 1989 that ranged between $8.7 and $14.2 billion.[5] Their combined revenues of $77.1 billion greatly exceeded the size of the cable industry.

The administration in Washington was thought to favor more competition between the cable and telephone systems, and the telephone companies had been lobbying vigorously to be allowed to carry TV signals. Regulations had already been relaxed to allow them to offer information services such as home banking and shopping. On October 24, 1991, the FCC took another step in easing restrictions when it issued a Notice of Proposed Rule to allow local telephone companies to carry "video dial tone." This meant they could carry video programs provided by others but would not be allowed to program or to edit programs themselves. Because the twisted pair of copper wires that telephone systems used to connect to homes had a relatively small bandwidth, the RBOCs were expected to transmit video using a new technology proposed by Bellcore called ADSL (asymmetrical digital subscriber loop). ADSL would provide one digital video channel to the home that the subscriber could switch at the TV set to the TV channel desired. The signal would be of VCR quality, which was not up to the level of good cable TV, and would require a converter to decode the signal.

The telephone companies seemed to regard the proposed rule as just another step toward their vision of the future. By the year 2000, the telephone industry visualized itself as providing a complete package of integrated digital entertainment, information, and educational and other household services to homes and businesses.

In the short term, however, there was considerable uncertainty about the impact of the proposed rule. Where would the telephone companies get their programming? Would the video signal provided be of adequate quality for subscribers? Would the opportunity to enter the video market prompt telephone companies to extend fiber optics to the home? Would the telephone companies use their switching capabilities to provide new services such as video on demand?

---

[5] Source: United States Telephone Association, *Phone Facts 1990.*

Future Opportunities for the Cable Industry

Various new video and communication services were on the horizon that could encourage the cable industry to switch to digital equipment. Keith Dawson was aware that the cable industry itself was seriously engaged in studies of digital compression standards. Three years ago, MSOs representing 80 percent of all cable subscribers agreed to establish and fund an industry R&D operation called Cable Laboratories. With a budget of $11 million in 1991, Cable Labs had a mandate to advise the industry on technical directions and to contract out R&D projects.

The digital compression project at the labs was one of its more important ventures and was being driven by two MSOs, Viacom Networks and TCI. A request had been issued for vendors to submit proposals for a digital compression system to be installed in two stages, beginning in 1992. The system selected would ideally set a standard for the cable industry that would be adaptable enough to evolve as digital standards for other services such as high-definition television emerged. The plan for the initial deployment of digital was almost identical to what Jack Terry had proposed to BNR. At first, digital was to be provided as an electronic overlay on analog systems using the frequency spectrum above 600 MHz. The number of digital channels would then expand gradually with demand.

Among the new services Keith Dawson noted were receiving much attention in the industry were the following.

High-Definition TV (HDTV)

HDTV would upgrade picture quality significantly by using about double the number of lines of present TV to create the image. The larger the television screen, the more noticeable the improvement would be. The picture, itself, would have a wide screen, movie-type format. The sound would be of CD quality.

It was estimated that analog HDTV would require at least the space of 1.5 to 2 standard TV channels. In Japan, analog HDTV signals were already being broadcast and the receiving sets were being sold for around $30,000. HDTV was not yet available in the United States, but the FCC had requested and received proposals for standards. From the initial proposals, three had been selected for final consideration and all three involved digital signal formats.

Others saw HDTV as only a stepping stone in the evolution of video. At the Multimedia Lab at the Massachusetts Institute of Technology, digital techniques were being demonstrated that could vary the degree of picture definition according to the application. Thus, small TV sets need not have the same degree of definition as large screens. The Multimedia Lab was extremely concerned that the standard adopted by the FCC be flexible enough to accommodate new forms of digital compression that could provide other new capabilities in addition to scalable picture definition.

Enhanced Pay per View (EPPV)

To gain better revenues from PPV, EPPV aimed to make it more convenient to watch a movie by starting it at different times on different channels. For instance, the same movie might start at 15-minute intervals on six different channels. To show four different movies simultaneously that way would require 24 channels. Existing analog technologies could provide enough channels to make EPPV feasible, but digital could provide even more channels.

Impulse Pay per View (IPPV)

Some cable systems already offered IPPV using a fast polling system to query subscriber orders entered via a keypad on their set-top converters. People could then decide to watch at the last minute instead of having to order ahead by telephone. The cable system needed an upstream communication ability to transmit the orders. Most systems had upstream capacity but needed to install the right kind of system components, such as amplifiers, to use it. Switching to digital would make upstream signaling much easier.

Video on Demand (VOD)

To compete with video stores, the cable industry was discussing the possibility of offering video on demand. With 70 percent of households in the United States owning a VCR, the video rental market had grown to an estimated annual volume of $14 billion. A VOD service would essentially turn the TV set into a video store. From the library of movies shown on the screen a subscriber could select, at any time, one to view immediately and be billed for later. There was even the possibility of providing VCR-type controls where the movie could be stopped, reviewed, and fast-forwarded.

To offer VOD, cable operators had to provide a dedicated channel to each household. Fiber optic trunks, combined with digital technology and some switching, could potentially make that possible.

In the short term, MSOs were more concerned with improving revenues from PPV than with developing VOD. However, a major trial of VOD was being arranged using 450 customers on TCI's system in Denver. The technical equipment for the experiment was being provided by AT&T, and a local telephone company, US West, was making the switching capacity of its system available. The trial would use analog rather than digital signals, because it aimed to explore consumer demand rather than to test new technologies. Two trials were planned—one to gauge consumer appetite for VOD with 1,000 movies and events; the other to assess the merits of EPPV by showing 15 movies and other events per day.

It was not common for a MSO and a telephone system to cooperate as they were doing in this experiment. Many analysts believed future services could be provided most economically by the two systems combining their respective strengths. Their different styles of operation, however, could make it difficult for them to cooperate. The MSOs were free-wheeling and entrepreneurial, whereas the telephone companies with their many standards, interconnections, and more regulated environment were cautious and conservative.

Personal Communication Services (PCS)

An Arthur D. Little report estimated that the revenue from this wireless cellular system using wallet-sized phones and small 200-foot radius cells would be $20 to $25 billion within five years of deployment. A portion of that, possibly major, would derive from cannibalization of existing telephone markets. Cable companies were very interested. Cable Labs had two major research projects started and MSOs had applied for 22 PCS licenses from the FCC. Four had been awarded.

MSOs connected to homes with coax cable, which had a much wider bandwidth than the twisted pair of wire connectors used by the telephone companies. The MSOs, therefore, believed they were better able to collect and transmit PCS messages. Because they lacked the switching capabilities of the telephone companies, the MSOs were forming alliances with cellular systems that were not part of the traditional telephone industry. TCI was involved in trials with McCaw Cellular that would use McCaw's switches. In another planned trial, Comcast, Motorola, and General Instruments were going to connect Comcast's cable network to the switches in Comcast's cellular system.

It was expected that PCS would be digital. As yet no standards existed. Three or four different modes were in use in a small way in the United States and Europe, none of which were compatible with each other.

Reduced Signal Theft

The cable industry believed it could boost its revenues by as much as $2 billion dollars annually by reducing signal theft. A common form of theft was the reception of pay programming with unauthorized decoders. Digital could solve such problems because an encrypted digital signal was virtually impossible to decipher by unauthorized users.

Interactive Video

New applications were foreseen where video would be transmitted in both directions between the receiver and the sender. Some interactive services using text only were already in service for applications such as home shopping or home banking. Subscribers had shown only low, or at best, moderate interest in them. Also in place on some systems were home security and home monitoring systems, which tended to be expensive.

Video Conferencing

For business applications there seemed to be a growing interest in video conferencing and video telephone applications so people in distant locations could work more closely together. Digital compression was required. The telephone companies were providing most of the early applications.

Alternative Access Carrier

It was possible for cable companies to compete directly with the local telephone companies (local exchange carriers) by using their fiber networks to connect large businesses to long-distance carriers.

■ Consumer Interests

Keith Dawson searched for information on how cable subscribers viewed their future needs for cable services. Judging by trade media news items, the MSO's believed subscribers were much less interested in interactive services than in new entertainment offerings. Media items also indicated that subscribers wanted cable systems to be responsive, and were concerned about their abuses of monopoly power.

A study conducted by the McGannon Communications Research Center at Fordham University in 1989 surveyed opinions of 189 community leaders on future cable service needs of the community. Included in the sample were people representing consumers, media activists, handicapped and minority groups, religious organizations, and a wide variety of special interest groups. Of 32 services queried, those rated most highly in terms of need were the following (listed in order of most to least needed):

- Emergency/safety (911 two-way services),
- Access to libraries and information banks without a computer,
- Home security and fire protection,
- Two-way hookup with a physician,
- Ability to plug into any new service without worrying about compatibility,
- Monitoring the elderly at home, and
- TV picture quality.

Various educational and information services received moderate ratings. Low, or very low, ratings were given to video phones and all the on-demand entertainment services. Also rated low were new consumer services such as meter reading, two-way shopping, and real estate listings.

The survey did not ask respondents to give reasons for their ratings. However, the authors speculated that the low need they saw for new entertainment services was possibly because the leaders' high education level caused them to underestimate the interest of others in entertainment.

Cable Equipment Suppliers

Most equipment needs of the MSOs were supplied by a small group of manufacturers, with whom they had very close relationships. The largest of these suppliers was General Instruments (through its Jerrold Division), with sales in 1990 of $1.2 billion. The market share of its Jerrold Div. was thought to exceed 60 percent. Much smaller was Scientific Atlanta with sales in 1990 of $614 million. Another competitor, Anixter Corporation, had 1990 sales of $1.3 billion but acted more as a distributor than a manufacturer. Supplementing these larger suppliers were a variety of smaller component and technology vendors.

Almost everything in the way of electronic equipment, including addressable boxes and descramblers for subscribers, could be provided by the major suppliers. Both GI's Jerrold Div. and Scientific Atlanta were at the leading edge of digital compression developments for applications such as HDTV. Both were members of different consortia that submitted HDTV proposals to the FCC. However, their development work depended heavily on technology obtained through licensing and joint ventures. Their independent R&D activities were limited; in 1990, Scientific Atlanta's R&D budget was $40 million.

AT&T was also involved in the cable equipment market through its links with Anixter's Optical Networks International, which supplied 80 percent of the fiber optic equipment bought by MSOs. More recently, AT&T formed a new division to focus on video-oriented digital products. Information on its Cable Services Integrated Network products for MSOs had already been released as a statement of intent. This was to be a fiber-optic-oriented system using a standard developed by telephone companies. It would support all anticipated voice, data, and video services. AT&T was also actively involved, through an alliance with Zenith Electronics Corp., in the FCC's activities to set an industry standard for HDTV. Their proposal was one of the final three being considered.

Within the telephone industry there was speculation that AT&T's overtures to the cable industry could antagonize its main telephone equipment customers, the RBOCs.

Future Evolution of Cable and Telephone Systems

Whether cable, or telephone systems, or both could offer potential services such as VOD and PCS depended on how their respective systems developed in the future. At the moment, each system was optimized for its particular task: Cable systems provided a very economical mode of one-way transmission of the same video signals to many subscribers; telephone systems, in contrast, excelled at highly reliable two-way transmission of voice and data between many one-on-one subscriber connections. Telephone systems needed very sophisticated switching capabilities to connect callers; cable systems did not. Cable systems, on the other hand, needed broader bandwidth connectors (coax cable) to deliver 50 or more video channels to each home.

Since VOD and PCS required the switching and two-way capabilities of telephone systems, as well as the broader bandwidth connectors of the cable companies, the ideal solution might be for both systems to cooperate with each other. However, fiber optics combined with digital signals raised the possibility that each system could develop independent capabilities. To consider that possibility, it is necessary to examine the structure and operation of each system in more detail.

Cable Systems

A cable company distribution system (Exhibit 7) began with the headend, which received video signals from transmission sources such as satellites, or a super-trunk from another headend. Main lines, called trunks, then carried the signals to the community. The length of a trunk line was limited by the number of

Exhibit 7

Tree and Branch Cable System Configuration (Coax from Headend to the Subscriber)

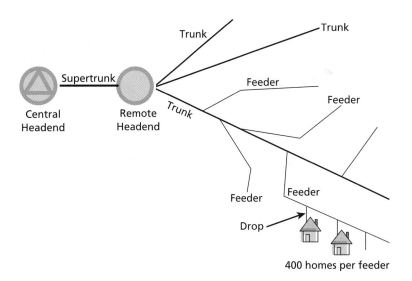

amplifiers required to boost the signal as it weakened due to losses in the cable. Each amplifier in series in an analog system introduced signal distortion and the effect was cumulative.

From the trunks, feeders branched off to carry the signal into neighborhoods. A feeder typically served 200 to 400 homes. Individual homes were connected to the feeder by drops.

This "tree and branch" configuration was a very economical way of distributing the same set of channels to many subscribers. New cable systems were estimated to cost around $300 per subscriber, with over 80 percent of the total investment consumed by the cost of the feeders and drops. The trunks, where fiber was being installed, represented only 18 percent of system investment. Because of their need for expensive switches, and higher reliability standards, telephone systems required larger investments of between $500 and $1,500 per subscriber to install. A comparison of the distribution of investment in typical cable and telephone systems is shown below:

Cable		Telephone	
Headend	1%	Switching	40%
Trunk	18	Interoffice connections	11
Feeder	62	Feeder	19
Drop	19	Drop	25
		Other	5

Source: Bruce L. Egan and Douglas A. Conn, 1990, Capital budgeting alternatives for residential broadband networks, in Stuart N. Brotman (ed.), *Telephone Company and Cable Competition* (Norwood, Mass.: Artech House).

Before fiber was installed, the whole cable system, from the headend to the home, utilized coax cable. This gave it a frequency bandwidth of 1 GHz[6] if the appropriate amplifiers were used. Such a system could deliver as many as 150 TV channels to each home, with each channel using a bandwidth of 6 MHz. Most systems, however, were still using amplifiers that limited the usable frequency range to less than 500 MHz.

Because of the unused capacity of their coax lines, cable systems had only recently begun to upgrade their trunks to fiber and were doing so to reduce maintenance costs rather than to gain additional capacity. For cable systems, the additional cost of installing fiber instead of coax in the trunks was not considered to be large. On extensions and rebuilds, many cable companies were assuming the costs to be equivalent. However, some published estimates showed variations. Thus in 1988, ATC installed fiber for an additional $36 per subscriber, whereas Jones in 1989 had costs of $250. Rogers in Toronto expected to realize a cost of $190.[7] These estimates were not prepared the same way and did not include the same cost items. Estimates also varied between installations due to factors such as the density of subscribers on the system, the extent of fiberization, and how and when the fiber was installed.

---

[6] The bandwidth of a system is measured in the range of frequencies it can carry. 1 GHz (Gigahertz) represents a bandwidth of 1 million hertz or 1,000 megahertz (MHz). The wider the bandwidth, the greater the number of signals, or amount of information, that can be transmitted simultaneously.

[7] Source: Bruce L. Egan and Douglas A. Conn, 1990, Capital budgeting alternatives for residential broadband networks, in Stuart N. Brotman (ed.), *Telephone Company and Cable Competition* (Norwood, Mass.: Artech House).

Exhibit 8

Star and Bush Cable System Configuration (Fiber Trunks; Coax Feeders and Drops)

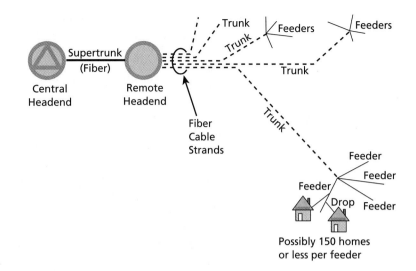

In 1991, MSOs were expected to deploy 5,000 route miles of fiber, a 50 percent increase over 1990. In 1990 there was an estimated 963,057 miles of cable plant, which included the feeders and drops. Trunk lines might account for 20 percent, or less, of that. Total cable industry spending on fiber was about $50 million per year and was expected to rise to about $100 million. In 1988, total cable industry spending on new construction was in the vicinity of $1.6 billion.

When cable systems installed fiber on the trunk lines, they could convert the system from its "tree and branch" configuration to what was referred to as a "star and bush" (Exhibit 8). When combined with switching capabilities at the headend, and digital compression, this configuration could distribute VOD and telephone-type services.

The star and bush arrangement arose because the "fiber backbone" trunk cable contained a number of fiber strands, each of which could be a trunk. These individual trunk fibers could be split off, star fashion, to different parts of the service area and each could be run considerably longer distances than was possible with coax. Much shorter feeders then branched out in a "bush" from the end node of the fiber trunk. Where a feeder in a tree and branch configuration might serve 400 or more subscribers, a feeder in a star and bush system could be connected to fewer than 150 homes. To provide VOD, each subscriber would require a dedicated, two-way switched channel, resulting in 150 channels in the feeder. Normal cable video service would add another 50 or more channels. The total of 200 channels would exceed the analog capacity of the coax feeder but was well within the capability of compressed digital transmission.

With these considerations in mind, Jack Terry predicted that cable systems would evolve in a series of stages. At first, fiber backbone systems would be installed to cut maintenance costs and to improve the quality and reliability of the video signal. Systems would continue to use analog until new services required system capacities that could only be provided by upgrading to digital technology. Then a digital overlay would be added. About 80 digitally compressed channels would be located in the 600-MHz to 1-GHz frequency spectrum of the coax to provide new services such as HDTV. Below that frequency range would be 70 analog video channels to carry normal programming. Terry expected this hybrid form of cable system to migrate gradually to an all-digital format.

The switch to compressed digital would have to be driven by the prospects of new revenues, because the cost of changing was not trivial, even after fiber was installed in the trunks. Components throughout the system would have to be changed and each home would require a digital-to-analog converter to be able to use the compressed digital signals. These converters alone could be a major portion of the per-subscriber cost. It was uncertain whether they could be manufactured for less than $200 each, and at that level could amount to as much as 50 percent of the total cost of upgrading. By upgrading to compressed digital, however, the cable companies could probably avoid the cost of replacing their coax feeders and drops with fiber. With compressed digital, the bandwidth of coax was adequate for the foreseen applications.

As this evolution occurred, Northern Telecom would be able to sell PCS equipment (not fully developed yet), switching equipment (not developed yet for video), and components related to digital modulation (not developed yet for video). The market for digital and optical systems devices could be very large. Another significant portion of the market would be accounted for by digital-to-analog decoders for subscribers. Management at BNR believed this could be an opportunity for Northern to greatly expand its presence in the U.S. customer-premises equipment market.

Telephone Systems

Instead of the tree and branch or star and bush configurations of the cable systems, telephone system made their one-on-one connections between subscribers using a star, or double star, arrangement (Exhibit 9). At the center of the star was a switch that made the connections for each telephone conversation. Radiating from the switch were the many lines connecting the switch to local subscribers and to other exchanges. Each local subscriber was, therefore, connected directly to the switch by a loop of twisted copper wire, which averaged 21,000 feet in length.

Because voice required a frequency bandwidth of only 3 KHz (2,000 times less than color video) the limited bandwidth of a twisted pair of copper wires was quite adequate for current telephone needs. To offer video services, however, the telephone companies were faced with the likelihood of having to upgrade their twisted-pair feeders to fiber. It seemed unlikely that the 1.5-Mbps ADSL standard being promoted by Bellcore to transmit regular video over a twisted pair would suffice for HDTV. An upgrade to fiber would be expensive. Current estimates of fiber to the home (FTTH) for telephone systems were in the range of $2,000 to $3,000 per subscriber. It was believed that the regulated RBOCs could only justify such a large investment by obtaining major new revenues from broadband video services. FTTH also required the development of inexpensive devices to transform the optical signals to electrical at each home.

An even greater problem for the telephone companies was the heavy switching demand posed by TV viewers. Unlike cable systems, ADSL could only deliver one or two channels to the home simultaneously. Therefore, most channel switching requests would have to be handled by the central office telephone switch. As viewers browsed the channels at peak times, the central office switch could be flooded and overwhelmed by the demand.

Exhibit 9

Telephone System Star
Configuration

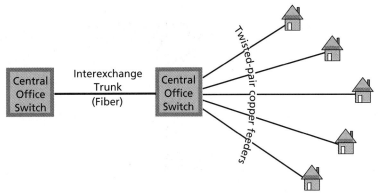

As many as several hundred thousand
lines handled by one central office switch.

■ Options for BNR

Just to resolve the basic technical issues would require a budget of at least several million dollars per year for three to five years. In the short term, development money would have to be allocated from BNR's budget for exploratory projects. Once basic technical issues were resolved, the design of specific digital products would require large amounts of additional funding. Some work of this kind was already in process through other BNR projects. One such project was working on PCS; another was developing video systems for telephone company networks.

Keith Dawson's report was not to be directed at any particular manager, or management group, for decision purposes. Instead the report would be fairly widely distributed through BNR's technical management as a means of informing and influencing opinion. Keith knew he was not an expert on the cable TV industry. He thought he had enough information, however, to sketch future scenarios and to make some clear recommendations. He knew that within BNR there were a variety of opinions on what BNR and Northern should do. Some wanted to pursue the cable opportunity aggressively and strive for technical leadership. Others felt there was too much uncertainty about future markets to invest heavily in R&D yet. There was also an opinion that it might be better to stay within the telephone industry and concentrate on developing technologies for telephone systems to carry video signals.

Given BNR's limited budget for exploratory projects, proposals for further funding would have to present a good case for any of the many possible options. Should Northern target the cable TV industry? If so, what would be the best way to proceed? And when?

■ CASE 5 Ben & Jerry's Homemade Inc.: "Yo! I'm Your CEO!"

Katherine A. Auer
Indiana University

Alan N. Hoffman
Bentley College

"Ben & Jerry's Grows Up"—*The Boston Globe*
"Ben, Jerry Losing Their Values?"—*The Washington Times*
"Ben & Jerry's Melting Social Charter"—*The Washington Post*
"Life Won't Be Just a Bowl of Cherry Garcia"—*Business Week*
"Say It Ain't So, Ben & Jerry"—*Business Week*

The headlines said it all. Ben & Jerry's, the company that built its success as much on its down-home image and folksy idealism as on its super-rich ice cream, was at a crossroads. Having been started in 1978 in a renovated Vermont gas station by childhood friends Ben Cohen and Jerry Greenfield, the unconventional company soon grew into a $140 million powerhouse that was rivaled only by Haagen-Dazs in the superpremium category of the ice cream market. With its many donations and policies promoting corporate responsibility, Ben & Jerry's took great pride in its success combining social activism with financial viability. But in mid-1994, the outlook was not so rosy. Sales were flat, profits were down, and the company's stock price had fallen to half of what it was at the end of 1992. In its 1993 annual report, Ben & Jerry's admitted that some flavors of its "all natural" ice cream included ingredients that were not, in fact, all natural. And staffers within the company reportedly criticized it for lack of leadership.

On June 13, 1994, Ben & Jerry's announced that Ben was stepping down as CEO, and that it would abandon its longtime cap on executive salaries in order to help it find a new one. The message was clear: Ben & Jerry's was no longer the company it once was. For many, the question then was, what would it become?

■ The Contest

With a marketing flair befitting its tradition of wacky promotional tactics, Ben & Jerry's set out to find its new leader by announcing the "Yo! I'm Your CEO!" contest. Customers were asked to send in a lid from a container of their favorite Ben & Jerry's ice-cream flavor along with a 100-word essay explaining "Why I Would Be a Great CEO for Ben & Jerry's." The winner would become the new CEO, the runner-up would receive a lifetime supply of ice cream, and the losers would receive a rejection letter "suitable for framing."

"We have never had an experienced CEO and we have reached the point in our life when we need one," said Ben, adding that he planned to continue with the company as chairman and concentrate on "fun stuff" like product development.

But the search wasn't all fun and games. Ben & Jerry's also announced that it would abandon its longtime policy that no executive be paid more than seven times the salary of the lowest paid employee, and hired an executive recruiting firm to help find the right person. Under the old policy, Ben was paid $133,212 in 1993 and no bonuses; the going rate for executives at companies of like size was $300,000 to $500,000.

"I think we are looking for a rare bird," said Ben. "I guess there are about five or ten executives who will be interested and have the skills." The key, he added, is experience in keeping "everyone aligned and moving the same direction" as the company grows—something he admitted he was learning but not good at. "I haven't found the happy medium between autocratic and laissez-faire," he explained.

Some 22,500 aspiring leaders around the world flooded the company with their responses, which were as varied as the flavors in its ice cream line. Entries came from places as far away as Australia, Thailand, East Africa, and Saudi Arabia. An entire fifth-grade class sent in letters, with offers from some of the students to develop new flavors. One woman sent in a near-nude photo of herself, while an advertising executive attached his resume to a Superman costume.

An Indiana schoolteacher scrawled her essay on a painting of a woman reading a book, while Allen Stillman, head of New York restaurant chain Smith & Wollensky, put a full-page ad in *The New York Times*. "I propose a whole new line of flavors," he wrote. "Red Meat Swirl, Potato Gravy Chunk, Starchie Bunker." Stillman also proposed a merger and a new name: Ben Smith & Jerry Wollensky Steaks and Shakes.

Other response tactics included a resume written entirely on a giant sheet cake, another engraved on a brass plaque and mounted on marble, and one written in crayon by a hopeful couple's $2\frac{1}{2}$-year-old son. A Milwaukee car salesman sent a mock two-foot-wide lid of a New York Super Fudge Chunk carton, folded in half. When the lid was unfolded, an electronic device made a sound like a telephone ring; the opener then read "Please call me—I'm the one you want to be your CEO."

"Some of them may not be right for the CEO's job, but they sure would be right for marketing jobs," Ben said. "We may not have to advertise for people for the next several years."

The Winner

On February 2, 1995, Ben & Jerry's announced that they found the leader they wanted: Robert Holland Jr., a former partner at management consultancy McKinsey & Co. By taking the helm of Ben & Jerry's, the 55-year-old MBA became one of the most visible African-American chief executives among the nation's publicly traded corporations.

Holland was selected not through the essay contest, but through New York executive recruiter Russell Reynolds. Some 500 candidates were initially considered by that firm, and Ben & Jerry's board members ultimately reviewed about 15 applicants. The race was eventually narrowed to six competitors (one of which came from the essay contest), and from there, it came down to two finalists, both of whom spent considerable time over dinner and ice cream with Ben, Jerry, and board members. Rumor had it that his competitor preferred frozen yogurt, while Holland was a passionate ice cream fan.

Having grown up in Michigan, Holland spent 13 years as an associate and partner at McKinsey, where he worked with consumer and industrial clients including the soft drink division of Heineken. He left McKinsey in 1981 to become an independent consultant and businessman. Among his subsequent roles were chairman of Gilreath Manufacturing Inc., a plastic injection-molding company, and chairman and CEO for Rokher-J Inc., a White Plains, New York, consulting and takeover firm. Holland earned his MBA at Baruch College in New York.

His experience in turning troubled companies around was important, however, more important were Holland's social values. He was chairman of the board of trustees at Spelman College in Atlanta, a school traditionally attended by black women, as well as the founder of a dropout-prevention program for Detroit high school students and a board member of the Harlem Junior Tennis program for inner city youth.

"We were very impressed not only with Bob's operational expertise, but with his social commitment, as expressed in both his business experience and his active involvement with the nonprofit sector," said Ben.

Holland's salary was set at $250,000 plus options on 180,000 shares of stock and a bonus of up to $125,000 if he met certain financial goals. Though significantly higher than what Ben had been earning, it is low compared to the pay scale for CEOs at midsized manufacturers, and reportedly less than what Holland had been earning as a management consultant.

Though he didn't submit an essay as part of the contest, Holland did submit something—a poem—upon request after he was chosen. The poem, entitled "Time, Values and Ice Cream" (see Exhibit 1), reflected his background in poor, working-class, south central Michigan. Though his appointment at Ben & Jerry's made Holland one of just a few African-American CEOs at public companies, Holland declined to be called a role model for other blacks, calling the term "too presumptuous." Nevertheless, he said, "I'm looking forward to dispelling whatever concerns people have."

Holland faced a formidable challenge at Ben & Jerry's, however. The company posted its first quarterly loss for the fourth quarter of fiscal 1994, and when Holland's appointment was announced, Chuck Lacy, the company's longtime president, resigned.

While Holland won the executive slot, what some may say was the better prize—a lifetime supply of ice cream—went to three runners-up. Among them

---

Exhibit 1   Time, Values and Ice Cream*
by Robert Holland

Born before the baby boom
as war drums raged cross distant waters—way
beyond my family's lore since our 1600s coming to this far off land called
America.

T'was a simple time, as I grew tall.
Shucks! Uncle Sam really wanted you (so the poster said)—pride
in work, parades and proms, company picnics 'tween eve'ns spent with "Suspense,"
"The Shadow," and everybody's "Our Miss Brooks."
Good ole days in the summertime, indeed! . . . in
America.

Yet, some nostalgia stayed 'yond one's grasp,
like Sullivans,
the ice cream place on Main—swivel stools, cozy booths, and sweet,
sweet smells with no sitting place for all of some of us.
Could only dream such humble pleasure. Sometimes, dear 'Merica,
of thee I simply hum.

Much, so much has changed in twenty springs. Sputnik
no longer beeps so loud;
Bay of Pigs, Vietnam and contentions in Chicago. . .
come and gone. . .
All that noise almost drowning out "One small step for man. . ."
and ". . . Willie, time to say goodbye to baseball."
Confusing place, this melodious mix,
called America.

Now I sit by eyeing distant twilight,
Engineer and MBA,
smiling wide on M.L.K.'s day,
CEO of Cherry Garcia and Peace Pops' fountain
having not forgotten the forbidden seats of Sullivans',
with miles to go before we sleep. . .
and time left yet to get there.
Only in America!

*Only 100 words before translation from the language of Chunky Mandarin Orange with Natural Wild Brazil Nuts.

---

was Taylor James Caldwell, the toddler, by then three years old, who had submitted an entry for his parents. In addition, about 100 honorable mentions received limited edition T-shirts.

■ The "Good Old Days"

The birth of Ben & Jerry's can be traced to a $5 correspondence course in ice cream making taken by Ben Cohen and Jerry Greenfield. The duo, friends since early childhood in Merrick, New York, then gathered $12,000 ($4,000 of which was borrowed), and in May 1978 opened an ice cream shop in a renovated Burlington, Vermont, gas station. Featuring an antique rock-salt ice cream freezer and a Volkswagen squareback for its delivery van, the shop soon became popular for its innovative flavors made from fresh Vermont milk and cream.

At the heart of Ben & Jerry's is the distinct business philosophy shared by its founders. In essence, they believe that companies have a responsibility to do good for society, not only for themselves. This philosophy is best explained by the company's three-part mission statement, formally stated in 1988 and reproduced here in its entirety:

> Ben & Jerry's is dedicated to the creation and demonstration of a new corporate concept of linked prosperity. Our mission consists of three interrelated parts:
> Product Mission: To make, distribute, and sell the finest quality, all-natural ice cream and related products in a wide variety of innovative flavors made from Vermont dairy products.
> Social Mission: To operate the company in a way that actively recognizes the central role that business plays in the structure of society by initiating innovative ways to improve the quality of life of a broad community—local, national, and international.
> Economic Mission: To operate the company on a sound financial basis of profitable growth, increasing value for our shareholders, and creating career opportunities and financial rewards for our employees.
>
> Underlying the mission of Ben & Jerry's is the determination to seek new and creative ways of addressing all three parts, while holding a deep respect for the individuals, inside and outside the company, and for the communities of which they are a part.

This unconventional philosophy touched everything the company did, from the way it treated its employees to the way it dealt with its suppliers.

The company enjoys a strong team- and family-oriented atmosphere; for example, it has progressive family leave, health insurance, and other benefit plans. Reasoning that happy employees reduce stress and improve the workplace in general, Ben & Jerry kept the culture extremely casual and relaxed, and formed a "Joy Committee" to spread joy among their employees. Some of the spontaneous events coordinated by the Joy Committee include an Elvis Presley recognition day, with an Elvis look-alike contest, a Barry Manilow appreciation day, and a car race derby in which employees raced their own toy cars. Pranks abounded at all gatherings, including the annual shareholders' meetings, and most were followed by entertainment such as 1960s musicians Richie Havens, Livingston Taylor, and dozens of other bands. In essence, Ben and Jerry truly seemed to live by their motto: "If it's not fun, why do it?"

Yet in their desire to create a healthy and equitable workplace, Ben & Jerry's did more than just promote fun and games: Their longtime cap on executive salaries required that no executive be paid more than seven times the salary of the lowest paid employee. Typical staff meetings included all employees, and issues affecting women, minorities, and gays in their workforce were always discussed openly.

In choosing suppliers for the ingredients of their products, Ben & Jerry's tried to be equally responsible. For example, the brownies used in its Chocolate Fudge Brownie ice cream are bought from a bakery in Yonkers, New York, that hires undertrained and underskilled workers and uses its profits to house the homeless and teach them trades. Ben & Jerry's Rainforest Crunch ice cream features nuts grown in South American rain forests; the firm pays the harvesters directly, and donates a portion of the proceeds from sales of the ice cream to environmental presevation causes. Wild Maine Blueberry ice cream is made with blueberries grown and harvested by the Passamaquoddy Indians of Maine. Fresh Georgia Peach ice cream is made from Georgia-grown peaches as part of the company's policy of supporting family farms.

Similarly, for the milk and cream that forms the bulk of its products, Ben & Jerry's is committed to buying from Vermont dairy farms, to whom it pays above-market prices. When rBGH, a genetically engineered drug to increase cows' milk production, was approved by the FDA, Ben & Jerry's declared it would buy only from farms not using the drug, citing health concerns and a desire to protect smaller farms. To ensure that its products remain wholesome and pure, the company pays a premium to suppliers in exchange for their written assurance that they will not use rBGH.

Finally, the company also established the Ben & Jerry's Foundation, which donates 7.5 percent of its pretax profits to nonprofit organizations. These causes included the American Wildlands in Montana; Burch House in New Hampshire (a safe house); the Burlington Peace and Justice Coalition in Vermont; the Citizens Committee for Children in New York (aid for drug-addicted pregnant women); Natural Guard (an environmental group for school-age children and teens); the Brattleboro Area AIDS Project (providing free services to HIV-positive individuals and their families); and the Massachusetts Coalition for the Homeless.

Such efforts won the hearts of scores of like-minded consumers, many of whom had grown up in the same socially conscious generation as Ben and Jerry. Indeed, because of its values and its unconventional nature, the company has done very little marketing: Media coverage of its various antics has been virtually guaranteed on a regular basis, providing free publicity for the company, its products, and its values. Thanks in part to the size of the "baby boomer" generation of which its leaders were a part, Ben & Jerry's flourished in the 1980s, growing to more than 100 franchises. In 1984 the company went public in Vermont, and by 1986 it had achieved 100 percent growth.

Recent Troubles

While Ben & Jerry's thrived during the 1980s, the 1990s presented a very different picture. One of the primary reasons was that the baby boomer generation—Ben & Jerry's primary target market—was entering middle age and becoming more health conscious. Whereas, during the 1980s these consumers enjoyed the socially conscious self-indulgence of Ben & Jerry's ice cream, they became averse to high-fat foods such as superpremium ice cream. At the same time, new labeling requirements imposed by the FDA meant that customers could see with painful clarity the amount of fat each scoop of Ben & Jerry's ice creams contained, thus showing their less-than-healthful nature.

To respond Ben & Jerry's introduced a reduced-fat, reduced-calorie ice milk, called Ben & Jerry's Lite. That line failed, reportedly due to poor quality, but the subsequent introduction of a low-fat, low-cholesterol frozen yogurt line met with much better success. In addition, the company introduced the first flavors in its nonfat yogurt line in the summer of 1995. Nevertheless, the fact remains that ice cream sales are slowing.

Ben & Jerry's also faced increased competition from the deep-pocketed Haagen-Dazs, which expanded its selection of flavors to better rival Ben & Jerry's (including its chunky "Extraas," a low-fat ultrapremium ice cream as well as frozen yogurt) and started a price war by reducing its prices and offering a variety of promotions and discounts. During the weakened economy of the 1990s, competing on price was common.

Indeed, the superpremium category as a whole witnessed increased competition from lower cost, lower fat premium ice creams. Among those are Edy's, manufactured by Dreyer's, which produces roughly half of Ben & Jerry's output. Also, Dreyer's recently received a huge cash infusion from Nestle, giving it increased competitive muscle.

Despite the fact that U.S. ice cream exports had tripled in recent years, and that Haagen-Dazs had begun exporting (even opening a factory in France), Ben & Jerry's paid little attention to markets outside the United States. Chuck Lacy, the company's president, stated "It's something that we're starting to think about, but we've got a lot of work to do here in the U.S." Sales to restaurants was another option for growth outside of the heated grocery store market, but again, Lacy said, while "there's huge potential, it's a completely different business. It requires completely different distributors and sales staff, a completely different head."

Software glitches, meanwhile, repeatedly delayed the opening of Ben & Jerry's new $40 million ice cream plant in St. Albans, which was planned to increase production significantly. But with sales down, it was not clear that the company would be able to use much of the plant's capacity when it opened.

Management problems also plagued the firm, reducing morale and drawing criticism from employees, who said there was a lack of direction. By the end of 1994, the mood reportedly became so dark that the company asked author Milton Moskowitz to remove them from the most recent edition of *The 100 Best Companies to Work for in America*.

Finally, on December 19, 1994, Ben & Jerry's announced an expected loss of $700,000 to $900,000 for the fourth quarter of 1994 — its first since going public in 1984.

■ The Industry Landscape

The packaged ice cream industry includes ordinary, premium, and superpremium products. These types are distinguished primarily by their butterfat content and density, as well as the freshness of their ingredients and the way they were blended and treated.

Ordinary ice creams typically contain the minimum of 10 to 12 percent butterfat and the maximum proportion of air; one four-ounce scoop contained 150 calories or less. Premium ice creams contain 12 to 16 percent butterfat and less air than regular types; a four-ounce scoop usually contained 180 calories. Superpremium ice creams, which include Ben & Jerry's, generally contain about 16 to 20 percent fat (excluding add-ins) and less than 20 percent air. The caloric value of a four-ounce scoop is generally about 260 calories. This type of ice cream is characterized by a greater richness than the other types, and is sold in packaged pints priced between $2.29 and $2.89 each.

The total annual sales in U.S. supermarkets for the ice cream and frozen yogurt market as a whole were more than $3.6 billion in 1994. The superpremium market (ice cream, frozen yogurt, ice milk, and sorbet) accounted for about $415 million. Ninety-three percent of American households consumed ice cream, but demand is seasonal, with summer levels as much as 30 percent higher than those in the winter. Sales for frozen yogurt (superpremium and regular) were $550 million in supermarkets in 1994; at this time, Ben & Jerry's was clearly ahead of Haagen-Dazs in the superpremium frozen yogurt market.

Gross margins in the ice cream industry as a whole are about 30.6 percent, compared with only 20 percent for the frozen food department as a whole. Premium and superpremium varieties outperform other ice cream types, accounting for 45.8 percent of sales and 45.9 percent of profits of the ice cream category as a whole, and earning a gross margin of 31.5 percent.

The superpremium ice cream and frozen yogurt business is highly competitive. Ben & Jerry's principal competitor is The Haagen-Dazs Company, Inc., which roughly matches Ben & Jerry's 42 percent share of the market; others, including Columbo, Dannon, Healthy Choice, Simple Pleasures, Elan, Frusen Gladje, Yoplait, Honey Hill Farms, and Steve's, constituted less than 10 percent of the market.

Haagen-Dazs is owned by The Pillsbury Company, which in turn is owned by Grand Metropolitan PLC, a British food and liquor conglomerate with resources significantly greater than those of Ben & Jerry's. Haagen-Dazs entered the market well before Ben & Jerry's, and also became well established in certain markets in Europe and the Pacific Rim. And to compete with Ben & Jerry's, it introduced in 1992 its Extraas line of products that included a variety of add-ins like cookies, candies, and nuts.

Ben & Jerry's also competed with several well-known brands in the ice cream novelty segment, including Haagen-Dazs and Dove Bars, which are manufactured by a division of Mars, Inc. Both Haagen-Dazs and Dove Bars achieved significant market share before Ben & Jerry's entered their markets.

■ Market Share

The total U.S. sales for superpremium ice cream, frozen yogurt, ice milk, and sorbet were more than $415 million in 1994. The market was dominated by Haagen-Dazs and Ben & Jerry's: In 1993, the former held 62 percent of the market while Ben & Jerry's held 36 percent, but by early 1995, both held roughly 42 percent.

Haagen-Dazs entered the superpremium market back in 1961. Though success was not achieved overnight, the brand remained on the market and became the industry leader. Early success was linked to word-of-mouth advertising, but by 1983 Haagen-Dazs spent $14 million on advertising, while average ice cream manufacturers spent less than one percent of sales on advertising.

When new competitors began entering the market in the early 1980s, namely, Ben & Jerry's, Haagen-Dazs attempted to keep them out by threatening distributors. Ben & Jerry's fought back with a lawsuit and a campaign including bumper stickers and T-shirts displaying the statement, "What's the Pillsbury Doughboy Afraid of?" The litigation was settled and the campaign brought to an end within about a year.

Between 1989 and 1993, overall growth in the market was sluggish, increasing by only 14 percent. During that same time period, however, Ben & Jerry's market share rose by 120 percent, while Haagen-Dazs' share decreased by 10 percent. In 1992, Ben & Jerry's increased its U.S. market share by 10 percent; Haagen-Dazs, on the other hand, lost 8 percent. Thus, while Ben & Jerry's entered late into the mature, low-growth ice cream market, it gained substantial market share, primarily at the expense of Haagen-Dazs.

Ben & Jerry's products are distributed primarily by independent regional ice cream distributors. With certain exceptions, only one distributor was appointed to each territory. In some areas, subdistributors are used. Ben & Jerry's trucks also distributes some of the ice cream and frozen yogurt sold in Vermont and upstate New York. Ben & Jerry's has a distribution agreement with Dreyer's whereby Dreyer's has exclusivity, in general, for sales to supermarkets and similar accounts of Ben & Jerry's products in most of its markets outside New England, upstate New York, Pennsylvania, and Texas. Net sales to Dreyer's accounted for about 54 and 52 percent of Ben & Jerry's net sales for 1993 and 1994, respectively.

While Dreyer's markets its own premium ice cream, as well as frozen dessert products made by other companies, it does not produce or market any other superpremium ice cream or frozen yogurt. Were it to begin doing so, Dreyer's would lose its exclusivity as a Ben & Jerry's distributor.

Because of instances of legal action over distribution agreements, manufacturers and distributors generally opted for verbal rather than written contracts. In recent years, two independent distributors claimed that Ben & Jerry's and Dreyer's had squeezed them out of the business, and at least three others claimed they had lost access to the brand after building it for years. Furthermore, Amy Miller, founder of Amy's Ice Creams in Austin, Texas, claimed that Ben & Jerry's pressured the best distributor in that area to not carry Amy's pints or risk losing the immensely popular Ben & Jerry's. But Ben and Jerry categorically denied any such involvement, and was supported by the distributor. There were also a few other instances in which distributors claimed that they had been pressured not to carry brands competing with Ben & Jerry's. Said one retailer, who sued Ben & Jerry's after it stopped sales to his firm, "corporately, they are absolutely vicious."

Ben & Jerry's admitted that while its relationships with Dreyer's and other distributors have been generally satisfactory, they were not always easy to maintain. But alternatives are few: According to the company, the loss of one or more of the related distribution agreements could have a material adverse effect on the company's business.

When it came to choosing suppliers, Ben & Jerry's insistence on social responsibility earned it much acclaim, but developing such relationships was not always easy. Its search for the perfect coffee bean, for example, took more than five years and led to one of its most complex, yet successful, supplier relationships. The company's goal is to give much of the profits back to the grower, rather than to a middleman broker; accomplishing this requires a significant commitment of time and resources to learn each party's needs and expectations.

Because working directly with suppliers requires so much energy, Ben & Jerry's plan to establish only one or two new relationships each year. The R&D, quality assurance, finance, and manufacturing departments all are involved in the evaluation and education of each new supplier. Although the work involved is much more than would have been required if it simply made calls to existing suppliers, Ben & Jerry's felt the result made it worthwhile.

Finance

Ben & Jerry's sales steadily increased from 1988 through 1992, but then slowed dramatically in 1993. Sales increased by about 30 percent annually from 1990 to 1992, but that dropped to 6 percent in 1993. Furthermore, the company indicated that virtually all of its growth in 1993 came from its frozen yogurt line the sales of which increased by 35 percent during that year. Sales for fiscal 1993 were $140 million and $149 million for fiscal 1994.

Exhibit 2   Five-Year Financial Highlights (In thousands except per share data)

	Year Ended				
Summary of Operations:	*12/31/94*	*12/25/93*	*12/26/92*	*12/28/91*	*12/29/90*
Net sales	$148,802	$140,328	$131,969	$96,997	$77,024
Cost of sales	109,760	100,210	94,389	68,500	54,203
Gross profit	39,042	40,118	37,580	28,497	22,821
Selling, general and administrative expenses	36,253	28,270	26,243	21,264	17,639
Asset write-down	6,779				
Other income (expense)-net	229	197	(23)	(729)	(709)
Income (loss) before income taxes	(3,761)	12,045	11,314	6,504	4,473
Income taxes	(1,893)	4,845	4,639	2,765	1,864
Net income (loss)	(1,868)	7,200	6,675	3,739	2,609
Net income (loss) per common share[1]	$(0.26)	$1.01	$1.07	$0.67	$0.50
Weighted average common shares outstanding[1]	7,148	7,138	6,254	5,572	5,225
	Year Ended				
Balance Sheet Data:	*12/31/94*	*12/25/93*	*12/26/92*	*12/28/91*	*12/29/90*
Working capital	$37,456	$29,292	$18,053	$11,035	$8,202
Total assets	120,295	106,361	88,207	43,056	34,299
Long-term debt	32,419	18,002	2,641	2,787	8,948
Stockholders' equity[2]	72,502	74,262	66,760	26,269	16,101

[1]The per share amounts and average shares outstanding have been adjusted for the effects of all stock splits, including stock splits in the form of stock dividends.
[2]No cash dividends have been declared or paid by the Company on its capital stock since the Company's organization. The Company intends to reinvest earnings for use in its business and to finance future growth. Accordingly, the Board of Directors does not anticipate declaring any cash dividends in the foreseeable future.

Net income grew steadily along with sales growth, and exceeded that pace during 1991 and 1992. While sales grew at 26 and 36 percent during 1991 and 1992, respectively, net income grew at 42 and 81 percent. During 1993, sales grew 6 percent while net income grew at 7 percent. For 1994, however, the company reported a net loss of $1.87 million (see Exhibits 2 and 3).

The company's net profit margin was 5.1 percent, compared with the industry average of 3.4 percent. The net loss per share for 1994 was ($0.26); during previous years, earnings per share had risen steadily, from $0.32 in 1988 to a high of $1.07 in 1992, then falling to $1.01 in 1993. Consequently, its stock price fell nearly 50 percent from its 1993 high of $32 by investors impatient with the company's lack of momentum. On February 1, 1995, the company's stock price was $12.125.

Marketing

Product

Ben & Jerry's "product" is a carefully orchestrated combination of premium ice cream products and social consciousness—"Caring Capitalism"—created through bottom-up management and cause-generated marketing and public relations efforts. The physical products include superpremium ice cream, in both chunky and smooth flavors, low-fat frozen yogurt, and ice-cream novelties. The

Exhibit 3 Consolidated Balance Sheets		
Assets		
	12/31/94	**12/25/93**
Current Assets:		
Cash and cash equivalents	$20,777,746	$14,704,795
Accounts receivable, less allowance for doubtful accounts:		
$504,000 in 1994 and $229,000 in 1993	11,904,844	11,679,222
Inventories	13,462,572	13,452,863
Deferred income taxes	3,146,000	1,689,000
Income taxes receivable	2,097,743	
Prepaid expenses	534,166	847,851
Total current assets	51,923,071	42,373,731
Property, plant and equipment, net	57,980,567	40,261,538
Investments	8,000,000	22,000,000
Other assets	2,391,465	1,725,316
	$120,295,103	$106,360,585
Liabilities & Stockholders' Equity		
	12/31/94	**12/25/93**
Current Liabilities:		
Accounts payable and accrued expenses	$13,914,972	$12,068,424
Income taxes payable		344,519
Current portion of long-term debt and capital lease obligations	552,547	669,151
Total current liabilities	14,467,519	13,082,094
Long-term debt and capital lease obligations	32,418,565	18,002,076
Deferred income taxes	907,000	1,014,000
Commitments and contingencies		
Stockholders' equity:		
$1.20 noncumulative Class A preferred stock - $1.00 par value, redeemable at the Company's option at $12.00 per share; 900 shares authorized, issued and outstanding, aggregate preference on voluntary or involuntary liquidation - $9,000	900	900
Class A common stock - $.033 par value; authorized 20,000,000 shares; issued: 6,290,580 shares at December 31, 1994 and 6,266,772 shares at December 25, 1993	208,010	207,224
Class B common stock - $.033 par value; authorized 3,000,000 shares; issued: 932,448 shares at December 31, 1994 and 947,637 shares at December 25, 1993	30,770	31,271
Additional paid-in capital	48,366,185	48,222,445
Retained earnings	25,316,309	27,185,003
Unearned compensation		(19,815)
Treasury stock, at cost: 69,032 Class A and 1,092 Class B shares at December 31, 1994 and 66,353 Class A and 1,092 Class B shares at December 25, 1993	(1,420,155)	(1,364,613)
Total stockholders' equity	72,502,019	74,262,415
Total Liabilities and stockholders' equity	$120,295,103	$106,360,585

company operates in the focused niche of superpremium ice cream products, with the driving competitive factor traditionally being diversity and uniqueness of flavor.

As such, the primary marketing goal at Ben & Jerry's is to develop and deliver great new products and flavors. It maintains a full-time R&D team dedicated to the development of unconventional, cutting-edge flavors. It is this strength that has placed Ben & Jerry's at the forefront of the superpremium ice-cream market, with 6 of the Top 10 and 13 of the Top 20 Best Selling Flavors.

In its traditional line, Ben & Jerry's distinguishes its flavors and products through "chunkiness," maintaining specifications not only for chunk size, but for number per spoonful and quality of the fruits and nuts they contain. Although such requirements add a great deal more to the cost of the finished product, the enhancement in taste differentiates Ben & Jerry's product from the competition.

The company also distinguishes its product by its use of pure, natural, and socially conscious milk from Vermont dairy farmers who agree not to use rBGH. The FDA allowed the voluntary labeling of dairy products made from non-rBGH treated cows, so Ben & Jerry's aggressively promotes its products' purity on its packaging.

Ben & Jerry's products are sold by the pint in recycled paper board cups, a standard practice in the superpremium market. Ben & Jerry's arrived at that strategy based on the demographics of its target market: 25- to 40-year-old consumers in the upper middle class sector who had no children. People in this segment do not need to purchase larger quantities of ice cream at one time.

Ice cream pints accounts for only about 13 percent of supermarket ice cream sales. Nonetheless, Ben & Jerry's strategy has been to obtain an increasingly large piece of a shrinking pie, but that is becoming more difficult as the competitive landscape has changed.

It became apparent that the company would have to work harder to continue success based on its "new flavor" strategy because competitors are increasingly imitating its flavors. While originally it could count on about six months before imitations arrived, Ben & Jerry's now solely "owned" a flavor for only about 60 days. As a result, the company revised its marketing goal to establish a standard of product quality that cannot be imitated, to introduce more "euphoric" new flavors and to improve the selection of the company's flavors in grocery stores.

In March 1994, Ben & Jerry's introduced its line of Smooth, No Chunks flavors in response to market research indicating that a large portion of the superpremium market did not like chunks. The company targeted the segment that was "just too tired to chew" at the end of a busy day and who would rather "experience their ice cream without having to exert too much energy." That move placed Ben & Jerry's in a fortified position in its battle with Haagen-Dazs.

Other product innovations include novelty items such as Brownie Bars, which failed, and Peace Pops, which were marginally successful. Peace Pops were wrapped in a message to redirect one percent of the military budget to social programs; they did well only at convenience stores, suggesting to the company that they were primarily impulse buys. Recently, 70 percent of Peace Pops were sold in convenience stores.

■ Place

Ben & Jerry's markets its superpremium ice cream products to supermarkets, grocery stores, convenience stores, and restaurants that demonstrate corporate consciousness in the way they do business. Roughly 105 Ben & Jerry's franchises or licensed "scoop shops" exist across the United States, in addition to some in Canada and Israel and a 50–50 joint venture in Russia. In addition, in March 1994 the company began shipping a small amount of its products to small specialty stores in the United Kingdom.

The company also attempted to increase its distribution channels by offering gifts by mail. This concept featured a brochure advertising earthy, tie-dyed gifts, as well as ice cream, coffee, and candy, and offered consumers the ability to have the ice cream dry-ice packed and delivered overnight anywhere in the country. The concept met with limited success, due in part to limited promotion.

Restaurants represent another venue the company explored to maintain growth, but to date, Ben & Jerry's has not made this opportunity a primary goal. The same is true for global expansion. The company was successful abroad, but efforts had been haphazard and outcomes were based solely on luck. The company admitted that it did not have an international strategy and that true commitment to global exporting would require that it learn much more about the market—something it had not made a current priority.

■ Price

Ben & Jerry's ice cream products are premium priced at the high end of the ice cream market. A pint of its ice cream retails for approximately $2.69. Although this pricing strategy worked extremely well within the exploding market of the late 1980s and early 1990s, it experienced some difficulty in recent years, as demand shifted toward lower priced and/or private-label products in grocery stores. Price elasticity declined, whereas in the past, Ben & Jerry's could impose significant price increases (8 percent in 1991, 4 percent in early 1993).

Pricing pressure also resulted from the apparent consolidation of sales in a few players' hands and the stagnation of the market, with new forms of pricing competition coming into play. Until recently, all superpremium ice cream and frozen yogurt makers had roughly equivalent prices for their products. But Haagen-Dazs, the "sleeping giant" that allowed Ben & Jerry's to gain market share at its expense during the late 1980s, recently awakened and began "throwing dollars and incentives at the marketplace."

Haagen-Dazs is much larger than Ben & Jerry's and is capable of waging a significant price war without fear of any lasting harm. The result was 2-for-1 sales and discounts in certain parts of the country. Ben & Jerry's guardedly followed suit with price discounts and store coupons for $1.49 pints, recognizing that the battle had become primarily financial.

■ Promotion

Ben & Jerry's product promotion relies primarily on cause-generated marketing. It is the company's belief that marketing should not be performed simply to sell the product, but to have an effect on society. This marketing theory is called "Edible Activism."

The company's cause-related events included such things as traveling vaudeville shows in buses with solar-powered freezers—the more unconventional and politically correct, the better. The largest part of Ben & Jerry's promotion budget goes to major music festivals around the country, including the Newport Folk

Festival in Rhode Island. In addition, the company's own plant is the largest tourist attraction in Vermont, hosting 275,000 visitors annually; thus, just by opening its own doors, Ben & Jerry's is promoting its products.

The company's socially conscious practices also earned it regular publicity, thereby saving it millions in public expenditures annually. As Ben once said, "The media can supply the ink and Ben & Jerry's will supply the wackiness."

Responsibility for marketing is not farmed out to outside design and advertising firms. Rather, the company maintains control of this function in-house. In March 1994, for example, Ben & Jerry's created its first 30-second commercial to sell its new Smooth, No Chunks flavors; directed by Spike Lee, the ad featured socially minded stars who received nothing but a lifetime supply of ice cream for their efforts. The $6 million campaign to launch the line also included print ads featuring high-profile activists such as Carlos Santana, Bobby Seal, and Pete Seeger.

As competitive pressures increased and market growth slowed, Ben & Jerry's was forced to reexamine its exclusive use of socially oriented promotion. Many publicity events were abandoned so that funds could be diverted to promotional priorities such as store coupons and price discounts. While apparently rational, such a shift also garnered criticism that the company was simply using the "world's ills and social needs to sell a product."

■ Operations

In February 1995, Ben & Jerry's had two manufacturing plants located in Waterbury and Springfield, Vermont; its St. Albans plant, whose opening had been delayed several times, was scheduled to come on line in the second half of 1995. The company's main factory, in Waterbury, is located just over the hill from company headquarters, and generally operates two shifts a day, six days a week. Production averages about 4.7 million gallons a year. The Springfield plant is used for the production of ice cream novelties, bulk ice cream and frozen yogurt, and packaged pints; its production averages about 1.2 million dozen novelties, 2.3 million gallons of bulk ice cream and frozen yogurt, packaged pints and quarts per year. It, too, operates six days a week. Overall, the company has a maximum manufacturing capacity at its own facilities of about 10.2 million gallons per year of packaged pints.

During 1992 and 1993, Ben & Jerry's increased its manufacturing capacity to support its phenomenal sales growth. After a surge in sales in the winter of 1991, the company added pint production lines at its Springfield plant and at the St. Albans Cooperative Creamery, in space loaned to the company by the site's family farmer owners.

The new St. Albans plant has a maximum ice cream and yogurt production capacity of about 17 million gallons per year when operated six days a week. It was built with energy-efficient lighting, motors, and compressors to reduce the total amount of energy required for production. At the same time, Ben & Jerry's invested $2 million in the Waterbury plant to improve efficiency. In the early 1990s the company was fined for dumping too much waste into the Waterbury system; since then, it launched a pilot cleanup product using a solar greenhouse to treat sewage.

The production equipment used at Ben & Jerry's is not highly efficient; in fact, the only new machine added in recent years is a wrapping machine, which replaced an antiquated predecessor. The company felt that increased automation might eliminate jobs, which would undermine its philosophy of social responsibility. In discussing the labor-intensive nature of the packaging line, the company stated that it would choose versatility over speed, should the choice be necessary. Executives admitted that there were several faster machines available than what they currently used: It took the company about two hours to change from one size packaging capability to another.

Until the new plant was finished, Ben & Jerry's had a manufacturing and warehouse agreement with Edy's Grand Ice Cream, a subsidiary of Dreyer's Grand Ice Cream Inc., to manufacture certain pint ice cream flavors at its plant in Fort Wayne, Indiana. The agreement was in accordance with Ben & Jerry's quality control specifications, and used dairy products shipped from Vermont. About 5 million gallons, or 40 percent of the packaged pints, were manufactured under this agreement in 1994, compared with about 37 percent in 1993. For 1995, the company expected it to be 2 million gallons.

Human Resources

Since its inception, Ben & Jerry's has been managed entrepreneurially by Ben and Jerry and "built on the cult of these two counter-cultural personalities." As the company grew to almost 600 employees, the challenge was to maintain the original spirit while managing an increasingly large organization.

The key to Ben & Jerry's human resources success is keeping employees at all levels involved in the decision making. The company attempts to create ownership at all levels and follows the New Age management model of worker empowerment. Because they have the power to make decisions and influence how things were done, employees are energized and committed.

Of course, as the company grew, it became difficult to preserve the small company atmosphere in which people matter amid the firm's transformation into an immense corporate entity. Both Ben and Jerry receive considerable praise from those inside as well as outside the company for their efforts to achieve this, and are viewed by many as the company's two biggest assets.

At the same time, however, there are those who criticize the company for "not walking its talk" in terms of employee treatment. Despite the firm's much hailed and publicized politically correct culture, for instance, employees nonetheless hold less than half of one percent of company stock. And while Ben and Jerry frequently drew attention to the fact that their own salaries are a relatively paltry $130,000 per year, they failed to note that their combined stock is worth in excess of $50 million.

Finally, known for occasionally getting bored with the daily grind and going off on some sabbatical, Ben and Jerry do not enjoy an untarnished reputation on Wall Street. The company's stock consistently underperforms the market and irritates many investors, largely as a result of the firm's insistence on putting its principles—the promotion of charity, peace, and environmental preservation—ahead of its public shareholders.

The benefits offered to employees at the company are widely regarded as cutting edge. Tuition reimbursement, flexible spending accounts, opinion surveys, evaluate-your-boss polls, paid health club fees, 12 unpaid weeks of maternity, paternity, and adoption leave, child care centers, free body and foot massages, sabbatical leave, profit sharing, paid adoption expenses, wellness plans, an insurance plan covering unmarried heterosexual and homosexual domestic partners, and free ice cream are among the offerings employees have. Ben & Jerry's management also reflects a commitment to minorities and women: Of the five senior positions filled in 1990, four were women or minorities.

Minimum wage at Ben & Jerry's is $8 per hour. While top salaries were capped at roughly $150,000 (the sum earned in 1993 by Charles Lacy, president and COO), that policy was abandoned with the hiring of Holland. Nevertheless, while the average per capita income of Vermont residents was $17,436, the lowest paid employee at Ben & Jerry's earned salary and benefits worth roughly $22,000.

Not surprisingly, the result of all its attention to employees has earned Ben & Jerry's a generally happy workforce; its turnover rate is only 12 percent.

The Challenge

When Robert Holland took the helm as CEO, Ben & Jerry's future direction was far from clear. While the company built its success by selling high-fat ice creams to consumers who were willing to pay more for the unique flavors and for Ben & Jerry's social causes, those days are gone. Health concerns, increased competition, pressure on prices and its own massive size suggest that Ben & Jerry's had to change. For Holland, the question is not "if" but "how."

Epilogue

After the highly publicized and unusual search and hiring process for Ben & Jerry's new CEO, Robert Holland, another change is in the offing. Robert Holland announced his resignation from the CEO position effective October 31, 1996. Holland had been CEO for only two years but stated that he had taken the firm as far as he could.

Earnings were down from the previous year as Ben & Jerry's faced increasing competition and challenges in marketing its products. While the stock price reached a high of $20.00 per share in 1995, the share price closed at $12.50 on the day of Holland's resignation announcement. Holland stated that the firm now needs a CEO with expertise in consumer products. Unfortunately, because of the slowing sales and marketing problems, large investors (e.g., institutional investors) have been unloading their holdings in Ben & Jerry's.

Source: D. Canedy, 1996. Ben & Jerry's is losing chief, in addition to market share. *The New York Times*, September 28. http://www.nytimes.com/yr/mo/day/news/financial/ben-jerry.html

Selected Sources

Allen, Robin Lee. "Demographics Changing, Shaping Industry." *Nation's Restaurant News*, October 28, 1991, p. 42.

Annual Report, Ben & Jerry's Homemade Inc.

"Ben & Jerry's: A Firm with a View." *Packaging Digest*, January 1993, p. 50.

"Ben & Jerry's Finally Scoops Up New CEO." *The Chicago Tribune*, February 2, 1995, p. 1.

"Ben & Jerry's Names Cream of the Crop." *The Washington Post*, February 2, 1995, p. D11.

"Ben & Jerry's Projecting Loss for Fourth Quarter." *Ice Cream Reporter*, January 20, 1995, p. 1.

"Ben, Jerry Losing Their Values?" *The Washington Times*, June 27, 1994, p. A17.

Bittman, Mark. "Ben & Jerry's Caring Capitalism." *Restaurant Business Magazine*, November 20, 1990, p. 132.

Britt, Bill. "Haagen-Dazs Pushes Cold Front Across World." *Marketing (UK),* October 4, 1990, pp. 30–31.

Bryant, Adam. "Ding-a-Ling Marketing; an Ice Cream Truck Not Just for Kids." *The New York Times,* August 21, 1992, p. 3.

Calta, Marialisa. "Ice Cream Sorcerer." *The New York Times,* March 21, 1993, p. 66.

Carlin, Peter. "Pure Profit; For Small Companies That Stress Social Values as Much as the Bottom Line, Growing Up Hasn't Been an Easy Task." *The Los Angeles Times,* February 5, 1995, p. 12.

Carton, Barbara. "A Ben & Jerry's Principle Hits a Melting Point; Seeking New CEO, Firm To Scrap Pay Ceiling." *The Boston Globe,* June 14, 1994, p. 1.

Collins, Glenn. "Ben & Jerry's Talent Hunt Ends." *The New York Times,* February 2, 1995, p. D1.

Feder, Barnaby J. "Ben Leaving as Ben & Jerry's Chief." *The New York Times,* June 14, 1994, p. D1.

Forseter, Murray. "Ben & Jerry's Caring Capitalism." *Chain Store Age Executive with Shopping Center Age,* December 1991, p. 12.

Glassman, James K. "Inside Scoop." *The Washington Post,* June 19, 1994, p. H1.

Henriques, Diana B. "Ben & Jerry's—and Dreyer's?" *The New York Times,* June 16, 1991, p. 27.

Hitchner, Earl. "We All Scream for Ice Cream; Ben and Jerry's Homemade Inc. *National Productivity Review,* December 22, 1994, p. 114.

Horwich, Andrea. "Ice Cream Still America's Favorite Dessert?" *Dairy Foods,* August 1990, p. 42.

Hwang, Suein L. "Marketscan: While Many Competitors See Sales Melt, Ben & Jerry's Scoops Out Solid Growth." *The Wall Street Journal,* May 25, 1993, p. 1.

"Ice Cream Firm Names New CEO; Ben & Jerry's Uses Traditional Search." *The Houston Chronicle,* February 2, 1995, p. 2.

"The Ice Cream Market Grows Up." *Frozen and Chilled Foods,* April 1992, p. 25.

Katz, David M. "How Ben & Jerry's Mingles Conscience with Profit Motive." *Property & Casualty/Risk & Benefits Management Edition,* June 3, 1991, p. 9.

Kuhn, Mary Ellen. "Ben & Jerry's Suffers Some Growing Pains; Ben & Jerry's Homemade Inc." *Food Processing,* September 1994, p. 56.

Laabs, Jennifer J. "Ben & Jerry's Caring Capitalism; Ben and Jerry's Homemade Inc." *Personnel Journal Optimas Award,* November 1992, p. 20.

LaFranchi, Howard. "Haagen Dazs Invades Europe, Sans Bowl." *The Christian Science Monitor,* August 19, 1993, p. 7.

Lager, Fred "Chico." *Ben & Jerry's: The Inside Scoop.* New York: Crown Publishers, 1994.

Larrabbe, Kathryn. "Ben Cohen Runs a Business with a Mission." *Business Insurance,* T27, April 1990.

Linsen, Mary Ann. "Slow Going for Ice Cream." *Progressive Grocer,* March 1991, p. 117.

Lowery, Mark. "Sold on Ice Cream." *Black Enterprise,* April 1995, p. 60.

Mann, Ernest J. "Ice Cream, Part 1." *Dairy Industries International,* July 1991, p. 15.

Manor, Robert. "Ben, Jerry Aren't Above Making a Profit." *Star Tribune,* July 5, 1994, p. 6B.

Maremont, Mark. "Say It Ain't So, Ben & Jerry." *Business Week,* June 13, 1994, p. 6.

Maremont, Mark. "They're All Screaming for Haagen Dazs." *Business Week,* October 14, 1991, p. 121.

Mathews, Jay. "Ben & Jerry's Melting Social Charter; Ice Cream Maker Abandons Progressive Pay Policy to Find New CEO." *The Washington Post,* June 14, 1994, p. D3.

"More than an Ice Cream . . . Ben & Jerry's Is Social Responsibility." *Chain Store Age Executive,* August 1991, p. 81.

Norris, Floyd. "Market Place: Low-Fat Problem at Ben & Jerry's." *The New York Times,* September 9, 1992, p. 6.

O'Donnell, Claudia Dziuk. "The Story Behind the Story: Two Dairy Processors Tell a Tale of Fruits, Flavors and Nuts; Dean Foods Co.; Ben & Jerry's Homemade Inc." *Dairy Foods Magazine,* May 1993, p. 53.

Palmer, Thomas. "News in Advertising." *The Boston Globe,* November 11, 1990, p. A4.

Pandya, Mukul. "The Executive Life: Ice-Cream Dream Job Is Tempting Thousands." *The New York Times,* July 10, 1994, p. 21.

Pereira, Joseph, and Joann S. Lublin. "Ben & Jerry's Appoints Holland President, CEO." *The Wall Street Journal,* February 2, 1995.

Rosenberg, John S. "Growing Pains: After a Remarkable Adolescence, Is Ben & Jerry's Settling into Middle Age?" *Vermont Magazine,* November–December 1993, p. 44.

Ryan, Nancy Ross. "Frozen Assets." *Restaurants & Institutions,* March 25, 1992, pp. 118–126.

Saulnier, John M. "Ice Cream Serves Up Sweetest Profits of All in Retail Frozen Food Cabinet." *Quick Frozen Foods International,* January 1992, p. 134.

Seligman, Daniel, and Patty de Llosa. "Ben & Jerry Save the World." *Fortune,* June 3, 1991, p. 247.

Shao, Maria. "A Scoopful of Credentials: CEO Holland Brings an Activist's Blend to Ben & Jerry's." *The Boston Globe,* March 1, 1995, p. 1.

Shao, Maria. "Ben & Jerry's Grows Up." *The Boston Globe,* July 3, 1994, p. 65.

Shao, Maria. "The New Emperor of Ice Cream." *The Boston Globe,* February 2, 1995, p. 35.

Smith, Geoffrey. "Life Won't Be Just a Bowl of Cherry Garcia." *Business Week,* July 18, 1994, p. 42.

Sneyd, Ross. "Ben & Jerry's Set to Appoint New CEO." *The Associated Press,* January 31, 1995.

Stableford, Joan. "Ben & Jerry's Sweetens Its Success by Helping Others." *Fairfield County Business Journal,* March 4, 1991, p. 1.

Wallace, Anne. "Ben Cohen to Step Down as CEO of Ben & Jerry's." *The Associated Press,* June 13, 1994.

Windle, Rickie. "Ben & Jerry's Creams Amy's." *Austin Business Journal,* October 4, 1993, p. 1.

"World Screams for America's Ice Cream." *The Christian Science Monitor,* September 28, 1990, p. 8.

■ CASE 6 The Body Shop, Inc.

Ann Carlson
Angela Ely
Kathy Groff
Clint Harrington
Chris Hellman
Julie Humphries

We will be the most honest cosmetic company in the world.
—Mission Statement, The Body Shop (see Exhibit 1)

No decision is ever made without first considering its social and environmental implications. Although it makes our life at The Body Shop far more difficult and troublesome, it is infinitely richer in every sense. It's that constant search for a better way, a more ethical way, that gives my company its morale and sense of purpose and its enormous sense of fun.
—Margot Franssen, president of The Body Shop Canada

■ http://www.the-body-shop.ca/
■ http://www.think-act-change.com/

Because she produces and sells skin and beauty products while simultaneously trying to save the world from environmental and social ills, Anita Roddick has her hands full. What initially began as her attempt to earn some extra money has now become a model for social and political change. With locations around the world, The Body Shop International has sold everything from peppermint foot cream to tangerine beer shampoo, creating a multi-million dollar company in the process. Along the way, the U.K.-based firm has been shaped by the personal philosophy and convictions of its creator, Anita Roddick.

With Roddick's guidance, every business decision made by The Body Shop includes a strong social message. It is this social awareness that has helped to distinguish The Body Shop from other cosmetic companies. However, recent rumors of animal testing and chemical dumping have surfaced and threaten to damage The Body Shop's image. With expansion into new markets, the company faces criticism from environmentalists and consumers alike. It also cannot escape the threat of lost market share from closely matched competitors. As Anita Roddick determines the next step, she is not likely to forget the tough times and hard work that made The Body Shop successful.

Case prepared under the direction of Professor Robert E. Hoskisson for class discussion purposes only.

Exhibit 1   The Body Shop's Mission Statement

Our Reason for Being:

To **CREATIVELY** balance the financial and human *needs* of our stakeholders: employees, customers, franchisees, suppliers, and shareholders.

To **COURAGEOUSLY** ensure that *our* business is ecologically sustainable; meeting the needs of the *present* without compromising the *future*.

To **MEANINGFULLY** contribute to local, national and international communities in which we trade; by adopting a code of conduct which ensures *care, honesty, fairness,* and *respect*.

To **PASSIONATELY** campaign *for* the protection of the environment and human and civil rights, and *against animal testing* within the cosmetics and toiletries industry.

To **TIRELESSLY** work to narrow the gap between principle and practice; while making fun, *passion* and *care* part of our daily lives.

The Body Shop International: A Brief History

At age 50, Anita Roddick has become one of the richest women in England and one of the best known personalities around the world due to the corporate philosophies and strategies she has successfully implemented at The Body Shop International. In approximately two decades, Roddick and her husband, Gordon, have expanded their operations from a rustic, single store to a booming global industry. Today, Roddick, former housewife, down-to-earth world traveler, and social activist, has created a company that stands for social and environmental responsibility.

To better understand the strategic intent of the charismatic Roddick, it helps to take a look at her background. After teaching at the elementary level and working as a library researcher, Roddick became a member of the United Nations International Labor Organization focusing on the rights of women in the Third World. During travels through Africa, Asia, and the Middle East she encountered many women and was fascinated with the simple, yet effective, methods by which they purified and attended to their hair and skin.

In 1974, Roddick came back to England, met and married her husband Gordon, had children, and settled down. Soon after their marriage, Gordon announced his plans to take a solo, two-year long trip horseback riding from Buenos Aires to New York City while Anita stayed home with their daughters. To finance this journey, the Roddicks sold a hotel and restaurant business they had started. To support the family during Gordon's absence, Anita opened a shop selling some of the cleansing and moisturizing products she had discovered on her Third World travels. After raising $12,000 from bank loans and private investors, she developed about 20 different products consisting of all-natural ingredients. She originally made the products in her kitchen and stored them in urine-sample receptacles in an effort to minimize costs.[1] To this day, the much expanded product line still has the same handwritten labels with a logo that was designed by an art student for about $35.

An intrigued and loyal client base began to grow for The Body Shop's unique products. As demand for her products grew, Anita realized that she needed to open more stores, but was financially limited in doing so. Gordon suggested that she franchise her operations, and soon after two new stores were opened in nearby towns. Other potential franchisees became interested as a result of this success, and the business rapidly exploded.

By 1978, The Body Shop expanded outside the United Kingdom for the first time, which inspired the Roddicks to strive to become a multinational corpora-

> **Exhibit 2   Group Structure of The Body Shop International PLC**
>
> Exercises control of the Group and provides a number of services including product development, environmental, legal, design and corporate communication functions.
>
> | Retail Subsidiaries | Operating Subsidiaries | Other Subsidiaries |
> |---|---|---|
> | **The Body Shop Worldwide Ltd**
Responsible for all retail activities outside the UK and USA | **The Body Shop Supply Company Ltd**
Manufactures bottle products and controls distribution to all retail outlets | **Jacaranda Productions Ltd (80% owned)**
Video production for the Group and third parties |
> | **The Body Shop UK Retail Company Ltd**
Responsible for all UK retail activities | **Cos-tec Ltd**
Manufactures colour cosmetic, skin care and toiletry products | |
> | **The Body Shop Inc. (90% owned)**
Responsible for all US retail activities | **Soapworks Ltd**
Manufactures soap products | |
> | **The Body Shop (Singapore) Pte Ltd**
Responsible for retail activities in Singapore | **Colourings Ltd**
Controls marketing of colour cosmetic products | |
> | **The Body Shop Norway A/S**
Responsible for company shops in Norway | | |

tion. This goal was quickly realized; by 1994, there were 1,140 shops across 45 countries (operating in 23 different languages), with global profits reaching approximately $12.3 million. Of these shops, 125 were company owned and the rest operated as franchises.[2] The company also operates numerous subsidiaries (see Exhibits 2 and 3). Over the years, the company's impressive performance awarded it the following distinctions:

- Company of the Year in the United Kingdom, 1985
- United Kingdom Retailer of the Year, 1989
- Roddick—Veuve Cliquot Businesswoman of the Year, 1985
- Roddick—UK Communicator of the Year, 1987
- Roddick—Order of the British Empire, 1988
- Roddick—International Banksia Achiever Award, 1993
- Roddick—National Audobon Society Medal, 1993
- Roddick—Environmental Achiever Award, 1993

Anita Roddick has generated five simple principles that have been incorporated into the culture of the company[3]:

1. To sell its products with inexpensive packaging and no hype.
2. To emphasize health over glamour, and reality over false promises.

Exhibit 3	Where in the World		
	Number of Shops		**First Shop**
	Feb 1994	Feb 1993	Opening
Europe			
Austria	9	8	1979
Belgium	11	8	1978
Cyprus	1	1	1983
Denmark	15	11	1981
Eire	10	10	1981
Finland	17	15	1981
France	25	16	1982
Germany	43	37	1983
Gibraltar	1	1	1988
Greece	28	23	1979
Holland	47	40	1982
Iceland	2	2	1980
Italy	38	37	1984
Luxembourg	2	2	1991
Malta	1	1	1987
Norway	14	15	1985
Portugal	8	8	1986
Spain	52	33	1986
Sweden	40	34	1979
Switzerland	21	19	1983
	385	321	
UK	*239*	*233*	*1976*
Asia			
Bahrain	1	1	1985
Brunei	1	—	1993
Hong Kong	9	8	1984
Indonesia	4	2	1990
Japan	22	11	1990

3. To make products from natural and organic ingredients, with as little chemical processing as possible.
4. To refuse to participate in or to condone any kind of animal testing.
5. To act in an environmentally sound manner.

These standards stemmed from Roddick's personal convictions about how to conduct business and life. With them in mind, The Body Shop established rigorous quality control procedures and works continually to ensure that its products meet the highest standards. For example, throughout the production process there are up to four independent laboratory sites where merchandise is tested for microbial contamination and proper ingredient balance. If a product ever makes it to the store shelf and is later discovered to be defective, it is

Exhibit 3	Where in the World—Continued		
	Number of Shops		**First Shop**
	Feb 1994	**Feb 1993**	**Opening**
Kuwait	2	2	1986
Macau	1	—	1993
Malaysia	11	10	1984
Oman	2	2	1986
Qatar	1	1	1987
Saudi Arabia	13	10	1987
Singapore	9	11	1983
Taiwan	6	5	1988
Thailand	2	—	1993
UAE	4	2	1983
	88	65	
Australia and New Zealand			
Australia	48	43	1983
New Zealand	9	7	1989
	57	50	
Americas excluding USA			
Antigua	1	1	1987
Bahamas	3	4	1985
Bermuda	1	1	1987
Canada	106	104	1980
Cayman Islands	1	1	1989
Mexico	2	—	1993
	114	111	
USA	*170*	*120*	*1988*
Grand Total	*1,053*	*900*	

Our company shops are located as follows: USA, 51; UK, 38; Singapore, 9; Norway, 2.

Number of countries: **45**.

Number of languages we trade in: **23**.

immediately removed from the shelves, and the entire product batch is recalled from all the shops.

The Body Shop operates with a "no exception" policy against animal testing. The company claims that it has never tested a product or ingredient on animals. The Body Shop has been active in fighting against international and domestic regulations that dictate successful animal testing results before the product can be approved for distribution. It also has provided generous funding to seek alternative methods for product qualification. Currently, the company utilizes some of these alternative methods in the testing of its own products. Specifically, it uses Eyetex human patch testing, SPF testing, and analytical procedures. Volunteers are taken from within the company and the community to participate in testing sessions.[4]

Anita Roddick has also established a policy of using Body Shop stores as promotion centers for programs for social change. Examples of these programs include the following:

1. In 1990, The Body Shop started a relief drive to fund volunteers to renovate orphanages in Romania.
2. Founded *The Big Issue,* a monthly newspaper sold by and for the homeless.
3. In 1993, The Body Shop Foundation donated $162,000 to Rights and Wrongs, a weekly human rights television series.
4. Created The Body Shop Charitable Foundation to fund community groups and grassroots organizations working in the areas of the environment, youth programs, women's issues, and human rights with an emphasis on the rights of indigenous peoples.
5. Opened community stores situated in economically disadvantaged communities. These stores donate a percentage of profits back into the community to fund programs to improve the quality of life.

The Body Shop operates with strict environmental standards to maintain its reputation and ecological image. Examples of these standards include the following:

1. Issues an environmental audit with its financial reports; all stores contribute data.
2. Operates a product recycling and refill system; limits unnecessary packaging.
3. Uses least environmentally damaging products.
4. Designed buildings with environmental specifications.

The issue of fair trade is also vital to The Body Shop, as it seeks to deter the exploitation of animals and humans and their habitats. This principle is highlighted in the company's Trade Not Aid policy. Through this effort, direct trading links are established with less developed communities in other countries, as these communities generate products that can be sold in Body Shop stores. Through its Trade Not Aid program, The Body Shop intends to prove that environmental preservation and social progress can occur simultaneously. Its theory is that if these communities can finance their own economic growth, then concerned outsiders can efficiently funnel their money to philanthropic needs. This, in turn, leads to growth that is more sustainable. The Trade Not Aid program has also brought together various indigenous people to create a joint effort to protest the deterioration of their lands. Overall, Anita Roddick created this program to promote fair trade instead of free trade and conservation instead of consumption. These are some tangible examples of this policy:

1. Profits from foot massagers produced in India help support health care and education programs in that area.
2. The Nepalese Paper Project in Nepal contributes to a community action fund for education, health care, and environmental initiatives.
3. Sustainable trading links with Kayapo communities in Brazil help fund health care programs and provide alternative sources of income to the logging and mining industries that threaten their rain forest.

4. In the Mesquital Valley in Mexico, 350 Nanhu Indian women trade with The Body Shop.

5. The Body Shop manufactures more than 90 percent of its soaps in Easterhouse, an economically depressed postwar housing project in Glasgow, Scotland, and donates after-tax profits to the community.

The Body Shop's unusual social programs have created a great deal of publicity that the company has used as a low cost means to promote its merchandise.[5] This marketing strategy has been merged with other innovative schemes to foster growth in its customer base. The company has historically relied on lavish window displays, catalogs, and point of purchase advertising to market its products, ignoring traditional marketing approaches. Traditional advertising is deemphasized in order to focus on health over glamour and reality over false promises. Roddick intentionally excluded advertising from her original company strategy because she believed that "the best advertising is a good shop and a good product."[6]

The Body Shop has traditionally positioned its stores in large malls or shopping districts with high consumer traffic. Each store features natural wood floors, green walls and bright lights that facilitate the "natural" feel of the organization. Window and in-store displays emphasize the purity of the products and the social and environmental campaigns that The Body Shop supports.

In the past, The Body Shop's products were mainly focused toward women's needs, but recently the store has begun to develop products that appeal to men also (or are at least non–gender based). Skin cleansing products, soaps, and varieties of bubble baths are targeted to assorted market segments.

The Bath and Beauty Industry

The Body Shop is attributed with much of the credit for spurring the booming international popularity of bath and body products in the 1990s. By 1992, total sales for this market segment had grown to almost $1.1 billion (up from $890 million in 1988), and were expected to grow at a rate of 2.6 percent annually between 1992 and 1998. Bath and shower additives (gels, oils, salts, and bubble baths) made up the most dynamic growth area within the bath and shower products market, growing 49 percent in the period 1988–1993.[7] Additionally, per capita expenditures on bath and shower products have grown consistently during the past few years, increasing from $8.82 in 1988 to $10.49 in 1992.[8]

According to industry analysts, two significant trends affected cosmetic sales in the mid-1990s: the aging of America and the growth of green consumerism.[9] As graying baby boomers spend more and more money on anti-aging products (alphahydroxy acid and vitamin-based products in particular), many younger consumers are leaning towards "cosmetics with a conscience." Once thought to be a short-lived trend, many now expect environmental awareness to represent a permanent shift in social values, and predict continued growth in this market category.

A recent survey found that one-third of all skin care and makeup dollars comes from consumers described as female "ecologists," generally consumers between the ages of 18 and 30 who count themselves as highly sensitive to environmental issues and deeply concerned about animal rights. These consumers demand products that are environmentally safe in terms of formulas, testing, packaging, and manufacturing practices, and look for cruelty-free products that contain natural ingredients.[10] They are not especially price sensitive, because they prefer product benefits and attributes over cost savings. They value the peace of mind that comes with knowledge of product ingredients and company philosophy.

| ■ Recent Developments | ■ Increased Competition |

When the first U.S. Body Shop opened in 1988, the idea of marketing "green" cosmetics was a new concept. By 1994, The Body Shop had over 33 copycat competitors, each trying to capitalize on the Body Shop's enormously popular earth-friendly niche. The company's most serious competitors included Bath & Body Works, H₂O Plus, Garden Botanika, Goodebodies, and Estee Lauder's Origins line.[11] By 1994, its four major competitors had a combined total of over 400 stores worldwide. These new products and retail chains make similar claims of using natural ingredients, environmentally safe packaging, and limited animal testing.

The success of environmentally aware product lines has even begun to filter down to the department store level. Such well-known retailers as JC Penney, Macy's, and Federated Department stores have greatly increased their retail space devoted to environmentally conscious bath and body lines. The Body Shop also faced an onslaught of natural-style products from companies ranging from supermarket chains to such beauty giants as L'Oreal and Procter & Gamble.

The Body Shop's most serious competitor is Bath & Body Works, a retail chain of cosmetics and toiletries stores started by The Limited Inc. The Bath & Body Works stores are very similar in atmosphere and product line to The Body Shop, and are often mistaken for one another in many U.S. markets. This chain is growing rapidly in shopping malls across the United States with approximately 220 stores nationwide (within four years of its introduction) and operating margins of about 20 percent higher than most British retailers. The franchise's sales are expected to grow to $250 million during 1994 (up from $18 million in 1991), with 200 store openings planned for the next 12 months.[12]

Most recently, The Limited has made a powerful move into the international marketplace by teaming up with Britain's Next PLC in a joint venture to launch its Bath & Body Works throughout Britain and other European markets.[13] It will compete directly with The Body Shop, who it sees as its main rival, consistently using similar ambiance, product lines, and pricing strategies to gain a piece of The Body Shop's market share. The movement of Bath & Body Works into the British market comes at a particularly delicate time, as The Body Shop attempts to recover from negative publicity that sheds doubt on its "green" credentials.

While The Body Shop has withstood threats from numerous competitors in the past in the United Kingdom (including the now defunct Body & Face Place stores and Nectar), it regards Bath & Body Works as a more serious threat. It has realized that the combined expertise of The Limited and Next will ensure that the Bath & Body stores are attractively merchandised and well promoted, and that the joint venture has vast financial resources to finance continued growth. It has also worried that its franchising system could prove to be a hindrance in an increasingly competitive market.

Other key competitors include these:

- *Garden Botanika:* a health and beauty aid chain based in Redmond, Washington; best known for its Spa Botanika range of body products.
- *H₂O Plus:* a Chicago-based skin care shop, known for selling water-based (rather than oil-based) products. As of 1993 it operated 51 free-standing stores in the United States (not including 25 shops within The Parisian department stores), 2 stores in Canada, and 4 in Argentina. The company plans to open 200 stores by 1996.[14]
- *Goodebodies:* As of April 1993, there were 80 Goodebodies bath and body shops located in department stores across the United States. The company has a line of 450 products, all of which are made without animal by-products, and most contain botanical extracts and natural scents. In addition to soaps, cleansers, moisturizers, bath oils, gels, shampoos, and conditioners, the company has an aromatherapy line with more than 60 products.
- *Origins Natural Resources:* a division of Estee Lauder, its products are sold primarily in department stores. Products are priced at a level almost twice as high as The Body Shop's.

■ New Management Structure

To accommodate its rapid growth and increasing international emphasis, The Body Shop realized in 1994 that it needed to redesign its management structure to increase operating efficiency. Problems in the company's structure had become apparent through communication and control problems that had emerged in different levels of the organization. Corporate expansion exposed downfalls in the loosely defined structure of the company's top management and problems resulting from lengthy absences of Anita Roddick (who spends much of her time traveling to remote areas generating new product ideas).

The major issue that the company faced with restructuring was how to protect the unique corporate culture and values that defined the strategy of the organization. While it wanted to improve efficiency, it did not want to dilute the socially responsible business values, which emphasized human, animal, and environmental rights.

Gordon Roddick turned to an Israeli management consultant who had the philosophy that when a business has grown to a certain stage, it needs to create a balance between creativity and bureaucracy, an idea that seemed to fit with the objectives of The Body Shop's reorganization. A significant development from the implementation of this philosophy included the separation of the bureaucratic and creative aspects of a given function to keep the everyday demands of the administrative factors from interfering with the more creative facets.

In August 1994, The Body Shop announced its new organizational structure. Distinctive features of this new structure include prominent roles defined to direct cultural and ideological aspects of the firm, such as an executive responsible for "values and vision" and another responsible for corporate culture. These positions were created specifically to protect The Body Shop's entrepreneurial culture and its ecological philosophy. The company also expanded its board by hiring a new managing director to take responsibility for much of the company's day-to-day management. In addition, the company appointed two nonexecutive directors to its board for the first time. These appointees included Penny Hughes, president of Coca-Cola Great Britain and Ireland, and Aldo Papone, former chairman and CEO of American Express Travel Related Services Company. These nonexecutive directors were hired for their expertise in consumer marketing, branding, and franchising.[15]

■ Environmental Spill

In early 1994, several claims were made against The Body Shop regarding shampoo and chemical spills from its New Jersey plant. Four separate releases of liquids were cited by local U.S. environmental authorities, contradicting statements supporting environmental responsibility made by The Body Shop to protect its waning "green" and ethical image.[16] Specifics of the spillage differ between company and governmental records, as do perceptions of the significance of each incident. The authorities claimed that The Body Shop assured them that they would make systems improvements after the first incident, but two additional spills resulted. Furthermore, officials of the Hanover Sewage Authority recognized each occurrence and traced the liquid releases back to The Body Shop. Authorities believed that the spills were readily preventable and that there was ample time for The Body Shop to have taken action.

Negative Publicity

On September 1, 1994, an article was published in *Business Ethics* magazine accusing The Body Shop of hypocrisy in its business practices and ecological claims. Written by former ABC News producer Jon Entine, the article claimed that The Body Shop's charitable contributions, environmental standards, efforts to support developing nations through materials purchases, and use of ecologically sound ingredients in products failed to meet its claims to the public. Further, the article publicized a Federal Trade Commission investigation regarding disputes with The Body Shop's U.S. franchises over high product markups and earnings promises.[17]

Effects of the Accusations

The prerelease publicity that surrounded the *Business Ethics* article had highly detrimental effects. Word of Entine's disparaging claims was leaked to the public several weeks in advance of the article's publication. Speculation about the actual contents of the article stimulated a 24 pence fall in stock price, and a loss of investor confidence in the company. Some specific results are discussed next.[18]

Loss of Investor Support

Soon after the publication of the article, Franklin Research and Development (a Boston-based investment fund that invests on behalf of clients who are concerned with organizational social responsibility) dropped its 50,000-share holding of Body Shop stock and encouraged its clients to do the same.[19] Franklin claimed that the decision to sell was based on concerns that The Body Shop's sales growth was slowing and that the fully valued stock left no room for growth. Franklin also worried that the negativity surrounding the publication of Entine's article would depress the stock's value. Increased competition from Bath & Body Works also influenced the decision to sell. It is important to remember, however, that Franklin's holding in The Body Shop was minor compared to the total 188 million shares in circulation (less than 1%),[20] and that since the time of the sale, The Body Shop has since been backed by other ethical investment funds. Franklin did not specifically comment on its belief of Entine's claims, but it did undertake its own investigation into The Body Shop's business practices to decide if it lived up to its socially responsible standards.

Franklin's Report

Franklin's investigation concluded that some of the criticisms of The Body Shop were justified. The report commented on a gap between the company image and reality. Additionally, the defensiveness of the company was criticized. The Body Shop was said to utilize "bombastic and offensive tactics" in responding to Entine's accusations.[21] Franklin expressed frustration with the fact that The Body Shop refused to provide information to those trying to verify the claims. However, Franklin's conclusions clearly contrasted those of other organizations, in that many other companies argued that the criticisms of The Body Shop were unfair. In response to the report, Gordon Roddick stated that Franklin had a "vested interest in taking a shot at us."[22]

On a more positive note, the report stressed that The Body Shop's problems were "quite correctable" and that the company was "currently making improvements in almost all areas." The report cited the company's overall record of environmental auditing and disclosure as being impressive, but mentioned several areas for improvement. It suggested that the packaging of the company's products include the source of their ingredients. Additionally, the report argued that the language used to describe "Trade Not Aid" required revision to reflect accurately the scale of the projects the company supports.

Resignation of Business Ethics Board Member

Ben Cohen resigned from the advisory board of *Business Ethics* magazine prior to the article's release. Cohen was the cofounder of Ben & Jerry's, the socially responsible ice cream maker referred to as The Body Shop's brother company. His resignation from the board was in direct protest to the magazine's decision to publish the article critical of The Body Shop. Cohen called the article a "diatribe" that "reputable media outlets had refused to publish." He went on to say the article was "an unbalanced questionable piece of journalism that does not advance a constructive dialogue about social responsibility."[23]

Effects on Profitability

Overall, the negative publicity had little long-term effect on The Body Shop's earnings. Initially, the company's share price fell more than 20 percent, from 264 pence to 212 pence during the summer of 1994 due to the speculation that its environmentally conscious image was about to suffer an attack.[24] The Body Shop's response to the accusations seemed to meet investor approval, in that the stock price has experienced a complete recovery from the fall it originally encountered. The Body Shop can look forward to strong growth as its international business expands—the number of shops operated around the world is planned to rise to 2,000 by the end of the century.[25]

Exhibit 4 Body Shop International Balance Sheet			
Year to February	**1992**	**1993**	**1994**
Freeholds	0.7	3.3	4.9
Other tangibles	55.7	61.4	63.0
Investments	2.3	5.3	3.7
Fixed Assets	58.7	70.0	71.6
Stocks	38.5	35.3	34.6
Debtors	36.1	33.6	37.2
Current Assets	74.5	68.9	71.8
Trade creditors	−10.1	−8.9	−7.9
Provisions & other creditors	−16.0	−18.8	−26.8
Current Liabilities	−26.1	−27.7	−34.7
Cash	0.5	14.0	24.9
Borrowing	−33.1	−12.5	−36.7
Net borrowings	−32.6	−28.5	−11.8
Net Assets	74.5	82.7	96.9
Share capital reserves	9.4	9.4	9.4
Reserves	64.8	72.8	87.5
Shareholders' funds	74.2	82.2	96.9
Minority interests	0.3	0.5	0.0
	74.5	82.7	96.9

At the end of August 1994, The Body Shop's half year results indicated exceptional growth for the company (*see Exhibits 4, 5, and 6*). Overall, the company performance was in the top range of market expectations. These results reflect the stability provided by having operations in 45 countries. During the first half of 1994, the company experienced a 23 percent increase in interim pretax profits with little impact on sales. The Body Shop saw a small drop in customer numbers for the United Kingdom at one point with an immediate recovery. In the United States, sales were relatively unaffected, due to the fact that the *Business Ethics* controversy was not widely reported outside of the financial press. Total sales increased 18 percent, while sales through company-owned shops experienced 13 percent growth. During this time period, 83 new shops were opened bringing the total to 1,136 with 80 more planned for the second half of the year. The interim dividend increased from .75p to .9p, with earnings up from 3.4p to 4.2p per share. Currently, second half trading is following a similar trend.[26]

The Body Shop's Response to the Accusations

> *Why am I always measured against the standard of Mother Teresa—a standard by which even saints will fail—and not against those chairmen of companies who create huge corporate crimes?"—Anita Roddick, after The Body Shop came under attack in 1992 over its environmental standards*

Exhibit 5   Body Shop International Profit and Loss Statement

Year to February	1990	1991	1992	1993	1994
Sales	84.5	115.6	147.4	168.3	195.4
Gross profit	47.6	65.2	79.2	90.3	105.9
Gross Margin (%)	56.4	56.4	53.7	53.7	54.2
Selling expenses	−19.7	−27.5	−32.0	−37.5	−43.0
Admin. expense	−11.0	−15.7	−19.3	−28.5	−32.8
Operating Profit	16.9	22.0	27.9	24.3	30.1
Operating margin	20.0	19.0	18.9	14.4	15.4
Sales by Country					
UK	56.9	73.4	86.0	83.5	91.1
USA	5.8	13.4	23.5	37.8	50.4
Europe	10.9	16.0	22.3	28.2	30.9
Canada	5.9	8.7	7.3	8.8	8.6
Australia	3.5	2.1	4.0	4.1	6.3
Asia	1.5	2.1	4.3	5.9	8.1
Total	84.5	115.6	147.4	168.3	195.4
Operating Profit					
UK	13.5	14.8	16.5	11.2	11.4
USA	−1.9	−0.6	1.5	2.1	6.2
Europe	2.6	4.2	5.5	5.6	5.9
Canada	1.5	2.5	2.0	2.5	2.4
Australia	0.9	0.6	1.1	1.1	1.8
Asia	0.4	0.6	1.3	1.8	2.4
Total	16.9	22.0	27.9	24.3	30.1
Interest payable	−2.4	−2.0	−2.7	−2.8	−1.5
Pretax profit	14.5	20.1	25.2	21.5	28.6
Taxation	−5.5	−7.3	−8.7	−7.6	−9.4
Tax Rate (%)	34.5	35.3	32.9	34.0	32.9
Minority	−0.5	−0.6	−0.1	−0.1	−0.2
Profit after tax	8.5	12.2	16.4	13.8	19.0
Dividends	−1.5	−2.3	−3.0	−3.2	−3.8
Retained Profit	7.0	9.9	13.5	10.6	15.2
EPS	5.0	6.7	8.8	7.4	10.1
Operating Margins					
UK	23.7	20.1	19.1	13.4	12.5
USA	−33.2	−4.8	6.4	5.6	12.3
Europe	23.9	26.3	24.7	19.9	19.1
Canada	25.3	28.4	27.7	28.4	27.9
Australia	26.1	28.8	28.2	26.8	28.6
Asia	26.6	29.1	29.8	30.5	29.6

Exhibit 6 Body Shop International Cash Flow Statement

Year to February	1991	1992	1993	1994
Cash Flow from Operations	22.0	27.9	24.3	30.1
Operating profit	3.5	4.7	7.2	9.5
Depreciation	0.0	0.1	0.4	0.4
Profit/(loss) on fixed assets	−10	−5.0	3.3	−0.5
Change in stocks	−8.0	−7.6	3.9	−4.6
Change in debtors	2.3	0.2	1.0	5.1
Change in creditors	−3.1	−1.6	−1.5	0.3
Others	6.7	18.7	38.6	40.3
Returns on Investment & Servicing of Finance				
Net interest	−2.0	−2.6	−2.3	−1.5
Dividends	−1.8	−2.6	−3.0	−3.3
Total	−3.8	−5.2	−5.3	−4.8
Taxation				
Corporate tax paid	−5.7	−7.6	−7.5	−6.6
Investing Activities				
Purchase of fixed assets	−18.0	−17.2	−19.6	−12.7
Sale of fixed assets	0.0	0.4	0.2	2.2
Purchase of subsidiaries	−0.3	−5.6	−1.8	−3.9
Others	0.0	0.0	0.0	0.0
Total	−18.3	−22.4	−21.2	−14.4
Net Inflow/Outflow Before Financing	−21.1	−16.5	4.6	14.5
Financing				
Issue of ordinary shares	29.6	1.3	0.0	2.2
Increase/decrease in net debt	8.5	−15.2	4.6	16.7
Year End Net Debt	−17.9	−33.1	−28.5	−11.8
Gearing%	27.0	45.0	35.0	0.0
Interest coverage(times)	11.0	11.0	11.0	42.0
Free cash flow	−7.0	0.0	17.0	13.0

As environmental groups, financial analysts, and journalists attempted to determine the truth behind Entine's allegations, The Body Shop scrambled to diffuse the latest threat to the company's "green" image. Company spokespeople complained that the article contained "distortions, shoddy reporting, and views of several unqualified or biased sources or so-called experts," and threatened lawsuits if the article were published outside of the United States.[27] The company repeatedly blasted the international news media for firing pot shots at Anita Roddick's unconventional management style and for threatening the integrity of The Body Shop's products.

On September 2, 1994, The Body Shop International issued a 32-page press release attacking the legitimacy of each of Mr. Entine's allegations. In this release, The Body Shop questioned the motives of the editors of *Business Ethics* magazine, and accused them of orchestrating a prepublication publicity campaign designed to put itself "on the map" with the publication of controversial accusations against a popular company. It charged that in a letter to the magazine's financial backers, *Business Ethics*' publisher personally promised to stimulate interest in and generate publicity for The Body Shop story by telephoning dozens of journalists herself.[28] In addition to these charges, the company challenged the credibility of many of Entine's "expert" sources, claiming that two current competitors were cited as independent experts without any reference to possible conflicts of interest.

After the story was published, The Body Shop sent a 10-page letter to all *Business Ethics* subscribers discrediting its allegations. Later, Marjorie Kelly, publisher and editor-in-chief of *Business Ethics,* claimed that the company obtained the magazine's mailing list under false pretenses. Angela Bawtree, The Body Shop's head of investor relations, confirms that this letter was sent, but denies that the list was obtained through questionable methods through a consultant.

In its lengthy press releases, The Body Shop categorically denied most of the accusations made against the company. One of Entine's main allegations concerned the thoroughness of the company's quality control procedures, and alleged that a certain type of eye gel could possibly be contaminated. The company disputed this claim by describing in detail its microbial testing procedures, which include four different series of tests done by two different laboratories and apply to both domestic and imported products. In addition, the company described its policy of immediately removing any questionable products from the shelves of all of its stores.

In response to criticism of its animal testing procedures, the company reiterated its policy of never commissioning or testing any of its cosmetic products or ingredients on animals. In addition to funding research into alternative testing methods and campaigning to ban animal testing, the company maintains a "five-year rule" purchasing policy, by which it will not buy ingredients for its products that have been tested on animals in the past five years. The Body Shop cites that it has received support for this policy from several leading animal rights organizations, including the British Union for the Abolition of Vivisection, the International Funds for Animal Welfare, and many member-organizations of the European Coalition to End Animal Tests.[29]

The company countered claims that its Trade Not Aid program isn't as beneficial to disadvantaged regions as it is marketed to be by arguing that through this initiative, the company bought $1.85 million worth of goods from less developed areas in 1993. The Body Shop cites its dedication of six full-time staff members to the operation of this program as evidence of its long-term commitment to it, and argues that Entine never visited a single Trade Not Aid project site, making him unqualified to judge its success.

Additionally, The Body Shop disputed reports of poor relations with franchisees by citing a letter of support signed by 95 percent of its American franchisees that Anita and Gordon Roddick received within 24 hours of the publication of Entine's article. The company also argued that many franchisees who were quoted in the article have since sent the company letters saying that their words were twisted or misquoted. The company argued that it has terminated only one franchisee in its entire history, and that was only after British court had found that she had in fact caused considerable damage to the company.

The Body Shop confirmed only one of the allegations made by Entine—the accusation that in 1992, 60 gallons of shampoo and shower gel were spilled at

The Body Shop's former warehouse and factory in New Jersey—but denied that this spill was damaging to the environment. The company said that in its history, it has never had any serious toxic emissions or spills, which is unusual for a company of its size and scope.

The Body Shop has been criticized for its aggressive and seemingly hostile handling of the negative publicity surrounding the publication of Entine's article. An editorial in London's *Financial Times* argued that the company's actions, and especially its lengthy press releases, "painted a picture of a company with much to fear,"[30] and that the company seemed more concerned with discrediting the author of the article than rebutting the charges he made. The article goes on to call the company naive and immature for its attempts to discredit Mr. Entine. Interestingly, however, is the fact that despite its numerous attacks on Entine, The Body Shop made no attempts to enact publicity campaigns or promotional materials at the consumer level or to meet with British financial analysts to calm the fears of skittish investors. It did, however, seek an injunction against *Vanity Fair* magazine to prevent further publication of the article.

Response to New Competition

When the managers of The Limited's Bath & Body Works chain first announced their decision to go into a joint venture with a British fashion retailer and establish operations in the United Kingdom, Gordon Roddick initially seemed unconcerned. He argued that The Body Shop had successfully competed with this chain in U.S. markets, and that U.S. retailers have traditionally had problems establishing themselves successfully in the United Kingdom. He also questioned the logic of Bath & Body Works' pricing strategy, noting that its prices are 20 percent higher than The Body Shop's.[31] He did concede that "it will be interesting to see what they do over here, and we will watch them closely. They may show us a few good ideas."

However, since that time the company has changed its tune considerably. In response to the negative publicity surrounding Entine's article, sluggish sales, and a market survey that showed that most U.S. shoppers could not distinguish The Body Shop from such competitors as Bath & Body Works and H_2O, the company has drastically changed its marketing strategy. In the past, the company said that it would not "fritter away the customers' money on advertising," and communicated with customers only through window displays, catalogs, and point-of-purchase product descriptions. Recently, however, the company has leaned towards more mass marketing, and has even hired an influential public relations firm, Chiat Day, to promote its products.

In an unusual marketing move, Anita Roddick appeared recently in an American Express retail ad campaign that also featured Toys 'R Us CEO Charles Lazarus and Southwest Airlines CEO Herb Kelleher. The company also recently paid an undisclosed amount to run an eight-page "advertorial" in a popular European magazine (*Marie Claire*), and is currently investigating the possibility of producing infomercials for television. The Body Shop insists that it has no moral problem with the use of advertising itself, only the use of glamorous images or cure-all claims. One British financial analyst, however, noted that "they always used to say they would rather cut off their right arm than advertise. But now it is something they would consider doing."[32]

■ Implications for the Industry

The dynamics of the bath and beauty industry are constantly evolving to include new players, new products, and new formats. With the entrance of Bath & Body Works into the British market, and the success of H$_2$O, Origins, and Garden Botanika, The Body Shop cannot ignore the threat of tough competition and potential loss of market share. The recent addition of many smaller "natural" cosmetics companies within department and grocery stores suggests that The Body Shop and bath and beauty industry itself is open to new competitors and copy-cat formats. While each of these companies sells similar products, they may provide other extra services that set them apart. The Body Shop will remain at the forefront only as long as consumers value their concern for social and environmental issues.

Body Shop patrons who value their altruistic motives will remain loyal to its products, while those seeking direct product benefits may be led away by competitors with intriguing claims and similar products. However, the nature of the industry suggests that high switching costs exist for consumers who put faith in the bath and cosmetic products they use. Generally, they are not price sensitive because specialized products generate extreme loyalty. However, with so many similar products on the market, consumers have a wide variety from which to choose and will not hesitate to switch if they become displeased with a particular brand.

With The Body Shop's attempts to create useful, environmentally sound products comes the strict expectations for itself and its colleagues. The Body Shop utilizes its strict policy of no animal-tested products within the past five years to ensure that products and ingredients are tested without harm to animals. This and other policies allow The Body Shop to carefully control its suppliers. Those wishing to do business with The Body Shop are forced to operate according to Body Shop, or Anita Roddick's expectations.

■ Where Do They Go from Here?

Now that The Body Shop has altered its stance on advertising, consumers are left to wonder what is next. With its product testing measures in question, it faces not only potential lost market share and customer loyalty, but also the possibility of reduced employee morale and loss of company vision. With many similar cosmetic companies entering the market, The Body Shop will struggle to remain on top. Can it retain its socially conscious image amid a flurry of accusations and confusion? If The Body Shop loses its distinction as the company with a global perspective, will they become just another cosmetics company?

■ Notes

1. Christopher A. Bartlett, K.W. Elderkin, and K. McQuade, 1991, The Body Shop International, *Harvard Business School*, 2.
2. The Body Shop International, 1994, *Annual Report and Accounts*.
3. Bartlett, Elderkin, and McQuade, 1991, The Body Shop International, 3.
4. The Body Shop International, 1994, *Green Book*.
5. Bartlett, Elderkin, and McQuade, 1991, The Body Shop International, 8.
6. Bartlett, Elderkin, and McQuade, 1991, The Body Shop International, 7.
7. *Research Alert*, August 15, 1994.
8. Ibid.
9. New U.S. body products emphasize nature and innovation, *Cosmetics International,* November 11, 1993.
10. Susan Sargisson, 1994, Current of change in the cosmetics business, *Drug and Cosmetic Industry,* June, 39.

11. Body and bath turns it on, *Women's Wear Daily,* October 30, 1992, 5.
12. Rod Whitehead, 1994, The Body Shop—fighting fit, *U.K. Research* (publication of Goldman Sachs), October 19.
13. Susan Gilchrist, 1994, U.S. chain launches Body Shop rival in U.K., *The Times,* October 10.
14. Soren Larson, 1993, H2O Plus to flow into UK in September, *Women's Wear Daily,* July 30, 4.
15. Vanessa Houlder, 1994, The passage into adulthood—as it grows, The Body Shop is striving to balance convention with creativity, *Financial Times,* August 11, 11.
16. Andrew Jack, 1994, Body Shop spillage details revealed, *Financial Times,* August 26, 16.
17. Ellen Neuborne, 1994, Body Shop in a lather over ethics criticism, *USA Today,* August 29, 3B.
18. Richard W. Stevenson, 1994, The Body Shop's green image is attacked, *The New York Times,* September 2, D1.
19. Ibid.
20. Whitehead, The Body Shop.
21. Andrew Jack, 1994, Franklin defends Body Shop stance, *Financial Times,* September 24.
22. Ibid.
23. Neil Buckley, 1994, Protests grow over Body Shop article, *Financial Times,* September 31.
24. Stevenson, The Body Shop's green image is attacked.
25. The Lex Column, 1994, Body Shop, *Financial Times,* October 14.
26. Neil Buckley, 1994, Body Shop profits up despite ethics row, *Financial Times,* October 14.
27. The Body Shop reaffirms its commitment to ethical business and fends off cynical and unwarranted attacks on its good works, Canada NewsWire, September 7, 1994.
28. The Body Shop International responds to misleading media reports, Canada NewsWire, September 2, 1994.
29. The Body Shop adheres to rigorous quality controls and is against animal testing, Canada NewsWire, September 2, 1994.
30. Ethical report threatens blow to the Body Shop, *The Financial Times Limited Investor's Chronicle,* September 2, 1994.
31. James Fallon, 1994, The Body Shop International is digging in its heels, *Women's Wear Daily,* September 2.
32. Charles Siler, 1994, Body Shop marches to its own drummer but competitors push it nearer standard marketing, *Advertising Age,* October 10.

■ CASE 7 The Boeing Company: How Do We Get There from Here?

Michael Andress
Bulent Erkmen
Paul Miller
Lisa Milligan
Ali Ozkazanc

■ http://www.boeing.com/

Approaching retirement, CEO Frank Shrontz reflected on the changes Boeing and the aircraft industry were facing, and he wondered how his protégé, President Philip Condit, could top the company's last 75 years of success. Since its founding in 1917, Boeing had grown to become the world's leading manufacturer of commercial airplanes and one of the United States' leading exporters. The company was also recognized as a major player in the defense industry, with capabilities ranging from helicopters and missile systems design to information systems management. Philip Condit was a 54-year-old, 30-year Boeing veteran who had witnessed much of the company's growth firsthand. He entertained the philosophy that productivity improvements would enable Boeing to control its own destiny. Boeing had recently incorporated this emphasis on increased productivity and reduced cost into its strategy of technological leadership. Shrontz knew that this new mentality had strengthened the company's ability to compete today, but he was uncertain if it would be enough to carry Boeing successfully into the next century.

■ Company History

The Boeing Company originated in Washington State during the early part of this century. It was named for William E. Boeing, a Yale graduate and Seattle area timber merchant who took his first airplane ride in 1915, a dozen years after the Wright Brothers' first flight. Boeing and a friend, Conrad Westervelt, quickly decided that they could build a better plane, and in 1916 they launched the first of two B&W models.[1] Their first design was a single-engine seaplane, with a top speed of 75 mph. Boeing was soon taking delivery orders from both the civil

Case prepared under the direction of Professor Robert E. Hoskisson for class discussion purposes only.

aviation industry and the U.S. Navy. The enterprise was registered as the Boeing Airplane Company during 1917. Boeing's business expanded rapidly during the 1920s and 1930s, primarily due to the growing market for mail delivery.

The company committed itself to technological development early on, building the first low-wing, multiengine transport in 1930, the Pan American "Clipper" flying boat during 1938, and the first pressurized cabin later that same year.[2] This know-how allowed Boeing to play a key role in the Allied war effort of World War II, which depended heavily on the company's B-17 and B-29 bombers. After the war, Boeing set the standard for jet bombers with the B-47 and the B-52, the latter of which is still flown today. The company also foresaw the huge market for commercial jet aircraft, launching the first of its 700 series of planes with the 707 during 1957. Since that time, Boeing has continued to build safer, more efficient planes for both the commercial and defense markets. Although this strategy of technological leadership has provided Boeing with tremendous success, the company still faces significant hurdles from its customers in the commercial airline industry, from strict government regulation and declining defense spending, and from deep-pocketed competitors.

The Commercial Airline Industry

The commercial airline industry sets the pace for aircraft manufacturers. Airlines first gained this influence over manufacturers during the 1960s, a period that has been labeled the "Decade of Prosperity." This decade followed the introduction of the jet age in 1957 and brought great expansion to the airline industry: (1) Passenger travel increased from 56.3 million passengers to 158.4 million over the 10-year period; (2) American Airlines implemented their SABRE system to handle passenger reservations; (3) airlines began running shuttle services, while local services modernized their fleets; and (4) intrastate carriers emerged in states such as California and Texas.[3] These improvements led to dramatic growth for aircraft manufacturers.

The airline industry began to decline after 1970, as domestic passenger travel dropped, airlines posted losses, and the need for new planes fell. From 1974 to 1983, the industry experienced "stagflation." This situation was further complicated by the Airline Deregulation Act, which President Carter signed in 1978, leading to industry-wide price wars. Deregulation also led to the entry of many new players into the airline industry, most of which either failed, filed for bankruptcy, or merged, as the industry suffered losses nearing $1.2 billion. American, Delta, and United Airlines surfaced as the three major long-term survivors. The lower margins faced by these airlines forced aircraft manufacturers, such as Boeing, to concentrate on improving aircraft operating efficiency.

The 1990s brought new challenges to both the airline and aircraft industries. Passenger miles again increased, while revenue per mile began to fall. Airlines quickly cut orders for new aircraft and refurbished older models instead, in an effort to cut costs and reverse this trend. They also demanded that aircraft manufacturers help them reduce purchase and upkeep costs on new planes.

This pressure to cut costs forced aircraft manufacturers to reevaluate their own development programs. As a result, manufacturers looked to their suppliers to cut costs and began to move some operations to countries with lower costs of labor. One area that was particularly attractive was Asia. Besides its cheap labor pool, demand was also emerging there for an 80- to 100-seat airplane. Many

Asian countries, however, were demanding joint production facilities in exchange for market entrance. They used this requirement as a bargaining tool to stimulate competition between manufacturers. The technology transfer that would occur through such an alliance worried manufacturers and their employees. They feared that joint assembly would open the door for smaller, state-owned producers, as well as manufacturers of large turboprop-driven aircraft, like Saab and Bombardier, to enter the market for jet aircraft. Continued downsizing of the defense industry during the mid-1990s raised the additional possibility that government contractors would also seek new markets in the commercial aircraft industry.

Despite these concerns, aircraft manufacturers expected continued long-term growth. They pinned their hopes on industry-wide forecasts, such as one 20-year forecast released in 1995, which projected airline passenger travel to expand at an average annual rate of 5.0 percent and new-aircraft sales to reach $1 trillion by 2014.[4] These predictions were based on (1) continued growth in passenger traffic, (2) aging fleets in need of replacement, and (3) a return to profitability by the airline industry as a whole.[5]

Boeing and its competitors knew that they would need faster, more efficient airplanes in order to capitalize on any future growth. With the industry already committed to the burgeoning Asian market, however, few competitors had the resources to spare on new-plane development. As a result, companies began collaborating on several models. Boeing and Airbus Industrie, for example, teamed up to research and build a 600- to 800-seat airplane. Manufacturers also began talks with the National Aeronautics and Space Administration, in order to determine the feasibility of a second-generation supersonic transport to succeed the Concorde already in passenger service with British Airways and Air France. The success of these projects hinged not only on degree of cooperation between companies, but also on the amount of support that those companies received from their local governments.

Government Regulation of the Industry

The U.S. government has always been a key player in the aircraft industry. It began to lay the economic foundations for the airlines during the mid-1920s. In 1925, Congress passed the Air Mail (Kelly) Act, which gave the aircraft industry a boost through airmail subsidies. The Air Commerce Act of 1926 gave the Secretary of Commerce the power to designate and establish airways, license pilots and aircraft, and investigate accidents.[6]

One of the most important pieces of legislation for the aircraft industry was the Federal Aviation Act of 1958, which created the Federal Aviation Agency (FAA) to promote airspace safety control procedures.[7] Today, the FAA is one of the most important players in the aircraft industry, enforcing safety standards and regulations, conducting inspections, investigating accidents, and making recommendations to prevent accidents from occurring. The agency is so powerful that it can order entire fleets of planes to remain on the ground, as it did in late 1994 after an American Eagle ATR-90 crashed on approach to Raleigh/Durham International Airport in North Carolina. ATR-90s around the country were taken out of service until the plane's manufacturer, Avions de Transport Regional (ATR) of France, could ensure that the crash was not the result of a design flaw.

Europe's counterpart to the FAA is the Joint Aviation Authority, or JAA. The FAA and JAA have unified their standards, so that a plane certified by one agency will also be certified by the other. The first aircraft to win joint certification was the Airbus A-330, followed by Boeing's 777 in April 1995.[8] Governmental actions and regulations, whether in the United States or Europe, impact Boeing in two different fields: the commercial plane industry and the defense and space industry.

■ Commercial Plane Industry

Every commercial plane in flight is required to meet current FAA standards. This poses quite a challenge for manufacturers like Boeing. A recent example of this is the mitigation of jet aircraft noise, commonly known as Stage 2 Phase-Out, which was federally legislated by the Airport Noise and Capacity Act of 1990. The FAA began enforcing this act in January 1994. Boeing and other plane manufacturers subsequently reduced engine noise on their planes coming off the production line, but planes already in service were also affected. Domestic carriers and even air cargo carriers were forced to buy new planes, reengineer existing ones, or install them with hush kits to meet phase-out standards.[9] Another important FAA regulation mandated the installment of new digital data recorders on Boeing's 737-series aircraft before December 31, 1995. U.S. airlines operating the 737 considered this schedule unattainable and feared that a large amount of aircraft would be out of service during 1996.[10]

The U.S. government influenced the development of new commercial planes through the granting of subsidies to aircraft manufacturers. Thus, the success of any new design often depended on government acceptance. The second-generation supersonic transport plane (STT) illustrated how much control the government had. Boeing actually built a prototype for the first STT, which was capable of speeds approaching 1,600 mph, but never produced it because the government refused to subsidize the project.[11]

Governments can also be a source of comparative advantage. Twenty-five years ago, Congress voted to end all federal funding for passenger airplanes. Development costs for Airbus Industrie, on the other hand, continue to be subsidized by European governments. In 1992, the U.S. government worked with the European Community to limit this advantage through the General Agreement on Tariffs and Trade (GATT). As a result, direct subsidies from European governments were limited to 33 percent and government production loans and subsidized sales agreements were prohibited.[12] However, while becoming less direct, there remains a strong government influence.

■ Defense and Space Industry

Throughout the history of the defense and space business, the U.S. government has been Boeing's major customer. Boeing has designed and sold aircraft to the U.S. military establishment since before World War I. Currently Boeing has a share in two important military programs: the F-22 Advanced Tactical Fighter for the U.S. Air Force and the V-22 tilt-rotor Osprey for the Marine Corps. A third project, the Comanche helicopter for the Army, had its maiden flight on January 4, 1996. In addition, the Pentagon is planning to modernize its airlift fleet, by replacing the old C-17 and C-141 transports and KC-135 tankers currently in service. Boeing is trying to convince military brass that the most cost-efficient replacement option for the C-141 and KC-135 includes the company's 767ER (extended range) model.[13] Boeing is also NASA's prime

Exhibit 1   Boeing Company's Product Segment

Commercial Transport

737	Short to medium-range two-engine jet; 100 to 168 seats
747	Long-range four-engine jet; 420 to 566 seats
757	Medium-range two-engine jet; 185 to 230 seats
767	Medium- to long-range two-engine jet; 181 to 325 seats
777	Long-range two-engine jet; 300 to 440 seats

Defense and Space Products

Avenger air defense systems

B-2 bomber

Communications and reconnaissance equipment

Computer services

E-3 Airbone Warning and Control System (AWACS)

F-22 fighter program

Inertial upper stage (IUS) booster rockets for the space shuttle and Titan rockets

Living and work quarters for the Space Station Freedom

Minuteman ICBM engineering support, maintenance, and updating services

V-22 Osprey Tiltrotor aircraft

Source: *Hoover's Handbook of World Business 1995–1996.*

contractor for the international space station. The company has completed the exterior structure of a pressurized module, which will allow the space shuttle to dock to any future space station (see Boeing Company product segment data in Exhibit 1).[14]

Defense contracts play an important role in the company's sales, but this industry is currently shrinking, and it is predicted to remain small in the future. Downturns in the defense industry and spending cutbacks have already forced the company to begin a large-scale downsizing. This represents another challenge for Boeing, since only a few financially and technologically strong companies are expected to survive. As a result, Boeing is trying to increase its sales to foreign nations. Japan, for example, recently purchased two of the company's 767 AWACS (airborne warning and control system) planes. Japan's army is also studying plans to enhance its airlift capabilities, which may lead to sales of Boeing's CH-47J heavy-lift helicopter to the country. Additionally, Turkey agreed to buy four KC-135 tanker planes, a military version of Boeing's 707 design.

Although sales of the company's aircraft products and services declined over the last two years, Defense and Space segment revenues have actually increased (see Exhibit 2). Revenues for this segment reached $4.7 billion in 1994, compared with $4.4 billion in 1993 and $5.4 billion in 1992. The Defense and Space segment accounted for 22, 12, and 19 percent of total operating revenues for 1994, 1993, and 1992, respectively. Space station-related work was the major contributor to higher sales in 1994. The company's business is broadly diversified, however, and no program accounted for more than 20 percent of its total 1992, 1993, or 1994 defense and space segment revenues. Despite its key position on several defense programs, Boeing was only the eleventh largest U.S. defense contractor in terms of sales. Its two major competitors, McDonnell Douglas and Lockheed, ranked first and second, respectively.[15]

Exhibit 2   Boeing Company's Product Segment Data

| | 1994 | | | | 1993 | | | |
| | Sales | | Operating Income | | Sales | | Operating Income | |
	$ mil.	% of Total	$ mil.	% of Total	$ mil.	% of Total	$ mil.	% of Total
Commercial aircraft	16.851	77	1.022	67	20.568	81	1.646	88
Defense and space	4.742	22	0.303	20	4.407	17	0.219	12
Other industries	0.331	2	0.2	13	0.463	2	0.016	1
Total	21.924	100	1.525	100	25.438	100	1.881	100

Source: The Boeing Company Form 10-K for the year ended December 31, 1994.

Exhibit 3   Commercial Jet Airplane Producers

	1990[a]	1992[b]	1995[c]
1. Boeing	0.62	0.586	0.697
2. McDonnell Douglas	0.15	0.087	0.099
3. Airbus Industries	0.21	0.327	0.148
4. Others	0.02	0	0.056

[a]Ranked by percent of new order for commercial jets in 1990. Sources: Industrial Distribution December 1991, p. 25.

[b]Market shares are shown in percent. Sources: Investext, Thomson Financial Network, February 4, 1993, from Shearson Lehman Brothers Inc.

[c]Ranked by percent of new order for commercial jets in 1995. Sources: The Boeing Company Press Release, January 4, 1996.

Major Competitors

The market for commercial jet aircraft is dominated by three key players: Boeing, McDonnell Douglas, and Airbus Industrie. Together, these three producers hold over 98 percent of the worldwide market for new jetliners (see Exhibit 3). Their planes accounted for 8,565 of the 10,843 jets (79 percent) in service during 1993 (see Exhibit 4). This dominance is expected to continue; 1,278 of the 1,575 planes on order at the end of 1993 (or 81 percent) were contracted to these manufacturers. Between 1990 and 1992, Airbus Industrie saw its share of this market jump from 21 to 33 percent. Much of this gain came at the expense of Boeing and McDonnell Douglas.

McDonnell Douglas Corporation

McDonnell Douglas has been producing aircraft in the United States since the early 1920s. In that time, it has come to offer a variety of products, ranging from helicopters, missiles, aircraft, and military navigation systems to commercial jet aircraft for the airline industry.[16]

Exhibit 4 World Airliner Fleet		
	Aircraft in Service	On Order Year-End
Jets	*1993*	*1993*
1. Boeing	5300	901
2. McDonnell Douglas	2288	134
3. Lockheed	193	0
4. Other U.S.	35	0
5. Canadair	13	57
6. Airbus	977	243
7. Other European	2037	240
Total jets	10843	1575
Other Aircraft		
Turboprops	3938	163
Piston engines	521	0
Helicopters	59	0
Other	19	0
Total other aircraft	4535	163
Total aircraft	15378	1738

Source: *Hoover's Handbook of World Business 1995–1996.*

McDonnell Douglas depends on the U.S. government for the majority of its operating revenues. (Exhibit 5 shows the percentage of revenues for different segments of the company.) Recent cutbacks in defense spending and increased competition, however, have reduced the demand for its products. The government's cancellation of the $4.8 billion A-12 Stealth attack plane was also a major setback. McDonnell Douglas has been able to withstand these blows through its economies of scale and scope. And even though the industry is in a downturn, the company continues to dominate the defense sector in the United States. Its redesigned C-17 transport plane is one example of this. During November 1995, the Department of Defense ordered 80 new C-17s from the company, a deal valued at about $18 billion. This order dealt a huge blow to Boeing, who had hoped to sell the Air Force at least some converted 747-400F cargo planes. It also helped McDonnell Douglas pave the way for potential sales to foreign governments and perhaps even to large commercial users.[17]

The commercial aircraft market has provided McDonnell Douglas with just as many ups and downs. During the 1960s and 1970s, McDonnell Douglas developed and produced two major airframes that eventually became the backbone of its fleet. These planes were the short-range DC-9 and the medium to long-range DC-10. Both planes were well built and highly respected, leading to strong sales for the company. After the late 1970s to the present, though, this sector of the company came under attack from increased competition and decreased demand. Companies such as Airbus, which originally targeted the DC-9, have continued to eat away at McDonnell's market share. Its DC-10 program faced strong competition from another manufacturer, Lockheed and its L-1011. This competition cost the company precious profitability.[18]

Exhibit 5   McDonnell Douglas Corporation's Product Segment Data

| | 1993 | | | | 1994 | | | |
| | Sales | | Operating Income | | Sales | | Operating Income | |
	$ mil.	% of Total	$ mil.	% of Total	$ mil.	% of Total	$ mil.	% of Total
Military aircraft	6,852	47	83	17	7,804	59.29	708	66.35
Commercial aircraft	4,760	33	40	8	3,155	23.97	47	4.40
Missiles, space & electronic systems	2,575	18	338	69	1,877	14.26	262	24.55
Financial services & other	287	2	31	6	326	2.48	50	4.69
Adjustments	13	—	—	—	—	—	—	—
Total	14,487	100	492	100	13,162	100	1,067	100

Source: McDonnell Douglas Corporations Form 10-K report in 1995.

In the late 1970s, McDonnell Douglas decided it was time for new development. With little capital to start an extensive development program, management decided to build on the technologies of its existing DC-9 to develop the all-new MD-80. This model was a short-to-medium-haul aircraft that was configurable to meet a wide variety of passenger handling requirements. The MD-80 quickly became the company's most popular aircraft. At this time, McDonnell Douglas also proposed its MD-11 design, which was meant to be an improvement of the DC-10. During development, orders poured in for the new design. Unfortunately, with the delivery of the first new planes came many problems. American Airlines, who was McDonnell's largest customer at the time, experienced several complications. Besides being forced to accept deliveries months behind schedule, American realized that the plane was not capable of meeting its promised maximum range when filled to capacity. These problems infuriated customers and lowered their confidence in McDonnell Douglas. During early 1995, McDonnell Douglas announced that it was considering scaling back or even halting the plane's production for 1996, due to a lack of orders.[19]

As a result of these problems, McDonnell Douglas decided that it needed to look globally for answers. As a result, the company began discussions with Airbus Industrie to form a strategic alliance in order to better combat Boeing. This proposal involved production of McDonnell Douglas aircraft in Europe with the use of Airbus facilities. In return, Airbus airframes would be produced in California at McDonnell's facilities. The two companies also proposed the production of the "McAirbus," a 500-seat combination of an MD-11 fuselage with an A-330 wing. This plane would be the first major competitor to enter the market against Boeing's 747. Fortunately for Boeing, the two companies could not decide on who would produce the cockpit and discussions of an alliance quickly dissolved.

A merger with Boeing was also a strong possibility. Such a combination would shake markets worldwide. With Boeing's dominance in commercial aircraft and McDonnell Douglas's leading position in sales of military airplanes, the combined company would completely redefine the buying and selling of almost every type of aircraft. It would also distract European competitors, such as Airbus

Industrie, which had recently increased its market share at McDonnell's expense. Both companies seriously explored the possibilities. Although Boeing was pushing for an outright merger, many industry insiders felt that a major asset exchange was more likely.[20]

Airbus Industrie

Airbus Industrie was formed in 1970 as a Groupement d'Interet Economique (GIE). A GIE is a French-based entity in which a group of separate companies pool their interests and activities for mutual benefit and profit. The main players in the Airbus consortium are France's Aerospatiale, Germany's Daimler-Benz Aerospace, British Aerospace, and Spain's CASA. The purpose of this consortium was to create a strong European presence in the aerospace industry.[21]

In the early days of Airbus, the partners focused almost exclusively on the medium-range aircraft market, since most worldwide flights at that time were less than 2,500 miles in length. More recently, Airbus has come to realize the importance of having a range of aircraft available for its customers. For this reason, Airbus has been expanding its product offering to include short-range and longer range aircraft. This decision was prompted by the emergence of many new low-cost, low-capacity airlines in the United States and Europe. These airlines require smaller seating capacities and lower costs. This, along with the use of the hub and spoke system by most major airlines, gave rise to the need for short-haul, high-efficiency aircraft. Airbus also reacted to a predicted rise in intercontinental air travel. To meet this demand, the company began developing its A-330 and A-340, which compete with the MD-11 and Boeing's 747.[22]

Airbus recently started a campaign to attack McDonnell Douglas and Boeing on another front. In mid-1995, the company announced a plan to develop military planes, including the Future Large Aircraft (FLA). This plane, and others like it, would be competing directly against American-produced military aircraft.[23]

Airbus has been very successful in identifying the current and future needs of its customers. Its success, though, is not all due to great planning and luck. One of the company's greatest assets has been its huge investment in R&D and the resulting technological advances. These expenditures have placed little strain on Airbus' budget, since 70 to 90 percent of all R&D costs before 1992 were financed by the participating nations' governments. Even with GATT's limitations, Airbus retains a strong advantage: None of its major competitors can expect this same level of governmental assistance.[24]

Lockheed Martin

Although it is not currently a major player in the commercial sector, Lockheed has demonstrated that it is capable of competing with Boeing for the airlines' business.[25] Its recent merger with Martin Marietta provides additional resources that may eventually be targeted at the commercial aircraft industry.

Other Sources of Competition

Other defense contractors may present additional sources of competition, since many of them are experienced in the production of large aircraft. Shrinking demand in the defense sector may push some of these manufacturers to seek new sources of revenue in the market for commercial aircraft.

Manufacturers of turboprop-driven aircraft are also expected to change the shape of the industry, even though they do not compete directly with jet aircraft. Turboprops serve mostly regional airlines, with plane sizes approaching a 70-seat capacity. Growth in this sector is expected to outstrip that of the major airlines in the key North American and European markets over the next decade.[26] State-run Industri Pesawat Terbang Nusantara of Indonesia, for example, recently introduced its N250 prototype aircraft, which it hopes will fill an expected demand of 3,300 aircraft in the over-45-seat turboprop market through 2012.[27] Bombardier has launched production of its 70-seat de Havilland Dash 8 Series 400 aircraft and is likely to go ahead with a similarly sized version of its Canadair Regional Jet model. Other manufacturers, such as Fokker, ATR, and Saab, are taking advantage of new technologies that improve both the safety and comfort of turboprops to target long-term growth in the industry. Russia's Aviastar is another potential player.[28]

Corporate Strategy

Boeing has dealt with these external factors by becoming an early-mover in the aircraft manufacturing industry. As a result, Boeing has been able to almost continuously upgrade its customers' fleets with larger, more efficient, technologically advanced airplanes. This strategy has helped the company achieve a high level of customer satisfaction among the commercial airlines. Boeing's correspondingly strong safety record has allowed it to build a close working relationship with the FAA, which helps minimize delays in obtaining flight approvals for its new project development programs. Together, these capabilities have given Boeing a reputation for high-quality manufacturing and a dominant market position in the industry.

Boeing employees see their manufacturing plants as laboratories for the latest technologies. This mindset grew out of a statement issued by William Boeing before he left the company in 1934:

> Our job is to keep everlastingly at research and experimentation, to adapt our laboratories to production as soon as possible, and to let no new improvement in flying and flying equipment pass us by.

This challenge was met early on through vertical integration. Boeing manufactured its own aircraft, supplied them with engines built by its Pratt & Whitney subsidiary, and flew them through its United Air Lines division. The Air Mail Act of 1934 broke up the divisions, leaving the company to concentrate solely on aircraft production.[29]

Boeing's continued focus on manufacturing and know-how led the company to develop a capability in applied technology. The company maintained an ongoing process to develop new technologies in areas such as aircraft structures, flight systems, and aerodynamics. Breakthroughs were incorporated into its products only if Boeing's engineers could provide positive answers to three questions: (1) What is its ultimate value to the customer? (2) Is it an acceptable technological risk? (3) Can it be incorporated within schedule and cost? Boeing often worked with its suppliers and customers in assessing new technologies and soliciting their ideas for additional developments.[30]

Management capitalized on this strength in applied technology by diversifying into space systems, helicopters, and military airplanes, building a portfolio of core competencies in high-quality manufacturing. Today, the Boeing Company consists of its Commercial Airplane Group, Defense & Space Group, and a separate Information & Support Services division. The Commercial Airplane Group is the company's most visible business, employing nearly 70,000 employees, primarily in the Puget Sound area of Washington State. This group has accounted for more than 7,700 of the roughly 13,000 commercial jets produced since the jet age began.[31]

Manufacturing Strategy

In the Commercial Airplane Group, the development process for a new airplane requires a lengthy, multibillion dollar investment. Risks, as well as rewards, are considerable. Boeing has moved to share these risks by partnering with outside contractors, who develop and build the components that Boeing later assembles. Over 50 percent of the parts that make up an airplane are typically outsourced; the primary exceptions are the nose section and wings, which Boeing continues to build in-house. This risk sharing strategy grew out of the near bankruptcy that followed Boeing's introduction of the 747, the industry's first widebody jet, in 1969. At that time, management problems, declining productivity, steep development costs, engine problems, and cutbacks in commercial and government orders led to a severe cash crunch, nearly crippling the company.[32] Although the ultimate success of the 747 allowed Boeing to recover, additional manufacturing obstacles remain. For each new development program, Boeing faces up-front development costs approaching $1.5 to $2 billion, lead times of up to four years, uncertain learning curves, and the qualification and management of thousands of subcontractors.

Competitive pricing from McDonnell Douglas and Airbus Industrie makes it harder for Boeing to recoup this investment. During October 1995, for example, ValueJet Airlines awarded an order for fifty 100-seat jets with a range of up to 1,500 miles to McDonnell Douglas for its MD-95 model, at a price below $19 million per plane. This compared with a price of $22 million, which Scandinavian Airlines paid for Boeing's similarly-sized 737 model only six months earlier. Boeing normally listed this model at $35 million.[33]

Boeing has attempted to deal with these problems through its "family of planes" concept, which allows it to position its products across the entire commercial aircraft market while keeping manufacturing costs low. This strategy involves creating each new generation of aircraft with several variations in mind: standard, long-range, freighter, cargo/passenger convertible, and/or stretched fuselage. By using this approach, Boeing has been able to install a more efficient design and development process, utilize a common assembly line, and continue moving down the learning curve while still meeting market demand. The family of planes concept has also led to a rapid accumulation of experience and knowledge. Boeing's families currently offer a complete product line, with anywhere from 100 to 600 seats and enough payload, range, and operating flexibility to fill every market need.[34]

737 Family

Other competing jet transports were well established in the short-haul market by the time the first 737 rolled out in 1967. The 737, however, quickly earned respect for its rugged dependability in all types of operations, even on remote gravel airstrips. Convertible versions could be quickly reconfigured to carry people, cargo, or both. Today, the 737 family consists of three sizes of virtually the same airplane, seating from 100 to 168 passengers. Because all three models share the same cockpit, any flight crew trained on one model can fly all three.

■ 747 Family

During the 1960s, Boeing anticipated a huge increase in air traffic growth. The company developed the 747 "Jumbo Jet" in order to meet this expected passenger demand. Instantly recognized by passengers around the world, the 747 is now in a class by itself. Seating from 420 to nearly 570 passengers, the 747 continues to revolutionize air travel with economics and performance that make intercontinental transportation affordable. Passenger comfort surveys consistently rate the 747 higher than any other airplane. Its shape, which places the flight deck above the passenger cabin to allow for container loading through the nose section, also makes it popular for freighter service.

■ 757/767 Family

The 757/767 is the only family to offer both standard and widebody models sharing a common flight crew rating. The 757, which was introduced in 1982, is unsurpassed in fuel efficiency and can climb faster and fly higher than any other single-aisle twin-engine jet. Its performance allows it to serve airports limited by runway length, high altitude, hot weather, and weight restrictions. Shippers worldwide rely on the 757 to deliver both large container shipments and overnight express packages. The double-aisle twin-engine 767, which was developed at the same time as the 757, shares common advances in propulsion, aerodynamics, avionics, and materials. Although its design targets transcontinental markets, its operating efficiency allows it to serve domestic routes as well. This family offers capacities ranging from 180 to 325 seats.

■ 777 Family

The 777, which is the world's largest twin-engine jet, is Boeing's first all-new model in more than a decade. It represents other firsts as well, being the company's first "fly-by-wire" jet, in which parts are controlled electronically with no cable connections, and the first plane to be designed entirely on computer. For markets requiring between 300 and 440 seats, the 777 family offers the most efficient solution at any range with virtually the same airplane. The plane made its maiden commercial voyage in June 1995.

■ Possible Additions to the Family

Boeing's commercial customers have expressed interest in many potential airplanes, including these types[35]:

- an airplane smaller than the 737, seating 80 to 100 passengers,
- an airplane larger than today's 747 "Jumbo Jet,"
- a capable and cost-effective supersonic jetliner, and
- continued support and new derivatives of its existing models.

Any new development that occurred in these areas would almost surely have to target the rapidly developing countries of Asia. Boeing's declining sales,

Exhibit 6	Boeing Company's Commercial Jet Transport Deliveries by Model			
	1995	**1994**	**1993**	**1992**
737	89	121	152	218
747	25	40	56	61
757	43	69	71	99
767	36	40	51	63
777	13	—	—	—
Total	260	270	330	441

Source: The Boeing Company Form 10-K for the year ended December 31, 1994.

however, may be hard pressed to support the development of any new models without the sacrifice of one or more of its existing families of planes. The prospect for joint overseas production might also raise labor issues in Boeing's domestic manufacturing facilities.

■ Recent Performance

Boeing's commercial jet transport deliveries for the years 1992, 1993, and 1994 are shown in Exhibit 6. The 737 family accounted for the majority of orders each year, although its share of total production has dropped recently. Total production has also declined, with only 270 planes completed in 1994 versus 441 in 1992. During 1996, Boeing plans additional production cuts. Expected deliveries per model are shown below.[36]

Plane Model	Estimated 1996 Production
737	66
757	42
767	42
747	30
777	30
Total	210

Exhibit 7 displays Boeing's geographical segment data. During the past five years, sales outside the United States accounted for more than 70 percent of total commercial aircraft sales; over 60 percent of the contractual backlog at the end of 1994 was with non–U.S. airlines. This moved Boeing into second place among U.S. exporters in terms of 1993 sales, after only General Motors (McDonnell Douglas and Lockheed ranked fourteenth and twentieth, respectively).[37] Access to global markets would continue to be extremely important to the company's future stability and the realization of its sales potential and long-term investments.

Exhibit 7 Boeing Company's Geographical Segment Data					
	1994 Sales		1993 Sales		1992 Sales	
	$ mil.	% of Total	$ mil.	% of Total	$ mil.	% of Total
US	10,800	49	10,822	43	12,698	42
ASIA	7,403	34	8,870	35	7,108	24
Europe	3,277	15	4,698	18	7,165	24
Oceania	877	4	635	2	1,911	6
Africa	135	1	264	1	430	1
Western Hemisphere	142	1	149	1	872	3
Total	21,924	100	25,438	100	30,184	100

Sources: The Boeing Company Form 10-K for the year ended December 31, 1994.

Despite its recent short-term production cuts, Boeing remained upbeat about its medium- and long-term prospects. The company was counting on process improvements, which were expected to provide shorter production cycle times, to help position itself for any upturn in demand.

Culture

Any process improvements needed by Boeing in order to survive a shrinking market would be delivered by its manufacturing operations. In this area, Boeing had built a distinct corporate identity through its heavy reliance on teamwork. Interfunctional cooperation was especially valued. Employees were expected to be both competent and capable of working as members of a team. This culture was woven into the company's product development programs, which require close cooperation among managers over a period of 5 to 10 years, often under intense time pressures and 60- to 70-hour workweeks. Once selected, teams were often granted considerable autonomy. A disciplined decision-making process, as well as detailed planning, and regular communication, however, were required to ensure success.[38]

Boeing's culture was weighted just as heavily on after-market service. The company had built long-term relationships with the airlines through credibility, commitment, and proven dedication to customer service. Anytime, anyplace that a Boeing plane broke down, for example, the company dispatched AOG (airplane-on-the-ground) teams, free of charge to the customer. If repairs were necessary, Boeing immediately dispatched the required spare parts, which it sold at only a modest markup.[39] Boeing also relied heavily on two-way communication with the airlines, in order to gauge the performance of its existing fleet of planes and to help it design new models. The 777, for example, incorporated more than 1,000 customer design ideas. Boeing was also recognized as the industry leader in promoting aviation safety, another extremely important area for the airlines. This focus on delivering value to the customer has led Boeing to maintain the industry's only full line of products and services.

As the year 2000 approaches, Boeing is having trouble balancing these two cultures. Its commitment to customer service encouraged its designers to focus on the increasing demand for a new 80- to 100-seat airplane. With the expected growth of regional aviation throughout much of the world, as many as 6,000 of these planes could be sold by 2020.[40] A large part of this market, however, would be derived from Asian carriers. Boeing, like its competitors, hoped to build these planes through partnerships with manufacturers in that region, in order to enhance its marketing efforts there and strengthen its relationships with foreign governments. These governments, after all, were potential buyers of the company's defense products. Additionally, lower labor costs in these countries would help Boeing meet the lower prices demanded by the airlines. Workers at Boeing's domestic facilities see this potential transfer of jobs overseas as a major threat. They also worry about the technology that these partnerships would provide to foreign aircraft manufacturers. These concerns threaten to weaken the company's internal culture of teamwork.

The Challenge of Change

Despite its past success, Boeing still lacked a strong competitor to benchmark against. As a result, the company had become the highest cost manufacturer in the industry. Part of its cost problems were derived from Boeing's lavish commitment to customer service. Additional cost problems resulted from the company's World War II era tracking system that linked manufacturing and engineering. This system utilized 800 different, incompatible computer systems to track the millions of parts that went into each airplane. The system also relied on separate drawings for each individual part. Design changes often required these drawings to be corrected manually, in order to keep customer identification codes accurate. Corrections sometimes tripled the time required for even a simple design change. Draftsmen spent over two years in training before they fully understood the system, and even then a third of their paperwork contained at least one error.[41]

High manufacturing defect rates were an additional problem. This rate averaged 52 defects per seat during 1993. Boeing estimated that it spent approximately $1 billion repairing these defects, almost as much as its corporate profit of $1.2 billion that year. The company set a target of 26 defects per seat by 1996, which represented roughly half of the 49 defects per seat averaged during 1994.[42]

Boeing also suffered from smaller rates of improvement in the design of its aircraft. The new 777, for example, which had a maximum cruising speed of 757 miles per hour, flew only marginally faster than the 707 did 40 years ago. New plane prices, on the other hand, had continued to rise. The new 777 model, which had a list price of up to $138 million, cost twice as much as its functional equivalent, a seven-year-old 747 that carried more passengers. Boeing was counting on the new plane's technology and efficiency to help it fill orders.[43] The 777, for example, was the first twin-engine airliner ever certified by the FAA at market introduction to fly for up to three hours over water (most new models required a trial period of several years before gaining approval). And 1998 versions of the plane were expected to require 40 percent less maintenance and burn a third less fuel than a comparably sized 747.

Boeing's overall operating revenues for 1994 fell to $21.9 billion, compared with $25.4 billion in 1993 and $30.2 billion for 1992 (see the income statement and balance sheet in Exhibits 8 and 9). The decline in revenues was due to

Exhibit 8   Boeing Company Income Statement

At December 31	1994	1993	1992	1991	1990	1989	1988
Net sales	21924000	25438000	30184000	29314000	27595000	20276000	16962000
COGS	16801000	19959000	24105000	23826000	23355000	17302000	14316000
Gross income	3981000	4454000	5118000	4662000	3562000	2347000	2079000
Depr. exp.	1142000	1025000	961000	826000	678000	627000	567000
Sell & admin. exp.	2830000	2763000	3078000	2708000	2032000	1766000	1631000
Total oper. exp.	20773000	23747000	28144000	27360000	26065000	19695000	16514000
Operating income	1151000	1691000	2040000	1954000	1530000	581000	448000
Non operating intr. income	122000	169000	230000	263000	448000	0	0
Extra-credit-pretax	0	0	0	0	0	347000	0
other inc/exp-net	0	0	0	0	0	0	378000
Interest expense	217000	139000	80000	57000	28000	24000	11000
Interest capitalized	87000	100000	66000	44000	22000	18000	5000
Pretax income	1143000	1821000	2256000	2204000	1972000	922000	820000
Income taxes	287000	577000	702000	637000	587000	247000	206000
Net inc. after income taxes	856000	1244000	1554000	1567000	1385000	675000	614000
Extra items	0	0	-1002000	0	0	298000	0
Net inc bef prev div	856000	1244000	552000	1567000	1385000	973000	614000
Net income	856000	1244000	1554000	1567000	1385000	675000	614000
Earnings per share ($)	2.51	3.66	4.57	4.56	4.01	1.96	1.79
Stock price-high ($)	47	44.75	54.63	53.00	61.88	41.27	30.08
stock price-low ($)	43.25	33.38	32.13	41.25	37.77	25.74	16.63
stock price-close ($)	47	43.25	40.13	47.75	45.38	39.6	26.97
P/E ratio	20	12	12	12	15	21	17
P/E low	17	9	7	9	9	13	9
Dividends per share ($)	1	1	1	1	0.95	0.78	0.69
Book value per share ($)	28.46	26.41	23.73	23.71	520.3	17.74	15.69
Employees	115,000	123,000	142,000	157,700	160,500	163,900	153,000

Source: Compact Disclosure Data Bank (1995)

Boeing's Company Vertical Commonsize							
Net sales	100	100	100	100	100	100	100
COGS	76.6	78.5	79.9	81.3	84.6	85.3	84.4
Gross income	18.2	17.5	17.0	15.9	12.9	11.6	12.3
Depr. exp.	5.2	4.0	3.2	2.8	2.5	3.1	3.3
Sell & admin. exp.	12.9	10.9	10.2	9.2	7.4	8.7	9.6
Total oper. exp.	94.8	93.4	93.2	93.3	94.5	97.1	97.4
Operating income	5.2	6.6	6.8	6.7	5.5	2.9	2.6
Non operating intr. income	0.6	0.7	0.8	0.9	1.6	0.0	0.0
Extra-credit-pretax	0.0	0.0	0.0	0.0	0.0	1.7	0.0
other inc/exp-net	0.0	0.0	0.0	0.0	0.0	0.0	2.2
Interest expense	1.0	0.5	0.3	0.2	0.1	0.1	0.1
Interest capitalized	0.4	0.4	0.2	0.2	0.1	0.1	0.0
Pretax income	5.2	7.2	7.5	7.5	7.1	4.5	4.8
Income taxes	1.3	2.3	2.3	2.2	2.1	1.2	1.2
Net inc bef income taxes	3.9	4.9	5.1	5.3	5.0	3.3	3.6
Extra items	0.0	0.0	-3.3	0.0	0.0	1.5	0.0
Net inc bef prev div	3.9	4.9	1.8	5.3	5.0	4.8	3.6
Net income	3.9	4.9	5.1	5.3	5.0	3.3	3.6

Source: Compact Disclosure Data Bank (1995)

Exhibit 9   Boeing Company Balance Sheet (000's)

At December 31	1994	1993	1992	1991	1990	1989	1988
Assets							
Current Assets							
Cash & equivalents	2643000	3108000	3614000	3453000	3326000	1863000	3963000
Net receivable	1914000	1833000	1657000	2099000	2057000	1809000	1651000
Raw materials	0	0	0	1145000	0	0	0
Finished goods	11269000	10485000	11073000	12597000	0	0	0
Prog. pymnts & oth	−6290000	−7051000	−8372000	−10465000	0	0	0
Inventories	4979000	3434000	2701000	3277000	3332000	4942000	2947000
Other current assets	878000	800000	115000	0	55000	46000	0
Total current asset	10414000	9175000	8087000	8829000	8770000	8660000	8561000
Other investments	61000	184000	211000	242000	253000	0	0
Long term receivables	3071000	2959000	2066000	567000	490000	0	0
Net PP&E	6802000	7088000	6724000	6146000	5078000	3481000	2703000
Accum depreciation	6786000	6144000	5569000	5196000	4633000	4109000	3682000
Deferred charges	1115000	0	0	0	0	0	0
Other tangible assets	0	981000	847000	0	0	0	0
Other assets	1115000	981000	847000	0	0	1137000	1344000
TOTAL assets	21463000	20387000	17935000	15784000	14591000	13278000	12608000
Liabilities and Stockholder's Equity							
Current Liabilities							
Account payable	3207000	2731000	2869000	2335000	2586000	4932000	0
St debt & current LTD	6000	17000	21000	4000	4000	5000	7000
Accr. payroll	1062000	1005000	997000	1554000	1405000	0	0
Inc. taxes payable	281000	434000	232000	139000	479000	291000	0
Other curr. liabil.	2271000	2344000	2021000	2244000	2658000	1445000	6698000
Total Cur. Liab.	6827000	6531000	6140000	6276000	7132000	6673000	6705000
Long term debt	2603000	2613000	1772000	1313000	311000	275000	251000
Defered taxes	51000	−63000	−327000	102000	161000	199000	0
Other liabilities	2282000	2148000	2004000	0	14000	0	248000
Total liabilities	11763000	11229000	9589000	7691000	7618000	7147000	7204000
Common stock	1746000	1746000	1746000	1746000	2327000	0	0
Capital surplus	586000	413000	418000	583000	0	0	0
Retained earnings	7696000	7355000	6451000	6064000	4840000	0	0
Treasury stock	328000	356000	384000	300000	194000	0	0
Shareholder's equity	9700000	9158000	8231000	8093000	6973000	6131000	5404000
Total Liab. & Equity	21463000	20387000	17935000	15784000	14591000	13278000	12608000

worldwide economic conditions and airline industry overcapacity, which resulted in fewer airplane deliveries (see Exhibit 10 for annual growth rates). Throughout this period, Boeing maintained a market share of approximately 60 percent in terms of sales value.

In addition to these internal problems, Boeing also faced obstacles in the airline industry. Frequent fare wars there contributed to weaker financial

Exhibit 10 Growth Rate Annual							
	1994	1993	1992	1991	1990	1989	1988
Net sales growth	−13.81	−15.72	2.97	6.23	36.1	19.54	10.47
Operating growth	−31.93	−17.11	4.4	27.71	163.34	29.69	114.35
Net inc grwth	−31.19	125.36	−64.77	13.14	42.34	58.47	27.92
Tot assets growth	5.28	13.67	13.63	8.18	9.89	5.31	0.33
Equity growth	5.92	11.26	1.71	16.06	13.73	13.45	8.36
Tot employment grwth	−8.37	−15.55	−4.56	−2.69	0.5	8.08	8.23
Eps. growth	−31.42	−19.91	0.22	13.72	104.59	9.7	29.68
Div/share growth	0	0	0	−16.67	54.29	12.9	10.71
Book vl/shr grwth	−13.8	36.14	2.26	16.84	14.48	13.87	7.8
Net margin growth	−20.16	167.41	−65.79	6.51	4.59	32.57	15.8
Reinvstmntrate/share	4.57	10.97	15.05	17.54	15.85	7.59	7.6
Reinvstment rate/tot	5.63	10.98	2.62	17.55	17.24	13.03	7.56

Source: Compact Disclosure Data Bank (1995)

positions among the airlines, forcing them to consider refurbishing their existing planes rather than buying new ones. Along with the longer-than-expected life of many models, this contributed to a surplus of used airplanes in the market. Decreased defense spending, meanwhile, increased the company's reliance on its commercial aircraft business.

CEO Shrontz cited the challenge of competing with the used airplane as a rallying call to his employees, but he realized that the saturation of the U.S. market and the possible emergence of new aircraft manufacturers would continue to change the competitive environment after he was gone. Shrontz was determined to maintain Boeing's commitment to customer satisfaction, but what advice could he give to Condit? Which new family of planes should be developed? Any new development that did occur would surely have to target the rapidly developing countries of Asia. The transfer of jobs to these countries, however, would not sit well with Boeing's unionized labor force. In addition, Boeing's declining sales would not allow the development of a new model without the sacrifice of one or more of its existing families of planes. The company's manufacturing inefficiencies also required full-time attention at the corporate level. Shrontz wondered in what direction Condit would take the company after his departure.

Notes

1. Bill Gunston, 1993, *World Encyclopedia of Aircraft Manufacturers* (Annapolis, Md.: Naval Institute Press), 51.
2. *The Boeing Company home page,* http://www.boeing.com.
3. William M. Leary (ed.), 1992, *The Airline Industry, Encyclopedia of American Business History and Biography* (New York: Facts on File), xxiii–xxiv.
4. The Boeing Company, 1994, 10K Report, 25.
5. Pamela Sebastian, 1995, Business bulletin: A special background report on trends in industry and finance, *Wall Street Journal*, June 22, A1.
6. Leary, *The Airline Industry.*
7. Ibid.
8. Paul Proctor, 1994, Work accelerates on joint certification, *Aviation Week and Space Technology* June 20, 49.
9. Debra Skyes, 1994, Carriers turn down the volume of aircraft noise, *Global Trade and Transportation*, July, 30.

10. Edward H. Phillips, 1995, US airlines snub DFDR proposals, *Aviation Week and Space Technology*, May 1, 33.

11. Pamela S. Zurer, 1995, NASA cultivating basic technology for supersonic passenger aircraft, *Chemical and Engineering News*, April 24, 10–16.

12. The Boeing Company, 10K Report.

13. David A. Fulghum, 1994, USAF chief favors C-17s As C-141s retire early, *Aviation Week and Space Technology*, December 12, 20.

14. Boeing completes exterior of first station module, *Aviation Week and Space Technology*, April 10, 1995, 68.

15. *Hoover's Handbook of World Business 1995–1996*, (Austin, TX: The Reference Press), 98.

16. Jeff Cole, 1993, McDonnell finds it ever harder to cope . . ., *Wall Street Journal*, January 28, A1.

17. Jeff Cole, 1995, C-17 contract is door-opener for McDonnell, *Wall Street Journal*, November 6, A3.

18. *Douglas Aircraft Company home page*, http://www.dac.mdc.com.

19. Jeff Cole, 1995, McDonnell may halt MD-11 production. . ., *Wall Street Journal*, February 6, A3.

20. Jeff Cole, and Stephen Lipin, 1995, Boeing and McDonnell Douglas discuss merger of aircraft giants, *Wall Street Journal*, November 16, A3.

21. Christopher Bartlett and Ghoshal Sumantra, 1992, *Transnational Management* (Homewood, Ill.: Irwin), 255–272.

22. Michael Westlake, 1995, Your order, please, *Far Eastern Economic Review*, August 17, 70.

23. Howard Banks, 1995, Superjumbo, *Forbes*, October 24, 180–186.

24. Edward Heath, 1995, A triumph for European unity—birds of prey, *Management Today*, May, 33.

25. *Lockheed Martin home page*, http://www.lockheed.com.

26. Carole A. Shifrin, and Pierre Sparaco, 1995, Bombardier launches Dash 8-400, plans stretched regional jet, *Aviation Week & Space Technology*, June 19, 32–34.

27. Michael Mackey, 1995, IPTN N250 rolls out, *Air Transport World*, January, 70.

28. Brian Coleman, 1993, Russia's Aviastar intends. . ., *Wall Street Journal*, January 27, A12.

29. David A. Garvin, Lee J. Field, and Janet Simpson, 1988, The Boeing 767: From concept to production, Harvard Business School case 668-040, 377.

30. Ibid., 381.

31. *The Boeing Company home page*, http://www.boeing.com.

32. Garvin et al. The Boeing, 767, 378.

33. Howard Banks, 1995, Profitless prosperity, *Forbes*, November 6, 64.

34. *The Boeing Company home page*, http://www.boeing.com/value/homepage.html.

35. Ibid.

36. *The Boeing Company home page*, http://www.boeing.com/news.releases.html.

37. *Hoover's Handbook of World Business*, 98.

38. Garvin et al. The Boeing, 767, 378.

39. Alex Taylor, III, 1995, Boeing—sleepy in Seattle, *Fortune*, August 7, 94.

40. Banks, 1995, Profitless prosperity, 65.

41. Taylor, Boeing—sleepy in Seattle, 96.

42. Ibid.

43. Ibid.

■ CASE 8 Cadbury Schweppes PLC and Dr Pepper/7UP Corporation

Sherman Corbett
Erik Eichinger
Kathy Emerson
Dimitri Filippov
Mike Kuvlesky
Chris Petro

■ http://www.drpep.com

In the spring of 1995, Cadbury Schweppes PLC secured a controlling interest of Dr Pepper, its largest acquisition ever. Cadbury, the British confectionery company, had achieved the coveted third-place position in the U.S. soft drink market, becoming a formidable threat to Coca-Cola and PepsiCo. Its ownership in Dr Pepper has fluctuated dramatically in a seven-year period. After holding a 34.4 percent interest in 1986 and dropping to a 5.7 percent stake just two years later, in October 1993, the vacillations ceased at 25.9 percent equity ownership.

Dr Pepper was an insignificant player in the international arena whose primary limitation was distribution reliance on external bottlers. Despite this firm's agile nature, its size, or lack thereof, had stood as the one impediment to full-scale global penetration. The large European "candy" company, which was desperately seeking a more significant presence in the largest soft drink market in the world, could have removed this limitation and helped this American company to new heights. However, there was more to consider than just what each company could do for the other.

The meshing of a highly bureaucratic, culturally segmented British confectionery company with an entrepreneurial, internally trusting, and cohesive American soft drink firm presents both great challenges and opportunities for the new union. What will be the chemistry between these two proud and culturally diverse firms? Furthermore, Coke and Pepsi have long dominated the soft drink distribution facilities domestically and abroad. Their brands are among the most recognized in the world. Will Cadbury's new, stronger presence in the U.S. market pose a threat to these industry giants? How will Cadbury prepare for their strategic actions if confronted with competitive responses from Coca-Cola and PepsiCo? Last, after the transition period of this new marriage is over and many Dr Pepper executives leave, who will assume the leadership of Dr Pepper's

Case prepared under the direction of Professor Robert E. Hoskisson for class discussion purposes only.

operations? Will Cadbury's management allow Dr Pepper the freedom it has had in the past? These are critical issues that stakeholders in the newly formed company must consider. The historical evolution of these once separate entities frame the great challenge faced by its leaders of building a successful and strategically competitive corporation.

Dr Pepper/7UP[1]

Exhibit 1 Dr Pepper/7UP—Principal Brands, 1993

Dr Pepper
7UP
Diet Dr Pepper
Diet 7UP
Cherry 7UP
Diet Cherry 7UP
Welch's Grape
Welch's Strawberry
Welch's Fruit Punch

As of January 1995, Dr Pepper/7UP, was the industry's largest producer and the third largest maker and marketer of carbonated soft drinks in the United States. It was also the industry's fastest growing major soft drink enterprise that, for the past five years, had exceeded industry growth by 1.5 to 2 times. The principal business of the Dallas-based company was the manufacture of soft drink concentrates, extracts, and syrups that were sold to licensed bottlers (see Exhibit 1).

Dr Pepper was divided into five business units: Dr Pepper USA (40 percent of 1994 sales), 7UP USA (31 percent), Foodservice (20 percent), Welch's/IBC (8 percent), and International (1 percent). Sales in 1994 had increased 8.7 percent to $769 million from $707.4 million in 1993. Operating profit was up 11.2 percent to $203.6 million while operating cash flow increased 9.2 percent to $219.6 million. Net income was $67 million before an extraordinary charge of $11.2 million (see Exhibit 2 for 1992 and 1993 data).

Dr Pepper's Beverage History

In 1885, Charles Alderton, assistant to Dr. Wade B. Morrison, took a personal interest in carbonated water—an interest sparked by an opportunity to sell water from artesian wells as a health drink. In Dr. Morrison's absence, his assistant began combining flavors used in Morrison's Old Country Drug Store for medicine and fruit drinks with carbonated water. Eventually, he discovered a mixture he liked and began selling it to the store's customers. Dr Pepper, the first nationally distributed soft drink, was born.

A few months later, the small drugstore could no longer handle the 8,000 Waco, Texas, residents' demands for the product, so the company made its first distribution expansion under the name of the Artesian Manufacturing and Bottling Works. Sales soon outpaced growth, so the company moved to Dallas in 1923 in order to expand and distribute from a growing city. Dr Pepper then took on 50 licensed franchises in 1925 to meet the new demand.

During the next decade, Dr Pepper continued to respond to its customers' demands. For example, when customers began to complain that the 24-bottle packs Dr Pepper was delivering were not of a manageable size, it changed to 6-packs. Then it changed again to 6-packs of 12-ounce bottles, a move up from the 6.5-ounce bottles that were being sold. This decision spurred continued growth and Dr Pepper soon captured 25 percent of the soft drink market, ranking second among consumers. To improve further, Dr Pepper began using metal and electric coolers in its distribution process in place of the wooden ice barrels that had been used. This allowed both distributors and customers more storage flexibility. Dr Pepper also began to sell premixed powders and postmix equipment, cutting costs by decreasing the weight of its shipped product.

During World War II, the bottling plants, owned primarily by small businessmen and located in 35 states, were run by women in order to make wise use of

Exhibit 2 Dr Pepper/7UP Companies, Inc., Consolidated Balance Sheets
(in thousands, except shares data)

	1993 $	1992 $
Assets		
Current assets:		
Accounts receivable, less allowance for doubtful accounts of $1,737 in 1993 and $1,573 in 1992	70,255	57,267
Inventories	14,550	12,685
Prepaid advertising	16,872	16,748
Deferred income taxes	24,175	—
Other current assets	16,801	1,140
Total current assets	127,460	87,840
Property, plant and equipment, net	19,012	18,253
Intangible assets		
Franchises	459,988	459,988
Goodwill, formulas, trademarks and other	142,872	142,872
	602,860	602,860
Less accumulated amortization	111,434	96,357
Total intangible assets, net	491,426	506,503
Deferred debt issuance costs, less accumulated amortization of $8,711 in 1993 and $1,508 in 1992	31,313	42,979
Other assets	10,812	12,521
Total assets	680,023	668,096
Liabilities and Stockholders' Deficit		
Current liabilities:		
Accounts payable	25,060	21,112
Accrued marketing expenses	67,026	77,810
Other accrued expenses	17,266	15,708
Current portion of long-term debt	85,274	75,433
Total current liabilities	194,626	190,063
Long-term debt, less current portion	790,540	1,091,956
Deferred credits and other	28,805	27,139
Deferred income taxes	86,156	69,559
Redeemable Senior Preferred Stock, at redemption value	—	96,792
Stockholders' deficit		
Common stock, $.01 par value, authorized 145,000,000 shares, issued 60,796,377 shares in 1993	608	385
Additional paid-in capital	406,728	96,012
Accumulated deficit	(827,672)	(904,005)
Foreign currency translation adjustment	232	195
	(420,104)	(807,413)
Less treasury shares (148,152 in 1993), at cost	—	—
Total stockholders' deficit	(420,104)	(807,413)
Commitments and contingencies		
Total liabilities and stockholders' deficit	680,023	668,096

Exhibit 2	Dr Pepper/7UP Companies, Inc., Consolidated Statement of Cash Flows (in thousands, except shares data)		
	1993 $	1992 $	1991 $
Cash flows from operating activities:			
Net income (loss)	77,925	(140,148)	(37,505)
Adjustments to reconcile net income (loss) to net cash provided by operating activities:			
Depreciation and amortization of intangibles, debt discounts and deferred debt issuance costs	59,634	90,289	92,884
Debt restructuring charge	8,844	24,664	10,391
Cumulative effect of accounting change	—	74,800	—
Preferred stock dividends of subsidiary	—	11,119	10,499
Other	(1,438)	726	2,375
Changes in assets and liabilities:			
Accounts receivable	(12,988)	(6,565)	(2,359)
Inventories	(1,865)	(466)	(1,585)
Prepaid advertising and other assets	1,117	(7,068)	(933)
Accounts payable and accrued expenses	(7,720)	7,823	6,497
Net cash provided by operating activities	123,509	55,174	80,264
Cash flows from investing activities:			
Capital expenditures	(3,754)	(1,861)	(2,180)
Sales (purchases) of marketable securities with maturity less than three months, net	—	31,166	(31,166)
Purchases of marketable securities	—	(312,108)	(147,053)
Sales of marketable securities	—	366,733	92,428
Other	—	(2,000)	93
Net cash provided by (used in) investing activities	(3,754)	81,930	(87,878)
Cash flows from financing activities:			
Proceeds from long-term debt	831,000	1,266,001	315,800
Payments on long-term debt	(1,156,960)	(1,269,407)	(313,117)
Proceeds from sale of common stock	305,366	—	—
Issuance of preferred stock	—	—	50,000
Repurchase of preferred stock	(98,383)	(120,744)	—
Payments of refinancing costs	(4,381)	(53,149)	(17,885)
Increase in cash overdraft	2,442	5,181	—
Other	1,161	469	(290)
Net cash provided by (used in) financing activities	(119,755)	(171,649)	34,538
Net increase (decrease) in cash and cash equivalents	—	(34,545)	26,924
Cash and cash equivalents at beginning of year	—	34,545	7,621
Cash and cash equivalents at end of year	—	—	34,545

Exhibit 2 Dr Pepper/7UP Companies, Inc., Consolidated Statement of Operations (in thousands, except shares data)			
	1993 $	1992 $	1991 $
Net sales	707,378	658,718	600,941
Cost of sales	115,981	126,002	118,757
Gross profit	591,397	532,716	482,184
Operating expenses:			
Marketing	362,484	329,706	302,192
General and administrative	30,816	27,312	26,621
Amortization of intangible assets	15,077	15,112	15,155
Total operating expenses	408,377	372,130	343,968
Operating profit	183,020	160,586	138,216
Other income (expense):			
Interest expense	(85,560)	(150,245)	(147,957)
Preferred stock dividends of subsidiaries	(1,744)	(17,538)	(12,294)
Recapitalization charge	—	(6,026)	—
Other, net	495	4,627	3,174
Total other income (expense)	(86,809)	(169,182)	(157,077)
Income (loss) before income taxes, extraordinary items and cumulative effect of accounting change	96,211	(8,596)	(18,861)
Income tax expense (benefit)	2,087	(182)	1,100
Income (loss) before extraordinary items and cumulative effect of accounting change	94,124	(8,414)	(19,961)
Extraordinary items:			
Benefit from utilization of net operating loss carryforwards	—	—	(1,022)
Extinguishments of debt, less applicable income taxes	16,199	56,934	18,566
Cumulative effect of accounting change	—	74,800	—
	77,925	(140,148)	(37,505)
Preferred stock dividend requirements	—	12,941	11,882
Net income (loss) attributable to outstanding common stock	77,925	(153,089)	(49,387)
Income (loss) per common share:			
Income (loss) before extraordinary items and cumulative effect of accounting change	1.46	(0.60)	(0.90)
Extraordinary items	(0.25)	(1.60)	(0.49)
Cumulative effect of accounting change	—	(211.00)	—
Net income (loss)	1.21	(4.31)	(1.39)

available labor. The company was then able to continue its growth despite the war-ravaged workforce, build a new headquarters in Dallas, and even go public on the New York Stock Exchange in 1946. From here, the company moved into Mexico City and furthered its innovative marketing and distribution practices by installing vending machines in schools. The drink was then introduced in more states, bringing the total to 44 states. By 1962, Dr Pepper was canned as well as bottled, and a 24-ounce throwaway bottle had been introduced.

The popularity of the drink led the executives of Dr Pepper to establish a set of Dr Pepper basics. These included point-of-sale promotions, advertising, a perfect product, sampling, and distribution. Apparently, the easiest of these to accomplish was the perfect product, because the flavor was already set. Inherent in this idea was consistency in both the manufacture of the syrup and the eventual combination with carbonated water. Marketing and advertising also came easy because the company began advertising nationally on American Bandstand. Soon, fountain sales broke records and bottling plants were added in Canada. Distribution was changed when the company began to produce a concentrate that could be added to carbonated water and packaged by bottlers in order to produce the final product. A problem soon developed, however, when the Federal Trade Commission (FTC) began to claim that the territorial restrictions placed on bottlers was in violation of antitrust laws. In hopes of avoiding a court judgment, Dr Pepper CEO W.W. Clements gave a presentation to the U.S. Senate Committee, Judiciary Subcommittee on Antitrust and Monopoly. As a result of this presentation, the committee dropped its charges, allowing Dr Pepper to continue its practice of franchising the bottling and distributing of its drink. The two-liter bottle was also introduced and metric labeling was used first in Europe. By the mid-1970s, only 0.5 percent of the bottling was not franchised.

The next decade was characterized by growth of a different form: mergers and acquisitions. Dr Pepper played a large role in the industry; it issued a franchise to Welch's in 1981 and Canada Dry in 1982. Forstmann Little then purchased Dr Pepper in 1984 through a leveraged buyout. This again made Dr Pepper a privately-owned company. Dr Pepper then sold Canada Dry. In 1993, the company again went public, and competitors began to eye it as a possible purchase for differentiation purposes. Coca-Cola had attempted to do just that in 1986 but was denied by the FTC as part of a ruling that required Coke to have all purchases of franchises within the soft drink industry approved. This was the beginning of a series of acquisitions by Dr Pepper as its managers attempted to make the company into a national rather than a regional soft drink producer.

■ Corporate Strategy

Dr Pepper revealed a different strategy than its competition when it sold off the last of its bottling facilities in the early 1980s because of the increased competition from Coke- and Pepsi-owned operations. The company decided to utilize other companies' state-of-the-art facilities as a means for bottling its soft drinks.[2]

Today, Dr Pepper grants licenses to bottling companies, who must in essence lease its trademark to put on the final package. The biggest difference between the company and Coke or Pepsi is in the companies' respective customers. Dr Pepper considers bottlers as its direct customers; Coke and Pepsi, on the other hand, consider its direct customers to be the ultimate consumers. In light of this, Dr Pepper's bottlers are brought together once a year for meetings that relate the company's plans for advertising and marketing. In addition, numerous incentives exist for bottlers who effectively promote Dr Pepper products through such concepts as display promotions and priority branding. Examples of such incentives include Outstanding Salesperson of the Year, travel rewards for domestic bottlers, and Partners in Excellence (rewarding international bottlers for sales).[3]

As indicated, a large percentage of Dr Pepper's bottlers are owned by Coke or Pepsi. In 1990, the company wanted to move a 7UP license in New York City from a 7UP bottler to a Pepsi bottler. The FTC barred Dr Pepper from distributing 7UP in New York for three years until the issue was resolved. The company has had to deal with the FTC in instances such as this in order to transfer bottling licenses from one distributor to another, and often must strive to regain the ground lost in these battles.[4]

Internationally, Pepsi owns the rights to 7UP while Dr Pepper is sold on a comparatively minimal basis through various bottlers, none of which it owns.[5] Incentive programs designed to spur international growth are intended to improve the company's presence overseas, where sales are approximately one percent of total sales.

■ Corporate Structure

Dr Pepper's unique corporate strategy has been supported by an equally unique corporate structure. To avoid the tremendous financial pressures that can be levied by the two soft drink giants—Coca-Cola and Pepsi—Dr Pepper has been known to move quickly and effectively. This was first seen in 1904 when Dr Pepper had the foresight to open a manufacturing plant in St. Louis, the sight of that year's World's Fair Exposition. Twenty million people were in attendance, and by making this move, Dr Pepper was able to capitalize on its first opportunity for national exposure. Today, Dr Pepper's modern, efficient production and technical center (known as the Waco Manufacturing Company) is the company's lone producer of concentrates and syrups. This aggressive strategy is still embedded in Dr Pepper's culture and seems to be paying off for the firm, because it is the fastest growing soft drink enterprise.[6]

Dr Pepper's cultural edge emphasizes entrepreneurship rather than "arm's length financial control." Employees utilize an aggressive "do-it, fix-it" process of empowerment.[7] Dr Pepper's culture is sustained through an extremely flat organizational structure. The firm employs about 950 people, with 475 serving in its headquarters and 300 employees serving as field sales personnel. This structure includes 17 corporate officers, all of whom report to a CEO and a board of directors. This board consists of eight members, two of whom are current corporate officers and two who are retired corporate officers. The other four are from outside of the company, giving the firm unique and, to some extent, unbiased viewpoints. The corporate officers and the employees in general have a high stake in the company, largely through stock options yielding ownership percentages that are above the industry average. Such incentives may improve company loyalty and dedication while reducing the potential for a conflict of interest between managers and shareholders. The firm's aggressive strategy and responsive culture have allowed it to build distribution strength and create marketing momentum.

■ Cadbury Schweppes PLC

Cadbury Schweppes PLC is one of the oldest and largest family-run businesses in the world. Although confectionery Cadbury Limited merged with the carbonated drinks company Schweppes Limited in 1969, Cadbury Schweppes is still run by members of the Cadbury family. The history of Cadbury dates back to 1824, when John Cadbury opened his grocery business in Birmingham, England. From the beginning, cocoa for drinking and chocolate were his most popular products.

In 1847, John took on his brother Benjamin as a partner. But the business began to decline, and in 1860 the brothers dissolved their partnership. The business was left to John's sons, Richard and George, who continued to struggle for several years. But, in 1866, the new Cadbury brothers introduced an improved process for pressing cocoa butter, which resulted in purer drinking cocoa and cocoa butter that could be made into eating chocolate.[8]

In 1868, Cadbury Brothers began marketing its own lines of chocolate candy. In 1906, the brothers introduced a new recipe for milk chocolate, marketing it under the name Cadbury Dairy Milk, which has remained a mainstay of its product line ever since. After World War I, innovations in industrial technology made the manufacture of chocolate cheap enough to price chocolate candy for a wider market, and the company accordingly retooled its factory for mass production. Throughout the postwar years, Cadbury maintained its position as the leading chocolate manufacturer in the world's leading per capita candy-consuming nation, Great Britain. During that time and continuing today, the company remains a family business. Its chairman has always been a direct descendent of John Cadbury.[9]

In direct contrast, Schweppes Limited has not been guided by a Schweppe for almost 200 years. The company bears the name of Jacob Schweppe, a German-born jeweler and amateur chemist, who in 1790 formed a partnership with pharmacist Henry Gosse, engineer Jacques Paul, and his son Nicholas. Together, they formed Schweppe, Paul, and Gosse, which devoted itself to producing artificial mineral water. The Schweppe's brand was popular during the time because carbonated water was believed to have medicinal value. In 1799, Schweppe sold a 75 percent interest in his business, but the company continued to use the Schweppe name. Schweppes introduced new product lines with ginger ale in the 1870s, tonic water, its most famous product, around the same time, and a carbonated lemonade in 1885.[10]

During the interwar years and throughout World War II, Schweppes continued to consolidate its overseas operations as the company's sales declined. In 1948, Schweppes regained its strength through the shrewd marketing of new managing director Sir Frederick Hooper, who renewed the focus on overseas businesses. Schweppes management realized that overseas expansion was the key to its future and continued this mission throughout the 1960s. But, unfortunately, its capital base was too small compared to that of the American conglomerates with which it would have to compete. In 1968, chairman Lord Watkinson met with Cadbury chairman Adrian Cadbury who had similar concerns about his own company. Schweppes and Cadbury began merger talks soon thereafter and reached an agreement in January 1969. The two companies consolidated some of their operations, but they maintained autonomy in the matter of distribution, since bottling franchises controlled local distribution in the soft drink business. By the 1990s, Cadbury Schweppes had become a major global company as a maker and distributor of confectionery (chocolate) and beverage products whose quality brands and products are sold in over 170 countries (see Exhibit 3). In 1993, the company reported sales of £3,725 million ($5,513 million), an increase of 10.4 percent over 1992, and pretax profits of £416 million ($616 million), a 25.1 percent increase from the previous year (see Exhibit 4). Confectionery products accounted for 44.6 percent of the total sales while beverages accounted for 55.4%.[11] These percentages remained relatively unchanged from 1992 (see Exhibit 5).

Exhibit 3   Cadbury Schweppes—Balance Sheets at January 1, 1994 (exchange rate 1.5 dollars to 1 pound)

	Group		Company	
	1993 £ m	1992 £ m	1993 £ m	1992 £ m
Fixed Assets				
Intangible assets	545.8	385.1	—	—
Tangible assets	1,288.2	1,241.3	9.0	14.6
Investments	196.0	41.6	1,552.8	1,608.6
	2,030.0	1,668.0	1,561.8	1,623.2
Current Assets				
Stocks	358.4	362.6	—	—
Debtors - due within one yr	586.5	559.6	358.1	109.6
-due after one yr	41.6	39.7	14.8	29.1
Investments	121.9	237.3	—	—
Cash at bank and in hand	128.5	95.9	0.2	—
	1,236.9	1,295.1	373.1	138.7
Current Liabilities				
Creditors: amounts due within one yr				
Borrowings	(221.3)	(294.4)	(209.6)	(329.7)
Other	(1,036.9)	(934.9)	(135.2)	(123.6)
Net Current Assets (Liabilities)	(21.3)	110.8	28.3	(314.6)
Total Assets less Current Liabilities	2,008.7	1,778.8	1,590.1	1,308.6
Noncurrent Liabilities				
Creditors: amounts due after more than one year				
Borrowing	(386.4)	(462.0)	(52.6)	(70.5)
Other	(14.3)	(20.1)	(281.0)	(347.5)
Provisions for liabilities and charges	(98.5)	(82.7)	(1.4)	(0.6)
	(499.2)	(564.8)	(335.0)	(418.6)
	1,509.5	1,214.0	1,255.1	890.0
Capital and Reserves				
Attributable to Equity Interests				
Called up share capital	207.5	185.4	207.5	185.4
Share premium account	704.4	385.1	704.4	385.1
Revaluation reserve	95.3	104.4	1.5	1.6
Profit and loss account	199.0	250.9	183.4	159.6
Attributable to Nonequity Interests				
Called up share capital	0.3	0.3	0.3	0.3
Share premium account	158.0	158.0	158.0	158.0
	1,364.5	1,084.1	1,255.1	890.0
Minority interests	145.0	129.9	—	—
	1,509.5	1,214.0	1,255.1	890.0

Exhibit 3 Cadbury Schweppes—Balance Sheets at January 1, 1994 (exchange rate 1.5 dollars to 1 pound)

Group Cash Flow Statement, 52 weeks ended January 1, 1994

	1993 £ m	1992 £ m
Operating activities		
Net cash inflow from operating activities	607.0	499.3
Returns on investments and servicing of finance		
Interest paid	(73.8)	(83.1)
Interest received	28.8	31.1
Dividends paid to shareholders	(102.7)	(92.9)
Dividends paid to minorities in subsidiary undertakings	(3.0)	(1.9)
Dividends received from associated undertaking	5.4	6.9
	(145.3)	(139.9)
Taxation		
UK corporation tax paid	(45.3)	(43.8)
Overseas tax paid	(48.7)	(45.3)
	(94.0)	(89.1)
Investing activities		
Purchases of tangible fixed assets	(202.9)	(191.1)
Disposals of tangible fixed assets	19.6	21.2
Purchases of long term investments	(157.9)	(2.8)
Disposals of long term investments	12.3	1.3
Purchases of short term investments	(6.9)	(3.2)
Disposals of short term investments	2.3	5.0
Expenditure on post-acquisition restructuring	(13.5)	(18.3)
Acquisitions of businesses	(320.1)	(229.8)
	(667.1)	(418.7)
	(299.4)	(148.4)
Net cash outflow before financing		
Financing		
Issues of ordinary shares	337.3	155.6
Long term debt issued	19.0	21.4
Long term debt repaid	(142.9)	(72.9)
Finance leases initiated	2.7	16.8
Finance leases repaid	(23.9)	(31.2)
Short term borrowings repaid	(1.3)	(6.5)
Loans repaid to minorities in subsidiary undertakings	(19.4)	—
Net cash inflow from financing	171.5	83.2
Decrease in cash and cash equivalents	(127.9)	(65.2)

Exhibit 4 Cadbury Schweppes—Group Financial Record, 1993					
Sales and Profits					
	1993 £ m	1992 £ m	1991 £ m	1990 £ m	1989 £ m
Sales					
United Kingdom	1613.7	1546.2	1506.0	1476.0	1257.5
Europe	741.5	700.9	655.8	638.0	479.7
Americas	643.6	512.9	438.3	403.7	372.4
Pacific Rim	508.0	448.3	491.2	495.5	545.7
Africa & Others	218.0	164.1	141.0	132.9	121.4
	3724.8	3372.4	3232.3	3146.1	2776.7
Operating Profit					
United Kingdom	194.9	172.6	160.2	143.1	99.4
Europe	50.1	55.4	79.6	68.2	58.6
Americas	101.6	72.1	42.5	43.0	36.5
Pacific Rim	68.8	55.9	63.9	57.5	61.0
Africa & Others	34.0	28.6	24.9	18.2	17.8
	449.4	384.6	371.1	330.0	273.3
Profit on sale of operations	—	—	—	—	13.7
Profit on sale of investment	11.9	—	—	—	—
Profit/(loss) re properties	(1.5)	(1.3)	0.6	3.8	2.8
Net interest	(43.5)	(50.6)	(57.0)	(57.2)	(31.1)
Profit Before Taxation	416.3	332.7	314.7	276.6	258.7
Taxation	(129.1)	(94.2)	(87.9)	(77.9)	(69.6)
Minority interests	(44.2)	(35.7)	(25.1)	(22.1)	(17.0)
Preference dividends	(6.2)	(7.2)	(9.0)	(3.4)	0.0
Profit for the Financial Year	236.8	195.6	192.7	173.2	172.1
Dividends to ordinary shareholders	(116.4)	(98.0)	(88.0)	(80.2)	(76.3)
Profit Retained for the Year	120.4	97.6	104.7	93.0	95.8

■ Cadbury's Beverage Business

Most of Cadbury Schweppes' involvement in the world soft drink industry during the 1970s was small in scale and generally unsuccessful. In the 1980s, Cadbury Schweppes remained focused on the American market. In 1986, it acquired Sodastream Holdings, a British company that produced equipment for making carbonated drinks at home, as a way of trying to capture American customers without competing head-on with Coke and Pepsi. Cadbury Schweppes held one percent of the American market during this time. This changed in July 1986 when it acquired the Canada Dry worldwide soft drink business for $230 million, putting the company in direct competition with the two soft drink giants Coke and Pepsi. At this point Coke and Pepsi held 41 percent and 31 percent market share, respectively. This acquisition also included rights to the Sunkist brand within the United States. During the same year, Cadbury also participated in a buyout of Dr Pepper, landing a 34 percent share in the company. In early

Exhibit 5	Financial Highlights of Cadbury Schweppe's Business Units					
1993	Total £ m	United Kingdom £ m	Europe £ m	Americas £ m	Pacific Rim £ m	Africa & Others £ m
Sales						
Confectionery	1660.1	826.9	312.3	53.0	311.5	156.4
Beverage	2064.7	786.8	429.2	590.6	196.5	61.6
	3724.8	1613.7	741.5	643.6	508.0	218.0
Operating Profit						
Confectionery	211.3	94.2	33.3	12.3	53.9	17.6
Beverage	238.1	100.7	16.7	89.3	14.9	16.5
	449.4	194.9	50.0	101.6	68.8	34.1
Operating Assets						
Confectionery	743.2	332.0	129.3	30.8	174.6	76.5
Beverage	627.7	223.1	181.5	141.5	75.1	6.5
	1370.9	555.1	310.8	172.3	249.7	83.0
Trading Margin	%	%	%	%	%	%
Confectionery	12.5	11.4	10.7	23.2	17.3	8.9
Beverage	11.1	12.8	2.7	15.1	7.6	19.5
	11.7	12.1	6.0	15.8	13.5	11.9
1992	Total £ m	United Kingdom £ m	Europe £ m	Americas £ m	Pacific Rim £ m	Africa & Others £ m
Sales						
Confectionery	1469.2	785.9	268.7	31.7	273.2	109.7
Beverage	1903.2	760.3	432.2	481.2	175.1	54.4
	3372.4	1546.2	700.9	512.9	448.3	164.1
Operating Profit						
Confectionery	175.8	83.0	25.5	9.2	45.2	12.9
Beverage	208.8	89.6	29.9	62.9	10.7	15.7
	84.6	172.6	55.4	72.1	55.9	28.6
Operating Assets						
Confectionery	685.9	340.1	134.6	9.0	152.5	49.7
Beverage	682.1	249.1	223.2	124.1	69.6	16.1
	1368.0	589.2	357.8	133.1	222.1	65.8
Trading Margin	%	%	%	%	%	%
Confectionery	11.8	10.6	9.5	29.0	16.6	9.6
Beverage	10.4	11.8	5.4	13.2	6.1	18.2
	11.0	11.2	7.0	14.2	12.5	12.4

1988, Dr Pepper merged with 7UP, and in April of that same year, Cadbury sold all but a 5.7 percent stake in Dr Pepper for $90 million, $18 million in securities, and an 8 percent equity in the Dr Pepper/7UP merger concern. At this point, Cadbury held 3.4 percent of the U.S. market. Cadbury continued to acquire soft drink companies and purchased the Crush International soft drink business from

Procter & Gamble Company for $220 million. Included in the acquisition were the Crush, Hires, and Sundrop citrus soda lines in the United States and Crush, Gini bitter-lemon soda, and fruit-flavored soft drinks outside the United States.[12]

Entering 1992, Cadbury Schweppes Group chief executive David Wellings recognized that the lingering recession in Europe had caused Cadbury's overall profits to flatten out in its most important market. Mr. Wellings envisioned that further expansion in the United States would nicely increase the company's geographic diversification and cushion it against future downturns in any one region. The opportunity came in August, 1993 when Cadbury announced its intentions to buy root beer maker A&W Brands, Inc. On October 13, 1993, Cadbury acquired A&W Brand for $334 million, equal to $24.50 a share. Though A&W accounted for only a 2.2 percent share of the overall U.S. soda market, this included 30 percent of the U.S. root beer category. This meshed perfectly with Cadbury's Hires Root Beer line, which had 10 percent of the category. To Cadbury's surprise, another opportunity presented itself even before the A&W acquisition was final. Prudential Insurance announced its intention to cash out on its long held 20.2 percent stake in Dr Pepper/7UP. Prudential was still financially strapped due to Hurricane Andrew, which had struck Florida in August 1992, and was being forced into a "fire" sale in order to produce much needed cash. Cadbury was an eager buyer for $231 million, approximately $19 a share, since it could add to its existing 5.7 percent, giving the company a total 25.9 percent share of Dr Pepper. More importantly, these acquisitions were consistent with Cadbury's global growth strategy by making it a potential third-place competitor in the $47 billion U.S. soft drink industry with approximately 5.0 percent of the U.S. market.

▉ Cadbury's Global Focus

Cadbury's corporate strategy is built on its traditions of quality and value to provide brands, products, financial results, and management performance that meets the interests of shareholders, consumers, employees, customers, suppliers, and the communities in which it operates.[13] Cadbury's global focus is exemplified by Chairman Dominic Cadbury in the 1993 annual report. He states:

> We [Cadbury] are committed to growing profitability, brand strength and volume on a global basis within our focus on the confectionery and beverage markets. Our development will continue through a combination of organic growth, targeted acquisitions, and partnerships. We have made substantial further investments in 1993 to broaden the geographic reach of our brands while adding significantly to our brand portfolio.

> About one third of all soft drinks are consumed in the U.S. In 1993 we made two important moves [acquisition of A&W Brands and increased investment in Dr Pepper/7UP] to increase our involvement in that market. . . .[14]

This increased presence in the U.S. market was also supported by David Wellings when he commented on the outright purchase of A&W Brands and its increased stake in Dr Pepper/7UP. According to Wellings:

> There are sound reasons that the U.S. soft drink market is an especially high priority for us. It is an enormous market, totaling perhaps 34% by volume of world sales. It is so large that it tends to be a kind of cradle, the genesis of new development. If you don't have a significant presence in this market, then I can't see how you can claim to be a global player. We want to be—have to be—a global player.[15]

This philosophy of being a global player was seen by Cadbury to be right in line with its international goals and objectives. First, volume in soft drink sales would increase since Cadbury was now more than a bit player in the U.S. market, where 34 percent of all soft drinks are sold. It also offered an accessible test market to launch new beverages. Second, through Cadbury's acquisitions of Canada Dry, A&W Brands, and Dr Pepper/7UP, it became a major player in the non-cola segment of the U.S. soda market. From 1990–1993, the non-cola market grew at quadruple the rate of the soda market as a whole. Third, Cadbury could reduce its financial risks through diversification away from its predominant European market. These risks included lost potential profits by not being more involved in the large U.S. market and its lack of geographic diversification, which made it vulnerable to downturns in the European market. This was the case during the 1990s when Cadbury's beverage operations showed profits of less than 4 percent because of continuing hard economic times in Germany, Spain, and France. Another risk included its lack of critical mass and financial muscle, which weakened its ability to negotiate better deals and lower prices with larger bottlers that it relied on for the manufacturing, bottling, and distribution of its products. But, an enlarged Cadbury was now in a better position to "offer bottlers a strong stable of high margin uncola brands—and, as a result, demand better store displays, better promotions and better terms. It was just possible that in the non-cola market, Cadbury could beat Coke and Pepsi."[16] Cadbury executives sounded ready for the challenge. Frank Swan, its managing director of Beverage Stream, said, "I am duly respectful of their size and ability, but I'm not frightened. We have been in this end of the business longer than they have and we know it better. I think we can be faster on our feet than Coke and Pepsi."[17]

■ Cadbury's Business Structure

As a natural result of Cadbury Schweppes' acquisition growth strategy, it is essentially a confederation of acquired corporations, and is attempting to develop a cultural image that is built on that of its English headquarters. Decision making is largely centralized within a top-down management structure, and previous acquisitions have been effectively assimilated.[18]

Cadbury Schweppes focuses on two product streams: Beverages and Confectionery, each of which has its own management structure. The Beverages Stream operates through Cadbury Beverages and Coca-Cola Schweppes Beverages Ltd. (CCSB). It is comprised of five principal operating divisions: Cadbury Beverages North America, Mott's North America, Cadbury Beverages International, Cadbury Beverages Europe, and Schweppes Cottee's in Australia. In addition, there are beverage interests within Cadbury Schweppes (South America) Ltd. The Beverage Stream brands are sold in cans, glass and plastic bottles, and aseptic packages at stores, fountain outlets, and vending and dispensing machines. Entering 1995, Cadbury owned 415 brands of soft drinks (see Exhibit 6).

Cadbury's bottling and distribution system consists of a global network of principal subsidiaries, affiliates, and licensing agreements. In the United Kingdom, CCSB, 51 percent owned by Cadbury and 49 percent owned by Coca-Cola Company, bottles, cans, and distributes Coca-Cola and Cadbury beverages. In the United States, Cadbury did not produce any of its own beverages. The rights to produce its products are licensed to independent bottling companies across the United States.[19] The two biggest licensees are Dr Pepper and Coca-Cola. In fact, Dr Pepper's state-of-the-art facility in St. Louis manufactures soft drink concentrates

---

Exhibit 6   Cadbury Schweppes—Major Beverage Stream Brands, 1993

Schweppes
Canada Dry
Crush
Rose's
Kia-Ora
Sunkist
Hires Root Beer
A&W Root Beer
Sundrop
Squirt
Mott's Apple Brand
Clamato Juices
Solo (Australia)
Hepburn Spa (Australia)
Cottee's (Australia)
Gini (Europe)
Oasis (Europe)
TriNaranjus (Europe)

and provides technical assistance for approximately 150 flavors, many of which were Cadbury brands.[20] These companies are then responsible for licensing the distribution operations. Consumers of Cadbury beverage products can contact the company directly concerning any questions or comments. The distributors, whose names are found on the bottle cap or on the side of the container, are always documented in any correspondence. This way, Cadbury can keep record of responses that provide insight into the relationship it has with its bottlers and distributors.[21] The company also has principal subsidiaries in France (Schweppes France SA), Spain (Schweppes SA), Mexico (Cadbury Aquas Minerales, SA de CV), Australia (Cadbury Schweppes Pty Ltd), and Zambia (Cadbury Schweppes, Zambia Ltd.)[22] (see Exhibit 7). In these principal markets, sales are made either through Cadbury's or independent bottlers' sales forces.[23]

Exhibit 7	Cadbury Schweppes Beverage Stream—Wholly or Partially Owned Principal Subsidiaries and Principal Affiliates, 1993	
Details of Principal Associated Undertakings	Country	Proportion of Shares/Capital If Not 100%
Schweppes (Central Africa) Ltd (listed)	Zimbabwe	46%
Apollinaris & Schweppes GmbH & Co.	Germany	28%
Amalgamated Beverages Industries (pty) Ltd (listed)	South Africa	19%
Details of principal other investments		
Dr. Pepper/Seven-Up Companies, Inc. (listed)	U.S.A.	25%
Details of principal subsidiary undertakings		
Operating Companies		
United Kingdom:		
Coca-Cola & Schweppes Beverages Ltd	Great Britain	51%
Sodastream Ltd	Great Britain	
Europe:		
Schweppes France SA	France	
Schweppes SA	Spain	
Citricos y Refrescantes, SA	Spain	
Schweppes Belgium SA	Belgium	
Cadbury Schweppes Bebidas Portugal, SA	Portugal	
Americas:		
Cadbury Beverages Inc.	U.S.A.	
A&W Brands, Inc.	U.S.A.	
Cadbury Beverages Canada Inc	Canada	
Cadbury Aguas Minerales, SA de CV	Mexico	
Other overseas:		
Cadbury Schweppes Pty Ltd	Australia	
Cadbury Schweppes (South Africa) Ltd (listed)	South Africa	53%
Cadbury Schweppes (Zambia) Ltd	Zambia	
Export and franchises:		
Schweppes International Ltd	Ireland	
Canada Dry Corporation Ltd	Ireland	

As Cadbury looked to the future, it remained committed to growing profitability, volume, and brand strength on a global basis. Dominic Cadbury and David Wellings believed that significant opportunity remained to develop further by innovation, effective brand marketing, and increased distribution. The company continued to move aggressively to obtain major ownership in subsidiaries in which it possessed a minority interest, in establishing joint ventures in attractive, developing markets (i.e., China and Vietnam), and in strengthening licensing arrangements.[24] This was due to Cadbury's concern that Coca-Cola, one of its major competitors, was also its partner in its most profitable market (United Kingdom—42 percent). Confidential strategic actions were not always easy to maintain. Therefore, the possibility of a complete buyout of Dr Pepper looked very appealing. With its promising income growth rate and efficient manufacturing plant, this was one opportunity that neither Coke or Pepsi could do much about—due to antitrust laws and the FTC's 1986 ruling.

The Soft Drink Industry and Distribution

The soft drink industry as a whole is composed of various complicated distribution channels consisting of soft drink companies, bottling companies, wholesalers, and retailers. The following sections provide some insight into the functioning of these entities.

Bottling and Canning Operations

Bottling and canning operations combine syrup produced by soft drink manufacturers with carbonated water or combine concentrate produced by manufacturers with sweeteners and carbonated water. The finished product, packaged in cans, refillable and nonrefillable glass bottles, and plastic containers, is then distributed to supermarkets, convenience stores, warehouse outlets, and vending machines.[25] Bottlers must create different sales and distribution methods for each of these selling points. Warehouse outlets purchase in bulk, resulting in lower profit margins for the bottling companies. Vending machines represent 15 percent of U.S. soft drink sales and provide instant gratification for consumers who want soft drinks "cold and now." The most successful bottlers in the United States have made long-term investments in full-service vending locations.[26]

Fountain/Postmix Wholesalers and Retailers

Fountain/postmix wholesalers and retailers combine syrup produced by soft drink manufacturers with carbonated water. The soft drink is dispersed through fountain outlets to be consumed in cups or glasses. For the most part, syrups are sold to wholesalers, who add the carbonated water and sell it to retailers. Only a few retailers purchase syrup directly from soft drink manufacturers.[27] Fountain outlets are found just about anywhere, including fast-food restaurants, supermarkets, stadiums, and convenience stores. At such fountain locations, customers have their choice of beverage that is, for the most part, free of pricing, packaging, and promotional ploys. Therefore, purchase decisions here are based purely on taste preferences of the various consumers.[28]

As mentioned, Coke and Pepsi hold a large majority of market share in the soft drink industry, and the rivalry between them extends deep into their respective distribution channels. As will be seen, Coke and Pepsi have quite a different relationship with their bottlers than any other soft drink manufacturers, Dr Pepper included.

▪ Coca-Cola

Chartered in 1919, the Coca-Cola Company is presently the world's largest producer and distributor of soft drink syrups and concentrates. Its products are sold through bottlers and fountain wholesalers and distributors in more than 195 countries. In 1993, company products represented approximately 44 percent of total flavored carbonated soft drink unit case volume consumed worldwide, including the former Soviet Union, China, and India.[29]

Coke has significant ownership interests in vast distribution networks both in the United States and abroad. The number of independent bottling and canning operations that distribute Coke's products is small and diminishing even further. The company holds a 43.5 percent ownership interest in Coca-Cola Enterprises Inc., the world's largest bottler of soft drink products, and it owns 49 percent of Coca-Cola Beverages, the principal bottler in Canada. Furthermore, the company holds a 51 percent ownership interest in Coca-Cola Amatil Limited, an Australian-based bottler of company products. Coke owns approximately 49 percent interest in Coca-Cola Schweppes Beverages Ltd., the leading marketer in Great Britain. Additionally, Coca-Cola possesses ownership interests in countless bottling companies around the world, such as the Netherlands, Mexico, Brazil, Germany, Colombia, and India. Thus, with the Dr Pepper acquisition, Cadbury may be directly in competition with its central market partner in the United Kingdom.[30]

Over the last few years, Coca-Cola's bottling investments have been significant as a proportion of its capital investments. The company believes that these investments ensure strong and efficient production, distribution, and marketing systems:

> Through these investments, the Company is able to help focus and improve sales and marketing programs, assist in the development of effective business and information systems and help establish capital structures appropriate for these respective operations.[31]

▪ Pepsi

Pepsi-Cola has been in existence just 10 years less than Coke; however, it was not until the late 1930s that it was positioned for long-term competitiveness. Sixty years later, PepsiCo, Inc., is a mammoth multinational supplier of soft drinks, snack foods, and fast foods.[32] Its soft drinks are sold in 166 countries. Pepsi-Cola is America's second best selling soft drink, capturing 16.5 percent of the market in 1993, up 1.4 percent from 1992 data.

PepsiCo also owns most of its bottling companies, and like Coca-Cola, possesses distribution channels not enjoyed by its competitors. For instance, the company was able to stimulate growth through creative packaging, introducing the Big Slam (a one-liter, wide-mouth bottle) and The Cube (a 24-pack that fits in a refrigerator) in 1993. Without its distribution network, Pepsi would not have a cost-effective means of transporting these differing products to its global customers. The company's philosophy regarding its bottlers is revealed by its chairman: "As our business has grown, we've gained tremendous production efficiencies. . . . In the U.S. that's meant great prices."[33]

Pepsi is also pursuing this strategy in its emerging international markets by establishing company-owned bottling and distribution operations in France and Eastern Europe and forming alliances with powerful bottlers in Latin America.[34] Despite such investments, the company has been losing market share the past couple of years. To improve its weakening position, Pepsi is focusing on increasing vendor penetration with a concentration on the workplace.[35]

Overall, there is little to distinguish between the quality, variety, and taste of Coke and Pepsi; thus, the long-time rivals have been forced to compete on the basis of price, advertising, and distribution. They do, however, each have a tremendous following and brand loyalty. Because Coke and Pepsi are never offered at restaurants together, customers generally accept the one that is available; if asked, though, they would likely have a preference for one or the other. These two companies rely on their brand equity, capitalizing on this massive consumer following not only in their marketing approaches but in their negotiations with international bottlers.

■ The Merger

As previously stated, Cadbury sold its 34.4 percent interest in Dr Pepper in 1988, leaving it with a 5.7 percent interest in the company.[36] At this point, Cadbury held 3.4 percent of the U.S. market. The company, however, was not satisfied with this minor presence in the biggest soft drink market in the world. Consequently, Cadbury became interested in acquiring Dr Pepper. In 1988, it tendered an offer of $.10 per share, which was immediately turned down by Dr Pepper. Four years later, Dr Pepper again rejected Cadbury's offer of $1.25 per share. In both instances, Dr Pepper management believed the offers did not account for its ongoing debt refinancing or growth potential and, subsequently, were not fair value offers.[37]

These offers only served to offend Dr Pepper's management, planting the first seed of tension between the two companies. As mentioned, Cadbury's buyout of Prudential's interest increased its stake in Dr Pepper to 25.9 percent. The move brought a negative reaction from Dr Pepper, especially from chief executive John Albers. Based on previous buyout attempts, he believed this was a committal move on Cadbury's part that would lead to an eventual controlling ownership in the firm. He did not want to have any part in such a merger and, in fact, had been thinking more along the lines of his company taking over Cadbury's U.S. beverage operations. Citing the nature of Cadbury's ownership interest, Dr Pepper refused Cadbury any board representation and quickly adopted a shareholder rights plan (i.e., a poison pill) that would make it difficult—and expensive—for Cadbury to launch a hostile takeover.[38]

For the next several months, the two companies were at a stalemate. Dr Pepper refused to initiate talks with Cadbury, yet the latter was waiting anxiously for the right time to commence negotiations. Despite the posturing, it was common knowledge that both companies agreed that a merger made good commercial sense. By merging operations, in which Cadbury and Dr Pepper already had considerable production overlap, great potential existed to realize substantial cost savings through manufacturing and distribution synergies and economies of scale. Frank Swan, the London-based managing director of Cadbury's beverage operations, admitted their fundamental strategic goal: to create value for both companies by working together and building a close relationship. *Beverage Digest* publisher Jesse Meyers foresaw an end to this impasse by claiming, "At the end of the day, cool heads will prevail and it is inevitable that they will get together. This is a pact made in heaven. Critical mass is critical."[39]

After several prior shutouts, the timing and manner of Cadbury's final approach to Dr Pepper was critical. If it decided to play the waiting game and slowly romance Dr Pepper into an agreed-on deal, it must accept the fact that a wait could be costly. As of November, 1993, Dr Pepper's stock was trading at just over $20 per share. Including debt of close to $1 billion and assuming an offer of $25 a share, the price tag would have been about $2.1 billion for the share Cadbury did not already own. That equaled about 40 percent of Cadbury's $5.20 billion market capitalization, a stretch by any standards. Furthermore, Dr Pepper did not pay a dividend, and for as long as Cadbury could hold on, the British company would not earn a cent on its stake. Given the continued strength of the non-cola segment, it was likely that Dr Pepper would continue to report profit gains that could only strengthen its stock.[40]

On the other hand, if Cadbury had launched a hostile bid, a move that Group Chief Executive Wellings said was not in the ethics of the company, it could also prove costly. Dr Pepper's poison pill would drive the price sharply higher. More importantly, a hostile move would more or less guarantee that senior Dr Pepper managers would take their handsome golden parachutes, further raising the costs and depriving Cadbury of needed expertise.[41] These were the delicate issues Cadbury's management was weighing at this juncture.

Finally, in January, 1995, Cadbury Schweppes began its tender offer to acquire the remaining Dr Pepper shares for $1.7 billion, or $33 a share. The strategic importance for the British-owned company was threefold: (1) The purchase negated Dr Pepper's "poison pill," which ensured that Cadbury could not buy more stock piecemeal; (2) it eliminated the opposition to Cadbury having no seats on the Dr Pepper board with its existing 25.9 percent share; and (3) the acquisition further diminished the importance of its chocolate and confectionery business by increasing its presence in the U.S. soft drink market. The move to obtain the remaining 74 percent stake Cadbury did not already own would make the firm the third-largest soft drink company in the U.S. market. Michael Bellas, president of New York beverage consultant Beverage Marketing Corporation, stated:

> If you're going to be a global soft-drink company you can't bypass the biggest soft-drink market in the world. It [the acquisition] gives both companies scale where they need some—Cadbury needed scale in the U.S. and Dr Pepper to gain additional presence overseas.[42]

On March 6, 1995, the acquisition was finalized. Cadbury bought the remaining 74 percent of Dr Pepper's stock for $35 per share,[43] emerging as the third largest soft drink company in the world and capturing 17 percent of the $47 billion U.S. market.[44] Ending a 110-year period of American ownership, this marriage would mark the beginning of change for Dr Pepper.

For Cadbury, the acquisition had many benefits, even some that positively affected Dr Pepper. First, the purchases of A&W in 1993 and of Dr Pepper in

1995 supported its existing long-term plan for international expansion. Second, Cadbury now possessed volume and capital strength to negotiate better deals and lower prices with bottlers. Third, the deals presented the opportunities for cost savings from the rationalization of common brands and the consolidation of manufacturing soft drink concentrates.[45] Therefore, Dr Pepper could possibly gain marketing and distribution muscle to boost its brand in international markets. In fact, it was Cadbury's intention to eventually export Dr Pepper through its already existing international distribution channels in the United Kingdom, Europe, Australia, and other countries.[46]

However, Cadbury's U.S. products were bottled by companies that were owned, wholly or partly, by Coca-Cola and PepsiCo and whose main business came from bottling Coke and Pepsi. Cadbury had to continue to worry about the tremendous leverage the giants had. If they chose to use it, they could push their own brands and encourage bottlers to drop smaller rivals.

Challenges for the Future

It is clear that the union between Cadbury and Dr Pepper will have major implications for the entire soft drink industry. Substantial worldwide influence over soft drink distribution channels rests with Coke and Pepsi; likewise, these companies hold dominant market shares. Both are capable of matching price cuts made by private-label soft drinks and of undercutting the pricing capabilities of Cadbury and Dr Pepper under current conditions. Will Cadbury's attempt to increase its presence in the soft drink industry backfire in the form of a stronger strategic reaction by Coke and/or Pepsi? Will these cola giants begin restricting the newly-formed company's distribution outlets or redirect their marketing attacks away from each other and instead to Cadbury/Dr Pepper's non-cola products? Despite Coke's and Pepsi's significant investments in bottling systems, most income comes from their manufacturing of concentrates.[47]

Another issue centers on that of leadership. Who will assume the reins of the new soft drink powerhouse? Dr Pepper CEO John R. Albers and CFO Ira M. Rosenstein will both retire after helping to facilitate the transition. Some observers believe the top spot will go to John F. Brock, the 46-year-old president of Cadbury Beverages North America, who moved to the United States in May, 1994, after heading up the company's European operations. True H. Knowles, the 57-year-old president and chief operating officer of the Dr Pepper division, is the next highest ranking executive and could be enticed to run the soft drink company. Knowles has had "far more responsibility than anybody at Cadbury Beverages North America," one analyst said.[48] Cadbury has expressed interest in retaining Dr Pepper's key managers, although it is unclear in what capacity.

Dr Pepper's entrepreneurial culture has resulted in steady growth and success by producing collaborative relationships with its partners. But how will Dr Pepper's entrepreneurial culture mesh with Cadbury's centralized decision making? John Quigley, Dr Pepper's vice president of administration, stated:

> What they've [Cadbury] acquired is three times larger than what they had before [in the U.S. market]. This may force them to evaluate the culture Dr Pepper had with more validity than what they have had because there won't be many more acquisitions like this. Instead of growing by buying big boxes, they are going to have to start building things. It's going to be a change for both environments.[49]

The marriage of these two companies presents many opportunities, but at the same time elicits questions that management must consider. Can a British company like Cadbury ever truly feel at home in the U.S. soft drink industry? Considering Cadbury's ambitions to expand its newly-acquired brands abroad, how will Cadbury market Dr Pepper in international markets, where it has not been successful in the past? What will happen to 7UP, whose international rights belong to Pepsi? Can two companies, each with its own unique culture, peacefully coexist and strategically align their goals for the betterment of the firm? The leaders of this merged company must respond effectively to these formidable challenges.

■ Notes

1. This discussion of Dr Pepper's history is based on *Clock Dial,* Centennial Issue, 1885–1985, Dr Pepper Company; G.W. Prince, Coke must acquire FTC's approval to purchase large soft drink firms, *Beverage World* 113, July 31, 1994.
2. L. Cassner, Telephone interview by Chris Petro, February 23, 1995.
3. *Clock Dial,* Winter 1994, 12, 19.
4. Dr Pepper/7UP, *Annual Report,* 1993.*
5. Cassner, Telephone interview.
6. Cassner, Telephone interview.
7. J. Quigley, Telephone interview conducted by Chris Petro, April 12, 1995.
8. L. Mirabile, ed. "Cadbury Schweppes," *International Directory of Company Histories,* Vol. II (1990): 476.
9. Ibid.
10. Ibid., 476–477.
11. E. B Lusk, "Cadbury Schweppes," *Value Line* 1995: 1534.
12. "Cadbury Schweppes PLC," *Standard and Poor's* 1995: 3992–3993.
13. Cadbury Schweppes, *Annual Report,* 1993, 1.
14. Ibid., 4.
15. J. Palmer, Has Cadbury gone crazy? *Barrons,* November 8, 1993, 10–11, 32.
16. Ibid., 10–11, 32.
17. Ibid., 11.
18. Quigley, Telephone interview.
19. C. Dawson, "Telephone interview concerning Cadbury's distribution," *Cadbury Beverages,* March 3, 1995.
20. J. Quigley, *vice president of administration, Dr Pepper,* Guest speaker at Texas A&M University concerning merger of Cadbury and Dr Pepper/Seven-Up," February 28, 1995.
21. Dawson, "Telephone interview."
22. Cadbury Schweppes, *Annual Report,* 1993, 68–69.
23. Cadbury Schweppes, *Annual Report,* 1993, 14.
24. Cadbury Schweppes, *Annual Report,* 1993, 7.
25. Coca-Cola Company, *Annual Report,* 1993.
26. G.W. Prince, "Right here, right now," *Beverage World,* February, 1992, 54–58.
27. Coca-Cola Company, *Annual Report,* 1993.
28. "Soft drink all-star review," *Beverage World,* March, 1994, 54.
29. Coca-Cola Company, *Annual Report,* 1993.
30. Coca-Cola Company, *Annual Report,* 1993.
31. Coca-Cola Company, *Annual Report,* 1993.
32. *International Directory of Company Histories,* 276.
33. R. Emproto, "Two and three trying harder," *Beverage World,* February, 1994, 34.
34. PepsiCo, *Annual Report,* 1993.
35. Emproto, Two and three trying harder, 34.
36. "Cadbury Schweppes PLC," 3993.
37. Quigley, "Telephone interview."
38. Palmer, Has Cadbury gone crazy? 11.
39. Ibid.
40. Ibid.
41. Ibid.
42. T. Parker-Pope, Cadbury confirms talks to acquire rest of Dr. Pepper, *Wall Street Journal,* January 24, 1995, B4.
43. Quigley, Guest speaker.
44. Parker-Pope, Cadbury confirms, B4.
45. Palmer, Has Cadbury Gone Crazy 11.
46. Cadbury Schweppes PLC, 3992.
47. B. Oman, Here we go again, *Beverage World,* April 1994, 95.
48. B. Ortega, Cadbury seeking a new king of pop to oversee No. 3 soft-drink business, *Wall Street Journal,* January 30, 1995, B2.
49. Quigley, Telephone interview.

---

*Notes with no page numbers are from CD-ROM databases, which often do not provide page numbers.

Cap Gemini Sogeti

Marcus J. Hurt

Ecole deHautes Studes Commerciales duNord
EDHEC Graduate School of Management

■ Introduction

■ http://www.mvlti-com.fr/cgs/
■ http://www.cgs.fr

It was Spring 1992 and Serge Kampf, executive chairman of the Cap Gemini Sogeti Group, the European leader in information technology services, was facing some difficult choices. Two years before, he and his management team had laid the groundwork for a strategy to position the group among the three or four world leaders in its profession. The strategy had been prepared, then adopted by the group's executive committee with the support of the shareholders, and finally voted on by CGS's 550 top managers at the 17th Cap Gemini Sogeti General Meeting of Management or "Rencontres" at Marrakech in June 1990. Since then, much progress had been made in translating those decisions into actions. Yet in 1992 a growing number of problems were appearing both in the industry and in the group that could not be overcome without a major revamping of Cap Gemini's traditional business lines and operating structure. The high growth rate that had long been characteristic of the group had slowed considerably, and net income was down. The time had come to finalize decisions concerning both the group's businesses internationally and the organizational structure best suited to help it meet its strategic goals.

The 18th CGS Rencontres was scheduled for June 1992. It would bring together some 600 to 700 managers of all the different companies of the group in Prague, Czechoslovakia. If the group's ambitions were to be fulfilled, the further changes needed should be announced then. The Marrakech Rencontres of 1990 had seemed to mark a major crossroads for the group more important than the Rencontres of Rome in 1987, but Prague promised to mark an even greater commitment to a path of change for the future. And the future was approaching fast. It seemed that the road from Marrakech to Prague, which had first seemed so long, was becoming increasingly short, and there was much to accomplish.

This case was written with the assistance of Gilles Serpry, of the Cap Gemini Sogeti Group. It is intended to be used as a basis for class discussion rather than to illustrate either effective or ineffective handling of an administrative situation. Best European Case Study, European Foundation for Management Development, 1996.

The Information Technology Services Industry

The industry that is now labeled *information technology services,* or IT, started in the 1960s as the data processing industry to assist corporations with their computerization efforts. It grew up alongside, and sometimes overlapped, the developing computer industry. Like the computer industry, which by 1980 was already overlapping with the telecommunications, integrated circuits, and information support industries, the IT industry had never been very homogeneous. The very rapid developments in what might be considered corporate "information" and computer-based systems had caused a wide variety of products and services to be assimilated to the IT segment. The relative importance of hardware, software, and human inputs in computing had caused the IT industry to have very blurred frontiers. This was due partly to the number and kinds of competitors. So many IT offerings called for related services upstream that competitors from neighboring industries had been drawn in, at least on a temporary basis, further confusing the picture.

Before the mid-1980s, with the major impact of personal computers and the desktop revolution, off-the-shelf PC-based software packages, and local-area networks, the general data processing industry had been mainframe technology based and could be broken down into the following segments:

- *The major hardware manufacturers:* Some 15 corporations were competing on the world market. About 80 percent of market share had been captured by American manufacturers. This industry segment could be further subdivided into mainframe and minicomputer producers, workstation manufacturers, and the developing PC segment. Some manufacturers like IBM were highly integrated into all levels of the business and delivering overall solutions including services. Most manufacturers would at least offer start-up services for a data processing (DP) system. A special niche of supercomputer manufacturers like Cray Research had developed. This niche later attracted other major players from the United States and Japan.

- *Manufacturers of IT components, peripherals, terminals, systems, and specialized products:* Several hundred companies were operating in this very dynamic market linked to the rapid technological development of the computer in its various forms, producing storage disks, drives, memories, microprocessors, modems, printers, etc. Special niches linked to desktops, videotex, and CAD-CAM systems were particularly fast growing. CAD-CAM engineering and other specialized products could be considered as overlapping into IT services.

- *IT services:* This was a very large and fast-growing industry but highly fragmented, with a vast number of companies providing services of greatly differing scope. The industry developed in the late 1960s and through the 1970s around companies with computer centers based on mainframes and terminals. The need for interfaces, operating systems, and technical personnel evolved faster than the hardware itself. Design, installation, management, and upkeep of customized information systems for corporations and public administrations were beyond the capability of many companies' personnel. Many also hesitated to incur the cost of developing the skills in-house. This caused a large number of small IT companies, often one-office businesses, to spring up and serve small, local companies. Larger IT companies developed to provide services to national corporations. Some of the larger organizations with a great need for information services developed their own departments, competencies, and computer centers. These departments were later perceived as an opportunity for high-margin diversification into a new business and were spun off as independent divisions, selling services to the market as well as providing in-house service for the parent company.

The IT industry could be categorized into two subsegments with many companies like Cap Gemini Sogeti operating in both areas:

- *IT machine-based services:* Throughout the 1980s, several thousand IT companies were operating throughout the world selling time-sharing on mainframes to companies that did not have their own central computer or needed extra capacity. Often, such machine-based service companies would provide complete solutions to management problems of their customers. At Cap Gemini this was called the "Service Bureau." CGS would provide a complete payroll, complete accounts, or similar services for a client. The fastest growing segments were network services and data bank access services. Simple keypunching services and data tabulation could also be attached to this segment.

- *IT "intellectual deliveries":* Only slightly less fragmented than machine-based services, the "intellectual deliveries" segment included needs and systems auditing, consulting, basic and applications software, systems engineering, project management, and technical assistance. Technical assistance could be considered the renting out of programmers and other IT personnel to corporations who hesitated to invest in building up their own staff for short-term projects. In the industry jargon it was often referred to as "body shopping," comparing it to the business of temporary work agencies. Yet, unlike temporary work agencies this "rented" staff was always on the providers' payroll and trained by him. "Body shopping," or technical assistance, might best be described as "time and materials contracting," in which there was commitment by the provider to quality of service but no guarantee of results or of continuity of personnel. The IT provider reserved the right to shift programmers to another job where their skills were needed and replace them with other staff suited to the assignment.

By the beginning of the 1990s technology shifts had begun radically altering the nature of the DP industry. Major IT component manufacturers like Intel, Motorola, and NEC had increased the speed and capacity of desktop computers 100-fold and over, to the point where PCs were becoming powerful workstations that could be linked on networks. This was contributing to the gradual decline of the company computer center and the mainframe solution to corporate information processing needs. The growing availability of standardized off-the-shelf components moved power away from proprietary technology, top-down computer builders to computer assemblers and marketers around the world. Software editing giants like Microsoft and Novell also appeared. They provided other standardized products—software—that could carry out a variety of very common business tasks, be customized for specific needs, and link independent PCs in more flexible systems. Their possibilities contributed to further dismantle the large computer builders' offerings.

It was in the early 1990s that "enabling technologies" set up client–server networks permitted by the new, highly intelligent client PCs. Servers were powerful PCs with great storage capacity that acted like relays between the client PCs, but unlike mainframes did not perform the processing for the PCs, which were independent units. This evolution brought about a crisis and gradual restructuring, because companies found it very expensive to make the transformation from their costly legacy systems based on DP centers. The shift to fleets of PCs saw the rise of third-party maintenance specialists who often took over upkeep of these fleets as well as the client company's applications.

These developments led to the declining popularity of body shopping, as in-house DP centers were decentralized, and to an increasing importance for two of the major offerings by IT service providers: systems integration and completely outsourced solutions. Fixed-price contracts grew in importance as clients came to prefer ordering guaranteed results rather than the delivery of components for a do-it-yourself solution.

- In systems integration the IT provider took over, planned, designed, and carried through the implementation of a complete information system solution. As PCs and software packages became simple components to tie together, integrators could call on many vendors to build their systems, rather than purchase the hardware or software of one manufacturer.

- Outsourced solutions took either the form of outsourcing itself or facilities management. Outsourcing made available to client companies large, off-premises DP centers on which to run their software. The outsourcing provider offered a cost per byte of storage and mps (million instructions per second) of CPU time that was lower than the client would pay if he ran his own center. It was the "mutualization" of resources that produced the economies of scale. In facilities management, the IT provider provided a guaranteed result, but not the means. The provider would buy a client's whole DP center and put all the DP personnel on its payroll, then evolve the system from mainframe to PCs, guaranteeing up-to-date applications, technology, and service. This would have the effect of turning the client's previously high-fixed-cost DP center into a flexible cost solution.

The tendency was growing for companies to expect IT service providers to more clearly understand their business problems and link their IT solutions with their strategy needs. IT services could no longer be considered a mere appendage added on to the company. The IT consultant increasingly needed to act as a management consultant.

■ Competition

■ The World Market

In the early 1990s, IT services worldwide was a very fragmented market characterized by national industry leaders rather than world industry leaders, but globalization was under way. Companies offering IT services ranged in size from little "shops" serving small businesses at the local level, to major corporations, increasingly multinational, providing services to giant corporations at both the national and international level. Some offered specialized services while others provided the full range of services shown in Exhibit 1. The largest companies were American and yet performed only about 13 percent of their sales outside the United States, whereas the French companies did some 18 percent abroad. In

Exhibit 1

Exhibit 1

The Global IT Professional
Services Market — 1990

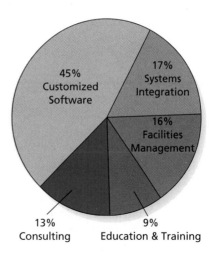

1990, total worldwide DP spending reached $330 billion. For the first time, spending on IT services alone, at $170 billion, topped the $160 billion spent on hardware. Industry growth was very rapid and estimations for the end of the decade suggested spending on services alone would reach $600 billion. Yet sales by the 10 leading IT companies in the world accounted for less than 10 percent of total world volume in IT. CGS itself estimated that the $1 billion club included only Cap Gemini, EDS, Andersen Consulting, IBM, and Computer Sciences Corporation.

■ World Competitors

Some of the competitors who could be said to compete globally included Electronic Data Systems (EDS), Computer Sciences Corp., IBM, Andersen Consulting, and Cap Gemini Sogeti.

EDS.   The world leader in IT services was Electronic Data Systems. EDS was founded by Ross Perot in 1962 and was acquired and made an independent division by General Motors in 1984 primarily to manage GM's own information services. In 1984 the company also set up its first European operation and by 1991 was established in 16 countries in Europe. In 1990, EDS reached $6.1 billion in sales worldwide, 47 percent of which was in services performed outside GM. It was expected to reduce its dependence on the captive business from GM in the coming years to less than 30 percent, particularly if it could bring its European operations to 20 percent of its global volume. To do this it was strengthening its position in the European market every year, challenging CGS's leadership through an aggressive strategy targeting major accounts and gaining market share through some important acquisitions. By the end of 1990, it ranked as the third leading IT services company in Europe. Its specialty was outsourcing, in which EDS set up large data processing centers to which it shifted all the client's processing, selling the client a lower cost DP service based on economies of scale. One of EDS's annual reports defined its practice of outsourcing: "EDS offers customers a complete range of tested proven computing and communication capabilities, fulfilling long-term contracts (5–10 years) at competitive prices. Project after project, year after year, EDS is the single point of responsibility." It also offered services in management consulting, systems development, systems integration, process management, and systems management. Its customers in Europe included Heineken, Caterpillar Belgium, Saab, and the Crédit Lyonnais Bank in France.

Computer Sciences Corporation.   Although only ranking in the top 25 in Europe, CSC was the third leading IT industry company in the world in software and services with over 500 offices worldwide. It had been operating in Europe since the 1960s and ran its operations through CSC Europe. Most of its European business was done in Northern Europe with Great Britain accounting for 50 percent and Belgium 31 percent. Only 9 percent was done in Germany, 6 percent in the Netherlands, and 4 percent in France. Sales breakdown by industry was 34 percent in public administrations, 15 percent in industry and retailing, 16 percent in financial services, and 35 percent in the rest. Fifty-seven percent of its sales was in consulting and technical assistance, 14 percent in systems integration, 12 percent in facilities management, and 17 percent in turnkey projects. It was concentrating on growth in reengineering and outsourcing. Its clients included the U.S. Social Security Administration, the Dutch Tax Office, Holiday Inn Worldwide, and the National Library of Australia.

IBM.   The biggest computer company in the world and one of the most integrated companies in the world, IBM had always been in IT services. From its very beginnings in the computer business, it had a solutions approach, in which it designed and delivered a complete DP system, including software, services, and maintenance. Nevertheless, as its overall package solution—based on mainframes, systems, and peripherals plus services—was attacked by competitors at every level over the years, IBM was obliged to disassemble its activities and create separate division strategies, making IT services a separate offering. In the United States, it set up Integrated Systems Solutions Corporation (ISSC), which concentrated on systems integration, application development and maintenance, client/server-distributed systems management, custom networking services for telecommunications, data center services, and business recovery services for recovering lost IS data. In Europe these services were offered under the IBM name directly.

Andersen Consulting.   Arthur Andersen's auditing and accounting activities had expanded into computer-based projects in 1952 and had grown quickly with the expansion of information technology. Andersen had used its favored position with corporate boards to develop its IT consulting business. Although most of its IT clients had originally come from the audit business customer base, by 1990 their share had declined to 20 percent. Andersen Consulting was spun off from the auditing branch in 1988 as an independent division and by 1990 had emerged not only as the world's largest specialist in information systems consulting but the largest consulting firm in the world. Andersen Consulting in Europe, the Middle East, Africa, and India (EMEAI) had emerged as a separate entity and had offices in 18 countries. It was well known for its specific, highly standardized methodology and tools set. At the beginning of the 1990s, Andersen Consulting was evolving from systems integration into business integration activities, thus strategy and change management consulting, as it had previously expanded from auditing into IT consulting. Andersen's particular strengths lay in its project teams, which could draw on capabilities worldwide through the personal networks of the firm partners. This permitted Andersen to target multinational clients and provide an integrated, even worldwide solution. As a partnership, Andersen's culture—as well as limited financial resources—made it shun acquisitions as a growth mechanism.

■ The European Market

The European market was very fragmented with some 13,000 IT service companies. No one player took more than 10 percent of market share. As a whole, Europe was considered weak in hardware infrastructure compared to the Americans, yet very different situations existed in the various markets.

- **France** was the most developed market, spending a greater part of its GDP on IT services than any other European country. Traditionally, most spending by French companies had traditionally been on technical assistance services. The in-house IT manager had never developed the stature of a top manager charged with helping the company integrate its business and IT strategies, as was more the case in the United Kingdom. Thus, he ran his department with little interference and tended to farm out services in a way that would secure him control of his department. This may have assisted the development of French IT companies, but limited their access to top management strategic decision makers. French companies like CGS held strong positions at home and had sought market share abroad. France had the most complete range of services available through its many IT firms. Half of the 25 leading IT service companies in Europe in 1990 were French.

- In the **United Kingdom,** telecommunications was a very developed industry, unlike many countries in Europe. U.K. companies proved more willing than companies in other parts of Europe to subcontract part or all of their DP management. The leaders in this market were Hoskyns, Sema Group, and EDS.

- Growth in IT services in the **Netherlands** was the fastest in Europe, with IT consulting leading the other offerings. Systems integration was the least well developed service and the audit and consulting firms such as McKinsey, Arthur Anderson, and Coopers and Lybrand dominated this segment. The IT leader on the Dutch market was Volmac with 50 percent of its billings done in customized software development and body shopping.

- In **Germany,** the major development had been in desktop computers rather than in mainframes. Germany also possessed two national champions in PC manufacturing, Siemens and Nixdorf. There was nevertheless the undeniable presence of IBM and DEC. German companies were generally reluctant to let outsiders have access to company information, thus technical assistance had never really become established as in France. They were also reluctant to subcontract their DP management. Information systems were usually developed in-house and purchases concentrated on applications software. Thus most IT business was in applications development and, on the average, most IT firms were smaller than their French counterparts. Germany was also a strongly regionalized country, with strong local identities, and this made it difficult to form larger national groups. The leader in IT was Debis, a subsidiary of Daimler-Benz motor company and with whom Debis did 75 percent of its business.

- In the wake of 15 years of general economic and industrial development, IT services in **Italy** were undergoing great growth and there were numerous major projects, particularly in the public sector, telecommunications, transportation, and banking. Subcontracting of services was a distinct new trend. Finsiel, a government-created company, was the Italian leader in IT but worked only on its home market. Olivetti also had an important IT branch.

- DP industry development in **Spain** was two-thirds greater in hardware than in software and services. Major IT projects were beginning to appear, particularly in banking, but no important calls for tender on the German, French, or British model had been made.

■ European Competitors

Some of the major competitors in Europe were Hoskyns, Sema Group, Sligos, Debis, and Volmac.

Hoskyns. Apart from the truly global players, British companies were the most frequently met nonlocal competitors in European countries. They could be found in Holland, Scandinavia, and Italy. In the United Kingdom, most continental European companies seeking a foothold were dwarfed by British or American companies on the market and chose acquisitions as a way of gaining market share. Hoskyns was one of the leaders on the U.K. market having developed traditional activities like systems integration and technical assistance, but particularly focusing on the high-growth segment of facilities management. In facilities management, Hoskyns would take over the data center of the client company as well as its personnel, leasing back the equipment and possibly refinancing the whole IT system.

Sema Group. Sema Group was born of the merger between the French company Sema and Cap UK. Cap UK had separated from Cap Europe when Serge Kampf took over Cap France/Cap Europe and formed Cap Gemini Sogeti. In 1990, the fourth-ranking IT group in Europe, Sema Group was similar to CGS in its business lines operating on both U.K. and French markets but with a much larger market share than CGS in the United Kingdom. It was to strengthen CGS's foothold in the United Kingdom that CGS had acquired approximately 30 percent of Sema Group's equity.

Debis Systemhaus gmbh. Debis AG, located in Stuttgart, Germany, was the interservices subsidiary formed by Daimler-Benz to handle financing for car purchases and leasing contracts. It also performed marketing research activities, and through its Systemshaus division, IT services in Germany. Debis Systemshaus processed all the work for the Daimler-Benz group, as EDS did for General Motors, and then contracted other work for outside clients. Its services included consulting for manufacturing operations, project management, tax consulting, computerization of production systems, air transport, and transport logistics.

Sligos. The core business of Sligos had always been bank transaction processing since its creation from the merger of a subsidiary of the Credit Lyonnais bank and a management information systems company in 1973. Its major activities had developed in banking information and clearing services. These included bank and credit card design and production, bank card transaction processing, check design and clearing, plus check guarantee services for retailers. Sligos also had a microcomputer retailing business whose sales had been declining in the late

1980s. The company had also moved from early service bureau activities and information systems design and integration activities into facilities management as well as outsourcing on its own data centers. Sligos had followed a strategy of acquisitions to position itself as a European player in the United Kingdom, Italy, Spain, and Germany. With more than 50 percent of its sales performed on the French market, it ranked only marginally as a European-level competitor—although second to CGS among French IT companies.

Volmac. Volmac Software Groep n.v. was a sound and profitable group and leader on the Dutch market, but only did 9 percent of its business in foreign countries, mostly Belgium. Volmac was, above all, a specialist in custom-designed software for corporate clients and also in technical assistance through fixed-price rentals of programmers and other technical staff. Half of its business was in these fields. IT consulting and analysis activities accounted for an additional 18 percent.

Cap Gemini Sogeti: The Road to Marrakech

The Early Years of the Group

Serge Kampf created Sogeti, S.A., at the end of 1967 in Grenoble, France, to provide computer-based management services to local corporations. The company underwent spectacular growth with its sales volume soaring from FF 1.5 million in 1968 to FF 30.3 million in 1974 with a net income maintained at over 10 percent of sales. This permitted Sogeti to quickly expand geographically by setting up branches in Geneva in 1968, Lyon in 1969, Paris and Zurich in 1970, and Marseilles in 1971. It gradually widened its range of services to include IT consulting, programming, basic software, and distribution of software packages. This widening of service lines took place within what Sogeti considered to be its core business of "intellectual deliveries" for information management. It also set up divisions specialized in more personnel-intensive fields like data processing and keypunching.

Acquisitions and Partners

Serge Kampf soon started the strategy that was to characterize the group over the next 25 years. The goal was to acquire a market presence on all attractive information services markets in Europe and overseas: first, through the direct establishment of Sogeti branches, and, second, by "assembling" competencies and market positions through a long series of mergers and acquisitions on the domestic French market and transnationally. The underlying philosophy was that an ambitious growth strategy was the only way to maintain market share in a fast-growing market. This acquisitions policy included seeking partners to buy into the group's capital to provide funds to fuel growth or provide access to skills and markets. The strategy followed created a globally aggressive IT services company unlike any other European group in the industry. Whether or not the acquisitions proved totally successful, and without taking into account a multitude of smaller takeovers over the years—particularly in the 1980s—the landmarks of this strategy of reaching critical size and scope were the partnership with CISI and the acquisition of Cap France/Cap Europe, Bossard Consulting, Gemini Computer Systems, and Sesa Group.

CISI.   In 1973, the French Atomic Energy Commission's newly established CISI division, which managed the scientific applications and hardware of the commission, took a 34 percent holding in Sogeti. CISI was a public company and the government was deeply involved in computer technologies. The director of the "délégation de l'informatique"[1] had great admiration for Serge Kampf. Kampf had bought the first French CII machines for the data processing part of Sogeti's business, whereas CISI was using American equipment and not French equipment. The délégation thus encouraged CISI to buy into CGS, which provided a bridge between CISI and the French manufacturer CII. For Sogeti, this partnership was also to assist in a certain diversification of its business. CISI was very experienced in scientific information services, which was very different from Sogeti's specialization in management information services. Over the years, however, CISI followed a strategy that competed with Sogeti, and cooperation between the two became very difficult. In the early 1980s, CGS bought back the CISI-held shares to sell them to another acquirer and the two companies separated. Later, CGS bought 36 percent of CISI's equity. Having become very successful CGS felt it could support a large government agency and hoped for cooperation with CISI on large contracts, profiting from CISI's capability in systems design and development, particularly in the military business where CISI and CGS were competitors. However, major cooperation projects between the two groups never really appeared.

Cap France and Cap Europe.   In 1974–1975 the basis of the group that was to become Cap Gemini Sogeti was brought together by the acquisition by Sogeti of Cap France/Europe and then Gemini Computer Systems in the United States. Sogeti, despite its newly launched partnership with CISI, was still very much a provincial French company based in Grenoble with a couple of offices outside France in Switzerland. It was still a very French-oriented company. Cap France was twice as large as Sogeti although not as profitable and with a very different management approach. Cap France had a jointly held subsidiary with Cap UK called Cap Europe, with offices in Belgium, Sweden, the Netherlands, Switzerland, Spain, and Italy. Serge Kampf was very interested in the international flavor and presence that Cap France and its subsidiary offered to the Sogeti group. The money raised through the sale of Sogeti shares to CISI was used to acquire a controlling interest in Cap. Kampf had hoped to acquire Cap UK as well in order to create a major European group. Cap UK countered with an attempt to take complete control of Cap Europe. In the negotiations Cap staff was allowed to choose, and the continental staff chose to stay with Cap France. Cap UK was left on its own as a British company and Cap Europe became a part of Cap Sogeti Group. This constituted the beginning of the internationalization of the group but left Cap Sogeti without a major position in the UK.

Bossard Consulting.   At the end of 1976, CGS acquired a minority holding in the French Bossard Group. Bossard specialized in corporate advertising and marketing communication consulting. It also had a well-developed organization and management consulting practice. Consultancy was not really part of the CGS's business, but Kampf perceived a potential synergy between the consulting and IT services. Bossard was also quite profitable and personal friendship linked Kampf with the Bossard CEO. When the opportunity presented itself, Kampf bought a

---

[1] Computer Technologies Commission.

49 percent stake in the group. This major diversification proved to be premature: Joint actions were very limited in number and Bossard's organizational consulting was shifting CGS further and further away from its core business in information technology services. The organization of the client was done by management consultants, who, on the other hand, did not do any of the IT work. The merging of management consulting with IT services would not take place for another decade. The Bossard and CGS groups also had very different philosophies and cultures. Bossard was very turned toward the French market and was barely English speaking. CGS was aiming at a global, or at least, European orientation and was increasingly English speaking. The equity holding was maintained with Bossard as an affiliated company, but the two groups operated independently. Over the years, Kampf made repeated offers to acquire the remaining 51 percent but was refused. CGS maintained the holding as a good financial investment.

Gemini Computer Systems. The acquisition of American Gemini Computer Systems in the late 1970s proved synergistic and completed the formation of Cap Gemini Sogeti, giving the newly formed group a presence in Germany, the Netherlands, Switzerland, and Iran. Thirty-five percent of Gemini was held by Gemini's CEO, who offered his holding to Serge Kampf. Other manager-owners followed and the company was soon acquired and restructured. Little by little, Gemini operations were merged into Cap's and American management left. In the Netherlands Gemini's division was called Pandata and Cap Europe's was called Cap Nederlands. After the acquisition, they both operated under separate company names but were held by the same holding company. Yet, the Gemini acquisition, like others, failed to deliver its full potential. Gemini UK was spun off by its management and kept operating under the Gemini name. This meant that, once again, CGS had not managed to acquire a solid foothold in the United Kingdom. In Germany, with the departure of the Americans, the originally quite substantial Gemini operation slowly decayed and was finally phased out. In Italy an operation with Olivetti called Syntex also slowly decayed. Nevertheless, the acquisition did add considerable European and American market presence and added competencies in the fields of major public administration projects, turnkey systems, and the marketing and maintenance of standard software packages.

By the end of the 1970s, only a few companies among the 10 leading IT companies worldwide had reached sales of between $100 and $200 million dollars per annum of a total estimated world demand of some $13 billion and most of them were American. The European market was about 70 percent the size of the American one and about three times the size of the Japanese. CGS, with 19 percent of the French market and 34 percent of its sales abroad, had clearly already reached a leadership position in Europe.

Sesa. The major acquisition by CGS in the 1980s was the French group Sesa. Sesa Group was a very strong competitor in the high end of the business—fixed-price contracts and systems integration. Sesa was 51 percent owned by the Compagnie Général d'Electricité with the remaining equity held by its managers and founders. Sesa's top management was having difficulty with its major shareholder and the CEO decided to leave and take over the management of the French computer maker Bull. His 30 percent holding in Sesa was offered to Kampf. Other managers of Sesa followed suit and joined the CGS management team, which increased CGS's holding to about 42 percent. A few years later the management changed at the Compagnie Général d'Electricité, which permitted CGS to acquire total control in the early 1990s.

The Sesa addition to the group was very important in that it provided CGS with a major position in telecommunications software and systems. Sesa specialized in this field and had built the Transpac network for France Telecom while CGS had built the computerized screen-based telephone directory for the French videotext system, Minitel. Sesa had also built a competing system to the CGS one. The decision was made to merge the two systems as well as the contracts and know-how. Telecom software thus became one of the dominant offerings of the group. The merger also moved CGS into a more financially oriented management of fixed-price contracts, which was a skill relatively undeveloped in the group. Sesa introduced CGS to their accounting mechanisms and to their management of such contracts. Many of the Sesa executives stayed on with the group.

One executive of the group summarized the strategy of these years by saying that from Sogeti the group took Kampf and his charisma, his financial engineering ability, and his management talent for reporting, finances, motivation, and human assessment, and that from Cap and from Sesa CGS took its technical structure, which underlay all the achievements of the group. The shareholders backed the group's ambitious strategy and stood behind CGS with belief and assistance whenever it was in difficulty.

Cap Gemini Sogeti's Business Lines

Business Lines 1980

By 1980 Cap Gemini Sogeti had developed the following business lines (see Exhibit 2):

- *Consulting and technical assistance:* This included drawing up complete specifications for an information system for the customer, including choice of equipment, data security, operational training, and providing technical personnel to run the system.

- *Design and production of systems:* CGS would design and deliver a complete customized system including hardware, if desired, for accounting, finance, sales, personnel administration, and industrial management applications. It produced office automation applications including in-house mail, word processing, and electronic scheduling; scientific applications for simulations; and industrial applications for line automation, quality control, process control, and CAD.

- *Major projects:* CGS would manage any major project that brought together a variety of equipment and techniques that needed to be linked.

- *Basic software:* CGS would design software for public administrations and operating systems for European hardware manufacturers.

- *Training:* Intensive short courses or continuous education programs were offered in introductory data processing for non-DP staff as well as state-of-the-art specialized courses to update the skills of DP staff. Such courses could be delivered in-house or at the CGS Computer College.

- *Software products:* Sales of licensed American software packages or CGS-designed products. Although CGS did design some software products, it

Exhibit 2   Clients of Cap Gemini Sogeti

The number of services and products furnished by Cap Gemini Sogeti over the 25 years of its existence varied greatly. In the mid 1980s it was estimated that some 20% of its business worldwide came from government contracts. Its clients were also extremely varied, some examples of services and clients follow:

Stockholm Securities Exchange	Trading system
Mazda	Vision system for designing prototypes
Minitel (the French electronic telephone directory and videotex system)	The electronic directory
Electricity of France	Computerization of transmission and remote control of electrical energy production
Polish DP managers	Training
Swedish Customs Service	DP management system
Luxembourg Ministry of Agriculture	Wine production system
Soviet Union	Production control management system, information system for meat packing plant
Airbus Industrie	Cabin configuration CAD system
Microsoft	Development of Windows solutions
Akzo Nobel Chemicals, Netherlands	Systems management
Total	Risk management and decision support system for refinery
Eureka (EU 7 country project)	'Membrain' project (Management of Major Emergencies)—software-based resource and evacuation management procedure for handling national emergencies
U.K. Royal Navy	Logistics support system to improve aircraft availability and reduce support costs
Seven former member countries of the USSR	Extension of the international communications network
Dutch Social Insurance Bank	Modernization of information systems to administer pensions and sickness benefits
Intel Corporation	Vogue, a prototype professional multimedia application for travel agencies to plan travel packages
Egyptian Ministry of Agriculture	Agricultural management support, satellite data analysis tool
Woolworth's UK	Facilities management of IBM mainframe computer system
U.K. Ministry of Defense	Operational control of Operations West Data Center
Eurotunnel (the tunnel construction project to connect Great Britain and France under the English Channel)	Establishing computing infrastructure and international systems
U.S. Air Force	Mobile ground station for reception and processing of Spot satellite imagery data
ITV, U.K. independent TV station	Financial management system for airtime sales accounting

Others include manufacturers of all kinds, banks, brokerage firms, and insurance companies

considered its own business to be in custom-designed products and not standardized packages.

- *Computer center management:* Services included consulting or the running of corporate computer departments or the actual management of the client company's department.
- *Machine-based services:* Keypunching plus processing services, time-sharing, and the Service Bureau.

Redefinition of Business Lines by the Late 1980s

During the decade culminating with the acquisition of Sesa, the business lines were redefined and consolidated to accompany changes in the market. There was a "weeding out" of hardware-linked and low-grade human resource activities characterized by low-added-value skills and products with little CGS content. The 1980s was a "a period of building a group with the common identity of Cap Gemini Sogeti and getting rid of 'bits and pieces.' " Two major business lines, one that had been strong at Sogeti and one that had been strong at Cap, were sold off, and the movement from body shopping-like activities to fixed-price contracts was strengthened.

In Sogeti the business that was to be sold off was external processing for firms, which was considered too capital intensive for the group at the time. This included the Service Bureau, which was performing services for clients on CGS machines, and selling time-sharing on CGS computers for business applications, where the group simply took over what one executive called the grinding of the data. It was felt that CGS had chosen the wrong machines and that IBM could do it better. The group was also competing with its own clients, the manufacturers. CGS preferred to expand geographically in its core business—systems services, like programming and analysis—rather than invest in capital goods. This business, under the company name of Eurinfor, was sold off to CISI, as were later the data acquisition activities like keypunching.

In Cap a strong business activity had been started in software product distribution. Cap France had been among the first to introduce American products in France. CGS did not develop products but took over representation for American companies such as Applied Data Research and others, selling nonapplication systems products—sorts and library products. Management felt there were several reasons to move out of this business: First, it was not proprietary; the group was just acting as a sales representative and developing a market for the vendors and not for the group. Second, CGS was led to develop its own systems products, which it was tempted to sell in competition with its own clients' products. Third, it was felt that selling products was a different culture and that CGS was not very good at it.

CGS's core business was refocused on systems design, systems analysis, and applications programming. The farming out of people and their skills under the form of time and materials billing increasingly gave way to fixed-price contracts. CGS was interested in moving up the quality of its people and guaranteeing their quality. Body shopping had been the initial business of both Sogeti and Cap. It was a business based on keeping large numbers of people on the payroll full time, keeping them trained for assignments, and billing for their services on the basis of a daily charge-out rate. Performance of the branches was largely measured by the utilization rate of this personnel. But Cap had gradually moved into fixed-price contracts where it predetermined the number of personnel to assign to the contract. There was a whole range of intermediary services moving toward applications management and responsibility contracts. This shift toward fixed-price contracts had started very early but developed very strongly with the acquisition of Sesa in 1987.

■ **Cap Gemini Sogeti: Marrakech**	■ **Decisions at the Marrakech Rencontres**

■ Decisions at the Marrakech Rencontres

The Marrakech Rencontres of June 1990 were the 17th such general meeting of the group's managers since its founding. The Sesa company had been part of the group for three years and CGS was a financially sound, profitable European leader about to truly embrace the changes the 1990s would bring to the industry. The decisions announced at the Rencontres would certainly shape the evolution of the company for a decade, a decade in which it would either become a global player in the industry or become relegated to the rank of a second-level competitor facing major world competitors.

The three days of the Rencontres were marked by a series of addresses and conferences led by top management, followed by votes by the 550 managers of the group attending on various development scenarios under consideration. The decisions taken were to reflect a consensus of opinion concerning the analyses of industry evolution, the values and resources of the group management as a whole.

The major topics dealt with were strategy, CGS's objectives, the business environment, strengthening company resources, developing the scope of the business, and scenarios for development of the group.

Strategy.   Serge Kampf opened the conference by reminding the audience that the broad directions outlined in 1987 in Rome on the eve of the entry of Sesa into the group had been followed. He went on to sketch his conception of corporate strategy as the art of combining resources to achieve objectives. Strategy therefore presupposed setting explicit objectives and seeking resources. Patience was needed as well as determination. Decentralization of responsibility and decision making, he reminded them, was a management principle and should not be confused with a corporate objective.

CGS's Objectives.   Kampf stressed that his own objectives for the group in order of importance were independence, money, power, and durability—making CGS a permanent entity that would live on after their departure. These objectives were put to the audience for a vote. Kampf admitted that he was surprised to see that the managers present ranked independence second and that the executive committee had ranked it fourth. Although he had always placed great importance on independence and freedom of control, he understood that now that CGS was a world leader, its managers wanted something else.

The Business Environment.   There was general consensus at the Rencontres that the IT business was relatively difficult to describe. It had been shunned or underplayed by the media because of its impalpable nature and because they had concentrated on computer and software developments. Despite its evolutionary nature, it was felt a typology of a "complex but foreseeable" business could be

Exhibit 3

Analysis of Industry in 1990,
Marrakech Rencontres

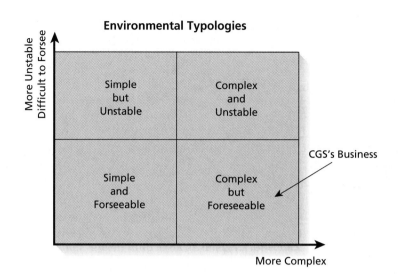

Environmental Typologies

applied (see Exhibit 3). True, binary technology was a basically complex undertaking and IT was a service business, where demand, as in all service businesses, depended greatly on behavior. Yet this complexity was offset by DP being strongly embedded in the basic mechanisms of companies, which made it relatively foreseeable.

IT services would be technology driven for the next five years at least, which would prevent it from stabilizing and becoming a commodity business. The high sustained growth and increasingly good net margins would keep the industry attractive. Clients were increasingly global companies struggling with global issues and looking for global solutions. Most world-class competitors were working with one methodology and one set of techniques and tools. The market, however, would continue to encourage low-rate, low-cost, low-margin services, so small body shops and freelancers would continue to exist. The large new entrants were appearing whose core business had been elsewhere. The managers present were polled about where they felt the greatest competition would be coming from over the next five years (see Exhibit 4).

"Surrogate offers," which offered competitors an unpredictable way of penetrating the market by taking an opposing and daring position, were discussed. In the language of CGS, these were offers from competitors who "switched" the client away from tailor-made solutions to standard products or software packages, focusing on installation and training rather than design. Such competitors broke down the total solution into standard modules and then tried to bid away business from CGS. However, CGS managers felt that connection of the modules offered a huge opportunity for consulting services at both local and departmental levels. Another surrogate offer came from facilities management (FM) providers who could make any offer from a non-FM IT service supplier useless, unless they subcontracted a part of the contract. The last form of surrogate offer was to reformulate the client's needs, usually into an upstream offer of consulting on strategy or productivity levels rather than a strictly IT offering. Two-thirds of the managers present felt FM was a real threat but were reluctant to move into the business. Despite the risks in the industry, there was general agreement that the environment was very favorable.

Exhibit 4	CGS Managers' Perception of Competitor Evolution, 1990 Marrakech Rencontres		
MOST FREQUENTLY ENCOUNTERED COMPETITORS		Today 1990 (%)	Future 1995 (%)
Midsize professional service companies		48.8	19.2
Small professional service companies		15.4	3.1
Large professional service companies		12.2	22.7
Accounting companies and other Big Six companies		7.9	16.5
IBM and other manufacturers		6.5	23
Systems integrators		4.6	13.2

Strengthening Company Resources.   Human resources were the key to the IT services business at both the technical level and the management level. It was decided that there would be an increasing need for project managers and "integrators" working with a stronger educational background than had previously been the case. The high rate of turnover among technical people was attributed to the lack of career plans, a lack of consideration, and uninteresting assignments with the group. Training should particularly be invested in the branch manager who was seen as the "prime mover" of his agency's development. A deputy branch manager to assist with the heavy reporting responsibility was envisaged. CGS university and management seminars would also contribute to the branch managers' development. A manager could also draw on the CGS management system with career committees, compensation grids, and personalized training plans to assist in running his or her branch efficiently.

Improvement needed to be made in the revenue per capita ratio. This could be done by the time-honored high utilization rate, which meant keeping down the number of staff relative to the number of contracts under way. Quoting high fixed-price deliveries and performing high quality would also avoid delays and cost-generating problem projects that "killed" revenue. Above all, capacity for more valuable work needed to be created and qualified people needed to be moved up into consulting work. Cap Gemini International Support could provide assistance through legal support in negotiations or contract implementation as well as project review and audits to help avoid overruns.

Developing the Scope of the Business.   Emphasis was given to the need for a single quality system for the group, cross-fertilization between divisions, and a strengthening of Cap Gemini's quality image through external communication, as was practiced by Andersen Consulting. In systems integration, the group should aim at responsibility contracts with ever expanded content, including long-term after-sales service but keeping away from the capital-intensive third-party maintenance business. The latter, which often meant buying a client's fleet of machines and taking over the upgrading of his applications, was very much like facilities management (FM) and had proved to be a heavy burden for the Cap group years before. Thus, there was much disagreement over moving into businesses like FM, outsourcing, and so on. Facilities management was considered by many managers to be only a surrogate offering very different from the traditional CGS business, calling for a marketing approach and proposal design capabilities that CGS did not have. It also required an international network and infrastructure like processing centers, which would call for far greater financing for the group. The options for CGS were either to reject FM, go into an alliance with a major player, or acquire an FM professional.

Diversification into strategic and organizational consulting through the acquisition of Gamma and United Research consulting firms was announced. This was meant to keep CGS from becoming dependent on upstream consulting firms, with its concomitant danger of CGS companies becoming mere subcontractors. This was seen as a logical diversification from the group's well-developed IT consulting activities and should provide business opportunities downstream in the continuum from strategic consulting to implementation. Yet, it was a different business with a different culture and should be kept separate. The group was to keep out of the software package business, because its skills were not in software authoring or distributing; they were not industrialists.

Development Scenarios.   In Marrakech three scenarios for development were presented:

1. Enhancement of CGS's professional services core business through the coordinated use of differentiators to allow billing rates based on value rather than basic labor costs, i.e., utilization rate. This would complement the CGS heritage of local authority and require no dramatic change in group culture or structure. This would increase business in squares 3 and 4 (see Exhibit 5).

2. Developing a total service approach from management consulting to systems operations, including on-site FM in all countries where CGS had even a slight presence. This would require changes in group structure to enable

Exhibit 5

Scenarios and Choices, 1990
Marrakech Rencontres

Cap Gemini Sogeti
Possible Strategic Components 1990

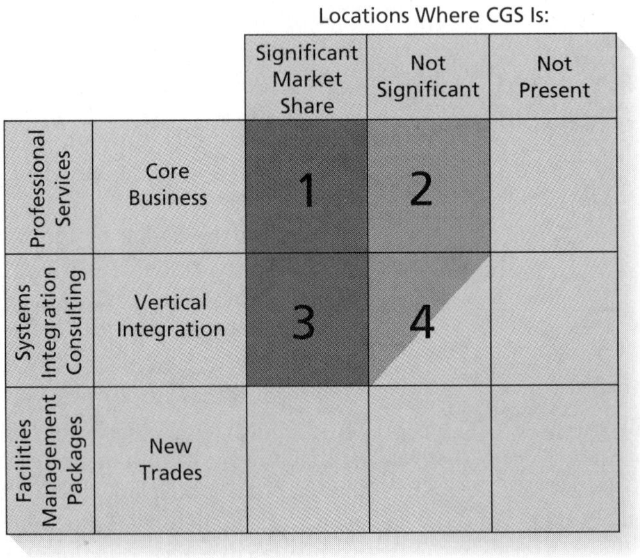

Locations Where CGS Is:

		Significant Market Share	Not Significant	Not Present
Professional Services	Core Business	1	2	
Systems Integration Consulting	Vertical Integration	3	4	
Facilities Management Packages	New Trades			

both systems integration and consulting companies in the group to operate outside their current geographic area. This would move CGS into the "New Trades" square.

3. The third scenario was the most ambitious and would aim at global leadership, based on enhancing the core business, moving into integrated solutions, enhanced systems integration, and extended FM services. This would be followed by network services as a logical follow-up to FM, and advanced technologies like parallel computing, pattern recognition, and image computing. This scenario would require very heavy financing and a low rate of profitability for a limited period.

Scenario 3 gathered the majority of votes and was thus adopted as the group's strategy. The matrix shown in Exhibit 5 was used at Marrakech to demonstrate the avenues for development for CGS in the future.

- In squares 1 and 2 core business with dark gray for heavy commitment and light gray means very small market share and an average, unsophisticated set of services, still in the core business
- In square 3, strong presence in systems integration in an extremely limited number of countries along with small presence in consulting
- Square 4, significant presence in consulting in United States and United Kingdom but overall market share is small—this is United Research
- Now we need to build scenarios corresponding to different combinations of the nine segments of this model

Conclusion. Serge Kampf closed the Rencontres by saying he applauded the vote for global leadership and that it was important for the managers to vote for what was best for the whole group and not just the group they were in charge of. He also announced that a project would be under way to define the structures of the group by January 1, 1993, because the structures would have to be adapted to CGS's ambitions. There was still much to do to increase the group's technical skills, to acquire leadership positions in countries where CGS market share was small, and to fully integrate Sesa's systems integration business into the CGS range of services worldwide. He announced the creation of SKIP (Serge Kampf Investissement Participation) as another holding company level, which would permit the entry of new capital into the group without losing control, freeing him from the constraint imposed by his desire to maintain 51 percent of the capital. The door could be opened to new shareholders at either the CGS level or to Sogeti itself.

Kampf went on to say that strategy was "well and good" but it was not everything. It was worthless without ambition, courage, intuition, and gut feeling. Ambition meant having the same ambition for oneself and one's team that he had for the group. Courage was being able to accept change when one did not really want it. Intuition did not mean making irrational choices, since the group tried indeed to choose its development path rationally, but "sensing" dangers and "sniffing" opportunities that might escape the group's strategic analysis. "Gut feeling," which he likened to "heart" and "soul," meant companies had to use their basic corporate values as the mainspring of their actions. He reiterated CGS's basic values of honesty, solidarity, freedom, daring, confidence, simplicity, and fun.

Cap Gemini Sogeti: From Marrakech to Prague

The two years following the Marrakech Rencontres in June 1990 were devoted to carrying through the ambitious objectives laid out at the meeting. Serge Kampf used his 51 percent control of the new SKIP holding company to bring in fresh capital into Sogeti and yet maintain control of the group with only 20 percent of the equity (see Appendix E). This capital went into the acquisition and establishment of companies with positions and skills needed to make the group a global player. During this time the group's total workforce grew from 13,500 to nearly 17,000 by early 1992. The major IT acquisitions were German Scientific Control Systems and Hoskyns in July 1990, and Programator in January 1992. Also in early 1992, through major new partnerships, two subsidiaries were set up: Cap Debis in Germany and Cap Volmac in the Netherlands. Finally, the creation of Gemini Consulting in 1990, after the acquisition of three consulting firms, marked an upstream move for CGS just as the Hoskyns acquisition marked a downstream diversification.

Hoskyns. Whereas the acquisition of German Scientific Control Systems gained CGS a stronger position in Germany in one of the two IT businesses it had targeted for growth, the 70 percent stake (later 100 percent) in Hoskyns, the European leader in facilities management, gave it both diversification into FM and an IT leadership position in the U.K. market. This U.K. stronghold had been denied to CGS since the partitioning agreement between Cap UK and Cap France 15 years earlier. Facilities management had been singled out by the top management and this choice had been validated at Marrakech. Cap Sesa Exploitation in France was already receiving a growing portion of its revenue in a similar activity, operations management, but Hoskyns, with its 25 years of experience, brought CGS a fully developed business that it hoped to spread to other European countries. A new joint company was set up called Cap Sesa/Hoskyns to open the door to large accounts and international opportunities.

Programator. Another acquisition furthered the group's ambition of leadership in the Nordic countries (Sweden, Norway, Denmark, and Finland). A friendly takeover bid launched on the Stockholm Stock Exchange on February 7, 1992, led to the group's acquisition of Programator, which was then merged with CGS local subsidiaries under the name Cap Programator.

Volmac. Also in early 1992, CGS organized an equity swap that gave it control of Volmac Software Groep, the Dutch IT leader. A new subsidiary, Cap Volmac, with 58 percent of the equity held by CGS, was established, bringing together CGS Belgian and Dutch subsidiaries with the computer services subsidiaries of Volmac. Quoted on the Amsterdam Stock Exchange, Cap Volmac became the largest IT services company in the Benelux, with a total workforce of 4,500 and revenue of FF 2.5 billion.

Cap Debis. On July 23, 1991, an agreement was signed between CGS and the German motor giant Daimler-Benz. Under the terms of the agreement, Daimler-Benz, through its IT subsidiary Debis Systemhaus, took a 34 percent stake in the holding company Sogeti, S.A. and not directly in CGS (see Appendix D). This brought much-needed capital into the group and, in January 1992, led to the creation of a jointly held subsidiary in Germany called Cap Debis, with 51% being held by the CGS's German partners. CGS already had a company in Germany called Cap Gemini Deutschland but whose development had not been very successful. Cap Debis brought together Cap Gemini SCS and the professional services arm of Debis Systemhaus.

A number of observers felt the agreement with Daimler-Benz marked the end of an era for Cap Gemini Sogeti, which had always maintained its independence, and for Serge Kampf, who had always kept financial and strategic control of the group. Was a world leadership position compatible with independence? Many questioned the capacity of Cap Gemini Sogeti's managers to counterbalance the weight of such a partner. Daimler-Benz was the leading European industrial group, with revenues approaching $59 billion and 380,000 employees. Kampf answered that Daimler-Benz's IT subsidiary Debis Systemhaus was only one-fourth the size of CGS and operated only in Germany. Nevertheless, the agreement with the German giant left a big question hanging over the future of CGS. Although the creation of SKIP seemed to grant Kampf secure control, Daimler-Benz had also paid FF 250 million for an option to become Sogeti's major shareholder in 1995, unless Kampf and his fellow shareholders bought back the option in late 1994. It was felt Kampf would seek other partners to help boost CGS's position and possibly dilute Daimler's influence. Talks were rumored to be under way with France Telecom, among others.

Gemini Consulting.   The event that most signaled CGS's diversification away from pure IT services was the creation of Gemini Consulting in late 1990. A project carried out with the parent company Sogeti, who held 66 percent of the new company, Gemini Consulting was born of the acquisition of the French consultant Gamma International, which specialized in organization and information systems, and two U.S.-based groups: United Research, which specialized in change management, and the MAC Group, which specialized in strategy formulation. Although operating separately from CGS, Gemini Consulting proved to be a very successful diversification, reaching $270 million turnover globally by 1992, and ranked as one of the largest independent management consultancies worldwide. The hoped-for and never realized synergy with Bossard Consulting had finally occurred through Gemini Consulting. This caused the group to redefine its business lines from the parent company's (Sogeti) standpoint in its 1991 annual report in order to include management consulting in its offerings (see Exhibit 6).

▧ Management and Structure

Management Style

Serge Kampf, like most company founders, had marked the management style of the group with his own values and personality. When he set out in 1967, the

Exhibit 6

CGS Business Lines, 1991

The Four Businesses of Sogeti

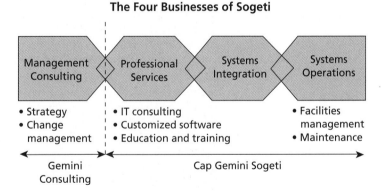

brash straightforwardness about competing, winning, and making money that characterized his company still shocked what some called the "genteel and prudish world of French business." A former inspector for the French telecommunications authority and then sales director for the Bull computer group in Grenoble, Kampf had an appetite for a free hand. The frustration he suffered from the inability to get anything done at Bull made him quit the computer group and start his own IT services company in the area. The transformation of this little provincial company into a dynamic fast-growing multinational over the next 25 years was founded on a single-minded commitment to certain strategic principles: daring; in-house entrepreneurship by operating companies and branch managers; decision making pushed down to the divisions and branches where success was measured by profitability at the local level; in-group competition to establish record performance; and tight financial control at the corporate level. The keyword was financial performance as a way of assessing the validity of acquisitions and thus maintaining profitability to finance further growth.

Entrepreneurship did not necessarily mean democracy. Kampf was known for gathering around himself a tight-knit group of senior managers who had often joined the group from the companies he acquired. Senior management remained virtually unchanged through most of the 1980s and general management turnover averaged only two to three percent. Kampf had a hands-on approach, spending a great deal of his time with his managers to ensure they understood what was expected of them. He was said to take a personal interest in his managers' families and careers. In exchange, he was enormously demanding about their commitment to the group. Each spring and autumn he went over the quarterly review with the management of each division and attempted to visit each branch twice a year. Much of the group's success was credited to Kampf's personal responsibility for and influence on his managers.

Company Organization in Early 1992

The entrepreneurial culture of CGS was perhaps best reflected in its highly decentralized structure, which itself was the outcome of the strategy of bringing together so many companies under one holding. In this structure clients and group professionals worked together in the closest possible proximity. These full-charge core units then became part of larger operational groups. There was only one management level between the CEO and the foreign subsidiaries, or operational companies. One journalist likened the CGS structure to "Roman legions" in that they waged war on their local markets and administered for the group.

In essence the over 100 branch offices around the world operated like autonomous small or medium-sized companies although the group itself had reached the size of a multinational. The branches set their own prices, recruited their own personnel, found their own clients, and determined their own marketing strategies. As Bob Sywolski, chairman of Cap Gemini of America, said, "we encourage the entrepreneurial concept that says a business is best managed by the people closest to the market," and CGS's success was based on being German in Germany, French in France, etc. Given the very different expectations of clients for IT services in the many countries where CGS was present, the freedom of the local branch seemed perfectly adapted to satisfying local needs. Throughout the 1980s the clients were the corporate DP center managers and not the managers of companies. The DP managers were happy to receive a customized service without worrying if it had been done before and the CGS IT technical staff were happy to rebuild it all over again with their own sizable staff and "ivory tower" departments that nobody else in the company understood.

Exchanges of staff were infrequent, and when staff was moved around the group, it was not on the basis of their knowledge of clients' problems and the specificities of clients' businesses, but on the basis of the staff's knowledge of IT problems. Monday meetings between companies in the group arranged these transfers of personnel for contracts, but the "lending" or "supplier" branches themselves were neither interested in what these personnel would be doing, nor participants in the projects they would be handling. This system constituted a kind of in-house body shopping with transfers of people but not of skills to the "borrowing" branch. All of the different CGS populations were used to doing everything for themselves. Group management became aware that throughout all the subsidiaries the same programs must have been created many times over.

All the subsidiaries had their own working methods and quality standards. There was no policy for a method common to the group nor a common language to describe methods used and deliveries to the clients of the different divisions. In France the method used was called Expert, in Holland STM, Logic in Scandinavia, PQS in the United States, Prism by the Hoskyns group in the United Kingdom, and Reflex for Programator in Sweden. In 1991, PERFORM, a new combined methodology, borrowing the best elements of the various approaches used in the group, was adopted by all CGS companies in an effort to unify the group's project management and quality control methods. PERFORM was "to make it easier to manage international projects, conduct technical audits of these projects, reuse certain modules on other projects, distribute high-quality technical documentation, and so on."[2]

In the words of one CGS executive, the branch structure was a " 'do-it-yourself,' cottage industry type of activity federated by a financial and controlling group, with nothing going through from one group to the other." It was above all an organization based on national markets and built for administrating. The branch manager was the key person with strong across-the-board responsibility for a whole territory whose offerings were technology based on his own resources. This generated a spirit of competition between branches whose vision was based on the annual budget.

The five-division structure of Cap Gemini Sogeti was set up in 1990 and reflected the strength of the Cap Sesa and Hoskyns divisions strategically. Cap Gemini Europe was composed of 27 companies located in 11 European countries exclusive of France and Great Britain (see Exhibit 7). The national companies were further restructured into five areas: Benelux, Nordic, Germany/Austria, Italy, and Switzerland/Spain. Geographically related companies were to share technical, marketing, and communications support as needed. Cap Sesa was the French holding company that combined all the operational companies in France, specialized by type of customer (banks, industry, etc.) or technique (training, maintenance, etc.) (see Exhibit 8). Hoskyns conducted business throughout the United Kingdom and Ireland in three large professionally specialized divisions: consulting and assistance, systems integration, and facilities management.

In each of four of the European countries—the Netherlands, Sweden, Italy, and Germany—a national holding company was established to cover several

[2] Cap Gemini Sogeti S.A. Board of Directors Report, General Shareholders Meeting of May 13, 1992.

Exhibit 7

CGS, Spring 1992

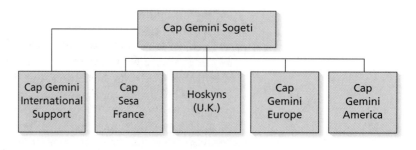

Exhibit 8

Cap Sesa: An Example of a CGS
Operational Group

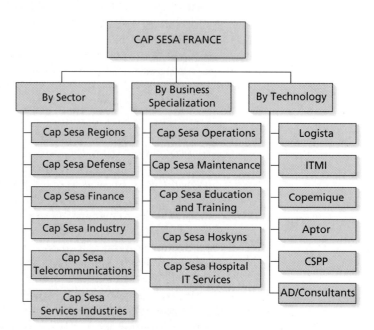

subsidiaries. For example, the various independent Italian companies of the group were merged to form one entity, Cap Gemini Italia, with four market-specialized operational units: finance and distribution, aerospace and defense, public sector and telecommunications, and industry. In Germany, three operational units were set up devoted to specific market sectors: financial services, trade transportation and regional authorities, and telecommunications.

The Cap Gemini International Support division was set up in 1989 to provide a threefold European support function for all companies in the group: in technical development assistance, including quality assurance and R & D programs through Cap Gemini Innovation; in marketing development by business sector, and to aid in cooperation within the framework of international projects; as a central support in managing the group's references; and in monitoring relations with hardware manufacturers.

Human Resource Management

CGS, like other IT service companies, suffered from a shortage of adequately trained skilled technical personnel. Universities in Europe were generally good at producing academics, scientists, and researchers but, from the point of view of the industry, had always been poor in providing people for business and industry. Their graduates had received a theoretical rather than operational, immediately applicable training. They lacked experience on the kinds of machines most used in industry—that is, IBM or IBM-standard machines—as well as in programming languages, which were dominated by IBM, such as FORTRAN and COBOL. This was due to the enticement exercised on universities by state governments to buy locally produced computer hardware. In France and the rest of Europe, throughout the 1960s, 1970s, and 1980s governments were supporting their own national computer industry champions. In Britain it was ICL, in Germany it was Siemens, in Holland it was Philips, in Italy it was Olivetti, and in France it was Bull. There were also minor players such as Nixdorf in Germany, Data Central in Denmark, and Eriksson in Sweden.

Throughout the 1980s CGS had to retrain entry-level graduates in IBM-based languages if they were to be useful to the company's clients. Typically junior programmers were hired directly out of university and trained at CGS's programming school and in the field. They would be assigned to a contract and their services not billed for approximately three months. CGS, who had very low turnover in management, nevertheless experienced some 15 to 20 percent annual turnover in technical staff, which was not unusual in the computer industry, where the shortage of qualified personnel was chronic.

When universities became aware of the need to train students for IT services, they concentrated on the polytechnic-style, two-year educational programs. With the growing systems integration market, which required people who understood business problems and could integrate technologies for customer needs, these undergraduate programs failed to produce the high-grade programmers needed by IT companies. Increasingly, CGS turned to the graduates of engineering schools. In France it was estimated that the domestic computing services industry as a whole hired 40 percent of all engineering graduates.

In consultancy, apart from the activities of Gemini Consulting, CGS's offerings were all in IT services rather than industry-specific services, and CGS consultants were generally older programmers. The market had not developed to require sector-specific consultants. Yet, there was an increasing trend for corporations to expect services more in phase with strategic objectives and guaranteeing outcomes more than operational means, requiring IT service providers to develop methodologies for designing systems that were more secure, faster, more reliable, and more cost effective. CGS managers began to acquire new types of skills in managing high-tech people and high-tech contracts, with more detailed contractual terms entailing far greater risk.

In 1989, the group launched CGS University. Although, Cap Gemini had always provided training, the university was a recognition of the need to bring together managers from the many companies and aid in building cohesion. CGS University provided courses and seminars for which employees with current or anticipated management responsibilities could register, according to their specific needs. The university's objectives were to provide a forum for exchanges between managers from different national cultures and leadership experiences, develop management ability within a specific context, and demonstrate the similarity of functions and problems from one country to another to stimulate common solutions.

Cap Sesa, the French operational group of CGS, had launched several career management initiatives and set up Cap Sesa Carrières (Careers). It was felt that employee aspirations could best be understood through the branch manager, who was put in charge of his own staff. Nevertheless, employee opinion surveys were conducted at regular intervals to provide feedback on CGS personnel

concerns and expectations. This polling style also characterized the CGS Rencontres, where all managers were asked to vote on the major issues. As part of a
career evaluation interview, Cap Sesa employees determined with their managers
the types of training to be followed over the next few years and a plan was drawn
up. These plans were then updated annually. Cap Sesa Carrières informed
employees of the availability of jobs and assignments within the group, using the
electronic mail system.

The Information Technology Services Industry at the Beginning of 1992

The Economy and Business

Since 1989, the global economy had been in recession, striking even Japan and
Germany—which was suffering the aftershocks of its reunification with Eastern
Germany. The revival of the American economy forecast for early 1992 never
happened. For two years in a row Western Europe had recorded a drop in gross
domestic product. There was a continuing recession in Great Britain, worsening
problems in Sweden, and austerity measures being implemented in Southern Europe.

Certain key industries had particularly suffered. The chemical industry had
experienced a major cutback in orders, especially for plastics and base chemicals.
Consumer electronics sales were dropping as were the industry's profit margins.
Public works projects were declining everywhere. Both European and Japanese
car manufacturers had been hard hit by falling registrations for top-of-the-line
automobiles, with even Japan experiencing a fall-off in home demand for the first
time since WWII.

The service sector, which had been a net job creator during the past few years,
was also afflicted. Banks had been weakened by shocks to the financial system
and declining property values. Insurance companies saw their investment portfolios decreasing in value with an unstable stock market situation. Tourism and
travel industries were also victims of the general slump. Service providers to the
hard-hit manufacturing, processing, and service industries had to adjust to the
slowdown. They included accounting practices, executive search firms, temporary employment agencies, office equipment suppliers, advertising agencies, and
IT service companies.

A record number of bankruptcies was recorded in France alone—some
60,000. The fall of Pan Am, Macy's department stores, and the shake-up at
Lloyd's of London were other signs of economic hard times. Governments in
many countries adopted painful austerity policies which started to cut deeply into
defense and public spending. New patterns in consumer behavior showed
consumers growing more cautious, adopting a wait-and-see attitude when it
came to laying out sizable sums on nonessential purchases. Serious reductions in
consumer spending coupled with cutbacks in public spending left companies with
great overcapacity in many industries, which put a brake on investments.

Strategic restructuring was a widespread outcome. The general trend of
companies refocusing on their core activities witnessed in the 1980s was
strengthened by the crisis. Companies were making every effort to reduce costs,
rethinking all make-or-buy decisions and subcontracting functions that turned
money and staff time away from their primary line of business. Increasingly they
were offloading their risks upstream, asking their suppliers to contribute to their
competitiveness by increasing their own productivity, quality, and flexibility and
shortening their delivery times. Corporate efforts were turned in many directions

to beef up declining margins: narrowing of product lines, new sales techniques, adding services to bring added value to the customer.

■ Technological Developments

In technology, it was becoming obvious that computer potential was well ahead of actual user needs and that this potential was increasing its lead. Faster and faster processing speeds and seemingly endless increases in memory capacity coupled with parallel architectures promised delivery of unprecedented computer power. From the ideal of a PC on every desk linked to the company system over a client–server architecture run by man–machine communication software, the world was moving toward a concept of multimedia applications, high-traffic transmissions with well-defined standards, and client–server architectures facilitated by network, application, and system management software. Also a new generation was growing up with the computer and that mind-set would be integrated into the corporate environment.

■ Political Backdrop

There was much confusion and pessimism concerning the European Union (EU) and its evolution toward common foreign and security policies as well as a single European currency, as were called for in the Treaty of Maastricht. When the treaty was resoundingly rejected by the Danish voters, received only lukewarm support from the French, and was met with outright coldness from the British, it only added to the pessimism. Also, Germany's role as the motor of the European economy seemed jeopardized by the current economic difficulties it was suffering due to reunification, dropping productivity, and the effects of an outdated wage policy. This augured badly for economic convergence of the EU countries within the time limit set, all the more so because bringing their deficits down to the three percent of GDP required for monetary union seemed difficult in a period of economic recession.

■ The Changing Nature of the IT Business

In Marrakech, CGS managers had felt that the IT industry was rather complex but rather foreseeable. Now it appeared that the industry had lost none of its complexity but was no longer rather foreseeable. Major changes seemed to have taken place overnight.

In the generally sluggish economic conditions, hardware vendors were suffering and bearing huge restructuring costs. In the United States, 100,000 people lost their jobs in the computer industry in 1991. Expenditure on PCs had outstripped expenditure on mainframes to a point of $2 for every $1. A movement toward standardization and open systems was making hardware itself a commodity. In 1991, total hardware expenditure had fallen from $117 billion to $110 billion. There was a general equipment overload and worry over the pace of technological development and the risk of investing in rapidly outdated machines. The fall-out for IT services was a slowdown and even a drop in growth, causing a reduction in CGS's performance. A number of its current competitors were also in financial difficulty.

At the same time, new competitors were appearing, moving into the business from other areas of the industry as well as from other industries, grabbing at CGS's market share. Manufacturers like IBM were looking to offset their declining hardware revenues in less capital-intensive services, and the big accounting firms like Arthur Andersen were using their power in boardrooms to influence company IT strategy decisions and develop the downstream business. Large telecom operators were beginning to leverage their vast infrastructure of communications to compete in IT services. Large banks were starting to see the attraction of the industry. Major IT users were realizing that the market was a lucrative one. In the field of software, exports of high-quality software from India had increased by 40 percent in 1991.

How could this arrival of new players be explained if there was generally such intense competition? Despite the currently difficult marketplace, global demand was forecast to double as we move toward the end of the century. Many new areas remained to penetrate in the Far East, Eastern Europe, and Latin America. New business sectors were developing, using information technology extensively for the first time. There was also the development of new needs—like in the area of personal communications, with pocket portable phones. A general restructuring of the industry was taking place, changing the rules of the game and breaking down traditional industry frontiers. Many niche players were surviving and growing. Yet, a concentration movement was taking place, as large players became even larger though acquisitions and consolidation of their positions, providing global services to global customers. This meant that, to a large extent, major positions in major countries were no longer available. Also, the Americans were taking the 1993 single-market watershed date seriously. EDS, Arthur Andersen Consulting, and Computer Sciences Corporation were investing heavily to acquire IT market share on the European Continent.

■ Changes in Customers

The industry's customers had also become more IT literate, which meant a far more sophisticated buyer public. They were no longer ready to invest in IT as an end in itself, but required the investment to help them meet specific needs. In the field of IT management, customers proved particularly demanding as well as cautious. IT should be a strategic variable to be handled like any other business variable and it should contribute to competitiveness. It should provide savings in personnel and efficiency in administration by lightening structures through dependable information, thus assisting in reengineering efforts. Innovation in the field should concentrate on user friendliness of software and systems integration for greater productivity.

The IT service provider was increasingly expected to know the user's business and needs, to understand the functioning of the latter's legal department and business processes as much as he was expected to be an expert in IT. More and more, the IT service provider found his contact in the client organization was not the EDP manager but the end user, more interested in solutions than resources. Constantly increasing IT budgets would no longer be accepted. The provider should be a partner completely involved in the client's objectives, accountable for and, at least partly, paid on results.

As Geoff Unwin, president of CGS Regions, put it: The new IT manager was no longer a craftsman but a strategic planner who oversaw the building of the whole organization, setting standards common throughout it to permit integration. His function would increasingly be that of procurement, finding the best service for the money to meet the specifications of the client. Continual reskilling would be needed to enable him to evolve side by side with his customer.

■ Cap Gemini Sogeti: Facing Challenges

In Marrakech in June 1990 the 550 managers of the group had voted to make CGS rank among the leading four or five information technology service companies in the world. To do this, the company had to broaden its range of services, strengthen its European position, and consolidate its financial structure. By the beginning of 1992, Serge Kampf felt that these objectives had been attained: the addition of FM and consulting skills; doubling the personnel over two years; and the addition of a new major shareholder—Daimler-Benz.

Yet the real mission had not yet been accomplished; in the words of Serge Kampf, who likened the challenge of creating an integrated international offer to that of crossing a dangerous river, the company "was in the middle of the ford." Such rapid growth required great adapting and assimilation. "Investments don't stop the day the check has been written, giving control of the share capital. Time, money and energy are needed for differences to fade away, synergies to appear and develop, and strategies and teams to be established."

Kampf perceived problems appearing at a variety of levels that were threatening the group's expansion:

- The growth rate of some 30 percent or more that the group had experienced through most of the 1980s had dropped to 9 percent in 1991. After 23 years of uninterrupted growth, the group's profits had fallen for the first time, sliding 10 percent. Since 1989, operating margins had shrunk from almost 12 to 7.9 percent.

- The group's image was weak globally. Almost 40 percent of the group's profits still came from France. And CGS's presence in the United States was totally inadequate, hovering at less than 1 percent of the market.

- There was a lack of coherence and consistency in the Group's offerings. From region to region there were different interpretations of service offerings—outsourcing did not include the same services everywhere in CGS. Multinational customers were getting different messages in their contacts with different CGS branches.

- There was not enough management concentration on selling, which, now that demand had slumped, was crucial.

- The traditional branch structure of the group was proving inadequate in providing access to national and multinational clients. A number of the branches were too often acting like local fiefdoms.

- The identity of the group was not really global. Clients all over the world referred to Cap Gemini Sogeti using one of its companies' names rather than the group name.

- Competition between different units in the group, which had always contributed to strong growth, had its downside when multidisciplinary and multinational teams needed to be set up. Cohesion was suffering. Geoff Unwin, the executive chairman of Hoskyns and group president in charge of CGS Regions, told of two examples of lost opportunities for the Group:

1. One was of an international public administration which had put out a call for tender in their official journal as well as in selected daily newspapers in major capital cities around the world. This call for tender was spotted by three alert CGS offices in three different companies, all of whom decided to respond. A manager in one of the offices realized that other parts of the Group might be involved and wished to coordinate efforts. However, he

was on a sales training course for the following three days and when he returned to the office, he was drafted to develop a particularly delicate sales opportunity. Although he made a note in the bid file, there was no clear handover of responsibility. As tendering was a very long and drawn out process, no one took over full responsibility for the proposal for some time. Two weeks before the proposal submission deadline all three entities on the deal were struggling to find relevant sales support and the required references. Unable to cope, they called on Cap Gemini International Support, but it was too late to put together a coordinated proposal. A high-level decision was made not to proceed.

2. The second example was of a project where the Group submitted three proposals. In one of the proposals, the company was a subcontractor for a vendor in the country where the customer company was based. In another, two CGS companies had formed a consortium to submit a joint bid. In the third, a larger company of the Group with great experience in systems integration decided to submit a proposal in which it acted as prime contractor with yet another Group company and a small, niche supplier acting as subcontractor. Although all proposals had their merits, CGS lost credibility with the caller for tender, who considered the lack of coordination unprofessional and felt it portended badly for future implementation. The contract was lost with considerable waste of sales effort and lost spin-offs for other parts of the Group.

■ The new group international quality system, PERFORM, with its standards, methods, techniques and tools, was not being applied systematically in all the companies in the group and hundreds of millions of francs were being lost.

■ There was felt to be a growing bureaucratization in CGS that was stifling initiative and slowing reaction time.

■ Although cultural diversity might be a creative force, the national differences were overshadowing lateral cooperation within the company. Serge Kampf characterized it by saying that:

The French were interested more in petty local quarrels and defense of their privileges.

The English felt that what was good for them was good for the world.

The Germans believed all businesses should be run the way they did it.

The Dutch showed an aversion to everything outside their borders.

The Americans were hardly interested in anything going on in those strange European countries where most of their ancestors had come from.

Even within one country like the Netherlands, CGS companies were being run the American, German, or French ways.

To "globalize" the company, profound changes in its culture, systems, and structures had to be carried out! In the summer of 1990, after the Marrakech Rencontres, Serge Kampf and his team had instituted a project to work out a complete revamping of the traditional organization of CGS that would enable the group to reach its strategic goals. It was to be unveiled on January 1, 1993, for the new Europe. It was to be ready to launch at the next CGS Rencontres scheduled in Prague in June 1993.

Appendix A Glossary

Applications software	Any software that performs a specific application such as accounting, word processing, etc. Applications for businesses might include financial control systems, personnel payroll systems, CAD systems, transport and logistics systems.
Body shopping	Originally an expression used relating to temporary work agencies who delivered personnel on an "as-needed" basis to companies, without making these personnel full-time employees of the agency. Extended in the IT services jargon to mean technical assistance, although the IT company personnel were full-time employees of the provider firm.
CAD-CAM	Computer-assisted design/computer-aided manufacturing.
Charge-out rate	An expression used by CGS to refer to the selling price per day of their services in technical assistance.
Client PC	A personal computer linked to a server, which acts as a powerful date storage unit and switchboard to communicate with other computers.
DP manager	The manager in charge of a centralized data processing department of a company.
Enabling technologies	A general expression meant to refer to the fact that technological advances brought man more control over information technology and made it more user friendly.
Facilities management	A service whereby the IT provider buys the computer facilities of a company, hires its DP personnel, and delivers back a complete information service of guaranteed quality.
Fixed-price contracts	Contracts in which the company guarantees a result and quotes one price for the whole service—profitability for the provider then depends on very careful assessment of risks and costs for itself.
Keypunching	A service whereby the IT provider's own personnel keyed in data for tabulation for other companies.
Mainframe	A large central computer, usually linked to terminals.
Mutualization	An expression used by "outsourcing" service providers that suggested that data processing costs were lower for companies sharing one large DP center.
Outsourcing	A business in which the IT service company provides a large off-premises center, which takes over the processing of a company's information.
Reengineering	Redesigning in-house processes in a company for greater efficiency, often streamlining old ways of doing things.
Server	A small computer acting as a storage unit and switchboard for communications between other computers.
Service Bureau	CGS's expression for providing services like payrolls, accounting reports, etc., for clients.
Software packages	Standardized software that might be adapted by each company to its own needs—word processors, spreadsheets, accounting packages, etc.
Solutions	An approach that addressed the client's business problems and offered a complete interlinked system to help him manage his business, rather than selling him components for him to assemble and adapt.
Systems auditing	Checking the suitability or efficiency of an information system for the client's needs.
Systems engineering	Designing and implementing a complete information system for a client.
Systems integration	The prime contract and project management of the planning, design, and implementation of complete information systems solutions by integrating into the system components—hardware, software, communications, etc.—from different suppliers.
Technical assistance	Cap Gemini Sogeti's expression for supplying skilled personnel to program and run a data processing department.
Third-party maintenance	Similar to facilities management, it called for the taking over of the client's fleet of machines and applications.
Time and materials pricing (contracting)	As opposed to fixed-price contracts, time and material pricing sold personnel's time and equipment on a unit basis with guarantee of quality but not of results—it was up to the client to determine their use.
Utilization rate	Percentage of personnel time really invoiced or really sold at any one time.

Appendix B   CGS Financial Statements

	1987		1988		1989		1990		1991	
	Amount	%	Amount	%	Amount	%	Amount	%	Amount	%
(expressed in thousand of U.S. dollars) Total Operating Revenue	700501	100,0	975779	100,0	1294562	100,0	1682905	100,0	1774868	100,0
Purchases	83794	12,0	131930	13,5	178186	13,8	186496	11,1	221778	12,5
Traveling expenses	28900	4,1	36056	3,7	66739	5,2	78175	4,6	97609	5,5
Other external charges	67302	9,6	84315	8,6	102306	7,9	200557	11,9	186980	10,5
Local taxes	6468	0,9	8496	0,9	13741	1,1	19321	1,1	28484	1,6
Salaries & social security charges	402168	57,4	561164	57,5	750991	58,0	956667	56,8	1046469	59,0
Goodwill amortization					11327	0,9	10940	0,7	12293	0,7
Depreciation	14488	2,1	22163	2,3	18127	1,4	36661	2,2	48112	2,7
Provisions	2907	0,4	3683	0,4	9470	0,7	6722	0,4	4915	0,3
Total Operating Expenses	606027	86,5	847807	86,9	1150887	89,0	1495539	88,8	1646639	92,8
Operating Income	94474	13,5	127972	13,1	143675	11,0	187366	11,2	128228	7,2
Financial revenue	12660	1,8	12960	1,3	32235	2,5	47814	2,8	33048	1,9
Financial expense	−15756	(2,2)	−24569	(2,5)	−36628	(2,8)	−65629	(3,9)	−47043	(2,7)
Net Financial Items	−3096	(0,4)	−11609	(1,2)	−4393	(0,3)	−17815	(1,1)	−13996	(0,8)
Exceptional revenue	5511	0,8	5532	0,6						
Exceptional expense	−14163	(2,2)	−15512	(1,6)						
Net Exceptional Items	−8652	(1,4)	−9980	(1,0)	−394		−6743	(0,4)	15586	0,9
Equity Interests & Income Before Taxes, Minority Interest	82726	11,7	106383	10,9	138888	10,7	162808	9,7	129819	7,3
Provision for Income Taxes	−38248	(5,5)	−42671	(4,4)	48849	3,8	51396	3,1	−28718	(1,6)
Net Income Before Equity Interest & Minority Interest	44478	6,2	63712	6,5	90039	6,9	111412	6,6	101101	5,7
Equity in undistributed earnings of affiliates	3571	0,5	3851	0,4	6856	0,5	8143	0,5	2356	0,1
Minority interest in net income	−1038	(0,1)	−40	0,0	−647	(0,1)	−5269	(0,3)	−4414	(0,2)
Net Income	47011	6,6	67523	6,9	96248	7,3	114286	6,8	99043	5,6
Net Income per Common Share (in US $)										
On the basis of average number of shares, option & equity warrants outstanding:										
−number of shares	3781766		4266159		24975758		29497139		35321725	
−net income per share	12,4		15,8		3,9		4,2		17,4	
On the basis of average shares outstanding as of December 31:										
−number of shares	3891890		4570463		25251046		27939313		37472775	
−net income per share	12,1		14,8		3,8		4,1		14,9	

Group Cap Gemini Sogeti Consolidated Balance Sheets					
Assets	1987	1988	1989	1990	1991
Current assets					
Cash	34312	58195	48521	99514	102046
Short-term investments	83450	147463	203905	77069	106761
Accounts and notes receivables, net	252946	336035	501381	675194	645039
Other receivables	13430	15898	29124	34938	54988
Other current assets			24848	64967	44244
* deferred income taxes	−2768	5024			
* other	18168	17315			
Inventories and work in progress net	43577	2257	3757	8912	7646
Total Current Assets	443115	582187	811536	960594	960726
Noncurrent assets					
Investments			226128	318759	325512
* Equity investments in affiliates	25363	29256			
* Other investments in affiliates	1310	161026			
Other noncurrent assets	2362	4314			
Property, plant & equipment net of accumulated depreciation	62536	74960	74817	161320	129040
Intangible assets			227202	859022	848126
* Goodwill	136017	168546			
* Other intangible assets	854	1391			
Total Noncurrent Assets	228442	439493	528147	1339101	1302678
Total Assets	671557	1021680	1339683	2299695	2263403
Guarantees given by third parties	14839	16793	23513	20274	5766

Group Cap Gemini Sogeti   Consolidated Balance Sheets

Liabilities & Shareholders' Equity	1987	1988	1989	1990	1991
Current liabilities					
Financial debt	43442	60384	78220	164492	175455
Operating debt	232574	263294	384551	486294	460528
Other current debt	19716	39011			
* deferred income taxes			4876	7733	4426
* other current liabilities			51425	78329	26112
Total Current Liabilities	295732	362689	519072	736848	666522
Debenture loan	98532	98532	107752	107752	
Convertible bonds				280571	279918
Other long-term liabilities	52108	175645	214998	451020	122863
Deferred income taxes	8057	10083	6091	1278	
Minority interest	3472	248	2541	145052	142524
Shareholders' equity					
* Common stock	13060	15337	185329	205059	275030
* Retained earnings	153585	291623	207652	257829	673870
* Share capital					
* Additional paid-in capital					
Total Shareholders' Equity	166645	306960	392981	462888	948899
Net Income/Loss for the Year	47011	67523	96248	114286	102677
Total Shareholders' Equity					
Before appropriation of income/loss	213656	374483	489229	577174	1051577
Total Liabilities and Shareholders' Equity	671557	1021680	1339683	2299695	2263403
Commitments	28562	33897	72958	417649	641750

Appendix C

Companies in the Group—1992

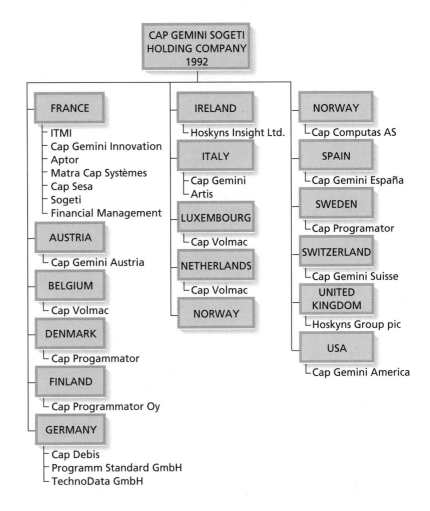

Appendix D   CGS Affiliated Companies—1992

French Subsidiaries	%
Cap Sesa Defense	100
Cap Sesa Operations	100
Cap Sesa Finance	100
Cap Sesa Training and Education	100
Cap Sesa Hoskyns	100
Cap Sesa Hospital IT Services	100
Cap Sesa Maintenance	100
Cap Sesa Regions	100
Cap Sesa Telecommunications	100
Cap Sesa Service Industries	100
Aptor	100
Copernique	74
ITMI	100
Logista	100
Cap Gemini Innovation	100
Cap Gemini International Support	100
Cap Gemini Sogeti University	100
European Subsidiaries (Apart from France)	
Cap Debis and its subsidiaries	49
Cap Gemini Austria	100
Cap Gemini España	100
Cap Gemini Suisse	100
Cap Programator and its subsidiaries (Nordic countries)	100
Hoskyns and its subsidiaries (United Kingdom)	73
Cap Volmac and its subsidiaries (the Benelux)	58
American Subsidiary	
Cap Gemini America	100
Investments Accounted for on the Equity Basis	
Gemini Consulting	34*
CISI	36
Bull Ingenierie	46
Carelcomp (Finland)	50
AU System Invest (Sweden)	50

*The remaining 66% is held by the group's parent company, Sogeti S.A.

Appendix E

CGS Shareholders—April 1992

*Serge Kampf Investissement Participation.

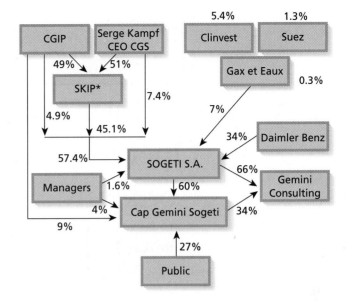

Appendix F

Evolution of Staff Distribution in CGS between 1990 and 1992

**CGS Staff 1990
14,000**

**CGS Staff 1992
24,500**

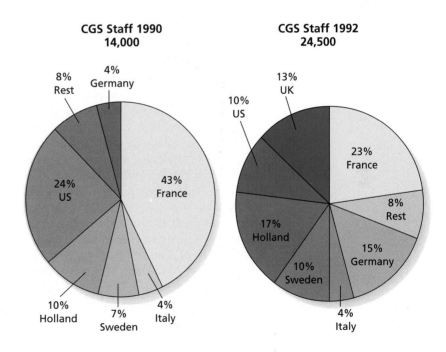

Chrysler's International Operation: Beijing Jeep Company

Justin Tan
California State University–San Marcos

■ http://www.jeepunpaved.com
■ http://www.chryslercars.com/

In late 1989, Chrysler Chairman Lee Iacocca found himself in the midst of political controversy with Chrysler's Chinese ventures, the Chrysler's engine plant and the Beijing Cherokee Jeep project. Following the June 4th incident in which the Chinese government used military force to quell student demonstrations, human right groups protested and urged Chrysler to close down its China operation, and to slow down or stop any new investment in China. Some of Chrysler's American vendors—small companies supplying parts to Beijing Jeep—called the company to say they had no desire to do business in China anymore. Chrysler officials also discovered in the weeks after the Beijing incident that some shipping companies were unwilling to carry cargo to China.

The Beijing Jeep Company, Ltd. (BJC), is a joint venture inherited from American Motor Corp. AMC was formed in 1954 by the merger of two failing car companies, Hudson Motor Car Company and Nash Kelvinator Corporation. AMC was at its strongest in the years immediately after the merger, under the leadership of George Romney, AMC's president from 1954 to 1962 and later governor of Michigan. Yet AMC never achieved more than 7.5 percent of the American car market (Exhibit 1). By the mid-1970s, the company was being sustained largely by a single, highly profitable product, the Jeep. In 1970 AMC purchased Kaiser Jeep Corporation from Kaiser Industries, the company that made the famous four-wheel-drive utility vehicles. AMC overhauled the design of the car, gave it a sporty look, and started to market it as a recreational vehicle for private use—a high-priced substitute for the passenger car or station wagon. Marketing was made easier by the fame and recognition of the Jeep name.

A few features distinguish the auto industry from other industries: (1) economies of scale, which is the minimum efficiency size (MES) required to compete in the market (Exhibit 2 shows the increase of MES with reference to

This case was prepared as a basis for class discussion rather than to illustrate either effective or ineffective handling of a managerial situation.

Exhibit 1

Market Share (1953–1988)
Based on U.S. Car
Registrations—Big Four

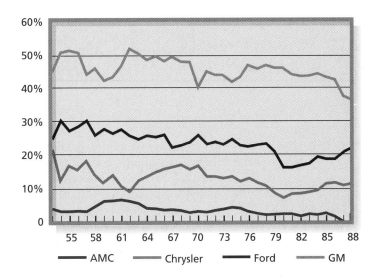

Exhibit 2   Minimum Efficient Scale (MES) of Production
(Selected Years with Reference to British Data)

Year	Largest Firm's Share	Total Market	Estimate of Largest Firm's Production	MES	MES Estimate
1947	21%	287,000	60,000	150,000	0.4
1954	38%	769,000	292,000	600,000	0.5
1960	36%	1,352,000	486,000	750,000	0.6
1967	45%	1,552,000	700,000	1,000,000	0.7
1974	48%	1,543,000	740,000	1,250,000	0.6
1977	49%	1,315,000	651,000	2,000,000	0.3

Source: D. P. Quinn, Jr., 1988, *Restructuring the Automobile Industry: A Study of Firms and States in Modern Capitalism* (New York: Columbia University Press). (Some analysts suggest that MES varies among elements of a car.)

British data. Firms with production levels below the MESs for cars and their component parts operate at a per-unit-cost disadvantage compared to companies that exceed the MESs.); (2) high barriers to entry and to exit; (3) technological changes that shape the industry; (4) high unionization; (5) government regulation, and (6) distribution network, service, warranty, and financing programs. These elements along with fierce domestic competition prompted automakers to seek global expansion.

In the late 1970s, AMC's domestic market share in the United States fell to about 2 percent. In the meantime, the People's Republic of China started to attract worldwide attention because of its large potential market, low labor cost, newly introduced economic reforms, and its strategic location for exporting to the rest of Asia and competing with the Japanese. Mercedes-Benz, Fiat, British Leyland, Volkswagen, Ford, etc., following Japanese companies such as Toyota,

Nissan, Mitsubishi, and Daihatsu, all sent emissaries to evaluate business prospects in China. In May 1983, after four years of negotiation, AMC and the Beijing Automotive Corp. agreed to form a joint venture, the Beijing Jeep Company, Ltd., to produce jeeps in Beijing, the Chinese capital city.

Making the Deal

The deal was a landmark, the largest manufacturing agreement up to that time between a foreign corporation and China. AMC and Beijing Automotive Corp. would form a new joint venture called Beijing Jeep Co. AMC would own a 31.35 percent stake by contributing $8 million in cash and another $8 million in technology. The Chinese agreed to put up to $35 million in cash and assets for 68.65 percent of the new company. The board of directors of BJC would include seven Chinese representatives, one of which would serve as chairman, and four Americans. For the first three years an American would hold the title of president and CEO. After that time the job would rotate between the Chinese and Americans.

Wall Street and the American media anticipated nothing less than enormous sales. Jerry L. Sloan, AMC's vice president who orchestrated the news coverage, summed up the significance of the joint venture: ". . . portrayed AMC as having an innovative international presence, gave credit to AMC for pulling off a business coup, and added a new dimension to American Motors." From 1980 to 1983, AMC reported a total loss of $491 million , and $66.1 in the first quarter of 1983. Following the announcement of the deal, AMC's stock jumped 40 percent in two weeks, from $7.50 a share to $10.50. At the press conference in Beijing, Joseph E. Cappy, AMC's executive vice president, said AMC would reinvest profits earned from BJC to increase AMC's equity share to as much as 49 percent, and was confident that BJC would be able to export Cherokee Jeep from China to other countries in Asia. "For American Motors, [Beijing Jeep] has meant not only an entry into the Chinese market, but the establishment of a strategic manufacturing base in the Pacific rim of Asia," Cappy said.[1]

Early Operation at BJC

Bringing the two sides together was not an easy task, because the partners came from very different societies with different economic conditions and historical backgrounds. In addition, the two sides do not always share the same goals. The Chinese hoped to digest the sophisticated technology and eventually rank among the world's most advanced auto producers, while the Americans hoped to establish a base in a foreign country that would enable them to manufacture cars at low cost and compete in Asia.

After the venture started in January 1984, the two sides clashed over the nature of the new jeep and the method by which it would be manufactured, because the vague language of the agreement did not spell out what kind of new jeep the venture would develop. According to the agreement between AMC and Beijing Automotive Corp., BJC was to make the Chinese BJ212 while developing a new generation of Jeeps, known as the BJ213, based on AMC technology, but designed jointly by AMC and the Chinese. The Americans wanted it to be as similar to other AMC jeeps as possible so that parts would be interchangeable.

BJC's Chinese officials wanted a military jeep for the army, historically Beijing Automotive Corp.'s most important customer. The military purchases at least 10 percent of all jeeps produced, and during war time, the military is entitled to purchase all of the products. The army wanted a four-door vehicle with a soft convertible top so that soldiers could open fire from inside the car and quickly hop in and out. Such a vehicle could not be designed based on AMC's existing jeeps, and developing the vehicle would cost at least $700 million.[2] Neither China nor AMC had the money. Several AMC vice presidents visited Beijing later in 1984 to convince the Chinese to accept the idea of assembling AMC's newest product, the Jeep Cherokee, from parts kits imported from the United States. This was a fundamental change in plans and allowed AMC to make money by selling kits. The Chinese accepted the idea but had not completely abandoned the idea of eventually producing a new Chinese-made jeep. BJC expected to reach annual production of 40,000 Cherokees in 1990. AMC seemed to be misleading China with a sales technique commonly known to American consumers as bait-and-switch, which reshaped AMC's commitment in China, yet it failed to foresee a serious problem: Where does BJC obtain the continuous foreign exchange to buy Cherokee kits?[3] Whenever such large-scale use of foreign exchange is involved, it needs import licenses. Cherokee was not formally cleared with the government.

There was tension between the Americans and the French within AMC's top management regarding the BJC project. In September 1984 Paul Tippett, AMC's CEO who signed the China deal, was replaced by Jose J. Dedeurwaerder, a Renault official who had never been enthusiastic about AMC's move into China and was known in American Motors for saying that the China project was crazy. To make matters worse, Dedeurwaerder had an especially frosty relationship with Tod Clare, formerly AMC's vice president for international operations, who negotiated the BJC deal and directed the China operation. Dedeurwaerder refused to visit China.[4] In addition there was tension between AMC's domestic manufacturing people and its international division, headed by Clare.

Some cultural differences were also unfolding on both sides. At AMC's 1985 annual dealer show in Las Vegas, the company planned to unveil its new Comanche truck, which AMC also hoped to introduce eventually in China. The show was held at approximately the same time as a scheduled meeting with the Chinese delegation. Hoping to "educate" the Chinese partners in the American lifestyle and ways to market its new products, the company held a series of meetings at Las Vegas' MGM Grand Hotel, and arranged to have a one-night overlap with the dealer show, in which two red Comanche trucks were introduced, accompanied by two girls in bikinis and the Beach Boys, the rock group selected especially for its appeal to AMC's middle-aged dealers. For the Americans, the show was a big affair and an epic production, one on which the company spent lavishly to impress the dealers. Not impressed by the scene, BJC's Chinese Chairman, Wu Zhongliang, was dissatisfied with AMC's unwillingness to pursue new investments at BJC while spending $1 million on the dealer show and an open confrontation with Dedeurwaerder resulted.

More problems arose when BJC ran out of foreign exchange later in 1985. AMC had hundreds of Cherokee kits piled up to be shipped to China, but BJC had trouble getting a government import license and had no hard currency to buy them. Moreover, housing costs for AMC's expatriate staff had risen 38 percent when luxury hotels increased their rents. The company was virtually broke, and the plant was shut down for two months in early 1986.[5] Don St. Pierre, then

BJC's American president, appealed to the top Chinese leaders. After intervention by then-Premier Zhao Ziyang, large loans, new capital funds, and foreign exchange were provided. Stockpiled Jeeps were purchased by the government. BJC resolved the problem and was back in production. BJC was also given preferential treatment on import tariffs, and was allowed to convert AMC's share of dividends into U.S. dollars and send back to the United States.

Major Product Lines

Cherokee is considered to be a high class vehicle. In his public statement on the day Chrysler announced its takeover of AMC, Lee Iacocca made it clear that some of AMC's assets were more important than others, and that AMC's Jeep was on the top of the list. "For Chrysler, the attractions are Jeep, the best-known automotive brand name in the world. . .," Iacocca said. The Jeep Division gave Chrysler an instant entry into the booming 4WD truck market.

The new Cherokee (1985) being assembled in China is powered by a 2.5-liter AMC petrol engine from the United States. There is a question, however, of whether the Cherokee is really suitable for China, or whether the more basic BJ212 is better. BJC engineers have already found it necessary to make design changes on the chassis frame and suspension. In fact, the Cherokee has been modified to suit the Chinese market. Optional extras have been deleted, and the vehicle is not as luxurious as the U.S. version. It was agreed that for seven years exports were to go through AMC—now Chrysler—outlets. Inside China there was a black market for the Cherokee. A Cherokee was a commodity: A Chinese municipality could buy it then trade it for something else.

Beijing Jeeps are produced in different versions, but they are all based on a relatively heavy-gauge chassis frame, which gives the vehicle strength and a stiff base on which to mount the sturdy mechanicals: engine, a three-speed manual gearbox, 4WD transmission, long travel, semi-elliptic leaf spring suspension, and a high- and low-speed transfer box. Both the BJ212 and the civilian version BJ212A are not fuel efficient. The BJ212 has been exported from China to the Netherlands, France, and Australia in small numbers. Some had to be modified and upgraded to meet current safety regulations applying to those export markets.[6] The original BJ212 design was later replaced by a modified version, BJ212L.

Derived from this Beijing Jeep, which was originally a Soviet commander car, is the BJ121A. The BJ121K version has all the features of the BJ121A plus a canvas top with side windows, which cover the whole vehicle; it can double as a 10-seat rural bus.

The Chinese Market

Tod Clare believes that the volume of cars sold in the United States is stable, about fifteen million or so a year. Western Europe was the same, a totally saturated market. In either place one can only sell more cars for his company by stealing another firm's market share. Latin America's economies were bad, and Africa is worse. China and the Soviet Union are the two last large-scale automotive markets in the world with potential for huge growth in volume that have yet been hardly explored.[7] It presents both a challenge and an attraction to the West. The potential is great, for China covers about 20 percent of the world's land mass and about a quarter of the world's population lives there. China has about 200 million families. If each year 0.1 percent of them bought cars, the number of private vehicle sales in China would reach 200,000 annually.[8] No matter how much Chinese state enterprises wanted to protect their market from the foreign competitors, they will be unable to do so.

With a heavy emphasis on agriculture, China may be the world's biggest potential market for 4WD vehicles. With Japan holding about 97 percent of the (100,000 a year) 4WD market in the Pacific Basin, the attractions of this opportunity to the U.S. company are clear.[9] AMC is the first foreign company to establish operations in this part of the Chinese automotive sector. It has enabled a cheap wage manufacturing foothold to be established in the Far East with the potential to compete with Japanese producers.

Most cars in China are publicly owned. Of those, half are imported models. The proportion of old vehicles still in daily use is much higher than in Western countries, and the government intends to replace them soon to improve safety and energy efficiency. There are about 1.7 million township enterprises and 150,000 urban collectively owned enterprises that are more autonomous than state-owned enterprises. As these enterprises develop, more vehicles will be needed. Currently, owners of private cars are mainly businesspeople, especially private entrepreneurs. At least 1.5 to 2 million cars will be needed by the year 2000.[10] Due to shortages, there are long waiting times for private cars or vans. In many cities there is no commercial showroom. Agents buy wholesale from factories and display on blackboards the inventory of what they have to offer. Thus vehicles are often bought "unseen and uninspected." After placing an order, prospective private individuals may have to wait up to a year for delivery. Consequently, the price is high. Exhibit 3 lists prices of some selected models made in China.

There is an immediate need for vehicles for the 1990 Asian Games to be held in Beijing. At least 1,500 cars and 1,000 vans and trucks will be needed, plus an as-yet unspecified number of luxury coaches. While the Chinese hope that they can step up the manufacture of locally built vehicles, there will be large imports of such vehicles.

The Political and Economic Environment

The Chinese economy has experienced a period of dramatic change. As a result of economic reforms and the introduction of market mechanisms, provincial and local administrators and managers have acquired more decision-making abilities, and new profit-sharing incentives have encouraged the use of these added capabilities. Provincial governments have been given a great deal of financial independence from the central authority. Some provinces are getting rich at the expense of central government, and these provincial governments have gained increasing bargaining power over the central government. Even though economic activities are still subject to a substantial amount of state intervention, these changes have moved some sectors of the Chinese economy a step closer to a market system. An overhaul of the Chinese government was announced in March 1988 that was aimed at cutting red tape, ending inefficiency, and expediting economic reforms. In 1989, however, a return to centralized economic planning was announced. The new general secretary of the Chinese Communist Party,

Exhibit 3   Official and Market Prices of Cars in China (March 1989, in U.S. $)

Make and Model	Official Price	Market Price
Audi 100, 4 cyl 2,203cc, 96 bhp	94,990	97,630
VW Shanghai Santana 1,800cc, 4 cyl, 88 bhp	31,520	41,080
Beijing Jeep 212 L 4×4 2,245cc, 4 cyl, 71 bhp	9,830	10,370
Tianjin Daihatsu Charade 993cc, 3 cyl, 71 bhp	22,900	26,940
Tianjin Daihatsu Minibus 843cc, 3 cyl, 56 bhp	13,470	14,820
Peugeot 505 Estate 1,971cc, 4 cyl, 93 bhp	30,710	41,755
Peugeot 504 Pickup 1,971cc, 4 cyl, 93 bhp	22,090	25,320
Shanghai SH 760 A 2,232cc, 6 cyl, 90 bhp	16,160	21,930

Source: A. Hope and M. Jacobson, 1989, China's motor industry: Risks and opportunities to 2000. *The Economist Intelligence Unit, Special Report No. 2008*, November.

Jiang Zemin, is a China and Soviet Union trained automotive and electrical engineer and has an in-depth knowledge of the automobile industry.

It is predicted that there will be political conflict between the hardliners and the reformers, especially during the transition of the power structure, and there may be political and social unrest during this process.[11]

While industrial enterprises have acquired more autonomy than ever before, the central government still has substantial power and influence over business activities, because it controls the majority of raw materials and the distribution system. It also remains the largest customer and product distributor.

In Chinese industrial enterprises, union membership is basically universal. The primary concern of labor unions is workers' welfare. The union's role becomes more important in joint venture companies, where the Communist Party and government do not have direct involvement.

About Government Regulations

Compared to the United States, China has less rigid emission control and safety standards. As in other parts of the world, the Chinese government has tried to regulate car sales by raising or lowering taxes. The Chinese recognize that there are subtle differences between a law and rules and regulations. A law has to be obeyed, whereas rules and regulations can often be interpreted in different ways and hence be observed in part or even be ignored.[12] Many foreign businesspeople have learned that it is important to build long-lasting relationships with Chinese business partners.

All foreigners and foreign companies owning cars or any other vehicles in China have had to take out third-party motor vehicle insurance since February 15, 1989. Chinese individuals who own vehicles must also insure them for third-party risks.

■ Foreign Competition for Presence

Trade between China and South Korea is rising. It is only a matter of time before China officially does business with South Korea rather than through middlepersons in Hong Kong or elsewhere. South Korea auto manufacturers have shown interest in joint ventures in China. Kia Motor Corporation is considering setting up a plant in Shandong Peninsula. Daewoo is also interested in a joint venture. China is critical about the Japanese tendency to transfer obsolescent know-how and its reluctance to build factories in China, suggesting that it welcomes South Korea investments.

Due to lack of maintenance and difficulty in obtaining spare parts, many of the taxis in China need to be replaced. The government is considering lifting the ban on imports from Eastern Europe. According to the Ministry of Material Supply, China will import 10,000 Volga and 10,000 Lada cars from the Soviet Union, 5,000 Polonez and 5,000 Fiat 126p cars from Poland, and some Dacias from Romania.[13] Trade with the Soviet Union and Eastern Europe might not provide the most advanced technology, but since China has the consumer goods these Eastern European countries need, and most of these countries do not have sufficient foreign exchange, most imports have taken the form of "compensation trade," or barter trade.

In his first speech as Communist Party general secretary in 1985, Soviet leader Mikhail Gorbachev declared that improving relations with China would be one of his highest priorities. Under Gorbachev, the Soviet Union quickly became China's fifth largest trading partner. The Soviet visited Beijing Jeep in 1988 and proposed a new idea—a joint venture between Beijing Jeep and the Soviet Union, allowing the new technology to be transferred to the Soviet Union, from which the Chinese obtained the design for its first jeep over three decades ago.[14]

Japanese automakers have been selling into China since the early 1970s. Toyota decided that China was beginning to prosper and began to sell trucks, buses, luxury cars, taxis, and motorcycles. Soon after, Nissan, Daihatsu, Suzuki, and Mitsubishi, and others followed. Between 1983 and 1984, Japan's car and truck exports to China increased sevenfold, from 10,800 to 85,000, and China became the second largest foreign car market after the United States. The massive imports of vehicles resulted in rapid depletion of foreign currency reserves and resulted in cancellations of further import licenses. Following their disenchantment with the Japanese and particularly the steadfast refusal of Japanese car, truck, and bus manufacturers to get involved in joint ventures in China, the Chinese government showed intentions to shift its interest to the Western Europe and the United States.

Since about 1983, the Chinese government has encouraged greater involvement by foreign partners in major automotive projects. This usually involves both manufacturers and financial institutions. There are two basic types of joint ventures:

- Equity joint ventures, in which the Chinese and the foreign firm(s) jointly invest and manage. The minimum foreign investment is generally 25 percent of the total equity.

- Contractual/cooperative joint ventures, which can take any form agreed on by both sides. Most of the thousands of recently concluded joint ventures in a variety of Chinese industrial enterprises fall into this category. The Chinese side will usually provide labor, land, and factory buildings, while the foreign partner will provide the technology, equipment, and financing.

The Chinese government has established some additional incentives, including taxes, bank loans, and foreign exchange, to encourage foreign companies to reinvest earnings or export their product. For instance, the new tax law allows a joint venture company to apply for a waiver of import tariffs when 40 percent of the parts are made in China. Whereas there are many joint ventures in other industrial fields, in the automotive sector there are relatively few true joint ventures in which both the foreign and Chinese partners fully share the commercial risk. Exhibit 4 introduces some selected foreign investments and joint ventures in China's automobile industry. Exhibit 5 is a Chinese national map that indicates locations of some selected major Chinese auto manufacturers and their foreign partners, as of 1985.

Besides these ventures in automobile manufacturing, there are numerous such projects with heavy-duty truck and auto parts manufacturers.

BJC Before the Takeover

As of 1989, Beijing Jeep had 4,300 employees, including 800 administrators, engineers, and technicians. Its main manufacturing activities were producing chassis frames and body panels, welding, painting, and final assembly.

Labor costs were low. Initial wage costs at the BJC plant were put at 60 cents an hour, compared to labor costs (including fringe benefits) of about $22 an hour in the United States and $12 an hour in Japan. There were other hidden costs, however, including medical care, educational expenses, etc., that were traditionally paid by the employer. Clare believed that regardless of these hidden costs, it would be nowhere near the U.S. rate of $22. In 1986, the approximate average expense for an AMC staff member in China added up to about $220,000, including salaries, $70,000-a-year rents, and their three trips a year back home plus vacations. Some of the tasks could be handled by the Chinese. For example, some AMC employees read novels or always seemed to be asleep in their offices.[15]

BJC adopted the American management style. Traditionally employees were guaranteed lifelong employment in China, and they were basically paid the same regardless of their performance. This system was discarded at BJC. The company offered strong incentives for high performance, and the names of those who violated work rules were put on the "mistake list." If they were listed three times, they were in danger of being fired. Since its inception, BJC had fired nine Chinese and eight American middle managers. St. Pierre lobbied but failed to win the Chinese support for a more fundamental reform of the salary system, which

Exhibit 4   Major Foreign Participation in China's Motor Industry

Products	Partners	Date and Contract Type
Dump truck	Terex, UK Inner Mongolia No 2 Machinery	1987 20-year joint venture
Dump truck	Aveling Barford, UK Beijing Dump Truck Plant	April 1986 7-year coproduction
Forklifts	Toyo Umpanki, Japan China Machinery & Equipment Import & Export Corp.	1986 Technology transfer
35-seat medium-sized buses	Hino Motors, Japan China Shenyang Aircraft Corp.	1986 Technology transfer
Charade cars	Daihatsu Motors, Japan Tianjin Auto Industry Corp.	November 1986 7-year licence
Light commercial vehicles	Mitsubishi Motors, Japan CNAIC, Liuzhou Auto Industry Corp.	1986 Coproduction
Pickup	Isuzu Motors, Japan Chongqing Automotive Industry Corp.	August 1984 Joint venture
Small trucks	Isuzu Motors Ltd. & T Ito Commercial Co. Nanjing Auto Plant	1983 Technology transfer
Light trucks	Fiat Group, Italy Nanjing Auto Plant	September 1986 Technology transfers
Passenger cars	Volkswagen, W.G. Shanghai Tractor Auto Co. & Others	November 1982 Joint ventures
Diesel engines	Perkins Engines Beijing Jeep Corp.	April 1982 Cooperation and production agreement (lapsed)
4 × 4 vehicles	AMC–Chrysler Motors Beijing Jeep Corp.	January 1979 Joint venture
Light duty truck, then other passenger vehicles	Peugeot Automobiles, French CITIC, Guangzhous Auto Man. IFC & Banque International de Paris	Joint venture
Light trucks	Hong Kong Shortridge CITIC Beijing No 2	Joint venture
Passenger cars	Volkswagen, W.G. 1st Automobile Corp.	Equipment transfer from New Jersey
Passenger cars	Citroen, French (30%) 2nd Automobile Corp. (70%) (GM also interested)	February 1989 Joint venture

Source: A. Hope and M. Jacobson, "China's Motor Industry: risks and Opportunities to 2000." *The Economist Intelligence Unit, Special Report No. 2008,* November 1989.

would increase Chinese workers', especially BJC's Chinese managers', salaries substantially, because the Chinese felt that too large a difference in pay among Chinese employees might backfire.

Apparently both sides were satisfied with the success of the joint venture, now that some of the problems of 1986—when the joint venture company temporarily ran out of the foreign exchange allocation required to import essential components—had been resolved. The Chinese abandoned their hope of making a

Exhibit 5

Vehicle Production in China

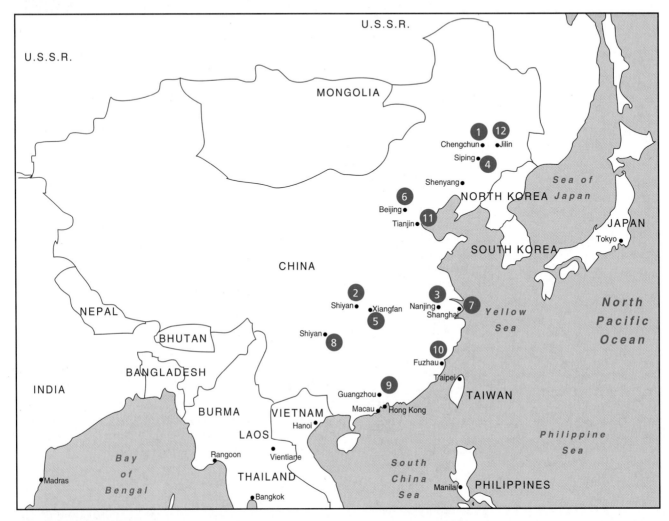

1. China's largest commercial vehicle plant, output 80,000 per year
2. China's second largest commercial vehicle plant
3. China's third largest commercial vehicle plant
4. Truck plant
5. Truck plant, Nissan Diesel negotiating deal for additional 20,000 trucks per year
6. Commercial vehicles, AMC Jeeps, Cars, Suzuki license for 4WD vans and pickups
7. Car plant
8. Honda mopeds
9. Peugeot 504 pickups, Mitsubishi opens second parts depot in October 1984
10. Proposed joint venture with Isuzu for light commercial vehicles
11. Daihatsu to supply CKD kits for 4WD micro trucks
12. Vehicle plant. Suzuki providing technical assistance

RECENT AND FORECAST VEHICLE PRODUCTION
IN CHINA.

1982	196,000	
1983	230,000	Vehicles in use in 1983
1984	290,000	100,000 cars
1990	700,000	1.7 mn Commercial vehicles
2000	1 million	

new military jeep, the BJ213, and promised that whenever sales inside China did not generate enough foreign currency, Beijing Jeep could keep on importing the Cherokee kits by converting earnings from the BJ212 into dollars, and China would guarantee $120 million in foreign exchange to pay for them. AMC would make money both by selling the American kits to BJC and by selling the assembled Cherokee inside China. The preferential treatment also allowed AMC to convert its dividends from BJC and send them back to the United States. The deal was beyond AMC's expectations since the provision would allow AMC to share the profits from the Chinese-designed and manufactured BJ212, which was selling well in China, without costing AMC anything. Furthermore, the BJ212 Jeep was made more attractive to customers after BJC persuaded the government to reduce taxes on it because the BJ212 was entirely Chinese made. This favorable pricing policy reduced the price of the BJ212 from $8,700 to $7,000.[16] China also agreed to finance major new capital projects at Beijing Jeep. The Chinese side had contributed $70 million to modernize the plant, while the Americans had added virtually no new capital beyond the original investment.

All Cherokees assembled were sold, with the government as the largest customer. Up to 1987, BJC earned $59 million in profits. BJC was elected as one of the 10 best performing joint venture companies in China.[17] BJC sold its BJ212 and Cherokee well in China and started to export Cherokees to other Asian countries. In addition to having money to reinvest, the two partners shared higher dividends.

The Transition of BJC from AMC to Chrysler

The takeover of AMC by Chrysler created some strange haggling over finances. When AMC sent one expert to China to investigate some malfunctioning American parts, it suddenly asked Beijing Jeep to pay the man's hotel bills and advance him $2,000 for living expenses—even though the Americans had already assured their Chinese partners that AMC would take responsibility. AMC began delaying its payments to Beijing Jeep for the Cherokees it was buying for export, and Beijing Jeep had to pay AMC well in advance of shipment for the Cherokee parts kits.

Chrysler bought AMC in 1987. Tod Clare became one of the first AMC people to leave, and it is believed he was ousted. Several others living in China found themselves out of work. While overseas they had lost both their positions and their contacts back home. At the beginning of 1988, according to the agreement, St. Pierre handed over the presidency of BJC to Chen Xulin, his hand-picked successor. In March 1988, St. Pierre accompanied a large Chinese delegation from BJC for meetings at Chrysler headquarters. He believed that he was close to convincing the Chinese to accept a 6 percent price increase in the Cherokee kits that BJC would buy from Chrysler in 1989. While in Detroit, Peter Badore, the executive in charge of the China project at Chrysler headquarters, had lunch with the Chinese delegation out of St. Pierre's presence. Following the lunch, the Chinese announced that Badore had accepted a Chinese offer of a 2.5 percent raise, with another 2.5 percent in another six months. St. Pierre was infuriated with Badore, the Chrysler official for whom he was supposed to be working. The two men did not get along and soon it became clear that there was no way St. Pierre would stay in China, reporting to Badore, for the remainder of the year. St. Pierre later became the Hong Kong-based director of China operations for another multinational corporation. Chrysler sent an American expert in manufacturing to China to work under Chen Xulin as vice president of Beijing Jeep. The Chinese were extremely concerned about what this takeover would mean to BJC since they had little knowledge of Chrysler.[18]

■ BJC Under Chrysler

When Chrysler bought AMC it announced that it had no intention of altering operations. The acquisition gave Chrysler rights to the Jeep name and expanded Chrysler's operations to include facilities in Egypt, Venezuela, and China. Immediately following the takeover of AMC, Chrysler had held out the prospect of big new plans for China. In the summer of 1987 Chrysler's vice president Bob Lutz signed a deal with the First Automotive Corp. in Changchun under which Chrysler sold new engine technology to China. Chinese officials were talking to foreign auto companies about the possibility of manufacturing passenger cars in Changchun, and Chrysler also hoped to land that contract. Top Chrysler executives, such as Gerald Greenwald, head of the Chrysler Motor division, traveled to China in pursuit of the passenger car deal.

Meanwhile, Chrysler officials began talking with authorities in Beijing about the possibility of a major expansion of Beijing Jeep. There was talk of having the Beijing joint venture start manufacturing trucks, a project of which AMC had once dreamed. At one point the Chinese side suggested that Chrysler should invest as much as $80 to $100 million in new capital for the proposed expansion. Chrysler made it known that AMC was a small company, but Chrysler had more financial resources and more people at its disposal, and it was willing to investment more. Yet Chrysler officials moved cautiously on the idea of expanding Beijing Jeep, avoiding any commitment to invest new money in the joint venture. The First Automotive Corp. of Changchun gave the contract for passenger cars to Audi, a subsidiary of Volkswagen.

In October 1988, Lee Iacocca visited China. He and his aides had expected to be received by China's top leaders, especially the paramount leader Deng Xiaoping and the Party General Secretary Zhao Ziyang, who was the former premier. Both of them had met with most prominent American business executives visiting China in the past. But while in Beijing for several days, the Chrysler delegation was only able to have a dinner session with Premier Li Peng. During the session, Iacocca said he felt China had made a mistake in choosing to link up with Audi, rather than Chrysler, for production of the passenger car. The premier did not press Iacocca for additional investment by Chrysler in China.[19] Lee Iacocca inspected BJC and said "I really have a feeling that they are creating history."[20]

When a general contract was signed, a foreign partner was limited to a 35 percent stake; in 1985 the limitation was changed to 49 percent, and then in 1988 the limit was removed, 100 percent foreign ownership now being possible. Whether Chrysler will take up this option of increasing its shareholding partly depends on when the U.S. reaction to the suppression by the Chinese authorities of the prodemocracy movement will soften. Many Japanese firms bought round-trip tickets for their employees in China during the Beijing turmoil. While Chrysler was among the first to evacuate executives and their families from China when the army assault started, it was also among the earliest Western companies to send them back, after directing its Chinese operations from Chrysler's Tokyo office.

◼ Notes

1. J. Mann, 1990, *Beijing Jeep: The Short, Unhappy Romance of American Business in China* (New York: Simon & Schuster).
2. J. Mann, "One Company's China Debacle," *Fortune*, November 6.
3. Mann, *Beijing Jeep*.
4. Mann, *Beijing Jeep*.
5. N. Fletcher, 1989, Chrysler China venture finds road to success, *Journal of Commerce and Commercial*, May 12, 1A.
6. A. Hope and M. Jacobson, 1989, China's motor industry: Risks and opportunities to 2000, *The Economist Intelligence Unit, Special Report No. 2008,* November.
7. Mann, *Beijing Jeep*, 280.
8. Hope and Jacobson, China's motor industry.
9. *Motor Business. No. 1, 1985. Economist Intelligence Unit, No. 121.*
10. Hope and Jacobson, China's motor industry.
11. China against the tide: The succession struggle and prospects for reform in China after the Peking spring. *The Economist Intelligence Unit, Special Report No. 2025,* February 1990.
12. Hope and Jacobson, China's motor industry.
13. Hope and Jacobson, China's motor industry.
14. Mann, *Beijing Jeep*.
15. Mann, *Beijing Jeep*, 202.
16. X. Zhou, 1990, Beijing Jeep back in gear, *Beijing Review,* April 2.
17. Fletcher, Chrysler China.
18. Mann, *Beijing Jeep*.
19. Mann, *Beijing Jeep*.
20. Q. Wang, 1989, Developing the Beijing Cherokee Jeep, *China Pictorial,* September.

■ CASE 11 Daimler-Benz

Joe Canterbury
Susanne Lauber
Vincent Marijon
David Thoumieux
Jim Var

■ http://www.daimler-benz.com

At the Daimler-Benz* shareholders' meeting on May 24, 1995, when former CEO Edzard Reuter passed the reigns of Germany's largest conglomerate to Juergen Schrempp, shareholders' confidence and the health of the firm appeared restored and secure for the future. Reuter boasted of returns of $750 million in 1994, after losses of $1.2 billion in 1993 and promised even better outcomes for 1995. Mercedes-Benz* seemed to be reaping the benefits of massive restructuring and new product introductions. The past difficulties and losses of the electrical and aerospace business units, AEG and DASA, appeared to be ebbing and the financial services arm of Daimler, Debis, had experienced continual profit growth since its 1990 inception.

A mere month later on June 29, 1995, Daimler's stock plunged 45.5 deutsche marks (DM) or 6.5 percent after Juergen Schrempp announced that Daimler-Benz would experience heavy losses for 1995. Following a month of internal dissension, worsened outlooks for 1995, and a blitzkrieg of negative publicity, the largest German weekly news magazine, *Der Spiegel,* displayed a broken Mercedes star on its cover and posed the question: "Intrigen, roter Wein und rote Zahlen: Was ist los bei Daimler-Benz?"[1] (Intrigue, red wine and red numbers: what is wrong at Daimler-Benz?). Juergen Schrempp, who had recently been involved in a minor scandal, contemplated both what went wrong and what immediate and long-term actions should be undertaken to rectify the situation.

■ History

■ Emergence of a Car Manufacturer

The history of Daimler-Benz began in 1883, when Karl Benz founded the auto manufacturing firm Benz & Co. in Mannheim, Germany. He invented the world's first conventional motor car in 1886. In 1890, Gottlieb Daimler founded the Daimler-Motoren-Gesellschaft (DMG) in Bad Cannstatt, near Stuttgart. In 1893, the "Benz Velo," the world's first standard production automobile, appeared on the

Case prepared under the direction of Professor Robert E. Hoskisson for class discussion purposes only.
*Throughout this case, Daimler-Benz and Daimler are used interchangeably as are Mercedes-Benz and Mercedes.

market, and in 1894 the first bus was developed. In 1902, DMG took over the vehicle and engine-making factory Motorfahrzeug- und Motorenfabrik Berlin AG in Berlin-Marienfelde, in what was a very sizable merger for that time period. In 1907, it acquired the Süddeutsche Automobilfabrik Gaggenau GmbH and later also branched out into manufacturing of aeroengines, winning the Imperial Prize for the best German aeroengine in 1913. With the outbreak of World War I, both Benz and DMG had to convert plants for war production.[2]

After the war, both companies were affected by the world economic crisis and hyperinflation in Germany, which made automobiles too expensive for the average consumer. Realizing the need to diversify, the firms began producing typewriters and bicycles. The troubled economic climate and the large number of vehicle manufacturers contending for a share of the market forced companies to form alliances. In 1924, DMG and Benz merged and began marketing their cars under the trade name Mercedes-Benz. Mercedes was the name of the daughter of Karl Benz's most valued customer.

From 1933 onward, Daimler-Benz began to profit from the upsurge in armament production under the Nazis and the state-sponsored boom in the vehicle industry. With the outbreak of war in 1939, the company had to again convert machinery for armaments production. Car and commercial vehicle output was cut back, while production of large industrial engines was stepped up. Aerial bombardment of the Daimler-Benz plants in the following years led to the destruction of up to two-thirds of the buildings and facilities in Sindelfingen, Untertürkheim, and Berlin by 1945.[3]

■ Birth of a Multinational

Only a few months after the end of the war, vehicle production began again, initially for the sole purpose of the allied forces. By 1946, car production had resumed at the Sindelfingen plant with an output equivalent to the prewar era. In 1950, exports soared from DM6 million to DM66 million. At the same time, Daimler-Benz AG extended its manufacturing activities to the South American continent, establishing its first foreign production facility in Argentina. This was followed a few years later by the founding of Mercedes-Benz of Brazil and, in 1955, of Daimler-Benz of North America.

An important foreign investment in Iran, the Tabriz engine factory founded in 1970, soon became a springboard for sales of commercial vehicles to countries in the Middle and Far East. The year 1973 marked the first in which the company's foreign business exceeded sales in Germany. Then 1980 and 1981 saw heavy investments in the United States. In Hampton/Newport, a truck plant was erected that had the capacity to assemble 6,000 trucks annually, and the leading American manufacturer of heavy-duty trucks, Freightliner Corporation of Portland, Oregon, was acquired.

■ Acquisitions and Adaptive Corporate Structure

In 1985, the board of management and the supervisory board decided to make substantial investments in a number of German companies and to expand the size and scope of the organization (see Exhibit 1 for a time line). In 1985, the Daimler-Benz group, which still was mainly comprised of Mercedes, paid DM680 million to increase its holding of the motor and turbine company MTU (Motoren and Turbinen Union) from 50 to 100 percent. In the same year,

Exhibit 1

Daimler-Benz Stock Prices
Overlaid Against Company
Time-Line

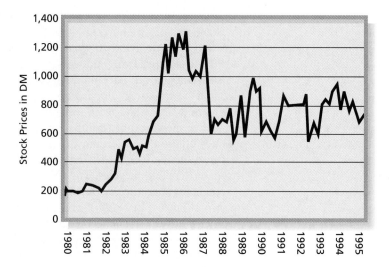

Source: Translated and adapted from "Schock für die Aktionäre," *Der Spiegel,* July 31, 1995, 31: 28–29.

Jan. 1980 Reuter becomes CFO of Daimler-Benz.

Aug. 1984 Reuter recommends new strategy for a broadly diversified holding company.

Feb. 1985 100% ownership of MTU.

May 1985 Majority ownership (66%) of Dornier GmbH.

July 1985 Herrhausen, speaker of the Deutsche-Bank, appointed Chairman of the Board (Daimler).

Oct. 1985 Acquires shares of AEG valued at DM 1.6 billion.

Sept. 1987 Reuter appointed CEO.

Sept. 1989 63% ownership of MBB.

Nov. 1989 Herrhausen killed.

1988 80% ownership of AEG.

Apr. 1989 Restructuring of Daimler-Benz AG into three business units:
• Mercedes-Benz AG
• Dasa
• AEG

July 1990 Debis founded as the fourth business unit.

Mar. 1991 Acquires 10% of Metallgesellschaft.

July 1991 Acquires 34% of Cap Gemini Sogeti, a French software company.

1993 AEG suffers a loss of DM 1.2 billion

May 1995 Reuter retires as CEO.

Daimler spent DM500 million to purchase a majority share (66 percent) in the Schwabian (southwestern German region) airplane manufacturer Dornier. The workforce increased to 231,000 (+16 percent), sales to DM52.4 billion (+11 percent), and net income to some DM1.7 billion (+52 percent).

In late 1985 Daimler-Benz paid out DM1.6 billion to purchase a 56 percent partnership in the large German electrical concern Allgemeine Elektrizitäts Gesellschaft (AEG). It was the largest acquisition in German history. As a result, the total workforce of the group rose by 33 percent and sales increased by 20 percent.

After becoming CEO of Daimler in 1987, Edzard Reuter began an aggressive drive to increase the holdings of Daimler through further acquisition. Although Mercedes was extremely profitable at this time, Reuter foresaw a bleak future in the auto industry and was determined to forge a large conglomerate centered around transportation: road, rail, and air. He repeatedly expressed his vision of a harmonious group of electrical and transportation companies increasing the value of one another through technology and know-how transference. Reuter envisioned significant potential benefits that would be realized through synergy among different companies and businesses.

In the late 1980s, AEG was experiencing serious difficulties and was contemplating turning to the German government for assistance. The German government was not interested in subsidizing AEG but also did not want to see one of Germany's largest and best known companies go under. With a considerable amount of prodding from the government, Daimler decided to increase its stake in AEG to 80 percent. At this time, AEG consisted of rail and subway systems, battery production, postal distribution systems, and household appliances. In 1989, Reuter pulled his biggest coup with the purchase of a majority share (66 percent) of the large Bavarian plane and weapons manufacturer Messerschmitt-Bölkow-Blohm GmbH (MBB). The price tag of DM1.7 billion had created the most powerful German industrial firm since the end of World War II.[4]

■ Restructuring for the 1990s

In 1989, Daimler began restructuring its integrated high-technology concern. Daimler-Benz AG became an executive holding company, with the primary task of ensuring the optimal use of the group's resources. All vehicle businesses were placed under the roof of Mercedes-Benz AG, and the aerospace and defense companies [Dornier, MTU, Telefunken Systemtechnik (TST), and MBB], along with Germany's share of the Airbus Industrie, were grouped into Deutsche Aerospace AG (DASA). In addition to the third business unit, AEG, Daimler decided to create a fourth corporate unit, Daimler-Benz InterServices (Debis) AG. This organization offers customers a wide range of services including software products, computer communication services, financial services, an insurance brokerage, and marketing services. Each of the four group subsidiaries has its own individual logo, reflecting the fact that they are now independent companies accountable for their own results. In 1990, a new lavish corporate headquarters was officially opened in the Stuttgart suburb of Möhringen.

■ Corporate Structure

In 1990, Daimler-Benz reportedly paid "millions of deutsche marks" to McKinsey Consulting to help design a new company structure (the structure developed by McKinsey and described later was altered in August 1995). At the top of the structure sits the *Vorstand* (the managing board), which consists of the *Vorstandsvorsitzende* (CEOs) of Daimler-Benz and the four business units—Mercedes, AEG, DASA and Debis (Exhibits 2 and 3). In addition, the Vorstand consists of the heads of personnel, finance, and R&D. The areas of law, strategy, corporate development, public relations, and environmental protection report directly to the *Vorstandsvorsitzender,* Schrempp. The finance department includes the tax, financial planning, treasury, and accounting divisions. The personnel department handles the traditional functions of training and development, hiring, employee relations, and strategic human resource management. A separate division of the Vorstand comprises just one person, the official art collector, who holds the same hierarchical position as the other CEOs.

In August 1995, the personnel and finance departments were merged into one entity. Of the 3,000 employees in the corporate headquarters, 1,700 work in the corporate R&D department, which is subdivided into five different functional

Exhibit 2   Daimler-Benz AG

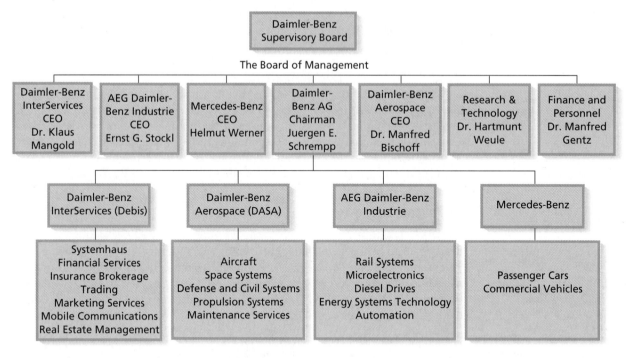

Source: Daimler-Benz, 1995, *Annual Report.*

areas: street vehicles, air and space, microelectronics, rail vehicles, and information and communication technology. In addition to the corporate R&D function, Mercedes, AEG, and DASA each have their own R&D facilities which employ 13,000, 4,100, and 14,500, respectively.

The Daimler Vorstandsvorsitzender must attain a consensus from the other Vorstand members and the *Aufsichtsrat* (supervisory board—discussed in further detail under corporate governance) before implementing any action or plan. Many incidents have exemplified how the business units' CEOs often are more concerned with their own units than with the entire corporation. Although top managers of the four units receive performance-related bonuses, no one receives stock options from Daimler-Benz (as of August 1995, only three companies offered stock options in Germany: Continental, SAP Software, and BFG Bank). Many executives at Mercedes, which contributes 67 percent of Daimler's revenue, are known to consider only Mercedes' viewpoint and to eschew cooperation with the money-losing AEG and DASA units.

■ Corporate Governance

By German law, all companies must have a dual board: supervisory *(Aufsichtsrat)* and management *(Vorstand)*. Besides large shareholders, the supervisory boards must also include some employees and labor union representatives. In addition all German firms must also have a separate workers' council, *(Betriebsrat),* which has the right to monitor and authorize all corporate plans and actions. A downsizing plan must be agreed on by the members of the Vorstand, then

Exhibit 3   Daimler-Benz AG Business Units and Subsidiaries

Mercedes-Benz A.G.

Mercedes-Benz Espana S.A. (Spain)
Mercedes-Benz (United Kingdom) Ltd. (U.K.)
Mercedes-Benz Nederland B.V. (Netherlands)
Mercedes-Benz Belgium S.A./N.V. (Belgium)
Mercedes-Benz France S.A. (France)
Mercedes-Benz Italia S.p.A. (Italy)
Mercedes-Benz (Schweiz) AG (Switzerland)
Freightliner Corp. (U.S.)
Mercedes-Benz of North America, Inc. (U.S.)
Mercedes-Benz Mexico S.A. de C.V. (Mexico)
Mercedes-Benz do Brasil S.A. (Brazil)
Sociedade Tecnica de Fundicoes Gerais (Brazil)
Mercedes-Benz Argentina S.A. (Argentina)
Mercedes-Benz of South Africa (South Africa)
Mercedes-Benz Tuerk A.S. (Turkey)
Mercedes-Benz Japan Co. Ltd. (Japan)
Mercedes-Benz (Australia) Pty. Ltd.
Maschinenfabrik Esslingen AG
Holzindustrie Bruchsal GmbH
NAW Nutzfahrzeuggesellschaft Arbon & Wetzikon AG (Swiss)
Mercedes-Benz Osterreich GmbH (Austria)
Mercedes-Benz Hellas S.A. (Greece)
Mercedes-Benz Portugal S.A. (Portugal)
Mercedes-Benz Danmark AS (Denmark)
Mercedes-Benz Canada, Inc. (Canada)
Anambra Motor Manufacturing Co. Ltd (Nigeria)
P.T. German Motor Manufacturing (Indonesia)
P.T. Star Motors Indonesia (Indonesia)
Iranian Diesel Engine Manufacturing Comp. (Iran)
Tata Engineering & Locomotive Comp. Ltd. (India)

Holding and Finance Companies

Daimler-Benz Holding France S.A. (France)
Daimler-Benz Holding Belgium S.A. (Belgium)
Daimler-Benz Holding Nederland B.V. (NL)
Daimler-Benz Holding AG (Swiss)
Daimler-Benz North America Corporation (U.S.)
Daimler-Benz UK plc (U.K.)
Daimler-Benz Coordination Center S.A. (Belgium)

Joint Venture Companies

Temic Telefunken microelectronic GmbH
Temic MBB Mikrosysteme GmbH
Temic Bayern-Chemie Airbag GmbH
Siliconix Inc. (U.S.)
Mercedes-Benz Charter Way GmbH
AEG Schneider Automation (France)
Mercedes-Benz India (India)
MC AG (France)

AEG Daimler-Benz Industrie

AEG Aktiengesellschaft
AEG Hausgeraete AG
AEG Bahnsysteme GmbH
AEG Westinghouse Transportation Inc. (U.S.)
AEG Schienenfahrzeuge GmbH
MODICON, Inc. (U.S.)
AEG ETI Elektrik Endustrisi A.S. (Turkey)
AEG Starkstromanlagen Dresden GmbH
AEG Iberica de Electricidad S.A. (Spain)
AEG Austria Gesellschaft m.b.H. (Austria)
AEG Fabrica de Motores S.A. (Spain)

Daimler-Benz Aerospace (DASA)

Deutsche Aerospace AG
Dornier GmbH
Daimler-Benz- und Raumfahrt Holding AG
Deutsche Aerospace Airbus GmbH
Eurocopter Holding S.A. (France)
ERNO Raumfahrttechnik GmbH
MTU Motoren- und Turbinen GmbH
MTU Maintenance GmbH
N.V. Koninklijke Nederlandse Vliegtuigenfabrik Fokker (NL)
Dornier Luftfahrt GmbH
Dornier Medizintechnik GmbH

Daimler-Benz InterServices

Daimler-Benz InterServices AG
Debis Systemhaus CCS GmbH
Mercedes-Benz Credit Corp. (U.S.)
Mercedes-Benz Finanz GmbH
CAP debis Software und Systeme GmbH
Diebold Deutschland GmbH
Debis Assekuranz Vermittlungs GmbH
Debis Industriehandel GmbH
Debis Marketing Services GmbH
Debitel Kommunikations-technik GmbH KG
Sogeti S.A. (France)

Source: Daimler-Benz, 1995, *Annual Report.*

approved by the Aufsichtsrat, and finally presented to the Betriebsrat before the powerful Metallgesellschaft labor union, Germany's largest and most influential union, has its opportunity to review the plan.

Of the 20 members on Daimler-Benz's Aufsichtsrat, 4 are bank representatives, 7 are employed by Daimler-Benz, and 3 represent the labor union. The remaining 6 members are all outsiders (from Bayer, IBM, private law firms, and a former French government minister). The most influential member of the Daimler-Benz's supervisory board is the head of the Deutsche Bank, which owns 24 percent of Daimler-Benz (14 percent is owned by the state of Kuwait). The former Deutsche Bank CEO, Alfred Herrhausen, had worked in industry and was well versed in management and strategy. He played a very active role in monitoring and advising Daimler's operations and partially constrained Reuter's rapid growth through diversification strategy. In 1989, Herrhausen was murdered by left-wing terrorists and replaced by Hilmar Kopper. From the beginning, Kopper acted as a mere observer of Daimler and rarely raised a voice or asked a question. During the difficult times of the early 1990s and the more recent problems, Kopper has remained silent. In August 1995, *Der Spiegel* said: "To consider the misery at Daimler-Benz without considering the role of Kopper is inconceivable."[5]

The Four Business Units

■ Mercedes-Benz AG

The motor vehicle business with its traditional brand, Mercedes, was restructured as a separate business unit in July 1989. Mercedes-Benz is divided into a Passenger and a Commercial Vehicle Division and is headquartered in Stuttgart, Germany. Mercedes operates more than 50 production and assembly plants, of which 12 are located in Germany. Approximately 98 percent of the passenger cars and 50 percent of commercial vehicles are made in Germany. The foreign passenger car plants are mostly small final assembly operations. Mercedes-Benz owns 6,164 sales and service outlets worldwide, which sell cars in more than 170 countries. The business has established an enviable reputation as a producer of high-quality luxury automobiles. For years the company has promoted itself as "the car engineered like no other in the world."

Earning an annual average of DM60,500 based on 36.6 hours per week ($42,907 based on an exchange rate of $1/DM1.41), German auto workers earn about 75 percent more than their U.S. counterparts. Because of the high cost of labor, Mercedes has established assembly plants in the Far East, South Africa, and South America and is building production plants in other parts of the world. The company has engaged in new globalization activities to protect itself against currency fluctuations (see the section on globalization for more information). In 1993, realizing the huge growth potential that exists in North America (sales grew in the U.S. market by 18 percent to DM11.8 billion in 1994) and recognizing the need to produce in the dollar realm, Mercedes began construction of a new U.S. factory in Tuscaloosa, Alabama. The new plant, which will go on line in 1997, will produce a new sport utility vehicle (SUV). Sixty percent of the planned annual output of 60,000 units will be sold in the United States.

In 1994, Mercedes entered a joint venture with the Swiss manufacturer of Swatch to build a new microcompact car, which will be equivalent in size to the tiny Japanese Daihatsu "Tonka." Production plants will be located in France and the Mercedes logo will not appear on the car. Mercedes is also planning production of another compact car, the new A class, which will be produced in Germany and Brazil. In 1993, Mercedes experienced a loss of DM1.2 billion. However, extraordinary revenue and income transferred to Daimler-Benz boosted this loss to a profit of DM340 million. In addition, the loss was related to the recession in Europe, which affected sales of luxury cars, and to accounting changes necessary for the listing of Daimler's share on the New York Stock Exchange (NYSE). In 1994, Mercedes was able to increase its world production and sales and showed a profit of DM1.8 billion. Mercedes was again expecting profits for 1995 to be over DM1 billion (see Exhibits 4 through 8).

■ AEG Daimler-Benz Industrie

AEG Daimler-Benz Industrie supplies various industrial systems. As of 1995, it consisted of five divisions: rail systems, microelectronics, diesel drives, energy systems technology, and an automation division. The name AEG is best known in Europe for consumer goods ranging from washing machines to radios and blenders. This consumer goods and heavy manufacturing division along with the office communications division was sold in 1989/1990. AEG has only had one profitable year since 1989, when Daimler increased its holding to 84 percent. Despite restructuring efforts of DM600 million and layoffs of 14,000 employees, AEG still experienced a loss of DM357 million in 1994. This loss had to be absorbed by other profit-making business units.

The rail systems division encompasses complete transport systems for long-distance, regional, and local rail traffic as well as industrial rail systems. In March 1995, AEG announced a 50:50 joint venture with Asea Brown Boveri AG (ABB). If this venture is approved by the European Cartel Office, it would create the world's leading supplier of rail systems.

The microelectronics division offers products that range from semiconductors and microsystems technology to vehicle electronics systems and airbag components. Despite a substantial increase in vehicle electronics systems sales, AEG still lost money in this industry during 1994. In an effort to reduce these losses, AEG sold off its Hausgeräte division (household appliances) to the Swedish giant Electrolux. The other divisions that are combined under AEG Daimler-Benz Industrie provide a variety of products, such as high-quality drive and propulsion systems, engines, decentralized power generation and transmission, and automation technology systems. The one subunit of AEG that has been consistently profitable is the postal distribution system business-unit. In fact, the U.S. Postal Service buys postal processing equipment from this business-unit.

■ Daimler-Benz Aerospace (DASA)

Deutsche Aerospace, known as DASA, was formed in 1989 and is based in Bavaria near Munich. In an attempt to promote the corporate name and downplay its German location, Deutsche Aerospace was later renamed Daimler-Benz Aerospace. In 1994, DASA employed about 75,000 people, down 14 percent from 1993 and had sales of DM17.4 billion. DASA was forged primarily out of the fusion of three large firms (MBB, MTU, and Dornier). MBB, the maker of the famous Me-109 fighter of World War II, was Germany's largest weapons

Exhibit 4

Revenue and Operating Profits

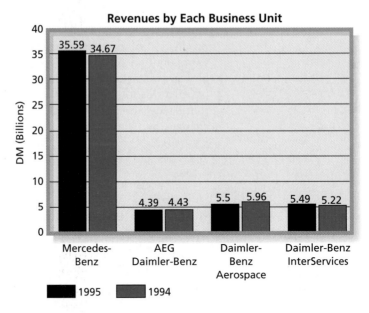

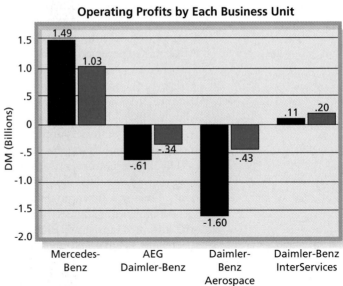

Source: Daimler-Benz, 1995, *Annual Report.*

Note: Figures are based on 1994 and 1995 half-year results.

producer. At the time of the MBB investment, Daimler was anticipating a surging market for defense systems and armaments. The fall of the Berlin Wall and the end of the Cold War strongly altered this forecast. The DASA unit MTU manufactures propulsion systems and diesel engines.

The negotiations surrounding the takeover of Dornier, a producer of aircraft, satellites, and medical equipment, have resulted in negative repercussions for present-day DASA and Daimler. When Daimler paid DM500 million in 1985 for a 66 percent stake in Dornier, the firm allowed the Dornier family to retain extensive voting and consent rights. The family had the right to block any DASA moves within the airplane industry. In addition, the family was guaranteed a very

Exhibit 5

Mercedes-Benz Total		
DM Amounts in Millions	1994	1993
Revenues	70,715	64,696
Employees	197,568	209,933
Net Income	1,849	(1,198)

AEG Daimler-Benz Industrie Total		
DM Amounts in Millions	1994	1993
Revenues	10,294	11,012
Employees	44,769	58,921
Net Income	(357)	(1,190)

Daimler-Benz Aerospace Total		
DM Amounts in Millions	1994	1993
Revenues	17,394	18,626
Employees	75,581	86,086
Net Income	(438)	(694)

Daimler-Benz InterServices Total		
DM Amounts in Millions	1994	1993
Revenues	10,804	9,491
Employees	9,226	8,812
Net Income	86	18

Source: Daimler-Benz, 1995, *Annual Report.*

magnanimous dividend. In 1989, Reuter, together with the Daimler CFO and Mercedes CEO, met in a local Stuttgart hotel with a female representative of the Dornier family (Frau Dornier-Tiefenthaler) to negotiate Daimler's purchase of the family's generous rights. After an exhausted and frustrated Reuter departed at 4:00 A.M., the other gentlemen continued bargaining until 8:00 AM, when Frau Dornier-Tiefenthaler left the hotel DM570 million richer. Every year DASA must make large payments to the Dornier family for the controlling rights to the money-losing Dornier firm. Other executives, the business community, and the shareholders did not respond favorably to the deal.

As CEO of DASA, Schrempp was responsible for the purchase of Fokker, a plane manufacturing company based in the Netherlands. Schrempp was determined to make DASA Europe's largest aerospace firm and a viable global competitor. Daimler paid DM500 million in 1992 for the Dutch manufacturer of regional aircraft. Fokker, which is still partially owned and controlled by the Dutch government, has lost money consistently since the DASA takeover.

After the amalgamation of the numerous individual firms into DASA, the company divided its operations into four groups: propulsion systems, space systems, aircraft, and defense and civil systems. The propulsion systems division is responsible for the development and manufacture of aeroengines for passenger and cargo aircraft, helicopters, turboprops, and combat and training aircraft. The space systems group is a leader in the European Orbital program for which it provides the space infrastructure and satellite systems. The aircraft group is engaged in the manufacture of large passenger aircraft through Daimler-Benz Aerospace Airbus GmbH, which holds 37.9 percent of shares in the European Airbus consortium. Besides regional aircraft that are provided through the acquisitions of Dornier and Fokker, the aircraft group also produces military aircraft and helicopters. Finally, the defense and civil systems division operates in the fields of defense and protection, information and communication systems, and sensor systems. In 1990, the French company Aerospatiale and DASA formed the new joint venture Eurocopter S.A., to which DASA transferred its helicopter activities.

Exhibit 6			
Daimler-Benz AG	*1994*	*1993*	*1992*
		(DM in Millions)	
Revenues	104,075	98,534	98,549
Germany	39,015	38,526	42,572
Europe (without Germany)	26,225	25,523	27,031
North America	19,609	17,431	13,881
Latin America	6,021	5,238	3,850
Other Markets	13,205	11,816	11,215
Employees	330,551	366,736	376,467
Germany	251,254	284,576	302,464
Foreign	79,297	82,160	74,003
Research and Development	8,692	9,043	9,312
Cash Flow from Operating Activities	11,282	9,913	5,328
Cash Flow Used for Investment Activities	(10,591)	(10,523)	(7,523)
Cash Flow from Financing Activities	3,383	679	3,072
Working Capital	16,035	20,170	21,868
Operating Profit	2,708	(3,299)	2,026
Net Income	895	615	1,451
Net Income per DM 50 Share	21.57	12.78	30.12
Net Income/Loss by U.S. GAAP	1,052	(1,839)	1,350
Net Income/Loss by U.S. GAAP per DM 50 Share	21.53	(39.47)	29.00
Net Income/Loss by U.S. GAAP per ADS	2.15	(3.95)	2.90
Daimler-Benz AG			
Capital Stock	2,565	2,330	2,330
Net Income	565	390	703
Total Dividend Amount	564	373	604
Dividend per DM 50 Share	11.00	7.91	12.85

Source: Daimler-Benz, 1995, *Annual Report.*

As a partner of Airbus Industrie, DASA assembles the Airbus A321 and A319 in Hamburg. However, the division faces difficulties in being competitive because of the decreased demand for military fighters on the one hand and the restrictions of building commercial passenger planes on the other hand. Because DASA is a partner of Airbus, it is not allowed to compete with Airbus by building large passenger airplanes. The tendency of customers to purchase smaller aircraft from the same firm that sells them larger planes (i.e., Boeing and Airbus) has also eroded DASA's competitive ability.

Most damaging to competitiveness, however, has been the precipitous decline of the dollar against the deutsche mark, which makes it extremely difficult for DASA to price its planes competitively against those of U.S. and other international firms. DASA's financial department based all 1995 projections on a $1/DM1.65 exchange rate. During March 1995, the dollar had hit a postwar low of $1/DM1.35. Although the operating loss of DASA went down from DM694 million in 1993 to DM438 million in 1994 (see Exhibits 5 through 8), DASA faced a DM1 billion loss for 1995 due to the unexpected decline of the dollar. DASA planned to close some manufacturing facilities and lay off some 15,000 workers in Germany (based mostly in Bavaria).[6]

Exhibit 7   Daimler-Benz AG Financial Statements

	1985	1986	1987	1988	1989	1990	1991	1992	1993	1994
Number of Employees (At Year-End)										
Daimler-Benz Group	231,077	319,965	326,288	338,749	368,226	376,785	379,252	376,467	366,736	330,551
of which: Germany	186,652	257,538	262,658	268,277	298,199	303,404	305,295	302,464	284,576	251,254
Foreign	44,425	62,427	63,630	70,472	70,027	73,381	73,957	74,003	82,160	79,297
Mercedes-Benz	—	—	—	—	223,219	230,974	237,442	222,482	209,933	197,568
AEG Daimler-Benz Industrie	—	78,199	80,499	89,585	77,722	76,949	76,338	60,784	58,921	44,769
Daimler-Benz Aerospace	—	—	—	—	62,959	61,276	56,465	81,872	86,086	75,581
Debis						4,879	6,203	8,258	8,812	9,226
Major Balance Sheet and Income Figures (in Millions of DM)										
Non-Current Assets	10,209	10,857	12,202	17,342	20,084	23,448	29,198	33,633	35,354	36,239
Current Assets	25,571	31,168	34,336	34,589	42,653	43,891	46,516	52,551	55,572	57,297
Capital Stock	1,699	2,118	2,118	2,118	23,330	2,330	2,330	2,330	2,330	2,565
Total Paid-In Capital and Retained Earnings	8,070	7,742	6,778	8,075	13,314	14,059	15,301	15,557	14,881	16,971
of which: Paid-In Capital		368	370	370	2,114	2,117	2,117	2,117	2,117	4,904
Retained Earnings	—	7,374	6,408	7,705	11,200	11,942	13,184	13,440	12,764	12,067
Minority Interests in Subsidiaries	330	1,251	768	626	767	881	1,214	1,228	561	151
Stockholder's Equity	9,769	11,111	9,663	10,819	16,411	17,270	18,845	19,115	17,772	19.687
% of Total Assets	27	26	21	21	26	26	25	22	20	21
% of Non-Current Assets	96	102	98	79	109	102	89	80	76	79
Long and Medium-Term Liabilities	11,201	17,696	22,744	24,485	24,331	25,529	28,045	33,833	37,118	36,144
Stockholders' Equity Plus Long and Medium-Term Liabilities	20,970	28,807	32,407	35,304	40,742	42,799	46,890	52,948	54,890	55,831
Balance Sheet Total	35,780	42,025	46,538	51,931	62,737	67,339	75,714	86,184	90,926	95,536
Total Investment	5,492	5,580	3,736	7,007	7,620	6,857	9,579	8,363	6,804	8,109
% of Revenues	11	9	6	10	10	8	10	9	7	8
of which: In Property, Plant, Equipment										
and Intangible Assets	4,014	5,385	3,834	6,628	7,242	6,539	7,231	8,047	6,515	5,858
Germany	2,753	3,891	3,392	6,038	6,459	5,680	6,115	7,284	4,061	4,264
Foreign	1,261	1,494	442	590	783	859	1,116	763	2,454	1,594
In Financial Assets (net)	1,478	195	(98)	379	378	318	2,348	316	289	2,251
Total Depreciation	2,375	3,361	2,560	3,086	3,218	3,780	4,328	4,990	5,821	5,401
of which: In Property, Plant and Equipment										
and Intangible Assets	3,242	3,239	2,505	3,074	3,138	3,670	4,213	4,907	5,523	5,148
Germany	2,514	2,575	2,192	2,708	2,620	3,071	3,639	4,269	4,858	4,389
Foreign	728	664	313	366	518	599	574	638	665	759
in Financial Assets	33	122	55	12	80	110	115	83	298	253
Cash Flow	5,012	6,214	6,626	6,130	5,991	6,711	7,814	5,328	9,913	11,282
% of Revenues	10	10	10	8	8	8	8	5	10	11

Source: Daimler-Benz, 1995, *Annual Report*.

Exhibit 8   Daimler-Benz AG Financial Statements

	1985	1986	1987	1988	1989	1990	1991	1992	1993	1994
(In Millions of DM)										
Revenues	*52,409*	*65,498*	*67,475*	*73,495*	*76,392*	*85,500*	*95,010*	*98,549*	*97,737*	*104,075*
of which: Germany	18,706	27,838	28,064	29,094	29,562	36,674	44,443	42,572	38,319	39,015
Foreign	33,703	37,660	39,411	44,401	46,830	48,826	50,567	55,977	59,418	65,060
Foreign Revenues in %	64	58	58	60	61	57	53	57	61	63
Mercedez-Benz	—	—	—	—	54,969	57,872	65,317	64,849	61,728	68,239
of which: Passenger Cars	25,549	31,405	31,472	31,833	31,865	34,142	38,331	38,650	36,370	40,107
Commercial Vehicles	20,204	17,755	19,454	23,063	23,104	23,730	26,986	26,199	25,358	28,132
AEG Daimler-Benz Industrie	—	11,070	11,480	1,352	11,852	12,721	13,573	11,184	10,733	10,034
Daimler-Benz Aerospace	3,194	4,882	4,421	4,976	7,489	12,168	11,974	16,735	18,173	17,053
Debis						2,739	4,146	5,781	7,103	8,749
Total Average Annual Revenues										
Per Employee (in DM)	229,119	207,559	207,128	218,102	224,765	228,477	249,036	257,555	263,366	304,397
Purchases of Goods and Services	27,245	32,467	33,701	37,646	39,552	44,477	49,456	49,084	51,076	56,289
Personnel Expenses	13,657	19,367	20,670	22,371	23,199	26,890	29,372	32,003	33,790	30,108
Average Annual Personnel Expenses										
Per Employee (in DM)	59,846	60,581	63,451	66,388	68,257	71,857	76,989	83,639	91,052	88,060
Results from Ordinary										
Business Activities	—	5,880	5,297	5,197	10,096	4,221	4,027	2,533	−1,083	2,077
% of Revenues	—	9.0	7.9	7.1	13.2	4.9	4.2	2.6	−1.1	2.0
Extraordinary Results	—	—	—	—	—	—	−544	—	2,603	—
Taxes	4,341	4,113	3,515	3,495	3,287	2,426	1,541	1,082	905	1,182
Net Income	1,682	1,767	1,782	1,702	6,809	1,795	1,942	1,451	615	895
% of Revenues	3.2	2.7	2.6	2.3	8.9	2.1	2.0	1.5	0.6	0.9
Daimler-Benz AG										
Net Income	1,252	1,404	1,403	1,382	1,120	1,120	1,194	703	390	565
Total Dividend Amount										
(Paid/Proposed)	491	507	503	504	555	557	603	604	373	564
Dividends for Each DM 50										
Par Value Share (in DM)	12+2.5	12	12	12	12	12	13	13	8	11
Tax Credit for Each DM 50										
Par Value Share (in DM)	8.2	6.8	6.8	6.8	6.8	6.8	7.3	7.3	3.4	4.7
Dividend for Each DM 50	11.3	11.5	11.5	11.5	11.9	11.9	12.9	12.9	7.9	11.0
Tax Credit for Each DM 50										
Par Value Share Adjusted (in DM)	6.4	6.5	6.5	6.5	6.7	6.7	7.2	7.2	3.4	4.7

Source: Daimler-Benz, 1995, *Annual Report.*

Originally, the German government approved the merger between Daimler-Benz and MBB in an attempt to make the German space and aircraft industry more independent from state subsidies. However, DASA is still subsidized and therefore prevented from moving its manufacturing plants out of Germany into a low-labor-cost country.

■ Daimler-Benz InterServices (Debis)

Daimler-Benz InterServices (Debis) was founded in July 1990. Debis provides in-house services for the Daimler-Benz group and its divisions. The services include finance and leasing, real estate management, mobile communications services, an insurance brokerage, software development, and various marketing and trading services. In 1991, Debis acquired a 34 percent share in Sogeti S.A., the parent company of Cap Gemini Sogeti, Europe's largest software company. Headquartered in Berlin, Debis is a decentralized organization that also offers solutions to outside clients and individuals. The international network consists of more than 200 branches with regional centers and is represented in 22 countries around the world. The goal is to become the largest service company in Europe. In 1994, Debis had 9,226 employees and showed a net income of DM86 million. This business unit of Daimler has posted increasing profits each year since its inception.

■ Globalization

Although Mercedes-Benz has had an extensive sales and service network for decades (4,722 of Mercedes' 6,164 sales and service centers are located outside of Germany), 98 percent of all passenger car production in 1992 was within Germany. In addition, approximately 85 percent of Mercedes' suppliers were German firms.[7] Realizing the need to defend itself against currency fluctuations and high labor costs in Germany, Mercedes set a goal in 1993 to increase foreign production 10 percent by the year 2000.[8] Since this time, Mercedes has begun construction on the new SUV plant in Alabama, decided to build the new microcompact car in France, signed an agreement with the Chinese government to build minivans in China, and announced plans to simultaneously produce the new A class in both Germany and Brazil. In contrast to the passenger car division, almost one-half of the 241,606 Mercedes commercial vehicles (busses, trucks, etc.) produced in 1993 were manufactured abroad. Twenty-six percent of Mercedes' 188,215 workers were based outside of Germany.[9] As a symbolic gesture of its commitment to becoming a global firm, Mercedes has replaced its "Made in Germany" slogan as a guarantee for high-quality products with the new slogan "Made by Mercedes-Benz."

In 1993, 41 percent of AEG's sales and 24 percent of its 56,864 employees were based abroad. AEG has a strong manufacturing presence in the Philippines, the United States, and Austria. Before the purchase of Fokker, DASA was primarily a German company. About two-thirds of DASA's 1993 revenues (DM18,626 million) came from abroad.[10] DASA is the only Daimler unit with a non-German Vorstand member: John Tucker of the United States. Debis, with 15 percent of its workers located abroad, earned approximately one-half of its sales outside of Germany.

Of the 330,551 Daimler-Benz employees at the end of 1994, about 25 percent were employed abroad: 25,926 Daimler employees worked in other EU countries besides Germany, 18,325 worked in Brazil, and 16,527 were based in the United States.[11] Daimler-Benz AG corporate-wide has endorsed a commitment to global vision and expansion. The company has communicated this vision to all shareholders in its 100-page book *Going Global,* which outlines the reasons and plans for continued globalization.

To help facilitate a corporate global outlook, Daimler attempts to instill a global perspective in all managers through training, job rotation, and multinational team projects. Daimler has a training center, called *Haus Lämmerbuckel,* near Stuttgart, which is dedicated to bringing employees together from worldwide to discuss differing cultures, trade policies, management and production practices, and global market trends. Daimler is trying to become more locally responsive by beginning to adapt products and marketing campaigns to local markets. After years of obstinately refusing to alter the interior of its autos, Mercedes recently yielded to the desires of American consumers by installing cup holders in models to be exported to the United States.

Besides focusing on further globalization of operations, Daimler-Benz has also identified a need to globalize its finances. Until 1989, the Daimler-Benz stock was listed only on the German and Swiss exchanges. Since then it has been listed on the Tokyo, Vienna, Paris, Singapore, and New York exchanges. After arduous months of negotiations with the U.S. Securities and Exchange Commission (SEC), Daimler became the first German company, on October 5, 1993, to be listed on the NYSE. Daimler has pursued access to foreign financial markets for these reasons: the desire for a broader shareholder base, easier and broader access to capital, international name recognition, and the problem of limited capital in Germany (so much capital is tied up in projects in the former East Germany).[12]

■ Competition

Because Daimler-Benz operates in so many arenas, competition should be analyzed on a divisional level (divisional revenues are shown in Exhibits 4 and 5). The following competitive analysis focuses on Daimler's largest global competitors. On a global level, Mercedes' major competitor is Munich-based BMW (Bayerische Motoren Werke). Each class of Mercedes competes directly with a similar model (price and features) from BMW on a worldwide basis. In 1992, BMW announced the opening of its first U.S. plant in South Carolina. In 1994, BMW acquired the British company Rover in order to enter the SUV market. BMW has benefited greatly from surging sales of the Range Rover and from the synergy created by the merger of the two distribution networks on the U.S. market. Mercedes has responded by building a plant in Tuscaloosa, Alabama, to produce a SUV. In 1990, BMW's stock was selling at DM630 compared to Daimler's share at DM930. By August 1995, BMW was selling around DM850 compared to Daimler at DM670. In 1993, BMW, which produces only cars and motorcycles, had a much higher profit margin, ROE, and ROA than Mercedes.[13]

Mercedes also vies with other luxury car makers in certain vehicle niches: Audi, Jaguar, Volvo, Saab, and Porsche on premium models. The success of the relatively inexpensive Japanese luxury cars in the United States has forced Mercedes to rethink its strategy and to quickly restructure its operations. Full-line automobile manufacturers could also be considered as potential competitors, especially for Mercedes' C class, the least expensive and smallest car of Mercedes' present line.

Mercedes' trucking operations compete directly with the three largest European truck producers: Volvo and Saab-Scania of Sweden and Renault Vehicle Industriel (R.V.I.) of France. In the American truck market, Mercedes' Freightliner Corp. is successfully competing against the U.S.-based truck producers Kenworth and Mac Truck (R.V.I.).

DASA is engaged in various European programs such as Airbus Industrie and Arianespace. Through Airbus, DASA is competing with the world leader in aircraft production, Boeing Co., which controls approximately 60 percent of the civil airline market. Airbus Industrie, which has about 30 percent of the market, is aiming to control 50 percent of the world market by the year 2000.[14] The remaining 10 percent is shared between other competitors such as McDonnell Douglas Corp., Bombardier and Lockheed Martin Corp. Concerning the satellite and space equipment operations, major competitors are NASA, the French companies Thomson CSF and Aerospatiale, and British Aerospace. The French–German helicopter partnership, Eurocopter Holding S.A. (40 percent is owned by Daimler-Benz), is already the world leader in civil helicopter building. Its new military "Tiger" will compete directly with McDonnell-Douglas' AH 64 Apache.[15]

DASA's small twin-jet division Fokker NV is by far the most unprofitable unit of the aerospace activities.[16] The competition in the regional aircraft industry is very intense and congested. The European market is currently dominated by the French–Italian "Avions de Transport Régional" (ATR), who offers cheap and easy to operate twin-turboprop aircraft. DASA's aircraft engines division is competing mainly against Saab-Scania, General Electric, SNECMA (Société Nationale d'Etude et de Construction des Moteurs d'Avion), BMW Motors Division, and Rolls Royce.

Although AEG is currently involved in various activities ranging from automation technology to microelectronics, its two major activities are rail transportation systems and automation technology. The rail transportation division is competing on a worldwide basis against other European firms, who compete in every major field of the rail transportation system: subway, electrical and diesel locomotives, signaling systems, maintenance services, trains, and high-speed trains. The AEG/ABB merger, announced in the summer of 1995, constitutes the world's largest rail systems provider with $4.5 billion in sales and an estimated 12 percent of the world market. The next largest competitors, with about 8 percent of the world market each, are France's GEC-Alsthom and Siemens AG of Germany. AEG's automation technology division provides a large variety of automated systems, ranging from a hydrolic distribution control systems to airport automated systems to mail distribution software.[17] In these various fields AEG is competing with GE Fanuc Automation North America, Allen Bradley, Siemens Industrial Automation, and Klockner Moeller.

Debis competes with numerous telecommunication, insurance, financial services, and software firms. In the telecommunication industry, particularly cellular phones, debis is competing against France Telecom, Deutsche Telekom, and British Telecom, all much larger and established firms. Debis has increased its market share in the software service industry by acquiring 34 percent of France's leading computer and software services company, Cap Gemini Debis Sogeti (CSG). Both companies are competing against software service giants IBM and Microsoft.

Communication and Culture at Daimler-Benz

Vertical and horizontal communication within Daimler-Benz is influenced strongly by German culture. Like many foreign languages, German has a formal and informal address to denote the single English word "you." Traditionally, when one is speaking to a stranger, elder or superior the term *Sie* is used and when speaking to a friend or peer the word *Du* is used. At Daimler business peers that have worked 20 years together will often still use the *Sie* form of address and only utter the last name. When an employee is speaking with his or her boss it is inconceivable that the first name or *Du* form would be invoked. Other cultural factors affecting communication include closed doors, heavy use of euphemisms and indirect language, and insistence on scheduling any informal discussion.

The languages of the four business units often sound quite different: literally. This is because the units have their roots and headquarters in different regions of Germany, where various dialects are spoken and differing mentalities have evolved over the centuries. (Before 1871, Germany was a hodgepodge of numerous small kingdoms, city-states, and principalities.) Attitudes towards open communication, external information disclosure, and a strict Lutheran work ethic are quite different for the congenial Bavarians at DASA as opposed to the more rigid and work-focused Schwabians (the indigenous people of the state Baden-Württemberg) at Mercedes. According to Michael Ondrashek, vice president of acquisitions: "The Schwabians find it easier to work with and understand many non-Germans than the Bavarians."[18]

In 1990, the Daimler-Benz corporate headquarters was moved from its plain surroundings in Untertürkheim, a Stuttgart suburb where Mercedes has been based for 100 years, 20 miles south to the remote suburb Möhringen. A very comfortable multimillion DM complex was erected to house the *crème de la crème* of Daimler-Benz. In addition to the in-house art gallery (as mentioned, the art collector sits on the management board of Daimler) and numerous sculptures, the complex was also aesthetically enhanced through the construction of ponds, streams, and walking trails. Stressing a desire to facilitate and expedite communication, Daimler paid Siemens over DM1 million to install a mechanical internal postal distribution system. Employees at Möhringen dine in a plush cafeteria, which serves three gourmet offerings per day (subsidized by Daimler) and then can relax by going to the separate coffee room for a wide variety of gourmet pastries and coffees or take a stroll through the pastoral grounds. Other Daimler employees outside of Möhringen (especially at Mercedes, where blue-collar and white-collar workers rub shoulders in the drab century-old canteen) have nicknamed the Daimler complex "Bad Möhringen," meaning Spa Möhringen.

Daimler-Benz does have a company-wide (i.e., worldwide) communications system known as Memo. The system, which can be used in English, French, Spanish, or German, is DOS based and approximately nine years old. Because the system is quite slow and user unfriendly, many departments within the four corporate units have had local area networks, Lotus Notes, and MS-Mail installed. Because many employees have stopped utilizing the Memo system, it has become increasingly difficult to send colleagues questions or ideas.[19]

Daimler-Benz has no corporate information technology (IT) department, opting instead to allow individual divisions within the units to formulate their own IT strategies and implement their own systems.

A Wave of Negative Publicity

During the summer of 1995, Daimler-Benz was plagued by a wave of negative publicity that was seen and heard by most Europeans. The wave began June 29 when Stuttgart newspapers carried identical front-page headlines: "Daimler schreibt rote Zahlen" (Daimler in the red). Feeling misled by Reuter's encouraging words only a month beforehand, many investors began crying foul play and threatened Daimler with lawsuits. Realizing that further job cuts were imminent and believing that Daimler's problems were caused by mismanagement and not the fate of the dollar, numerous employees began raising defiant voices. Days later Germany's newspapers reported that numerous Mercedes employees in Eastern Europe had been involved in underpriced and illegal sales of autos to the Japanese.

In late July, a popular German business magazine, *Manager Magazine,* published a 72-page diatribe of the former Daimler CFO, Gerhard Liener, in which he adamantly denounced the diversification strategy of Daimler and past actions of other top executives. He attacked the personal character and integrity of Edzard Reuter, saying "Things said by Reuter were so full of untruths they made me sick to my stomach; he should be ashamed of himself."[20] Liener was even more verbose in his appraisal of Daimler's diversification strategy:

> The integrated technology concern of Reuter is a flop, it exists only in the heads of the executive officers. In the day to day work the numerous daughter firms not only do not cooperate, they are at battle with one another.[21]

Within hours Daimler's leaders were pointing fingers at each other and trying to save their own face. Reuter, who now sits on the Aufsichtsrat (the supervisory board), remained silent. Schrempp fired Liener from a lucrative Daimler consultancy contract.[22]

At this time, reports focusing on the plethora of problems at Fokker, believed by the media to be DASA's destructive parasite, derided the Fokker deal as a colossal error and placed the blame on the former DASA chief, Juergen Schrempp. In the midst of this damaging press, Herr Schrempp himself offered the papers one of the biggest stories of the summer, when he was brought into a local Rome police precinct at 2 A.M. for questioning. Apparently intoxicated, Herr Schrempp and two colleagues, drinking red wine near the Spanish steps, were not very receptive to a policeman's request to see their identification papers. After a brief altercation, in which an officer's wrist was supposedly injured, the group was taken into custody. An embellished version of the story appeared on the front pages of Italian and German papers the following day.

One prominent German business professor, Ekkehard Wenger, summarized his opinions of Daimler's activities of the past year in interviews with *Der Spiegel* and *Wirtschaftswoche* (a German business magazine) by saying:

> Reuter was the greatest capital annihilator and Herr Schrempp will be the greatest job destroyer in German history. Schrempp must somehow create order out of the diversified scrap pile created by Reuter . . . .[23]

During this barrage of bad news for Daimler, there was some very good news for Mercedes-Benz after Chinese President Jiang Zemin chose the Stuttgart auto concern over Ford and Chrysler to enter into a joint venture to build minivans in China.[24] The deal was worth $1 billion. It appeared that Mercedes once again came out shining while other units and the overall corporation were ailing.

■ Conclusion

Apparently, Mercedes' globalization and restructuring strategies were paying off as the business unit announced expected 1995 profits of DM1 billion. What lessons could be transferred to DASA and AEG? Many critics and analysts were suggesting in mid-1995 that Daimler should sell off all or parts of AEG and large chunks of DASA. When addressing these considerations, Juergen Schrempp reflected on the vision of his predecessor—a vision of a global integrated transportation and technology firm gaining competitive advantages in numerous diverse markets through the benefits of synergy. Did this synergy exist and could the envisioned benefits be fully realized?

Believing that a strong German currency would not fluctuate lower soon, Schrempp realized that he had to act quickly to help Daimler further defend itself against currency fluctuation. Globalization of operations was a clear remedy, but numerous questions loomed: Where, when, and how fast should Daimler continue to globalize? On the other hand, Daimler may need to concentrate more on existing operations and problems. One thing was quite certain: Schrempp was not enjoying an easy "honeymoon" period as the new CEO of Germany's largest conglomerate.

■ Notes

1. Intrigen, roter wech und rote Zahlen: Was ist los bei Daimler-Benz?, *Der Spiegel* July 31, 1995, 31.
2. History of Daimler-Benz, Internet, http://www.daimlerbenz.com (Daimler-Benz home page) Oct. 10, 1995.
3. Ibid.
4. Shock für die Aktionäre, *Der Spiegel,* July 31, 1995, 31: 28.
5. Wir pflegen zu heucheln, *Der Spiegel,* July 31, 1995, 31: 24.
6. Rexdroht verweigert DASA weitere Finanzspritzen, *Die Welt,* September 29, 1995, 1.
7. Interview with Dr. Specht, Mercedes-Benz AG, manager of the *Sindelfingen Plant* in Sindelfingen, Germany, April 25, 1995.
8. S. Marquardt, 1994, German auto industry on the rebound, *Automotive Industries,* September, 78–80.
9. *Daimler-Benz: Einblick* (Daimler publication), Supplement: Mercedes-Benz, 1994, 9.
10. Ibid., 21.
11. Ibid., 9–25.
12. *Daimler-Benz: Going Global,* Churchill Murray International, May 1994, 16–18.
13. Daimler-Benz, Annual Report, April 1994; BMW, 1993, Annual Report, Fall 1994.
14. Compétition entre deux géants, Boeing vs. Airbus, *Capital,* September 1994, 34–42.
15. Ibid.
16. Weinen Hilft Nicht, *Der Spiegel,* June 21, 1995, 27: 88.
17. Daimler-Benz, 1994, Annual Report, April 1995.
18. Personal Interview with Mr. Ondrashek, vice president of acquisitions, Daimler-Benz AG, Stuttgart, Germany, September 15, 1995.
19. Interview with Herr Gerhard Herrstein, Personnel Research, Daimler-Benz AG, Stuttgart, Germany, November 8, 1995.
20. Wir pflegen zu heucheln, *Der Spiegel,* July 31, 1995, 31: 25.
21. Ibid., 26.
22. J. Templemann, 1995, The shocks for Daimler's new driver, *Time,* August 21, 38.
23. "Shock für die Aktionäre," *Der Spiegel.*
24. B. Mitchener, 1995, Mercedes-Benz seals $1 billion China deal, *International Herald Tribune,* Frankfurt, July 13, 1.

■ CASE 12 **Dow Corning and the Silicone Breast Plant Implant Controversy**

Anne T. Lawrence
San Jose State University

■ http://seamless.com/alexanderlaw/txt/dow.html
■ http://www.legalseminars.com/breasthp.html

The corporate jet lifted off from Washington's National Airport, en route to Dow Corning Corporation's headquarters in Midland, Michigan. February 19, 1992, had been a grueling day for Keith R. McKennon. Named chairman and chief executive officer of Dow Corning less than two weeks earlier, McKennon had just testified before the Food and Drug Administration's Advisory Committee on the safety of the company's silicone gel breast implants. Although not the only maker of mammary prostheses, Dow Corning had invented the devices in the early 1960s and had been responsible for most of their medical testing. Now, the company was faced with the task of defending breast implants against numerous lawsuits and a rising tide of criticism from the FDA, Congress, the media, and many women's advocacy organizations.

The company's potential liability was large: as many as two million American women had received implants over the past three decades, and perhaps 35 percent of these implants had been made by Dow Corning. In December 1991, a San Francisco jury had awarded a woman who claimed injuries from her Dow Corning implants an unprecedented $7.3 million in damages. Although the company believed its $250 million in product liability insurance was adequate to meet any possible claims, some felt that the company's liability exposure could be much, much larger.

The hearings had been contentious. Critics had repeated their allegations, heard often in the press in recent weeks, that the implants could leak silicone into the body, causing pain, scarring and—most seriously—debilitating autoimmune diseases such as rheumatoid arthritis and scleroderma. They also charged that the

Originally presented at a meeting of the Western Casewriters' Association, March 1993. Research was supported in part by the San Jose University College of Business. This case was written from public sources, including internal company documents released by Dow Corning Corporation in February 1992, solely for the purpose of stimulating student discussion. All events and individuals are real.

Copyright © 1993 by the *Case Research Journal* and Anne T. Lawrence.

silicone prostheses could interfere with detection of breast cancer by mammography. In response, McKennon had testified that implants served an important public health need and did not pose an unreasonable risk to users. On the job less than a month, however, McKennon had had little time to sort through the thousands of pages of relevant documents or to talk with the many managers who had been involved with the product's development over the past 25 years.

The breast implant controversy would surely be a litmus test of McKennon's crisis management skills. Recruited from Dow Chemical Corporation, where he had been executive vice president and head of domestic operations, McKennon came to his new position with a reputation as a "seasoned troubleshooter."[1,2] At Dow Chemical (which owned 50 percent of Dow Corning), McKennon had earlier managed his firm's response to charges that its product Agent Orange, a defoliant widely used during the Vietnam War, had caused lingering health problems for veterans. Later, he had managed Dow Chemical's problems with Bendectin, an antinausea drug alleged to cause birth defects. At the time of his appointment as chairman and CEO, McKennon had served on Dow Corning's board of directors for nearly six years.

The unfolding breast implant crisis showed every sign of being just as difficult—and potentially damaging—as any McKennon had confronted in his long career. Would Dow Corning become known as another Johnson & Johnson, renowned for its skillful handling of the Tylenol poisonings in the 1980s? Or would it become another Manville or A. H. Robins, companies that had declared bankruptcy in the wake of major product liability crises? McKennon was well aware that the future of the company, as well as his own reputation, might well hinge on decisions he and his top managers would make within the next weeks and days.

Dow Corning, Inc.

Dow Corning was founded in 1943 as an equal joint venture of Dow Chemical Company and Corning Glass Works (later known simply as Corning, Inc.) to produce silicones for commercial applications. The term *silicone* was coined by British chemist F. S. Kipping to describe synthetic compounds derived from silicon, an abundant element commonly found in quartz and sand. In the 1930s, Corning researchers working on possible applications of silicone in glassmaking developed a number of resins, fluids, and rubbers that could withstand extremes of hot and cold. In 1940, Corning approached Dow Chemical with a proposal for a joint commercial venture, and by 1942 a small plant in Midland, Michigan (Dow's hometown), had begun production. In an important early success, the fledgling venture produced a sealant that prevented the ignition systems of Allied fighter planes from failing at high altitudes. Dow Corning also made products used by the U.S. military in radio and radar systems, aboard Navy ships, and in wartime factories.

At the close of World War II, Dow Corning moved successfully to develop multiple commercial applications for silicone. Within a decade, the company had introduced more than 600 products and doubled in size three times, making it one of the fastest growing firms in the booming chemical industry. Its varied product line included specialty lubricants, sealants, and resins as well as a variety of consumer items ranging from construction caulk to adhesive labels to Silly

Putty. When astronaut Edward H. White walked in space in 1965, he was connected to the space capsule by a hose made of Dow Corning Silastic silicone rubber. By 1992, the company was producing nearly 5,000 separate products based on silicone.[3-5]

Dow Corning soon developed a reputation as an innovator in organizational design as well as research and development. In 1967, the company reorganized from a conventional divisionalized structure to a global-matrix form of organization, which the company called "multidimensional." At the time pathbreaking, this structure was featured in an article in the *Harvard Business Review* and received considerable attention from management theorists and other practitioners. Under the multidimensional form, the company had ten "profit centers," or basic businesses, each with its own manager and Business Board. Within each profit center, cross-functional product management groups (PMGs) were vested with responsibility for individual product families. Most professionals within this system were in dual authority relationships, reporting both to business group and functional managers. The company was further organized by geographic region, with area managers around the world enjoying significant autonomy. The effect of the company's multidimensional structure was to decentralize authority, push decision making down, and put a premium on cross-functional teamwork and communication. The culture of Dow Corning became known as open, informal, and relaxed.[6]

Development of the First Breast Implant*

Although most uses of silicone were industrial, by the mid-1950s Dow Corning scientists had become interested in possible medical applications and developed several implantable devices, including a heart pacemaker and a hydrocephalic shunt. In the early 1960s, a physician working for the company, Thomas Cronin, became intrigued by the possibility of using silicone to make a breast prosthesis for mastectomy patients. Building off Cronin's preliminary ideas, Dow Corning engineers developed the first prototype of a breast implant by encapsulating a firm-density silicone gel within an elastomer (silicone rubber) bag. First marketed in 1963, this device—known as the Cronin implant—was used initially almost exclusively in reconstructive surgery performed on breast cancer patients following mastectomies.[a]

When Dow Corning first developed and marketed breast implants (as well as its other medical products), the company was operating with virtually no government oversight. Unlike pharmaceutical drugs, regulated since 1906 under the Pure Food and Drug Act and its several amendments, medical devices—even those designed for implantation in the body—were for all practical purposes unregulated. Under the Food and Drug, and Cosmetics Act of 1938, the FDA had the authority to inspect sites where medical devices were made and could seize adulterated or misbranded devices. The agency could not require premarket approval for safety or effectiveness, however, and could remove a product from the market only if it could demonstrate that the manufacturer had broken the law.[7]

---

*The superscript letters refer to explanatory notes that are found at the end of the article, preceding the references.

Although not required to prove its implants safe by law, Dow Corning—in accord with standard "good manufacturing" practices at the time—attempted to determine the safety of its own medical products before releasing them for sale. In 1964, Dow Corning hired the Food and Drug Research Laboratories, an independent contractor, to undertake several studies of the safety of medical-grade silicones, including those used in breast implants. Several different kinds of silicones were injected or implanted in experimental animals. No evidence was found that the silicones caused cancer, but one study found that silicone fluid injected in dogs created "persistent, chronic inflammation." Company scientists dismissed this finding, concluding that the test animals had experienced a "typical foreign body reaction" that was "not material specific," that is, not specific to silicone.

More troubling were the results of another study conducted by the same lab and reported to the company in 1969. Silicone fluids injected into mice and rats had spread widely, becoming lodged in the lymph nodes, liver, spleen, pancreas, and other organs of the test animals. Again, the company appeared unconcerned, noting that it did not advocate the direct injection of silicone. By the late 1960s, the company had in hand evidence that silicone might cause chronic inflammation and scarring and that, in fluid form, it could migrate widely within the body. The company's responses to the studies, however, suggested that it firmly believed silicones to be biologically inert and safe for internal use.

In the early 1970s, Dow Corning's breast implant business for the first time experienced a serious competitive threat. In 1972, five young men—all scientists or salesmen at Dow Corning—left the company to work for Heyer-Schulte, a small medical devices company in Goleta, California, where they used their experience with silicones to develop a competing breast implant. Two years later, the group—led by Donald K. McGhan—left Heyer-Schulte to form their own company, McGhan Medical Corporation, based in Santa Barbara, California. Their idea was to modify the basic technology developed over the past decade by Dow Corning to make a softer, more responsive implant that more closely resembled the natural breast. In this effort, they relied completely on prior research and development done at Dow Corning; McGhan's group apparently undertook no independent tests of the safety of silicone materials used in their products. By 1974, both Heyer-Schulte and McGhan Medical had competing products on the market.[b]

The Heyer-Schulte and McGhan implants quickly gained favor with plastic surgeons, and Dow Corning's market share began to erode. By 1975, Dow Corning estimated its market share had declined to around 35 percent, as plastic surgeons switched allegiance to products offered by the small company start-ups. Dow Corning managers became alarmed.

The Mammary Task Force[c]

In January 1975—responding to the challenge from its California competitors—Dow Corning dedicated a special cross-functional team, known as the mammary task force, to develop, test, and bring to market a new generation of breast implants. The group's main goal was to reformulate the silicone gel to create a softer, more pliable implant competitive with the new products recently marketed by McGhan and Heyer-Schulte. The task force also aimed to develop implants with varying "profiles" and improved sterile packaging. The group of about 20—all men—hoped to have the new implants ready for shipment by June 1975. The company believed it was justified in bringing the new implant to market quickly, without extensive medical testing, because the new product would be based on materials substantially similar to those used in the older Cronin implants. The safety of the existing line, management maintained, had already been satisfactorily documented on the basis of earlier studies and the history of their use.

One of the questions that quickly arose in the task force's deliberations—as reported in the minutes of its January 21, 1975, meeting—was: "Will the new gel . . . cause a *bleed through* which will make these products unacceptable?" (emphasis in original). Dow Corning scientists clearly recognized that a more watery gel (dubbed "flo-gel")—while softer to the touch—might also be more likely to permeate its elastomer envelope and "bleed" into surrounding tissue. Two product engineers, Thomas D. Talcott and William Larson, were assigned to investigate this issue. A week later, task force leader Arthur Rathjen reminded the group in forceful terms:

> Per the Task Force Time Table, there is only a two week period before the new "flo-gel" is scheduled to be formulated and filling begins. A question not yet answered is whether or not there is excessive bleed of the gel through the envelope. We must address ourselves to this question immediately, determine what the facts are, and decide whether the plant is to proceed with the filling of the current inventory [of envelopes]. . . . Question—does the proposed mammary bleed any more than our standard product? If the product does bleed more, is it substantial enough that it will affect the product acceptance? A "go or no go" decision will have to come from the Business Board. The stakes are too high if a wrong decision is made. (January 28, 1975)

On February 4, Talcott and Larson reported that their two- and three-week experiments "*to date* indicate that the bleed with new gel is no greater than what we measure from old gel controls." They also added, however, that they viewed their early results as inconclusive, and they remained concerned about "a possible bleed situation."

Biomedical tests were contracted out to an independent laboratory, which proceeded with tests in which the new gel was injected into experimental rabbits. Early reports back from the lab on February 26 showed "mild to occasionally moderate acute inflammatory reaction" in the test animals around the injected gel, but the pathologist concluded it was probably due to the trauma of insertion, not the product itself. The task force expressed exasperation at the ambiguity of the lab report:

> G. Robertson wants a clarification on their definition of "mild to occasionally moderate acute inflammatory reaction." Suggested he call Biometrics. (February 26, 1975)

The task force also ordered biomedical testing on migration of gel into the vital organs of monkeys. The laboratory results showed "some migration of the [flo-gel] formulation. . . ." However, the task force agreed that the bleed was still not any more or less than standard gel.

The task force continued to move along at a breakneck pace. On February 20, Rathjen praised the group:

> Mel Nelson and the Business Board members, along with the PMG, were very complimentary of the Task Force/Consultant progress in the mammary program. This

has been possible because of your cooperation and open channels of communication. Certainly this last month has demonstrated what can be accomplished when we all pull together. Let's keep it going.

The pace of product development, however, seemed to overwhelm the group's ability to conduct conclusive research on safety, particularly on the issue of whether or not the more liquid-like gel would bleed through the envelope and into body tissues. The March 7 minutes include the following notation:

> T. Talcott still not satisfied [with the elastomer envelope]. A. Rathjen challenged Talcott—if there is something TS&D can do to assist in improving envelopes, do it. We are past the point of discussion about getting together to look into it. (emphasis in original)

"The Best We Have Ever Made"

Development proceeded so rapidly that by March 31, 10,000 new flo-gel mammaries were ready for packaging. The task force minutes reported that the products were "beautiful, the best we have ever made." Now six weeks ahead of schedule, the company was able to ship some samples of the new product to the West Coast in time for the California Plastic Surgeons meeting on April 21. However, early demonstrations did not go flawlessly. The task force got back the following report:

> In Vancouver, and elsewhere on the West Coast introduction, it was noted that after the mammaries had been handled for awhile, the surface became oily. Also, some were bleeding on the velvet in the showcase. (May 12, 1975)

The task force asked that the high-bleed samples be returned, and Talcott and Larson set about testing them. Tom Salisbury, a marketing representative on the task force, wrote the company's sales force on May 16 to advise them on how to handle "oily" implants:

> It has been observed that the new mammaries with responsive gel have a tendency to appear oily after being manipulated. This could prove to be a problem with your daily detailing activity where mammary manipulation is a must. Keep in mind that this is not a product problem; our technical people assure us that the doctor in the O.R. [operating room] will not see any appreciable oiling on product removed from the package. The oily phenomenon seems to appear the day following manipulation. You should make plans to change demonstration samples often. Also, be sure samples are clean and dry before customer detailing.

The task force ordered samples from the West Coast for examination, but no further discussion of this issue appeared in subsequent minutes.

As the flo-gel implants came on line, the focus of the task force's discussion shifted from production issues to marketing strategy. The task force debated various aggressive marketing approaches, such as rebates, distribution by consignment, price breaks for "big users," and free samples for surgeons known to perform augmentations. Noting that June and July were the "peak months" of the "mammary season," managers called for a big push to grab back some of Dow Corning's eroding market share. Rathjen exhorted his troops:

> With the changes in the plastic surgery business that are happening, RIGHT NOW (McGhan Medical, Heyer Schulte, etc.) it was felt that aggressive development and

marketing activity in the next four months will make a tremendous difference in Dow Corning's position in this market. The time to act is NOW. (May 12, 1975)

The group felt that their market share, which they estimated had eroded to around 35 percent, could be lifted back to the 50 to 60 percent range if they moved aggressively.

By September, Dow Corning was producing 6,000 to 7,000 units per month and aimed to phase out the older Cronin models by early 1976. However, many bugs in the production process remained to be ironed out. The reject rate at inspection was high—as high as 50 percent on some lots. Among the problems: floating dirt, weak bags, and thin spots in the envelopes. Doctors had returned some unused mammaries, citing breakage and contamination. Overall, however, plastic surgeons liked the product. One task force member later recalled that when plastic surgeons saw and felt the new material, "their eyes got big as saucers."[8] Besides feeling more natural to the touch, the new softer devices were easier to insert and were more suitable for small-incision, low-trauma cosmetic procedures.

In 1976, engineer Thomas D. Talcott, who had been an active member of the mammary task force, quit his 24-year job at Dow Corning in protest, citing the company's decision to market a product of unproven safety. He later said that he felt Dow Corning was conducting "experimental surgery on humans." Talcott later testified as an expert witness for the plaintiff in several trials in which women sued Dow Corning for product liability. The company dismissed his charges, saying that he "left as a disgruntled employee. You've got to question to some degree his motives."[9,10]

■ A Boom in Busts

Although breast implants first became available in the 1960s, it was only in the late 1970s and 1980s that the rate of implant surgery took off. The increase was due entirely to a fast rise in the number of so-called "cosmetic" procedures; by 1990, fully 80 percent of all implant surgeries performed in the United States were to increase the size of normal, healthy breasts, rather than for reconstruction following mastectomy.

One cause of the rise in cosmetic augmentations, of course, was the availability of the softer, more pliable implants, which could be inserted through smaller incisions with less trauma to the patient in less expensive, outpatient procedures. In 1990, 82 percent of all breast augmentation procedures were performed on an outpatient basis. Other, broader trends within the medical profession and the wider culture also played important roles, however.

One factor behind the boom in breast augmentation surgery was the growth of the plastic surgery profession. Although procedures to graft tissue from a healthy part of the body to another that had been damaged or mutilated were developed early in the century, plastic surgery as a distinct subdiscipline within surgery did not emerge until the 1940s. During World War II, military surgeons struggling to repair the wounds of injured soldiers returning from the front pioneered many valuable reconstructive techniques. Many of these surgeons reentered civilian life to start plastic surgery programs in their home communities. Within a couple of decades, plastic surgery had become the fastest growing specialty within American medicine.[11] Between 1960 and 1983, the number of board-certified plastic surgeons quintupled, during a period when most other medical specialties were growing much less quickly (and the U.S. population as a whole grew by just 31 percent). The draw for newly minted M.D.s: regular hours, affluent customers, and high incomes—averaging $180,000 per year after all expenses in 1987.

As their numbers soared, plastic surgeons faced an obvious problem: developing a market for their services. Demand for reconstructive surgery was not fast growing, and cosmetic procedures were often elective and typically not fully covered by medical insurance. In 1983—following approval by the Federal Trade Commission—the American Society for Plastic and Reconstructive Surgery (a professional association representing 97 percent of all board-certified plastic surgeons) launched a major advertising (or, as the society called it, "practice enhancement") campaign.[12] Other ads were placed by individual surgeons. In one appearing in *Los Angeles* magazine, a seductive, well-endowed model was shown leaning against a sports car. The tag line: "Automobile by Ferrari. Body by [a prominent plastic surgeon.]"

Plastic surgeons also campaigned to redefine female flat-chestedness (dubbed "micromastia" by the medical community) as a medical disease requiring treatment. In July 1982, the ASPRS filed a formal comment with the FDA that argued that:

> There is a substantial and enlarging body of medical opinion to the effect that these deformities [small breasts] are really a disease which in most patients results in feelings of inadequacy, lack of self confidence, distortion of body image and a total lack of well-being due to a lack of self-perceived femininity. The enlargement of the underdeveloped female breast is, therefore, often very necessary to insure an improved quality of life for the patient.[13]

The ASPRS later officially repudiated this view.

By 1990, breast augmentation had become the second most common cosmetic procedure performed by plastic surgeons, exceeded only by liposuction. Since it was a more expensive procedure, however, breast augmentation was the top money maker for plastic surgeons in 1990. That year, ASPRS members collected almost $215 million in fees from women for breast implant surgery (Exhibit 1).

For a variety of reasons, plastic surgery has not been subject to the same degree of oversight as most other medical specialties. Cosmetic procedures are often carried out on an outpatient basis, thus escaping oversight by hospitals. Elective procedures that are not considered medically necessary usually are not reimbursed by insurance, thus avoiding review by another external agency. Although plastic surgery patients typically return to their surgeons for follow-up treatment related to complications of the surgery itself, they rarely return for long-term care. Thus, complications that arise months or years later are more often seen by internists or family physicians, who may be unaware of earlier surgical procedures. Thus, as plastic surgeons moved increasingly into cosmetic procedures, they operated with less institutional oversight than many other specialists.

Another factor contributing to the rise in cosmetic augmentation may have been changing cultural standards of feminine beauty in the 1980s, a decade characterized by social conservatism and, according to some commentators, by a backlash against feminism and female liberation.[d] In the 1970s, women appearing in the glossy pages of fashion magazines were often tall and lanky, with long, straight hair tied at the nape of the neck, menswear "dress-for-success" suits, and distinctly boyish figures. The 1980s ideal woman was very different: the typical

Exhibit 1 Number and Average Fees of Cosmetic Surgery Procedures Performed by ASPRS Members, 1990*

Procedure	Number	Average Fee	Total Fees (000s)
Liposuction	109,080	$1,480	$161,438
Breast augmentation	89,402	2,400†	214,565
Collagen injections	80,602	250	20,151
Eyelid surgery	79,110	1,360‡	107,590
Nose reshaping	68,320	2,590	176,949
Facelift	48,743	3,880	189,123
Retin A	37,338	45	1,680
Tummy tuck	20,213	3,430	69,331
Dermabrasion	16,969	1,260	21,381
Forehead lift	15,376	1,980	30,444

*Only the ten most common procedures are included. These figures do not include operations by the many physicians who perform plastic surgery procedures without receiving specialized residency training in the field. In most states physicians certified in general surgery may perform cosmetic surgery; in some states, any licensed physician may do so. Thus, this table significantly underestimates the total number of procedures performed and the total fees collected in the U.S. each year.

†Fees for a breast implant operation in 1990 ranged from $1,000–5,500.

‡Uppers only. Some eyelid surgery involves both lids, which is more expensive.

Source: "Estimated Number of Cosmetic Surgery Procedures Performed by ASPRS Members in 1990" and "Treatment Locations and Surgeons' Fees for 1990," fact sheets distributed by the American Society for Plastic and Reconstructive Surgery, 1992.

fashion model by this time was more likely to sport 1940s retro-look fashions, thick, full curls, sweetheart lips—and lots of bosom. A number of top movie actresses and celebrities—including Mariel Hemingway, Cher, and Jenny Jones—spoke openly of their surgically enhanced breasts. In a special 100th anniversary edition published in April 1992, *Vogue* magazine summed up current standards of female beauty in this sentence:

> And in women's bodies, the fashion now is a combination of hard, muscular stomach and shapely breasts. Increasingly, women are willing to regard their bodies as photographic images, unpublishable until retouched and perfected at the hands of surgeons.[14]

Ironically, the same issue also ran an ad, placed by trial attorneys, in which "silicone breast implant sufferers" were invited to come forward with legal claims.

A Stream of Sick and Injured

As the rate of implant surgeries rose in the 1980s, so did the number of unfortunate and unintended results. Women who were sick, injured, and in pain from their breast surgery began appearing in the offices of doctors and product liability attorneys. Their stories began to be told—at medical conferences, in legal briefs, and by women's and consumer's advocacy organizations. Dow Corning and other implant makers were forced to respond to a growing crisis of confidence in their products.

The most common adverse side effect of implant surgery was a phenomenon known as "capsular contracture," a painful hardening of the breast that occurred when the body reacted to the implant by forming a wall of fibrous scar tissue around it. In severe cases, the breast became as hard as a baseball and painful to the touch. The FDA has estimated that severe contracture occurred in about 25 percent of all patients; some hardening may have occurred in up to 70 percent. In fact, capsular contracture was so common that the journal *Plastic and Reconstructive Surgery* advised its physician readers to refer to the phenomenon as an "expected result" or "consequence," rather than a "complication," of implant surgery.

Implants could also rupture, spilling silicone gel into the body and often necessitating repeat surgery to replace the damaged implants. Dow Corning's data, based on voluntary reporting by surgeons, showed a rupture rate of only 1 percent. These figures were challenged by researchers who pointed out that ruptures often are asymptomatic and do not show up on mammograms. Scientists at Washington University in St. Louis and the University of Pittsburgh, for example, estimated rupture rates of 5 to 6 percent; individual doctors reported rates as high as 32 percent, according to evidence presented to an FDA panel.[15] Ironically, rupture was sometimes precipitated by a procedure called "closed capsulotomy," in which physicians attempted to treat capsular contracture by exerting force to the breast, manually tearing the scar tissue capsule. In many cases, the procedure inadvertently broke the implant. Ruptures could also be provoked by programs of strenuous massage recommended by some surgeons to prevent formation of fibrous scar tissue. Once the device had ruptured, silicone could and did travel via the lymphatic system throughout the body, lodging in a woman's spleen, liver, and other internal organs.

Also worrisome was the tendency of silicone implants to obscure cancerous tumors that otherwise would be revealed by mammography. Dr. Melvin Silverstein, a surgical oncologist, conducted studies from 1986 to 1991 showing that mammograms performed on women with implants had a "false-negative" rate almost four times as high as those among women without implants; in 39 percent of implant recipients with tumors, the tumor was completely obscured by the implant.[16]

More controversial and less well documented were allegations that silicone implants could lead to so-called autoimmune disorders—diseases in which the body's immune system attacks its own connective tissue. According to the FDA, by 1991 around 600 cases of autoimmune disorders—such as rheumatoid arthritis, scleroderma, and lupus erythematosus—had been reported in women with implants.[17] Some scientists speculated that some women were, in effect, allergic to silicone and that their bodies had attacked their own tissues in an attempt to rid itself of the substance. Such reactions were most likely in the presence of ruptures, but even small amounts of gel bleeding through the envelope—or silicone in the envelope itself—could provoke an autoimmune response. Other physicians believed, however, that the appearance of autoimmune disorders in women with implants was wholly coincidental. In any substantial population—and two million women with implants was clearly substantial—a certain number would develop autoimmune disease purely by chance. Peter McKinney, a plastic surgeon and professor at Northwestern University, articulated this view in an interview in the *Journal of the American Medical Association* in which he called the association between autoimmune disorders and breast implants a "crock of baloney. . . . People get immunological diseases and they just happen to have breast implants."[18]

The question, clearly, was an epidemiological one that could be resolved only with long-term controlled studies of the incidence of autoimmune disorders in populations of women with and without implants. The problem was that absolutely no studies of this type were initiated or even contemplated until 1991. In fact, no comprehensive registries of women with implants existed. Data submitted to the FDA by implant manufacturers in 1991 included no studies that had lasted more than two years, and none that included any questions on autoimmune disease. All relied on the records of plastic surgeons, who were, in any case, unlikely to treat or know about subsequent immune disorders. The question about the relationship between implants and autoimmune disease was, on the basis of existing data, wholly unanswerable. Congressman Ted Weiss (D–New York), who reviewed data submitted to the FDA in 1991, later angrily concluded: "For thirty years, more than one million women have been subjects in a massive, uncontrolled study, without their knowledge or consent."[19]

Victims Seek Redress

Some women who had suffered from breast implants sued. In 1984, Maria Stern of Nevada was awarded $1.5 million by jurors in a San Francisco court, who concluded that Dow Corning had committed fraud in marketing its implant as safe. Stern claimed that her implants had caused joint pain, swollen lymph glands, fatigue, and weight loss. The case was later settled for an undisclosed amount while on appeal, and the court records were sealed. In a post-trial ruling, a federal judge who had reviewed the case records called Dow Corning's actions "highly reprehensible." In the wake of the Stern case, Dow Corning changed its package insert to include a warning that mentioned the possibility of capsular contracture, silicone migration following rupture, and immune system sensitivity.

As other cases slowly made their way through the courts, some victims spoke out publicly. One of the first was Sybil Goldrich, a doctor's wife who had received implants after undergoing bilateral mastectomy for breast cancer in 1983. In an article published in *Ms. Magazine* in 1988, entitled "Restoration Drama," Goldrich told of her experience with silicone implants:

> After two mastectomies, I made every effort to learn about breast reconstruction. . . . Nothing in my research suggested that this "simple" procedure [reconstruction with silicone implants] would turn into five operations, over a period of 10 months, requiring more than 15 hours under anesthesia and countless days of pain and discomfort. The implants hardened, became misshapen, changed position ("migrated" is the word generally used for that) so that they never matched. . . . At one point, the implants nearly passed through the weakened skin, and had to be surgically removed. After this last set of implants failed, I was no closer to restoration than when I started; I simply had several more glaring scars on my disfigured torso.[20]

Goldrich later joined with Kathleen Anneken, a nurse who had experienced a failed augmentation procedure, to found the Command Trust Network, an advocacy organization that became instrumental in providing information, support, and legal and medical referrals to implant victims.

Other women's and public health advocacy groups also played a role in publicizing the risks of breast implants. One of the most active was the Health

Research Group (HRG), a Washington-based spin-off of Ralph Nader's Public Citizen. Headed by a consumer activist, Dr. Sidney M. Wolfe, the HRG in 1988 began a systematic effort to pressure the FDA to ban silicone breast implants. The group petitioned the FDA, testified before Congress and other government agencies, issued regular press releases, and distributed information to consumers. The HRG also initiated an information clearinghouse for plaintiffs' attorneys.[21,22] Another active advocacy organization was the National Women's Health Network, a public interest group that widely distributed information on silicone-related issues.

■ Devising Regulation for Devices

The agency in charge of regulating implants—and thus the object of these and other advocacy organizations' pressure—was the U.S. Food and Drug Administration. In 1976—the year after Dow Corning's mammary task force developed its new generation of flo-gel implants—Congress passed the Medical Amendments Act to the Food and Drug Act. Enacted in the wake of the Dalkon shield controversy—in which thousands of women claimed they had been injured by a poorly designed intrauterine device—the amendments for the first time required that manufacturers of new, implantable medical devices prove their products safe and effective before release to the public.[e] Devices already on the market were ranked by risk, with the riskiest ones—designated "Class III"—required to meet the same standards of safety and effectiveness as new devices.

In 1978, during the initial review of the 1,700 known existing devices, the FDA's General and Plastic Surgery Devices Advisory Panel—which was dominated by plastic surgeons—recommended that breast implants receive the less restrictive Class II designation. The FDA disagreed and, in 1982, proposed a Class III rating. For six years, however, the agency failed to take action on its own recommendation. The commissioner later explained that the agency had simply been overwhelmed by the sheer volume of premarket approval applications it had received from manufacturers; he told reporters that reviewing devices in over 130 different categories had been "an enormous undertaking." Finally, in January 1989, the FDA identified silicone implants as Class III devices and gave their manufacturers 30 months—until July 1991—to submit safety and effectiveness data to the agency.

Four breast implant manufacturers submitted premarket approval applications (PMAs) to the Food and Drug Administration in July 1991: Dow Corning, INAMED (formerly McGhan Medical), Mentor (formerly Heyer-Schulte), and Bioplasty. Surgitek, a unit of Bristol-Meyers Squibb, withdrew from the implant business, saying it was unable to meet the FDA's deadline.[f] Together, the four PMAs filled 15 large file boxes; Dow Corning's application was by far the most extensive. On August 12, the head of the FDA Breast Prosthesis PMA task force submitted a review of Dow Corning's clinical studies, stating that they were "so weak that they cannot provide a reasonable assurance of the safety and effectiveness of these devices." He noted:

> [The studies] provide no assurance that the full range of complications are included, no dependable measure of the incidence of complications, no reliable measure of the revision rate and no quantitative measure of patient benefit. . . . [Physicians surveyed were instructed] to report only complications associated with the implant. As a result

the only complications reported are those at the implant site. This prevents these investigations from detecting systemic adverse effects. . . . [This] causes an underestimate of both the types and incidence of complications.[23]

Staff reviews of the PMAs submitted by other manufacturers were, if anything, even more scathing. On September 25, the FDA ordered implant makers to give doctors more information about the risk of implants as an interim measure while its PMA reviews continued.

Finally, on November 13, the FDA convened its advisory panel to consider the PMAs and to take further testimony. The hearings were highly contentious. The panel heard, once again, arguments concerning the dangers of implants. But the FDA hearings also generated intense support for implants from plastic surgeons, satisfied implant recipients, and breast cancer support and advocacy organizations. Among the most vocal defenders of the implants were women who had experienced successful reconstruction following mastectomies, including representatives of such peer support organizations as Y-Me and My Image after Breast Cancer. Several spoke of the positive psychological benefits of reconstruction, and warned that if the FDA took implants off the market, some women—knowing that reconstructive surgery was unavailable—would delay regular checkups for breast cancer, endangering their lives.[g] Other witnesses argued that women should be free to choose implants, so long as they were fully informed of the benefits and risks of the devices.

The advisory panel debate was, by all accounts, heated. In the final analysis, the panel split hairs: It voted that although breast implants "did not pose a major threat to the health of users," the data submitted by manufacturers was "insufficient to prove safety." However, citing "a public health need," the panel recommended that the devices be left on the market.

The regulatory decision, at this point, passed to the FDA commissioner, Dr. David A. Kessler.[b] Appointed just a few months earlier, Kessler had brought a new commitment to regulatory activism to an agency marked by what some viewed as a pattern of weak government oversight during the Reagan administration.[24] Now, the fledgling commissioner had two months—until mid-January—to rule on the panel's recommendation on breast implants.

Unauthorized Leaks

Unfolding events, however, forced Kessler's hand sooner. In December, a San Francisco jury returned a verdict in *Hopkins v. Dow Corning*, awarding Mariann Hopkins $7.3 million—by far the largest victory ever for a plaintiff in a breast implant suit. Hopkins' attorney claimed that his client's implants (made by Dow Corning in 1976) had ruptured and spilled silicone gel, causing severe joint aches, muscle pain, fatigue, and weight loss. Hopkins had been disabled by a disorder her doctors diagnosed as "mixed connective tissue disease." The woman's attorney told the jury that "this case is about corporate greed and outright fraud." Dow Corning immediately moved to have the legal records in the case—which included hundreds of pages of internal company memos Hopkins' attorney had subpoenaed—sealed.

Somehow, however, the documents from the Hopkins trial ended up in Commissioner Kessler's hands.[i] Their contents evidently alarmed him. On January 6, 1992, Kessler abruptly reversed the FDA's November decision and called for a 45-day moratorium on all sales of silicone gel breast implants pending further study of their safety, and he recalled the advisory panel to consider "new evidence." Both the plastic surgeons and Dow Corning were furious. Dr. Norman Cole, president of the American Society of Plastic and Reconstructive Surgeons, took the unusual step of calling a press conference to brand Kessler's action as "unconscionable—an outrage." Cole said that the sudden moratorium on implant sales had "created hysteria, anxiety, and panic" and called on Kessler to reconstitute the advisory panel, which he called unqualified to judge the safety of the devices. For its part, Dow Corning demanded publicly to know what "new evidence" Kessler had obtained and restated the company's intention to block any release of "nonscientific" internal memoranda. Robert Rylee, chief of Dow Corning's health care business, called a press conference to repeat the company's contention that "the cumulative body of credible scientific evidence shows that the implants are safe and effective."[25,26]

Ranking "Right Up There with the Pinto Gas Tank"

Dow Corning's efforts to block release of the Hopkins documents, however, failed. On January 13, *New York Times* reporter Philip J. Hilts—saying only that he had obtained the material from "several sources"—broke the Hopkins case memos in a page one article, under the headline "Maker is Depicted as Fighting Tests on Implant Safety."[27] In a summary of the contents of several hundred internal company memos, Hilts charged that Dow Corning's safety studies were "inadequate" and that serious questions raised by its own scientific research and by doctors' complaints had not been answered.

More damaging revelations were yet to come. Over the next several weeks, newspaper readers learned of the following incidents, drawn from the company's internal documents:

- In a 1980 memo, Dow Corning salesman Bob Schnabel had reported to his marketing manager that he had received complaints from a California plastic surgeon who was "downright indignant" because the implant envelopes were "greasy" and had experienced "excessive gel bleed." "The thing that is really galling is that I feel like I have been beaten by my own company instead of the competition. To put a questionable lot of mammaries on the market is inexcusable," Schnabel wrote his manager. "It has to rank right up there with the Pinto gas tank."

- In 1985, Bill Boley, a company scientist, had warned that a particular formulation of the gel could cause cancer, and called for further testing. "Without [it ...]," he argued, "I think we have excessive personal and corporate liability exposure."

- Marketing manager Chuck Leach had reported in a memo that he had told a group of doctors that he had "assured them, with crossed fingers, that Dow Corning had an active study [of safety issues] under way." (Leach later angrily disputed the interpretation given his remarks by the media, saying in a letter to the Associated Press that he had meant the term "crossed fingers" in a "hopeful" rather than a "lying" sense.)

- Dr. Charles Vinnik, a Las Vegas plastic surgeon, had had an extensive correspondence with the company reporting his dissatisfactions with the product. In one letter, he charged that he felt "like a broken record" and told of an incident in which an implant has ruptured and spilled its contents—which he described as having the "consistency of 50 weight motor oil"—onto the operating room floor.

Whether wholly justified or not, the memos created a strong impression that Dow Corning had been aware of safety concerns about its implants for many years and had failed to act on this knowledge. The press moved in aggressively, attacking Dow Corning for its "moral evasions"; a widely reprinted cartoon depicted a Dow Corning executive apparently deflating as silicone gel oozed from his body.

A Model Ethical Citizen

That Dow Corning was being labeled publicly as "a company adrift without a moral compass"—as one *New York Times* columnist put it several days after the internal memos broke in the press[28] —struck many in and around the company as deeply unjust. Ironically, Dow Corning Corporation was widely regarded in the business community as a model for its efforts to institutionalize ethical behavior.

At the center of Dow Corning's efforts was a formal code of conduct and an unusual procedure for monitoring compliance. In 1976—the first full year of sales for its new-generation breast implants—the company's board of directors had appointed a three-person Audit and Social Responsibility Committee and charged it with developing a corporate code of ethical conduct. Top managers were motivated, in part, by a breaking scandal at that time in which several large companies had been accused of questionable payments to foreign heads of state to secure contracts. With a substantial portion of its operations overseas, Dow Corning wanted its behavior to be above reproach.[j]

In 1977, the company published its first corporate code of conduct (Appendix A), laying out a comprehensive statement of ethical standards. In order to ensure compliance, the company initiated a series of annual audits, in which top managers would visit various cities around the globe to evaluate corporate performance against code standards. Audits typically involved 5 to 15 people and lasted a full day. Issues covered in the audits were wide ranging, including, for example, competitor and customer relations, distribution and purchasing practices, employee welfare, and product and environmental stewardship. In addition, the company held training programs on the code, and its semiannual employee opinion survey included a section on business ethics.[k]

Yet, for whatever reason, the company's widely admired procedures had failed to flag the safety of breast implants as an ethical concern. A routine 1990 ethics audit of the Arlington, Tennessee, plant that manufactured silicone implants, for example, did not bring to light any concerns about the product's safety. When later questioned about the apparent failure of the audit procedure, Jere D. Marciniak, chairman of the conduct committee, pointed out that normally product safety issues would come before the relevant business board, not the ethics review. "It wouldn't have been necessary to bring up [the implants' safety] inside a code-of-conduct meeting unless an employee thought the [Medical Device Business Board's] process wasn't working well and wanted to raise the issue," he noted.[29,30]

A "Hardball" Strategy

As the controversy widened, Dow Corning's response, in the words of one *Wall Street Journal* reporter, was to "play hardball."[31] On January 14—eight days after the FDA had announced its moratorium on implant sales and one day after the first leaked documents appeared in the press—Dow Corning took a $25 million charge against fourth quarter 1991 earnings to cover costs of its legal liability, unused inventory, and efforts to prove implants safe. The company also suspended implant production and placed workers at the company's manufacturing facilities on temporary layoff, with full pay and benefits. Investors, apparently alarmed by this turn of events, knocked down the stock price of both Corning, Inc., and Dow Chemical as they contemplated the parent firms' potential liability.

Implant recipients and trial lawyers were also contemplating the liability question. During the week following the FDA's decision to place a moratorium on implants, one prominent plaintiff's attorney reported he was fielding phone calls from 50 to 60 potential clients a day. By March, as many as 600 lawsuits had been filed against Dow Corning and other breast implant makers, according to Karen Koskoff, cochair of the breast implant litigation group of the Association of Trial Lawyers of America. The National Products Liability Database estimated that Dow Corning had been sued at least 54 times in federal court and possibly more than 100 times in state courts. Frank C. Whiteside, Dow Corning's attorney, disputed these figures, saying that there were far fewer than 200 cases pending against his client.[32]

The unauthorized leaks created tremendous pressure on Dow Corning to release its own documents to the public. The FDA publicly called on the company on January 20 to release the material so that women and their doctors could evaluate the new evidence for themselves, rather than simply relying on news reports. (The agency, although in possession of the documents, could not release them because they were still protected under court order.) The company responded two days later by releasing a group of scientific studies—but not the infamous "Pinto" memo and other internal materials that the company dubbed "unscientific."

Suspension of breast implant sales and release of the scientific studies did not slow down the crisis engulfing the company. On January 29, in an apparent acknowledgment of the severity of the situation, the company hired former attorney general Griffin B. Bell—who had performed a similar role at Exxon Corporation following the Valdez oil spill and at E. F. Hutton following the check-kiting scandal—to investigate its behavior in making implants.

Finally, on February 10—following a top-level intervention by the chairmen of Corning, Inc., and Dow Chemical, both of whom sat on Dow Corning's board—the board of directors executed a stunning management shakeup. Dow Corning demoted chief executive Lawrence A. Reed to the position of chief operating officer and forced longtime board chairman John S. Ludington to retire. Keith R. McKennon was named chairman and CEO. Simultaneously, the board announced that it would release to the public 15 scientific reports and 94 nonscientific memos or letters from company files, including the "Pinto" and "crossed fingers" memos, as well as other potentially damaging materials that had not yet been reported by the media.

Several top executives, including Robert Rylee and Robert LeVier, technical director of Dow Corning's Health Care Businesses, met the press the same day to present the company's perspective. Rylee defended the company's decision not to release the documents earlier, saying:

> Our motives are simple. First and foremost, these memos do not answer fundamental questions and concerns that women have about breast implants. And by focusing attention on the memos rather than the science that supports the device, we do nothing but further raise the anxiety level of women and physicians and scientists.

Rylee told the packed press room that "while we are not happy with the memos, we have nothing to hide, and we believe that each memo put in its proper context can be understood and explained." For example, in the case of the infamous "Pinto" memo, Rylee stated:

> The memo was written by a salesman who had an unhappy customer, so obviously he, as a salesman, was unhappy. . . . We believe the doctor was unhappy about the way the implant appeared, rather than the safety or effectiveness of the product. . . .

Rylee categorized many of the memos as "sensational and anecdotal reports, versus true science." Many, he said, were best understood as part of the normal give and take that occurs within a technical organization, "one part of a multifaceted dialogue or communication or discussion that goes on," and did not reflect fundamental problems. By pulling various statements out of context, Rylee implied, the press had misrepresented questions scientists might legitimately raise in the course of their inquiry as final conclusions.

He closed the press conference by denying categorically that implants could cause autoimmune disease or cancer.[33]

Facing a Crucial Decision

On February 20, the day after his testimony before the FDA, McKennon received word from Washington. After three hours of tense debate, the FDA advisory panel had voted just after 5 P.M. to recommend that implants be taken off the market, except for women needing reconstruction following mastectomies or to correct serious deformities. All implant recipients would be required to enroll in clinical studies. Cosmetic augmentations would be strictly limited to those required by the design of the clinical trials. Commissioner Kessler would have 60 days to rule on the panel's recommendation.

McKennon would have to lay a plan of action before his board soon—he certainly could not wait another two months for the FDA's next move. The breast implant business, he had learned, had not made any money for Dow Corning for the past five years. Even in its heyday, it had contributed no more than one percent of the company's total revenues. Some of his top executives had urged him just to get out of the implant business altogether and let the attorneys mop up the liability problems. Many in the company felt that the huge settlement in the Hopkins case would be greatly reduced on appeal, and the company's $250 million in insurance would be sufficient to cover their liability. McKennon reflected on these issues as he contemplated his next actions. Certainly, he needed to act decisively to stem Dow Corning's financial losses. But, he pondered, did the company not also have—as he had put it to a reporter a few days earlier—an "overriding responsibility . . . to the women who have our implants"?[34] And what of the company's reputation, so carefully nurtured, for always upholding the highest standards of ethical behavior?

Appendix A

■ Dow Corning Corporation Corporate Code of Business Conduct, 1977

A Matter of Integrity

Dow Corning believes in private enterprise. We will seek to establish an atmosphere of trust and respect between business and members of society, an atmosphere where business and the public understand, accept, and recognize the values and needs of each other.

To establish and promote this atmosphere of mutual trust and respect, Dow Corning accepts as our responsibility a recognition, evaluation and sensitivity to social needs. We will meet this responsibility by utilizing our technological and management skills to develop products and services that will further the development of society.

The watchword of Dow Corning worldwide activities is integrity. We recognize that due to local differences in custom and law, business practice differs throughout the world. We believe that business is best conducted and society best served within each country when business practice is based on the universal principles of honesty and integrity.

We recognize that our social responsibilities must be maintained at the high standards which lead to respect and trust by society. A clear definition of our social responsibilities should be an integral part of our corporate objectives and be clearly communicated to every employee.

Statement of General Conduct

We shall not tolerate payments in any illegal or questionable form, or non-standard commissions or other compensation, given or received, that may influence business decisions.

We shall not make any political contribution nor participate in partisan political activity as a company, recognizing however the rights of employees to participate in legal political processes as private citizens.

We shall be knowledgeable of local laws and customs and operate within them. On the other hand, when we are not being treated legally or ethically we will pursue whatever legitimate recourses are available to us.

Responsibilities to Our Employees

Relations with employees are based on the understanding that attracting and retaining talented and dedicated employees is vital to the accomplishment of financial and social objectives.

Our responsibilities to our employees are:

To manage our activities in such a way as to provide security and opportunities for our productive employees.

To hire, train, evaluate, and advance on the basis of individual ability, contribution, potential, interest and company needs without distinction as to nationality, sex, age, color or religion.

To compensate in accordance with local, national or industry practice.

To provide a safe and healthy work environment that at least meets the applicable governmental laws and regulations.

To provide a work environment that encourages individual self-fulfillment, open communication and free interchange of information and ideas.

Responsibilities to Host Countries in Which We Operate

Activities in host countries are based on the premise that we can and wish to contribute to the economic objectives of the host government while concurrently meeting our corporate objectives.

Our responsibilities to host countries are:

To preserve and, where possible, enhance the environment through elimination or control of pollution.

To conserve natural resources.

To design and modify facilities which meet or exceed current and anticipated environmental and safety laws and regulations.

To hire, train, and qualify host country nationals for positions of responsibility consistent with their demonstrated capabilities.

To pay our required share of taxes and duties but resist inequitable or double taxation between countries.

To resolve any government relations problems or conflicts among overlapping jurisdictions through prompt, direct and open discussions with responsible government officials.

To follow responsible monetary and credit practices and conduct foreign exchange operations not for speculative purposes, but in accordance with normal business requirements and to protect our exposure fluctuations.

To encourage the flow of our technology across borders to the extent needed and appropriate in our local operations and markets, and to receive adequate compensation and protection of this technology.

Appendix B

Time Line

1940s: Dow Chemical Corporation and Corning Glass Works form a joint venture to develop and produce military applications for silicone as lubricant, sealant, and coolant.

1950s: Dow Corning develops numerous commercial applications for silicone.

1962: Dow Corning invents the silicone breast implant.

1975: Dow Corning develops and markets new generation of softer, more responsive breast implants.

1976: Congress gives the FDA power to regulate medical devices. However, breast implants are excluded because they are already on the market.

1976: Materials engineer Thomas Talcott quits Dow Corning in protest, citing company inattention to safety concerns with the new implants.

1976: Dow Corning establishes an ethics program, publishes its first Code of Conduct, and initiates annual ethics audits.

1984: Maria Stern successfully sues Dow Corning, claiming foreign body reaction to silicone.

1985: Dow Corning warns doctors and women of possible side effects, including capsular contracture and inflammation.

1989: FDA reclassifies breast implants as Class III devices and orders their makers to provide evidence of implants' safety within 30 months.

September 1991: Surgitek drops out of the breast implant business, saying it cannot meet the FDA deadline.

November 1991: FDA panel finds safety data submitted by the industry inadequate, but recommends silicone breast implants be left on the market to meet "a public health need."

December 1991: Mariann Hopkins receives $7.3 million judgment against Dow Corning in San Francisco federal court.

January 6, 1992: FDA calls for a 45-day moratorium on the sale and use of silicone breast implants, citing insufficient evidence of their safety, and asks its advisory panel to examine new evidence.

January 13, 1992: The New York Times publishes unauthorized leaks from internal Dow Corning documents.

January 14, 1992: Dow Corning suspends production of breast implants and takes a $25 million charge against fourth quarter 1991 earnings to cover costs of legal liability, unused inventory, and efforts to prove implants safe. Workers at the company's manufacturing facilities are placed on temporary layoff.

January 20, 1992: The FDA asks Dow Corning to make public documents on implants so that women and their doctors can evaluate evidence for themselves.

January 22, 1992: Dow Corning releases a group of scientific studies to the public.

January 29, 1992: Dow Corning hires former attorney general Griffin B. Bell to investigate its behavior in making implants.

February 10, 1992: Dow Corning names Keith R. McKennon chairman and chief executive officer, demoting CEO Lawrence A. Reed, who becomes chief operating officer. John S. Ludington, chairman, retires.

February 10, 1992: Dow Corning releases to the public several hundred additional pages of internal documents, annotated by the firm, including the "Pinto" memo.

February 18, 1992: FDA opens three days of hearings to reconsider whether or not silicone breast implants should remain on the market.

February 20, 1992: FDA panel recommends that silicone breast implants be limited to women who have had mastectomies or who have seriously deformed breasts, and that all implant recipients be required to participate in clinical trials. FDA Commissioner David Kessler has until April 20 to make a final decision on the panel's recommendation.

Notes

a. Although Dow Corning did not introduce its first breast implant until 1963, silicones may have been used for breast augmentation as early as the late 1940s. Shortly after World War II, transformer coolant fluid made of silicone was said to be disappearing from the docks in Japan, apparently for use by cosmeticians who injected it into prostitutes to enlarge their breasts. To prevent the silicone from migrating in the body, the Japanese added cottonseed or croton oil to cause scarring, containing the silicone at the site of injection. Shortly thereafter, the technique apparently spread to the United States. During the 1950s, perhaps as many as 50,000 American women—mostly exotic dancers in Nevada, California, and Texas—and a handful of gay men were injected with liquid silicone. At the time, the procedure was totally unregulated. Later, some of the first medical evidence of the adverse health effects of silicones in the body came from studies of these early recipients of breast augmentation procedures. (Statement of Dr. Norman Anderson, Hearing before the Human Resources and Intergovernmental Subcommittee of the Committee on Government Operations, House of Representatives, December 18, 1990, Is the FDA protecting patients from the dangers of silicone implants?, pp. 30–31.)

b. The corporate successors to both Heyer-Schulte and McGhan Medical continued in the breast implant business. In 1977, McGhan and his partners sold their company to Minnesota Mining and Manufacturing (3M), which operated a breast implant division until it sold the company back to McGhan and a group of private investors in 1984. McGhan and his associates continued to manufacture implants under the name INAMED Corporation. In 1984, a portion of Heyer-Schulte—including its breast implant business—was purchased by the Mentor Corporation of Santa Barbara, becoming Mentor's plastic surgery subsidiary. Mentor, which has said it purchased the assets—not the liabilities—of Heyer-Schulte, later became the second largest manufacturer of implants, following Dow Corning. Other manufacturers that later entered the breast implant field included Bioplasty, of St. Paul, Minnesota, and Surgitek, a division of Bristol-Meyers Squibb. (Thomas M. Burton, Several firms face breast implant woes, *Wall Street Journal,* January 23, 1992, B1, B7.)

c. The following two sections are based on internal Dow Corning documents released to the public in February, 1992, following intense pressure from the Food and Drug Administration and several public health and women's advocacy organizations. All quotations are from internal company memoranda and minutes.

d. This argument has been most fully articulated in Susan Faludi, *Backlash: The Undeclared War Against American Women,* New York: Crown, 1991. For further discussion of changing standards of feminine beauty in the 1980s, see Naomi Wolf, *The Beauty Myth: How Images of Beauty Are Used Against Women,* New York: Doubleday, 1991.

e. For a full account of the Dalkon shield case, see Richard B. Sobol, *Bending the Law: The Story of the Dalkon Shield Bankruptcy,* Chicago: University of Chicago Press, 1991.

f. Surgitek had manufactured an implant coated with a layer of polyurethane foam. This foam was later discovered to break down over time in the body, producing as a by-product minute quantities of 2-toluene diamine, or TDA, a known animal carcinogen. Surgitek stopped selling the product in April 1991.

g. FDA advisory hearings held in Gaithersburg, Maryland, *Command Trust Network Newsletter,* Winter 1991–1992. For another view by a representative of a breast cancer survivors' organization, see the statement of Rosemary Locke, Hearing before the Human Resources and Intergovernmental Subcommittee of the Committee on Government Operations, House of Repre-

sentatives, December 18, 1990, Is the FDA protecting patients from the dangers of silicone implants?, pp. 11–12.

h. For a statement of his regulatory philosophy, see David A. Kessler, The basis of the FDA's decision on breast implants, *New England Journal of Medicine,* 18 June 1992: 1713–1715.

i. According to one account, Seth Rosenfeld, a reporter for the *San Francisco Examiner,* offered copies of the Hopkins documents to the FDA, which refused them. Rosenfeld then gave the documents to Dr. Norman Anderson, a consultant to the FDA advisory panel and a prominent breast implant critic. Anderson reportedly hand delivered the documents to Kessler's home on January 3, 1992. (Michael Castleman, The enemy within, *California Lawyer,* March 1993, 106.)

j. This scandal later led to passage of the Foreign Corrupt Practices Act of 1977, in which payments by U.S. corporations to foreign politicians or political parties to secure or retain business were ruled illegal.

k. This account of Dow Corning's ethics program is based largely on Kenneth E. Goodpaster with David Whiteside, Dow Corning corporation: Business conduct and global values," Parts A, B, and C, Harvard Business School, 1984–1989.

◼ References

1. Lois Ember, Silicone breast implants: New Dow Corning chief to tackle crisis, *Chemical and Engineering News,* 17 February 1992: 4–5.
2. Larry Reibstein, Fighting the implant 'Fire,' *Newsweek,* 24 February 1992: 9.
3. Don Whitehead, *The Dow Story: The History of the Dow Chemical Company* (New York: McGraw-Hill, 1968).
4. Eugene G. Rochow, *Silicon and Silicones* (Berlin: Springer-Verlag, 1987).
5. Barnaby J. Feder, P.R. mistakes seen in breast implant case, *The New York Times,* 29 January 1992.
6. William C. Coggin, How the multidimensional structure works at Dow Corning, *Harvard Business Review,* January/February 1974: 54–65.
7. Office of Technology Assessment, *Federal Policies on the Medical Devices Industry* (New York: Pergamon Press, 1984).
8. Philip J. Hilts, Implant maker is depicted as fighting tests on implant safety, *The New York Times,* 13 January 1992: A1, A12.
9. Tim Smart, This man sounded the silicone alarm—in 1976, *Business Week,* 27 January 1992: 34.
10. Leslie Berkman, Implant whistle blower says he warned Dow, *Los Angeles Times,* 19 February 1992.
11. Bradford Cannon, The flowering of plastic surgery, *Journal of the American Medical Association,* 263(6), 1990: 862–864.
12. Susan Faludi, *Backlash: The Undeclared War Against American Women* (New York: Crown, 1991), pp. 217–218.

13. American Society of Plastic and Reconstructive Surgeons, Comments on the proposed classification of inflatable breast prosthesis and silicone gel filled breast prosthesis, July 1, 1982, pp. 4–5, reported in Joan E. Rigdon, Plastic surgeons had warnings on safety of silicone implants, *Wall Street Journal,* 12 March 1992: A8.
14. Marsha F. Goldsmith, Image of perfection once the goal—now women just seek damages, *Journal of the American Medical Association,* 267(18), 1992: 2439.
15. Philip J. Hilts, Studies see greater implant danger, *The New York Times,* 9 February 1992.
16. Felicity Barringer, Many surgeons are reassuring their patients on silicone implants, *The New York Times,* 29 January 1992.
17. Philip J. Hilts, Panel to consider what sort of rules should control gel implants, *The New York Times,* 18 February 1992: A14.
18. Goldsmith, Image of perfection.
19. Hilts, Panel to consider.
20. Sybil Niden Goldrich, Restoration drama, *Ms. Magazine,* June 1988.
21. Marilyn Chase, A consumer crusader with an M.D. is a pain to the health industry, *Wall Street Journal,* 7 April 1992: A18.
22. Public Citizen Health Research Group, *Health Letter,* various issues.
23. Diana Zuckerman, Memo to Congressman Ted Weiss, PMA applications for silicone breast implants, 12 September 1991.
24. Christine Gorman, Special report: Can drug firms be trusted? *Time,* 10 February 1992: 42–46.

25. Philip J. Hilts, Maker of silicone breast implants says data show them to be safe, *The New York Times,* 14 January 1992: A1, A13.
26. Felicity Barringer, F.D.A. accused of creating panic over breast implants, *The New York Times,* 16 January 1992.
27. Hilts, Maker is depicted as fighting tests.
28. Steven Fink, Dow Corning's moral evasions, *The New York Times,* 16 February 1992: F13.
29. John A. Byrne, The best laid ethics programs . . . couldn't stop a nightmare at Dow Corning, *Business Week,* 9 March 1992: 67–69.
30. Feder, P.R. mistakes seen in breast implant case.
31. Thomas M. Burton and Joan E. Rigdon. Management shake-up at Dow Corning signals a more conciliatory attitude, *Wall Street Journal,* 18 February 1992: A3, A10.
32. Don J. DeBenedictis, FDA action spurs implant suits, *American Bar Association Journal,* March 1992: 20.
33. Federal News Service, News conference: Dow Corning Corporation regarding breast implants, February 10, 1992.
34. Thomas M. Burton and Scott McMurray, Dow Corning still keeps implant data from public, despite vow of openness, *Wall Street Journal,* 18 February 1992.

CASE 13   Eastman Kodak Company: A New Image

Paul Hines
Ken Wollin
Rick Truscott
Leni Kantono
Uzma Suboohi
Andrew Callaway

■ http://www.kodak.com/

George M.C. Fisher became CEO of Eastman Kodak Company in December 1993, replacing Kay Whitmore, who was forced to step down by angry shareholders and an impatient board. Kodak has been spending billions on diversification and repeated restructuring. However, Kodak earned less in 1993 than it had in 1982. The restructuring had failed to streamline the company and achieve the desired profitability. The Standards & Poor's 500 Stock index has outperformed Kodak's stock by more than 200 percentage points since 1982.

Fisher took over knowing there were several problems concerning Kodak's balance sheet, its earnings, its growth, and its management and organizational functions (see Exhibits 1 and 2). Realizing the failures of the past decade's diversification strategies and the resulting financial dilemma, the new CEO announced a new corporate strategy on May 3, 1994, that would focus the company's resources and management attention exclusively on its imaging business:

> Imaging offers Kodak tremendous opportunities for long-term success and growth. It is the business Kodak knows best, built on over a century of brand strength, marketing know-how, and technological leadership," said George M.C. Fisher, Kodak's Chairman, President, and CEO. "To achieve maximum success, we have concluded that we must commit our entire resource base to imaging opportunities and divest non-core businesses.[1]

Case prepared under the direction of Professor Robert E. Hoskisson for class discussion purposes only.

Exhibit 1 Balance Sheet ($000)

	1994	1993	1992	1991	1990	1989	1988	1987	1986	1985
Assets:										
Cash	2,020,000	1,635,000	361,000	783,000	735,000	1,095,000	848,000	702,000	145,000	161,000
Marketable securities	48,000	331,000	186,000	141,000	181,000	184,000	227,000	290,000	468,000	652,000
Receivables	3,064,000	3,463,000	3,433,000	4,348,000	4,333,000	4,245,000	4,071,000	3,144,000	2,563,000	2,346,000
Inventory	1,480,000	1,913,000	1,991,000	2,311,000	2,425,000	2,507,000	3,025,000	2,178,000	2,072,000	1,940,000
Other current assets	1,071,000	679,000	466,000	675,000	934,000	560,000	513,000	477,000	563,000	578,000
Total current assets	7,683,000	8,021,000	6,437,000	8,258,000	8,608,000	8,591,000	8,684,000	6,791,000	5,811,000	5,677,000
Property, plant, equipment	12,299,000	13,311,000	13,607,000	19,034,000	17,648,000	16,774,000	15,667,000	13,789,000	12,919,000	12,047,000
Accumulated depreciation	7,007,000	6,945,000	6,843,000	9,432,000	8,670,000	8,146,000	7,654,000	7,126,000	6,643,000	6,070,000
Net property, plant, equipment	5,292,000	6,366,000	6,764,000	9,602,000	8,978,000	8,628,000	8,013,000	6,663,000	6,276,000	5,977,000
Other noncurrent assets	872,000	1,271,000	5,667,000	1,961,000	2,102,000	1,854,000	1,657,000	820,000	815,000	488,000
Deferred charges	505,000	481,000	1,473,000	4,349,000	4,448,000	NA	NA	NA	NA	NA
Intangibles	616,000	4,186,000	NA	NA	NA	4,579,000	4,610,000	424,000	NA	NA
Total assets	14,968,000	20,325,000	20,341,000	24,170,000	24,136,000	23,652,000	22,964,000	14,698,000	12,902,000	12,142,000
Liabilities:										
Notes payable	371,000	655,000	1,732,000	2,610,000	2,956,000	NA	NA	NA	NA	NA
Accounts payable	3,398,000	3,630,000	3,127,000	3,835,000	3,457,000	6,073,000	5,277,000	3,614,000	3,440,000	2,989,000
Income taxes	1,701,000	460,000	524,000	292,000	588,000	338,000	411,000	380,000	209,000	156,000
Other current liabilities	365,000	165,000	163,000	162,000	162,000	162,000	162,000	146,000	142,000	180,000
Total current liabilities	5,735,000	4,910,000	5,546,000	6,899,000	7,163,000	6,573,000	5,850,000	4,140,000	3,791,000	3,325,000
Deferred charges	95,000	79,000	568,000	1,490,000	1,830,000	1,690,000	1,565,000	1,420,000	1,209,000	1,048,000
Long-term debt	660,000	6,853,000	5,402,000	7,597,000	6,989,000	7,376,000	7,779,000	2,382,000	911,000	988,000
Other long-term liabilities	4,461,000	5,127,000	2,268,000	2,080,000	1,406,000	1,371,000	990,000	743,000	603,000	219,000
Total liabilities	10,951,000	16,969,000	13,784,000	18,056,000	17,388,000	17,010,000	16,784,000	8,685,000	6,514,000	5,580,000
Equity:										
Common stock net	966,000	948,000	936,000	934,000	934,000	934,000	934,000	933,000	622,000	621,000
Capital surplus	515,000	213,000	26,000	9,000	7,000	6,000	1,000	NA	314,000	312,000
Retained earnings	4,485,000	4,469,000	7,721,000	7,225,000	7,859,000	7,802,000	7,922,000	7,139,000	6,533,000	6,710,000
Treasury stock	1,957,000	2,039,000	2,041,000	2,052,000	2,059,000	2,059,000	2,059,000	2,059,000	1,081,000	1,081,000
Other equities	8,000	(235,000)	(85,000)	(12,000)	7,000	(41,000)	(18,000)	NA	NA	NA
Shareholder equity	5,974,000	3,356,000	6,557,000	6,104,000	6,748,000	6,642,000	6,780,000	6,013,000	6,388,000	6,562,000
Total liabilities and net worth	14,968,000	20,325,000	20,341,000	24,170,000	24,136,000	23,652,000	22,964,000	14,698,000	12,902,000	12,142,000

Exhibit 2 Income Statement ($000)

	1994	1993	1992	1991	1990	1989	1988	1987	1986	1985
Net sales	13,557,000	16,361,000	16,545,000	15,951,000	18,908,000	18,398,000	17,034,000	13,305,000	11,550,000	10,631,000
Cost of goods	7,325,000	8,063,000	8,018,000	7,729,000	9,637,000	9,822,000	9,727,000	8,037,000	7,613,000	7,129,000
Gross profit	6,232,000	8,298,000	8,527,000	8,222,000	9,271,000	8,576,000	7,307,000	5,268,000	3,937,000	3,502,000
R&D expenditures	859,000	1,301,000	1,419,000	1,337,000	1,329,000	1,253,000	NA	NA	NA	NA
Selling, general, & administrative expenses	3,711,000	4,989,000	5,280,000	5,049,000	5,098,000	4,857,000	4,495,000	3,190,000	3,213,000	2,378,000
Income before depreciation & amortization	1,662,000	2,008,000	1,828,000	1,836,000	2,844,000	2,466,000	2,812,000	2,078,000	724,000	1,124,000
Nonoperating income	(249,000)	(520,000)	103,000	(1,516,000)	(775,000)	(646,000)	121,000	87,000	129,000	(411,000)
Interest expense	142,000	635,000	713,000	754,000	812,000	895,000	697,000	181,000	255,000	183,000
Income before taxes	1,271,000	853,000	1,218,000	(434,000)	1,257,000	925,000	2,236,000	1,984,000	598,000	530,000
Provision for taxes	448,000	381,000	491,000	(132,000)	554,000	396,000	839,000	806,000	224,000	198,000
Net income before extraordinary items	823,000	475,000	727,000	(302,000)	703,000	529,000	1,397,000	1,178,000	374,000	332,000
Extraordinary items/discontinued operations	(266,000)	(1,990,000)	419,000	319,000	NA	NA	NA	NA	NA	NA
Net income	557,000	(1,515,000)	1,146,000	17,000	703,000	529,000	1,397,000	1,178,000	374,000	332,000
Outstanding shares	335,700	330,566	325,916	324,933	324,638	324,577	324,414	324,371	226,033	225,677
Earnings per share	1.66	-4.58	3.52	0.05	2.17	1.63	4.31	3.63	1.65	1.47

Company History

Early History[2]

George Eastman lived a tough childhood, growing up in Rochester, New York, in the 1860s. His father died when George was young, leaving the family financially distressed. George went to work as a messenger boy at an insurance company to help support his family. On his own initiative, he became a junior bank clerk by studying accounting at night school. At the age of 24, George Eastman became interested in photography while planning for a vacation. A coworker suggested that George make a photographic record of his vacation. George discovered that the camera, film, and wet-plate developing chemicals and equipment were too bulky, and he decided to devote the rest of his vacation to making photography more convenient. In three years, George Eastman obtained a patent for a new dry glass plate process technology and a machine that produced more than one plate at a time. He began selling the plates to photographers. Henry Strong, a local businessman, became interested in George's work and convinced him to form Eastman Dry Plate Company on January 1, 1881.

In 1883, Eastman introduced a new film using gelatin-coated paper packed in a roll holder that could be used in almost every plate camera available. The company continued to create new products and reorganized as Eastman Dry Plate and Film Company. In 1888, Eastman introduced the first portable camera with enough film for 100 pictures for five dollars. This was the birth of snapshot photography. At this time, Eastman trademarked "Kodak." Along with the trademark, George created a slogan that promised "You push the button, we do the rest."

In 1889, Eastman Photographic Materials was incorporated in London with a manufacturing plant built outside of London and distribution sites in France, Italy, and Germany. In the following year, the company's name was changed to its present name, Eastman Kodak Company. George Eastman established Kodak under four main business principles:

1. mass production at a low cost,
2. international distribution,
3. extensive advertising, and
4. focus on the customer.

Beyond his inventive genius, George blended human and democratic qualities into building his business. He believed his employees should have more than good wages; they should have a promise of future employment and regard the company as a family. To help his employees, Eastman set up "wage dividends" (the first of any type of profit sharing), retirement plans, life insurance policies, and disability benefits. George Eastman was a modest man, patriotic citizen, and philanthropist. His kindheartedness went beyond his employees to society as well. Eastman contributed large sums of money to the Rochester Institute of Technology, MIT, the Eastman School of Music, and the Rochester Symphony.

Eastman Kodak Company proceeded to introduce numerous photographic innovations. In 1902, the company introduced a new developing machine that processed film without the use of a darkroom. A research center, built in Rochester in 1912, produced many new products including 16mm Kodacolor motion picture film, the 16mm Cine-Kodak motion picture camera, and the Kodascope projector. During the World War I, Kodak devoted its efforts to helping the military by developing aerial cameras and training U.S. Signal Corps photographers in their use.

After the war, Kodak returned to producing consumer products. Sadly, when in his seventies, George Eastman committed suicide in 1932. His final note said, "To my friends. My work is done. Why wait? G.E."[3] Thereafter, Kodak attempted to follow the strategy practiced by George Eastman. It introduced, in 1932, the first 8mm motion picture system consisting of the cameras, film, and projectors. In 1935, Kodak made available the first amateur color film, 16mm Kodachrome. One year later, color film was introduced for 35mm slides and 8mm home movies.

■ Post–World War II

In 1951, a low-priced Brownie 8mm movie camera was brought to market, while the accompanying projector was introduced the following year. In 1953, Kodak formed Eastman Chemical Products to market alcohols, plastics, and fibers for industrial use. The substances had been previously manufactured by Tennessee Eastman and Texas Eastman, which had been formed in 1920 and 1952 because of Kodak's use of chemicals in its film manufacturing and processing.

Until this point in time, Kodak had always included the cost of film processing in the cost of the film. However, a consent decree filed in 1954 forced Eastman Kodak to forgo this practice. This provided Kodak an opportunity to serve a new market of independent photofinishers with its film developing products. Also at this time, Kodak was making significant advances in 35mm color slide technology, and in 1958, manufactured the first completely automatic projector, the Kodak Calvacade. Three years later, the line of Kodak Carousel projectors proved to be successful. In 1962, astronaut John Glenn used Kodak film to record his orbit around the earth. In that same year, the Instamatic camera, which used a film cartridge instead of a film roll, became a commercial success because of its ease of use. By 1972, five different models of a pocket version of the Instamatic had become popular. In the same year, Eastman Kodak formed Eastman Technology and acquired Spin Physics, a producer of magnetic heads used in recording equipment, in order to expand into unrelated businesses.

Antitrust concerns and other developments such as the industry trend to diversify, caused Kodak to believe it needed to compete in other markets. In 1975, it introduced the Ektaprint Copier-Duplicator, putting Kodak in direct competition with Xerox and IBM. The new product fit well with the existing microfilm business because the copier used a wet process similar to that used in film processing. The wet process allowed production of numerous copies at high speeds, while collating them during duplication, which was a unique feature at the time. Unfortunately, due to slow market entry, Ektaprint lost millions of dollars in its first five years.

This was not the only time Kodak took on well-established companies. In 1976, it went head to head against Polaroid's 30-year lock on the instant photography market. Kodak attacked Polaroid with a new line of instant cameras and film that developed outside the camera within a few minutes. Kodak had always thought Polaroid's product was a "toy" of poor quality and was convinced it could produce a better product to protect its overall photographic market leadership. Within four years, Kodak began marketing an instant camera, but it was continually plagued with problems. Kodak's emphasis on long-term product development over quick market entry proved to be a major obstacle. Polaroid's ownership of hundreds of patents propagated Kodak's problems even further. Polaroid stifled Kodak with lawsuits and product innovation, thus establishing and maintaining a strong position in the market.

The year 1980 marked Kodak's 100th anniversary, which was celebrated by the introduction of the Ektachem 400 blood analyzer. The Ektachem blood analyzer provided entry into the health sciences market and represented a natural application of Kodak's film manufacturing technology. It also reinforced the company's strong position as a supplier of x-ray film to hospitals and other health care facilities.

■ Kodak Leadership

■ The Chandler Years, 1977–1990

In 1977, Kodak went through a change in leadership when Colby H. Chandler became president. Chandler had been with Kodak since 1951 and as head of the U.S. and Canadian Photographic Division, he was directly responsible for both the instant camera and the Ektaprint copier. In 1983, he was selected as the chief executive officer and chairman of the board.

At this point Kodak faced stiff challenges from Japanese and U.S. suppliers in the photographic paper market. Fuji Photo Film Company and 3M were undercutting Kodak's prices for paper. In addition, Kodak's photographic equipment sales were eroded by the rapid introduction of competitive products from Japan. Chandler believed that the answer to Kodak's challenges was to diversify through acquisitions and joint ventures. He also believed that Kodak should place a stronger emphasis on nonphotographic products with high profit potential and should take a more aggressive approach to protecting the firm's chemical imaging business. His diversification strategy was to build the existing businesses through both horizontal and vertical integration.

Colby Chandler also saw new development in the area of electronics that would provide Kodak with much-needed sales growth. Chandler formed a new electronics division, which included the Spin Physics subsidiary. Kodak made a number of acquisitions (see Exhibit 3) to support this objective. The acquisitions were not limited to electronic imaging equipment, but also included diversification into the rapidly growing computer industry. This was demonstrated by the partial acquisition of Sun Microsystems, Mead Digital Systems, and Kusuda Business Machine. Kodak also entered into a joint venture to develop a camcorder with the Matsushita Electrical Industrial Company of Japan. The camcorder was introduced in 1984, and represented Kodak's first electronic product.

Also in 1984, Kodak came out with a complete line of videotape cassettes for all video formats, and floppy disks for use in personal computers. To further enhance its computer data storage capabilities, Verbatim Corporation was acquired. Unfortunately, this venture proved to be disappointing due to cost management inefficiencies and was subsequently sold to Mitsubishi Kasei Corporation of Japan in 1990 (see Exhibit 4).

In 1986, Kodak formed Eastman Pharmaceuticals Division in order to establish a stronger presence in the health care industry. To further strengthen its position, Kodak acquired Sterling Winthrop in 1988 for $5.1 billion. Sterling

Exhibit 3   Acquisitions

1984

—Acquired Sun Microsystems Inc. $20 million partial stock purchase in this electronic computers firm.

1985

—Acquired the assets of Mead Digital Systems. Kodak paid $10 a share in this partial acquisition.

—Full acquisition of Verbatim Corp, a manufacturer of data storage media. The offer was for $7.55 a share or $175 million.

—Acquired three units of Kusuda Business Machine. Three units were division for Kodak Product, Kusuda Micro Systems Service, and Nippon Information Publishing. Kodak paid $143.50 per share.

—Acquired Eikonix Corporation for $56 million. Eikonix Corp provides image processing equipment and R&D in the same area.

1986

—Acquired Fox Photo through its wholly owned subsidiary Rochester Holdings for $95.5 million. Fox Photo provides Kodak with a large share of photofinishing laboratories in the United States.

—Acquired Bell & Howell's Pasadena, California, plant for $26 million. Bell & Howell provide information products and services.

—Acquired Neo Rx Corporation, which operates health care facilities. Eastman acquired equity interest and acted as financial supervisor.

—Acquired the Wafer Inspection Equipment Business of Aeronca Inc.'s Aeronca Electronics unit for $12.75 a share.

—Acquired Bioimage Corporation, which manufactures scientific instruments. The amount paid was undisclosed. Bioimage manufactures intelligent analytical systems for digital image interpretation used by medical and biotechnology researchers to analyze protein and nucleic acid.

1987

—Full acquisition of International Biotechnologies for $16.5 million. International Biotechnologies manufactures systems for biomedical research.

—Acquired 18.7 percent interest in Enzon for $5 million. Enzon is a biochemical research firm.

—Acquired American Photo Group Corporation. American Photo is a private company with 20 wholesale photofinishing labs in 17 states. The purchase complements its acquisition of Fox Photo to regain its place as the largest photofinisher in the United States.

—Acquired Yourdon Inc., which is a software company. Yourdon was a unit of Keller Graduate School of Management.

—Acquired a minority interest in Viratek Inc. and in its parent company ICN Pharmaceuticals.

—Raised its 16 percent stake to 25 percent in Genecor Inc. This move puts Kodak at equal level with other partners.

1988

—Acquired CX's photofinishing assets. CX operates three wholesale photofinishing laboratories.

—Acquired IBM Copier Service business and existing copier sales agreements in the United States.

—Acquired Interactive Systems, which supplies UNIX services and products to the computer industry.

Continued

Winthrop manufactures and markets prescription drugs and over-the-counter medicines. Sucrets throat lozenges, Tums antacid tablets, and the U.S. rights to the Bayer aspirin brand name and trademark were part of the assets acquired. Sterling Winthrop was the second largest pharmaceutical company in France and Italy and had an established position in the Pacific Rim countries. The acquisition of Sterling Winthrop was viewed unfavorably by industry analysts. This negative perception proved correct as sales decreased due to increasing competition within the pharmaceutical industry. Kodak had moved away from

Exhibit 3	Acquisitions—*Continued*

1989	—Acquired Les Laboratories Associes of France. Les Labs has 25 photofinishing labs and estimated annual sales between $100 million and $150 million. It was acquired by the French subsidiary of Eastman Kodak Co, Kodak-Pathe.
	—Acquired Sterling Drug for $5.1 billion. Kodak was a white knight against hostile takeover bids. Sterling Drug is a manufacturer of medicine and household products.
	—Increased its ownership in Nagase Kodak KK of Tokyo from 50 to 51 percent. The transaction was valued at $37.9 million.
1990	—Interactive Systems Corp., a unit of Eastman Kodak, acquired Lachman Associates Inc.
	—Sterling Drug, a subsidiary of Eastman Kodak, acquired Pharma Investi, a Spanish manufacturer of pharmaceuticals.
1991	—Kodak Canada Inc. acquired Direct Film for 2.7 million. Kodak Canada sold the assets after the acquisition in order to collect on outstanding debt owed by Direct Film.
	—Acquired Jamieson Film Co., a Dallas based manufacturer of cineradiography film processors commonly used in cardiac catherization laboratories.
	—Acquired Vortech, a supplier of medical image management systems.
	—Acquired Genencor Biotechnology Co. and renamed it Genencor International.
1992	—Acquired all the stock of Vanguard Instruments, which manufactures 35mm cineangiogram projectors and microcalcium ventricular volumes and other heart parameters.
	—Atex, a unit of Eastman Kodak, acquired the entire product line of Ctext Inc. The acquisition included Ctext's DOS and OS/2 based editorial and classified advertising systems.
	—Eastman Chemical, a division of Eastman Kodak, purchased a polymer plant in Hartepool from the Thakral Group of Hong Kong. Kodak will manufacture polyester plastics for packaging at the plant.
	—Acquired Image Bank, Inc. for $24.91 million. Image Bank is a photography agency that reproduces rights to photographers and other images for editorial and promotional purposes.
	—Acquired 5% interest in Fuisz Technologies Ltd. as part of R&D agreement. Fuisz was involved in R&D of polymer materials processing use, imaging, and *in vitro* and *in vivo* diagnostics.
	—Acquired assets of Systepo Sypress Oy and worldwide rights to advertise products of this Finland-based advertising agency.
	—Acquired Genentech Vitamin C Business Unit for Genecor International to end antitrust charges of decreased competition in the vitamin market. Genentech Inc. discovers, develops, and manufactures human pharmaceuticals.

Source: Mergers and acquisitions database, IDD Information Services, Inc.

its core competencies, venturing into the health care industry and was unable to compete with its rivals competently.

The acquisition of Fox Photo in 1986, for $95.5 million, and the subsequent acquisition of American Photo Group Corporation, CX Photofinishing, and Les Labs of France, represented Eastman Kodak's expansion into the wholesale photofinishing industry. These acquisitions were meant to take advantage of Kodak's business of producing the supplies and equipment used within the photofinishing industry.

Exhibit 4   Divestitures

1986

—Textile dye business sold to Ciba-Geigy.

1987

—Photoresistor business sold to Union Carbide Corporation.

1988

—Kodak beta physics polyester film operations sold to Rhone-Poulenc SA.

1989

—The Estek unit, a manufacturer of semiconductor equipment such as spin-rinse dryers, megasonic cleaning systems, and solvent processing equipment, was sold to Verteq Inc.

—The Kodak Video Program unit, holding the rights to 135 special interest films, sold to Wood Knapp and Co.

1990

—Sayett Technologies sold to Sayett Acquisition Co., Inc.

—Pathtek, a supplier of selective plating service for making of custom plastic molded circuits, sold to Mitsui Petrochemical Inc.

—Verbatim Corporation, a manufacturer of removable magnetic data storage media, sold to Mitsubishi Kasei. The sale did not involve the small-format optical disk or other tape programs.

—Fastek, division of Eastman Technologies, sold to Osmonics.

Yourdon Inc., a software consulting and training services firm, sold to CGI Info-France.

—Acquidneck Data, a computer software and system development firm, sold to Systems Engineering Associates Corporation, a subsidiary of Day and Zimmerman Inc.

1991

—Ultralife Battery business including manufacturing equipment, technologies, inventory, and brand name sold to an investment group.

1992

—Eastman Kodak Credit business, with assets of $1 billion serving 12,000 Kodak customers and $600 million of Kodak's $10.3 billion debt, sold to GE Capital Corporation.

—Videk, manufacturer of optical scanners for medical, industrial, and scientific applications, sold to Performance Technologies.

—Atex Inc., a manufacturer of publishing systems and software, was sold to a European acquisition group.

—Interactive Systems, a supplier of UNIX services and products, sold to SHL Systemhouse, Inc.

—PhisoHex skin-cleaner product line of Sterling Winthrop sold to Bausch and Lomb.

—Estek, a manufacturer of equipment utilized in the semiconductor industry to detect and analyze contamination on silicone wafers, sold to ADE.

1993

—Eastman Chemical spin off resulting in a $1,8 billion reduction of Eastman Kodak's debt.

1994

—Sterling Winthrop's prescription business sold to Sanofi SA of France for $1.68 billion.

—Sterling Winthrop's over-the-counter medicines, including Sucrets throat lozenges and Tums antacid tablets, sold to SmithKline Beecham plc for $2.93 billion.

—Lehn and Fink's household product lines, including Lysol and Mop and Glo floor cleaner, sold to Reckitt and Colman plc of London for $1.55 billion.

—Kodak's clinical diagnostic business sold to Johnson and Johnson for $1.01 billion.

—Lehn and Fink's consumer products businesses, including MinWax wood finishes, Red Devil paints and Thompson's water seal waterproofers, sold to Forstman Little and Co. for $700 million.

Source: Mergers and acquisitions database, IDD Information Services, Inc.

In addition to diversification, Chandler's tenure was characterized by extensive downsizing. The effects of downsizing on Kodak's earnings were mixed. Kodak cut 7,006 jobs in 1982, only to see its earnings slip to $1.65 per share the next year. In 1985, 8,670 jobs were eliminated, but this time the earnings per share increased by $0.18 to $1.63 per share after peaking at $4.31 per share in 1988.[4] In addition, the debt had reached $7 billion in 1990, as a result of Kodak's acquisition activities.

■ The Whitmore Years, 1990–1993

Upon Chandler's retirement in 1990, President Kay Whitmore took over as CEO after an open struggle for succession with Vice Chairman Phillip Samper.[5] Whitmore began his career with Kodak as an engineer in film manufacturing in 1957. In 1978, he was named vice president of the company and became president in 1983.

As president, Whitmore's objectives were to reduce costs, divest noncritical assets, and reallocate resources to those key businesses that offered Kodak the best opportunity for long-term growth.[6] Whitmore continued the diversification strategy, but streamlined Kodak's operations, focusing his efforts on the imaging, health care, and chemical industries. In the imaging area, both the traditional silver-halide photofinishing business and the emerging digital imaging industries were emphasized.

As CEO, Whitmore divested Eastman Kodak of many of its smaller units, such as the Ultralife battery business; the Atex company, a publishing systems and software business; and the Phiso-Hex skin cleaner product line of Sterling Winthrop. In addition to these divestitures, Kodak undertook the acquisition of the Spanish pharmaceutical firm, Pharma Investi, to strengthen its pharmaceutical operations in Europe. The clinical diagnostic testing businesses were also strengthened by the acquisition of Amerlite Diagnostic LTD, Vanguard Instrument Corporation, and Vortech Data Inc.

This strategy met with disapproval from Kodak's stockholders. Industry analysts and stockholders alike believed that Kodak needed to divest itself of a major asset in order to reduce its high debt. The embattled information systems business, which makes copiers, was a possible divestiture.[7] This division experienced poor earnings, sluggish growth, high costs, and faced antitrust lawsuits.

By 1993, the stockholders began applying pressure through the board of directors. They felt that the actions taken by Whitmore were not drastic enough to bring the necessary changes. The company's $10.5 billion debt that had been taken on during the acquisition strategy of the 1980s and Kodak's "bloated" structure were the issues that the stockholders felt needed attention.[8] In response to these pressures Whitmore hired Christopher Steffen as the chief financial officer in 1993. This represented a break in tradition because Steffen was the first outsider to be hired for a top management position at Kodak.

Mr. Steffen was considered a turnaround artist who had previously orchestrated the successful turnaround of Chrysler and also Honeywell's revitalization. Announcement of his appointment resulted in a jump of $1 billion in stock value.[9] However, Mr. Steffen resigned only 11 weeks after his arrival on the job. It was rumored that Mr. Steffen had clashed with Kay Whitmore over the actions necessary to restore Kodak to profitability. The stock market reacted strongly by reducing Kodak's stock price by $5.125 per share.

Whitmore then divested Kodak of its credit services business. Eastman Kodak Credit Corporation, with $1 billion of assets and $600 million of Kodak's $10.3 billion total debt, was sold to GE Capital Corporation. Nonetheless, Kodak's earnings fluctuated dramatically during Whitmore's tenure as CEO, culminating in a $4.58 loss per share for 1993. Events such as the unsuccessful introduction of the photo CD in 1992 simply added fuel to the fire. Apparently, Whitmore's actions were not rapid enough to satisfy Eastman Kodak's stakeholders, and he was replaced by George Fisher in October 1993.

■ The Fisher Years, 1993–Present

George M.C. Fisher began his career as a highly educated technologist, having earned a master's degree in engineering and a doctorate in applied mathematics. After working for several years in research and development for Bell Telephone Laboratories, Fisher moved to a management position with Motorola in 1976. In 1988, Fisher became CEO of Motorola and proceeded to guide the company to five consecutive years of phenomenal sales and earnings growth. Motorola's stock appreciated at a compound rate of 26 percent during Fisher's tenure as the company assumed worldwide leadership in pagers and cellular telephones.[10]

In October 1993, Fisher shocked observers by accepting an offer to become CEO, president, and chairman of Eastman Kodak. He had previously declined an offer to become CEO of IBM, partly because IBM did not share his belief in slow cost reduction. In his own words, Fisher was "already a success" at Motorola and welcomed the chance to help turn Kodak around.[11] Fisher believes that Kodak will regain its stature by emphasizing technological innovation and marketing vision, the same principles that led to the success of Kodak's founder, George Eastman.[12]

Following his appointment as CEO, Mr. Fisher immediately increased the level of divestiture (see Exhibit 4) to lead Kodak back to a strategy focused on its core business of imaging. Eastman Chemicals was spun off on the last day of 1993. In 1994, the divestiture trend was continued as approximately $5.2 billion of its $16.4 billion 1993 revenues were sold. In June and August, Sterling Winthrop was sold in two separate transactions for $4.6 billion. Kodak's clinical diagnostic business sold for $1.01 billion in September, and the household products business, Lehn and Fink, was sold in two separate transactions for $2.25 billion in September and October. However, Kodak retained health care products related to imaging such as its x-ray film, and electronics-based medical, cardiology, and dental diagnostic imaging equipment. At the end of 1994, the only nonimaging assets remaining were a research lab and Nanosystems, a technology development center. In addition, Kodak had lowered its debt from $6.7 billion with a long-term debt ratio of 58 percent to a much lower 35 to 38 percent or $660 million debt.[13]

Although Kodak had taken numerous steps toward economic success, analysts pointed out that many actions were still required before Kodak would be completely healthy. A disappointing third quarter 1994 earnings announcement highlighted Kodak's continuing problems. Industry experts observed that "Kodak is hindered by a lack of new products because it hasn't invested in copier technology since the early '80s."[14] This was demonstrated in the third quarter earnings report by its commercial imaging segment, where earnings fell 39 percent from 1993 results.

Kodak employment fell from 110,400 to approximately 92,000 employees as a result of 1994 divestitures. But the expected restructuring program was expected to cut at least another 10,000 people before it was finished. Analysts believed that Kodak needed to make even more changes. "The measures the company is taking now aren't enough. It has to do some structural realignment."[15] Summary of Kodak's financial results over time are shown in Exhibits 5, 6, 7, 8, 9, and 10.

Exhibit 5

Revenues

Source: Kodak annual reports.

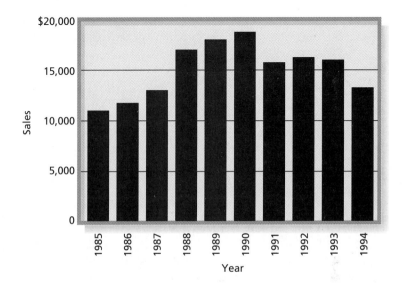

Exhibit 6

Net Income

Source: Kodak annual reports.

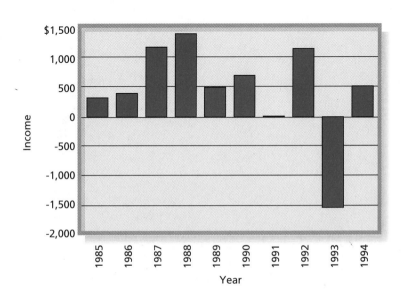

Exhibit 7

Long-term Debt

Source: Kodak annual reports.

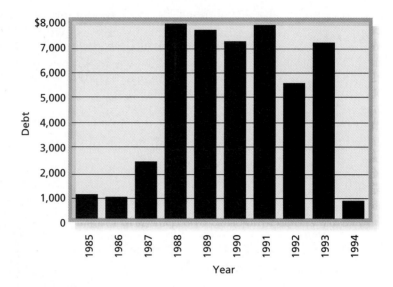

Exhibit 8

Earnings per Share

Source: Kodak annual reports.

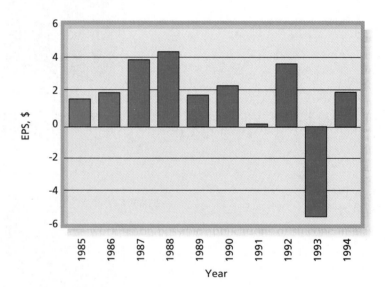

Exhibit 9

Business Segment Revenues, 1993

Source: Kodak annual reports.

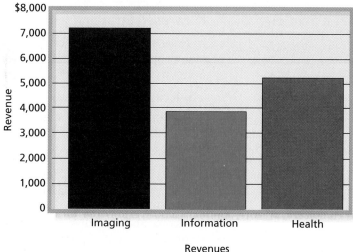

Exhibit 10

Business Segment Income

Source: Kodak annual reports.

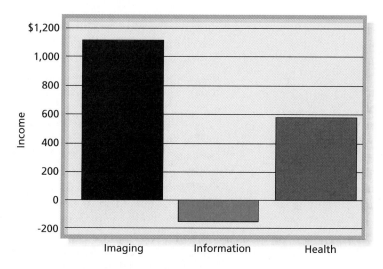

Fisher's Strategy

Focused Strategy

In order to realize George M.C. Fisher's strategy of focusing Kodak's resources and management attention exclusively on its imaging business, divestitures were necessary. Kodak's divestitures of nonimaging businesses serve three purposes:

- First, Kodak can move quickly to achieve significant debt reduction.
- Second, Kodak can commit its management attention to improving the current performance of its core imaging business.
- Third, the company can strategically attack a broader array of imaging opportunities.

Fisher stated that Kodak will focus on profitable participation in the five links of the imaging chain: capture, processing, storage, output, and delivery of images for people and machines anywhere in Kodak's worldwide market. Under the new strategy, Kodak's imaging business can be divided into the traditional silver-halide photoimaging business and the digital imaging business.

Traditional Silver-Halide Imaging

Silver-halide is the main chemical used in film to capture the image in conventional photography. For Kodak, silver-halide photofinishing is a mature and slowgrowing industry. Although critics believe that this traditional film business is a mature market with slow growth prospects, Fisher believes the future of the company will continue to rely mostly on the silver-halide business. He believes the resolution of silver-halide cannot be duplicated with electronics economically today. Therefore, the challenge facing Kodak is to show the customer the value added in the silver-halide technologies.[16]

Kodak's worldwide research laboratories have set new performance standards in film speed, grain, sharpness, and color reproduction. In the early 1990s, the company had a breakthrough development in silver-halide technology called Kodak T-GRAIN emulsion technology. By manipulating the molecular structure of silver-halide crystals to produce tabular grains of silver, Kodak scientists were able to "flatten" them to more efficiently gather light. This technology allows for higher speed films with sharper, more compelling pictures. T-GRAIN technology has also created improvements in motion picture production, diagnostic imaging, graphic arts applications, and business documentation.

Eastman Kodak formed a partnership to develop a new photographic technology, Advanced Photo System (APS), with Fuji Photo Film Company, Canon Inc., Nikon Corporation, and Minolta Camera Company. APS is a completely new camera, which uses technologically advanced film known as "smart film." This new technology could eventually surpass conventional 35mm film sales. Around 90 percent of conventional photographs taken by U.S. consumers in 1994 were shot on 35mm film. George Fisher and other industry leaders insisted that the new system would coexist with the 35mm technology.[17]

Kodak researched and partially developed the new technology for APS, but realized that it needed support from competitors in order to create an industry-wide standard. Although the companies shared patents in developing the system, each will most likely name, manufacture, and market its own products. In the end, the companies will still compete against each other in the marketplace.[18]

The new technologies will allow new cameras to be produced that are smaller and thinner than ever before, and the smart film will come in tiny cartridges. The film is "smart" because it has magnetic strips, which can record data that will later be read and translated onto prints by compatible photofinishing equipment. Additionally, the film can be shot in three different formats, perhaps even on the same roll. The companies hope that the new technology will generate enthusiasm for picture taking in a video era.[19]

■ Digital Imaging

To focus special attention on both traditional and digital growth opportunities, Kodak formed a new worldwide business unit, Digital and Applied Imaging, in March 1994. An outsider, Carl Gustin, a former employee of Digital Equipment and Apple Computers, was hired to head this division. It was believed that Gustin would add much-needed marketing expertise to the business in order to alleviate problems concerning the transfer of technology to successful products. The target market for the imaging business was divided into four different segments, consisting of professional image producers (professional photographers), large businesses, small office and home users, and personal computer users. The units comprising Digital and Applied Imaging included Applied Imaging, CD (Compact Disk) Imaging, Printer Products, and the Equipment and Software Platform Center.[20]

In July 1994, Kodak introduced the CopyPrint in an attempt to apply digital imaging technology to amateur photography. The machine was able to scan photographs and make true color reproductions in a few minutes. Since 98 percent of photos taken are never copied or enlarged, the CopyPrint has allowed Kodak to enter this lucrative untapped market.[21] Pictostrat, a copy machine made by Fuji, was the closest substitute to the CopyPrint. It also made images of three-dimensional objects such as jewelry or baby shoes. Fuji's system, although not digital, was chemical free and needed only a small amount of water. An 8×10 copy on a CopyPrint retailed at $10 as opposed to Pictostrat at $5.

The new business unit was expected to introduce new digital products by early 1995. In addition to the $1,000 thermal printer, the unit was aiming to introduce a $300 digital scanner and a camera in the $300 range. Apple's QuickTake digital camera, made by Kodak, is among the cheapest now on the market, at $700. Kodak also planned to relaunch photo CD, targeting the PC user, in March 1995. By adding software to each photo CD platter, Kodak planned to make it easier to retrieve photos and use them in electronic documents.[22]

■ Competition[23]

In the imaging business Kodak is just one of the players in a hypercompetitive industry. According to Yeaple, the executive professor of Marketing and Business Policy at University of Rochester's Simon school of Business Administration, "Kodak faces two types of competition . . . conventional-film makers and technical innovators in electronic imaging."[24] In the digital imaging business, Kodak is just one of many in an emerging industry. Kodak faces no fewer than 599 global competitors working on optical storage technology that could challenge its photo CD. In addition, other rivals are chasing after the emerging digital market. Kodak also faces giant competitors such as Canon, Fujitsu, Konica, Polaroid, Nikon, Minolta, Sony, and Hewlett Packard in other niches ranging from scanners to printers[25] (see Exhibit 11 for industry statistics).

Exhibit 11   Industry Statistics

Top Camera Brands

Brands	Sales ($000)	% of Group
Polaroid	1,400	25.8
Kodak Star	850	15.7
Kodak	841	15.5
Vivitar	631	11.6
Olympus	430	7.9
Ansco	321	5.9
Keystone	314	5.8
Canon Sure Shot	219	4.0
Pentax	215	4.0
Fuji	205	3.8

Source: *Non-Food Merchandising,* June 1994, 16, from Nielson Marketing Research.

Film Brand Preferences

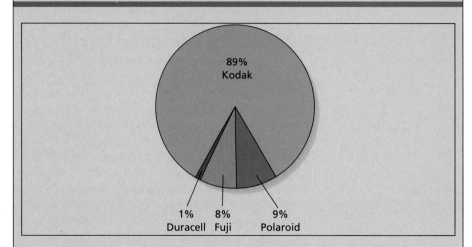

Discount outlets' leading film brand preferences are shown in percent based on a survey of discount store shoppers and managers.

Kodak	89.0%
Polaroid	9.0%
Fuji	8.0%
Duracell	1.0%

Source: *Discount Store News,* October 18, 1993, 61, from Leo J. Shapiro & Associates.

Continued

■ Single-Use Cameras

In 1993, Kodak had about 72 percent of the domestic unit sales for single-use cameras, followed by Fuji at 16 percent, Konica at 9 percent, and 3 percent for others, including Polaroid and private labels. In the international market, it was estimated that Kodak's share of 35mm film (including single-use cameras) was 36 percent, just ahead of Fuji's 34 percent, followed by Konica at 16 percent.[26] Even

Exhibit 11   Industry Statistics—*Continued*

Film Market

Sales are shown based on movement in:	Vol. ($ mil.)	Mkt. Share
Kodak Gold Plus	$ 207.8	56.7%
Polaroid 600	38.0	10.4
Fujicolor	33.6	9.2
Kodacolor Gold	13.6	3.7
Kodak Fun Saver	13.3	3.6
Other	60.5	16.5

Source: *Non-Foods Merchandising,* February 1994, 36, from Nielson Marketing Research.

Photographic Film by Type

Percent of rolls purchased in the U.S. in 1993 is shown by film type.

35mm	80.0%
110 camera	7.7
One-time use	4.5
35mm slide	3.2
Instant	2.7
Disc	1.9

Source: *Photo Marketing Magazine,* January 1994.

Exhibit 12

Sales of One-Time-Use Cameras

Source: Kodak 1994 Annual Report

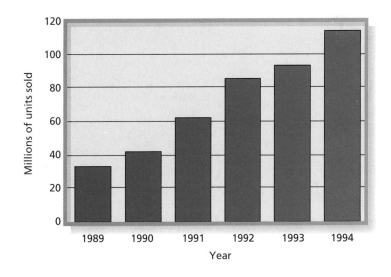

though the film sales are plateauing, sales of the single-use cameras have been increasing since 1989. The market for single-use cameras is relatively young and not considered to be fully developed. Therefore, the single-use camera market is considered advantageous for achieving growth in the future. Exhibit 12 shows Kodak's sales of single-use cameras for 1989–1994.

■ Photo Film Market

In the photo film business Kodak faces stiff competition from AGFA and Fuji films. Nationally, Kodak has about 70 percent of the film market, with Fuji garnering approximately 13 percent and AGFA having 5 percent.[27] Globally Fuji is strongest in Japan where it has approximately 70 percent of the market share, and AGFA is considered the Kodak of Europe.[28]

■ Major Competitors

Canon Inc.

Canon Inc. is a Japanese company that makes copiers, laser beam and bubble jet printers, image scanners, fax machines, calculators, cameras, camcorders, and optical products. In 1994, 36.7 percent of the sales revenue was generated by its copiers and consumables; printers and scanners accounted for 30.1 percent; computers, faxes, word processors, and other business machines, 18 percent; cameras and camcorders, 8.5 percent; and optical products, 6.7 percent.

Financial information for Canon is as follows:

Currency—Japanese—Yen (millions) Summary Financials—12/30/94	
Total assets	2,226,855
Current assets	1,464,168
Total liabilities	1,445,699
Current liabilities	942,599
Long-term debt	311,002
Stockholders' equity	781,156
Total income	1,933,310
Net income	31,024
Net income per share (calc.)	35.84
Average shares outstanding	885
Year-end shares outstanding	830
———— Profitability ————	
ROE	3.97%
ROA	1.39%
Profit margin	1.61%
———— Liquidity ————	
Current ratio	1.55
Working cap./total assets	0.23
———— Debt Management ————	
Current liab./equity	1.21
Long-term debt/equity	0.40
Total liab./equity	1.85
———— Asset Management ————	
Total income/total assets	0.87
Total income/working cap.	3.71

Polaroid Corporation

Polaroid Corporation is an American company best known for its instant photo cameras. Polaroid makes and markets various products for use in instant image recording fields, including instant photo cameras, film, magnetic media, light polarizing filters and lenses, and diversified chemical, optical and commercial products. Products are used by amateurs and professionals in photography, industry, science, medicine, and education. Polaroid's photographic products include color and black-and-white films, cameras, and accessories (flash units, flash guns, cases, cable releases, tripods, mounts, and self-timers).

AGFA

The German company Bayer AG makes AGFA film.[29] Bayer Ag makes several products related to various industries. It is the second largest chemical manufacturer in the world and produces developing equipment and other imaging systems, health care products, industrial products, organic products, and agrochemicals. In 1993, 16 percent of its net sales were from its imaging technologies while 23 percent came from health care products, 18 percent from industrial products, and 13 percent from agrochemicals. Of total 1993 group net sales Europe yielded 67.5 percent; North America, 22.4 percent; Latin America, 4.4 percent, and others, 5.7 percent.

AGFA's strategy, within Europe, has resembled that of Kodak in the United States. Both companies diversified into several industries such as imaging, health care, and chemicals. Interestingly, Miles Inc. (a subsidiary of Bayer AG) recently acquired the over-the-counter drugs division of Sterling Winthrop. AGFA intends to increase its market share within the United States. The company is using television commercials and newspaper inserts for a free roll of film as a part of its initial entry into the U.S. market.[30]

A *financial summary follows* for AGFA-GEVAERT N.V.

Currency—Belgian—Francs (thousands) Summary Financials—12/31/93	
Total assets	55,804,859
Current assets	24,291,370
Shareholders' equity	40,900,893
Debts	11,468,002
Operating income	55,997,171
Net profit for the year	2,117,820
Earnings per share (calc.)	3,958.54
Average shares outstanding	
Year-end shares outstanding	535
——— Profitability ———	
ROE	5.18%
ROA	3.80%
Profit margin	3.78%
——— Debt Management ———	
Debts/equity	0.28
——— Asset Management ———	
Oper. income/total assets	1.00

The *financial summary for Bayer A.G.* is given here:

Currency—Deutsche—Marks (millions) Summary Financials—12/30/94	
Total assets	42,363
Current assets	25,280
Total liabilities	25,308
Shareholders' equity	17,055
Total operating income	44,609
Net income for the year	1,970
Consolidated income	
Income per share (calc.)	28.55
Average shares outstanding	
Year-end shares outstanding	69
———— Profitability ————	
ROE	11.55%
ROA	4.65%
Profit margin	4.42%
———— Debt Management ————	
Total liab./equity	1.48
———— Asset Management ————	
Tot oper inc./Total assets	1.05

Fuji Photo Film Company

A Japanese company that produces and markets photographic film and paper, cameras and related equipment, chemical and x-ray products, graphic arts products, microfilm products and supplies, motion picture film, video, audio and memory tapes, floppy disks, carbonless copying paper, and photofinishing equipment. Fuji is perhaps Kodak's leading rival and the competition between the two is characterized by severe legal battles.

In 1988, Fuji had only a small foothold in the United States and gross margins on Kodak's little yellow boxes were as high as 80 percent. Unfortunately for Kodak, Fuji and private label film makers have become fierce competitors by undercutting Kodak's prices and reducing its marketshare from 80 to 70 percent in five years. Kodak managed to halt the slide in 1993, mostly by lowering prices in special promotions. A year later, to further protect its market share, Kodak introduced Funtime films, which were priced 20 percent below the standard Gold brand, to serve the low end of the market.

Here is *current financial information* for Fuji:

Currency—Japanese—Yen (millions) Summary Financials—9/30/94	
Total assets	1,714,559
Current assets	1,064,046
Total liabilities	558,982
Current liabilities	376,694
Long-term debt	61,497
Stockholders' equity	1,155,577
Total income	1,066,748
Net income	63,771
Net income per share (calc.)	123.92
Average shares outstanding	
— Profitability —	
ROE	5.52%
ROA	3.72%
Profit margin	5.98%
— Liquidity —	
Current ratio	2.83
Working cap./total assets	0.40
— Debt Management —	
Current liab./equity	0.33
Long-term debt/equity	0.05
Total liab./equity	0.48
— Asset Management —	
Total income/total assets	0.62

Immediately after arriving at Kodak in 1994, George Fisher hired top Washington attorney Allen Wolff to file a petition in Washington claiming that Fuji unfairly dominates the Japanese photography market.[31] Fuji responded by submitting a 585-page document called "Rewriting History," which states that Kodak's allegations of Fuji's unfair business practices is in reality the case of the pot calling the kettle black. The two companies seem to be going into battle against each other in both the marketplace and the courtrooms.[32]

In 1994, Fuji announced a plan to create a new U.S. division to focus solely on digital imaging, mimicking a similar move made by Kodak. The move will allow Fuji to boost its digital sales force and cultivate alliances with computer companies to market its various products such as filmless cameras, printers, and digital devices for image display on television and computers. With the new division, Fuji will be able to market the wide range of products it already sells in Japan. Furthermore, Fuji plans to "hook-up" with the Apples and IBMs of the world with the view that Fuji already has products to offer them that are better than the competition's.[33]

Kodak is not sitting still while Fuji makes the move to increase market shares in the United States. Mr. Fisher recently bought the rights to the 1998 Winter Olympics in Naggano, Japan, increased advertising, and lowered prices on products in the Japanese market.[34]

It is interesting to note that while both of these companies engage in a competitive battle, they are also collaborating on a few projects such as the APS. It seems that both companies are realizing a future in digital imaging, and analysts also predict that future growth opportunities for Kodak are believed to exist within the digital imaging area. Filmless photography is quickly becoming very popular among law enforcement officials, photo ID centers, photojournalists, real estate listing agencies, and insurance claims adjusters.[35] The digital imaging market is growing significantly faster than the conventional silver-halide–based photography market. Therefore, in order for Eastman Kodak to capitalize on this growth, it must be successful in exploiting its own technology in the marketplace.[36]

■ Bringing Products to Market

Kodak has traditionally been a company with strong technical resources and is currently a leader in silver-halide and digital imaging technologies. However, Kodak has had a problem with bringing technology to market. The photo CD debacle, which occurred under Kay Whitmore in 1992, illustrates that difficulty. The photo CD was originally designed to allow users to transfer photographs to a digital disk at a cost of approximately $20 per roll. These photographs could then be displayed on a television screen using a special CD player, priced at about $400.[37] Kodak mistakenly marketed photo CD to home users of photography without convincing these consumers of the need for the product or of the superiority of photo CD to traditional Photography.[38] As a result of this poor marketing strategy, the photo CD product was unsuccessful. George Fisher has revived the product, however, marketing it toward desktop personal computer users, and plans to relaunch photo CD in early 1995.[39]

Fisher believes that marketing is probably the biggest hurdle for Eastman Kodak. Fisher wants to change Kodak from an engineering-driven company to a market-driven company by focusing on the customer. Kodak has retained John Scully, former CEO of Apple, as a marketing advisor and hired Carl Gustin to help remedy its marketing inefficiencies.

■ Reigniting Growth

Fisher believes one way to achieve growth in the marketplace will be through strategic alliances or acquisitions, especially in the digital imaging area:

I really believe the future of the company is more in silver-halide, but we are spending a lot of time in the electronics area. There are so many good strong players sitting there already with a lot of good capabilities, some of which are competitive with us, some of which are complementary to us. It is going to be necessary for us to have a clearly delineated strategy, which we probably wouldn't make public, by the way. Then in the context of that strategy, we could look at what our strategic strengths are, our core competencies, that we don't want to let out or give to others. We can look at what we want to do, in the context of those, and say, "Well, what do we need, who do we need to work with in order to be a complete something in the marketplace?" And as a result of that, you're going to see a combination of alliances, maybe acquisitions.[40]

The company has been attempting to get other industry players to adopt its technologies as standards in the computer and multimedia worlds. George Fisher met with leaders of computer giants like Microsoft's Bill Gates, and Scott McNealy, of Sun Microsystems, to discuss licensing and partnership deals. Microsoft's new Windows 95 operating systems would include Kodak's color management standards. IBM had also teamed up with Eastman Kodak to utilize Kodak's photo CD technology in IBM's newest operating systems. Kodak was also working with telephone companies to make sending images over telephone lines easier.[41] On an international level, Kodak has released little information about its strategy, but Fisher has made three trips to China. He also appointed one of Kodak's most senior executives, Executive Vice President William Prezzano, to head a new thrust into Asian countries like China, Taiwan, and Hong Kong.[42]

■ Leveraging the Corporate Culture

Although he recognizes the monumental task set before him, namely, the turnaround of a company facing mature markets and increased competition, Fisher is not intimidated. His quick, decisive actions have won him praise from a variety of analysts. Fisher subscribes to the 80/20 rule, which holds that being right 80 percent of the time is acceptable as long as decisions are acted on quickly.[43] He hopes that his view of decision making will bring about changes in Kodak's culture, which has been described as "lethargic."[44]

Like past Kodak CEOs, Fisher possesses a technical background, although his style differs substantially. Kodak's past CEOs tended to be unapproachable, while Fisher is characterized as being relaxed, informal, and accessible.[45] Despite his low-key nature, Fisher promotes clearly defined areas of responsibility and accountability. At Motorola, he was known for his skill in motivating employees, decentralizing decision making, and choosing promising technologies to pursue.[46] Fisher is attempting to utilize these skills at Kodak while establishing a culture based on five principles:

- respect for the individual,
- uncompromising integrity,
- trust,
- credibility, and
- continuous improvement.[47]

In addition, Fisher believes that in order to become more aggressive and faster moving, Kodak has to earn customers' respect and maintain its right to be in the marketplace. Therefore, with the help of the five principles in the new culture, Kodak strives to be the best in quality, product development, and cycle time. All of these actions will create a company that is innovative yet can still remain customer focused.

Not everyone shares the confidence in Fisher's ability to dramatically change Kodak's culture. As one institutional investor put it, "Fisher is a great manager in a tough environment. In a situation like that, very often the environment wins."[48] Nonetheless, Fisher remains excited about the challenge, even casting it in Machiavellian terms by quoting from *The Prince*: "There is nothing more difficult to take in hand, more perilous to conduct, or more uncertain in its success, than to take the lead in introduction of a new order of things."[49]

Future Growth Opportunities

One of the biggest challenges facing Fisher and Kodak is to realize significant revenue growth. Kodak divested $6.5 billion of its debt in Fisher's first year on the job. This reduced debt level provided flexibility to enable Kodak to implement growth strategies. "Hopefully, in the three to five year time frame, you will see growth resulting from our various initiatives whether they be in China or other parts of Asia-Pacific, in Latin America, Eastern Europe, or whether they be from digital imaging, equipment business, product differentiation and traditional silver-halide business or service business. All of those areas are going to be major thrusts for growth."[50] To bring in appropriate expertise, Fisher hired another outsider, Harry L. Kavetas, as chief financial officer in 1994. He was formerly the CEO of IBM's Credit Corporation. In the same year, Jesse J. Greene, another former IBM employee, was hired as treasurer. In 1995, Kodak brought in a fourth outsider to top management, when David J. Fitzpatrick, a former employee of General Motors, was hired as controller.

Upon his arrival at Kodak, Fisher promised something that hasn't been delivered in years: "Kodak has a great franchise, and my hope is to build on that to get exciting growth." This promise has sparked controversy. It pumped up morale among employees who, prior to Fisher's arrival, had feared for their jobs. However, the promise angered many stockholders and disappointed financial analysts who are convinced that the fast growth at Kodak—promised but undelivered by both Chandler and Whitmore—is nothing more than false hope. According to an analyst at Prudential, B. Alex Henderson, "Making Kodak grow is not like teaching an elephant to dance. It's like cloning an elephant into a mouse." The critics felt that the company should be run as a mature cash cow: cutting costs to generate as much cash flow as possible, buying back shares, and paying big divivends.[51]

"Developing" the New Strategy

As Kodak entered the end of 1994, it had divested itself of approximately $5.2 billion of its $16.4 billion 1993 revenues and reduced its debt to $660 million. The debt reduction has placed Kodak in a more stable financial position. These represented the first of many steps needed to reverse Kodak's ill-fated diversification strategy of the 1980s. George Fisher decided to focus Kodak's strategy on its core imaging business. The principle problems facing Kodak are how to achieve growth and profitability in a mature silver-halide industry, which has shown little growth for several years, and how to achieve and sustain a dominant position in the emerging digital imaging market.

Kodak plans to use its strong technical development abilities with a coherent marketing strategy to develop new digital imaging processes based on its competencies in the traditional silver-halide technology and, in time, possibly supplant it.

■ Notes

1. Paul McAfee, 1994, Kodak's CEO unveils new corporate strategy, *The PR Newswire,* May 3.
2. The company history was excerpted from two main sources: (1) Adele Hast, Eastman Kodak Co., in *International Directory of Company Histories,* Vol. 3 (Chicago, Ill.: St. James Press), 474–477; and (2) Kodak's home page, http://www.Kodak.com.
3. Hast, Eastman Kodak Co.
4. Phil Johnston, 1991, Kodak observes split in reaction to latest strategy, *Rochester Business Journal,* August 19, 1.
5. John Holusha, 1989, Click: Up, down, and out at Kodak, *The New York Times,* December 9, Sec. 1, 33.
6. Moody's reviews Kodak's credit unit for possible upgrade, proprietary to United Press International, November 24, 1992.
7. Joan E. Rigdon and Randall Smith, 1993, Kodak chairman reassures investors, promises plan to sell a 'major asset,' *Wall Street Journal,* April 30, A4.
8. Ibid.
9. Joan Rigdon, 1993, Kodak selects C. J. Steffen for senior post; turnaround artist to be firm's first outsider in 20 years in a top spot, *Wall Street Journal,* January 12, A3.
10. Martin Dickson and Louise Kehoe, 1993, Fisher aims to give Kodak a sharper focus—the appointment at the photographic group, *Financial Times,* October 29, 24.
11. Mark Maremont, 1995, Kodak's new Focus, *Business Week,* January 30, 64–65.
12. Ibid., 62.
13. *Kodak 1994 Annual Report.*
14. Joan Rigdon, 1994, Kodak's third quarter 1994 results, *Wall Street Journal,* October 26, A3.
15. Ibid.
16. Paul Ericson and Catherine E. Salibian, 1994, George Fisher's vision for Kodak, *Rochester Business Journal* May 27, 4.
17. Wendy Bounds, 1994, "Marketing & media: Kodak to change marketing strategy for low-end film," *Wall Street Journal,* December 9, B3.
18. Wendy Bounds, 1994, Technology: photography companies hope people smile over 'smart film,' *Wall Street Journal,* July 25, B1.
19. Ibid.
20. Paul McAfee, 1994, Kodak announces new digital imaging organization, *The PR Newswire,* March 28.
21. Maremont, Kodaks new focus, 68.
22. Ibid, 67.
23. Some of the information on competitors was obtained from Standards & Poor's Corporations Publications.
24. Catherine E. Salibian, 1994, Fisher's film strategy puzzles some observers, pleases others, *Rochester Business Journal,* June 24, 1.
25. Maremont, Kodak's new focus, 64.
26. Laura Loro, 1994, Single-use camera snaps the photo industry awake, *Advertising Age,* September 28, 28.
27. David Milstead, 1994, No. 3 brand of film goes after market share, *Cincinnati Business Courier,* July 4, Sec. 1, 3.
28. Ibid.
29. All financial information on the competitors was obtained from *Moody's International Company Data Report,* Moody's Investor Services, Inc., 1995.
30. Milstead, No. 3 brand of film, 3.
31. Bounds, Marketing & media, B9.
32. Wendy Bounds, 1995, Corporate focus: George Fisher pushes Kodak into digital era, *Wall Street Journal,* June 9, B1.
33. Bounds, Marketing & media, B6.
34. Bounds, Corporate focus, B1.
35. Photography: Negative vibes, *Economist,* August 26, 1995, 4.
36. McAfee, Kodak announces new digital imaging organization.
37. Alex Taylor, III, 1993, Eastman Kodak; higher rewards in lowered goals, *Fortune,* March 8, 75.
38. Eastman Kodak's chairman hypes new products, CNN Transcripts, August 25, 1992, Transcript # 102-2.
39. Maremont, Kodak's new focus, 64.
40. Ericson and Salibian, George Fisher's vision, 4.
41. Maremont, Kodak's new focus, 62.
42. Ibid., 68.
43. Ibid., 65.
44. Ibid., 65.
45. Ibid., 64.
46. Ibid., 64.
47. Kodak statement on new corporate strategy, Reuters, May 3, 1994.
48. Maremont, Kodak's new focus, 64.
49. Ibid., 68.
50. Ericson and Salibian, George Fisher's vision, 4.
51. Peter Nulty, 1994, Kodak grabs for growth again, *Fortune,* May 16, 77.

■ CASE 14 Euro Disney: The Theme Park Mold

Scott Reynolds

■ Introduction

■ http://www.disney.com

For years, Walt Disney Company has been a leader in several high-impact, high-visibility industries, and has often been the benchmark for excellence in many fields. Particularly in the theme park industry, Disney has pushed the envelopes of development and fantasy to raise the worldwide standards of amusement quality, excellence, and creativity.

The development around the world of Disneyland-esque parks with Walt's signature surprised no one who has experienced the success of Disney's earliest ventures into the theme park industry. A consistent strategy and implementation schedule guided Disney through three decades of development and growth and pushed the company to the frontiers of progress. However, the 1990s held some surprises for Disney, and those surprises uncovered what some labeled as holes and tears in the Disney master strategy. Disney's self-discovery process was painful and costly, both financially and socially. To a company where image is everything, Euro Disney proved to be a bittersweet experience. In many ways, Euro Disney testified of the success of Walt Disney's original vision, and yet in many other, more distressing ways, Euro Disney awakened Disney officials and the public to the shortcomings of the Disney theme park mold.

■ Disney's Initial Strategy

Although it may be difficult to convince a 10-year-old otherwise, Disneyland was somewhat of an embarrassment to founder Walt Disney. Disney had created Disneyland in Anaheim, California, as an off-shoot of his incredibly successful animated motion picture enterprises. His movies depicted fairy tales, fantasies, and childlike wonder, and he had hoped that Disneyland would be more than just images of those ideals, but hands-on experiences for the old and young alike.

For the most part, Disney succeeded. With the opening of Disneyland in 1955, breathtaking roller coaster-style rides such as the Matterhorn and Pirates of the Caribbean became the standard of adventure and fun. Bigger and better attractions such as the Small World and Bear Country exhibits made the park seem like a living dream, and employees were trained to be as helpful and

Exhibit 1

Walt Disney's Money

Source: Walt Disney Co.

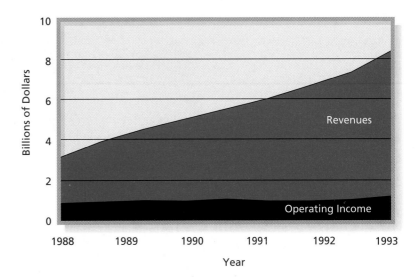

courteous as Snow White herself. Albeit the concept of a theme park was not new, Disney took the concept to new levels of development.

Although the majority of Disney's revenue (over $9 billion in 1993) is generated from theme parks (see Exhibits 1 and 2), Walt Disney's original success in the animated motion picture industry served as a strong complement to his theme parks and became the driving force of their development; children raced to the park to see characters they knew and with whom they were familiar, and visitors gobbled up the products of fantasy from Mickey Mouse ears to Goofy T-shirts. The success of the theme park spurred further success with more animated motion pictures, which, in turn, created new ideas for the theme park and even greater receptivity by the public. By creating a theme park, Disney successfully marketed the last frontier of the consumer's dreams: the vacation. Disney built success on the notion that there was profit in helping adults to become children again, or at least to visit their childhood once more.

For all purposes, the inside of the park lived up to Disney's original vision. Frontierland allowed tourists to escape to the past, and Tomorrowland propelled dreamers into the future. Unheralded ticket sales in every aspect of Disney's empire confirmed the success of his all-encompassing marketing strategy. Mickey Mouse quickly evolved into the foremost of world figures, and Anaheim became the Mecca of many families, first in the United States, and then across the world.

However, Walt Disney was extremely disappointed at what occurred outside of his theme park. Anaheim quickly closed in on Disneyland and began to peck at the image of wholesomeness and fantasy. Hotels and cheap restaurants crept up to the park's borders, and the lure of naive tourists brought a seedy crowd to the outskirts of the park. Disney took as much action as possible by purchasing property and building fences, but his ability to affect the environment was limited. For the most part, he simply took note of his mistakes, and quietly laid out a new plan for correcting those problems.

The fulfillment of those plans, the opening of Walt Disney World near Orlando, Florida, in 1971, was preceded by careful planning. The Disney Company purchased acres of land for the creation of its theme park, and then

Exhibit 2

Disney's Sources of Income

Source: Walt Disney Co.

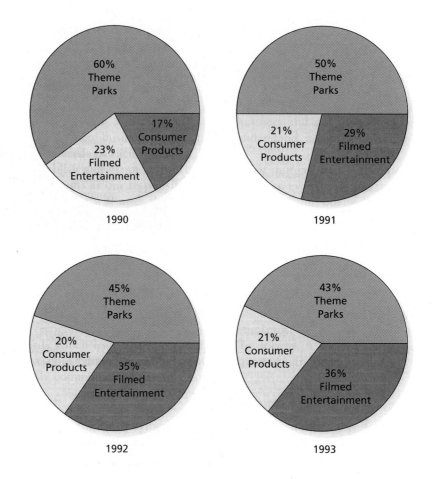

1990

1991

1992

1993

continued buying until the firm owned everything within miles of the site. From the beginning, Disney World was designed to be more than just a theme park, but an actual world unto itself catering to every need of the consumer. The essentials of life, entertainment, and business priorities could all be handled without leaving Disney property, and by purchasing the surrounding acreage for miles, the consumer was actually faced with few other options. The Disney Company felt that it had created the perfect escape/adventure experience for customers.

From a business point of view, creating a world unto itself required a greater coordination of activities and a deeper strategy of vertical integration. In California, Disney had not been greatly concerned with the subsistence of his visitors. Disneyland Hotel had only been somewhat of a token venture into the hotel industry, and Disneyland had relied to some degree on outside sources for food and souvenirs. However, Walt Disney World, the world's largest resort with a total of three resorts on 27,000 acres (about the size of Orlando), had to be much more self-sustaining simply as a result of its sheer size. To create a more vertically integrated system, Disney World specifically contracted with hotel chains and food companies who met their own standards of quality and service. Disney developed its own transportation systems to meet the needs of their huge investment, and created a completely self-sustaining environment. In this way, the visitor to Disney World found all of his needs taken care of without ever leaving Disney property. This plan became a stunning success as Disney capitalized on the successful strategy and culture of Disneyland while rectifying its problems with the environment.

In 1983, Disney's first move outside of the United States, Tokyo Disney, opened with the exact same strategy of self-sustainment as Walt Disney World, and it was also a tremendous success. The management team of the parent company faced new obstacles such as poor weather and language barriers and made the necessary adaptations (more indoor shops and covered walkways, and translators for every major department).[1] In the end, Tokyo Disney's success seemed practically unhindered. Disney officials saw this success as the green flag to enter other foreign markets. The development of a European Disney theme park was the next logical step.

A European Disneyland

In the mid-1980s, Disney made it known to the European community that Walt Disney corporation was interested in creating a Disneyland-type theme park in Europe. Originally, intense lobbying had propelled Britain into the foreground as a possible site (Rainham Marshes in Essex) for construction. Disney executives foresaw a battle with the British government over ownership and control as unavoidable if not impassable, so the site was passed over. Quickly, the French government responded with a proposal that, for three reasons, Disney could not refuse.[2]

The Offer

First, the French government proposed to purchase 51 percent of the venture and to be responsible for the selling of those stocks. Second, the government offered incredible tax breaks for Disney's park and all aspects of the theme park industry in which Disney would be involved. And third, the government offered 5,000 acres of land (one-fifth the size of Paris) to the parent company at rock bottom prices.[3]

Disney officials acknowledged not only the financial merit of the French offer, but they also recognized the proposed location as an ideal center place for their predicted tourist springs: Germany, France, and the United Kingdom. Disney projected that 17 million people lived within a two-hour drive of the site and that 109 million people were only six hours away. Also, the flat tracts of Marne-la-Vallee were only 20 miles from Europe's biggest tourism magnet, Paris, and therefore unlimited numbers of people were within hours of the site via the Orly and Charles de Gaulle airports.[4]

As another sign of France's eagerness to welcome Disney, the government diagnosed possible problems in other areas and acted quickly with proposals and suggestions. As an example, despite the projected completion of the Channel Tunnel in 1993, the French government foresaw potential transportation difficulties and worries for Disney; the French voluntarily offered to not only extend Paris's subway system to Marne-la-Vallee, but also to build a station for the high-speed Train a Grande Vitesse at the proposed entrance of the theme park.[5] The extension of the subway line made a trip from Paris to the park a reasonable $6 journey,[6] and the rail station connection established a three-hour link to London and a 90-minute link to Brussels.[7]

■ Complete Integration

Despite all of Disney's tremendous success in Orlando, the parent company learned yet another valuable lesson from its efforts. *Planning* on vertical integration and *profiting* from vertical integration were two different concepts. The hotels at Disney World had served the purposes of caring for much of the tourists' total out-of-the-park needs, but Disney found that most of that revenue went to hotel chains with whom they had contracted, and not into its own pockets.

Upon accepting France's offer, Disney announced a 30-year plan for the site at Marne-la-Vallee hoping to correct the vertical integration problem. Phase I of the plan required the completion of the theme park and 5,600 hotel rooms fully owned and operated by Walt Disney corporation by 1992. Phase II of the plan called for the creation of a second theme park, the Disney MGM Studios–Europe, with 2,700 additional hotel rooms. The entire 30-year plan foresaw 18,000 guestrooms by the year 2017.[8]

Besides the increased financial draw of park-owned living accommodations, Disney officials saw an opportunity for further vertical marketing. Hotels such as the Hotel Cheyenne, Hotel New York, and the Camp Davy Crockett were designed to further the adventurous experience of the visitor. "There is a strong commitment within the company to give guests the same experience in their hotel as they have in the park," reported Daniel Coccoli, vice president of resort hotel operations. "The most exciting thing about Euro Disney Resorts is that guests will be able to walk from the park to a hotel that allows them to continue the fantasy, instead of going to a hotel that interrupts that fantasy."[9]

■ Physical Developments

Following the completion of negotiations with France's government in 1985, Disney set out, in essence, to re-create Disneyland in Europe without its prior mistakes. Nearly $4.5 billion was invested over seven years to re-create the Magic Kingdom in Europe. The project became the second largest construction project in European history, second only to the Channel Tunnel.[10] Many of the attractions that were successful at Disneyland and Disney World were painstakingly re-created, only bigger and better. Duplicate attractions such as the Swiss Family Robinson Treehouse, Big Thunder Mountain, and Sleeping Beauty's Castle caused visitors to ask themselves if they were in France or California.[11] Responding to this strategy and several complaints from unimpressed American visitors, Disney spokesman Charles Ridgway said, "The park was built mostly for Europeans, and we went for attractions tried and true."[12] Food was also copied from other Disney theme parks to include hot dogs, chicken nuggets, and bagels, and "California" merchandise such as Mickey Mouse ears and Pluto dolls were on sale at every turn.[13]

■ Social Developments

As with all other aspects of the Magic Kingdom, Disney wanted the same atmosphere to exist at Euro Disney as at its other theme parks. Thus, employees were forbidden to smoke, chew gum, dye their hair an unusual shade, grow facial hair, or go without deodorant or underwear, and alcohol was not sold in the park.[14] Disney wanted its image to be communicated not only from the park, but from the employees as well. Disney's selection process therefore focused on "Disney's" qualities.

All of these aspects were drawn together quickly, and just as had been planned, French sugar beet fields became Disneyland IV. On April 12, 1992, complete with a 500-piece marching band and a drill team parade down Main Street, U.S.A., Euro Disney opened its doors to the public, and Europe would never be the same.

■ Euro Disney Opens

Disney's investment in Euro Disney was a unique blend of control and coordination. The French government owned 51 percent of Euro Disney (which was eventually sold to the public in 1989 at FFr72[15]), and the Disney parent corporation owned 49 percent, the most allowed by a foreign firm under French law.[16] Disney, however, held all of the cards of managing Euro Disney for the first seven years and had negotiated a management fee. This management fee was 3 percent of gross revenues until 1997, and then the proportion was scheduled to increase to 6 percent. The parent company also received a 10 percent royalty on admissions and a 5 percent royalty on food.

Also included in the initial negotiations was "an incentive management fee" that increased over the first few years from 30 to 50 percent of pretax cash flow. Stanley Morgan estimated that by 1997, 57 percent of Euro Disney's total operating profit would go to the parent company.[17] And so it was that even if the parent company reduced its share of ownership to 17 percent, regardless of whether or not Euro Disney lost money in a bad year, the parent company would come out ahead.[18] Even if the parent company decided to sell its interest, the Walt Disney corporation originally paid only FFr10, or 15 percent of the market value for its stocks, and would, therefore, make a profit even in the event of a major devaluation.[19] The parent company was preparing for great financial success.

■ Euro Disney's Losses

Euro Disney was expected to be a big success, and the entire situation appeared to be a gold mine for the parent company; that is until Euro Disney began to experience major losses. Managers at Euro Disney surfaced in the summer of 1993 to announce what most experts had already supposed: Euro Disney was in red ink. The theme park management announced a loss of $201 million (FFr1.1 billion) and commented that they were "exploring potential sources of financing."[20] The managers issued a statement about their difficulties blaming the losses on a recession, currency devaluation, low-spending visitors, and soaring costs. The statement read, "Tourism in France has been adversely affected by the economic downturn in Western Europe and by the devaluation of the U.K., Italian and Spanish currencies. In addition, the real estate market in the Paris region has remained depressed, preventing the company from realizing anticipated revenues from real estate development."[21] Analysts around the world began to ask questions such as "How real are the external difficulties Euro Disney is facing?" and "How much of the problem is internal?"

■ Visitor Spending

As a result of its losses, one of Euro Disney's primary concerns was the apparent discrepancy between the projected spending figures of visitors to the park and the actual money passing hands.[22] Initial projections had supposed that 11 million tourists would make their way to Euro Disney, and that number had proven to be very reliable, making Euro Disney the biggest attraction in France, surpassing the Louvre and even the Eiffel Tower[23] (the most successful of French leisure parks, Euro Disney's direct competition, only attracts 1.3 million[24]). However, it was also projected that each of those 11 million tourists would purchase $33 worth of products ranging from food to souvenirs. That spending was down 12 percent and was making deep cuts into Euro Disney's bottom line.[25]

Several possible explanations for this low spending were suggested. First, it was proposed that initial prices on products, services, admission, and accommodations were too high. The admission price to Euro Disney was unusually high, a full 30 percent higher than at Disney World in Orlando.[26] Food prices were also out of sight, nearly twice as expensive as the same food at Disney World.[27] Hotels, operating at a disappointing 69 percent occupancy rate,[28] cost anywhere from $200 to $300 a night, and guests whose arrangements had been made as part of group plans were voicing their complaints and their intentions not to return.[29]

With all of these high prices, most analysts suggested that the majority of visitors were more interested in getting the most for their money, and that translated into taking as many rides as possible. Therefore, if the visitors were spending more time on the rides, then they were spending less time in the theme shops and the restaurants, and therefore spending less money overall.[30]

■ The European Economy

Referring back to Disney's official statement, the strength of the French franc had an adverse affect on the state of Euro Disney. In a time of recession when Disney was first shopping for a site for their theme park, France looked wonderfully attractive, but over the years as the French franc grew stronger and the rest of the European community began to sink, France's allure dissipated. Translated, this meant that ticket, food, and souvenir prices for non-French visitors rose almost 15 percent, and it became almost more economical for British tourists to go to Orlando for a vacation than to Paris.[31]

Not only did non-French visitors feel the shift of currency levels in their ticket prices, but also in their hotel accommodations as well. Reacting to the situation, visitors slowly turned to the subway and headed in to Paris for their overnight accommodations where rooms were typically half the price. Hotel occupancy rates slowly began to drift down until eventually with slow seasons coming, Disney announced the seasonal closing of Euro Disney's largest hotel, the Newport Bay Club, a hotel the firm had hoped to keep open year-round.[32]

The Europeans were not the only ones affected by a stronger franc. The parent company as well found that interest rates on its debts initially incurred to build Euro Disney became much steeper than expected. The huge payments put a dent into all profits and diminished the amount of funds available for future investment. Therefore, phase II of Disney's 30-year plan was in real jeopardy,[33] and most analysts agreed that Disney could never really turn a profit without the completion of the second phase.[34]

Disney's Culture in France

One aspect of working in France that Disney officials had not prepared for was the shock wave of trying to transfer American ideals to a European market. For instance, Euro Disney's financial forecasters expected Europeans to spend like Americans, and based most of their predictions on past American experiences. However, Euro Disney officials quickly learned that Americans and Europeans have different paradigms regarding vacations. On the average, Americans vacationed from one to two weeks, while Europeans vacationed from four to six weeks, yet each family had comparatively the same amount of money to spend. Consequently, Americans tended to spend more money per vacation day as compared to Europeans who had to see their vacation funds last upwards of an entire month. These spending habits were reflected in the sale of souvenirs and treats that many Europeans considered an excessive expense on a limited budget.

In addition to being ignorant of European vacation habits, Euro Disney did not prepare for European tastes. The park did not attempt to serve European eating habits with such staples as bread and cheese. Wine, the French equivalent of water, or any type of alcoholic beverage for that matter, was not sold or even allowed in the park. Many families either skimped on a meal in the park until they could eat somewhere else, or others who were more prepared carried lunches with them from home and ate them picnic-style just outside the gates of the park.[35] Also, smoking, which is not the social enigma in France that it is in the United States, was harshly frowned on. Visitors were often found smoking while waiting for rides, sitting at the outdoor cafes, or while strolling around the park, but cigarettes could not be purchased anywhere in the park.[36] Smokers and nonsmokers, visitors and employees alike, all complained about the policy's double standard.

Disney's attitudes regarding European consumers carried over into its human resource practices. American strategies with Euro Disney workers were not initially very productive. Euro Disney had originally recruited 12,000 workers from around Europe. Of that number, 75 percent were French, and the rest were of various nationalities. Regarding the staff, Coccoli proudly proclaimed, "We have 600 managers representing 38 different nationalities and 24 spoken languages."[37] Euro Disney management envisioned its philosophy of clean-cut, wholesome employees as a unifying bond among their workers. "The Disney Look," a rigid code of employee appearance regarding hairstyles, fashion choices, and personal hygiene, was a plan that management hoped would be accepted across the board and provide the common link among employees. Coccoli commented, "With everyone coming from different backgrounds and cultures, our set of rules is essential. Otherwise, we won't make it."[38]

Problems followed "The Disney Look." Disney officials expected its employees, who were mostly French and notorious for their rudeness and blatant honesty, to greet their visitors with the friendliness of Snow White. The banning of smoking and moustaches was seen as insensitive to French men who traditionally recognize both as symbols of masculinity. Throughout the confrontation, Disney executives argued that all of these standards were necessary to maintain the Disney "magic," which was the center of the firm's image.[39] Workers began to tell stories of enforcement tactics such as spying by managers and their stoolies, whom the workers satirically labeled the Magic Kingdom "Mouseschwitz."[40]

Euro Disney also had difficulty simply caring for its employees. The development of Marne-la-Vallee real estate was hampered by a sluggish French property market. As a result, development was slow, and on opening day many employees were still struggling to find a place to sleep.[41] The apparent lack of planning for employees' needs and the disenfranchisement resulting from "The Disney Look" caused a rift between management and the employees. Turnover rates were high from top to bottom, but the figures were skewed due to a November 1993 mass layoff, based on financial reasons, of approximately 10 percent of its employees.[42]

■ The Cultural Backlash

In the early stages of growth, managers simply were not concerned with developing into an European organization. Euro Disney's early attempts at culturalization were architectural designs and bilingual signs. As leisure industry analyst Nigel Reed commented, "The Americans didn't assess European tastes sufficiently, or take on board European seasonality or vacation habits."[43]

This apparent lackluster concern with the European market led to a tremendous backlash from the economic and scholarly European community. Walt Disney Company as a whole (as well as Euro Disney) suffered attacks in the public press from all over Europe, particularly France, regarding the cultural packaging of Euro Disney. Editorials maliciously charged the Americans with "Cultural Imperialism," or marketing American culture under the guise of European fairy tales and stories rehashed and retold in a sellable fashion. Writer Ariane Mnouchkine, a noted French intellectual, remarked that Euro Disney was a "cultural Chernobyl" in that the explosion of American culture was leaking into European markets and into European homes, contaminating the people and destroying their own culture.

With the continual quarterly announcement of extreme financial losses and growing public concern, stock prices began to tumble. In 1989, Euro Disney stocks floated onto the market at FFr72 ($11) and had steadily climbed to a Euro Disney opening day high of nearly FFr165 (see Exhibit 3). However, with growing criticism, confusion, and rumors of substantial losses and refinancing, stock prices plummeted radically over a four-month period until they reached rock bottom: FFr68.[44] The time for action had arrived.

Exhibit 3

Euro Disney Share Price

Sources: Datastream, Stanley Morgan.

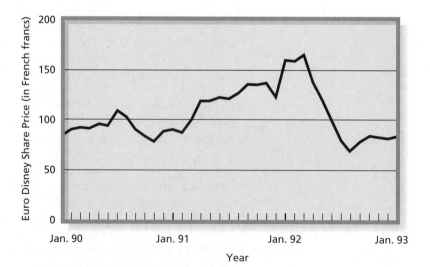

A Case of Realignment

Following the disappointing 1992 annual report, changes began to take place within Euro Disney. Originally, every aspect of Euro Disney was controlled by Americans with little to no foreign experience. Most strategy and design plans were carried out by managers in America and 300 expatriates in Paris.[45] After the grand opening in April 1992, nearly all of those expatriates returned home. In September 1993, Frenchman Philippe Bourguignon replaced American Robert Fitzpatrick first as president and then as chairman of Euro Disney. Quickly, Bourguignon developed a management team consisting of young people, roughly one-third French, one-third American, and the rest representing the U.K., Ireland, and the Netherlands.[46]

Changes in Practice

Following the changes in managerial staffing, Euro Disney's practices were modified. Rather than waiting until the proposed opening dates, management opened six new attractions ahead of schedule with the hope that lines would be reduced around the park, thus putting a halt to customers' complaints and increasing the cash flow. Also, a total product overhaul was initiated to reduce restaurant and merchandise prices by an average of 15 percent.[47] To woo the disillusioned French consumer, marketing disposed of the high-impact American-oriented advertisements on French television and radio ("California is only 20 miles from Paris"[48]) in favor of a more descriptive and subtle campaign appealing to the French style of marketing.[49]

Euro Disney struggled to cater to its visitors in many other ways as well. Alcohol was sold at various spots around the park. More European-style foods such as bread, cheese, and chocolates were offered side by side with the traditional theme park staples of burgers and fries. The park moved from recognizing the American calendar to recognizing a more European calendar; the seasonal commemoration of American holidays was deemphasized and celebrations of European holidays such as Bastille Day and Oktoberfest were carefully planned, marketed, and exploited.[50]

Following these trends toward European customs, Euro Disney then tried to kill two birds with one stone. Visitors had often complained about the high prices of admission and hotels, and the park management was worried regarding the high seasonality of their consumers. Disney theme parks had historically enacted standard year-round prices in an effort to control the market, but in a highly unusual move, Euro Disney broke Disney tradition and announced the offering of cut-rate entry and room rates for the off-season. Management even introduced an "After 5" evening entrance program aimed at Parisians looking for a fun-filled evening of entertainment. Steve Burke, Bourguignon's right-hand American deputy, commented that "Our job now is to figure out what the market wants and provide it, rather than being ideological about what's done in the U.S."[51]

Besides adapting to the consumer, Bourguignon recognized the need for flexibility with his own employees. Shortly after his appointment, Bourguignon started to cope with his French laborers. To promote peace and reduce turnover, Bourguignon eliminated American compensation procedures in favor of French human resource practices. Gone were the long hours and poor pay. In their place were French job classifications, a maximum work week, and annual salaries for hourly employees. Through the negotiation and implementation of these practices, a new respect for management began to evolve, and the initially high turnover rate began to subside.[52]

Of particular importance to Bourguignon and his management team was the external tour operators. In the beginning, Euro Disney expected that 60 percent of its visitors would be free-traveling individuals and families on vacation, and that 40 percent of their consumers would be part of package tours and groups either on business or on vacation.[53] For various financial and cultural reasons, the tour operators were falling short of their commitments to fill hotel rooms from the very beginning, and Euro Disney failed to offer any help in their struggle. The tour operators promptly became disenfranchised with the arrangements and collectively clamored for renegotiations. Euro Disney was slow to respond, but eventually, under Bourguignon's leadership, the theme park renegotiated the deals and put on the hat of cooperation. "We didn't realize the importance of catering to groups and tour operators initially. They play a much larger role here than in the U.S. We now pay a lot more attention to them," said Burke regarding management's new attitude toward the firm's tour operating partners.[54]

■ Changes in Financing

Although the changes in social practices of Euro Disney seemed drastic, financially, Euro Disney made changes that some would call desperate. Most analysts predicted a first fiscal year report of a FFr1.7 billion debt. Instead Euro Disney reported a debt of FFr5.3 billion (nearly $1 billion) which included the start-up costs of the park.[55] Traditionally, companies (Disney theme parks included) amortize such costs over a 20- to 30-year period, but Euro Disney management decided to list the bulk of the debt early for two reasons. First, the new management team hoped to start with a clean slate, and by paying off the debt in the first year, the team could blame the huge deduction on the predecessors and enact new policies without having to compensate for the obstacles of the past. Also, Disney's unfortunate start required a new strategy for financing. Disney wanted to refinance many of its debts with French banks, and discovered that the firm could best do so if the French banks believed the worst of the financial news was part of the past.[56]

Throughout the early economic problems, the parent company provided the most short-term financial support to Euro Disney. However, most analysts agreed that the parent company would also cause the most damage in the long term. In the winter of 1993, Walt Disney agreed to postpone its three percent management fee until Euro Disney made a profit, and also loaned Euro Disney $175 million to help them through the spring of 1994. However, as explained earlier, the parent company's management fee, as well as the "incentive management fee," were designed to increase with time; therefore, the long-term fees owed to the parent company by Euro Disney hung over the park and cast a dark shadow on the future of its profits and development (see Exhibit 4). Most analysts agreed that Euro Disney's future (5 to 10 years) revenue would not be strong enough to compensate for the fees of the demanding parent company.[57]

Recognizing that without profits its own future was at risk, the parent company announced a rescue package in March 1994. According to the offer, Walt Disney Company agreed to spend about $750 million, more than quadruple the initial investment, to push the park over some of its financial hurdles. As part

Exhibit 4

Euro Disney's Revenue

Sources: Datastream, Morgan Stanley.

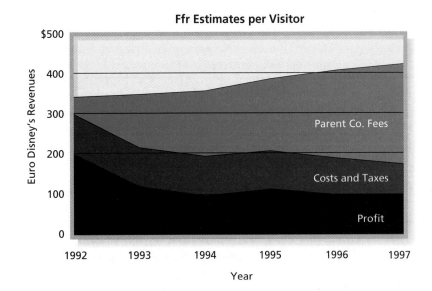

Ffr Estimates per Visitor

of the financial restructuring, Euro Disney's lead banks also agreed to contribute their share: $500 million aid and other concessions such as erasing 18 months of interest payments of Euro Disney's debt.[58] The deal not only cut Euro Disney's debt in half and paved the way for profitability by the fall of 1995, but it also sent a message regarding the confidence of Disney officials in their theme park, and suggested to the world that Euro Disney was there to stay.

■ It's All Part of the Plan

Although most analysts charged that Euro Disney had been way off base in its management practices since it started, Bourguignon and Burke disagreed. Euro Disney's management duo argued that the problems of Euro Disney were not based in Disney's culture or strategy, but were simply the growing pains of any new organization. Euro Disney's initial management team was established with one goal: to get Euro Disney started quickly and efficiently. Each of the initial Euro Disney managers had experience in one of the other theme parks, and these managers were then brought together to transfer those things that worked well from other parks into Euro Disney. When Euro Disney opened, the experienced managers turned the management over to the locals. Burke commented, "Our priority was getting the park up and running by April 1992. That left no room for innovation. But we always knew that afterwards we would have to make adjustments."[59] Bourguignon claimed to be living proof of this system, and suggested that he replaced his American counterpart only when the time to fine-tune the organization had arrived.[60]

Bourguignon suggested that Euro Disney was not faced with a crisis, only a stage of development. According to Bourguignon, Euro Disney developed a core strategy and culture of Disney, and then had to work to Europeanize its theme park. He argued that with time Euro Disney would develop its own managerial culture independent of Disney and Europe. "We will apply the U.S. experience in our own way, creating a hybrid. In the end, the test of whether our management works is not the park's initial difficulties. The test is how quickly we react to resolve them."[61]

■ Conclusion

For Euro Disney, the future held many uncertainties. Management and analysts alike had no experience in such a venture and could only guess about the ramifications of new policies, new financing, and new attitudes. Could Euro Disney officials simply "fine-tune" their organization and continue on toward a profitable destination, or were the problems and difficulties of the European market unsolvable? Would Disney's magic help or haunt them?

Walt Disney Co. officials, on the other hand, struggled not only with Euro Disney's situation, but with the firm's entire resort strategy, as well. Was a theme park template capable of carrying the Disney magic around the world, or were the pains experienced by Euro Disney indicative of the grief the parent company would encounter again and again with such a strategy? Walt Disney Co. officials were uneasy because they did not know if their theme park mold—the basis of Disney's entire worldwide expansion strategy—had created an exception or the rule.

■ Notes

1. G. Wagner, It's a small world after all, *Lodging Hospitality,* April 1992, 26.
2. Mouse trapped in France, *New Statesman & Society,* August 20, 1993, 6.
3. Ibid.
4. Wagner, It's a small world.
5. Ibid.
6. J. Popkin, M. Williams, and E. C. Baig, 1993, Summer in Europe, *U.S. News & World Report,* May 18, 68.
7. Wagner, It's a small world.
8. Ibid.
9. Ibid.
10. Euro Disney theme park near Paris is Europe's second-biggest project, offers opportunities for U.S. business, *Business America,* December 2, 1991, 21.
11. Popkin et al., Summer in Europe.
12. Ibid.
13. Ibid.
14. A. Phillips, Where's the magic? Problems plague Euro Disney's first year, *MacLean's,* May 3, 1993, 47.
15. Euro Disney: The not-so-magic kingdom, *The Economist,* September 26, 1992, 87.
16. Wagner, It's a small world.
17. Euro Disney: The not-so-magic kingdom.
18. Euro Disney: Ducking doom, *The Economist,* July 10, 1993, 72.

19. Euro Disney: The not-so-magic kingdom.
20. Euro Disney: Ducking doom.
21. M. Williams, Euro Disney awash in red ink, *Variety,* July 19, 1993, 38.
22. C. Fisher, Parks still spark Disney imagination, *Advertising Age,* November 22, 1993, 31.
23. Phillips, Where's the magic?
24. A profitable theme, *The Economist,* May 1, 1993, 74.
25. S. Toy, P. Oster, and R. Grover, The mouse isn't roaring, *Business Week,* August 24, 1992, 38.
26. Euro Disney: The not-so-magic kingdom.
27. Popkin et al., Summer in Europe.
28. Williams, Euro Disney awash.
29. Popkin et al., Summer in Europe.
30. Euro Disney: The not-so-magic kingdom.
31. Toy et al., The mouse isn't roaring.
32. Ibid.
33. Euro Disney: Ducking doom.
34. Euro Disney: Waiting for Dumbo, *The Economist,* May 1, 1993, 74.
35. Popkin et al., Summer in Europe.
36. Ibid.
37. Wagner, It's a small world.
38. Ibid.
39. Phillips, Where's the magic?
40. Ibid.

41. Wagner, It's a small world.
42. W. Echikson, Sacre Bleu! American dinosaurs, *Fortune,* November 29, 1993, 16.
43. J. Sasseen, Disney's bungle book, *International Management,* July/August, 1993, 26.
44. Euro Disney: The not-so-magic kingdom.
45. Sasseen, Disney's bungle book.
46. Ibid.
47. Ibid.
48. Toy et al., The mouse isn't roaring.
49. Sasseen, Disney's bungle book.
50. Phillips, Where's the magic?
51. Sasseen, Disney's bungle book.
52. Ibid.
53. Wagner, It's a small world.
54. Sasseen, Disney's bungle book.
55. Fisher, Parks still spark.
56. Of mice and money, *The Economist,* November 13, 1993, 79.
57. Euro Disney: The not-so-magic kingdom.
58. B. Coleman and T. R. King, Euro Disney rescue package wins approval, *Wall Street Journal,* March 15, 1994, 3A.
59. Sasseen, Disney's bungle book.
60. Ibid.
61. Ibid.

■ CASE 15 Glaxo PLC: Medicine, Management, and Mergers

Renato Garcia
Richard Kight
Manuel Lugo
James McMiller
Pravin Nayar
Joel (Rick) Porter

■ http://www.glaxowellcome.co.uk/

In late 1994, the pharmaceutical industry (Exhibit 1) witnessed the launching of yet another major takeover bid as Glaxo's Sir Richard Sykes made a $15 billion tender offer for Wellcome PLC (both firms are headquartered in the United Kingdom). While acquisitions were on the rise at this time in the industry, Glaxo's high dollar, hostile bid attracted unusual attention. Glaxo's competitors such as Merck and SmithKline Beecham had adopted the strategy of acquiring drug distributors. These purchases were an attempt to wrestle the power back from the "managed care" firms such as Columbia/HCA that in recent years had taken the health care industry by storm. It appeared that Sir Richard had chosen an alternate means of achieving the same end. The addition of Wellcome, a major competitor in the drug industry, would make the merged firm the largest pharmaceutical company in the world.

The pharmaceutical industry, which is populated by hundreds of firms, has proven to be one of the most lucrative major industries in the past two decades. In 1993 pharmaceutical revenues topped $60 billion in the United States and $200 billion worldwide, and despite the large number of firms, profits have been equally as desirable.[1] One reason for the above-average returns is the fragmented nature of the industry. The substantial research costs required to identify and develop breakthrough formulas has led most firms to concentrate on a particular therapeutic class of drugs. Secondly, once a company discovers a new drug, patent protection, in effect, guarantees product differentiation over the life of the patent. Such protection allows the company to charge a premium on its new drugs. These above-average returns are reinvested into the company to continue research and development and to build an effective sales force.

Once the patent expires, however, other companies can gain access to the formula, obtain U.S. Food and Drug Administration (FDA) approval (in the

Case prepared under the direction of Professor Robert E. Hoskisson for class discussion purposes only.

Exhibit 1

The Pharmaceutical Industry

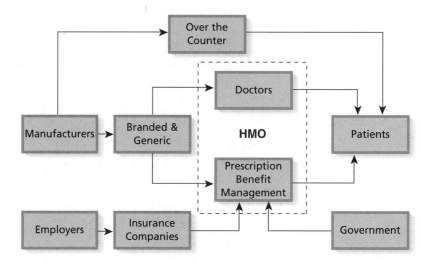

U.S.), and begin to compete typically with a lower priced generic substitute. Nevertheless, the branded product can continue to command a premium beyond the patent period due to relatively inelastic demand. Prescribing doctors have a tendency toward brand loyalty given the threat of malpractice suits and the belief that the patient's health should not be compromised for cost savings. Brand-name companies reinforce this belief in the superiority of their branded product through a large, proactive sales force, making it difficult for doctors to justify switching to the generic product. In addition, prior to the Waxman–Hatch Act of 1984, U.S. pharmacists were unable to substitute a generic for a branded product without the authorization of the physician.[2]

Waxman–Hatch was an attempt on the part of Congress to mitigate these anticompetitive forces. The effect of the legislation was to facilitate the FDA approval process for generics, thereby greatly reducing R&D requirements for generic companies. However, generics did not rise in popularity until cost conscious, volume-based buyers entered the picture.

Toward the end of the 1980s new pressures started to form in the industry that would completely change the nature of the relationship between pharmaceuticals and their buyers. Historically, hospitals engaged in little bargaining with pharmaceuticals because they practiced independent purchasing and bought in relatively low volumes. Even though two hospitals were part of the same group, because they bought supplies independently, they were unable to leverage the size of the group against the giant drug companies. As drug prices increased rapidly throughout the 1970s and especially the 1980s, affiliated hospitals and hospital chains began to consolidate their purchasing departments with the intention of increasing their bargaining power.[3]

The managed care concept also surged during this time. Cost conscious managed health care started because of pressure from government and insurance companies, which were under pressure from employers to decrease the cost of health care. Health maintenance organizations (HMOs), created for the purpose of providing preventive as well as quality care at the lowest possible cost, began to flourish. HMOs contracted with employers to provide health care for their employees for a fixed monthly charge. Often prescription medicine coverage was included in the arrangement.

Prescription benefit management companies (PBMs) were another organization that came to the forefront during this time. PBMs design and manage consumers' pharmaceutical benefits by processing claims, creating rebates and discounts from drug manufacturers, and developing pharmacy networks. They reach millions of drug users, thereby increasing their bargaining power tremendously. PBMs also serve to deliver drugs via mail order making sure that the patients, typically elderly, are taking their drugs correctly. With the incentive of reducing their costs, PBMs work directly with physicians to encourage them to authorize the substitution of branded drugs with generics. As a result, these institutions have introduced price competition into some segments of the market. Both sales and profit growth have slowed sharply as cost conscious managed care institutions gained control over a greater portion of the prescription business. The influence on the market by managed care companies has been so substantial that by 1994 generics accounted for 37 percent of the U.S. prescription drug market. Generics have become so profitable that some pharmaceutical companies have acquired their own generic division to cushion the blow once their patent runs out. Exemplifying this trend is Bristol-Myers Squibb's takeover of Purepac Pharmaceutical Co., a generic drug company with $70 million in revenues.[4]

Further supporting the push for generics was the passage of the Omnibus Budget Reconciliation Act in 1993. This legislation enabled the states to use restrictive formularies, which mandate use of the lowest effective pharmaceutical alternative in state health care systems in order to hold down drug benefit costs. States immediately included generics in these restrictive formularies as an option to the brand-names products.[5]

History of Glaxo

Named after its founder, Joseph Nathan, the New Zealand–based Joseph Nathan and Company began as a merchant trader in 1873. However, after stumbling across a milk drying process the company opened a subsidiary that produced and sold dry milk. At the time, the only viable market for dry milk was in the baby food business. Demand for the company's milk and soon other baby food products increased once Nathan's son, Alec, wrote and published the *Glaxo Baby Book*. The *Glaxo Baby Book* was a child care book that quickly gained widespread readership and also served as a marketing tool for the company's products. Additionally, the demand for Glaxo's dry milk grew remarkably with the outbreak of World War I. Glaxo's success made possible the opening of its own research laboratory. After the war, Glaxo continued its growth by exporting its baby food products to Third World countries.

In 1923 Glaxo licensed a Vitamin D extracting process, realizing the market potential of vitamin D fortified baby foods. Building on its success with vitamin D, the company produced its first pharmaceutical product, Ostelin Liquid, a vitamin concentrate. World War II spurred demand for the company's vitamin concentrate as well as penicillin and anesthetics. Glaxo responded by increasing its focus on pharmaceuticals through the opening of an independent research laboratory in India, Glaxo Laboratories Ltd. Following the retirement of the founder's son, Louis Nathan, after the war, Glaxo's lead chemist assumed the role of chairman of the company. The holding company, Joseph Nathan and Company, was dissolved and Glaxo became an independent public company headquartered in London. A series of successful breakthrough products through the 1950s and 1960s helped Glaxo achieve strong growth. Glaxo also grew with the acquisition of a chemical company, a medical supply company, and a competing British pharmaceutical firm, Allen and Hanbury's.

All the same, the product that propelled Glaxo, now named Glaxo Holdings, to one of the largest in the pharmaceutical industry was Zantac, an anti-ulcer drug. Zantac, introduced in the late 1970s, would eventually contribute $1 billion to the company's profits and earn the title of the largest selling prescription drug in the world. Under the marketing efforts of CEO Paul Girolami, Sir Richard's predecessor, Zantac gained 25 percent of the anti-ulcer market by 1984. To facilitate the distribution of Zantac and other products in the United States, the company built a $40 million plant in North Carolina. Most recently Glaxo's extensive research and development capability brought to market 3TC, a drug used for the treatment of AIDS.[6]

Glaxo's Current Strategy

With Zantac as a prime example, Glaxo has successfully discovered, developed, and produced drugs for the prescription market. Glaxo's strategy has been to launch new drugs globally in the largest markets, while at the same time maintaining and improving the sales of long-standing products.

One of the keys to Glaxo's success is the ability to get new products approved and launched in major markets. Glaxo has successfully employed a technique known as *comarketing* to expedite the distribution of a product. Comarketing involves the licensing of a patented drug formula to another pharmaceutical company that might have superior marketing expertise in a particular market. Zantac was introduced in the United States under a comarketing agreement with Hoffmann-La Roche. Examples of more recent new product introductions include Serevent, an inhaled long-acting bronchodilator, which was introduced in the United States in 1994, and Flixotide, an inhaled steroid, which was introduced in the United Kingdom in 1993 and in 11 other major markets in 1994. In fact, 12 percent of Glaxo's 1994 net sales (Exhibit 2) were generated by newly introduced products. Financing the large upfront expenses involved in the launch of these new products is the $965 million in profits from Glaxo's established drugs such as Zantac.

However, as the profitability of Zantac inevitably declines over the next few years, Glaxo must seek to overcome its dependence on this significant source of revenue and profit. The company hopes that acquiring Wellcome will improve the likelihood of producing more winning drugs, thereby delivering a sustained competitive advantage and above-average returns.

More products implies market power for Glaxo. The industry has traditionally been dominated by the large drug makers, but the demand for lower health care costs and the subsequent introduction of managed health care providers has shifted the balance of power within the industry. Although the post merger company (Glaxo and Wellcome combined) would command less than 6 percent of the market, it would be the largest drug maker in the world. Furthermore, with the acquisition of Wellcome, Glaxo would immediately increase its market shares in particular therapeutic classes. For example, Glaxo would control approximately 70 percent of the antiviral market, 35 percent of the gastrointestinal market, and 25 percent of the antibiotic market.[7]

Exhibit 2: Glaxo PLC's Financial Statements (Fiscal year from July 1 to June 30)

Income Statement	1994	1993	1992	1991
Net sales	$5,656,000	$4,930,000	$4,096,000	$3,397,000
Cost of goods	$1,004,000	$874,000	$724,000	$590,000
Gross profit	$4,652,000	$4,056,000	$3,372,000	$2,807,000
R&D expenditures	$858,000	$739,000	$595,000	$475,000
S, G & A expenses	$1,972,000	$1,795,000	$1,492,000	$1,231,000
Inc. before dep. and amort.	$1,822,000	$1,522,000	$1,285,000	$1,101,000
Dep. and amort.	NA	NA	NA	NA
Nonoperating income	$18,000	$153,000	$142,000	$182,000
Interest expense	NA	NA	NA	NA
Income before tax	$1,840,000	$1,675,000	$1,427,000	$1,283,000
Prov. for income taxes	$525,000	$461,000	$386,000	$359,000
Minority int. (inc)	$12,000	$7,000	$8,000	$12,000
Net income before extraordinary items	$1,303,000	$1,207,000	$1,033,000	$912,000
Extraordinary items and disc ops.	NA	NA	NA	($31,000)
Net income	$1,303,000	$1,207,000	$1,033,000	$881,000
Outstanding shares	3,049,397	3,031,294	3,010,247	1,499,602
Balance Sheet				
Cash	$55,000	$63,000	$24,000	$34,000
Marketable securities	$2,708,000	$2,434,000	$1,725,000	$2,095,000
A/R	$908,000	$916,000	$720,000	$655,000
Inventories	$575,000	$595,000	$475,000	$494,000
Other current assets	$402,000	$430,000	$365,000	$357,000
Total current assets	$4,648,000	$4,438,000	$3,309,000	$3,635,000
Prop., plant, and equip.	$3,184,000	$2,959,000	$2,341,000	$2,081,000
Acc. dep.	NA	NA	NA	NA
Net prop. and equip.	$3,184,000	$2,959,000	$2,341,000	$2,081,000
Invest and adv. to subs.	$55,000	$61,000	$32,000	$28,000
Total assets	$7,887,000	$7,458,000	$5,682,000	$5,744,000
Liabilities:				
Notes payable	$400,000	$597,000	$366,000	$871,000
A/P	$188,000	$178,000	$162,000	$146,000
Income taxes	$382,000	$336,000	$265,000	$294,000
Other current liabilities	$1,160,000	$1,089,000	$775,000	$716,000
Total current liabilities	$2,130,000	$2,200,000	$1,568,000	$2,027,000
Deferred charges inc.	$146,000	$204,000	$190,000	$161,000
L-T debt	$272,000	$212,000	$137,000	$140,000
Other L-T liabilities	$173,000	$185,000	$148,000	$134,000
Total liabilities	$2,721,000	$2,801,000	$2,043,000	$2,462,000
Equity:				
Minority interest (liab.)	$123,000	$111,000	$64,000	$74,000
Common stock (net)	$762,000	$758,000	$753,000	$750,000
Capital surplus	$229,000	$151,000	$77,000	$39,000
Retained earnings	$4,052,000	$3,637,000	$2,742,000	$2,419,000
Shareholder equity	$5,043,000	$4,546,000	$3,572,000	$3,208,000
Total liabilities and equity	$7,887,000	$7,458,000	$5,682,000	$5,744,000

Concerned, on the other hand, that Glaxo has not taken part in a major acquisition in more than 15 years, some analysts doubt Glaxo's management capabilities in integrating Wellcome into the firm, especially considering that intangible assets constitute a large part of the overall value of both firms. R&D department mergers often combine unique cultures. There is no guarantee that these distinct cultures will merge effectively, leading to more hit products. In addition, difficulties in merging the cultures will probably not be limited to the R&D department.

Furthermore, while R&D has been Glaxo's strength in the past and may need to carry the firm into the future, R&D may be somewhat different within the industry due to the increased pressure from managed health care institutions to control costs. The days of spending whatever it takes to find new "wonder" drugs are past, and R&D departments are becoming increasingly cost conscious. Glaxo's planned spending for fiscal year 1995 will grow approximately 6 percent compared to an average annual growth of over 15 percent in the previous decade.[8] There is a need to reach a balance between innovation and creativity and the need to be fiscally responsible. Currently, it is estimated that it costs, on average, $359 million (including overhead and the costs associated with products that never reach production) to bring a drug to the market.[9] Firms that are best able to control these costs while maintaining innovation will likely be future pharmaceutical industry leaders. This seems to be the rationale behind the acquisition of Wellcome. Glaxo believes that efficiencies can be gained through pooling R&D resources, namely, scientists. Management feels that they would also be able to combine facilities to further reduce costs.

In addition to the transition, Glaxo's drug pipeline is not developing as expected. Glaxo's Imitrex, a drug for treating migraines, has not been as successful as first expected. European governments are pressuring Glaxo to reduce the price, which currently stands at about $30 a pill. The French government has rejected the drug until the price is reduced. Zofran, an antinausea drug for chemotherapy patients, is suffering from strong competition and price pressures. These two drugs were to be the replacements for Zantac once its patent expires in 1997. Glaxo's new product pipeline includes 3TC for HIV patients and Lamivudine for hepatitis B. Expectations are high, but there are no sure bets in the pharmaceutical industry. However, the risk associated with the development of 3TC and Lamivudine is reduced because they were developed through strategic alliances with biochemistry research firms.[10] Strategic alliances are likely to be a continuing trend as drug makers seek other ways to contain costs and gain efficiencies.

■ Distribution

Marketing has been very expensive for all pharmaceuticals and Glaxo is no exception. In fact, in Glaxo's case expenses for marketing exceed those for R&D. Glaxo has more than 16,000 salespeople in place to push its products. This might suggest that another possible benefit of the proposed merger would be the potential cost savings through a merging of distribution capacity.

With regard to distribution strategies, other firms such as Merck have chosen vertical integration. In November 1993, Merck & Co. acquired Medco Containment Services, a mail-order pharmacy and PBM company for $6.6 billion. The aim is to have these distribution channels push the drugs of the drug maker. Such a situation will not excuse the drug maker from the need for cost efficiency, however, because the vertically integrated managed health care organizations may not be able to promote the parent's products in a cost-effective manner. Glaxo's distribution strategy focuses on the end consumer. The acquisition of Wellcome would bring Glaxo highly recognized consumer brand names (e.g., Actifed). Glaxo may be hoping that as consumers become better informed, they will develop more brand loyalty and thus pull the products through the channels.

Another marketing approach is the extension by drug makers into the over-the-counter (OTC) market. Price pressure is allowing more drugs into the OTC market and Wellcome will also be beneficial in this area due to its partnership with U.S. pharmaceutical giant, Warner-Lambert (WL). If Zantac or other drugs are approved as OTC drugs, WL could be an invaluable resource.

The bottom line for Glaxo is to make sure that the firms are integrated in such a way that synergy is fully realized. The firms that are able to retain their innovation while cutting costs will improve their competitive advantage.

Wellcome PLC

Wellcome PLC, a $3.2 billion British pharmaceutical firm, was formed in 1880 when Silas M. Burroughs offered partnership in his promising pharmaceutical company to Henry S. Wellcome, a fellow graduate of the Philadelphia College of Pharmacy. Wellcome began by marketing products for U.S. producers of novel powders and pills. However, it did not take long before the ambitious partnership was manufacturing products on its own. The partnership's first factory was acquired in 1883 on the Thames River in Wandsworth. Wellcome proved quite successful in the early years, and it achieved a reputation for a high standard of quality and precise, innovative product formulation. In 1894, the company founded the Physical Research Laboratories and within one year the lab had developed an antidiphtheria serum. Following Burrough's death in 1895, Wellcome began to expand the company's international presence. Associate houses were opened in Asia, North and South America, Continental Europe, and South Africa.

Wellcome would lead the company until his death in 1936, after which the company experienced a period of decline for several years as a result of ineffective leadership. In the early 1950s the company began to renovate its outdated line of products and focus its energies on R&D. Wellcome introduced a variety of winning products in the years to come. In the 1960s the firm commercialized Septrin, an antibacterial treatment, and Zyloric, and antigout product. The 1970s saw the introduction of Actifed, the now famous OTC allergy medicine. All of these proved quite successful for the company.[11] Today, Wellcome has 16,400 employees worldwide, and is best known for Retrovir or AZT, which is widely recognized as the most effective treatment for the symptoms of AIDS. Despite its relatively small size, Wellcome is a truly multinational corporation with the lion's share of its sales coming from Europe, North America, and Asia (see Exhibits 3 and 4). The company's primary operations and R&D facilities are located in the Research Triangle Park in North Carolina and at Beckenham in Kent, United Kingdom.

Exhibit 3   Wellcome's Sales by Geographic Region (pounds sterling—millions)

Europe	1111.4
North America	1010.9
Australia and Asia	271.7
Africa and Middle East	48.7
Central and South America	25.5

Source: Annual Report.

Exhibit 4: Wellcome PLC's Financial Statements As of August 29, 1992, and August 31, 1993 ($ in millions)

Income Statement	1992	1993
Sales	$2,766.34	$3,203.90
Cost of goods sold	($616.23)	($562.37)
Selling, general and administrative	($986.27)	($1,141.55)
Research and development	($399.72)	($511.04)
Gross profit	$764.12	$988.94
Share of profits of affiliates	$1.57	$0.63
Operating profit	$765.69	$989.57
Discontinued operations (loss)/profit	($74.89)	NA
Release of provisions from prior years	NA	$26.69
Income on ordinary activities before int.	$690.80	$1,016.26
Net interest income	$26.69	$31.09
Income from ordinary activities before tax	$717.49	$1,047.35
Taxation on income from ordinary activities	($302.07)	($377.59)
Income from ordinary activities after tax	$415.42	$669.76
Minority interests	($10.05)	($14.13)
Net income	$405.37	$655.63
Distributions to shareholders	($175.68)	($235.19)
Income retained for the financial year	$229.69	$420.45
Balance Sheet		
Assets		
Cash and cash equivalents	$608.69	$1,036.20
Investments	$322.32	$185.42
Receivables and prepaid expenses	$575.41	$727.54
Inventories	$308.66	$373.82
Total current assets	$1,815.08	$2,322.97
Noncurrent investments	$3.45	$3.61
Property, plant and equipment	$1,284.26	$1,582.56
Total assets	$3,102.79	$3,909.14
Liabilities and shareholders' equity		
Short-term borrowings	$140.83	$179.77
Accounts payable and accrued liab.	$675.10	$785.79
Total current liabilities	$815.93	$965.55
Long-term debt	$146.32	$152.45
Provisions for liabilities and charges	$243.51	$219.64
Other liabilities	$6.75	$4.08
Minority interests	$41.76	$32.03
Total liabilities	$1,254.27	$1,373.75
Shareholders' equity	$0.00	$0.00
Ordinary shares	$337.86	$339.91
Premiums paid in excess of par	$101.27	$118.38
Income retained	$1,409.39	$2,077.11
Total shareholders' equity	$1,848.52	$2,535.39
Total liabilities and shareholders' equity	$3,102.79	$3,909.14

■ Wellcome's Strategy

Wellcome is led by a very dynamic CEO, John Robb, whose articulated vision is to expand Wellcome's global market share such that it becomes one of the 15 largest producers in the world. In a global market characterized by rising price sensitivity and an industry dependent on heavy R&D expense, size brings much needed economies of scale.

Although AZT receives the most headlines, it accounts for only 10 percent of Wellcome's sales. In reality Wellcome is highly dependent on its antiherpes drug, Zovirax, which accounted for 39 percent of sales in the first six months of 1994. Such singular dependence has been disturbing to management given the fact that Zovirax's patent will expire in 1997. Other offerings in the current product pallet include an antiepileptic medicine, Lamictal, and neuromuscular blocking agents such as Tracrium and Wellbutrum. The latter is a relatively new area for Wellcome, but it is showing promising growth: Sales in the first six months of 1994 increased 26% from the previous year.

Wellcome's R&D portfolio is remarkably similar to that of Glaxo with three-quarters of its current expenditures in the areas of anti-infective, anticancer, and cardiovascular drugs. One experimental drug, 311C, promised to offer substantial competition to Glaxo's current market-leading migraine treatment. Wellcome feels that many of its best efforts in this area will come from extensions of its current products. Two herpes treatments were under development to follow Zovirax, as Wellcome moved to maintain dominance in the anti-herpes market. A follow-up to AZT is also in the works.

Wellcome employs 3,500 people in R&D. Many analysts feel this is an optimal size. Wellcome is known for its willingness to develop new drugs in its R&D program, even if the potential markets for them are relatively small. The firm's philosophy is based on the belief that "cross-fertilization" will occur, i.e., that research in one product area will create opportunities for additional product extensions that might prove to be more lucrative. The department has been criticized at times, however, because of the concern that Wellcome's R&D leadership is reluctant to drop projects whose commercialization is infeasible.

Wellcome has a sales force of 4,500, which is responsible for marketing Wellcome products to the various buyers. The marketing function is currently being reviewed with the goal of improving productivity and devising more effective ways to market products to bulk health care providers. In one way Wellcome has responded to the cost conscious movement in the industry by forming an alliance with U.S. pharmaceutical giant Warner-Lambert, the makers of Listerine antiseptic mouthwash. The stated objective in the cooperation with WL is to facilitate the marketing of OTC versions of Wellcome's products, most notably Zovirax, in the United States and Canada. The enterprise, which is to be named Wellcome-Warner Consumer Health Products, is expected to immediately generate sales of $1.65 billion. Management feels the partnership is also a wise move strategically because it will allow Wellcome to market itself to the end consumer, thus building brand loyalty.

Wellcome is 39.5 percent owned by the Wellcome Trust, a medical charity that was founded soon after the death of Henry Wellcome. It was for this reason that analysts felt the successful company had not fallen prey to a hostile takeover in the past, and would likely resist offers to merge with another company despite the industry trend toward consolidation. Insiders said that the board at Wellcome would likely demand a high premium in the event of a takeover bid; some estimates ran as high as 25 times earnings or around $15.6 billion.

Competitive Dynamics

According to Roy Vagelos, former Merck & Co. CEO, "The pharmaceutical industry is highly fragmented. No competitor has more than 5% of the market worldwide, so the competition is fierce and the battlefield is crowded."[12] (Exhibits 5 and 6 show the leading companies' market shares in the world and the United States, respectively.) In spite of the large number of competitors, the prescription pharmaceutical industry has been one of the most profitable in U.S. manufacturing for the past two decades. As mentioned earlier, competition has been mitigated by a therapeutic class structure (the natural market segmentation), with no single company manufacturing a leading product in every major category. The top 3 classes—antibiotics, cardiovascular treatments, and central nervous system therapies—accounted for approximately 36 percent of industry revenues in 1993. The top 10 classes accounted for about 68 percent. (Exhibit 7 includes the top 9 drugs, Exhibit 8 includes a comparison between branded and generic products, and Exhibit 9 includes the leading growth categories.) Differentiation of products within segments helps blunt competition on price. Moreover, obtaining access to markets is also made difficult because new drugs are protected by patents. However, the attractiveness of the industry began to deteriorate in the late 1980s and early 1990s, with the development of PBMs (Exhibit 10).

Merck & Co. Inc.

Merck & Co. is the worldwide leader in prescription pharmaceuticals. It sold $10.5 billion in 1993 with net income of $2.2 billion. (Exhibit 11 includes financial data on the main manufacturers of pharmaceuticals.) Merck's pretax margin of 35 percent is above the other pharmaceutical companies. It spends around 11 percent of sales on R&D. Merck has always been viewed as the industry's best managed and one of the best positioned to weather the expected stormy periods. In 1993, the firm was named the most admired corporation for the seventh year in a row in a *Fortune* magazine survey. However, even Merck's profit growth is slowing and the future seems uncertain. Its product line is under siege from competition. Competition is threatening its cardiovascular drugs, which account for almost half of the company's sales. Its two main products, the heart drug Vasotec and its cholesterol-lowering Mevacor, have been losing ground to new, but similar, products.

A series of significant patents will expire later in the decade. Furthermore, Merck's R&D department has not developed the expected breakthrough to sustain its growth. In fact, the company has not announced any drug in advanced testing. Its latest introduction, Proscar, which is used to treat enlarged prostate glands, has largely been a failure. Proscar is still expected to fuel the company's revenue growth through the end of the decade.

Merck's acquisition of Medco set off a firestorm within the pharmaceutical industry when competitors followed Merck's lead by acquiring their own PBMs. In the words of Dr. P. Roy Vagelos, "Merck decided to acquire Medco to create a new model for the pharmaceutical industry that would simultaneously improve the quality of the health care, help contain costs, and increase Merck's market share."[13] Merck believed that to achieve these goals it was critical to expand its information base. Medco's database on 38 million patients would allow Merck to learn a lot more about how its drugs are prescribed and used and, ultimately, how effective they are in fighting diseases. "The company that best controls the

Exhibit 5   Share of the World Pharmaceutical Market, 1993–1994

		Percentage
1	Glaxo Wellcome*	5.9
2	Merck	4.2
3	Bristol-Myers Squibb	3.1
4	Roche	2.7
5	Pfizer	2.6
6	SmithKline Beecham	2.5
7	Johnson & Johnson	2.0
8	Hoechst	2.0
9	Eli Lilly	2.0
10	Sankyo	2.0

*If the acquisition is completed.
Source: *The Economist*, January 28, 1995, p. 58.

Exhibit 6   Share of the U.S. Market, 1992–1993

		Percentage
1	Merck	15.0
2	Bristol-Myers Squibb	11.7
3	Glaxo	10.9
4	American Home Products	10.9
5	Eli Lilly	10.5
6	Johnson & Johnson	8.9
7	Pfizer	8.9
8	SmithKline Beecham	8.5
9	Marion Merrell Dow	7.7
10	Upjohn	6.9

Source: *New York Times*, August 5, 1993, p. C1.

Exhibit 7	Top 9 Drugs, 1993 Sales ($ in millions)
1	Cardiovascular	$9,075
2	Internal medicine	$7,125
3	Anti-infective	$6,750
4	Central nervous system	$4,225
5	Pain control	$4,050
6	Respiratory	$2,025
7	Nutritional	$1,775
8	Topical	$1,525
9	Others	$3,200

Source: *Chemical Week*, April 20, 1994, p. 36.

Exhibit 8   Branded Versus Generic, 1992 and 1993 Sales ($ in millions)

	1992	1993
Generic	2,822.7	3,523.7
Branded	43,365.4	45,098.2
Total	46,188.1	48,621.9

Source: *Business & Health*, November 1994, p. 43.

Exhibit 9   Leading Growth Categories, 1992–1993 Sales Growth

		1993/1992
1	Anti-infectives	115%
2	Cardiovascular	78
3	Ophthalmic	78
4	Antidepressants	50
5	Vitamin E	50
6	Cough preparations	30
7	Respiratory	29

Source: *Business & Health*, November 1994, p. 43.

information flow from doctor to patient to pharmacist to plan sponsor has the best chance of succeeding in the industry,"[14] states Dr. Vagelos. The pharmaceutical industry is a complex marketplace: "the people who pay for the products—the sponsors—are not the people who prescribe the drugs—the doctors. And doctors are not the people who dispense them—the pharmacists. Moreover, . . . doctors and pharmacists don't take the medication, patients do." Merck has traditionally marketed its products by sending salespeople to doctors' offices to tell them about new drugs. The emergence of PBMs like Medco has introduced a whole new dimension to pharmaceutical marketing. Having salespeople visit doctors' offices does not allow firms to reach PBMs, HMOs, or plan sponsors, all major players in the changing industry.

Industry observers who are aware of Merck's limited new-drug pipeline argue that the acquisition of Medco may cause Merck to lose its focus on product development. Merck contends that R&D is the source of competitive advantage, and that "losing it would rob society of its very best source of new medicines."[15] Dr. Vagelos believes only a few pharmaceutical companies will survive the restructuring that has already begun, and that the ones that do will have to excel at both research and the new distribution methods. "You cannot succeed without mastering both."[16]

▨ Bristol-Myers Squibb Co.

Bristol-Myers, the No. 2 pharmaceutical firm in the United States (see Exhibit 11), is an $11.4 billion company, with net income of almost $2 billion. The company is a close competitor to Merck & Co. It is the leading marketer of cancer drugs, which account for 25 percent of its sales. Its cholesterol-lowering product, Pravachol, competes directly with Merck's Mevacor and Zocor. In addition, the firm owns Clairol, a major hair care products distributor. However, Brystol-Myers is not isolated from the changes taking place in the pharmaceutical industry. As is the case with Merck, some of Bristol-Myers most important products will soon lose patent protection.

Bristol-Myers has formed a joint venture with Axion pharmaceuticals, a six-year-old, privately held distributor specializing in sales to cancer treatment clinics. Axion provides value-added services such as extended payment terms, simplified procurement procedures, and quick deliveries, which allow for better inventory management. As Donald Hayden Jr., vice president and general manager of Bristol-Myers' Oncology Divisions said, "Brystol-Myers didn't have the expertise to service thousands of small accounts"; the joint-venture will provide that expertise.

Bristol-Myers is also acquiring Purepac Pharmaceutical Co., a generic drug company with $70 million in revenues. Moreover, it negotiated a multibillion-dollar, five-year deal with American Health Care Systems, a leading HMO, which will give Bristol-Myers access to more than 1,000 hospitals. The pact includes pharmaceuticals, infant formulas, and diagnostic agents. This contract is highly unusual because it covers a broad range of products. In fact, it is one of the first contracts of its kind and certainly the largest.

▨ American Home Products Corp.

Although American Home Products (AHP) is a highly diversified company, pharmaceutical sales account for more than half of total company sales (see Exhibit 11).

Exhibit 10 Top 10 PBMs, Plans in Millions of Subscribers	
1 PCS Health Systems Inc.	51.0
2 Medco Containment Services Inc.	40.0
3 Diversified Pharmaceutical Services	14.0
4 Diagnostek Inc.	14.0
5 Caremark Inc.	13.0
6 ValueRx Pharmacy Program Inc.	8.0
7 Wellpoint Pharmacy Management	7.0
8 Express Scripts	5.2
9 America's Pharmacy	4.0
10 Prescription Solutions	2.2

Source: *Business & Health*, November 1994, p. 56.

It manufactures such "on-every-shelf" products as Anacin, Advil, Chapstick, Robitussin, Chef Boyardee, Preparation H, and Pam cooking spray.

AHP agreed to buy the giant American Cyanamid Co. for $9.7 billion. The acquisition will increase its revenues by 50 percent, and will make it the world's fourth largest pharmaceutical company, just behind Merck & Co., Glaxo Holdings PLC and Bristol-Myers. The bid for Cyanamid appears to reflect another basic strategy that pharmaceutical companies are pursuing: less risky growth through acquisition and horizontal integration.

However, AHP is probably the pharmaceutical firm with the biggest problems, which size cannot solve. It has 50,000 employees, but its chairman, John R. Stafford, who is also president and chief executive officer, has to approve expenditures of as little as $1,500. Its management structure maintains huge amounts of responsibility, resulting in a day-to-day bureaucracy in the hands of its chairman. Its products are hardly cutting-edge. Advil faces a potentially draining marketing war against Procter & Gamble's Aleve pain reliever. Its most profitable product, Premarin, used for the treatment of menopause, is an old drug likely to face competition from generic versions. "AMH is in trouble not because they are small or inefficient," says an analyst, "they're in trouble because they have the wrong drugs." [17] Some believe its R&D is weak. AHP has been one of the lowest R&D spenders in the industry, committing about 8 percent of sales, while the industry average is 13 percent. As serious as AHP's situation may be, some analysts think the problem with the takeover is that Cyanamid suffers many of the same difficulties as AHP. Once a premier drug research house, Cyanamid's laboratory has not produced a major drug in years. Neither has AHP's R&D division, and it is not likely to contribute much anytime soon.

Cyanamid might give AHP some short-term help. A broader product line would bring greater negotiating power with PBMs, and the combination could allow costs to be decreased by eliminating duplicate sales and administrative staff. The merger would also allow plant closures. Analysts believe AHP will sell its food units to help finance the acquisition of Cyanamid's, which will allow it to focus more on its core business. [18]

■ Eli Lilly & Co.

Eli Lilly is another important participant in the pharmaceutical industry with sales in 1993 of $6.5 billion and net income of $480 million (see Exhibit 11). The firm is also a victim of the major changes taking place in the pharmaceutical industry. For the past two years the company has suffered a painful restructuring process, which resulted in 4,000 layoffs and the discontinuation of its research on the HIV virus.

In November 1994, Eli Lilly learned that the Federal Trade Commission approved its $4 billion offer for McKesson Corp.'s PCS Health Systems, the largest U.S. PBM. While the bid is 131 times PCS' earnings and 23 times PCS' revenues, the alliance will give Eli Lilly new leverage. PCS Health System, Medco Containment Services (acquired by Merck), and Diversified Pharmaceutical Services (acquired by SmithKline Beecham) share about 80 percent of the managed drug benefit market, while more than 35 other companies divide the remainder (Exhibit 10 shows the top 10 PBMs). The importance of PCS was highlighted when Glaxo Holdings PLC tried to set a three-way joint venture with Johnson & Johnson and McKesson to run PCS, which did not work. Analysts

Exhibit 11   Annual Income Statements Selected Manufacturers ($ in thousands)

American Home Products Corp.

Fiscal year ending	31-Dec-93	31-Dec-92	31-Dec-91	31-Dec-90
Net sales	8,304,851	7,873,687	7,079,443	6,775,182
Cost of goods	2,723,902	2,568,690	2,390,463	2,453,469
Gross profit	5,580,949	5,304,997	4,688,980	4,321,713
R & D expenditures	662,689	552,450	430,519	NA
Sell gen & admin exp	2,922,579	2,846,365	2,541,422	2,806,045
Inc bef dep & amort	1,995,681	1,906,182	1,717,039	1,515,668
Non-operating inc	−3,016	−182,112	42,771	312,610
Income before tax	1,992,665	1,724,070	1,759,810	1,828,278
Prov for inc taxes	523,365	573,332	384,537	597,681
Net inc bef ex items	1,469,300	1,150,738	1,375,273	1,230,597
Ex items & disc ops	NA	310,104	NA	NA
Net income	1,469,300	1,460,842	1,375,273	1,230,597
Outstanding shares	310,326	313,048	315,623	NA

Bristol-Myers Squibb Co.

Fiscal year ending	31-Dec-93	31-Dec-92	31-Dec-91	31-Dec-90
Net sales	11,413,000	11,156,000	10,571,000	9,741,000
Cost of goods	3,029,000	2,857,000	2,717,000	2,665,000
Gross profit	8,384,000	8,299,000	7,854,000	7,076,000
R & D expenditures	1,128,000	1,083,000	983,000	873,000
Sell gen & admin exp	4,353,000	5,229,000	4,087,000	3,770,000
Inc bef dep & amort	2,903,000	1,987,000	2,784,000	2,433,000
Non-operating inc	−332,000	NA	NA	NA
Income before tax	2,571,000	1,987,000	2,784,000	2,433,000
Prov for inc taxes	612,000	449,000	793,000	742,000
Net inc bef ex items	1,959,000	1,538,000	1,991,000	1,691,000
Ex items & disc ops	NA	424,000	65,000	57,000
Net income	1,959,000	1,962,000	2,056,000	1,748,000
Outstanding shares	511,906	517,984	519,517	523,819

Eli Lilly & Co

Fiscal year ending	31-Dec-93	31-Dec-92	31-Dec-91	31-Dec-90
Net sales	6,452,400	6,167,300	5,725,700	5,191,600
Cost of goods	1,959,000	1,897,000	1,717,700	1,586,300
Gross profit	4,493,400	4,270,300	4,008,000	3,605,300
R & D expenditures	954,600	924,900	766,900	702,700
Sell gen & admin exp	1,713,500	1,624,200	1,472,800	1,363,200
Inc bef dep & amort	1,825,300	1,721,200	1,768,300	1,539,400
Non-operating inc	−1,123,400	−538,900	110,900	59,600
Income before tax	701,900	1,182,300	1,879,200	1,599,000
Prov for inc taxes	210,800	354,700	564,500	471,700
Net inc bef ex items	491,100	827,600	1,314,700	1,127,300
Ex items & disc ops	−10,900	−118,900	NA	NA
Net income	480,200	708,700	1,314,700	1,127,300
Outstanding shares	292,748	292,686	292,623	277,064

Continued

Exhibit 11   Annual Income Statements Selected Manufacturers ($ in thousands)—*Continued*

Johnson & Johnson

Fiscal year ending	2-Jan-94	3-Jan-93	29-Dec-91	30-Dec-90
Net sales	14,138,000	13,753,000	12,447,000	11,232,000
Cost of goods	4,791,000	4,678,000	4,204,000	3,937,000
Gross profit	9,347,000	9,075,000	8,243,000	7,295,000
R & D expenditures	1,182,000	1,127,000	980,000	834,000
Sell gen & admin exp	5,771,000	5,671,000	5,099,000	4,469,000
Inc bef dep & amort	2,394,000	2,277,000	2,164,000	1,992,000
Non-operating inc	64,000	54,000	3,000	−168,000
Interest expense	126,000	124,000	129,000	201,000
Income before tax	2,332,000	2,207,000	2,038,000	1,623,000
Prov for inc taxes	545,000	582,000	577,000	480,000
Net inc bef ex items	1,787,000	1,625,000	1,461,000	1,143,000
Ex items & disc ops	NA	−595,000	NA	NA
Net income	1,787,000	1,030,000	1,461,000	1,143,000
Outstanding shares	642,981	655,396	666,331	333,076

Merck & Co Inc

Fiscal year ending	31-Dec-93	31-Dec-92	31-Dec-91	31-Dec-90
Net sales	10,498,200	9,662,500	8,602,700	7,671,500
Cost of goods	2,497,600	2,096,100	1,934,900	1,778,100
Gross profit	8,000,600	7,566,400	6,667,800	5,893,400
R & D expenditures	1,172,800	1,111,600	987,800	854,000
Sell gen & admin exp	2,913,900	2,963,300	2,570,300	2,388,000
Inc bef dep & amort	3,913,900	3,491,500	3,109,700	2,651,400
Non-operating inc	−811,200	72,100	57,000	47,400
Income before tax	3,102,700	3,563,600	3,166,700	2,698,800
Prov for inc taxes	936,500	1,117,000	1,045,000	917,600
Net inc bef ex items	2,166,200	2,446,600	2,121,700	1,781,200
Ex items & disc ops	NA	−462,400	NA	NA
Net income	2,166,200	1,984,200	2,121,700	1,781,200
Outstanding shares	1,253,935	1,144,695	1,159,529	386,991

Pfizer Inc

Fiscal year ending	31-Dec-93	31-Dec-92	31-Dec-91	31-Dec-90
Net sales	7,477,700	7,230,200	6,950,000	6,406,000
Cost of goods	1,772,000	2,024,300	2,200,600	2,259,400
Gross profit	5,705,700	5,205,900	4,749,400	4,146,600
R & D expenditures	974,400	863,200	756,800	640,100
Sell gen & admin exp	3,066,000	2,899,300	2,739,100	2,452,700
Inc bef dep & amort	1,665,300	1,443,400	1,253,500	1,053,800
Non-operating inc	−707,400	194,800	120,300	182,000
Interest expense	106,500	103,400	430,100	132,500
Income before tax	851,400	1,534,800	943,700	1,103,300
Prov for inc taxes	191,300	438,600	218,400	297,900

Continued

Exhibit 11   Annual Income Statements Selected Manufacturers ($ in thousands)—*Continued*

Minority int (inc)	2,600	2,700	3,200	4,200
Net inc bef ex items	657,500	1,093,500	722,100	801,200
Ex items & disc ops	NA	−282,600	NA	NA
Net income	657,500	810,900	722,100	801,200
Outstanding shares	320,922	325,141	329,647	165,122

SmithKline Beecham plc

Fiscal year ending	31-Dec-93	31-Dec-92	31-Dec-91	31-Dec-90
Net sales	6,164,000	5,219,000	4,685,000	4,764,000
Cost of goods	2,065,000	1,763,000	1,647,000	1,703,000
Gross profit	4,099,000	3,456,000	3,038,000	3,061,000
R & D expenditures	575,000	478,000	432,000	393,000
Sell gen & admin exp	2,344,000	1,905,000	1,549,000	1,701,000
Inc bef dep & amort	1,180,000	1,073,000	1,057,000	967,000
Non-operating inc	55,000	47,000	4,000	3,000
Interest expense	15,000	31,000	59,000	110,000
Income before tax	1,220,000	1,089,000	1,002,000	860,000
Prov for inc taxes	378,000	351,000	329,000	286,000
Minority int (inc)	14,000	11,000	11,000	9,000
Other income	−15,000	−16,000	−24,000	−21,000
Net inc bef ex items	813,000	711,000	638,000	544,000
Ex items & disc ops	NA	NA	NA	201,000
Net income	813,000	711,000	638,000	745,000
Outstanding shares	2,679,785	2,670,215	676,511	654,752

Upjohn Co.

Fiscal year ending	31-Dec-93	31-Dec-92	31-Dec-91	31-Dec-90
Net sales	3,611,180	3,548,570	3,320,249	3,032,746
Cost of goods	919,667	904,756	804,955	823,227
Gross profit	2,691,513	2,643,814	2,515,294	2,209,519
R & D expenditures	642,033	581,534	522,875	427,197
Sell gen & admin exp	1,409,149	1,389,734	1,301,400	1,120,261
Inc bef dep & amort	640,331	672,546	691,019	662,061
Non-operating inc	−118,413	55,414	44,490	24,443
Interest expense	31,496	31,253	19,956	30,954
Income before tax	490,422	696,707	715,553	655,550
Prov for inc taxes	89,001	153,300	178,700	193,400
Minority int (inc)	−1,062	−1,034	2,685	4,083
Net inc bef ex items	402,483	544,441	534,168	458,067
Ex items & disc ops	−10,086	−220,119	3,251	−2,386
Net income	392,397	324,322	537,419	455,681
Outstanding shares	173,432	174,581	175,215	183,927

Source: Annual reports.

expect Eli Lilly to sell its 40 percent interest in Dow Elanco, a joint venture with Dow Chemical, to finance the acquisition.

■ Pfizer

Although a smaller player, Pfizer has an interesting future. It has a relatively youthful family of pharmaceuticals and is committed to research.[19] It spends annually almost 13 percent of revenues on R&D, and a profitable stream of new products has resulted. Its product UK-92,480, a new drug for treating impotence, is only one of a dozen new drugs that the firm hopes to get approved in the next 10 years. The company, with sales of $7.5 billion (see Exhibit 11), is boosting its R&D budget from $1.1 billion in 1994 to $1.3 billion in 1995. Pfizer's chairman William Steere states that competitors are paying too much for their mergers, business will come to the producer with unique, useful products.

However, Pfizer has also tried to respond to the new competitive dynamics. It established an alliance with Value Health Inc., whose ValueRX unit is a leading PBM (see Exhibit 10). Pfizer has also formed a strategic alliance with the French company Rohne-Poulenc Rorer, Inc., as well as Caremark International Inc., a provider of home care, a prescription drug benefits service, and other health services. Of particular interest was Caremark's ownership of a prescription drug database, covering about 28 million people. The objective is to work with Caremark's database to develop strategies to provide cost-effective drug benefits to its customers.

■ Johnson & Johnson

Johnson & Johnson (J&J) is a huge consumer products firm. It operates 33 major lines of business, with 168 operating companies in 53 countries. It is the world's biggest health care products company (see Exhibit 11). "The company sells a lot more than baby oil. It makes artificial cornea lenses, multi-million-dollar blood testing machines, gallbladder removers, 50 types of prescription drugs, artery openers, brain surgery equipment, and hundreds of other products."[20] It is developing an osteoporosis drug to compete against AHP's Premarin and is investing $30 million to introduce its arthritis painkiller. A new J&J medicine may revolutionize the treatment of schizophrenia; it reduces the emotional withdrawal that afflicts many schizophrenics and has no side effects. Introduced in the United States in January 1994, it already has reached $100 million in sales, making it the fastest starting J&J drug ever.

J&J is a "consumer-marketing juggernaut, spending half a billion dollars a year on consumer advertising to promote products such as Tylenol, J&J Baby Powder, and Reach toothbrushes."[21] Its Monistat 7 and Imodium A-D brands have come from behind and are now first in their categories for yeast infections and diarrhea, respectively.

J&J is divided into three major segments: consumer, pharmaceutical, and professional. The professional sector sells mostly to doctors and hospitals. It receives a third of its revenues and half of its earnings from pharmaceuticals. Tylenol, its biggest consumer brand, has maintained its market share relative to generic products. In the highly competitive U.S. painkiller business, Tylenol is still the biggest selling brand by far, with more than $1 billion in sales. "Decades after Tylenol switched from prescription-only to over-the-counter, the company still has salesmen touting its virtues, such as minimal side effects, directly to doctors and hospitals."[22]

Johnson & Johnson has mastered the art of decentralized management. "They operate with deliberately redundant operations and amazingly independent management."[23] Research reflects this management style: "Rival Merck has 3,000 research scientists. . . . But because J&J's research is so decentralized, units are smaller and are forced to specialize in niche areas. And being a niche player has turned out to be the perfect thing to be for a drug company in the 1990s."[24]

■ SmithKline Beecham PLC

SmithKline (SK) manufactures several OTC products such as the oral care Oral-B line. It sells Tagamet, an ulcer drug that competes successfully with Glaxo's Zantac. Recently, it successfully introduced its antidepressant Paxil, which competes with Eli Lilly's Prozac.

SK purchased Diversified Pharmaceutical Services (DPS) for $2.3 billion from United Healthcare Corp. DPS is considered among the most aggressive marketers to managed care buyers, and is the third largest PBM, after Eli Lilly's PCS Health Systems and Merck's Medco Containment Services (see Exhibit 10). Furthermore, in late summer 1994 its bid for Eastman Kodak's OTC pharmaceutical unit, Sterling Winthrop, for $2.9 billion, made SK the world leader in OTC products. Sterling will add to SK's consumer health portfolio brands like Panadol, Bayer, Stridex, and the Phillip's line of laxatives. With the acquisition, SK will derive 30 percent of its sales from OTC products and 52 percent from prescription drugs.

■ Upjohn

Upjohn, with $3.6 billion in sales (see Exhibit 11), is expected to be acquired by a major firm within a year. The firm lost patent protection on four major products, which represented more than $1 billion in sales per year, during 1993. One of them alone, a tranquilizer called Xanax, represented more than 20 percent of Upjohn's pharmaceutical revenues. "Going off patent means a loss of 50% to 80% of market share to generic versions, sometimes within a year."[25] The company has new products in the pipeline. The newest, called Freedox, treats head and spinal column injuries and could sell for a healthy premium if approved. "Trouble is, the company missed the FDA's 1993 deadline to begin testing, a further delay for its potential debut, which is yet a few years away."[26] Nine other products and product extensions were expected to receive approval in 1994.

Financial analysts say Upjohn's shares are cheap now because expectations are low. The next couple of years will be very disappointing until large commercial opportunities materialize. As an analyst said, "We view Upjohn's current valuation as an excellent opportunity to accumulate longer term positions."[27] It has attractive assets and its distribution network in the United States is very attractive for foreign companies. It is possible that Upjohn is being considered for either a buyout or a merger by the German giant Bayer AG.

Glaxo Management: Looking to the Future

As Sir Richard anxiously awaited the outcome of the tender offer, he knew there were many questions that remained unanswered. Was the $15 billion tender offer, more than 25 times Wellcome's earnings, too much? Additionally, Glaxo's lack of experience in acquisitions could further complicate the situation. Assuming the price was fair, would the culture of the two R&D departments be integrated to become a productive leader in the pharmaceutical industry? There was also the issue of whether Glaxo's attempt at horizontal integration would prove to be a better strategic move than the vertical integration that was so common within the industry. Was purchasing Wellcome the best way to deal with the increased market power of the managed health care groups? All of these questions would ultimately decide the fate of not only Glaxo-Wellcome, but possibly the competitiveness of Great Britain's strength in the pharmaceutical industry.

Notes

1. Anita M. McGahan, Industry structure and competitive advantage, *Harvard Business Review,* November/December, 1994, 115-124.
2. Henry G. Grabowski and John M. Vernon, Brand loyalty, entry, and price competition in pharmaceuticals after the 1984 drug act, *The Journal of Law and Economics,* October, 1992, 115–124.
3. McGahan, Industry structure and competitive advantage.
4. Ibid.
5. Learning to live with formularies, *Drug Topics,* February 21, 1994.
6. *International Directory of Company Histories* (Chicago: St. James Press, 1991), Vol. 3, pp. 713–714.
7. Waging Sykological warfare, *The Economist,* January 28, 1995, 57–58.
8. Glaxo 1993 Annual Report.
9. McGahan, Industry structure and competitive advantage, 117.
10. J. Flynn, J. Weber, and S. Chandler, That burning sensation at Glaxo, *Business Week,* October 3, 1994, 76.
11. *International Directory of Company Histories.*
12. Nancy A. Nichols, Medicine, management and mergers: An interview with Merck's Roy Vagelos, *Harvard Business Review,* November/December, 1994, 105–114.
13. Ibid.
14. Ibid.
15. Ibid.
16. Ibid.
17. Elyse Tanouye and Greg Steinmetz, Growth initiative: Takeover would ease, not end, American Home Products' bind, *Wall Street Journal,* Aug. 5, 1994, A1.
18. Ibid.
19. Robert Stovall, Keep an eye on R&D, *Financial World,* October 11, 1994, 84.
20. Brian O'Reilley, J&J is on a roll, *Fortune,* December 26, 1994, 178–192.
21. Ibid.
22. Ibid.
23. Ibid.
24. Ibid.
25. Debra Sparks, Upjohn: Empty shelves, *Finance World,* April 12, 1994, 17.
26. Ibid.
27. Ibid.

■ CASE 16 Goodyear: The Gault Years

Bernard A. Deitzer
Alan G. Krigline
Thomas C. Peterson
The University of Akron

■ http://www.goodyear.com/

In June 1991, The Goodyear Tire and Rubber Company announced that its board of directors elected Stanley C. Gault, an outside member of the board since 1989, as chairman and chief executive officer to succeed Tom H. Barrett who retired after 38 years of service with Goodyear. The board of directors, in a statement released after the election meeting, commented:

> Goodyear is exceedingly fortunate that Stan Gault has agreed to lead the company for at least the next three years. In addition to being one of America's most able corporate managers, with an outstanding record of accomplishment at Rubbermaid, he brings to Goodyear the unique advantage of having both the perspective of an outsider as well as a thorough knowledge of the company's businesses gained from his service as Goodyear director.[1]

Acknowledging his election to Goodyear's prestigious top management positions, Gault responded:

> I am very pleased to be joining the team at Goodyear, which is the greatest name in the rubber industry. It has a superior brand franchise, high-quality products, state-of-the-art technology and manufacturing facilities, broad distribution, and very promising new products scheduled to be introduced later this year. Although the rubber business is experiencing industry-wide problems, I am confident that Goodyear shareholders can look forward to a bright future. As a strong believer in hands-on management and open communication between corporate managers and the investment community, I intend to keep our lenders and shareholders fully informed about the company's progress.[2]

■ Background

Goodyear Tire and Rubber Company, in the fall of 1986, under the leadership of then chairman of the board and chief executive officer, Robert Mercer, operated in a mature, concentrated, and highly competitive global market.

At the same time, Goodyear had incurred $3.7 billion in crippling long-term debt, a legacy of both the 1986 successful takeover defense against Anglo-French financier Sir James Goldsmith and of Celeron, a money-losing California–to–

Texas oil pipeline, that was the last vestige of Goodyear's mid-1980s attempt to diversify from rubber into defense and oil.[3] Until then, Goodyear was the world's largest and most profitable tire and rubber products business, selling original equipment tires to the automotive industry. The company was now positioned behind Michelin/Uniroyal Goodrich in the world tire market.

During the period from 1982–1986, Goodyear's principal business was the development, manufacture, distribution, and sale of tires for most applications. The company also manufactured and sold a broad array of rubber, plastic, and metal products for the transportation industry and various government, industrial, and consumer markets. Goodyear was a multiproduct, diversified conglomerate. Goldsmith, however, changed all that.

Pre-Goldsmith Grand Strategy

Goodyear's grand strategy was to maintain its position as the world's No. 1 tire manufacturer while reducing its dependency, roughly 80 percent, on the uncertain demand for original equipment tires and related products supplied to the cyclical new-car industry.

Goodyear planned to generate one-half of its sales volume from tires and rubber products, one-quarter from sales volume of its subsidiary Goodyear Aerospace, and another quarter from its Celeron oil and natural gas operations. Additionally, Goodyear planned for above-average rubber industry returns to stockholders, while reducing its dependence on the automotive industry.

Meanwhile, in 1985, Chairman Mercer emphatically enunciated Goodyear's approach to go "global." This meant a marketing and distribution approach involving a single strategy for the world, a global strategy, instead of tailoring products and distribution to individual national or regional markets.[4]

Two areas most affected by the Goldsmith takeover attempt were financial and structural. It included buying back 43 percent of its outstanding shares, while long-term debt was increased by $2.6 billion to 72 percent of total capitalization. In restructuring, Goodyear sold its oil and natural gas reserves for $685 million; it also sold the assets of two Arizona subsidiaries involved in agricultural products, real estate development, and a resort hotel for $220 million. It sold Goodyear Aerospace to Loral Defense Systems for $588 million and sold Motor Wheel Corporation in a leveraged buyout to its management. Goodyear also closed plants in Cumberland, Maryland, and Toronto, Canada. Other casualties of this change included reduced R&D spending, the loss of 6,786 jobs, and the placement of the ill-fated Celeron All American hot-oil pipeline up for sale, after its completion, for $1.3 billion.[5]

At this juncture in 1988, Goodyear was reorganized into two major divisions, tire and nontire products, each operating independently of the other. Formerly separated geographic business units were combined into global units. Goodyear's management was now flatter with fewer layers of middle management between top and bottom. The idea was to improve performance in overall corporate operations and services.

Goodyear's Business in 1995

Goodyear's business in 1995 was comprised of three major business segments: tires, general products, and oil transportation. The company also has the Kelly-Springfield Tire Company, a wholly owned subsidiary.

Tires

The tire segment develops, manufactures, distributes, markets, and sells tires and rubber supplies to both automotive, original equipment, and replacement markets. This segment had sales of $10.5 billion in 1994.

General Products

The general products division, which generated $1.7 billion in sales in 1994, is separated into two divisions: engineered products and chemical products.

The engineered products division makes vehicle components and industrial rubber products, such as belts, hose, pipe lining, tank treads and shoe products. The chemical products division supplies synthetic rubber and organic chemicals used in rubber and plastic processing to Goodyear itself, as well as other customers.[6]

Oil Transportation

The All-American Pipeline subsidiary segment was profitable for the first time in 1994. Goodyear's Celeron subsidiaries are engaged in the operation of the All-American Pipeline systems, a crude oil pipeline that extends from Gaviota, California, to McCamey, Texas, and related crude oil transportation and trading activities.

Service and Distribution

Goodyear also provides vehicle repairs and other services at its approximately 1,900 retail tire and service centers and other worldwide distribution centers. The company manufactures its products in 33 plants in the United States and 39 plants in 27 other countries. In addition, Goodyear operates two rubber plantations in Southeast Asia.[7]

Kelly-Springfield

The Kelly-Springfield subsidiary serves the replacement tire market by manufacturing and marketing radial passenger tires, radial and bias light truck tires, radial and bias medium truck tires, and radial and bias farm tires for both front and rear.

Headquartered in Cumberland, Maryland, the subsidiary operates with approximately 7,000 associates and has the capacity to produce 123,000 tires daily. Kelly-Springfield is generally considered to be the industry's largest producer of private-label tires for independent distributors and mass marketers. Strategically, Kelly brand, associate brand, and private-brand tires provide Goodyear with total market coverage at virtually all price points.[8]

The Goodyear Challenge

When asked the reason for undertaking the enormous challenge confronting him at Goodyear, Gault answered:

> Well, frankly, the decision was 98 percent emotional because Goodyear is the last American-owned tire company. All the other brands, with the exception of a much smaller Cooper, are now owned by foreign companies, and they will never return to this country.
>
> Therefore, I decided that I was willing to change my life for three years if there was any way I could lead the charge to rebuild Goodyear. It was mentioned to me more than once that I was a prime candidate for the Maalox moment.[9]

Gault While at Rubbermaid

Gault had retired in May 1991 as chairman and chief executive officer of Rubbermaid, Inc., of Wooster, Ohio, which he joined in 1980 after a 31-year career with General Electric. When Gault became CEO of Rubbermaid in 1980, Rubbermaid was a slow-growth consumer products business with rising overhead costs, declining productivity, and complacent personnel. Product development lagged, profit margins were depressed, and relations with retail customers flagging.

Gault wasted no time in restructuring Rubbermaid's operations and installing a new management team. As leader, he set the tone and pace, defined objectives and strategies, and demonstrated what he expected from both management and staff.

Gault strategically eliminated unprofitable lines of business and searched for complementary acquisitions. He engineered a strong focus on product quality, insisted on higher standards of job performance, revamped an in-place corporate culture, and reorganized Rubbermaid into nine decentralized units.

Under Gault's hands-on administration, Rubbermaid sales rose from $241 million in 1980 to $1.8 billion in 1992. During the same period, net income increased from $21 million to $163 million in 1991 and $184 million in 1992. Total corporate assets in 1980 were $255 million and $1.3 billion in 1992. In sum, Gault had transformed Rubbermaid from a parochial manufacturer of a limited line of mundane household utensils to a celebrated world-class marketer of more than 2,000 consumer-directed products.[10]

Gault's Initial Strategy at Goodyear

Shortly after accepting the greatest challenge of his already illustrious career, Gault communicated to both Goodyear associates and the business community his personal business philosophy, slated to underscore the company's operations in the 1990s. "A tremendous change was needed at Goodyear," Gault believed, "a cultural change involving everyone in the organization. When you're in this kind of jam, time is not on your side."[11]

Exhibit 1   Gault's Basic Business Concepts

- Do we have a mission? What statement or messages does my company portray to my potential customers and to my associates? What sets my company apart from my competition?

- What are the key environmental factors in the area in which we operate? Are we protecting the environmental conditions for the area in which we are located?

- What is the nature of our competition? Do we know our competitor's product line and policy strategy, their financial strengths and weaknesses?

- What are our long-term objectives? Do we have a business plan? Do we work this plan? Does my supplier interact with my long-term objectives with products, training, business systems, brand and retail advertising?

- Do we have strategies to accomplish our objectives? Has competition changed product lines and pricing strategies? Has our customer base shifted geographically or demographically? How are we going to reach new markets?

- What resources do we now have? What are needed for the future? What are future job requirements and how are we going to get them?

- And last, do we have a contingency plan? What might go wrong? What impact will it have on my business and how can we counteract it?

Source: Remarks by Stanley C. Gault in 4th Annual CEO Report, "Tire Review," December 1991.

"Furthermore, there is no quick fix or instant formula for success," remarked Gault. "It is a matter of returning to basic business concepts that in today's high technology-driven society often get forgotten."

"Included necessarily," said Gault, "are the company's operational plans, its overall essential objectives and supporting strategies, its critical resources and competition. All the factors taught in Business Management 101"[12] (Exhibit 1). "What we needed," Gault strongly insisted, "was a road map for our journey and then to explain that map to everyone of our 107,000 Goodyear associates throughout the world."[13]

These were the bedrock fundamentals Gault wanted to establish firmly at the onset. After accomplishing these fundamentals, Gault planned to review all company operations; reduce costs, identify corporate assets to sell in order to reduce debt; and, most of all, eventually create a world-class, market-driven, customer-oriented tire manufacturing operation—all while serving as the implacable strategist and consummate representative of Goodyear.

In addition, Gault serves on the boards of directors of Avon Products, International Paper Co., PPG Industries, Rubbermaid, Inc., the Timken Company, and the New York Stock Exchange. Gault is also chairman of the Board of Trustees of the College of Wooster, and has served on the Board of Trustees of the Ohio Foundation of Independent Colleges. He is a director and honorary vice chairman of the National Association of Manufacturers, having served as the 1986–87 chairman of the board.

He was appointed by President Reagan, and subsequently President Bush, to the Advisory Committee for Trade Policy and Negotiations. He is chairman of the Task Force on Industrial Subsidies. Gault also serves on the executive committee of the Board of Trustees of the National Invention Center.[14]

■ Gault's Principles

These are a simple set of business principles that I have honored throughout my career—essential elements that contributed to my prior and personal success. Some say I'm a zealot on these points.

They are low cost, high quality, and customer satisfaction. They are new product development, aggressive merchandising and new-customer and new-business development. Undeniably, they are the prudent management of assets entrusted to us; good communications and sound human relationships with all associates; and a commitment to a total quality culture which by itself will be the single-most important force for success in the 1990's and beyond.[15]

■ Gault's Twelve Objectives

After reviewing everything he could, and in as much detail as possible for 45 days, Gault developed 12 objectives to lead Goodyear out of its internal depression and onto the road to success. He termed them "How to Manage Goodyear Successfully in the 90s" (Exhibit 2). "Our objectives are extremely ambitious but are doable. We attacked debt reduction through asset sales and an equity offering, while achieving working capital reductions and capital expenditures below depreciation."[16]

■ Gault's Teachable Moments

Gault enjoys a compelling instinct for making the appropriate "teachable moment." His approaches are legendary. The day the new CEO moved into his spacious Goodyear office, he was handed a fistful of keys to the numerous beautifully paneled cabinets built into the walls. "I don't want these, I like things unlocked" Gault reacted. "But sir," came the reply, "a lot of people come in here at night for cleaning, you understand: union people." "I don't give a damn," said a seemingly irritated Gault. "This company should be run on the basis of trust."[17]

Exhibit 2   Gault's Twelve Objectives for the 1990s

1. Achieving significant debt reduction.
2. Increasing the company's financial performance.
3. Holding a quality leadership position.
4. Striving to be a low-cost producer.
5. Providing superior satisfaction in meeting customer expectations.
6. Increasing market share.
7. Introducing new exciting customer-oriented products.
8. Strengthening merchandising, advertising, and distribution programs.
9. Enhancing shareholder value.
10. Expanding the company's global presence.
11. Being a socially responsible corporation.
12. Maximizing the company's human resource capability.

Source: Stanley C. Gault remarks to Avon Products Financial Conference, New York, September 1994.

Gault describes his management style as very involved. He wants to know what is going on in every part of the company and is known to read every report that crosses his desk. Yet he is most concerned with what is going on in the marketplace. Gault regularly browses in stores on Saturdays, both Goodyear's and rivals as well—testing the tire market and talking with Goodyear managers and customers.

Gault is not only a blizzard of activity, but his presence seems to permeate Goodyear headquarters. A Goodyear associate for human resources observed that he never heard Gault give a direct order. "But we all know exactly what he expects of us."[18]

At Goodyear, he deliberately discontinued using the word "employee" and instituted the word "associate" company-wide because "that was a leveling action." An African-American employee, a mill worker with 35 years of service, questioned its application to him as well. Gault assured him that it did, absolutely, apply to him, as well as to Gault as chairman of the board and chief executive officer. In affirmation, Gault later visited the associate's workstation. With support from Goodyear's grapevine and electronic mail, the incident was around the world in 60 seconds.[19]

Goodyear's Partnerships

A strong segment of Gault's business philosophy is the premise that meaningful partnerships are the foundation for success. "Partnerships," Gault explained, "is what enables us to make continuous improvements. It is the willingness of people to look at something and say, 'If we meet each other halfway, we can work cooperatively together, we can improve everything together.' It is those partnerships between people, between companies, with customers and with suppliers, that create greater value for all concerned."[20]

Gault insisted his compensation be tied to the price of Goodyear's stock, an unprecedented arrangement at the firm. "If we can do the job together, as a team, and can show earnings growth, it makes sense for me to benefit in an equal fashion with other shareholders. My ship will rise or fall with the value of the stock and the performance of the company."[21]

Goodyear Restructured

Goodyear, under Gault, in early 1995 was a leaner and more profitable business. It had slashed costs and improved operating performance, boosted overall quality production, and reduced once-strangling debt in an attempt to best its international adversaries like Bridgestone/Firestone, Inc., Continental AG, and Michelin S.A.

Structurally, it had replaced a formal hierarchical and engineering-directed focus with more emphasis on innovative product development and broadened sales and marketing services in a globally oriented environment.

Goodyear trimmed its workforce from 108,000 in 1991 to 85,000 in 1995. It sold billions in noncore assets. Strategically preparing for the twenty-first century, the firm had expanded its presence in the world's growing tire market. In the process, Goodyear restructured the organization into eight strategic business

Exhibit 3

SBU Chart

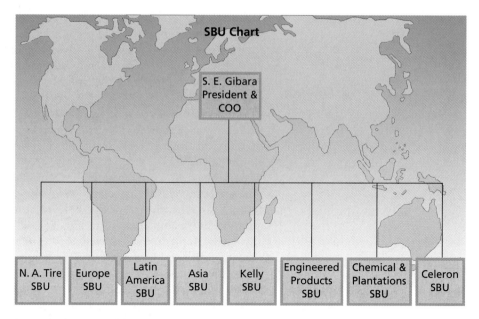

Source: Goodyear Tire and Rubber Co. 1994 *Annual Report.* p.4.

units (SBUs) (Exhibit 3). The SBUs, organized by product and market, are responsible for sales growth, profitability, and customer satisfaction. Objectives of the SBUs are firmly linked with Goodyear's corporate objectives.

Multifunctional teams comprising R&D, engineering, production, distribution, finance, human resources, and other functions cooperate to deliver the quality product or service.[22] Regional tire operations serve auto, truck, aircraft, farm specialty, and construction markets. The nontire business units provide rubber and plastic products for automotive and industrial markets and crude oil transportation services (Exhibit 4).

■ Goodyear's Debt Reduction Initiatives

In July 1991, shortly after accepting his greatest managerial challenge, Gault's initial strategy for Goodyear's reconstruction was to center on two major objectives: reducing corporate debt and cutting costs. Goodyear, according to Gault, would accomplish these by increasing revenues and by the expansion and enhancement of the firm's marketing, sales, merchandising, and advertising effort to gain a larger share of the market. It would, furthermore, seek to improve operations performance.

Oppressively, total debt in 1990 had reached $3.7 billion, and was costing the company $1 million daily in interest. Gault candidly outlined his options. "We have to go through and review every asset that we have and look at disposing of some, particularly those that do not relate directly to the tire business. We are a tire company. Nothing is sacred. We'll look at everything, research and development, capital expenditures, the company's 1200 retail stores, even the Goodyear Blimp"[23] (Exhibit 5).

"One of the things that's different here from my past experience, even at G.E., is the debt," recalled Gault. "At G.E., we were very thrifty people. And at

Exhibit 4

Serving Customers Worldwide

	Goodyear strategic business units are organized to meet customer requirements and global competition. Regional tire operations serve auto, truck, aircraft, farm, specialty and construction markets. The non-tire business units provide rubber and plastic products for automotive and industrial markets and crude oil transportation services.	
Strategic Business Unit	Products and Markets	Geographic Markets Served
North American Tire	Original equipment, replacement tires for autos, trucks, farm, aircraft, construction	United States, Canada, Export
Kelly-Springfield	Replacement tires for autos, trucks, tractors	United States, Canada, Export
Goodyear Europe	Original equipment, replacement tires for autos, trucks, farm, construction	Europe, Africa, Middle East, Export
Goodyear Latin America	Original equipment, replacement tires for autos, trucks, tractors	Central, South America, Export
Goodyear Asia	Original equipment, replacement tires for autos, trucks, farm, aircraft, construction	Southeast, Western Asia, North Pacific Rim, Export
Engineered Products	Auto belts, hose, body components, industrial products	Worldwide
Chemicals	Synthetic and natural rubber, chemicals for internal, external customers	Worldwide
Celeron	Crude oil transportation, related services	Operates only pipeline from U.S. West Coast to Texas
Goodyear Racing	Tires for all major motor racing series	Worldwide

Source: Goodyear Tire and Rubber Co. 1994 *Annual Report,* p.5.

Rubbermaid, we drove debt down to where it was 5% of total capitalization. So, I'm not used to spending more than a million dollars a day for interest, every day of the week, even on Saturdays, Sundays and holidays. That we cannot live with."[24]

Gault's Panache

While attacking corporate debt, Gault symbolically removed more than 25 light bulbs from wall scones, lamps, and chandeliers in his suite, leaving him to work in a comfortable, clublike dimness that he calculates, by way of his GE experience, saves Goodyear $230 a year. After that, lights were turned out in halls and offices all over the company.[25] Gault created quite a stir around Akron when he suggested using low-cost overhead transparencies instead of high-cost slides. That idea saved $1,500 per meeting with no loss in the information presented.[26]

"Associates in one department carefully looked at their lighting needs and learned they could save $5,000 a year by turning off unnecessary fixtures,"

Exhibit 5   Goodyear's Debt Reduction Initiatives

1991	Sold 12 million shares common stock at $50 per share. Gault, in fourth quarter, made 39 personal presentations in 13 days in 13 cities in Europe and the States.
1991	Scottsboro, Alabama, tire cord textile plant sold in fourth quarter to Akzo N.V. for $95.0 million.
1991	Goodyear's New York apartment sold.
1991	Goodyear's corporate aircraft sold.
1991	Houston blimp base closed and for sale.
1991	Corporate limousines replaced with inexpensive models.
1992	Madison, Kentucky, specialty tire plant sold in third quarter.
1992	Closed Celeron Corporation's subsidiary office in Texas.
1992	Closed European headquarters and relocated its top executives to Akron as part of reshuffling European operations. Laid off 100 associates.
1992	Blown and cast film business assets sold to Huntsman Holdings Corporation for $105.5 million.
1992	Sold the industrial and commercial films business in second quarter for a gain of $9.1 million.
1992	Sold polyester resin business assets in fourth quarter to Shell Oil Company for $308.4 million. Consisted of a plant in West Virginia and a technical center in Akron, Ohio. Approximately 700 production, marketing, and administrative associates were employed.
1993	Sale pending on Reneer Films subsidiary in first quarter.
1993	Sold rubber roofing business in first quarter.
1993	Air Trends subsidiary sold. Aircraft Wheel and Brake closed its Kingston, Ontario, facility in second quarter for a $3.1 million reduction.
1993	Lowered debt to $1.4 billion from $1.9 billion in 1992 and $3.7 billion in 1990.
1994	Employment continued downward to approximately 89,000 associates from 91,000 in 1993 and 108,000 in 1991.

Source: Adapted from Goodyear Tire and Rubber Company, Akron, Ohio, Annual Reports and Corporate Documents, 1991–1994.

---

allowed Gault. "If each associate saves just one dollar a day in the way he or she performs their work, we will save more than $25 million a year. I'll get the debt down in every way I can." To reduce operating expenses, Gault is known to bring along stationery and postage stamps to his office for personal use.[27]

Goodyear Sells Stock to Reduce Debt

In October 1991, Goodyear announced plans to sell 10 million shares of common stock to raise an estimated $400 million to retire a portion of its burdensome debt load of $3.6 billion. Analysts pointed out that Goodyear is reselling 20 percent of the stock it bought back in early 1987 after financier Sir James Goldsmith agreed not to take over the company. Goodyear then paid $50 a share in the buyback of 50 million shares.[28]

Gault's Performance Record

In Gault's first year of leadership, there was a positive savings of nearly $135 million between 1991 earnings and a loss in 1990. Earnings were $96.6 million, which included a $43.2 million gain from a divested asset sale, compared with a loss of $38.3 million in 1990. Debt was reduced by approximately $1 billion with the sale of nontire-related businesses. Goodyear's Scottsboro, Alabama, textile facility was the first divested.

In a slack economy, 1991 Goodyear sales were $10.9 billion, slightly below its prior-year sales record of $11.3 billion. Earnings per share for 1991 were $1.61 compared with a loss of $0.66 during 1990. Operating margin was 7.2 percent in 1991, compared to 5.4 percent. The debt-to-debt-plus-equity dropped significantly to 49.2 percent at year-end from 63.3 percent in 1990.

Improved results reflected the benefits of personnel reductions, cost-reduction programs, productivity improvement, price increases, and lower material costs.[29]

■ Turnaround Year

For 1992, Gault again planned to improve operating margins, reduce debt, and interest expense, and control capital spending. Under Gault, the firm led the tire industry in all-time quarterly sales records and exceeded its 6 percent growth objective. Operating income increased by $327 million, compared with 1991. Debt, concurrently, was reduced by $697 million to below $2 billion, originally a 1994 forecasted objective. Sales in 1992 reached $11.8 billion, the highest in Goodyear's 94-year history. Consolidated debt dropped to $1.9 billion against $2.6 billion in 1991.

The operating margin was 9.4 percent in 1992, compared with 7.2 percent the previous year. Goodyear's annual stock dividend was increased to $1.00 per share from $0.40 in order to share the company's improved financial performance. Goodyear's stock appreciably outperformed Standard & Poor's 500 Index during 1992; as its capitalized market value approached $5 billion, compared with $3.8 billion in 1991 and $1.1 billion in 1990.

Consistent with its debt-reduction plans, Goodyear continued to sell operations not directly related to the tire business. Sold were an interest in a chemical facility in Brazil, the industrial and commercial films unit, and the polyester operation. These asset sales, coupled with improved operating performance, enabled the firm to reduce debt by $697 million during 1992 and slash interest payments by $85 million over the period.[30]

■ Goodyear's 1993 Financial Performance

A resuscitated Goodyear in 1993 outpaced the industry as it recorded a third consecutive year of improved financial performance. The company validated its commitments to greater profitability, debt reduction, industry leadership, growth, customer needs, and greater performance.

Record sales of $11.6 billion were achieved compared with 1992's $11.4 billion, which excluded the sales from divested assets. Earnings in 1993 surpassed those of all other major global tiremakers. Combined income before extraordinary charges increased to $488.7 million, or $3.33 per share in 1993, including a $0.10 per share nonrecurring gain on the sale of assets, compared with 1992 income before extraordinary charges of $367.3 million or $2.57 per share.

Goodyear's common stock in 1993 again outperformed the Standard & Poor's 500 Index, while its market value grew almost 40 percent, and nearly seven times since year-end 1992. A two-for-one stock split doubled the number of authorized shares to 300 million. There was a 20 percent dividend increase, raising the quarterly dividend to $0.15 a share on the split shares.

Continuing its commitment to debt reduction, Goodyear lowered debt to $1.4 billion from $1.9 billion in 1992, and $3.6 billion three years ago. Major debt rating agencies correspondingly upgraded the firm's long- and short-term debt ratings to investment grade. Debt reduction in 1993 resulted from improved operating performance, divestment of certain noncore businesses, and the redemption of Euro convertible debentures, $117 million of which was converted into common stock. Debt to debt-plus-equity ratio reduction to nearly 38 percent, coupled with lower interest rates, lowered 1993 interest expense by almost one-third, compared to 1992.

The All-American Pipeline subsidiary entered into long-term crude oil transportation agreements with several major offshore California oil producers. These agreements are scheduled to produce significant cash flow beginning in 1996.

As a percent of sales, Goodyear's cost of goods sold declined 3.3 points during the past three years, through higher capacity utilization and lower material costs. Sales, administrative and general (SAG) expenses as a percent of sales declined one percentage point on growing sales. Goodyear's employment levels continued downward to 92,000 associates from 108,000 in 1990, while output per person-hour improved.[31]

Performance Plan Plus Objectives

During 1994, Gault initiated ambitious plans to strengthen Goodyear's strategic focus on growth consistent with earnings improvement. The Performance Plan Plus objectives (Exhibit 6) were to encourage greater geographic and business diversification, establish higher expectations for business unit revenue, and provide additional capital and technology to support aggressive growth plans.

Significant earnings improvement in 1994 derived from Goodyear's greater commitment to geographic diversity through global expansion. International operations accounted for a significant increase in revenues, unit sales of tires and rubber products, and segment operating income.

Exhibit 6   Gault's Performance Plan Plus (PPP)

1. We will increase sales between 4.5 and 5 percent per year . . . twice the projected industry growth rate.

2. Our operating margin at the segment level will reach 12 percent . . . never before accomplished. We were at 10 percent in '93 . . . but at 6 percent in 1990.

3. Capital expenditures will range between $500 and $700 million annually . . . a significant increase.

4. We will lower our sales, administrative and general expenses to below 14 percent of sales . . . we were over 18 percent earlier.

5. Our debt to debt-plus-equity ratio will decline to 25 to 30 percent . . . down from 63 percent in 1991.

6. Our dividend policy guideline will be to ask our board to pay out 20 to 25 percent of prior-year earnings.

Source: Goodyear Tire and Rubber Company, Corporate Document.

Since the second quarter of 1991, Goodyear achieved 15 consecutive quarter-to-quarter improvements in net income. Income from continuing operations in 1994 reached an all-time high of $567 million, a 16 percent increase over 1993.[32]

Goodyear's 1994 Achievements

At Goodyear's annual stockholder's meeting, Gault recalled that "the year 1994 was truly remarkable as we recorded significant progress in our quest to be the best tire and rubber products company in the world."[33]

"For the fourth consecutive year," he proudly announced, "we achieved improved financial performance and in the process, broke every performance record in the Goodyear history book."[34] (See Exhibits 7 through 10 for a summary of Goodyear financial progress from 1992 to 1994.) The 1994 results:

- Sales of $12.3 billion were the highest in Goodyear history.
- Income of $567 million from continuing operations was at an all-time high, surpassing 1993 by 16 percent.
- Every geographic region reported record tire unit sales.
- Tire segment sales for the first time exceeded $10 billion.
- Rating agencies raised Goodyear's rating for commercial paper and senior debt.
- A new four-year financial plan—entitled "Performance Plan Plus"—was launched.
- Interest expense was the lowest since 1986.
- Debt declined to the lowest level in a decade.
- Celeron became the turnaround story of the year.
- Successful negotiation of U.S. labor agreements.
- Celebrated the 300th victory on the Formula One Grand Prix circuit; 300 consecutive victories in Indy Car racing.[35]

At the meeting, an exuberant Gault hailed Goodyear's achievements for 1994, during which Goodyear made significant progress in its quest to be the best tire and rubber products company in the world.

Goodyear's Marketing Mission

Many American businesses are struggling to survive because of the failure to focus effectively on their marketing and sales objectives.

The science of sales and marketing is an American creation served by the free enterprise system and we cannot allow it to become stagnated by reluctance to adjust to a changing environment of more demanding and more resistant consumers.[36]

Gault envisioned Goodyear's marketing mission to be a three-pronged challenge. First, to do the complete marketing job by applying proven tenets of good marketing better and sooner than smart aggressive competitors. Second, to serve as a catalyst for change—to motivate and encourage the entire organization to

Exhibit 7 Consolidated Balance Sheet ($ in millions)		
December 31,	**1994**	**1993**
Assets		
Current Assets:		
Cash and cash equivalents	$ 250.9	$ 188.5
Short term securities	15.4	39.2
Accounts and notes receivable (Note 3)	1,524.7	1,314.2
Inventories (Note 4)	1,425.1	1,349.8
Prepaid expenses	406.6	371.1
Total Current Assets	3,622.7	3,262.8
Other Assets:		
Investments in affiliates, at equity	133.4	107.2
Long-term accounts and notes receivable	208.5	173.6
Deferred charges and other miscellaneous assets	775.9	604.6
	1,117.8	885.4
Properties and Plants (Note 5)	4,382.8	4,287.9
Total Assets	$9,123.3	$8,436.1
Liabilities and Shareholders' Equity		
Current Liabilities:		
Accounts payable—trade	$1,013.9	$ 870.0
Compensation and benefits	745.2	657.1
Other current liabilities	259.8	269.6
United States and foreign taxes	326.2	373.1
Notes payable to banks and overdrafts	213.0	313.1
Long term debt due within one year	13.9	41.0
Total Current Liabilities	2,572.0	2,523.9
Long Term Debt and Capital Leases (Note 6B)	1,108.7	1,065.9
Compensation and Benefits	2,173.4	2,101.0
Other Long Term Liabilities	322.1	321.8
Minority Equity in Subsidiaries	143.9	122.7
Shareholders' Equity:		
Preferred stock, no par value:		
Authorized, 50,000,000 shares, unissued	—	—
Common stock, no par value:		
Authorized, 300,000,000 shares		
Outstanding shares, 151,407,285 (150,515,374 in 1993)	151.4	150.5
Capital surplus	918.5	878.0
Retained earnings	2,194.5	1,740.9
	3,264.4	2,769.4
Foreign currency translation adjustment	(421.7)	(422.4)
Minimum pension liability adjustment (Note 11)	(39.5)	(46.2)
Total Shareholders' Equity	2,803.2	2,300.8
Total Liabilities and Shareholders' Equity	$9,123.3	$8,436.1

Source: Goodyear Tire and Rubber Company, Akron, Ohio, *Annual Report*, 1994, p. 25.

Exhibit 8	Consolidated Statement of Income ($ in millions, except per share)		
Year Ended December 31,	1994	1993	1992
Net Sales	$12,288.2	$11,643.4	$11,784.9
Cost of Goods Sold	9,271.4	8,713.0	8,971.8
Selling, Administrative and General Expense	1,958.2	1,922.1	1,997.3
Interest Expense (Note 14)	129.4	162.4	232.9
Other (Income) and Expense (Note 2)	(37.9)	(79.1)	(147.3)
Foreign Currency Exchange	77.6	113.1	77.1
Minority Interest in Net Income of Subsidiaries	23.8	27.0	23.2
Income before Income Taxes, Extraordinary Items and Cumulative Effect of Accounting Changes	865.7	784.9	629.9
United States and Foreign Taxes on Income (Note 15)	298.7	296.2	262.6
Income before Extraordinary Items and Cumulative Effect of Accounting Changes	567.0	488.7	367.3
Extraordinary Item—Early Extinguishment of Debt (net of tax $6.1 in 1993, $6.4 in 1992)	—	(14.6)	(15.3)
Cumulative Effect of Change in Accounting for Postemployment Benefits (net of tax of $55.2) (Note 13)	—	(86.3)	—
Transition Effect of Change in Accounting for Non-Pension Postretirement Benefits (net of tax of $617.0) (Note 13)	—	—	(1,065.7)
Cumulative Effect of Change in Accounting for Income Taxes (Note 15)	—	—	55.1
Net Income (loss)	$567.0	$387.8	$(658.6)
Per Share of Common Stock:*			
Income before Extraordinary Items and Cumulative Effect of Accounting Changes	$3.75	$3.33	$2.57
Extraordinary Item—Early Extinguishment of Debt	—	(.10)	(.11)
Cumulative Effect of Change in Accounting for Postemployment Benefits	—	(.59)	—
Transition Effect of Change in Accounting for Non-Pension Postretirement Benefits	—	—	(7.46)
Cumulative Effect of Change in Accounting for Income Taxes	—	—	.39
Net Income (loss)	$3.75	$2.64	$(4.61)
Average Shares Outstanding*	151,203,885	147,086,828	142,808,424

*1992 has been restated to reflect the two-for-one stock split in May 1993.

Source: Goodyear Tire and Rubber Company, Akron, Ohio, *Annual Report*, 1994, p. 24.

support their marketing plans by serving the customer in a truly market-driven manner. Third, to be involved in the external activities that affect marketing's ability to perform, to assume a greater role in influencing economic, social, and political policies affecting those businesses, and to study and understand issues and then to participate in their resolution.[37]

Exhibit 9   Consolidated Statement of Shareholder's Equity ($ in millions, except per share)

	Common Stock Shares	Common Stock Amount	Capital Surplus	Retained Earnings	Foreign Currency Translation Adjustment	Minimum Pension Liability Adjustment	Total Shareholders' Equity
Balance at December 31, 1991							
after deducting 52,328,368 treasury shares	70,663,515	$ 70.7	$639.1	$2,208.5	$(187.2)	$ —	$2,731.1
Net loss for 1992				(658.6)			(658.6)
Cash dividends 1992—$.275 per share				(39.3)			(39.3)
Common stock issued (including 1,580,945 treasury shares):							
Dividend Reinvestment and Stock Purchase Plan	45,281		3.1				3.1
Stock compensation plans	1,535,665	1.5	46.3				47.8
Foreign currency translation adjustment					(153.8)		(153.8)
Balance at December 31, 1992							
after deducting 50,747,423 treasury shares	72,244,461	72.2	688.5	1,510.6	(341.0)	—	1,930.3
Net income for 1993				387.8			387.8
Cash dividends 1993—$.575 per share				(84.9)			(84.9)
Stock dividend 1993	72,689,064	72.6		(72.6)			—
Common stock issued (including 5,584,285 treasury shares):							
Dividend Reinvestment and Stock Purchase Plan	66,589	.1	3.0				3.1
Stock compensation plans	2,605,544	2.7	74.8				77.5
Conversion of debentures	2,909,716	2.9	111.7				114.6
Foreign currency translation adjustment					(81.4)		(81.4)
Minimum pension liability adjustment						(46.2)	(46.2)
Balance at December 31, 1993							
after deducting 45,163,138 treasury shares	150,515,374	150.5	878.0	1,740.9	(422.4)	(46.2)	2,300.8
Net income for 1994				567.0			567.0
Cash dividends 1994—$.75 per share				(113.4)			(113.4)
Common stock issued (including 891,911 treasury shares):							
Dividend Reinvestment and Stock Purchase Plan	96,691	.1	3.5				3.6
Stock compensation plans	795,220	.8	37.0				37.8
Foreign currency translation adjustment					.7		.7
Minimum pension liability adjustment						6.7	6.7
Balance at December 31, 1994							
after deducting 44,271,227 treasury shares	151,407,285	$151.4	$918.5	$2,194.5	$(421.7)	$(39.5)	$2,803.2

Cash dividends per share for 1992 have been restated to reflect the two-for-one stock split in May 1993.

Source: Goodyear Tire and Rubber Company, Akron, Ohio, *Annual Report*, 1994, p. 26.

Exhibit 10   Consolidated Statement of Cash Flows ($ in millions)

Year Ended December 31,	1994	1993	1992
Cash Flows from Operating Activities:			
Net Income (loss)	$567.0	$387.8	$(658.6)
Adjustments to reconcile net income (loss) to net cash provided by operating activities:			
Depreciation	410.3	392.9	445.8
Deferred tax provision	99.8	(36.3)	(36.0)
Accounts and notes receivable	(192.4)	(10.9)	(219.6)
Inventories	(63.9)	(100.2)	(71.9)
Accounts payable—trade	139.7	(48.1)	124.2
Domestic pension funding	(238.8)	(82.2)	(172.7)
Other assets and liabilities	42.9	117.8	162.1
Accounting changes	—	86.3	1,065.7
Asset sales	—	(24.7)	(164.2)
Workforce reductions and other non-cash charges	—	—	120.3
Early extinguishment of debt	—	20.7	21.7
Total adjustments	197.6	315.3	1,275.4
Net cash provided by operating activities	764.6	703.1	616.8
Cash Flows from Investing Activities:			
Capital expenditures	(523.0)	(432.3)	(366.6)
Asset dispositions	19.0	83.6	425.3
Short term securities acquired	(287.1)	(157.5)	(121.1)
Short term securities redeemed	310.6	214.2	95.8
Other transactions	(15.7)	9.8	10.5
Net cash (used in) provided by investing activities	(496.2)	(282.2)	43.9
Cash Flows from Financing Activities:			
Proceeds from sale of foreign currency exchange agreements	—	4.1	44.5
Short term debt incurred	385.6	324.8	442.8
Short term debt paid	(395.7)	(487.6)	(325.6)
Long term debt incurred	52.9	2.7	124.4
Long term debt and capital leases paid	(166.4)	(385.8)	(909.3)
Common stock issued	41.4	195.2	50.9
Dividends paid	(113.4)	(84.9)	(39.3)
Net cash used in financing activities	(195.6)	(431.5)	(611.6)
Effect of Exchange Rate Changes on Cash and Cash Equivalents	(10.4)	(8.4)	(5.0)
Net Increase (Decrease) in Cash and Cash Equivalents	62.4	(19.0)	44.1
Cash and Cash Equivalents at Beginning of the Period	188.5	207.5	163.4
Cash and Cash Equivalents at End of the Period	$250.9	$188.5	$207.5

Source: Goodyear Tire and Rubber Company, Akron, Ohio, *Annual Report,* 1994, p. 27.

Distribution's New Kid on the Block

In Gault's opinion, "the retail tire marketer is in the midst of great change. The way tires were sold yesterday isn't necessarily the way we'll be selling tomorrow."

"For example," he continued, "there's a totally new kid on the block—the warehouse clubs. Just 10 years ago, this channel of distribution for tires didn't even exist. Today, 6 percent of all replacement tires are sold in those outlets. And, this trend is only starting. Moreover, tires sold through service stations, department stores, and even tire dealerships, are continuing to lose market share."[38]

"The customer," conceded Gault, "wanted convenience in buying; quick service, low prices, a large selection from which to choose, and in the case of Sears, to use a specific credit card."[39]

Goodyear's New Distribution Strategy

Attempting to regain market share, Gault's first steps were to centralize Goodyear's sales organization, narrow its existing structure, and to increase local and national advertising (Exhibit 11). Alone among U.S. tire manufacturers, Goodyear's channels of tire distribution originally were to original equipment (OE) manufacturers or to affiliated dealerships, whether franchised or company owned.

However, in spring of 1992, Goodyear in a strategic marketing move to reclaim a share of the U.S. replacement car-tire market, announced it would sell Goodyear brand tire lines through Sears Roebuck & Co., Kmart, Wal-Mart, and others like Big O. Goodyear hoped to sell up to 2.5 million additional tires each year through Canadian Tire and Discount Tire, and the new distribution channels. Market share had fallen from about 15 to 12 percent since 1987. A major reason for the loss of market share was that Goodyear was not stocking tires that customers would buy. As Gault saw it "we're not serving the market with what the customers wanted, but what the manufacturing plant wanted to build."[40] Increasingly, it appears, consumers were buying tires at multibrand discount outlets, as well as warehouses (Exhibit 12).

Sensing potential hostility of Goodyear dealers, Chairman Gault addressed the company's 600 franchises and 4,000 independent dealers at their Las Vegas convention. "Goodyear dealers," he guaranteed, "can only lose if we don't generate more funds to support you. Actually, you should be critical of us if we don't take action to expand our business so we can provide the necessary support to our dealer structure."[41]

Exhibit 11 Goodyear's Advertising Expenditures ($ in millions)			
	1992	1993	1994
1. Sales	$11784.9	$11643.4	$12288.2
2. Advertising costs	$266.5	$248.2	$248.2
3. Advertising costs as a percent of sales	2.26%	2.13%	2.02%

Source: Goodyear Tire and Rubber Company, Akron, Ohio, *Annual Reports*, 1992–1994.

Exhibit 12   Estimated Share of the Domestic Passenger Tire Retail Market (based on retail sales)

	1994 (%)	1993 (%)	1992 (%)	1991 (%)	1990 (%)	1985 (%)
Tire dealerships*	54.0	54.0	54.0	54.0	54.0	55.0
Chain/department stores	19.0	19.0	19.0	19.0	18.0	19.0
Tire company stores	11.5	12.0	12.0	12.0	13.0	10.0
Warehouse clubs†	8.5	8.0	8.0	7.0	6.0	2.0
Service stations	5.0	5.0	5.0	6.0	7.0	9.0
Auto dealerships	1.0	1.0	1.0	1.0	1.0	2.0
Miscellaneous outlets	1.0	1.0	1.0	1.0	1.0	3.0

*Large dealers defined as independent dealers with 30 or more retail outlets, make up 29% of this total, or 15.5% of the entire replacement passenger tire market.

†Warehouse clubs have increased their U.S. unit total by 80% in the last five years.

Distribution Channels—How Passenger Tires Reach the Domestic Retail Supplier

	1994 (%)	1993 (%)	1992 (%)	1991 (%)	1990 (%)	1985 (%)
Independent dealers	66.0	66.0	66.0	67.0	67.0	68.0
Chain, department, and discount stores, clubs, miscellaneous	20.0	20.0	20.0	19.0	18.0	17.0
Tire company stores	12.0	12.0	12.0	12.0	13.0	12.0
Oil companies	2.0	2.0	2.0	2.0	2.0	3.0

Of an estimated 169.5 million replacement passenger tires handled directly in 1994 (both retail and wholesale, but counted only once):

- Independent dealers accounted for 111.9 million units.
- Chain and department stores and warehouse clubs handled 33.9 million units.
- Tire manufacturer-owned stores handled 20.3 million units.
- Oil companies supplied their dealers with 3.4 million units.

Source: *Modern Tire Dealer Facts Issue*, 29th ed. (Akron, OH: Bill Communication, January 1995).

Gault's Success Formula

Goodyear's chief strategist was committed to create value for shareholders by generating consistent earnings growth and delivering high value-added products to the customer. "It's no secret," Gault declared, "success comes from the development of market-driven products combined with brand name associated with high quality and offered at true value price."[42]

With a bit of chutzpah, as he did while at Rubbermaid, Gault shops competitive stores and asks people why they bought competitive products or why, in this case, they didn't buy Goodyear tires. "Selling isn't just the role of sales and marketing people. Communicating the benefits of our product is everybody's job in a company."[43] At a recent plastic industry convention, he asked the audience to please check their tires. If they didn't have Goodyear, then please get a set. He didn't want them driving around on inferior, competitive products.[44]

Goodyear's Blimps

For over 25 years Goodyear's blimps, synonymous with Goodyear itself, have been deployed nationwide for the purpose of community relations, providing broadcast quality pictures. Central to the firm's worldwide promotional efforts, the omnipresent blimps, Spirit of Akron, based in Akron, Ohio; the Eagle, based in Los Angeles, California; and the Stars and Stripes, based in Pompano Beach, Florida, not only advertise Goodyear tires but have emerged as aerial participants in dramatic events that overwhelm their commercial mission.

The blimps have provided more than 2,000 telecasts, including 15 Superbowls, 15 World Series, the 100th Anniversary of the Statue of Liberty, and broadcasts for the *Today Show* and *Good Morning America*. The blimp was invited to the farewell salute to *Cheers* in California. The popular TV program was charging $650,000 for 30 seconds on the show. It had 91 million viewers. Goodyear had its most enduring corporate image name recognized for free.

They were witness to the October 1989 earthquakes during the Candlestick Park World Series. And the Stars and Stripes was a familiar image in the skies over South Florida in the aftermath of Hurricane Andrew, flashing vital messages in Creole, Spanish, and English. Surprisingly, Goodyear does not charge for blimp coverage. It is free in return for any free advertising the sight of the blimp might generate.

While the existence of the blimp was threatened because of the hostile takeover attempt by Goldsmith, it was Stanley Gault who envisioned the importance of the blimp. He changed its colors to blue, silver, and gold and originated the idea of putting "#1 in TIRES" on its sides.[45]

Goodyear's Marketing Performance

Apparently, Gault's marketing strategies were paying off. In 1994, Goodyear held first position in the estimated U.S. replacement passenger tire brand shares (Exhibit 13) and first in the estimated 1994 U.S. replacement light truck brand shares[46] (Exhibit 14).

Goodyear, in 1994, consistently ranked high in achieving its brand share of the U.S./Canadian OE passenger and light truck vehicle market (Exhibit 15), and Goodyear regularly held first place in the U.S./Canadian OE passenger and light truck tire market share from 1990–1994[47] (Exhibit 16).

Goodyear in 1994 was third among the world leaders in new tire sales (Exhibit 17). Evidently the company suffered a 26.5 percent drop in its stock price from year-end 1993 to year-end 1994 from $45.75 to $33.62, a result of lower sales. Bridgestone, Michelin, and Pirelli, meanwhile, experienced increases in their stock prices while Continental suffered a decrease.[48] Goodyear, however, in 1994 held the first position among the U.S./Canadian leaders in new tire sales[49] (Exhibit 18).

Exhibit 13   Estimated 1994 U.S. Replacement Passenger Tire Brand Shares (based on 169.9 million shipments)

Brand	%	Brand	%
Goodyear	16.0	Patriot	1.5
Michelin	8.0	Summit	1.5
Firestone	7.5	Yokohama	1.5
General	4.5	Delta	1.0
BFGoodrich	4.0	Laramie	1.0
Cooper	4.0	Lee	1.0
Kelly	4.0	Monarch	1.0
Sears	4.0	Montgomery Ward	1.0
Bridgestone	3.5	National	1.0
Multi-Mile	3.0	Regul	1.0
Uniroyal	2.5	Remington	1.0
Cordovan	2.0	Sigma	1.0
Dayton	2.0	Spartan	1.0
Dunlop	2.0	Star	1.0
Pirelli	2.0	Stratton	1.0
Sentry	2.0	Toyo	1.0
Falls Mastercraft	1.5	Others	9.5
Hercules	1.5		

Source: *Modern Tire Dealer Facts Issue*, 29th ed. (Akron, OH: Bill Communications, January 1995).

Exhibit 14   Estimated 1994 U.S. Replacement Light Truck Tires Brand Shares* (based on 25 million shipments)

Brand	%	Brand	%
Goodyear	13.0	Falls Mastercraft	2.5
BFGoodrich	8.5	Lee	2.5
Michelin	7.0	Sears	2.5
Firestone	6.5	Remington	2.0
Cooper	5.5	Road Tamer	2.0
Kelly	5.5	Toyo	2.0
General	5.0	Summit	1.5
Multi-Mile	5.0	Hankook	1.0
Bridgestone	4.0	Kumho	1.0
Armstrong	3.0	Monarch	1.0
Cordovan	3.0	Sigma	1.0
Dunlop	3.0	Star	1.0
Uniroyal	3.0	Yokohama	1.0
Dayton	2.5	Others	5.0

*Because numbers are rounded to the nearest one-half percent, total may exceed 100%. Brands must have at least 1% of market in shipment numbers to be listed at 1%.

Source: *Modern Tire Dealer Facts Issue*, 29th ed. (Akron, OH: Bill Communications, January 1995).

Exhibit 15   Estimated 1994 brand shares (U.S./Canada passenger/LT vehicles)*

Chrysler	%	Mazda	%
Goodyear	85.0	Firestone	40.0
Michelin	15.0	Bridgestone	27.0
		Goodyear	20.0
Ford		Dunlop	10.0
Firestone	36.5	Michelin	3.0
Goodyear	25.0		
Michelin	25.0	Nissan	
General	11.5	Goodyear	26.0
Uniroyal	2.0	Firestone	22.0
		Michelin	22.0
General Motors		General	15.0
Goodyear	33.0	Dunlop	9.0
Uniroyal	26.0	Uniroyal	6.0
Michelin	16.0		
General	15.0	Nummi	
BFGoodrich	6.0	Goodyear	41.0
Firestone	4.0	Firestone	30.0
		Dunlop	15.0
BMW		Bridgestone	14.0
Michelin	100.0		
		Saturn	
CAMI		Firestone	100
Goodyear	84.0		
Uniroyal	16.0	Subaru	
		Bridgestone	80.0
Diamond Star		Goodyear	20.0
(Chrysler-Mitsubishi)			
Goodyear	71.0	Toyota	
Bridgestone	29.0	Dunlop	330.0
		Goodyear	22.0
Honda		Firestone	17.0
Michelin	44.0	Bridgestone	14.0
Goodyear	30.0	Michelin	11.0
Dunlap	15.0	Yokohama	2.0
Bridgestone	11.0	General	1.0
Isuzu		Volvo	
BFGoodrich	75.0	Goodyear	80.0
Uniroyal	15.0	Michelin	20.0
Goodyear	10.0		

*Excluding imports.

Source: *Modern Tire Dealer Facts Issue*, 29th ed., (Akron, OH: Bill Communications, January 1995).

Exhibit 16	U.S./Canadian OE Passenger/LT Tire Market Share (excluding Imports)			
	1994 (%)	**1993** (%)	**1992** (%)	**1990** (%)
Goodyear	40.0	40.0	38.0	36.5
Michelin	18.0	18.0	17.0	15.7
Firestone	15.7	15.4	15.0	17.0
General	9.7	10.0	10.3	12.0
Uniroyal	9.5			
		12.0*	14.0*	17.0*
BFGoodrich	2.0			
Dunlop	2.5	2.5	2.5	1.5
Bridgestone	2.5	2.0	3.0	.3
Yokohama	.1	.1	.2	—

*The Uniroyal and BFGoodrich brands were calculated as one before 1994.

Source: *Modern Tire Dealer Facts Issue*, 29th ed. (Akron, OH: Bill Communications, January 1995).

Exhibit 17	World Leaders in New Tire Sales ($ U.S. in billions)	
	1994*	1993
Groupe Michelin	11.5	10.87
Bridgestone Corp.	10.7	10.64
Goodyear Tire & Rubber	10.4	10.0
Continental AG	4.0	3.8
Sumitomo Group	3.4	3.3
Pirelli	3.3	3.0
Yokohama	2.6	2.56
Toyo	1.2	1.3

*MTD estimates.

Source: *Modern Tire Dealer Facts Issue*, 29th ed. (Akron, OH: Bill Communications, January 1995).

■ Goodyear's Aquatred

During the fall of 1991, Goodyear launched the Aquatred, a radically different, all-season, wet traction tire, with a 60,000-mile treadlife guarantee. The Aquatred has a deep center groove and unique tread design that squirts water from the tire. The system helps prevent cars and light trucks from hydroplaning.

While introducing Aquatred, Gault assured, "Customers want safety and reliability. And they will buy features. We're bringing out a tire that truly addresses aquaplaning. Someone might say 'I live in Phoenix, that surely isn't my problem.' Oh yes it is. Three days a year in Phoenix it rains like crazy. You hit the intersection. You're not used to the wet road, and you're taking off. That is a salable characteristic."[50]

The Aquatred qualifies as a "pivotal product" in Goodyear's history as well as the tire industry itself. It is a highly important and integral part of a strategic plan to revitalize Goodyear and inject new life into a mature commodity industry.[51] According to Goodyear sources, the Aquatred was in development for almost a decade, mostly because of its unusual appearance. It has a large, rounded indentation in the center of the tread that helps channel water from under the tire. John Fiedler, former executive vice president of the North American tire division, critically remarked, "Around here, we called it the baby's butt, and you don't want to put an ugly tire on the market."[52] Gault, nonetheless, ended the snail-like product development of the tire and ordered that three other tires in the pipeline be introduced at the same time.

Almost simultaneously, Goodyear issued a new stock offering. Gault, the irrepressible marketer, visited 13 cities in 13 days, holding 39 meetings with potential investors. At the conclusion of his tour, the stock had reached $50, and he had sold 12 million shares instead of the intended 10 million, raising more than $170 million more than planned.

Exhibit 18	U.S./Canadian Leaders in New Tire Sales ($ U.S. in billions)	
	1994*	1993
Goodyear/Kelly	6.0	5.4
Michelin North America	4.2	4.0
Bridgestone/Firestone	3.1	2.7
Continental General	1.2	1.3
Cooper	1.1	.95
Dunlop	.65	.6
Pirelli Armstrong	.6	.7
Yokohama	.41	.40
Toyo	.265	.26

*MTD estimates.
Source: *Modern Tire Dealer Facts Issue*, 29th ed. (Akron, OH: Bill Communications, January 1995).

Best-Managed Brand

Goodyear owns one of the "best-managed" and most-valuable brand names in the world according to *Financial World* magazine's fourth annual trade name evaluation and ranking (Exhibit 19). By comparing brand value with an estimated industry average, the magazine determined the Goodyear name is the 20th best-managed brand.

Based solely on estimated monetary value, the Goodyear brand ranked 24th with a value of $4.66 billion among the 282 trade names considered, the Bridgestone brand 32nd at $3.76 billion; the Michelin brand, 49th at $2.66; the Pirelli brand, 197th at $299 million; and the Continental brand, 225th at $179 million.

Other Tire Lines

The pioneering Aquatred was followed by the Intreped, a lower priced version for more price-conscious consumers.[53] The next introduction was the Eagle Aquatred for high-performance tires, a market segment where wide, high-adhesion tires are the vogue. But, wider tires are more susceptible to hydroplaning so a performance tire with dual aqua channels became a big hit.

Most recently, Goodyear introduced the Aquatred II, an updated version of the original Aquatred. The Aquatred II offers a deeper aqua channel and a longer treadlife warranty. The newest member of Goodyear's aqua-channel family, the Wrangler Aquatred for sport-utility vehicles, was unveiled in a 1995 Superbowl commercial.[54]

Run-Flat Tires

By mid-1993, Goodyear, Bridgestone, and Michelin had all engineered and marketed run-flat tire systems. The complete system, including tires, special wheels, and electronic sensor system, then cost about $5,000.

Exhibit 19	Comparative Value of Tire Brands						
		BRAND					
Tire Brand	Company	Current Value (Mil.)	One-Yr. Change in Value	1994 Sales (Mil.)	1994 Operating Income (Mil.)	Margin	Ratio of Brand Value to Brand Sales
Goodyear	Goodyear Tire & Rubber	$4,660	4%	$7,320	$653	9%	0.6
Bridgestone	Bridgestone	3,762	7	6,626	683	10	0.6
Michelin	Michelin	2,656	41	8,080	553	7	0.3
Pirelli	Pirelli	299	65	2,503	100	4	0.1
Continental	Continental	179	30	1,316	59	5	0.1
Category	Average	—	29	—	—	—	0.4

Source: *Financial World*, August 1, 1995, p. 69.

Goodyear's tire, which does not require a special rim, the Eagle GS-C EMT, is an option on all 1994 Chevrolet Corvette models. Bridgestone's Expedia 5-01 A/M Run Flat is sold only as an option to the Callaway Corvette, a customized version of the Chevrolet sports car.[55]

Goodyear EMT

Goodyear's EMT (extended mobility tire) run-flat option was scheduled for the 1995 model year. It is capable of traveling at least 50 miles at 55 mph, with zero air pressure. At reduced speeds, the range could be as much as 200 miles.[56]

Just Tires

In another strategic move, Goodyear in 1993 inaugurated Just Tires, a tire-sales-only group of company stores. Just Tires offers no auto repair service, provides tires only, and those services directly related to mounting, balancing, and alignment. Goodyear's new logo: "Just Tires . . . Fast Service . . . and Low Prices."[57]

Goodyear planned to expand its Just Tires chain of retail stores by more than 250 locations nationwide during the next several years. In May 1994 Goodyear converted 31 retail stores to the Just Tires format and planned to expand Just Tires primarily through conversion of existing retail stores.

Goodyear's Research and Development

Early on, Gault sensed that if Goodyear was to prosper and eventually survive, it must develop a total commitment to R&D and to quality products and services. For many years, in Gault's opinion, "Goodyear's management viewed R&D as an upstream link in the value chain. There was a linear model involving research, development, engineering, distribution, and marketing. Products evolved at one end and then filtered down to the customer. The product development effort really came out of R&D and not out of the marketing function."

"All too frequently," he concluded, "we wanted customers to buy what we wanted to make or what we wanted to sell rather than saying: 'Tell us what you want and need and we'll supply it for you.' Now, Goodyear has a new model for business. First marketing establishes customer needs. Then, the team members comprising R&D, engineering, production, distribution, finance, and human resources work together to deliver the product or service."[58]

Goodyear's policy on R&D expenditures is directly related to its sales (Exhibit 20).

Despite the rubber industry's recovering sales in 1993, R&D budgets for 1993 remained flat. Industry analysts surmised that R&D is experiencing a flattening out that is probably reflective of modern scientific equipment—you can do more with a lot fewer people. There's less model building and prototyping.[59]

Goodyear's TQC Program

Underscoring Goodyear's research and development efforts is its total quality culture. "I am known as a zealot (at Rubbermaid a 'sonofabitch') on quality," confessed Gault. "And, I won't tolerate shoddy merchandise. I expect our products to be the best in the industry. Every department in this entire global

Exhibit 20   Goodyear's R&D Expenditures ($ in millions)

	1991	1992	1993	1994
1. Sales	$10,906.8	$11,784.9	$11,643.4	$12,288.2
2. R&D expenditures	330.0	325.9	320.0	340.0
3. R&D as a percent of sales	3.0%	2.8%	2.8%	2.8%

Source: Goodyear Tire and Rubber Company, Akron, Ohio, *Annual Reports*, 1991–1994.

Exhibit 21   Continuous Quality Improvement Program

Implementing Goodyear's total quality control program is its Continuous Quality Improvement Program (CQI). Seen as "a systematic, organization-wide approach for continually improving all processes that deliver quality products and services."

While pursuing CQI, Goodyear's management and associates are urged to stick to four basic principles:

- Develop a strong customer focus, including the needs of both external end users and internal co-workers, and other departments.
- Continually improve all processes. Identify those processes that are a sequence of repeatable steps that lead to some desired end or output. Improve the processes by use of planning, doing, checking, acting cycle.
- Involve employees. Encourage teams—train them—support them—use their work—celebrate their accomplishments.
- Mobilize both data and team knowledge to improve decision making. Use graphically displayed numbers and word data. Develop team consensus on root cause(s) of a problem and plan for improvement. Provide a safe and efficient outlet for ideas at all levels.

Source: Goodyear Tire and Rubber Company, Corporate Document.

company is developing a total commitment to quality in every aspect of its operations."[60]

Presently, 51 percent of Goodyear's tire sales are now from tires on the market for less than five years, which continues to increase from the emphasis that Gault has placed on new product development.[61]

Goodyear has monthly meetings in Akron open to all associates where teams of fellow associates explain how this commitment to quality has solved seemingly insolvable problems, bettered working conditions, reduced costs, improved product quality, and brought associates together. Every meeting is videotaped, and tapes are distributed to the company's 88 plants around the world. Gault also chairs bimonthly meetings at which employees demonstrate improvements they have made and receive awards.[62]

Supporting Goodyear's commitment to its TQC program are its mission statement and guiding principles, which provide a foundation for its applications to the company's quality improvement program[63] (Exhibit 21).

Exhibit 22	Goodyear's Emerging Markets			
	China	India	Indonesia	Commonwealth of Independent States
Economic growth (real GDP)	9.5%	4.4%	6.0%	Undergoing economic reform
Population (millions)	1,193	875	195	294
Percent of world population	22%	16%	3.6%	5.4%
Persons per car	663	356	151	22
Vehicles in use (millions)	6.1	4.7	2.9	28.0
Tire market in 2000 (millions)	66	12	10	61

Source: Goodyear Tire and Rubber Company, Akron, Ohio, *Annual Report,* 1993, p. 5.

Goodyear: A Global Player

In early 1995, an optimistic Gault feels that "Goodyear is less vulnerable to regional swings in product demand than in the past. The firm's continued strategic focus is that of a growth company capable of consistent earnings improvement in world-wide emerging markets"[64] (Exhibit 22).

More than 40 percent of Goodyear's record 1994 revenues and 45 percent of unit sales of tires and rubber products were achieved outside the United States, and more than 50 percent of segment operating income came from international operations. (Exhibits 23 and 24 present industry and geographic segment data.)

The business is strategically poised not only to increase its market leadership in North America, but also to grow faster than the industry around the world. It intends to increase sales by twice the industry rate—about 2.5 percent—in the United States and plans revenue growth in Europe of about 5 percent.[65]

Goodyear's Global Progress

The company's increasing progress reflects its regional trade agreements in Latin America, which stimulated the growth of export sales and enabled Goodyear plants to regionalize production for high capacity utilization. Goodyear Latin America remains the quality tire leader for the region. Goodyear Brazil is an export leader, shipping tires to 83 countries from its modern Americana export center.

Goodyear's expansion in the Asian growth market advanced as the Chinese government granted approvals for the Goodyear Dalian joint venture to manufacture tires in China. Production began at an existing plant in Dalian, Liaoning Province, in the first half of 1995. Other joint tire ventures are being sought in the world's most populous nation. The performance of the Asia region has improved since new capacity came on stream in Thailand. Construction began on expansions in Malaysia and Indonesia.

The joint venture with CEAT Ltd. in India for a new tire plant is proceeding on schedule. Production is scheduled to begin early in 1996.

Exhibit 23 Industry Segments ($ in millions)			
	1994	**1993**	**1992**
Sales to Unaffiliated Customers			
Tires	$9,427.6	$8,853.3	$8,661.4
Related products and services	1,080.6	1,110.2	1,108.7
Total Tires	10,508.2	9,963.3	9,770.1
General products	1,700.9	1,618.0	1,953.9
Oil transportation	79.1	61.9	60.9
Net Sales	$12,288.2	$11,643.4	$11,784.9
Income (loss)			
Tires	$1,010.6	$998.5	$763.4
General products	170.9	177.8	362.7
Oil transportation	11.8	(11.6)	(15.8)
Total operating income	1,193.3	1,164.7	1,110.3
Interest expense	(129.4)	(162.4)	(232.9)
Foreign currency exchange	(77.6)	(113.1)	(77.1)
Equity in net income of affiliated companies	25.7	17.6	10.5
Minority interest in net income of subsidiaries	(23.8)	(27.0)	(23.2)
Corporate revenues and expenses	(122.5)	(94.9)	(157.7)
Income before income taxes, extraordinary items and cumulative effects of accounting changes	$865.7	$784.9	$629.9
Assets			
Tires	$5,490.7	$5,127.9	$5,049.8
General products	636.4	566.9	615.6
Oil transportation	1,398.6	1,413.2	1,487.7
Total identifiable assets	7,525.7	7,108.0	7,153.1
Corporate assets	1,464.2	1,220.9	1,302.9
Investments in affiliated companies, at equity	133.4	107.2	107.7
Assets at December 31	$9,123.3	$8,436.1	$8,563.7
Capital Expenditures			
Tires	$425.4	$356.5	$291.4
General products	90.2	67.7	65.7
Oil transportation	7.4	8.1	9.5
For the year	$523.0	$432.3	$366.6
Depreciation			
Tires	$309.4	$305.0	$348.4
General products	55.1	47.5	56.2
Oil transportation	45.8	40.4	41.2
For the year	$410.3	$392.9	$445.8

Source: Goodyear Tire and Rubber Company, Akron, Ohio, *Annual Report*, 1994, p. 40.

Exhibit 24   Geographic Segments ($ in millions)

	1994	1993	1992
Sales to Unaffiliated Customers			
United States	$7,130.5	$6,777.4	$6,787.3
Europe	2,279.8	2,233.3	2,476.1
Latin America	1,512.5	1,403.5	1,325.1
Asia	711.6	644.9	654.0
Canada	653.8	584.3	542.4
Net Sales	$12,288.2	$11,643.4	$11,784.9
Inter-Geographic Sales			
United States	$373.9	$296.9	$290.4
Europe	92.5	78.4	66.5
Latin America	159.2	107.7	87.4
Asia	490.7	346.6	325.9
Canada	269.1	233.6	195.3
Total	$1,385.4	$1,063.2	$965.5
Revenue			
United States	$7,504.4	$7,074.3	$7,077.7
Europe	2,372.3	2,311.7	2,542.6
Latin America	1,671.7	1,511.2	1,412.5
Asia	1,202.3	991.5	979.9
Canada	922.9	817.9	737.7
Adjustments and eliminations	(1,385.4)	(1,063.2)	(965.5)
Total	$12,288.2	$11,643.4	$11,784.9
Operating Income			
United States	$591.5	$590.5	$654.3
Europe	212.0	221.5	216.8
Latin America	278.2	271.1	155.5
Asia	81.3	70.0	82.9
Canada	30.3	12.0	4.0
Adjustments and eliminations	—	(.4)	(3.2)
Total	$1,193.3	$1,164.7	$1,110.3
Assets			
United States	$5,467.3	$5,113.4	$5,143.0
Europe	1,541.3	1,433.8	1,462.0
Latin America	809.4	799.2	854.6
Asia	645.4	471.6	466.0
Canada	538.9	521.8	541.4
Adjustments and eliminations	(12.4)	(10.9)	(11.0)
Total identifiable assets	8,989.9	8,328.9	8,456.0
Investments in affiliated companies, at equity	133.4	107.2	107.7
Assets at December 31	$9,123.3	$8,436.1	$8,563.7

Source: Goodyear Tire and Rubber Company, Akron, Ohio, *Annual Report,* 1994, p. 41.

In Europe, Goodyear is pursuing acquisitions and business development in the new market economies of the former communist countries.[66]

Gault remains convinced that "all these actions translate into growth in financial sources in technical capability, in competitive ability, and growth as a stronger supplier for its customers worldwide."[67]

■ Goodyear's New President

In April 1995, at the annual shareholder's meeting, Gault ended months of speculation when he announced Samir F. Gibara as Goodyear's new president and chief operating officer. Gibara previously had been vice president of strategic planning and business development, as well as acting chief financial officer. Egyptian-born Gibara, fluent in several foreign languages, worked in a variety of international management positions to improve the firm's standing as a global competitor. "The board," he pledged, "made an outstanding choice in the selection of Sam Gibara who has all the credentials and experience to lead and successfully manage a global enterprise, such as Goodyear, today and into the future."[68]

Gault retired at year-end and refused to name a successor to his role as chairman and chief executive officer.

■ Notes

1. Goodyear Tire and Rubber Company, Public relations release 06155-91, June 1991.
2. Ibid.
3. Jung Ah Pak, Gault on fixing Goodyear's flat, *Fortune,* July 15, 1991, 104.
4. Goodyear Tire and Rubber Company, Akron, Ohio, *Annual Reports,* 1982–1988.
5. Adapted from Bernard A. Deitzer, Alan G. Krigline, and Thomas C. Peterson, Goodyear: Beyond Goldsmith—A strategic management case, The University of Akron.
6. Goodyear Tire and Rubber Company, Akron, Ohio, *Annual Reports,* 1991–1994.
7. Ibid.
8. Goodyear Tire and Rubber Company, Corporate Document.
9. Jacqueline M. Graves, Leaders of corporate change, *Fortune,* December 14, 1992, 104.
10. Rubbermaid Inc., Wooster, Ohio, *Annual Reports,* 1992–1993.
11. Graves, Leaders of corporate change.
12. Stanley C. Gault remarks in 4th Annual CEO Reports, "Tire Review," December 1991.
13. Ibid.
14. Goodyear Tire and Rubber Company, Corporate Document.
15. Graves, Leaders of corporate change.
16. Stanley C. Gault remarks to Avon Products Financial Conference, New York, September 1994.
17. Peter Nulty, The bounce is back at Goodyear, *Fortune,* September 7, 1992, 71.

18. Ibid.
19. Graves, Leaders of corporate change.
20. Excerpted from Stanley C. Gault's comments at Goodyear's Vendor Awards Program, Akron, Ohio, September 1991.
21. Ibid.
22. Adapted from Stanley C. Gault's remarks at the Industrial Research Institute Annual Meeting, Virginia, May 1993.
23. Jonathon P. Hicks, The Wall Streeter who runs TLC Beatrice, *New York Times,* June 9, 1991, C5.
24. Ah Pak, Gault on fixing Goodyear's flat.
25. Nulty, The bounce is back at Goodyear.
26. Hicks, The Wall Streeter who runs TLC Beatrice.
27. Ibid.
28. Donald Sabath, Goodyear to issue more stock, *Cleveland Plain Dealer,* October 3, 1991, C1.
29. Goodyear Tire & Rubber Company, Akron, Ohio, *Annual Report,* 1991, pp. 2–4.
30. Ibid.
31. Ibid, 2–4.
32. Stanley C. Gault remarks at Annual Meeting of Shareholders, Akron, Ohio, April 1995, pp. 2–4.
33. Ibid.
34. Ibid.
35. Ibid.
36. Excerpted from Stanley C. Gault remarks before the Timken Corporate Forum, Canton, Ohio, April 26, 1993.
37. Ibid.

38. Adapted from Stanley C. Gault's presentation to the Harvard Business School Club of Cleveland, Cleveland, Ohio, May 13, 1993.
39. Ibid.
40. Gault, Harvard Business School Club of Cleveland.
41. Zachary Schiller, Goodyear is gunning its marketing engine, *Business Week,* March 16, 1992, 42.
42. Nulty, The bounce is back at Goodyear.
43. Stanley C. Gault's remarks at an Investor Presentation, New York, November 1991.
44. Nulty, The bounce is back at Goodyear.
45. Abe Zaiden, Executive strives for free TV, *Cleveland Plain Dealer,* June 27, 1993, 2.
46. *Modern Tire Dealer* Facts Issue.
47. Ibid.
48. Ibid.
49. Ibid.
50. Ah Pak, Gault on fixing Goodyear's flat.
51. Nulty, The bounce is back at Goodyear.
52. Ibid.
53. Goodyear Tire and Rubber Company Corporate Document.
54. Ibid.
55. Stuart Drown, The race to drive with a flat, *Akron Beacon Journal,* June 28, 1993, D1.
56. Jim McCraw, Throw away the spare, *Popular Science,* May 1993, 88.
57. Goodyear Tire and Rubber Company, Akron, Ohio, *Annual Report,* 1994, p. 4.

58. Remarks by Stanley C. Gault at Avon Products Financial Conference, New York, September 1994.

59. Bryan Kodish, R&D expenditures flat in 1993, *Rubber and Plastic News,* July 4, 1994.

60. Adapted from Stanley C. Gault's address to the Industrial Research Institute Annual Meeting in Hot Springs, Virginia, May 1993.

61. Nulty, The bounce is back at Goodyear.

62. Goodyear Tire and Rubber Company, Corporate Document.

63. Adapted from Stanley C. Gault's address to the Industrial Research Institute Annual Meeting in Hot Springs, Virginia, May 1993.

64. Glenn Gamboa, New Goodyear becomes a global player, *Akron Beacon Journal,* April 16, 1995, C1.

65. Goodyear Tire and Rubber Company, Akron, Ohio, *Annual Report,* 1994, p. 5.

66. Ibid., 13.

67. Ibid.

68. Donald Sabath, Goodyear picks a new CEO, *The Cleveland Plain Dealer,* April 11, 1995, C1.

CASE 17 The Greensboro Housing Authority

Lew G. Brown
William M. Kawashima
Diana H. Carlin
Margaret K. Craig
University of North Carolina at Greensboro

■ http://www.hvd.gov/cpes/nc/
greensnc.html

Elaine Ostrowski, executive director of the Greensboro Housing Authority (GHA), closed her front door and walked to the end of her driveway to pick up the morning newspaper. She noticed that the North Carolina air had a touch of fall about it this morning, but she knew that September still held more summer-like days. "You have to get used to the heat in this job," she mused as she slipped the paper out of its plastic bag. Elaine glanced quickly at the front page. "Well, at least we're not on the front page," she thought. "I think I'll wait until I get to the office to tackle the letters to the editor."

In April 1992, the authority had announced that it was seeking a 10- to 12-acre site on which to build a 50-unit public-housing community. Responding to a request from the Greensboro City Council, the authority had said that it would focus its search on areas in the city's western sections. The city council had previously encouraged the GHA to locate public-housing communities in city areas where there were fewer such developments.

In August, the GHA announced that it had selected a site near the Adams Farm community, a predominantly white, upper-middle-class neighborhood in southwest Greensboro. Area residents had quickly voiced their opposition. Several hundred residents had attended a community meeting where Elaine and other GHA officials presented their development plans. Elaine had shown slides of the city's newer public-housing developments. One area resident, however, had responded by saying, "Who cares what they look like? We are worried about the people you are going to put there." Two days later at a GHA Board of Commissioners' meeting, residents voiced their concerns over the proposed site's cost and topography, the development's effect on their property values, and the site's lack of convenient access to shopping and public transportation. The board, however, voted to approve the plan and to forward it to the U.S. Department of Housing and Urban Development (HUD) for approval.

Elaine arrived at her office early, hoping to get some things done before the day became hectic. She sat at her desk and opened the newspaper to the editorial page. As she expected, she quickly spotted a letter to the editor that carried the headline "Public housing would ruin property values." Three paragraphs from the letter read:

> To make matters worse, when Ostrowski was asked did she think the surrounding property values would be affected, she said she didn't know. This is not the kind of answer one would expect from a person who has been on the job for over 10 years.
>
> What she was really saying is that the GHA couldn't care less about the value of homes located around public housing. The presentation the GHA made was a complete sham and insulted the intelligence of all those in attendance.
>
> The homeowners are not going to stand idly by and let some city employee spend our tax dollars to devalue our property. We have all worked very hard to build our homes for ourselves and our families and we will all work twice as hard to ensure that the value is maintained.

Elaine slumped in her chair and gazed out the window. Every public official knew what it was like to have members of the public attack their program or to attack them personally. It still hurt, especially when the attack was wrong. She had not said that she didn't know. She had said that the authority did not have any information that suggested that property values around scattered-site housing declined. She had stated that, in fact, the GHA had done studies that indicated that property values continued to increase. She and the authority did care, and they understood property owners' concerns. However, the letter reminded her that perceptions are reality and that the public's perceptions were often clouded by preconceived ideas.

When Elaine had accepted her position, she made a conscious effort to keep the authority out of the news because a scandal involving her predecessor had created unfavorable publicity. Now, a decade later, she realized that she had made a mistake in maintaining a silent presence.

On one hand, Elaine knew that GHA had been very successful. The authority had won national and regional recognition for some of its innovative programs, such as the Police Neighborhood Resource Centers (PNRC) and its youth programs. Many civic and business leaders admired GHA's effective management. Yet, despite these accomplishments, Elaine felt that many members of the public still held a largely negative opinion of public housing and its residents, or they did not know anything about the authority and its programs.

Several blocks away, Jerry Lawson sat at his desk in a well-appointed office. Although he was president of Baron Financial, Inc., Jerry pondered his other career as a member of the GHA Board of Commissioners. Jerry's ability to work in two very different worlds, financial services for the upwardly mobile and public housing for low-income families, often puzzled his business colleagues.

Lately, Jerry had been thinking about people's attitudes toward public housing. Every time business colleagues made comments such as "It must be awful working with all those welfare people," it would remind him of some of the misconceptions he had about public housing before joining the board. He wished more people had the chance he had to meet the many hardworking, decent, public-housing residents.

Jerry had read the same letter to the editor that Elaine had seen. He recalled that a week ago the Guilford County Board of Commissioners, which had no formal relationship with GHA, had voted 6–1 to ask the authority to hold another public hearing on the new site. One commissioner had voiced the opinion that "I've never seen a housing project yet, I don't care how new and how well planned, that ended up in six months' time looking like anything but a damned housing project." He then added, "Those places invariably become slums and everybody knows it."

Jerry thought that this all seemed too familiar. A little over two years ago, GHA had proposed building a 50-unit development in a northeast Greensboro community. This development represented the first new public-housing community in over seven years. The city desperately needed the housing to help the more than 800 families on the waiting list. Then, too, area residents had raised similar objections to the project. But the city council had approved rezoning the site, and HUD had approved the project. That development, Laurel Hill, had just opened.

"We've got to do a better job," Jerry thought. "We can't keep fighting the same battles. We need to educate the community about public housing. GHA needs a marketing strategy just like any other business."

■ History

The City of Greensboro (1992 population of 190,000) established the Greensboro Housing Authority in 1941, shortly after Congress passed the National Housing Act, which provided communities with federal funding for public housing. The 1930s depression had left many cities with inadequate housing for low-income citizens. For example, Greensboro's civic leaders then estimated that one-third of the city's housing was substandard and that 45 percent lacked sanitary facilities. As a result, the mayor appointed GHA's first Board of Commissioners, and the board made plans to build 2,500 housing units during the following 10 years.

Unfortunately, World War II intervened, and GHA did not complete the first two 400-unit community developments until 1952. By 1992, the authority had constructed a total of 2,435 housing units in 16 public-housing communities that served approximately 6,500 residents.

Congress had passed the National Housing Act with the goal of providing *temporary* housing for low-income families. These families would eventually move out of public housing as their financial situation improved. GHA pursued this goal also, and many of its residents succeeded in moving into the private-sector housing market.

However, socioeconomic changes during the last several decades made it difficult for many families to make the transition from public to private housing. In the 1950s and 1960s, many low-income families migrated from rural areas into the cities. Simultaneously, urban renewal projects depleted the supply of affordable, low-income housing. Due to these factors, some low-income families and individuals became permanent public-housing residents. Either the families or individuals lacked the education, skills, or training to improve their financial status, or there were simply no adequate houses that they could afford.

Before the 1970s, GHA, like other authorities, built large public-housing communities. The authority located these densely populated 200- to 400-unit complexes in southeast Greensboro. Most citizens thought of these communities when they thought of public housing.

In the late 1970s, GHA adopted the scattered-site concept and built smaller, 50-unit housing complexes in locations throughout the city. GHA purposely designed scattered-site communities to blend in with the surrounding neighborhood. As a result, the public often did not realize that these were public-housing communities.

During the 1980s, the federal government severely reduced public-housing funding. The cutbacks halted new construction for almost a decade. However, approval of new capital funding in the late 1980s allowed GHA to develop the Laurel Hill community. Because the authority expected very little funding for new housing construction, it was renovating many older, large complexes to improve the public's image of these neighborhoods and to help preserve the existing housing stock.

In 1992, the Authority had the following mission statement:

It is the mission of the Greensboro Housing Authority to provide decent, safe, and sanitary housing for the low-income residents of the City of Greensboro. To fulfill this mission, the Greensboro Housing Authority has adopted the following objectives:

1. Provide for the responsible management of Greensboro Housing Authority's programs.
2. Improve the public perception of Greensboro Housing Authority's public-housing communities.
3. Assist Greensboro Housing Authority families to attain self-sufficiency.
4. Seek opportunities to increase the supply of affordable rental units.

■ Organizational Structure

As a public corporation (much like an airport authority), GHA administered low-income housing programs, including public housing and rental assistance. GHA had a contractual agreement with the federal government through HUD to deliver these services. HUD provided the subsidies needed to offset the deficits resulting from the below-market rent that public-housing residents paid. HUD subsidies provided approximately two-thirds of GHA's operating budget, and rental income accounted for one-third. City, county, and state governments had, in the past, provided limited funds for capital improvements. Exhibit 1 presents GHA's 1990, 1991, and 1992 operating budgets. These budgets do not include special grant monies HUD provided for specific programs, such as the Drug Elimination Program.

Greensboro's mayor appointed the seven-member Board of Commissioners that governed the housing authority. However, the housing authority operated as an independent agency and was not part of city government. Its employees were not city employees. Each commissioner served five-year terms without pay. At least one public-housing resident served on the board. The board met monthly to review the agency's operations, such as its new construction plans, operating budgets, and policies.

The Board of Commissioners also hired the executive director, who managed the authority's daily operations and its 123 employees. The executive director's

Exhibit 1 Greensboro Housing Authority Operating Budgets			
	1992	**1991**	**1990**
Income:			
Rental Income	$2,360,670	$2,687,810	$3,531,840
Other Income	170,940	195,470	201,990
Operating Subsidy (HUD)	4,335,090	3,367,420	2,574,846
Total Income	$6,866,700	$6,250,700	$6,308,676
Operating Expenses:			
Administration	1,396,500	1,337,070	1,292,990
Tenant Services	127,110	104,700	111,560
Utilities	1,053,450	994,180	1,442,900
Maintenance	2,820,850	2,576,120	3,013,480
General	1,188,710	1,280,380	1,270,210
Total Operating Expenses	$6,586,620	$6,292,450	$7,131,140
Capital Expenditures:	$192,070	$158,250	$134,090
Total Expenses	$6,778,690	$6,450,700	$7,265,230
Provision for Operating Reserve:	$88,010	($200,000)	($956,554)
Operating Reserve Account:			
Beginning Balance	$1,198,975	$1,398,975	$2,355,529
Ending Balance	$1,286,985	$1,198,975	$1,398,975

Source: Greensboro Housing Authority.

immediate staff consisted of the deputy executive director, the director of administration, the director of capital improvements, and the director of housing services (see Exhibit 2).

The Residents

GHA's 16 communities housed 2,262 families (see Exhibit 3). Most of the communities served families, although GHA designated three developments (Hall Towers, Gateway Plaza, and Stoneridge) for elderly, handicapped, and disabled residents only.

The authority charged rent on a sliding-scale basis to make housing affordable for families who did not have sufficient income to rent in the private market. Resident families paid 30 percent of their annual adjusted income for rent. The mean gross monthly rent was $137, substantially below the private-market rate of approximately $550.

Exhibit 2

**Greensboro Housing Authority
Organizational Chart**

Village Green is a retirement
community that is owned and
operated by GHA, but is not
federally subsidized. However, this
complex with its own staff and
budget is operated separately from
GHA's public housing communites.

Source: Greensboro Housing Authority.

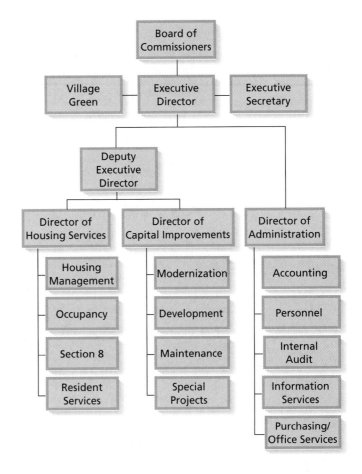

The average resident family had a $6,350 mean gross annual income, with 94
percent of the families earning less than $13,000 annually. About one-third of the
resident families received public assistance (welfare) besides subsidized public
housing. About two-thirds of the resident families had at least one wage earner.
Those residents who had jobs generally earned the minimum wage.

Of the 6,500 residents, about one-third were male and two-thirds were
female. Fifty percent of the residents were minors (less than 17 years old), and 15
percent were elderly (over 61 years old). Of the 2,262 families, 55 percent were
one-parent, female-head-of-household families. Exhibits 4, 5, and 6 provide
additional information about the families living in GHA's communities.

Other Housing Programs

The Greensboro city government and other organizations had become increasingly concerned with the need for low-income housing. Recently approved bond
issues provided housing opportunities for families whose incomes were too high
to qualify for public-housing assistance but too low to qualify for private-sector
mortgages. These bond issues supported programs that provided affordable
housing through the renovation of existing substandard, dilapidated facilities;

Exhibit 3   Greensboro Housing Authority Communities

Community	Number of Residents	Number of Units	Percent of Minority Residents
Large Complexes			
Morningside Homes	964	380	99%
Smith Homes	837	430	96%
Ray Warren Homes	651	236	99%
Hampton Homes	884	275	97%
Claremont Courts	755	250	97%
Elderly Complexes			
Hall Towers	159	156	21%
Gateway Plaza	226	221	46%
Stoneridge	55	50	14%
Scattered Sites			
Hickory Trail	377	127	82%
Baylor Court	64	11	88%
Woodberry Run	120	39	88%
Applewood	113	50	73%
Pear Leaf	132	50	85%
Lakespring	137	60	81%
Silver Briar	108	50	75%
Laurel Hill		50	
Totals		2435	83%

Source: Greensboro Housing Authority.

Exhibit 4

GHA Household Sizes

In 1992, there were 2,262 families residing in GHA's communities.

Source: Greensboro Housing Authority.

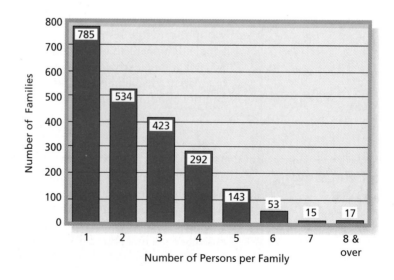

Exhibit 5

Residents' Length of Residence and Public Assistance Status

Source: Greensboro Housing Authority.

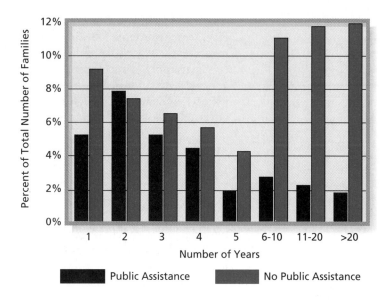

Exhibit 6

Age and Sex of Head of Household

Source: Greensboro Housing Authority.

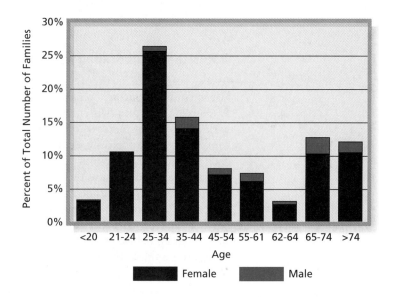

provided funds to help first-time buyers with down payments and initial mortgage payments; provided housing counseling to aid first-time home buyers; and provided building lots for nonprofit groups to construct housing. The City Housing Foundation, Habitat for Humanity, the Episcopal Housing Ministry, and a group called HOME all worked to create more affordable housing. These organizations worked closely with the GHA, helping some public-housing families attain home ownership.

Observers felt that the city and the housing authority were progressive and innovative in the housing field. GHA had many programs in place that did not exist in many other cities. However, these combined initiatives addressed only a small part of low-income families' housing needs. According to Greensboro's Five-Year Affordable Housing Plan, the city needed 12,000 low-cost rental units to serve the 12,000 families earning less than $10,000 annually. The total existing supply of such units (including public housing) was 6,725 units, leaving an unmet need for 5,275 low-cost rental units. The GHA had a current waiting list of 1,882 unduplicated families for its public-housing and Section 8 (another government-assisted program) units.

Support Services for Residents

Over the years, many public and private agencies provided traditional support services to Greensboro's public-housing families, including counseling, health care, tutoring, and a variety of other services. In addition, the GHA began several new and award-winning programs and initiatives. Some of the most recent awards it has received include the Youth Sports and Cultural Program Award (for achievements in the development of children's programs), the Public Housing Agency Performance Award (for recognition of the excellence of GHA's PNRC program) awarded by HUD Region IV; and first place for the Master Kids program and second place for the PNRC program, both awarded by the Southeast Regional Council of the National Association of Housing and Redevelopment officials.

Police Neighborhood Resource Centers (PNRCs)

A few years ago, most of Greensboro's drug trafficking occurred in the four largest public-housing communities (Smith Homes, Morningside Homes, Ray Warren Homes, and Claremont Courts). These older public-housing complexes, with their large number of units and high population density, provided a convenient place for drug dealers to hide. Most of the residents, who were not drug users or participants in drug-related activities, were horrified that their communities had become the sites for these activities.

In response to the residents' concerns, the Authority, working closely with the police, initiated the PNRC program. The Greensboro Police Department permanently assigned two police officers to patrol each of the four communities on foot. This program helped eradicate much of the illegal drug activity; and, in addition, it helped to establish an improved relationship between the residents and the police. In particular, the police provided good role models for the children.

Furthermore, the PNRC's combined on-site law enforcement activities and drug prevention and education services produced a comprehensive drug elimination program. A variety of organizations, both public and private, provided the wide range of services and resources necessary to support this comprehensive approach to drug elimination (see Exhibit 7). GHA also obtained HUD funding to support both a drug prevention coordinator and a youth activities coordinator. These individuals helped to recruit volunteers and coordinate the activities of the many agencies that provided services through the PNRC offices.

Youth Services

Many of GHA's programs targeted the young people who lived in its communities. GHA had initiated the Salvation Army Boys' and Girls' Clubs. The Salvation

Exhibit 7	Support Services for Residents—Selected Participating Community Agencies and Organizations

Drug Education/Prevention:
Substance Abuse Services of Guilford, Inc.
Guilford County Area Mental Health, Mental Retardation, and Substance Abuse Services
Youth Focus, Inc.
Southeast Greensboro Council on Crime and Delinquency
The National Association for the Advancement of Colored People (NAACP)
National Black Child Development Institute (NBCDI)
Planned Parenthood of the Triad, Inc.
The Greensboro Pulpit Forum
Juvenile Services Division of the Courts

Family and Other Support Services:
Guilford County Department of Social Services (DSS)
Guildord County Department of Public Health
The Salvation Army
Greensboro Urban Ministry Clinic
Greensboro City Schools
United Services for Older Adults, Inc.

Economic/Educational Opportunities:
Employment Security Commission
Guilford County Private Industry Council
Job Corps
Guilford Technical Community College (GTCC)
Guilford County Community Action Program, Inc.

Youth Services:
Salvation Army Boys' and Girls' Clubs
Agricultural Extension Service
City of Greensboro Parks and Recreation Department
The Boy Scouts of America
The Girl Scouts of America
North Carolina A&T State University
National Conference of Christians and Jews
Achievements Unlimited Basketball School

Facilitators:
Greensboro Agency Transportation Express, Inc. (GATE)
Greensboro Jaycees
Greensboro Junior League

Source: Greensboro Housing Authority.

Army provided personnel to plan and supervise these on-site youth activity clubs that furnished educational, leadership, recreational, drug prevention, and enrichment programs for young people between the ages of 6 and 18.

Frank Cuthbertson, the chairman of GHA's Board of Commissioners, established the Southeast Council on Crime and Delinquency. This agency provided educational and cultural enrichment activities for at-risk young people.

The Master Kids program, an academic incentive program started by the drug prevention coordinator, rewarded and recognized students who had achieved "Master Kid" status by improving their schoolwork.

Resident Councils and Resident Services

Each public-housing community established Resident Councils that included all persons 17 years of age or older living in the particular community. Each council elected officers, including a president who met monthly with the executive director and the administrative staff to maintain a good working relationship between the GHA staff and residents. Resident Councils sponsored educational, social, and recreational programs for their communities and worked closely with the PNRCs.

GHA's Resident Services Unit provided technical assistance for the Resident Councils and coordinated resident group activities. GHA's Resident Services staff helped residents deal with health problems, family matters, and financial matters. This staff also worked closely with local service agencies that were available to offer help.

Resident Management

Many Resident Councils in the public-housing communities had entered agreements with GHA to maintain their communities' grounds and manage their PNRC offices. GHA provided these residents with management training. It had assisted one Resident Council in obtaining a resident management grant from HUD to work toward further increasing its management responsibilities.

In addition, GHA was developing a self-sufficiency program that would help public-housing residents in obtaining the services and skills needed to make the transition into the private-housing market. GHA also started a small business program to identify and support residents who wanted to start their own small businesses.

Image Problems and Misconceptions

During the next several weeks, Jerry Lawson continued to read the letter-to-the-editor exchanges between the development's supporters and opponents:

As taxpayers, we feel we should have a say in the way our money is being spent; why was a public hearing denied?

Why doesn't the government give us statistics on these nice public housing units, showing average number of arrests made, domestic disputes reported, drugs and thefts, compared to other communities?

After HUD builds this project, will they (or anyone) pay us the true value of our property as it was before the valuation decrease due to the location of this complex on Hilltop Road?

What will be the next undesirable surprise for our neighborhood? Public transportation? Shopping centers?

To characterize legitimate concerns, such as property values, security, and use of tax dollars as racist is ridiculous.

In late September, Jerry had lunch with some business associates, Joe Phillips and Paul Conners, who both worked in advertising. He shared his frustrations over the public's poor image of public housing.

Stereotypes and Prejudices

Minorities comprised the largest portion (83 percent) of public housing's residents. In the five largest and best known communities, roughly 98 percent of the residents were minorities. Thus, to the extent that members of the general population held racist attitudes and stereotypes, these attitudes would potentially negatively affect GHA's and public housing's images.

Low-income status carried with it another stereotype. Many people believed that all residents were lazy and on welfare, allowing "the system" to keep them. In reality, public-housing residents paid rent, and about 65 percent of these families had at least one employed family member. However, with the average family income of only $6,350, these people represented the city's "working poor."

Crime and Media Coverage

The public also associated public housing with high crime rates. Drug dealing, murder, and violent crimes did occur in these communities. The older, more densely populated sites were once popular havens for drug sales. However, the Greensboro Police Department's Division of Crime Analysis reported that the per capita rate of violent crimes against persons and property (the crime index) was *lower* for the GHA communities than for the city as a whole. For example, in 1990, only 1 of the 21 murders in Greensboro occurred in a public-housing community.

The newspaper and television media unintentionally encouraged the connection between public-housing communities and crime. When someone committed a crime near a GHA community, the media identified the location as "in or around Morningside Homes" or "near Smith Homes." In reality, "in or around" or "near" were not precise location descriptions but only indicated that someone committed a crime somewhere in the vicinity of a particular housing community. In contrast, the media identified the locations of crimes committed in more affluent neighborhoods by street name rather than by a community name. As a result, the names of public-housing communities became strongly associated with criminal activity. Unfortunately, the "good" side of public housing (the Salvation Army Boys' and Girls' Clubs, the Master Kids program, etc.) remained largely unreported by the media. Thus, there was little positive information to counterbalance the negative.

Awareness and Reputation

The public often used the terms "projects" and "tenants" to refer to public housing and its residents. GHA wanted to eliminate these terms because of their negative connotations. Unfortunately, the media continued to use these terms partly out of habit and partly because the residents themselves used them. These terms perpetuated images of dilapidated slums and negative attitudes toward the people who lived there, creating inaccurate perceptions of public housing.

Ironically, many people were unaware of the smaller, more modern scattered-site public-housing communities. Just recently, Elaine had been talking with the mayor about a particular 50-unit complex, and even he had not realized that this community was part of public housing.

On the other hand, due to extensive media coverage of the older communities in southeast Greensboro, citizens were quite familiar with those housing communities. As a result, most people associated public housing only with the older, larger complexes although they made up only half of GHA's housing stock.

Nevertheless, if one were a public-housing resident, one lived "in the projects" regardless of what type of community it was. The residents carried this stigma with them. For the children, it was an embarrassment. In school, students and even teachers referred to individuals as "Johnny from Morningside Homes," for example.

Organizational Image

Public housing in Greensboro also suffered from public housing's nationwide reputation. Some major cities had poorly administered or unethically operated housing authorities. These abuses and negative images spilled over to both GHA's residents and its administration. Some city residents probably brought negative views of public housing from experiences in other cities.

On the other hand, those few community leaders who were familiar with GHA's operations held it in high regard as an effectively managed organization. However, most people did not understand GHA's organizational or operational structure, nor did they completely understand the relationship between GHA and the public-housing communities.

The Effect of Public Image on the Residents

As the lunch continued, Jerry discussed how these image problems and misconceptions affected the residents.

"If people have decent housing, they have a better opportunity to become contributors to the community and society," Jerry observed. "Living in public housing is not the cause of the residents' problems but instead a result of being poor, unskilled, insufficiently educated, or unemployable. People in these situations seek public housing.

"Probably 90 to 95 percent of the residents are good, decent people who were trying to do the right things and to raise their children. It frustrates me to think that less than 5 percent of the residents shape the community's view of public housing and its residents. As a result, I believe many residents do not have pride in where they live because they do not think the community has pride in them.

"As I've told you before," Jerry continued, "before I became involved, I had many of the same misconceptions. I've noticed that others who become directly involved change their opinions also. Take the police officers who started the PNRC program, for example. Some police officers sympathized with them for having to pull 'awful duty.' In reality, we found just the opposite result. Many residents practically 'adopted' the officers, and the officers became both supportive of and complimentary about many residents. In the process, the residents developed a much better opinion of the police."

Is Marketing in GHA's Future?

"I realize that GHA has more than just an image problem," Jerry continued as the group finished lunch. "We've got to continue to build new projects, although I expect the budget situation will make federal funding for new projects difficult to obtain. We also need to continue to renovate our existing units."

"I saw in Saturday's paper that the Guilford County Commissioners had voted to delete its $84,000 contribution to the authority from its 93–94 budget," Joe Phillips interjected.

"Yes," Jerry responded, "that's one reason I wanted to have lunch with you two. The commissioners took that action in response to citizens' outcries about the new community. But the commissioners' action just hurts the people we are trying to help. We use that money to renovate existing housing units. Their action just points out that we need to take action to deal with our marketing problem."

"Well, you certainly have a marketing problem!" Paul Conners exclaimed. "It seems to me that it is more than just a public relations or a public image problem."

"That's exactly my point," Jerry answered. "We need to look at the authority from a marketing perspective, not just focus on promotion."

"But do you think marketing is appropriate for public agencies," Joe Phillips asked. "Many people don't feel that governments or public agencies should be involved in marketing."

"Yes. You hear statements like that occasionally," Jerry noted. "There may even be members of our board who feel that way. That just makes it more important that we educate them about the need for marketing in its broadest sense."

"Do you have any money to support a marketing effort?" Paul asked.

"Not really," Jerry responded. "We've never had a marketing budget. We don't even have a brochure! We are not going to have much money to support marketing efforts. So, I need to be creative and see what we can do that will not cost much money.

"I know a marketing professor at the university. I think I'll give Elaine a call and see if I can set up a meeting with the three of us. Perhaps he will have some ideas to get us started. Meanwhile, if you two have any ideas, I'd surely appreciate them."

Later that afternoon, Jerry telephoned Elaine to tell her of his lunch meeting and his idea about meeting with the professor. Elaine liked the idea, and Jerry agreed to set up the meeting.

After the conversation, Elaine sat in her office, and thought about recent events. She, too, had been thinking about GHA's image and its marketing problems. She wondered exactly which image was the most important: the housing authority's, the residents', or the idea of public housing. It seemed that the Greensboro Housing Authority needed to improve its image, but the real benefactors she hoped would be the residents, especially the children. There needed to be a way to raise their self-esteem and make them less ashamed of their living conditions. Some adults would remain in public housing. However, the children needed to see a future with more possibilities.

Elaine grabbed a note pad and jotted down several key groups in the city that already affected or could affect GHA's and public-housing's image, including the media, local government, public and social service agencies, business and civic groups, volunteer and charitable organizations, schools and universities, and the public-housing residents themselves. She decided that she needed to do some thinking about the issues that Jerry Lawson had raised before their meeting.

Before continuing, Elaine reached across her desk and picked up a copy of a letter to the editor from an area property owner and read again the key paragraphs:

> For too long, those of us with means and education have built communities outside the inner city and have left those in poverty with very little resources to rise above their situation. My work has taken me into many public housing projects and other poverty areas in Greensboro and I have learned that, like us, most residents do not want to live near drug dealers or live in substandard housing.

> I believe with a little bit of community involvement from the successful people contained within Adams Farm, Oaks West and the Hilltop Road area, this public housing project will not be an area that attracts drug dealers, it will not raise crime and it will not lower property values.

> Just imagine what could happen if we became friends and neighbors with this housing community. It may become instead an area where people recapture a dream, learn valuable skills from their neighbors and become partners in building a better community.

As Elaine picked up her pad to make more notes, she thought, "We need more people who feel like that."

Not far from the GHA's administration building, Mary Wilson stood at the kitchen window of her Ray Warren Homes apartment. She watched her son Kevin walk down the street on his way home from school. "That silly kid's late getting home again," she thought to herself. Although she needed him to arrive home on time to watch her two younger children so she could go to work, she couldn't get too angry with him. He had made some really good friends at school this year. However, every day he got off the bus three blocks before his designated bus stop so he could be like the other "middle-class" kids and so they wouldn't know where he lived.

Harley-Davidson, Inc.

Charles Darnell
Jerry Rumpf

■ http://www.harley-davidson.com/

In 1992, Harley-Davidson embarked on an ambitious $80 million expansion to increase its motorcycle production capacity 24.4 percent by 1996.[1] Combined with implementation of cross-functional assembly teams and other internal strategies, Harley achieved its capacity goals in 1995, one full year ahead of schedule. Faced with an ever growing demand, and a strong interest in the European and Asian markets, Harley is considering plans for increasing production capacity from 115,000 units to 200,000 units annually by the year 2003.[2]

After facing near bankruptcy in the early 1980s, Harley is a financially sound public corporation with gross sales exceeding $1.5 billion.[3] Today, Harley enjoys an excellent reputation for product quality, which partly accounts for a demand that is much larger than supply. The typical lead time for a newly purchased motorcycle is 10 months. This delay helps to stimulate a secondary market, where a one-year-old motorcycle typically sells for a 30 percent premium over its original purchase price.[4] Also in 1995, the recreational vehicle subsidiary of Harley-Davidson, Holiday Rambler, returned to profitability.

However, amid the internal optimism, several significant issues regarding production capacity and market share continue to plague the company. As of June 1995, the price of Harley-Davidson stock had slumped 7 percent.[5] While motorcycle demand has remained strong, this sluggish stock market performance could reflect persistent complaints by market analysts that Harley's subsidiaries are a drain on its corporate resources.[6] Likewise, Harley's inability to meet demand may be jeopardizing its relationship with customers and hurting the company's reputation.

■ The Corporate Harley-Davidson

In its 90-year history, Harley-Davidson has endured two world wars, the Great Depression, and other significant economic downturns. However, throughout the 1970s and early 1980s, it barely survived its corporate ownership by the conglomerate AMF. During this period, emphasis was placed on meeting market demand without regard for product quality and customer service.[7] Accordingly, quality declined to the extent that new motorcycles often had to be rebuilt by the

This case was prepared under the direction of Professor Robert E. Hoskisson. This case was written for the purpose of stimulating class discussion and is not intended to convey any judgment on the administrative decision–making of the firm.

Exhibit 1   Harley-Davidson, Inc., Officers—March 1995

Name	Age	Title	Remuneration
Vaughn L. Beals, Jr.	67	Chairman of the board	NA
Richard F. Teerlink	58	President and CEO	$1,207,923
Jeffrey L. Bleustein	55	Subsidiary officer	$607,973
James M. Brostowitz	55	Vice president, controller, treasurer	NA
Thomas A. Gelb	59	Vice president	$490,508
William C. Gray	53	Vice president	$367,719
Timothy K. Hoelter	48	Vice president, legal counsel, secretary	NA
Martin R. Snoey	51	Subsidiary officer	$367,071
James L. Ziemer	45	Vice president, CFO, Assistant to the treasurer	NA

dealer before they could be sold. Many first-time motorcycle buyers turned to Honda and Yamaha, as the Harley reputation became synonymous with unreliability. Market share declined to 23 percent in 1983, down from a historical high of 73 percent in 1973. As Harley-Davidson teetered on the verge of extinction, AMF initiated plans to divest the division.[8]

Early in 1981, AMF Chairman Vaughn Beals persuaded 11 other Harley executives to join him in taking over the company in an $81.5 million leveraged buyout.[9] Current CEO Richard Teerlink left AMF, joining the other 11 buyers within a few months of the buyout as chief financial officer of the new company. The group found a willing lead lender in Citicorp, and after several months of tough bargaining with AMF, the independent Harley-Davidson Motor Company began business on June 16, 1981.[10] In 1984, Citicorp became disenchanted with Harley's projected profitability. Concerned about the prospects for a weakening economy and the impending end of tariff protection against Japanese big bikes, Citicorp began looking to unload the Harley debt. Harley negotiated out of its arrangement with Citicorp and acquired financing from Heller Financial Corp. Harley-Davidson returned to public ownership in July 1986, raising $20 million in a stock offering, thus enabling the refinancing of its debt.[11] After struggling throughout the early 1980s, Harley-Davidson was able to improve the quality of its product and reassert itself as the market leader in a prominent segment of the U.S. motorcycle market.

Executive Officers and Ownership

Exhibit 1 sets forth, as of March 21, 1995, the name, age, title, and remuneration of the executive officers of Harley-Davidson. All of these individuals have been employed by the company in an executive capacity for more than five years, except William C. Gray and Martin R. Snoey.

Harley-Davidson, Inc., currently has 77,269,617 shares outstanding as of October 10, 1995 (see Exhibit 2). These shares are divided between institutional investors (51 percent), general investors (45.45 percent), and insiders (3.55 percent; see Exhibit 3).

Exhibit 2   Harley-Davidson, Inc., Ownership—October, 1995

Shares held by institutions	39,409,000	51.00%
Shares held by insiders	2,741,000	3.55%
Remaining shares outstanding	35,119,617	45.45%
Current total outstanding shares	77,269,617	

Exhibit 3   Harley-Davidson, Inc., Insider Ownership—October 1995

Name of Insider	Shares	Relationship	Filing Date	Last Trade
Richard F. Teerlink	450,400	President and CEO	Feb-95	—
Vaughn L. Beals, Jr.	312,630	Chairman of the board	Feb-95	—
Jeffrey L. Bleustein	270,112	Subsidiary officer	Feb-95	—
Timothy K. Hoelter	200,000	Vice president, legal counsel, secretary	Feb-95	—
Harold W. Dahl	180,088	Director	May-93	—
William G. Davidson	173,000	Vice president	Dec-91	—
James H. Peterson	173,000	Vice president	May-93	—
Mark G. Tuttle	126,160	Vice president	Apr-91	—
Robert R. Miller	112,672	Vice president	Sep-91	—
John H. Campbell	88,464	Officer—Holiday Rambler	Nov-92	(9,628)
Bernard J. Witczak	80,120	Retired	Jan-91	—
Thomas A. Gelb	75,944	Vice president	May-95	—
James L. Ziemer	68,133	Vice president, CFO, assistant to treasurer	Feb-95	—
Jerry G. Wilke	67,968	Vice president	Apr-91	—
Stanley R. Kulp	67,269	NA	Apr-91	—
Clyde Fessler	66,112	Vice president	Apr-91	—
Kathleen A. Demitros	65,200	Vice president	Apr-91	—
James M. Brostowitz	45,104	Vice president	Feb-95	—
Richard E. Bond	44,712	Vice president	Dec-93	—
Donald A. James	20,000	Director	Dec-92	—
Michael R. Myers	18,056	Officer—Holiday Rambler	Jul-93	(13,902)
Frederick L. Brengel	8,000	Director	Dec-92	—
Michael J. Kami	8,000	Director	May-92	—
Barry K. Allen	4,000	Director	May-95	100
William F. Andrews	4,000	Director	Dec-94	—
Fred T. Deeley	4,000	Retired	May-91	—
R. J. Hermon-Taylor	4,000	Director	Dec-94	—
Richard G. Lefauve	2,000	Director	May-95	2,000
James A. Norling	2,000	Director	Dec-94	—
Ronald M. Hutchinson	88	Vice president	Dec-93	—
	2,741,232			(21,430)

The AMF Years

In 1968 the conglomerate American Machine & Foundry (AMF) prevailed in a bidding war with Bangor Punta to acquire Harley-Davidson. The deal converted each Harley-Davidson share to 1.5 AMF shares, which netted original owners of Harley stock an estimated 700 percent return in just under a five-year period. This opportunity motivated some Davidson and Harley family members to liquidate their holdings. By 1971 Walter Davidson had departed the company, and board chairman William Davidson's position was primarily a facade, because the Harley board of directors had been disbanded. A company that was once considered so stable that it was accused of "throwing away calendars after 1936," entered a period of great turbulence. In the decade to follow, Harley had six different presidents. Lack of decision-making autonomy at the division level and disagreements with corporate AMF personnel clearly prompted some of the departures.[12]

Not all AMF contributions to Harley Davidson can be viewed as bad for the company. AMF contributed millions of research and development dollars to Harley, which were largely credited for the advent of the Super Glide as well as various other product innovations. AMF also invested a staggering $4.5 million to mass produce Harley's five-speed transmissions. However in retrospect, James Paterson, one of the original 12 buyout partners has stated that "one of the problems during the AMF years was the fact that the company went for a long while without a corporate strategy." William Davidson concluded further that AMF's miscalculation was that "they thought Harley-Davidson could become another Honda." "We were never meant to be a high-production company" said Davidson, who in 1982 scoffed at the idea that Harley might ever be capable of duplicating Honda's 3.5 million units produced in that year.[13]

The American Market for Heavyweight Motorcycles

Harley-Davidson competes in the heavyweight motorcycle market class, which is defined by engine displacements in excess of 751 cc. As the last surviving American company to manufacture and assemble motorcycles, Harley commands a dominating 56 percent share of the domestic market in the heavyweight motorcycle class.[14] The company currently manufactures 20 models of motorcycles, which range in selling price between $5,000 and $17,500. For the past nine years, Harley sales have been robust. While domestic registration of heavyweight motorcycles increased by 17 percent in 1993, and 15 percent in 1994, the company is projecting slower overall market growth in the near future.[15] Over this same two-year period, the company's market share declined slightly from 57.9 to 55.7 percent.[16]

The typical Harley purchaser is a male in his early forties with a mean family income of $65,200.[17] The common interests of a Harley purchaser are recreational rather than transportation oriented.[18] Harley's main competitors in the heavyweight class include Honda, Kawasaki, Yamaha, BMW, Motoguzie, and Suzuki.

The International Motorcycle Market

International motorcycle sales account for approximately 28 percent of Harley-Davidson total net sales and are anchored by market shares of 17 percent in the Asia/Pacific region and 11 percent in Europe. Sales in Germany, Japan, Canada, and Australia account for approximately 60 percent of all export sales for Harley. Harley-Davidson is determined to increase market share in Europe, estimating that the total market is approximately 9 percent larger than the U.S. market. Likewise, Harley believes that the Asian/Pacific region is potentially the world's largest developing market for heavy motorcycles. Even though Harley maintains full-service motorcycle dealerships in Japan, Singapore, and Malaysia, other Asian countries such as Thailand and Taiwan are closed to the company because of government import restrictions. With a market potential in excess of two million registered motorcyclists in Thailand alone, each of these areas represents tremendous growth potential for the company. Harley continues to work with U.S. and foreign government agencies in an effort to ease import restrictions and other trade barriers. In an effort to prime these potential markets, Harley has opened Motorclothes boutiques in Taipei, Taiwan, and Bangkok, Thailand. By making its presence known through offerings of licensed Harley-Davidson clothes and accessories, the company hopes to stimulate a demand for its motorcycles in these otherwise closed markets.

In the face of unmet domestic demand, Harley has initiated policies that limit export allocations to 30 percent of total production. Furthermore, Harley has refused numerous license bids by foreign firms to produce and assemble Harley-Davidson motorcycles outside the United States. To enhance international market growth in Europe, Harley has implemented new strategies for improving distribution systems by consolidating and centralizing distribution in Amsterdam. Studies that led to improvements in dealership networks and customer service in Europe are now being duplicated to determine how best to serve the characteristic needs of customers in the Asian/Pacific Region.

Harley-Davidson's Failure in Lightweight Motorcycle Markets

In 1960 Harley-Davidson, acquired 50 percent of Aermacchi of Italy and from 1961 to 1978 produced a variety of small-displacement lightweight motorcycles. While some models competed directly with Honda lightweights, the Aermacchi/Harley line could not overcome persistent reliability problems or the perception of high relative pricing. While a Treasury Department ruling in 1978 agreed with AMF's contention that the Japanese had been "dumping" their products on the American market, the International Trade Commission ruled that Harley lightweight motorcycle sales had not been harmed by this activity. Many believe that this ruling came about after commissioners interviewed Harley dealerships directly. When queried about Aermacchi/Harley models, dealers indicated that the small Harley-Davidson's were obsolete and could not compete with the state-of-the-art Japanese bikes. The Aermacchi interests were sold by Harley-Davidson in 1978, which resulted in a significant write-off in that year.[19]

Related Product Markets

Harley-Davidson licenses its trademark for use on jewelry, clothing, leather goods, and numerous other products. The parts and accessory division helps to improve the brand image of Harley-Davidson. Moreover, this approach helps to recruit potential customers and stimulates brand loyalty through its appeal to a customer's individualism. This Harley-Davidson division grew by 97.3 percent in the three years following 1992, and now accounts for approximately 17 percent of net sales. Accordingly, the company intends to expand its licensing activities in the United States and abroad. Licensing of the trademarks has also provided an effective mechanism for policing unauthorized use of the Harley-Davidson name, thereby protecting its brand recognition. While licensing revenues only account for approximately 2 percent of net sales, the profitability of this business is extremely lucrative for the company. More importantly, however, it fosters the image of its brand, which is a valuable intangible resource.

Harley-Davidson Motorcycle Division

Manufacturing

Harley-Davidson has progressed significantly from the days when its motorcycles were often derided for poor quality. Adoption of just-in-time inventory techniques, employee involvement, and statistical process control have been the foundation of Harley's continuous improvement program.[20] Cross-trained teams consisting of three "builders" incorporated into its assembly line complete construction of an entire motorcycle.[21] Builders are paid at two grades higher than other assemblers. While the pay differential is not substantial, worker pride and a sense of identity provide for a level of motivation that makes the entire assembly system work effectively. Assembly line improvements have resulted in production rates of one Sportster every 45 minutes totaling 130 per day, which far exceeds earlier production rates of only 20 motorcycles per day.[22] Improvements were largely achieved by working "smarter, not harder"; only one additional worker was added to the line to increase production output substantially. The three-member teams rotate job duties at the end of the assembly line to reduce monotony and promote cross-training. These methods have been so effective that team flexibility helps to reduce some of the more typical assembly line problems such as absenteeism and boredom. While these improvements typify the company's efficiency efforts, these concepts have yet to be applied to more than just one assembly line. Three older lines used by the company have yet to be converted.

Empowerment of the workforce has been an important objective of CEO Richard Teerlink. "We hope to [empower] by recognizing that the primary responsibilities of the leaders is to create an environment where people want to do great things," says Teerlink.[23] Teerlink continues, "Figuring out ways to help people in the organization" and "balancing employee empowerment with value creation and stakeholder interests" are key elements for creating that environment.[24] Examples of the organization's cultural philosophy is seen at the York, Pennsylvania, plant, where assembly line workers have embraced a goal of trimming current production cycle times of just over three minutes, to three minutes flat.

In the early 1980s, Harley management visited a Honda assembly plant in Marysville, Ohio, with the intent of learning how the Japanese were capable of building better bikes at a lower price. According to then acting CEO Vaughn Beals, "We were being wiped out by the Japanese because they were better managers. It wasn't robotics, or culture, or morning calisthenics and company songs—it was professional managers who understood their business and paid attention to detail."[25] Soon after their bench marking visit, Harley replaced its computer-based control and elaborate 3.5-mile overhead conveyor system with a push cart just-in-time (JIT) inventory system. Opting for a low-tech material handling system improved manufacturing reliability because parts were more easily located and arrived at workstations in tact. Likewise Harley all but abandoned a broad strategy to compete directly in Japanese-dominated markets, favoring instead the heavyweight market niche.[26]

Domestic Labor Relations

At the beginning of 1995, the motorcycle division of the company had 4,300 employees. Production workers at the Wisconsin manufacturing facilities are generally represented by the United Paperworkers International Union (UPIU), which is part of the AFL-CIO. Other positions at the Wisconsin facilities and most workers at the York, Pennsylvania, plant are represented by the International Association of Machinists and Aerospace Workers (IAM). The collective bargaining agreements with the IPIU and the IAM will expire in early 1997, at all company locations.[27]

The emphasis on training programs and a strong employee involvement approach are largely credited with creating value in Harley-Davidson's human resources. The company's union contract stipulates that when promoted to a new position, an employee must learn the skills involved in 20 days, or relinquish the position.[28] In redesigning its planning and assembly processes, Harley brought together management, engineering, and maintenance groups to work toward consensus decision making. Conversely, during the time when Harley was plagued with quality control problems, an adversarial relationship existed between Harley's engineering and assembly functions. According to Mr. Vaughn Beals regarding assembly line changes, "Engineering would make its usual number of errors, and the typical employee reaction was "those dummies screwed up again." Mr. Beals continues, "And worse yet, the employees wouldn't have lifted a finger to help solve the problems."[29]

Supplier Relations

Because of the high demand for its products, Harley maintains close partnerships with its raw material suppliers. The company has reduced the number of suppliers in recent years, and generally offers more of its business to companies that employ similar manufacturing strategies as does Harley. In this informal "partnership", Harley-Davidson directly assists its suppliers in the implementation of manufacturing techniques employed by Harley through training sessions and plant evaluations.

Approximately 80 percent of Harley's suppliers are located within 180 miles of Milwaukee, Wisconsin, making it easier to manage the JIT system while simultaneously reducing transportation costs.[30] The company purchases all of its raw material, principally steel and aluminum castings, forgings, sheet and bars, and certain motorcycle components, including carburetors, batteries, tires, seats, electrical components, and instruments. Certain of these components are secured from one of a limited number of suppliers. Interruptions from certain of these suppliers could adversely affect the company's production pending the establishment of substitute supply arrangements. The company anticipates no significant difficulties in obtaining raw materials or components for which the source of supply is limited.

■ Marketing and Distribution

Harley-Davidson's primary distribution channels consist of more than 600 independently owned, full-service dealerships. The company sells directly to each of its dealers, of which approximately 75 percent sell Harley-Davidson motorcycles exclusively. Each dealer sells genuine Harley-Davidson parts and provides full maintenance and repair services. The company has also implemented a Designer Store Service, which helps its dealers upgrade the appearance of their businesses. Through this program, the company provides expert assistance to the dealer for creating a more inviting and comfortable retail environment. Of the 1,033 worldwide dealerships, approximately 465 (45 percent) are classified as designer stores. Combined with intense dealer and sales force training, Harley believes that the upgraded stores have accounted for a significant increase in the dealers' success. The company believes the program has been so successful that it now requires all new dealerships, as well as any changes in store ownership, to implement its designer store concept.[31]

For the three years beginning in 1992, Harley spent an average of $55 million on domestic (U.S.) marketing and advertising. The company's marketing efforts include dealer promotions, customer events, magazine advertising, and public relations.

To hold on to its market share in the United States, Harley perpetuates the image of independence that is often credited for making the country great. "I think that we represent the adventurous pioneer spirit, the wild west, having your own horse, and going where you want to go—the motorcycle takes on some of the attributes of the iron horse. It suggests personal freedom and independence," Teerlink asserts.[32] Customer loyalty also accounts for the company's steady demand. As Teerlink notes, "The power of Harley-Davidson is the power to market to consumers who love the product."[33]

Perhaps the most visible example of Harley-Davidson, Inc.'s close-to-the-customer marketing philosophy can be found in its enthusiast organization— Harley Owners Group (HOG). HOG is the largest company-sponsored club in the motorcycle industry. One of Harley's most useful marketing tools is its steadfast participation in the annual road rallies cosponsored by HOG and Harley-Davidson. HOG members and company employees participate in these rallies to show off their bikes and socialize with other riders. In 1994, more than 60,000 HOG members were entertained in four U.S. national rallies, one "touring" rally, and 41 state rallies. In addition, there was record attendance at rallies held in the Czech Republic, Germany, England, France, Norway, Canada, New Zealand, and Australia. Worldwide HOG membership reached 270,000 members in 1994, up from 250,000 in 1993. Local chapters increased to 858, up from 800. Roughly 20 percent of HOG members live outside the United States. By "pressing the flesh and sharing stories," Harley managers not only endear themselves to the customer, but receive valuable insights that enable them to better satisfy customers' needs.

■ Harley Davidson Subsidiaries

■ Holiday Rambler

The recreational vehicle (RV) section of Harley-Davidson is known as the Transportation Vehicle Division. This division manufactures Class A motorhomes in the midrange and premium market segments. Prices range from $166,000 in the premium quality range, and $53,600 to $113,000 in the midrange market. The division also manufactures travel trailers designed to be towed by a passenger vehicle. Called towables, these products sell for prices ranging from $46,800 to $72,500. Additional production includes general utility-type vehicles manufactured under the Utilimaster trade name. These vehicles are designed as delivery and service trucks and are purchased under large fleet contracts with Federal Express, Frito Lay, and Ryder Truck Rental Inc.[34]

In 1994, the Transportation Vehicle Division accounted for $382.9 million (sum of Recreational, Commercial and other vehicles), or 25 percent of net corporate sales (see Exhibit 4). During the past few years, the entire RV market has experienced double-digit growth. In 1994, the Endeavor motorhome, which is priced in the company's midrange, was named a "Best Buy" by *Consumer's Digest* magazine. To meet increasing demand, the Travel Vehicle Division has initiated expansion plans for its Class A motorhomes, towables, and its Utilimaster line. The commercial division is currently running second shifts to keep up with demand. While the RV division sales have increased by 40 percent in the two years beginning in 1992, competition within this market is significant. During this period, the RV division held a 5.5 percent market share, and a 2.2 percent share, in Class A RVs and towables, respectively. This performance had Holiday Rambler ranked fourth and tenth in each of these markets behind the industry leader, Fleetwood Enterprises, Inc.[35]

Exhibit 4	Harley-Davidson, Inc., Motorcycle Unit Shipments & Consolidated Net Sales		
	Year ended December 31,		
	1992	1993	1994
Motorcycle unit shipments	76,495	81,696	95,811
Net sales (in millions):			
Motorcycles	$667.2	$734.3	$902.6
Motorcycle parts and accessories	$155.7	$199.0	$256.3
Recreational vehicles	$202.1	$192.7	$274.5
Commercial vehicles	$67.9	$78.9	$95.1
Other	$12.4	$12.5	$13.3

The commercial vehicles produced by the Utilimaster division account for approximately 25 percent of the total revenues of the transportation vehicle division. Competition in commercial utility vehicles is lead by Grumman-Olsen Corporation, Union City Body Company Inc., and Supreme Corporation. Competition is based on price, quality, and responsiveness to design requirements and speed of delivery.[36]

As of early 1995, the Transportation Vehicle Division employed approximately 2,400 employees. None of these employees is currently represented by labor unions.

There have been persistent complaints by market analysts that the Transportation Vehicle Division is a drain on Harley Davidson's corporate resources.[37] A 7 percent decline in the company's stock price between June 1993 and June 1994 may well reflect these concerns. CEO Teerlink believes that the RV market is on the verge of more explosive growth, as baby boomers begin to reach retirement age. Much of Harley-Davidson's investment in the division is geared to position it for taking advantage of this market growth.

Buell Motorcycle Company

During 1993, Harley acquired a 49 percent interest in Buell Motorcycle Company, a manufacturer of performance motorcycles. This investment in Buell offers the company the possibility of gradually gaining entry into select niches within the performance motorcycle market. Buell began distribution of a limited number of Buell motorcycles during 1994 to select Harley-Davidson dealers. Since that time, Harley's Buell Motorcycle Company joint venture has produced better than expected results, with the new S2 Thunderbolt motorcycle gaining positive reviews in major motorcycle publications.[38] With increased promotion and dealer support in 1995, Harley expected further demand for Buell products in the sport/performance motorcycle market.

Financial Characteristics

Except for its Holiday Rambler, Harley Davidson has a very narrow market focus compared to its principal competitors. Harley's motorcycle sales account for more than 75 percent of its revenues as compared to 14 percent for Honda, 55 percent for Yamaha, and 16 percent for Suzuki. These competitors also compete across market classes, selling different sizes and styles of motorcycle, whereas Harley competes predominantly in the heavyweight market. This lack of market diversity makes financial comparisons with competitors difficult. Given the characteristics of demand for Harley-Davidson motorcycles, there is an expectation that the company's return on assets would exceed those of its competitors. However, a review of Exhibit 5 reveals that the firm's performance was only roughly equivalent to the industry average. This performance only slightly improved after adjustments were made for the write-off of goodwill attendant to its acquisition of Holiday Rambler. Neither the profit margin nor return on equity ratios portray a company capitalizing on its popularity much beyond that of its closest competitors (see Exhibit 5).

Harley-Davidson maintains minimal levels of long-term debt financing. At the year ending December 31, 1994, the company had acquired only $17 million of

Exhibit 5	Harley-Davidson, Inc., Return on Assets, Profit Margin, and Return on Equity		
Year ended December 31,	1992	1993	1994
Return on Assets			
Harley-Davidson	10.0%	−2.0%	14.0%
Industry average	8.0%	4.0%	14.0%
Profit Margin			
Harley-Davidson	5.0%	−1.0%	7.0%
Industry average	8.0%	1.0%	6.0%
Return on Equity			
Harley-Davidson	16.0%	−4.0%	24.0%
Industry average	28.0%	16.0%	47.0%

an estimated $46 million from available lines of credit. As of the first quarter of 1995, there were 28,135 shareholders of record. The company paid dividends of $0.14 and $0.06 per share of stock in the years 1994 and 1993, respectively. Prior to these periods the stock had not paid dividends.[39]

Planning for the Future

After pouring over financial statements (see Exhibits 6 and 7), growth projections, and other company performance data, it appears clear to Harley management that the opportunity for continued and significant company growth is likely. Opportunities in the European and Asian regions appear particularly strong within its core heavyweight motorcycle market. Because of its experiences in the 1970s, Harley-Davidson is resolute in its promise not to expand capacity at the expense of quality. Similarly, the company has rejected foreign production opportunities in order to maintain its made in America image. Yet, how perilous is Harley's market position given the lengthy lead time for its products? Is the company's recent decline in market share an expression of customer frustration?

These concerns are perhaps best summarized by CEO Teerlink when questioned about the company's capacity constraints: "Fortunately we have regained a very strong market position, so we're sold out. We can't make enough motorcycles. But that's a double edge sword: it means we've got customers out there who are unhappy with us because they can't share in the enjoyment of the product."

Will Harley-Davidson be able to continue enjoying a market where customers are willing to wait more than 10 months for a motorcycle? What if Harley's competitors are able to imitate the desirable features of its products, yet offer them more quickly, and at potentially lower prices? How stable is Harley's core market, and how difficult will it be for the company to recruit customers that do not already love the product?

Exhibit 6   Harley-Davidson, Inc., Consolidated Statements of Operations

Year ended December 31,	1992	1993	1994
Net sales	$1,105,284	$1,217,428	$1,541,796
COGS	$808,871	$880,269	$1,120,332
Selling, administrative and engineering expenses	$199,216	$210,329	$261,157
Goodwill and restructuring changes*		($57,024)	
Income from operations	$97,197	$69,806	$160,307
Interest expense net	($4,912)	($831)	$44
Lawsuit judgment	$2,200		
Other income (ezxpense), net	($5,676)	($2,460)	$1,718
	($8,388)	($3,291)	$1,762
Income from operations before extraordinary items and accounting changes	$88,809	$66,515	$162,069
Provision for income tax	$34,636	$48,072	$57,797
Discontinued operations, net of tax	$0	$0	$0
Extraordinary items, net of tax	($388)	$0	$0
Cumulative effect of accounting changes, net of tax	$0	($30,328)	$0
Net income (loss)	$53,785	($11,885)	$104,272

*Includes a $57.0 million charge related primarily to the write-off of goodwill at the Transportation Vehicles segment (Holiday Rambler).

Should Harley-Davidson divest Holiday Rambler, or will Teerlink's intuition regarding the impending retirement of baby boomers prove eminent? Will Teerlink's intuition alone prove sufficient, or will Harley have to increase its level of support to that division? Are there lessons Harley should apply regarding its subsidiaries that it might have learned from its own experiences at AMF?

Is Harley's investment in Buell a wise move for them? Will introduction of Harley-Davidson motorcycles in the high-performance class be well received by the market, or will this diversion outside of Harley's market niche sap corporate resources?

In summary, Harley-Davidson's management is faced with many key decisions that are capable of creating conflicts in corporate objectives. What strategies Harley-Davidson management employs to balance these pressures will no doubt play an important role in the future success of this company.

■ Appendix

Harley Davidson has authorized 0.5 million shares of Series A Junior Participating preferred stock. Each share has a par value of $1, and no shares are currently outstanding. The allocation of preferred stock satisfies the firm's outstanding preferred stock purchase right. This option conveys to the owner a one-quarter right for each share of common stock held. Under certain conditions, the owner of common stock may purchase one one-hundredth of a share of preferred stock at a price of $100, which is subject to adjustment. The preferred stock holder is

Exhibit 7 Harley-Davidson, Inc., Consolidated Balance Sheet

Year ended December 31,	1992	1993	1994
Assets			
Cash and cash equivalents	$44,172	$77,709	$59,285
Accounts receivable	$93,178	$86,031	$143,396
Inventories	$94,428	$140,151	$173,420
Prepaid expenses	$9,617	$9,571	$9,424
Other current assets	$24,120	$20,296	$20,111
Total current assets	$265,515	$333,758	$405,636
Property, plant, and equipment (net)	$183,787	$205,768	$262,787
Other assets	$72,912	$43,759	$70,792
Total assets	$522,214	$583,285	$739,215
Liabilities and Stockholders' Equity			
Accounts payable	$58,004	$56,350	$63,988
Salaries payable	$25,612	$41,226	$62,882
ST debt and current LTD	$16,965	$21,369	$18,303
Other current liabilities	$68,652	$71,817	$71,105
Total current liabilities	$169,233	$190,762	$216,278
Long-term debt	$7,224	$12,612	$29,422
Deferred taxes	$10,327	$0	$0
Postretirement health care benefits	$0	$54,999	$60,283
Total liabilities	$186,784	$258,373	$305,983
Common stock, net	$385	$385	$772
Additional paid-in capital	$131,053	$137,150	$150,728
Retained earnings	$204,213	$188,774	$283,010
Unrealized foreign exchange GN/LOS	$757	$186	$303
	$336,408	$326,495	$434,813
Less: Treasury stock	$1,028	$1,583	$1,581
Total shareholders' equity	$335,380	$324,912	$433,232
Total liabilities and shareholders' equity	$522,164	$583,285	$739,215

entitled to 400 votes per share. These rights are subject to adjustment and together with other rights should approximate the value of common stock at a ratio of one share preferred to four shares common. The rights can only be exercised if an individual or group has acquired, or announced its intention to acquire, 25 percent or more of the outstanding common stock.[40]

Notes

1. Harley-Davidson Inc., 1994, *Annual Report.*
2. L. Croghan, 1995, Customers for life: How to hang on to your core market the Harley-Davidson way, *Finance World,* September 26, 26–31.
3. Harley-Davidson Inc., 1994, *Annual Report.*
4. Croghan, Customers for life.
5. R. D. Hylton, 1995, Finding bargains among stock market laggards, *Fortune,* June 26, 164.

6. Croghan, Customers for life.
7. How Harley beat back the Japanese, 1989, *Fortune,* September 25, 155–164.
8. Ibid.
9. Ibid.
10. Ibid.
11. Ibid.
12. Wright, David K., 1983, *Harley-Davidson Motor Company* (Osceola, Wisconsin: Motorbooks International), 244–267
13. Ibid
14. Harley-Davidson Inc., 1994, *Annual Report.*
15. Ibid.
16. Ibid.
17. Harley-Davidson Inc., 1994, Form 10-K.
18. Ibid.

19. Wright, *Harley-Davidson Motor Company*, 85, 86, 249–251.
20. Circles and cycles, 1995, *Executive Excellence,* September, 6–7.
21. R. Y. Bergstrom, 1995, Take three people, and build a motorcycle, *Production,* November, 60–63.
22. Ibid.
23. Circles and cycles.
24. Ibid.
25. How Harley beat back the Japanese.
26. Ibid.
27. Harley-Davidson Inc., 1994, Form 10-K.
28. Bergstrom, Take three people, and build a motorcycle.

29. How Harley beat back the Japanese.
30. S. Cayer, 1988, Harley's new manager–owners put purchasing out front, *Purchasing,* October 13, 50–54.
31. Harley-Davidson Inc., 1994, *Annual Report.*
32. Circles and cycles.
33. Ibid.
34. Harley-Davidson Inc., 1994, Form 10-K.
35. Ibid.
36. Ibid.
37. Croghan, Customers for life.
38. Harley-Davidson Inc., 1994, *Annual Report.*
39. Harley-Davidson Inc., 1994, Form 10-K.
40. Ibid.

■ CASE 19 The Hue-Man Experience Bookstore

Joan Winn
University of Denver

■ http://www.denver-rmn.com/insid/
guide/books/huebook.htm

I began telling everyone who came in the store that this was the largest African-American bookstore in the country. I really didn't know if that was true, but it was the largest one I had ever seen in my travels and everyplace I go I'm always looking for bookstores. Maybe eventually I'll uncover one that's larger and I'll have to acknowledge it, but until then I won't say anything different. So I began to create that image in people's minds, nationally as well as locally. —Clara Villarosa

What began in 1984 as an attempt to set up an independent business targeted to affluent African-Americans was by 1992 a 3000-square-foot retailing establishment and North Denver community landmark. The Hue-Man Experience Bookstore specialized in books, cards, jewelry, and artwork by and for people of color (hence the "Hue" in "Human"). While most patrons lived within five miles of the bookstore, the Hue-Man Experience Bookstore had gained a national reputation, attracting frequent out-of-town visitors. By 1994, Clara Villarosa was looking at expansion. The availability of the building next door kindled her dream of creating an Afrocentric retail and cultural center.

■ History

The Hue-Man Experience Bookstore grew out of the dream of a woman who had already made it in corporate America. Clara Villarosa started out professionally as a psychiatric social worker, working in an outpatient (nonresidential) clinic in Chicago, after receiving a master's degree in social work in 1954. Like many women of her generation, she dropped out of the workforce when her children were born. In 1968, when her daughters were five and nine years old, Clara and her husband moved the family to Denver. Clara soon took a position in the department of behavioral sciences at Denver's Children's Hospital. By the time

This case was originally presented at the Case Critique Colloquium at the Academy of Management Conference, August 1994. The author thanks the management and employees for their cooperation in the field research for this case, which was written solely for the purpose of stimulating student discussion.
Copyright © 1995 by the *Case Research Journal* and Joan Winn.

she left the hospital in 1980, she had become the director of the department of behavioral sciences and assistant hospital administrator. After entering a doctoral program in social work and law, she started a consulting business.

> I wanted to help African-Americans move up the corporate ladder and I thought I could sell that idea to large corporations. As a social worker I had some skills, but I didn't know how to knock on doors, to get a business off the ground. When I ran out of money I took a temporary job at United Bank. I started out in employee relations and moved quickly up the corporate ladder, becoming the vice president of Human Resources within two years. Again I found myself in the position of being the highest African-American on the payroll. But, as often happened in those times, I hit the glass ceiling. People were extremely resentful and angry about African-Americans and affirmative action and I received a significant backlash. So I left the bank. But left the bank with some money. I think they *wanted* me to quit.

Her consulting business had taught her that she wanted to sell something tangible, and at the same time, something that would relate in a positive way to the African-American community.

> And I came up with books, because I've always been a reader. My father was a reader and I grew up immersed in books. We [the African-American community] had had a bookstore in Denver, but there wasn't one now, so my dream was to create the largest African-American bookstore in Denver.

This time, Clara researched her market and wrote a business plan, outlining the financial and marketing requirements of her ethnic bookstore concept. With the help of two friends and her severance from the bank, she got together $35,000 and secured a lease on a two-story row house in a rundown residential/commercial area north of downtown Denver in a predominantly African-American area. The Hue-Man Experience Bookstore opened in 1984. In 1986, realizing that business and friendship don't always mix well, Clara arranged to buy out her partners' shares over a two-year period by selling shares of the business to interested friends and customers. In 1993, the Hue-Man Experience Bookstore was governed by a nine-member board of directors, elected annually by Clara, who owned 58 percent, and 31 shareholders. Financial data for the Hue-Man Experience Bookstore for 1990–1993 are given in Exhibits 1 and 2.

■ The Bookselling Industry

In 1992, book sales in the United States exceeded $16.1 billion, according to the Association of American Publishers. The American Book Trade Directory estimated that there were about 27,000 retailers of books in the United States, 15,700 of which were privately owned independent bookstores. The largest book retailers were general bookstore chains, which had sales of $2.9 billion in 1992 from a total of 2768 outlets. Exhibit 3 contains sales information for the largest bookstore chains in 1991 and 1992.

Major chain expansion began in the late 1970s to mid-1980s. Mall outlets carrying 1,000 to 20,000 titles proliferated toward the end of the 1980s. As mall growth slowed, the focus changed to superstores, huge discounters that averaged 200,000 titles, 5 to 10 times the number offered by specialty or mall stores. Barnes & Noble opened its first superstore in September 1990, in a Minneapolis suburb. The 15,000-square-foot store was patterned after such well-known

Exhibit 1   The Hue-Man Experience Bookstore Income Statements for 1990—1993 (Period Ending 12/31)

	1990	1991	1992	1993
Revenue				
Books	$181,134	$216,922	$272,542	$269,751
Cards	26,024	26,517	25,811	23,106
Prints	13,503	15,579	13,994	9,616
Jewelry	3,903	2,152	1,759	1,438
Miscellaneous	17,274	16,967	14,712	7,154
Catalogue	13,098	18,268	21,338	6,828
Tapes and magazines	3,924	2,724	4,342	5,310
Reimbursed postage	1,428	3,070	3,345	2,433
Total revenue	260,289	302,198	357,841	325,635
Cost of sales				
Books	121,719	143,793	196,666	152,104
Cards	14,613	12,769	17,603	14,583
Prints	6,146	11,100	8,487	3,453
Jewelry	956	612	1,435	325
Miscellaneous	8,942	6,396	2,665	5,946
Tapes and magazines	3,568	2,437	8,319	4,044
Catalogue	3,336	5,661	779	120
Freight and postage	1,733	2,770	6,663	740
Framing supplies	1,815	590	1,379	538
Inventory (increase)/decrease	(1,094)	5,617	(4,047)	8,034
Total cost of sales	161,732	191,743	239,947	189,885
Gross margin	98,557	110,455	117,894	135,750
Administrative expenses				
Officer salary	26,000	26,814	29,599	24,973
Salaries	20,874	27,193	27,647	26,706
Employee benefits		160	169	3,454*
Advertising	3,848	4,406	4,740	3,309
Promotional	2,677	1,364	758	13
Accounting and legal	4,008	4,101	3,389	4,256
Vehicle expense	2,822	3,010	3,433	4,517
Bank and credit card service charges	3,791	2,208	6,407	1,175
Janitorial/cleaning expenses	276	164	240	
Consulting/contract labor	2,568	2,510	328	676
Contributions	864	900	229	293
Dues and subscriptions	907	1,242	933	1,977
License and fees		10	26	95
Depreciation	3,015	4,453	4,027	3,997

Continued

Exhibit 1   The Hue-Man Experience Bookstore Income Statements for 1990—1993 (Period Ending 12/31)—*Continued*

	1990	1991	1992	1993
Entertainment	971	257	1,409	3,299
Travel/conferences	4,011	1,530	1,576	2,082
Rent	9,078	7,677	7,350	12,495
Repairs and maintenance	869	662	2,008	2,609
Security	322	520	458	556
Telephone[1]	5,147	7,689	9,995	7,577
Utilities	2,445	2,722	2,636	3,055
Insurance		1,462	1,164	173
Office supplies and equipment	4,082	3,345	4,259	4,667
Printing			598	2,194
Store supplies	1,686	3,681	2,722	3,264
Taxes—personal property	148	284	486	
Taxes—payroll	4,156	4,826	4,970	4,409
Freight and postage	4,242	357	1,254	5,280
Miscellaneous	1,284	319	1,254	436
Total expenses	111,561	113,583	122,655	127,755
Other income (expenses)				
Interest earned	348	283	168	105
Other income	5,000	325	779	7
Interest expense	(566)	(297)	(2,145)	(155)
Bookstore net income (loss)	(8,222)	(2,817)	(5,960)	7,952
Rental income		2,066	16,950	19,536
Administrative expenses				
Depreciation—building		440	2,643	4,423
Repairs and maintenance		900	1,682	4,737
Utilities		125	1,046	235
Miscellaneous				575
Insurance—property			2,964	1,226
Taxes—real property		134	820	1,948
Interest income—building			35	131
Interest expenses—building		(1,140)	(2,252)	(6,001)
Total building income (expense)		(639)	5,674	390
Total other income (expense)	4,781	(328)	4,475	347
Net income/(loss)	(8,222)	(3,456)	(286)	8,342

*In 1993, Clara added health care coverage for the employees. Due to the prohibitive costs, this was discontinued by the end of the year, in favor of increased wages.

†Includes Yellow Pages advertising and 1–800 phone lines.

Exhibit 2 The Hue-Man Experience Bookstore Balance Sheets for 1990–1993 (Period Ending 12/31)

	1990	1991	1992	1993
Assets				
Current assets				
Cash and cash equivalents	$6,401	$14,675	$11,891	$13,787
Accounts receivable—trade			681	1,998
Prepaid employee benefits			1,134	
Inventory—merchandise	61,153	55,536	59,583	65,579
Total current assets	67,554	70,211	73,289	81,364
Property and equipment				
Building		79,260	79,260	79,260
Construction in progress			8,900	8,900
Leasehold improvements	6,701	6,701	6,701	6,701
Furniture and fixtures	3,323	3,323	3,323	3,323
Machines and equipment	16,888	21,888	23,943	25,917
Less accumulated depreciation	(13,994)	(18,887)	(25,557)	(33,977)
Other assets				
Organizational expense	5,056	5,056	5,056	5,056
Less accumulated amortization	(5,056)	(5,056)	(5,056)	(5,056)
Total fixed assets	12,919	92,286	96,571	90,125
Total assets	80,473	162,497	169,860	171,489
Liabilities and Stockholders' Equity				
Current liabilities				
Accounts payable	11,847	12,060	19,686	14,219
Security deposits		870	870	370
Payroll taxes payable	3,429	2,960	2,606	107
Sales tax payable	2,618	3,357	4,596	3,886
Property taxes payable		806	792	2,413
Deferred revenue	100	100	2,209	100
Interest payable—SBA loan		1,140	1,140	498
Officer loans	4,400	4,400	4,400	4,400
Accrued interest—shareholder			2,097	2,383
Total current liabilities	22,395	25,694	38,396	28,377
Noncurrent portion—SBA loan		72,000	66,948	70,255
Total liabilities	22,394	97,694	105,344	98,631
Stockholders' equity				
Common stock	46,102	56,282	56,282	56,282
Paid in capital	47,902	47,902	47,902	47,902
Retained earnings	(23,201)	(35,925)	(39,381)	(39,669)
Dividends	(4,502)			
Net profit (loss)	(8,222)	(3,456)	(287)	8,342
Total equity	58,079	64,803	64,515	72,858
Total liabilities & equity	80,473	162,497	169,860	171,489

Exhibit 3	U.S. Bookstore Chain Sales (Sales of 11 Largest Trade Bookstore Chains, 1992–1991)				
Chain	Ownership	'92 Sales*	'91 Sales	% Change	No. Stores at Year End
Waldenbooks	Kmart	$1146.0	$1139.0	.06	1260
Barnes & Noble	public (in 1993)	1086.7	920.9	18.00	916
Crown Books	Dart Group	240.7	232.5	3.50	247
Borders Books	Kmart	116.0	82.5	40.60	22[†]
Books-A-Million	public	95.1	72.8	30.60	107
Encore Books	Rite-Aid Corp.	65.2	52.3	24.70	103
Lauriat's[‡]	Chadwick-Miller	49.0	46.0	7.00	56
Tower Books[‡]	MTS Inc	33.0	29.0	13.80	15
Kroch's & Brentano's[†]	Waldenbooks	30.0[§]	33.0	−9.00	20
Rizzoli Bookstores[†]	private	24.0	21.0	14.30	11
Taylor's Inc.[†]	private	20.0	17.5	14.30	11
Totals		$2905.7	$2646.5	9.8%	2768

*Sales in millions. Figures are for calendar 1992 or most current fiscal year.

[†]Store totals do not include nine Basset Books transferred to Borders at year-end.

[‡]Estimated sales.

[§]Sales estimate is a projection for year ending June 30, 1993.

Source: *Publishers Weekly,* June 14, 1993.

independent booksellers as Oxford Books in Atlanta, Powell's Books in Portland, the Tattered Cover in Denver, and Waterstone's in Boston.

The hallmark of the chain superstores was discounting, selling mainly fiction, celebrity biographies, and other books that appeal to the general public. Increasing competition was coming from mail-order catalogs, warehouse clubs, discount retailers, and nonbook specialty stores (such as the Nature Company, Sutton Place Gourmet, and Toys 'R' Us). In addition, university bookstores had expanded their stock to include popular books and sidelines such as cards and clothing, and, more recently, books targeted to young adults, known as "generation X" or "13th Gen" books. Both chain and independent bookstores had been increasing their use of book catalogs and newsletters, which promoted bestsellers or discount specials and also served as promotional tools to get more people in the stores.

Profit margins among the large chains were estimated at less than 1 percent, which made volume critical to this business. Exhibit 4 shows estimates of financial performance for 1991 or 1992 based on *Publishers Weekly* data compiled from Barnes & Noble, Books-A-Million, and Crown Books (for chain-store estimates) and American Booksellers Association ABACUS survey results, based on reports from 199 independent bookstore operations.

Fiscal 1993 reports from the large chains showed revenue increases of 19 percent. Profit margins and operating income were similar to 1992 levels, resulting in operating margins for each of the two years at 3 percent, nearly twice the independents' 1.62 percent.

Exhibit 4   Comparison of Independent and Chain Bookstore Profitability
(Estimates of Bookstore Expenses as % of Total Sales*)

	Chains Composite Dollars (millions)	Chains (%)	Sample Independents Composite Dollars	Independents (%)
Net sales	$1197.8	100.0	$170.5	100.0
Receipts from books[†]	1078.1	90.0	136.4	80.0
Receipts from sidelines[†]	119.7	10.0	34.1	20.0
Cost of goods sold	816.3	68.2	106.4	62.4
Gross profit	381.5	31.8	64.1	37.6
Operating, selling, and administrative expense	317.8	26.5	61.4	36.0
Occupancy costs			12.3	7.2
Advertising			4.9	2.9
Depreciation and amortization	27.6	2.3		
Operating profit	36.1	3.0	2.8	1.6
Interest expense	29.9	2.5	.34	0.2
Income before tax	6.2	0.5	2.42	1.4
Income tax	5.5	0.4	.68	0.4[†]
Net income	0.7	0.1	1.7	1.0

*Calendar year 1991 or fiscal year ending 1992. (Most independents operate on a calendar year; chains report earnings on a fiscal year basis.)

[†]Estimate from anecdotal reports.

Source: *Publishers Weekly,* October 18, 1993.

Barnes & Noble attributed a 144 percent increase in sales in 1992 to its new superstores. In 1993, 30 percent of Barnes & Noble sales were from its 135 superstores, 77 of which were added in 1993. Another 75 stores were planned for 1994 and for 1995. Encore Books, which operated only one superstore in 1993, planned to open four more by mid-1994. Waldenbook's superstore operations were under the name of Borders, a previously independent 19-store chain purchased by Kmart in the fall of 1992. Borders (which also included Walden's Basset Book Shops) had 30 superstores in 1992 and planned to open 20 more by the end of 1993. Crown planned to increase its 22 superstores to 40 by the end of 1993. Books-a-Million, with 10 superstores in 1992, expected to open 5 more in 1993. Tower books had 15 stores by the end of 1992; Lauriat's was positioning its new Royal Discount Bookstores as superstores.

Many independent bookstore owners were concerned that the industry was going the way of hardware stores and neighborhood pharmacies. According to John Mutter of *Publishers Weekly,* there was fear that superstores were creating "a concentration of power that threatens the diversity of what gets published and what is available for the public to read."[1] The American Booksellers Association was cooperating with the Federal Trade Commission in investigating business practices and pricing policies that appeared to threaten the small independent book retailers.

While chains offered cheap prices, few could offer the personal service of independents who knew their customers. This was particularly true in the growing breed of specialty book stores. Some specialty booksellers focused on a particular subject, such as Armchair Sailor in New York, which specialized in nautical books; Victor Kamlin, Inc., in Rockville, Maryland, which specialized in Russian literature; Books of Wonder in New York, which specialized in children's books; Sports Central: The Ultimate Sports Bookstore in Palo Alto; or Books for Cooks in Baltimore. Others, like Salt of the Earth Bookstore in Albuquerque, Midnight Special in Santa Monica, California, and Odyssey Bookshop in South Hadley, Massachusetts, prided themselves on community involvement by promoting multicultural authors. Some stores focused on one particular market group, such as Charis Bookstore in Atlanta, which positioned itself as a feminist bookstore; OutBooks in Fort Lauderdale and A Different Light in San Francisco, which targeted lesbians and gays; and Shrine of the Black Madonna in Detroit and Hue-Man Experience Bookstore in Denver, which catered to an African-American clientele.

Bookselling and publishing by and for African-Americans had surged since 1988. An increasing interest in African-American culture, aided by school curriculum reforms, fueled a growth in bookstores catering to African-Americans. According to Wade Hudson, who ran Just Us Books in New Jersey, "African-Americans are hungry for knowledge and understanding about their experience, so they are looking for books that provide it."[2] Until recently, these books had been published by small independent publishing operations or by the authors themselves, and sold out of car trunks at book conventions. More recently, the major publishers and national distributors had entered this market, providing easier access to booksellers through mainstream distribution channels.

"Bookstores used to assume there was no market because blacks didn't come in asking for titles like these, but that's because they assumed the stores wouldn't stock them," Mr. Hudson commented. Kassahun Checole, president of the Red Sea Press, the largest distributor of African-American titles, had spent his career in the publishing business. Early in 1992, he told *Publishers Weekly,* "The Red Sea Press now distributes titles from about sixty publishers, approximately half of them African-American."[3]

Bookseller and publisher Haki Madhubuti, who had founded the African-American Publishers and Booksellers Association (AAPBA) in 1989, believed that "A good 30 to 35 percent of the people who buy our books aren't black."[4] The AAPBA held trade meetings and special sessions at the American Booksellers Association convention. This group became the first specialty segment within the ABA. As of 1992, there were several such segments, including a travel group and a mystery group, which held roundtable discussions at national and regional meetings and put together newsletters targeting specialty bookstore owners.

■ The Denver Market

According to the 1990 census, Colorado had almost 3.3 million residents; nearly 2 million lived in the greater metropolitan Denver area, of whom 460,000 lived within the city limits. While only 4 percent of Colorado's population was black, the city of Denver was nearly 13 percent black; 60 percent of these lived north of downtown.

According to Scarborough Research Corporation, Denver ranked 10 percent above the national average in the popularity of reading in 1993, ranking twenty-second out of 209 surveyed metropolitan areas. Forty-three percent of metropolitan Denver households were considered "avid readers." Both Denver and Boulder, 35 miles away, boasted independent superstores, which had been in existence for more than 20 years.

The Tattered Cover, a Denver landmark, was located in a former department store in Cherry Creek North, an established shopping area with nearly a million square feet of retail and service businesses. The Tattered Cover had 40,000 square feet of selling space on four floors, and boasted more than 220,000 titles. Across the street was the prestigious Cherry Creek Shopping Center. The Cherry Creek center, which had opened in August 1990, was a 1 million square foot mall comprised of luxury and specialty stores (including Doubleday Book Shop and Travelday's Book Shop, both owned by B. Dalton, and Brentano's, owned by Waldenbooks). Recent competitors, located in suburban areas, included five Barnes & Noble superstores, each with approximately 10,000 square feet of selling space. A sixth Barnes & Noble superstore was planned in a renovated theater building about two miles east of the Tattered Cover.

There was a wide variation in retail lease rates in Denver, depending on the location. Rents in Cherry Creek North averaged between $17 and $28 per square foot (calculated on a yearly basis). Rates for the Cherry Creek Shopping Center, immediately south of Cherry Creek North, were about twice that rate.

The Denver area had more than 100 independent retailers of new and used books. Specialty bookstores included Murder by the Book, which specialized in mystery fiction; Astoria Books and Prints, which specialized in rare books and artwork; Hermitage Antiquarian Bookshop, which specialized in collectibles and first editions; Isis Metaphysical Bookstore, which specialized in books on metaphysics, crystals and jewelry, and new-age music; Category Six Books, specializing in gay and lesbian literature; Cultural Legacy, which specialized in books in Spanish; and numerous children's bookstores and religious specialty stores.

The Hue-Man Experience bookstore was located on Park Avenue West, a well-traveled thoroughfare about a mile north of downtown, bordering the area known as Five Points, named for the five tramway lines that once intersected there. Five points was one of Denver's largest residential areas, encompassing more than 1,000 acres. Five Points had once been known as a cultural center for African-Americans, with more African-American–owned businesses than any other place in the United States except for Harlem. This began to change in 1959 with the passage of Colorado's Fair Housing Act. During the 1960s and 1970s, many of the more affluent African-Americans moved to other, more integrated, neighborhoods. In 1993, the Five Points area was populated with small service and retail establishments and rundown houses. According to 1990 census data, the average household income in Colorado was $36,015 (the U.S. average was $29,199). Half of the residents in the vicinity of Five Points had an annual household income under $35,000; nearly 30 percent of the households reported an annual income under $15,000.

Walking in the vicinity of Five Points was not considered advisable, especially after dark. In 1993, this area had the third highest crime rate in Denver, with 315.2 crimes reported per 1,000 population. In 1992, Five Points had ranked second. The highest crime area (consistently since 1989) was North Capital Hill, which bordered Five Points to the south, with 413.2 crimes reported per 1,000 population in 1993. These numbers included car thefts and petty robbery as well as gang violence and homicides, and Five Points was generally viewed as a undesirable part of town.

Hue-Man's Operations and Layout

The Hue-Man Experience Bookstore began operations in a two-story row house, one of four attached residential apartments. Within two years, Clara had expanded her store into the adjacent row house, convincing the landlord to do renovations to connect the two. She thought that with 4,200 titles occupying 3,000 square feet, the Hue-Man Experience was, very likely, the largest African-American bookstore in the United States.

Two cash registers, or point-of-sale computer terminals, were located just inside the door. Afrocentric greeting cards and note cards were located in a separate room adjacent to the checkout area. Afrocentric art created a backdrop for the checkout area, which was surrounded by a glass case displaying ethnic jewelry. An employee was always on hand to greet people and offer assistance. Each room was arranged around a particular theme or subject. Popular titles and classics were on the main floor, in what was once a living room. Upstairs, there were rooms devoted to sports, religion, music, and children's books.

Specialty cards, calendars, and jewelry comprised approximately 20 percent of sales. Fine art prints and ethnic artwork by local artists were displayed on the walls throughout the store and in two browsing racks. Calendars featuring African-American history and African-American art were also prominently displayed. During the holiday season, two rooms upstairs were full of distinctive boxed Christmas and Kwanzaa cards. People who bought books as gifts could also purchase gift wrapping and gift bags with African designs. As with most specialty stores, these sidelines were an integral part of the store's identity, geared specifically to the African-American market. Cards and jewelry typically have a bigger markup than books, and bring added traffic into the store.

Industry insiders recognized that books are often an impulse purchase, bought on a whim for personal reasons or to be given as a gift. Both small mall boutiques and large chain stores understood the importance of lighting and displays for enticing people to walk in the door to browse. Location and name recognition were also important, especially for independent booksellers.

Because of the fixed maximum price of most items, inventory control was critical to profitability. Computerized inventory control systems attached to point-of-sale (POS) terminals were considered essential for the success of large stores. These computer programs ranged in price from around $400 (for software that runs on most PCs) to over $5,000 (for systems that included POS terminals, cash registers, and scanners). Some of the more expensive computer systems available could be connected to on-line electronic ordering systems with wholesalers or major distributors to expedite reorders and returns. Others could tie into banking networks for credit card authorization and check scanning. Hue-Man Experience used a program called Booklog, a menu-driven system that was easy to use, even for "noncomputer" people. Booklog kept track of purchases and sales, and these records could be used to track fast- and slow-moving items. Booklog also kept a customer file, which was used for identifying frequent buyers and sending out announcements or newsletters.

Employees were critical to the success of independent booksellers, whose customers relied on service. Many booksellers had difficulty finding qualified employees, people who read and who were knowledgeable about books, who were personable, and who were willing to work hard. Wages in most bookstores ranged from $4.50 to $5.50 per hour, far less than most full-time employment. Despite this, and even given Denver's strong economy, booksellers such as the

Tattered Cover and Hue-Man Experience had had no trouble finding competent, well-educated employees who liked their work.

There were four full-time employees at the Hue-Man Experience Bookstore. Turnover was low, with employees typically staying over a year, a rarity in minimum-wage positions. The employees at the Hue-Man Experience Bookstore conveyed a sense of belonging, not only to the bookstore, but also to the cultural community. One employee at Hue-Man Experience Bookstore, a college graduate who majored in African-American studies, had stayed at the store for over a year because she enjoyed learning more about her culture and interacting with African-Americans in her community.

Marketing

Clara commented:

> I started out with a marketing plan, but there were many flaws because it was based on Anglo book purchasing behavior. We were unable to anticipate the difficulty in getting African-American people to buy books. I had to go back and reevaluate my marketing strategies. We thought people would come because the idea was unique. It was an upscale store with ambiance, patterned similar to Tattered Cover, which really has a national presence. And we thought that people would come—particularly middle-class people with disposable incomes and a higher education level, because that was the population that I was close to. But it took a lot more marketing to get people in. The variable we didn't count on is that the store sells not just books, but culture. The customers we attract have to be culturally connected.

Clara originally put out fliers and took out ads to publicize her store, but quickly realized that she wasn't reaching her market. And she soon understood that the people who came into the store were not the well-to-do clientele that she had envisioned.

> We found out that our market was the working class. So we had to direct our advertising to these people. Unfortunately, they don't belong to a lot of groups. They belong to churches, but marketing from churches is very difficult because pastors do not want you to come into their congregation to sell something—other than what they sell. So we've tried to determine what our people buy and why they buy what they buy. We've studied the psycho-demographics of our population and tried to create a presence in the community. And we have tried to create a national presence. People make purchases based on prestige, so the bookstore had to develop prestige.

Clara Villarosa began telling everyone who came in the store that Hue-Man Experience was the largest African-American bookstore in the country. She became an influential figure in the African-American community. She did book reviews on the radio. She was active in community and civic affairs. She was appointed to the governor's council for business development and served on the Board of Directors of the Small Business Development Center and the Metro Denver Visitors and Conventions Bureau. She was a "friend of the library," she worked with the Denver Center for Performing Arts (DCPA), the Cleo Parker Robinson Dance Company, and Eulipions Cultural Center. As Clara put it, she was willing to be involved in

> . . . anything that's culturally related, because I enjoy ethnic events. I like the theater and the ballet and all of that, so I get involved. DCPA currently performs one black play a year, and maybe someday they'll do two. I host the director and cast for a

reception here in the store and I invite my customers in so that they can touch and feel the cast and it advertises the show and helps sell tickets. Cleo Parker Robinson—her dance troupe is an African-American dance troupe, and I work with her and find out what she's doing. Eulipions is an African-American theater company. I was a founding member of their Board of Directors and served for 8 years. If an author—an African-American author—is coming to town to make a speech or presentation, I ask if they want their book sold at the event where they are appearing, and if they would like to come to the store for a signing. And of course they do and of course they will! I'm not stupid! But I really have to hustle and seek out opportunities. And so I've been nominated for a zillion awards and won most of them. I'm a small business, I'm retail, I'm a minority-owned business.

In the 10 years since the store had opened, Clara felt she had become much better at marketing. By the end of 1993, the only paid advertising was in the form of courtesy ads, ads placed in local programs or newsletters. These ads generated goodwill, but Clara did not believe that they generated new business. Word of mouth was the main source of advertising, but it was a sophisticated type of word of mouth, cultivated through sophisticated public relations. Clara had been featured in *Ms. Magazine, Executive Female,* and *Publishers Weekly.* She was on the board of directors of the American Booksellers Association and was a member of the Mountains and Plains Booksellers Association. In 1990, she was instrumental in putting together a feature exhibit entitled "Black and Read: Books by African-American Authors and Illustrators" at the ABA convention, which met in Denver that year.

> African-Americans come to Denver for many conventions, but how do I locate them? By serving on the board [of the Denver Metropolitan Visitors and Conventions Bureau]. I am instrumental in putting together a fact sheet of things to do and places to go in Denver for African-American visitors. For example, there's a convention of African-American educators in Denver this week, and I'm hosting a group of them here on Friday. I'm also learning about other industries, like the hotel industry. Everything becomes part of my marketing strategy.

In 1989, at the suggestion of many out-of-town customers, Clara put together a 64-page mail-order catalog. "They said, 'Send me the booklist.' They like to read it but they don't order. It's a different motivation to pick up the phone and order a book. But the catalog appears to create a feeling of connectedness, and brings them back to the store." Clara financed the newsprint catalog largely through co-op advertising, whereby publishers paid for most of the printing cost of ads for their books.

By 1992, Clara's catalog had been streamlined down to 16 pages. The catalog was professionally produced, in a format similar to those found in upscale bookstores such as the Tattered Cover. In 1993, she began negotiating with Ingram's, a major book distributor, to jointly produce a catalog that would be distributed to other bookstores. The new catalog would be a glossy version of her newsprint catalog that other bookstore owners could use for their customers.

> My name would appear as a by-line and Ingram's would do the layout and pick up the printing costs. Individual bookstores would put their name and address on it for their own customers, which would help them publicize current titles. I know it's a lot of work to design this, but I've already done the work for my own catalog. This way Hue-Man Experience will get national publicity.

Clara also published a quarterly newsletter, highlighting author signings and community events. A reduced copy of the newsletter appears in Exhibit 5. This

Exhibit 5   Sample Newsletter (Front and Back of Flier)

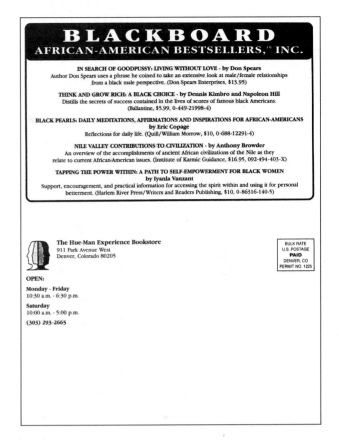

newsletter was typically one page, printed on both sides, which could be mailed easily when folded and stapled. Regular customers were on the mailing list; customers who spent at least $10 were added to this list. Clara had found out the hard way that sending out unsolicited newsletters was not an efficient way to bring in new customers. As she put it, regular customers were "the ones most likely to come back and most likely to come to store-sponsored events. They pay for the newsletter."

PR is critical in this business—community connections. It's interesting, because that's what we built this store on—a community presence. Local people say that we have something of value and this creates pride and ownership. And we perpetuate that image by showing them that we care about them as individual customers and that we care about their community. We find that our customers expect to be treated well, everyone is greeted, everyone is treated warmly, nurtured. We have to recognize our history, based on segregation, discrimination.

You still hear of sales people demanding IDs and avoiding eye contact with African-American customers. It happens every place. Not as often as before, but people are still uncomfortable around African-Americans. Even in Denver, which is a city that's pretty well mixed, an integrated city. There's no central African-American community because Denver was developed as an integrated city and people have dispersed to all areas of the city. People have moved to the suburbs, outlying areas, Aurora, Littleton.

These people aren't inclined to drive the distance to the store very often. We have to create a destination place for them. There's no other traffic around here.

Plans for the Future

In November 1992, Clara Villarosa bought the four houses that comprised the building which contained the bookstore, with financing backed by the U.S. Small Business Administration. She was able to buy the building for $79,000. With her track record as a successful retailer, she was able to secure a $72,000 24-year loan on the building, which appraised for $120,000. Her store occupied two units; the other two were rented to an art gallery and an ethnic apparel retailer.

Clara viewed her business as more than a bookstore. To her, it was a cultural center. She observed, "People who come here are culturally connected." She feared that, in 1993, Denver's African-American population was too dispersed to support a cultural center. She also recognized that there was strength in numbers: a larger concentration of attractive African-American businesses could serve as a catalyst for cultural connections.

> I'd like to create an Afrocentric Marketplace and position it as a minimall. So I bought this building 2 years ago. The other rented spaces in this building are complementary product lines. One sells African clothing and cloth and accessories and the other is an Art Gallery. I'd eventually like to work with them to make it a coffee shop also. The rent is fixed, it's stable, so they aren't going to deal with escalating rent costs. I offer limited services; I maintain the property, but we work cooperatively. I know the bookstore is the anchor. They each have their own customer base, but we feed off of each other. We want to create a synergy that will create more traffic for everyone. I'm working on joint PR [with the clothing store and the art gallery].

Around the corner from the Hue-Man Experience Bookstore was another row-house building, which faced the side street. The first floor of this building housed an artists' co-op, a store that sold blues tapes, a custom hat shop, and a caterer. Rents were about $4 per square foot (per year), or $400 per month for each tenant. Three of the leases were month-to-month contracts. The second floor was boarded up and uninhabitable due to fire damage several years before.

In September 1993, this building went up for sale. By December 1993, the asking price had been reduced from $150,000 to $95,000. The roof had recently been repaired, but needed replacement. The building would need extensive renovation, estimated as high as $200,000, for the upstairs to be used for retail space. One prospective buyer estimated that a new floor could be put in for about $50,000, after which the upstairs could be used as storage.

The Mayor's Office of Economic Redevelopment had targeted the Five Points area for low-interest redevelopment loans. Clara believed that there was potential for a lot of retail activity in this area, but that it would be slow in coming. A light-rail transit system, connecting Five Points to downtown, was scheduled to open in October, 1994.

> I had hoped that the catering operation [around the corner] would also serve food, but she just wants to cater, and my suspicion is that they're not stable tenants. The top floor of the building needs to be renovated for retail or office space. I think the purchase is still an option.

Clara Villarosa was confident that she could get financing for expansion without diluting her ownership in the business. Business loan rates were going for as low as 10 percent. But, even if she could obtain the building at less than the current asking price, she was not sure that this would be a prudent investment. At this point in her life, Clara was particularly concerned about the income potential of any expansion effort. At the same time, she didn't want to give up her dream of creating an Afrocentric Marketplace with national recognition.

■ Notes

1. J. Mutter, 1993 Heated competition gets hotter, *Publishers Weekly,* January 4, 43.

2. C. Goddard, 1992, Aiming for the mainstream, *Publishers Weekly,* January 20, 29.

3. Goddard, Aiming for the mainstream, 30.

4. Goddard, Aiming for the mainstream, 30.

■ CASE 20 Japanese-American Seating Inc.

Joyce Miller
University of Western Ontario

J. Michael Geringer
California Polytechnic University

In mid-January 1991, Jim Needham was facing one of the first challenges of his new position as general manager at Japanese-American Seating Inc. (JASI). Located in southwestern Ontario, JASI was a joint venture between a Japanese seat manufacturer and a Michigan-based seat assembler. When Needham arrived at the beginning of the year, the JASI plant had been through 20 months of commercial production under his predecessor, Bill Stanton. After several hours of discussion in a recent meeting about how to strengthen project management, Needham's Japanese managers had finally gotten his agreement to hire a project coordinator who would report to the materials manager and schedule and control engineering projects. But the more he considered the situation, the more uneasy Needham felt about enlarging the role of the materials department. Could he renege on his earlier decision, or should he just let this one go?

■ The North American Automotive Industry

The automotive industry accounted for a large part of manufacturing activity in both Canada and the United States, and contributed significantly to the expansion and recession of these economies. In the past decade, the Big Three U.S. automakers had experienced an unprecedented decline in market share and profitability, and they continued to battle against foreign car companies (Exhibit 1). A recent study noted that sales of vehicles made by North American manufacturers had dropped dramatically as the popularity of overseas models increased, particularly those from Japan, Taiwan, and South Korea. In the 1984–89 period, annual North

This case was prepared for the sole purpose of providing material for class discussion. Certain names and other identifying information may have been disguised to protect confidentiality. It is not intended to illustrate either effective or ineffective handling of a managerial situation. Copyright 1992 © J. Michael Geringer and The University of Western Ontario 1/27/92

Exhibit 1	The Big Three Automakers and the North American Automotive Industry				
	1973	1978	1987	1988	1989
General Motors Corporation					
Quality (defects per 100 cars)	—	—	176	165	158
Productivity (cars per person per year)	11.4	12.1	11.3	12.9	12.6
Inventory turns	5.4	6.7	18.0	18.8	20.0
Profit per unit ($)	490	684	435	692	645
Return on sales (%)	6.7	5.5	3.5	4.4	3.8
Market share (%)	51.5	47.3	34.7	34.9	35.0
Ford Motor Company					
Quality (defects per 100 cars)	—	—	156	169	143
Productivity (cars per person per year)	13.7	13.8	18.7	19.9	20.9
Inventory turns	5.3	6.5	15.6	17.3	18.0
Profit per unit ($)	260	360	1023	1014	663
Return on sales (%)	3.9	3.7	6.4	5.7	3.9
Market share (%)	29.8	26.5	23.1	23.7	24.6
Chrysler Corporation					
Quality (defects per 100 cars)	—	—	178	202	169
Productivity (cars per person per year)	13.0	13.1	16.2	18.0	19.5
Inventory turns	5.6	6.3	16.8	21.6	26.3
Profit per unit ($)	127	(129)	853	649	649
Return on sales (%)	2.1	(1.5)	4.5	3.0	1.0
Market share (%)	15.6	11.2	12.3	13.9	13.7

Source: Annual reports and industry sources.

American vehicle production was relatively flat at about 13 million units, roughly 30 percent of global production. Captive imports represented a growing phenomenon, and accounted for nearly 5 percent of North American motor vehicle sales in 1990. Pure imports accounted for an additional 24 percent of 1990 sales. Captive imports were vehicles imported by American companies. For instance, Chevrolet marketed the Isuzu I-Mark as the Spectrum, General Motors' LeMans and Optima were manufactured in Korea by Daewoo, and Chrysler imported several products made in Thailand by Mitsubishi.

Overall, foreign nameplates had captured about a third of the North American automobile market, despite trade barriers designed to keep them at bay. Honda now claimed 10 percent of the North American passenger vehicle market, and Toyota had a 7.5 percent share. These companies beat the quotas by agreeing to voluntary restraints, and building plants in North America, sometimes in conjunction with domestic producers. These operations were called "transplants." The total transplant production in Canada for 1991–92 was forecast at 460,000 units or 16 percent of Canadian capacity, an explosive increase since 1988, when transplants represented only 3 and 9.5 percent, respectively, of total Canadian and U.S. production capacity. Under the Auto Pact, vehicles manufactured in Canada and having at least 50 percent Canadian or U.S. content could be exported duty-free to the United States. This also applied to vehicles built by transplant operations.

In response to the challenge posed by foreign manufacturers, the Big Three had invested over US$8 billion in the past five years to upgrade capacity and launch quality programs aimed at matching the Japanese. As well, they were streamlining the manufacturing process by using just-in-time (JIT) principles and contracting out subassemblies. Outsourcing was part of an industry-wide effort to reduce costs. Where car makers used to retool and redesign components almost annually, they were now pushing the burden of design and engineering down to parts suppliers.

These developments had a dramatic impact on organizations supplying seats to the automotive manufacturers. Until the early 1980s, the seat industry was highly fragmented, and could be described as a series of hand-offs, from engineering through to marketing. Each supplier concentrated on one or two areas, such as headrests or suspension systems. The automakers handled most of the "cut-and-sew" activities in house. By 1991, however, 40 percent of seat production was being outsourced to suppliers who designed and manufactured complete seating systems. A complete system included the frame, foam pads, cover, seat tracks, lumbar support, recliner, headrest, and trim. At this time, to cut overhead and increase quality control, the automakers were reducing the number of suppliers, and the seat industry was becoming more competitive.

Japanese-American Seating Inc.

In 1987, Kasai Kogyo Ltd., a seat manufacturer based in Tokyo, and Banting Seat Corporation, a seat assembler headquartered in a Detroit suburb, formed a 65–35 joint venture to exclusively supply seats on a JIT basis to Orion Manufacturing Corporation. JASI was one of several companies established in southwestern Ontario as dedicated suppliers to Orion. Located 15 km away, Orion was a recently negotiated Japanese–American joint venture, which expected to begin producing four-cylinder subcompact cars in early 1989. The Orion plant would have the capacity to produce 200,000 vehicles annually, most of which would be shipped to the United States. Actual production volumes would depend on the market's acceptance of these vehicles as well as cyclical movements of the industry.

Banting and Kasai were leaders in automotive seating in their respective countries. Banting employed about 5,000 people in their North American operations and another 2,000 abroad. The firm was an established supplier to the Big Three with over $1 billion in annual revenues. After several years of reorganization, Banting had shed all of their nonautomotive businesses, and were focused exclusively on seating (approximately 70 percent of revenues) and other automotive interior parts. Banting's objective was to attain a position of leadership in the automobile seating industry. During the late 1980s, it had invested heavily in R&D and manufacturing facilities in the United States, as well as acquiring several smaller European producers of automotive seating and interior components.

Kasai employed about 4,200 people and had $1.5 billion in annual sales. Nearly 80 percent of Kasai's revenues were from the automotive industry, with the remainder coming from office and communications equipment, chemical products, building materials, and miscellaneous machinery. Overall, while heavily involved in its traditional business of automobile parts, Kasai's objective was to achieve greater growth and stability through product diversification and overseas market expansion.

While Banting relied on a myriad of raw materials suppliers to assemble its seating systems, Kasai had a more vertically integrated operation. Kasai owned 12 plants and 26 affiliated companies in Japan, most of them involved in auto-related activities. By applying JIT principles to seat production, Kasai had gained a strong reputation within the Japanese auto parts industry. In the 1980s, in an effort to follow its customers and to increase penetration of international markets, Kasai had aggressively expanded its sales network throughout the world, with regional sales headquarters in the United States, Canada, Spain, Brazil, Taiwan, and Thailand. Although Kasai had also pursued international manufacturing through 11 joint ventures worldwide, the JASI operation marked the company's entry into North American production. The JASI venture was initiated, in part, to help Kasai maintain its supplier relationship with the Japanese firm which was the majority partner in Orion.

The venture was to be run as a profit center. Banting held the minority participation, and JASI would supply Orion on an exclusive basis for a five-year period. The contract called for three to five percent annual price cuts. Construction on the 120,000-square-foot facility began in mid-1988, and was completed in early 1989. An investment of $20 million was required and breakeven was expected within four years. The plant had the capacity to produce 245,000 seats annually and would eventually employ 220 people on two shifts.

JASI's Start-up

Under the terms of the joint venture agreement, Banting would design the plant, contribute a general manager, and negotiate the purchase of major raw materials and components. Kasai would contribute its expertise in production and process technology and provide a president to head the venture. Orion placed great value on having an important representative from Japan on site.

The start-up team was composed of Sumio Imai, president, Bill Stanton, general manager, Akira Hoshino, finance, Tadashi Abe, Orion design engineer, Katsuhiko Ito, engineering, and Yuji Yamanaka, manufacturing/quality director. (Exhibits 2 and 3 show organization charts for mid-1989 and January 1991, respectively.) This was the first time any of the Japanese managers had worked in North America. The Japanese who went abroad were typically on a five-year rotation. Rotating people to gain a cross-section of experience within a company was a widely accepted practice and was, in fact, the foundation of management training and development in Japan. Lifetime employment was still the common practice in Kasai.

Except for Imai, all the Japanese managers brought their families to Canada. Imai, who chose to return to Tokyo three to four times a year for three-week periods, commented:

> My children have finished university and are working; it made sense to do it this way. I go back regularly to spend time with my family and to maintain business connections. The biggest challenge of going on rotation is actually returning. I mean this in a couple of ways. First, companies are dynamic, always changing, and it is important to know

Exhibit 2

Organization Chart, May 1989

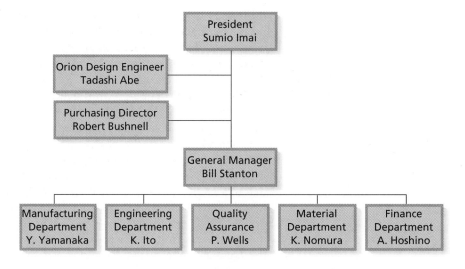

Exhibit 3

Organization Chart, January 1991

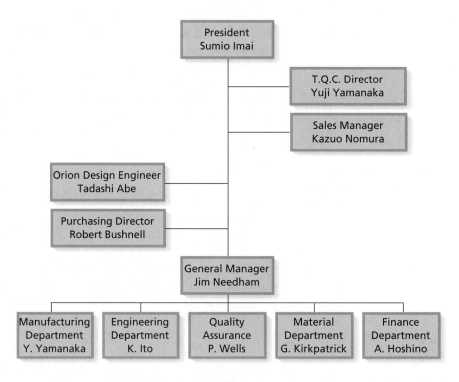

the organization. This takes time. It is not uncommon for people to spend many evenings after work socializing with colleagues, building up networks. Second, those who relocate their families to another country often find returning quite an adjustment. They get used to the lower cost of living and the bigger houses. Some people have difficulty getting their children back on track for the best universities. There is a sense that they have gained "bad habits" abroad.

JASI adopted the principles of the JIT production system known as "kanban," which was considered to be Toyota's invention. As one Japanese manager remarked, "Toyota has been doing it for 30 years and is seen as the master of the kanban system. In Japan, everybody likes and lives under kanban." Where the conventional production system was built on an earlier process continuously forwarding products to a later process regardless of its requirements, the kanban system was built on reversing this concept. To supply parts used in assembly under this system, the later process traced back to an earlier process, and withdrew materials only when they were needed. In this way, wasteful inventory could be eliminated. Imai was an early champion in applying the kanban system to the production of seats at Kasai.

In JASI's case, the kanban referred to a triangular vinyl envelope, which accompanied parts and products as they moved through the plant. The kanban provided information about picking up or receiving an order so that only what was needed would be produced. The kanban controlled the flow of goods by serving as a withdrawal order, a work order, and an order for conveyance. Associates picked and replaced parts in small batches according to the kanban.

Work cells contained several machines designed for quick, easy changes and short setup times so that a single operator could do a series of tasks. At any one time, there was no more than 4 to 8 hours of inventory in the plant, from parts through to the seats waiting on the rack for shipping. Seat storage and shipping were geared to the "live broadcast" of cars coming out of Orion's paint section, which fixed the order through final trim and assembly. To meet JIT requirements, units were shipped sequentially based on material and other options according to Orion's production schedule. JASI typically had a 3.5- to 4-hour window to deliver a particular seat set to Orion. There was a substantial financial penalty for late or incorrect delivery. Incoming seats were transferred directly to the final assembly line in the correct position without having to sort through an entire truckload to locate a specific unit. An industry analyst observed:

> Kanban systems require a lot of training: training workers to monitor inventory levels and training suppliers to operate under JIT principles. Suppliers have to understand the concept of delivering 50 pieces at 10 a.m.; not before, not after, and not 49. It's about supplying the right quantities of the right product at the right time. It's changing the philosophy away from protecting business behind the delivery door; it's about partnerships.

JASI had approximately 100 suppliers of small stampings, nuts and bolts, cloth, foam, frame, recliners, and other raw materials. At some point, certain activities like manufacturing foam might be brought in house in a separate facility.

In September 1988, Kazuo Nomura joined the company as materials manager. Following the Japanese model, Nomura had both purchasing and sales responsibilities, and oversaw all aspects of cost, material, and production control. In addition to being a liaison with Orion, handling suppliers, and scheduling incoming materials, he controlled engineering projects. However, expediting materials was taking up an extraordinary amount of his time. Nomura explained:

> North American suppliers don't give us the kind of support we're used to in Japan. I'd end up having regular quarrels with suppliers just trying to explain the kanban process. It was taking longer than I expected to get them to buy in, to deliver small quantity shipments on a JIT basis, and I was getting frustrated. It was hard to handle everything. Our reputation with Orion was key, and I was dedicated to building this relationship. In January 1990, I became sales manager, and JASI hired a Canadian, George Kirkpatrick, to take over materials. By this time, many of my responsibilities had been parcelled out to other departments. Kirkpatrick would schedule parts in and products

out, keep suppliers onstream, ensure manufacturing had the materials to keep the plant going, and interact with Orion regarding product sequencing and shipping.

During start-up, the management team generally worked well together despite some differences in management style. Stanton had designed the plant, knowing nothing about Japanese management and production principles that would be used to operate it. Over a six-month period beginning in November 1988, three groups of two to three salaried managers and technicians went to Japan to learn about Kasai's production system, and see the same seats they would be making being built at the Tokyo facility. Throughout this time, JASI was producing pilot seats, programming and debugging the numerically controlled metal benders and robot welders, and training people how to properly fit seat covers.

Overall, there were few technical problems or difficulties with the nonunionized workforce. The area had an abundant labor pool, particularly with the recent influx of East European and Southeast Asian immigrants. Stanton's policy was to recruit young people without industry experience, and have them work in teams and cross-train. With a monthly absenteeism rate of three percent, where the industry average was five percent, JASI was considered a highly successful venture, especially on the interpersonal side.

JASI began commercial production in April 1989, coinciding with Orion's start-up. Over the next 20 months, the company made steady progress in training their workforce and suppliers, containing costs, and meeting the price cuts scheduled into the contract with Orion. From the start, JASI had adopted the Japanese concept of "kaizen." Literally translated, this meant continuous improvement. This philosophy encouraged associates to submit ideas for new methods, rationalized setups, more efficient ways of operating machinery, and so on.

The Japanese managers considered that JASI operated relatively autonomously from both parent companies, particularly Kasai. Their communications with Kasai were principally about issues of product quality; major problems with customers, especially regarding product quality issues; engineering changes, and the development and testing of prototypes; and proposed investments. For example, in response to model changes at Orion, they would send samples of parts prototypes for testing in Kasai's labs, since JASI lacked the required capabilities. Interactions with Banting often involved operational details such as purchasing materials, changing suppliers, and introducing new products. They also communicated with Banting regarding cultural issues that the Japanese managers were unfamiliar with, such as donations to a local charity, or staging a company party for employees and their families.

On a monthly basis, both parent companies received a statement outlining the venture's general financial status. While Kasai had never requested additional detailed financial data, Banting had occasionally asked for figures on overtime, production costs and output, particularly during the venture's start-up. JASI's managers were strictly required to consult with both parents, including detailed documentation, whenever funding was required for new investments. One Japanese manager noted that requests for investment funds had never been rejected, and parent inquiries associated with these requests had diminished substantially as the venture became more established. However, he noted that where Kasai would allow the venture to have a negative cash flow for five years, Banting had a significantly shorter horizon and seemed to require stricter budgetary control.

As a sole supplier of a major component, quality or delivery problems on JASI's part could shut down Orion's plant. Of all of Orion's suppliers, JASI believed it faced the greatest potential for problems; the fabric, foam, and weave of the knit all affected the final product. Most returns were because of variances within tolerances. Nomura was the key liaison between the two companies, and he met daily with Imai to report current issues. He traveled frequently to the Orion site, and was in daily contact with the purchasing, engineering, and quality departments to feed information back into the JASI plant. Nomura explained:

> For minor problems, Orion's quality department talks directly with our quality area. If problems are deeper, I get involved. I'll set up a meeting with people from both sides to analyze the current system and get at the root cause, then I report back to Orion about how we're implementing improvements. Everyone has their mind on corrective action and there's a lot of informal communication. We're still small enough to respond fast. When significant new investment is required, I'll get the president and general manager involved. Otherwise, it's up to me.

Showing a high degree of responsiveness and taking quick action to correct returns had enabled JASI to build an excellent reputation to the extent that the company had recently been taken off Orion's regular quality audit list, which meant that performance reviews would only be conducted every six months. By this time, a strongly knit culture had developed, in both management and on the plant floor.

When Orion geared up production in September 1990, JASI brought on a second shift, which added 100 people to the payroll. Work groups had to be split up to train the new associates. Defects increased and productivity deteriorated significantly during this period. At this time, the Canadian Auto Workers (CAW) made a successful bid to unionize the workforce. In October, the CAW was certified as the official bargaining unit and began negotiations with JASI management.

Jim Needham's Arrival

In fall 1990, Banting finalized a deal to acquire a German seat assembler, giving the firm entry into the country, which represented about one-third of the automotive manufacturing market in Europe. European seat makers had traditionally sold foam and metal components, but there was increasing pressure from the car makers to deliver complete seating systems on a JIT basis. Stanton was asked to take over the management of the plant in Germany, and Jim Needham was offered the general manager position at JASI, a promotion from his current position managing a seat assembly plant in Michigan. Needham, age 41, expected to spend at least three years at JASI. He reflected:

> Bill took the job in Germany because he felt he couldn't do much more here; he was ready to take on a new challenge. I accepted the job in mid-November and started commuting back and forth several times a week. A lot of my time was taken up with paperwork and immigration matters. I had to buy a house, move my family here at the beginning of the year, and get my two kids settled into new schools. My wife and 12-year-old son seemed to make the transition okay. But my 16-year-old daughter wasn't exactly thrilled about moving to a small rural town in another country. At first, it seemed like there was just one brick on my back after another.

Needham had worked for Banting for the past six years, coming up through the ranks from manufacturing manager. He continued:

> I'm an old factory nut, and I was really impressed with the JASI plant: how well it was laid out, the robotics and metal bending capabilities, the high tech product testing. JASI was making all their own frames whereas the plants I'd worked in before were building seats with purchased parts. I'd been through some consensus training but I had limited experience working with the Japanese. In Michigan, we were doing JIT, we had cards on the seats and were scheduling the replacement of batches. We thought we were doing a lot, but I've never seen kanban worked as thoroughly through the production process as here. It's hard to learn how to make kanban work, and making it work right is a real trick.
>
> Right now, I'm concerned about the union negotiations. I'd worked with the United Auto Workers in the past but the CAW has the reputation of being a more militant organization. I hope that we won't get into the typical adversarial relationship. JASI's wage structure is good and the benefits package is solid. We have a progressive-thinking union rep who seems open to a different approach. I'm not anticipating a lot of restrictions; the union knows our relationship with Orion, that the company will be growing.
>
> I think Bill took the decision to unionize quite personally. Bill put everything he had into this plant, and he had a strong feeling of personal ownership here. He was into all the details. Once he was convinced of something, he went all out to make it happen. He has quite a forceful personality with a decisive, direct style, even authoritarian at times.

Needham did not have a lot of preparation before taking on his new position. He remarked:

> I only had 3-4 days with Bill, and I spent that time trying to get down the mechanics of the organization. I knew that I was coming into a tightly knit group. And I was coming into a situation where I couldn't even speak directly with my own boss and some of my key managers. Nomura and Hoshino had a working knowledge of English, but I'm not sure how much the other Japanese comprehend. They spend a lot of time together interpreting for each other. I suspect that Imai understands more than what he can express in English. Whenever Imai has a meeting with an Anglo, he'll always have someone else there, usually Nomura, to interpret. Still, I have to be careful. What gets said may be just the best way someone knew how to say it and not necessarily their intent.
>
> It's hard to figure out the dynamics of the management group. Imai is gregarious and outgoing while Yamanaka gravitates towards the role of the "keeper"; he keeps situations in control, he's more grounded. Nomura seems to be the linking pin in the whole operation. Bill tried not to tell me too much; he didn't want to predispose me to certain individuals. One thing Bill emphasized was the need to maintain operational control, especially in order to achieve better cost/benefit ratios. He gave the example that the Japanese continually look for improvements and might request that eight people be assigned to the task of rearranging a work cell. They'll justify it as being for the good of the company, but the benefit might not come until four or five years later. Bill noted that this could generate problems at Banting, since Mr. Begar, an Executive Vice President at Banting and their senior representative on JASI's board, as well as other executives at headquarters would expect me to regularly report key production data as Bill had done, and they would not be pleased if the figures varied substantially from budget.
>
> I'm mostly learning as I go along. I realize that I can't do things the same way I did before. I didn't think people could tolerate an American coming in swinging. The last

thing I want anyone to think is that I'm a dictator; I've worked for those types before, and it never works. I want to take the long view; changes will come over time. At the beginning, the important thing is to not make too many quick judgments or life-threatening decisions, to just get involved where you really need to.

I'm starting to have some interaction with Hoshino on the budget, and it's possible that he could be a window into the Japanese group, someone who I can put the sticky questions to and find out about personalities and political ramifications in Japan. At the moment, I'm very much the new guy. I have a sense that people might be looking for changes in the way things get done. I bring a new set of ears, and ideas that didn't get through before will be resubmitted. People are redefining relationships, and this isn't necessarily a bad thing. There are good reasons for making changes at this level: there's the saying that you can't change the players but you can sometimes change the coach. Maybe I'll have a chance to make the improvements my predecessor couldn't crack.

Shortly after Needham's arrival, the media reported that early January 1991 sales of North American vehicles had plunged as worries about the faltering economy and the Persian Gulf crisis continued to erode consumer confidence.

<table>
<tr>
<td>

Managing in a Cross-Cultural Environment

</td>
<td>

Needham knew that his job at JASI would be more difficult, at least initially, than those he had gone into previously. He recounted:

> I'm used to reading a situation quicker. I come from a system where a good boss listens to his managers, then makes a decision; his people understand it and follow it. The Japanese look for consensus, and this is hard to get to. Management meetings are long. Recently, we spent an hour only to find that we had two versions of the same vacation policy, one for the Japanese and one for the North Americans. We spent another two hours trying to hammer out a single policy. There's always a risk that everyone will nod their heads, and then the Japanese will go off and run the business their way and the North Americans will go off and do things differently. People forget that they're supposed to be learning from each other; there's always some tension, and sometimes it's hard to get over the humps. The North Americans aren't familiar with the kanban system and sometimes they don't go far enough; they had something that worked before. Put that against the Japanese guys who know and believe in their system.
>
> I see my role as bringing up issues for discussion. If I walked in with the solution to a problem, there would be immediate resistance. We need the extra step here, and I'm patient enough to go through it.

</td>
</tr>
</table>

Through a series of conversations, Needham discovered that the Japanese were used to relying heavily on their technicians. In Japan, once these people were told the rules, there was apparently little need to follow up. However, he noticed that JASI's floor technicians were not consistently enforcing such simple things as wearing safety glasses. Shop rules and discipline seemed to be foreign ideas to his Japanese managers. Needham elaborated:

> The Japanese don't seem to recognize that the workforce might slip; they aren't trained to look for such problems. Even if they become aware of something, they appear to overlook it. I don't know if it's just a cultural difference, a case of not feeling comfortable dealing with the situation. For instance, it recently happened that someone was stealing and my Japanese guys didn't seem to realize that a person who behaved this way would have to be fired.

Another difference between the Japanese and North American systems was the role of the materials department. In Japan, this department was a large, central hub, which ran new engineering and information programs, and scheduled and controlled all aspects of projects. In North America, these activities were typically handled by engineering or manufacturing. As a whole, JASI's Japanese management group felt strongly that the company needed to get better at project management to achieve continuing quality improvements and cost reductions.

The January Meeting

On January 11, 1991, Jim Needham convened a two-hour meeting with virtually the entire management team, including Imai, to discuss the project management situation. Project management was intimately linked with costs. The decisions made in this meeting would affect everyone. The Japanese managers felt strongly that the materials department should enlarge its role and regain its original status. As the venture had moved toward commercial production, many of the responsibilities Nomura originally had as materials manager had been dispersed across departments as he dedicated more of his time to building JASI's relationship with Orion. The Japanese felt that the key to better project management was to centralize this function back in materials. They argued adamantly that a project coordinator needed to be hired.

Reporting to the materials manager, the project coordinator would launch projects and follow them through to completion. For example, if an engineering study proposed joining three pieces to bolt onto a seat, the project coordinator would find parts suppliers and obtain quotes to facilitate a make or buy decision. This person would also interact with engineering, quality, and manufacturing to ensure each department carried out its responsibilities on the project. The Japanese contended that creating such a position would mean that everyone was informed of the status of ongoing projects. Starting up new projects would be smoother, less costly, and better quality. Needham responded:

> I kept telling people I wasn't convinced that we needed to add an extra person. This hadn't been slotted in and I didn't want to bastardize the budget within the first month. I thought that the job could be handled by someone else already in the organization. I had recently talked to the quality manager, Paul Wells, and he was willing to schedule and follow up projects. This wouldn't make for as big a role for the materials department as the Japanese wanted: the real responsibility would still be with the pieces, but I didn't feel comfortable giving up some of my own authority when I still didn't completely understand the operation. My Japanese managers persisted. One even remarked that when I went to Japan in April, I'd learn why project management should be done in materials. After several hours of discussion, I finally relented.

> I suspected that Imai and the others were pleased with the outcome. They were comfortable that I went after consensus, and I had a feeling they would like JASI to operate even more like a Japanese organization.

A few days after agreeing to hire a project coordinator, Needham was having serious second thoughts. Besides concerns that the company was still too small to warrant this additional person and the accompanying costs, he did not feel that the materials department was ready to take on this level of responsibility, and ultimately, he was not comfortable defining the department as largely as it was in

Japanese operations. Delegating this additional authority to lower level managers before he was comfortable in his new position might also limit his own decision-making authority in the future. But what could he do now?

Needham was to meet with Imai at 8 A.M. tomorrow for their weekly meeting, and the agenda which Imai had sent to him was quite full. In addition to addressing several important strategic and operational issues, such as improving integration of local suppliers within JASI's kanban system, production planning and quality control issues, and finalizing a strategy for upcoming negotiations with union representatives, Needham and Imai had been asked by the materials manager to formally approve the proposal to hire a project coordinator, including funding to retain a personnel recruiting firm and placement of position advertisements. In fact, this latter issue was the first item on their agenda, along with review of the quality control report for the prior two weeks, which showed a continuing decline in production defects. Could he change his mind? And how would he even go about doing it?

■ CASE 21 Johns-Manville and Riverwood-Schuller

Arthur Sharplin,

Institute for International Business Studies, Pordenone, Italy, and McNeese State University

■ http://www.schuller.com/

Blood and bones are more important than bricks and mortar.
—U.S. Bankruptcy Judge Burton R. Lifland

In 1898, Henry Ward Johns, inventor of many asbestos products and founder of Johns-Manville Corporation (J-M), died of scarring of the lungs, presumably asbestosis.[1] But his company survived, and for most of the next century it would be the world leader in mining and distributing the fiber and developing, manufacturing, and marketing asbestos goods. By mid-1992, some 200,000 former asbestos workers had filed asbestos health (A-H) lawsuits against the company. Fewer than 1 in 10 of these had received compensation (averaging about $20,000 each); new plaintiffs could not hope to receive compensation for 23 years.

Also in mid-1992, a revitalized Manville Corporation, rich in assets and reorganized as two new, independent companies—Riverwood International and Schuller International—was preparing to emerge from 10 years of bankruptcy court protection. The new firms, free of liability for asbestos health damages, would rejoin the ranks of respectable American corporations.

Exhibit 1 discusses asbestos applications and health issues.

■ Overview

By 1930, a second generation of J-M managers had taken over from the colleagues of H. W. Johns, and would remain with the company into the 1960s. A third generation of J-M managers and directors was installed about 1970 and started to diversify the company and change its image. Four events made the strategy more urgent: J-M lost its first major A-H case (to Clarence Borel) in 1973; a steep recession in 1974–75 cut profits in half; in 1976, the former

All rights reserved jointly to the author and the North American Case Research Association (NACRA). Copyright © 1993 by the *Case Research Journal* and Arthur Sharplin.

Exhibit 1   Asbestos Applications and Health Issues

Asbestos is a mineral fiber, obtained by crushing asbestos-containing rock, mainly from open-pit mines, and sifting and blowing away the unwanted material. The fine strands are fireproof and almost impervious to most acids, to body fluids, and to oxygen. Before about 1978 (and even after that in many countries), asbestos cloth was used to make such household items as drapes, rugs, pot holders, and ironing board covers. Asbestos was mixed into slurry and sprayed onto building walls and ceilings. It was used in most industrial insulations, in roofing and floor tiles and wallboards, in a wide range of putties and sealants, and in automobile brakes, clutches, and mufflers. The substance was present in practically every ship, automobile, airplane, home, factory, and school completed before the mid-1970s, and many completed afterward. As asbestos products are worked or disturbed, they exude dust containing microscopic pieces of fiber. Ingested, the fibers cut and penetrate moving tissue, especially in the lungs. Intense or prolonged exposure leads to asbestosis, a progressive and irreversible scarring, thickening, and calcification of the lungs and their linings (the pleura). Mesothelioma, a rare and fatal cancer that usually strikes the pleura but sometimes also affects the peritoneum, the lining of the abdomen, is strongly connected with prolonged occupational exposure to asbestos, as are increased incidence and severity of lung cancer and many other respiratory ailments. The first symptoms of asbestos disease typically appear 10 to 30 years after exposure begins. But early damage is easily detectable by x-rays and some cancers and respiratory deficiencies show up after only a year or two. Cigarette smokers are several times more susceptible to respiratory diseases, especially those related to asbestos, than are nonsmokers. It is widely agreed that as long as asbestos is "encapsulated"—as in floor tiles or painted insulating blocks—the danger of disturbing it in the process of removal exceeds that of leaving it in place.

---

medical director admitted the firm's 1940s and 1950s knowledge of asbestos dangers; and in 1977, A-H lawyers found a batch of incriminating correspondence among industry officials of the 1930s and 1940s.

Lawyer John A. McKinney became chief executive in 1976. He arranged to acquire Olinkraft Corporation, a large wood products firm, paying half in cash and half in preferred stock. In 1981, J-M was renamed Manville Corporation and reorganized. By August 1982, the number of A-H claims totaled 20,000, and some juries were awarding punitive damages. Also, Manville's businesses were losing money.

On August 26, 1982, the company filed for bankruptcy reorganization. No A-H claims would be paid for over six years, although commercial creditors were soon assured of full payment. A plan to emerge from Chapter 11 protection was approved by the court in 1986 and became final in 1988. Bankruptcy judge Burton R. Lifland issued an injunction directing the A-H claims to a trust, to be funded with $150 million from the company and $695 million from its insurers. The trust also received common and preferred stock, but could not trade or vote the shares for several years. (Exhibits 4 to 12, at the end of the case, provide financial data.)

Shielded by the bankruptcy court, the managers and directors got improved pay and benefits, continued indemnity against the A-H claims, and added tenure to retirement. Some set up groups to buy assets out of the bankruptcy, including the main asbestos mine and factories. By 1988, remaining third-generation executives chose successors and retired, several with large severance checks as well as pensions.

The fourth-generation managers set about sorting Manville's $3 billion in assets and cash into divisions to be renamed Riverwood International and

Exhibit 2	Outline of the Manville Story
1898	Founder, Henry Ward Johns, dies of asbestosis.
1920s	Early lawsuits; second generation of managers in charge.
1930s	Incriminating correspondence among industry officials.
1970s	Third-generation managers take charge; Borel case; diversification efforts; Olinkraft acquisition.
1981	J-M renamed Manville and reorganized.
1982	A-H claims total 20,000; punitive damages awarded; businesses losing money; Chapter 11 filing in August; asbestos claims, other debts, stayed.
1984–86	Manager pay and benefits increase; asbestos mine, other assets, sold free of asbestos claims; Chapter 11 plan approved by court.
1987–88	Manville begins public relations campaign; Chapter 11 plan becomes final; unsecured creditors receive full value; injunction directs asbestos claims to trust.
1989	A-H trust runs short of funds within three months of paying first claim.
1991–92	A-H trust in disarray and expected to sell Manville shares to survive; 16,000 A-H claims have gotten an average $20,000 each; 12,000 more promised payment by the year 2020; 160,000 claims await processing; Manville, with $3 billion in assets, prepares to divide itself and break free of past.

Schuller International. They began a public relations campaign. Soon, CEO W. Thomas Stephens expressed confidence that the company would escape the asbestos mess altogether.

The A-H trust paid its first claim in 1989 and ran short of funds three months later. By late 1991, the chief executive of the trust and all but one trustee had resigned. Sixteen thousand A-H claimants had gotten an average of about $20,000 each (after attorneys' charges). Payment of another 12,000 claims was promised by the year 2020. But 160,000 still awaited processing,[2] and new claimants were told to expect their first payment in 23 years.[3] At that time, average life expectancy of claimants was estimated at 17 years.[4]

Lifland reaffirmed the injunction. Company legal chief Richard B. Von Wald said, "That's the kind of certainty we were after. Manville is a company which has put the asbestos risk questions behind us." But many victims faced a less favorable certainty, the one Henry Ward Johns himself had confronted nearly a century before. Exhibit 2 outlines the Manville story, which is told in more detail in the pages that follow.

■ "The Evil Is Very Insidious . . ."

The year Johns died, a British factory inspector had described a common fate of asbestos textile workers: "In the majority of cases the evil is very insidious. . . . The worker falls into ill-health and sinks away out of sight in no sudden or sensational manner."[5] And in 1918, Prudential Insurance Company's chief actuary wrote, "[I]n the practice of American and Canadian life insurance companies asbestos workers are generally declined on account of the assumed health injurious conditions of the industry."[6]

Studies reported in the medical literature in 1924, 1928, and 1930 began to show the nature of the A-H problem. The 1930 research revealed 26.3 percent of the workers studied had fairly serious asbestosis, a name given the disease in 1927.[7]

A "Principal Defense"

By 1929, J-M was defending lawsuits for asbestos deaths. In court, the company claimed that employees assumed the risks of employment, knew or should have known the dangers, and were contributorily negligent. Legal documents in these cases bore the signatures of senior J-M officials who would remain with the company until the late 1960s. Through the 1950s, most A-H claimants were present and former J-M employees who had been exposed in the company's mines and factories—later claimants were mainly asbestos insulation workers employed by others.

Prominent among J-M's insurers was Metropolitan Life Insurance Company. In 1930, Dr. A. J. Lanza of Metropolitan began a 4-year study on the effects of inhalation of asbestos dust on the lungs of asbestos workers.[8] His preliminary report, written the next year, showed that 87 percent of the workers with over 15 years' exposure and 43 percent with under 5 had x-ray-visible fibrosis.[9] J-M vice president Vandiver Brown reviewed a draft of Dr. Lanza's report and wrote him:

> All we ask is that all of the favorable aspects of the survey be included and that none of the unfavorable be unintentionally pictured in darker terms than the circumstances justify. I feel confident that we can depend upon you and Dr. McConnel to give us this "break."[10]

Although the insurers had some liability, J-M remained primary defendant in the lawsuits. In 1934, J-M's chief outside attorney, George Hobart, wrote Brown:

> [I]t is only within a comparatively recent time that asbestosis has been recognized by the medical and scientific professions as a disease—in fact one of our principal defenses in actions against the company on the common law theory of negligence has been that the scientific and medical knowledge has been insufficient until a very recent period to place on the owners of plants or factories the burden or duty of taking special precautions against the possible onset of the disease in their employees.[11]

A half century later, Brown successor John A. McKinney would be claiming to have just recently learned that asbestos "can sometimes cause certain lung diseases."[12] And McKinney would hire Hobart's firm, then called Davis Polk Wardwell, to defend the company.

"The Minimum of Publicity"

In October 1935, Brown wrote Raybestos-Manhattan Corporation president Sumner Simpson, "I quite agree that our interests are best served by having asbestosis receive the minimum of publicity."[13] He was commenting on Simpson's response to the editor of the industry journal *Asbestos,* who had written:

> You may recall that we have written you on several occasions concerning the publishing of information, or discussion of, asbestosis. . . . Always you have requested that for certain obvious reasons, we publish nothing, and, naturally your wishes have been respected.[14]

Brown and Simpson convinced nine other asbestos companies to provide an average of $450 each per year for the industry's own 3-year study of the effects of asbestos dust on guinea pigs and rabbits. Brown wrote the researcher, Dr. LeRoy U. Gardner, "In the event it is deemed desirable that the results be made public, the manuscript of your study will be submitted to us for approval prior to publication."[15] Gardner later advised the companies of "significant changes in guinea pigs' lungs within a period of one year" and "fibrosis" produced by long fibers and "chronic inflammation" caused by short fibers.[16] He made several requests for funding but died in 1946 without reporting final results.

■ Let Them "Live and Work in Peace"

World War II brought J-M upward-spiraling sales. Thousands of tons of asbestos were used in building war machines, mainly ships, thus exposing hundreds of thousands of shipyard workers and seamen to the fiber. Many would die of asbestos diseases decades later.

In 1947, a study by the Industrial Hygiene Foundation of America found that from 3 to 20 percent of asbestos plant workers had asbestosis. A J-M plant employing 300 was reportedly producing "5 or 6 cases annually that the physician believes show early changes due to asbestos."[17]

In 1950, J-M chief physician Dr. Kenneth W. Smith gave superiors a report showing that of 708 workers he studied only 4 had "essentially normal and healthy lungs" and 534 had "fibrosis extending beyond the lung roots," "advanced fibrosis," or "early asbestosis."[18] Concerning the more serious cases he wrote:

> The fibrosis of this disease is irreversible and permanent so that eventually compensation will be paid to each of these men but as long as the man is not disabled it is felt that he should not be told of his condition so that he can live and work in peace and the company can benefit from his many years of experience.[19]

Dr. Smith later said he tried to convince senior J-M managers to put caution labels on the bags of asbestos in 1953. In a 1976 deposition, he characterized their response: "We recognize the potential hazard that you mentioned [and] the suggested use of a caution label. We will discuss it among ourselves and make a decision." Asked why he was overruled, Smith said, "Application of a caution label identifying a product as hazardous would cut our sales."[20]

By 1952, John A. McKinney, Fred L. Pundsack, Chester E. Shepperly, Monroe Harris, and Chester J. Sulewski had all joined the company in various capacities. They would be the firm's top five officers as it prepared for bankruptcy 30 years later.

■ "Disassociate This Relationship"

In 1956, the Board of Governors of the Asbestos Textile Institute (made up of J-M and other asbestos companies) met to discuss the increasing publicity about asbestos and cancer and agreed that, "Every effort should be made to disassociate this relationship until such a time that there is sufficient and authoritative information to substantiate such to be a fact."

The next year, the Asbestos Textile Institute rejected a proposal by the Industrial Health Foundation that asbestos companies fund a study on asbestos and cancer. Institute minutes reported, "There is a feeling among certain members that such an investigation would stir up a hornet's nest and put the whole industry under suspicion."[21]

■ "Not Until 1964 Was It Known . . ."

An increasing number of articles connecting asbestos with various diseases appeared in medical journals over the next few years. And in 1963, Dr. I. J. Selikoff of Mt. Sinai Medical Center in New York presented his study of asbestos insulation workers to the American Medical Association. Like the earlier research, the Selikoff study implicated asbestos in many thousands of deaths and injuries. Selikoff would soon estimate that at least 100,000 more Americans would die of asbestos diseases before the year 2000.

In later congressional testimony, Selikoff told a group of 632 insulation workers he had followed from 1942 through 1962:

> During these years, 27 men have died of asbestosis, of a total of 367 deaths. . . . [In addition,] while we would have expected approximately six or seven deaths due to lung cancer among these men, there were 45. While we would have expected nine or ten cancers of the stomach or colon, there were 29. . . . Incidentally, since 1963 the figures have been, if anything, even worse. While we would have expected approximately 50 of the remainder of these men to have died in the past five years, there have been 113 deaths. And while we would have expected 3 to have died of cancer of the lungs or pleura, 28 have died of this disease.[22]

J-M officials claimed Selikoff's 1964 report was their first knowledge of the danger, a position they would consistently maintain over the next two decades. For example, on August 27, 1982, McKinney wrote:

> Here's the bottom line. Not until 1964 was it known that excessive exposure to asbestos fiber released from asbestos-containing insulation products can sometimes cause certain lung diseases.[23]

And the 1982 *Annual Report* and Form 10-K would state, "The company has maintained that there was no basis for product warnings or hazard controls until the results of scientific studies linking pulmonary disease in asbestos insulation workers with asbestos exposure were made public in 1964."[24]

In 1964, J-M placed its first caution labels on certain asbestos products. The labels read, "Inhalation of asbestos in excessive quantities over long periods of time may be harmful" and suggested that users avoid breathing the dust and wear masks if "adequate ventilation control is not possible." The company's most profitable product, bags of asbestos fiber for distribution to other manufacturers and insulators throughout the world, would not be caution-labeled for another five years.

Use of asbestos in the United States had risen from around 200,000 metric tons a year in the 1930s to about 700,000 tons during the 1950s, 1960s, and early 1970s. Then it dropped sharply, to just over 100,000 in the 1980s.[25] Worldwide, production plateaued at about 4.6 million metric tons a year in the mid-1970s. This would drop only a little in the 1980s, as increased shipments to developing countries offset declining usage elsewhere.[26] Canada, the world's dominant marketer of asbestos in the 1980s and early 1990s, sold an estimated 42 percent of its output to Asia in 1988, up from just 16 percent in 1979. Other leading producers were Russia, Zimbabwe, and Brazil.[27]

■ The "Smoking Gun"

Always lucrative, the asbestos trade became even more so as the industry came under suspicion during the sixties and seventies. For example, sales of the raw fiber alone produced 41 percent of J-M's operating profit in 1976, though it accounted for just 12 percent of revenues. By that time, J-M had accumulated about $3.0 billion (1992 dollars) in assets and $1.6 billion in book value net worth, practically all from asbestos and asbestos products.*

Like R. J. Reynolds and American Tobacco, J-M had already begun to invest its wealth in "clean" businesses, first fiberglass, then a variety of unrelated enterprises. A prestigious new slate of directors had taken over in the late sixties. Among them were college deans at Princeton and New York Universities, the chief executive of Ideal Basic Industries and former three-time governor of Colorado, the head of Phelps-Dodge Corporation, and the top managers of three other firms.

The directors installed psychologist-consultant Richard Goodwin as president in 1970. Goodwin promised to diversify the company and change its image. He moved J-M headquarters from its old Madison Avenue brick building to a new, modern structure in the Denver countryside and arranged 20 or more small, diverse acquisitions. But he would not have time to finish his program.

In 1972, J-M and its codefendants lost their first big A-H case, to Clarence Borel, a Texas asbestos victim. According to a later news report, this loss "triggered the greatest avalanche of toxic tort litigation in the history of American jurisprudence."[28] A short, steep recession in 1974–75 cut J-M's profits in half. It made matters worse when, in 1976, former J-M medical director Smith told of his earlier knowledge and research on asbestos and health. Later that year, the directors fired Goodwin and replaced him with long-time J-M lawyer John A. McKinney. A later chief executive would claim Goodwin had been a womanizer and an alcoholic,[29] but Goodwin would deny that and say he was not given a reason for his firing.[30]

Then, in April 1977, A-H attorneys found what they called J-M's "smoking gun," the Raybestos-Manhattan correspondence. Included were many letters and memoranda among Manville officials and other asbestos industry executives. Most were written during the 1930s. A South Carolina judge reviewed the material and wrote:

> The Raybestos-Manhattan Correspondence very arguably shows a pattern of denial of disease and attempts at suppression of information which is highly probative [and] reflects a conscious effort by the industry in the 1930s to downplay, or arguably suppress, the dissemination of information to employees and the public.[31]

By April 1978, J-M was a defendant in 623 A-H lawsuits asking as much as $4 million for each plaintiff—but the annual report did not mention the lawsuits.[32]

A liberal new bankruptcy code, which would provide J-M a way out, was passed by Congress that October. Chapter 11 of the law so favored big debtors that public-company assets in bankruptcy would soon increase more than tenfold.[33] Exhibit 3 describes bankruptcy reorganization under the new law.

---

*Conversion to 1991 dollars, here and elsewhere, employs the Consumer Price Index for All Urban Consumers (CPI-U), not seasonally adjusted, as reported in Ibbotson Associates, *Stocks, Bonds, Bills and Inflation: 1992 Yearbook*. Chicago: Ibbotson Associates, 1992, esp. 84.

Exhibit 3   Chapter 11: Bankruptcy Reorganization

A voluntary Chapter 11 petition acts as an order to stay all legal and administrative proceedings against the debtor, which becomes Debtor in Possession (DIP). Neither good faith nor insolvency is required. Unless removed for cause, the DIP may pursue the ordinary course of business and has the powers and duties of a trustee. Except as modified by the court, the stay remains in effect throughout the proceeding. Often, a secured creditor requests the stay be lifted with respect to its claim. The DIP can usually prevent this by showing the liened asset is needed and providing "adequate protection" of the secured claim.

Reorganization is accomplished through implementation of a written plan. At first, only the DIP may file a plan. But if a plan is not submitted within 120 days and accepted in 180 days, any party with an interest in the case may file one. Both time limits may be extended or shortened for cause. A committee is appointed to represent unsecured creditors. A stockholders' committee and other representatives may also be appointed.

A confirmed plan binds all parties. Here are the main requirements for confirmation:

1. The plan must be proposed in good faith and disclose "adequate information" (done by means of a written "disclosure statement").

2. Each holder of a claim or interest who has not accepted the plan must receive at least as much value, as of the plan's effective date, as Chapter 7 liquidation on that date would provide.

3. Each class of claims or interests which is "impaired" under the plan must have "accepted" the plan unless the judge rules the plan "does not discriminate unfairly and is fair and equitable with respect to the class." The DIP, or the trustee if one is assigned, sorts claims and interests into classes, usually when a plan and disclosure statement are filed. A class of claims or interests is unimpaired if reinstated and the holders compensated for damages, or if paid in cash. Acceptance of a plan by a creditor class requires approval by over half the voting claimants, representing at least two-thirds in amount of allowed claims in the class. For classes of interests, such as shareholders, the requirement is two-thirds in amount of interests which are voted. Imposition of a plan on a class of impaired claimants which has not accepted it is called "cramdown," and is only allowed if at least one class of claimants (equity is an "interest," not a "claim") has accepted the plan.

4. Confirmation must not be deemed likely to be followed by the need for further financial reorganization or liquidation.

Executory contracts, except financial accommodations (e.g., agreements by banks to extend additional borrowing), may be assigned, assumed, or rejected by the debtor at any time before plan confirmation—or in an approved plan. "Executory" means neither party has completed its legal obligations under the contract. The rejection of executory contracts may create allowable claims, which are usually treated as prefiling, unsecured claims. While collective bargaining agreements are executory contracts, Code Section 1113 sets special requirements for their assumption or rejection.

In 1984, the U.S. Supreme Court ruled, "The *fundamental* purpose of reorganization is to prevent the debtor from going into liquidation, with an attendant loss of jobs and possible misuse of economic resources" (*NLRB v. Bildisco & Bildisco*, 108 S. Ct. 1188, 1984). Ideally, the company will remain viable and will propose to pay its creditors more than they could get through liquidation. The first claim to payment goes to administrative costs of the proceeding and any postfiling obligations, especially any assigned "superpriority" status by the judge. It is generally believed that any remaining value should be distributed to the claimant and interest groups in order of their prebankruptcy entitlements: (1) secured debt (up to the value of respective collateral as of the effective date of the plan), (2) unsecured debt (including nominally secured debt above the value of respective collateral), and (3) equity interests in order of preference (e.g., preferred, then common).

Claimants within each group, again ideally, share pro rata according to the value of their respective claims. The value may be distributed as cash, securities, or other real or personal property. Negotiation among stakeholders and court intervention often result in departures from such an "ideal" distribution. In general, claims not provided for in the plan or the order confirming it are discharged. Unlike debt forgiveness, the discharge of debts in bankruptcy does not create income.

■ Aggressive Defense and a Substantial Acquisition

Upon taking office, McKinney had vowed "aggressive defense" of the A-H lawsuits and a "substantial acquisition." J-M purchased Olinkraft Corporation in late 1978. The price was $595 million ($1.2 billion in 1991 dollars), over twice recent market value. But only half was to be cash; the remainder was debt-like preferred stock, required to be repurchased at par starting in 1987. The repurchase requirement would be canceled by the bankruptcy filing in 1982. W. Thomas Stephens, who would later become Manville chief executive, was Olinkraft's chief financial officer at the time and was an early advocate of the sale. Olinkraft's main assets were several paper mills and 600,000 acres of prime timberland, with many trees over 50 years old. J-M soon doubled the division's plywood capacity and increased the harvest rate of timber by adopting a 32-year life for the tree farms, enhancing the subsidiary's cash-producing capability.

In 1981, J-M changed its name to Manville Corporation and reorganized itself, segregating its various businesses in separate divisions. Also that year, juries began awarding Manville A-H claimants punitive damages, over $1 million each in some cases. Actually, J-M paid few A-H claims—such expenses never amounted to even a half percent of sales—but the operating businesses were in trouble. In real terms, the company's sales fell 20 percent from 1978 to 1982 and profits disappeared. Manville's auditor, Coopers and Lybrand, qualified its opinion on the company's 1980 and 1981 annual reports.[34] Of course, Standard & Poor's and Moody's downgraded Manville's debt.[35]

Manville's insurers stopped paying for most of the asbestos claims by 1981, and generally could not pay punitive damages anyway.[36] The firm's insurers of the 1970s and 1980s, when many A-H problems appeared, argued that the claims should be paid by insurers from decades earlier, when most of the claimants were exposed. The insurers from the earlier period took the reverse position. This "manifestations versus exposure" debate was used by the insurers as a rationale for refusing to pay claims.[37]

Recording the A-H liabilities on Manville's balance sheet would justify a bankruptcy filing, but accounting rules required that claims be reasonably estimable to be recorded. A committee of directors assessed the liabilities with the help of consultants. In mid-1982, the committee reported that the A-H liabilities would total "at least $1.9 billion." Selikoff's associates said that was "a serious underestimate." The directors suggested as much, by saying the estimate involved "conservative assumptions favorable to Manville."[38] By mid-August 1982, Manville's stock dropped below $8, less than one-fourth its 1977 high.

In Full Readiness for Chapter 11

There were five main reasons to consider the company well prepared for bankruptcy.[39] First, assets were dispersed in separately incorporated divisions. The divisions could file joint or separate petitions and reorganization plans.

Second, a large part of Manville, the former Olinkraft, had never been in the asbestos business. And the company had other nonasbestos divisions, such as fiberglass. This would be a public relations advantage, at least.

Third, management was tough, long-tenured, rich with lawyers, and cohesive in the face of attacks from without. The company had opposed asbestos claims since the 1920s and had a reputation for effectiveness in court. Eight of the 11 prefiling directors had been with the firm since the fifties and sixties. They were distinguished in business, government, and academe. McKinney and four others were attorneys. The top five officers in 1982 each had at least 30 years' tenure. Only one, President Fred Pundsack, objected to the forthcoming Chapter 11 filing, and he resigned. The number of A-H claims totaled 20,000 by then, and three new ones were being filed per business hour.[40]

Fourth, the firm had competent counsel, resolute leadership, and access to the nation's preeminent pro-debtor bankruptcy court. McKinney retained top bankruptcy lawyer Michael Crames as well as New York law firm Davis Polk Wardwell and investment banker Morgan Stanley and Company. The latter two firms had been Manville allies since the thirties. McKinney insisted on one fundamental principle: The reorganized Manville must not have asbestos liabilities. McKinney later wrote that his resistance to compromise was considered stubbornness, adding, "In this context, I am proud to be called stubborn."[41] The company met requirements for filing in the Southern District of New York, where Burton R. Lifland was chief bankruptcy judge. Lifland administered more bid cases than any other bankruptcy judge and was known for favoring debtors.[42]

Finally, the firm's debt was practically all unsecured and the debt-like preferred stock would not have to be repurchased, assuring plenty of cash and borrowing capacity. McKinney would soon boast of "nearly $2 billion in unencumbered assets." The company's "cash portfolio" would increase to $760 million during bankruptcy. And cash would exceed $300 million even after implementation of the reorganization plan.[43]

■ The Bankruptcy Reorganization

On the evening of August 25, 1982, the directors met in New York and were briefed on bankruptcy. A Chapter 11 petition had been prepared and was filed the next day. The required committee of unsecured creditors was formed. The Committee of Asbestos-Related Litigants and/or Creditors, composed of 19 contingent-fee attorneys and one victim, represented present A-H claimants. New York lawyer Leon Silverman was appointed to represent future claimants.

The usual, but optional, committee was set up for shareholders. Some shareholder members of the committee demanded a special meeting of Manville stockholders, at which they might elect new corporate directors. In response, Judge Lifland disbanded the shareholders' committee and ejected shareholders from the proceedings. The Committee of Asbestos-Related Litigants continued in force.

Leading A-H attorney Ronald Motley spoke of criminal prosecution of the company or its executives. Other A-H attorneys called for liquidation, which Manville later said would yield $2 to $2.4 billion ($3.0 to $3.6 billion in 1992 dollars).[44] The directors and officers consistently opposed liquidation.

The largest division, Manville Forest Products Corporation (MFP—formerly Olinkraft), emerged from Chapter 11 on March 26, 1984. MFP paid its commercial debt, but was ordered immune from asbestos claims.[45] Various other units, notably the main asbestos fiber subsidiaries and certain asbestos-cement pipe operations, were sold that year, also shielded from asbestos liabilities.[46]

■ The Manville Plan for Reorganization

A reorganization plan for the remaining divisions was filed in 1986. It promised commercial creditors full payment with 12 percent interest. A trust was to be set up to pay A-H claims, and Lifland issued an injunction which shielded Manville; its past, present, and future managers and directors; its insurers; and even its codefendants from asbestos claims. Morgan Stanley affirmed that Manville's plan was feasible—but added elsewhere in its report: "No representations can be made with respect to the accuracy of the projections. . . . Morgan Stanley did not independently verify the information considered in its reviews." To explain its plan to the A-H claimants, Manville distributed 100,000 copies of a 550-page information packet accompanied by brief, glossy "Vote yes" fliers provided by the A-H committee and emphasizing its members' trustworthiness. Later, the A-H attorneys voted claimant proxies overwhelmingly for the plan. Judge Lifland confirmed the plan just before Christmas 1986. It survived two appeals and became effective two years later.

The plan promised the A-H trust a "$1.65 billion bond." That number was the sum of 44 semiannual payments which would start six years later. Discounted at 16 percent, the 44 bond payments were worth just over $200 million. In 1987, Stephens would estimate the value of the bond at $350 million.[47]

The trust was to own 50 percent of Manville's common stock. Manville would vote these shares until November 1992, and the stock could not be traded until a year later.[48] The trust would also get 7.2 million preferred shares convertible to bring common stock ownership to 80 percent. A description of the stock would say it "does not pay a dividend; has no maturity or mandatory sinking fund; has restrictions on convertibility, transferability, and voting rights; is nonredeemable by Manville; and has a liquidation preference of $89 per share."[49]

Shortly after the bankruptcy filing, many property damage (PD) claims—mostly for asbestos removal and abatement in buildings—had poured in, soon totaling $90 billion. McKinney's successor, W. Thomas Stephens, later said the PD claims had been his main reason for opposing liquidation.[50] A trust set up to pay these PD claims soon ran out of money and ceased operating. Judge Lifland rationalized the limited funding for PD claims as compared to A-H ones: "Blood and bones are more important than bricks and mortar."

By 1992, the practical results of bankruptcy for Manville's main stakeholders were becoming clear.

■ Benefits for the Managers and Directors

The third generation of Manville executives and directors retired in the mid-1980s, some with bonuses in addition to their pensions.[51] For example, McKinney left in 1986 with $1.3 million in severance pay. His annual cash compensation had gone from $408,750 in 1982 to $638,005 in 1985, his last full year of employment. And legal chief G. Earl Parker got $1.2 million after he stepped down. McKinney was replaced by his protege W. Thomas Stephens and Parker by his, Richard B. Von Wald.

Other managers arranged to buy company assets. A group headed by the chief of J-M Canada, which owned the world's largest asbestos mine, bought that division in 1983.[52] All but a small, borrowed down payment was to be paid "out of 85.5% of available future cash flows."[53] Payment took less than four years, prompting division president Peter Kyle to remark, "As far as leveraged buy-outs go, I don't think there are any as good as this one."[54] John Hulce, Manville president for a short while in 1986, retired and paid $7 million for Manville plants with annual sales of $17.5 million.[55]

Staying behind with the fourth-generation managers was long-time board chairman and Stephens mentor George C. Dillon. Dillon signed a consulting agreement with Manville and stepped down to director and chairman of the executive committee. He later compared Manville to such companies as Johnson & Johnson, whose handling of the Tylenol scare made it the nation's most respected firm; to Union Carbide, whose chief executive was arrested when he rushed to India after a disastrous gas leak at a subsidiary's plant there; and to Perrier, which discovered a trace of benzene in its mineral water and soon

Exhibit 4   Comparative Income Statements, 1976 to June 1982 (Dollar Amounts in Millions)*

	1982 6 mos.	1981	1980	1979	1978	1977	1976
Net sales	$949	$2,186	$2,267	$2,276	$1,649	$1,461	$1,309
Cost of sales	784	1,731	1,771	1,747	1,190	1,066	983
Sell, G&A	143	271	263	239	193	174	166
R&D & engineering	16	34	35	31	33	28	25
Operating income	6	151	197	259	232	193	135
Other income	1	35	26	21	28	2	1
Interest expense	35	73	65	62	22	20	15
Income before tax	(28)	112	157	218	238	175	121
Income tax	(2)	53	77	103	116	89	48
Net income	(25)	60	81	115	122	86	73
Preferred stock dividends	12	25	25	24			
Net income for common stock	$(37)	$ 35	$ 55	$ 91	$ 122	$ 86	$ 73

*Totals may not check, due to rounding.

corrected the problem. Dillon ended by quoting his "granddaddy," who said, "If you ain't got a choice, be brave."[56]

Stephens surrounded himself with loaves and fishes and posed as Jesus Christ for the cover of *Corporate Finance.* The article inside expressed wonder at Stephens's "miracle."[57] *Fortune* featured him as one of 1988's "25 most fascinating business people" and proclaimed the company "Free at Last." The cover of *CFO* featured chief financial officer John Roach under the caption "Redeeming Manville." The text inside the magazine articulated a recurrent theme: "Manville is out to redress past wrongs—by growing big enough to repay its victims."

The 15 executive officers' cash pay went to an average of $359,826 in 1990—Stephens's went from $330,000 in 1985 to $866,583 in 1990.

Benefits for Unsecured Creditors and Insurers

The unsecured commercial (as opposed to asbestos-related) creditors received full value of their claims, with 12 percent interest. The secured debt was variously paid or reinstated. And Manville's insurers settled billions in contingent liabilities by contributing about $695 million for the A-H trust.

Results for the Asbestos Victims

The asbestos claimants were often painted as opportunists, even charlatans—represented by "ambulance chasing lawyers." Several thousand of the 1982 claimants died before 1989, when the A-H trust made its first payments. Many surviving plaintiffs were old and sick. Smoking had multiplied the risk of asbestos disease for many. Few knew who to blame, since most had been exposed to asbestos from several companies.

The claimants had generally discovered their diseases after years of declining health. Most had fared poorly in state courts. Manville had usually been able to

Exhibit 5   Comparative Business Segment Information, 1976–1981 (Dollar Amounts in Millions)*

		1981	1980	1979	1978	1977	1976
Revenues	Fiberglass products	$625	$610	$573	$514	$407	$358
	Forest products	555	508	497	—	—	—
	Nonfiberglass insulation	258	279	268	231	195	159
	Roofing products	209	250	273	254	204	171
	Pipe products and systems	199	220	305	303	274	218
	Asbestos fiber	138	159	168	157	161	155
	Industrial and specialty products	320	341	309	291	301	309
	Corporate revenue, net	12	9	11	20	12	(22)
	Intrasegment sales	95)	(84)	(106)	(94)	(74)	(56)
	Total	$2,221	$2,292	$2,297	$1,677	$1,480	$1,291
Income from	Fiberglass products	$90	$91	$96	$107	$82	$60
Operations	Forest products	39	37	50	—	—	—
	Nonfiberglass insulation	20	27	27	35	28	18
	Roofing products	(17)	9	14	23	14	8
	Pipe products and systems	0	(5)	18	26	24	(3)
	Asbestos fiber	37	35	56	55	60	60
	Industrial and specialty products	50	55	43	36	25	19
	Corporate expense, net	(23)	(38)	(23)	(23)	(24)	(49)
	Eliminations and adjustments	3	11	(2)	1	3	2
	Total	$198	$223	$280	$260	$212	$116

*Totals may not check, due to rounding.

delay A-H lawsuits if not to win them. The company had employed top law firms and had certain valid defenses, as suggested earlier. Few large judgments against the company had come down, and fewer yet had been paid.

Finding the Raybestos-Manhattan papers had promised to change that. But it had taken A-H attorneys several years to get them before juries. The first big awards remained unpaid when Manville filed its bankruptcy petition—which McKinney said "preserved the position of the victims as equal creditors (virtually all unsecured) in the event of a financial calamity."[58] And prefiling A-H claimants were soon joined in line by thousands of new ones. Many of these had been recruited by Manville, which in 1986 advertised nationally for potential claimants. The Committee of Asbestos-Related Litigants assisted with the advertising program. Whatever the committee's purposes, its members thus obtained thousands of potential new clients—and as many proxies which would be voted for Manville's plan.

Representatives of both present and future victims appear to have been preempted in the bankruptcy court. In the five months from September 1983 to January 1984, the A-H committee tried to dismiss the bankruptcy,[59] rejected Manville's plan,[60] requested that management be replaced with a trustee,[61] and asked the court to cut executive pay.[62] In November 1983, Manville pronounced the asbestos attorneys' contingent fee contracts "completely unconscionable."[63]

Exhibit 6   Comparative Balance Sheets, December 1976-June 1982 (Dollar Amounts in Millions)*

					December 31			
		June 30 1982	1981	1980	1979	1978	1977	1976
Assets	Cash	$10	$14	$20	$19	$28	$39	$25
	Marketable securities	17	12	12	10	38	121	66
	Accounts and notes receivable	348	327	350	362	328	263	239
	Inventories	182	211	217	229	219	149	144
	Prepayments	19	19	20	31	32	30	26
	Total current assets	$576	$583	$619	$650	$645	$601	$501
	Land and improvements	—	119	118	114	99	64	64
	Buildings	—	363	357	352	321	264	259
	Machinery and equipment	—	1,202	1,204	1,161	1,043	642	598
	Total fixed assets	—	$1,685	$1,679	$1,627	$1,462	$970	$921
	Accrued depreciation and	—	(525)	(484)	(430)	(374)	(337)	(327)
	depletion		$1,160	$1,195	$1,197	$1,088	$633	$594
	Timber and timberland		406	407	368	372	0	0
	Total plant, property, and equipment	$1,523	$1,566	$1,602	$1,565	$1,460	$633	$594
	Other assets	148	149	117	110	113	99	93
		$2,247	$2,298	$2,338	$2,324	$2,217	$1,334	$1,188
Liabilities and	Short-term debt	$0	$29	$22	$32	$23	$18	$20
Stockholders'	Accounts payable	191	120	126	143	114	69	58
Equity	Accrued compensation and benefits	0	77	80	54	45	37	32
	Income tax	0	30	22	51	84	57	32
	Other liabilities	149	58	61	50	63	54	48
	Total current liabilities	$340	$316	$310	$329	$329	$235	$189
	Long-term debt	499	508	519	532	543	203	208
	Other noncurrent liabilities	93	86	75	73	60	23	11
	Deferred income tax	186	185	211	195	150	130	108
	Total liabilities	$1,116	$1,095	$1,116	$1,129	$1,083	$591	$516
	Preferred stock	$301	$301	$300	$299	$299	$—	$—
	Common stock	60	59	58	56	55	54	54
	Capital above par	178	174	164	152	142	134	134
	Retained earnings	642	695	705	692	643	561	492
	Current transactions, adjustments	(47)	(22)	0	0	0	0	0
	Treasury stock	(3)	(3)	(4)	(4)	(6)	(7)	(9)
	Total stockholders' equity	$1,131	$1,203	$1,222	$1,196	$1,134	$742	$672
		$2,247	$2,298	$2,338	$2,324	$2,217	$1,334	$1,188

*Totals may not check, due to rounding.

Exhibit 7   Comparative Income Statements, 1982-1988 (Dollar Amounts in Millions)*

	1988	1987	1986	1985	1984	1983	1982
Net sales	$2,062	$1,935	$1,803	$1,880	$1,814	$1,729	$1,685
Cost of sales	1,545	1,440	1,368	1,473	1,400	1,370	1,329
Sell, G&A	203	206	213	246	238	224	256
R&D & engineering	36	32	35	36	36	35	28
Restructuring costs	139	(3)	47	153	2	—	—
Other income (loss)	69	50	39	63	61	61	32
Income from operations	207	310	180	36	200	161	104
Interest expense	40	25	20	23	21	26	52
Chapter 11 and A-H cost	12	15	28	61	43	39	18
Disposition of assets	—	—	—	—	—	(3)	46
Income tax	66	113	54	(2)	58	40	8
Income, continuing operations	89	157	78	(45)	77	60	(21)
Income, discontinued operations	7	7	4	—	—	7	(77)
	96	164	81	(45)	77	67	(98)
Extraordinary charge	(1,288)	(91)	0	0	0	0	0
Accounting change	(107)	0	0	0	0	0	0
Net income	$(1,299)	$73	$81	$(45)	$77	$67	$(98)

*Totals may not check, due to rounding

(In general, such contracts give attorneys a third of gross receipts. The attorneys' expenses are reimbursed out of the other two-thirds, with the remainder going to clients.) In January 1984, a hearing was set on Manville's motion to void these contracts.[64] Lifland later made it clear that he would have cut the fees, complaining that the victims were not told how to contest them.[65]

In March 1984, the A-H Committee withdrew its motion to cut management salaries.[66] Manville stopped questioning the attorneys' fees. For the ensuing two years, the committee filed no action in opposition to management.[67] In fact, the committee appeared to become a management ally, providing glossy brochures to promote the company's plan.[68] In defense of his committee, chairman Ronald Motley wrote, "[The] intimation that there is some relationship between Manville's withdrawal of its objection to contingency fees in exchange for the A-H Committee's not opposing certain management decisions is both false and insulting."[69] The future claimants' representative, Leon Silverman, got $2.3 million and a commendation from Judge Lifland for helping design the payment plan, which would essentially disenfranchise future victims.

The A-H trust spent millions on salaries, offices, and expert help. Lifland had appointed the Executive Director of the U.S. Trial Lawyers Association, Marianna S. Smith, to head the trust, at $250,000 a year. She hired three assistants, at salaries above $150,000 each. The six lifetime-tenured trustees received $30,000 each per year, plus expenses and $1,000 a day for meetings. The trustees together received $440,555 plus expenses before any A-H claim was paid[70] and Smith was paid at least $500,000. In addition to directors' and officers' insurance, $30 million of trust funds was set aside to indemnify the trustees and others. The trust

Exhibit 8	Comparative Business Segment Information, 1982–1988 (Dollar Amounts in Millions)*							
		1988	1987	1986	1985	1984	1983	1982
Revenues†	Fiberglass products	$937	$877	$809	$803	$780	$720	$609
	Forest products	678	596	541	459	451	427	436
	Specialty products	501	506	494	674	254	248	285
	Nonfiberglass insulation	—	—	—	—	203	209	232
	Roofing products	—	—	—	—	190	228	211
	Corporate and eliminations (net)	15	6	−2	8	(4)	(41)	(55)
	Total	$2,131	$1,985	$1,842	$1,943	$1,873	$1,791	$1,717
Income From	Fiberglass products	$123	$151	$120	$69	$115	$97	$75
Operations	Forest products	127	100	62	34	63	53	48
	Specialty products	38	36	27	(38)	22	18	28
	Nonfiberglass insulation	—	—	—	—	16	9	11
	Roofing products	—	—	—	—	(11)	(10)	(6)
	Corporate and eliminations (net)	(81)	23	(29)	(28)	(4)	(5)	(15)
	Total	$207	$310	$180	$36	$200	$161	$141

*Totals may not check, due to rounding.

†Income includes net sales and other income, net.

leased 32,038 square feet of Washington, D.C., office space for $26.50 annually per square foot. During 1990 and 1991, trust expenses would average $3.5 million a month—about 50 percent more than would be paid to A-H claimants in those years.[71] Claims payments would average $4.7 million a month, of which perhaps $2.2 million a month would go to claimants. Again, the calculations assume standard contingent fees and expenses totaling 20 percent of gross payments.

The trust ran short of money three months after paying its first claim. Attorney Silverman remarked, "This recent flurry of publicity should not lead to disquiet. All of these problems were anticipated in the original plan and should not result in diminution of payments to claimants."[72] And Smith told a reporter, "Based on current projections over the life of the trust, there will be enough money to pay all the claimants, although there will be temporary cash short-falls."[73]

By the end of 1991, the trust had received over $900 million. It had dispensed $696 million for 15,864 A-H claims, an average of $43,902 each. A-H attorneys presumably got a third, $232 million, plus estimated expenses of $140 million. This left perhaps $325 million for claimants, an average of $20,487 each for the 1 in 10 who got paid. "Settled" but unpaid claims totaled $523 million—to be paid by the year 2020. Over 160,000 claims were waiting to be processed,[74] and prospective new claimants had been told they might expect their first payment 23 years after filing a claim.[75]

By March 1992, the A-H trust was in chaos. The directors' and officers' insurance had not been renewed by the trustees, who cited Judge Lifland's complaint about its cost. Smith and all but one trustee had resigned.[76] New trustees were hired in early 1992, but Smith's job remained vacant. Lifland's

Exhibit 9   Comparative Balance Sheets, 1982-1988 (Dollar Amounts in Millions)*

		December 31						
		1988	1987	1986	1985	1984	1983	1982
Assets	Cash and equivalent	$219	$210	$137	$7	$9	$19	$11
	Marketable securities	54	385	307	314	276	240	206
	Accounts and notes receivable	298	309	292	314	285	277	310
	Inventories	146	160	153	153	164	141	152
	Prepayments	14	27	24	29	17	22	17
	Total current assets	731	1,091	914	817	752	700	696
	Land and improvements	95	97	99	95	96	97	108
	Buildings	253	261	312	304	308	303	332
	Machinery and equipment	1,366	1,330	1,234	1,156	1,121	1,056	1,090
	Accrued depreciation and depletion	(645)	(597)	(586)	(538)	(513)	(472)	(547)
	Timber and timberland	357	367	376	385	392	395	402
	Plant, property, and equipment, net	1,427	1,458	1,434	1,402	1,405	1,379	1,385
	Other assets	235	204	165	174	182	174	154
	Total assets	$2,393	$2,753	$2,513	$2,393	$2,339	$2,253	$2,236
Liabilities and	Short-term debt	$77	$21	$30	$26	$20	$14	$12
Stockholders'	Accounts payable	103	104	93	84	102	94	86
Equity	Accrued compensation and benefits	97	101	103	94	81	65	63
	Income tax	31	14	16	12	18	10	32
	Other accrued liabilities	113	73	62	69	35	26	29
	Total current liabilities	421	312	304	286	256	208	221
	Long-term debt	869	223	80	92	84	4	12
	Liabilities subject to Chapter 11	0	547	575	578	574	713	736
	Other noncurrent liabilities	208	101	118	115	67	61	60
	Deferred income tax	97	198	161	144	162	136	140
	Total liabilities	1,595	1,381	1,239	1,214	1,142	1,122	1,170
	Preferred stock	$418	$301	$301	$301	$301	$301	$301
	Preference stock	89						
	Common stock	0	60	60	60	60	60	60
	Capital above par	761	178	178	178	178	178	178
	Retained earnings	(479)	821	749	667	713	635	568
	Current transaction adjustments	8	12	(11)	(26)	(53)	(41)	(39)
	Treasury stock	0	(2)	(2)	(2)	(2)	(2)	(2)
	Net worth	798	1,370	1,275	1,178	1,197	1,131	1,066
	Total liabilities and stockholders' equity	$2,393	$2,753	$2,513	$2,393	$2,339	$2,253	$2,236

*Totals may not check, due to rounding.

Exhibit 10	Comparative Income Statements, 1989-1991 (Dollar Amounts in Millions)*		
	1991	**1990**	**1989**
Net sales	$2,025	$2,127	$2,081
Cost of sales	1,640	1,649	1,553
Sell, G&A	220	212	206
R&D and engineering	36	41	39
Restructuring costs	(64)	(27)	4
Other income (loss)	10	34	21
Income from operations	76	232	308
Interest expense	74	83	76
Profit sharing	10	0	0
Disposition of assets	—	—	—
Income tax	22	61	75
Income, continuing operations	(30)	88	157
Income, discontinued operations	(18)	22	39
Income before charge	(13)	111	197
Extraordinary charge	0	0	0
Accounting change	47	0	0
Net income	$35	$111	$197

*Totals may not check, due to rounding.

superior, district judge Jack B. Weinstein, had ordered claims processing suspended until the existing "first-come, first-served" waiting line could be rearranged and payments cut further. Under the new system, the "most urgent" claims would be paid first. Initial payments would be 12 percent of *settlement* value, and payments could never total more than 45 percent of that amount. The new chief trustee said, "That could create a lot of heat and fire. But I'd rather it come to the surface now."[77]

New Divisions: Riverwood and Schuller

Manville allocated its assets into new divisions named Riverwood International (Paperboard and Packaging Products, formerly Forest Products—see Exhibit 11) and Schuller International (Engineered Products and Building Products—see Exhibit 11). The consolidated company would have $307 million in "deferred tax assets" (see Exhibit 12), created by nuances of the Bankruptcy Code and a large special charge in 1988.

The managers were confident they would be free of the A-H trust before November 1992, when the trust could vote its shares. Stephens remarked:

> We know the change in ownership is going to happen. What we've tried to do is have the maximum flexibility, in case the market puts more value on the pieces than the whole.[78]

"Change of ownership" was interpreted to mean a sale of Manville stock or of one or both divisions by the A-H trust.

Exhibit 11	Comparative Business Segment Information, 1989-1991 (Dollar Amounts in Millions)*		
		1991	**1990**	**1989**
Revenues†	Paperboard and packing	$1,019	$906	$789
	Engineered products	486	581	631
	Building products	568	720	725
	Corporate and eliminations	(37)	(46)	(42)
	Total	$2,036	$2,161	$2,103
Income from	Paperboard and packing	$145	$159	$186
Operations	Engineered products	34	90	109
	Building products	(39)	54	68
	Corporate and eliminations	(63)	(71)	(55)
	Total	$76	$232	$308

*Totals may not check, due to rounding.

†Income includes net sales and other income, net.

But a management-led buyout was an obvious possibility. Stephens himself had strong connections with Riverwood. The division's main plant was in his hometown of West Monroe, Louisiana, where he had been Olinkraft's chief financial officer before the 1978 acquisition. Plans were made in April 1992 to restructure Riverwood and for it to buy Macon Kraft, Inc., for $210 to $220 million, which was to include assumption of $175 million in debt. Macon Kraft had an annual capacity of 525,000 tons of corrugated paperboard. Stephens said, "If the transaction is successfully completed later this year [1992], we would expect to make substantial investments to equip the Macon mill to produce our proprietary coated boxboard grades of paperboard." Stephens expected to fund the project through a "primary public offering of up to 20 percent of Riverwood International's common stock and a concurrent offering of long-term debt."[79] This would further shield Riverwood from possible A-H trust control. In early 1982, Manville owned all the stock of Riverwood, and the trust was to gain control of Manville (and therefore Riverwood) in November 1992—if it resisted pressures to sell its interest. After the restructuring, outsiders were expected to own 18 percent of Riverwood.

Preparing for the 1991 Annual Meeting

At the 1991 annual meeting, Stephens had said:

> The situation with the Trust has been stabilized and while our businesses are operating in a recessionary environment, the situation is under prudent control. . . . Manville is a company where 18,000 skilled and hard working people have committed themselves to making your company a special place to invest their careers as well as your money.

At the 1992 meeting, scheduled for June 5, Stephens was expected to map the company's corporate strategies for the next year and to set forth, with finality, the firm's attitude toward the asbestos claims.

Exhibit 12	Comparative Balance Sheets, 1989-1991 (Dollar Amounts in Millions)*			
		December 31		
		1991	1990	1989
Assets	Cash and equivalent	$ 127	$ 88	$ 280
	Marketable securities	36	37	47
	Accounts and notes receivable	251	295	277
	Inventories	190	192	162
	Prepayments	10	25	18
	Deferred tax assets	61	6	0
	Total current assets	675	642	785
	P, P&E, net	1,437	1,483	1,295
	Timber and timberland	347	353	354
	Deferred tax assets	246	14	0
	Other assets	297	304	210
	Total assets	$3,003	$2,796	$2,645
Liabilities and	Short-term debt	$41	$60	$137
Stockholders'	Accounts payable and accruals	401	382	386
Equity	Accrued dividends, common stock	128	0	0
	Total current liabilities	570	442	523
	Long-term debt	823	870	802
	Accrued dividends	267	0	0
	Other long-term liabilities	564	343	326
	Total liabilities	2,223	1,655	1,651
	Preferred stock	418	418	418
	Preference stock	100	119	103
	Common equity	262	604	472
	Net worth	780	1,141	994
	Total liabilities and stockholders' equity	$3,003	$2,796	$2,645

*Totals may not check, due to rounding.

Notes

1. David Ozonoff, 1988, Failed warnings: Asbestos-related disease and industrial medicine, in Ronald Bayer (ed.), *The Health and Safety of Workers: Case Studies in the Politics of Professional Responsibility.* (Oxford: Oxford University Press), 151.
2. Manville Personal Injury Settlement Trust, 1992, Financial statements and report of Manville personal injury settlement trust for the period ended December 31, 1991, *Stockholders & Creditors News Re. Johns-Manville Corp, et al.,* March 11, 12614–12625.
3. Your check is not in the mail, 1990, *Time,* September 17, 65.
4. Author's calculation based on conversations with Dr. Irving J. Selikoff, of Mt. Sinai Medical Center in New York, and standard mortality tables.
5. Quoted in Ozonoff, Failed warnings. 155–156.
6. Quoted in Ozonoff, Failed warnings. 157.
7. Ozonoff, Failed warnings. 155, 167.
8. Vandiver Brown to A. J. Lanza, December 10, 1934.
9. Ozonoff, Failed Warnings. 167.
10. Vandiver Brown to A. J. Lanza, December 21, 1934.
11. George S. Hobart to Vandiver Brown, December 15, 1934.
12. Manville Corporation, 1982, Beleaguered by asbestos lawsuits Manville files for reorganization, News release, August 27.
13. Vandiver Brown to Sumner Simpson, October 3, 1935.
14. Anne Rossiter to Sumner Simpson, September 25, 1935.
15. Vandiver Brown to LeRoy U. Gardner, November 20, 1936.
16. LeRoy U. Gardner, M.D., 1939,"Interim report on experimental asbestosis at the Saranac Laboratory." Enclosure to letter from Vandiver Brown to Sumner Simpson, December 26, 1939.

17. W. C. L. Henderson, 1947, Industrial Hygiene Foundation of America, Inc.: Report of preliminary first investigation for Asbestos Textile Institute, June 18, 2, 15.

18. Kenneth W. Smith, 1949, Industrial hygiene— Survey of men in dusty areas, Enclosure to memorandum marked "Confidential" from A. R. Fisher (J-M president) to Vandiver Brown, February 3, 2.

19. Ibid., 3.

20. Kenneth W. Smith. Discovery deposition, *Louisville Trust Company, Administrator of the estate of William Virgil Sampson, v. Johns-Manville Corp.*, File no. 164–122 (Court of Common Pleas, Jefferson County, Kentucky, April 21, 1976).

21. David A. Shaw, 1988, Memorandum in opposition to motions for summary judgment filed by the Wellington defendants and defendant Raymark Industries, Reprinted in *Asbestos Litigation Reporter*, November 18, 18051.

22. Irving J. Selikoff, Testimony before House of Representatives, Select Committee on Labor, Committee on Education and Labor, U.S. Congress, March 7, 1968.

23. Manville Corporation, Beleaguered by asbestos lawsuits.

24. Manville Corporation, 1982, *Annual Report* and Form 10-K, December 31, 49.

25. Barry I. Castleman, 1987, *Asbestos: Medical and Legal Aspects* (Clifton, NJ: Prentice-Hall), 614.

26. Ibid., 636–637.

27. Alan Freeman, 1989, Canadian asbestos mining enjoys a modest recovery, *Wall Street Journal*, March 10, B2.

28. Arkansas plane crash kills Marlin Thompson, Robin Steele, four others, 1988, *Asbestos Litigation Reporter*, December 2, 18086–18087.

29. W. Thomas Stephens. Conversation with author, October 16, 1987.

30. Richard Goodwin. Conversation with author, January 21, 1988.

31. Amended Order (Survival and Wrongful Death Actions), Bennie M. Barnett, Administrator, for *Gordon Luther Barnett, deceased, v. Owens-Corning Fiberglass Corporation, et al.* (Court of Common Pleas, Greenville County, South Carolina, August 23, 1978), pp. 10, 5.

32. Manville Corporation, 1977, Form 10K, December 31, 26–27.

33. Christopher McHugh, ed. 1992, *The 1992 Bankruptcy Yearbook and Almanac* (Boston: New Generation Research), 40.

34. Manville Corporation, 1980, *Annual Report*, 21; 1981, *Annual Report*, 15.

35. See, for example, Manville ratings cut by Standard and Poor's, 1982, *Wall Street Journal*, June 11, 36.

36. Manville Corporation, U.S. Securities and Exchange Commission Form 10-Q, June 30, 1982, pp. II–11–II–14.

37. An argument for the conspiracy theory is found in Shaw, Memorandum in opposition to motions for summary judgment filed by the Wellington defendants and defendant Raymark Industries.

38. Manville Corporation, 1982, *Annual Report* and Form 10-K, 9.

39. See Arthur Sharplin, 1989, Chapter 11: A Machiavellian analysis, in Samuel M. Natale and John B. Wilson (eds.), *The Ethical Contexts for Business Conflicts* (Lanham, MD: University Press of America), 23–28.

40. G. Earl Parker, 1983, The Manville decision, Paper presented at the symposium "Bankruptcy Proceedings—The Effect on Product Liability," conducted by Andrews Publications, Income, Miami, March 1983, p. 3.

41. John A. McKinney, 1989, Letter to editor. *Business Month*, February, 5.

42. See, for example, Beth Lubove, 1991, A bankrupt's best friend, *Forbes*, April 1, 99–102.

43. John D. C. Roach, 1990, Reshaping corporate America: Chapter 11 forced Manville to reexamine the way it did business, *Management Accounting*, March, 22.

44. Manville Corporation, 1986, *First Amended Disclosure Statement, Second Amended and Restated Plan of Reorganization, and Related Documents*, August 22, p. M–399.

45. Manville Corporation, 1983, *Annual Report* and Form 10-K, 13.

46. Manville Corporation, 1983, *Annual Report* and Form 10-K, 15.

47. Speech at National Conference on Business Ethics, October 1987.

48. A-H Trust, 1991, *Annual Report*.

49. A-H Trust, 1991, *Annual Report*.

50. Conversation with author, October 1987.

51. A sympathetic story of several of the departing executives is told in Greg Barman, 1989, Life after Manville, *Colorado Business Magazine*, November, 15–23.

52. Hearing on sale of J-M Canada scheduled for August 30, 1983, *Stockholders and Creditors News Service*, August 15, 1315.

53. Ibid.

54. Alan Freeman, 1989, Canadian asbestos mining enjoys a modest recovery, *Wall Street Journal*, March 10, B2.

55. 3 Manville manufacturing plants sold to former President Hulce, 1988, *The Denver Post*, January 5, 2C; Manville sells three plants for $7 million, 1988, *Stockholders and Creditors News Service*, January 11, 7, 261–262.

56. George C. Dillon, 1991, Does it pay to do the right thing? Not necessarily. But for Manville Corporation, that's the wrong questions to ask, *Across the Board*, July, 15–17.

57. Stephen W. Quickel, 1987, Miracle at Manville: How Tom Stephens raised the bread to overcome bankruptcy, *Corporate Finance*, November, (no page numbers; reprint of article provided by Manville Corporation). Jesus' miracle of the loaves and fishes is described in Matthew 14:15–21.

58. John A. McKinney to Arthur Sharplin, May 11, 1987.

59. Committee of asbestos related litigants again asks bankruptcy court to dismiss Johns-Manville bankruptcy, 1983, *Asbestos Litigation Reporter*, September 23, 7148.

60. Asbestos claimants committee rejects plan, 1983, *Asbestos Litigation Reporter*, November 25, 7416.

61. Asbestos-related litigants move to have bankruptcy court appoint trustee, 1984, *Asbestos Litigation Reporter*, January 6, 7625.

62. Committee of asbestos-related litigants and/or creditors withdraws its motion to reduce salaries of Manville officers, 1984, *Asbestos Litigation Reporter*, March 16, 7999.

63. Johns-Manville asks court to void asbestos-claimants attorney fees, 1983, *Asbestos Litigation Reporter*, November 25, 7411.

64. Hearing set on replacement for plaintiff contingency fee arrangements, 1984, *Asbestos Litigation Reporter*, February 3, 7785.

65. Judge Lifland refuses to stop trust payments to claimants, 1989, *Stockholders and Creditors News Re. Johns-Manville Corp., et al.*, May 8, 8799.

66. Committee of asbestos-related litigants and/or creditors withdraws its motion to reduce salaries of Manville officers, 1984, *Asbestos Litigation Reporter*, March 16, 7999.

67. In re Johns-Manville Corp, 1987, *Asbestos Litigation Reporter: Eight-Year Cumulative Index, February 1979–July 1987*, August, 37–38.

68. The Committee of Asbestos-Related Litigants and/or Creditors Representing Asbestos-Health Claimants of Manville Corporation, 1986, Questions and answers on asbestos-health claims and the Manville reorganization plan and A very important message for people with asbestos-related diseases, undated, distributed in August–October 1986.

69. Ronald L. Motley to Arthur Sharplin, April 1, 1988.

70. Manville personal injury settlement trust financial statements, 1989, *Stockholders and Creditors News Re. Johns-Manville, et al.*, March 6, 8639–8655.

71. A-H Trust, 1991, *Annual Report*.

72. Stacy Adler, 1989, Payouts do not imperil Manville trust: Director, *Business Insurance*, February 13, 2.

73. Ibid.

74. Ibid.

75. Your check is not in the mail, 1990, *Time*, September 17, 65.

76. Marianna S. Smith resigns as executive director of trust, 1991, *Stockholders and Creditors News Re. Johns-Manville Corp., et al.*, December 9, 12279. Smith said she was resigning because the directors' and officers' insurance was not being renewed.

77. Manville trust to hold regional meetings on claims process, 1992, *Stockholders and Creditors News Re. Johns-Manville Corp., et al.*, March 25, 12638.

78. Marj Charlier, 1992, For Manville, a sale or breakup appears imminent, *Wall Street Journal*, March 3, B4.

79. See Marj Charlier, 1992, Manville's rating on debt and stock is cut by Moody's, *Wall Street Journal*, April 13, C 15; W. Thomas Stephens, letter to shareholders, Manville Corporation, *MvL* (1992 Summary Annual Report Issue), 1–4.

CASE 22 Kitchen Made Pies

James J. Chrisman
University of Calgary

Fred L. Fry
Bradley University

Charles W. Hofer
University of Georgia

In late 1981, Paul Dubicki, owner and president of Kitchen Made Pies (KMP), was faced with a difficult problem. Company sales had stagnated since 1975, and the firm was about to suffer its fourth straight year of losses (see Exhibit 1). Further compounding this problem were unfavorable economic and industry conditions, both locally and nationally, as well as difficulties with certain customers and creditors. In addition, KMP's balance sheet showed a deficit equity position (see Exhibit 2), which limited the range of feasible alternatives available to turn the situation around. In spite of these concerns, Mr. Dubicki was determined to return the business to profitability, and was confident that this task could be accomplished if he could only get away from day-to-day decision making.

When commenting on the current situation at Kitchen Made, Mr. Dubicki emphasized that volume was the key to success:

> We must increase our customer base and we must somehow encourage our present distributors to provide the promotional support retailers need to sell our products. One well-publicized special can sell more pies in one day than can be sold in a normal week without one. That's what I'd like to concentrate on, but every day something else comes up around here.

Management cooperated in the field research for this case, which was written solely for the purpose of stimulating student discussion. All events and individuals are real. All rights reserved jointly to the authors and the North American Case Research Association (NACRA). Copyright © 1993 by the *Case Research Journal* and James J. Chrisman, Fred L. Fry, and Charles W. Hofer.

Exhibit 1   KMP Operating Results 1971–1981 (in thousands of dollars)

Year	Sales ($)	Profits		Materials		Production Labor		Overhead*		Selling*		Administration	
		$	%	$	%	$	%	$	%	$	%	$	%
1971	844	14	1.7	432.1	51.2	253.2	30.0	64.1	7.6	24.5	2.9	83.6	9.9
1972	955	8	0.8	482.3	50.5	279.8	29.3	67.8	7.1	26.7	2.8	90.7	9.5
1973	1246	24	1.9	656.6	52.7	306.5	24.6	110.9	8.9	34.9	2.8	114.6	9.2
1974	1453	18	1.2	828.2	57.0	324.0	22.3	135.1	9.3	36.3	2.5	111.9	7.7
1975	1604	110	6.9	864.6	53.9	332.0	20.7	150.8	9.4	35.3	2.2	110.7	6.9
1976	1580	109	6.9	771.0	48.8	363.4	23.0	178.5	11.3	41.1	2.6	116.9	7.4
1977	1642	7	0.4	802.9	48.9	426.9	26.0	221.7	13.5	44.3	2.7	139.6	8.5
1978	1608	−24	−1.5	818.5	50.9	422.9	26.3	204.2	12.7	35.4	2.2	151.2	9.4
1979	1601	−58	−3.6	810.1	50.6	432.3	27.0	209.7	13.1	44.8	2.8	160.1	10.0
1980	1506	−91	−6.0	772.6	51.3	426.2	28.3	192.8	12.8	49.7	3.3	155.1	10.3
1981	1635	−178	−10.9	887.8	54.3	452.9	27.7	220.7	13.5	67.0	4.1	183.1	11.2

Note: All cost figures are not strictly comparable due to changes in allocation procedures, although these changes were not substantial in nature.
*Includes both fixed and variable costs.
Source: KMP internal data, 1981.

Exhibit 2   KMP Balance Sheet 1981 (in thousands of dollars)

	Assets			Liabilities & Equity	
Current Assets	Cash	$ 2	Current Liabilities	Accounts payable	$291
	Accounts receivable	163		Unsecured bank note	70
	Inventory	137		Accrued payroll & taxes	25
	Prepaid expenses	17		Note—F. Dubicki	8
	Total current assets	$319		Total current liabilities	$394
Fixed Assets after Depreciation	Leasehold improvements	$ 1	Long-Term Liabilities	Bank note on truck	$ 15
	Machinery and equipment	48		Bank note on equipment	12
	Autos and trucks	28		Total long-term liabilities	$ 27
	Total fixed assets	$ 77		Total Liabilities	$421
				Equity (deficit)	$(25)
		$396			$ 396

Source: KMP internal data, 1981.

■ Company History

In 1981, Kitchen Made Pies was a regional producer of a wide variety of pies and other bakery products. Located in Peoria, Illinois, the firm traced its history back 30 years. The company was founded by Frank Dubicki, the father of the current owner, and had been run by the Dubicki family throughout its existence.

Paul Dubicki grew up and worked for his father in the bakery business, but in his youth was not very interested in pursuing a career with the firm. After leaving the business to attend college and work on his own, Paul returned in 1968 to work for his father and later become, along with his brother, David Dubicki, a minority stockholder. During this time, Paul was dissatisfied because he never seemed able to get away from line operations and other day-to-day aspects of the business. Furthermore, he felt that the true market potential of the firm had never been realized due to his father's persistent reliance on one customer, Dean's Distributing, for the bulk of KMP's sales. Paul did not believe Dean's served Kitchen Made's needs particularly well, and he was convinced that future growth depended on an expanded, and perhaps more selective, customer base. However, the elder Dubicki remained firm in his conviction, and the status quo at KMP was maintained throughout the 1970s.

In early 1981, Paul persuaded his father to sell out, though the elder Dubicki did retain ownership of the company's land and facilities. This sale was accomplished through a redemption of Frank Dubicki's stock by the corporation in a transaction that also eliminated his sizable debt to the corporation. At the same time, David voluntarily gave his shares of the business to his brother, leaving Paul as the sole owner. In this context it should be noted that David Dubicki had never showed much interest in the business and was not directly involved in its operation at the time of his exit.

Upon assuming full control, Paul Dubicki immediately set about changing and updating the firm's various operational procedures, and, for the first time, he made a firm commitment to strategic planning. Unfortunately, difficulties such as delinquent accounts and lagging sales, which had built up over a long period of time, had become very serious problems.

■ The Baking Industry

■ General Description

The baking industry can be divided into two broad SIC code categories: bread, cakes, and related products (SIC #2051), which includes pies (SIC #20515), and cookies and crackers (SIC #2052). According to the 1977 *U.S. Census* of manufacturers:

> This industry [SIC #2051] comprises establishments primarily engaged in the manufacture of bread, cakes, and other "perishable" bakery products. Establishments manufacturing bakery products for sale primarily through one or more nonbaking retail outlets are included in this industry. (page 20E-2)

Baked goods have been produced and consumed by individuals all over the world for hundreds of years. Traditionally, baking has been a trade occupation, with nearly every community having at least one local baker in the area. Baking has also been done in the home for many generations. Thus, the baking business

Exhibit 3	Bread, Cake, and Related Products Industry Statistics 1977 (SIC #2051) (dollar figures in thousands)		
Establishments	1–19 employees	1,945	
	20–99 employees	561	
	100 or more employees	556	
		3,062	
	Total number of employees (office, production, etc.)		178,000
	Total payroll		$2,335,800
	Cost of materials		$3,909,000
	Value of shipments		$9,274,900

Inventory		*Beginning*	*Ending*
	Total	$220,600	$235,100
	Finished goods	22,000	25,000
	Work in process	2,100	3,700
	Raw materials	196,500	206,400
	Capital expenditures	$303,800	

Source: *U.S. Census of Manufacturers*, 1977, p. 20E-10.

has always had a distinctly local flavor and orientation. In fact, it was not until around the turn of the century that technological advances, such as refrigeration and food preservatives, permitted baked goods (and other food products) to be transported any distance.

Even in 1981 transportation costs and the perishable nature of baked goods were significant barriers to industry consolidation. As a result, the baking industry remained fragmented, although less so than in earlier periods. Thus, in the bread, cake, and related products industries there were only moderate increases between 1972 and 1977 in the concentration ratios for the top four firms (29 to 33 percent), top eight firms (39 to 40 percent), and top fifty firms (62 to 68 percent). Furthermore, during the same period, the number of establishments employing fewer than 20 workers increased, while the total number of competitors decreased almost 8 percent. These trends, which resulted in fewer medium-sized bakers, implied that large firms, with internal delivery capabilities, and smaller firms, which emphasized local business, possessed certain cost and/or market advantages. Some industry observers felt that recurring energy shortages would accentuate this development.

Exhibit 3 provides a composite of the bread, cake, and related products segment of the baking industry as of 1977.

■ Current Conditions*

Though the outlook for the baking industry was helped considerably in 1981 by softening sugar prices and stabilized wheat prices, overall prospects were

---

*The majority of the discussion in this section was drawn from the *U.S. Industry Outlook,* 1980 and 1981.

Exhibit 4   Producer and Consumer Price Index for Commodities 1970, 1975–1981

		1970	1975	1976	1977	1978	1979	1980	1981
Producer Price Index (1967 = 100)	All commodities	110.4	174.9	183.0	194.2	209.3	235.6	268.8	293.4
	Processed food and feeds	112.1	182.6	178.0	186.1	202.6	222.5	241.2	248.7
	Cereal and bakery products	107.7	178.0	172.1	173.4	190.3	210.3	236.0	255.5
	Grains (including wheat)	98.8	223.9	205.9	165.0	182.5	214.8	239.0	248.4
	Processed fruits and vegetables	110.6	169.8	170.2	187.4	202.6	221.9	228.7	261.2
	Sugar and confectionary	115.8	254.3	190.9	177.4	197.8	214.7	322.5	275.9
Consumer Price Index (1967 = 100)	All items	116.3	161.2	170.5	181.5	195.4	217.4	246.8	272.4
	Food	114.9	175.4	180.8	192.2	211.4	234.5	254.6	274.6
	Food at home	113.7	175.8	179.5	190.2	210.2	232.9	251.5	269.9
	Food away from home	119.9	163.0	169.4	175.4	189.4	208.5	231.1	254.9
	Sugar and sweets	115.1	246.2	218.2	229.4	257.5	277.6	341.3	368.3
	Cereal and bakery products	108.9	184.8	180.6	183.5	199.9	220.1	246.4	271.1

Source: *U.S. Statistical Abstract*, 1982, p. 456.

Exhibit 5   Value of Shipments of Bread, Cake, and Related Products (SIC #2051) 1975–1980 (in millions of dollars)

	1975	1976	1977	1978	1979	1980
Industry value of shipments*	$9,059	$9,512	$9,275	$9,504	$10,360	$11,500
Product value of shipments[†]	7,727	8,084	7,966	8,170	9,000	9,930
Change in producer price index	+1.6%	+2.8%	+1.3%	+13.4%	+12.1%	+12.4%

*Value of all products and services sold by SIC #2051 industry.

[†]Value of all shipments of bread, cake, and related products produced by all industries.

Source: *U.S. Industrial Outlook*, 1981, p. 391.

somewhat uncertain due to the recessionary conditions in the U.S. economy and recent shortages of certain essential ingredients such as sugar. Exhibit 4 provides producer and consumer price indexes for selected commodities for the years 1970 and 1975–1981. The baking industry (with the possible exception of breads), and particularly the pie and cake segment, seemed likely to suffer because purchase of these products tends to be more discretionary in nature than purchases of other foodstuffs. When the economy declines, consumers usually cut back on discretionary items first. Indeed, as Exhibits 5 and 6 indicate, sales in the mature bread, cake, and related products segment had been somewhat erratic during the 1975–1980 time period, and the pie industry had done even worse.

Several other emerging trends also threatened to upset whatever balance currently existed in the industry. More and more consumers appeared to be cutting down on sweets and sugar intake for health and weight reasons. Additionally, the average age of the population was increasing due to the demographic changes resulting from the 1950s and 1960s baby boom. Since

Exhibit 6 Value of Shipments of Pies, Fruit and Custard, Except Frozen (SIC #20515) 1967, 1972–1977 (dollar figures in millions; quantities in thousands of tons)

	1967	1972	1973	1974	1975	1976	1977
Product value of shipments*	226.7	224.2	254.8	326.0	319.0	347.6	297.1
Quantities shipped	N/A	574.5	N/A	N/A	N/A	N/A	498.0

*Value of all shipments of fruit and custard pies (except frozen) produced by all industries.
Source: *U.S. Census of Manufacturers,* 1977, p. 20E-18.

Exhibit 7 Household Demographics for the United States 1960–1981

Households	1960	1970	1980	1981
Total number	52,600,000	62,900,000	80,800,000	82,400,000
1-person	13.1%	17.0%	22.7%	23.0%
2-person	27.8%	28.8%	31.4%	31.3%
3-person	18.9%	17.3%	17.5%	17.7%
4-person	17.6%	15.8%	15.7%	15.5%
5-person	11.5%	10.4%	7.5%	7.4%
6-person	5.7%	5.6%	3.1%	3.1%
7 or more person	5.4%	5.1%	2.2%	2.0%
Average number of persons per household	3.33	3.14	2.76	2.73

Source: *U.S. Statistical Abstract,* 1982.

people's eating habits and preferences tend to change as they grow older, this trend could significantly affect the industry's sales and product mix.

Other factors that could affect the outlook and subsequent performance of the baking industry were recent trends toward eating out and the emerging popularity of prepared foods. In the fast-paced world of the 1980s, people no longer had as much time to cook their own meals. Increases in the numbers of single households (see Exhibit 7) and the growing participation of women in the workforce had exacerbated these trends. According to the *U.S. Industrial Outlook,* 1981:

> The growing trend among Americans toward eating out has been good for the bakery foods industry because all types of restaurants serve bakery foods. Fast food outlets are major users of buns and rolls but also serve other bakery goods. Conventional restaurants serve all types of bakery foods including buns, rolls, variety breads and sweet goods. (page 392)

However, according to Mr. Dubicki, fast-food chains, which were gaining in popularity, usually purchased desserts on a nationwide basis and did not like to buy from local dessert manufacturers.

Government regulation was also a potentially serious concern for bakers. Recent controversies included the issue of what "natural" and "organic" foods really were

Exhibit 8   1979 Sales Records of Frozen Foods

Categories	Millions of Dollars	% Change vs. 1974	% Change vs. 1978	% of Total
Total, all frozen foods	$7,643.8	+73%	+9.9%	100%
Baked goods	860.8	+70.8%	+10%	11.2%
Sweet goods	437.0	+50.2%	+6.1%	5.7%
Pies	229.9	+66.6%	+14.5%	3.0%

Source: Grocery retailing in the 1980s, 1980, *Progressive Grocer*, 96.

(and when foods could be advertised as such), as well as product labeling regulations. No specific projections on the effects of these legislative activities could be made in regard to industry participants, although costs were expected to increase as a result, and hence inefficient producers might face difficulties.

Frozen bakery products were yet another area of concern for industry participants. Though the overall trend had been one of increasing sales of frozen bakery goods (see Exhibit 8), and many grocers expected significant advances for a number of frozen products in the 1980s (see Exhibit 9) at least two factors threatened to constrain frozen food sales growth. First of all, consumers seemed to view frozen foods as more expensive than fresh or canned items. Secondly, grocers were hesitant to expand frozen food sections in the supermarket due to high energy costs, which, on average, actually exceeded the cost of rent in 1980 (*Progressive Grocer*, April 1981). Therefore, the future of frozen food sales in general, and frozen pie sales in particular, remained in doubt.

■ Value-Added Chain in the Baking Industry

The value-added chain in the baking industry starts, of course, with the farmer who grows the grains, fruit, and other food products which make up the baked goods, in this case, pies. Farmers represented the closest facsimile to a purely competitive market existing in the U.S. economy; thus, farmers were price takers rather than price makers. As a result, the effects of farmers' activities on conditions in the baking industry were limited to the quantity of goods brought to market (which in itself largely determines prices, but was uncontrollable by the individual farmer unless one or more decided to withhold their produce—an infrequent occurrence) and the overall quality of these goods.

The farmers sold their products to food processors such as sugar refineries and flour mills, who transformed the raw foodstuffs into the actual material used in the bakeries. Due to economies of scale and the fragmented nature of the baking industry, these suppliers tended to be larger than many of their customers (though this was not always the case) and hence enjoyed relative power in regard to price and service agreements. It should be noted that many of the larger firms involved in the baking industry were vertically integrated backward into the food-processing business, thus enjoying potential cost advantages over nonintegrated rivals.

The processed foodstuffs were the basic raw materials for the competitors in the baking industry. Once the baked product was produced it had to be transported, distributed, and sold to the consumer. Usually, two distribution links

Exhibit 9   Frozen Food Predictions for the 1980s
(Survey of Buyers/Merchandisers)

"Outstanding Advances"*
  Boilable pouch products
  Pizza
  Frozen meats, poultry
  Premium quality
  Private label
  Vegetables, regular poly
  Fish, seafood
"Good Advances"*
  Single dish entrees
  Single serving
  Orange juice
  Froz. meat, poultry
  Diet/low calorie
  Family servings
  Potatoes
  Nationality foods
  Breakfast items
  Entrees
  Ice cream
  Vegetables, prep.
  Dairy toppings
  Vegetables, regular box
  Sweet goods
  DESSERT PIES
  Non-orange juices

"Average Advances"*
  Pot pies
  Fruits
  Bread, rolls
  Margarine
  Miscellaneous desserts
  Snacks
  Regular dinners
  Pet foods
"Decline Anticipated"*
  Generic labels

*Products ranked in descending order.
Source: Grocery retailing in the 1980's, 1980, *Progressive Grocer,* 92.

(distributors and retailers) appeared in the value chain before the goods reached the consumer. In the baking industry, some competitors were forward-integrated into distribution and even retail.

Producers of baked goods usually sold their products to distributors (75 percent of sales according to *Progressive Grocer,* 1980), although some made direct deliveries to retail or institutional customers. Since distributors contributed so substantially to the value-added chain, it is useful to understand the types of distribution, their cost structures, and their basic strategies.

There were three basic types of independent distributors or wholesalers.

1. *Voluntary* wholesalers sponsored retailers who belonged to voluntary merchandising groups such as IGA (Independent Grocers Association) or Red and White, and did virtually all business with this related buying group.

2. *Cooperative* wholesalers were actually owned (wholly or partially) by (generally independent) retail grocers and specifically served the needs of these customers. Certified Grocers and Associated Grocers were two examples of wholesale buying groups organized by retailers.

3. *Unaffiliated* wholesalers, as the name suggests, did business with unaffiliated independent grocers and served some of the needs of the large food chains as well.

All these types of distributors provided grocers with a wide range of food products, including pies. Some smaller concerns concentrated on certain food lines such as baked goods, but many dealt with the full range of food products sold in grocery stores. Exhibit 10 provides statistics on wholesaler operating characteristics in 1980.

Distributors used two basic methods to sell products to grocers. Some sold on a guaranteed basis, with unsold products returned to the dealer at no charge. Others sold products unguaranteed; i.e., grocers assumed full responsibility for all products they bought. As might be expected, profit margins for the two methods differed. Grocers usually made about 23 to 25 percent on guaranteed sales, while unguaranteed sales yielded margins of approximately 35 to 40 percent. However, because of the inherent risks involved in unguaranteed

Exhibit 10   Wholesaler Operations Review—1980

	Voluntary	Co-op	Unaffiliated
Distribution centers per firm	1.6	1.7	1.3
Average size, ft²	226,000	227,000	38,000
Annual turnover, %	15.9	16.1	11.0
Service level to store, %	94.9	94.9	88.3
Manufacturing service level, %	93.9	89.9	86.7
Sale per ft²	$509	$472	$187
Average sales	$187,495,000	$223,329,000	$9,614,000
Gross margin, %	7.4	6.5	9.2
Net before-tax profits, %	1.6	1.4	1.6
Expenses (% of sales)			
Payroll	3.74	4.08	6.15
Transportation	0.15	0.17	0.25
Utilities	0.22	0.20	0.40
Interest	0.36	0.37	0.50
Insurance	0.17	0.16	0.55
Goods	92.6	93.5	90.8
Business (% of sales)			
Supermarkets	63	68	26
Convenience stores	16	9	11
Small stores	21	23	63

Source: *Progressive Grocer*, April 1981.

purchases, some grocers preferred the lower but safer profit margins of guaranteed arrangements, especially when dealing with unaffiliated "door-to-store" distributors. Nonguaranteed sales were most commonly used by bread bakers.

Whereas door-to-store distributors accumulated individual orders daily and delivered merchandise direct from the baker to the grocer, *drop shipments* involved larger orders, which were taken first to warehouses for later delivery to individual stores. For example , drop-ship distributors such as Eisner's (a current customer of KMP) sold direct to their own or an affiliated grocery chain and thus enjoyed profits on both the delivery and retail end. According to Mr. Dubicki, this was an important competitive advantage, since 40 to 50 percent of the retail product cost was in distribution. Another feature distinguishing drop shippers from door-to-store distributors was the greater willingness of the former to provide the promotional support necessary to sell the food products. This in part explained the willingness of grocers to make unguaranteed purchases with drop shippers. Due to these factors, Mr. Dubicki expressed a desire to concentrate on doing business with this type of distributor.

Although many pies were sold to institutional customers and restaurants, the last link in the value-added chain for the baking industry was usually the retail grocer, who sold the bakery product to the ultimate consumer. Grocers sold pies to the consumer in at least three ways. Some supermarkets depended on sales of prepackaged pies, which were bought from an outside supplier and sold on the premises. Prepackaged pies could be either fresh or frozen, though frozen pie purchases were more common due to the limited shelf life (approximately two to four days) of fresh pies.

Many stores had taken different approaches. In-store bakeries were gaining popularity not only because of the higher profit margins available but also because they attracted consumers into the store, where they bought other things in addition to baked goods. Some grocers ran "scratch" operations, i.e., bakery goods were made and baked at the store, while other grocers ran "bake-off" operations, i.e., baked foods were bought from an outside supplier (prebaked or unbaked) and baked or rebaked on the premises. Although some supermarkets employed either one method or the other, it was not uncommon to find pies or other bakery products sold via a combination of these methods in a single store (*U.S. Industrial Outlook*, 1980). In-store bakeries with scratch operations made their own pies and thus were not customers for firms such as KMP. In-store bakeries with bake-off operations, however, did buy pies (mainly fresh).

The overall trend for in-store bakeries had been on the upswing, but 1981 saw a reversal to this trend. Bakery departments and delicatessens offered grocers the highest profit margins, but their percentage contribution to total sales fell in 1981 compared to 1980 (see Exhibits 11 and 12) according to statistics compiled by the National Association of Retail Grocers. Furthermore, among respondents to *Progressive Grocer's* annual survey of supermarket operations, the percentage of supermarkets operating on-premise bake-off bakeries had declined from 26 percent in 1979 to 24 percent in 1980 and the percentage operating scratch bakeries had declined from 17 percent in 1979 to 15 percent in 1980.

■ Competition

Pie-baking competitors seemed to follow either a full-line or a limited-line approach. Additionally, most seemed to concentrate on either fresh or frozen

Exhibit 11   Grocery Sales and Profit Mix 1980–1981

		1981	1980	Trend
Sales Mix, %	Grocery	65.9	66.1	(0.3)
	Meat	19.9	20.6	(3.5)
	Produce	6.6	6.3	4.8
	Bakery	2.9	3.8	(31.0)
	Delicatessen	3.3	3.6	(9.1)
Gross Profit, %	Grocery	18.8	17.9	5.0
	Meat	20.8	19.9	4.5
	Produce	28.7	27.7	3.6
	Bakery	41.9	39.3	6.6
	Delicatessen	40.1	36.7	9.3
	Total store	20.2	19.6	3.1

Exhibit 12   Bakery Sales and Gross Profit 1979–1981

		1981	1980	1979
Bakery Sales, % of Total Sales	High	5.0	5.4	3.7
	Low	1.4	0.9	2.1
	Average	2.9	3.8	2.9
Bakery Gross Profit, %	High	55.6	52.5	54.6
	Low	34.3	16.7	40.8
	Average	41.9	39.3	48.1

Source: 1981 Financial Analysis, National Association of Retail Grocers of the U.S., 1, 12, 16.

products. For the most part, larger firms offered a full line of frozen pies nationally, while smaller firms emphasized limited lines of fresh pies in regional markets. No matter what strategy was employed, efficiency in production and purchasing was extremely important, since the cost of raw materials (42 percent of sales in 1972 and 1977) and labor (28 percent of sales in 1972, 35 percent in 1977) amounted to over two-thirds of total pie revenues (see Exhibit 13). Since the larger firms had facilities for long, simultaneous product runs of many pies, of many flavors and sizes, and could take advantage of purchasing economies, a full-line strategy was feasible. Smaller firms without such capabilities were generally content with serving niches in the marketplace, both in varieties and customer coverage, because in order to be reasonably cost competitive they had to be able to match to a certain degree the economies of their more powerful competitors. The only way this could be accomplished was by concentrating on a limited-line strategy.

Exhibit 13   Pies, Fruit and Custard, Except Frozen (SIC #20515) 1977 Summary Statistics

	Number of Establishments	Number of Employees	Payroll	Cost of Materials	Value of Shipments ($000,000)
Establishments with this product class primary	44	3700	$47.9	$101.7	212.3
Establishments with 75% specialization or more in class	26	2000	$26.3	$48.3	109.8

Source: *U.S. Census of Manufacturers*, 1977, p. 20E-15.

Exhibit 14   Peoria Area Demographics (population figures in thousands)

	Census*			Preliminary Census	Projected Total	
	1950	1960	1970	1980	1990	2000
City	111.9	103.2	127.0	121.4	126.0	129.7
Metro area	271.8	313.4	342.0	360.6	380.2	401.2

Population Characteristic[†]	Metro Peoria	Total United States
Male	48.6%	48.7%
Female	51.4%	51.3%
Children under 18	34.9%	34.3%
Median Age	28.2 years	28.1 years

Labor Data—Peoria Metropolitan Area (March 1980)

Civilian labor force	172,250
Unemployment	12,725
Percent unemployment	7.4%
Manufacturing	51,500
Nonmanufacturing	83,400
Total government employees	17,200
Agricultural employees	3,700
Retail trade	26,800

*Data from "Peoria Profile," Peoria Area Chamber of Commerce, September 1980.

[†]Data from *Journal Star* research, cited in "Peoria: Illinois' Other Prime Market," 1980.

The Peoria Area Environment

The Peoria area, like most midwestern cities, had shown little or no growth in the past decade, as the U.S. population shifted to the southwest. Peoria itself showed a population decline according to the 1980 census, although the number of households increased. Exhibit 14 provides summary demographic statistics for the Peoria area. The economy in Peoria had traditionally been solid due to the dominant influence of Caterpillar Tractor Company, a Pabst Brewing plant, a

---

Exhibit 15   Peoria Area Employers

200–299 employees

Allied Mills	Lexington House
Belwood Nursing Home	Libby, McNeil & Libby
Carson, Pirie, Scott & Co.	Limestone High School, Bartonville
Central Telephone	McDougal-Hartman
Commonwealth Edison	Montgomery Ward
East Peoria City	Morton Building
Equitable Life	Morton Schools, Morton
Federal Warehouse	L. R. Nelson
First Federal Savings	Ozark Airline
First National Bank	Pekin Insurance, Pekin
Great Central Insurance	UNARCO
H. C. Products	Venture Stores
Chris Hoerr & Co.	Zeller Zone Center
Hopedale Hospital	
Illinois Mutual Insurance	*400–499 employees*
IBM	Bemis Co.
Jefferson Bank	Bergner's Inc.
V. Jobst	Fleming & Potter
Jumer's Castle Lodge	Journal Star
Lum's, Inc.	Pekin Schools, Pekin
Metamora Woodworking, Metamora	U.S. Regional Lab
Morton Metalcraft, Morton	
Natkin Co.	*500–599 employees*
J.C. Penney, Pekin	American Distilling
J.C. Penney, Peoria	Commercial National Bank
Pekin City	Foster-Gallagher
Peoria Library	Pekin Memorial Hospital
Peoria Hilton Hotel	Peoria & Pekin Union
Ramada Inn	Sears, Roebuck & Co.
Rock Island Lines	
Ben Schwartz Markets	*600–699 employees*
Sealtest	Bradley University
Sprinkman Industries	C. Iber & Sons
Szold's, Inc.	C.P.C. International
Thompson Food Basket	Illinois Bell Telephone
Toledo, Peoria & Western R.R.	Illinois Central College
West Central Utilities	Kroger Co., E. Peoria
Zaborac Electric	City of Peoria
	Proctor Hospital
300–399 employees	U.S. Post Office
Ashland Chemical	
Cohen Furniture	*Over 699 employees*
Cullinan & Sons	Caterpillar Tractor Co.
East Peoria High School	Central Illinois Light Co.
East Peoria Schools	Keystone Steel
Farm Supply Services	Methodist Hospital
Interstate Bakeries	Pabst Brewing
	Peoria Dist. #150 Schools
	St. Francis Hospital
	Wabco

Source: *Journal Star* research, cited in "Peoria: Illinois' Other Prime Market," 1980.

Hiram-Walker distillery, a number of other medium-sized manufacturing facilities, and a host of smaller plants—many of which were suppliers of Caterpillar (see Exhibit 15). As a result, Peoria wage rates and median income had consistently ranked in the top 20 cities in the nation. Many Peorians believed that "Peoria doesn't have recessions."

Exhibit 16 Peoria Area Major Grocery Wholesalers, Food Brokers, and Retail
Food Chain Stores

Grocery Wholesalers:

Calihan Co.	Pavey & Co.
Chris Hoerr & Son Co.	Peoria Marketing Corp.
Illinois Fruit & Produce Corp.	Pioneer Foods Sales
Leu Collins Inc.	Professional Marketers, Inc.
Geo. O. Pasquel Co.	E. Skinner, Inc.
Peoria Cash & Carry	M.L. Underwood
Peoria Packing Co.	James A. Woodhouse Co.
Rashid Provision Co., Inc.	
Schmidt Brothers Produce	*Food Chains Stores*
SuperValu Stores, Inc.	*(number of stores):*
Waugh Frozen Food Co.	A&P (1)
Winkler's Meats	Ben Schwartz (IGA) (6)
	Cardinal (4)
Food Brokers:	Convenient Food Mart (15)
Block & Lieb, Inc.	Del Farm (4)
Calkins & Co.	Eagle (3)
Conneely Brokerage Co.	IGA (10)
Glatz Bros., Inc.	Kroger (10)
Hockenberg-Rubin Co.	Mr. K's (3)
M.J. Holland, Inc.	Randall's (1)
R. Kinsinger Co.	Red Fox (22)
E.L. Menges Brokerage Co.	Thompson Food Basket (8)
Mid American Marketing	Vogels (2)
Myles Young, Inc.	

That appeared to have changed in the last few years, however. A 12-week strike in the fall of 1979 idled many of the over 30,000 Peoria-area Caterpillar workers and caused substantial harm to the many suppliers and other businesses that depended either directly or indirectly on the firm. In addition the Hiram-Walker plant and a Colonial Baking (bread) facility closed in 1981, the Pabst plant was scheduled to close in March 1982, and Caterpillar, for the first time in 20 years, laid off substantial numbers of workers in 1981. As a result, Peoria, which had escaped the impact of the extended recession which started around the end of the 1970s, began to suffer. Unemployment rates reached double-digit levels, and there was no relief in sight.

These events could have significant impact on the sales of pies and other desserts in the Peoria area. For instance, Caterpillar (not a customer of KMP) used less than half as many pies in 1981 as it had 10 years before. Similar problems were expected in regard to other institutional, and possibly retail, markets in the future. Exhibits 16, 17, and 18 provide statistics and listings of the major wholesalers and retail grocers in the Peoria area, respectively.

Kitchen Made Pies' Current Operations

Product Line

Kitchen Made Pies, as the name implies, was primarily engaged in pie baking. The company made a full line of pies, some on a regular basis, some seasonally. Exhibit 19 lists all major sizes and flavors of pies produced by Kitchen Made, as well as other bakery products which the firm made.

Exhibit 17   Statistics on Customers of Peoria Area Food Wholesalers

Type of Customer	Total Number	Unincorporated Sole Proprietorships	Partnerships	Number of Establishments with Payroll (Number of Employees)
Food stores	332	151	30	261 (3198)
Grocery stores	207	91	19	175 (2666)
All other	125	60	11	86 (532)
Eating and drinking places	640	343	55	538 (4934)
Eating places	384	195	31	344 (4239)

Source: "Peoria: Illinois' Other Prime Market," Peoria Area Chamber of Commerce, 1980.

Exhibit 18   Peoria Area Retail Sales by Store Group (dollar figures in thousands)

Metropolitan Area	Total Retail Sales*	Total Food Stores	Supermarkets	Eating and Drinking Places
Peoria S.M.S.A.	$1,372,088	$246,732	$229,337	$117,013
Peoria County	894,761	129,410	121,930	74,185
Tazewell County	407,459	103,601	95,499	37,057
Woodford County	69,868	13,721	11,908	5,771

*In the Peoria S.M.S.A. retail sales of groceries and other foods in all stores were $215,334,000 and retail sales of groceries and other foods in food stores were $202,892,000.

Source: "Peoria: Illinois' Other Prime Market," Peoria Area Chamber of Commerce, 1980.

Kitchen Made sold both fresh and frozen pies, though the former were preferred by Mr. Dubicki due to better turnover and more predictable ordering by customers. One factor limiting frozen pie sales was limited freezer space. Kitchen Made had only enough capacity to store 3,500 pies at one time. Since this represented the maximum amount of pies per day it could freeze, frozen pie sales could not exceed this volume. Due to current sales mixes, KMP did not usually utilize its full storage capacity.

The Dubickis had long been proud of the fact that they used only the highest quality ingredients in Kitchen Made products. Mr. Dubicki strongly believed that Kitchen Made Pies tasted better than competitors' products and that customers recognized this difference. Although Mr. Dubicki viewed KMP's product quality as a major strength, especially to generate and maintain a repeat business, he conceded that many times customers were more concerned with price. In the end, however, Mr. Dubicki believed KMP's superior quality would be more important than price in the development of loyal KMP customers.

Kitchen Made Pies were usually more expensive than the competition, although prices at KMP had remained stable over the last several years, and in fact, were the same in 1981 as they were in 1980. Exhibit 20 shows the prices for the various types of pies made by Kitchen Made. Management was particularly

Exhibit 19	Kitchen Made Pie Products		
	Pies		**Other**
4-inch	*8-inch*	*9-inch*	
Apple*	Apple*	Apple*	8-inch cakes
	Applecrum	Applecrum	10-inch cakes
Blackberry*		Blackberry*	Sheet cakes
	Black raspberry	Black raspberry	Shortcake
		Boston	
Cherry*	Cherry*	Cherry*	
Chocolate*	Chocolate*		
		Chocolate Boston	
Coconut*	Coconut*		
Lemon*	Lemon*		
Peach*	Peach*	Peach*	
Pineapple*	Pineapple*	Pineapple*	
	Pumpkin	Pumpkin	
		Walnut	
	Banana meringue (HT+R)	Banana meringue (R)	
	Chocolate meringue (HT+R)	Chocolate meringue (R)	
	Coconut meringue (HT+R)	Coconut meringue (R)	
	Lemon meringue (HT+R)	Lemon meringue (R)	
		Banana Whip	
		Chocolate Whip	
		Coconut Whip	
		Lemon Whip	
		Pumpkin Whip	

*Made on a regular basis
HT = high tops, R = regular

pleased with their high-top meringue pie. Because of its superior looks and acceptance by consumers, the price charged was much higher than the price charged for the regular meringue, while costs were almost identical. Thus, profit margins were significantly higher.

■ Markets and Consumers

The majority of Kitchen Made's sales were made to food and bakery distributors who basically supplied two major markets. One was the institutional market which consisted of restaurants, as well as university, hospital, corporate, and government cafeterias. The other was the retail market, which included grocery stores and convenience outlets. The retail segment of KMP's market was susceptible to change in the economy, as was the institutional side. However, some segments of the institutional market, such as hospital cafeterias, did not always reflect economic variabilities.

Kitchen Made's total sales were almost evenly split between the two markets. The institutional market accounted for the majority of cake and 9-inch pie sales, while the retail market bought mainly 4- and 8-inch pies. Most distributors concentrated on one market or the other, thus determining the type of products they purchased. Buying motives for both markets varied depending on the

Exhibit 20	KMP Products Wholesale Pie Prices				
4-inch	**8-inch**		**9-inch**		
$0.25	Regular meringue	$0.90	Fruit pies	$1.30	
	High-top meringue	$1.40	Whips	$1.30	
	Fruit pies	$1.00	Meringue	$1.25	
			Specialty	$1.60	
			Walnut	$2.00	
			Cherry	$2.25	

Exhibit 21	Breakdown of KMP Sales by Distributor and Market Served	
Distributor	**Market Served**	**% of KMP Sales**
Dean's Distributing	Institutional	40
McCormick Distributing	Institutional	10
Lowenberg	Retail	11
Eisner's	Retail	8
Master Snack and New Process	Retail	13
Edwards	Retail	4
Other	Retail	14

customer and market area involved. Some customers were very conscious of price, especially in institutional markets, while others—most notably restaurants and grocers—were sometimes more interested in quality or promotional support.

Kitchen Made's products were sold in the Peoria and St. Louis areas, but the firm also served customers in other parts of Missouri and Illinois, as well as in Iowa and Wisconsin. Major distributors of Kitchen Made products, as well as their served markets, are listed in Exhibit 21.

Besides the differences in buying motives and the type of products purchased by the two end markets, there were several other features which differentiated them from each other. Institutional markets frequently preferred frozen pies because of buying habits which prevented extensive use of fresh varieties. (Institutional customers often bought to satisfy monthly needs.) In contrast, turnover was a way of life in the grocery business. Thus, retail customers usually preferred to make weekly or biweekly purchases. Mr. Dubicki believed retail customers liked fresh pies better because they could be put directly on the shelf, which eliminated storage, thawing, and the extra work involved in moving and stocking products twice. However, fresh pies in the grocery stores sold best through in-store bakeries, which connoted greater "freshness" to the ultimate consumer than other store locations.

In addition, retailers depended heavily on promotional assistance for sales. In fact, one of the primary reasons Dean's Distributing, which at one time accounted for almost all of KMP's sales, became a less important customer for

Kitchen Made and was not a factor in the Peoria retail market was that it refused to offer grocers this type of support. Since Dean's still accounted for 40 percent of KMP's sales as of 1981, the result was that Kitchen Made had virtually no representation in the local retail market. Mr. Dubicki saw this as a major problem because he viewed retail customers as more desirable than institutional customers and therefore wished to focus on the former. Mr. Dubicki had also been attempting to attract business from drop-ship distributors because of their reduced price for retailers, and hence consumers. This, he felt, could help circumvent the higher prices charged for Kitchen Made products on the whole-sale end. Furthermore, since drop-shippers usually ordered larger quantities, Mr. Dubicki believed that longer production runs, and therefore lower costs, were possible.

In addition to sales to bakery wholesalers, Kitchen Made operated its own delivery truck which was used primarily to deliver specialty or rush orders. No plans had been made to expand this portion of the operation.

■ Competitors

Kitchen Made Pies competed against a variety of firms who did business both regionally and nationally. Some rivals made a full line of pies. Additionally, some firms were also diversified into breads and other bakery products. Others had been successful concentrating on specific sizes or types of pies, which allowed longer production runs, lower inventories, and thus, in some cases, lower costs. Mr. Dubicki felt, however, that Kitchen Made's full-line strategy gave the firm an advantage over competitors in attracting new customers and protected sales from changes in consumer taste.

Kitchen Made had no direct competition located in the Peoria area, although they did compete against a variety of firms for local as well as regional business. In some cases the firm also competed against its own customers who possessed in-house baking capabilities. Most independent companies primarily engaged in pie production were relatively small (see Exhibit 14 for summary statistics on establishments providing fresh pies). Other competitors were either divisions, or parts of divisions, of large, diversified food manufacturers.

By far the largest competitor for KMP was Mrs. Smith's Frozen Food Company, a division of Kellogg's. Mrs. Smith's produced and distributed frozen dessert pies (usually 8- or 10-inch sizes), pie shells, and frozen dessert and entree crepes nationwide, and in some areas fresh-baked pies and other pastries. Other products included Eggo frozen waffles and nondairy whipped toppings. These products were sold to both retail (grocers, restaurants) and institutional (hospitals, universities) customers. Mrs. Smith's was based in Pottstown, Pennsylvania, and had plants in Morgantown, York, and Philadelphia, Pennsylvania; McMinnville, Oregon; Atlanta, Georgia; San Jose, California; Silver Spring, Maryland; Blue Anchor, New Jersey; and Arlington, Tennessee. Total sales in 1981 were approximately $150 million, and the company employed about 2300 individuals.

Chef Pierre was another nationwide producer of frozen 8- and 10-inch pies. Owned by Consolidated Foods Corporation (1981 corporate sales $5.6 billion, profit $140 million) since 1978, Chef Pierre also prepared other frozen desserts sold through independent brokers and distributors. Chef Pierre's primary market was the midwestern United States, which was mainly served by the company's 270,000-square-foot facility in Traverse City, Michigan. Though no sales figures were obtainable for Chef Pierre alone, Consolidated's frozen food operations, of which Chef Pierre was a part (along with Booth Fisheries Corp., Idaho Frozen Food Corp., Popsicle Industries, Inc., and Kitchens of Sara Lee, Inc.), registered 1980 and 1981 sales of $598 million and $643 million, respectively. Pretax income in 1981 for Consolidated's frozen foods division was $28 million, down from $32 million in 1980.

KMP also competed against at least three significant regional rivals for its pie business. Shenandoah Pies, with its location and markets in St. Louis, Missouri, was one of KMP's chief rivals in this area. Shenandoah made a full line of fresh pies, which it sold to both retail and institutional customers.

In the Chicago, Illinois, area, KMP competed against Fasano Pies, which supplied retail and institutional customers east of the Rocky Mountains with fresh 9-inch pies and 8- and 10-inch frozen pies. Fasano employed approximately 200 persons and had 1981 sales of $12 million. Fasano, like Kitchen Made, had been experiencing financing difficulties.

Blue Bird Baking Co., located in Dayton, Ohio, was a regional producer of 4- and 8-inch fresh pies, which it sold to midwestern retail customers. Blue Bird was the largest of KMP's regional rivals; in 1981, Blue Bird registered sales of $15 million and employed approximately 200 workers.

■ Production

Baking and production techniques at Kitchen Made were relatively simple, though not without their own special problems. In most instances, pie crusts and fillings were made on KMP's only assembly line. One person operated the dough machine, which flattened the dough and rolled enough out to make one crust. Next, the dough was passed to a second person, who placed it into a pie pan. The machine then pressed the dough into the pan. Afterward, the crust passed under a filling machine, which was set according to the size of pie being made. After the crust was filled with the desired ingredients, the pie moved to another station, where the top crust was molded onto the sides of the pie pan and the excess dough removed. This excess was transported by conveyor back to the dough machine.

All fruit pies were put together by the method described above, but cream pies were filled by hand. Mr. Dubicki intended to make all of Kitchen Made's pie products on the assembly line in the near future.

A major problem associated with production was the frequent conversions required each time the size or the flavor of the pies was changed. It took approximately 15 to 20 minutes to change over to a different size pie, and 4 to 5 minutes to change the type of ingredient. Size changes usually occurred twice a day (from 4 inches to 8 inches to 9 inches), but ingredients had to be changed 20 to 25 times per day depending on the production schedule. A more efficient pie machine could be purchased for $150,000, but Mr. Dubicki said that the efficiency advantage could not be realized without longer production runs. However, no explicit cost analysis had been conducted.

Once the pies were assembled, they were placed on racks and wheeled over to the ovens for baking. All fresh pies were baked. However, whether frozen pies were baked or not depended on customer preference. After baking, the pies were again placed on racks and wheeled over to the appropriate packaging area. All pies were packaged in plain paper boxes with the Kitchen Made logo printed on the sides and top. Once packaged the pies were stacked within easy access of the shipping docks for convenient loading.

Production costs could have been reduced by limiting the numbers of different types of pies made. However, Mr. Dubicki felt that this move might hurt the firm; he believed that many retail and institutional buyers preferred to buy full lines of products from the same supplier. Despite this perceived concern, it was undeniable that limiting pie varieties could achieve substantial savings. For example, with full crews, Kitchen Made baked a little more than $30,000 worth of pies and cakes per week. In cases in which the firm received a special order, a half crew would be brought in on an unscheduled shift. On those days, production reached as high as $10,000.

Recently, the first production manager who was not related to the Dubicki family had been appointed from off the shop floor. Despite creating this new position, Mr. Dubicki had continued to spend a significant portion of his time in the shop. The production manager helped mainly in a supervisory role. Mr. Dubicki expressed overall confidence in her ability, but was concerned with her failure to delegate work assignments and responsibilities.

One positive recent development was the reduction of raw materials inventory by Mr. Dubicki. Though done as much out of necessity as out of design, the move nonetheless helped in many respects. In the past, ingredients such as fillings, flour, sugar, etc., had often been bought in six-month quantities. In 1981, the firm tried to buy only what it needed for one or two weeks, except in special cases when supplies were hard to find or favorable price breaks could be obtained.

Exhibit 22 provides a rough sketch of KMP's plant layout in 1981.

■ Financial Information

Given Kitchen Made's current product mix, sales of approximately $35,000 per week ($1,820,000 per year) were needed to break even, according to Mr. Dubicki. Variable expenses (materials and labor) were estimated to be about 85 percent of sales revenue. Exhibit 23 provides a rough breakdown of sales and operating profits by product line in percentages and dollar amounts. The 4-inch pies and the cakes were the biggest money makers, according to Mr. Dubicki, with margins on the 8-inch and 9-inch varieties substantially lower.

Because of weak sales over the past several years, the financial condition of Kitchen Made had deteriorated. Exhibit 1 provides the operating results for the years 1971 through 1981. Exhibit 2 shows the balance sheet for 1981. Exhibit 24 presents the computable financial ratios for Kitchen Made as compared to industry averages for SIC #2051 businesses (bread, cake, and related products) with sales of under $50 million.

Several events served to increase the seriousness of the liquidity and solvency problems indicated by these statements. The most immediate problem concerned the bank note that had come due. Kitchen Made had an agreement with a local banking institution which allowed the company to borrow $70,000 on a program resembling revolving credit. Kitchen Made paid only interest on this loan, and the principal was due in a lump sum at the end of the borrowing period. Mr. Dubicki had hoped to refinance the loan, but he was greatly dissatisfied with the bank's attitude. One major complaint was that despite sometimes keeping as much as $20,000 to $30,000 in cash in its checking account at the bank, KMP received no interest relief. Furthermore, when

Exhibit 22

Layout of the KMP Plant

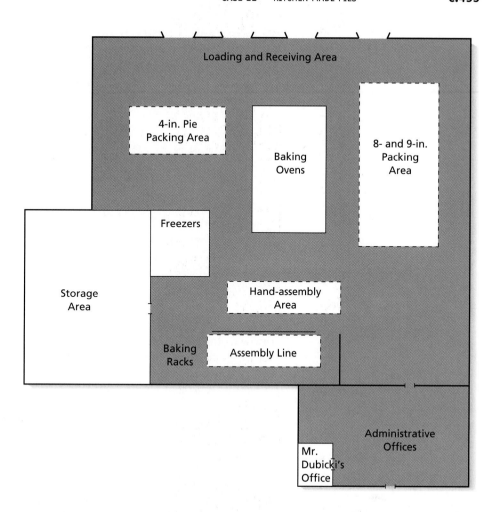

Exhibit 23	Sales and Operating Profits by Product Lines (dollar figures in thousands)				
	Sales		**Operating Profits**		
	%	$	%	$	Profit Margin (%)
4-in.	33.5	$536	61.5	$147.6	27.5
8-in.	18.5	296	10.3	24.7	8.3
9-in.	44.0	704	21.0	50.4	7.2
Other	4.0	64	7.2	17.3	27.0
Total	100.0	$1600	100.0	$240.0	15.0

Source: Mr. Dubicki's estimates, 1981.

discussing the possibility of refinancing the loan, Mr. Dubicki was informed that in the future he would be required to sign a second mortgage on his house to secure the note. Without renewal, the firm would be faced with a considerable liquidity problem. However, Mr. Dubicki was hopeful that other Peoria area banks would welcome Kitchen Made's business if his present bank did not

Exhibit 24   1981 Company and Industry Financial Ratios

	SIC #2051	Kitchen Made Pies
Current ratio	.76	.81 (without Dean's .66)
Net profit/sales (%)	3.8%	−10.91%
Net profit/total assets (%)	6.5%	−44.9%
Net profit/equity (%)	19.5%	−65.4%
Sales/total assets	2.5	4.1
Collection period (days)	14	36 (without Dean's .23)
Sales/working capital	8.8	−21.8
Sales/inventory	53.3	11.9
Fixed assets/equity (%)	131.6%	−308%
Total debt/equity (%)	201.7%	−1684.0%

Source: *Key Business Ratios 1980*, Dun & Bradstreet.

choose to continue their current relationship. The present note was not secured in any way, and arrangements to place the bank in a secured position with options for renewal were possible, though not a certainty.

Another problem causing concern was slow payments by some customers. Most firms paid on time, and some, such as Lowenberg and Eisner's consistently took advantage of discounts for early payment (usual terms were 2%/10 days, net/30 days). The major delinquent was Dean's Distributing. Dean's currently owed back payments amounting to $60,000. Mr. Dubicki felt most of this account was uncollectible, but had not yet written the amount off the company's books. Mr. Dubicki had expressed a desire to eliminate or substantially cut back on the business done with Dean's, but since, despite its poor payment record, Dean's still accounted for a large portion of sales, Mr. Dubicki felt Kitchen Made needed to continue to do business with this customer to maintain sales levels. However, all dealings with Dean's were being conducted strictly on a cash basis, and at least a portion of the overdue account was being gradually paid off.

In spite of these financial difficulties, Mr. Dubicki indicated that Kitchen Made had been able to keep up to date on most of their current payables and pay small amounts on older accounts. Thus, although Mr. Dubicki knew the situation was far from ideal and the firm was highly vulnerable to unforeseen events, he believed liquidity was probably not a life-or-death concern at the moment. However, he did realize that any further decline in liquidity could be extremely hazardous and potentially fatal.

■ Management and Organization

Most of the managerial activities at Kitchen Made Pies were handled directly by Mr. Dubicki. Besides the production manager, Ms. Barbara Britt, the only other management personnel were Ms. Charolete Watson, office manager, and Mr. Lonnie Beard, the sales promotion manager. Mr. Beard was responsible for making sure products were stocked and advertised properly at the individual stores, which he visited periodically. Mr. Dubicki, besides being president and owner, also acted as general manager and sales and distribution manager, prepared projected cash-flow statements, searched for new accounts, and handled many other day-to-day activities. About the only activity he was not directly involved with was the actual assembly of the pies.

Kitchen Made currently employed about 30 production workers whose responsibilities were more or less evenly split among preparation and assembly, baking, packaging, and other duties such as shipping and receiving. The shop was unionized and paid wages (about $7.25 per hour) comparable to other area firms of comparable size. In addition to production and office personnel, Kitchen Made also employed several maintenance workers, a truck driver, and six office workers.

■ Mr. Dubicki's View of the Future

Though the current situation at Kitchen Made Pies was far from ideal, Mr. Dubicki had expressed a commitment to planning and had made some long-needed improvements in operations, such as inventory reduction. Furthermore, he believed that the good employee relations which he had developed would facilitate some of the changes being considered. Naturally, Mr. Dubicki recognized that there were many questions yet to be answered and that the answers to these questions could determine the company's fate. Despite all the problems, however, Mr. Dubicki remained confident. In his own words:

> We have been actively soliciting new accounts, reduced our dependence on Dean's and improved production methods and controls. I'm optimistic about our future. But then again, isn't that the only way I can feel?

Liz Claiborne, 1993:
Troubled Times for the
Women's Retail Giant

Sharon Ungar Lane
Patricia Bilafer
Mary Fandel
Barbara Gottfried
Alan N. Hoffman
Bentley College

In 1986, Liz Claiborne, Inc., became the first company started by a woman to make the *Fortune* 500. Described by *Working Woman* magazine as "the wizard of the working woman's wardrobe,"[1] Liz Claiborne, Inc., provides quality career and casual clothing, accessories, and fragrances at prices working women can afford. In fact, the company's philosophy, to produce "simple, straightforward fashion designed for women who have more important things to think about than what to wear,"[2] has made it the largest women's apparel manufacturer in the world. In 1993, Liz Claiborne sold 65 million garments, and more than 20 million accessories.

■ The Early Years

The daughter of a banker at Morgan Guaranty Trust Company, Liz Claiborne spent her early childhood in Brussels before moving with her family to New Orleans in 1934. She never finished high school, but after the War, her father sent her to Europe to study at the Art School in Brussels, and then to the Academie in Nice, France, to study fine arts. She returned to the United States only to discover that her family opposed her desire to work in the fashion industry. Nevertheless, Liz entered a sketch of a woman's high-collared coat in a design contest sponsored by *Harper's Bazaar*, and won. At 21, she began her career as a sketcher, model, and, later, designer on "Fashion Avenue," the insiders' name for New York's Seventh Avenue garment district, where much of America's ready-to-wear is designed and was, at one time, produced. Soon afterward, while

The authors would like to thank Jane Moreno, Jeffrey Shuman, and Sally Strawn for their valuable contributions to this case. Photographic contribution by Scott Lane.

working at Rhea Manufacturing Company in Milwaukee, she met Arthur Ortenberg, a design executive, whom she married in 1957.

In 1960, Liz Claiborne embarked on a 15-year career as the chief designer for Youth Guild, the junior dress division of Jonathan Logan. It was during these years that the seeds of Liz Claiborne, Inc., were sown: More and more women were entering the workforce, and Liz perceived that there was an opening in the market for tasteful, moderately priced career clothes. She could not sell Youth Guild on her vision of a mix-and-match sportswear line to fill that gap, so she decided to set up her own company.

Liz Claiborne, Inc., was launched on January 19, 1976. Financed by $50,000 in personal savings and $200,000 from family, friends, and business associates, the company began small, with Liz Claiborne as president and head designer, and her husband, Arthur Ortenberg, an expert in textiles and business administration, as secretary and treasurer of the corporation and, later, chairman. A third partner, Leonard Boxer, contributed production expertise, and in 1977, Jerome Chazen, a personal friend, was named vice president of marketing. Within its first year, the company was operating in the black, with sales of more than $2 million. In 1985, sales reached the half billion dollar mark; the next year, retail sales surpassed $1.2 billion, and Liz Claiborne, Inc., made it into the *Fortune* 500.

In February 1989, Liz Claiborne and Arthur Ortenberg announced their retirement from active management of the company to pursue environmental, social, and other interests. Jerome Chazen, one of the company's original partners, was named CEO, and Jay Margolis was hired as vice chair and president of Women's Sportswear, Liz Claiborne, Inc.'s core division. Committed to taking Liz Claiborne into the 1990s debt free, they and a team of designers expanded product lines, adding accessories and fragrances to meet customer demand. They also purchased Russ Togs company to sustain company growth. Today Liz Claiborne can claim a full two percent of the women's apparel market—more than any other publicly held company.

The Fashion Industry

The fashion industry is highly competitive. The maturing market for women's clothing is dominated by Liz Claiborne and its major competitors: Jones New York, Chaus, Evan Picone, JH Collectibles, and VF Corporation. Retailers, the interface between the fashion industry and the consumer, have suffered in recent years from the recession and volatile consumer tastes, necessitating major restructuring, which has had a significant effect on the fashion industry. Mergers, acquisitions, and bankruptcies of major retailers have created powerful retail rivals with the financial resources to create large economies of scale and withstand new entrants, strict governmental regulations, and technological advances. For instance, when Macy's, which had accounted for a significant percentage of Liz Claiborne sales, went bankrupt in 1992, Liz Claiborne's sales figures suffered in the ensuing bankruptcy settlement.

The retail clothing industry is also highly vulnerable to shifting tastes. Predicting fashion is risky and expensive because what is considered stylish today may be unappealing to consumers tomorrow. Yet significant lead time is required to bring new styles to market. A company may invest a year or more in the design and production stages of a new design concept only to have the line fail upon introduction. In fact, clothing lines are usually either complete successes or fail altogether; yet, at the same time, inventory levels for successful lines must be adequate to meet consumer demand, which doesn't leave much margin for error. Establishing name recognition is a priority for designers. Consumers consistently shop their favorite designers, and remain loyal to those whose clothes fit best. Indeed, strong designer loyalty dominates the retail industry. Thus fashion industry marketing strategies must take many contingencies into account at all times, while remaining flexible enough to respond to continually shifting consumer tastes.

Product Lines

Liz Claiborne's principal lines are designed to meet the work and leisure clothing needs of working women. Today, 57.7 percent of all women in the United States work outside the home; and women with children under the age of six are the fastest growing segment of the workforce. The dual-income family has become the norm, and stay-at-home moms the exception rather than the rule. Consequently, many women no longer have the kind of leisure time they once had to shop; rather, they prefer to maximize any shopping outing. Liz Claiborne, Inc., has carved out a niche for itself by targeting these women as its primary constituency, designing mix-and-match coordinating outfits, rather than separates, that can be variously combined to suit individual needs and tastes, simplifying both shopping and dressing for the busy lifestyles of working women. To market this concept, Liz Claiborne was one of the first companies to merchandise their clothing lines as outfits rather than single items, arranging them on the display floor to demonstrate that they can dress the customer from head to toe, rather than displaying single garments by classification. Furthermore, the clothes are modern classic rather than trendy and are designed with practicality, style, and fashion longevity in mind. Liz Claiborne's goal is to offer clothing and accessories that are not only aesthetically and technically well designed, but that make the customer feel confident, addressing all the needs of her busy life.

As of 1993, Liz Claiborne, Inc., had 18 divisions (Exhibit 1) offering various products aimed at specific target markets and covering a wide range of career, active wear, and accessories for women and for men. The company is continually adding new products to its apparel line, such as the women's suits introduced in 1991, not simply to increase sales, but to garner more department store space. Their perfume, "Liz Claiborne," has been particularly successful. The versatile scent was conceived to be worn around the clock, at work or out on the town, and was based on Liz Claiborne's instinctive preferences rather than on market research, as was the triangle-shaped logo and the red, yellow, and blue color scheme for the packaging.

The company also carved out a niche for itself marketing to the "forgotten" woman. More than 30 percent of adult women are overweight. Liz Claiborne, Inc., entered the large-sized women's clothing market with its "Elisabeth" line, which successfully serves a long-neglected group of consumers by offering large-sized sportswear that provides the excellent fit, fashion, and quality of its regular sportswear lines. This marketing effort has been successful, and Liz Claiborne, Inc., has plans to continue extending the Elisabeth line. In yet another strategic action to extend its markets and increase its sales, Liz Claiborne, Inc.,

---

Exhibit 1   Liz Claiborne, Inc.'s Product Line Overview

SPORTSWEAR: *Includes Collection, Lizsport, Lizwear, and Petite Sportswear.*

Liz Claiborne, Inc., launched into the fashion industry with its sportswear line in 1976. Designed to be modern classic rather than trendy so as to ensure fashion longevity, the sportswear division divided into three distinct lines. The first, COLLECTION, is primarily a career-oriented, tailored, and professional line. LIZSPORT provides sportswear for leisure time as well as for more casual work environments, while LIZWEAR is a highly denim-driven sportswear division. Our PETITE sportswear was developed in 1982 to fulfill an unmet need in the market for the 5'4" and under customer. Petite sizes are offered in all three sportswear lifestyles.

DRESSES: *Misses and Petite*

Misses dresses were launched in 1982, followed by petite in 1985. Our dresses include a wide range of fabrications and styles, from career to knit to social occasion dresses. Furthermore, the dress division offers a large selection of dresses that can be worn from day-to-dinner, encompassing the ease and professionalism necessary for a work environment with the style and fun for an evening on the town.

SUITS:

In 1991 Liz Claiborne, Inc., ventured into the Suits market. The division differentiates itself by offering a wide variety of skirt and jacket lengths, seasonless fabrics, pantsuits, and day-to-dinner designs.

LIZ & CO.:

Liz & Co., launched in 1989, consists primarily of comfortable and coordinated knitwear separates with a relaxed fit and a youthful attitude.

DANA BUCHMAN: *Sportswear, Petite Sportswear, and Dresses*

Founded in 1987, Dana Buchman is our bridge sportswear division with prices that range from better sportswear to designer merchandise. It offers sophisticated styles of the highest quality fabrics with an exceptional attention to detail. Dana Buchman's distribution is selective.

ELISABETH: *Sportswear, Petite Sportswear, and Dresses*

In response to a previously neglected market, Liz Claiborne, Inc., developed its large size division called Elisabeth in 1989. The line includes a wide range of products from activewear to career clothing to evening dressing in sizes 14–24 and 14P–22P. Through Elizabeth's high attention to design, quality, and fit, it has become a market leader.

CLAIBORNE: *Men's Sportswear and Men's Furnishings*

Liz Claiborne, Inc., launched into the men's market in 1985 with our Claiborne sportswear division and in 1987 with men's furnishings. Furnishings include men's dress shirts and ties, while our men's sportswear incorporates the same high level of fashion and quality as offered in our women's sportswear areas.

---

has ignored the industry standard of four seasons and opted for six seasonal lines to offer women clothes they can wear right away and to allow for a constant flow of new merchandise to generate consumer interest. The net result of the company's versatility and market savvy: Liz Claiborne outfits more women than any other designer.

To stay on top of its huge volume of business, Liz Claiborne uses both direct customer feedback, and a unique computerized system, SURF (System Updated Retail Feedback), which provides weekly sales trends reports on what is and isn't selling nationwide. At the end of each week, data on sales, styles, sizes, and colors are reviewed by division heads to determine both short- and long-term planning needs. Most importantly, SURF allows the company to respond quickly to mistakes. For example, for the spring 1988 season, Liz Claiborne had decided

---

Exhibit 1   Liz Claiborne, Inc.'s Product Line Overview—*Continued*

CRAZY HORSE:

Acquired in 1992, Crazy Horse is a casual line with a young and modern attitude that is merchandised in department and specialty stores. Its fashion-forward appearance appeals to a younger customer.

RUSS:

Also acquired in 1992, Russ offers career as well as casual dressing and is displayed in the moderate areas of department stores.

THE VILLAGER:

The Villager, acquired in 1992 along with Crazy Horse and Russ, focuses on career clothing but offers some casual wear as well. It will be distributed to national and regional chain department stores. Thus, with these three new labels, Liz Claiborne, Inc., has expanded both its product offerings and its distribution to include moderate career and casual dressing.

ACCESSORIES: *Includes Handbags, Small Leather Goods, and Fashion Accessories*

Our fashion accessories, organized in 1980, include scarves, belts, hats, tights, socks, and hair accessories. Also introduced in 1980 were Liz Claiborne handbags and small leather goods. Many of the Liz Claiborne accessories are designed and developed to coordinate with our sportswear and can be used for anything from work to play. Recently, the Accessories division launched our bodywear, offering the same fit, fashion, and quality of all Liz Claiborne products.

SHOES: *Shoes and Sportshoes*

Also designed to coordinate and complement our sportswear, Liz Claiborne, Inc., moved into the shoe market in 1981. This division includes casual shoes, dress shoes, and as of 1991, fashionable and athletic sport shoes. Of course, like all our apparel divisions, all styles are comfortable and of the highest fashion sense.

JEWELRY:

Liz Claiborne, Inc., also offers a wide range of fashion jewelry designed for both casual and go-to-work. Many of the designs coordinate with the seasonal apparel trends and color ways. Introduced in 1990, this division offers a full range of jewelry including earrings, necklaces, bracelets, and pins.

COSMETICS:

Our Cosmetics division was launched in 1987 and consists of a collection of fragrances that captures and completes the whole Liz Claiborne attitude. The first, our signature fragrance, is entitled LIZ CLAIBORNE and is bottled in Liz Claiborne's trademark triangle. CLAIBORNE for men was developed in 1989, followed by REALITIES in 1990. In the fall of 1993, Liz Claiborne, Inc., will be launching its new fragrance, VIVID. Various complimentary fragrance items are also carried in the lines, including shampoo, conditioners, and body lotion to name a few.

---

to fall in line with current trends—and market miniskirts. When it became obvious through SURF that the company's regular customers had no intention of baring their thighs, Liz Claiborne was able to adjust their fall 1988 designs quickly and order longer skirts for the fall fashion season to avoid losing loyal customers.

Nevertheless, Liz Claiborne, Inc., has had a few disappointments, such as its girls line for 5 to 12 year olds begun in 1984, but phased out in 1987. Also, 1992 sales of men's sportswear and furnishings lines were a big disappointment, falling 24.6 percent; as a result, the "Claiborne" collection of men's sportswear, originally styled for young customers, has shifted to a more upscale, conservative look.

While saturation is always a possibility, especially as the core sportswear line matures, Liz Claiborne works hard to stay one step ahead of the game. Recently the company perceived the potential for new business and a broadened customer base in the moderate market. The moderate market targets working women with more sophisticated, yet reasonably priced clothes than those at the Gap or Limited stores. In 1992, Liz Claiborne entered the moderate women's sportswear market by acquiring Russ Togs (Russ, Crazy Horse, and The Villager labels), which broadened the firm's distribution by expanding its position in both national and regional chain department stores, in addition to the moderate areas of traditional department stores.

Liz Claiborne: 1993

Liz Claiborne, Inc., markets its various lines primarily through 3,500 leading department stores such as Bloomingdale's, Filene's, Lord & Taylor, Macy's, and Jordan Marsh, delivering a consistent product at a fair price. The company usually sets up Liz Claiborne boutiques within these stores, which carry the full line of Liz merchandise to allow for one-stop shopping for women who don't have time to shop (the store within a store concept pioneered by Ralph Lauren).

However, because many of its best retailers were in financial trouble, Liz Claiborne made an ambitious move into retailing. By 1993, the company had opened 16 Liz Claiborne company-owned retail stores, 39 First Issue stores, and 55 outlet stores nationwide. The 16 company-owned retail stores help give "Liz Claiborne" fashions a unique identity, and play an important role in testing new products and new merchandising ideas, functioning as "laboratories" to observe consumer taste and measure reactions to such elements as fit, selling, size, group, and fabric. The company also owns three Elisabeth retail stores.

The 39 First Issue stores, opened in 1993, are designed to compete with retailers such as The Limited and The Gap. The stores exclusively market First Issue merchandise, related separates and basics similar to Liz Claiborne sportswear but less career oriented, designed by a separate team and priced approximately 15 percent lower than the Liz Claiborne label lines.

Liz Claiborne also has 55 outlet stores in which they sell unsold merchandise from previous seasons, providing the company with control over the disposition of unsold inventories. The outlets are deliberately located at some distance from the department and specialty stores where Liz products are regularly sold in order to preserve brand image.

Because many segments of the U.S. fashion industry are maturing, overseas markets represent new and substantial sources of growth for U.S. designers. An internationally recognized brand name and worldwide advertising campaign are critical to competing successfully in European and Asian markets. To market its products effectively outside the United States, Liz Claiborne, Inc., is tailoring its sales strategies specifically for each country. To date, Liz Claiborne has met with some success in Canada and England, where women tend to shop and dress like Americans, but less success in other parts of the world. One problem lies in the fact that Liz Claiborne is essentially a department store line in the United States, while in Europe most business is done in small boutiques. In some British stores, Liz Claiborne is leasing space and selling their goods themselves. In Japan the company is selling through a mail-order catalog in addition to the two Liz Claiborne stores that were opened in Tokyo during fall 1993. International expansion has, however, suffered the adverse impact of recessions in both Europe and Japan.

International Manufacturing

Currently, 100 percent of Liz Claiborne's product lines are manufactured overseas. Global outsourcing is widespread in the textile industry capitalizing on lower labor and production costs at overseas manufacturing sites. Outsourcing creates the flexibility to shift production to various sites depending on wage differentials. Yet many of these sites are high risk due to the political and economic instability of developing and Third World countries. Nevertheless, very few firms have manufacturing facilities in the United States, so they vary their sources by using a combination of domestic, Caribbean and foreign sources to ensure minimal instability. However, scattered production sites can jeopardize quality control. In addition, reliance on foreign suppliers is not without its disadvantages, because those suppliers are not always consistent, and cannot be easily relied on to operate on the tight schedules necessitated by the time pressures of an industry that turns around four to six seasonal lines a year.

United States' import regulations are currently favorable for retailers, which further contributes to the marketing of goods made overseas; however, these conditions are subject to change. As imports rise, quota restrictions are more strictly enforced; and recently, the government has shifted to a more protectionist policy. The garment industry has been criticized both for exporting U.S. manufacturing jobs and for exploiting foreign labor. Indeed, the shift of clothing production to overseas sites has been economically significant for the United States because "apparel production alone employs more people than the entire printing and publishing field and more than the automobile manufacturing industry."[3]

Women's Work

Liz Claiborne, Inc., has a long-standing commitment to the welfare of others, especially women. In the past, the Liz Claiborne Foundation, funded by company profits, actively assisted organizations involved in social welfare programs, e.g., helping the homeless, serving people with AIDS and their families, and enhancing opportunities for underprivileged children. The company also strongly encourages its employees to volunteer and support local nonprofit organizations.

Over the years Liz Claiborne has learned a great deal about the lives of the women who buy their products—about their careers, their dreams, and their struggles outside of work. The company wanted both to give something back to the millions of women who had contributed to the company's success, and to contribute to social change by making a difference in peoples lives. To do so, Liz Claiborne, Inc., recently developed "Women's Work." Women's Work develops and funds multiyear, nationwide programs designed to heighten awareness of social problems and encourage positive social change with regard to issues of particular concern to women and their families, such as domestic violence and work–family conflicts.

The specific Women's Work project supported in each target community is based on issues of particular concern to that community: domestic violence in San Francisco, Boston, and Miami; the needs and concerns of working mothers in Chicago. In each city, Liz Claiborne builds innovative, collaborative partnerships with organizations active in confronting domestic violence and the concerns of working women. In Chicago, a local artist and children from a local elementary school published a book that addresses the impact of working mothers on their families, especially their children. All proceeds resulting from the sale of the book are donated to literacy programs nationwide.

In 1993, to coincide with National Domestic Violence Awareness Month, Liz Claiborne launched domestic violence awareness programs in Boston and Miami, and formed a partnership with the Jane Doe Safety Fund sponsored by the Massachusetts Coalition of Battered Women. To raise money for the fund, Claiborne solicited the help of Barbara Kruger, a contemporary artist whose work advocates social change. The fund's public awareness campaign on domestic violence includes billboards, city bus signs, transit stop posters, and educational brochures, as well as broadcast and print public service announcements. Additionally, Liz Claiborne launched a collection of special commemorative products, which can be purchased at local Liz Claiborne stores, participating department stores, or through a special toll-free number, whose proceeds will be donated to domestic violence programs such as the Jane Doe Safety Fund in Boston. Liz Claiborne has also donated money to establish the first centralized 24-hour domestic violence hot line, which the company hopes will become permanent with the support of local foundations and organizations.

Women's Work is a way for Liz Claiborne, Inc., to give something back to the communities and the American women who have contributed to Liz Claiborne's success by funding programs for the future welfare of women. In addition, Liz Claiborne, Inc., is exploring the possibility of sponsoring educational programs about the detection and treatment of breast cancer, and already offers free mammograms to all its women employees. While the company acknowledges that they do not expect sales to increase as a result of the Liz Claiborne Foundation or Women's Work, they hope that by responding to concerns important to women and their families, Women's Work will reinforce Liz Claiborne, Inc.'s reputation as a company that cares.

1993: The Wrong Product—and Too Much of It

By the late 1980s, Liz Claiborne had branched beyond clothes for working women into petites, large sizes, accessories, fragrances, men's clothing, and other lines. With so much to control and coordinate, managers began to lose their focus on the core merchandise. Customers yawned at many outfits, which too often repeated past styles. Retailers, who had allowed Liz Claiborne's presence in their stores to reach King Kong-like proportions, say top managers were slow to admit the problem. According to a former senior Claiborne executive: "If the product didn't sell, it was always someone else's fault. The buyers didn't show it right, or it wasn't delivered in the right way. They didn't allow themselves to think that maybe they just weren't listening to the customer."[4]

The year 1993 was a difficult one for Liz Claiborne. A weak retail environment, conservative buying by customers, the start-up costs associated with the Russ Division, and the surprise resignation of Jay Margolis in July 1993 led industry analysts to question the strength of Liz Claiborne, Inc. Sales were flat for the first nine months of 1993 and earnings dropped by 40 percent in the third quarter after double-digit declines in the first and second quarters. The consensus opinion on the problem: the wrong product and too much of it.

The following excerpt appeared in the January 1994 edition of *SmartMoney* magazine:

> In late 1992, Louis Lowenstein, a Claiborne director, bragged that the apparel maker's balance sheet was so solid it would bring tears to [his] mother's eyes. Save the hanky. Investors watched Liz's earnings slide all year. The company overestimated shopper's appetites after a strong 1992 Christmas season and made too many clothes. Then its uninspired 1993 fashion collections failed to entice thrift shoppers. The inventory overload prevented Liz from being able to react quickly to the slow retail environment, causing profits to slide an estimated 40% for the year. Liz Claiborne's stock traded at $42.38 on January 7, 1993 and was $18.13 on October 21, 1993.[5]

Clearly, 1993 was a disappointing year for Liz Claiborne, Inc. (Exhibits 2, 3, and 4).

Exhibit 2 Liz Claiborne, Inc., and Subsidiaries Consolidated Statements of Income (all dollar amounts in thousands except per common share data)

	Fiscal Years Ended		
	December 25, 1993	December 26, 1992	December 28, 1991
Net Sales	$2,204,297	$2,194,330	$2,007,177
Cost of goods sold	1,453,381	1,364,214	1,207,502
Gross Profit	750,916	830,116	799,675
Selling, general and administrative expenses	568,286	507,541	471,060
Operating Income	182,630	322,575	328,615
Investment and other income—net	16,151	19,349	22.133
Income Before Provision for Income Taxes and Cumulative Effect of a Change in Accounting Principle	198,781	341,924	350,748
Provision for income taxes	73,500	123,100	128,000
Income Before Cumulative Effect of a Change in Accounting Principle	125,281	218,824	222,748
Cumulative effect of a change in the method of accounting for income taxes	1,643	—	—
Net Income	$ 126,924	$ 218,824	$ 222,748
Earnings per Common Share:			
Income Before Cumulative Effect of a Change in Accounting Principle	$ 1.54	$ 2.61	$ 2.61
Cumulative effect of a change in the method of accounting for income taxes	.02	—	—
Net Income per Common Share	$ 1.56	$ 2.61	$ 2.61
Dividends Paid per Common Share	$ .44	$ .39	$ .33

The accompanying notes to consolidated financial statements are an integral part of these statements.

Exhibit 3   Liz Claiborne, Inc., and Subsidiaries Consolidated Balance Sheets (all amounts in thousands except share data)

	December 25, 1993	December 26, 1992
Assets		
Current Assets:		
Cash and cash equivalents	$104,720	$130,721
Marketable securities	204,571	294,892
Accounts receivable—trade	174,435	200,183
Inventories	436,593	385,879
Deferred income tax benefits	15,065	13,907
Other current assets	69,055	55,384
Total current assets	1,004,439	1,080,966
Property and Equipment—net	202,068	145,695
Other Assets	29,831	29,647
	$1,236,338	$1,256,308
Liabilities and Stockholders' Equity		
Current Liabilities:		
Accounts payable	$141,126	$138,738
Accrued expenses	97,765	87,330
Income taxes payable	15,547	22,109
Total current liabilities	254,438	248,177
Long-Term Debt	1,334	1,434
Deferred Income Taxes	2,275	8,922
Commitments and Contingencies		
Stockholders' Equity:		
Preferred stock, $.01 par value, authorized shares—50,000,000, issued shares—none	—	—
Common stock, $1 par value, authorized shares—250,000,000, issued shares— 88,218,617	88,219	88,219
Capital in excess of par value	56,699	55,528
Retained earnings	1,123,413	1,034,280
Cumulative translation adjustment	(1,279)	(1,410)
	1,267,052	1,176,617
Common stock in treasury, at cost—9,371,217 shares in 1993 and 5,436,864 shares in 1992	(288,761)	(178,842)
Total stockholders' equity	978,291	997,775
	$1,236,338	$1,256,308

The accompanying notes to consolidated financial statements are an integral part of these statements.

The Outlook for the Future

Consumers today are demanding more and are adamant about paying less. A global economy has given them a "sultan's power to command exactly what they want, the way they want it, when they want it, and at a price that will make[companies] weep."[6] Companies will have to either meet these expectations or be forced out of business by those competitors that do.

Exhibit 4   Liz Claiborne, Inc., Five-Year Sales, Net Income, and EPS Summary (dollars in thousands)

Year	Sales	Net Income	EPS
1993	$2,204,297	$126,924	$1.56
1992	$2,194,330	$218,824	$2.61
1991	$2,007,177	$222,748	$2.61
1990	$1,728,868	$205,800	$2.37
1989	$1,410,677	$164,591	$1.87
Five-year growth rate	11.8%	−6.2%	−4.4%

The prolonged recession, low consumer confidence, a four-year national decline in per capita clothing spending and numerous bankruptcies among several of the nation's largest department stores have wreaked havoc in the apparel industry. Many companies are cutting costs through sophisticated inventory control systems and computer-aided design and manufacturing, as well as enhanced fabric production systems. But the industry must also comply with federal legislation, which regulates competition and requires product labeling with content and care instructions designed to protect consumers, both of which contribute to higher costs.

At the same time, Americans are changing the way they shop. Many designers, including Liz Claiborne, rely on large department stores located in shopping malls for a large percentage of their sales. However, the appeal of shopping malls is diminishing and the trend is toward specialty stores. Consumers, especially women, have less time to shop, so convenience is becoming even more important.

Clearly, for 1994 and beyond, questions abound. Liz Claiborne, Inc., must rethink both its product lines and its entire marketing strategy, considering whether it has grown too fast, spread itself too thin, and/or set itself up to compete with itself by branching out into retailing lines under other labels that are too similar to its own name-brand lines. The company must also consider how best to fill the void left by the departure of Liz Claiborne herself, clearly a visionary who carved out a fashion empire that may now be on the brink of decline.

■ Notes

1. Michele Morris, 1988, The wizard of the working woman's wardrobe," *Working Women,* June, 74.
2. Nancy Marx Better, 1992, The secret of Liz Claiborne's success, *Working Women,* April, 68.
3. Miraim Guenciro and Jeannette Jarnow, 1991, *Inside the Fashion Industry,* 5th ed. (New York: Macmillan Publishing Company), 5.
4. Susan Caminiti, 1994, Liz Claiborne: How to get focused again, *Fortune,* January 24, 85.
5. Underachiever's club disappointments of 1993: These Wall Street favorites burned investors bad, 1994, *Smart Money,* January, 29.
6. Rahul Jacob, 1993, Beyond quality and value, *Fortune,* Autumn/Winter, 8.

■ Bibliography

Agins, Teri, 1993, Liz Claiborne seems to be losing its invincible armor, *Wall Street Journal,* July 19.

Applebaum, Cara, 1991, Stepping out (Liz Claiborne company profile), *Adweek's Marketing Week,* November 18.

Better, Nancy Marx, 1992, The secret of Liz Claiborne's success, *Working Women,* April.

Black, Jeff, 1992; US seen high on high tech at bobbin, *Daily News Record,* September 11.

Braithwaite, Alan J., 1990, Far East dragons changing their spots, *Bobbin,* November.

Caminiti, Susan, 1994, Liz Claiborne: How to get focused again, *Fortune,* January 24.

Ciampi, Thomas, 1991, Liz Claiborne: A $2 billion phenomenon, *Women's Wear Daily,* May 8.

Ciampi, Thomas, 1991, In the stores: The Claiborne clout, *Women's Wear Daily,* May 8.

Darnton, Nina, 1992, The joy of polyester (Liz Claiborne Inc.)", *Newsweek,* August 3.

Deveny, Kathleen, 1989, Can Ms. Fashion bounce back, *Business Week,* January 16.

Dumaine, Brian, 1992, Exporting jobs and ethics, *Fortune,* October 5.

Esquivel, Josephine R., 1992, The pains and gains of '91, *Bobbin,* June.

Fallon, James, 1991, Claiborne speeding up its invasion of Europe, *Women's Wear Daily,* February 5.

Farnsworth, Steve, 1990, Urge stores to prepare for aging Americans, *Daily News Record,* October 24.

Feldman, Amy, 1992, Lean and debt free (Liz Claiborne, Inc.), *Forbes,* January 6.

Fiedelholtz, Sara, 1993, Liz Claiborne's moderate maneuvers, *Women's Wear Daily,* March 10.

Friedman, Arthur, and Chuck Struensee, 1992, Wary consumers give classics a boost, *Women's Wear Daily,* January 14.

Guenciro, Miriam, and Jeannette Jarnow, 1991, *Inside the Fashion Business,* 5th ed. (New York: Macmillan Publishing Company).

Hartlein, Robert, 1992, Claiborne's Chazen speaks on pricing and customer importance, *Women's Wear Daily,* January 16.

Hartlein, Robert, 1991, Claiborne to back a program of community art projects, *Women's Wear Daily,* October 9.

Hass, Nancy, 1992, Like a rock (Liz Claiborne), *Financial World,* February 4.

Jacob, Rahul, 1993, Beyond quality and value, *Fortune,* Autumn/Winter.

Klapper, Marvin, 1992, Claiborne, Ge-Ray to open new plant, *Daily News Record,* February 25.

Lipman, Joanne, 1992, Fashion ads aim at abuse, *Wall Street Journal,* September 8.

Liz Claiborne, 1992, *Annual Report.*

Liz Claiborne, 1992, Company overview.

Liz Claiborne, June 1989, *Current Biography.*

Lockwood, Lisa, 1992, Claiborne's media blitz, *Women's Wear Daily,* April 3.

Lockwood, Lisa, 1991, Vendors: In the ring with Liz, *Women's Wear Daily,* May 8.

Lockwood, Lisa, 1991, Claiborne's complete image, *Women's Wear Daily,* September 25.

Moin, David, 1993, Claiborne sees retail as growth solution, *Women's Wear Daily,* April 22.

Morgensen, Gretchen, 1993, The fall of the mall, *Forbes,* May 24.

Morris, Michele, 1988, The wizard of the working woman's wardrobe, *Working Women,* June.

Online Industry Information: Dow Jones News Reports, Bloomberg Industry Reports, First Call Industry Reports.

Ostroff, Jim, 1991, Caribbean sourcing hasn't lost its luster, *Daily News Record,* March 4.

Reese, Jennifer, 1993, America's most admired corporations, *Fortune,* February 8.

Rowlands, Penelope, 1992, Claiborne ads hit home, *Women's Wear Daily,* August 7.

Smith, Adam, 1986, How Liz Claiborne designed an empire, *Esquire,* January.

Sprinkle, Stephen D., Paula Charles, and Jerry Chepaitis, 1992, Computing new solutions: 1992 Bobbin's industry specific annual computer software survey; apparel industry specific software suppliers directory, *Bobbin,* July.

Zinn, Laura, 1990, Liz Claiborne without Liz: Steady as she goes, *Business Week,* September 17.

Zinn, Laura, 1990, Liz Claiborne's rag trade-off, *Business Week,* August 13.

■ CASE 24 Matsushita Industrial de Baja California

Stephen Jenner
California State University

■ Can Mexico
Compete with
Asia?

■ http://www.mei.co.jp/

Making his daily crossing from San Diego to Tijuana to the offices of Matsushita Industrial de Baja California (MIBA), Mitsuharu Nakata, subdirector administrativo, was personally concerned about the fate of the Mexican plants after the start of the North American Free Trade Agreement (NAFTA) on January 1, 1994. Before this assignment, Nakata lived in Central America for 6 years working for Matsushita in Guatemala and Costa Rica. After San Diego/Tijuana, he knew that he would move wherever the company sent him; the idea of leaving Matsushita was unthinkable. As he swung his car to avoid the potholes in the road leading to Ciudad Industrial just across the commercial border crossing from the United States, he saw the gleaming glass and steel factories belonging to Sanyo, Matsushita's neighbor and worldwide competitor. He had been living in San Diego for 10 years, and he was concerned that after another 5 to 7 years, production of televisions in Mexico would no longer be competitive.

Compared to low-cost Asian producers, Mexico in 1994 offered a 2 percent savings in transportation as a location supplying the U.S. market. There was also a 5 percent duty imposed by the United States on assembled televisions. Together, these two items represented 7 percent; if an Asian country such as Malaysia, Indonesia, or China had a 10 percent labor cost advantage, then they could compete with Mexico. NAFTA's rules of origin stipulate that automobiles must be 62.5 percent North American, but televisions need only a picture tube worth about 33 percent to qualify as North American products. If the picture tube (or CRT) is made in the United States, the duty saved is 5 percent compared to a CRT fixed in a cabinet with a tuner or a TV assembled with its chassis. Importing the CRT alone results in a duty of 15 percent; it was the possibility of importing the CRT duty-free into Mexico via Long Beach, California, and bringing it back to the United States as an assembled TV that brought Japanese producers to

This case was prepared as a basis for class discussion rather than to illustrate either effective or ineffective handling of administrative situations.

Tijuana in the first place. Now it was possible that Matsushita and Sanyo would buy CRTs from Samsung in Tijuana.

Nakata wondered why the U.S. government didn't seem to care about the television industry in the same way it nurtured the automobile industry. "I guess the car is closer to what America is all about," he said. "The U.S. government should assist in the development of TV component manufacturing; it's like a growing tree which needs water and help to reach the size that will allow it to survive a storm. But I guess they don't care about TVs." Any company making TVs has to be concerned about costs and price competition, and production can move to the country with the most competitive cost structure.

Mexico was special to Japanese producers of TVs because of its proximity to the United States, its good government relations and its low wages, according to Nakata. "But salaries for indirect employees in Mexico are just as high as in the U.S., and there are no sources of transistors, integrated circuits (ICs), registers, or raw materials nearby," complained Nakata. "When the U.S. lost competitiveness, it moved production to Asia, including component manufacturing, which requires three to five times the investment of an assembly plant. Now Motorola and Texas Instruments have excellent factories in East Asia, and it makes sense to buy from them. Mexico is very far away from Singapore, Taiwan, Malaysia, Hong Kong, and Japan where Matsushita sources its components."

Should Matsushita make the decision in 1995 to relocate to China or Indonesia where wages are much lower than in Mexico and component plants are close at hand (See Exhibits 1 and 2)?

The Big Picture

Matsushita's long-term response to the appreciation of the yen was to relocate manufacturing outside Japan. In 1994, the company produced 20 percent of its goods abroad, and the goal for 1995 was 25 percent. Nevertheless, many overseas factories rely heavily on imported components from Japan, and there were concerns about Matsushita's ability to maintain quality.

Although Matsushita's *Annual Report* for 1994 (see the Appendix) was optimistic, its sale of MCA in April 1995 at a big loss after five years was evidence of a strategic disaster. The assumption of hardware makers Matsushita and Sony (Matsushita's main rival) was that they could gain a competitive advantage by controlling audio and video software. According to industry analysts, Hollywood's entertainment products will increasingly be distributed electronically through cable systems and television networks, which are much more strategically important than the boxes that play the music and movies. Due in part to the changes in U.S. regulations that allowed television broadcasters to enter into program production, Matsushita would have to consider strategic alliances with communications companies and cable television if it were to stay in the movie and music production business.

Matsushita plans to spend the money from the sale of MCA to implement a revitalization plan that will focus more on multimedia and manufacturing key components, such as semiconductors. To avoid converting the proceeds back into yen at unfavorable exchange rates, Matsushita plans to spend much of the money in the United States.

Exhibit 1 International Network: U.S., Mexico, China, Indonesia (As of April 1, 1994)

THE AMERICAS

U.S.A.
Matsushita Electric Corporation of America
Matsushita Avionics Systems Company
Matsushita Compressor Corporation of America
Matsushita Floor Care Company
American Matsushita Electronics Corporation
Matsushita Semiconductor Corporation of America
Matsushita Communication Industrial Corporation of America
Matsushita Electronic Components Corporation of America
Matsushita Microwave Oven Corporation of America
Matsushita-Ultra Tech. Battery Corporation
Matsushita Battery Industrial Corporation of America
Matsushita Refrigeration Company of America
Kyushu Matsushita Electric Corporation of America
America Kotobuki Electronics Industries, Inc.
Solbourne Computer, Inc.
AMAC Corporation
Panasonic Advanced TV-Video Laboratories, Inc.
Panasonic Technologies, Inc.
Matsushita Avionics Development Corporation
Panasonic Finance, Inc.
Panasonic Capital Corporation
MCA Inc.

MEXICO
Panasonic de Mexico, S.A. de C.V.
Matsushita Electric de Mexico, S.A. de C.V.
Matsushita Industrial de Baja California, S.A. de C.V.
Matsushita Electronic Components de Baja California, S.A. de C.V.
Kyushu Matsushita Electric de Baja California, S.A. de C.V.

CHINA
Beijing-Matsushita Color CRT Co., Ltd.
Hangzhou KIN MATSU Washing Machine Co., Ltd.
Beijing Matsushita Communication Equipment Co., Ltd.
Matsushita-Wanbao (Guangzhou) Electric Iron Co.
Matsushita-Wanbao (Guangzhou) Air-Conditioner Co.
Matsushita-Wanbao (Guangzhou) Compressor Co.
Shunde Matsushita Seiko Co., Ltd.
Beijing Matsushita Electronic Components Co., Ltd.
Shanghai Matsushita Battery Co., Ltd.
Qingdao Matsushita Electronic Components Co., Ltd.
Zhuhai Matsushita Electric Motor Co., Ltd.
Matsushita Audio (Xiamen) Co., Ltd.

INDONESIA
P.T. National Gobel
P.T. Matsushita Gobel Battery Industry
P.T. Kotobuki Electronics Indonesia
P.T. Asia Matsushita Battery
P.T. Panasonic Gobel Electronic Components
P.T. National Panasonic Gobel
P.T. MET & Gobel

Exhibit 2 Financial Highlights
Matsushita Electric Industrial Co., Ltd. and Subsidiaries
Years ended March 31, 1994 and 1993

	Millions of yen, except per share information		Millions of U.S. dollars, except per share information
	1994	1993	1994
Sales	¥6,623,586	¥7,055,868	$ 64,307
Percentage of previous year	93.9%	94.7%	93.9%
Income before income taxes	¥ 128,223	¥ 162,207	$1,245
Percentage of previous year	79.0%	45.4%	79.0%
Net income	¥ 24,493	¥ 37,295	$ 238
Percentage of previous year	65.7%	27.9%	65.7%
Per share of common stock:			
Net income	¥ 11.67	¥ 17.66	$ 0.11
Cash dividends	13.50	12.50	0.13
Per American Depositary Share, each representing 10 shares of common stock:			
Net income	¥ 117	¥ 177	$ 1.14
Cash dividends	135	125	1.31
Total assets (at end of period)	¥8,192,632	¥8,754,979	$ 79,540
Stockholders' equity (at end of period)	3,288,945	3,406,303	31,932
Capital investment	¥ 266,522	¥ 309,097	$ 2,588
R&D expenditures	381,747	401,817	3,706
Employees (at end of period)	254,059	252,075	254,059

Operations in Tijuana, Baja California, Mexico

In 1994, MIBA employed 1,700 workers in six buildings in Ciudad Industrial (Tijuana, Baja California, Mexico's industrial city on Otay Mesa adjacent to the U.S. border). Another 700 workers manufactured tuners and other components in an industrial park several miles west overlooking the Pacific Ocean. In addition, there were 550 workers making components and cellular telephones at another, newer Matsushita plant in Tijuana (see Exhibits 3 and 4).

Matsushita's goal for the U.S. market was to expand local content, with 50 percent to be manufactured locally, and a 70 percent local content ratio overall. In the low end of the market, the television was Matsushita's loss leader, and the U.S. market was supplied almost entirely by maquiladoras (twin manufacturing operations on both sides of the U.S. and Mexican border). Tijuana TV producers accounted for five million sets annually in 1993, or about half of all TVs sold in the United States. If Toshiba, Thompson-RCA, Zenith, and Philips in Ciudad Juarez (opposite El Paso, Texas) are also included, they accounted for most U.S. TV sales. But with the passage of the North American Free Trade Agreement (NAFTA), the future location of TV component manufacturing and assembly might be in East Asia.

Exhibit 3

San Diego and Tijuana
Industrial Map

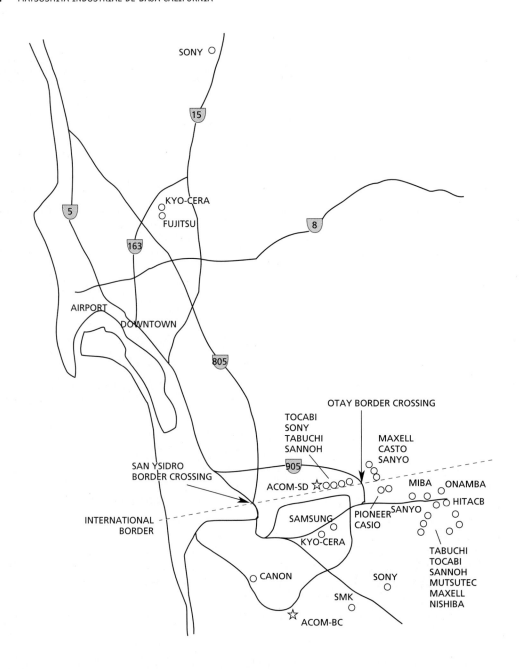

The Early Years: The Nelson Era and the Decision to Locate in Tijuana

Chuck Nelson was "very special" compared to other U.S. managers because he spent five years in Japan after World War II and "he knew the culture." He was also married to a Mexican and knew the Spanish language, and he had experience managing a maquiladora/in-bond assembly plant before he came to MIBA. Nelson managed what was once the largest maquiladora in Tijuana, Warwick Electronics, a division of Whirlpool, with 1,500 workers assembling Silverstone TVs sold in Sears stores. In 1973, Matsushita bought a Motorola

Exhibit 4

Matsushita Group Chart

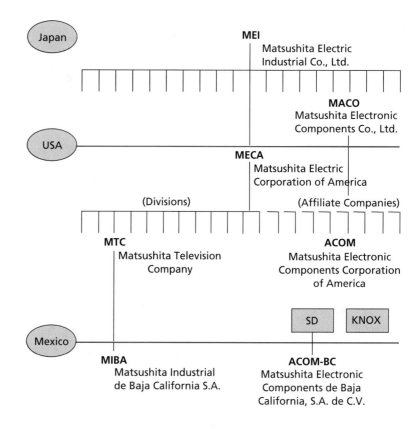

plant in Franklin, Illinois. It was not profitable, and the company sent people to all the U.S.–Mexican border cities, because RCA and Zenith already had maquiladoras. Matsushita needed to produce TVs at a competitive price. Tijuana could take material and components from Japan, Malaysia, Taiwan, and Singapore; assemble one standard, high-volume model TV in Mexico; and send it to the plant outside Chicago to finish it. Matsushita began in Mexico City with a joint venture, and considered a location in Reynosa, Tamaulipas, Mexico (near McAllen, Texas) before deciding to locate in Tijuana.

In 1979, Tijuana was more attractive due to lower transportation costs and proximity to Asian sources of components, although a location along the Texas border was closer to major U.S. markets and distribution centers in the East. According to Nelson, Reynosa also had militant labor unions, and the quality of life for Japanese people living in San Diego, California, was considered far superior to the border region of Texas. However, Tijuana had the disadvantages of higher costs of labor, energy, and sites, as well as a poor telecommunications infrastructure and delays crossing the border. There was also the problem in Tijuana of extremely high employee turnover of around six percent per month.

After locating in Tijuana, Nelson reported in 1985 that "overall MIBA encountered very few problems" and it was expected that there would be expansion. Nelson added that the use of the maquiladora resulted in a net decrease in the total number of Matsushita U.S. employees during the first seven years of operations, "but it saved jobs, and perhaps increased jobs in the U.S. in the long-run" by allowing Matsushita to be more price competitive.

The Evolution of Japanese Investment

According to Yasuo Sasaki, a Brazilian of Japanese ancestry who was deeply involved in Sanyo's move to Tijuana, the location decisions by Japanese TV producers began with the oil crisis in the early 1970s. These Japanese multinationals began investing in the United States and Mexico as part of a trend toward local manufacturing in foreign markets. This globalization was also due to the appreciation of the Japanese yen from 250 to 200 per U.S. dollar, and a shortage of labor in Japan; college graduates did not want factory assembly jobs. Initially Japanese factories moved to Hokkaido and other more remote islands.

The Japanese pattern of entry into Mexican maquiladoras was different than that of U.S. firms. "The Japanese start inside and directly by asking questions, starting with other Japanese companies and Mexican local real estate professionals. They test people's credibility by asking the same questions over and over again," Sasaki noted. In contrast, U.S. companies began "outside and indirectly, working through lawyers in Mexico City and New York," according to Sasaki. The Mexican government was unknown to most Japanese corporations, and harder to deal with than the U.S. government. Compared to U.S. decision making, the Japanese are faster, especially in the final analysis when the implementation stage is included. Japanese companies plan "who will do what when, and are ready once the decision is made—at that point, it's irreversible, and all are aboard the ship," explained Sasaki.

In the case of Sanyo, the original plan was to establish a factory in Mexico City with the involvement of the Mexican government and a Mexican company. Instead, Sanyo decided to go it alone, and originally considered Reynosa just across the Texas border as a location. Zenith was the first TV maker to move to Mexico. Sony established a plant in San Diego, and set up a maquiladora in Tijuana, followed by MIBA in 1979.

Whereas all of the other Japanese multinationals opted for a wholly owned Mexican subsidiary, Sony chose to work through an intermediary or "maquiladora shelter" program. Unlike international subcontracting in which the foreign manufacturer is responsible for making the product and managing the people, shelter arrangements offered only administrative services such as payroll and transportation. The shelter company also dealt with the Mexican governmental agencies.

Sanyo followed Sony and Matsushita to Tijuana, as did Hitachi. "It's part of the Japanese culture and psychology," explained Sasaki, "like the way they play golf together, or go on vacation in Hawaii, always in a group. The fact that the others were there was reason enough—there must be something there."

Japanese companies also chose Tijuana because of its neighbor, San Diego, California, "the only place in the border area with sushi and Japanese schools," he added. "This is important to younger Japanese general managers, production managers, engineers and technicians working in Mexico," noted Sasaki. According to Sasaki, Japanese investment is always "a one-way ticket." There is a long-term commitment, although it may begin very gradually. "For example, Japanese maquiladora buildings were very simple at first, and they could have pulled out easily. Gradually they upgraded."

As they became more successful and stronger, Japanese maquiladoras increased their level of technology from "screwdriver" assembly operations to manufacturing, and they brought their other divisions and suppliers. "You must keep pedaling the bicycle," says Sasaki, "It's not just profits, but survival."

According to one of the top real estate professionals in Tijuana and landlord for one of Matsushita's factories, Beatrix Sanders, 95 percent of Japanese companies own the land their maquiladora is built on, whereas only 50 percent of U.S. companies own their land. Foreigners may "purchase" Mexican land through a trust held by a Mexican bank that is renewable after 30 years. "The Japanese companies want to be around for 200 years," she explained.

The Impact of NAFTA and U.S.–Mexican Relations in 1994

NAFTA was implemented on January 1, 1994, and immediately reduced tariffs and nontariff barriers on many products. Other reductions are to be gradually made over 5 to 10 years. By 1999, two-thirds of U.S. exports were expected to enter Mexico duty-free, up from one-half in 1994. NAFTA's rules of origin (requiring 33 percent North American content, including TV picture tubes) and the restriction of duty drawback (which exempts third-country imports from customs duty) were specific provisions of NAFTA that affected television production (and displays for computers).

NAFTA increased trade and led to a modest increase in U.S. foreign direct investment in Mexico in 1994; there were also massive capital flows into the Mexican stock and bond markets. U.S. exports to Mexico increased 25 percent (including more than 50,000 U.S.-made cars and trucks, a 500 percent increase) as did Mexican exports to the United States. President Clinton boasted that more than 100,000 new U.S. jobs were created by NAFTA. Japanese and South Korean television producers made massive investments in Tijuana during 1994 (see Exhibit 5).

In December 1994 the United States, Mexico, and Canada announced that Chile would be joining NAFTA, and the heads of all the countries of the Western Hemisphere (except Cuba) agreed to work toward a free-trade agreement.

The General Agreement on Tariffs and Trade (GATT) was ratified by the United States late in 1994; this created a new World Trade Organization and was expected to lead to more economic growth by reducing tariffs and nontariff barriers worldwide. International trade was expected to account for 80 percent of U.S. growth by the year 2000.

However, there were also serious concerns about public safety and political stability in Mexico throughout 1994 because of several stunning events. The rebellion in the Mexican state of Chiapas began on January 1, 1994, to coincide with NAFTA's implementation. Mexican presidential candidate Luis Donaldo Colosio was assassinated in Tijuana, and a ruling political party leader in Mexico City was also assassinated. The number of kidnappings of businessmen continued to grow, and included a maquiladora owner/manager in Tijuana in November.

Most importantly, there was a sudden 40 percent devaluation of the Mexican peso in December, the "Christmas Crisis" for the Mexican government. The Chiapas rebels were still threatening, and it was their false statement to the media that they had broken out of an encirclement by the Mexican Army that precipitated (but did not cause) the devaluation. The greatest challenge of the decade was to restore the confidence of foreign investors, while responding to the growing popular demands within Mexico for human rights and political reform.

On the positive side, the Mexican elections of August 1994 were the cleanest ever, which was attributed in part to the Chiapas rebellion by a small band of

Exhibit 5   New Investments in the San Diego/Tijuana/Mexicali Border Region After NAFTA Was Implemented in January 1994

Name of Firm	Type of Facility
Matsushita	Manufacturing and assembly (200 more workers on car audio, plus 140 more making batteries in addition to 3,000 in Tijuana)
	Research and development for hemisphere (140 engineers plus administrative/support staff in addition to 150 in San Diego)
Sanyo Electric Co.	TV Assembly (200 more workers in addition to 1,300 in Tijuana and 6 purchasing in San Diego)
Sony Electronics	Picture tube production (100 more workers in addition to 2,000 in San Diego and 3,000 in Tijuana TV assembly)
Samsung	Picture tube manufacturing ($400 million; 5,000 workers in Tijuana by 1997)
	Assembly (600 workers in Tijuana)
Goldstar	TV assembly (400 workers in Mexicali)
Daewoo	TV assembly (800 workers near Mexicali)
JVC (announcement expected)	TV assembly (1,000 workers in Tijuana)
Hitachi (existing operation)	TV assembly (1,050 workers in Tijuana and 85 support staff in San Diego)

Source: *San Diego Union Tribune* as of December 31, 1994.

Mexican Indians, and also to the introduction of better voter identification cards with photos. There were still instances of unfair tactics by the ruling party, and the election results in the third largest Mexican city, Monterrey, and in the state of Chiapas were both reversed after an electoral review. Most of the improvements in election processes were at the top or the bottom, with many abuses still prevalent in the middle level of the government apparatus.

The issue of border environmental regulation of maquiladoras led to a side agreement to NAFTA and the creation of the Border Environmental Cooperation Commission with $8 billion in funding, and a North American Development Bank (NADBank) to provide additional funding for a deteriorating cross-border infrastructure. However, little was accomplished in the first year of NAFTA, and critics predicted that increased industrialization on the border would only make things worse. In November 1994, the U.S. Environmental Protection Agency (EPA) took steps to enforce U.S. environmental laws against 95 U.S.-owned companies operating in Mexicali, Baja California, Mexico. One of the petitions came from a citizens group in the Chilpancingo neighborhood of Tijuana, which for years had complained about chemical waste dumped on them by maquiladoras above them on Otay Mesa. The EPA issued subpoenas ordering the companies to identify the chemicals that the facilities made, processed, or otherwise used that were likely to be released into water. Along with Mexican sewage and chemical runoff from farms from both sides of the border, these industrial discharges contaminated the New River region in California (immediately north of Mexicali, the Rio Bravo, flows north from Mexico into the United States where it is called the New River). The 95 companies included microelectronics firms, and most of the parent firms were based in Southern California;

their maquiladoras in Mexico were supposed to return the waste products to their country of origin, although many apparently did not, disposing of the waste in Mexico or simply storing it on site. The EPA also urged the Mexican government to take action against the Mexican companies operating along the border.

In the long term, NAFTA was also expected to cause a diversion of U.S. trade and investment from China, Thailand, the Philippines, Malaysia, Indonesia, and other low-wage areas to Mexico. Nevertheless, Asian countries were often more attractive than Mexico to foreign investors, especially Japanese transnational corporations, because they may offer more favorable government investment incentives, trade administration regimes, and networks for supplying components and other production inputs.

■ The Mexican Crisis of 1995

Mexico's worst crisis ever began in December 1994 following the Chiapas uprising, the Colosio assassination, kidnappings, the national elections, and another assassination, along with several increases in U.S. interest rates. According to the Mexican government, their mistake was to think that temporary capital inflows would continue to come. "People like to live in a democracy and invest in a dictatorship," complained Alejandro Valenzuela, director general of international affairs, Secretaria de Hacienda y Credito Publico (Mexico's IRS). Valenzuela argued that investors did not like the increasingly democratic trend in Mexican politics, with effective opposition challenges to the ruling party demonstrated in the elections of August 1994.

However, after paying off holders of bonds denominated in U.S. dollars ($29 billion in January dropped to $14 billion in April 1995, paid with the help of the U.S. Treasury dollar stabilization fund), and increasing Mexican interest rates to bolster the peso, he felt that the worst was over. The United States had the security of a "payment mechanism" that would tap Mexican oil revenues in the event of a default. A futures market for the Mexican peso opened in April 1995, allowing investors to hedge their bets. In 1994, Mexican exports surged by 32 percent (over 40 percent for manufacturing), while imports remained flat. Valenzuela's forecasts for 1995 (as of April) were 42 percent inflation and $8 billion in foreign investment.

Critics argued that the poor people of Mexico and the U.S. middle class would be forced to bail out a few New York banks. The most fragile segments of Mexican society also included small to medium-sized companies and the middle class. There were concerns that the Mexican economy might not emerge from the 1995 recession in 1996, possibly leading to social unrest in Mexico and more migration to the United States.

■ Appendix: Excerpts Matsushita Annual Report Fiscal Year Ended March 31, 1994

■ Profile

Matsushita Electric Industrial Co., Ltd., was founded in Osaka in 1918 as a small producer of home electric products. Today, the company is one of the world's premier manufacturers of electronic products for home, industrial, and commercial uses. Matsushita's products are marketed under such well-known brand names as National, Panasonic, Technics, and Quasar in more than 160 countries.

In response to far-reaching changes in the world's political and economic structures and in anticipation of the challenges of the twenty-first century, Matsushita has established the revitalization plan. This plan emphasizes the importance of returning to the company's basic philosophy, namely, that Matsushita is committed, as an industrial concern, to contributing to social progress and the well-being of people the world over through its business activities. The essential strategies of the revitalization plan are outlined in this year's annual report.

Through the revitalization plan, Matsushita is striving to consolidate its reputation worldwide as a contributing member of society and as a vital, strong corporation.

■ Financial Highlights

In 1994, net sales declined 6 percent (see Exhibit 6), largely reflecting reduced demand and the impact of yen appreciation on overseas revenues when translated into Japanese currency. Although we worked to minimize manufacturing and overhead costs, earnings were negatively affected by lower sales of audiovisual equipment and seasonal products, a shift in consumer preference toward lower priced items, and the strong yen. Income before taxes fell 21 percent, and net income dropped 34 percent.

There was brisk demand for home facsimile machines and compact read-only (CD-ROM) drives in Japan, and in overseas markets, sales of telephones, hard-disk drives, and factory automation equipment were firm. Sales of electronic components achieved a level close to that of 1993 as a result of improved demand, especially for semiconductors.

Exhibit 6   Matsushita Sales and Income, 1990–1994

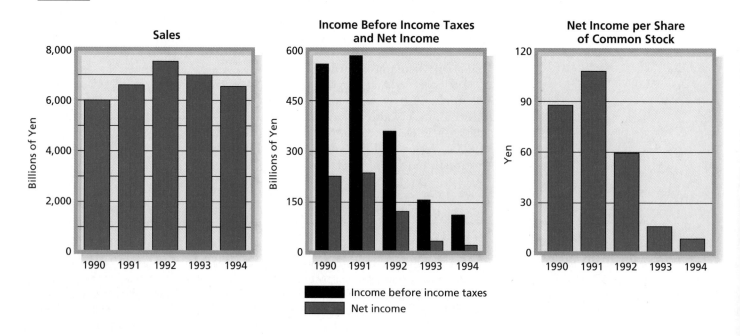

▪ Revitalizing Matsushita—Responding to the Changing Environment

The past several years have seen far-reaching changes in the world's political and economic structures following the crumbling of the Cold War political framework. In Japan, we have seen the collapse of the bubble economy and the end of brisk growth. These transformations, as well as the continued appreciation of the yen, have necessarily modified consumer preferences and have propelled us into a new economic era.

Difficult business conditions during this period of immense change hindered the performances of many Japanese companies, including Matsushita. However, we cannot simply blame external factors for our results. Rather, as the new era unfolds we must seek to develop innovative management practices by more closely tracking social developments.

In line with this objective, we have established the revitalization plan. The basic goal of this three-year plan is a return to the company's original principle, namely, that our primary purpose is to contribute to social progress through our business activities. In other words, Matsushita aims to provide products and services that are truly of use to society. Our reward for doing so will be growth in sales and earnings.

▪ Ten Principal Business Areas

To meet the goal of the revitalization plan, we have sought to clarify our future direction (see Exhibit 7). To this end, we have identified 10 principal business areas that the Matsushita Group worldwide will develop. These business areas are AV hardware, information and communications, home appliances, housing products, air-conditioning equipment, manufacturing and industrial equipment, components and devices, environmental protection and health care products, systems and networks, and AV software.

Rapid technological advances have prompted us to target three of these areas-AV hardware, information and communications, and components and devices-for intensive, coordinated development by the entire Matsushita Group.

AV Hardware

The transition from analog to digital technology is changing the nature of AV hardware. In the years ahead, high-definition TV, digital videocassette, and digital videodisk equipment will lead us into a new era of fully developed digitization.

▪ Specific Strategies and Objectives

As a guideline, we have determined that at the end of 1997 nonconsolidated recurring profit should be equivalent to five percent of annual net sales, the same level as before the collapse of Japan's economic bubble.

▪ Strengthen Division Management

Divisions will no longer depend on an upper layer of management, but will be entirely responsible for generating their own profits. As well, divisions will be

Exhibit 7

Matsushita at a Glance

Product Category	Percentage of Total Sales	Major Products
Video Equipment	20% 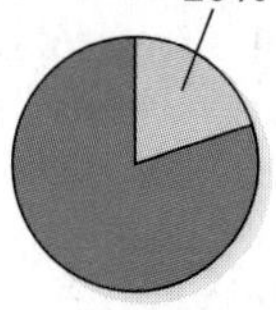	Videocassette recorders, video camcorders and related equipment, color TVs, TV/VCR combination units, projection TVs, liquid crystal display TVs, videodisc players, satellite broadcast receivers, satellite-communications-related equipment.
Audio Equipment	8% 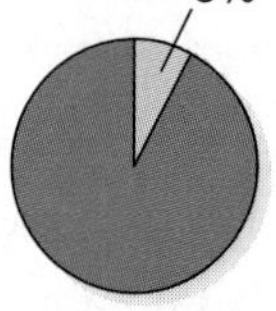	Radios, radio cassette recorders, tape recorders, compact disk players, digital compact cassette players, stereo hi-fi and related equipment, car audio products, electronic musical instruments.
Home Appliances	13% 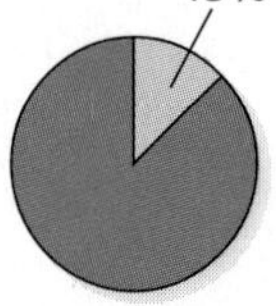	Refrigerators, room air conditioners, home laundry equipment, dishwashers, vacuum cleaners, electric irons, microwave ovens, rice cookers, electric fans, electric and kerosene heaters, infrared-ray warmers, electric blankets, electrically heated rugs.
Communication and Industrial Equipment	25% 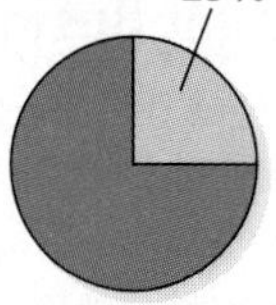	Facsimile equipment, word processors, personal computers, copying machines, CRT displays, telephones, PBXs, CATV systems, measuring instruments, electronic-parts-mounting machines, industrial robots, welding machines, air-conditioning equipment, compressors, vending machines.
Electronic Components	12% 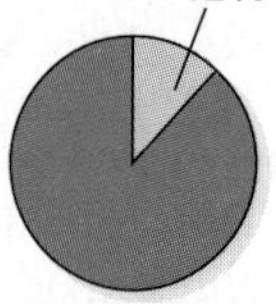	Integrated circuits, discrete devices, charge coupled devices, cathode-ray tubes, image pickup tubes, tuners, capacitors, resistors, speakers, magnetic recording heads, electric motors, electric lamps.
Batteries and Kitchen-Related Products	5% 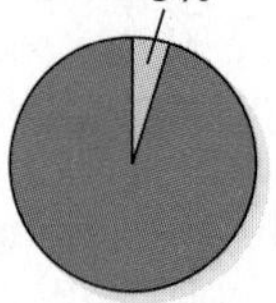	Dry batteries, storage batteries, solar batteries, solar energy equipment, gas hot-water supply systems, gas cooking appliances, kitchen sinks, kitchen fixture systems, bath and sanitary equipment
Other	8% 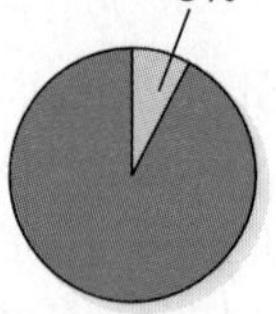	Bicycles, cameras and flash units, electric pencil sharpeners, water purifiers, imported materials and products such as nonferrous metals, lumber, paper and medical equipment.
Entertainment	9% 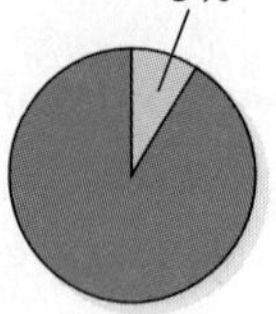	Filmed entertainment, music entertainment, theme parks, book publishing, gift merchandise, pre-recorded video and audio tapes and discs.

expected to conduct their operations with enthusiasm and an entrepreneurial eye to future growth.

◼ Select Business Areas for Expansion and Concentration of Resources

It is no longer possible to take constant growth for granted in every business area. We will reassess operations company-wide and in each division, choosing specific business areas to develop and strengthen. At the same time, consistently unprofitable businesses will be targeted for restructuring or downsizing.

◼ Improve the Productivity of Administrative and Support Departments

We will thoroughly reevaluate administrative and support departments to streamline the organization, reduce redundancy, and improve efficiency. By doing so, we aim to make these departments responsive to the needs of a rapidly changing society. We have summarized our vision for these departments as "simple, small, speedy, and strategic."

◼ Restructure R&D Activities

In February 1994, Matsushita thoroughly reorganized its R&D structure, one of the most immediately important tasks the company had set for itself as part of the revitalization plan. The reorganization involved replacing the corporate engineering divisions, formerly the heart of Matsushita's R&D structure, with two new core divisions: Corporate Research and Corporate Product Development. At the same time, the company consolidated the more than 20 research centers previously under the jurisdiction of the corporate engineering divisions into seven laboratories and two development centers.

The Corporate Product Development Division handles the integration of strategically important AV, computer and communications technologies, as well as the development of key devices and software applications, thus concentrating the company's ability to transform new technologies into market-creating products and systems. This division is expected to continue playing an important role in strengthening high-potential business areas as Matsushita enters the multimedia age.

An important feature of Matsushita's new corporate R&D structure is its emphasis on closer coordination of the activities of the two R&D divisions. Also important is President Morishita's establishment of R&D themes for the entire company and effective allocation of resources. Matsushita believes that improved teamwork will accelerate the transformation of new technologies into the products and businesses of tomorrow.

◼ Toward the Multimedia Age

The company's response to technological and social change will be to build new businesses around imaginative and innovative products that integrate AV, computer, and communications technologies. In the AV field, for example, Matsushita has to date marketed a broad selection of compact disk (CD) and digital compact cassette (DCC) products. The company is currently employing its advanced technologies to develop next-generation HDTV, DVC, and DVD equipment.

Matsushita is also a leader in the information and communications equipment field. Matsushita is Japan's top manufacturer of cellular communications office- and home-use facsimile machines, cordless telephones, personal computers (PCs), word processors, displays, and disk drives.

Matsushita capitalized on its accumulated expertise in the AV, computer, and communications fields in fiscal year 1994 to market the Panasonic REAL 3DO Interactive Multiplayer, a 32-bit home entertainment machine that has raised the curtain on the multimedia age, and a notebook-sized PC with built-in CD-ROM drive.

As Matsushita seeks new business opportunities, it will make full use of the extensive resources of the Matsushita Group worldwide. In line with its commitment to strengthening its multimedia technologies, the company has designated software as a key business area to be cultivated and promoted.

■ Coexistence with the Earth

Matsushita places great importance on environmental protection in its technological and product development activities. Coexistence with the earth and harmony with the natural concerns are goals in the years ahead as the company strives to adhere to its philosophy of contributing to society through its business activities.

In 1970, Matsushita established the Environmental Control Office, subsequently renamed the Environmental Protection Promotion Office. Since then, we have broadened our environmental protection efforts. In 1991, the company published the Matsushita Environmental Control Policy, and we have subsequently set forth environmental rules and procedures to be followed at Matsushita Group sites worldwide.

In line with the tenets of the Matsushita Environmental Control Policy, the company has devoted considerable effort to developing technologies that are contributing to the fight against environmental deterioration.

In addition, Matsushita has garnered acclaim from all sectors for its revolutionary no-mercury-added alkaline batteries. Since 1990, the company has manufactured and marketed these cells, which pose fewer disposal hazards than conventional batteries. Matsushita has also made this technology available to overseas battery manufacturers in the belief that the benefits of such technology should be shared.

Matsushita incorporates concern for the environment into all aspects of production, from product development to waste-conscious packaging practices. A particular focus has been the elimination of CFCs and other ozone-depleting substances from manufacturing processes. CFCs have traditionally been used for washing semiconductors and other electronic components, and Matsushita has devoted significant resources to develop production facilities that do not require CFCs. The company's achievements have earned praise both in Japan and overseas. The U.S. Environmental Protection Agency selected Matsushita as a winner of the 1993 Stratospheric Ozone Protection Award in recognition of the company's efforts to eliminate the use of CFCs.

Matsushita will step up efforts to apply new technologies to the development of products that are safe for the environment and people. By doing so, the company aims to enhance its contribution to tomorrow's society.

Matsushita is manufacturing environmentally conscious products. All of the company's domestically produced batteries are no-mercury-added cells. Matsushita's overseas subsidiaries are rapidly switching to this type of battery.

■ Operations in China

In line with its strategy to localize production in the markets where its products are used, Matsushita plans to conclude a formal contract with the government of the People's Republic of China to establish a joint venture to manufacture VCR mechanisms. Production facilities incorporating the newest technology are already in place. Matsushita is also localizing all aspects of its TV operations, from product planning and design to manufacturing and marketing, in selected major markets to enhance the autonomy of its overseas companies.

In September 1993, Matsushita established its first audio equipment production facility in China for minicomponent systems, radios, radio/cassette recorders, and portable headphone players. Matsushita will enhance its local presence in the future by having this facility also function as a procurement and supply center for Chinese-manufactured components.

In China, operations progressed smoothly at a joint venture production plant for fully automatic washing machines established in April 1992. Matsushita continues to solidify its operating base in the promising Chinese market: at another joint venture, the company began manufacturing electric steam irons for the local market in April 1994.

Matsushita is expanding offshore component and material production to bolster overseas procurement and to capitalize on the appreciation of the yen. Following on the success of Beijing Matsushita Color CRT Co., Ltd., Matsushita's first joint venture in China, the company established two component production joint ventures during the year. One of these companies will manufacture electronic tuners, demodulators, and remote control units for TVs and VCRs; the other will make feather-touch switches for consumer electronic products.

During the year, Matsushita established a joint venture in Shanghai to produce and market no-mercury-added manganese batteries, primarily for the Chinese market.

■ Joint Venture with Philips

Matsushita Electronics Corporation (MEC), a joint venture with Philips Electronics, became a wholly owned subsidiary of Matsushita in May 1993. MEC is currently trying to expand its operations in international markets for such key devices as semiconductors, cathode-ray tubes (CRTs), and electric lamps.

■ Battery Production

As a leading international battery manufacturer, Matsushita is expanding production overseas to better meet the needs of its customers in each region where it makes batteries. In fiscal 1994, Belgium-based Philips Matsushita Battery Corporation N.V. started manufacturing nickel-cadmium (NiCd) cells locally. Matsushita Storage Battery Company, a division of Matsushita Battery Industrial Corporation of America, began full-scale production of sealed lead-acid batteries, while P.T. Asia Matsushita Battery in Indonesia commenced making NiCd batteries. Additionally, Matsushita announced its intention to set up a joint venture in Poland with Philips Electronics to manufacture manganese batteries.

Matsushita is concerned about the global environment and is striving to popularize no-mercury-added cells. All of the Company's domestically produced manganese and alkaline batteries are now no-mercury-added cells, and overseas plants are rapidly switching to this type.

■ CASE 25 Mercedes-Benz: In the Race to Win

Todd Barber
Michael Kuban
Kristi Rickman
Mark Thompson
Uzma Suboohi
Michael Grundmeyer

■ http://www.mercedes-benz.com/

Mercedes has long stood as the ultimate symbol of success for many automobile owners. Particularly in the U.S. luxury car market, Mercedes has enjoyed great success. However, since the 1980s, Mercedes management has been plagued by declining sales, loss of market share, stiffer competition, stagnant market growth, changing consumer trends, rising production costs, and a negative dollar-to-duetsche mark exchange rate, resulting in shrinking profits. In response, Mercedes is attempting to reduce operating costs while broadening its product line to enter into new markets and market segments. Recent globalization due to relaxed import barriers and industrialization of developing countries is opening up new and lucrative markets for the automobile manufacturers. Mercedes plans to establish its presence in these emerging markets via its extended product line. Furthermore, Mercedes is cutting costs and changing its image from a German automobile manufacturing company to a global one by establishing several production facilities worldwide. The major questions are:

1. How successfully can Mercedes enter into the new market segments?
2. How will Mercedes perform in the emerging new markets?
3. How will consumers respond to Mercedes' recent changes in its product line?

The Mercedes name has been synonymous with expensive, but prestigious, luxury cars that emphasized superb German engineering and safety designs. However, now Mercedes is extending its product line to cater to market segments effectively dominated by other competitors. As such, Mercedes is entering into new markets and market segments where it has little or no experience.

The C Class compact car (priced at approximately $30,000), the A Class car (priced in the $20,000 range), the new "Swatchmobile" minicar (priced in the

Case prepared under the direction of Professor Robert E. Hoskisson for class discussion purposes only.

C.485

$10,000 range), and the yet-to-be-named sports utility vehicle (priced in the $40,000 to $50,000 range) are the recent product line extensions by Mercedes. Mercedes management plans to market these new products under the Mercedes brand name and the Star symbol. Mercedes' prestigious image could be "tarnished" by this move. The customers of its $130,000 range S Class sedans may react adversely if the Mercedes symbol and Star symbol grace the economically priced $10,000 Swatchmobile. Furthermore, by entering into these segments, Mercedes is progressively moving farther away from its area of expertise and dominance. Does the environment surrounding the auto industry demand such bold moves? Can Mercedes adapt its position and its image to suit these markets segments and new markets? Or, is the luxury market segment alone large enough to sustain the company?

■ History[1]

Mercedes Benz is the largest of five divisions of Stuttgart-based Daimler-Benz AG (see Exhibit 1). The company emerged as a result of a merger in 1926 between companies founded by German automobile pioneers Gottlieb Daimler and Karl Benz.

■ Carl Benz (1844–1929)

The Mercedes-Benz saga begins with Carl Benz, who operated a machine shop in Mannheim, Germany. In 1879, Benz successfully completed the two-cylinder, internal combustion engine. In 1883, Benz and two other financial backers founded Benz et Cie, Rheinische Gasmotoren-Fabriks, to manufacture internal-combustion engines. In 1885, Benz demonstrated his "velocipede," the first self-propelled vehicle powered by an internal-combustion engine, to his town's people. He promptly scored another first by crashing into a brick wall. He received a German patent for the velocipede in 1886. In 1893, Benz patented a steering mechanism for a four-wheeled vehicle called the Viktoria. In 1894, Benz introduced the Benz Velo, a newer model of the Viktoria. By the end of 1901, Benz had sold approximately 2,700 vehicles and became the leading automobile maker in the world.

■ Gottlieb Daimler (1834–1900)

Gottlieb Daimler, the other half of Daimler-Benz, was the first of his family in four generations not to become a baker. Instead he became an engineer. In 1882, Daimler joined with Wilhelm Maybach to develop an engine small enough to drive a vehicle. Though they lived only 60 miles apart, Daimler and Benz never met. In 1885, the same year that Benz rolled out his velocipede, Daimler and Maybach mounted an engine on a wooden bicycle, thus creating the first motorcycle. In 1888, Daimler and Maybach created an engine-driven propeller system for hot-air balloons.

■ Emile Jellinek (1853–1918)

An unlikely collaborator in the Mercedes-Benz story was Emile Jellinek, a wealthy Austrian banker and consul general in Nice, France. It was Jellinek who

Exhibit 1   Daimler-Benz AG

Corporate Unit Mercedes-Benz
Mercedes-Benz AG, Stuggart
Mercedes-Benz Espana
Mercedes-Benz (U.K.)
Mercedes-Benz Nederland
Mercedes-Benz Belgium S.A.
Mercedes-Benz France
Mercedes-Benz Italia
Mercedes-Benz (Schweiz) AG
Freightliner, Portland, United States
Mercedes-Benz Mexico
Mercedes-Benz de Brasil
Sofunge S.A., Sao Paolo
Mercedes-Benz Argentina
Mercedes-Benz of South America
Mercedes-Benz Turkey, Istanbul
Mercedes-Benz Japan Co. Ltd.
Mercedes-Benz (Australia)

Corporate Unit AEG
AEG Aktiengesellschaft, Berlin and Frankfurt am Main
AEG Hausgerate AG, Nuremburg
AEG Westinghouse Transport-Systeme GmbH, Berlin

Corporate Unit Deutsche Aerospace
Deutsche Aerospace A G, Munich
Deutsche Aerospace Airbus GmbH, Hamburg
Domier, Friedrichschafen
MTU Motoren-und Turbinen-Union Munchen, Munich

Corporate Unit Daimler-Benz InterServices (debis)
Daimler-Benz InterServices (debis) AG, Berlin
Mercedes-Benz Lease Finanz, Stuttgart
Mercedes-Benz Finanzaria S.P.A., Rome
Mercedes-Benz Credit, Norwalk, United States

Regional Holding and Finance Companies
Daimler-Benz Holding, AG, Zurich
Daimler-Benz U.K., London
Daimler-Benz Holding France
Daimler-Benz Holding Nederland B.V.
Daimler-Benz Holding Belgium
Daimler-Benz Coordination Center S.A.
Daimler-Benz North America Corporation, New York

convinced Daimler to position the engines at the front of the car "because that was where the horse used to be." Jellinek also pressured Daimler to create faster, more powerful automobiles. In 1900, Jellinek asked Daimler to design a racer with a longer wheelbase, a lower center of gravity, and an engine capable of generating speeds of at least 30 mph. Jellinek also promised to purchase 36 of the cars—a big order in those days—in return for exclusive rights to distribute Daimler automobiles in Austria-Hungary, France, Belgium, and the United States. Jellinek had one other stipulation: He wanted the car named "Mercedes," in honor of his one-year-old daughter, Maria de las Mercedes Adrenne Manuela Ramona. In 1902, Daimler-Motoren-Gesselschaft registered the name "Mercedes" as a trademark, and the name "Daimler" faded from use. Jellinek's association with Daimler-Motoren-Gesselschaft came to an acrimonious end in 1908. During World War I Jellinek was accused of spying for Austria and he died in prison in 1918. His daughter Mercedes died impoverished in 1929.

■ Daimler-Benz

During the late 1800s and early 1900s, Mercedes gained an unparalleled reputation for manufacturing racing automobiles. When World War I ended in 1918, there were 86 German car makers competing in a devastated market. In 1924, Benz et Cie and Daimler-Motoren-Gesselschaft agreed to an "association of common interest." The informal agreement became a merger in 1926 with the formation of Daimler-Benz Aktiengesellschaft. The Daimler star apparently originated with Gottlieb Daimler's sons, who recalled that their father had once sketched a star to symbolize his rising fortunes. The star stood for air, sea, and land—the elements dominated by Daimler engines. The star became the radiator emblem in 1921. The circular emblem used by Benz began in 1903 as a gear wheel with "Original Benz" printed inside. It was changed to a wreath in 1909.

■ World War II

The Mercedes-Benz passenger cars produced by Daimler-Benz AG between 1926 and the beginning of World War II are considered among the most magnificent automobiles ever created. Even with its success, Mercedes remained reluctant to expand production to passenger cars. Finally, in the mid-1930s, the company introduced its first diesel-powered automobile at the Berlin automobile show. The 260D quickly gained worldwide recognition and soon put Mercedes in the position of No. 1 manufacturer of diesel automobiles. With the outbreak of World War II in 1939, Daimler-Benz turned its attention to producing airplane engines and vehicles for the German Third Reich. From 1930 until 1943, the company also produced the Mercedes-Benz 770K, some of which were for Hitler's personal use.

■ Post–World War II

Daimler-Benz factories were heavily damaged by the war so the company did not introduce its first post-war passenger car until 1949, when it launched the Mercedes-Benz 170S. The 170S was followed by the Mercedes 220 and the Mercedes 300. In 1952, Daimler-Benz returned to the international racing circuit with the Mercedes 300SL, the legendary gullwing coupe. Mercedes enjoyed rapid expansion of its exports in the 1950s. From 1954 to 1957, Daimler-Benz produced 1,485 production model gullwing coupes, most of which sold in the United States. In 1965, Mercedes-Benz North America (MBNA) was founded in order to facilitate increased sales in the United States.

MBNA can attribute its success specifically in the United States market to two important developments. First, the company adopted a standard equipment policy. Mercedes was the initial car company to include features such as radios and air conditioners in the car's sticker price; previously the buyer would have been assessed an additional charge for each item. Second, Mercedes enjoyed a rapid expansion upon the introduction of the five-cylinder diesel-engine automobile in 1975. The company was already proficient in the production of diesel engines, which allowed Mercedes to eclipse the competition by producing superior diesel cars.

For almost two decades, beginning with the Mercedes-Benz 600 in 1963, Daimler-Benz focused on building full-size luxury sedans. Every model was bigger, more advanced, and more expensive than the last. Sales continued to increase as the appeal for high-quality, luxury cars grew. Mercedes, along with a few other luxury car makers, was spared the decline in car sales due to the oil crises of the 1970s because their customers were less price sensitive to the gasoline price increases. By the mid-1980s, Mercedes-Benz was generally considered the finest manufacturer of passenger cars in the world.[2]

The Baby Benz

In 1982, Daimler-Benz introduced the Mercedes-Benz 190, a sleeker, less expensive automobile, which soon became known as the "Baby Benz." It sold in the United States for about $25,000, which placed it in the luxury class but was half the cost of the next best Mercedes-Benz. The Mercedes 190 signaled another change in the policy for Daimler-Benz. For years, the firm had deliberately allowed production to lag behind demand. This helped establish Mercedes-Benz as a prestigious marque and kept prices high. But the 190 was the first Mercedes-Benz meant to be mass produced—up to 200,000 cars per year. However, the Mercedes 190 was never as popular as Daimler-Benz had hoped. In the late 1980s, Daimler-Benz began offering pricier models and moved even more strongly toward the upper end of the luxury market. Unfortunately, new taxes in the United States on luxury items and the entrance of Japanese competitors in the luxury market soon began cutting into the large sales and profits. To make matters worse, the BMW, from Bayerische Motoren Werke AG, passed Mercedes-Benz in 1989 to become the best-selling luxury car in Europe after 30 years as runner-up. In 1992, BMW also passed Mercedes in the critical U.S. market. Faced with competition from BMW and the aggressive new entrance of the Japanese, Mercedes was forced to reexamine its methods for serving the automobile consumer and to reassess the luxury car market.

Industry Background

North America, and particularly the United States, has been the largest market for automobiles. For the full-year 1993, vehicle sales in the United States and Canada totaled 15.39 million units (9.26 million passenger cars and 6.13 million trucks).[3] Approximately six percent of these sales are in the luxury car segment. The luxury cars are characterized by high levels of comfort, a pleasurable driving experience, and hefty price tags. Large price tags accompany the specialty cars such as Porsche and Ferrari but they fall into the sports category. The luxury car segment is the market leader in technical advancements. Most new innovations are first introduced in the luxury models and, then, as the cost of manufacturing decreases, are placed in the regular car models. The overall luxury category was expected to grow by about seven percent in 1994, and about eight percent in 1995.[4] However, during the past few years, the real growth in the U.S. auto market has come in the light-truck category—big, rugged sports utility vehicles and pickups. Many of them cost as much as luxury cars, and a surprisingly large number of traditional luxury car buyers are switching. Those who are still buying fancy cars these days are opting for so-called near-luxury cars. These sedans, such as the Nissan Maxima and the Toyota Avalon, can come equipped with most of the gadgets offered on larger, more traditional luxury models. But they cost about $30,000—some $10,000 to $20,000 less than the fancier fare. Even in the luxury segment itself, much of the growth during the past five years has been in the low-end vehicles such as the BMW 325, Mazda Millenia, Mitsubishi Diamante, Infiniti G20, and the Lexus ES300.[5] While automakers still earn large profits from luxury cars, the profit margins have been depressed since the Japanese jumped into the U.S. luxury market in the late 1980s.

Until the late 1980s, Mercedes-Benz and BMW regarded the United States as their own private hunting preserve, stocked with big game almost exclusively for their pleasure. Year after year, they rolled out new models, raised prices, and earned sizable profits.[6] A few American car manufacturers also competed in this market. American luxury cars such as Cadillac and Lincoln typically catered to the lower end of the luxury car market, whereas European manufacturers concentrated on the higher end. Certain European automobile companies such as Rolls Royce developed cars for the very high luxury market. Thus, each company catered to a niche market. However, these markets overlapped to a large extent, resulting in some competition. This situation changed drastically with the entrance of Japanese automobile manufacturers.

■ The Japanese Invasion

The Japanese automakers had become the leading automobile manufacturers by the early 1980s (see Exhibit 2 for car production statistics). Their success in overtaking the Big Three is paralleled only by the speed with which they accomplished this feat. In the 1960s, Japan's auto exports were considered the worst in the world in terms of quality. In less than 20 years, Japan's auto manufacturers had completely revamped their production facilities, quality controls, and distribution channels.

Most of their success is due to the implementation of Dr. Deming's management techniques and the strong keiretsus. Dr. Deming taught the Japanese about the importance of quality and efficient production. Through the use of just-in-time (JIT) production, Japanese automakers were able to decrease their inventory costs substantially while simultaneously increasing their quality. Keiretsus are groups of organizations that cooperate on all aspects of strategy. The Japanese automakers have developed these keiretsus, which include their suppliers and their banking organizations. These two factors enabled the Japanese to excel quickly.[7]

By 1980, Japan was the leading exporter of quality automobiles. Japan was able to discount their low-end automobiles more than the competition because of

Exhibit 2	Trade and Transportation World Motor Vehicle Production, 1950–1992 (in thousands)			
Year	U.S.	Japan	World Total	U.S. % of World Total
1992	9,702	12,499	47,377	20.5
1991	8,811	13,245	46,496	19
1990	9,783	13,487	48,345	20.2
1989	10,874	13,026	49,101	22.1
1988	11,214	12,700	48,210	23.3
1987	10,925	12,249	45,903	23.8
1986	11,335	12,260	45,297	25
1985	11,653	12,271	44,811	26
1984	10,925	11,465	42,058	26
1983	9,225	11,112	39,755	23.2
1982	6,986	10,732	36,113	19.3
1981	7,943	11,180	37,230	21.3
1980	8,010	11,043	38,514	20.8
1970	8,284	5,289	29,403	28.2
1960	7,905	482	16,488	47.9
1950	8,006	32	10,577	75.7

Source: American Automobile Manufacturers Association.

the strength of their domestic market. Japan's import barriers (formal and informal) have allowed the Japanese market to remain protected from foreign manufacturers. The two main barriers to imports were the complexities in distribution within the Japanese market and government taxes. The Japanese have set up a complex system of distribution that discourages imports, due to the costs of entering the market and the difficulty of succeeding in this market. At the same time, the Japanese government strongly discouraged the production of large automobiles. Large cars are taxed an extra 23 percent in order to keep the size down in the small streets of Tokyo. These incentives compelled the Japanese automakers to refrain from producing large, luxury cars up until the mid-1980s. The economies of scale that these producers achieved were the key to their success in the United States.[8]

Although the Japanese had great success in the U.S. automotive market, as their exports of low-end, low-priced automobiles increased, they experienced several problems. First, as their consumer base became older, the owners of the Toyota Cressidas, Nissan Maximas, and Honda Accords became wealthier. With this wealth, these consumers wanted more luxurious cars that portrayed their success, and accordingly purchased German or American luxury automobiles. This gap in their product line had to be filled if the Japanese wanted to maintain the customer loyalty that they had built in the lower end segments.[9] Second, because of their success in the U.S. market, Japan had established a large trade surplus with the United States. This caused an uprising of projectionist fears within the United States, which led to trade agreements limiting Japanese

Exhibit 3	Currency Exchange Rates		
Year	French Franc	Deutsche Mark	Japanese Yen
1970	5.52	3.65	357.6
1975	4.49	2.62	305.1
1980	4.52	1.96	203.0
1985	7.56	2.46	200.5
1987	5.34	1.58	123.5
1989	5.79	1.70	143.5
1991	5.18	1.52	125.2
1993	5.92	1.71	108.9

Source: Compiled from *International Financial Statistics Yearbook*, 1993.

exports. During this same period, the Japanese yen became stronger against the dollar (see Exhibit 3 for exchange rates). This caused the prices of Japanese automobiles within the United States to increase. Third, due to the rapid weakening of the dollar, Japan was unable to increase its prices as fast as the yen increased, resulting in the shrinking of profit margins. As such, Japan was unable to maintain its growth within the low-end segment.[10] Thus, the Japanese were encouraged to enter into new segments.

The market they targeted was the high-end luxury segment. Honda was the first to make the move and was followed quickly by Nissan and Toyota. This attack by the Japanese has changed the face of the competition in the high-end luxury car market segment significantly.

Competition

Since the late 1980s, the luxury car segment has been characterized by severe competition (see Exhibit 4). Companies such as General Motors (Cadillac), Ford (Lincoln), Mercedes-Benz, BMW, Saab, Jaguar, Volvo, Honda (Acura), Toyota (Lexus), and Nissan (Infiniti) all compete for the large returns generated by this segment. (See Exhibit 5 for a listing of top 10 luxury cars in the United States.) The market share for each of these companies for 1993 is shown in Exhibit 6.

Cadillac[11]

Throughout most of its history, Cadillac has been known for its style, performance, innovation, and luxury in the automotive industry. The first Model A Cadillac rolled out in 1902. In 1909, Cadillac Motor Company was acquired by General Motors. Cadillac pioneered such innovations as the electric starter and the overhead-valve engine. Since 1927, when the LaSalle was introduced, Cadillac has been known as both a designer's and an engineer's automobile. In 1948, Cadillac incorporated a new design, the hugely popular tail fin. In 1959, the total volume of Cadillac sales was more than twice the volume sold by all other luxury cars combined. However, in 1973, when the first energy crisis hit,

Exhibit 4

Market Share in 1986 and 1990

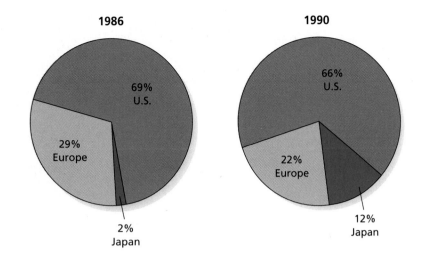

Exhibit 5 Top 10 Luxury Cars

Rank	Brand	% Share of Market–1993	% Share of Market–1992
1	Cadillac	22.8	24.1
2	Lincoln	19.4	18.2
3	Acura	12.1	13.5
4	Lexus	10.6	10.5
5	BMW	8.7	7.4
6	Volvo	8.2	7.6
7	Mercedes	6.9	7.1
8	Infiniti	5.6	5
9	Saab	2.1	3
10	Jaguar	1.4	1
	Total Top 10	97.9	97.4
	Total Market in Units	894,481	888,454

Source: *Automotive News Market Data Book, 1994 and 1993.*

the fuel inefficient Cadillacs suffered an enormous amount of adverse publicity. By 1986, a year in which Cadillac had redesigned the Seville and Eldorado in hopes of regaining its reputation, sales had plummeted 60 percent. Quality, the one factor on which Cadillac's reputation had been built, was slipping, and it was showing in sales. In 1987, Cadillac reorganized with the goal of stressing quality and style for its luxury cars. Despite the increase in competition, Cadillac continued to hold the No. 1 position in the luxury car market, with a 27.3 percent market share. In 1993, Cadillac introduced its integrated powertrain-suspension system called the Northstar engine. Although overall (including fleet) sales dropped 4.7 percent, Cadillac improved its retail sales performance by 7.4 percent and retained its position as the best-selling American luxury car.

Exhibit 6

Market Share for Luxury Cars, 1993

Source: Automotive News Market Data Book.

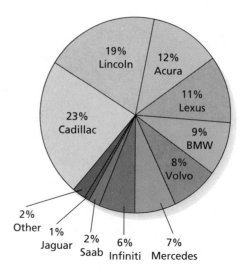

Lincoln[12]

The Lincoln automobile is manufactured by a division of Ford Motor Company. The first Lincoln was introduced in 1920. The early Lincolns made their debut in the midst of a declining economy, and therefore sold poorly. By 1930, the Lincoln lineup included touring cars, roadsters, coupes, sedans, limousines, Broughams, Town Cars, Phaetons, and Cabriolets. In 1953, Lincoln first offered power-assisted optional equipment such as power steering, power brakes, and power front seats. In 1955, Lincoln introduced its exclusive new automatic transmission, the turbo-drive. In 1971, the Lincoln Town Car, known as the "Golden Anniversary Continental," was introduced. In 1973, a Town Car was presented as a gift by President Nixon to the Soviet Party Secretary Brezhnev during a state visit. Despite the Arab oil embargo of the early 1970s, Lincoln experienced its third best production year in its history in 1974.

Almost since its inception, Lincoln has placed second in luxury car sales to its chief domestic rival and market leader, General Motors' Cadillac. But in 1990, Lincoln actually tied Cadillac in sales for the first time in its history. Despite the economic recession of the early 1990s, Lincoln continued to improve the comfort and handling of its cars. The 1994 Town Car included dual air bags, an antitheft alarm system, hands-free cellular phone, and programmable memory seat in the signature series. The 1994 Mark VIII offered the highest level of standard equipment ever available on a Lincoln, including such features as remote keyless entry and memory outside mirrors. Options included such features as voice-activated cellular phones, trunk-mounted CD changer, electronic traction assist, and chrome directional wheels. A 1994 Lincoln could be purchased for $20,000 to $40,000.

BMW[13]

BMW is considered the most direct competitor of Mercedes-Benz. Based in Munich, BMW is the 15th largest producer of cars in the world. BMW is a global company, operating 10 plants in Germany, Austria, and South Africa. It has 12 subsidiaries in Germany, as well as subsidiaries in 15 other countries. BMW conducts business in 20 countries around the world. In Germany, the BMW car is viewed as a high-quality domestic product, but in the United States, BMW cars are prestigious luxury imports.

The company began in 1913, as an aircraft engine manufacturer and produced its first luxury car, the Dixi, in 1926.[14] Auto production ceased during World War II because the company was forced to build aircraft engines for the Luftwaffe, the German Air Force, instead. From 1956 to 1959, BMW made sports cars. In 1967, BMW introduced the sport sedan to the American drivers with the 1600, a two-door sedan called the "Bubbletop." Exports to the United States increased dramatically in the 1970s. From 1971 to 1975, the 3.0 CS coupe was marketed, offering luxury performance and smooth six-cylinder engines. In 1975, BMW introduced a midsize four-door sports sedan known as the 530i with a powerful six-cylinder engine. In 1976, the 3 series debuted as a compact sports sedan.

In the early 1990s, there were four BMW series of cars available to American drivers, each having its own line of models. The 3 series, made up of sedans, coupes, and convertibles, included the smallest cars and was the most affordable. The 5 series was the middle-line and included larger sedans and sports wagons. In 1991, BMW entered the exotic car market with the 8 series, introducing an exotic sports coupe known as the 850Ci. Large luxury sedan models followed in the 8 series. The cars ranged in price from about $25,000 for the 3 series to $85,000 for the 8 series. In June 1992, BMW announced plans to build an assembly factory in Spartanburg, South Carolina, in part to avoid the high cost of German labor. BMW also planned to enter the luxury small car market in 1996 with a subcompact model. This car would be less expensive and targeted for less affluent buyers.

■ Acura[15]

American Honda conceived of the Acura line during the recession of the early 1980s, when the luxury car market was one of the few to report continued healthy sales. American Honda decided to market Acuras separately to "build the snob appeal needed to sell luxury performance cars in the United States."[16] Creating the Acura brand allowed Honda to broaden its customer base without diluting its identity. Honda dealerships could continue to be associated with reliable, economical cars, whereas Acura dealerships, catering to a more affluent clientele, could benefit from Honda's reputation for quality. In 1986, Acura was born. Acura introduced two styles, the Legend and the Integra. The Legend sedan, selling for $20,000 in 1986, was intended to compete with cars made by German automakers BMW and Mercedes-Benz. Meanwhile, the Integra sports sedan gave customers a powerful engine but less elbow room and sold for between $9,300 and $11,800.

Acura quickly became the highest volume seller of imported luxury cars. By 1987 Acura surpassed its sales goal of 105,000, selling 109,470 cars. That year Acura sold more cars than BMW, Mercedes-Benz, Volvo, or Audi. Acura had a 3.5-year lead on other Japanese automakers in the luxury car market when Nissan Motor Corp. and Toyota Motor Corp. announced they would both enter upscale cars into the market in 1989. The introduction of Lexus and Infiniti caused the first dip in Acura sales, as Legend revenues dropped 8.7 percent from the previous year. To compete more effectively with new luxury vehicles, Acura introduced an updated Legend in 1990.

The second-generation Legend was completely redesigned to be larger and less angular. The body panels were made thicker, which made the Legend's chassis rigidity comparable to the Mercedes 300E and BMW 535i. To broaden sales, Acura developed a model between the Integra and the Legend called the Vigor. The five-cylinder Vigor was positioned in the near-luxury car market to capture consumers who wanted a more luxurious sports sedan but not the plushness of the Legend. The Vigor was the first car to offer digital sound processing, an eight-speaker system that can simulate six different environments, including a concert hall and a cathedral. In 1994, Acura announced that it would move part of its production process into the United States to avoid the losses due to the rising yen. Customer satisfaction has been one of Acura's most renowned traits and Acura's sales proved that Americans were willing to pay a premium price for Japanese cars. The success prompted Toyota Motor Corp. and Nissan Motor Corp. to enter the market.

■ Infiniti and Lexus

By late 1989, Nissan (Infiniti) and Toyota (Lexus) had entered the luxury car market. Toyota introduced the Lexus and Nissan produced the Infiniti. Introduced during the fall of 1990, Lexus quickly proved to be a formidable contender in the highly competitive American market. Within a year, it threatened the position of Honda Motor Company's Acura as the best-selling Japanese luxury car in the United States and outsold Infiniti two to one. Lexus had positioned its new line as an exclusive entry into the luxury car market, with sticker prices considerably below those of other luxury car makers.[17] According to a Lexus senior vice president, "without question we're going to get a share of the BMW and Mercedes buyers who have been priced out of the market."[18]

Both Infiniti and Lexus competed with other luxury car makers on price, and imitated designs from competitors instead of originating new designs. However, price and design were not the only things these car makers targeted. Beginning in early 1989, both companies started active advertising campaigns to promote their entry into the segment. Infiniti began with a very subtle advertisement, not showing the car until late 1989. The Lexus campaign touted their "relentless pursuit of perfection." Once in operation, both companies pushed for the best quality service. One Infiniti owner was ecstatic after having her oil changed. When she arrived at the dealer, they loaned her a new Q45. When she picked up her car the next day, the car had been cleaned, inside and out. To top off this complete package, as she was driving out of the parking lot, she noticed that her gas tank had been filled.[19] By competing on quality service as well as price, Lexus and Infiniti were able to differentiate their product from the rest of the luxury car makers. These factors enabled Lexus and Infiniti to show excellent sales, even in their first year.

Lexus faced a critical problem in early 1990. They had to recall a majority of their automobiles shortly after introduction. Although this would represent a serious problem for most companies, Lexus saw an opportunity. To rectify the situation, Lexus sent out its technicians to the homes of every owner to fix the minor problem. This display of service served only to strengthen their growth.[20]

Exhibit 7	Relevant Financial Performance										
	1993	1992	1991	1990	1989	1988	1987	1986	1985	1984	1983
Sales (DM million)	64,696	66,480	67,104	85,880	76,392	73,495	67,475	65,498	52,409	43,505	40,005
Net income	[1198]	849	1,872	1,684	1,700	1,675	1,787	1,805	1,735	1,145	1,034
Income as % of sales	−1.90%	1.30%	2.80%	2.20%	2.30%	2.60%	2.80%	3.30%	2.60%	2.60%	2.60%
Earnings per share	[25]	18	40	36	36	40	42	43	41	27	25

Source: Mercedes Benz annual reports and compact disclosure.

In the first eight months of 1989, Lexus and Infiniti had not sold one car, while Mercedes had sold 49,444 automobiles. Comparatively, in the first eight months of 1990, Lexus sold 40,146 cars and Infiniti sold 13,303. Mercedes-Benz, during this period, dropped slightly to sales of 48,991 vehicles. In its first full year of production, Lexus came close to outselling the premier automobile company in the world, namely, Mercedes. In the United States, the Japanese had moved from holding 1.9 percent of the luxury market segment in 1986 to 11.8 percent in 1990 (see Exhibit 4). By 1993, as Exhibit 5 shows, Lexus owned a 10.6 percent share, pushing Mercedes into seventh place with 6.9 percent, only slightly ahead of Nissan's Infiniti at 5.6 percent.[21]

The combined force of Lexus, Infiniti, and Acura, all introduced within a six-year period in the later 1980s, took a large percentage of Mercedes' German and BMW's American market share and severely threatened the position of American luxury cars such as Cadillac and Lincoln.

■ Current Situation

Throughout the 1980s, Mercedes-Benz's designers were motivated to create the best possible car without regard to cost. Model changes came slower for the company, often taking more than 10 years to accomplish. This strategy was effective through the mid-1980s because of little or no competition. However, the increased market pressure of the late 1980s forced Diamler-Benz to reevaluate its business strategy for Mercedes.

In 1990, Mercedes announced that it would introduce a "fundamentally new model" every year for the next five years.[22] In 1991, Mercedes introduced a new version of its 10-year-old, ultraluxury S Class automobile with the sticker price ranging from $70,000 to $130,000. In 1992, the midsized C Class was selected to replace the Mercedes 190 series.[23] In 1992, Mercedes sold about 63,300 automobiles in the United States—a marked drop from the 99,300 sold in 1986.[24] The bad news for Mercedes continued with 1993 operating losses of $790 million on sales of $40 billion.[25] (See Exhibit 7 for relevant financial performance.) In early 1994 Mercedes cut its prices up to 15 percent to spur sluggish sales for the year. Furthermore, by 1994, approximately 70,000 employees had been laid off from the peak of 400,000 in 1992.[26] However, these measures were not enough. According to Michael N. Basserman, president of MBNA, "Mercedes-Benz must go into different market segments of the vehicle market. That's because the traditional luxury segment has been stagnating in the U.S. while sales of sports-utility-vehicles, minivans, and pickup trucks have been skyrocketing."[27]

The most startling and risky news for Germans has been Daimler-Benz Chairman Edzard Rueter's plan to internationalize the car manufacturer. According to Edzard Rueter, Mercedes-Benz will not only expand its product line, but will move production facilities abroad to cut manufacturing costs.[28] Rueter will begin by hiring foreign managers into the Mercedes culture. Another aspect to Rueter's international plan is to extend manufacturing facilities abroad. The company is completing plans for car assembly plants in Mexico and the United States. This includes the sports utility vehicle plant in Alabama. Mercedes will begin production of a luxury minivan in Spain later this year. Mercedes has licensed the Asian production of its minivan to Sang Yong Motor Company of South Korea. As well as these locations, Werner, CEO for Mercedes-Benz, is considering Eastern Europe and other Asian locations. Germany remains the core of its production facilities, accounting for 43 percent of Mercedes' output.[29] However, high labor costs may force a larger part of the manufacturing to be relocated (see Exhibit 8).

Due to Edzard Rueter's and Helmut Werner's efforts, Mercedes-Benz appears to be regaining the lost market shares. In late 1994, the company reported increases in productivity of 21 percent resulting from cost cutting and higher volume due to the improved design. However, Werner is not yet satisfied and has plans to continue cutting costs. He intends to reduce costs by between 45 and 55 percent during the next few years to be competitive with the Japanese, who currently enjoy a 35 percent cost advantage over Mercedes. The company has also successfully lowered its research cycle to eight years.

The reduced cycle times and production costs were the core of the organizational changes for Mercedes. The next step for the company was to produce a product that could change the world view of Mercedes to a more value-oriented focus. Mercedes engineers had to produce an automobile that was world class in quality and value. The result was the new Mercedes C Class cars.

■ C Class

The C Class car was introduced in Europe in June 1992, and marketed in the United States in late 1993. The C Class replaced the 190 model. However, the new car is larger and better equipped, yet similarly priced. The C Class is intended to be a change of focus for the company, a change to a more value-oriented customer. Mercedes also emphasized environmental sensitivity by including such features as CFC-free air-conditioning and more efficient engines.

The C Class is a return to the leading edge of technology for Mercedes. The car possesses a certain engine that was not present in the smaller E Class. The design is more dignified and subtle. The wider body and the longer wheel base make it look more like the S Class (the top of the line Mercedes sedan, starting at $65,800), which is appealing to consumers. In almost every category from safety, performance, styling, handling, and fuel efficiency to comfort, the C Class is superior to the E Class, but is equally priced.[30]

The target market for the new Mercedes is 30- to 50-year-old individuals earning approximately $95,000. Most are expected to be young, married executives with an even mix of both men and women. The C Class has nine

Exhibit 8	Average 1993 Hourly Labor Costs in Manufacturing (in dollars)
Western Germany	$24.87
Japan	$16.91
United States	$16.40
France	$16.26
Britain	$12.37
Spain	$11.73
Taiwan	$ 5.46
South Korea	$ 4.93
Hong Kong	$ 4.21
Mexico	$ 2.41
Czech Republic	$ 1.14
Thailand	$ 0.71
Romania	$ 0.68
China	$ 0.54

Source: DRI McGraw-Hill; Morgan Stanley Research.

variations to appeal to a wide variety of customer tastes and lifestyles. The three major types of C Class cars are the Classic, Elegance, and Sport (each intended to appeal to a different market segment).[31]

The original C Class cars, introduced in 1993, came in two versions: the C220 and C280. The C220 sedan includes a 2.2-liter, 16-valve, in-line four-cylinder engine, which is able to produce 148 horsepower at 5,500 rpm. The car features antilock brakes, heated windshield wipers, air bags, and dual heated, electrically operated outside mirrors. This model has a base price of $30,950. The C280 is similarly equipped, but has a larger engine. The C280's in-line, six-cylinder, 2.8-liter engine has 24 valves and is capable of producing 194 horsepower at 5,500 rpm. The C280 starts at $36,300.[32]

The C Class strategy has worked well against Lexus and Infiniti. Mercedes experienced an 18 percent climb in sales in 1994, to 73,000 units sold in the United States. The U.S. sales were overwhelmingly led by the new car with almost 23,500 cars sold. Overall in 1994, Mercedes sold 585,000 vehicles, compared to less than 520,000 in 1993. The move to the C Class is a distinct strategy change for the company and is not seen as a defensive tactic to those at Mercedes. In fact, Mercedes executives see it as an offensive move. Werner said, "We are not retreating to the ivory tower of some mega-luxury class. We are attacking the Japanese niches with technically superior, customer-oriented products."[33]

■ A Class Car

Facing lackluster sales of its luxury cars in the United States, and environmentally aware and cost-conscious consumers, Mercedes set out to develop a small compact "city car" that would target the young urban consumer. It was designed to be smaller than anything currently on the roads, and was the answer for the older, smaller, and congested European city streets. Navigating these streets, as well as parking in tight spaces, would be the car's forte. Mercedes planned to market this car only in Europe, with possibly an electric version only to be sold in the United States. California's zero-emission mandates provide the incentive for the development of the electric version.

Because of the weak sales in its traditional luxury market, Mercedes has now decided to sell the non-electric-powered A Class cars in the United States beginning in 1997 or 1998. Although the car will be smaller than both the Chrysler Neon and the Volkswagen Golf, it will have the same interior space as the Mercedes C Class compact car. With four doors, a liftback, and room for four, it also boasts the Mercedes standards for safety. This is achieved by having the engine and the power train positioned below the passenger compartment, rather than in front. This also provides the driver with superior visibility. Priced just under $20,000, Mercedes expects to sell between 5,000 and 10,000 A Class cars in the United States.[34]

Mercedes was able to design the A Class engine and complete the all-aluminum block, which weighs only 40 pounds, in only 5 weeks, compared to the normal 40 to 50 weeks, by using the latest software and parts-building technologies. A first for Mercedes-Benz, the A Class will be a front-wheel-drive model, powered by either gas or diesel 16-valve four-cylinder engines, producing 115 and 90 horsepower, respectively. Fuel consumption estimates are around 50 miles per gallon. Top speed should be 125 mph, and the car should be able to register a 10-second 0–60 mph time. Aluminum will be used in many places, but cost considerations should dictate that the inner structure and body be made of steel.[35]

■ Swatchmobile

The "high-class" city car Swatchmobile is Mercedes' response to the slowing sales of luxury cars, and the increased purchases of specialty vehicles such as minivans, sports utility vehicles, and pickups. Mercedes has joined forces with Nicholas Hayek, who was responsible for the successful Swatch wristwatch, to design an even smaller city car than the A Class, dubbed by the media as the Swatchmobile. This microcompact car was originally designed for the European commuter. The car seats just two people, is only five feet wide, and just over eight feet long. The car will be priced at less than $10,000 but will have the safety and crash-worthiness of a Mercedes.[36]

The Swatchmobile concept will test whether Mercedes, with the style and manufacturing expertise of Swatch, will be able to combine style, strength, and affordability in a car while keeping a cap on the development and production costs of the car. Mercedes hopes to harness Hayek's creative abilities, as well as his "extraordinary gift for promotion." After his much publicized turnaround of the Swiss watch industry, analysts are looking to see if his abilities can be transferred to the automobile industry. "Calling cars an item, like watches, to which consumers become emotionally attached, he says he is a genius at exploiting that vulnerability."[37]

To keep production costs low, Mercedes has decided to produce the Swatch-mobile in France because of the lower labor costs (close to one-third lower than in Germany; see Exhibit 8). These savings will amount to approximately 500 marks ($318) per car. Mercedes' current plan is to build 200,000 units a year to sell throughout Europe beginning in 1998.[38] Critics are questioning whether the price, which is comparable to that of Volkswagen's and Renault's four-seaters, is low enough to warrant these kinds of sales predictions. Both VW and Renault have been successful in attacking the small car market, and have well-established distribution networks, and more than a few years experience. Even Volkswagen, which has this kind of small car experience, abandoned its planned cooperative efforts with Swatch.

■ Market Segments

In addition to the declining sales in the luxury car segment, particularly in the United States, Mercedes is responding to the increase in sales of specialty vehicles such as minivans, sports utility vehicles, and pickups by extending its product line. Mercedes is completing a plant in Alabama to produce its own sports utility vehicle and the Swatchmobile and A Class cars, addressing the "city car" segment. One of the reasons for entering these market segments is to increase sales volume. In 1995, Mercedes expects to increase sales from 70,000 to about 75,000 cars. An infusion of 5,000 to 10,000 units a year of the A Class cars in the United States in addition to what the company hopes to be much stronger European sales (for which it was originally designed) would boost sales significantly in a market where Mercedes comes only somewhat close with the C Class.[39]

Other reasons for entering the city car segment in the United States include California's zero-emissions mandate. The law will require that 2 percent of the vehicles sold by large automakers reach zero emissions (i.e., be electric) for the 1998 model year. By the 2003 model year, California will require 10 percent of all automakers' sales in their state be zero emissions.[40] The A Class electric version will address this requirement for Mercedes. This driving force toward efficiency is also prevalent in Europe where $4 per gallon of gasoline and high energy taxes are pushing consumers' preferences toward energy-efficient automobiles.

■ Conclusion

To achieve its goals in the small car market, Mercedes will be forced to balance cost constraints against revolutionary technologies and to weigh constraints and efficiency against the safety standards and performance synonymous with the Mercedes brand name. Mercedes' traditional image of heavy, safe, rear-wheel-drive luxury sedans with powerful engines and supreme engineering will be changed when Mercedes markets the intended line extension. The new generation of lighter, fuel-efficient, front-wheel-drive city cars that must come under a strict cost ceiling will cater to a market in which Mercedes has little or no experience. The impending question is whether or not entrance into these markets will increase Mercedes' market share and, if so, whether it will be at the expense of its long-standing reputation.

The stiffer competition from the Japanese in the luxury car segment has led to increasingly poor sales for Mercedes during the past several years and forced the firm to enter new market segments. Although Mercedes has no experience in the compact and city car industry, the company plans to attack these niche markets with the same dedication, quality, and technical superiority that served to make them the leader in luxury cars for several decades. Significant changes in the firm's cost structure, as well as new directions for meeting the market needs, are important strategic considerations. In attacking the compact and city car segments, Mercedes must consider the negative effects on its traditional, prestigious image.

■ Notes

1. The company history is excerpted from two main sources: Dean Boyer, 1994, Mercedes-Benz, *Encyclopedia of Consumer Brands,* Vol. 3, pp. 331–334; Thomas Derdak (Ed.), 1988, Mercedes-Benz, *International Directory of Company Histories,* p. 136.
2. Beverly Rae Kimes, 1986, *The Star and the Laurel* (New Jersey: Mercedes-Benz Publishing).
3. Autos—Autoparts, April 1994, *Industry Surveys,* A79.
4. Fara Warner, 1994, Marketing & media—advertising: Lexus, sales skidding 10%, hopes campaign can re-tool its identity, *Wall Street Journal,* November 14, B4.
5. Angelo B. Henderson, and Gabriella Stern, 1995, Producers of luxury autos still face a tough market, *Wall Street Journal,* June 29.
6. Greg Farrell, 1995, Where roads diverge, *Adweek* 136, no. 4: 24–34.
7. Richard Chase and Nicholas Aquilano, 1989, *Production and Operations Management,* Homewood, Ill.: (Irwin Publishing), 186.
8. Marc Beauchamp, 1988, Here they come again, *Forbes,* February 8, 76.
9. Ibid., 77.
10. Ibid., 76.
11. Information excerpted from Maura Troester, 1994, Cadillac, *Encyclopedia of Consumer Brands,* Vol. 3, pp. 56–60.
12. Information excerpted from Dorothy Kroll, 1994, Lincoln, *Encyclopedia of Consumer Brands,* Vol. 3, pp. 294–296.
13. Information excerpted from Dean Boyer, 1994, BMW, *Encyclopedia of Consumer Brands,* Vol. 3, pp. 40–42.
14. Thomas Derdak (Ed.), 1988, BMW, *International Directory of Company Histories,* p. 138.
15. Sara Pendergast, 1994, Acura, *Encyclopedia of Consumer Brands,* Vol. 3, pp. 1–4.
16. Stewart Toy, "The Selling of Acura—A Honda That's Not a Honda," *Business Week,* March 17, 1986, pg. 93.
17. Information excerpted from Maura Troester, 1994, Lexus, *Encyclopedia of Consumer Brands,* Vol. 3, pp. 292–293.
18. Ken Gross, 1990, First round to Lexus, *Automotive Industries,* June, 21.
19. Amy Barrett, 1988, After sales service: Infiniti, *Financial World,* April 14, 49.
20. Alex Taylor, 1990, Here come the hot new luxury cars, *Fortune,* July 2, 60.
21. It's tough at the top, 1994, *Asian Business,* May, 54.
22. Boyer, BMW, 334.
23. Ibid.
24. Ibid.

25. Robert L. Simison, 1994, Mercedes fans face a new landscape: Start thinking small; car maker plans to sell A Class in the U.S. in late 1990's, aiming to broaden line, *Wall Street Journal,* December 12, 8A.

26. John Templeman, 1992, Downshift at Daimler, *Business Week,* November 16, 48.

27. Simison, Mercedes fans face.

28. Mercedes-Benz, 1993, *Annual Report,* 10.

29. Ibid., 12.

30. Whose the most pampered motorist of all? 1991, *Business Week,* Industrial Edition, June 10, 109.

31. Raymond Serafin, 1990, Upscale stretching to Infiniti, *Automotive Marketing,* January.

32. Dealernet, World Wide Web Site.

33. *Annual Report,* 36.

34. Robert Simon, 1994, Mercedes face a new landscape, *Wall Street Journal,* December 12, 8A.

35. New Quickcast 1.1 now available to commercial markets, 1995, *PR Newswire,* February 3.

36. Kevin Helliker, 1994, Swiss movement, *Wall Street Journal,* May 4, 1A.

37. Ibid.

38. Ashley Seager, 1994, Swatchmobile faces tough road to profit, *Reuter European Business Report,* December 21.

39. David Lawder, 1994, Mercedes to bring A-Class small car to U.S., *Reuter European Business Report,* December 9.

40. Cacilie Rohwedder and Robert Simison, 1993, Electric cars stay on agenda in Europe, *Wall Street Journal,* February 1, B7.

■ CASE 26 The National Financial Planners Association

Raymond M. Kinnunen,
James F. Molloy, Jr.,
Northeastern University
John A. Seeger,
Bentley College

Dan Crosby, executive secretary of the National Financial Planners Association (NFPA), shook his head. It was clear he'd been taken for at least $100,000—maybe for two or three times that amount. The question was what to do about it.

Dan was assessing what he had learned about potentially incriminating practices by the management company that had served as "the office" of NFPA for more than a decade. Twelve years earlier, as volunteer president of the then-fledgling trade association, Crosby had hired Pamela Gardner, president and co-owner of Program Management, Inc. (PMI), to handle the administrative details of running NFPA. Looking back, Crosby commented:

> All the members and officers of the association held full-time jobs; we all contributed time to NFPA on a volunteer basis. Nobody had time to negotiate with hotels and suppliers, to arrange meetings outside New York.

> If NFPA was to grow into a meaningful organization, as all the officers wanted it to, it had to have professional administrative help. Somebody knew of Pam Gardner. I talked with the other associations she was arranging meetings for, and they were delighted with her work. So we found the help we needed. Now I wonder how much help it's been.

Originally presented at a meeting of the North American Case Research Association in November 1994. Management of NFPA cooperated in the field research for this case, which was written solely for the purpose of stimulating student discussion. All events and individuals are real, but names of the officers and "Program Management, Inc." have been changed at the organization's request. The association has been disguised and placed in the financial services industry.

NFPA Profile

NFPA was founded in New York in 1962 by a handful of sales executives associated with the insurance industry. In the beginning, NFPA was a small organization that was run informally by several members as a means of exchanging ideas and information. There were a president, vice president, and a secretary-treasurer who had all the records in cardboard boxes at his office. They did not meet frequently, but communicated with each other over the telephone. NFPA's secretary arranged all the meetings including the meals, the guest speaker, the hotel, promotion, and collection of the registration fees.

The mission of the association was to facilitate and promote leadership and innovation within the operations sector of the financial planning industry by:

1. Encouraging a free exchange of ideas among companies.
2. Developing improved methods and practices to meet current and future needs.
3. Advocating uniform procedures and standard practices to take advantage of telecommunications and applications technologies.
4. Providing a medium through which members could confer, consult, and cooperate with government, the public, and other industry groups.
5. Maintaining a high standard of ethical conduct while providing service to our members.

During small, informal dinner meetings, these charter NFPA members shared information and developed solutions to common operational problems. People from the mutual fund industry and financial planners began to join the original insurance industry members as word of their periodic meetings spread. The association grew slowly and in the 1970s began to organize regional meetings, where industry experts and leaders would gather to talk about current issues. As many as 100 people would attend a Boston meeting, while 250 might attend one in New York.

Association annual dues at the beginning were $25 per company regardless of the company size. The only membership rule was that the members be employed as financial planners. People with only partial or tangential involvement in the industry could become an associate (nonvoting) member by paying $15. As the financial industry began to grow, bringing with it new members, dues rose. By the mid-1980s dues for full membership had increased to $350 per year. At the same time, the rules for becoming a full member were relaxed and companies in other industries became involved. By 1992, with membership in NFPA approaching 250 member companies, dues reached $1,000 per year. The association's evolution was typical of many not-for-profit trade groups.

The Association Industry*

According to *National Trade and Professional Associations of the United States* (Columbia Books, 1990), a trade association was defined by the late C. Jay Judkins, chief of the Trade Association Division of the U.S. Department of Commerce as:

---

*Data in this section were drawn from *National Trade and Professional Associations of the United States,* Columbia Books, Inc., New York, 1990.

. . . a nonprofit, cooperative, voluntarily joined organization of business competitors designed to assist its members and its industry in dealing with mutual business problems in several of the following areas: accounting practice, business ethics, commercial and industrial research, standardization, statistics, trade promotion, and relations with Government, employees and the general public.

There have been three periods of pronounced growth in the number of U.S. national trade associations. The first occurred during World War I, as the number grew from about 100 associations in 1900 to more than 1,000 in 1920. The second period of growth occurred during the Depression in the 1930s, when the National Industrial Recovery Act of 1933 encouraged the formation of trade groups to help stimulate the economy. Some 800 new associations were formed under this law, although many disappeared when the Supreme Court in 1935 declared the law unconstitutional. The third period of growth occurred during World War II as companies had to share information in order to produce at peak efficiency. By 1943 there were about 1,900 trade groups; some closed in the years just after the war, but the total has risen gradually ever since.

Trade associations were formed by individuals who come together to solve, through concerted action, a problem they could not solve acting alone. An example was the standardization of time zones, which resulted from joint action by the nation's railroads. Trade associations promoted research on new products, new uses for by-products, and improved methods of manufacturing. They also provided training seminars, collected market or cost data in order to compile industry statistics, and published quality and certification standards. They often sponsored exhibits, contests, awards, and cooperative advertising.

Perhaps the most important function of trade associations was keeping members informed of governmental developments that could affect the industry and representing the industry viewpoint to governmental agencies. Virtually no major law passed through Congress or the state legislatures without some lobby or trade association having had a hand in the process.

In 1990, there were 3,400 national trade associations in the United States. The total number of national offices, their local chapters, and independent local or regional groups was estimated at around 40,000. According to the U.S. Department of Commerce, more than 35 percent of those were retail trade groups; about 20 percent represented services; and about 15 percent were in manufacturing. An example from the service sector was the American Society of Association Executives, with a membership of 20,000 paid employees of associations and societies. Founded in 1920 and renamed in 1956, by 1990 the association had a budget of $14.5 million. A 1984 survey of 170 not-for-profit groups in the District of Columbia/Maryland/Virginia area showed an average salary for top officers of associations at $98,500; the range was from $25,500 to $258,000. Staff size for associations varies from one person to several hundred. The usual staff size was 6 to 10 people.

A growing number of management companies handled operations for trade associations on a contract basis. In 1990 there were 264 such management firms operating in the United States, serving more than 500 national and 1,000 local or regional organizations. The typical large firm handled administrative work for a number of associations, providing a range of skills and services beyond the means of most small trade groups. To the volunteer officers of many trade associations, management companies presented a very attractive option for conducting their business.

Association revenues were derived primarily through members' dues. In most cases dues were based on a percentage of annual sales of the member company (usually ranging from 0.01 to 0.1 percent) or based on a flat fee. Associations typically had several classes of memberships, with different dues and privileges for each class. Associate members were vendors or suppliers of goods and services, with no voting rights. Only full members usually had the right to vote and hold office.

■ NFPA Growth

In the 1980s, the president and the board of directors had decided that in order to bring in more members, NFPA would have to expand the services it offered. They decided that the association should offer an annual conference in San Francisco in the month of February. The conference would offer panel discussions and workshops to all NFPA members, spread over an entire week.

President Dan Crosby realized that neither he nor any other officer had the time to put together all the details of a major out-of-town conference. He decided to hire an outside management company to run the event. After investigation, the board decided to retain the services of Program Management, Inc.

PMI employed three full-time staff, headed by Pamela Gardner, to take care of the records and organize the meetings for its eight other clients. Gardner, a poised and sophisticated Smith College graduate, had 12 years of experience managing other associations. NFPA agreed to pay PMI $5,000 per month or $60,000 a year plus expenses (copying, mailing, etc.) to organize and handle all the details of the annual meetings (hotels, meals, accommodations, audio visual equipment, etc.); to set up regional conferences and seminars and arrange board meetings; to create and send out notices to NFPA members about meetings and upcoming events; to develop an annual membership directory; and to collect member dues for deposit into NFPA's account. PMI negotiated terms for all meetings, conferences, and seminars and paid all the bills after being reimbursed by the association.

With a sigh of relief, Crosby and the NFPA secretary-treasurer carried their seven cartons of records into PMI's office. Henceforth, this would be the headquarters address of the National Financial Planners Association.

The first annual meeting under PMI's management took place in San Francisco in February 1982. Approximately 200 people—evenly split between exhibitors and members—attended, and the administrative details went smoothly. Although this first conference was not viewed as a huge success by NFPA's leaders, it showed that the association had a strong base for national expansion.

Between 1982 and 1988 NFPA's membership grew steadily and annual meetings and conferences attracted greatly increased attendance. Seeing great potential for growth, NFPA leaders recognized that the association needed to become more formal and better controlled. The association needed to ensure professionalism yet retain management control as it grew.

In 1988, Al Dugan, an officer of a large bank, became NFPA's president. As the first president who was not himself in the financial planning industry, Dugan brought a new perspective to the association's leadership. He was less concerned with organizational control than prior presidents had been. Dugan focused

---

Exhibit 1   NFPA Long-Range Planning Workshop, January 19–20, 1990

Objective

To identify strategic issues that will face NFPA in the early 1990s and to plan appropriate actions that will enable NFPA to reach its full potential in membership benefits.

Process

1. Examine the mission of NFPA in light of its stakeholders and specify modifications.
2. Recognize the opportunities and threats that will become manifest in the early 1990s.
3. In the context of item #2, identify the current strengths and weaknesses of NFPA.
4. Clarify the strategic issues of the early 1990s that must be addressed by NFPA.
5. Identify and evaluate alternative actions that address the strategic issues, then decide on an action plan.
6. Specify what resources are necessary, who has responsibility for specific actions, when those actions will be taken, what results will be seen, and how accountability will be established.

---

instead on a long-term strategy for the association. He decided to convene a two-day strategic planning seminar for NFPA leadership in 1991 (Exhibit 1).

The president invited approximately 30 members he thought would be active participants and contributors during the seminar and would be most likely to play an active role in implementing any changes. The seminar was conducted in a group format with two local consultants acting as facilitators. The two days resulted in consensus on a wide range of strategic issues and the commitment of many key people to specific actions.

At that point, the only people familiar with NFPA's inner workings were Pamela Gardner and the employees of PMI. They ensured that the association ran smoothly and professionally, and was financially sound. For 10 years, NFPA officers had been highly satisfied with conference arrangements, including meals, meeting rooms, lodging, etc.

PMI provided a monthly statement to the NFPA board of directors that included revenues, expenses, and the balance in the checking account. There was little detail in the reports, but NFPA's leaders could see the organization was struggling financially to provide its promised services. When asked about the apparent problem with cash flow, however, Gardner responded "Not to worry—everything will be fine. Compared to most trade associations, NFPA is in great shape."

■ Professional Management for NFPA

One result of the 1991 seminar was a decision to hire an executive secretary, who would be paid to work part time for the association to ensure that the association was being run in the best long-term interest of the members. Dan Crosby, past president of NFPA and still a regular (although nonvoting) participant at board meetings, was hired to fill this position.

Crosby, formerly a line manager of Metropolitan Life Insurance Company, was considered to be a hardnosed leader and an ideal executive secretary. He had served NFPA continuously for 15 years, and still consulted on the annual renewal of the PMI management contract. He held an MBA degree and taught courses in strategic management at a local university. Looking back at his accepting the job, Crosby commented on the time required for doing it:

> I told the board I would spend at the most 6 hours a day working; everybody knew that was all NFPA could afford. Actually, I would be there for 10, maybe 12 hours, but I'd only charge them for 6. The board would say, "don't charge us a lot." But at the same time, they would call and say "Dan will you do this? Would you do that?" Suddenly my hours were escalating because at the same time the association was growing, the board's involvement became greater and greater.

A Sense of Suspicion

One of Crosby's initial undertakings was to review the way PMI was managing the association's business. He watched all aspects of the 1992 conference in San Francisco. Because of his prior relationship with association members and Pamela Gardner, Dan could see how things were run at the conference without attracting attention. He saw some things that made him wonder, but nothing he could pinpoint. After returning from the 1992 conference, Dan learned from PMI's statement that the event had produced $300,000 of revenue from registration fees. This was offset by $298,000 in expenses. He commented,

> It just didn't make sense that our annual conference, with that kind of revenue, only had a surplus of $2,000. After spending a considerable amount of time probing and analyzing the situation, I could understand how the system worked. But that still didn't explain why it was so close to breakeven.

The limited profitability, if true, meant that NFPA needed to revise its policies, procedures, and records in order to improve cash levels. This led Dan to examine receipts and billings of recent New York meetings. For the big meetings in New York, the association would collect revenues of $30,000 to $35,000 and lose money. These meetings attracted 300 to 400 people at $80 per person for a one-day meeting. Because the association was losing money on these events, Dan asked to review expenses with Pamela. It was difficult, however, to schedule a meeting with her. Her other work interfered with efforts to prepare the special expense reports Dan requested. "Our office is set up to produce the routine reports automatically," Pamela said. "But special reports are something else. It's not ready yet, but will be soon."

When Crosby asked Pamela for a specific receipt, she responded, "It's around somewhere." When he sought assurance that PMI was bonded, she gave positive sounding answers. When asked again, Pamela said they "couldn't find the certificate and we're all looking for it." NFPA's annual audits, performed since the organization's inception by a Big Six firm whose managing partner had once served as association president, gave little help in understanding the situation. As with most small business and not-for-profit audits, the annual CPA letter included the passage:

> . . . All information included in these financial statements is the representation of the management of the National Financial Planners Association.

> A review consists principally of inquiries of company personnel and analytical procedures applied to financial data. It is substantially less in scope than an audit in

accordance with generally accepted auditing standards, the objective of which is the expression of an opinion regarding the financial statements taken as a whole. Accordingly, I do not express such an opinion.

Dan received the routine March reports from PMI, and still didn't like what he saw. His instincts told him something was wrong. "I am seeing numbers that don't make sense," he said, "and I am dealing with a woman who appears not to be in touch with reality". Even though Al Dugan, president of the association, was a close friend, Dan felt it was premature to convey his suspicions to Al.

In April 1992, Pamela visited Crosby and requested an advance check for $5,000 for expenses for the New York Hilton, in connection with the association's May meeting. Dan was perplexed because he was quite sure that advances had never been required in the past. He asked why she needed it. Pamela responded, "We have to give them [the Hilton] an advance. I tried to get around it. They may be in trouble. They told me that they need the advance within three days." Dan asked if she had spoken to the hotel's general manager. She said "yes."

> I said "fine." After the meeting, I picked up the phone and spoke to the president of Hilton Hotels, in Seattle, Washington. I said, "I need your assistance with a problem. Either the Hilton Corporation must be in serious trouble, or you are trying to blow customers away." He said, "Neither. We are in great shape and we want customers." I told him what had happened. He said, "That's strange. We don't normally require advances from good customers." He inquired how long NFPA had used Hilton. When I said six or seven years, he said, "stranger still. I'll call you back."

From Suspicion to Conviction

That night, while sitting in his office at the local university, Dan received a telephone call from the president of the Hilton. He had looked into the matter and said that the NFPA problem was not unusual. He asked Dan if a management company handled the association's business, and went on to say the hotel had asked for an advance because the association's last bill had not been paid for 120 days and even then, the check bounced. Dan couldn't believe what he was hearing. "I sign the checks myself. We pay in 10 days. I sometimes pay within a week because when a supplier performs a service for us I want them to get their money. I want NFPA to be known as a choice customer—one vendors will fight to keep." The Hilton president said, "this is not all that unusual, Mr. Crosby. We've been through cases like this before. Let me do this for you. Whatever you need, you let me know and I'll find it for you. My New York people are alerted to help; if there's anything more you need, call me."

After hanging up, Dan was on a mission. He pulled out all the PMI bills, to search again for an answer.

> It's 11:30 at night and I become an obsessed animal. I'm doing all kinds of reviews—looking and looking, and suddenly I realize these are Xerox copies of the bills. Where are the original copies of the bills? Why am I looking at Xeroxes? I approved a Xerox copy of a bill. We had all approved Xerox copies of bills, for twelve years. I said, "wait a minute. Wrong!" I called the Hilton at 11:30 at night and asked for accounting. The accounting manager wasn't in, of course, but the night manager told me he usually arrived by 7:00 A.M. and I should call back then.

The next morning at 7:00 A.M., Dan called the accounting manager at the New York Hilton. Dan discussed his problem and said he needed to see the original bills. The accounting manager told Dan, "Come on in. I'll even validate your parking. Sounds like you're in a rush."

During the meeting with the hotel accountant, Crosby found that the original invoice requested an advance of $2,000; Pamela Gardner asked him for $5,000. Crosby decided to investigate further by reviewing three years worth of bills for regional one-day meetings. At the Hilton he compared his checks to the original hotel bills. He found $35,000 in NFPA payment overcharges in the New York Hilton invoices alone. Back at home, working by telephone with the San Francisco Hilton on the 1992 annual meeting, he found $40,000 extra had been paid to PMI.

Crosby consulted the law firm that occasionally helped the NFPA, and learned that any accusations against Pamela Gardner or her firm would have to be handled with caution because a countersuit for defamation of character would be a likely response. Gardner might claim ignorance of any malfeasance: Perhaps some one of her employees was fiddling with the books. Filing suit against PMI would probably cost $50,000 to $75,000 in legal fees, and it might take several years to get a judgment. Even if a judgment was won in court, the association would still need to get the money back from Gardner and PMI.

Crosby felt the prospects of actually collecting anything from PMI were doubtful at best, because the firm had few apparent assets. He also felt that if PMI was siphoning money, it undoubtedly would not be left in PMI. This meant charges would have to be made against individuals, and it might be difficult to prove who in fact took the funds. For example, if Pamela Gardner were charged she could claim she knew nothing and it was the accountant who did it without her knowledge.

Another concern for Crosby was the other trade associations that were serviced and perhaps victimized by PMI and Pamela Gardner. Crosby considered another option—contacting PMI's other customers privately to suggest they be alert to potential fraud. He was unsure, however, of the risks associated with this option. It was very possible that this course of action might open NFPA and himself to a lawsuit for defamation of character. On the other hand, if he did nothing PMI could continue to practice fraud.

Criminal charges might also be a possibility, of course. The state's attorney general, or the city police, or the U.S. Postal Service mail fraud investigators might prosecute if it saw the case as attractive. The U.S. Postal Service, not NFPA, would be the accusers.

A fraud audit would also have to be conducted by an outside auditing firm, which would require studying every invoice received by NFPA over the past three to five years, identifying where it came from, what was done with it, and how it was paid by NFPA, and also contacting the vendor to verify the original bill amount and what actually had been received from PMI. The accounting cost alone was estimated to be between $25,000 and $35,000. Crosby estimated that PMI had diverted $100,000 to $200,000 from the association.

Armed with this information Crosby pondered the ramifications of his discovery. It was time to involve Al Dugan and the board of directors, but Dan was unsure what to recommend. He shook his head again. This was not what he'd expected when he took the NFPA job.

Novell: Expanding the Network

Janice Mills
Jeffrey Brown
Todd Kucker
Puu Subruangthong
Len Koster
Hyejoon Park

■ http://corp.novell.com/

Robert Frankenberg smiled to himself as Raymond Noorda walked out of his office in August 1994. It was another beautiful summer day in Provo and the two men had been discussing several items that had come up in the board meeting that week at Novell. Noorda was now on his way to the golf course that stretched out invitingly beside the company whose success was largely credited to Noorda's leadership during the past 11 years. Many industry experts had questioned whether Novell would survive without its dynamic, hands-on leader and the last few years had been full of speculation regarding possible successors. As late as March 1994, the *Wall Street Journal* had reported that "Novell is currently searching for a successor, but no obvious candidates have surfaced."[1]

Just two weeks later, in early April, 46-year-old Frankenberg had been tabbed as heir apparent to the world's leading network software company. After 25 years with Hewlett-Packard, Frankenberg brought broad experience in software, big information systems, and personal computing to his new position. At the August board meeting, Noorda had passed the chairmanship to Frankenberg with the comment, "In the four months since Bob joined Novell his perspective and leadership have given timely focus to the strengths of our increasingly diverse organization. The company is in good hands with Bob. . . ."[2] Now, as Frankenberg sat ensconced in his new office,[3] he knew that he would have to use all his acquired knowledge and then some to shape Novell's second decade and continue Novell's leadership position in the volatile industry.

With emphasis turning to the Information Superhighway, Frankenberg felt confident that the future of computing would be network based, which spelled numerous opportunities for Novell to expand its business. Still there were also numerous challenges he now faced as head of Novell—chief among these was

Prepared by graduate students under the supervision of Professor Robert E. Hoskisson, Department of Management, Texas A&M University.

how to quickly integrate Novell's recent purchases of WordPerfect Corporation and the spreadsheet business (Quattro Pro) of Borland International. Novell was also still struggling to absorb its 1993 acquisition of Unix Systems Laboratory. On every front, Novell seemed to be at a critical juncture, with Microsoft Corporation looming ominously on the horizon even in Novell's core networking business. Even though Noorda remained on the board of directors, Frankenberg realized that he was now in the driver's seat and the next few decisions he made would be critical in determining the company's course in the near and distant future.

Brief History of Novell

Based in Provo, Utah, Novell Data Systems originally produced computer terminals, printers, and other hardware components. Raymond J. Noorda, a 20-year veteran of General Electric, joined the company in 1983 when it was on the verge of collapse. Believing that "computer networks would one day link the world,"[4] Noorda ignored the skeptics and redirected the firm from hardware components into software products for networking DOS-based PCs. The company was incorporated as Novell, Inc., on January 25, 1983. Under Noorda's helm, the firm emerged from near bankruptcy in 1983 to become the world's leading networking company with $1.1 billion in sales in 1993. (See Exhibits 1 and 2 for selected financial data.)

Market Leader

Although the initial move to software was made to reverse the company's downward income trend, Novell's strategy soon became the most focused in the industry: build and broadly distribute network operating system (NOS) software. The company developed, marketed, and serviced specialized and general-purpose operating system products and application programming tools. Novell's first products focused on basic printer-and-file sharing capability; however, as revenues grew, Novell added functionality by spending aggressively on R&D and by purchasing small software companies that enhanced its own technology. By 1990, Novell had become the leader in group and department networks with an array of products under the name "NetWare" (see Exhibit 3). Novell's family of products provided matched software components for distributing information resources within local-area, wide-area, and internetworked information systems. By 1994, Novell commanded 72 percent of the overall networking market (see Exhibit 4) and sold its products domestically and internationally through 33 U.S. sales offices and 31 foreign offices.

Co-opetition

Novell's global leadership in the PC network software industry was largely attributed to Noorda, who not only changed the focus of the company from hardware to software, but also introduced the concept of "co-opetition" at Novell. Noorda stressed the need to cooperate with competitors and vendors in order to accelerate the growth of the network computing industry. This philosophy opened the door to many informal as well as formal partnerships with

Exhibit 1 Novell and WordPerfect Consolidated Balance Sheets (in thousands of dollars)

	WordPerfect Corporation			Novell, Inc.			Combined		
	4/30/94	12/31/93	12/31/92	4/30/94	10/31/93	10/31/92	4/30/94	FY1993	FY1992
ASSETS									
Current Assets									
Cash & Cash Equivalents	$ 51,194	$ 55,127	$ 86,569	$ 427,396	$ 328,469	$ 259,933	$ 478,590	$ 383,596	$ 346,502
Short-term Investments	–	–	–	502,158	335,601	285,327	502,158	335,601	285,327
Net Receivables	56,058	63,672	39,670	290,797	331,662	264,920	346,855	395,334	304,590
Other	93,566	86,404	29,078	72,460	56,474	55,805	166,026	142,878	84,883
Total Current Assets	$200,818	$205,203	$155,317	$1,292,811	$1,052,206	$ 865,985	$1,493,629	$1,257,409	$1,021,302
Property, Plant & Equipment	180,244	186,903	175,157	225,799	216,849	181,765	406,043	403,752	356,922
Other Assets	9,102	9,376	3,305	60,619	74,800	48,946	69,721	84,176	52,251
Total Assets	$390,164	$401,482	$333,779	$1,579,229	$1,343,855	$1,096,696	$1,969,393	$1,745,337	$1,430,475
LIABILITIES & SHAREHOLDERS' EQUITY									
Current Liabilities									
Notes Payable	$ 28,447	$ 8,640	$ –	$ 324	$ 796	$ 1,979	$ 28,771	$ 9,436	$ 1,979
Accounts Payable	21,618	37,472	37,448	34,033	37,998	33,198	55,651	75,470	70,646
Accrued Salaries & Wages	19,284	15,305	13,884	43,692	53,756	33,827	62,976	69,061	47,711
Accrued Marketing Liabilities	20,517	21,661	24,222	32,959	29,892	25,252	53,476	51,553	49,474
Other Accrued Liabilities	43,507	61,638	39,127	46,431	41,566	17,896	89,938	103,204	57,023
Income Taxes Payable	7,302	5,001	6,371	67,081	50,588	28,277	74,383	55,589	34,648
Deferred Revenue	33,038	17,949	23,230	16,152	15,839	9,523	49,190	33,788	32,753
Total Current Liabilities	$173,713	$167,666	$144,282	$ 240,672	$ 230,435	$ 149,952	$ 414,385	$ 398,101	$ 294,234
Deferred Income Taxes	–	–	–	11,711	–	–	11,711		
Long-term Debt	91,763	84,289	12,256	–	–	–	91,763	84,289	12,256
Minority Interests	–	–	–	12,759	10,205	8,938	12,759	10,205	8,938
Put Warrants	–	–	–	–	106,716	–	–	106,716	–
Shareholders' Equity									
Common Stock	5,138	5,138	5,138	31,060	30,805	30,064	36,198	35,943	35,202
Additional Paid-in Capital	74,189	74,189	74,189	545,963	411,064	306,420	620,152	485,253	380,609
Retained Earnings	46,490	73,313	97,056	739,964	562,238	601,078	786,454	635,551	698,134
Unearned Stock Compensation	–	–	–	(7,007)	(9,814)	–	(7,007)	(9,814)	–
Cumulative Translation Adjustment	(1,129)	(3,113)	858	4,107	2,206	244	2,978	(907)	1,102
Total Shareholders' Equity	$124,688	$149,527	$177,241	$1,314,087	$ 996,499	$ 937,806	1,436,775	1,146,026	1,115,047
Total Liabilities and Shareholders' Equity	$390,164	$401,482	$333,779	$1,579,229	$1,343,855	$1,096,696	$1,969,393	$1,745,337	$1,430,475

Exhibit 2 Novell and WordPerfect Consolidated Income Statements (in thousands of dollars)

	WordPerfect Corporation			Novell, Inc			Combined		
	Six mos. ended 4/30/94	FY 1993	FY 1992	Six mos. ended 4/30/94	FY 1993	FY 1992	Six mos. ended 4/30/94	FY 1993	FY 1992
Net Sales	$305,233	$707,515	$579,118	$717,975	$1,122,896	$933,370	$1,023,208	$1,830,411	$1,512,488
Cost of Sales	77,173	178,071	142,531	172,001	224,531	184,176	249,174	402,602	326,707
Gross Profit	$228,060	$529,444	$436,587	$545,974	$898,365	$749,194	$774,034	$1,427,809	$1,185,781
Operating Expenses									
Sales & Marketing	111,429	254,064	148,209	141,452	258,658	219,399	252,881	509,722	367,608
Product Development	56,110	125,379	100,168	110,350	164,860	120,849	166,460	290,239	221,017
General & Administrative	41,009	83,127	67,602	45,382	80,122	52,084	86,391	163,249	119,686
Nonrecurring Charges	14,969	36,001	46,324	—	320,500	—	14,969	356,501	49,324
Total Operating Expenses	$223,517	$498,571	$362,303	$297,184	$824,140	$392,332	$520,701	$1,319,711	$757,635
Income from Operations	$ 4,543	$ 33,873	$ 71,284	$248,790	$ 74,225	$356,862	$ 253,333	$ 108,098	$ 428,146
Other Income									
Investment Income	—	—	13,205	18,861	28,131	21,340	18,861	28,131	34,545
Other, Net	(545)	236	—	(394)	1,692	(884)	(939)	1,928	(884)
Total Other Income	$ (545)	$ 236	$ 13,205	$ 18,467	$ 29,823	$ 20,456	$ 17,922	$ 30,059	$ 33,661
Income before Taxes	$ 3,998	$ 34,109	$ 84,489	$267,257	$104,048	$377,318	$ 271,255	$ 138,157	$ 461,807
Income Taxes	(9,100)	(41,771)	11,541	89,531	139,208	128,288	80,431	97,437	139,829
Net Income	$ 13,098	$ 75,880	$ 72,948	$177,726	$ (35,160)	$249,030	$ 190,824	$ 40,720	$ 321,978
Wtd. Avg. Shares Outstanding	54,125	53,491	51,380	314,154	314,409	308,104	368,279	367,900	359,484
Net Income per Share	$ 0.24	$ 1.42	$ 1.42	$ 0.57	$ (0.11)	$ 0.81	$ 0.52	$ 0.11	$ 0.90

Exhibit 3	NetWare Major Products	
Product	**Market Segment**	**Number of Users**
NetWare 4.01	Enterprise	Up to 1,000 each server
NetWare 3	Group Department	5, 10, 20, 50, 100, 250
NetWare 2.2	Group	2–10
NetWare Lite 1.1	Group	2

NetWare products also include operating system products, network services products, communications products, internetworking products, UNIX connectivity products, network management products, and NetWare development tools.

Source: *Novell Products and Program Guide*, 1994.

Exhibit 4

Network Software Market Share

Source: Novell advertising copy, *Wall Street Journal*, September 1994.

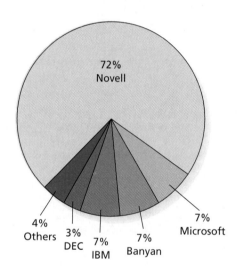

competitors over the years. While advocating cooperation, Noorda nevertheless emphasized competition as the chief motivator to keep employees on their toes and to make the whole company better.

■ Building the Industry

To stay ahead of the competition and to provide "responsible leadership" in the industry, Novell made investments in some technology companies while acquiring others in order to maintain the leading edge technologies necessary to keep the company at the forefront of the industry.[5] The WordPerfect and Quattro Pro deals brought the number of Novell's acquisitions to 15 between the fall of 1986 and the spring of 1994. Novell issued common stock or paid cash for each acquisition, invested cash in other technology companies, and formed several strategic alliances with still further companies (see Exhibit 5). According to Novell's 1993 annual report, these transactions were undertaken to "promote the growth of the network computing industry, and . . . also broaden the Company's business as a system software supplier."[6]

Exhibit 5   Novell's Acquisitions, Joint Ventures, and Investments

ACQUISITIONS			Fair Market Value at Date of Acquisition (in thousands of dollars)
6/94	WordPerfect Corporation, Orem, UT	Applications software	$855,000
6/94	Quattro Pro, Scotts Valley, CA	Spreadsheet application	$125,000
7/93	Fluent Inc., Natick, MA	Multimedia for networks	$17,500
6/93	Software Transformation, Inc., Cupertino, CA	Programming tools for cross platforms	$21,800
6/93	Serius Corp, Salt Lake City, UT	Object-based tools	$17,250
6/93	Univel, San Jose, CA	Developer of UnixWare	Not Disclosed
6/93	Unix System Laboratories, Summit, NJ	Developer of UNIX	$321,900
6/92	Annatok Systems, Inc., Boulder, CO	Developer of automated software distribution services	$10,000
4/92	International Business Software, Ltd., Sunnyvale, CA	Developer of virtual server	$5,200
10/91	Digital Research, Inc., Monterey, CA	Developer of operating system, including DR DOS	$135,750
10/90	Indisy Software, Inc., Toronto	IBM host messaging	Not Disclosed
6/89	Excelan, Inc., San Jose, CA	UNIX, Apple, and Stds-based networking	$155,620
3/87	Softcraft, Inc., Austin, TX	Developer of database and programming tool software	$5,346
3/87	CXI, Inc., Sunnyvale, CA	Developer of LAN-to-host systems	$34,879
10/86	Santa Clara Systems, Inc., Mt. View, CA	Manufacturing of storage subsystems	$4,068

JOINT VENTURES		% Novell Ownership		Joint Venture Partners
10/92	Onward Novell Software India PVT Ltd., Bombay	50%	NetWare Products in India	Onward Technologies
4/90	Novell Japan, Ltd., Tokyo	63%	Kanji-based NetWare products	Canon, Fujitsu, NEC, Sony, Toshiba, and Softbank

INVESTMENTS IN TECHNOLOGY			Investment (in thousands of dollars)
1/93	Beyond Inc., Cambridge, MA	Workgroup applications and messaging software	Not disclosed
1/93	HyperDesk, Westborough, MA	Object-based services interface	Not disclosed
11/92	Reach Software Co., Sunnyvale, CA	Workflow automation software	Not disclosed
12/91	Serius Corp., Salt Lake City, UT	Object-based applications tools	Not disclosed
12/91	Co-op Solutions, Inc., Summit, NJ	On-line transaction processing	Not disclosed
7/91	DaVinci Systems Corp., Raleigh, NC	Messaging software and Windows front- ends	Not disclosed
4/91	Unix System Labs., Summit, NJ	Developer of UNIX	$14,950
4/90	Gupta Technologies, Inc., Menlo Park, CA	SQL database, Windows front-ends, and IBM DB2 gateway technology	$10,359
6/88	Dayna Comm., Inc., Salt Lake, UT	Macintosh connectivity software	Not disclosed

Source: Novell, June 1994.

■ Alliances

Novell had been able to forge successful alliances with many software companies through the years and Noorda had been viewed as a grandfatherly figure in the industry. Most software companies felt safer sharing technical information with Novell than with Microsoft because Noorda had forsworn getting into the applications business. Now, with the purchases of two strong applications, many analysts questioned whether Novell had "compromised its position as the neutral 'Switzerland' of the industry."[7]

■ The WordPerfect and Quattro Pro Acquisitions

In March 1994, when Novell announced that it would acquire WordPerfect Corporation and the spreadsheet business (Quattro Pro) of Borland International, most analysts wondered aloud if Novell had made a serious misstep. Although the acquisitions vaulted Novell into the position of third largest software company (behind Microsoft Corporation, which focused on microcomputer/PC software, and Computer Associates, which sold mainframe software) and second largest PC applications company (behind Microsoft), Novell's projected revenues were still less than half of Microsoft's projected revenues (see Exhibit 6). Novell exchanged 59 million shares of stock (valued at $855 million) for WordPerfect and paid $125 million in cash for Quattro Pro. Critics were quick to say that the acquisitions amounted to "overpaying for damaged goods."[8] After enjoying many years as the leader in the word processing market, WordPerfect had slipped to number two behind Microsoft's Word. Quattro Pro was a very distant third (8 percent) in the spreadsheet market behind Microsoft's Excel (48 percent) and Lotus Corporation's 1-2-3 (42 percent). Novell had outbid Lotus for the WordPerfect acquisition.

Exhibit 6

Projected Revenues for Novell and Microsoft

Source: Value Line.

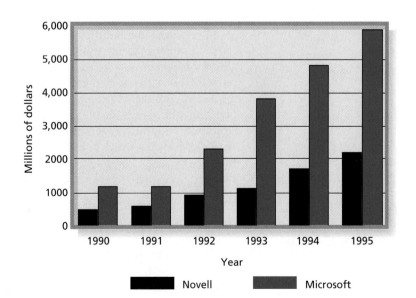

■ Reactions

Heidi Dix, a software strategy analyst at Forrester Research, Inc., in Cambridge, Massachusetts, made the point that "Novell is eating something larger than its head. They are investing in too many companies and not doing enough with the ones they have."[9] The acquisitions resulted in a net loss for the company's second quarter with another loss anticipated in the third quarter due to restructuring charges associated with the acquisitions. Still others questioned whether Novell had become too obsessed with attacking Microsoft by trying to match Microsoft's diversity while losing sight of their core networking business. Wall Street, too, seemed to echo these doubts as Novell's stock price slipped 25 percent in the days immediately following the announcement of the acquisitions on March 22 (from $23.75 on March 22 to $20 on March 23, sinking to $16.875 by April 4). Exhibit 7 summarizes Novell's stock trading range over the company's last 11 quarters.

■ Novell's Response

Novell executives countered that the acquisitions were a logical step in their overall networking strategy. Terri Holbrooke, Novell vice president for corporate communications, said, "the basic premise for the merger" was creating 'networked applications' which would build on the strengths of Novell's network products and WordPerfect's desktop applications so computer users in different locations could work together more easily."[10] Soon after the acquisitions were completed, Novell announced that it would launch a suite of software products called PerfectOffice.

Novell's vow to deliver true networked applications was seen as promising by many customers. Others praised the potential for consolidated network and desktop application support. WordPerfect had a strong customer support program in place, which had been a weak area for Novell. Many observers saw significant cross-marketing possibilities in the merger although Novell had been criticized for ". . . failing to convey a clear corporate vision"[11] in its advertising. Novell had never depended heavily on advertising and some thought Novell could benefit from WordPerfect's more aggressive communication strategy.

In addition, the cultures of the two Utah companies were very similar with both companies being run largely by members of the Mormon church. The Mormon influence stressed business ethics and a strong work and family ethic, which Noorda had promoted during his tenure at Novell. Frankenberg was also affiliated with the Mormon church. The relative ease of blending similar cultures was thought to be a big plus in speeding the merger process and, from the human resources end, the merger appeared to be a good fit. In a fast-paced industry that was experiencing much consolidation, this was thought to be a large advantage.

■ The Computer Software Industry

In the 1980s and 1990s, the computer software industry continued to be one of the fastest growing segments of the overall computer industry. Product development and sales were often tied to the technological growth and innovation in the computer hardware industry. As a result, fierce competition for market share emerged among the numerous companies. Many firms marketed only a single product or service. This had begun to change in the early 1990s as more narrow

Exhibit 7

Novell's Stock-Trading Range, 1992–1994

Source: Novell Report to Shareholders, Third Quarter 1994.

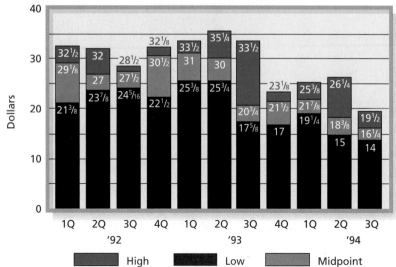

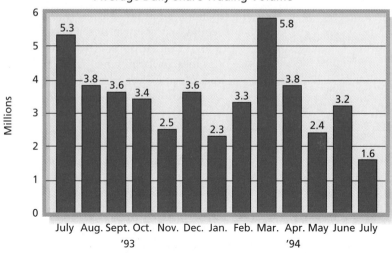

gross margins forced many companies to consolidate for financial reasons. The volatility of the industry marked by rapid technological change also put smaller companies at a severe disadvantage because they lacked the resources to compete. The increasing dominance of Microsoft Corporation in all areas of the software industry also fueled the trend toward massive consolidation within the industry. The industry was also characterized by frequent litigation regarding copyright, patent, and other intellectual property rights. Technical expertise was highly sought and competition for qualified personnel was intense among all companies.

■ Networking Software

Novell competed in the smaller networking software segment of the computer software industry. In the beginning, many firms had developed and sold peer-to-peer products to connect IBM-compatible PCs. Increasing customer demand for more complex products, distribution channel problems, and fierce competition had reduced the market to a mere handful of major competitors by 1994: Novell, Banyan, Microsoft, and IBM. Of these, Novell had the lion's share of the market with 72 percent in 1994, but Microsoft and other competitors had begun to be a serious threat. In 1991, Microsoft had targeted the network operating system segment and began spending approximately $50 million a year to catch up to Novell. Microsoft CEO William Gates declared at the time that he was ready to "weather losses for as long as it took to win."[12] Microsoft's growing dominance in all sectors of the software business was seen as increasingly problematic to Novell.

■ Market Segments

Network software suppliers identified three major market segments: group (small groups of users, typically fewer than 10 PCs), department (networks serving up to 100 or more users), and enterprise (networks connecting departments and groups throughout an organization and often across wide geographical areas). Although an organization might contain customers in each segment, the needs of each segment were different and the products that had been designed to fulfill those needs each represented significantly different complexity and price (see Exhibits 3 and 4). Novell was the leader in two of the three segments, lagging behind only Banyan in the enterprise segment.

By 1994, Novell's growth had slowed considerably, however, and Novell faced a unique problem when its customers showed stubborn reluctance to adopt the upgrade of one of Novell's flagship products. Even customers who acknowledged the superiority of the upgrade grumbled that Novell "could've made it (the transition) smoother."[13] Other competitive factors Novell identified in the market for network operating systems included hardware independence and compatibility, the availability of software applications for any given network operating system, system performance, customer service and support, reliability, ease of use, price/performance, and connectivity with minicomputer and mainframe hosts. The key elements of Novell's overall business strategy (see Exhibit 8) were designed to address these specific competitive factors.

■ Competitors

■ Microsoft Corporation

The biggest threat to Novell's future success in the software industry was Microsoft. By concentrating on developing software to run on microcomputers, Microsoft had grown exponentially from its inception in 1975 to become a $5-billion-a-year business in 1993. Microsoft's founder, 38-year-old Bill Gates, was by virtue of his 40 percent stake in the company the youngest billionaire in the world. Microsoft's success was fostered by MS-DOS, the *de facto* operating system standard for PC compatibles during the early and mid-1980s. The firm introduced the Windows graphical operating system in the late 1980s. This product, in conjunction with MS-DOS, gave Microsoft a presence on approximately 120 million computers worldwide in 1993. In comparison, IBM had only three million OS/2 users.

Exhibit 8   Key Elements of Novell's Business Strategy

To meet the needs of its customers, over the past year Novell has embarked on a strategy to combine the industry's most proven network operating system with the industry's most proven application platform—UNIX. This "matched pair" combines the best network services with the best application services to deliver to customers the best computing platform on which to run their businesses. These strong operating systems combine with Novell's innovative client/server application platform to deliver a total system software solution.

Novell's mission is to accelerate the growth of the network computing industry through responsible leadership. The Company accomplishes this by delivering an overall networking environment which includes industry leading product technology, programs, and partnerships. The key elements of the Company's overall business strategy are:

Technological Leadership.

Integration Platform.   Novell's NetWare network operating system provides a platform for the integration of multiple technologies. This includes the seamless integration of multiple desktop systems and host environments. Novell believes that the customer environments are inherently heterogeneous and therefore require an information system that integrates dissimilar technologies. The goal of Novell's strategy of integrating various desktop systems is to allow IBM and IBM-compatible, Apple Macintosh, and UNIX-based PCs and workstations to access and share simultaneously a common set of network resources and information. This gives customers the freedom to choose the desktop and application server systems that best fit their application requirements. In addition to the integration of desktops, host environments from vendors such as IBM, DEC, H-P, and Olivetti are integrated into the NetWare network so that users can access host-based resources and information from their desktops across the network. Novell continues to extend this hardware and infrastructure integration to other communication devices such as PBXs and imbedded systems such as cash registers and process control devices. The overall objective is to seamlessly connect users by shielding them from the underlying network technology used to share resources and information across heterogenous systems.

Network Services.   Novell delivers advanced network services on top of the integration platform. These services enhance the functionality available to users on the network. In the first release of NetWare eleven years ago, those services were file and print only. While Novell has continued to enhance NetWare file and print services, the services provided by Novell and third parties have expanded significantly to include communications, network and systems management, messaging, directory, software licensing and distribution, imaging and document management, and telephony services. Novell continues to add network services through internal development efforts, partnerships, and acquisitions.

Application Framework: AppWare.   In addition to the programming interfaces that Novell provides for application developers, Novell has begun delivering AppWare—a set of development tools that significantly eases the development of true client/server applications. AppWare allows application developers and internal IS development teams to deliver distributed applications that integrate and take advantage of all of the network services available in NetWare and UnixWare.

Directory Services.   With the introduction of NetWare 4 in March 1993, Novell began to deliver an industry leading distributed naming service—NetWare Directory Services (NDS). NDS allows administrators and users to view the information and resources on the network in a simple and integrated way. It provides for one common view of the network rather than having to track resources by knowing on which server the resource resides. NDS allows the user to login once into the network and access information and resources independent of physical location. While this simplifies both the administration and use of the network, NDS also improves the security of network information with the use of encryption technology. The NetWare Directory Service will continue to become the centerpiece of network services and client/server applications for the next several years.

Source: Novell, 1993, Form 10-K.

Broad Product Line

While Microsoft dominated the operating system market for PCs, the firm was noted for its broad product line, claiming 43.6 percent of the $8.3 billion PC software market in 1993. The firm developed products that were the leaders or front-runners in their respective product lines. Products such as Word (word processing), Excel (spreadsheet), and Powerpoint (presentation software) were very popular among Windows users. These programs all shared similar graphic interfaces that made learning a new program relatively simple to an experienced Microsoft user.

In the last year, Microsoft had formed a Consumer Products Division specifically targeting the growing home computer market, significantly increased its advertising and R&D budgets, and entered into a number of joint ventures with other companies in the areas of wireless communications, interactive television, and other leading edge technologies. Microsoft was a relatively late entrant in the networking software field; however, the company had determined that network software and client-server applications were vital to its strategy of establishing the standards for the overall PC software industry.

Application Suites

In the early 1990s, Microsoft began combining (or "bundling") programs (Word, Excel, Microsoft Mail, and PowerPoint) together into a product called Microsoft Office. The introduction of Office ushered in a new type of software called application suites. Office extended the similar look and feel of the core software it contained to include greatly improved interaction between the programs. Office users could combine sections created with any of the different programs into one document. Links between programs were made possible by what is called object linking and embedding (OLE). OLE allows users to edit objects in place, without having to quit one application and start the application in which the object was created. With OLE, when a user working with a Word document clicked on a graph created in Excel, Excel would open and the user could make changes to the graph.

The evident popularity of Office with PC users was easily explained. Microsoft offered all of the core software that a home or small-office user needed in a package that was discounted some 40 to 50 percent off the prices of the stand-alone applications. Microsoft was also working on creating a standard called "Microsoft Office Compatible" that would let programmers create small add-in packages to complement the Office suite. If this strategy proved successful, Microsoft could effectively lock out producers of stand-alone business software, and create what would amount to an "office operating system."

Network Strategy

Although Microsoft's LAN Manager had failed to make a serious dent in Novell's lead, Microsoft was actively pursuing an additional plan of attack by incorporating the network operating system into the desktop operating system. Microsoft's Windows for Workgroups had built-in peer-to-peer networking and Windows NT had both client and server software for LAN Manager built into it at no additional cost to the consumer. Microsoft's intentions to build networking software into its next Windows upgrade (Windows 95) would effectively eliminate the need for a separate network operating system such as NetWare.

Litigation and Antitrust Questions

Known for its aggressive marketing tactics, Microsoft had been under investigation by the FTC for alleged anticompetitive practices for much of the 1990s. In July 1994, the U.S. Justice Department had ended its investigation with no more than a slap on the wrist to Microsoft. Microsoft had also been able to rack up significant gains in the first two quarters of 1994 despite having to take a $120 million charge in the second quarter for a lost patent infringement lawsuit by another software company. Novell was acutely aware of Microsoft's power, stating that ". . . (Novell) does not have the product breadth or market power of Microsoft. Microsoft's dominant position provides it with enormous competitive advantages including the ability to unilaterally determine the direction of future operating systems and to leverage its strength in one or more product areas to achieve a dominant position in new markets."[14]

■ Lotus Development Corporation

Lotus was another veteran in the microcomputer software industry. The company had single-handedly started the PC explosion in the early 1980s with the introduction of Lotus 1-2-3, a spreadsheet program. Lotus 1-2-3 brought powerful accounting software applications to the PC that previously had been available only for minicomputers or mainframes. The program also introduced an ease of use that had been unheard of in mainframe accounting software packages. After the success of 1-2-3, Lotus branched out to offer a word processor (Ami Pro), a database (Approach), and a presentation package (Freelance Graphics).

Failed Merger

In the spring of 1990, Lotus and Novell announced a tentative merger that took the rest of the industry by surprise. After six weeks of discussions, the negotiations broke down when Noorda insisted that the merged entity split its board of directors with four representatives from each company. Lotus maintained that the two companies had agreed to a board that would have favored Lotus by a split of 4–3. The two companies continued to do business with each other despite some "hard feelings," which were quoted in the press immediately following the end of merger talks.

SmartSuite and Lotus Notes

Noting the popularity of Microsoft Office, Lotus decided that they should offer a suite of their own. In 1992, the firm introduced SmartSuite, which combined Lotus 1-2-3, Ami Pro, Approach, and Freelance Graphics into one package. Like Microsoft Office, SmartSuite offered users enhanced interaction between programs, and a similar look and feel between programs. Lotus decided to adopt the OLE standard advanced by Microsoft to help their programs work together better. While Lotus had the potential to gain market share with SmartSuite due to the loyalty of millions of 1-2-3 users, its late entry into the market had left them (in mid-1994) with a relatively meager portion of the suite market (Microsoft had roughly 80 percent of the Windows market). However, Lotus had the potential to combine SmartSuite with its very popular network communication software, Lotus Notes, to create a network-friendly suite. Microsoft had largely neglected this aspect of the market, and Lotus could effectively increase market share with successful integration of these two products.

■ Banyan Systems

Formed in 1983, Banyan developed a network operating system based on UNIX that enabled different types of computers running different operating systems to be connected to local-area and wide-area networks. Banyan was the undisputed leader in enterprisewide networks although both Microsoft and Novell were seen to be making some gains in this area by developing their own products to mimic Banyan's successful "Vines" software. In 1990, Banyan suffered a blow when it lost its chief technologist to Microsoft.

That same year, CEO David Mahoney summed up the difference between Banyan and Novell: "We address the needs of the corporate office . . . we solve problems with a skilled and direct presence at the customer."[15] Banyan emphasized its highly skilled and experienced representatives who met directly with corporate MIS managers with sales completed through 150 resellers. While the selling cycle often was in excess of 12 months, Banyan received on average $8,000 per copy of Vines while Novell received only an average of $1,000 per copy of NetWare, which was distributed through 12,000 resellers.

■ IBM

Long known for its customer service, IBM offered PC networking software to customers and distributors as part of its PC hardware and software product line. IBM's chief network products in 1990 relied on Microsoft technology and were distributed under the name LAN Manager and LAN Server. Then in 1991, IBM and Novell announced an agreement whereby IBM would support Novell's PC network software, surprising Microsoft, which had been its traditional software partner.

■ Products

The idea to connect computers together originally got its start when it was seen that it was much cheaper for a group of computers to use one printer. For as little as $200 per computer, 10 or more users could share one $10,000 printer. Eventually users began to see other benefits from networking such as sharing software or files among different computers. Novell used its position as market leader to point out these benefits in its advertising.

The economies of networking software were similar to other segments of the software industry. Vendors usually experienced huge upfront R&D expenditures. After these sunk costs, production costs were negligible so software programs usually generated gross margins of close to 80 percent.

Novell's products were grouped into three operating groups: NetWare Systems Group (NSG), UNIX Systems Group (USG), and AppWare Systems Group (ASG). NetWare products accounted for 75 percent of Novell's revenues in 1993, but the latest version of NetWare had not been selling well and most observers felt Novell should concentrate on improving NetWare's features.[16] Novell's separation of its UNIX (operating system) products into a separate group was seen by some as evidence that Novell had not fully committed to its 1993 acquisition. Jamie Lewis of the Burton Group said, "Novell is treating Unix as a side bet" and Novell's handling of Unix "reflects a confused strategy about operating systems."[17] In March, 1994, Sun Microsystems had bought a permanent UNIX license from Novell for $83 million—getting essentially the same access to the software for which Novell had paid $350 million.[18]

■ Distribution

To distribute its products in the United States, Novell relied on 12,000 resellers of various types [original equipment manufacturers (OEMs), distributors, value-added resellers, systems integrators, and major end users]. Novell owed much of its success to its broad product line and distribution. Novell's traditional weakness had been its distribution to the corporate segment. Its strategy of relying on resellers made it difficult to sell more advanced networks inside larger companies. End users of all products often felt that Novell did not offer sufficient post-purchase support. Because of reseller and customer complaints, Novell had instituted a program in 1990 to classify the resellers into five categories with the highest skilled resellers in the Platinum group. While this directed customers to the most skilled resellers, it did not reduce distributors' complaints because resellers received little benefit from the status designation.

Export Sales

Export sales had increased during the last three years from 44 percent of net sales in 1991 to 48 percent in 1993. International customers were primarily distributors and no one country (except for Germany's 11 percent in 1993) accounted for more than 10 percent of net sales in any period. Export sales were expected to reach 50 percent by 1995.

Suppliers

Novell, like most other software companies, faced intense competition for highly skilled programmers. The company followed the industry lead in offering an attractive salary/stock option plan to attract and retain employees with the desired expertise. Once developed, Novell's products (primarily software diskettes and manuals) were duplicated by outside vendors to minimize the company's need for expensive capital equipment.

Opportunities

The business community was rapidly climbing onto the network "train" in 1994. Both *Business Week* and *Fortune* magazines had featured several issues dealing with the proliferation of network technology and how it was changing the way companies did business in the 1990s and suggesting that non-networked companies would be left behind in the dust. The global computer network market was expanding in 1994 with only 60 percent of all computers networked in the United States. Foreign markets reflected even greater potential with only 50 percent of all computers networked in Europe and only 11 percent of the computers in Japan were linked in 1994. The competition for these new and expanding global network markets was expected to be intense, but Novell had the market leader advantage and the merging of the Novell and WordPerfect marketing teams had increased Novell's presence in eight additional countries and significantly increased its presence in Eastern Europe.

The acquisitions of WordPerfect and Quattro Pro provided the opportunity to Novell to offer its own application suite, PerfectOffice. The combined companies of WordPerfect and Novell also provided Novell everything it needed to compete effectively in the enterprise market: applications, tools, network services, and operating systems. Novell felt it could differentiate its products from its competitors by "wedding" networking services with stand-alone applications. Critical to this combination was the need to make applications with the capability to access network services with great ease. Novell envisioned the creation of intelligent agents that would retrieve and organize E-mail and faxes and infrared connection of notebook computers to the network. Users would have unlimited, instant access to information, which Novell termed "pervasive computing." To achieve this aim, Novell felt that the network, not the operating system or application, was the point of convergence for all users. The key points of the pervasive computing model would include the infrastructure, access, and applications.

■ Infrastructure

Novell felt the infrastructure of the pervasive computing model would be provided by two of its core products, NetWare and UNIX. With more than 40 million users, NetWare was the most popular network operating system in the world. NetWare provided users the ability to link 2 to 250 computers to shared file servers and printers. With the acquisition of UNIX, Novell gained an inroad to larger computers. UNIX ran on 30 million computers worldwide on a wide range of machines from workstations to minicomputers to large file servers. To create an infrastructure to better serve the concept of pervasive computing, Novell planned to combine NetWare and UNIX to create a new operating system that would have key networking functions built in. By the end of 1994, Novell planned for NetWare and UNIX to have common symmetric multiprocessing interfaces. By 1995, they would share common management, security, and directory services. In 1996, Novell would deliver the super network operating system (Super NOS) that would be fully distributed, modular, and fault tolerant. Super NOS would allow Novell to create specialized solutions that shared a common look and feel, and a common code base.

■ Access

To make the network easier to access and use, future versions of NetWare would include an advanced client-server package with a three-dimensional graphical user interface and a navigational tool for searching the network and its services. Novell would include advanced mobile links as part of its future networks, including cellular, data radio, infrared, and telephony links. The final key access point was called netware embedded systems technology (NEST). NEST would allow hardware vendors to embed NetWare technology into office equipment, peripherals, and televisions to make network access very easy.

■ Applications

As networks expanded, Novell believed users would need intelligent network applications to increase productivity on the pervasive network. Novell would create applications that automated network access. PerfectOffice would be "network enabled," permitting network management and task integration. Additional products were designed as either part of PerfectOffice or as separate applications that would work toward enhancing group productivity. GroupWise, part of PerfectOffice, would include E-mail, calendaring, scheduling, fax, and paging capabilities. Novell InForms, a separate product, would allow forms processing and workflow automation. Novell branched into the high-growth home software segment in 1994 with the introduction of its WordPerfect Main Street line of consumer "edutainment" products.

■ PerfectOffice

Mark Calkins, vice president of product marketing at WordPerfect, summed up PerfectOffice by saying, "[It] is the first suite to integrate network services with desktop applications, making it the best solution for end users, and system administrators who manage software across an enterprise."[19]

PerfectOffice consisted of several mainstream business applications as well as several new network-enabled applications built in. PerfectOffice Standard consisted of:

- WordPerfect (word processor),
- Quattro Pro (spreadsheet),
- WordPerfect Presentations (presentation graphics), and
- InfoCentral (personal information manager).

These were stand-alone products incorporated into a suite. However, Novell introduced several new programs as well. The first was called Envoy, a workgroup publishing tool. Envoy allowed users to electronically view, annotate, and distribute documents across the network while keeping all graphical elements intact. Envoy also compressed documents to one-third their normal size, thereby preserving network bandwidth. PerfectOffice was the only suite to offer a feature such as Envoy. Another new addition was Symmetry. This component was accessible from any PerfectOffice application, and allowed users easy access to E-mail, personal scheduling, calendaring, and group assignments.

Following the lead of Microsoft, Novell offered PerfectOffice in three versions: standard, professional, and select. Standard included all of the items just mentioned. The professional version added Paradox (database), and a new component called AppBuilder. This was another innovation by Novell, allowing nonprogrammers to create custom applications out of PerfectOffice capabilities such as the WordPerfect text editor, the Quattro Pro spreadsheet module, and the WordPerfect Presentations bit map editor. Select added the capability to create an entire custom suite from PerfectOffice applications, WordPerfect Main Street applications, and third-party products.

In June 1994, Novell and WordPerfect announced the PerfectFit Partners initiative. In an attempt to counter Microsoft's Office Compatible program, Novell initiated PerfectFit to encourage third-party developers to design, build, and market products that supported PerfectOffice. Novell would allow products that met its criteria to include the "PerfectFit With PerfectOffice" label on their packaging and marketing materials. At the outset of the program, Novell had commitments from:

- Calera, an optical character recognition (OCR) developer,
- Intel ProShare, a videoconferencing product,
- Jurisoft, legal market software developer, and
- Kurzweil, speech recognition software.

Novell also invited the 900+ developers that were part of the Working With WordPerfect program to join as PerfectFit Partners.

Industry watchers predicted that Novell had about a 12-month window of opportunity to integrate its products. Microsoft's Windows 95 was anticipated to be released mid-1995 after several prior release dates had slipped by. Most of Novell's new or integrated products (NetWare 4.1, PerfectOffice 3.0, first generation of AppWare network application development tools) were expected to be released in early 1995. Jesse Burst, in writing for Windows experts in *Windows Sources* magazine, was quick to state his opinion that "Novell's vision for the future is more complete and more compelling than the one from [Microsoft]."[20] He felt the combination of Novell and WordPerfect had resulted in "the best combination of networking services available anywhere."[21] Summing up the potential of the Novell vision, Burst said:

> Are you starting to see how neatly the Novell vision fits together? Each piece works separately. If the new operating system doesn't succeed, Novell can still sell its apps, tools, and network services. But the pieces are even stronger when combined. The apps provide modules for the tools. The tools build and connect to network services. The network services work seamlessly with the operating system. The operating system meshes perfectly with the apps. And around we go.[22]

Novell's New Leader

Robert Frankenberg was the son of a watchmaker/jeweler who started working in his father's business at age eight. Following high school, he spent four years in the Air Force before joining Hewlett-Packard full time. He finished two years of college via correspondence while in the Air Force and then completed his degree in computer engineering at San Jose State University while working full time for H-P. He graduated with more than 180 units (much more than was required) because he "kept taking fascinating courses in software, history, psychology, and just about every other subject."[23]

Frankenberg had married a high school sweetheart in 1967 after a two-year long-distance relationship. He and his wife had been married for 27 years and had two children. Frankenberg considered himself an avid fisherman, gourmet cook, and voracious reader. He slept only four to six hours a night spending another two to four hours each night reading "anything from science fiction to mysteries to textbooks and user manuals."[24]

When Frankenberg was named to succeed Noorda, those who knew him declared that he was "one of only a handful of executives with the technical breadth and management expertise necessary to lead Novell."[25] Frankenberg had spent 25 years with Hewlett-Packard, rising through engineering, R&D management, and marketing positions to become general manager of H-P's Commercial Systems Division in 1982. After a year's stint as business unit manager of Office Systems in 1986, he was named general manager of the Information Systems Group in 1987 with responsibilities encompassing all office applications, PC applications, and PC-integrated software. In 1989, Frankenberg became general manager of the Information Network Group responsible for all applications, hardware, and software for network products. In 1991, he had been named head of the Personal Information Products Group where he had achieved a dramatic turnaround in H-P's PC-related business (personal computers and network servers, PC networks, PC software, mobile products, and interactive television).

In assessing Novell, Frankenberg had said, "There is tremendous talent at Novell and a vast array of technologies, both developed and acquired. To move forward we need more focus and coherence in what we're doing. Today we're kind of a cacophony of voices, and we need to be a bit more like a symphony. We need to focus on the areas Novell can be the world's best at rather than spreading ourselves three molecules thick over the entire networking space."[26]

Exhibit 9	Novell's Vision
Novell will drive the evolution of pervasive computing by connecting people to other people and the information they need, enabling them to act on it anytime, anywhere.	
Source: Novell Strategic Direction White Paper, September 1994.	

One of the first assignments Frankenberg had given his top executives was to list the top 10 issues Novell needed to address. These were compiled, prioritized, and a "dirty dozen" list was developed. Executives were then assigned problems and charged with developing proposed solutions to the problems. Frankenberg envisioned a new "dirty dozen" list being generated each time problems were successfully solved.

Next Frankenberg and the executive staff met to review Novell's values, purpose, vision, mission, and objectives. This process included identifying Novell's core competencies, establishing what capabilities were necessary to accomplish its mission, reviewing Novell's strategies, examining the organizational structure for necessary improvements or changes, and developing a clear business plan. Through a participatory process, Frankenberg hoped to promote the vision for a "greater" Novell (see Exhibit 9).

■ Other Management Concerns

In 1993, Noorda had quietly reorganized the top management of Novell by creating an Office of the President consisting of himself, Mary Burnside, chief operating officer (COO), and James Tolonen, chief financial officer (CFO) and handing off many of the day-to-day responsibilities to the other two. Burnside had been with Novell since 1988 and oversaw Novell's three product groups. Tolonen had come to Novell in 1989 following Novell's acquisition of Excelan where Tolonen had been Excelan's CFO. Tolonen was responsible for fiscal matters, but also oversaw human resources, sales, and customer service and support. Both had been considered likely successors to Noorda.

Many of Novell's executives were former executives of the companies that Novell had acquired over the years. In fact, the WordPerfect and Quattro Pro businesses were combined to form a new WordPerfect/Novell Applications Group headed by Ad Rietveld, WordPerfect's former CEO. Rietveld also became a member of the Office of the President. One of Frankenberg's ongoing challenges would be in managing so many "former chiefs." He would also need to look at Novell's organizational structure to ensure that Novell's business and corporate strategies could be effectively carried out.

■ Layoffs

Under Noorda, Novell had grown both in revenues and in employees over the years. The biggest growth in employees had resulted from the acquisitions made in the last several years of Noorda's tenure with the number of employees increasing from 2,120 in 1989 to 4,429 in 1993 and to over 10,000 in 1994 following the WordPerfect and Quattro Pro acquisitions. One of Frankenberg's immediate goals was to reorganize and streamline Novell, which meant laying off as much as 15 percent of the workforce in the short term. It was anticipated that the WordPerfect staff would take the brunt of this reduction since its productivity was less than half that of Novell.

Other Options

Frankenberg knew he would also have to look at shedding marginal products such as Novell DOS (a PC operating system), which had only a minute fraction of the market, and even entire divisions to help cut costs and improve operating efficiencies. Some wondered whether Frankenberg would cut or eliminate Word-Perfect's famed free customer service.[27] Further outsourcing of functions was another possibility.

Recent Alliances

Meanwhile, Novell had continued to enter into numerous strategic alliances with smaller technology companies throughout the summer of 1994. These included a licensing agreement with Artisoft whereby Artisoft would license key NetWare tools providing Novell with a steady revenue stream, a deepening of the partnership with 3Com with the two companies cross-licensing routing technologies, and a deal with Proginet Corp. to jointly develop and sell a line of products that will bring NetWare services to IBM mainframes.

Frankenberg's Challenge

In May, Frankenberg had been asked why he had chosen to come to Novell. The answer then had been "I . . . love a challenge, and leading Novell into what it can become is a great challenge."[28] Now the "great challenge" had begun in earnest as he looked at:

- integrating the WordPerfect and Quattro Pro acquisitions,
- managing a multitude of cooperative agreements/strategic alliances,
- timing products relative to Microsoft and other competitors,
- managing a complex, multiproduct, multisegment strategy,
- merging the technologies from previous acquisitions,
- managing multiple development groups at multiple locations,
- teaching Novell's dealers/resellers to sell a new line of products, and
- becoming an overall better marketer so consumers better understood the benefits of Novell's technologies.

Notes

1. G. Pascal Zachary, 1994, Novell pact with WordPerfect followed a secret bidding war initiated by Lotus, *Wall Street Journal,* March 24, A6.
2. Novell news release, 1994, Robert J. Frankenberg named chairman of Novell board of directors, August 11.
3. According to Cindy Parsay, Frankenberg's administrative assistant at Novell, Mr. Frankenberg was still living in California at the time of the case, but was commuting back and forth to Provo during August.
4. Larry Armstrong and Sandra D. Atchison, 1992, Two rising stars, *Business Week,* April 3, 62.
5. Novell, 1993, *Annual Report,* 8 and 21.
6. Ibid., 21.
7. Evan I. Schwartz, Robert D. Hof, and Kathy Rebello, 1993, A Novell approach for striking at Microsoft, *Business Week,* January 1, 28; Richard Brandt, Amy E. Cortese, and Gary

McWilliams, 1994, How sweet a deal for Novell?, *Business Week,* April 4, 38.

8. Bradley Johnson, 1994, Novell wagers on Word-Perfect, *Advertising Age,* March 28, 8+.

9. Lynda Radosevich and Elisabeth Horwitt, 1994, New desktop leaders face off—Novell to buy WordPerfect, Quattro Pro, *ComputerWorld,* March 28.

10. Johnson, Novell wagers on WordPerfect.

11. Ibid., 38.

12. Sandra Atchison and Evan I. Schwartz, 1991, Can LAN lord Novell extend its territory?, *Business Week,* September 2, 78–79.

13. G. Pascal Zachary, 1994, Novell finds new products can be a mixed blessing, *Wall Street Journal,* March 14, B6.

14. Novell, 1993, *Annual Report,* Form 10-K, 13.

15. David B. Yoffie and Toby Lenk, 1991, Note on the PC network software industry, 1990, Harvard Business School case, 7.

16. Brandt et al., How sweet a deal for Novell?

17. G. Pascal Zachary, Novell finds new products can be a mixed blessing.

18. Brandt et al., How sweet a deal for Novell?

19. Novell news release, 1994, WordPerfect announces PerfectOffice 3.0 for Windows, June 28, 5.

20. Jesse Burst, 1994, This paper tiger has real claws, *Windows Sources,* July, 1.

21. Ibid., 2.

22. Ibid., 2.

23. Robert Frankenberg interviewed by Muriel O'Flynn Giroux, 1994, A conversation with Novell's CEO and president, Bob Frankenberg, *Net-Words* (Novell company newsletter), June, 4.

24. Ibid.

25. G. Pascal Zachary, 1994, Novell picks Hewlett-Packard veteran, Frankenberg, to succeed CEO Noorda, *Wall Street Journal,* April 5, B6.

26. Robert Frankenberg interviewed by Giroux, 7.

27. Richard Brandt, 1994, Tackling the bloat at Novell, *Business Week,* August 8, 28.

28. Robert Frankenberg interviewed by Giroux, 6.

CASE 28 Perdue Farms Inc., 1995

George C. Rubenson
Frank Shipper
Franklin P. Perdue School of Business
Salisbury State University

Jean M. Hanebury
Texas A & M University, Corpus Christi

Background and Company History

I have a theory that you can tell the difference between those who have inherited a fortune and those who have made a fortune. Those who have made their own fortune forget not where they came from and are less likely to lose touch with the common man. (Bill Sterling, 'Just Browsin' column in *Eastern Shore News*, March 2, 1988)

In 1917, Arthur W. Perdue, a Railway Express agent and descendent of a French Huguenot family named Perdeaux, bought 50 leghorn chickens for a total of $5 and began selling table eggs near the small town of Salisbury, Maryland. A region immortalized in James Michener's *Chesapeake*, it is alternately known as "the Eastern Shore" or the "Delmarva Peninsula" and includes parts of *DEL*aware, *MAR*yland and *Virgini*A.

Initially, the business amounted to little more than a farm wife's chore for "pin money," raising a few "biddies" in a cardboard box behind the woodstove in the kitchen until they were old enough to fend for themselves in the barnyard. But, in 1920, when Railway Express asked "Mr. Arthur" to move to a station away from the Eastern Shore, at age 36 he quit his job as Salisbury's Railway Express agent and entered the egg business full time. His only child, Franklin Parsons Perdue, was born that same year.

"Mr. Arthur" soon expanded his egg market and began shipments to New York. Practicing small economies such as mixing his own chicken feed and using leather from his old shoes to make hinges for his chicken coops, he stayed out of debt and prospered. He tried to add a new chicken coop every year. By the time young Frank was 10, he had 50 or so chickens of his own to look after, earning money from their eggs. He worked along with his parents, not always enthusi-

The authors are indebted to Frank Perdue, Jim Perdue, and the numerous associates at Perdue Farms, Inc., who generously shared their time and information about the company. In addition, the authors would like to thank the anonymous librarians who routinely review area newspapers and file articles about the poultry industry—the most important industry on the Delmarva peninsula. Without their assistance, this case would not be possible.

astically, to feed the chickens, clean the coops, dig the cesspools, and gather and grade eggs. A shy introverted country boy, he went for five years to a one-room school, eventually graduated from Wicomico High School, and attended the State Teachers College in Salisbury for two years before returning to the farm in 1939 to work full time with his father.

By 1940, it was obvious to father and son that the future lay in selling chickens, not eggs. But the Perdues made the shift to selling broilers only after careful attention to every detail—a standard Perdue procedure in the years to come. In 1944, "Mr. Arthur" made his son Frank a full partner in what was then A. W. Perdue and Son, Inc., a firm already known for quality products and fair dealing in a toughly competitive business. In 1950, Frank took over leadership of Perdue Farms, a company with 40 employees. By 1952, revenues were $6,000,000 from the sale of 2,600,000 broilers.

By 1967, annual sales had increased to about $35,000,000 but it was becoming increasingly clear that additional profits lay in processing chickens. Frank recalled in an interview for *Business Week* (September 15, 1972) ". . . processors were paying us 10 cents a live pound for what cost us 14 cents to produce. Suddenly, processors were making as much as 7 cents a pound."

A cautious, conservative planner, Arthur Perdue had not been eager for expansion and Frank Perdue himself was reluctant to enter poultry processing. But economic forces dictated the move and, in 1968, Perdue Farms became a vertically integrated operation, hatching eggs, delivering the chicks to contract growers, buying grain, supplying the feed and litter, and, finally, processing the broilers and shipping them to market.

The company bought its first plant in 1968, a Swift and Company operation in Salisbury, renovated it, and equipped it with machines capable of processing 14,000 broilers per hour. Computers were soon employed to devise feeding formulas for each stage of growth so birds reached their growth potential sooner. Geneticists were hired to breed larger breasted chickens and veterinarians were put on staff to keep the flocks healthy. Nutritionists handled the feed formulations to achieve the best feed conversion.

From the beginning, Frank Perdue refused to permit his broilers to be frozen for shipping, a process that resulted in unappetizing black bones and loss of flavor and moistness when cooked. Instead, Perdue chickens were (and some still are) shipped to market packed in ice, justifying the company's advertisements at that time that it sold only "fresh, young broilers." However, this policy also limited the company's market to those locations that could be serviced overnight from the Eastern Shore of Maryland. Thus, Perdue chose for its primary markets the densely populated towns and cities of the East Coast, particularly New York City, which consumes more Perdue chicken than all other brands combined.

During the 1970s, the firm entered the Baltimore, Philadelphia, Boston, and Providence markets. Facilities were expanded rapidly to include a new broiler processing plant and protein conversion plant in Accomac, Virginia; a processing plant in Lewiston, North Carolina; a hatchery in Murfreesboro, North Carolina; and several Swift and Company facilities including a processing plant in Georgetown, Delaware; a feed mill in Bridgeville, Delaware; and a feed mill in Elkin, North Carolina.

In 1977, "Mr. Arthur" died at the age of 91, leaving behind a company with annual sales of nearly $200,000,000, an average annual growth rate of 17 percent compared to an industry average of 1 percent a year, the potential for processing 78,000 broilers per hour, and annual production of nearly 350,000,000 pounds of poultry per year. Frank Perdue, who says without a hint of self deprecation that "I am a B-minus student. I know how smart I am. I know a B-minus is not as good as an A," said of his father simply "I learned everything from him."

Stew Leonard, owner of a huge supermarket in Norwalk, Connecticut, and one of Perdue's top customers, describes Frank Perdue as "What you see is what you get. If you ask him a question you will get an answer." Perdue disapproves the presence of a union between himself and his associates and adds, "The absence of unions makes for a better relationship with our associates. If we treat our associates right, I don't think we will have a union." On conglomerates, he states, "Diversification is the most dangerous word in the English language." His business philosophy is "I'm interested in being the best rather than the biggest. Expansion is OK if it has a positive effect on product quality. I'll do nothing that detracts from product quality."

Frank Perdue is known for having a temper. He is as hard on himself, however, as he is on others, readily admitting his shortcomings and even his mistakes. For example, in the 1970s, he apparently briefly discussed using the influence of some unsavory characters to help alleviate union pressure. When an investigative reporter in the late 1980s asked him about this instance, he admitted that it was a mistake, saying ". . . .it was probably the dumbest thing I ever did."

In 1981, Frank Perdue was in Massachusetts for his induction into the Babson College Academy of Distinguished Entrepreneurs, an award established in 1978 to recognize the spirit of free enterprise and business leadership. Babson College President Ralph Z. Sorenson inducted Perdue into the academy, which at that time numbered 18 men and women from four continents. Perdue had the following to say to the college students:

> There are none, nor will there ever be, easy steps for the entrepreneur. Nothing, absolutely nothing, replaces the willingness to work earnestly, intelligently towards a goal. You have to be willing to pay the price. You have to have an insatiable appetite for detail, have to be willing to accept constructive criticism, to ask questions, to be fiscally responsible, to surround yourself with good people and most of all, to listen. (Frank Perdue, speech at Babson College, April 28, 1981)

The early 1980s proved to be a period of further growth as Perdue diversified and broadened its market. New marketing areas included Washington, D.C.; Richmond, Virginia; and Norfolk, Virginia. Additional facilities were opened in Cofield, Kenly, Halifax, Robbins, and Robersonville, North Carolina. The firm broadened its line to include value-added products such as "Oven Stuffer" roasters and "Perdue Done It!," a new brand of fresh, prepared chicken products featuring cooked chicken breast nuggets, cutlets, and tenders. James A. (Jim) Perdue, Frank's only son, joined the company as a management trainee in 1983.

But the latter 1980s also tested the mettle of the firm. Following a period of considerable expansion and concentric diversification, a consulting firm was brought in to recommend ways to cope with the new complexity. Believing that the span of control was too broad, the consulting firm recommended that strategic business units, responsible for their own operations, be formed. In other words, the firm should decentralize.

Soon after, the chicken market leveled off and eventually began to decline. At one point the firm was losing as much as one million dollars a week and, in 1988,

Perdue Farms experienced its first year in the red. Unfortunately, the decentralization had created duplication of duties and enormous administrative costs. MIS costs, for example, had tripled. The firm's rapid plunge into turkeys and other food processing, where it had little experience, contributed to the losses. Waste and inefficiency had permeated the company. Characteristically, Frank Perdue took the firm back to basics, concentrating on efficiency of operations, improving communications throughout the company, and paying close attention to detail.

On June 2, 1989, Frank celebrated 50 years with Perdue Farms Inc. At a morning reception in downtown Salisbury, the governor of Maryland proclaimed it "Frank Perdue Day." The governors of Delaware and Virginia did the same.

The 1990s have been dominated by market expansion to North Carolina; Atlanta, Georgia; Pittsburgh, Pennsylvania; Cleveland, Ohio; Chicago, Illinois; and Florida. New product lines have included fresh ground chicken, fresh ground turkey, sweet Italian turkey sausage, turkey breakfast sausage, fun-shaped chicken breast nuggets in star and drumstick shapes, and BBQ and oven-roasted chicken parts in the "Perdue Done It!" line. A new "Fit 'n Easy" label was introduced as part of a nutrition campaign using skinless, boneless chicken and turkey products. By 1994, revenues had increased to about $1.5 billion, Frank Perdue was chairman of the executive committee, and Jim Perdue was chairman of the board.

In January 1995, Perdue Farms became the 3rd largest producer in the broiler industry when it bought Showell Farms, Inc., of Showell, Maryland, the 12th largest producer in the United States with about 8,000 employees and revenues of approximately $550,000. Thus, Perdue Farms estimates total revenue for fiscal year 1996 at more than $2.0 billion.

Sitting in the small unpretentious office that had been his dad's for 40 years, Jim looked out the window at the house where he had grown up, the broiler houses Frank built in the 1940s, his grandfather's homestead across the road where Frank was born, and a modern hatchery. "Dad would come home for dinner, then come back here and work into the early hours of the morning. There's a fold-out cot behind that credenza. He got by on three or four hours of sleep a night."

Mission Statement and Statement of Values

From the beginning, Mr. Arthur's motto had been to "... create a quality product, be aware of your customers, deal fairly with people, and work hard, work hard, work hard ..." In a speech in September 1991 to the firm's lenders, accountants, and Perdue associates, Frank reiterated these values, saying:

> If you were to ask me what was the biggest factor in whatever success we have enjoyed, I would answer that it was not technology, or economic resources, or organizational structure. It ... has been our conscious decision that, in order to be successful, we must have a sound set of beliefs on which we premise all our policies and actions. ... Central to these beliefs is our emphasis on quality. ... Quality is no accident. It is the one absolutely necessary ingredient of all the most successful companies in the world.

The centrality of quality to the firm is featured in its mission statement and its statement of values. To ensure that all associates know the company's mission, quality policy, values, and annual goals, managers receive a fold-up, wallet-size card with them imprinted on it (see Exhibit 1).

Exhibit 1   Perdue Farms, Fiscal Year 1994

Mission Statement

Our mission is to provide the highest quality poultry and poultry-related products to retail and food service customers.

We want to be the recognized industry leader in quality and service, providing more than expected for our customers, associates, and owners.

We will accomplish this by maintaining a tradition of pride in our products, growth through innovation, integrity in the management of our business, and commitment to Team Management and the Quality Improvement Process.

Quality Policy

We shall produce products and provide services at all times which meet or exceed the expectations of our customers.

We shall not be content to be of equal quality to our competitors.

Our commitment is to be increasingly superior.

Contribution to quality is a responsibility shared by everyone in the Perdue organization.

Statement of Values

Our success as a company, and as individuals working at Perdue, depend upon:

- Meeting customer needs with the best quality, innovative food and food-related products and services.
- Associates being team members in the business and having opportunities to influence, make contributions, and reach their full potential.
- Working together as business partners by implementing the principles of the QIP so that mutual respect, trust, and a commitment to being the best are shared among associates, customers, producers, and suppliers.
- Achieving the long-term goals of the company and providing economic stability and a rewarding future for all associates through well-planned, market-driven growth.
- Being the best in our industry in profitability as a low-cost producer, realizing that our customers won't pay for our inefficiencies.
- Staying ahead of the competition by investing our profits to provide a safe work environment; to pay competitive wages; to maintain up-to-date facilities, equipment, and processes; and to create challenging opportunities for associates.
- Serving the communities in which we do business with resources, time, and the creative energies of our associates.

FY 1994 Company Goals

1) PEOPLE—Provide a safe, secure, and productive work environment

- Reduce OSHA recordable incidents by 12%
- Reduce per capita workers' compensation by 28%
- Implement an associates satisfaction survey process
- Provide an annual performance evaluation for all associates.

2) PRODUCTS—Provide the highest quality products and services at competitive costs.

- Develop an improved measurement of consumer satisfaction
- Improve the "Customer Service Satisfaction Index"
- Improve our quality spread over competition
- Consistently achieve a plant weighted ranking score for product quality of 212 points
- Increase sales from new products

3) PROFITABILITY—Lead the industry in profitability.

- Achieve a 10% ROAE
- Broiler Agrimetrics Index to be equal to the Southeast Best Eight Average
- Turkey Agrimetrics Index to be equal to the Best Eight National Average
- Increase market share by growing at a rate which exceeds the industry.

■ Social Responsibility

To realize its corporate statement of values, Perdue Farms works hard to be a good corporate citizen. Two areas in which this is especially clear are its code of ethics and its efforts to minimize the environmental damage it causes.

■ Code of Ethics

Perdue Farms has taken the somewhat unusual step of setting forth explicitly the ethical standards it expects all associates to follow. Specifically, the code of ethics calls on associates to conduct every aspect of business in the full spirit of honest and lawful behavior. Further, all salaried associates and certain hourly associates are required to sign a statement acknowledging that they understand the code and are prepared to comply with it. Associates are expected to report to their supervisor dishonest or illegal activities as well as possible violations of the code. If the supervisor does not provide a satisfactory response, the employee is expected to contact either the vice president for human resources or the vice president of the employee's division. The code notes that any Perdue manager who initiates or encourages reprisal against any person who reports a violation commits a serious violation of the code.

■ Minimizing Environmental Damage

Historically, chicken processing has been the focus of special interest groups whose interests range from animal rights to repetitive motion disorders to environmental causes. Perdue Farms has accepted the challenge of striving to maintain an environmentally friendly workplace as a goal that requires the commitment of all of its associates, from Frank Perdue down. Frank Perdue states it best: "We know that we must be good neighbors environmentally. We have an obligation not to pollute, to police ourselves, and to be better than EPA requires us to be."

For example, over the years, the industry had explored many alternative ways of disposing of dead birds. Perdue research provided the solution—small composters on each farm. Using this approach, dead birds are reduced to an end product that resembles soil in a matter of a few days. This has become a major environmental activity. Another environmental challenge is the disposal of hatchery wastes. Historically, manure and unhatched eggs that make up these wastes were shipped to a landfill. Perdue produces about 10 tons of this waste per day! However, Perdue has reduced the waste by 50 percent by selling the liquid fraction to a pet food processor who cooks it for protein. The other 50 percent is recycled through a rendering process. In 1990, Perdue spent $4.2 million to construct a state-of-the-art waste water treatment facility at its Accomac, Virginia, plant. This facility uses forced hot air heated to 120 degrees to cause the microbes to digest all traces of ammonia, even during the cold winter months. In April 1993, the company took a major step with the creation of the Environmental Steering Committee. Its mission is "... to provide all Perdue Farms work sites with vision, direction, and leadership so that they can be good corporate citizens from an environmental perspective today and in the future." The committee oversees how the company is doing in such environmentally sensitive areas as waste water, storm water, hazardous waste, solid waste, recycling, biosolids, and human health and safety.

Jim Perdue sums it up as follows: ".... we must not only comply with environmental laws as they exist today, but look to the future to make sure we don't have any surprises. We must make sure our policy statement is real, and that there's something behind it, and that we do what we say we're going to do."

■ Marketing

In the early days, chicken was sold to groceries as a commodity, i.e., producers sold it in bulk and butchers cut and wrapped it. The consumer had no idea what company grew the chicken. Frank Perdue was convinced that higher profits could be made if Perdue's products were premium quality so they could be sold at a premium price. But the only way the premium quality concept would work was if consumers asked for it by name—and that meant the product must be differentiated and "branded" to identify its premium qualities. Hence, Perdue has emphasized over the years its superior quality, a higher meat-to-bone ratio, and a yellow skin (the result of mixing marigold petals in the feed), which is an indicator of bird health.

In 1968, Perdue spent $40,000 on radio advertising. In 1969, the company spent $80,000 on radio, and in 1970 spent $160,000, split 50–50 between radio and television. The advertising agency had recommended against television advertising, but the combination worked. TV ads increased sales and Frank Perdue decided the old agency he was dealing with did not match one of the basic Perdue tenets: "The people you deal with should be as good at what they do as you are at what you do."

That decision set off a storm of activity on Frank's part. To select a new ad agency, Frank studied intensively and personally learned more about advertising than any poultry man before him. He began a 10-week immersion on the theory and practice of advertising. He read books and papers on advertising. He talked to sales managers of every newspaper, radio, and television station in the New York City area, consulted experts, and interviewed 48 ad agencies. On April 2, 1971, Perdue Farms selected Scali, McCabe, Sloves as their new advertising agency. As the agency tried to figure out how to successfully "brand" a chicken—something that had never been done—they realized that Frank Perdue was their greatest ally. "He looked a little like a chicken himself, and he sounded a little like one, and he squawked a lot!" Ed McCabe, partner and chief copywriter of the firm, decided that Frank Perdue should be the firm's spokes-person. Initially Frank resisted. But, in the end, he accepted the role and the campaign based on "It takes a tough man to make a tender chicken" was born. Frank set Perdue Farms apart by educating consumers about chicken quality. The process catapulted Perdue Farms into the ranks of the top poultry producers in the country.

The firm's very first television commercial showed Frank on a picnic in the Salisbury City Park saying

> A chicken is what it eats . . . And my chickens eat better than people do . . . I store my own grain and mix my own feed . . . And give my Perdue chickens nothing but pure well water to drink . . . That's why my chickens always have that healthy golden yellow color . . . If you want to eat as good as my chickens, you'll just have to eat my chickens . . . Mmmm, that's really good!

An additional ad, touting superior quality and more breast meat read as follows:

> Government standards would allow me to call this a grade A chicken . . . but my standards wouldn't. This chicken is skinny . . . It has scrapes and hairs. . . . The fact is, my graders reject 30% of the chickens government inspectors accept as grade A. . . . That's why it pays to insist on a chicken with my name on it. . . . If you're not completely satisfied, write me and I'll give you your money back. . . . Who do you write in Washington? . . . What do they know about chickens?

> Never go into a store and just ask for a pound of chicken breasts. . . . Because you could be cheating yourself out of some meat. . . . Here's an ordinary one-pound chicken breast, and here's a one-pound breast of mine. . . . They weigh the same. But as you can see, mine has more meat, and theirs have more bone. I breed the broadest breasted, meatiest chicken you can buy. . . . So don't buy a chicken breast by the pound. . . . Buy them by the name . . . and get an extra bite in every breast.

The ads paid off. In 1968, Perdue Farms held about 3 percent of the New York market. By 1972, one out of every six chickens eaten in New York was a Perdue chicken. Fifty-one percent of New Yorkers recognized the label. Scali, McCabe, Sloves credited Frank Perdue's "believability" for the success of the program. "This was advertising in which Perdue had a personality that lent credibility to the product." Today, 50 percent of the chickens consumed in New York are Perdue.

Frank had his own view. As he told a Rotary audience in Charlotte, North Carolina, in March 1989, ". . . the product met the promise of the advertising and was far superior to the competition. Two great sayings tell it all: 'nothing will destroy a poor product as quickly as good advertising' and 'a gifted product is mightier than a gifted pen!' "

Today, the Perdue marketing function is unusually sophisticated. Its responsibilities include deciding (1) how many chickens and turkeys to grow, (2) what the advertising and promotion pieces should look like, where they should run, and how much the company can afford, and (3) which new products the company will pursue. The marketing plan is derived from the company's five-year business plan and includes goals concerning volume, return on sales, market share, and profitability. The internal Marketing Department is helped by various service agencies including:

- Lowe & Partners/SMS—advertising campaigns, media buys;
- R. C. Auletta & Co.—public relations, company image;
- Gertsman & Meyers—packaging design;
- Group Williams—consumer promotional programs; and
- various research companies for focus groups, telephone surveys, and in-home use tests.

Operations

Two words sum up the Perdue approach to operations—quality and efficiency—with emphasis on the first over the latter. Perdue more than most companies represents the total quality management (TQM) slogan, "Quality, a journey without end." Some of the key events are listed in Exhibit 2. The pursuit of quality began with Arthur Perdue in 1924 when he purchased breeding roosters from Texas for the princely sum of $25 each. For comparison, typical wages in 1925 were $1 for a 10-hour workday. Frank Perdue's own pursuit of quality is legendary. One story about his pursuit of quality was told in 1968 by Ellis Wainwright, the State of Maryland grading inspector, during start-up operations at Perdue's first processing plant. Frank had told Ellis that the standards that he wanted were higher than the government Grade A standard. The first two days had been pretty much disastrous. On the third day, as Wainwright recalls,

We graded all morning, and I found only five boxes that passed what I took to be Frank's standards. The rest had the yellow skin color knocked off by the picking machines. I was afraid Frank was going to raise cain that I had accepted so few. Then Frank came through and rejected half of those.

To ensure that Perdue continues to lead the industry in quality, it buys about 2,000 pounds of competitors' products a week. Inspection associates grade these products and the information is shared with the highest levels of management. In addition, the company's quality policy is displayed at all locations and taught to all associates in quality training (Exhibit 1).

Exhibit 2	Milestones in the Quality Improvement Process at Perdue Farms
1924	Arthur Perdue buys leghorn roosters for $25 each
1950	Adopts the company logo of a chick under a magnifying glass
1984	Frank Perdue attends Philip Crosby's Quality College
1985	Perdue recognized for its pursuit of quality in *A Passion for Excellence*
	200 Perdue managers attend Quality College
	Adopted the quality improvement process (QIP)
1986	Established corrective action teams (CATs)
1987	Established quality training for all associates
	Implemented error cause removal (ECR) process
1988	Steering committee formed
1989	First Annual Quality Conference held
	Implemented team management
1990	Second Annual Quality Conference held
	Codified values and corporate mission
1991	Third Annual Quality Conference held
	Customer satisfaction defined
1992	Fourth Annual Quality Conference held
	"How to" implement customer satisfaction explained for team leaders and QITs

Perdue insists that nothing artificial be fed or injected into its birds. The company will not take any shortcuts in pursuit of the perfect chicken. A chemical- and steroid-free diet is fed to the chickens. Young chickens are vaccinated against disease. Selective breeding is used to improve the quality of the chickens sold. Chickens are bred to yield more breast meat because that is what the consumer wants.

Efficiency is improved through management of details. As a vertically integrated producer of chickens, Perdue manages every detail including breeding and hatching its own eggs, selecting growers, building Perdue-engineered chicken houses, formulating and manufacturing its own feed, overseeing the care and feeding, operating its own processing plants, distributing via its own trucking fleet, and marketing. Improvements are measured in fractional cents per pound. Nothing goes to waste. The feet that used to be thrown away are now processed and sold in the Orient as a barroom delicacy.

Frank's knowledge of details is also legendary. He not only impresses people in the poultry industry, but those in others as well. At the end of one day the managers and engineers of a new Grumman plant in Salisbury, Maryland, were reviewing their progress. Through the door unannounced came Frank Perdue. The Grumman managers proceeded to give Frank a tour of the plant. One machine was an ink-jet printer that labeled parts as they passed. Frank said he believed he had some of those in his plants. He paused for a minute and then he asked them if it clogged often. They responded yes. Frank exclaimed excitedly, "I am sure that I got some of those!" To ensure that this attention to detail pays off, eight measurable items—hatchability, turnover, feed conversion, livability, yield, birds per man-hour, utilization, and grade—are tracked.

Exhibit 3

Perdue Farms Incorporated

Frank Perdue credits much of his success to listening to others. He agrees with Tom Peters that "Nobody knows a person's 20 square feet better than the person who works there." To facilitate the transmission of ideas through the organization, it is undergoing a cultural transformation beginning with Frank (Exhibit 3). He describes the transition from the old to the new culture and himself as follows:

> . . . we also learned that *loud and noisy* were worth a lot more than mugs and pens. What I mean by this is, we used to spend a lot of time calling companies to get trinkets as gifts. Gradually, we learned that money and trinkets weren't what really motivated people. We learned that when a man or woman on the line is going all out to do a good job, that he or she doesn't care that much about a trinket of some sort; what they really want is for the manager to get up from behind his desk, walk over to them and, in front of their peers, give them a hearty and sincere "thank you."

> When we give recognition now, we do it when there's an audience and lots of peers can see. This is, I can tell you, a lot more motivating than the "kick in the butt" that was part of the old culture—*and I was the most guilty!*

Changing the behavioral pattern from writing-up people who have done something wrong to recognizing people for doing their job well has not been without some setbacks. For example, the company started what it calls the "Good Egg Award," which is good for a free lunch. Managers in the Salisbury plant were all trained and asked to distribute the awards by "catching" someone doing a good job. When the program manager checked with the cafeteria the following week to see how many had been claimed, the answer was none. A meeting of the managers was called to see how many had been handed out. The answer was none. When the managers were asked what they had done with their award certificates, the majority replied they were in their shirt pockets. A goal was set for all managers to hand out five a week.

The following week, the program manager still found that very few were being turned in for a free lunch. When employees were asked what they had done with their awards, they replied that they had framed them and hung them up on walls at home or put them in trophy cases. The program was changed again. Now the "Good Egg Award" consists of both a certificate and a ticket for a free lunch.

Perdue also has a beneficial suggestion program that it calls "Error Cause Removal." It averages better than 1 submission per year per three employees. Although that is much less than the 22 per employee per year in Japan, it is significantly better than the national average in the United States of 1 per year per five employees. As Frank has said, "We're 'one up'. . . . because with the help of the quality improvement process and the help of our associates, we have *thousands* of 'better minds' helping us."

Management Information Systems (MIS)

In 1989, Perdue Farms employed 118 IS people who spent 146 hours per week on IS maintenance—"fix it"—jobs. Today, the entire department has been reduced to 50 associates who spend only 52 hours per week in "fix it," and 94 percent of their time building new systems or reengineering old ones. Even better, a six-year backlog of projects has been eliminated and the average "build-it" cost for a project has dropped from $1950 to $568—an overall 300 percent increase in efficiency.

According to Don Taylor, director of MIS, this is the payoff from a significant management reorientation. A key philosophy is that a "fix-it" mentality is counterproductive. The goal is to determine the root cause of the problem and reengineer the program to eliminate future problems.

Developer–user partnerships—including a monthly payback system—were developed with five functional groups: sales and marketing, finance and human resources, logistics, quality assurance, and fresh-poultry and plant systems. Each has an assigned number of IS hours per month and defines its own priorities, permitting it to function as a customer.

In addition, a set of critical success factors (CSFs) was developed. These include the following: (1) Automation is never the first step in a project; it occurs only after superfluous business processes are eliminated and necessary ones simplified. (2) The vice president for the business unit must sponsor major projects in its area. (3) Projects should be limited in size, duration, and scope. IS has found that small projects have more success and a cumulative bigger payoff than big ones. All major projects are broken into three- to six-month segments with separate deliverables and benefits. (4) A precise definition of requirements is necessary; the team must determine up front exactly what the project will accomplish. (5) Commitment from both the IS staff and the customer to work as a team.

Perdue considers IS key to the operation of its business. For example, IS developed a customer ordering system for the centralized sales office (CSO). This system automated key business processes that link Perdue with its customers. The CSO includes 13 applications including order entry, product transfers, sales allocations, production scheduling, and credit management.

When ordering, the Perdue salesperson negotiates the specifics of the sale directly with the buyer in the grocery chain. Next, the salesperson sends the request to a dispatcher who determines where the various products are located and designates a specific truck to make the required pickups and delivery, all within the designated one-hour delivery window that has been granted by the grocery chain. Each truck is even equipped with a small satellite dish that is connected to the LAN so that a trucker on the New Jersey Turnpike headed for New York can call for a replacement tractor if his rig breaks down.

Obviously, a computer malfunction is a possible disaster. Four hours of downtime is equivalent to $6.2 million in lost sales. Thus, Perdue has separate systems and processes in place to avoid such problems. In addition to maximizing on-time delivery, this system gives the salespeople more time to discuss wants and needs with customers, handle customer relations, and observe key marketing issues such as Perdue shelf space and location.

On the other hand, Perdue does not believe that automation solves all problems. For example, it was decided that electronic monitoring in the poultry houses was counterproductive and not cost effective. While it would be possible to develop systems to monitor and control almost every facet of the chicken house environment, Perdue is concerned that doing so would weaken the invaluable link between the farmer and the livestock, i.e., Perdue believes that poultry producers need to be personally involved with conditions in the chicken house in order to maximize quality and spot problems or health challenges as soon as possible.

Research and Development

Perdue is an acknowledged industry leader in the use of technology to provide quality products and service to its customers. A list of some of its technological accomplishments is given in Exhibit 4. As with everything else he does, Frank Perdue tries to leave nothing to chance. Perdue employs 25 full-time people in the industry's largest research and development effort, including 5 with graduate degrees. It has specialists in avian science, microbiology, genetics, nutrition, and veterinary science. Because of its research and development capabilities, Perdue is often involved in USDA field tests with pharmaceutical suppliers. Knowledge and experience gained from these tests can lead to a competitive advantage. For example, Perdue has the most extensive and expensive vaccination program among its breeders in the industry. As a result, Perdue growers have more disease-resistant chickens and one of the lowest mortality rates in the industry.

Perdue is not complacent. According to Dr. Mac Terzich, doctor of veterinary medicine and laboratory manager, Perdue really pushes for creativity and innovation. Currently, they are working with and studying some European producers who use a completely different process.

Exhibit 4   Perdue Farms Inc. Technological Accomplishments
■ Breed chickens with 20% more breast meat
■ First to use digital scales to guarantee weights to customers
■ First to package fully cooked chicken products on microwaveable trays
■ First to have a box lab to define quality of boxes from different suppliers
■ First to test both its chickens and competitors chickens on 52 quality factors every week
■ Improved on time deliveries 20% between 1987 and 1993

Human Resource Management

When entering the Human Resource Department at Perdue Farms, the first thing one sees is a prominently displayed set of human resource corporate strategic goals (see Exhibit 5). Besides these human resource corporate strategic goals, Perdue sets annual company goals that deal with "people." Fiscal year 1995's strategic "people" goals center on providing a safe, secure, and productive work environment. The specific goals are included on the wallet-size, fold-up card mentioned earlier (Exhibit 1).

Strategic human resource planning is still developing at Perdue Farms. According to Tom Moyers, vice president for human resource management, "Every department in the company has a mission statement or policy which has been developed within the past 18 months. . . . Department heads are free to update their goals as they see fit. . . . Initial strategic human resource plans are developed by teams of three or four associates. . . . These teams meet once or twice a year company-wide to review where we stand in terms of meeting our objectives."

To keep associates informed about company plans, Perdue Farms holds "state of the business meetings" for all interested associates twice a year. For example, during May 1994, five separate meetings were held near various plants in Delmarva, the Carolinas, Virginia, and Indiana. Typically, a local auditorium is rented, overhead slides are prepared, and the company's progress toward its goals and its financial status is shared with its associates. Discussion revolves around what is wrong and what is right about the company. New product lines are introduced to those attending and opportunities for improvement are discussed.

Upon joining Perdue Farms, each new associate attends an extensive orientation that begins with a thorough review of the Perdue Associate Handbook. The handbook details Perdue's philosophy on quality, employee relations, drugs and alcohol, and its code of ethics. The orientation also includes a thorough discussion of the Perdue benefit plans. Fully paid benefits for all associates include (1) paid vacation, (2) eight official paid holidays, (3) health, accident, disability, and life insurance, (4) savings and pension plans, (5) funeral leave, and

---

Exhibit 5   Human Resource Corporate Strategic Goals

- Provide leadership to the corporation in all aspects of human resources including safety, recruitment and retention of associates, training and development, employee relations, compensation, benefits, communication, security, medical, housekeeping, and food services.
- Provide leadership and assistance to management at all levels in communicating and implementing company policy to ensure consistency and compliance with federal, state, and local regulations.
- Provide leadership and assistance to management in maintaining a socially responsible community image in all our Perdue communities by maintaining positive community relations and encouraging Perdue associates to be active in their community.
- Provide leadership and assistance to management in creating an environment wherein all associates can contribute to the overall success of the company.
- Be innovative and cost efficient in developing, implementing, and providing to all associates systems which will reward performance, encourage individual growth, and recognize contribution to the corporation.

(6) jury duty leave. The company also offers a scholarship program for children of Perdue associates.

Special arrangements can be made with the individual's immediate supervisor for a leave of absence of up to 12 months in case of extended non-job-related illness or injury, birth or adoption of a child, care of a spouse or other close relative, or other personal situations. Regarding the Family and Medical Leave Act of 1993, although opposed by many companies because its requirements are far more than their current policies, the act will have little impact on Perdue Farms since existing leave of absence policies are already broader than the new federal law.

Perdue Farms is a non-union employer. The firm has had a long-standing open door policy and managers are expected to be easily accessible to other associates, whatever the person's concern. The open door has been supplemented by a formal peer review process. While associates are expected to discuss problems with their supervisors first, they are urged to use peer review if they are still dissatisfied.

Wages and salaries, which are reviewed at least once a year, are determined by patterns in the poultry industry and the particular geographic location of the plant. Changes in the general economy and the state of the business are also considered.

Informal comparisons of turnover statistics with others in the poultry industry suggest that Perdue's turnover numbers are among the lowest in the industry. Perdue also shares workers' compensation claims data with their competitors and incidence rates (for accidents) are also among the lowest in the industry. Supervisors initially train and coach all new associates about the proper way to do their jobs. Once trained, the philosophy is that all associates are professionals and, as such, should make suggestions about how to make their jobs even more efficient and effective. After a 60-day introductory period, the associate has seniority based on the starting date of employment. Seniority is the determining factor in promotions where qualifications (skill, proficiency, dependability, work record) are equal. Also, should the workforce need to be reduced, this date is used as the determining factor in layoffs.

A form of management by objectives (MBO) is used for annual performance appraisal and planning review. The format includes a four-step process:

1. Establish accountability, goals, standards of performance and their relative weights for the review period.
2. Conduct coaching sessions throughout the review period and document these discussions.
3. Evaluate performance at the end of the review period and conduct appraisal interview.
4. Undertake next review period planning.

The foundation of human resources development includes extensive training and management development plus intensive succession planning and career pathing. The essence of the company's approach to human resource management is captured in Frank Perdue's statement:

> We have gotten where we are because we have believed in hiring our own people and training them in our own way. We believe in promotion from within, going outside only when we feel it is absolutely necessary—for expertise and sometimes because our company was simply growing faster than our people development program. The number one item in our success has been the quality of our people.

■ Finance

Perdue Farms Inc. is a privately held firm and considers financial information to be proprietary. Hence, available data is limited. Stock is primarily held by the family and a limited amount by Perdue management. *Forbes* (December 5, 1994) estimates Perdue Farms revenues for 1994 at about $1.5 billion, net profits at $50 million, and the number of associates at 13,800. The January 1995 purchase of Showell Farms, Inc., should boost revenues to more than $2 billion and the number of associates to about 20,000.

The firm's compound sales growth rate has been slowly decreasing during the past 20 years, mirroring the industry, which has been experiencing market saturation and overproduction. However, Perdue has compensated by wringing more efficiency from its associates, e.g., 20 years ago, a 1 percent increase in associates resulted in a 1.3 percent increase in revenue. Today, a 1 percent increase in associates results in a 2.5 percent increase in revenues (see Exhibit 6).

Perdue Farms has three operating divisions: Retail Chicken (62 percent of sales, growth rate of 5 percent), Foodservice Chicken and Turkey (20 percent of sales, growth rate of 12 percent), and Grain and Oilseed (18 percent of sales, growth rate of 10 percent). Thus, the bulk of sales comes from the sector—retail chicken—with the slowest growth rate. Part of the reason for the slow sales growth in retail chicken may stem from Perdue Farm's policy of selling only fresh—never frozen—chicken. This has limited their traditional markets to cities that can be serviced overnight by truck from production facility locations, i.e., New York, Boston, Philadelphia, Baltimore, and Washington—which are pretty well saturated. (Developing markets include Chicago, Cleveland, Atlanta, Pittsburgh, and Miami.) On the other hand, foodservice and grain and oilseed customers are nationwide and include export customers in eastern Europe, China, Japan, and South America.

Perdue Farms has been profitable every year since its founding with the exception of 1988. Company officials believe the loss in 1988 was caused by a decentralization effort begun during the early 1980s. At that time, there was a concerted effort to push decisions down through the corporate ranks to provide more autonomy. When the new strategy resulted in higher costs, Frank Perdue responded quickly by returning to the basics, reconsolidating, and downsizing. Now the goal is to streamline constantly in order to provide cost-effective business solutions.

Perdue Farms uses a conservative approach to financial management, using retained earnings and cash flow to finance asset replacement projects and normal growth. When planning expansion projects or acquisitions, long-term debt is

Exhibit 6	Annual Compound Growth Rate—Revenues and Associates	
	Revenue Growth (%)	**Associate Growth (%)**
Past 20 years	13	10
Past 15 years	11	8
Past 10 years	9	5
Past 5 years	5	2

used. The target debt limit is 55 percent of equity. Such debt is normally provided by domestic and international bank and insurance companies. The debt strategy is to match asset lives with liability maturities, and have a mix of fixed-rate and variable-rate debt. Growth plans require about two dollars in projected incremental sales growth for each one dollar in invested capital.

The U.S. Poultry Industry

U.S. annual per capita consumption of poultry has risen dramatically during the past 40 years from 26.3 pounds to almost 80 pounds in 1990. Consumption continued to grow through 1994 according to a broiler industry survey of the largest integrated broiler companies. Output of ready-to-cook product increased 5.8 percent in 1991, 5.3 percent in 1992, 6.0 percent in 1993, and 7.9 percent in 1994 to 508 million pounds per week.

Recent growth is largely the result of consumers moving away from red meat due to health concerns and the industry's continued development of increased value products such as precooked or roasted chicken and chicken parts. Unfortunately, this growth has not been very profitable due to chronic overcapacity throughout the industry, which has pushed down wholesale prices. The industry has experienced cyclical troughs before and experts expect future improvement in both sales and profits. Still, razor thin margins demand absolute efficiency.

Fifty-three integrated broiler companies account for approximately 99 percent of ready-to-cook production in the United States. While slow consolidation of the industry appears to be taking place, it is still necessary to include about 20 companies to get to 80 percent of production. Concentration has been fastest among the top four producers. For example, since 1986 market share of the top four has grown from 35 to 42 percent (see Exhibit 7).

Although the DelMarVa Peninsula (home to Perdue Farms Inc.) has long been considered the birthplace of the commercial broiler industry, recent production gains have been most rapid in the southeast. Arkansas, Georgia, and Alabama are now the largest poultry producing states—a result of abundant space and inexpensive labor. The southeast accounts for approximately 50 percent of the $20 billion U.S. chicken industry, employing 125,000 across the region. Still, DelMarVa chicken producers provide about 10 percent of all broilers grown in

Exhibit 7 Nation's Top Four Broiler Companies, 1995*		
	Million Head	**Million Pounds**
1. Tyson Foods, Inc.	26.70	88.25
2. Gold Kist, Inc.	13.40	44.01
3. Perdue Farms, Inc.	10.97†	42.64†
4. ConAgra, Inc.	10.50	37.91

*Based on average weekly slaughter; Broiler Industry Survey, 1995.
†Includes figures for Showell Farms, Inc., which Perdue acquired in January 1995.3

Exhibit 8 Integrated Broiler Producers Operating on DelMarVa Peninsula*	
	National Rank
Tyson Foods, Inc.	1
Perdue Farms Inc. (includes Showell Farms, Inc., which Perdue acquired in January 1995)	3
ConAgra, Inc.	4
Hudson Foods, Inc.	7
Townsend, Inc. (headquarters in Millsboro, Delaware)	10
Allen Family Foods, Inc. (headquarters in Seaford, Delaware)	14
Mountaire Farms of DelMarVa, Inc. (headquarters in Selbyville, Delaware)	26

*DelMarVa Poultry Industry, Inc., May 1995 fact sheet.

the United States. This is due largely to the region's proximity to Washington, Baltimore, Philadelphia, New York, and Boston. Each weekday, more than 200 tractor-trailers loaded with fresh dressed poultry leave DelMarVa headed for these metropolitan markets.

Seven integrated companies operate 10 feed mills, 15 hatcheries, and 13 processing plants on the DelMarVa Peninsula, employing approximately 22,000 people and producing approximately 10 million broilers each week (see Exhibit 8).

The Future

Considering Americans' average annual consumption of chicken (almost 80 pounds per person in 1990), many in the industry wonder how much growth is left. For example, after wholesale prices climbed from 14 cents per pound in 1960 to about 37 cents per pound in 1989, the recession and a general glut in the market caused prices to fall back (see Exhibit 9). Although prices have rebounded somewhat in 1993 and 1994, in real terms the price of chicken remains at an all-time low. A pound of chicken is down from 30 minutes of an average worker's 1940 wage to only 4.5 minutes of a 1990 wage. While much of this reduction can be justified by improved production efficiencies, prices are clearly depressed due to what some consider overcapacity in the industry. For example, in 1992, ConAgra, Inc., temporarily stopped sending chicks to 30 Delmarva growers to prevent an oversupply of chickens, and several chicken companies have started to experiment with producing other kinds of meats—from pork to striped bass—to soften the impact (Kim Clark, *The Sun,* July 4, 1993).

The trend is away from whole chickens to skinless, boneless parts. Perdue has responded with its line of "Fit 'n Easy" products with detailed nutrition labeling. It is also developing exports of dark meat to Puerto Rico and chicken feet to China. Fresh young turkey and turkey parts have become an important product and the "Perdue Done It!" line has been expanded to include fully cooked roasted broilers, Cornish hens, and parts. Recently the company has expanded its lines to include ground chicken and turkey sausage.

Exhibit 9

Wholesale Price/Pound of Live Broilers as Received by Farmers

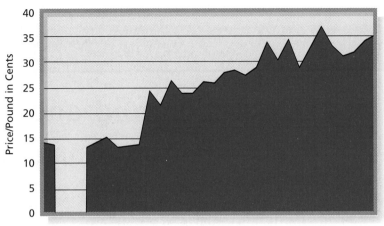

Frank Perdue reflected recently that "... we have a very high share of the available supermarket business in the Middle Atlantic and Northeastern United States, and if we were to follow that course which we know best—selling to the consumer through the retailer—we'd have to consider the Upper Midwest—Pittsburgh, Chicago, Detroit, with 25 to 30 million people."

■ Bibliography

Barmash, Isadore, 1992, Handing off to the next generation, *The New York Times,* July 26, 1.

Bates, Eric, and Bob Hall, 1995, Ruling the roost, *Southern Exposure,* Summer, 11.

Nation's broiler industry, 1995, *Broiler Industry,* January.

Clark, Kim, 1993, Tender times: Is sky falling on the chicken boom?, *The Sun,* July 4, 4F.

Facts about the DelMarVa broiler industry—1973, 1974, Industry Bulletin, February 25.

Facts about the DelMarVa poultry industry, 1995, DelMarVa Poultry Industry, Inc., May.

Fahy, Joe, 1989, All pain, no gain, *Southern Exposure,* Summer, 35–39.

Flynn, Ramsey, 1989, Strange bird, *The Washingtonian,* December, 165.

The 400 largest private companies in the U.S., 1994, *Forbes,* December 5.

Gale, Bradley T., 1992, Quality comes first when hatching power brands, *Planning Review,* July/August, 4–48.

Goldoftas, Barbara, 1989, Inside the slaughterhouse, *Southern Exposure,* Summer, 25–29.

Golden jubilee! Company honors Frank Perdue for his 50 years of service, 1989, *Perdue Courier,* special edition, July.

Hall, Bob, 1989, Chicken empires, *Southern Exposure,* Summer, 12–19.

In the money: Downhome retailer is nation's richest, Forbes says, 1986, *The Washington Post,* October 14.

MacPherson, Myra, 1975, Chicken big, *The Washington Post, Potomac Magazine,* May 11, 15.

Perdue chicken spreads its wings, 1972, *Business Week,* September 16, 113.

Perdue Farms Incorporated—Historical Highlights, 1992, Perdue Farms publication, September.

Perdue, Frank, 1981, Speech at Babson College, April 28.

Perdue, Frank, 1991, Speech to firm's lenders, accountants, and Perdue associates, September.

Poultry industry file; miscellaneous newspaper clippings from 1950 to 1994. The Maryland Room, Blackwell Library, Salisbury State University.

Santosus, Megan, 1993, Perdue's new pecking orders, *CIO,* March, 60–68.

Scarupa, Henry, 1973, When is a chicken not a football?, *The (Baltimore) Sun Magazine,* March 4, 5–12.

Silent millionaires in America, 1979, *Economist* 270 (7072), March 17.

Sterling, Bill, 1988, Just browsin', *Eastern Shore News,* March 2.

The Perdue Story. And the Five Reasons Why Our Consumers Tell It Best, 1991, Perdue Farms, publication, October.

Thornton, Gary, 1993, Data from broiler industry, Elanco Poultry Team, partner with the Poultry Industry, December.

Yeoman, Barry, 1989, Don't count your chickens, *Southern Exposure,* Summer, 21–24.

■ CASE 29 Polaroid and the Family-Imaging Market

Lew G. Brown
David R. Vestal
University of North Carolina at Greensboro

> *Don't do anything that someone else can do. Don't undertake a project unless it is manifestly important and nearly impossible.*
> —Edwin Land, Founder, Polaroid Corporation

■ http://www.polaroid.com/

At precisely 7:30 A.M. on a cold, blustery, New England winter day, Roger Clapp, project manager for the Joshua project, walked into the conference room near his office in Polaroid's Cambridge, Massachusetts, office complex known as Technology Square. The Joshua team leaders were already present: Vicki Thomas and Nick Ward from marketing; Rick Kirkendall, division vice president for consumer imaging; Roy Baessler, camera engineering; Howard Fortner, camera manufacturing; Ron Klay, film assembly manufacturing; Roger Borghesani, film assembly engineering; John Sturgis, film systems; Louise Reimenschneider, photographic systems; Bob Ruckstuhl, film programs; Harry Korotkin, finance; and Bob McCune, who served as the group's organizational development/team building facilitator. The group had been meeting every Tuesday morning since 1988 when Roger had assumed leadership of the Joshua project, the code name for Polaroid's newest camera for the instant photography market.

Roger and Hal Page, the Joshua leader before Roger, used the meetings as a way to coordinate the many disparate efforts that went into any high-technology product's development. At each meeting, each person discussed what was going on in his/her area and what problems he/she was encountering. Roger believed that if everyone had lots of information about all project areas and the project's overall direction, they would align their area's activities with that direction. The meetings would produce a self-aligning process.

The authors express their appreciation to Polaroid Corporation for its cooperation in this case's development and to Morgan Stanley and the Photo Marketing Association for providing data. Case is for classroom discussion purposes only. Copyright © 1994, by the *Case Research Journal* and Lew G. Brown. All rights reserved.

As Roger said good morning, he glanced around the room. He could tell the group members were tired. It was now early 1992, and the group had been working hard on Joshua for a long time. They had learned that he expected a lot from them. Five-day, 55-hour weeks were not enough. Most team members worked six-day weeks, often working into the night. But Roger was always there, too. He didn't ask them to do anything he didn't do.

From his previous work with project teams, Roger had realized that groups went through three stages. Initially, the group felt excited as it kicked off a multimillion dollar development project and faced the technological, marketing, and business challenges. Toward completion of the project, the group would experience the exhilaration of seeing its work come to fruition. However, the middle stage was the hardest. The group would go through an emotional "dip" when it seemed that every problem or delay brought more problems and delays. The group would feel that it would never complete the project. There would be much frustration.

Roger realized that he and Bob McCune faced the challenge of keeping the group moving through this middle stage. But he had to admit that even he sometimes felt the project was impossible. He knew, however, that the project was manifestly important to revitalizing Polaroid's instant camera sales.

"Well, let's get started," Roger began. "Besides our usual reports from each area, we have a meeting in three weeks with the corporate officers. We need to make a presentation on Joshua's status, so we need to begin to prepare for that today. We'll conclude today's meeting with a presentation from the marketing folks. First, however, let's start with reports of good news."

■ Polaroid's History

Edwin Land started Polaroid Corporation in 1937 in a Cambridge garage and developed the polarization process. In 1943, while on vacation with his family in Santa Fe, New Mexico, his three-year-old daughter asked why she could not see right away the picture of her he had just taken. Within an hour, Land had developed a mental picture of the camera, the film, and the chemistry that would allow him to solve the puzzle his daughter had presented.

In 1948, Land introduced the first Polaroid instant camera. By the time he stepped down as the company's chief executive officer in 1980, at age 70, he had built Polaroid into a $1.4 billion company. When he died in 1991, he left behind 537 patents, second only to Thomas A. Edison. (See Exhibits 1 through 3 for Polaroid's financial data.)

Land's single-minded pursuit of technology led to many successes, but also to his career's major failure. Convinced that he needed to take his instant photography concept from the portrait camera to the movie camera, Land and his engineers developed the Polavision instant movie system, launching it in 1977. Although Polavision met Land's criteria of being "nearly impossible," it was not quite "manifestly important." Polavision was too late—other companies had already invented videotape recording. Within two years, Polaroid had to write off the project at a cost of $68.5 million.

William McCune, Jr., Polaroid's president, felt that the company needed to move away from its dependence on amateur instant photography. Rather than

Exhibit 1   Consolidated Statements of Earnings and Balance Sheets (in millions, except per share data)

	Years ended December 31,		
	1991	1990	1989
Net sales			
United States	$1,113.6	$1,058.3	$ 1,091.8
International	957.0	913.4	812.9
Total net sales	2,070.6	1,971.7	1,904.7
Cost of goods sold	1,082.5	1,011.8	966.0
Marketing, research, engineering and administrative expenses	741.5	675.6	634.5
Restructuring and other expense	—	—	40.5
Total costs	1,824.0	1,687.4	1,641.0
Profit from operations	246.6	284.3	263.7
Other income/(expense)			
Litigation settlement, net of employee incentives	871.6	—	—
Interest income	25.6	19.7	37.2
Other	(2.2)	(4.7)	(2.1)
Total other income	895.0	15.0	35.1
Interest expense	58.4	81.3	86.2
Earnings before income taxes	1,083.2	218.0	212.6
Federal, state and foreign income taxes	399.5	67.0	67.6
Net earnings	$ 683.7	$ 151.0	$ 145.0
Primary earnings per common share	$ 12.54	$ 2.20	$ 1.96
Fully diluted earnings per common share	$ 10.88	—	—
Cash dividends per common share	$ .60	$ .60	$ .60
Weighted average common shares outstanding (000s)	49,943	51,519	57,568
Stock price			
High	$ 28⅛	$ 48⅛	$ 50⅛
Low	$ 19⅝	$ 20¼	$ 27¼

Source: Polaroid Corporation, 1991, *Annual Report.*

stand in the way, Land resigned in 1980, and McCune became chairman. McCune led Polaroid's diversification efforts, moving into disk drives, fiber optics, video recorders, ink-jet printers, and floppy disks. By the mid-1980s, however, some observers argued that the diversification effort was not paying off.

However, sales to amateur photographers and sales of instant cameras for business use were going strong. By 1986, these sales accounted for 55 percent of Polaroid's revenues. Consumers were still interested in instant cameras. To stimulate that demand, Polaroid introduced the Spectra camera in 1986, its first major new camera since the SX-70 in 1972. Some observers predicted that Spectra, priced at $150 to $225, was too expensive and would not sell. It sold anyway.

Exhibit 2   Polaroid Corporation and Subsidiary Companies Consolidated Balance Sheet (in millions)

	Years ended December 31, 1991	1990	1989
Assets			
Current assets			
Cash and cash equivalents	$ 162.9	$ 83.8	$ 131.2
Short-term investments	82.3	114.2	148.1
Receivables, less allowances	476.1	441.6	459.5
Inventories	524.3	519.0	529.9
Other assets	94.3	81.7	77.1
Total current assets	1,339.9	1,240.3	1,345.8
Property, plant and equipment			
Total property, plant and equipment	1,598.9	1,440.0	1,326.7
Less accumulated depreciation	1,049.5	979.0	895.8
Net property, plant and equipment	549.4	461.0	430.9
Total assets	$1,889.3	$1,701.3	$1,776.7
Liabilities and Stockholders' Equity			
Current liabilities			
Short-term debt	$ 145.9	$ 168.6	$ 299.0
Current portion of long-term debt	26.7	79.4	70.4
Payables and accruals	237.4	218.4	216.2
Compensation and benefits	131.8	123.8	143.9
Federal, state and foreign income taxes	102.8	41.0	44.7
Total current liabilities	644.6	631.2	774.2
Long-term debt	471.8	513.8	531.8
Redeemable preferred stock equity	—	348.6	321.9
Preferred stock	—	—	—
Common stockholders' equity			
Common stock, $1 par value, authorized 150,000,000 shares	75.4	75.4	75.4
Additional paid-in capital	379.5	379.5	379.5
Retained earnings	1,609.9	1,038.3	955.8
Less: Treasury stock, at cost	1,083.7	1,053.1	997.5
Deferred compensation—ESOP	208.2	232.4	264.4
Total common stockholders' equity	772.9	207.7	148.8
Total liabilities and stockholders' equity	$1,889.3	$1,701.3	$1,776.7

Source: Polaroid Corporation, 1991, *Annual Report.*

Edwin Land probably felt vindicated that Polaroid was refocusing on its core business, amateur instant photography. Polaroid had no direct competition in the U.S. instant photography market. The company had won a patent infringement suit against Kodak in 1985. The court ruling required Kodak to exit the instant photography business and pay Polaroid approximately $1 billion.

Exhibit 3	Income and Assets by Geographic Area (in millions)		
	Years ended December 31,		
	1991	1990	1989
Sales			
United States			
Customers	$1,113.6	$1,058.3	$1,091.8
Intercompany	438.5	421.4	407.7
	1,552.1	1,479.7	1,499.5
Europe			
Customers	624.6	598.5	504.5
Intercompany	287.3	159.6	167.4
	911.9	758.1	671.9
Asia/Pacific and Western Hemisphere			
Customers	332.4	314.9	308.4
Intercompany	51.0	11.0	9.1
	383.4	325.9	317.5
Eliminations	(776.8)	(592.0)	(584.2)
Net sales	$2,070.6	$1,971.7	$1,904.7
Profits			
United States	$ 120.9	$ 179.9	$ 150.2
Europe	94.4	97.7	115.0
Asia/Pacific and Western Hemisphere	40.3	23.8	31.5
General corporate expense	(18.0)	(13.4)	(13.0)
Eliminations	9.0	(3.7)	(20.0)
Profit from operations	246.6	284.3	263.7
Other income less interest expense	836.6	(66.3)	(51.1)
Earnings before income taxes	$1,083.2	$ 218.0	$ 212.6
Assets			
United States	$1,153.9	$1,055.0	$1,054.2
Europe	548.7	507.3	475.7
Asia/Pacific and Western Hemisphere	165.8	160.2	168.1
Corporate assets (cash, cash equivalents and short-term investments)	245.2	198.0	279.3
Eliminations	(224.2)	(219.2)	(200.6)
Total assets	$1,889.4	$1,701.3	$1,776.7

Source: Polaroid Corporation, 1991, *Annual Report*.

However, Land and Polaroid knew that the company faced severe competition in the larger photography market. Video camcorders, easy-to-use 35mm point-and-shoot cameras (often called 35mm rangefinders), and one-hour film developing were cutting deeply into Polaroid's market. Worldwide sales of instant cameras had fallen from a peak of 13 million units in 1978 to about 4 million in

1991. The new 35mm cameras were outselling instant cameras five to one. Polaroid realized that it had to do something to reinvigorate the amateur photography market and to expand its base.

How Instant Cameras Work

In black-and-white instant photography's early days, the camera user had to pull the exposed instant picture from the camera, wait about one minute, peel off a piece of paper, and use a small sponge to apply a chemical coating to the picture to stop its development. Then the picture had to dry before someone could safely handle it.

When Polaroid introduced color instant photography in 1963, the technology had advanced such that the user still had to time the picture's development and remove the print from the film sheet but did not have to apply any chemicals. The film was still "sticky" for several minutes.

In 1972, Polaroid introduced the SX-70 instant camera, which used what the company called "integral film." As the name implied, the new film was an integrated structure that did not require the user to do any timing or other treatment. There were no excess pieces of film or paper to discard. The one-piece unit contained all the chemicals necessary for development of the picture. The user still had to wait several minutes for the exposed picture to develop.

With integral film, within four-tenths of a second after the user has pushed the shutter release button and exposed the film, the camera partially ejects the exposed film unit. A battery contained in the film cartridge powers the camera and the motor that ejects the film. As the camera ejects the picture, the film passes between two metal rollers. These rollers squeeze the film, bursting a small pod at the leading edge of the film. This pod contains chemical reagents that spread between the film unit's receiving and negative layers. The chemicals react with the negative layers based on the nature of the layer and the amount of each layer's exposure to light during the exposure process (see Exhibit 4). These reactions determine the lightness, darkness, and color of each area of the final picture. This chemical process is what the user sees as he/she watches the film develop from the plain, grayish-green initial film color to the finished picture. All of this development takes place outside the camera in full light. Opacifying dyes in the reagent layer block additional light from entering the light-sensitive layers once the film exits the camera.

Because the user does not have to peel anything from the integral film unit or apply any chemical, he/she is technically able to take another picture immediately. However, because the camera only partially ejects the picture, the user must take the exposed picture from the camera and find a place to put it, usually a pocket or nearby table. If the user takes a second picture before removing the first, the second film unit will push the first out of the camera, causing it to fall to the floor. (See Exhibit 5 for a description of Polaroid's camera line.)

New Product Development at Polaroid

In the 1940s and 1950s, a product development process called "skunkworks" sprung to life a Polaroid. This process allowed maverick individuals or groups to pursue new product design ideas unofficially. These individuals or groups frequently generated technology-driven new product designs, giving little, if any, consideration to marketing or business strategy. Further, operating managers often had only limited influence over the design of machinery. Film and camera

Exhibit 4

How Polaroid Instant Film Works

Source: Neblette's Handbook of Photography and Reprography.

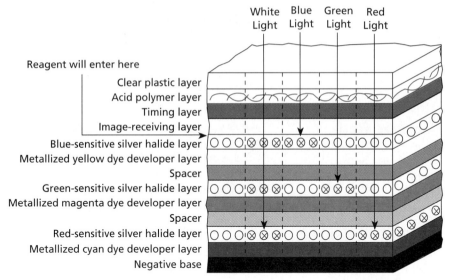

White Light   Blue Light   Green Light   Red Light

Reagent will enter here
Clear plastic layer
Acid polymer layer
Timing layer
Image-receiving layer
Blue-sensitive silver halide layer
Metallized yellow dye developer layer
Spacer
Green-sensitive silver halide layer
Metallized magenta dye developer layer
Spacer
Red-sensitive silver halide layer
Metallized cyan dye developer layer
Negative base

○ Unexposed silver halide
⊗ Exposed silver halide

(a) The Film at Exposure

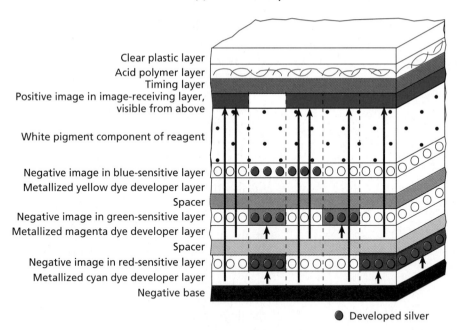

Clear plastic layer
Acid polymer layer
Timing layer
Positive image in image-receiving layer, visible from above
White pigment component of reagent
Negative image in blue-sensitive layer
Metallized yellow dye developer layer
Spacer
Negative image in green-sensitive layer
Metallized magenta dye developer layer
Spacer
Negative image in red-sensitive layer
Metallized cyan dye developer layer
Negative base

● Developed silver

(b) The Developed Film

development followed parallel paths. Development of the film pack occurred after development of the film components. This development process invariably resulted in major problems when managers tried to get all the parts to work together.

Exhibit 5   Guide to Polaroid Instant Cameras

Spectra Cameras

Spectra 2 AF Camera:
   Autofocus, range 2 feet to infinity.
   Auto exposure, flash range 2–15 feet.
   Uses Spectra instant color film.
   Pictures guaranteed for one full year after camera purchase (up to a limit of 10 packs of film).
   Camera folds to fit neatly in a briefcase.
   Easy to use, just point and shoot.
   Suggested retail: $79–$85. Dealer price: $74.

Spectra AF Camera:
   Has same features as Spectra 2 AF plus:
   Self-timer.
   Control panel allows user to turn off automatic features.
   Viewfinder displays symbols to help get best pictures.
   Suggested retail: $100–$110. Dealer price: $85.

Impulse Cameras

Impulse:
   Focus range 2 feet to infinity.
   Manual dual lens for close-up shots 2–4 feet.
   Pop-up flash, range 4–10 feet.
   Uses 600 PLUS instant film.
   Easy to use, just point and shoot.
   Suggested retail: $40–$45. Dealer price: $36.

Impulse AF:
   Has same features as Impulse plus:
   Autofocus.
   Self-timer.
   Flash range 2–14 feet.
   Suggested retail: $80–$85. Dealer price: $71.50.

OneStep Flash Camera:
   Built-in electronic flash folds down when not in use.
   Flash range 4–10 feet.
   Autofocus. Range 4 feet to infinity.
   Used 600 PLUS film.
   Easy to use, just point and shoot.
   Suggested retail: $27–33. Dealer price: $27.

Cool Cam Camera:
   Built-in electronic flash folds down when not in use.
   Flash range 4–10 feet.
   Autofocus. Range 4 feet to infinity.
   Uses 600 PLUS film.
   Easy to use, just point and shoot.
   Free matching camera bag with return of camera registration card.
   Suggested retail: $30–$35. Dealer price: $27.

Source: Polaroid Corporation.

Birth of a New Process

In 1984, a skunkworks team from camera engineering began discussing Polaroid's next camera, and a team from film research began to work on possibilities for a new film. The two groups met unofficially to share ideas. These "blue sky" meetings focused on the problems of picture quality, film cost, and camera size. The groups soon narrowed their discussions to a film that would fit a smaller camera.

Unlike some skunkworks groups, these two groups sought marketing's participation. In 1984 and 1985, Polaroid's internal market research group conducted focus groups to get consumer reactions to small, medium, and standard-sized instant cameras with picture-storage features. The results from these focus groups suggested that some consumers would be interested in the smaller camera and its smaller pictures. Polaroid president I. MacAllister Booth asked his assistant, Roger Clapp, to develop the idea.

The Joshua Story

Enter Joshua. Even as Polaroid introduced the Spectra camera in 1986, Booth, who had just assumed the CEO's position, realized that the company had to continue work on its next new camera. He appointed Peter Kliem as director of research and engineering, combining two departments that had traditionally had separate new product development responsibilities. Clapp took responsibility for camera engineering. Booth also asked Hal Page, Polaroid's vice president for quality, to become program manager for the next consumer camera. For the first time, Polaroid had a single, high-level program manager responsible for all aspects of new product development—for film as well as camera and for manufacturing as well as marketing.

Page began a year-long process of reexamination to generate ideas for a new camera. He started brainstorming sessions by showing a training film that featured a cartoon character named Joshua. In the film, Joshua finds himself trapped in a box and tries all the obvious ways to escape. Finally, in frustration, Joshua gently taps his finger against the box's wall and unexpectedly finds that his finger has poked a hole in the wall. He struggles to make the hole bigger and escapes.

Joshua sent a message to the hundreds of people from many functional groups who attended Page's brainstorming sessions. To generate truly innovative ideas for a new camera, the employees would have to attack new problems with new ways of thinking—"out-of-the-box" approaches. To create something other than an extension of Polaroid's existing cameras, people would have to think creatively and give up old prejudices, including, perhaps, their prejudice against smaller cameras. The brainstorming sessions also helped participants face the tension-filled question of whether new products should be "technology driven" or "marketing driven." Participants soon learned the answer: They had to be both.

Hal Page also showed the groups a film that dramatically illustrated the value of internal picture storage for the new camera. The film showed tourists at Disney World using 35mm automatic cameras to take picture after picture. Other tourists, however, stood around watching their one Polaroid picture develop and searching for a place to put it. Page and others thought consumers would take more pictures if they did not have to stop after each one to find a place to put it while it developed. Further, consumers would damage and lose fewer pictures.

This storage feature, however, required that the camera's film bend around a chute after exposure to enter the storage compartment. Engineers told Larry Swensen, a member of the marketing department, that Polaroid's standard film would not bend without breaking or coming apart. Swensen, however, refused to accept this conventional wisdom. He made a working model of a camera that allowed standard film to make a 180-degree U-turn during processing. The camera released the photographs into a built-in storage chamber where the user could view them as they developed. No longer would the user need to interrupt picture taking to find a safe place for each picture. Out-of-the-box thinking had begun to work.

Page also used outside marketing consultants. Based on studies of small cameras that Polaroid had conducted between 1984 and 1986, the consultants concluded that there would be a market for a smaller instant camera and that the camera would not cannibalize Polaroid's existing lines. Additional outside studies in 1987 and 1988 examined consumer preferences regarding camera size, camera price, and film price. Another study estimated the sales volume that Polaroid could expect from various feature combinations.

Polaroid had based these studies on the assumption that it would set the retail price of the new camera at $150. As the studies progressed, however, management concluded that the market at the $150 retail price would be too small and that it should price the camera so that its retail price would be about $100. This change required more market studies.

In 1988, Hal Page left Polaroid, and Roger Clapp took over what employees had dubbed the "Joshua project." Roger had been with Polaroid for 22 years, having earned a BS in chemical engineering at Northeastern University and an MBA from Harvard. Although Page and his groups had made much progress, many technical and marketing hurdles remained. Design engineers faced trade-offs between size and other features, such as performance and cost. As a result, the planned camera had become too large. Roger Clapp remarked that it looked like a "brick." Clapp stopped the design process and ordered the developers to reconsider all trade-offs. This planned four-week pause, however, turned into an eight-month interruption, as it opened the door for reconsideration of all the lingering issues.

As Clapp's managers reviewed the Joshua project, they realized that they needed to clarify the camera's market potential at a $100 price and to conduct new research to bring marketing fully behind the program. The managers agreed that the last market research hurdle would be an "assessor test" conducted by Professor Glenn Urban of MIT's Sloan School of Management.

The assessor test involved setting up mock stores at six geographically diverse sites in the United States. These "stores" offered 25 different cameras (both Polaroid's and competing models), with prices ranging from inexpensive to expensive. Each store had a real counter, a film rack, feature cards, and sales clerks to answer questions. As a part of the interview process, Polaroid's advertising agency created full-color sheets of print advertising for the new camera. Polaroid also developed realistic Joshua camera models. Over a one-month period, 2,400 people participated in market interviews and testing at the six "stores." Researchers carefully screened participants on factors such as age, sex, race, and economic status to make sure the group represented demographics of the U.S. population as a whole.

During this time, another camera design emerged from a one-man skunk-works. Although the Joshua project was well under way, Larry Douglas had continued to work on his idea. Douglas' camera offered an ingenious design for a camera that popped open to take a picture, then closed automatically. Polaroid ordered market research for Douglas' camera.

The two studies provided convincing evidence that there was a market for a smaller instant camera and that Joshua would be the preferred product. Polaroid's board of directors gave Joshua the go-ahead in late 1989.

■ Vision to Reality

Although Polaroid had devoted an extraordinary amount of time and energy to the Joshua project before its final approval, the camera and the film were still in the developmental stage. Polaroid employees throughout the company still had to solve many problems.

Manufacturing had to install a new computer-aided design (CAD) system and to select a new material and design for the camera's mainframe. The camera would employ through-the-lens viewing, the same viewing system found on millions of 35mm cameras. The picture storage compartment would have to hold up to all 10 of the pictures in a film package. And the camera would have to pass Polaroid's four-foot drop test and meet other aggressive quality goals.

Polaroid created a cross-functional steering committee to manage the film manufacturing process. This team addressed issues such as how to include the battery in the smaller film pack and how to design the film manufacturing process itself. Like Polaroid's other instant film, Joshua's film would come in a package of 10 exposures and would cost the consumer about $1.00 per picture, as compared to about $.40 for a conventional 35mm picture. The picture would be about 2-1/8 by 2-7/8 inches, a pocket-sized format that was smaller than conventional 35mm prints.

Electronics engineers designed a new microcontroller to be the heart of the Joshua camera. The new controller solved many long-standing technical and manufacturing problems. Using software, it provided "track and hold," "trim and speed," and "wink" features to measure the light available for the picture, set the exposure, and find the distance from the camera to the subject. In other words, like many 35mm cameras on the market, Joshua would have "automatic everything." In all these processes, managers insisted on meeting the highest quality and reliability standards.

By Labor Day 1991, the Joshua team had produced 24 Joshua prototype cameras for testing by Polaroid employees over the holiday weekend. Twenty-three cameras worked. The team continued to produce cameras for weekend tests and made a concentrated assault on any problems the tests identified. For Christmas 1991, the team produced 300 Joshua cameras for non-Polaroid employees from coast to coast to test. This test represented the earliest time in a product's development that Polaroid had ever placed cameras with outside users. Managers believed that they were making a new camera that met real customer needs, but they wanted to base their decisions on market research, not on instincts.

These field tests suggested that Joshua users took more vertical pictures and more close-ups than did users of other Polaroid cameras. Based on these reactions, engineers adjusted the camera's exposure systems to perform optimally in vertical format or close-up situations. Polaroid also conducted market tests in foreign countries. Polaroid calculated that, by the time it announced the camera, more than 2,000 Polaroid and non-Polaroid consumers would have made more than 55,000 images for picture analysis.

■ The Countdown

During 1990, Roger realized that he needed to create a sense of urgency in the team. The team had decided to have the camera ready for introduction in late 1992, but Roger worried that it was easy for team members to feel that they had plenty of time or that deadlines were flexible.

Therefore, he had a countdown clock constructed. The clock counted down the number of days and hours to "zero day"—the target day when everything had to be ready to meet the market introduction schedule. The clock ran on electricity and had a battery back up. One started the clock with a key. But once the clock had been started, no one could stop it. Roger wanted to make it clear to the group that there would be no on-again, off-again deadlines.

The group had agreed to start the clock in late 1990. Now it hung on the wall in the conference room, looming over their meetings and reminding them that time did not stand still.

■ The U.S. Family-Imaging Market

After each team member had made his/her initial status report, Roger turned to Vicki Thomas, senior marketing manager. Vicki had recently joined Polaroid from GTE. She had an undergraduate degree in political science from the University of Vermont and an MBA from the American Graduate School of International Management (Thunderbird).

"As you know, we have been focusing on camera and film manufacturing and on market research. It is now time for us to begin to develop our marketing strategy for the U.S. consumer market. At our last meeting we asked Vicki to prepare an overview of the market so we would have a background for the marketing plans she, Nick, and Rick will present later. Vicki."

"Thanks, Roger. I have prepared a series of overheads that summarize the U.S. market that I want to share with you now. This first overhead presents a U.S. economic overview. We feel that the recession is over and that economic conditions will improve slowly during 1992 and into 1993. Disposable income will increase about two percent over 1991 while the prime rate and inflation will remain relatively low. We also believe the unemployment rate will continue in the low seven percent range and that consumer confidence will remain relatively unchanged at about 65 on a 0-to-100 scale. There may be some higher taxes on individuals and corporations due to the federal government's budgetary problems. In summary, we feel that consumers remain cautious and that they are increasingly searching for value in the products and services they purchase. This concern with value puts pressure on instant photography because many consumers feel that instant film's price is very high compared with standard 35mm film.

"This overhead provides a societal overview and shows that we believe that the United States is becoming increasingly fragmented. Minority populations are

Exhibit 6   U.S. Camera Market Overview

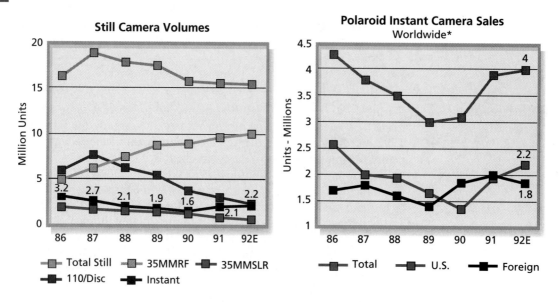

Still Camera Volumes

Polaroid Instant Camera Sales
Worldwide*

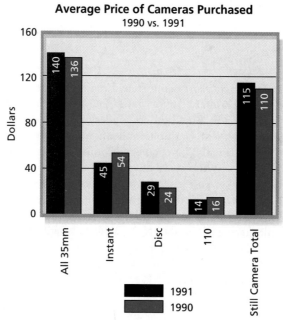

Average Price of Cameras Purchased
1990 vs. 1991

These Data Provided by Morgan Stanley & Co., not Polaroid. Its use here is for case purposes only.

Source: Photo Marketing Association

becoming more significant as is the mature population. Further, we are also seeing an explosion of specialized media and communication channels. The United States is becoming a 'salad bowl' instead of a 'melting pot.'

"We now turn to the U.S. camera market itself (Exhibit 6). This overhead uses Photo Marketing Association data and Morgan Stanley data to show that although the total still-camera market (not including camcorders) is flat, 35mm rangefinder camera sales (the so-called point-and-shoot 35mm camera without interchangeable lenses) are growing rapidly. The 35mm rangefinder has taken share from other camera types in the last six years. The rangefinders offer excellent photo quality, automated functions, ease of use versus traditional 35mm SLR cameras, compact size, built-in zoom lenses in some cases, and relatively low prices (as low as $19.95 for some simple versions). Vivitar, Olympus, and Polaroid have seen their total shares of the camera market grow in the past four years while Kodak's has fallen. Many major players are introducing new models.

"We estimate that about 90 percent of households own a still camera of some kind and about 20 percent own an instant camera. As you know, although our U.S. consumer business is reasonably healthy, our sales revenue has been flat since 1986 even though our shipments and market share are up. Average 35mm rangefinder camera prices have been in the $95 range for the past five years while average instant camera prices are falling into the low $40 range. The average price for 35mm SLR cameras is $333 today as compared with about $195 in 1986.

"I thought you would also be interested in camera distribution and prices, so I included these next two overheads (Exhibits 7 and 8) based on Photo

Exhibit 7

Still Cameras Purchased: Format Mix; by Outlet Type

Note: Other mass retailers include combination/hypermarket, supermarket, drug store, department store (not discount).

Base: Total still cameras purchased, except single-use cameras.

Source: Photo Marketing Association.

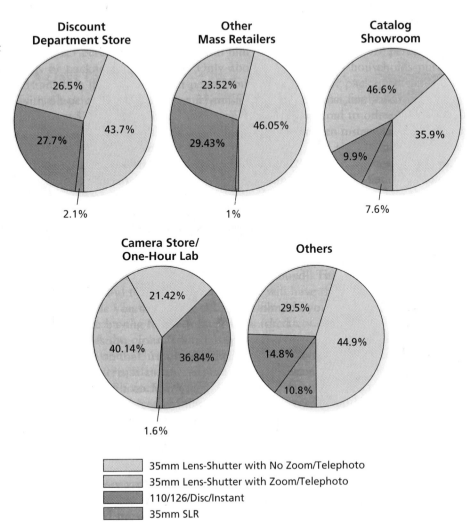

35mm Lens-Shutter with No Zoom/Telephoto
35mm Lens-Shutter with Zoom/Telephoto
110/126/Disc/Instant
35mm SLR

Exhibit 8   Camera Distribution and Prices, 1991

Average Number of Cameras Sold Per Firm*

Camera Type	All Speciality Retailers Combined	Camera Store No Minilab	Camera Store with Minilab	Stand-Alone Minilab	All Mass Retailers Combined
35mm SLR	122	84	174	42	22
35mm RF	359	253	665	90	2,662
110/Disc	194	12	324	13	165
Instant:					
Spectra	24	11	32	12	NA
Impulse	35	22	43	15	12
Cool Cam	68	12	105	11	NA
Other	37	13	50	13	2,050
Total inst.	82	32	118	23	1,371
Total still cameras	401	241	770	91	2,916

Average Price per Camera

Camera Type	All Speciality Retailers Combined	Camera Store No Minilab	Camera Store with Minilab	Stand-Alone Minilab	All Mass Retailers Combined
35mm SLR	$373	$413	$364	$391	$ 387
35mm RF	$205	$258	$200	$168	$ 37
110	$ 18	$ 25	$ 18	$ 22	$ 15
Instant:					
Spectra	$122	$143	$118	$136	NA
Impulse	$ 68	$72	$ 67	$ 86	$ 39
Cool Cam	$ 35	$40	$ 34	$ 54	NA
Other	$117	$62	$ 56	$ 75	$ 30
Total inst.	$ 82	$108	$ 67	$ 97	$ 30
Total still cameras	$179	$250	$170	$163	$ 35

*Numbers sold are per firm, not per outlet. A firm that sells a particular camera format may not do so in all of its outlets.

Source: Photo Marketing Association.

Marketing Association data. The major change since 1986 has been the almost one-third increase in our percentage distribution through discount stores, including stores such as Wal-Mart and Kmart. The Photo Marketing Association's research indicates that consumers purchase 58.1 percent of 110/125/disc/instant cameras in discount department stores and another 23.7 percent in other mass retail stores. Exhibit 7 shows that these cameras account for about 28 percent of the cameras sold in discount stores and about 29 percent in other mass retailers. Our top ten accounts generated about 60 percent of our sales in 1991 versus about 45 percent in 1986.

"Exhibit 8 reflects the importance of mass retailers (including discount stores) in the camera market. Camera sales through these outlets dwarf average sales in other outlets; but, as you can see, the average prices are much lower.

Exhibit 9   Film Market

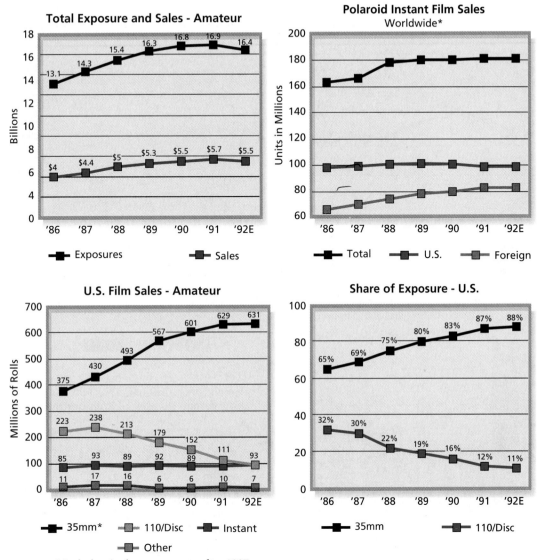

Source: Photo Marketing Association.

"Exhibit 9 uses data from the Photo Marketing Association and Morgan Stanley to describe the U.S. film market. You can see that total exposures are flat, as are our film shipments. However, 35mm film is taking a growing market share while our sales are relatively flat. As you know, film purchasing accounts for 18 percent of the $12 billion amateur camera/film market and film processing accounts for 45.5 percent. Still cameras themselves account for 13.3 percent of annual sales.

"This overhead (Exhibit 10) again uses Photo Marketing Association data to show that our dollar volume of film sales to the amateur market has been relatively flat since 1988, although the dollar volume will increase slightly this

Exhibit 10 Film Sales

Polaroid Film Sales to Amateur Market*

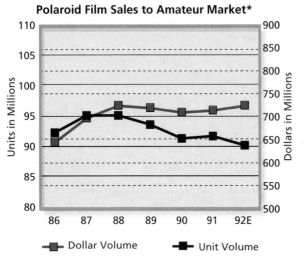

- Dollar Volume
- Unit Volume

Market Share of Film Purchased

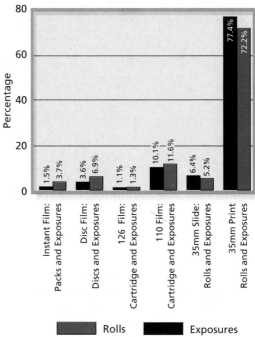

Rolls   Exposures

Price Paid Per Unit of Film
By Users of Individual Film Types and Exposure Counts

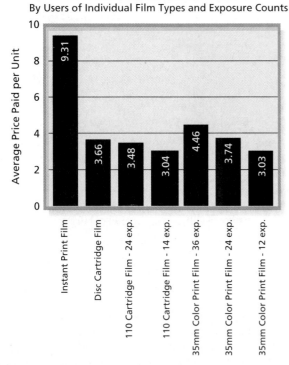

Percent of Households That Purchased Film, and Average Number of Rolls per Household
Total U.S. by Film Type

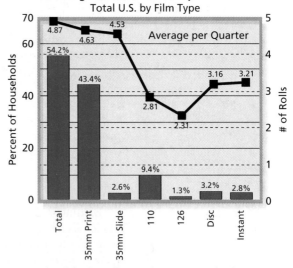

These data provided by Stanley Morgan & Co., not Polaroid. Its use here is for case purposes only.

Source: Morgan Stanley Research Estimates.

Source: Photo Marketing Association.

Base: All who purchased, received free, or used individual types of film in the past 12 months.

Note: Films defined as rolls, cartridges, instant packs, discs.

Source: Photo Marketing Association.

Source: Photo Marketing Association.

Exhibit 11   Minilab Processing

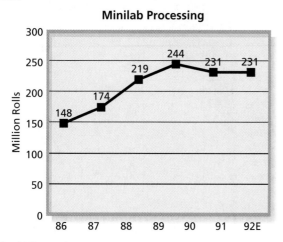

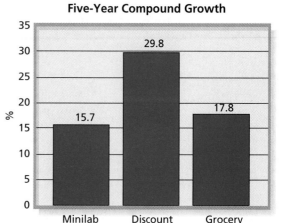

Source: Polaroid Corporation.

year. Unit volume, however has been declining since 1988. Instant film captures only a 1.5 percent share of the total film exposures and only 3.7 percent of the rolls or packages of film sold. Only about 2.8 percent of households purchase instant film in a three-month period, buying about three packs. This compares with 43 percent who purchase 35mm film, buying almost five rolls.

"I noted earlier that instant film is expensive compared to other film. Exhibit 10 shows this dramatically. In fact, the price gap between instant and 35mm film *per developed image* has been widening over the past six years. The cost per developed image for instant film will be about $.97 this year versus about $.39 for 35mm film. I analyzed some Photo Marketing Association data that indicated that consumers pay an average *premium* of almost 31 percent when they select "fast" processing versus regular processing at photo-processing outlets.

"While I'm discussing processing, this overhead (Exhibit 11) shows that the growth in minilab, one-hour processing seems to have peaked and that discount and grocery store processing is actually growing faster than minilab. Most grocery/discount stores offer one-day turnaround. This is where we feel the growth is."

"Vicki, while you are on the subject of film, do you have any data on where consumers are buying film?" John Sturgis asked.

"Good question, John," Vicki responded. "Let me see, I believe I have an overhead here on that. Yes, here it is (Exhibit 12). As I noted earlier, we have seen a significant increase in our camera sales in discount department stores. This chart based on Photo Marketing Association data shows that consumers purchased almost 37 percent of film in these stores, easily outdistancing drugstores and supermarkets. As in camera sales, our top ten customers now account for about half of our film shipments, up from about one-third in 1986."

"How are we doing on consumer awareness?" Howard Fortner asked.

"Another good question, and right on cue, Howard," Vicki responded. "I'll ask Nick to show you some overheads he prepared."

Nick Ward had only recently joined Polaroid as senior marketing research analyst. He had previously been with Kraft/General Foods and had a Ph.D. in

Exhibit 12

Percentage Breakdown of
Household Film Purchased in
the Past 12 Months, by Outlet
Type

Source: Photo Marketing Association.

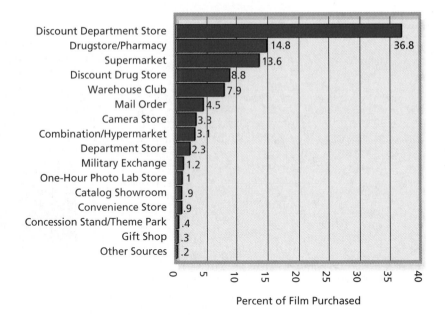

Percent of Film Purchased

experimental psychology from the University of Kansas and an undergraduate degree from UCLA in mathematical psychology.

"Howard, this overhead (Exhibit 13) shows some results from the Photo Marketing Association's most recent consumer tracking studies. As you can see, Kodak has tremendous consumer awareness in both cameras and film, while we hover in the 40 to 50 percent range. Our camera awareness is significantly below 50 percent in terms of top-of-mind awareness. As you know, our research shows that most Polaroid owners also have at least one other camera in their home. Our advertising tracking studies show that about one-third of consumers see instant cameras fitting their lifestyle. However, consumers' perceptions of our cameras' quality have fallen somewhat, probably due to our advertising our OneStep and Cool Cam cameras at less than $30, the 'under 30 clams' ads.

"I guess the next logical question relates to our advertising spending. So, this overhead also compares our U.S. advertising spending and share of voice with our awareness. There is some lag effect here from year to year. I've also included a graph showing our advertising and promotion expenses as a percent of worldwide sales.

"Exhibits 14 and 15 summarize some Photo Marketing Association information I've gathered about the knowledge and use of cameras. The first chart on Exhibit 14 indicates that 53 percent of the survey's respondents felt they knew almost nothing or just a little about photography. The second chart compares consumers' views of picture quality. Respondents gave instant prints the lowest rating. Our tracking studies also show that consumers see instant cameras as being more expensive and less flexible and compact than other camera types.

"Exhibit 15 again uses Photo Marketing Association data to reflect that consumers are taking fewer pictures because they feel they have fewer opportunities much more than because of their concern over the cost of film and processing. People cited their desire to preserve memories and share those memories later with others as their main reasons for taking pictures. Notice also

Exhibit 13 Advertising and Promotion

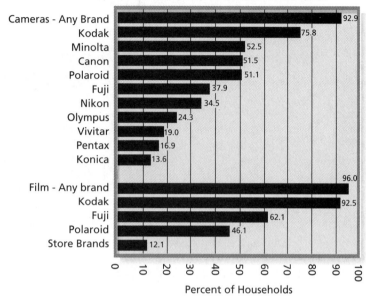

Which Photo Products/Brands Do You Recall Seeing or Hearing Advertised in the Past 12 Months?

	Percent of Households
Cameras - Any Brand	92.9
Kodak	75.8
Minolta	52.5
Canon	51.5
Polaroid	51.1
Fuji	37.9
Nikon	34.5
Olympus	24.3
Vivitar	19.0
Pentax	16.9
Konica	13.6
Film - Any brand	96.0
Kodak	92.5
Fuji	62.1
Polaroid	46.1
Store Brands	12.1

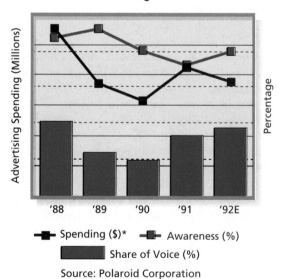

U.S. Advertising Awareness

('88 '89 '90 '91 '92E)

- Spending ($)*   - Awareness (%)
- Share of Voice (%)

Source: Polaroid Corporation

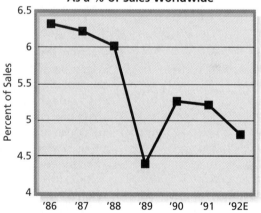

Advertising and Promotion Expenses As a % of Sales Worldwide

('86 '87 '88 '89 '90 '91 '92E)

Source: Morgan Stanley Research**

*Specific data points are not disclosed on the graph. Graph represents relative magnitudes of spending, awareness, and share of voice.

**Data for graph supplied by Morgan Stanley & Co., not by Polaroid. Use is for case purposes only.

Source: Photo Marketing Association.

Exhibit 14

How Respondents Described Their Knowledge About Photography

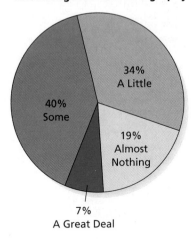

- 34% A Little
- 19% Almost Nothing
- 7% A Great Deal
- 40% Some

Source: Photo Marketing Association.

Household Rating of Picture Quality
By Individual Film/Camera Formats Household Uses

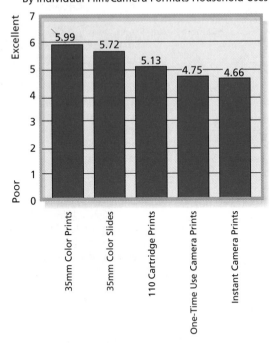

Format	Rating
35mm Color Prints	5.99
35mm Color Slides	5.72
110 Cartridge Prints	5.13
One-Time Use Camera Prints	4.75
Instant Camera Prints	4.66

Source: Photo Marketing Association.

that the instant camera's primary users are females. We also know that the average instant camera user is somewhat older than the average users of other cameras. For example, our average user is about 46 years old versus about 41 years old for users of 35mm rangefinders. The favorite subjects for picture taking are family celebrations and people. I should also add that we estimate that there are approximately 9.5 million households that have and use a Polaroid camera, about an equal number that have a Polaroid camera but don't use it, and about 75 million households that don't own a Polaroid.

"Finally, our research also shows that the Joshua camera has good product imagery; that is, compared to our other cameras, consumers see it as similar to a 35mm camera and as having a stylish appearance and contemporary design. Consumers also found it easier to handle, more full featured, and more fully automatic than our other cameras. Consumers also felt they would be more likely to use the camera for vacations, weekend and day trips, and sporting events more than our other cameras. Research also shows that consumers want a better camera that is easier to operate and that they can carry on trips in the U.S."

"Nick, did you find any commonalities among the consumers who liked the Joshua camera in your research?" asked Roy Baessler.

"Yes, Roy. At this time, we can say that the camera appeals to younger, upscale, career-minded people who are intelligent, stylish, adventurous, and friendly," Nick responded.

"Roger, that's all the background information we wanted to present today."

Exhibit 15 Camera Usage

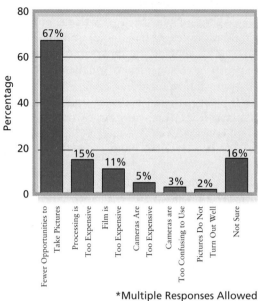

Reasons Why Currently Taking Fewer Pictures*

(Percentage)
- Fewer Opportunities to Take Pictures — 67%
- Processing is Too Expensive — 15%
- Film is Too Expensive — 11%
- Cameras Are Too Expensive — 5%
- Cameras are Too Confusing to Use — 3%
- Pictures Do Not Turn Out Well — 2%
- Not Sure — 16%

*Multiple Responses Allowed

*Among those who are taking fewer pictures now compared to five years ago.
Source: Photo Marketing Association.

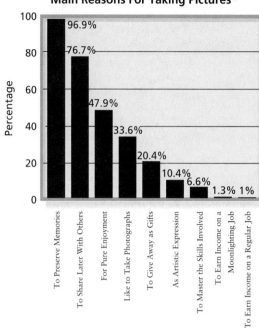

What Are Your Household's Main Reasons For Taking Pictures*

(Percentage)
- To Preserve Memories — 96.9%
- To Share Later With Others — 76.7%
- For Pure Enjoyment — 47.9%
- Like to Take Photographs — 33.6%
- To Give Away as Gifts — 20.4%
- As Artistic Expression — 10.4%
- To Master the Skills Involved — 6.6%
- To Earn Income on a Moonlighting Job — 1.3%
- To Earn Income on a Regular Job — 1%

*Multiple Responses Allowed

Source: Photo Marketing Association.
Base: All who own cameras/camcorders.

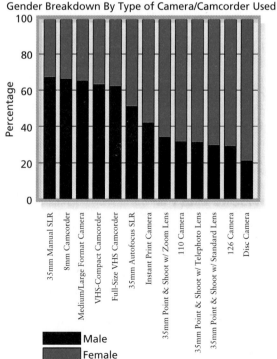

Primary Use of Each Camera Household Used in Past 12 Months

Gender Breakdown By Type of Camera/Camcorder Used

Camera types: 35mm Manual SLR, 8mm Camcorder, Medium/Large Format Camera, VHS-Compact Camcorder, Full-Size VHS Camcorder, 35mm Autofocus SLR, Instant Print Camera, 35mm Point & Shoot w/ Zoom Lens, 110 Camera, 35mm Point & Shoot w/ Telephoto Lens, 35mm Point & Shoot w/ Standard Lens, 126 Camera, Disc Camera

■ Male
▨ Female

Source: Photo Marketing Association.

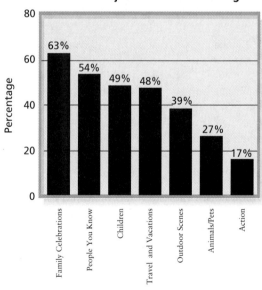

Favorite Subjects For Picture Taking*

(Percentage)
- Family Celebrations — 63%
- People You Know — 54%
- Children — 49%
- Travel and Vacations — 48%
- Outdoor Scenes — 39%
- Animals/Pets — 27%
- Action — 17%

*Multiple Responses Allowed

Source: Photo Marketing Association.

■ The Assignment

"Thanks, Vicki and Nick. As I said, we need to spend the time in these meetings over the next two weeks to prepare for our meeting with the corporate officers. I'd like to ask Vicki, Nick, and Rick to be prepared to present an outline of a U.S. marketing strategy for our family-imaging business at our meeting in three weeks. Meanwhile, if any of you have suggestions for them, please feel free to share them. I'm sure they'll appreciate your ideas."

As the meeting adjourned, Vicki gathered her overheads. She glanced at the countdown clock and then at Nick. "I'm starting to hate that clock," she announced. "We've lost seven days since our last meeting! There's just too much to do and too little time."

■ CASE 30 Service Corporation International

Ronald J. Salazar
Idaho State University

> *We have a strong competitor [from] Houston, Texas; they're about twice our size. They haven't got the same hands-on experience. The industry feels violated by them. They practice top-down management as opposed to our bottom-up management.*
> —Ray Loewen, President of The Loewen Group, May 1992

> *HOUSTON, TEXAS, February 9, 1993 ... Service Corporation International (SCI) today reported record-setting net income for the year ended December 31, 1992 of $86.5 million, representing an 18 percent increase over 1991. Revenues increased to an all time high of $772.5 million, up 20 percent over last year. Earnings per share increased to $1.13 in 1992 from $1.03 a year ago, after restatement for a 3-for-2 stock split in June 1992. Excluding a $4.8 million income tax benefit recognized in 1991, net income increased 26 percent and earnings per share increased 18 percent.*
> —SCI News Release

No matter what competitors say about Service Corporation International (SCI), the Houston-based firm is a dominant competitor in the funeral service industry in North America and, by some estimates, the world. Fueled by an impressive growth pattern spanning the 30 years since its founding in 1962, SCI has positioned itself for even greater success in the future. How have they done it and what lies ahead? What about the industry itself? What factors influence the funeral home business and what effects are these expected to have on SCI?

■ Industry History

Although many firms have experienced exceptional growth and profitability as a result of continuously improving and changing products and services, the funeral service business has not enjoyed success with innovation. The same types of products and services offered more than 200 years ago are still being offered today. Innovations have occurred gradually and have been rooted in social tradition. The last major funeral innovation occurred in the 1800s when

C.573

specialized houses, named parlors, were first used as gathering places for bereaved family members. At about the same time, men who "undertook" the tasks of handling deceased souls became known as "undertakers." This specialized and profitable profession evolved into the family-owned funeral service industry as we know it.

Today, as a result of increased operating costs, many owners are selling to large consolidators. One firm, Service Corporation International, has taken advantage of the favorable acquisition climate. Its corporate and business strategies have transformed the way the traditional funeral business is being conducted. By using a combined scale and scope economy approach, SCI has been able to gain competitive advantage and profit handsomely by acquiring and streamlining funeral home operations. Its pioneering concepts of clustering funeral homes and sharing operations and resources have contributed to the company's success as the world's largest owner and operator of funeral homes and cemeteries.

As with any business, however, continued competitive advantage and resulting profitability are not guaranteed. SCI's strategy is being copied by its largest competitors. Increasing federal regulations affecting the industry will likely increase costs. Some consider the funeral service business to be one of the least competitive in the U.S. economy. Others complain that funeral directors take advantage of their position and charge excessively for their work. As a result, governmental and consumer attention is focusing on the industry's cost structure and profits generated by the largest firms.

Industry Overview

According to government statistics, the death care industry generated more than $6 billion in revenues in 1992. The industry is highly fragmented with an estimated 22,000 funeral homes and 9,600 cemeteries in operation in North America. Half the 22,000 funeral homes host, on average, fewer than 100 funeral services annually. Another 7,500 annually host between 100 and 200 services, while the remainder host over 200 funerals per year (Exhibit 1). According to the National Funeral Home Directors Association (NFHDA), 85 percent of its active member funeral homes are family operated. The typical operation has been in business for 63.3 years, with almost 80 percent of an operator's business from families served previously.

Operators in the industry establish goodwill in their respective communities over long periods of time. A funeral home's reputation is closely associated with

Exhibit 1	Average Number of Services by Funeral Homes	
Number of Homes	**Number of Services**	**Percentage of Homes**
11,000	<100	50%
7,500	100–200	34%
3,500	>200	16%
22,000	N/A	100%

Source: 1992 Survey of Funeral Home Operations, NFDA.

the local funeral director, who is usually male (95 percent of all funeral directors are men), likely to be active politically, a leader in his local church or temple, and active in local groups such as B'nai B'rith or Knights of Columbus.

Roughly 85 percent of funeral customers contact only one funeral home when faced with a death in the family, and the typical family requires funeral home services every seven years. Funeral operators advertise their services subtly by providing fans, hymnals, and the like, for churches and temples. Word of mouth advertising is particularly vital for a funeral parlor to be successful. Operators actively cultivate relationships with local clergy.

■ Demand Characteristics

For the funeral service industry, demand for funerals and cemetery plots is predictable, seasonal, and recession resistant. Of all standard industrial codes (SICs), the funeral service industry has experienced the fewest business failures and the fewest start-ups. While there has been modest variation in the death rate over the years, the Bureau of the Census forecasts that the death rate will increase at an average annual rate of 0.8 percent through the year 2005. A number of factors impact the death rate, but the chief influences are the aging of the population and seasonal weather effects.

Aging of the Population

During the 1980s, the proportion of the population in America over age 65 reached 12 percent. Though average life expectancies continue to climb, the U.S. Census Bureau's demographic projections suggest that the number of deaths will maintain a modest rate of increase as the over-65 group reaches 13 to 14 percent of the total population during the next two decades. By 1996, the first of the 75 million people of the baby-boom generation will reach age 50.

Seasonality of Demand

On a short-term basis, demand for funeral services is seasonal; the winter months (December, January, and February) are the busiest months for the average funeral home because demand is closely related to the severity or mildness of the influenza season. As an example, the Influenza Research Center at Baylor College of Medicine in Houston estimated that some 50,000 flu-related deaths occurred in the United States from December 1989 through February 1990.

■ Types of Services

At-Need Funerals

The vast majority of funeral home services is sold on an at-need basis. Industry sources estimate that at-need services account for approximately 80 percent of a funeral home's business. The average customer, according to industry studies, makes his or her purchase while in a state of "emotional distress, operating within tight time constraints and with a general lack of prior experience." These elements tend to make the customer relatively insensitive to price. This insensitivity leads to high profit margins, especially for firms operating at low costs. However, since 1982, Federal Trade Commission (FTC) regulations have required funeral homes to make price lists of goods and services offered available

Exhibit 2	Average Prices Paid for Standard Funeral Items
Item or Service	**National Average Price**
Professional service charges	$716
Transfer of remains to funeral home	97
Embalming	263
Other preparation	92
Use of viewing facilities	201
Use of facilities for a ceremony	191
Hearse (local)	124
Limousine (local)	100
Casket, 18-gallon steel, sealer, velvet interior	1,958
Concrete vault	<u>751</u>
National Average Cost of a Standard Funeral	$4,493

Source: 1992 Survey of Funeral Home Operations, NFDA.

to customers. Recent studies by the FTC indicate that instead of increasing competition in the funeral service industry, the development of price lists has provided funeral home operators with more opportunities to charge for itemized services that might otherwise have been provided at no cost as part of a package. Typical itemized funeral cost components include the following:

1. transfer of remains to funeral home,
2. embalming,
3. other preparation (cosmetology, hairdressing, casketing),
4. use of viewing facilities,
5. use of facilities for a ceremony,
6. hearse,
7. limousine,
8. casket, and
9. concrete vault.

Exhibit 2 illustrates average prices paid for these items for 1990.

Pre-Need Services

The concept of pre-need funeral arrangements (the contracting for funeral services prior to death) originated in the 1920s. Industry participants began to promote pre-need funerals heavily in the 1970s as a way to gain market share. Today, approximately 32 percent of Americans have made specific funeral arrangements prior to death. On an ongoing basis, approximately 22 percent of funerals are arranged each year on a pre-need basis, and more than 90 percent of funeral homes offer some form of pre-need service. The industry has found that pre-need customers who are purchasing for themselves tend to be more thoughtful and conservative in their purchasing practices. Thus, such customers are more price sensitive. A more price sensitive customer makes pre-need funeral sales less profitable than at-need business.

Cremations

Another type of service offered by the industry is cremation. In 1960, the cremation rate in the United States was 3.56 percent of total deaths. By 1990, the rate exceeded 17 percent, and the estimated rate by the year 2000 is over 22 percent. Interestingly, the tendency to choose cremations varies greatly across the nation. The cremation rate is highest in the Pacific (including California) and the mountain regions, where cremations were chosen in more than 40 and 30 percent of all deaths, respectively, in 1992. Since cremations are approximately one-sixth the cost of traditional services, funeral providers face lower profit margins with the trend toward more cremation.

■ Cost Structure of a Typical Funeral Home

Direct costs of sales and personnel expenses (shown in Exhibit 3) account for more than 50 percent of revenues of the typical funeral home. The largest cost component is the casket, which represents over 14 percent of total revenues. Casket expense is the largest variable cost item, while personnel and facility expenses are the largest components of fixed costs. Consequently, unanticipated increases and decreases in case volume can result in significant changes in net profit margins.

■ Cemeteries

The cemetery business is much more sales oriented than the service-oriented funeral business. This is due to the inclination of the American consumer to buy a cemetery plot prior to actual need. Approximately 50 percent of cemetery plot and mausoleum crypt sales are arranged on a pre-need basis. A factor contributing to the high incidence of pre-need purchases in the cemetery business is the desire of family members to acquire plots adjacent to an interred relative. The average selling prices for plots in a given property increase substantially as the cemetery gradually becomes full. Scarcity value drives prices up; thus, the last sites sell for higher prices.

To ensure that a cemetery has sufficient funds to maintain its grounds, many states require establishment of perpetual care cemetery trust funds. Income produced by these funds is used to pay maintenance charges relating to the care of the property.

Exhibit 3   Average Funeral Home Profitability Analysis

Expense or Profit Item	Percentage
Total revenues	100.0
Cost of sales*	29.0
Personnel	26.2
Facilities	14.2
Business expenses	4.7
Automotive	4.2
Other expenses	8.9
Profit before taxes	12.8

*Includes caskets, which on average represent 14% of total revenues.
Source: 1992 Survey of Funeral Home Operations, NFDA.

■ Industry Competition

During the 1980s, a group of firms described as consolidators by Wall Street analysts developed in the funeral service industry. These firms recognized an opportunity to acquire funeral homes and cemeteries at modest prices and streamline operations to improve financial performance. Stand-alone independent operators began to sell their businesses as local and state agencies, OSHA, and the EPA became more active in regulating the industry. Smaller operators found profits squeezed as the costs of regulatory compliance increased. In addition, the aging population of funeral operators and the lack of desire by family members to continue operations also influenced many to exit the industry.

By January 1990, nine companies existed in the industry with more than 30 locations. Five of these firms have since been acquired by the remaining consolidators. The big four are the Loewen Group, Stewart Enterprises, Gibraltar Mausoleum, and Service Corporation International. Each has adopted an aggressive acquisition strategy, each with a different market focus.

■ The Loewen Group

The Vancouver-based Loewen Group was founded by Ray Loewen soon after he and his wife bought their first funeral home in 1967. By 1975, Loewen owned and operated 14 homes. The primary focus of the business was then on real estate development. After being approached by several small funeral home operators with businesses to sell in 1983, Loewen embarked on an aggressive acquisition strategy in Canada and the United States. By 1992, the company had bought 374 funeral homes, 29 cemeteries, and 13 crematoria. Today, it occupies the No. 2 position in the funeral service business behind industry giant SCI International.

In 1991, Loewen spent $98 million to acquire 98 more homes, two cemeteries, and one crematorium. The previous year, acquisition costs amounted to $201 million. Typical Loewen acquisition candidates are properties in small communities and rural areas. Loewen's focus on small properties resulted from earlier failed efforts to acquire larger and more attractive properties that were being sought by SCI. The average revenue generated by a Loewen funeral home ($393,000) is less than the average revenue generated by an SCI funeral home ($819,000). Loewen projects that most of its growth over the next few years will occur in the United States. The firm recently announced purchases of funeral home operations in Minneapolis and the southeastern United States. (See Exhibit 8, shown later, for financial data on Loewen.)

Loewen concentrates on developing middle managers and creating an atmosphere where its employees can advance in the profession. It promotes the notion that management's greatest responsibility is to develop its people: socially, professionally, spiritually, intellectually, and economically. The company encourages managers to dedicate themselves to community care programs and to be involved in their communities. Loewen continues to operate its facilities as if they were small independents, but with the security of a large conglomerate.

■ Stewart Enterprises

Founded in New Orleans in 1910, Stewart Enterprises is the oldest of the funeral home consolidators, and the newest publicly traded funeral service provider. The firm was privately held until October 1991. Stewart has regionalized its focus, operating principally in urban areas in Louisiana, Texas, and Florida. As of 1992, the firm owned 48 funeral homes and 35 cemeteries in eight states. Stewart's operations are concentrated in the New Orleans and Dallas markets. In recent years, Stewart has added several large combination facilities, e.g., funeral homes and mausoleums located adjacent to cemetery properties. In addition, Stewart heavily promotes prearranged funerals. Consequently, income from prearranged funerals represents as much as 50 percent of Stewart's currently reported operating income. Exhibits 8, 11, and 12, shown later, contain recent financial information for Stewart Enterprises.

■ Gibraltar Mausoleum

The fourth largest funeral service provider in North America is Indianapolis-based Gibraltar Mausoleum. This firm operates in small to mid-sized communi-

Exhibit 4	Average Annual Funeral Service Case Volume	
Type of Community	Population	Case Volume
Large city	500,000+	419.3
Moderate city	50,000 to 500,000	247.5
Small city	10,000 to 49,999	158.1
Town/rural	less than 10,000	83.0

Source: 1992 Survey of Funeral Home Operations, NFDA.

ties in the midwestern United States and does not typically compete with SCI in bidding for properties. Financial and operating data are not available for privately owned Gibraltar.

Service Corporation International

Started by its current chairman, Robert L. Waltrip, in Houston in 1962, SCI began as a family-owned funeral home business. Waltrip inherited a funeral home in 1957 and by 1962, he had acquired two more. At that time, he and a group of investors formed Southern Capital and Investment Company, later changing the name to Service Corporation. The company went public in 1969. Five years later the stock was listed on the New York Stock Exchange. Utilizing seller financing, SCI bought funeral home operations and cemeteries mainly in Texas and Louisiana in the early years. Waltrip believed that funeral operations could be effectively and economically run by using a "service center" or "clustering" concept. By consolidating funeral services in metropolitan areas, scope and scale economies could be achieved (See Exhibit 4).

Today, the company is the largest operator of funeral homes and cemeteries in the United States. According to the company's 1992 annual report to shareholders, SCI owned and operated 674 funeral homes, 176 cemeteries, 65 combination homes/cemeteries, 45 flower shops, and 64 crematoria. For 1992, SCI commanded an 8.8 percent market share of funerals conducted in the United States.

SCI's operations are diversified geographically, with facilities located in 505 cities, 39 states, the District of Columbia, and 4 Canadian provinces. The company is active in six of the eight states with the highest number of people over 65 years of age (New York, Ohio, Pennsylvania, Michigan, Illinois, Florida, Texas, and California). Key markets include California, Florida, and Texas.

Company Management

The SCI management team has broad-based funeral service industry management experience. A management roster is highlighted in Exhibit 5. William Heiligbrodt joined the company in 1988 and was elected president and chief operating officer in February 1990. Prior to joining the management team, Heiligbrodt had served on the SCI board of directors and had been chairman of Texas Commerce Bank.

The executive vice president of the company, John W. Morrow, Jr., sold his family-owned funeral home to SCI in 1970, and joined the company as a vice

	Position	Name	Age	Years with Company
Exhibit 5	**SCI Management Roster**			
Corporate Management	Chairman, CEO	R.L. Waltrip	61	30
	President, COO	William Heiligbrodt	51	5
	EVP, CFO	Samuel Rizzo	56	5
	EVP, Operations	Blair Waltrip	38	15
	EVP, Corporate Development	John Morrow	56	22
	VP, Prearranged Sales	Richard Sells	53	14
	Pres. Provident	Henry Neely III	48	5
	VP, Assistant to COO	George Champagne	39	5
Regional Management	VP, Eastern	Steve Mack	41	19
	VP, Southeast	Dan Garrison	42	20
	VP, Great Lakes	Paul Kuper	43	19
	VP, Gulf States	William Truscott	47	24
	VP, Northwest	Royal Keith	56	34
	VP, Western	Dave Anderson	57	28

Source: 1992 Survey of Funeral Home Operations, NFDA.

president. Morrow left SCI to become chairman, president, and chief executive officer of Pierce Brothers, another funeral service firm. This firm was acquired by SCI in 1991. Like Waltrip, Mr. Morrow is a licensed funeral director.

In 1987, SCI's board of directors added the 37-year-old son of the company's founder. After graduating from college in 1977, Blair Waltrip joined SCI as a management trainee. He subsequently moved to the Corporate Development Department where he was promoted to acquisition and merger manager, then to departmental vice president. Blair Waltrip has held many senior management positions since that time, and today he is chief executive officer of the Funeral Services Operation and chairman of the board of SCI Canada, Inc. The management team has been at the forefront of developing trends in the funeral service industry. SCI pioneered the movement toward consolidation and spearheaded the development of the prearranged funeral in the 1970s. In the mid-1980s, the firm focused on an aggressive acquisition strategy, shifted to vertically integrating its operations by purchasing an insurance company and a casket manufacturer, and established a financial arm to provide loans to independent funeral operators.

■ Insurance Services

SCI entered the burial insurance market in the late 1970s by purchasing an insurance firm. Sales personnel sold burial policies door to door, and by 1985, SCI had over $200 million in prearranged and insured funeral services. Although most purchasers chose the least expensive option offered under the plans, SCI management felt that a bereaved family could be persuaded to upgrade funeral services at the time a policy holder died. As the market for insurance for prearranged funerals grew, so did management's concern regarding casket price increases. This led to the purchase of the nation's No. 2 casket manufacturer, Amedco.

■ Casket Manufacturing

SCI entered the casket making business in 1986 by acquiring Amedco. Since SCI had developed a considerable prearranged funeral business of over $200 million, the firm had been vulnerable to casket price increases. SCI saw an opportunity to protect its margins generated by the prearranged funeral business and at the same time gain insight into competitor operations. By making its own caskets, SCI's funeral homes could be supplied at cost, thus ensuring higher profit margins. By supplying units to independent operators, SCI was presented with a unique advantage of acquiring competitor information. Simply stated, the quantity of caskets ordered by a funeral home equates to the volume of business conducted by that home.

Soon after SCI gained control of Amedco, however, sales declined dramatically as operators switched from Amedco to the No. 1 casket maker, Hillenbrand. Previously, one-third of Amedco's sales were to SCI with the remaining two-thirds to independent operators. After SCI's purchase, half its customers switched to Hillenbrand. Although SCI spent an average of $1 million per month during 1987 and 1988 to promote Amedco, the venture continued to lose money. This decline was exacerbated by the losses suffered in the supply business. As a result, management changes were made and reorganization was undertaken.

■ Restructuring

In early 1989, a senior management task force was formed by Bill Heiligbrodt, SCI's president and COO, to examine the company's performance and to recommend ways for improving the company. At the time of the study, five divisions existed within SCI. These were Funeral Operations, Cemetery Operations, Financial Services, Funeral Supply, and Insurance (see Exhibit 6). According to management, all divisions were profitable with the exception of the funeral supply segment. Losses in this division were offset by the gains in the insurance segment. By comparison, the funeral and cemetery segments accounted for over 80 percent of SCI's revenues. In September, 1989, the task force completed its analysis and recommended a restructuring to the board of directors. Suggested actions included a return to the company's core businesses (funeral services and cemetery operations), continued support of the financial services operation, divestment of the funeral supply and insurance segments, sale of 76 rural funeral homes, and a reduction in the number of company officers from 26 to 12. The board accepted the recommendations, and SCI began restructuring in late 1989 into its current form: two divisions, Funeral Services Operations, comprised of funeral home operations and cemetery properties, and Financial Services, made up of a fully owned subsidiary, Provident Services, Inc. (see Exhibit 7).

Exhibit 6

Pre-1989 SCI
Organizational Chart

Exhibit 7

Post-1989 SCI Organizational
Chart

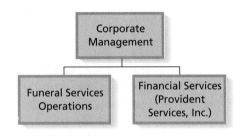

■ Funeral Services Operations

Funeral Homes

This operation is organized into six regional groups, each under the direction of a regional manager. Local funeral home and cemetery managers, under the direction of the regional managers, receive support and resources from Houston headquarters and have autonomy with respect to the manner in which funeral services are conducted.

SCI's management structure for Funeral Services Operations is decentralized. Headquarters personnel in Houston handle accounting, purchasing, human resources, and MIS functions. Regional performance standards focus on maintaining market share, generating 10 to 15 percent operating profit per year, and conducting a minimum of 250 funerals annually. Local managers are responsible for developing SCI's business strategy and conducting day-to-day operations. As long as the region achieves the set goals of profitability and market share, corporate management practices a hands-off philosophy. Regional personnel are rewarded with incentive bonuses for achieving performance goals.

SCI funeral homes provide personal and professional services relating to funerals, including the use of funeral facilities and motor vehicles. In addition, these funeral homes operate several crematoria and provide retail caskets, burial vaults, cremation containers, flowers, and burial garments. Funeral Services Operations owns 60 funeral home/cemetery combinations and operates 43 flower facilities engaged principally in the design and sale of funeral floral arrangements. These flower shops provide floral arrangements to some of SCI's homes and cemeteries. For the last three years, the funeral home segment of Funeral Services Operations has accounted for 70 percent of SCI's total revenues.

Cemeteries

SCI controls approximately 4,500 acres of cemetery land in the United States and Canada. This land is typically subdivided into 1,000 burial plots per acre. The company's cemeteries sell interment rights, mausoleum spaces, lawn crypts, and merchandise including stone and bronze memorials and burial vaults. Some locations also include crematory operations. SCI cemetery employees perform interment services and provide management and maintenance of cemetery grounds.

Because SCI owns a large inventory of undeveloped cemetery property, the company conducts an alternative-land-use program. Some alternate uses have included leasing property for mobile home parks, family recreation and golf centers, recreational vehicle storage, self-storage facilities, plant nurseries, agricultural uses, and oil and gas production. The alternative-use program generates approximately $3 million per year in revenues. In total, SCI's cemetery operations accounted for 28 percent of the firm's total revenue for the last three years.

Financial Services

In 1988, SCI established Provident Services, Inc., to provide loans to independent homes and cemeteries. The majority of Provident's loans are made to clients seeking funeral home or cemetery acquisitions. Additionally, Provident provides construction loans for independent funeral home or cemetery improvements and expansion. SCI had two primary reasons for entering this arena.

SCI's Growth Strategy

Since 1962, SCI has grown by buying or merging funeral providers. The company's current growth strategy has five main components: (1) acquisitions, (2) construction, (3) merchandising, (4) community service, and (5) financial services.

Acquisition Approach

SCI's past growth has centered on acquiring businesses, cutting costs, and streamlining operations. As the funeral service industry has entered the maturity stage of its life cycle and experienced no new growth, many operators have decided to exit the industry. The ready supply of available properties has fit well with SCI's acquisition strategy.

In evaluating potential acquisition candidates, SCI looks for established, well-known homes, which it classifies as "heritage properties." Names are not changed, and the former owners are typically retained as managers. Generally, the company does not acquire rural funeral parlors, but concentrates its efforts in metropolitan locations. Ideally, the firm pursues acquisitions where it can cluster a group of funeral homes. For example, the company will often buy the number one or two home in a community if it believes that the others may be available at a later date.

In targeting potential acquisitions and negotiating their purchase, SCI employs a systematic, research-based approach. Headquarters personnel analyze population growth as well as other demographic data. The company makes death rate projections by zip code throughout the United States.

SCI's acquisition strategy has centered around five basic criteria:

1. penetration into new markets,
2. metropolitan locations providing economies of scale,
3. opportunity to work in "clusters" with shared resources,
4. strong local management, and
5. ability to meet SCI business and financial requirements.

New Market Penetration. Until the mid-1980s, SCI primarily purchased single funeral homes and cemeteries in the southwestern United States. As more operators exited the industry, SCI began to acquire properties in new markets, especially in areas that the firm calls "God's waiting room." These areas, Southern California, Arizona, and Florida, for example, have a large population of older Americans. In addition, the company has targeted the Hispanic community. The company considers the Hispanic market attractive due to traditionally low cremation rates and relatively high spending for memorialization. These factors influenced SCI to enter the Miami market. Although SCI does not have any short-term plans to enter the European or Asian markets, the company has evaluated the Italian, French, British, Japanese, and Australian markets. Funeral services in these countries are traditional in nature and, as such, are similar to those occurring in North America.

Metropolitan Locations.   SCI has concentrated on owning and operating funeral homes and cemeteries in large metropolitan areas where economies of scale and scope can be realized. When compared to rural locations, cemeteries in large cities allow maintenance crews to move from one location to another. Urban areas allow for bigger funeral homes with the fixed costs spread over more funerals. Consequently, these costs can be recovered at a faster rate than the costs of operating rural mortuaries.

Clustering Concept.   SCI's clustering concept allows combining of operations of a number of funeral homes in certain areas and outlying locations. As a result, the need for personnel is reduced. In Houston, for example, 13 funeral homes are served by a central embalming facility. Bodies are transported to this operation, where a team prepares them for display, thus relieving the traditional funeral director of this duty. The assembly-line approach to body preparation gives rise to additional economies of scale in SCI's operations.

Other resources shared by SCI's funeral homes in large markets are limousines and hearses. This operation, like the embalming facility, is manned 24 hours a day. Vehicles needed for funeral services are pooled and dispatched when needed. This allows for better utilization of vehicles and lowers costs since each individual home does not need to purchase and operate its own fleet of vehicles.

Strong Local Management.   Because the relationships that the funeral director and other members of the funeral home management have established in the local community are a key factor in the success of a given location, SCI seeks to retain local personnel after acquiring a property. Local operators receive training from SCI on how to counsel families and sell more services, but the day-to-day duties of the location are controlled by the operators.

Construction Philosophy

An emerging tactic for SCI is one of locating new funeral homes in cemeteries. Such an arrangement eliminates land costs for a new facility, thus providing a quicker payback. The company refers to these groupings as "combos."

Another construction avenue involves establishing satellite funeral homes. The key is taking one of the better known funeral homes and setting up branches in outlying areas. By establishing satellites, SCI has addressed the migration of population from cities to suburbs. However, satellite areas are not limited to locations adjacent to SCI's metropolitan operations. For example, SCI branched one of its New York City funeral homes, Riverside-Gordon Memorial Chapel, to Delray Beach, Florida. The company recognized that many residents of the Florida city were former New Yorkers familiar with the mortuary's name.

Merchandising Emphasis

SCI works closely with manufacturers of funeral service supplies to keep them abreast of products that best suit SCI's client families. Since the firm controls approximately 9 percent of the funeral business in the United States, SCI receives volume discounts on most purchases. Such discounts allow the firm to realize better profit margins than operators unable to buy in bulk. SCI has developed a computer tracking program to monitor product demand throughout the country. Each regional manager is required to report product preferences and trends. This allows SCI's central purchasing group to minimize product inventories.

SCI has implemented a training program that prepares managers and funeral directors to handle clients in the most sensitive means possible. Through regional services and merchandise coordinators, SCI trains its personnel with intensive discussions and role-playing. The company provides to families videocassettes and books on coping with grief. As John Morrow said:

> It is a difficult chore for a firm to convey to the public that it would like to serve their funeral needs. All this is designed to make our firm come across as caring and empathetic.

Community Service Concept

According to R. L. Waltrip, SCI has never lost sight of what it considers the primary reason for its success: professional, quality service. The company stresses a commitment to community service by its funeral directors and managers. One such program is the "Toys for Tots" campaign in Southern California. Through its Pierce Brothers locations, SCI accepts local donations and distributes them to needy children. Another service project involves using funeral homes for nonfuneral activities. For example, some homes with large rooms have been used as art galleries, for town meetings, and as banquet facilities.

Financial Services

Provident Services, Inc., a fully owned subsidiary, developed a niche as a capital funding source for independent funeral homes and cemeteries. Although the unit competes with other lending institutions, Provident attempts to fill a void left by lenders unfamiliar with the funeral service industry. Lenders typically estimate the worth of a business only in terms of its liquidation value. As such, independent operators sometimes face obstacles to obtaining financing through traditional sources. Rather than relying on asset values in assessing credit worthiness, Provident focuses on the value of a business as a going concern. Cash flow, location, demographics, business philosophy, and community standing are among the factors considered to more accurately determine the potential for ongoing profits. By gaining insights into operators' business characteristics, SCI assesses loan prospects and future acquisition candidates.

■ Changing Regulatory Environment

SCI, like others in the funeral service business, is faced with rules and regulations promulgated by states, provinces, and federal governments. The most far reaching are the requirements at the federal level. One Federal Trade Commission (FTC) regulation requires funeral operators to publish price lists for items typically bought for funeral services. The intent of the regulation was to provide for more competition in the funeral service industry.

Recent action by the FTC suggests a stronger position is emerging, especially against industry giant SCI. In particular, the company agreed to pay $500,000 in 1991 for failing to comply with FTC rules about notification before attempting to acquire a competitor in 1986. Additionally, the company was recently forced by the FTC to sell some of its operations in Tennessee. The FTC decreed that SCI had monopolized the funeral service market in some areas of that state.

Management is keenly aware of these anti-competitiveness trends. For instance, when asked about the firm's extensive holdings in the Houston area, George Champagne, an upper level manager, said:

> We would love to own Earthman Funeral Homes [a large chain in Houston]. But the FTC wouldn't allow it. It would be anti-competitive in their view.

Additional action taken by the FTC regarding competitive issues centers on fees charged by funeral operators. Critics of the industry have asserted that the industry is still one of the economy's least competitive, despite its thousands of small firms. The most disputed action now before the FTC is the practice of charging as much as several hundred dollars to handle coffins that low-price retailers sell. Previously, some funeral home operators would not conduct services with caskets purchased from retail competitors. In one noteworthy case, the FTC fined an SCI-owned Memphis funeral home $25,000 for refusing service to a family who did not buy a casket from the home. Now, the fee policy is being examined, and already FTC staff has recommended that such fees be banned on the basis of being anti-competitive.

Occupational Safety and Health Administration (OSHA) regulations have been issued concerning handling of infectious disease-related cases, most notably hepatitis and AIDS. Operators are faced with investing in sanitized, tiled embalming rooms that contain a shower, eye-bath fountain, ventilation systems that replace formaldehyde fumes with fresh air, and splash-proof sinks to catch body fluids. In addition, embalmers are required to be outfitted with protective gear, called "moon suits" in the industry. This suit consists of a gown, double-thick gloves, boots, hairnet, goggles, and a welder-styled gas mask.

In addition to OSHA, the U.S. Congress has mandated certain actions, most notably the Americans with Disabilities Act (ADA), which affects not only the funeral service industry, but others as well. Like the FTC and OSHA requirements, compliance with ADA regulations will increase costs.

■ Major Competitor Initiatives

Both the Loewen Group and Stewart Enterprises have followed SCI's success in growing their operations by taking advantage of the favorable acquisition climate in the industry. Although each of SCI's competitors employs slightly different strategies and market segment focuses, the net effect is that these firms are gaining market share in the funeral service industry.

SCI's largest competitor, Loewen, operates 300 of its 374 funeral homes in the United States, although the firm is headquartered in Canada. Loewen has recently entered the Minneapolis market and, according to its 1991 annual report, plans to focus on the United States for additional acquisitions. Its move into U.S. metropolitan areas now puts it in direct competition with SCI.

Another competitor that is quietly gaining on SCI and Loewen is Stewart Enterprises. SCI management considers the firm essentially a cemetery operation with limited financial resources. Stewart has dominated the New Orleans and Dallas markets for some time.

SCI management has recognized the dominance of some foreign firms in their respective markets. While SCI has gained first mover advantages in the North American funeral service industry, these advantages may not be sufficient to keep foreign firms with capital resources from doing what SCI has done; that is, purchase existing operations. Although the public may be wary of having their local funeral home or cemetery owned by foreigners, the entry of foreigners into the North American funeral service industry may go relatively unnoticed.

■ Lending Service Competition

SCI's financial services subsidiary, Provident, faces·stiff competition in lending. Banks, pension funds, and insurance companies can typically lend at rates more favorable than Provident. This strains Provident's ability to compete in the lending arena. In addition, Provident has only been in operation for four years. Given that most loans have maturities of five to seven years, few loans have actually matured. A number of Provident's largest loans have been retired in the last 12 months as several large borrowers have been acquired either by SCI or the Loewen Group. Consequently, Provident's success as a lender is difficult to measure. Most of the income generated by this division has been from fee charges.

■ Trend Toward Cremations

SCI is already feeling the effects of the emerging trend regarding cremation. Even though the rate of cremation services in the United States stands at 17 percent, SCI is experiencing a rate of approximately 23 percent. This is due to the company's strong position in the California and western markets. Although SCI has realized revenues for cremation services that are twice the industry average, the firm's average revenues from all types of funeral services are approximately $800 lower than the national average. This reflects the higher proportion of its sales from cremation services. As this trend increases, the spread between SCI's funeral service revenues and the national average could widen.

■ Waltrip Family Influence

Since the company's founding, the Waltrip family has exerted considerable influence over SCI's operations and philosophy. Today, Robert Waltrip and his family own 14 percent of the outstanding stock. Robert, his son, and his mother are members of the board of directors. His son-in-law is president of a subsidiary company.

The senior Mr. Waltrip has developed a reputation as an astute businessman, due in part to SCI's history of acquisitions. Some Wall Street analysts said that before the current management team was in place, SCI was run like a family-owned funeral home. In fact, many of the firm's current senior managers are second- or third-generation funeral directors, and the company's balance of operations is tilted to the funeral side of the business.

Shareholders have brought legal action against Waltrip and some members of SCI's management team for attempts to take the company private. Specifically, charges were made that the firm was not releasing all financial information. Such nondisclosure actions could allow someone such as Waltrip to purchase the firm at less than fair market price. A strong indicator of the move to privatize may be SCI's aggressive program to repurchase outstanding stock and pay down debt from generated profits.

■ Financial Comparisons

Parallel financial statements for SCI, Loewen, and Stewart can be found in Exhibits 8 through 12.

Exhibit 8   Income Statement Highlights ($000)

Service Corporation International

Fiscal Year Ending	12/31/92	12/31/91	12/31/90	12/31/89
Net Sales	772,477	643,248	563,156	518,809
Cost of Goods Sold	550,422	464,740	413,236	386,032
Gross Profit	222,055	178,508	149,920	132,777
Sell Gen & Admin Exp	38,693	35,448	28,037	28,423
Inc Before Dep & Amort	183,362	143,060	121,883	104,354
Non-Operating Income	9,876	8,241	13,644	12,778
Interest Expense	53,902	42,429	36,095	32,514
Income Before Tax	139,336	108,872	99,432	84,618
Provisions for Income Taxes	52,800	35,500	35,900	31,000
Net Income Before Ex Items	86,536	73,372	60,218	46,721
Ex Items & Disc Ops	0	0	0	(94,935)
Net Income	86,536	73,372	60,218	(48,214)
Outstanding Shares	N/A	895,435	3,098,415	48,382,689

The Loewen Group

Fiscal Year Ending	12/31/91	12/31/90	12/31/89	12/31/88
Net Sales	217,816	136,500	75,712	49,634
Cost of Goods	134,334	81,755	43,499	28,810
Gross Profit	83,482	54,745	32,213	20,824
Sell Gen & Admin Exp	17,569	11,033	5,654	2,777
Inc Before Dep & Amort	65,913	43,712	26,559	18,047
Depreciation & Amort	14,609	7,766	4,301	2,863
Non-Operating Income	312	N/A	N/A	N/A
Interest Expense	19,710	14,425	9,486	6,498
Income Before Tax	31,906	21,521	12,772	8,686
Provisions for Income Taxes	12,840	8,657	5,571	4,166
Net Income Before Ex Items	19,066	12,864	7,201	4,520
Net Income	19,066	12,864	7,201	4,520
Outstanding Shares	N/A	28,391	N/A	N/A

Stewart Enterprises

Fiscal Year Ending	12/31/92	12/31/91	12/31/90	12/31/89
Net Sales	143,153	128,824	117,890	117,420
Cost of Goods	112,716	103,574	97,107	98,518
Gross Profit	30,437	25,250	20,783	18,902
Sell Gen & Admin Exp	5,030	5,249	4,342	3,499
Inc Before Dep & Amort	25,407	20,002	16,442	15,402
Non-Operating Income	971	2,869	1,580	1,758
Interest Expense	5,414	9,162	8,854	7,894
Income Before Tax	20,964	13,708	9,167	9,267
Provisions for Income Taxes	6,747	4,466	2,295	2,304
Net Income Before Ex Items	14,217	9,242	6,872	6,963
Ex Items & Disc Ops	20	195	117	N/A
Net Income	14,237	9,437	6,989	6,963
Outstanding Shares	98,843	9,884	7,000	6,804

Exhibit 9   Service Corporation International: Balance Sheet Highlights

Assets ($000)

Fiscal Year Ending	12/31/92	12/31/91	12/31/90	12/31/89
Cash	31,253	38,422	17,788	36,928
Receivables	182,272	153,809	128,529	96,906
Inventories	40,577	34,928	28,233	27,522
Other Current Assets	4,496	9,432	5,608	17,642
Total Current Assets	258,598	236,591	180,158	178,998
Property, Plant & Equipment	504,471	657,299	508,550	467,230
Invest & Avd to Subs	661,788	543,831	469,535	427,124
Other Non-Cur Assets	274,793	174,851	234,300	336,521
Deferred Charges	92,441	77,975	63,058	53,228
Intangibles	410,270	323,708	117,053	96,487
Deposits & Other Assets	110,515	109,197	81,035	41,880
Total Assets	2,571,474	2,123,452	1,653,689	1,601,468

Liabilities ($000)

Fiscal Year Ending	12/31/92	12/31/91	12/31/90	12/31/89
Accounts Payable	22,704	20,840	23,962	13,677
Current Long Term Debt	10,602	13,828	7,205	8,678
Accrued Expenses	70,150	45,540	32,288	35,961
Total Current Liabilities	103,456	80,208	66,767	58,316
Deferred Charges/Inc	362,917	247,343	220,085	167,988
Long Term Debt	980,029	786,685	577,378	485,669
Other Long Term Liabilities	477,951	393,440	355,136	331,718
Total Liabilities	1,924,353	1,507,676	1,219,366	1,043,691
Common Stock Net	75,261	50,654	45,867	48,383
Capital Surplus	220,497	395,269	264,895	372,040
Retained Earnings	220,497	168,371	133,443	135,413
Other Equities	(2,289)	1,482	(9,882)	1,841
Shareholder Equity	683,097	615,776	434,323	557,777
Total Liabilities & Net Worth	2,571,474	2,123,452	1,653,689	1,601,468

Exhibit 10   The Loewen Group: Balance Sheet Highlights

Assets ($000)

Fiscal Year Ending	12/31/91	12/31/90	12/31/89	12/31/88
Cash	21,194	12,830	23,711	N/A
Receivables	36,281	32,423	13,976	N/A
Inventories	10,792	8,434	3,857	N/A
Other Current Assets	2,972	2,395	1,264	N/A
Total Current Assets	71,239	56,082	42,808	N/A
Property, Plant & Equipment	307,679	230,859	109,144	N/A
Net Property & Equipment	307,679	230,859	109,144	N/A
Intangibles	115,710	96,461	33,521	N/A
Deposits & Other Assets	20,983	12,721	3,760	N/A
Total Assets	515,611	396,123	189,233	N/A

Liabilities ($000)

Fiscal Year Ending	12/31/91	12/31/90	12/31/89	12/31/88
Notes Payable	N/A	7,142	N/A	N/A
Accounts Payable	21,662	20,641	8,597	N/A
Current Long Term Debt	8,027	8,386	5,856	N/A
Income Taxes	964	N/A	778	N/A
Total Current Liabilities	30,653	36,169	15,231	N/A
Deferred Charges/Inc	1,868	509	1,802	N/A
Long Term Debt	250,848	199,762	92,322	N/A
Other Long Term Liabilities	4,389	3,768	N/A	N/A
Total Liabilities	287,758	240,208	109,355	N/A
Minority Int (Liab)	N/A	175	496	N/A
Capital Surplus	183,915	129,568	66,064	N/A
Retained Earnings	45,798	27,386	14,903	N/A
Treasury Stock	N/A	N/A	N/A	N/A
Other Equities	(1,860)	(1,214)	(1,585)	N/A
Shareholder Equity	227,853	155,740	79,382	N/A
Total Liabilities & Net Worth	515,611	396,123	189,233	N/A

Exhibit 11   Stewart Enterprises: Balance Sheet Highlights

Annual Assets ($000)

Fiscal Year Ending	12/31/92	12/31/91	12/31/90	12/31/89
Cash	6,391	8,006	10,506	8,787
Marketable Securities	5,945	6,088	6,009	6,222
Receivables	31,106	28,209	28,879	34,179
Inventories	8,511	7,417	6,118	6,007
Other Current Assets	1,301	1,046	1,096	727
Total Current Assets	53,254	50,766	52,608	55,922
Property, Plant & Equipment	167,250	129,793	122,452	94,591
Accumulated Depreciation	29,419	26,517	23,604	20,143
Net Property & Equipment	137,831	103,276	98,847	74,448
Other Non-Current Assets	63,904	52,335	64,587	53,932
Deferred Charges	22,679	17,857	16,204	16,163
Intangibles	21,849	13,585	9,147	1,982
Deposits & Other Assets	1,286	699	805	1,163
Total Assets	300,803	238,518	242,198	203,610

Annual Liabilities ($000)

Fiscal Year Ending	12/31/92	12/31/91	12/31/90	12/31/89
Accounts Payable	13,267	10,982	9,489	11,317
Current Long Term Debt	5,680	4,938	6,757	5,624
Income Taxes	4,243	3,765	3,014	4,304
Other Current Liabilities	2,969	3,041	3,110	3,105
Total Current Liabilities	26,159	22,726	22,370	24,350
Deferred Charges/Inc	44,042	31,648	32,348	28,574
Long Term Debt	82,740	53,139	93,381	65,214
Other Long Term Liabilities	4,728	3,051	22,792	21,390
Total Liabilities	157,669	110,564	170,891	139,528
Common Stock Net	51,014	50,225	2,944	1,515
Retained Earnings	92,880	78,742	73,988	66,925
Treasury Stock	N/A	N/A	4,359	4,359
Other Equities	(759)	(1,013)	(1,266)	N/A
Shareholder Equity	143,134	127,954	71,307	64,081
Total Liabilities & Net Worth	300,804	238,518	242,198	203,609

Exhibit 12	Five Year Summary		
Service Corporation International			
Year	Sales ($000)	Net Income	EPS
1992	772,477	86,536	1.84
1991	643,248	73,372	1.54
1990	563,156	60,218	1.28
1989	518,809	46,721	0.97
1988	417,530	55,133	1.17
Growth Rate	16.8%	12.5%	12.8%
The Loewen Group			
1992	N/A	N/A	N/A
1991	217,816	19,066	0.61
1990	136,500	12,864	0.51
1989	75,712	7,201	0.40
1988	49,634	4,520	0.30
Growth Rate	63.6%	58.0%	25.2%
Stewart Enterprises			
1992	136,141	14,217	1.44
1991	120,006	9,242	1.31
1990	107,138	6,872	1.00
1989	96,785	6,835	0.99
1988	89,836	12,768	1.83
Growth Rate	10.9%	2.7%	(5.8)%

■ CASE 31 Soft-Logik Publishing Corporation

Charles Boyd
Southwest Missouri State University

■ http://www.softlogik.com/

PageStream, the flagship product of Soft-Logik Publishing Corporation, enjoys a reputation as the premier desktop publishing software product for the Amiga computer. PageStream capitalizes on the Amiga's graphics capabilities to produce precise page layouts, mostly for professionals who write newsletters and advertisements for corporations.

Since operations began in 1985, Soft-Logik has sold 40,000 to 50,000 copies of PageStream. PageStream has been favorably reviewed in *Amiga World* and other major magazines for Amiga users. Despite this success, Soft-Logik stands at a strategic crossroads because of circumstances beyond its control.

In April 1994, Commodore, maker of the Amiga, filed for bankruptcy. The firm sold its assets and its name in May 1995 to Escom, a German retail store chain. Beginning in September 1995, Escom planned to sell a limited number of Amiga computers without marketing support. That strategy is not likely to revive the Amiga market. This effectively means the end of the line for firms such as Soft-Logik that write software only for the Amiga.

The effect of Commodore's demise on Soft-Logik was swift and dramatic. From mid-1994 to mid-1995, Soft-Logik sold 4,000 copies of its latest release of PageStream, version 3.0. By mid-1995, the firm had only 500 to 600 active customers buying upgrades of the product. Soft-Logik employed 11 people in mid-1994; there were only 4 employees in mid-1995. Future prospects were grim because as Amiga users' machines age, there will be no new Amigas to replace them. Soft-Logik's founder and CEO, Deron Kazmaier, knew that he must change his firm's strategy quickly if his product and his company were to survive.

■ The Desktop Publishing Industry

Before Apple Computer produced the first Macintosh in 1984, writers using a computer were confined to text produced by word processing programs. The Macintosh offered users the first popular graphical user interface (GUI), a screen on which both text and pictures (graphics) could be rendered, and on which a character font would appear on screen as it would on paper. This is known as WYSIWYG, what you see is what you get. The WYSIWYG screen gave rise to the development of desktop publishing (DTP) software that allowed the user to move text and graphic images about the screen, placing them precisely where wanted. This let graphical professionals such as magazine publishers and advertisers lay out each part of a page precisely. The Macintosh moved quickly to the forefront as the computer of choice for DTP work.

Commodore introduced its Amiga line of computers in 1987. Like the Macintosh, the Amiga was highly regarded for its GUI and WYSIWYG screen. It too became popular for DTP work, but not as popular as the Macintosh. The IBM and compatible personal computers did not offer a GUI until the introduction of Microsoft's Windows operating system in 1990. Windows made DTP possible for IBM-compatible computers, which already dominated the corporate market. Many users considered the first version of Windows to be a substandard GUI compared to those of the Macintosh and the Amiga. This was still generally true in 1992 when Windows 3.1 came on the market. Yet that version was improved enough that, with Microsoft's considerable marketing clout, it became the leading operating system. Microsoft's DOS and Windows operating systems were installed on 82 percent of personal computers by mid-1995, only a short time before a new, improved version called Windows 95 was due to ship.

As both the IBM and Macintosh DTP software markets developed, the market split into two segments: the high end and the low end. The high end of the market is served by a few products used mostly by professionals. Developed originally for the Macintosh computer, most high-end software products list from about $500 to $900, and are not found in most stores where individual users shop for software. When Windows came on the scene, versions of these products were written to run under that operating system. (Writing a version of a computer application program for a different operating system is called *porting* the application to the new system.) The low-end products list from about $60 to $200. They compete with high-end word processors, which had impressive DTP features by 1995. For the extra money, professionals using the high-end DTP programs get more precise control over page layout and more tools with which to manipulate text and graphics.

Low-End Desktop Publishing Packages

In 1995, the low-end DTP packages boasted impressive features for their price. Most of them offered extensive layout features, the ability to import text from major word processors, and to import graphic images in several popular formats. Some even offered color separation, considered an important DTP feature for materials to be printed in color. A brief review of the leading low-end products follows[1]:

- *PagePlus:* Offers about 80 percent of the functionality of high-end programs for 20 percent of the price. Especially noteworthy is its process-color separation ability. One review noted that this package is harder to learn than some competing low-end DTP products because some of its great features are buried three menus deep. Published by Serif Inc. Estimated street price: $120.

- *Easy Working Desktop Publisher:* A good value for the price, but does not have strong type and color controls. Published by Spinnaker Software Corp. $59.95.

- *Page Magic:* A powerful program with many features, but some quirks, according to one review. Seems especially hard to import text into this program. Published by New England Business Service,. Estimated street price: $50.
- *Publisher:* A powerful and easy-to-use program, according to one user test that rated it best in all categories of performance against PagePlus and Page Magic. Published by Microsoft. Estimated street price: $95.

The low-end products compete most directly with the three major word processing programs: Microsoft Word, WordPerfect, and Lotus Ami Pro. By 1995, the latest versions of these word processors were able to do basic DTP tasks with relative ease. They shipped with many templates for memos, letters, newsletters, and other documents that require combinations of fonts, graphics, and multiple columns. The prices of these products rivaled those for some low-end DTP packages in 1995. This made the word processors very attractive when one considered that they would do more common and less demanding writing projects with more ease than would the DTP packages and then would suffice for their DTP needs to boot. The strength of these word processors siphoned off some business from individual users while making the low-end DTP products good, cost-effective choices for small businesses with more modest publishing needs.

■ The High-End Desktop Publishing Market

There must be some good reasons why a company would pay the difference between a powerful DTP program selling from $50 to $120 and a high-end DTP program selling between $500 and $900. The benefit is precision. These programs are written for professionals who know how to take full advantage of precise layout controls. These controls include leading (the space between lines of text) and kerning (the space between letters). These programs also handle long documents better than do the low-end DTP programs. They can compile several document files into books, renumber pages accordingly, and create tables of contents. Many low-end DTP programs confine a long document to only one file. This limits the practical length of documents that those programs can handle. Hundreds of such differences separate the low-end from the high-end DTP packages.[2] That is why DTP professionals who work with long documents or design-intensive ones using much color material need a high-end package.

Soft-Logik clearly positioned PageStream for the professional DTP user at the high end of the market. Most high-end DTP programs were first written for the Macintosh, then ported to Windows when it became available. They now sell to both platforms. Exhibit 1 show sales and net income for Soft-Logik's leading professional DTP competitors.

The major high-end DTP programs in both the Macintosh and Windows markets during 1995 were QuarkXPress 3.3, Adobe PageMaker 5.0, Corel Ventura Publisher 5, and Framework's FrameMaker 5.0. QuarkXPress and PageMaker abound in layout tools and other features that are most useful in writing design-intensive documents. PageMaker best spans the range of DTP uses, but does not distinguish itself in any use. FrameMaker and Corel Ventura are better suited to developing long, complex publications. FrameMaker is strongest for this purpose. It also has the strongest collection of UNIX- and PC-based electronic publishing tools.[3]

Exhibit 1	Sales and Net Income of Major Desktop Publishing Firms, 1993 and 1994 (in thousands of dollars)	
	1993	**1994**
Adobe		
Sales	$520,237	$597,772
Net income	66,545	6,309
Corel		
Sales	105,020	164,313
Net income	20,853	32,503
Frame Technology Corp.		
Sales	56,093	72,413
Net income (loss)	(34,018)	9,705

Note: Quark Corporation is privately held and so does not publish its financial information. Quark's 1993 sales were $120 million according to IAC Company Profile. Note that Adobe did not have a DTP program until early 1995 when it purchased Aldus, the former owner of PageMaker.

Source: *Compact Disclosure,* Standard and Poor's, July 1995.

In January 1995, Soft-Logik published an advertising flyer showing a feature-by-feature comparison of PageStream 3.0 with QuarkXPress, PageMaker, and ProPage 4.1, its rival on the Amiga (see Exhibit 2). On the basis of this comparison, Deron and his staff believed that PageStream would be a very competitive product in the Macintosh and IBM markets. QuarkXPress, FrameMaker, and PageMaker each had list prices of $895; but, like most software, they were widely available through discount catalog sales for $580 to $600. Corel Ventura was discount-priced at $339.95 on CD-ROM and $399.95 on both CD-ROM and diskette.

After best-selling programs are on the market for a while, they attract other software vendors to write programs that work with them and provide additional functions beyond those offered in the original product. These programs are called third-party add-ons. Spreadsheet templates that work with the Lotus 1-2-3 spreadsheet program or macros (automated tasks) written for WordPerfect's word processing program are examples of third-party add-ons familiar to many users. High-end DTP programs also attract such add-ons. QuarkXPress is most blessed by other software vendors. Other companies publish utilities for QuarkXPress collectively called QuarkXTensions.[4] They help XPress users do such tasks as importing spreadsheet files, publish a database, link publication files into a book, create a table of contents, insert conditional headers, and generate an index.[5] About 100 XTension programs and utilities existed in 1995. A similar set of add-ons called Additions is available to PageMaker users. Also, a firm named Extensis publishes PageTools for PageMaker and XPress Tools for QuarkXPress. Having third-party add-ons increases the confidence users have in the future of the DTP product. They also enhance the product's functionality.

Exhibit 2 Comparison of Features of DTP Systems

PageStream 3.0

The complete feature comparison.

Interface

	PGS3	PP4.1	XP3.3	PM5
Maximum number of open documents	unlimited	1	25	unlimited
★ Maximum number of document views	unlimited	1	1	1
★ reveal/hide document views	●			
Moveable document view windows	●			●
☆ Load/save program defaults	●		○	○
Pasteboard surrounding pages	○	○	●	●
Moveable toolbox	●		●	●
★ change size and orientation	●			
★ Toolbar for common operations	●			
★ Edit palette (control/measurement)	●		●	●
★ Floating operation/selection palettes	●		●	●
☆ Number of view magnifications	13	5	6	8
user-specified view magnification	●	●	●	●
view magnification zoom	●		●	●
maximum view magnification	3000%	400%	400%	800%
★ Drag page to scroll	●			
★ Auto Scroll	●	●		●
★ Online context sensitive help	●		●	●
★ System clipboard support	●		●	●
☆ Undo levels	unlimited	1	1	1
★ Do math in text fields	●		○	○

Document Construction

	PGS3	PP4.1	XP3.3	PM5
☆ Number of pre-defined page sizes	20	6	5	13
Maximum page size (in inches)	2000"×2000"	48"×48"	48"×48"	42"×42"
change size of pages at any time	●	●	●	●
★ mix page sizes in a document	●	●		
☆ Maximum document size (in pages)	unlimited	9999	2000	999
★ Join pages into spreads	●	○	○	○
★ Maximum number of master pages	unlimited	0	127	2
hide master objects on normal pages	●			
edit master objects on normal pages			●	●
retroactive master column changes			●	●
★ Visual page arrangement	●	●	●	○ macro
Insert/Delete/Move multiple pages	●	●	●	●
☆ Automatic page numbering	●	○	○	○
★ Automatic page insertion	○		●	●
☆ Link and unlink columns	○	○	●	●
★ Chapters and subchapters	●		○	
★ Chapter numbering	●			
★ Automatic table of contents	○ macro			●
★ Automatic index generation	○ macro			●
★ Continued from/to numbers	○ macro		●	○ macro

Layout Aids

	PGS3	PP4.1	XP3.3	PM5
☆ Snap-to-guides	●		●	●
★ page (margin and column) guides	●	○	●	●
☆ ruler guides	●		●	●
★ adjustable guide strength	●			
show and hide guides	●		●	○
★ user-defined guide color	●			
☆ Snap-to-grid	●	●		○
★ adjustable grid strength	●			
show and hide grid	●	●		
★ user-defined grid color	●			

Layout Aids cont...

	PGS3	PP4.1	XP3.3	PM5
★ grid offset	●			
★ grid display interval	●			
☆ Rulers	●	●	●	●
show and hide rulers	●	●	●	●
★ adjustable ruler offset	●			
adjustable ruler zero point	●		●	●
★ adjustable ruler direction	●			
★ custom vertical and horizontal rulers	●			●
☆ Number of measurement system options	11	3	7	6
maximum precision	0.001 pts	0.001 pts	0.001 pts	0.05 pts
★ mix measurement systems in fields	●		●	○
☆ Cut, copy and paste text	●	○	●	●
☆ Find/replace text and text attributes	●	○	●	●
☆ search article and document	●	○ article only	●	○ article only
☆ Spelling checker	●	○	●	○
☆ user-defined spelling dictionaries	●		●	●
☆ check word, article and document	●	○	●	●
☆ Import/export formats	9/9	9/0	?/?	?/?
★ convert quotes and dashes	●		●	
★ Externally linked articles	●			
★ List articles in a document	●			
☆ Maximum number of tabs	unlimited	16	20	40
☆ number of alignment options	6	1	6	4
☆ place numerically or manually	●	○	●	●
☆ right indent tab	●		●	●
★ dot leaders (custom filled tabs)	●		●	●
★ Smart quotes and dashes	●		○	
★ Smart ligatures and bullets	●			
★ Show/hide invisible characters	●		●	
★ User-defined variables	●			

Style Tags

	PGS3	PP4.1	XP3.3	PM5
☆ Character style tags	●	●	●	
★ Paragraph style tags	●	●	●	●
★ Override styles	●		●	●
★ Next style; link style sequences	●		●	●
★ Base styles on other styles	●		●	
★ Find/replace styles	●			●
★ Object style tags	●			
★ Import style tags	●		●	●

Typography

	PGS3	PP4.1	XP3.3	PM5
☆ Number of font systems supported	3	1	2	2
☆ Number of included fonts	64	7	0	0
☆ Font sizes	1 to 50,000	2 to 720	2 to 720	4 to 650
☆ size increments	0.001 pts	0.125 pts	0.001 pts	0.1 pts
☆ horizontally scale text	1 to 655%		25 to 400%	5 to 250%
☆ Number of type styles	10	8	10	8
★ user-defined type styles	● 9		○ 4	○ 3
☆ Set text color, fill and stroke	●	○	○	○
☆ Rotate and skew text	●	○	●	●
☆ rotation increments	0.001°	1°	0.001°	0.01°

● Feature present   ○ Feature present/limited implementation   macro: included macro or extension   unlimited: Limited only by machine constraints
? unknown   ★ New in PageStream3   ☆ Improved in PageStream3

The choice is clear. PageStream 3.0 beats Xpress 3.3 and PageMaker 5.0. ProPage 4.1 isn't even in the running.

Note: Xpress and PageMaker are Macintosh and Windows programs. They are listed here to show that PageStream is not only the best Amigo DTP program, but the best for any computer.

Continued

Exhibit 2 Comparison of Features of DTP Systems—*Continued*

Typography cont ...

	PGS3	PP4.1	XP3.3	PM5
☆ edit rotated text	●	●	●	●
☆ Left/right/first indent/outdent	●	○	●	●
★ Inter-paragraph spacing	●	○	○	○
★ Widow and orphan control	●		●	●
★ keep paragraphs together	●		●	●
★ Automatic drop caps	●	○ macro	○	○ macro
★ Automatic bulleted paragraphs	●			○ macro
Paragraph rules			●	●
★ Column and page breaks	●		●	●
★ Auto and manual kerning	●	○	●	●
★ user-definable kerning tables	●	●	●	
★ hanging punctuation	●			
★ optical alignment	●			
★ automatic ligatures	●			
★ Auto tracing	●		○	●
★ min, max, opt character/word space	●		●	●
★ tracking tables	○		○	●
☆ manual tracking	●	○	●	
☆ Automatic and manual hyphenation	●	○	●	●
custom hyphenation dictionaries	●	○	●	
discretionary hyphens	●		●	●
☆ Absolute/relative leading	●	○	●	●
☆ increments	0.001 pts	0.01 pts	0.001 pts	0.1 pts
★ baseline grid	●		●	
★ List fonts used in document/chapter	●		●	● macro

Text Frames

	PGS3	PP4.1	XP3.3	PM5
★ Max number of columns in a frame	99	1	30	20
☆ Frameless text objects	●			
☆ Drag resize text	●		●	
★ Variable-shaped text frames	●		○	
★ Automatic text frame creation	●	●	●	●
Vertical justification			●	●

Graphics

	PGS3	PP4.1	XP3.3	PM5
☆ Bitmap picture import/export filters	6/5	5/0	?/?	?/?
☆ set frequency, angle and pattern	●		●	●
★ irregular picture cropping	●		○	
★ display pictures in color	●	●	●	●
☆ Structured drawing import/export filters	3/2	2/0	?/?	?/?
☆ dissolve drawings into paths & shapes	●			
☆ EPS import filter	●	●	●	●
show bitmapped previews	●	○	●	●
☆ Interpret EPS filters	3	3	0	0
☆ interpret Adobe Illustrator EPS	●	○		
★ interpret Aldus Freehand EPS	●	○		
★ Externally linked graphics	●	●	●	●
★ Export drawings as Adobe Illustrator EPS	●			
★ List all imported graphics in a document	●	●	●	●

Illustration

	PGS3	PP4.1	XP3.3	PM5
☆ Line tool	●	●	●	●
☆ Box tool	●	○	○	○
☆ Elipse/arc tool	●	○	○	○
★ Polygon/star tool	●			
☆ Pen tool	●		○ very limited	
☆ Freehand tool	●			

Object Editing

	PGS3	PP4.1	XP3.3	PM5
☆ Select multiple objects	●	○	●	●
☆ add/remove from selection	●		○	○
select behind	●		●	
☆ Proportional sizing constraint	●		●	●

Object Editing cont...

	PGS3	PP4.1	XP3.3	PM5
☆ Bring to front/send to back	●	●	●	●
☆ bring forward/send backward	●		●	●
☆ Cut, copy and paste objects	●	○	●	●
☆ Move and nudge objects	●		●	○
☆ Step and repeat duplication	●	○ macro	●	
☆ Merge and split paths	●			
☆ Rotate and skew objects	●	○	●	●
☆ rotation increments	0.001°	1°	0.001°	0.01°
☆ rotate about point	● macro			
Group/Ungroup objects	●	○	●	
Lock/Unlock objects	●	○	●	
Align and distribute objects	●	○ macro	●	
Text wrap around objects	●	○	○	●
wrap text around picture subject			●	●
Extend objects across page spreads	●	●	●	
Anchor objects to text	●		lb	●

Line & Fill

	PGS3	PP4.1	XP3.3	PM5
☆ Percentage (tint) fill precision	0.01%	0.1%	0.1%	1%
☆ Editable bitmap fill styles, number of	unlimited	16	0	0
★ Color gradient fills	●	●		
★ radial and shape fills	8	1	6	0
★ number of taper types	8	1	6	0
★ Screen types (spot functions)	6	1	4	1
☆ Max line width	1000 pts	27 pts	504 pts	800 pts
☆ increments	0.001 pts	1 pt	0.001 pts	0.1 pts
☆ Dash styles, number of	unlimited	9	11	8
★ Caps and joins	●			
★ Arrowhead styles, number of	14	0	3	0
★ Multiple line strokes per object	●			
★ Fill line strokes with a fill style	●			

Color

	PGS3	PP4.1	XP3.3	PM5
☆ Number of color models	6	3	8	8
★ PANTONE©	● (4 libraries)	○ (1 library)	● (4 libraries)	● (4 libraries)
TRUMATCH©			●	●
FOCALTONE©			●	●
☆ Create process and spot colors	●	●	●	●
☆ Shade increments	0.01%		0.1%	1%
★ Object level trapping	●		●	○
trapping values for each process plate			●	
☆ Angles/frequencies for each spot color	●	●	●	

Printing

	PGS3	PP4.1	XP3.3	PM5
☆ Actual size, percentage size, thumbnails	●	●	●	●
☆ Current page, page range, even/odd	●	○	○	○
☆ Print process separations	●	●	●	●
★ UCR/GCR	●	●		
★ Plate control	●			○
★ Booklet printing	● macro			● macro
☆ Tiling	●	○	●	
Crop and registration marks	●	○	●	
Print to disk	●		●	●
★ Suppress printout of selected items	●		●	●
Chain-print multiple documents				
★ Print empty pages option	●		●	●
★ Page independence	●		●	●
☆ Render to bitmap picture	●			
☆ Save pages as EPS illustrations	○	○		○
★ Mail merge	● macro	○ macro		
★ PPD support for PostScript printing	●		●	●
Create bleeds	●		●	●

● Feature present ○ Feature present/limited implementation macro: included macro or extension unlimited: Limited only by machine constraints
? unknown ★ New in PageStream3 ☆ Improved in PageStream3

The choice is clear. PageStream 3.0 beats Xpress 3.3 and PageMaker 5.0. ProPage 4.1 isn't even in the running.

Note: Xpress and PageMaker are Macintosh and Windows programs. They are listed here to show that PageStream is not only the best Amigo DTP program, but the best for any computer.

Exhibit 2   Comparison of Features of DTP Systems

	PGS3	PP4.1	XP3.3	PM5		PGS3	PP4.1	XP3.3	PM5
File Management					*Utilities cont...*				
★ Open document format other than own	• ProPage!				★ Picture (bitmap) editor	•	○ limited		
★ Revision control and log	•				★ effect filters	8	0		
★ Job numbering	•				★ autotracer	•			
★ Auto-save	•		○ macro	•	Table editor				•
★ Auto-backup	•			•	*Amiga Specific Features*				
Macro Scripts (ARexx)					☆ AmigaDOS 3 compatible	•	○ limited	n/a	n/a
★ Record macros	•				★ AGA compatible	•	○ limited	n/a	n/a
★ Edit macros	•		○ external		☆ Public & Workbench screen support	•		n/a	n/a
★ Internal macros	•				☆ Amiga standard menus and windows	•		n/a	n/a
★ External scripts (Flash macros, Genies)	•	•	○	•	☆ Amiga standard requesters and gadgets	•		n/a	n/a
★ Assign macros to function keys	• 80 keys	• 20 keys			☆ Amiga standard keyboard shortcuts	•		n/a	n/a
★ Add macros to menu	•			•	Price	$395	$299.95	$995	$895
Utilities									
★ Article (story) editor	•	•		•					

1-Logik Publishing has made every attempt to ensure the accuracy of this comparison; however, you should contact the other companies if you have questions about their programs. PageStream is a registered trademark of Soft-Logik Publishing Corp. Xpress is a registered trademark of Quark Inc. Pantone is a registered trademark of Pantone, Inc. PageMaker, PostScript and Illustrator are registered trademarks of Adobe Systems Inc. All other trademarks are the property of their respective owners.

New Trends in High-End Desktop Publishing

Two new trends in the DTP field were very evident in 1995: electronic publishing and workgroup publishing. Electronic publishing permits documents created in a DTP program to be read on a user's personal computer screen rather than printed on paper. The reader's PC does not need to have the DTP program on its hard disk to permit the user to read the file. The file is distributed with a reader program such as FrameMaker's Frame Viewer. The advantages of electronic publishing over conventional paper publishing include savings of storage space (diskette, hard drive, or CD-ROM versus paper files), saving paper and trees, and fast search and retrieval of information. The advantage of saved storage space is lost, of course, if the document recipient makes a paper copy of an electronic document for storage.

While Frame Viewer is a customized reader, other DTP programs use a more general program to prepare electronic documents and allow users to read them. In 1995 the professional DTP market was moving slowly toward the Standard Generalized Markup Language (SGML), which promotes easy document transfer among applications. Corel Ventura 5 offered SGML support. The disadvantage is that a user must be at the computer and have Corel loaded when a document is transferred. This is not always convenient.

Of the four competitors, it seems that FrameMaker and Corel Ventura could make best use of electronic publishing because it would enhance their strengths in handling long, complex documents rather than design-intensive ones. But there are other market opportunities for displaying graphic-intensive as well as text-intensive documents electronically. These opportunities attracted other competitors into the electronic publishing market. Key among them is Adobe, which publishes and sells PageMaker.

Early in 1994 Adobe Corporation established a 70-member interactive publishing unit to develop electronic-publishing and CD-ROM-authoring software.[6] Also,

Adobe and IBM were jointly developing printing and publishing systems based partly on Adobe's Acrobat Reader software. This effort is designed to make Acrobat the *de facto* standard for document and data exchange. Adobe will port Acrobat to two of IBM's operating systems: OS/2 Warp and OS/2 for the Macintosh PowerPC. IBM planned to preload Acrobat Reader onto most of its new desktop PCs beginning in the fall of 1995. Corel Ventura 5 offers full support for Acrobat features. And Acrobat also will be integrated into Netscape Navigator, the most popular program for browsing the World Wide Web on the Internet.[7] Investors reacted to Adobe's alliances with IBM and Netscape Communications by pushing Adobe Systems' stock to an all-time high in late March 1995. In April 1995, Adobe joined with Hearst, International Data Group, Knight-Ridder, TCI, and Times Mirror to purchase an 11 percent stake in Netscape Communications.[8]

The second recent trend emphasizes workgroup publishing. Workgroup publishing allows writers, editors, art directors, illustrators, layout artists, and production managers to perform their specialized tasks on a single document. Such group work has been handled mostly by workaround solutions in the past, but Quark Publishing System and the Metro System from Adobe will keep track of files across a network while different individuals do their part in creating and editing a document.[9]

Desktop Publishing on the Major PC Platforms

Different types of personal computers use different operating systems (OSs). The OS is the basic software that a computer must have to process instructions; a computer can do nothing if it cannot process instructions. The OS functions like a traffic cop to regulate the flow of instructions between an application program, such as a spreadsheet, word processor, or DTP program, and the computer's keyboard, monitor, central processing system, internal memory, hard disk, and printer. Because each OS is written in a unique way, an application program must be rewritten to be compatible with each OS. The combination of an OS and the type of hardware on which it runs is called a platform. A different version of an application program must be written for each platform on which it will be used.

Several platforms were in wide use in 1995. By far the dominant one was Microsoft's Windows and its underlying MS-DOS system for IBM compatibles, installed on 82 percent of personal computers. Other major platforms included Apple Computer's OS for the Macintosh, IBM's OS/2 for IBM compatibles, and the UNIX and Sun OSs, which were used mostly on higher powered workstation computers.

Most major software applications offered versions for more than one platform to increase sales and market share. This is the case in the high-end DTP market. While most major DTP programs started on the Macintosh, most were ported to additional platforms. QuarkXPress and PageMaker offered versions for both Windows and the Macintosh. FrameMaker sported four versions: Windows, Macintosh, Sun, and UNIX.

One 1994 survey showed that 78.7 percent of the desktop artists surveyed preferred the Macintosh platform because of its smooth interface. Most publishers responding to that survey planned to upgrade their systems soon, and they had average budgets of $30,000 for hardware and $4,600 for software with which to shop.[10] Despite this apparent good news for Apple Computer and its DTP vendors, an air of uncertainty surrounded the future of the Macintosh. Some felt that IBM-compatible computers would soon gain a larger share of the DTP market because they offered better price–performance ratios. Apple made major strides in closing the cost gap with IBM compatibles during the early 1990s by introducing new models at lower prices. In 1995, they made another major market move to close the price gap. It was a move that many analysts thought was years late in coming, and which they thought might be too late to do much good. Apple had always built all Macintosh computers, but decided to allow other vendors to build Macintosh clones.

Power Computing Corporation and Radius Incorporated were the first two companies to license the Macintosh for clone manufacturing. These two firms displayed their first models at the 1995 Macworld Expo trade show. Power Computing planned to offer low-cost machines that would undercut comparable Apple models by 10 to 20 percent. Radius took the high road, offering models aimed at the high-end DTP and digital video-editing market.[11]

Apple CEO Michael Spindler hopes that this cloning strategy will help the Macintosh gain market share against IBM compatibles. Cloning of IBM compatibles began soon after IBM introduced its PC in 1981. Many analysts think that the Macintosh would have sold many more models and that software writers would have produced many more programs for the machine if Apple had not kept the machine's architecture a proprietary secret for so many years. They are skeptical about the success of the cloning strategy now. Others see hope for Apple because the firm's clone strategy will be played much differently than that for IBM compatibles.

IBM did not have a strategy for clones, so the market developed some good machines and some that were not compatible with the standards. Apple will control clone development in a way designed to grow Apple in the market. Any company that licenses the Macintosh OS can market computers in any geographic area using any method of distribution it wants. This should ensure a broad range of licensees that guarantee a distribution channel for different markets, including the largest PC manufacturers. Apple will sell the OS at a price low enough to ensure that clone makers can keep the prices of their machines competitive against Apple Macintoshes and Windows PCs. Apple and the cloners will use generic PC equivalent parts to reduce supply costs. Apple also will offer peripherals to clone makers with or without the Apple logo. Some analysts predict that clone sales will take off when Macintoshes based on a new OS called Moccasin hit the market in 1996. Moccasin will be a converged-hardware reference platform (CHRP), meaning that it will read and write software files from other platforms. This should speed sales of Macintosh clones and relieve Apple of the burden of providing sole support for clone makers.[12]

With its clone strategy, Apple expects to reach greater sales success in its traditional markets: business publishing and graphics, education, and the home. Former vice president Ian Diery said, "You will see us focus our dollars and energies on these markets and customer uses that have made us successful, where we are the market leader. We will continue to stand out by being the best at the user interface, multimedia, graphics, communications, and collaboration."[13]

Some feel that to be really successful, Apple's clone strategy must include a major player to manufacture clones. This may not come until after Moccasin arrives to give the multiple-OS flexibility that may bring the economies of scale that a large manufacturer needs to enter this market. *Macworld* magazine identified the following companies as most likely to ship clones during 1995 and 1996[14]:

- Motorola,
- Acer,
- Toshiba,
- Zenith,
- Olivetti,
- Obis,
- NEC,
- Dell,
- Fujitsu,
- Canon, and
- FirePOWER.

Apple's bold competitive move into cloning was major news to the computer world in 1995. But the biggest computing news that year was due in August when Microsoft was scheduled to release Windows 95, its new OS for IBM compatibles. Microsoft promised that this significant upgrade, replacing the dominant Windows 3.1, would equal the Macintosh GUI for ease of use and that it would end some of the instability problems of Windows 3.1. Windows 95 may have been the most thoroughly tested new software ever to enter the market. In addition to extensive testing at Microsoft, the firm offered 400,000 copies of the beta (final test) version to any user willing to pay $32 for a copy. Microsoft sold out on this offer. The introduction of this improved OS spurred Apple to work hard to replace its existing System 7 OS for the Macintosh with Moccasin to keep competitive. There could be little doubt that Windows 95 would foster a raft of new upgrades of the major application software products, including the DTP applications.

These events in the computer industry during 1995 stimulated competitive actions among hardware and software firms. It was a year of opportunity to try a new product for the new operating systems about to be released. Yet it was a time of uncertainty in the fast-paced and increasingly competitive computer market. Events in the Amiga computer market were forcing Soft-Logik to test the competitive waters.

■ History of Soft-Logik

Soft-Logik is based in the St. Louis suburb of Ballwin, Missouri. Deron Kazmaier and Shawn Fogle started the firm in 1985 to develop and market a DTP program they named Publishing Partner for the Atari computer. Deron had the programming skills and Shawn was the firm's salesman. They did not have the cash necessary to enter the more competitive Macintosh or IBM PC markets, so they had to choose between the Atari and Amiga platforms. They chose the Atari because it was more capable of doing DTP work. They switched to the Amiga two years later when its technical capability surpassed the Atari's.

In 1987, Deron and Shawn were developing Publishing Partner 2.0 for both the Atari and the Amiga. Shawn wanted to release most of the seven sales and programming employees and work out of the home. Deron felt a stronger commitment to the employees, so he called Shawn to discuss the ownership arrangements. They had a 50–50 ownership arrangement that permitted either of them to freeze the firm's assets in the case of a disagreement they could not resolve. Deron threatened to invoke this privilege and freeze Soft-Logik's assets unless the two principals could agree not to retrench the firm. Deron had the leverage because Publishing Partner 2.0 had no value until it was finished, and only he had the programming technical knowledge to finish it. Deron offered Shawn a generous payout that Shawn accepted: almost half of 2.0's booked sales. Since then, Deron has owned 100 percent of the firm.

In 1988 Deron gave Publishing Partner 2.0 the product's current name, PageStream. Users and analysts quickly recognized PageStream as the leading professional desktop publishing program for the Atari and the Amiga. Commodore's Amiga computer was renown for its excellent graphics capability, which surpassed that of the Macintosh then. The sole competing DTP program for the Amiga was Professional Page, published by a firm named Gold Disk. After a few upgrades and enhancements, Soft-Logik released PageStream Amiga version 1.5 in March 1989.

In July 1991, Soft-Logik released PageStream 2.1. In 1992, this product received the Reader's Choice Award for Best Amiga Desktop Publishing Program from *Amiga World* magazine. Not resting on its laurels, Soft-Logik added about 1,000 new features to the program and introduced the improved PageStream 3.0 in January 1994 at a price of $395. Customers who purchased PageStream 2.1 after March 15, 1993, were eligible for a free upgrade to 3.0 for a $5 shipping and handling fee. Owners of PageStream 2.0 or higher could upgrade for $125, and owners of competitor Professional Page could switch to PageStream for $175.

Commodore, manufacturer of the Amiga, made some unfortunate market choices during the 1990s. The firm invested heavily in CD-TV, a player that displayed the contents of game and educational CD-ROMs on a TV screen. The firm developed a heavy inventory of CD-TV players for the 1993 Christmas gift season, but the product did not sell well. To many people, a personal computer with a CD-ROM drive was a more practical hardware choice for this use. Also, Commodore did not advertise the Amiga very much in the face of the increasingly competitive Macintosh and IBM PC markets.

In April 1994, Commodore filed for bankruptcy. The firm sold its assets and its name in May 1995 to Escom, a German retail store chain. Escom originally planned to use the Commodore name to market its own line of computers. To help recover the cost of the Commodore buyout, Escom decided to sell a limited number of Amigas, but with no marketing support. Deron expected that this feeble effort would do little to revive the flagging Amiga market. So Escom's purchase of Commodore marked the beginning of the end for the Amiga computer—and the end of the line for the few remaining Amiga-only software developers such as Soft-Logik. "Momentum behind the market is gone," said Deron. His words were supported by a decline in the number of Amiga magazines and the decrease in their content from 1994 to 1995.

The effect of Commodore's demise on Soft-Logik was swift and dramatic. From mid-1994 to mid-1995, Soft-Logik sold 4,000 copies of PageStream 3.0. By mid-1995 the firm had only 500 to 600 customers who were actively buying upgrades to the product. Soft-Logik employed 11 people in mid-1994; there are only 4 employees in mid-1995. Future prospects were grim because there will be no new Amigas to replace users' aging machines. And even though some still regard the Amiga as the leading graphics computer—many TV show producers use it to create special effects—the Amiga's lead in graphics is diminishing as the Macintosh, IBM PCs, and UNIX-based machines increase their graphics capabilities.

Soft-Logik After Commodore

With a shrinking customer base resulting from the end of the Amiga computer, it was clear to Deron that he must port PageStream to at least one other platform. Like most software firms, Soft-Logik did not rely on only one product, but had a line of related products. Soft-Logik's May 1995 product catalog described the following software line:

- *PageStream 3:* The firm's flagship product. Its features are detailed in Exhibit 2. $225
- *Wordworth 3.1:* A powerful word processor with features like kerning, text effects, and tables. This program offers extensive printer support and drag-and-drop text editing. It also has automatic spelling correction for common words, and can read text aloud. $135
- *Datastore 1.1:* A database that stores text, numeric, and graphic data. Comes with several templates for recipes, club memberships, a video library, and a home contents inventory. Users can create forms, sort records, print reports, and export data for mail merging with Wordworth and PageStream. $95
- *TypeSmith 2.5:* Allows users to convert fonts among PostScript, TrueType, Compugraphic Intellifont, and Soft-Logik formats. This allows customers to use their fonts for all major Amiga software packages. TypeSmith was highly rated by several Amiga user publications. $125
- *Organizer 1.0:* A personal information manager with the screen appearance of a spiral-bound organizer. Users can enter appointments and repeating events, and set reminder alarms. Also, they can create "to do" lists with priorities, keep an address book, and mail merge the addresses with PageStream, Wordworth, or export them into Organizer. The program prints pages in popular organizer formats. $95
- *Studio Fonts:* Fifty-three fonts that can be used with any Amiga program. $30
- *Amiga Computer Art:* A clip-art package containing 75 detailed, color drawings of Amiga computers and peripherals. $30
- *Serials TypeCollection:* A CD-ROM with 1,000 fonts from Brendel Type, one of the oldest names in European typeface design. $499
- *Flags of the World:* Clip art images of 190 national flags. $30

Exhibit 3 Soft-Logik Sales and Profits by Product, 1994 and 1995				
	Sales		**Cumulative Net Profit***	
Product	*1994*	*1995†*	*1994*	*1995†*
PageStream 3.0	$386,093	$47,612	$163,391	$160,910
Typesmith	107,849	19,804	130,837	138,426
Clipart (flags)	1,489	720	4,612	4,825
Artexpression (other clip art)	7,975	10	100,682	100,681

* Cumulative net profit (loss) since product began selling.
† January–July 1995.

Exhibit 4	Soft-Logik Sales and Profits from Digita Products, November 1994–July 1995
Product	**Sales**
Wordworth	$45,597
Wordworth Companion Book	910
Datastore	11,309
Organizer	9,195
Total sales	$67,011
Net profit	$23,163
Return on sales	35%

Wordworth, Datastore, and Organizer are programs supplied to Soft-Logik by Digita, a British software developer. Soft-Logik employees do not write code for these programs. All programs in the catalog are written to run exclusively on the Amiga platform, the operating system for which is AmigaDOS. Exhibits 3 and 4 show sales and profits for Soft-Logik's products. Exhibit 5 shows product lines for Soft-Logik's key competitors. Finally, Exhibit 6 shows Soft-Logik's overall sales and profits for 1993–1995.

Deron points out that there are advantages to having few programmers working on an application. In large software development firms where many programmers work on a program, one may write a sort routine or other module

---

Exhibit 5   Product Lines of Selected Soft-Logik Competitors

Adobe Pagemaker

- *Adobe Persuasion 3.0*: A presentation graphics software for professionals who deliver live presentations. It creates output for 35 mm slides, overheads, and on-screen presentations. $268.99

- *Adobe Premier 4.0*: Creates digital movies or videotapes. Includes movie editing tools and the ability to add stereo sound and special effects to the movies. $469.99

- *Adobe Type On Call 4.0*: Includes over 2,000 fonts, font tools, and Adobe Acrobat Reader. $48.99

- *Adobe Acrobat 2.0*: On-screen authoring and reading application. Allows users to read on-screen documents without the authoring application or hardware. $128.99

- *Adobe Streamline 3.0.1*: Lets users convert black-and-white or color bit-mapped graphic images to line art, then scale it in a drawing program. $124.99

- *Adobe Illustrator 4.0*: A professional illustration and page design tool. $429.95

- *Adobe Photoshop 3.0*: Gives users control of the image-making process. $139.99

Adobe also offers some combination packages of two or more of the products described above.

Corel

- *CorelDraw! 5*: A powerful graphics package that includes Corel Ventura 5. This package includes 22,000 clip art images and symbols, 825 fonts, 100 high-resolution photos, and Adobe Acrobat Reader. $446.99

- *Corel Photo-Paint 5+*: Power tools for painting, editing, and retouching images. $169.99 on CD-ROM and diskettes; $67.99 on CD-ROM only

- *Corel Flow 2.0*: Drawing program featuring drag-and-drop drawing, text and line editing, and other drawing tools. $66.99

- *Corel Gallery CD 2.0*: Image library with 15,000 clip art images, 500 photos, 500 fonts, 75 sound clips, 10 video clips, and a multimedia file manager. $64.99

Corel offers several more photo collections on CD-ROM that range in price from $14.99 to $699.99.

Frame Technology

The publisher of FrameMaker, Frame Technology, also makes Frame Viewer. Frame Viewer lets users distribute FrameMaker documents electronically. It is a proprietary product that competes with Adobe Acrobat Reader. Frame Viewer 5-Pack, $119.95

Source: Various catalog advertisements. Prices vary by vendor.

Exhibit 6	Soft-Logik Corporation Statement of Operations		
	For years ended June 30		
	1993	**1994**	**1995**
Net sales	955,136	592,052	609,988
Operating expenses:			
Selling expenses	260,056	69,679	134,918
General and administrative	677,813	515,556	461,085
Depreciation and amortization	19,380	18,443	11,867
Total operating expenses	957,249	603,678	607,870
Gain (loss) from operations	(1,959)	(11,626)	2,118

for the particular part of the program she or he is writing, while another programmer may write a similar routine for a different part of the program. One sort routine could serve both parts of the program, but because the programmers do not communicate and thus do not know what each other is doing, they write much redundancy of this type into programs. This is a major factor contributing to the increased size of new programs.

This is not a problem in Soft-Logik where only two or three programmers work on PageStream. They communicate and share program routines. This results in a smaller, more efficiently written program, and makes it easier to write upgrades, since they only need to rewrite or add certain modules of code. The downside of having few programmers is that a project takes longer to complete.

Years spent writing code for the Amiga also helped discipline Deron and his programmers to write more efficient code, because the Amiga always had less internal memory than did the Macintosh or most IBM-PCs. One can see the results by comparing the size and the hardware needed to run PageStream with the requirements of competing DTP programs. In its Macintosh version, QuarkXPress 3.3 needs eight megabytes of hard disk space; Deron expects PageStream to need only three megabytes when completed. For basic work, PageStream requires two megabytes of internal memory (RAM); QuarkXPress needs eight megabytes. The IBM PC tends to require even more disk space and internal RAM for a comparable program than does the Macintosh.

PageStream addresses the trend toward workgroup DTP with document revision control, tracking, and job numbering features. The program can use Adobe Acrobat even in its present Amiga version, so users can share documents electronically with people who do not have PageStream or who do not even use an Amiga computer.

Deron's plan was to port PageStream first to the larger IBM PC market, then to the Macintosh. He had two programmers, one working on each of these two projects. Deron worked on writing the functional code for PageStream itself. The programmer working on the code for the IBM PC version of PageStream left Soft-Logik in May 1995, temporarily halting that project. Deron and the remaining programmer focused on porting PageStream to the Macintosh. PageStream was close to running on the Macintosh in June 1995. Deron felt that it could be ready for market by October 1995. He planned to introduce it at a price of $575. The IBM PC version of PageStream would come later, after Deron hires another programmer to do the hard job of continuing the previous programmer's work in midstream and finishing it.

With the demise of the Amiga, Deron knows that Soft-Logik faces a critical juncture. He must choose the proper strategy to introduce PageStream into the market against its larger and better established, high-end DTP rivals. He says, "We will have one shot at this market."

■ Notes

1. Reviews of low-end packages are from William Harrel, 1993, Pick a publishing powerhouse, *Windows Magazine,* September, 180–195; Bob Weibel, 1995, Perfect pages made easy, *PC Computing* 8, no. 7(July): 164–172.
2. Harrel, Pick a publishing powerhouse.
3. Luisa Simone, 1994, Professional desktop publishing, *PC Magazine* 13(May 17): 167–189.
4. Kathleen Tinkel, 1994, XTraordinary XTensions, *MacUser,* November, 109–111.
5. Simone, Professional desktop publishing.
6. Erica Schroeder, 1994, Aldus taking digital route to interactive publishing, *PC Week* 11, no. 4: 1–2.
7. Lisa Picarille, 1995, Market rallies behind Adobe's partnerships, *Computerworld* 29, no. 14: 32.
8. Alison L. Sprout, 1995, The rise of Netscape, *Fortune* 132, no. 1(July 10): 140–142.
9. Simone, Professional desktop publishing.
10. Paul McDougal, 1994, Desktop survey: Publishers are doing it themselves, *Folio* 23, no. 14(September 1): 63–66.
11. Robert Hess, 1995, Power, Radius show Mac clones; Apple OEMs target different audiences, *PC Week* 12, no. 1: 1–2.
12. Apple's clone strategy: How Mac-compatibles will emerge, 1995, *Macworld,* April, 100.
13. *Ibid.*
14. Mac clones: Who's next?, 1995, *Macworld,* April, 101.

■ CASE 32 Susan's Special Lawns

David C. Snook-Luther
Grant L. Lindstrom
University of Wyoming

This has been a year for experience. We have done a lot of work, but we haven't made much money for all of our effort. We estimate jobs and put in competitive bids, but something always happens that makes the job take 20 to 40 percent longer than I planned. This means Susan and I have to work longer hours and we don't have time to do the planning and preparation we should be doing. I have learned a lot about planning a job and what I have to do to keep projects on schedule. I'm just glad we didn't get the contract for one of those really big jobs we bid on. We could have lost the business before we even got started with all of the extra labor we would have to hire and the equipment we would have to rent. But now we are ready to make a move and we have plenty of opportunities. (David Jensen speaking to Gerald Green)

■ The Beginning

Susan had been an avid gardener and flower lover all of her life. Having lived in prime growing areas on the West Coast and in the South, Susan now found herself in the ruggedly beautiful but very different growing region of the high Rocky Mountains. During the last few years, she had adapted to the growing climate of her new home in this moderate-sized university town. In the spring of 1988, she decided to remove the sod on part of her lawn that bordered the sidewalk and plant naturally growing wildflowers. By early summer the flowers were in full bloom.

We would like to recognize Craig Grenvik, Savyasachi Gupta, and Trent Kaufman for their help in data collection and company information. Originally presented at a meeting of the North American Case Research Association, November 1992. Management cooperated in the field research for this case, which was written solely for the purpose of stimulating student discussion. All events and incidents are real, but all names and financial information have been disguised at the organization's request. All rights reserved jointly to the author and North American Case Research Association (NACRA). Copyright ©1994 by the *Case Research Journal* and David C. Snook-Luther.

The response to her flowered border was amazing. As she worked in her flower beds, people often would stop to tell her how beautiful they thought her yard looked. Many people asked her where she had gotten her seed. She told them they could find wildflower seeds in just about any major retail outlet store such as Kmart, Target, or May's Department Stores.

1989

The following spring, she wanted to try something different. Since she was quite familiar with the individual species, Susan wanted to create a personalized garden where she could plant different flowers in different areas to achieve a color and size contrast. This was virtually impossible when buying seed from the major retailers because they only sold seed in generic mixes. She located the Applewood Seed Co., a wholesaler that sold individual species of wildflower seeds and obtained the individual varieties she wanted.

The response to her new flower beds was even greater than the previous year. Several people noticed flowers in her beds which they had never seen before. Susan explained which species she had in her beds, the blooming cycles of each, and the special planting and watering requirements. Susan realized many people had a deeper interest in these special flowers than just looking at their brilliant colors.

1990

The following spring, Susan decided to try to sell wildflowers as both individual species and in custom mixes. She spent $300 on seeds and another $100 on containers. She rationalized that even if she didn't make money, she would be introducing more people to "her" world of special flowers.

The seed sales exceeded her wildest expectations. People not only were buying for themselves, they were extensively buying the seeds as gifts for friends and relatives. Soon Susan had to order more seed. By the end of May 1990, Susan had sold $3,260 worth on an $850 investment in seeds and packaging. The amount of seed sold in two months would have covered nearly one and a half acres.

As people began to know Susan and her business, they started seeking her advice on many aspects of gardening. She began to do custom flower beds for many residences across town. In late April the owners of a local bank building requested her services to revitalize the lawn and flower beds on the premises. Susan soon found she had too much business to handle on just a part-time basis. Therefore, she took incompletes on her course work at the university where she was pursuing a master's degree in physics to devote all her time to the business.

In the beginning, Susan's husband David was less than enthusiastic about the seed business, thinking it would be a sure flop. To keep peace in the household he agreed to the venture. David has done quite well with his degree in statistics, specializing in geostatistics. David worked about 40 hours a week as a research associate in the statistics department, and the geology department wanted to hire him for another 30 hours a week if he was willing to do both jobs.

David had worked for a commercial landscaping company that specialized in golf course construction while he was in school. As Susan's customers' requests for help in landscaping grew, he realized the seed sales could act as a springboard into the lucrative landscaping business. David's interest and support of the business grew rapidly. His thorough knowledge of irrigation systems and landscape design added another dimension to the business.

By mid-June, they had diversified into small-scale landscaping projects including planting small trees and shrubs, laying sod, laying flagstone for walkways and patios, and shrub and small tree pruning. David prepared for expansion into irrigation systems. A milestone was reached in late July when Susan's Special Lawns was asked to do a complete landscaping job for a residence, starting from scratch. The job included the landscape design, a high-quality sprinkler system, laying sod for the lawn, tree and shrub plantings, and, of course, wildflower seed plantings. They bid the price of the job based on their time estimate, the costs for planting materials, and the price competitors were charging for high-quality sprinkler system installations. Within two days of starting the project, the Jensens realized they were going to need help to finish the project on time. Thus, Susan's Special Lawns hired its first part-time employee, Gerald Green, an MBA student at the local university.

During the fall of 1990, the company continued to sell wildflower seeds and do small landscaping projects. The seed sales entered a new era when Susan decided to try to sell her seeds through local retail dealers. A large local drug store and a popular local gift shop agreed to sell her seeds. At first, Susan used the same packaging as she had during the year. There were two types of packaging. Individual species were sold in small test tubes and mixes were sold in small plastic bags containing Susan's business card.

To spur sales during the Christmas Holiday season, Susan tried two different packaging techniques. The first consisted of putting five individual species in a wooden crate where the seeds were clearly visible. The process of building these crates was quite tedious and reaction to them was mixed. The second technique was quite successful. Susan bent glass tubing into the shape of a candy cane, melted one end creating a seal, and filled the cane with wildflower seeds.

As a percentage of the selling price, the glass candy cane package cost about twice as much as the standard package. However, the additional cost was worth it. Reaction to the candy canes was remarkable. Both of her retailers rapidly ran out of stock. With her last "production run" of the season, Susan was able to create and fill 20 canes an hour. At a wholesale price of $2.50/cane, she felt good putting in an hour a day working. By year's end the gamble of an initial $400 in start-up costs had grown to a business that produced $10,621 in revenues.

1991

The start of a new year brought high hopes for Susan's Special Lawns. They made several strategic moves. First, they found new suppliers for landscaping and irrigation products. They also purchased several new assets in anticipation of larger projects to come. Acquisitions included a computer-assisted design (CAD) software package, two 40-megabyte hard drives, and a laser printer for the computer system to create high-resolution drawings and blueprints. Another purchase was a professional composting device. Finally, they purchased two used trucks to haul larger loads of equipment and waste materials. They felt that these moves were necessary to establish Susan's Special Lawns in landscaping and lawn

Exhibit 1	Susan's Special Lawns Balance Sheet			
		As of 12-31-90	As of 3-31-91	As of 6-30-91
Assets				
Current Assets	Cash	775	275	275
	Accounts receivable	830	781	4947
	Office supplies	225	268	356
	Operating supplies	198	256	512
	Prepaid expenses	918	550	1378
	Inventory	2830	3053	5819
	Total current assets	5776	5183	13287
Fixed Assets	Office furniture	100	100	100
	Office electronic equip	1861	1861	2955
	Library	1089	1195	1245
	Machinery and equipment	2284	2300	3847
	Vehicles	5700	5700	7485
	Accumulated depreciation	−4193	−5074	−6208
	Total fixed assets	6841	6082	9424
	Total assets	12617	11265	22711
Liabilities & Owners' Equity				
Current Liabilities	Accounts payable	66	0	2006
	Notes payable	7848	9511	14808
	Payroll taxes payable	41	3	1062
	Sales tax payable	168	21	308
	Total current liabilities	8123	9535	18184
Long-Term Liabilities	Total long-term liabilities	0	0	0
	Total liabilities	8123	9535	18184
Equity	Jensen capital	7671	8345	9582
	Jensen drawing	−9767	−12063	−12063
	Retained earnings	1868	6590	5448
	Current earnings	4722	−1142	1560
	Total equity	4494	1730	4527
	Total liabilities and equity	12617	11265	22711

care. The balance sheet and income statement (Exhibits 1 and 2) show this expansion and the substantial business loan used to finance it. Both Susan and David considered this rapid expansion of assets necessary to pursue their expanded interests and sustain their growth. They were so sure of their decision, they were willing to commit their personal assets, including their house, to secure the loan.

A true friendship developed between the Jensens and their employee, Gerald Green. They respected Gerald's opinion and often discussed their business and plans with him. One evening late in the summer after an especially difficult week

Exhibit 2	Susan's Special Lawns Income Statement			
		Jan 1990 to Dec 1990	Jan 1991 to Mar 1991	April 1991 to June 1991
Income	Seed sales	10621	838	2893
	Irrigation system sales	3468	0	7045
	Landscaping services	12763	500	8523
	Net sales	26852	1338	18461
Cost of Goods Sold	Seeds	2658	54	1124
	Irrigation materials	1214	0	2466
	Landscaping supplies	3620	10	3426
	Total cost of goods sold	7492	64	7016
	Gross profit	19360	1274	11445
Expenses	Owners' salaries	1250	80	3750
	Contracted services	1285	23	328
	Payroll taxes	156	10	412
	Advertising	1130	130	701
	Mortgage for home office	1009	275	325
	Auto expense	1012	181	961
	Depreciation	4193	881	1134
	Insurance	578	225	299
	Research and development	84	0	0
	Licenses	342	0	50
	Office expense	517	120	129
	Equipment rental	163	17	412
	Telephone	268	92	48
	Utilities	143	72	42
	Total expenses	12130	2106	8591
	Net operating income	7230	−832	2854
	Interest expense	671	310	687
	Income before taxes	6559	−1142	2167
	Taxes	1837	0	607
	Net income	4722	−1142	1560

of long days to successfully meet a deadline on their biggest irrigation system installation to date, David started talking.

We must make a move! I can't continue to do all of my research work and keep up with the current demands of this business, too. We need to make the business large enough to support us comfortably without other sources of income.

I have three ideas about where the business should go. First, we can expand the number of retail outlets for the wildflower seed business. Susan has some good ideas for promotions throughout the year. Valentines, Easter, Thanksgiving, and Memorial Day are potentially as good as Christmas for seed promotions. With the right promotion we should be able to dramatically expand the number of retail outlets we have. Providing seeds and promotional materials to fund-raising groups should also be a good outlet.

Second, we can do a lot more with landscape planning, too. With the CAD software and the new computer equipment, we can make very attractive diagrams and elevations of custom landscape plans for people. Coupled with the attractive color photographs of our landscapes, people can get a clear idea of the dramatic effect the right use of wildflowers with other plantings has on outdoor spaces.

Finally, we have a terrific opportunity in designing and selling do-it-yourself irrigation systems. One of the regional distributors is so interested in the idea they gave me a CAD system developed by one of the major manufacturers. I am integrating the manufacturer's CAD system with our own CAD and accounting systems to provide a higher level of service to do-it-yourself customers than anything currently available. Combined with the laser printer we can quickly show potential customers a high-quality drawing of an overall irrigation system plan, a summary list of parts and prices, equipment required for the installation, and estimates of the installation time required. If they choose to buy the plans, we also would give them detailed construction plans, complete parts lists with current prices, and the specific skills, equipment, permits, and licenses required at different points of the installation. We can even incorporate a detailed landscape design showing the specific plantings set in locations with the proper light and water requirements. Then, depending on their interests and abilities, customers can contract with us for any part of the job from parts, seed, sod, and plants, to consulting advice, or a turnkey installation. We should be able to handle a fairly large geographic area with such a service.

Gerald was excited by David's vision, but also apprehensive for his friend. There were several points he felt David may not have considered adequately.

David, I think these are great ideas with a lot of potential. However, there are a few things that worry me. First, seed sales have not increased significantly since the first year. Second, our time is so tight that every time one of our big jobs takes longer, not only do we lose money on that job, but it forces Susan to delay some of the smaller jobs which provide a steady stream of income. Any misstep that substantially changes the planned time allocations for these moves could be very serious. I'm just not sure what the market potential for seeds, landscaping, and irrigation systems is in this geographic market, and how our competition is likely to respond to our moves.

David shared these concerns.

You're right, but I don't have the time to answer these questions—if they can be answered. Right now I'm doing well just to get the things done that I have to do. But we have to do something to generate enough profits to service the debt we have taken on. Can you help?

Gerald thought for a moment.

This is an interesting problem and not that difficult to deal with. It would be fun to try out some of the things I have been learning, and I have some friends in the MBA program that may be willing to help do part of the research for the experience. Let me see what we can do. I should be able to give you a fairly complete report in about four weeks.

Susan was intrigued by the ideas, but she also was thinking about how much work she had to get done in the next few weeks to be ready to supply her retailers for the gift season.

This is all very interesting, but I have a business to run. All of the landscape and sprinkler system work we have been doing lately has put me behind on preparing for the upcoming gift season. The drug store called yesterday to say that their seed display is getting low. These ideas sound like exciting opportunities, and I want to see what you find out. However, I seriously doubt that we are prepared to handle any more than we are doing now.

Several weeks later David and Susan were reading Gerald's report (see the Appendix) with great interest. They talked about it at length, but were having trouble arriving at a decision about what to do. Susan concluded, "I am impressed with how much information Gerald has been able to collect in such a short time, but I'm not sure what to make of it." David said he would have a talk with Gerald soon.

David talked to Gerald the next day while they were finishing up what they thought would be their last landscaping job for the season.

Your report is very impressive, and you certainly have given us a lot to think about. We have to make some decisions very soon or it will be too late to do anything this year. We think we have some ideas, but we would like to hear some of your specific recommendations before we go much further. We especially would like to hear how you think your recommendations can be implemented. Let's get together Saturday afternoon and start separating the wheat from the chaff.

Gerald started thinking about the methods they had covered in the strategy/policy class that he might use to organize and interpret all of this information for the Jensens. The problem was to decide which methods would reveal the greatest insights. He had to decide now and get started quickly!

Appendix: Study of Local and Regional Landscape, Lawn Care, and Wildflower Seed Markets by Gerald Green

I wish to express my appreciation to two of my colleagues in the MBA program, Jeff Bates and Les Barnes, who helped survey the businesses and potential consumers. The data in this study comes from three primary sources. The regional and local situation data are summarized from government reports, and reports compiled by chambers of commerce. Most of the consumer and competitor data comes from structured personal and telephone interviews of competitors and consumers. Finally, some of the detail regarding competitors' business practices reflects my judgments based on my experience selling sprinkler systems for two companies in this market for the last three years.

Regional and Local Situation

The central front range of the Rocky Mountains is dominated by one large metropolitan area, Denver, and several cities of approximately 100,000 population. The region covers a large geographic area with long distances between cities and a low population density. The economy is diversified and growing at a moderate rate even through a recession in the U.S. economy.

The population of the town is about 26,000 people. The population in the trade area is about 50,000 people. It is at least 70 miles to a major city. The town is characterized mainly by its service economy, with the two largest employers being a state university and a hospital. Other significant revenues come from agriculture, light manufacturing, and extractive industries. Extractive industries have produced boom and bust periods in the past. Most of the money reaped during boom periods was used for substantial personal, business, and government capital projects. Having survived a severe recession caused by a bust in the petroleum and uranium industries, the economy has grown at a modest inflation-adjusted annual rate of about three percent for the last five years. Business formations have been slightly above the rate of business closings. New housing construction is moribund, but sales of existing housing and remodeling are fairly brisk.

■ Local Industry Analysis

Residential Sprinklers

Area firms installed about 41 sprinkler systems in 1991, up from about 25 systems four years ago. With the average residential sprinkler system costing $3,500, the size of the current market is about $140,000. It is expected that this market will grow at about the same rate over the next four years to about 65 systems and $227,500, adjusted for inflation. Unlike some areas of the region and country that are severely affected by drought, water supplies and water costs in the city are not expected to be affected during the next 10 years.

Typical sprinkler system customers in the city fall into four groups: (1) convenience-minded home owners, (2) price-minded home owners, (3) real estate owners that do not occupy the premises, and (4) larger commercial and government projects. The team interviewed 10 people who fall into one of the first three groups, who shopped for average residential sprinkler systems, and who decided not to purchase one. Eight people said they would have purchased the system if the price had been less than $2,800. Additionally, four people said that they would be interested in installing part or all of their own system if there was a significant savings.

Based on my experience selling sprinkler systems in this city, about one-third of the qualified prospects eventually buy a system. Qualified prospects are ones who expressed a serious interest by developing rough plans for a system and getting a price estimate. Our data indicates that 80 percent of the people who did not buy a system would have bought one if the price had been less than $2,800. If the 41 systems sold last year were one-third of the total qualified prospects that year, then the potential market was about 123 systems, a potential increase of 82 systems. If systems had been priced at less than $2,800, then 80 percent of the additional 82 prospects may have purchased a system for a total market of 106 systems. Assuming the average sale at $2,700 rather than $3,500, I estimate the market would increase from the current $140,000 to $286,200, or about 51 percent. However, it seems likely that about 30 "premium" systems could be sold for an average price of about $3,500. If so, the total current market would be closer to $310,200. Clearly there are significant opportunities and profits if we can achieve significant savings in system costs.

Marketing costs currently run about 3 percent of sales. Overhead is dependent on the type of machinery the firm owns and ranges from about 6 to 11 percent. Labor costs can be quite different. Using labor intensive technologies, labor costs are about 40 percent of the selling price; however, these costs can be reduced to as low as 16 percent of the selling price by using specialized equipment. Finally, parts costs (e.g., sprinkler heads, timers, protectors) for the typical system range from about $640 to $800 depending on their quality. Firms can reduce this cost from 2.5 to 15 percent depending on the quantity they purchase and the quality of the parts. Quantity discounts on lower quality parts are not as great as they are on higher quality parts. Parts costs are in addition to materials such as pipe, fittings, and glue.

The competitive bidding procedures used for commercial and government installations result in high revenue contracts at much lower profits. Larger contractors use volume discounts on parts and materials, and costly, sophisticated equipment to achieve substantially lower costs in bidding for commercial installations.

The availability of low-cost, high-quality, part-time labor provided by the university students fits well with the highly seasonal nature of the business. This labor force also establishes an effective barrier to competition in residential sprinkler system installations from firms outside the city. Large outside contractors can successfully bid on large commercial projects in the area, but they cannot compete profitably in the residential sprinkler market. Also, given the presence of several good, local firms, the potential market is not great enough to attract large firms to make a substantial equipment investment in a local branch.

Landscaping

This industry segment includes landscape design, mowing and fertilizing, sodding and planting, tree trimming and spraying, and a corollary market for landscaping by-products as feedstock for mulch and compost. It has been very difficult to estimate the size of the landscape market in the area. The total sales of the leading firm in mowing and fertilizing are $200,000. They estimate their share of this market segment at 70 percent. Judging by the number of people employed by other firms doing some aspect of landscaping in the area, I estimate that the market is between $450,000 and $600,000. The market has grown moderately over the last five years, with firms adding one or two workers or a piece of major equipment each year.

Our telephone survey did not detect any major shifts in consumer tastes in the city. Xeriscaping using nonliving ground cover such as rocks and wood chips along with hardy species of flora is growing at an average rate of 250 percent in the desert Southwest and Southern California. With adequate rain and low water costs in the city, local residents will not benefit greatly by changing to this landscape. Although there will be some opportunities for market growth from yards switching to xeriscaping for aesthetic reasons, the growth will be moderate. Likewise, opportunities for growth from composting will be moderate since local landfills have plenty of space, and trash removal is cheap.

Economies of size are important in this market. A firm must achieve a minimum size before it can justify major equipment purchases such as bucket trucks for tree trimming, clam shells for transplanting mature trees, and power spraying equipment. Also, equipment that cannot be used for other purposes can only be employed during the short growing season (less than three months).

Judging by the number of workers employed, general lawn maintenance appears to be the fastest growing segment of the landscaping market in the city at about 10 percent per year. General lawn maintenance includes mowing, trimming, fertilizing, and deep feeding trees and shrubs. Summer contracts are priced by the size of the yard to be maintained and the other factors such as the number of trees to be fed. The average contract for the season is about $250 and gross margins often are about 50 percent. The largest cost component is labor, which is about 30 percent of sales. Marketing costs run from about 2 to 4 percent of sales, and materials costs are about 6 percent. Beyond an adequate number of contracts to support a power sprayer for fertilizing and deep feeding and a small associated cost saving in using liquid fertilizers, there are few economies of scale in this industry segment.

Wildflower Seeds

Wildflower seed planting is increasing nationwide. However, Susan estimates that the maximum for the local wildflower seed market is about $12,000. Although wildflower seed sales are highly seasonal with peak sales in the spring, significant markets exist at other times of the year. For example, Susan has found that a significant gift market for wildflower seeds exists at Christmas. No one knows how large other specialized markets for wildflower seeds may be.

Packaging costs can be negligible to several times the cost of the seeds for special gift packages, but typically are about 4 percent of the selling price. Unit sales revenue is from $2 to $10 depending on the number of seeds in the package and the type of package. The seeds usually are about 22 percent of the selling price. Marketing averages 4 percent and overhead 2 percent of the price.

The small unit sale price is the reason larger seed companies using inexpensive mass market distribution channels dominate the industry. Their control of the bulk of seed production and the mass marketing channels reduces the threat of large new entrants in the wildflower seed industry.

Outdoor Lighting

Our cost/revenue estimates for this market are about as poor as our estimates for lawn sprinkler systems are good. The only residential systems in town have been installed by the occupants. All of these systems used simple do-it-yourself packages.

Residential lighting systems range from about $2,000 to over $10,000. Roughly, 40 percent of the selling price is labor, and parts and material are 30 percent. One article we found said that a respectable gross margin is about 18 percent. In this geographic area, it is likely that once the business gets going, marketing costs will be about 3 percent.

■ Competitor Analysis

Residential Sprinklers

There are five firms in addition to Susan's Special Lawns that could sell and install residential sprinkler systems in the city: Green Lawns, Jack's Sprinklers, Aries, Pasque Flower, and Shaklee's. Retail stores such as Kmart, Wal-Mart, United Builders Co., Tru-Value, and others sell lawn hose, the accompanying sprinklers, and battery-operated spigot timers that can substitute for underground systems.

Competitive rivalry for residential sprinklers in the city is moderate. Because of the short installation season and the relatively small market, most of the residential firms use labor-intensive installation procedures supported by light equipment. When a job is large enough, or enough jobs are waiting to warrant it, they rent heavier equipment from out-of-town suppliers. This means that none of the firms has significant excess capacity and all of them seem to be content with the status quo.

(1) Green Lawns will try to build on its existing base of loyal lawn care customers who depend on them for mowing, fertilization, tree spraying, and sod laying. They probably will continue to focus only on the high margin residential market and avoid the lower margin commercial market. In part, this is because Green Lawns does not have the necessary licenses to do its own wiring and plumbing work. The cost of contracting with a licensed plumber and electrician is significant. Also, the company lacks the experience and expertise to design commercial projects which require detailed flow analyses such as water pound, pressure drop, and triangulation to calculate equivalent precipitation accumulation.

Green Lawns sells the second most expensive systems in the area, typically about $3,500, while using the poorest quality parts, materials, and designs. They compensate for the high cost and low quality by selling to loyal customers who want the extensive service the company provides. Their marketing reflects this approach. Green Lawns places only a few small ads in the local newspaper in the spring and a small ad in the Yellow Pages. Their primary marketing is through two newsletters sent to all of their current customers and customers from the previous year, and word of mouth referrals. The first newsletter is in early spring, announcing the services they will offer, their unit prices, and special rates for season contracts. This helps them keep a tight rein on past customers. A large percentage of their new customers is neighbors of existing customers who see the outstanding results the company delivers. Green Lawns will go to great lengths to protect its customer base from competitor advances.

(2) Pasque Flower has extensive experience installing systems in the city and has earned a reputation for excellent systems at somewhat higher prices, about $3,600 for the typical system. They use the highest quality parts, and pay about $325 for pipe and related materials after their discount which is as much as $150/job more than some high-volume competitors pay for lower quality pipe. Because of their choice of materials, Pasque Flower's labor costs can be nearly three times more than those firms using lower quality materials. The owner has a degree in civil engineering, designs and supervises all installations, and has all of the licenses required to install residential and commercial irrigation systems.

Pasque Flower has installed a number of systems for businesses and shopping centers in the community. However, for some reason they did not participate in bidding for the two largest contracts this year—two new schools and a large park.

The firm does little advertising, but its retail location is on the most heavily traveled street in the city and a few blocks from a large discount merchandiser, a large grocery store, and several fast food stores. This gives their logo excellent exposure and their lawn shows people the benefits of their services. In addition to irrigation systems which represent about 40 percent of its revenue, Pasque Flower does landscape design, and tree planting and trimming.

(3) Jack's Sprinklers specializes in sprinkler installations and completes more systems each year than any other firm in the city. The company also has more labor saving irrigation installation equipment than any other local firm, and runs two crews while other firms only run one. They use lower quality irrigation system components, but the price of the systems is attractive to customers, typically about $3,200.

Jack's has the experience and all of the necessary licenses to complete an installation. In addition he owns a line pulling machine that uses polyethylene pipe, which costs about half as much as the polyvinylchloride (PVC) pipe used by most of the other firms. Also, the line puller can install the pipe at a fraction of the cost of digging when laying the pipe through existing grass. The line puller makes a slit in the grass and lays a continuous length of flexible polyethylene pipe in a narrow groove in the soil. In addition to being faster, it also avoids having to replace sod which is necessary with the trench method. This gives Jack a significant cost advantage over the other firms. Jack's Sprinklers can be expected to vigorously protect its position in sprinkler installations.

(4) Aries is a general contractor for commercial buildings and houses. They bid aggressively on commercial irrigation projects and currently do not accept residential jobs. In past recessions they occasionally have taken residential work.

(5) Shaklee's may be going out of business. The founder died in 1989 and left a big vacuum in the organization. His children are trying to keep the business alive, but are struggling. They use low-quality parts and materials, and have next to the lowest market share. The typical price of their system is about $3,500. It would be wise to watch further developments with the company. Some useful assets may become available.

Landscaping

Three local companies do limited residential landscaping: Shaklee's, Pasque Flower, and Green Lawns. Services included in this market segment are sod laying, tree/shrub planting, flagstone walkways, and lawn maintenance services. A number of substitute sources of competition exist. Local nurseries and mass merchandisers sell flora directly to homeowners who do their own landscaping. A community college offers courses in landscape design and lawn care, and the university does soil analysis for a fee.

(1) Green Lawns has the strongest market position in the lawn maintenance segment. As noted earlier, they are recognized for their extensive, high-quality service in lawn maintenance, which includes about 70 percent of the market in power raking, mowing, and lawn and tree spraying. They also have a large share of the market for sod laying.

Green Lawn's strategy is to retain and monopolize its existing customers by providing every lawn care service that the customer could ask for. In return for this high level of service, they also charge the highest price in town for every service they provide. Green Lawns provides their customers with extensive advice, but their ability to provide customers with detailed plans for a design is limited. One of their strengths is that they suggest plans their customers can use to improve their yards over several years, and then follow up by reminding the customers about what improvements they were going to do for that year.

(2) Pasque Flower's primary landscape market is in tree planting and trimming. They have equipment that can handle the planting of trees of almost any size including mature trees. Pasque Flower also owns a bucket truck that allows them to efficiently trim large mature trees. The firm has about 80 percent of this market. They also do a substantial amount of sod laying. Most of Pasque Flower's landscape designs are developed for commercial projects.

(3) Shaklee's participation in the landscape market currently is limited to some sod laying. It is not clear whether it will continue in this business.

Wildflower Seeds

There are two large national suppliers of wildflower seeds who sell significant amounts of seed in the city. Burpee sells several wildflower mixes primarily through mail-order channels. High Altitude Gardens sells standard mixes through nurseries and major retailers such as Wal-Mart, Kmart, Target, etc. Susan's has a strong name recognition in the local area and sells through gift shops, and recently has started selling through nurseries and flower shops.

Green Lawn's attempted to preempt Susan's venture in wildflower landscaping by advertising seeds and providing the service to its customers in 1989. They also filed a complaint with the city charging Susan's Special Lawns with a zoning violation for placing a sign in their front yard advertising the name of the business. Susan was forced to remove the sign and subsequently suffered a substantial reduction in the number of customers that came to her house to purchase seeds. Green Lawns has since reduced its effort and sells only wildflower mixes as part of its landscaping projects.

Currently, there is little local competition. However, the remaining growth potential is limited. Susan will have to look beyond the city to find growth opportunities. In addition to gifts, it may be that wildflower seeds can be used by various nonprofit and not-for-profit organizations for promotional fund raising. Other niche opportunities may exist for mail-order sales by advertising in special interest publications. It is difficult to tell how large such markets may be, but many of these markets can be explored with minimal cost. Early successes can be used to support more market tests. At least for the short run, such efforts are unlikely to attract much attention or response from the national seed companies.

Outdoor Lighting

There does appear to be one significant opportunity in landscaping. No one in the city or the region advertises landscape design that includes outdoor lighting. Further, the Small Business Administration Office does not list a single landscaping company in the region that advertises outdoor lighting as a service. Currently, electricians are the only listed source for outdoor lighting installations. Installers of outdoor lighting must obtain a license by passing the state low-voltage electrical test, which serves as a barrier to most landscape firms. Susan's Special Lawns does possess such a license.

■ Conclusion

Overall I think we have some excellent opportunities. We now have to decide what we are going to be when we grow up.

■ CASE 33 Teléfonos de Mexico*

Jennifer Alexader
Tom Blackley
Linda Chen
Dru Ubben
John Economou
Sewardi Luis
Richard Martinez

On September 18, 1989, the president of Mexico, Carlos Salinas de Gortari, announced the privatization of TELMEX. The atmosphere throughout the offices of TELMEX had been electrified that day. Although privatization of Mexico's state-owned telephone services monopoly was intended to radically improve service for Mexican citizens, it also meant drastic changes in both the firm's structure and daily operations.

Following the privatization announcement, the government pledged to continue to maintain oversight of telecommunications within the country. This was to ensure that a smooth transition took place while transforming the company from public to private. Then, in December 1990, the Mexican government sold its controlling interest in TELMEX to a consortium of Mexican investors led by the Groupo Carso and two foreign telephone companies: France Télécom and Southwestern Bell International Holdings (headquartered in San Antonio, Texas). Under this agreement, the government granted TELMEX the power to be the exclusive provider of long-distance service through the end of 1996. Thereafter, competition would be allowed, and TELMEX was required to connect competing networks with its local networks at mutually acceptable rates, to be approved by government officials as well.

Since Salinas's announcement, TELMEX has expanded revenues at the rate of 18 percent per year, compared to the annual 6 percent expansion in the public sector in the early 1990s (see the financial statements given in Exhibits 1 through 5). Furthermore, phone lines had increased from 5 lines per 100 people to 8.7. TELMEX also replaced 80 percent of its obsolete exchanges with digital exchanges, and developed new microwave, optical fiber, and satellite systems.

---

*Case prepared under the direction of Professor Robert E. Hoskisson for class discussion purposes only.

Exhibit 1   Financial Data Highlights

	1993	1992	1991	1990
Consolidated*				
Revenues	24,602	22,363	19,675	16,248
Total expenses	14,320	12,657	11,085	10,383
Operating income	10,282	9,706	8,590	5,865
Net income	9,003	8,614	8,446	4,751
Total assets	52,902	47,031	45,233	40,831
Long-term liabilities	5,906	5,992	6,389	8,025
Net annual investment	7,087	7,914	7,303	7,751
Communities	18,281	15,738	12,869	10,221
Access lines in service (in thousands)	7,621	6,754	6,025	5,355
Kms. of LD circuits in service[†]	82,491	83,106	69,720	59,999
Domestic LD calls[†]	1,402,852	1,261,934	1,084,689	965,603
International LD calls[†]	387,462	351,258	257,749	211,786
Total liabilities total assets (%)	30.0	28.9	35.0	42.6
Data Per Share				
Earnings per share (N$)	0.85	0.81	0.80	0.45
Book value (N$)	3.49	3.15	2.77	2.21
Market value at year-end (N$)	10.450	8.775	7.150	2.030
Dividend per share (N$)	0.250[†]	0.150	0.075	0.025
Number of outstanding shares (in millions)	10,603	10,603	10,603	10,603

Note: Figures in million new pesos, unless otherwise indicated.

*The financial information for 1990 through 1993 has been updated according to the third reexpression document to Bulletin B-10 and, accordingly, it is stated in pesos with a purchasing power as of December 31, 1993.

†Proposed as of year-end 1993.

Source: Teléfonos de Mexico, 1993, *Annual Report.*

Although the TELMEX executive committee was aware of the effort already expended to achieve these results, they knew that TELMEX could—and must—continue to improve its service and operations if it wanted to remain the dominant long-distance telephone service provider in the Mexican market. An analysis of the financial statements of the company was all it would take to convince the executive committee members that long-distance service was, thus far, the most profitable aspect of the telephone business. However, given that current regulations in the Mexican telecommunications industry will allow for open competition in the long-distance market at the end of 1996, some analysts expect that TELMEX is likely to lose much of its market share to foreign competitors.

Against a backdrop of rapidly changing technology, a volatile and competitive global telecommunications industry, an unstable domestic economy and currency, and ambiguous customer demands, the executive committee faced a formidable challenge as it considered critical strategic decisions.

Exhibit 2 Operating Results

Year ended as of December 31	1993		1992	
	Millions of N$	% of Operating Revenues	Millions of N$	% of Operating Revenues
Operating Revenues				
Long-distance service				
International	4,850	19.7	4,746	21.2
Domestic	8,295	33.7	7,773	34.8
Local service	10,529	42.8	9,102	40.7
Other	928	3.8	742	3.3
Total revenues	24,602	100.0	22,363	100.0
Expenses				
Salaries and related costs	5,784	23.5	5,307	23.8
Depreciation	2,909	11.8	2,374	10.6
Other operating and maintenance	3,488	14.2	3,003	13.4
Telephone service tax	2,139	8.7	1,973	8.8
Total expenses	14,320	58.2	12,657	56.6
Operating Income	10,282	41.8	9,706	43.4

Source: TeléFonos de Mexico, 1993, *Annual Report.*

Worldwide Telecommunications

The Age of Privatization

Mexico was one of the first of the developing countries to privatize its telecommunications industry in the late 1980s. Prompted by the deregulation of AT&T, the global stock offering by British Telecom, and the lifting of the protected monopoly status of Japan's NTT in the mid-1980s, a wave of privatization surged in developing countries in Asia and Latin America. However, many of the more developed nations, for instance, Germany, had not privatized their phone companies by 1993 due to political opposition.

The economic arguments in favor of private enterprise are compelling. Additional financial, technical, and managerial resources (desperately needed in most emerging economies) could be provided by private telecommunications firms. Furthermore, as a result of increased competitive pressures in the industry, lower costs are expected. Private operators of telecommunications networks have been expected to restructure the workforce, introduce new technologies, and purchase components in larger volumes. Commercially minded firms could also increase their responsiveness toward customers and work to expand coverage of telecommunications services.

Because TELMEX is such a large part of the Mexican economy (upon privatization, TELMEX shares represented about one-third of the value of shares in the Mexican stock market), the executive committee understood that

Exhibit 3   Consolidated Statements of Income*

	1993	1992
Operating Revenues		
Long-distance service		
International	4,849,817	4,745,91
Domestic	8,294,563	7,772,517
Local service	10,528,765	9,102,152
Other	928,415	742,519
	24,601,560	22,363,098
Operating Expenses		
Salaries and related costs	5,783,780	5,307,171
Depreciation	2,908,681	2,373,735
Maintenance and other expenses	3,488,182	3,002,856
Telephone service tax	2,139,048	1,973,440
	14,319,691	12,657,202
Operating Income	10,281,869	9,705,896
Integral cost of financing		
Interest income	(1,434,560)	(1,543,859)
Interest expense	929,959	1,009,213
Exchange (gain) loss	(32,578)	64,270
Monetary effect	(28,062)	(251,402)
	(565,241)	(721,778)
Income before income tax and employee profit sharing	10,847,110	10,427,674
Provisions for:		
Income tax	1,197,716	1,199,049
Employee profit sharing	646,301	614,670
	1,844,017	1,813,718
Net Income	9,003,093	8,613,955

Source: TeléFonos de Mexico, 1993, *Annual Report.*
*Thousands of Mexican new pesos with purchasing power at December 31, 1993.

TELMEX's privatization strategy would serve as an example to the rest of the world. Even though partial privatization had taken place in many countries, completely open telecommunications markets existed only in a few countries such as Canada and the United States.

The TELMEX executive committee knew that some countries in Latin America had faced competition from newly licensed specialized service operators. Cellular networks, in particular, had grown quickly in Mexico, Venezuela, Argentina, and Chile. New service players, like Argentina's IMPSAT and Mexico's IUSACELL, the largest wireless cellular operator in the country, were taking their specialized service experience on the road and winning licenses in international markets. In late 1993, IUSACELL, allied with Bell Canada, led a

Exhibit 4 Consolidated Statements of Changes in Financial Position*

	1993	1992
Operating Activities		
Net income	9,003,093	8,613,955
Add: items not requiring the use of resources:		
Depreciation	2,908,681	2,373,735
Amortization	77,869	77,858
Changes in operating assets and liabilities:		
(Increase) decrease in:		
Accounts due from subscribers	(1,254,900)	(703,588)
Other accounts receivable	15,277	201,646
Prepaid expenses	(9,005)	(28,462)
Trust fund contribution	301,477	179,237
(Decrease) increase in:		
Employee pensions and seniority premiums		
Reserve	1,209,307	1,212,203
Contributions to trust fund	(890,505)	(981,938)
Payments to employees	(439,027)	(418,086)
Monetary effect of reserve	(76,444)	(139,261)
Accounts payable and accrued liabilities	(207,243)	696,661
Taxes payable	424,961	(673,022)
Deferred credits	83,945	20,245
Resources provided by operating activities	11,147,406	10,431,183
Financing Activities		
New loans	1,870,542	1,808,579
Repayment of loans	(1,083,101)	(2,497,033)
Reduction in purchasing power of debt	(651,112)	(164,062)
Application of advances on sale of receivables	(901,311)	(1,093,081)
(Decrease) increase in capital stock and premium on sale of shares	(76,721)	1,450
Cash dividends paid	(1,644,865)	(902,043)
Incorporation of Instituto Tenologico de Teléfonos de Mexico, S.C.		(648)
Resources used in financing activities	(2,486,568)	(2,846,838)
Investing Activities		
Investment in telephone plant	(8,356,371)	(7,961,053)
Reduction in telephone plant inventories	1,269,844	47,245
Resources used in investing activities	(7,068,527)	(7,913,808)
Net increase (decrease) in cash and short-term investments	1,574,311	(329,463)
Cash and short-term investments at BOY	3,981,245	4,310,708
Cash and short-term investments at EOY	5,555,556	3,981,245

*Thousands of Mexican new pesos with purchasing power at December 31, 1993.

Source: Teléfonos de Mexico, 1993, *Annual Report.*

Exhibit 5   Consolidated Balance Sheets*

	1993	1992
Assets		
Current assets:		
Cash and short-term investments	5,555,556	3,981,245
Accounts receivable:		
Subscribers	4,389,184	3,134,284
Interconnecting carriers	234,245	226,311
Advances to suppliers	286,908	229,641
Other	738,419	818,847
	5,648,756	4,409,083
Prepaid expenses	609,001	659,899
Trust contribution	236,278	537,725
Total current assets	12,049,591	9,587,952
Property, plant and equipment, net	36,189,632	34,200,627
Inventories, primarily for use in construction of the telephone plant	1,141,280	2,619,989
Other assets	3,521,308	622,913
Total assets	52,901,811	47,031,481
Liabilities and Stockholders' Equity		
Current liabilities:		
Current proportion of long-term debt	1,161,906	999,259
Accounts payable and accrued liabilities	1,889,529	2,096,722
Taxes payable	848,339	423,378
Total current liabilities	3,899,774	3,519,409
Long-term debt	5,905,719	5,991,940
Reserve for employee pensions and seniority premiums	3,845,811	1,066,216
Deferred credits	2,201,395	3,108,761
Total liabilities	15,852,699	13,596,326
Stockholders' equity:		
Capital stock:		
Historical	1,056,580	1,057,561
Restatement increment	15,557,484	15,557,263
	16,614,064	16,614,824
Premium on sale of shares	2,848,620	2,849,416
Retained earnings:		
Unappropriated earnings of prior years	24,789,899	17,895,625
Net income for the year	9,003,093	8,613,955
	33,792,992	26,509,580
Deficit from restatement of stockholders' equity	(16,206,564)	(12,538,665)
Total stockholders' equity	37,049,112	33,435,155
Total liabilities and stockholders' equity	52,901,811	47,031,481

*Thousands of Mexican new pesos with purchasing power at December 31, 1993.
Source: TeléFonos de Mexico, 1993, *Annual Report*.

consortium that garnered a coveted cellular operation concession in Ecuador. This move served as a signal of the increased competition that was to come. These same nonbasic service providers were also shaping up as potential competitors in the basic services market as the monopolies of privatized carriers expired.

The Telecommunications Industry Trends

Telecommunications systems consist of three components: customer equipment, such as telephones and private branch exchanges (PBXs, see Glossary); transmission equipment, such as the cables connecting individual phones to the local exchange and lines connecting one exchange to another; and the exchanges themselves, where telephone calls are completed by linking one telephone to another.

Recent changes in technology have affected all three of these components. Product lines have broadened customer equipment from the old rotary telephone to items such as push-button telephones, fax machines, answering machines, and networked computers. The medium for transporting calls has been upgraded from copper wires to fiber optic cables. Fiber optics has enabled more information to be transmitted with greater reliability than ever before. In addition, alternative methods of transmission, such as microwave and satellite systems, have also become available.

Originally, human operators acted as the exchanges that connected telephone calls. Operators were replaced by electromechanical switches, which were in turn replaced by electronic exchanges. The most recent innovation was digital exchanges. Each stage of advancement in exchange technology resulted in increased quality, reliability, versatility, and cost effectiveness.

The growing interdependence between the technologies for communication and computing has been another trend affecting the telephone industry. Business users required an integrated solution for their computing and communications needs in order to more freely input, transmit, and process messages of all kinds (e.g., voice, text, data, images) within a dispersed but interconnected computer system. In this context, then, "telecommunications" refers to systems that can handle this full range of message types. Telephone companies around the world have been struggling—and in some cases, failing—to satisfy these emerging needs.

As a result of this changing environment, telecommunications companies (private and state owned) in industrialized nations have invested heavily in converting to digital systems that are increasingly linked by fiber optic cables. In developing countries, on the other hand, the main dilemma has been to decide whether to extend *basic* service to a wider segment of the population or to offer more modern systems for existing business customers. TELMEX faces important decisions regarding these industry trends.

Mexico: Political and Economic Issues

H. Carlos D., director of marketing at TELMEX, had prepared a report (see the Appendix) for the executive committee detailing the state of the economy at the time of Salinas' privatization announcement. His analysis indicated that Mexico's political unrest and economic instability contributed to high inflation, declining savings and investment, capital flight, and excessive foreign and domestic debt. Mexico's era of privatization was undertaken as a method of economic reform.

As a result of Mexico's privatization program, during the last few years the state had sold much of the telephone, automotive, pharmaceutical and secondary petrochemical sectors, the state-owned steel industry, and other manufacturing interests. According to the Bank of Mexico, the number of *parastatals* (government-owned enterprises) had declined from 1,155 in 1982 to less than 200 in 1994.[1]

In addition, by December 1987, the government had entered into the Economic Solidarity Pact and the Pact for Economic Growth and Stability agreements with representatives of business and labor. These agreements were aimed at stabilizing the economy through restrictive fiscal and monetary policies and at "opening up" the economy in accordance with World Bank stipulations related to loans to Mexico. The pacts had far reaching effects, including a reduction in inflation from 159 percent in 1987 to 19 percent in 1989, decreasing external debt as a percentage of GDP from 75.8 percent in 1987 to 35.7 percent in 1991, and a decrease in interest rates on the 28-day cetes (government treasury bonds) from 77.3 percent in 1986 to 13.6 percent in 1992. Additional trade barriers were removed by decreasing the maximum tariff rate from 100 to 10 percent in 1987, and the introduction of NAFTA eliminated most tariffs for U.S. and Canadian goods and services in 1993. Furthermore, state control over the foreign exchange market was eliminated (although the Bank of Mexico had authority to devalue the peso in order to hedge against straying economic conditions).[2]

■ The Prelude to the 1994 Peso Devaluation

Mexico was plagued by much social unrest and economic uncertainty in 1994. Despite the hopes of Mexican businesses and foreign investors as a result of the implementation of NAFTA, the Mexican economy was not as stable as it seemed. Even as the December 1994 presidential election approached, the ruling political party in Mexico (the PRI) was under pressure to institute reforms that would open the country's political system to competing political parties. There had been allegations of political favoritism and abuses in the traditional one-party system for decades. Furthermore, rebels from the state of Chiapas in southern Mexico battled government troops and threatened terrorism in Mexico City.

By the time President Zedillo was inaugurated, Mexico's foreign reserves had been depleted from $30 billion in March to about $12 billion on December 1, 1994. On December 20, the government decided to alleviate this problem by devaluing the peso in order to gain foreign monies from increased exports. This action collapsed investor confidence in Mexico's "free market" economy, resulting in the loss of half of the remaining foreign reserves in one day. On December 22, in order to combat lost confidence, Mexico went to a free-floating currency exchange system.[3]

In February 1995, the Mexican economy had rebounded to some degree, due in part to the successful negotiation of a $20 billion loan guarantee from the United States. However, on February 15, Grupo Sidek, a Mexican conglomerate, defaulted on commercial payment papers. This situation caused greater uncertainty in the Mexican economy and the peso fell to a value of six pesos to the dollar, a 45 percent devaluation. After $50 billion in further loan guarantees from the United States and other financial institutions were secured, the peso recovered to a devalued rate of 35 percent during the spring of 1995.[4]

■ The Effects of the Mexican Economy on TELMEX

TELMEX's revenues and earnings are affected greatly by fluctuations in Mexico's monetary exchange rate. Exchange gains or losses included in the cost of financing are calculated by translating monetary assets and liabilities denominated in foreign currencies at the rates of exchange at the end of each month. Approximately 20 percent of TELMEX's revenues are derived from international long-distance charges (see Exhibit 2), which are stated in U.S. dollars. Additionally, about 80 percent of TELMEX's debt is in U.S. dollars. Thus, the recent devaluation of the peso had caused long-distance revenues to decrease in worth by half, and TELMEX expected constant-peso rates and settlement rates paid by U.S. long-distance carriers to decline further throughout 1995.[5]

The economic and political crisis of Mexico had also caused TELMEX's stock to suffer. The price of TELMEX ADRs (American Depository Receipts) on the NYSE on February 24, 1995, was $28; a substantial decline from its 52-week high of $70.[6] The effect of Teléfonos de Mexico's decrease in value on the Mexican economy was substantial because the drop in TELMEX's price carried worries over into the currency markets (TELMEX comprises one-third of the Mexican Bolsa), thereby causing the peso to fall further.[7]

The worries surrounding Mexican economic and political instability have caused applications for concessions of ownership of Mexican assets to decrease. However, in a development affecting TELMEX's potential competitors, government officials, in mid-April 1995, decided against charging a licensing fee for new entrants to the phone market. At a recent cabinet meeting, "Participants decided a fee would be counterproductive, reasoning that the current phone system is so far below world standards that it is a drag on the whole economy."[8]

■ The 1990 Concession Agreement

TELMEX operated under Mexican communications regulations and a license agreement referred to as a "Concession," granted by the Mexican Ministry of Communications and Transportation. The redefinition of the concession in 1990 was focused on providing the phone company with sufficient funds to accelerate line expansion, since limited access to telephone service, not cost, is the customer's primary complaint. Some key points and guidelines set under the Concession were as follows:

- The government had the right to take over the management of the company in cases of imminent danger to internal security or the national economy, and the company may not sell or transfer any of its assets without the government's right of first refusal.

- Establishment of a price cap system in order that the company would have the ability to increase local service rates to meet its costs and to reduce long-distance rates in anticipation of competition at the end of 1996.

- Excise taxes of 72 percent on local service charges have been replaced with a value-added tax (VAT) of 10 percent.

- Specific targets for service expansion and improvement, including overall installations (12 percent annual line increase), public phones, installation and repair delays.

- Long-distance telephone competition would commence in December 1996.[9]

Exhibit 6	Consortium Divisions		
Partner	Consortium Ownership	Equity	Voting
Grupo Carso	51.0%	10.4%	26.0%
France Télécom	24.5%	5.0%	12.5%
Southwestern Bell	24.5%	10.1%	12.5%
Total	100.0%	20.5%	51.0%

The Concession would remain in force until the year 2026, at which time it may be renewed for another 15 years. However, upon early or unnatural termination of the Concession, the telecommunications assets of TELMEX revert to the government free of charge. Therefore, any assets developed by others (foreign companies) risk being relinquished to the government upon termination of the Concession agreement. Even with all of these preparation clauses written into the Concession, as mentioned earlier, TELMEX faced strong challenges as the Mexican long-distance market opened up to foreign competition at the end of 1996.

The Consortium

In December 1990, the government of Mexico sold all of its TELMEX shares to a consortium of owners (see Exhibit 6). The consortium ownership was divided such that Mexican-conglomerate Grupo Carso owned 51 percent while France Télécom (FT) and Southwestern Bell International Holdings (SWBIH) each held 24.5 percent. This ownership consortium presented the winning bid of $1.758 billion.

All three entities in the consortium were active partners in TELMEX. Grupo Carso (GC) was a diversified conglomerate with proven business acumen. GC provided the majority Mexican ownership required for the sale of TELMEX,* and also represented the expertise in the consortium with regards to the Mexican political, cultural, and socioeconomic environment.[10] GC assumed responsibility for "financial and real estate matters; legal and government relations; human resources and labor relations; and general management of day-to-day operations."[11]

France Télécom has an international reputation for information systems development and deployment of digital technology. In addition, FT has "modernized the entire country of France, bringing it from 4 million access lines in 1971 to over 28 million [at the end of 1990]."[12] France Télécom's responsibilities included expansion and modernization of the network, international long distance, and expansion of the public telephone network.

Southwestern Bell was included in order to take advantage of its expertise in efficient operations. Southwestern Bell's capacity comprised operations and service quality, to include the substitution of digital equipment for analog

---

*Fifty-one percent of TELMEX is required by the government to be owned by Mexican Nationals.

Exhibit 7 Consortium Government			
Partner	Board of Directors	Executive Committee	Advisory Group
SWBIH	3	1	25
FT	3	1	25
SWBIH/FT roving	1		
Grupo Carso	12	2	3–4
TELMEX (CEO)	—	1	—
Total	19	5	~55

equipment, outside plant rehabilitation, operator services, marketing, wireless services, and directory/printing services.[13]

TELMEX operations were governed by a board of directors, executive committee, and advisory group composed as illustrated in Exhibit 7.[14] The advisory group has a support role for the executive committee to which it reports. Its primary function is to improve operations through investigating alternative strategies.

■ TELMEX's Primary Operations and Improvements

TELMEX's primary emphasis in 1993 was improving quality of service, increasing the number of lines in service (see Exhibit 8), and upgrading outside plant facilities (physical plant assets that are not located within buildings). To these ends, 1993 saw TELMEX replace 925,369 lines in exchanges, converting them to digital technology. In addition, 867,228 new lines were added (a 12.8 percent increase over 1992). In Mexico City, TELMEX replaced one central office each week, such that by the end of 1995, Mexico City's phone system was 100 percent digital. In 1993, its network was 65 percent digital, compared to 52 percent in 1992. This upgrading resulted in an overall penetration rate of 8.7 lines per 100 inhabitants. The following subsections describe the primary operations and additional improvements by TELMEX.

■ Long Distance

To increase the capacity and reliability of the long-distance network in 1993, 8,701 kilometers of fiber optic network were installed, resulting in a 64 percent increase in the 13,500-km network. These efforts were augmented by the beginning of construction on the submarine cable Columbus II, which was a fiber optic cable between Europe and America, which promised to improve telecommunications between the continents.

Included in the modernization of the long-distance network was the addition of digital operator positions in 39 traffic centers across Mexico. A total of 1,420 positions were created, which increased the capacity and the quality of service offered by operators of domestic and international long distance.

Exhibit 8

Number of Lines in Service (thousands)

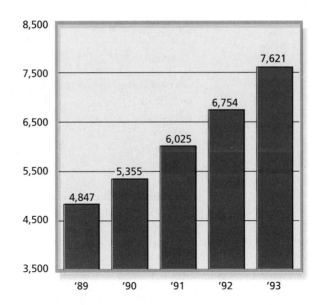

The opening of Mexican markets in numerous industries presented an increased load of international long distance as multinational companies increased their presence. As a result of the expansion of TELMEX's network and increased economic activity in 1993, a total of 1.4 billion domestic long-distance calls were handled, representing an increase of 11.2 percent over 1992. International long-distance calls reached 387.5 million, an increase of 10.3 percent. (See Exhibits 1 through 3 for the changes in the company's revenues from 1992 to 1993.)

Public Telephones

This lucrative market was attacked by TELMEX aggressively in 1993. During that year, 51,431 public telephones were put into service and the total grew to 177,995, a 122 percent increase since 1990. This increased access to two public telephones per 1,000 inhabitants, which was ahead of the schedule as required by the Concession agreements. In addition, TELMEX installed the latest technology in its public phones. The firm introduced the chip debit card, a technology developed by Alcatel (France) among others. It allowed users to purchase phone usage in advance with some measure of security.

Telcel

Mexico's cellular concessions have been divided into nine regions. There were two licenses for each region, one local and one national. TELMEX had the national concession, which it serves through its Telcel cellular unit. TELMEX offered cellular telephone services through its subsidiary, Radio Móvil Dipsa, under the trademark Telcel. At the end of 1993, Telcel offered its services to 195,409 users, a 43 percent increase over 1992. Telcel's coverage included 218 cities in Mexico as well as 1,220 rural communities. In addition, Telcel offered domestic and international roaming service with 1,200 cities in the United States and 36 cities in Latin America and the Caribbean.

▓ Other Products and Quality Improvements

New and Potential Services

The commercial offering of integrated digital network (see Glossary) services expanded from 1992 to 1993 with 218,635 total connections, up 39.3 percent. Large users were linked through fiber optic digital local networks, satellite networks, and private circuits. Meanwhile, the first steps were being taken to create specialized groups to handle middle- and small-sized users. In addition, TELMEX opened 19 new commercial information centers to serve customers by telephone, allowing the public to contact their business office about their telephone bills as well as to set up service for new lines. Furthermore, in 1994, TELMEX partnered with GTE Airfone to offer telephone services in domestic and international aircraft flying over Mexico.

Overall, TELMEX has an aggressive R&D program in developing new services. One of the ongoing projects is the intelligent network, which would provide the following features:

- *Advanced 800 service:* Provides selective access by telephone number and/or geographic area, programmable date and time service, and detailed statistics of calls received.
- *Service charged to telephone cards.*
- *Virtual private networks:* Offers the customer the facilities of a private network with domestic and international coverage, using the switched public network.
- *Universal number:* All calls from the customers of a user will reach the most convenient switching center, according to the origin of the call.
- *Personal number:* Allows the subscriber to receive his/her domestic and international calls on the telephone and at the date and hour he/she decides.

Furthermore, TELMEX was planning to implement a system called Videotex. This will allow data banks to be accessed for texts and images, including sources such as telephone directories, libraries, electronic newspapers, and banking services in the home. TELMEX was also expanding videoconferencing services both with regard to delivery of service to the public and in the training of personnel.

Administrative/Operational Improvements

Among the administrative/operational improvements and advances pursued by TELMEX was the creation of a network administration center, application of the synchronous digital hierarchy framework, and the creation of a technical institute for training its employees.

A network administration center (NAC) is the central control point from which a communications network is controlled and optimized. A communications network is a living entity because links are constantly in transition. Some links fail, while others are brought down for maintenance. This requires constant monitoring and optimization to ensure quality and reliable service as well as efficient utilization. TELMEX's equipment and systems that performed network administration (elements in the switching and transmission plant) were upgraded to facilitate greater network quality and coordination.

The application of an Integrated Services Digital Network (ISDN-see Glossary) framework increases the speed and expands the capabilities of transmission routes. In addition, an Intelligent Network (see Glossary) integrates an intelligent administrative system, such as TELMEX's NAC, which eases the input/output flow of information at any point in the route, without having to multiplex and demultiplex (see Glossary). These improvements make the network management and information handling more reliable.

Training is a vital part of TELMEX's ability to remain competitive. Created in 1991, the Technological Institute of Teléfonos de Mexico (Inttelmex) offers approximately 25,000 courses, with more than 200,000 participants. In 1992–1993, 70 training programs were developed in new technologies. This has significantly increased the development of core competencies within TELMEX.

■ TELMEX's Suppliers

Prior to privatization, TELMEX depended on two primary suppliers, Teleindustria Ericsson and Alcatel-Indetel, to meet its switching equipment needs. Teleindustria Ericsson, a Swedish company's local subsidiary, and Alcatel-Indetel, a subsidiary of a French company, had developed good relations with TELMEX because of their long-standing presence in the Mexican market. Both companies, however, had suffered to some extent since the privatization of TELMEX. In responding to customer demands and competitive pressure, TELMEX had increased demand on its suppliers by setting three priorities: price, quality, and delivery time.

Ericsson had been slow to adapt to the changes and especially slow in realizing that customer service was an essential component of quality. As a result, increased competition had reduced its market share and, in some cases, forced Ericsson out of select markets. Alcatel, on the other hand, had adjusted by restructuring its company to increase productivity and reduce costs. Consequently, Alcatel-Indetel not only remained competitive in the Mexican market, but also realized that many of its Mexican manufactured products could compete in global markets.[15]

AT&T, a major new supplier in Mexico, has been the only new vendor to penetrate Mexico's switching market, joining Ericsson and Alcatel. In 1991, after several previous rejections, AT&T was chosen to become TELMEX's third switching supplier due to its successful and speedy installation record with one of TELMEX's subsidiaries. Also, in mid-1994, AT&T signed an agreement with TELMEX to jointly provide value-added service to Mexican subscribers. The network will utilize AT&T equipment combined with the existing TELMEX infrastructure. AT&T's close relationship with TELMEX in the long-distance market (and now the value-added market) made it an unlikely candidate to be a supplier of equipment to any of TELMEX's future competitors in the long-distance market. This close relationship between the two partly accounts for market analysts' expectations that AT&T would match up perfectly with TELMEX, to the detriment of TELMEX's potential competitors, such as Grupo Alfa.[16]

Relative newcomers to Mexico, such as NEC, Siemens, Northern Telecom, and Phillips' Telecomunicaciones y Sistemas Profesionales, have chosen to compete in niche markets due to the dominance of Ericsson and Alcatel, as well as their inability to obtain contracts with TELMEX.

TELMEX's Competition

TELMEX's executive committee also concerned itself with the many companies vying for a chance to oppose TELMEX. Despite the uncertainty about Mexico's political and economic future, foreign telecommunications carriers have been flocking to Mexico, with U.S. carriers Bell Atlantic and MCI leading the pack. The next wave of alliances was already under way. Indeed, the stage was being set for long-distance and international service competition that would last well into the twenty-first century. Wildcard entrants included Telefónica de España, Latin America's most pervasive foreign carrier. Nonetheless, the Mexican market appeared to be shaping up as the exclusive breeding ground for U.S. telecommunications operators and their strong local partners. MCI, for instance, had created an alliance with Mexico's largest bank, and Sprint and Bell Atlantic both had partnerships with the cellular powerhouse Grupo IUSACELL.[17]

Government Action

To create an environment of competitiveness for the future, the Mexican government enacted legislation to "level the competitive playing field." Although TELMEX lobbied the government aggressively in order to establish barriers for the potential entrants in its industry, several new rules announced in late June 1994 disappointed the long-distance (LD) monopolist. The new rules state that there are no limits to the number of long-distance companies that could enter the industry in 1997 and that TELMEX had to connect 60 of its switches—significantly higher than the 10 switches originally requested by TELMEX—to the long-distance carriers. TELMEX also had to increase the availability of all its switches by January 1, 2001, and allow customers to sign up for a single LD carrier as opposed to specifying a carrier on each call. Finally, TELMEX would charge its competitors for handling the local portion of the long-distance calls based on its actual costs, without benefiting any LD carrier over another.

The relative uncertainty regarding new entrant rules for the long-distance industry had not seemed to deter potential entrants. As of December 1994, 40 Concession applications from companies and joint ventures had been accepted by the Mexican Communications and Transportation Secretariat (Secretaria de Comunicaciones y Transporte).

AT&T and Grupo Alfa

The announcement of an AT&T–Grupo Alfa joint venture on November 10, 1994, was a big blow to TELMEX and a major surprise to the analysts who thought that AT&T, the world's largest provider of global telecommunications services, would have great (and exclusive) synergies with TELMEX. Grupo Alfa, a conglomerate in high-growth industries such as food and petrochemicals, owned 51 percent and AT&T will own 49 percent of the $1 billion joint venture. The venture targeted mainly corporate customers for local and long-distance voice and data transmission services. These services were likely to be extended to residential subscribers, along with offerings of cellular phone services. Although it did not have any expertise in the communications industry, Grupo Alfa offered a deep knowledge of the Mexican market and contact with the Garza's of Monterey, one of Mexico's oldest and wealthiest families, which would help

AT&T in lobbying the Mexican government to provide more predictable and favorable regulations.

Analysts regarded the AT&T–Grupo Alfa joint venture as a major setback for TELMEX. News reports commented on TELMEX's missed opportunity to participate in a project that would span the Americas:

> One thing is clear: AT&T regards TELMEX as an inferior business partner compared to Alfa—even though Alfa has no telecommunications experience.[18]

The analysts' concerns were mirrored by the actions of public investors. The day after the joint venture announcement, TELMEX's stock price declined by about 10% whereas Grupo Alfa's increased by 6.5%.

■ MCI and Grupo Financier Banamex-Accival

MCI, the sixth largest global telecommunications service provider, has engaged in a joint venture with Mexican Grupo Financier Banamex-Accival announced on January 26, 1994. The $1 billion investment was split 45 percent MCI, 55 percent Banamex. Plans entailed linking the customers of Mexico City, Guadalajara, and Monterey, three of Mexico's largest cities, with fiber optic cables. This system would deliver advanced business requirements, voice, data, and video services.

As the largest financial group in Mexico, Banamex could provide MCI with a huge potential customer base from its 110,000 large business customers and two million retail banking clients. Furthermore, MCI could utilize Banamex's satellite and private microwave network to allow electronic funds transfers and use of automatic teller machines.

■ Bell Atlantic Corporation and Grupo IUSACELL

On December 2, 1993, Bell Atlantic completed a purchase of an initial 23 percent ownership stake in IUSACELL. This was increased to 42 percent, a total $992 million, on August 9, 1994. IUSACELL has the cellular concessions covering several regions of central Mexico. IUSACELL was considered tiny, compared to TELMEX, which had a national cellular concession through its Telcel subsidiary. However, with the investment of Bell Atlantic, IUSACELL could expand into local and long-distance services, in addition to its cellular service.

■ Sprint Corporation and TELMEX: An Opportunity

Sprint Corporation and IUSACELL were in negotiations for some time concerning an alliance to tap Mexico's LD market. Sprint, one of the three largest long-distance service providers in the United States, may have been a perfect match for IUSACELL, which offers advanced technology and services in the cellular industry. The negotiations were broken off, however, when Bell Atlantic invested so heavily in IUSACELL. Regulations require that Mexican interests have at least a 51 percent stake in the telecommunications partnership. As it stood, Bell Atlantic, an American company, already owned 49 percent.

The failure of the Sprint–IUSACELL alliance appears to have provided an opportunity for TELMEX to join with Sprint. In addition to protecting its market share in Mexico, a partnership with Sprint might provide TELMEX with access to other global markets, such as Europe, Brazil, Venezuela, and most of Central

America, in which Sprint already has operations. In fact, a nonequity strategic alliance between Sprint and TELMEX was announced on December 14, 1994.

Motorola Corp., Grupo Protexa, and Baja Cellular Mexicana

Motorola Corp., Grupo Protexa, and Baja Cellular Mexicana represent a recently formed alliance that is searching for a fourth partner (long-distance carrier) to round out the consortium. Motorola, recognizing the potential for growth in northern Mexico especially, has penetrated the market by developing a consortium with two North-Mexican cellular phone providers. This consortium linked up to extend service to all of the regions bordering the United States. The proximity of the United States could make it easy for the group to provide a U.S.–Mexico long-distance service. The long-term plan of this consortium was to provide cellular and long-distance service to compete directly with TELMEX.

Motorola maintained expertise in cellular transmission technology and hardware. In May 1995, it secretly purchased the license to operate in North Central Mexico. Baja Cellular controls two cellular regions, one in Baja California and another along Mexico's Northwest region. Motorola purchased 42 percent of Baja Cellular for a reported $100 million. Proceeds from the deal will be used to modernize Baja's cellular operations. Grupo Protexa, which controls two cellular regions covering central and northeastern Mexico, announced a $1.5 billion deal with Motorola to develop these franchises. Furthermore, Grupo Protexa and Sprint Corp. have recently failed in negotiations to develop long-distance service in Mexico, losing the chance to fill the fourth seat in the consortium. Upon filling this fourth seat, the consortium will likely become a formidable competitor. In the words of Baja Cellular co-founder Jose Manuel Villalvazo, this deal is:

> the first step toward something much more broad . . . we are missing a fourth seat, and that is the operator of a long-distance service.[19]

GTE Corp., Grupo Financier Bancomer, and Valores Industriales

On September 8, 1994, GTE Corp. agreed to form an alliance with two major Mexican companies to explore entering the Mexican local and long-distance phone market in 1997. Grupo Financier Bancomer is the second largest financial group in Mexico. Valores Industriales is the holding company for both Fomento Mexicano, a Mexican brewer, and the largest Coca-Cola franchise in Mexico. Although detailed information concerning the venture is not yet at hand, analysts suggest it will involve an investment of hundreds of millions of dollars. Projected ownership of the joint venture would be Mexican partners 51 percent and GTE 49 percent. While this venture enjoys significant technical and political clout, the partners do not appear to be moving as aggressively as others. Thus, they are considered a dark horse in the telecommunications race.

Challenges Ahead

The major questions facing the TELMEX executive committee were numerous. Should TELMEX seek out additional alliance partners besides Sprint? If so, what for? What areas of the Mexican telecommunications market can TELMEX hope to dominate after 1996, and how should it prepare for this? Where should TELMEX concentrate its investments in the meantime? How can the company balance its Concession responsibilities with the need to prepare for heavy competition, especially in long distance? What type of corporate strategy should TELMEX pursue? Should the company attempt to compete in its various segments on cost, differentiation, or otherwise? How might TELMEX diversify some of its risk? What sources of capital remain for TELMEX to utilize, especially since the devaluation of the peso, as it attempts to hold market share in the future?

Appendix

Demographic Environment of Mexico
In addition to the statistics given in Exhibit 9, note the following:

- Mexico is the 13th largest economy, yet ranks 83rd in lines per capita.
- Mexico covers 760,000 square miles.
- In telecommunications, Mexico has a promising future in data services. Having more engineers per capita than the United States makes Mexico an excellent resource for less expensive, sophisticated data services and data entry.
- TELMEX plans to spend some $8 billion through 1995 expanding and upgrading its network. By 2000, it expects to have 35 million phones wired in an all-digital network, up from 12 million.
- Since gaining certification as TELMEX's third supplier, AT&T has won a $150 million three-year contract to connect 54 Mexican cities and towns with more than 8,300 miles of fiber-optic cable and switching equipment.
- TELMEX does not offer discounts for 800-lines.
- In Mexico, 9 of every 100 inhabitants have a telephone; there are currently 7,621,000 lines.

Exhibit 9   Demographics of Mexico

	USA	Mexico
Per capita GDP	$22,340	$2,300
Population	250 million	85 million
Population growth	1%	2%
Urban population	74%	66%
% of population under 15	21	42
% of population 65 and over	12	4
Life expectancy	75	66
Fertility rate	1.9	3.8
Death rate, per 1,000	9	5
Telephones per 1,000	760	96
Radios per 1,000	2,120	241
Daily newspaper per 1,000	259	124
Literacy	97%	87%

- The cellular telephone is one of the most successful areas in telecommunications. It is already a market without barriers. The most important regions that use this service are Mexico City, Guadalajara, Monterrey, and Tijuana, having about 500,000 to 650,000 subscribers.

- One of the markets that represents the biggest telecommunications segment is the private network for banks, stock markets, and large corporations such as the following: Bancomer-Canadian Equipment NEC—controls 150 stations; Banamex—its network reaches 260 cities, including 10 outside of Mexico; Pemex—accounts for a network with unions of microwaves via satellite.

- Seventy percent of the calls from Mexico to the United States are made through AT&T and the same percentage from the United States to Mexico is also made through AT&T.

Glossary

Access line   A telephone line reaching from a telephone company's central office to a business or residence.

Central office   Switching facilities owned and operated by the local service provider.

Consortium   Collective equity body owning TELMEX, consisting primarily of SWBIH, FT, and GC.

Integrated digital network   Same as ISDN.

Intelligent network   Network consisting of three blocks: (1) intelligent processors that go beyond the digital switch, (2) common channel signaling, and (3) digital end-to-end connectivity.

ISDN   Integrated services digital network; provides end-to-end digital connection with standard user interfaces.

Multiplexer/Demultiplexer   Hardware that consolidates multiple lines into one, then at the other end reverses the process. This is done to maximize utilization of resources.

Private branch exchange (PBX)   Stored program-controlled customer-premises equipment that performs switching functions.

Notes

1. T. Kamm, 1994, Learning lessons from privatization in Latin America, *Business Forum,* Winter/Spring, 25–27.
2. Teléfonos de Mexico, 1993, *Annual Report,* 56–60.
3. R. L. Barthy, 1994, Mexico: Suffering the conventional wisdom, *Wall Street Journal,* October 5, A18; D. Solis and C. Torres, 1995, Mexico's move to quash Chiapas rebels carries a big risk to Zedillo, *Wall Street Journal,* February 13, A10.
4. A.B. Carroll, 1995, Mexico rejects phone market entry fees, *Wall Street Journal,* April 12, All.

5. TELMEX, 1993, *Annual Report,* 17.
6. Stock Tables, *Wall Street Journal,* February 24, 1995, C5.
7. P. B. Carroll, Mexico rejects phone market entry fees.
8. Ibid.
9. Lexus/Nexus, 1991, *1991 Mexico Service,* May 22.
10. Analyst questions re: TELMEX bid, D3. Hand dated January 1, 1991, received from John Atterbury.
11. Speaker's notes of presentation by John Atterbury, p. 2.

12. Analyst questions.
13. Speaker's notes, pp. 2–3.
14. Analyst questions, D1.
15. Internal study, Southwestern Bell International Holdings, 1995.
16. Ibid.
17. Ibid.
18. J. J. Keller and C. Torres, 1994, AT&T Corp. and Grupo Alfa plan venture, *Wall Street Journal,* November 10, A3.
19. Motorola to purchase 42% of Mexican cellular firm, 1994, *Wall Street Journal,* June 23, A11.

■ CASE 34 United Airlines' Global Strategy

A. J. Almaney
DePaul University

> *Come fly the airline that's uniting the world,*
> *Come fly the friendly skies.*

■ http://www.ual.com

Those were the words that ended United Airlines' TV commercial and which expressed the company's new global strategic thrust. They were also reflective of the frantic pace with which Stephen M. Wolf, United's chief executive officer (CEO), went about implementing the company's global strategy. Convinced that the opportunities for his company were much more significant in the international arena than in the domestic market, Wolf traveled to Hanoi to explore the possibility of starting a new service to Vietnam. He also held frequent meetings with company executives to discuss United's startup service from Los Angeles to Mexico City and from Washington, D.C., to Milan and Rome. In implementing its global strategy, United systematically built a strong system of hubs and spokes throughout the United States which later enabled it to expand its services internationally. As a result of this strategy, United emerged as the only U.S. airline with major operations in North America, South America, Europe, and the Far East.

As the company poured money into its international expansion, its losses began to mount. In 1991, the company lost $332 million, and in 1992 it lost $955 million. Reflecting on his company's dilemma, Wolf said: "It frustrates me that we're doing so many things correctly but losing so much money."[1] Meanwhile, United was facing a larger set of problems. In Europe, protectionist sentiment threatened to slow the carrier's expansion. A recession in Japan could impede United's success in the Pacific. Its operations there were battered in 1991 by the Gulf War.

This case is intended to be used as a basis for class discussion rather than to illustrate either effective or ineffective handling of the situation.

Presented and accepted by the refereed Society for Case Research. All rights reserved to the author and the SCR. Copyright © 1994 by A. J. Almaney.

History

In 1928, the Boeing Airplane Company, Boeing Air Transport, Pacific Air, and Pratt and Whitney formed a holding company called United Aircraft and Transport Corporation. Three years later, United Airlines was organized as a management company for commercial airlines. In 1934, United Airlines became a separate business entity, and in 1968 it emerged as the primary subsidiary of UAL Corporation, which was a holding company for Air Wisconsin Inc. and Mileage Plus Inc.

Soon after its inception in 1928, United became one of the largest carriers in the United States. In subsequent years, it overtook American Airlines as the No. 1 carrier. United played a leadership role in the airline industry. It was United that introduced the first flight attendants in 1930, the first flight kitchen for in-flight meals in 1936, and the first nonstop flights between New York and San Francisco in 1955. More recently, it was the first American carrier to offer services between the United States and Australia and between San Francisco and Hong Kong. The Flight Operations Division of United helped develop the Traffic Alert and Collision Avoidance System (TCAS) and was one of the first airlines to use the system.

In the mid-1980s, United underwent a severe crisis as a result of a strategy devised by Richard J. Ferris, the company's former CEO, to transform the carrier into an integrated travel services firm. United's pilots, enraged over the strategy, went on strike in 1985 and grounded it for 29 days. When the strike ended, the pilots sought to dump Ferris by buying the airline. Their $2.5 billion bid failed but Ferris was replaced by Stephen M. Wolf who was able to rebuild the company. In 1991, the pilots renewed their effort to buy the company by making a bid of $4.4 billion. Although the buyout, which would have cost Wolf his job, failed, the relationship between the restive pilots and Wolf continued to be tense. As a result, the pilots made another buyout bid in 1993 that appeared to be successful.

As a leading carrier in the United States, United provided passenger and cargo air transportation to 162 airports in 33 countries spanning five continents. In the United States, it was the largest carrier in each of its four hubs—Chicago, Denver, San Francisco, and Washington Dulles. It employed about 83,000 pilots, flight attendants, mechanics, and other service-related employees. In 1993, United's fleet of operating aircraft totaled 663 planes.

Board of Directors

United's board of directors was composed of 13 members, two of whom were insiders. These were Stephen M. Wolf, United's CEO, and John C. Pope, president and chief operating officer of United. The background of the 11 outside directors included banking and investment, electronics, academia, hotel management, electric power utility, car rental, and law. Three of the outside directors were active chairmen and CEOs of their own companies, two were active chairmen, one was a president, and the remainder were either partners, managing directors, or executive directors of their companies. Geographically, four directors were from New York, two from Seattle, and one each from Chicago, Hawaii, Minneapolis, and New Jersey. None of the directors, however, came from a foreign country. The board was organized into five committees: executive,

---

Exhibit 1   The Board of Directors of United Airlines

Stephen M. Wolf

Chairman of the board and chief executive officer, UAL Corporation, Chicago (1)

Neil A. Armstrong

Chairman, AIL Systems, Inc.

Deer Park, New York

(Electronic systems) (1) (3)

Andrew F. Brimmer

President, Brimmer and Company, Inc., Washington, D.C., (Economic and financial consulting) (2) and (5)

Richard P. Cooley

Chairman of the Executive Committee of the Board of Directors, SEAFIRST Corporation and Seattle First National Bank, Seattle (Banking and finance) (2) (5)

Keith R. Gollust

Managing Director, Gollust, Tierney and Oliver, Inc., New York (Investment banking) (3) (4)

Fujio Matsuda

Executive Director, Research Corporation, University of Hawaii, Honolulu (University-related research) (2) (4)

John F. McGillicuddy

Chairman and chief executive officer, Chemical Banking Corporation, New York (Banking and finance) (4) (5)

Harry Mullikin

Chairman emeritus, Westin Hotels and Resorts, Seattle (Hotel management) (2) (3)

James J. O'Connor

Chairman and chief executive officer, Commonwealth Edison Company, Chicago (Electric power utility) (3) (4)

Frank A. Olson

Chairman and chief executive officer, The Hertz Corporation, Park Ridge, New Jersey (Car rental) (1)

John C. Pope

President and Chief Operating Officer, UAL Corporation, Chicago

Ralph Strangis

Partner, Kaplan, Strangis and Kaplan, P.A., Minneapolis (Law firm) (1)

Paul E. Tierney, Jr.

Managing Director, Gollust, Tierney and Oliver, Inc., New York (Investment banking) (1) (2)

Committees: (1) Executive Committee, (2) Audit Committee, (3) Pension and Welfare Plans Oversight Committee, (4) Compensation Committee, (5) Nominating Committee

Source: UAL, 1992, Annual Report, 40.

---

audit, pension and welfare plans oversight, compensation, and nominating. For a list of the board members and their affiliations, see Exhibit 1.

■ Strategic Managers

Stephen M. Wolf, born in 1941 in Oakland, California, worked at various jobs while growing up in a blue collar environment. At the age of 18, Wolf entered San Francisco State College. Although he worked his way through college, taking tough jobs on the docks and in local factories, he graduated in four years. In 1966, Wolf began working for American Airlines and "battled through the trenches" to become a divisional vice president after 14 years. He moved to Continental Airlines as president and chief operating officer in 1982.

From 1984 to 1986, Wolf served as president and CEO of Republic Airlines where he implemented a turnaround strategy that transformed many years of corporate losses into record earnings. Then, from 1986 to 1987, Wolf served as president and CEO of Tiger International. He also served as president and CEO of its principal subsidiary, The Flying Tiger Line, Inc. At Flying Tiger, Wolf was once again successful in turning a money-losing company into a profitable airline. Much of his success at Republic Airlines and Flying Tiger was attributed to his ability to develop a rapport with labor. After leading two unusually successful turnarounds, Stephen Wolf was touted by many experts as an "industry boy wonder."[2]

In December 1987, with United Airlines facing labor problems, United's board of directors persuaded Wolf to take the helm as the company's CEO and chairman of the board. At United, he was able to restore the carrier's proud reputation with profits reaching record levels in 1988. In 1990, Wolf made *Fortune* magazine's list of "The 25 Most Fascinating People."[3] Wolf's tenure at United, however, was not altogether smooth as his relationship with labor began to sour. By late 1989, Wolf saw United go through four failed buyout attempts by the company's pilots. Wolf's 1990 $18 million compensation package—bloated by cashed-in stock options—made him a symbol of corporate greed. "The company's growth, however, helped heal the wounds,"[4] according to Wolf. So did his ability to lure talented managers.

Believing that the opportunities were in the international market, Wolf aggressively outbid rivals for choice routes and built the only airline worldwide with major operations in the North Atlantic, the Pacific, and Latin America. United was poised to become what no U.S. airline had ever been: a globe-girdling megacarrier with strong domestic routes to feed the system.

Although United began to lose money in recent years, Wolf remained fully confident of the company's future. "Our best days are before us,"[5] he said. He even placed a bet on it by buying 20,000 United shares at an average price of $150 per share for $3 million. Three months later, the stock price dropped for a paper loss of $433,000. Wolf was not worried, however, because, he said, he was in it for the long haul.

In the airline industry, the 6-foot, 6-inch Wolf was considered one of the hardest working CEOs who expected his employees to maintain his frantic pace. He was also affable and witty. Michael Derchin, an airline analyst, believed Wolf developed his personal style as an antidote to his imposing presence. Said Derchin: "He seems aware that he can be intimidating because of his size. He has bent over backwards to be personable."[6] He was also able to balance his hard work with regular exercise. He would get up at 4:45 A.M. every morning, read three newspapers, and then start exercising. Wolf was a self-described health nut who said: "In business, as in other walks of life, your physical condition is important. It gives you an edge in managing your life because you are sick less often."[7]

In terms of his decision-making style, Wolf relied on teamwork. Although he sometimes appeared to be aloof, he was not a loner. Since taking the helm at United, Wolf relied on a tiny coterie of advisers to help him run the airline. While running Republic Airlines in 1984 and later as CEO at Flying Tigers, he assembled close-knit management teams that helped revive the carriers. When he landed at United, Wolf tapped some of those colleagues including John Pope, vice chairman, Lawrence Nagin, senior vice president, James Guyette, executive vice president, and Joseph O'Gorman, executive vice president. Even his wife, Delores, whom he married in 1987, was a former executive at American Airlines. Whenever Wolf made a big decision, he leaned on this inner circle.[8] Team building was a Wolf watchword. According to him, "You win ballgames with good ballplayers."[9]

Members of Wolf's inner circle had complementary talents. Pope, considered by many the industry's aircraft finance guru, oversaw United's finance and marketing. Having built a solid reputation at American Airlines, "he had the most independent voice,"[10] said a former executive. Nagin, who worked on Robert F. Kennedy's 1968 presidential campaign, ran the carrier's legal and public relations activities and was considered the keeper of Wolf's image. George, a lawyer, managed employee relations and negotiated union contracts. (For a brief profile of the executive officers of United, see Exhibit 2.)

The team approach did not prevent Wolf from becoming involved in minute decisions. While his counterpart at American, Robert Crandall, preached "competitive anger" (if employees did not achieve their objectives, they should get angry with themselves) as the key to success, Wolf's philosophy of success rested on "doing the little things right."[11] For instance, he once participated in discussions about how big the closets should be in United's new Connoisseur Class. Wolf was also not shy about telephoning top managers at dawn to press for information about a project.

Exhibit 2   Brief Profiles of the Executive Officers of United Airlines

Stephen M. Wolf (age 51)

Wolf was elected chairman and chief executive officer of the company in 1992. He was elected chairman, president, and chief executive officer of United in 1988. Previously, he served as chairman, president and chief executive officer of Tiger International (1987) and chairman, president, and chief executive officer of The Flying Tiger Line Inc. (1986–1987).

John C. Pope (age 43)

Pope was elected president and chief operating officer of the company in 1992. He had served as vice chairman, chief financial officer, and treasurer since 1990. Pope was elected executive vice president, chief financial officer and treasurer of the company effective 1988. Previously, Pope was senior vice president, chief financial officer, and treasurer of American Airlines (1987–1988). He was also a director of Federal-Mogul Corporation.

James M. Guyette (age 47)

Guyette was elected executive vice president of the company in 1988. He was elected executive vice president for marketing and planning of United in 1992. He had served as executive vice president for operation of United since 1985.

Joseph R. O'Gorman (age 49)

O'Gorman was elected executive vice president of the company in 1991. He was elected executive vice president for operation in 1992. He had served as executive vice president for flight services since 1991. Previously, O'Gorman served as executive vice president for operation at US Air from 1990 until 1991. He served as United's senior vice president for maintenance operations from 1988 to 1990, and as United's senior vice president for corporate planning from 1986 to 1988.

Lawrence M. Nagin (age 52)

Nagin was elected executive vice president for corporate affairs and general counsel in 1992. He had served as senior vice president for corporate affairs and general counsel since 1990. Previously, he was elected senior vice president for corporate and external affairs of United in 1988. Prior to his service with United, Nagin served as senior vice president for administration and general counsel at the Flying Tiger Line Inc. from 1984 to 1988.

Paul G. George (age 41)

George was elected senior vice president for human resources in 1988. Previously, he was vice president for human resources of Pacific Southwest Airlines (1985–1988)

Source: UAL, 1992, Form 10-K, 28–29.

Mission and Objectives

As stated in the company's 10-K form, the mission of United Airlines "is to provide passenger and cargo air transportation to 169 airports in 33 countries on five continents." The airline's major hub operations are at Chicago; Denver; San Francisco; Washington, D.C.; London; and Tokyo.[12] The short and long-term objectives that Wolf set for United were to attain a commanding share of the transatlantic and the Pacific routes among U.S. carriers and to carve out a significant presence inside Europe.

Strategies

To achieve his profit objectives, Wolf pursued two strategies. The first involved cost reduction in the domestic market; the other consisted of aggressive expansion in foreign markets.

Wolf moved to bring down United's growing costs, which were higher than Delta's and American's. In February 1992, he deferred delivery of 122 planes, saving $6.7 billion and retired 29 Boeing 727s and 15 Boeing 737s. He also (1) modernized the fleet—leasing aircraft that hauled more passengers, burned less fuel, and required less maintenance; (2) sliced $400 million from the company's 1992 operating budget and imposed a hiring moratorium; and (3) reduced its workforce by 2,800 employees, about half from the ranks of management and salaried personnel. Further, the company planned on selling 17 flight kitchens in the United States. Wolf's global strategy was reflected in his statement: "Our ultimate focus will be on international expansion."[13] And Wolf allocated resources accordingly. While United deferred narrowbody aircraft ordered for domestic expansion, it accelerated delivery on widebody aircraft needed in foreign markets.

The carrier had huge success with its transpacific routes. Purchased for $750 million in 1985 by United's then-CEO Richard J. Ferris, the routes became a cash cow. Since 1986, United steadily increased its share of that market among U.S. carriers from 19.2 percent of passengers in 1986 to 36 percent in 1991, snatching high-paying business travelers from Northwest Airlines Inc. and competing Asian carriers.

Tightly controlled capacity on Pacific routes made them doubly attractive, and United's two biggest rivals were largely shut out. Robert Crandall, CEO of American Airlines, remained bitter over having lost out to United in late 1990 when the Transportation Department assigned a newly available Chicago-to-Tokyo route to United. "The fact is, there is only one market in Asia where people make money, and that's Tokyo," said Crandall. "And we can't get routes to Tokyo."[14]

Although a recession was developing in Japan, United was hopeful. Its executives noted that 48 percent of passengers who used United's North Pacific service flew beyond Japan or directly to other cities in the region, such as Singapore and Hong Kong. United was convinced the popularity of its Connoisseur Class for business passengers would help take more share from other carriers.

Wolf built an ambitious strategy in Europe. United had little presence there until 1990, when Wolf put down $400 million for Pan American's routes to and from London's Heathrow Airport. United began to fly to 11 cities. (For United's market share in the Pacific and European routes, see Exhibit 3.)

Exhibit 3	United's Market Share in the Pacific and Atlantic Routes			
	Atlantic		Pacific	
	1989 (%)	1991 (%)	1989 (%)	1991 (%)
United	0	14	35	36
American	10	19	1	2
Delta	6	11	2	3
Northwest	7	9	40	38

Source: Kevin Kelly, 1992, United wants the whole world in its hands, *Business Week,* April 27, 64–65.

But unlike American, which ran only direct flights between U.S. and European cities, United built hubs in London and Paris, with connecting flights, or spokes, across the continent. Crandall of American airlines called Wolf's strategy flawed. United was permitted only one connecting flight for each plane flown into its hubs. Such poor aircraft utilization made these flights almost certain money-losers, according to Crandall. But Wolf said the flights within Europe would channel enough people onto transatlantic flights back to the United States to make it all profitable. So Wolf used huge, 244- to 399-passenger Boeing 747s for about half of its transatlantic flights.

Even as the French government fought to roll back capacity increases, Wolf scrambled to build United's presence on the continent. In April 1992, United started service from San Francisco to Paris and added Paris to Athens, Milan, and Rome in June.

United also poured resources into starting up its new Latin American routes. In December 1991, Wolf outfoxed rival carriers American and Delta to snap up Pan American's routes for $135 million. A bankruptcy court blocked his acquisition of Pan Am's facilities or planes, though. So United had only four weeks to set up reservation offices and generate name recognition. Wolf assembled what he referred to as SWAT teams from Asia, Europe, and the United States to open offices. In Mexico, the crew managed to have a phone system for agents installed in 48 hours, an almost unheard-of feat for Teléfonos de Mexico. And the carrier hired local advisers to help avoid gaffes. When it started flying the Pacific in 1986, for example, United's workers wore carnations—a symbol of death in some Asian cultures. The carrier began running 11 flights to Latin America.

■ Strategic Alliances

United also relied on strategic alliances to implement its global strategy. Thus, it and Germany's Lufthansa entered into a partnership that would let travelers coordinate flights between both, making it relatively easy to reach destinations served by one airline but not the other. United extended its influence into the Middle East and the Caribbean by reaching agreements to coordinate flights with Emirates, the United Arab Emirates' carrier, and ALM Antillean Airlines, based in the Netherlands Antilles.

■ Operations

United was the largest U.S. international airline, with a route system that spanned 33 countries on five continents. About 35 percent of the airline's 1992 capacity (as measured in available seat miles) was flown in international markets, an increase from 17 percent in 1988 and only 4 percent in 1985. Since 1988, United's daily international departures rose from 44 to 180 in 1992.

As shown in Exhibit 4, United's operating revenues from foreign operations, as a percentage of total operating revenues, increased from 27 percent in 1990 to 33 percent in 1991, and to 38 percent in 1992. Exhibit 5 portrays the percentage change in the growth of foreign and domestic operations. Thus, whereas domestic operating revenues showed no growth, revenues from foreign operations grew by 38 percent between 1990 and 1992.

During 1992, international expansion focused primarily on Latin American and transatlantic markets where as recently as 1990 the carrier had virtually no service at all. In 1992, Latin America represented 4 percent of the carrier's total capacity and the Atlantic 9 percent. The Pacific Division, a part of the United route system since 1986, continued to be the company's largest overseas division with about 22 percent of capacity flown there in 1992. The U.S. market represented the company's largest market at 65 percent of total system capacity.

■ Atlantic Operations

United served 14 European destinations with 51 daily departures. Five of the destinations—Athens, Geneva, Milan, Rome, and Zurich—were added in 1992.

Exhibit 4	United Airline's Revenues from Foreign Operations As a Percentage of Total Operating Revenues			
Year	Total Revenues	Domestic Revenues	Foreign Revenues	% of Total Revenues
1992	$12,890	$8,027	$4,863	38
1991	11,663	7,793	3,870	33
1990	11,038	8,028	3,010	27

Source: UAL, 1992, *Annual Report*, 33, 39.

Exhibit 5	Percentage Change in United's Operating Revenues from Domestic and Foreign Operations (in billions)			
Operations	1992	1991	1990	% Change
Domestic	$8,027	$7,793	$8,028	0
Foreign	4,863	3,870	3,010	38
Total	12,890	11,663	11,038	14

Source: UAL, 1992, *Annual Report*, 33, 39.

United also began nonstop service in three new transatlantic markets—from Washington to Brussels and Milan, and from San Francisco to Paris.

United served Europe with nonstop flights from seven U.S. gateway cities, all representing strong markets for international travel: Chicago, Los Angeles, New York, Newark, San Francisco, Seattle/Tacoma, and Washington, D.C.

Intra-European flying was increased with services from Paris to three new destinations—Athens, Geneva, and Zurich. In total, United had access to nine destinations through its intra-Europe flying from Paris and London, allowing the carrier to carry incremental passengers for its long-haul international operation.

■ Latin American Operations

January 1992 marked the start-up of United's service to Latin America as a result of the company's $135 million acquisition of most Pan American World Airways' South and Central American route authorities.

In mid-January 1992, United began service from both New York and Miami to Caracas, Venezuela, with the New York flights continuing on to Port of Spain, Trinidad. These services were followed later the same month with nonstop service from both New York and Miami to Rio de Janeiro, Brazil, with continuing service to Sao Paulo, Brazil, and Buenos Aires, Argentina.

United acquired Pan Am's Los Angeles–Mexico City route authority with rights to several points beyond. Because the company purchased only route authorities in Latin America—not an ongoing business, which had been terminated in December 1991 with the cessation of Pan Am's operations—the start-up in Latin America was slower and more costly than anticipated. In Mexico City, United became the largest foreign carrier operating to 10 destinations.

In 1992, United served 16 destinations in Latin America with 69 daily departures, up from just two destinations, Mexico City and Cancun, in 1991.

■ Pacific Operations

United served 14 destinations in the Pacific with 60 daily departures, almost a 50 percent increase from 1988. Most of the increase was implemented in 1989 and 1990. (For United's number of daily departures on the Atlantic, Latin American, and Pacific routes, see Exhibit 6.) Demand in Japanese markets softened in 1992 due to weak Japanese economic conditions. However United's intra-Asian flying was good. By the end of 1992, United was the largest carrier operating across the

Exhibit 6	Number of United Daily Departures on the Atlantic, Latin American, and Pacific Routes					
Routes	1988	1989	1990	1991	1992	% Change
Atlantic	0	0	2	29	50	1667
Latin American	1	2	4	5	70	1429
Pacific	35	43	55	57	60	58

Source: UAL, 1992, *Annual Report*, 4–6.

Pacific. In July 1992, a new seasonal nonstop flight between San Francisco and Shanghai was launched.

North American Operations

The U.S. domestic market, representing 65 percent of United's capacity and 62 percent of its revenues, was United's largest market in 1992. In addition to providing transportation from point to point within the United States, the domestic network served an increasingly important need to feed traffic from cities within the United States to United's destinations in Europe, Latin America, Asia, and Australia. United's hub cities—San Francisco, Denver, Chicago, and Washington Dulles—were geographically well located for connecting traffic and represented major population centers.

Aircraft Fleet

In 1992, United Airlines' operating fleet totaled 663 aircraft, a net increase of 50 aircraft from 1991. The average age of the company's fleet declined to 10.3 years in 1992 from 11.2 years the year earlier, and 13.6 years in 1988. United's fleet, however, was older than that of American Airlines and Singapore Airlines whose average ages were 9 and 5 years, respectively.

The 1992 deliveries included twenty-five Boeing 737s, six 747s, twenty-five 757s, and ten 767s. The company retired eleven 727s, four 737s, and one 747. The company decided to reduce its capital spending for new aircraft significantly in the future.

Cargo

Worldwide cargo demand was projected to double by the year 2005, with growth in international markets exceeding growth in U.S. markets. United was the world's largest carrier of air cargo among passenger airlines without freighter aircraft.

Ground Facilities

In the vicinity of Chicago's O'Hare International Airport, United had its executive headquarters, a computer facility, and a training center. United operated reservation centers in 8 U.S. cities. It also operated 110 city ticket offices in the United States, plus offices in the Pacific and European countries.

United's Maintenance Operation Center (MOC) at San Francisco International Airport was used for all major aircraft and component maintenance. The company also began constructing a new major aircraft maintenance and overhaul facility in Indianapolis. In January 1992, the City of Denver and United entered into a 30-year lease agreement for space at the new Denver International Airport.

Exhibit 7	United's Fuel Expenses and Consumption				
	1992	**1991**	**1990**	**1989**	**1988**
Fuel expense, including tax (in millions)	$1,679	$1,674	$1,811	$1,354	$1,180
Gallons consumed (in millions)	2,529	2,338	2,253	2,128	2,106
Average cost per gallon	66.4c	71.6c	80.4c	63.6c	56.0c
% of total operating expenses	13%	14%	16%	15%	14%

Source: UAL, 1992, Form 10-K, 16.

Fuel

United's operations were significantly affected by the price and availability of jet fuel. Every $0.01 change in the average annual price per gallon of jet fuel caused a change of about $25.3 million in United's annual fuel costs. Exhibit 7 portrays United's fuel expenses and consumption for the years 1988 to 1992. United's average fuel cost per gallon in 1992 was 7.3 percent lower than 1991. Fuel prices decreased as the Middle East recovered from the effects of the Gulf War. Kuwait oil production returned to pre-war levels.

Changes in fuel prices were industry-wide occurrences that benefited or harmed United's competitors as well as United. Accordingly, lower fuel prices might be offset by increased price competition and lower revenues for all air carriers, including United. Fuel prices, however, may increase in the future. President Clinton's proposed tax on energy sources would, if enacted, cause the cost of fuel to United to increase.

To maintain adequate supplies of fuel and to provide a measure of control over fuel costs, United shipped fuel on major pipelines, maintained fuel storage facilities, and traded fuel to locations where it was needed. United purchased 98 percent of its fuel under contracts with major U.S. and international oil companies. These contracts were terminable by either party on short notice.

Marketing

United's marketing strategy was driven by three principal competitive factors: schedule convenience, overall customer service, and price.

United sought to attract travelers through convenient scheduling (particularly during peak demand periods) and high-quality service. In 1991, the company enhanced its international First Class product and introduced the luxurious Connoisseur Class. A new, more sophisticated inflight magazine was introduced to reflect United's worldwide route network. Called *Hemispheres*, the magazine featured more in-depth travel information, with articles and artwork of interest to cultures throughout the world.

Travel executives gave Wolf special praise for his recruitment in late 1990 of Adam Aron, as senior vice president for marketing. Creator of "the Hyatt touch" campaign with Hyatt Hotels Corp., Aron significantly improved service at United. Aron played a key role in creating the Connoisseur Class that won plaudits from international travelers. And although United's domestic service still lagged behind its competitors' service, Aron introduced improvements there as well. It was his brainstorm to serve McDonald's lunches for children traveling to Orlando.

United operated a frequent flyer marketing program known as "Mileage Plus" wherein credits were earned by flying on United or using the services of one of the other airlines, credit card companies, car rental agencies, and hotels (the "Partners") participating in the Mileage Plus program. The program was designed to enable United to retain and increase the business of frequent travelers. Credits earned under the program might be exchanged at certain plateaus for free travel or service upgrades on United or for use with one or more of the Partners.

On all of its routes, United's pricing decisions were affected by competition from other airlines, some of which had cost structures significantly lower than United's and could, therefore, operate profitably at lower fare levels.

■ Distribution

Travel agents accounted for a substantial percentage of United's sales. The complexity of the various schedules and fares offered by air carriers fostered the development of electronic distribution systems which displayed information relating to fares and schedules to travel agents and others. The use of such systems was a key factor in the marketing of airlines' products.

United developed the Apollo computer reservation system, which was one of the largest computer reservation systems in the United States. In addition, the system was also used in Canada, Mexico, and Japan. The Covia Partnership, in which United held a 50 percent interest, owned and operated Apollo.

The Galileo Company Limited, a U.K. corporation, provided computer reservation system (CRS) services, using a modified version of the Apollo software, to travel agencies in all countries other than the United States, Canada, Mexico, and Japan. United held a 26 percent interest in Galileo, with the remaining equity interests being held by nine European airlines.

■ Fares

Domestically, U.S. airlines were free to set their own domestic prices without any government regulations. Internationally, however, they were required to file and observe tariffs. The U.S. Department of Transportation established a standard industry fare which controlled the upward limit on international fares. The fare level was adjusted bimonthly based on average industry cost. International tariffs were also subject, in some cases, to the jurisdiction of, and approval by, the governments of the foreign countries served by the U.S. carriers.

■ Customers

United's customers basically consisted of any air traveler. The company's operations, therefore, were not dependent on a single customer or very few large customers. Thus, the loss of the few largest customers of United would not have a material adverse effect on the company.

■ Human Resources

In 1992 United had more than 83,000 employees. The relationship between management and employees could be described as turbulent. As a result, employee morale was very low, especially that of flight attendants. In summing up the morale problem, one flight attendant said, "Nobody likes to come to work anymore. Our morale can really kill this airline."[15] One reason for the low morale was that management imposed weight limits on its attendants. Also, the company planned to hire foreigners as attendants on some of its international flights and to open a flight attendant base in Taiwan, which the union saw as an attempt to rid the company of higher paid senior flight attendants.

United's wage and related costs accounted for 34 percent of its total operating expenses, which was higher than the 31 percent at low-cost carriers. The 1992 average employee salary at the largest carriers (including United) was $56,874. Although this was identical to the salary of Southwest Airlines' employees, Southwest employees had much higher productivity. At the low-cost carriers, including Southwest, pilots flew an average of 64 hours per month versus 48 hours per month at the largest carriers. High productivity provided smaller carriers a 38 percent labor-cost advantage and a bigger pricing advantage. Thus, a larger carrier such as United paid $1,200 more in total labor costs alone than a smaller carrier for a single flight between Baltimore and Chicago.[16] To enhance its competitive position, United planned various steps to reduce its unit costs, including the elimination of staff and support jobs, reduction in nonpersonnel expenses, and the redeployment of certain aircraft to more profitable airports. United requested representatives of its union employees to participate in the company's cost reduction program through various cost saving changes, in return for a profit sharing plan. The IAM and AFA representatives declined. The ALPA representatives requested more information.

■ Labor Unions

About 63 percent of United's employees were represented by the Air Line Pilots Association (ALPA), Association of Flight Attendants (AFA), and International Association of Machinists and Aerospace Workers (IAM). United's relationship with its labor unions had traditionally been rocky. The unions made four failed attempts at buying the company. The latest $5 billion employee bid, however, which was initially made in 1993 by the Air Line Pilots Association and the International Association of Machinists, seemed to have a better chance of succeeding, subject to the stockholders' approval. Under the buyout agreement, which was finalized in March 1994, United's pilots, machinists, and non-union and midmanagement employees would obtain 55 percent of the common stock in the company. In exchange, the employees would make wage and benefit concessions valued at about $5 billion over almost six years. The wage and benefit cuts would reduce United's unit costs by 4 percent to 7.4 cents per mile for every available seat. That would put United close to Southwest Airline's 7.2 cents per mile. The savings were also expected to enable the carrier to establish a low-cost, low-fare airline (within United) to compete with the growing number of low-cost carriers. Commenting on the agreement, Wolf said: "The transaction represents the best path to a competitive and successful future for United Airlines."[17] Of course, much of United's future success would depend on how cooperative the employees would be. Many rank-and-file employees were angry about the pay cuts they would have to take in exchange for their 55 percent stake in the company. Actually, the airline's 17,000 flight attendants refused to join the buyout agreement because they were unwilling to take a pay cut.

The stock-for-cuts swap, if successful, would make United the nation's largest employee-owned company, followed by Publix Supermarkets, Epic Healthcare, and Avis.[18] Four other airlines—America West, Delta, Northwest, and TWA—had some employee ownership.

■ A Possible New CEO

In anticipation of the employee buyout of United, the pilots and machinists unions selected nine new members for United's future board of directors. The two unions would get one board seat each and effective veto power over most major decisions. One of the newly nominated members was Gerald Greenwald, a former vice chairman with Chrysler Corp. Greenwald was chosen by the pilots and machinists unions to replace Wolf as United's chief executive if the buyout was approved by the shareholders.

Greenwald said he had "been preparing since college for this challenge."[19] The son of a Russian immigrant wholesale grocer in St. Louis, Greenwald studied economics and labor on a scholarship at Princeton University. He worked in St. Louis one summer as an organizer for the garment workers' union. "If you had asked me then to name my top heroes, half of them would have been labor leaders,"[20] he said.

Greenwald was a soft-spoken finance whiz who was key in saving Chrysler Corp. when it teetered on the brink of bankruptcy. But he had no airline experience and little record of dealing with hostile unions. Those who knew him said he was no born leader. Yet, Greenwald's easygoing manner was a reason United's unions chose him. They wanted a consensus builder to forge fractured groups into a harmonious team.

■ Finance

Although the company's international revenues showed a steady improvement, its total earnings declined. In 1992, the company, recorded a net loss of $956.8 million, or $39.75 per share, compared to the 1991 net loss of $331.9 million, or $14.31 per share (see Exhibits 8, 9, and 10). United's stock reacted negatively. Whereas the stock price was $171 in 1990, it dropped to $161 and $159 in 1991 and 1992, respectively.[21]

The company attributed its losses to the Gulf War, poor economic conditions, high oil prices, fluctuations in foreign currencies, competitive pressures, and international fare wars. The poor economic outlook in Japan and some European countries could continue to negatively affect the company's earnings. As a result, 1993 might be another difficult year for UAL.

Long-term debt and capital lease obligations incurred in connection with aircraft financing amounted to $1.032 billion in 1992. Cash used for payments of long-term debt and capital lease obligations was $164.5 million. As a result of its financing activities and net loss, the company's debt-to-equity ratio changed from 65:35 in 1991 to 86:14 in 1992. In March 1993, Standard and Poor's Corporation lowered United's ratings and debt securities to levels below investment grade. Such downgrades would increase the company's cost of raising capital.

Exhibit 8   Consolidated Cash Flows As of Year Ended December 31 (in millions)

	1992	1991	1990
Cash and cash equivalents at beginning of year	$449.0	$221.4	$465.2
Cash flows from operating activities:			
Net earnings (loss)	(956.8)	(331.9)	94.5
Adjustments to reconcile to net cash provided by operating activities:			
Cumulative effect of accounting changes	539.6	—	—
Deferred postretirement benefit expense	75.0	—	—
Deferred pension expense	165.0	75.2	4.2
Depreciation and amortization	725.6	603.8	559.6
Foreign exchange (gains) losses	(2.0)	19.7	7.2
Gain on disposition of property	(31.6)	(48.7)	(285.8)
Provision (credit) for deferred income taxes	(146.3)	22.0	21.7
Undistributed earnings of Covia Partnership	(27.4)	(3.7)	—
Decrease (increase) in receivables	(133.2)	0.5	(24.6)
Increase in other current assets	(66.7)	(90.7)	(139.5)
Increase in advance ticket sales	183.1	39.9	182.0
Increase (decrease) in accrued income taxes	164.2	(253.9)	24.3
Increase in accounts payable and other accrued liabilities	141.6	352.6	320.6
Amortization of deferred gains	(82.2)	(82.1)	(46.6)
Other, net	27.4	35.3	(1.8)
	575.3	338.0	715.8
Cash flows from investing activities:			
Additions to property and equipment	(2,518.6)	(2,122.4)	(2,575.9)
Proceeds on disposition of property and equipment	2,367.2	1,281.3	1,737.6
Decrease (increase) in short-term investments	(237.6)	248.4	(10.8)
Acquisition of intangibles	(149.6)	(358.4)	(34.4)
Other, net	1.2	(0.6)	8.7
	(537.4)	(951.7)	(874.8)
Cash flows from financing activities:			
Proceeds from issuance of long-term debt	197.8	687.4	—
Repayment of long-term debt	(114.8)	(66.6)	(68.0)
Principal payments under capital lease obligations	(49.7)	(31.5)	(22.9)
Proceeds from issuance of common stock.	—	247.2	—
Increase in short-term borrowings	1.2	1.3	1.0
Other, net	0.8	3.5	5.1
	35.3	841.3	(84.8)
Increase (decrease) in cash and cash equivalents	73.2	227.6	(243.8)
Cash and cash equivalents at end of year	$522.2	$449.0	$221.4

Source: UAL, 1992, *Annual Report*, 27.

Exhibit 9	Statement of Consolidated Financial Position As of Year Ended December 31 (in millions, except share data)		
		1992	1991
Assets			
Current assets:			
Cash and cash equivalents		$522.2	$449.0
Short-term investments		960.6	727.4
Receivables, less allowance for doubtful accounts (1992—$11.9; 1991—$13.1)		1,066.3	912.2
Aircraft fuel, spare parts and supplies, less obsolescence allowance (1992—$46.4; 1991—$67.3)		324.3	336.2
Refundable income taxes		63.6	166.9
Deferred income taxes		33.2	—
Prepaid expenses		328.1	290.2
		3,298.3	2,881.9
Operating property and equipment:			
Flight equipment		7,790.1	6,710.1
Advances on flight equipment		710.3	784.6
Other property and equipment		2,099.2	1,906.8
		10,599.6	9,401.5
Accumulated depreciation and amortization		(4,205.0)	(3,887.5)
		6,394.6	5,514.0
Operating property and equipment under capital leases:			
Flight equipment		959.2	682.3
Other property and equipment		100.7	100.3
		1,059.9	782.6
Accumulated amortization		(343.6)	(301.2)
		716.3	481.4
Other assets:			
Intangibles, less accumulated amortization (1992—$146.0; 1991—$91.4)		907.4	666.3
Deferred income taxes		588.8	27.2
Other		352.0	305.5
		1,848.2	999.0
		$12,257.4	$9,876.3

Continued

Exhibit 9   Statement of Consolidated Financial Position As of Year Ended December 31 (in millions, except share data)—*Continued*

	1992	1991
Liabilities and Shareholders' Equity		
Current liabilities:		
Short-term borrowings	$449.8	$448.6
Long-term debt maturing within one year	116.2	68.7
Current obligations under capital leases	53.7	39.3
Advance ticket sales	1,067.6	882.6
Accounts payable	645.9	580.1
Accrued salaries, wages and benefits	910.9	775.0
Accrued aircraft rent	715.0	526.3
Other accrued liabilities	885.9	762.7
	4,845.0	4,083.3
Long-term debt	2,800.7	1,826.6
Long-term obligations under capital leases	812.4	596.6
Other liabilities and deferred credits:		
Deferred pension liability	576.1	622.8
Postretirement benefit liability	960.0	—
Deferred gains	1,430.4	1,126.7
Other	127.2	22.4
	3,093.7	1,771.9
Redeemable preferred stock:		
5 1/2% cumulative prior preferred stock, $100 par value	—	1.1
Common shareholders' equity:		
Common stock, $5 par value; authorized 125,000,000 shares; issued, 25,284,670 shares in 1992 and 25,244,206 shares in 1991	126.4	126.2
Additional capital invested	340.4	304.0
Retained earnings	332.1	1,288.9
Unearned compensation	(11.4)	(17.2)
Pension liability adjustment	(7.9)	—
Common stock held in treasury—1,046,188 shares in 1992 and 1,486,100 shares in 1992	(74.0)	(105.1)
	705.6	1,596.8
Commitments and contingent liabilities		
	$12,257.4	$9,876.3

Source: UAL, 1992, *Annual Report,* 24–25.

Exhibit 10	Net Earnings per Share as of Year Ended December 31 (in millions, except share data)		
		1992	**1991**
Earnings or loss:			
Earnings (loss) before cumulative effect of accounting changes		$(417.2)	$(331.9)
Prior preferred stock dividend requirements		—	(0.1)
Interest on Air Wisconsin convertible debentures, net of income tax		1.6	—
Earnings (loss) before cumulative effect of accounting changes for fully diluted calculation		(415.6)	(332.0)
Cumulative effect of accounting changes		(539.6)	—
Net earnings (loss) for fully diluted calculation		$(955.2)	$(332.0)
Shares:			$(332.0)
Average number of shares of common stock outstanding during the year		24.1	23.2
Additional shares assumed issued at the date of merger for conversion of Air Wisconsin convertible debentures		0.1	—
Additional shares assumed issued at the beginning of the year for exercises of diluted stock options and stock award plans (after deducting shares assumed purchased under the treasury stock method)		0.3	0.5
Average number of shares for fully diluted calculation		24.5	23.7
Fully diluted per share amounts:			
Earnings (loss) before cumulative effect of accounting changes		$(16.96)	$(14.03)
Cumulative effect of accounting changes		(22.0)	—
Net earnings (loss)		$(38.96)	$(14.03)

Source: UAL, 1992, Form 10-K, 47.

■ **Industry**

The airline industry was in a continuous state of turmoil. The seeds of the turmoil were sown in 1978 when deregulation began an era of fierce competitiveness. Periodic price wars kept fares down and drove investors away. Between 1990 and 1993, the U.S. commercial carriers lost over $10 billion, far more than the industry earned during its entire 60-year history until then.[22] Among the major airlines, only Southwest managed to consistently make a small profit by keeping costs low and offering few-frills service. The airline industry's losses were caused by the economic recession, higher fuel prices, the adverse effect of the Persian Gulf conflict on international air travel, rising debt service costs, and persistent overcapacity, which fueled suicidal price wars as airlines battled to fill seats. As one observer of the industry said: "I knew the industry would be ruggedly competitive, but I did not expect its leaders to engage in extended kamikaze behavior."[23] In 1991, three large air carriers—America West, Continental, Midway—had filed for bankruptcy. Pan American Airways, and Eastern Air Lines ceased operating. Changes in the ranking and market share of the top 10 U.S. carriers are presented in Exhibit 11.

Many of the largest U.S. carriers became highly leveraged in the late 1980s, when they took on large amounts of debt to fund investment in new aircraft, to

Exhibit 11	Changes in the Ranking and Market Share of the Top Ten U.S. Carriers				
1992 Rank	Company	% Market Share	1985 Rank	Company	% Market Share
1.	American	20.7	1.	American	13.3
2.	United	19.7	2.	United	12.5
3.	Delta	17.1	3.	Eastern	10.0
4.	Northwest	12.4	4.	TWA	9.6
5.	Continental	9.2	5.	Delta	9.0
6.	USAir	7.5	6.	Pan Am	8.1
7.	TWA	6.1	7.	Northwest	6.7
8.	America West	2.9	8.	Continental	4.9
9.	Southwest	2.5	9.	People Express	3.3
10.	Alaska	1.2	10.	Republic	3.2
	Others	0.7		Others	19.4

Source: Aerospace and air transport, 1993, *Standard and Poor's Industry Surveys* 161, no. 7, Sec. 1, February 18, A3.

finance mergers and acquisitions, or to undertake financial restructuring. The long-term debt burden for the major carriers totaled $20.8 billion. In the meantime, stockholders' equity for these carriers totaled $7.1 billion which resulted in a debt-to-equity ratio of 2.9 (debt 2.9 times greater than equity).

One factor that influenced the industry structure was that some carriers were operating under Chapter 11 federal bankruptcy-law protection. Robert Crandall, chairman of American Airlines, claimed such companies had unfair competitive advantages over healthy carriers and were hurting the industry's efforts to rebound from the recession and the Mideast war. Crandall asked the Transportation Department to consider decertifying airlines operating under Chapter 11. Executives of the healthy airlines said that ailing companies did not have to pay all of their debt payments, including aircraft lease payments.[24] As a result, such carriers were able to offer bargain-basement fares, which forced the healthy carriers to cut their fares as well. Edwin Colodny, chairman of USAir Group, called bankruptcy court "a new form of federal subsidy."[25] The ailing operators maintained that the healthy giants were attempting to consolidate power, make it easier to boost fares, and scare fliers away from Chapter 11 companies.[26]

■ Seasonality and Cyclicality

The airline industry is seasonal. The first and fourth quarters of the year normally are affected by reduced travel demand in the winter and fall. United's operations, particularly at its O'Hare and Denver hubs, were often affected adversely by winter weather. Seasonality, however, resulted in better operating results in the spring and summer.

The air travel industry was also cyclical. The travel business fluctuated significantly in response to general economic conditions.

■ Industry Outlook

According to the Federal Aviation Administration (FAA), domestic airline traffic would increase at an annual rate of 4.1 percent until the year 2002, and international traffic at an annual rate of 6.4 percent. To support traffic growth and to replace aging aircraft, the industry would be required to spend an estimated $234 billion on new equipment during the next 15 years.

The outlook for the airline industry would depend on the state of the U.S. and world economy and whether fuel prices would remain stable. Following the 1990–1991 recession, the U.S. economy appeared poised for moderate growth. As the rate of inflation began to moderate, both short-term and long-term interest rates declined sharply. Fuel prices, which reached a high of 80 cents per gallon in 1990, dropped to 66 cents in 1992. However, the near-term financial prognosis remained highly uncertain for those air carriers that were either in poor financial shape or were being restructured under the supervision of the bankruptcy courts.

European Market

The outlook for the airline industry in Europe was not hopeful. With the economy of most European countries mired in recession, joblessness hovering at nearly 12 percent, and pending deregulation, the airline industry in Europe was expected to be chaotic for the foreseeable future.

Undoubtedly, deregulation was the single most important factor to affect air travel in Europe. In June 1992, the European Community (EC) passed a deregulation package that would remove most controls on airline capacity and fares and also abolish licensing rules to permit EC carriers greater access to markets in countries outside their home base. Under the new regulations, an airline from one country would be able to serve several cities in another country but only as a continuation of an international flight. British Airways, for example, could fly from London to Frankfurt and then on to Berlin. Even so, it could fill only 50 percent of its seats with new passengers for the last leg. Unrestricted flying rights within another country, known as cabotage, would not be granted until 1997. But the new rules gave EC member states plenty of loopholes to block the most serious forays of carriers from other European countries or from outside Europe; clauses and exceptions would permit governments to invoke fairness statutes and tie up invaders in red tape.

With respect to travel habits, Europeans differed from Americans in some ways. Whereas Americans often responded favorably to price promotions at the expense of service, Europeans seemed to value good service. As an executive at British Airways said: "The U.S. industry seems to have accepted the thought that aviation is a commodity business, but our experience is that the public likes being looked after."[27] In addition, Europeans typically took shorter flights within the continent. Thus, travelers always had the option of driving on modern superhighways or riding the fast, relatively cheap trains. Just 2 percent of travel between major European cities was by air, versus 14 percent in the United States.

Latin American Market

Latin America represented a lucrative market. Air travel between the United States and Latin America has grown at a rapid pace. The boom was sparked by Latin America's unprecedented political stability and economic strength. Latin stock markets hit new highs, inflation came under control, and trade barriers fell. The region also held promise as a vacation spot for North Americans. As a result, the region, which two decades ago comprised just 3 percent of global aviation, accounted for 5 percent in 1993, thus occupying a second place only to the Asia–Pacific region in projected growth through the 1990s. All the U.S. passenger carriers, except for latecomer United Airlines, were earning profits in the region.

Asian Market

The brightest spot for the airline industry was Asia, potentially the richest market on earth. Although traffic slackened in Japan due to the poor economy, the region as a whole was still the fastest growing market in the world. Asia, which accounted for 30 percent of the world air travel, could generate 50 percent of it within a decade. Air travel in Asia was expected to grow by 10 percent in the 1990s. Although this represented a decline from the 11 and 12 percent growth rate in the 1970s and 1980s, it still represented a healthy outlook. Growth of the gross domestic products, which almost always translated into increased air traffic, and the economies of several Asian nations were among the most expansive on earth. China was expected to grow by 10.7 percent, and South Korea, Taiwan, and Singapore were projected to grow by more than 6 percent.

Strategic Alliances

To bolster their nose-diving bottom lines and extend their reach, airlines increasingly were reaching out to one another across the Atlantic, entering into marriages of convenience.

Continental Airlines concluded an agreement with Air France and Air Canada. American Airlines attempted to link up with Canadian Airlines by obtaining a one-third stake in the airline. Delta Air Lines concluded an agreement with Swissair and Singapore Airlines. USAir had an agreement with British Airways that not only enabled the two carriers to coordinate their flights, but also gave the British carrier a 24.6 percent stake in USAir. Northwest Airlines had a similar alliance with KLM Royal Dutch Airlines, with the major difference being that their agreement gave KLM a 49 percent ownership interest in Northwest.

Creating alliances was even more frenzied among European carriers. European airlines, most of which were state owned, were gradually losing their government subsidies, in line with directions from the European Community to deregulate the industry. As a result, many European carriers were experiencing the same financial hardships that many U.S. airlines had faced.

Thus, Europe could experience the same deluge of bankruptcies and shutdowns that U.S. airlines eventually experienced after the 1978 deregulation. To prevent that, European carriers were rushing to achieve alliances among themselves, hoping such liaisons would provide them with the economies of scale needed to survive. Among the most important alliances under consideration was a merger of Swissair, KLM, SAS Scandinavian Airlines, and Austrian Airlines into a single airline. Such a merger would create the second largest airline in Europe after British Airways.

Partnerships between major U.S. and European carriers held the most promise for giving carriers on both sides of the Atlantic the global reach they needed. For European carriers, these linkups provided extensive access to the U.S. domestic airline market, the most lucrative in the world. It also gave them access to the growing operations some major U.S. carriers were developing in Latin America and the Pacific. Some U.S.–European alliances might end up becoming full-scale mergers of transatlantic carriers. However, U.S. law prohibited such unions. Foreigners could not own more than 49 percent of a U.S. carrier. But eventually mergers could be allowed, according to some industry analysts.[28]

On the other hand, alliances with European airlines gave U.S. carriers the ability to get their passengers to more European cities. It also extended their reach to destinations in far Eastern Europe, Africa, the Middle East, and the Asian subcontinent areas that European carriers served for years but which U.S. airlines barely covered.

The financial rewards resulting from the strategic alliances could be immense. United and Lufthansa officials were expecting significant gains in traffic as a result of their alliance. Each round-trip passenger that United won because of its links to Lufthansa would bring additional revenues of $650 to $700.

Such alliances represented "one of the most significant emerging trends in the global aviation industry today,"[29] said Stephen M. Wolf, United's CEO. The alliances provided a better customer service by making connections among various continents easier. But the reason behind such linkups was to ensure survival in a highly competitive industry that increasingly was becoming global. The carriers that served all continents would reap the biggest rewards. But extending operations to all points on the globe was virtually impossible for any one airline. For one thing, the cost was prohibitive. In addition, a host of restrictive air treaties existed between nations, limiting the number of flights and destinations that carriers could serve outside their own countries. To compete, airlines must have partners in different parts of the world.

One drawback of these alliances was a possible reduction in the quality of service. Consumers might be turned off because the quality of service provided by one partner was inferior to the level of service offered by the other. If the alliances were to succeed, the involved carriers would have to close any gaps in customer service.

Competition

Commenting on the competitive structure in the airline industry, Robert Crandall, American Airlines' CEO, said: "This business is intensely, vigorously, bitterly, savagely, competitive."[30] (For a list of the world's 20 largest airline companies, see Exhibit 12.)

United, and other U.S. carriers, had certain advantages over foreign air carriers in its ability to generate traffic from the United States because of their domestic route systems. However, United was in many cases constrained from carrying passengers to points beyond designated gateway cities in foreign countries. To the extent that foreign competitors could offer more connecting service to points beyond these gateway cities, they had an advantage in attracting traffic destined for these ultimate destinations and in attracting traffic from such cities for flights to U.S. gateway cities. In addition, some of the foreign carriers against which United competed on these routes were owned by government entities that subsidized their operations in various ways. Further, several foreign air carriers had sought access to the U.S. domestic market through substantial equity investments in U.S. airlines.

Exhibit 12	The World's 20 Largest Airline Companies				
Rank by 1992 Revenues	Company	Country	Revenues (in millions)	Profits (in millions)	Rank by 1992 Profits
1	American	U.S.	$14,495.0	($935.0)	45
2	United	U.S.	12,889.7	(956.8)	46
3	Air France	France	12,299.6	(616.8)	44
4	Lufthansa	Germany	11,074.6	(248.7)	33
5	Delta	U.S.	10,836.8	(506.3)	43
6	Japan	Japan	10,421.1	(383.6)	40
7	British Airways	Britain	9,416.0	(301.1)	3
8	Northwest	U.S.	7,963.8	(386.2)	41
9	All Nippon	Japan	7,158.8	(9.4)	16
10	USAir	U.S.	6,696.3	(1,228.9)	47
11	Scandinavian Airlines	*	5,909.1	N/A	—
12	Alitalia	Italy	5,672.6	(11.9)	17
13	Continental	U.S.	5,575.2	(125.3)	27
14	Swire Pacific	Hong Kong	5,029.5	570.9	1
15	KLM	Netherlands	4,662.8	(343.7)	37
16	Swissair	Switzerland	4,414.9	80.3	8
17	Iberia	Spain	4,389.2	(339.0)	36
18	TWA	U.S.	3,634.5	(317.7)	35
19	Singapore	Singapore	3,465.2	522.4	2
20	Quantas	Australia	3,104.1	105.6	6

*Half owned by the governments of Sweden, Denmark, and Norway.

Source: Adapted from Wilton Woods, 1993, Goodbuy hub and spoke? *Fortune*, December 13, 160–161.

In its international operations, United competed with a host of U.S., European, Latin American, and Asian companies.

U.S. Competitors

The major U.S. companies competing with United for international business were American Airlines, Delta Air Lines, Northwest Airlines, and USAir.

American Airlines

American airlines was the No. 1 airline in the world in passenger miles and total revenues. The company provided air travel service to customers throughout the world, serving airports in the United States, Canada, the Caribbean, Mexico, Europe, Central and South America, and Asia. American Airlines operated the Sabre Travel Information Network, which marketed the company's computerized reservation system to the travel industry. This division served travel professionals in more than 14,000 locations in the United States and in 57 countries around the world. Because of its large market share and aggressive management, American Airlines posed the biggest challenge to United.

Delta Airlines

Delta Airlines occupied the third position behind American and United in the domestic market and fifth among the world airlines. Delta was known for its premier customer service, ranking only second behind Alaska Airlines in customer satisfaction.

Northwest Airlines

Northwest Airlines lost about $1.9 billion from 1989 to 1992. Its financial situation was so dire that the company was prepared to file for bankruptcy. The company's problems stemmed from an inferior domestic route system, stiff competition in its crucial Asian routes, and an aging fleet of planes. In November 1992, Northwest and KLM Royal Dutch Airlines got preliminary approval to merge their operations—the first time that a U.S. and a foreign carrier were granted permission to act as one. In 1989, the Dutch airline had already paid $400 million for a 49 percent stake in Northwest. In October 1992, KLM offered $600 million in new financing. Without Northwest, KLM would have almost no presence in North America and would be doomed to remain a modest-size European airline. With KLM's access to the European market and Northwest's rich Pacific routes, the two carriers could be a powerful pair.

USAir

After entering into an alliance with British Airways, USAir was in a stronger financial position following the infusion of $300 million into the company by the British airline. The combination vaulted the seventh ranked British Airways and the tenth ranked USAir to a formidable position in the worldwide market. Together the two companies had a fleet of 676 planes with an average age of under 10 years.

■ European Competitors

The deregulation of the airline industry in Europe would likely create a chaotic situation among the continent's carriers, which historically operated under government protection. Except for British Airways, which was privatized in 1987, and as can be seen in Exhibit 13, all of Europe's big airlines were at least partially government owned.

Over the longer term, competition was sure to heat up. One sign of this was mounting pressure on governments to sell their shares in flag carriers. British Airways' success since getting out from under government ownership was encouraging others to try the same. The German government already indicated it would sell its 51.2 percent share in Lufthansa. The majority, if not all, of Europe's big carriers would be privatized eventually because politicians would want to stop the drain on their national treasuries. What follows is a brief profile of Europe's major carriers.

Air France

With its solid base at two airports in Paris, along with potential secondary hubs in Brussels, Lyons, and Prague, Air France had an enviable geographic reach. Its

Exhibit 13	Total Revenues of, and Percent Owned by Government, in Europe's Major Airlines	
Company	Total Revenues (in billions)	Percent Owned by Government
Air France	$11.8	99% (France)
Lufthansa	9.7	51 (Germany)
British Airways	9.1	0 (Britain)
SAS	5.3	50 (Denmark, Norway, Sweden)
Alitalia	4.7	81 (Italy)
Swissair	4.3	22 (Switzerland)
KLM	4.2	39 (Netherlands)
Iberia	3.8	100 (Spain)

Source: Kenneth Labich, 1992, Europe's sky wars, *Fortune*, November 2, 90.

virtual monopoly on traffic within France also ensured a steady revenue flow. But costs remained relatively high, and unions would not make it easy to trim labor rolls enough to make a strong impact. The airlines' biggest weakness was that management had been sheltered by an extremely protective government and was yet to be tested in an open marketplace.

Lufthansa

After piling up huge losses in 1991 and 1992, management finally tackled its inflated costs and unwieldy route structure. Labor outlays, which accounted for 32 percent of total costs compared with 24 percent at British Airways, would be the toughest nut to crack because of Germany's militant unions. By paring down its flight schedule, however, and continuing to add modern, fuel-efficient aircraft, the carrier was making some headway. Delta began to challenge Lufthansa's dominance at its prime international hub, Frankfurt, but secondary hubs at Munich and Berlin showed promise. Lufthansa was also well suited geographically to dominate Eastern European traffic, which promised to grow quickly in the latter part of the decade.

British Airways

BA brought some powerful weapons to the battlefield—the lowest cost structure and biggest profits of any of Europe's big airlines, a war chest brimming with well over $1 billion, and a seasoned management that had functioned without government interference or financial help for over five years. This carrier was a generation ahead of its rivals and would seem ready to dominate. But BA desperately needed a solid foothold on the continent to build secondary traffic bases, and so far it was unable to reach agreement with a merger partner.

Scandinavian Airlines System

Management was able to lower the company's sky-high costs while continuing to maintain a world-class reputation for efficiency and service. But the profit picture was particularly glum at SAS because recession battered both the airline and the string of international hotels owned by its parent company. Most crucial to SAS's long-term health was finding one or more viable merger partners. Because Scandinavia's relatively small population generated only limited traffic, the carrier could not remain a major player without tying in directly to major urban centers on the continent.

Alitalia

This airline had some geographical advantages. Rome remained a top collection point for international traffic, and both Milan and Turin showed promise as intra-European hubs. But negatives abound: high costs, an aging fleet, a reputation for indifferent service. Alitalia might best survive as a partner to a carrier based far to the north such as BA or KLM so that the two could bracket the continent and profit mutually from the traffic flow.

Swissair

The costs of this airline were high and its parent country's population was sparse, but Swissair had so far been able to charge premium prices and maintain reasonable profit margins because of ruthless efficiency and impeccable service. Despite the willingness of European travelers to pay for superior treatment, Swissair's positioning could be harder to maintain when the skies opened up and downward pressure on fares took over. Unless this airline joined up with one or more similar carriers in a solid financial partnership, it could be relegated to the uncertain status of high-quality niche player.

KLM Royal Dutch

With its superb international base at Amsterdam and its pending merger with U.S. giant Northwest, KLM should be able to grab a solid share of North Atlantic traffic. To keep its planes filled back and forth from North America, however, KLM needed to get traffic from elsewhere in Europe. That meant finding a merger partner, which would become harder to do after a while.

Iberia

The company's strategy of maintaining low costs and trying to fill its planes by charging relatively low fares produced mountainous losses during the recession. A merger partner based in central Europe could help the company, as would improvement in service. Iberia's financial links to several airlines in Latin America promised to pay off in increased traffic on lucrative long-range routes on the southern Atlantic.[31]

■ Latin America

Latin America emerged as a key battleground among U.S. airlines. Competition began in 1990. First American Airlines bought Eastern Airlines' southern routes before Eastern went down in bankruptcy. Then, United acquired routes from Pan American World Airways in Pan Am's liquidation. Meanwhile, Continental Airlines added flights to Mexico, Central America, and the Caribbean. Delta Airlines was considering similar moves. As a result, the number of flights from the United States to Latin America soared 69 percent from 1990 to 1992. Such changes hurt Latin America's mostly small, money-losing airlines. This spurred some calls to erect defenses. "We have to protect our own areas. American Airlines' great strides for the time being should be restrained,"[32] said an executive at newly privatized AeroPeru in Lima.

For the airlines, South America versus North America was a case of David and Goliath. Latin America's entire jet fleet consisted of only about 700 aircraft; American and United each had about that many planes. Despite lower labor rates, the Latin carriers' lack of buying power, small home markets, and bloated workforces rendered their costs 25 percent higher than those of their U.S. rivals. And for many Latin American airlines, their U.S. routes were among their most important and were most at risk.

Particularly vulnerable were airlines in countries that had embraced the same free-market aviation policies the United States espoused. Mexico, Chile, Costa Rica, Venezuela, and Guatemala all signed liberal aviation treaties with the United States. Other countries, including Colombia and Brazil, had more than one carrier serving the United States, meaning more than one U.S. airline could reciprocate.

Some Latin American airlines began to fight back by pursuing innovative strategies or by teaming up with other airlines in the region and beyond. But a growing number of airlines and governments were stiffening their opposition to what they saw as predatory practices by U.S. carriers. Airlines in such countries as Costa Rica, Bolivia, Guatemala, and Jamaica, at various times, accused U.S. carriers of price cutting, capacity dumping, and predatory scheduling, all charges the U.S. airlines denied.

■ Asia

Some of the world's biggest airlines were locked in combat in the skies over Asia. Many of Asia's airlines turned into powerhouses. Japan Airlines (JAL), All Nippon Airways (ANA), Cathay Pacific, and Singapore Airlines were all among the world's elite carriers. The region also supported a collection of national airlines that each had more than $1 billion in annual revenues and extensive international route systems. Among these were Quantas, Korean Air, Thai International, China Air of Taiwan, Malaysia Airlines, Garuda Indonesia, and Air New Zealand. Nearly 40 air carriers, founded by state-owned companies, sprang up in China alone.

Compared to United, Asian airlines suffered from a huge disadvantage, namely, labor costs. Even though United's labor costs amounted to more than 30 percent of overall fixed costs, they were about half those of its major Asian competitors. That was because Asian airlines generally had higher wage levels and needed more employees to provide the same capacity. To stay alive in the competitive deregulated U.S. market, United trimmed staffers and negotiated lower pay with their unions. Said Rakesh Gangwal, United's senior vice president for planning, "Unlike the Asians, we have gone through the hard-knocks school of deregulation."[33]

JAL and ANA

The falloff in traffic following the Gulf War, coupled with Japan's recession, hurt the Japanese carriers most. JAL, which the government privatized in 1987, expected to lose about $234 million in 1993. At ANA, a predominantly domestic carrier that had never been government owned, revenues tumbled nearly 5 percent in the first six months of 1993.

Japanese airline chiefs were outspoken about what they considered unfair competition from U.S. giants United and Northwest. They contended that aviation agreements between the United States and Japan, which dated to the early 1950s, no longer reflected market realities. In those years, the Japanese said, the passengers between the United States and Japan were Americans. As a result, U.S. airlines received liberal landing rights in Japan. The percentages were reversed in 1993, with Japanese accounting for the larger share.

Particularly nettlesome to Japan were the Americans' "beyond" rights, which allowed them more than 150 flights a week that stopped in Tokyo or Osaka to drop off then pick up passengers, and then go on to destinations like Hong Kong, Seoul, and Taipei. The United States did not allow foreign carriers to pick up and drop off passengers in one American city and then fly on to another. The U.S. executives countered by saying that the airline business was one of the few industries in which American companies competed successfully with Japanese companies. As the cochairman of Northwest Airlines said: "We respectfully would suggest to our Japanese friends that air transportation policy necessarily occurs in a broader trade context."[34]

Cathay Pacific

Cathay Pacific, Hong Kong's carrier, was relatively profitable with operating earnings of $112.6 million in 1993. Cathay managers, however, were unhappy over market opportunities lost because of overcrowded airports in Hong Kong. Meanwhile, Cathay made an attempt to stem costs. The airline moved some office functions to cheaper locations to save money on real estate. It also tried to bring down sky-high labor costs. Cathay senior pilots, mostly Britons and Australians, earned more than $150,000 a year and matched their basic salaries in expatriate housing and education benefits. Cabin attendants earned $50,000 or more in salary, plus about half that in various allowances. Cathay hoped to cut costs by basing some British pilots in London and Australians in Sydney to save on expatriate payments. In 1993, Cathay flight attendants struck for 12 days over new staffing rules aimed at boosting productivity.

Hong Kong returns to mainland China in 1997. The company already granted state-owned Chinese airlines a 22.5 percent equity stake. China was expected to provide Cathay with a heavy flow of passengers and air cargo. Air travel within China grew by 30 percent annually, and Cathay would likely be a big beneficiary through a subsidiary, Dragon Air, that flew into China from Hong Kong. Cathay was expected to score big gains from the rapid economic growth and rising middle-class populations throughout Southeast Asia. Hong Kong was located within a four-hour flight of one-half of the world's population.

Singapore Airlines

This airline was headquartered in Singapore, the third important aviation crossroads in Asia. Millions of Indians and Indonesians used the tiny nation on the top of the Malay Peninsula as a gateway for trips to Japan or on to North America. Japanese and Korean tourists funnel through, heading for holidays in Australia. Australians arrive on their way to Europe and North America.

Singapore Airlines was widely considered to be one of the very best air carriers in the world. It regularly topped the field in profit margins and was weathering the tough times better than most rivals. The airline, 54 percent owned by the government, earned an operating profit of nearly $250 million in the first six months of 1994. Its relatively healthy cash flow allowed it to maintain a fuel-efficient fleet that averaged five years of age without resorting to heavy borrowing or costly leasing deals. The fleets of most other international carriers were twice as old.

Conde Nast Traveler magazine named Singapore the best airline for international travel two years in a row. *Air Transport World* called Singapore the world's No. 1 airline over the last two decades. At the heart of the airline's service reputations were its smiling, willowy cabin attendants—outfitted in tight batik sarongs—unabashedly marketed as the Singapore Girls. New attendants typically underwent a rigorous four-month course that emphasized safety training and encompassed beauty tips, discussions of gourmet food and fine wines, and the art of conversation.

Regulations

Competition in international markets was subject to more extensive governmental regulation than in the United States. In these markets, United competed against foreign investor-owned and national flag carriers. U.S. carriers were granted authority to provide scheduled passenger and freight service between points in the United States and various overseas destinations. Operating authority between these points was subject to aviation agreements between the United States and the respective countries. Shifts in foreign government aviation policy could lead to alteration or termination of such agreements and could diminish the value of such routes. United recommended the U.S. Congress to consider developing an international aviation policy that sought enhanced access to international markets for U.S. carriers in return for access to U.S. markets by foreign carriers.

For international travel, the U.S. Department of Transportation established a standard industry fare that controlled the upward limit on international fares. The fare level was adjusted bimonthly based on average industry cost.

Protectionism

As the signs of growth in international travel were getting stronger, protectionist tendencies among some countries were increasing as well. This could frustrate U.S. carriers' efforts to have more open skies agreement with such countries. Germany, which was the most open aviation trading partner with the United States, moved to restrict access to its cities. France succeeded in dumping its bilateral agreement with the United States and began to reduce the U.S. carriers' flights to its cities. Meanwhile, Japan, which was already stingy with its air rights, wanted to disallow some services that its treaty with the United States explicitly allowed.

■ Conclusion

Exhibit 14	Stock Price of United Airlines During Employee Buyout Negotiations
Month	**Monthly Closes**
January 1993	$122
February	119
March	125
April	138
May	134
June	123
July	142
August	149
September	139
October	151
November	149
December	147
January 1994	148
February	135
March	129
April	130
May	120

Source: Stanley Ziemba, 1994, Plan is risky, but United is used to being a pioneer, *The Chicago Tribune,* July 10, Sec. 7, pp. 1, 8.

In his letter to the shareholders, Stephen M. Wolf said:

> The unacceptable losses reported last year by United Airlines and the U.S. air carrier industry at large reflect a deepening crisis in the country's aviation industry and, for United, the beginning of a watershed period.
>
> Weak economies at home and abroad, competition from bankrupt carriers operating with a court-approved lower cost base, and irrational pricing action initiated by competitors were contributing factors to UAL Corporation's 1992 loss of $957 million. With no clear signs that the difficult environment is easing as we enter 1993, we are determined to end this financial deterioration . . .[35]

By charting a global direction for the company, Wolf hoped to end the red ink. His challenge now was to implement the strategy without misstepping too dramatically—because he had little room for error.

In the meantime, the prospect of employee buyout presented the company with daunting challenges. Aside from restoring the company's competitiveness and profitability, the new management must strive to improve employees' sagging morale. Getting management and labor to work together as a team would be critical to the company's viability. Further, lowering the company's high operating costs would be far more difficult under employee ownership where layoffs would not be a palatable option. Perhaps the biggest challenge would be to allay investors' rising fears about United's uncertain future after the buyout. As can be seen in Exhibit 14, United's stock exhibited significant volatility during the buyout negotiations in 1993 and the first half of 1994.

The stock price dropped from a high of $151 in October 1993 to a low of $120 in May 1994 when management and labor became serious about reaching an accord. The stock volatility reflected the status of the buyout negotiations. When the negotiations seemed likely to lead to an agreement, the stock price dropped. When the negotiations hit a snag or broke down, the stock price rose. Standard and Poor's assessment of the buyout was negative. According to Standard and Poor, the buyout would "reduce management flexibility to undertake cost-cutting through layoffs or major asset sales."[36] Moody's assessment was also negative due to what it called "concern over the company's future financial flexibility."[37]

Finally, the big question that surrounded the possible employee buyout was: Would the new owners exhibit the same zeal and determination shown by Stephen Wolf in aggressively pursuing the company's global strategy?

■ Notes

1. Kevin Kelly, 1992, United wants the whole world in its hands, *Business Week,* April 27, 65.
2. Ibid.
3. Kenneth Labich, 1990, The year's 25 most fascinating business people, *Fortune,* January 1, 62–63.
4. Kelly, United wants the whole world, 68.
5. Ibid.
6. Labich, The year's 25 most fascinating business people, 63–64.
7. Sandra Greiner, 1992, Chicago executive profile: Stephen Wolf, *Chicago Executive Health and Fitness* 3(Summer): 1–3.
8. Kevin Kelly, 1992, He gets by with a lot of help from his friends, *Business Week,* April 27, 68.
9. Ibid.
10. Ibid.
11. Ibid.
12. UAL Corporation, 1992, Form 10-K, 2.
13. Kelly, United wants the whole world, 65.
14. Ibid.
15. Message for United's new chief: Fix morale, 1994, *The Chicago Tribune,* July 14, Sec. 3, p. 3.

16. Frank J. Dooley, 1994, Why airlines crash, *The Wall Street Journal,* March 30, A18.

17. Stanley Ziemba, 1994, United reaches final agreement with its unions on buyout details, *The Chicago Tribune,* March 26, Sec. 2, p. 1.

18. Stanley Ziemba, 1994, Well-known figures lined up for new United board, *The Chicago Tribune,* March 29, Sec. 3, pp. 1–2.

19. Susan Chandler, 1994, A United is still a ways off, *Business Week,* May 23, 32.

20. Ibid.

21. Moody's Investors' Service, *Moody's Handbook of Common Stock,* Winter 1993–1994.

22. Kenneth Labich, 1993, What will save the U.S. airlines, *Fortune,* June 14, 98.

23. Ibid.

24. Asra Q. Nomani and Bridget O'Brian, 1992, Healthy airlines lash out at their struggling rivals, *Wall Street Journal,* March 17, 4.

25. Ibid., 25.

26. Ibid.

27. Kenneth Labich, 1992, Europe's sky wars, *Fortune,* November 2, 89.

28. Stanley Ziemba, 1993, Airlines find marriage convenient, *The Chicago Tribune,* October 11, Sec. 4, p. 4.

29. Ibid., 1.

30. Wendy Zellner, Andrea Rothman, and Eric Schine, 1992, The airline mess, *Business Week,* July 6, 50.

31. Ibid., 91.

32. Susan Carey, 1993, U.S. airlines compete for Latin America, ruffle some feathers, *Wall Street Journal,* December 8, A1, A11.

33. Kenneth Labich, 1994, Air wars over Asia, *Fortune,* April 4, 94.

34. Wilson Woods, 1994, Unfriendly skies, *Fortune,* April 4, 96.

35. UAL Corporation, 1992, Annual Report, 2.

36. Michael J. MaCarthy, 1994, Holders of UAL approve bold buyout that gives workers majority control, *Wall Street Journal,* July 13, 4.

37. Ibid.

■ CASE 35 Will Whirlpool's Strategy Wash in Europe?

Matthew A. Ballard
Kendall E. Carr

> *We believe now is the time to further refine our organization in a manner which reflects the realities of the evolving marketplace and, in turn, improves the level of service to our customers and enhances our productivity.*—William D. Marohn, CEO

■ http://www.whirlpool.com

Just three years after acquiring the European appliance segment of Philips Electronics N.V., Whirlpool Corporation is posting higher profits and greater market share. The establishment of Whirlpool Europe B.V. (WEBV) has been a significant factor in this success: Despite a recessionary slump hampering the industry, in 1992, Whirlpool recorded profits of $205 million on revenue of $7.3 billion. Much of the company's success has resulted from a strong brand name and a quality image with consumers.

Recent trends, however, are presenting challenges. Although Whirlpool has reacted quickly to the changing environment, the competition is now doing the same. Hank Bowman, president of Whirlpool Europe, must now consider the development of WEBV's strategies. His immediate questions are whether the corporate strategy in Europe will allow Whirlpool to continue growth or whether WEBV should modify its strategy to ward off industry giants such as AB Electrolux, Maytag, and Bosch-Siemens.

■ Company History

Whirlpool Corporation began in 1911 as a small, hand-operated washing machine manufacturer called the Upton Machine Company. After several years of supplying washing machines for Sears Roebuck, the company merged with the Nineteen Hundred Washer Company and formed the world's largest washing machine business.

Nineteen Hundred Washer Company survived the depression and made it through World War II by producing for the war effort. The name Whirlpool appeared in 1947 when the company first marketed a washing machine under its own brand. The success of the brand prompted Nineteen Hundred to adopt Whirlpool as the company's name in 1950.

C.671

During the next two decades, Whirlpool continued to supply Sears with Kenmore brand machines. At the same time, the company developed a full line of its own Whirlpool products. The product line expanded further when Whirlpool added Seeger Refrigerator Company and the stove and air conditioning interests of RCA to its business in 1955.[1]

Whirlpool International B.V. (WIBV), the subsidiary that handled overseas sales and production, renamed Whirlpool Europe B.V. in 1992, was the result of a $500 million joint venture with Philips Electronics in 1989. Another $600 million put the venture under Whirlpool's complete control in 1991.

Whirlpool Financial Corporation (WFC) is also a part of the parent company. WFC provides financial services to dealers, distributors, and customers, with services including commercial lending, equipment leasing, and insurance premium financing.[2]

Company Management

As the company expanded in the European market, various managerial changes were made. At the end of 1992, Whirlpool Corporation's president, David R. Whitwam, said the following:

> Many of the changes we made in our senior management team during the year broadened its global perspective and further erased geographic and cultural borders. Bill Marohn, who had been president of [North American Appliance Group,] NAAG, assumed the head of Whirlpool Europe in January, then led the subsidiary through its most comprehensive strategic planning process ever. . . . Bill was succeeded at WEBV by Hank Bowman, who has 22 years of experience within our North American operation.[3]

Whirlpool prepared to be well positioned in Europe. Not only did new members of the board bring European experience, but new ideas were brought in through entrepreneurs, as explained by Whitwam:

> Along with Bill, two other new directors were added to the board during the year, expanding it to 14 members. Didier Pineau-Valencienne of France's Schneider S.A. brings European experience to the board, while Herman Cain of Omaha, Neb.–based Godfather's Pizza, Inc., offers a broad operating and entrepreneurial perspective.[4]

Whirlpool was indeed training its managers globally. Dan Miller, for example, became president of Whirlpool Brazil, and Ralph Hake was chosen to direct the NAAG after years of working with the Bauknecht Appliance Group in Europe.

Product Lines and Brand Names

Whirlpool Corporation has manufacturing facilities in 11 countries that support marketing of 10 major brand names in more than 90 countries.[5] In the United States, Whirlpool has become a leader in product depth, marketing the KitchenAid, Whirlpool, Sears Kenmore, Roper and Estate brands. KitchenAid is positioned at the high end, Whirlpool and Sears Kenmore labels are found in the broad middle, while the Roper and Estate names target the lower or "value" market segment. Whirlpool uses these same brands, except for Estate and Kenmore, in the Asian market.

Consistent with the rationalization of its operations, Whirlpool has centralized its marketing strategies. After changing the Philips brand name to Whirlpool, WEBV began implementing its plans to aim its brand names Whirlpool, Bauknecht, and Ignis at different segments of the market. Whirlpool is associated with high-value products, Bauknecht is a reliable and solid German brand in the middle segment, and Ignis, a 50-year-old Italian brand, offers products in the lower price ranges.[6]

In Europe, Whirlpool sells the brands Bauknecht, Ignis, Laden, and Whirlpool. The Bauknecht name is used in Asia as well. The only other European brand name used elsewhere is Whirlpool, which is used in all but the Brazilian market. The product line consists of automatic dryers, automatic washers, dishwashers, freezers, microwave ovens, ranges, and refrigerators. In 1981, Whirlpool celebrated its 25th anniversary of marketing a full line of Whirlpool brand products.

■ Corporate Strategy

With the No. 1 market position in North America, No. 3 position in Europe, and a leading presence in South America, Jerry Herman, of Kemper Securities Inc. in Chicago, calls Whirlpool "the best positioned appliance company for the 1990s."[7] As a part of its strategy, WEBV concentrated on customer satisfaction, diversity in brand lines, and quality maintenance.

Customer Satisfaction

Hank Bowman emphasized the consumers' importance to Whirlpool's success. Consumer services' expertise in such countries as the United Kingdom and Germany were soon shared with smaller operations. In 1992, Whirlpool Europe conducted 13,000 in-depth interviews on consumer satisfaction in the five largest European countries. To ensure the use of the results, the findings were fed directly into future product development. This new dedication to customer satisfaction resulted in the new extension of the VIP microwave line.[8]

Diversity of Brand Lines

By purchasing Philips' home appliance division, Whirlpool diversified its efforts away from the mature and slow-growing U.S. appliance market. According to an industry analyst with Merrill Lynch, "The saturation of most types of appliances is noticeably lower in European households than it is in American households."[9]

Quality Maintenance

Whirlpool's Worldwide Excellence System (WES) is the backbone of their total quality management system. WES is used to direct actions and track and report on results in terms of value creation, customer satisfaction, total quality, human-resources development, and financial performance.

■ Market and Environment

Whirlpool's recent strategy has focused on the developing single European market and the need for a global approach in Europe. Whitwam describes the process as follows:

> In 1988, Whirlpool forecasted and began acquiring the pieces needed to lead the globalization of the home-appliance industry. Events since then have only confirmed

our expectation that a relative handful of companies will, in time, dominate the manufacture and sale of home appliances.[10]

Some of the major market factors influencing Whirlpool's strategy include the Europe-wide recession, changes in demographics, the formation of the single market, and environmental concerns.

Europe-wide Recession

With a sluggish housing market, high unemployment, and a reluctance to pay by credit, the recession in Europe is likely to keep a hold on the white goods sector for some time.

Most sales improvements during the recession have been concentrated at the top and bottom segments of the product performance market. For premium brands, new technological developments, fueled by environmental concerns, have allowed manufacturers to add new features to models at profitable prices.

At the bottom of the market, sales have been maintained only as consumers trade down. Both the Hotpoint and Hoover brands have benefited greatly from offering budget price deals. Some firms in the industry have also seen moderate success in the secondhand market.

The recession has reduced sales competition to a variety of promotional offers, cash-back deals, and price discount schemes. Hoover even offered a free flight with the purchase of a vacuum cleaner,[11] which almost proved to be its undoing. Others are offering free small kitchen appliances with white goods purchases, or accepting late payments.

Demographic Changes

The last 20 years have seen a tremendous increase in the number of single-person households. Exhibit 1 summarizes the growth of this market segment.

The major purchasers of white goods are large family households. Consequently, the general reduction in household size is an unwelcome trend for white goods manufacturers. More single-person households may mean more households in total, but many of these households will have limited space, and possibly limited cash resources, so the general trend toward larger, more sophisticated machines may not produce the expected sales.

The Single European Market

Judging from the actions of major companies in the industry, individual national markets are gradually becoming merged into a single European market. The industry leaders (Whirlpool and Electrolux), have recently established pan-European strategies for their domestic appliances, with associated pan-European brands, marketing, and advertising.

Environmental Concerns

There are strong environmental pressures on manufacturers to develop improved machines that save energy, water, and detergents in the home laundry sector and replace compound fluorocarbons (CFCs) in refrigeration products.

Exhibit 1	Growth of Single-Person Households	
Year	Single-Person Homes (%)	Average Household Size
1971	18	2.89
1981	22	2.71
1991	26	2.48

Exhibit 2 Balance Sheets for Whirlpool Corporation ($ millions)

Assets	Dec 31, 1990	Dec 31, 1991	Dec 31, 1992	Mar 31, 1993	June 30, 1993	Sept 30, 1993	Dec 31, 1993
Current Assets							
Cash and equivalents	$78	$42	$66	$74	$59	$153	$88
Trade receivables—net	$784	$846	$851	$447	$859	$845	$866
Financing receivables—net	$1,102	$1,190	$980	$524	$1,010	$991	$814
Inventories	$801	$698	$650	$767	$829	$722	$760
Other assets	$135	$144	$193	$1,015	$159	$178	$180
Total Current Assets	$2,900	$2,920	$2,740	$2,827	$2,916	$2,889	$2,708
Investments	$281	$343	$346	$433	$441	$446	$502
Financing receivables—net	$647	$873	$912	$822	$792	$780	$793
Intangibles—net	$437	$909	$795	$794	$750	$768	$725
Property, plant and equipment	$1,349	$1,400	$1,325	$1,284	$1,263	$1,259	$1,319
Total Assets	$5,614	$6,445	$6,118	$6,160	$6,162	$6,142	$6,047
Liabilities and Stockholders' Equity							
Current Liabilities							
Notes payable	$1,268	$1,467	$1,453	$1,448	$1,300	$1,271	$1,160
Accounts payable	$580	$742	$688	$705	$767	$680	$742
Other current liabilities	$803	$722	$746	$765	$823	$902	$861
Total Current Liabilities	$2,651	$2,931	$2,887	$2,918	$2,890	$2,853	$2,763
Long-term debt	$874	$1,528	$1,215	$1,138	$1,089	$892	$840
Postretirement obligation	—	—	—	—	—	—	318
Other liabilities	$665	$471	$416	$688	$706	$719	$386
Stockholders' Equity	$1,424	$1,515	$1,600	$1,416	$1,477	$1,590	$1,648
Minority interest	—	—	—	—	—	$88	$92
Total Liabilities and Equity	$5,614	$6,445	$6,118	$6,160	$6,162	$6,142	$6,047

The pressure to produce environmentally friendly machines has increased development costs at a time when margins in the industry are being squeezed. However, once these new environmentally friendly products are in the market, many are sold at premium prices, thus boosting total market sales.

Whirlpool and Industry Competition

Whirlpool's Performance

The white goods industry has suffered in the past few years. As the third largest among some 100 appliance makers vying for business in Europe, Whirlpool faces stiff competition. A summary of Whirlpool's financial results is found in Exhibit 2. Whirlpool International B.V. showed signs of progress from its inception; WIBV outperformed industry shipment levels both for the fourth quarter of 1991 and

Exhibit 3   Sales and Income Figures for Whirlpool Corporation

	1992 Sales	1992 Operating Income	
Major home appliances	$7,097,000,000	$447,000,000	
Five Year Summary			
Year	*Sales*	*Net Income*	*EPS*
1992	$7,301,000,000	$205,000,000	$2.90
1991	$6,757,000,000	$170,000,000	$2.45
1990	$6,605,000,000	$ 72,000,000	$1.04
1989	$6,274,000,000	$187,000,000	$2.70
1988	$4,413,000,000	$ 94,000,000	$2.33
Five-Year Growth Rate	13.4%	21.5%	5.6%

for the total year of 1991. "WIBV improved its position in Germany, France and the U.K., the three largest markets in Western Europe," said Whitwam.[12]

Success continued as Whirlpool changed marketing strategies. Whirlpool Europe slowly began to replace the Philips brand name with the Whirlpool name in January 1992. This change led to some favorable results.

Although industry analysts deemed the white goods market flat, WIBV maintained a solid performance. Despite a $7 million restructuring charge from the compressor operations, WIBV improved its margins significantly during the second quarter of 1992. The third quarter saw slight unit-shipment growth. Overall, Whirlpool's 1992 appliance sales totaled $2.4 billion, up 6 percent over 1991 (see Exhibit 3). Operating earnings improved sharply, through a combination of growth and aggressive cost cutting.

"More than ever, we carefully examined our key processes and fine tuned them," commented Bowman.[13] Bowman attributed the success to a decrease in working capital needs. The decrease of 10 percent was accomplished by forming trade partnerships and enabling customers to place orders by accessing product schedules. Therefore, customers got more service due to reduced inventories and faster deliveries. Whitwam put it this way:

> In the quarter and during all of 1992, we used higher volumes to leverage that efficiency into an even greater return to our shareholders. . . . [W]e became more skilled at determining what customers want from us, incorporating those desires into our products and services, then measuring the extent to which Whirlpool meets and exceeds their expectations.[14]

Whitwam praised the performance of the WEBV. Although the industry's unit shipments had fallen, WEBV shipments were up, producing the best operating performance since the acquisition. Market share had also increased for four consecutive years. Even more noteworthy was that this performance occurred while Whirlpool Corporation was carrying out an aggressive strategy to reshape and expand the corporation into a global home-appliance manufacturer.

The next year, 1993, did not disappoint Whirlpool management either. According to Whitwam, the third quarter net profits of Whirlpool Corporation rose 27 percent from a year earlier due mainly to "particularly strong results"

Exhibit 4

Revenue 1990–1993

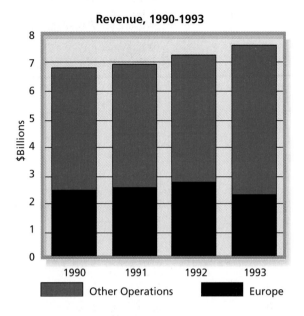

from the company's European business. The relative contribution of the firm's European operations to revenues and operating profit is displayed in Exhibit 4. European shipments rose nearly 5 percent, despite the economic slump. Favorable exchange rates and productivity improvements were quoted as reasons.

Positive effects of the structural changes were especially helpful. Global buying of parts reduced costs and led to a 40 percent reduction in the number of suppliers. The technology that had been shared led to further improvements. For example, the new Whirlpool European dryer, which had 22 percent fewer parts, was more efficient and of higher quality than previous models.

Exhibit 5   Selected Financials, Electrolux (in millions SEKM)

	1992	1993
Sales	48,902	58,888
Operating income	1,073	1,090
Net income	183	584
Assets:		
Current assets	44,251	47,670
Fixed assets	27,367	29,977
Total Assets	71,618	77,647
Liabilities & Shareholders Equity:		
Current liabilities	33,776	33,944
Long-term liabilities	20,755	26,460
Minority interests	315	390
Shareholders equity	16,772	16,853
Total Liab. & Shareholders Equity	71,618	77,647

During this time, WEBV completed the transition from the Philips-Whirlpool brand to the "stand-alone" Whirlpool label. The introduction of a pan-European television and print advertising campaign signified a step toward a global European home appliance strategy, stretching across 19 countries.

Whirlpool plans to invest hundreds of millions during the next few years to completely remake its European appliances. Simultaneously, it hopes to exploit the present gap in capability and price correlation that exists between the U.S. and European markets by working to further reduce costs.

The parent company could not complain during the fourth quarter of 1993 either. Although exchange rates did not prove as favorable, fourth quarter net earnings were $69 million, 13 percent higher than the $62 million level of the previous year. Revenues increased to $1.90 billion, an increase of 4 percent. Unit shipments were up for both the quarter and the year in North America, Europe, Latin America, and Asia. In addition, operating earnings reached record levels in the first three regions identified above.[15]

Whirlpool Europe's success was led principally by increased demand for Whirlpool brand products. The positive effects of this demand, as well as increased operating earnings in home appliances and compressors, overshadowed industry shipment decreases and unfavorable exchange rates. Despite improvements, the firm's European operating margin of about 5.6 percent is still far from its goal of 10 percent.

■ AB Electrolux and AEG

AB Electrolux is Whirlpool's largest and most aggressive competitor in the European market. Selected financial data is found in Exhibit 5. In the past, it has pursued an acquisition and restructuring strategy to obtain market positions and volume.

Recently, however, Electrolux has pursued a strategy focusing on increasing internal efficiencies, strengthening its core areas and structure, intensifying activities in new markets (such as Asia and Eastern Europe), and lowering cost levels while reducing capital already committed in other less profitable projects.[16] In the last two years (1992-1993), Electrolux has rationalized its operations and cut its worldwide workforce by 10 percent to improve performance.

Electrolux poses a further threat to Whirlpool as it develops new product lines. Besides product extensions such as forestry, garden, and car safety equipment, Electrolux has developed a completely new product range for the Frigidaire brand (in the United States). In 1993, it launched an environmentally aware CFC-free refrigerator-freezer that features low energy consumption.

The greatest threat, however, is the proposed merger of AB Electrolux and AEG AG. Whatever the original intentions, Electrolux is now pursuing a complete acquisition of AEG. AEG's parent company, Daimler-Benz, offered the remaining 90 percent of AEG Hausgeräte to the Swedish firm as Daimler-Benz launched a radical restructuring.

Less than 18 months after the original joint venture began, a full takeover may be programmed into the Swedish multinational's wash cycle. The acquisition would be the most important takeover in the European home appliance industry since Whirlpool acquired Philips. The takeover would enable Electrolux to challenge Whirlpool for the title of world's largest white goods producer.

Whirlpool, however, produces only white goods, and if appliances such as vacuum cleaners are included, the combined Electrolux–AEG group would clearly be the world's biggest appliance producer posting pro forma sales of $9.2 billion last year.

Strategically threatening to Whirlpool is the prospect of a third pan-European brand. Through this acquisition, Electrolux would be adding the AEG name to complement its Electrolux and Zanussi brands. While all three are well-known names across Europe, AEG is strongest in Germany and neighboring countries, Electrolux in northern Europe and Zanussi in southern Europe.

Although Electrolux was the leading supplier of the European white goods market as of February 1993, profits were down 3 percent. The company has been forced to cut dividends in half. With no upswing predicted in the future of the industry, Electrolux is also actively pursuing new strategies.

■ Maytag and Bosch-Siemens

Beyond the joint venture between Maytag and Bosch-Siemens Hausgeräte GmbH (BSHG), the competition between Whirlpool and Maytag has remained limited to the U.S. market. BSHG itself mainly targets the German market.

However, the actions taken by Whirlpool to rationalize and expand are being adopted by BSHG as well. Although BSHG has withdrawn an offer to buy the East German concern Scharfenstein GmbH (SG), SG's diligent efforts to make itself attractive to Western buyers has peaked BSHG's interest again.

After being deemed "fit only for liquidation" by the Treuhandanstalt (the body empowered to privatize East German businesses), SG released its plans for a CFC-free ecological refrigerator. Since then, SG changed its name to Foron Hausgeräte GmbH and won a federal prize for their environmental concerns.[17]

Whether it pursues this prospect, BSHG has dedicated DM 500 million for the Eastern market during 1993. It has laid the foundation of a new plant in Nauen with plans to increase the purchasing volume in the region to DM 875 million by the end of 1995.

In 1993, BSHG pursued plans to capture the eastern market by acquiring Gorenje MGA of Slovenia, a consumer durables producer. This active development of the white goods market in Eastern Europe may limit Whirlpool's ability to gain market share through its Slovakian venture with Tatramat a.s.[18]

Despite Maytag's focus on North America, the popularity of its brand-name Hoover appliances in Britain has opened up what management hopes is a loophole into Europe. In 1993, Maytag centralized its European marketing and operational structure in London. The structure now allows the Hoover European Appliance Group to work across all countries according to function.

Maytag's entry into the pan-European scene has been hesitant. Hoover had experienced some severe marketing failures as it attempted to appoint a single ad agency for Maytag's Hoover brands. Hoover Europe's president, Gerald Kamman, however, claims that the company will achieve "the total Hoover brand marketing potential throughout Europe with a highly efficient operating structure."[19]

Market Share

The development of market share is affected in large part by the rationalization of the white goods industry during the past 20 years. "In 1970, 400 companies had 80% of the European market, but soon only six or eight will control 80%," claims Mr. Vittorio Merloni, chairman of the Italian appliance manufacturer, Merloni.

In 1991, Whirlpool Europe, then WIBV, held approximately 15 percent of the European market. Though the industry suffered in Europe due to a pronounced economic slowdown, the combined market share of Whirlpool Europe brands increased for the fourth consecutive year in 1992.

If the European Community (EC) approves the Electrolux–AEG merger, however, Whirlpool's share will be threatened. Electrolux would strengthen its leadership in the European white goods market to a share of 30% (see Exhibit 6). This number compares very favorably (for Electrolux) against 15 to 19% for BSHG, 11 to 15% for WEBV, and 10% for Merloni of Italy.

Structural Changes

The formation of a single European market has spurred significant shifts in the white goods industry. Several leading firms are merging, rationalizing, and concentrating operations to gain cost advantages over competitors. Concentration will surely continue as existing products become more sophisticated and new appliances are developed.[20]

Industry trends have focused on improvements in productivity and flexibility. Following the example of the car industry, great efforts are being put into production processes. The flexibility of the industry is directed toward the still remaining differences in the European market. Although Whirlpool has reduced the number of production sites to 10, Electrolux has kept its 40 different sites while Bosch-Siemens, which concentrates mainly on the German market, has 12 sites of its own.

Exhibit 6 White Goods Market Shares in Western Europe, 1993	
Electrolux	20–25%
Bosch-Siemens	15–19%
Whirlpool Europe	11–15%
Merloni	10%
AEG Hausgerate	6%
Global White Goods Sales 1992 ($ billion)	
Whirlpool Corporation (excluding financial services)	7.1
Electrolux (75% of appliance sales)	5.8
AEG Hausgerate (85% of total sales)	1.3
	Electrolux and AEG—7.1
Electrolux	7.7
AEG Hausgerate	1.5
	Electrolux and AEG—9.2

Source: Industry.

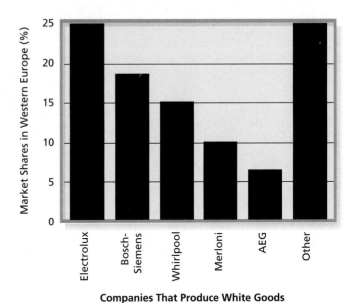

Companies That Produce White Goods

Whirlpool's European subsidiary was created to more fully leverage opportunities in the EC. Marohn considered the change "a further evolution from our former structure designed to improve efficiency."[21] Effectively, WEBV has regionalized sales and centralized logistics, marketing and information technology, and manufacturing and production technology. Exhibit 7 shows Whirlpool's manufacturing, sales, and parts distributions facilities as of 1992.

Exhibit 7   Whirlpool's European Facilities

Manufacturing Facilities

Amiens, France	Norrkeping, Sweden
Barcelona, Spain	Poprad, Slovakia
Calw, Germany	Riva di Chieri, Italy
Cassinetta, Italy	Schorndorf, Germany
Naples, Italy	Siena, Italy
Neunkirchen, Germany	Trento, Italy

Parts Distribution Centers

Comerio, Italy	Schorndorf, Germany

Sales Subsidiaries

Barcelona, Spain	Lisbon, Portugal
Brussels, Belgium	London, England
Budapest, Hungary	Nürnberg, Germany
Comerio, Italy	Osterhout, Netherlands
Dublin, Ireland	Oslo, Norway
Eindhoven, Netherlands	Paris, France
Espoo, Finland	Stuttgart, Germany
Herlev, Denmark	Vienna, Austria
Lenzburg, Switzerland	

Key: △ Parts Distribution Center ○ Sales Subsidiaries □ Manufacturing Facilities

Source: Whirlpool Corporation, 1992 *Annual Report*.

■ Sales

To meet environmental demands in the market, Whirlpool has replaced separate sales organizations in 17 countries with four regional sales offices. One region comprises Germany, Austria, Switzerland, the Netherlands, and Denmark. Another includes France, Spain, Portugal, and Belgium; the United Kingdom, Ireland, Norway, and Finland make up a third region. Italy continued to be managed separately while Eastern European interests were already managed regionally.

The new sales regions share resources and support services, take advantage of scope economies, and can respond to changing market expectations and increasing cross-border trade. Sales regions better meet the needs of customers.

■ Logistics

By centralizing the logistics function, WEBV hoped to better respond to disappearing trade borders and pending deregulation of the transport industry.

Regional WEBV distribution centers, therefore, were to take the place of a fragmented national network. It reduced the number of warehouses from 30 to 16. Management hopes to further reduce that figure to just 5 or 6.[22]

Marketing and Information Technology

Both the marketing and information technology functions were concentrated to focus on the end user. Marketing continued to search for similarities between national markets with unique, culture-based differences. It also presented the pan-European brands while remaining focused on the needs of the end user. Reorganization of the information technology areas was also intended to take the form of a borderless structure to expand the best practices of Whirlpool's previous national setup.

Manufacturing and Production Technology

By reorganizing manufacturing and technology according to product groups, WEBV developed a global technology platform and a worldwide supplier base. For example, WEBV separated laundry and dishwasher development centers in Germany from refrigeration and cooking centers in Italy to focus product development and better rationalize production processes.[23]

Through product redesign and massive cost cutting, Whirlpool aims to provide European customers with higher quality, while retaining more profits for itself. If European appliance businesses continue to consolidate, as expected, big players like Whirlpool stand a good chance of gaining significant market share.

By contrast, the stronger role of unions and political resistance to layoffs and plant closings in Europe makes the cost-cutting process longer than in the United States. Although WEBV is growing its business without expanding the workforce, the difficulty in consolidation efforts of administration, sales, and distribution organizations may frustrate some cost-cutting strategies.

Joint Ventures and Expansion

Czechoslovakia

In May 1992, Whirlpool Corporation announced that WEBV and Tatramat a.s. of Czechoslovakia had formed a joint venture. In an attempt to expand market share through expanding geographic spread in addition to volume, the agreement allowed Tatramat a.s., under the name Whirlpool Tatramat a.s., to manufacture and sell washing machines and market other major home appliances in Czechoslovakia.

Tatramat's contribution consisted of its current manufacturing assets. WEBV, holding only a 43.8 percent stake, agreed to modernize and expand the facilities while providing proprietary technology and equity. "By making and selling a more advanced model product, we expect to extend our market share even further, both in Czechoslovakia and through export to neighboring countries," said Martin Ciran, general manager of Whirlpool Tatramat.[24]

Hungary

A wholly owned sales subsidiary was established in Hungary by the parent company in April 1992. The manager of the new venture, Laszlo Gero, estimated that WEBV would be investing 50 million forints in Hungary.

WEBV's initial goal was 2.5 percent of the market for Philips-Whirlpool washing machines, dryers, refrigerators, freezers, and dishwashers. It aimed at a 10 percent share for microwave ovens. During 1992, the subsidiary tripled the number of trade customers previously served there. Within the next year, it hoped to increase its share further to 3.5 and 15 percent, respectively.[25]

■ Poland

Whirlpool's efforts to expand into Eastern European markets, particularly in the central area, continued with a sales subsidiary in Poland planned to open in the spring of 1993. Once again, the main purpose was to expand market share in the flat or even slightly shrinking industry.[26]

■ Divestitures

Whirlpool Corporation freed up capital by selling some of its assets. For example, Whirlpool sold some of its compressor business in Italy to a Brazilian business, Embraco S.A.

In June 1993, WEBV sold a refrigerator plant in Barcelona, Spain, to IAR/Siltal, an Italian home appliance maker. IAR/Siltal indicated it will continue to manufacture refrigerators at the factory and sell a part of the production to Whirlpool for distributing in Spain and elsewhere in Europe under a four-year supply contract.

For Whirlpool, these sales reflected a rationalization effort to meet customer needs and direct capital to operations best positioning WEBV for long-term growth.

■ Managerial Challenges

With Electrolux merging with AEG, WEBV executives wonder if they have positioned the firm appropriately to withstand increased competition. The slow market growth leaves them wondering whether they should expand quickly into eastern Europe. Perhaps WEBV needs to continue its rationalization efforts. But, how far can it rationalize? What kinds of shifts in population, consumer demand, and demographics can WEBV expect in the changing face of Europe? Finally, what can WEBV change (or continue doing) to maintain its growth in Europe?

■ Notes

1. *Hoover's Handbook of American Business,* 1993.
2. ICC Key Note Market Reports, 1993.
3. David R. Whitwam, 1992, President's letter to shareholders, *Whirlpool Corporation, Annual Report.*
4. Ibid.
5. Whirlpool Corporation—Board appointment, 1992, *Regulatory News Service,* September 14.
6. ICC Key Note Market Reports, 1993.
7. Robert L. Rose, 1994, Whirlpool is expanding in Europe despite the slump, *Wall Street Journal,* January 27.
8. At Domotechnica 1993 Whirlpool recaps 1992 performance and looks to the future, 1993, *Business Wire Service,* February 18.
9. Nicholas Platt, Jr., 1991, Talking point: Whirlpool Corporation, *Reuters,* June 6.
10. Whitwam, President's letter to shareholders.
11. Key Note Report on Household Appliances, ICC Key Note Market Reports, April 1993.
12. Whirlpool Corporation—4th quarter and final results, 1992, *Regulatory News Service,* February 10.
13. At Domotechnica 1993 Whirlpool recaps 1992 performance.
14. Whitwam, President's letter to shareholders.

15. Whirlpool Corporation—4th quarter and final results.

16. Electrolux—Final results, 1994, *Regulatory News Service,* March 2.

17. Foron Sees Demand for Its 'Eco-Refrigerators' Outstrip Production, 1993, *Süddeutsche Zeitung,* July 26.

18. Electrolux to increase Lehel investment, 1993, *Finance East Europe,* April 22.

19. Mat Toor, 1993, UK: Hoover builds European base, *Marketing,* August 19.

20. France: White goods sector likely to concentrate further, 1993, *L'Usine Nouvelle,* June 3.

21. Whirlpool Corporation—Board appointment, 1992, *Regulatory News Service,* September 14.

22. Rose, Whirlpool is expanding in Europe.

23. Whirlpool Corporation—Board appointment.

24. Whirlpool Corporation subs Czech joint venture, 1993, *Extel Examiner,* May 12.

25. Whirlpool International sets up subsidiary in Hungary, 1992, *AFX News,* April 6.

26. Whirlpool to open Polish sales subsidiary, 1993, *Reuters,* February 17.

■ CASE 36 **Wil-Mor Technologies, Inc.**

Andrew Inkpen
University of Western Ontario

In February 1991, David McNeil, CEO of Wilson Industries Inc. (Wilson), was meeting with Ron Berks, the president of Wilson's North American Automotive Division. "Ron, the situation with the Wil-Mor joint venture (JV) does not seem to be improving," said McNeil. "After three years it is still losing money. What's going on down there?" Berks, a JV board member and the Wilson executive who initiated the JV formation, realized there was a problem but was not sure what to do. Not only were the JV managers not concerned, they were talking about expansion. Wilson's Japanese JV partner did not even want to discuss profitability; all they seemed to care about was lowering costs and keeping the JV's largest customer happy. McNeil emphasized that something had to be done, adding, "When we formed this venture you predicted it would reach breakeven by the second year of operation. We are not even close to that after three years."

■ Wilson Industries Inc.

Wilson, a Detroit-based company founded in 1923, was a manufacturer of plastic and metal parts for the automotive and appliance industries. Total sales in 1990 were $360 million of which $210 million came from the North American Automotive Division. The Automotive Division produced plastic parts such as wheel trim covers, bumper reinforcements, plastic trim, and battery trays. Ford and Chrysler accounted for 80 percent of Wilson's sales with the remainder going to General Motors. For several years, the Automotive Division's sales had remained flat and profits had been decreasing.

In recent years, Wilson had taken steps to internationalize its automotive operations. In 1983, exports began to Germany and a small plant was purchased in England. Besides Wil-Mor, a JV was launched in 1988 to distribute Wilson products in Australia.

This case was prepared for the sole purpose of providing material for class discussion at the Western Business School. Certain names and other identifying information may have been disguised to protect confidentiality. It is not intended to illustrate either effective or ineffective handling of a managerial situation.
Copyright 1991 © The University of Western Ontario.

The Automobile Industry

The North American automobile industry changed dramatically in the 1980s. The primary impetus for much of the change was the emergence of the Japanese producers as leading competitors. In 1981, there were no Japanese assembly plants in North America. By 1990, there were nine Japanese-operated assembly plants in the United States and three in Canada. These plants produced 1.8 million cars in 1990, more than 20 percent of total North American production. By the end of 1990, the Japanese assembly plants, referred to as transplants, had combined capacity in place or announced to make 2.3 million vehicles per year. Transplant production, plus imports from all countries, accounted for more than 40 percent of the units sold in North America. With the growth in transplant capacity, some industry observers were projecting that North American automobile capacity could exceed demand by three million units or more during the 1990s.

The three largest Japanese companies, Honda, Nissan, and Toyota, were being referred to as the "other Big 3." They were becoming full-fledged North American producers capable of designing, engineering, and assembling vehicles entirely in North America. Toyota, for example, had an objective of 75 percent North American content in its cars by 1992. Nissan was in the process of completing a modern engineering center near Detroit that would have employment of 600 by 1992. Honda was sourcing about 75 percent of its parts and components in North America and 25 to 30 percent of its tooling and equipment. In 1990, Honda, for the first time, sold more cars in North America built domestically than imported from Japan.

Automotive Suppliers

The typical car is composed of more than 10,000 parts. In the initial years of the automobile industry, carmakers tried to produce as many parts in-house as possible. By the 1950s, outsourcing of parts from independent suppliers had become commonplace. Suppliers were given blueprints and asked to bid on parts contracts. The lowest bidder generally was awarded the contract, usually for one year. In the 1980s, the world's automobile companies were all using outsourcing to some degree. General Motors was the most integrated company with 70 percent of its parts made in-house. Saab, on the other hand, made only 25 percent of its own parts.

In the 1980s, the North American companies increased their outsourcing and made substantial cuts in the number of suppliers they dealt with. The customer–supplier relationship began to shift to a structure based on tiers of suppliers. The first tier suppliers dealt directly with the vehicle manufacturers and, increasingly, participated jointly in the design of new systems and parts. The first tier suppliers coordinated the operations of many smaller second tier suppliers who, in turn, worked with their own subsuppliers. The advantage of this multilayer approach, used by the Japanese producers for many years, was that the automakers could deal with a limited number of companies and work closely with them in design and engineering.

Besides the move toward outsourcing and multitiered supplier arrangements, several other trends characterized the supplier industry. One, automakers were pushing their suppliers toward just-in-time delivery systems and increased investment in design and engineering capabilities. Two, mergers were becoming prevalent in the supplier sector, largely because of the heavy demands for research and development, new equipment, and employee training. Three, suppliers were moving away from their traditional focus on home markets toward foreign investment. For example, more than 300 Japan-based supplier firms had operations in North America, most of which had arrived in 1987–1988.

The arrival of the transplant automakers was the major reason Japanese suppliers were locating in North America. However, many of these suppliers were making inroads into the domestic automakers as well. The implications were clear: Like the situation with automaking capacity, excess capacity at the supplier level was becoming a reality. The overcapacity and competition from foreign-based component suppliers were creating increasingly difficult conditions for North American automotive suppliers. One senior manager in a U.S. component supplier stated:

> The next five years are going to be horrible. With the new Japanese companies coming in, with peripheral capacity, and with component integration and the car companies all chasing the same market . . . a lot of suppliers are going to fall out.[1]

The Transplants

By the mid-1980s, with the traditional North American market eroding, many suppliers, including Wilson, saw a potentially lucrative market in supplying the transplants. The transplants were committed to North American content and were rapidly building up their manufacturing capacity. Unfortunately, becoming a supplier to a transplant firm was proving to be very difficult for many North American-based firms. North American companies were often unfamiliar with the rigors of Japanese just-in-time inventory systems and demands for flexible production. A further problem frustrating the efforts of North American suppliers was that unlike their North American competitors, the Japanese automakers rarely changed suppliers. For example, Toyota's supplier base had remained virtually unchanged since the 1950s. Many of the Japanese suppliers were partially owned by the automakers and, as part of a keiretsu, had a relationship that was much stronger than a North American supplier relationship. The president of Nissan's U.S. operations explained:

> Nissan's mix of U.S. suppliers and Japanese suppliers is not likely to change much. Given our philosophy, once you become our supplier you're our supplier forever on that part, unless you mess up so bad we can't fix you."[2]

The Japanese firms put much more emphasis on trust and cooperation in the supplier relationship. As one supplier executive commented:

> The North American supplier relationship is often adversarial. The supplier usually works with the blueprint provided by the automaker. You manufacture according to the blueprint and if the part doesn't fit, "you tell your customer to stuff it." With Honda our relationship is supportive as long as we deliver the product. And, the blueprint is only the starting point. The part must fit the car; if it doesn't Honda will say "what can we do together to make it fit?" If you ship 150 bad parts to General Motors, they will tell you that you have a problem and you better fix it fast. Honda may say you have a problem but they will also say "how can we help you fix it?" The Japanese customer will not use its power to threaten or harass the supplier. Once the marriage is formed they will try to make it work.

In North America, the threat that supplier contracts could be cancelled or moved in-house had created a system in which, according to some observers, neither party fully trusted the other. By contrast, the Japanese approach was based on long-term relationships, mutual discussion, and bargaining. While suppliers were expected to decrease prices over the term of the contract, joint activities between supplier and automaker were critical to the relationship. According to one study, "The [Japanese] system replaces a vicious circle of mistrust with a virtuous circle of cooperation."[3]

Of course, the Japanese automakers could, and did, fire their suppliers. When it became obvious that a supplier could no longer meet the exacting quality standards or improve on cost and quality, the Japanese customer was as likely to look for a new supplier as an American customer. The difference was that the Japanese automaker would expend more effort in assisting the supplier than was typical in the North American context. In addition, the Japanese companies usually kept their suppliers better informed about their performance relative to other suppliers.

■ The JV Formation

In 1983, Ron Berks was convinced that the transplant share of the North American market would continue to grow. He began to explore the possibility of becoming a supplier to the transplant firms. He made several trips to Japan and initiated discussions with Honda America in Ohio. However, after several years of fruitless efforts, he became convinced that access to the Japanese transplants was virtually closed to North American companies that did not have an established relationship with a Japanese firm.

In the meantime, the Japanese presence in the automobile industry continued to grow. The transplant automakers were encouraging their Japanese suppliers to build plants in North America in order to maintain established customer relationships and also, because of political pressure, increased domestic content was a priority. While some of the larger suppliers already had operations in North America, most did not. Trepidation about starting a new facility in North America and pressure from the Japanese automakers to involve local firms in the supply chain encouraged many Japanese suppliers to form JVs with American partners.

In late 1985, Berks first considered the feasibility of forming a JV. An obvious choice for a JV partner was Morota Manufacturing Company Ltd. (Morota). For several years, Wilson had been involved in a licensing agreement with Morota. Morota, founded in 1950, was a manufacturer of small electric motors for products such as sewing machines and small appliances and also produced various plastic components for the automobile industry. Morota had sales of $320 million in 1990 with $180 million to the automobile industry. About 70 percent of the automobile sales were to Toyota with the remainder going to Nissan, Honda, and Mitsubishi. Toyota owned 10 percent of the shares in Morota. Except for a JV in Korea, Morota had limited international experience.

Berks knew that Morota wanted a plant in North America. In early 1986, he contacted the president of Morota and set up a meeting in Japan for July. Berks learned at the meeting that Morota was being encouraged by Toyota to form a JV in North America. He also learned that Morota was "internationally naive and probably scared to death to come to the U.S. They were particularly worried about dealing with an American workforce." At the meeting, the two firms agreed to work toward forming a JV.

■ The JV Agreement

JV discussions between Wilson and Morota started in late 1986 and six months later a JV agreement was signed. The JV was named Wil-Mor Technologies, Inc. (Wil-Mor). Initially, Berks had hoped that Wilson would have about 70 percent ownership. However, although the Morota executives would not say so explicitly, Berks sensed that there would be problems with Toyota if Wilson had a majority position. Berks therefore agreed to 50/50 ownership. The JV agreement specified that Wilson would be responsible for locating a plant site and managing the workforce. Morota would be responsible for the equipment acquisitions and installation. Morota would provide initial engineering support and help train the workforce, both in Japan and the United States. Morota would also work with Toyota to ensure that the JV had contracts when the JV became operational.

The JV president would be nominated by Morota and the general manager would be nominated by Wilson. These two managers would be responsible for the JV startup. The JV board would include three executives from each firm. From Wilson, there would be Berks, an Automotive Division vice president, and the JV general manager. Morota's representatives would include Morota's president, its executive vice president, and the JV president.

Berks was very enthusiastic about the JV's potential. After the JV announcement in early 1987, his opinion was that the joint venture was a very important strategic move for Wilson. The JV was seen as an extension of Wilson's existing operation that would help increase market share and provide access to a growing segment of the market. The JV would also help Wilson learn from its Japanese partner. There was even some thought that in a few years, the JV would be able to export parts back to Japan.

■ Start-up

Berks thought that an experienced American manager should be general manager. He selected 58-year-old Dan Johnson, a Wilson employee for 30 years and most recently a plant manager. The president, Akio Sakiya, was 55 years old and had spent his entire career with Morota. Although an engineer by training, he was vice president of finance prior to becoming the JV president.

Johnson was given the task of selecting the plant site. He chose Elizabethtown, Kentucky, a small town south of Louisville and close to the new Toyota plant in Georgetown. The initial investment in the JV was $18.2 million. Each partner contributed $3 million; the other $12.2 million was borrowed by the JV and guaranteed by the partners.

The JV plant was based on the manufacturing system used by Morota. Most of the equipment in the plant was Japanese. Morota put together a Japanese team of engineers and technical specialists. This team was responsible for installing the equipment, getting the process started, and training the workforce. The workforce was hired by Johnson and Sakiya. Their emphasis was on young people with little or no manufacturing experience (from Morota's perspective, "no bad habits"). Both partners wanted to keep the JV union-free.

Exhibit 1

Wil-Mor Technologies, Inc.,
Organization Chart

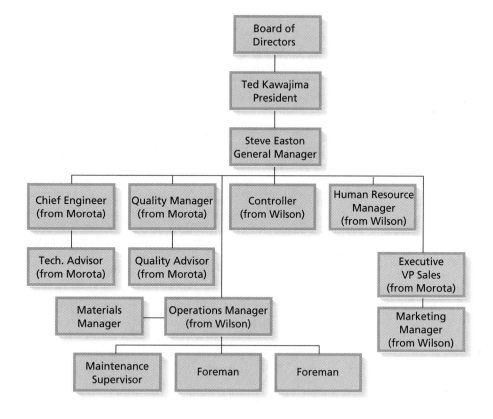

The JV began operations in early 1988 with contracts from NUMMI, the JV between General Motors and Toyota, and Toyota's new Georgetown plant, which would open later in the year. All contracts were for plastic trim parts, identical to parts made in Japan by Morota and very similar to parts made by Wilson for their Big Three customers. The initial start-up was done very slowly and for some months there was only enough work for about two to three days a week. The start-up, slower than Wilson would have liked, was based on Morota's attitude of "training before operating."

■ JV Management

Besides the president and general manager, JV management came from both partners. Wilson provided the operations manager, human resource manager, controller, and a marketing manager. None of these managers had any Japanese language capability or experience with the transplants. Morota provided the engineering manager, the quality manager, and a marketing manager (Exhibit 1 shows an organization chart). None of these managers had any prior international experience and except for the marketing manager, had only limited English language skills. The Japanese managers, including the president, had three-to five-year visas. At the end of the visa terms these managers would be rotated back to the Japanese parent. The American managers were in the JV for an indefinite period. The partners hoped that eventually, the Japanese managers could be replaced by American managers promoted from within the JV.

The JV did not begin smoothly. The Japanese managers insisted on complete technical responsibility. Johnson, the general manager, was not allowed to assist in the technical setup. This caused several problems because the Japanese were unfamiliar with many of the basic aspects of establishing a new plant, especially one in North America. The Japanese insisted on running the operation their way. They used a Japanese approach in selecting suppliers. Johnson estimated he could have saved the JV about $250,000 a year if a North American approach had been used to select suppliers. However, the Japanese insisted that if possible, suppliers should be selected not just on the basis of price but because they had established themselves as capable suppliers to Wilson or Morota.

When the JV started, the Japanese managers were initially skeptical about the ability of an American workforce to produce a quality product. They wondered: Can they run the machines properly? Do they know what a good product is? The Japanese managers drove the workers very hard at the outset. Several times Sakiya became furious with what he saw on the shop floor and berated the workers in Japanese.

Johnson became convinced that the Japanese managers were deliberately excluding him from the management process. The Japanese managers would regularly hold meetings and exclude the Americans. When meetings were held with both Americans and Japanese present they would last for hours because of the necessity to translate from English to Japanese. In addition, the Japanese managers corresponded daily by fax with their head office in Japan and would meet socially in the evenings and on weekends. The inevitable result was two distinct management "camps": the Americans and the Japanese.

By March 1989, it was obvious to Ron Berks that there were serious management problems in the JV. Although the contracts with Toyota seemed to be working out well, the plant was still running at far less than capacity. Very few decisions in the JV were "joint" because the Americans and Japanese rarely talked to each other. The American managers were looking after areas such as materials sourcing, human resources, accounting, and finance. The Japanese managers concentrated on product design, quality, pricing, and sales.

Berks discussed the situation with Morota's president. They decided to replace the JV president and the general manager. The new general manager, Steve Easton, was 46 and a former plant manager who had recently been working at Wilson headquarters in an international development position. The new president was 51-year-old Ted Kawajima, an engineer with several years of international experience and an excellent command of English.

■ The New Management Team

The new management team got off to a much better start than the previous one. Both Easton and Kawajima were avid golfers. They began playing golf together regularly and involved several of the other managers. Gradually, the tension between the American and Japanese "camps" began to ease. Although the regular faxing between the JV and Japan continued, meetings of Japanese managers became less frequent.

The JV was also successful in winning new contracts with Toyota and was quoting on some work for Mazda and Ford. Through the NUMMI relationship, initial contacts were established with General Motors. At first, General Motors was reluctant to deal with Wil-Mor. Because Morota was partially owned by

Toyota, there was a belief that buying from the JV was, in effect, subsidizing the competition. However, that belief was slowly disappearing as more and more Japanese suppliers became established in North America. By early 1990, Wil-Mor had successfully bid on several General Motors contracts. The JV customer mix was now about 80 percent Toyota, 10 percent General Motors, and 10 percent NUMMI. The JV was actively seeking new customers and was encouraged by Toyota to do so.

Annual sales in the JV were now close to $30 million. Employment had reached 300 and the plant was close to capacity. Although the JV was still losing money, Easton and Kawajima were considering a possible expansion.

■ Head Office Concerns

Ron Berks was pleased by the improved managerial situation in the JV but was troubled by a financial situation that did not seem to be improving. He knew at the outset that it would take a few years for the JV to become profitable. However, based on Morota's estimates, he thought that the JV could at least be at breakeven by the end of 1989 and making a profit by 1990. In early 1991 the JV was still losing about $100,000 a month.

Even more troubling was the fact that at the most recent JV board meeting in November 1990, the Morota executives did not seem concerned that the JV was losing money. In fact, they seemed pleased that the losses were not greater. At the board meeting, when Berks questioned the JV's performance, Kawajima replied that the JV was meeting expectations and was exceeding Toyota's quality standards. He went on to say that the JV still had to get its costs down and had some way to go before quality was at a level consistent with that in Morota's Japan plants. When Berks angrily asked how many years it would be before there was a profit, Kawajima replied that:

> Profit is obviously important but to achieve profitability there has to be a satisfied base of customers. We have achieved a good record with Toyota and now we are trying to build a relationship with General Motors. I think that we are in a very strong position.

Berks left the board meeting without a clear understanding of the Japanese expectations about profits in the JV. They seemed concerned only about the quality of the product and not about making money.

■ Easton's Perspective

Steve Easton knew that Berks, his boss, was concerned about the JV performance. He explained:

> There is an unresolvable conflict in the relationship between the partners. Morota is willing to lose money in the JV for as long as it takes to build up market share and quality in North America. Right now, their primary focus is on customer service and product improvement, not profit. They intend to be in this market for the long term and they know that Toyota plans to increase its North American capacity. Morota is determined to make money in North America but is willing to be patient. They believe that if there is a quality product and low costs, profit will take care of itself. They cannot answer the question about when the JV will be profitable because it is not consistent with their philosophy. Their approach is that prices are not the issue, costs must be improved first.

When the JV was formed, the partners thought that they were in sync about prices and profit margins that might be expected. Clearly, that was an incorrect assumption. Wilson wanted to make a quick buck; they were skeptical of making long-term investments. They saw the JV as a way to make some money. They expected a profit in two or three years. Morota expected the JV to lose money for about five or six years. However, they never communicated this to Wilson and no business plan was prepared.

Easton suspected that part of the problem was that Berks did not do his homework when the JV was formed. He commented:

The JV was started on blind faith. Each partner had some expectations about the other which have not been met. Wilson expected faster production and higher efficiency. The only thing certain at the outset was that Toyota would be a customer. Berks expected that a share of Toyota's business would be great to have and that it would be profitable. Unfortunately, nobody in Wilson had any idea of the potential profitability of supplying the transplants.

The reality is that we are unable to get the same kind of profit margins with Toyota as we can with the Big Three. We make more money on the parts we sell to GM than on the parts we sell to Toyota. A lot of suppliers are starting to say that transplant business is not good business because the prices are too low.

Easton also sensed that there was some resentment in Wilson toward the JV and an unwillingness to acknowledge openly that the JV provided an excellent learning opportunity:

I have given other Wilson managers an open invitation to visit the JV and see what we are doing. There has been some response to my invitations but there seems to be some resentment toward us. When I attend corporate meetings at Wilson, I show people what we are doing and it is clear that the JV is outperforming the other Wilson plants on a quality basis. In terms of reject rates, we beat Wilson by 10 times. Wilson talks about quality but we do it. I don't like to brag about our success in the JV but what I would like to see is an interest by the other Wilson managers in finding out why the JV is able to do so well.

The JV and the relationship with Toyota has put Wilson in a position to start questioning their capabilities. Berks would like to have Toyota as a customer so he invited Toyota purchasing managers to visit the Wilson plants. Toyota reported back to Wilson and the report was scathing. Berks's attitude was "these guys are just unreasonable."

Berks has acknowledged that some changes at Wilson may be necessary but he has avoided the serious questions. The reality is that Wilson would have to cross a lot of hurdles to get any Toyota business. However, the senior management at Wilson don't know that and would be surprised to find out. They have not addressed it and it is not a priority because of their existing business. My own belief is that Wilson has not grasped what world-class manufacturing is.

On the relationship between the partners, Easton commented:

Kawajima and the Morota executives realize that Berks is not pleased with the JV performance. However, they view their relationship with Wilson from a long-term perspective. They intend to succeed in North America and assume that Wilson thinks the same way. Should Wilson express some desire to end the JV, Kawajima and the other Morota executives would be shocked and take it as a serious affront. From their perspective, strengthening the relationship between the partners is critical to the success of the JV.

■ The Current Situation

The meeting with David McNeil left Berks in a difficult position. Berks was aware that at Wilson headquarters, there was growing opposition to the JV because it was not making money. Some managers were even starting to question Morota's capabilities, arguing that if they can't make money when they have a new plant and a guaranteed customer, how can we ever hope to learn anything from them?

McNeil wanted to see a JV return on investment at least as high as the other Wilson plants but Berks did not know when that would happen. At a meeting with Easton the previous week, Easton had assured him that Wil-Mor had the potential to be a leading supplier to both the transplants and the Big Three. Easton had also said that an expansion would soon be necessary. Berks knew that McNeil would never approve further capital investment until the JV started showing a profit. However, Easton argued that without expanding, the JV would lose market share and would probably take even longer to become profitable.

Ron Berks wondered what should be done about the JV. Maybe Wilson should cut its losses and get out of the JV. Or, perhaps it would be better if Wilson lowered its ownership interest to about 20 percent. That would reduce Wilson's share of the losses and would allow Wilson to maintain its relationship with Morota. Whatever the decision, Berks knew that McNeil was expecting something to be done very soon.

■ Notes

1. *Ward's Auto World,* 1989, no. 7, p. 37.

2. *Ward's Auto World,* February 1991, p. 29.

3. James P. Womack, Daniel T. Jones, and Daniel Roos, 1990, *The Machine that Changed the World* (New York: Rawson Associates), 150.

■ http://www.xel.com/

■ CASE 37 XEL Communications, Inc.

Robert P. McGowan
Cynthia V. Fukami
University of Denver

As he turned into the parkway that curves around his company's plant, Bill Sanko, president of XEL Communications, glanced at a nearby vacant facility that once housed a now-defunct computer manufacturer. During the next few months, in May 1995, XEL would be moving into this building. While this move was a sign of how far XEL had come in the last 10 years, Bill considered that they might have met the same fate as the previous tenant. He also wondered whether they would be able to sustain the same culture that enabled the company to succeed in a rapidly changing, highly competitive industry. At the same time, he realized that change could also create opportunities.

After parking and completing the short walk to his office, Bill grabbed a copy of today's *Wall Street Journal*. One article that caught his attention was titled, "Baby Bells Lobby Congress for Regulatory Freedom." As one of many suppliers of telecommunications equipment to the Regional Bell Operating Companies (RBOCs), this development posed some interesting issues for XEL Communications. If the RBOCs were allowed to pursue their own manufacturing (which they are currently prohibited from doing), how would this affect XEL's existing contracts? As telephone and cable companies develop more strategic alliances and partnerships, would this provide an opportunity for XEL? At the same time, it appeared that the telecommunications industry was becoming a global industry in which developing countries allowed outside companies the ability to establish and maintain telecommunications services. What role could XEL play in this rapidly growing market?

■ The Telecommunications Industry

A decade after the breakup of the telephone monopoly, the prospect of intense competition driving the telecommunications industry created some interesting scenarios.[1] The AT&T of old was the model for the telecommunications company of the future. "You're going to see the re-creation of five or six former AT&Ts—call them 'full-service networks'—over the next five years or more," said Michael Elling, first vice president at Prudential Securities. Marketing and

---

Presented at the Annual Meetings of the North American Case Research Association, Orlando, Florida, November 1995. Copyright © 1995 by the authors.

capital equipment dollars are invested more efficiently if distribution is centralized, he continued. "It could be that U S West, Time Warner, and Sprint get together. It could be that Bell Atlantic, Nynex, and MCI get together. It could be that GTE, AT&T, and a few other independents (local providers not affiliated with a regional Bell) get together."

The inevitability of such combinations was matched by the uncertainty over what form they would take. A business known for its predictability had suddenly found itself unpredictable. "I think you can't rule anything out in this industry anymore," says Simon Flannery, a vice president at J.P. Morgan Securities. "All the rules of the game are up for review."

In most cases, telecommunications systems transmitted information by wire, radio, or space satellite. Wire transmission involved sending electrical signals over various types of wire lines such as open wire, multipair cable, and coaxial cable. These lines could be used to transmit voice frequencies, telegraph messages, computer-processed data, and television programs. Another somewhat related transmission medium that had come into increasingly wider use, especially in telephone communications, was a type of cable composed of optical fibers. Here, electrical signals converted to light signals by a laser-driven transmitter carried both speech and data over bundles of thin glass or plastic filaments.

Radio communication systems transmitted electronic signals in relatively narrow frequency bands through the air. They included radio navigation and both amateur and commercial broadcasting. Commercial broadcasting consisted of AM, FM, and TV broadcasting for general public use.

Satellite communications allowed the exchange of television or telephone signals between widely separated locations by means of microwaves—that is, very short radio waves with wavelengths from 4 to 0.4 inches, which corresponded to a frequency range of 3 to 30 gigahertz (GHz), or 3 to 30 billion cycles per second. Because satellite systems did not require the construction of intermediate relay or repeater stations, as did ground-based microwave systems, they could be put into service much more rapidly.

Not only had the mode of delivery changed, but also the content. Modern telecommunications networks not only sent the traditional voice communications of telephones and the printed messages of telegraphs and telexes, they also carried images—the still images of facsimile machines or the moving images of video in video conferences in which the participants could see as well as hear each other. Additionally, they carried encoded data ranging from the business accounts of a multinational corporation to medical data relayed by physicians thousands of miles from a patient.

The U.S. telecommunications services industry was expected to continue to expand in 1994.[2] Revenues were expected to rise about 7.7 percent, compared with a 6 percent increase in 1993. In 1994, revenues generated by international services increased about 20 percent, and local exchange telephone service was expected to rise by 3 percent. Sales of domestic long-distance services were expected to grow more than 6 percent in 1994, depending on overall growth in the economy. Value-added network and information services were to climb an estimated 15 percent in 1994. Revenues from cellular mobile telephone services were to increase 39 percent in 1994; satellite service revenues in 1994 were to grow nearly 25 percent.

Local telephone services were provided by about 1,325 local telephone companies (telcos), including seven RBOCs, telcos owned by GTE, Sprint (United Telecom and Centel franchises), and independent local telephone companies. Many of these small, local companies operated as rural telephone cooperatives. Long-distance service was provided by AT&T, MCI, Sprint, WilTel, Metromedia Communications, Litel Telecommunications, Allnet, and more than 475 smaller companies.

In 1993, the local exchange telephone companies were confronted with increasing competitive pressures in certain local services they had monopolized for decades. In response to these pressures, and to possible future competition from cable TV companies and others for local exchange telephone service itself, the RBOCs stepped up their campaign to obtain authority to enter the long-distance and telecommunications equipment manufacturing businesses, and to offer video programming services.

The major long-distance carriers, meanwhile, focused their attention on wireless technologies and made plans to work with or acquire companies in the wireless market. This would enable them to provide long-distance services to cellular users and possibly to develop a more economical local access network to reach their own subscribers. Internationally, the large service providers continued to make alliances and seek out partners in efforts to put together global telecommunications networks and offer the international equivalent of the advanced telecommunications services available in the U.S. domestic market.

In terms of policy developments that affect the telecommunications industry, the Clinton Administration had focused its attention on the national telecommunications infrastructure, or the "information superhighway." Bills were introduced in both houses of Congress that addressed this and other key telecommunications policy issues. There was broad consensus that the federal government should not finance the construction of a national network. Rather, the government was being urged to help promote competition in network access, advance interconnection and interoperability standards, see that customers would have access to new services provided over the digital infrastructure at reasonable rates, and support pilot projects for applications in education and health care. Under proposed legislation, the digital infrastructure would be extended to tap information resources at libraries, research centers, and government facilities. Congress was to consider major telecommunications legislation in the future and then face how it would resolve the contentious issues involved that concerned so many large and powerful interests. There were also signs that some states would also open up their exchange and local service markets to competition.

Cable TV companies were likely to become another group of competitors the local telephone companies would face in the near future. Cable companies already had connections with 60 percent of U.S. households, and cable facilities extended into areas where another 30 percent of the households were located. New digital and fiber optic technologies would allow them to provide telephone services over their networks, something cable companies already were doing in Britain.

XEL Communications: The Beginning

XEL Communications was born not only with an opportunity but with a challenge as well. Bill Sanko started with General Telephone and Electronics (GTE) as a product manager after spending six years in the U.S. Army.[3] He was chosen in 1972 to help establish the GTE Satellite Corporation. After he was successful with this enterprise, GTE then selected Bill for another start-up business called Special Service Products in 1980.

The Special Service Products division (SSPD) was established to manufacture certain telecommunications products to compete with small companies who were making inroads into GTE's market. These products ranged from voice and data transmission products to switches customized to specific business needs. After two previous failures, it was GTE's third (and perhaps final) try at starting such a division. Company officials granted Sanko almost full autonomy to build the division, including recruiting all key executives, establishing a location in Aurora, Colorado, a rapidly growing region east of Denver, and in designing the division's overall operating philosophy.

By 1984, the division realized its first year of break-even operations, but it wasn't enough to win over GTE executives. Despite its initial success and the prospect of a fast-growing market, SSPD found itself heading toward orphan status in GTE's long-range plans.[4] After divestiture in telecommunications, GTE opted to concentrate primarily on providing telephone service rather than hardware. (GTE has subsequently divested all of its manufacturing divisions.) "Even though we were doing the job expected of us in building the business," Sanko said, "GTE's and SSPD's strategic plans were taking different directions." They opted to close the division. Sanko lobbied and ultimately persuaded GTE to sell the division.

The result was an action as unlikely as it was logical. On July 3, 1984, appropriately one day before Independence Day, Sanko and fellow managers from SSPD signed a letter of intent to buy the division from GTE. Two months later, the bill of sale was signed and XEL Communications, Inc., became an independent company. Sanko gathered a group of managers and raised the money—some through second mortgages on homes. GTE loaned Sanko and his colleagues money, and the rest was supplied by venture capitalists. In fact, just before the new company was scheduled to begin operations, one of the banks backed out of the arrangement. According to Julie Rich, one of the cofounders and vice president for human resources, "we didn't have any money lined up from September to December of 1984. Making the first payroll for a company of 180 employees was one of the major challenges. Christmas that first year was particularly lean."

The financing was eventually arranged, and XEL was under way. Sanko reflected on the perils and rewards of leaving the corporate nest to seek one's fortune: "In the end, it was the right thing to do, but it wasn't an easy decision to make. After 17 years with GTE, I had achieved vice president status; and I was more than a little nervous about leaving the corporation."[5]

■ Early Years

One of the more interesting exercises in starting any new company is what to name it. John Puckett, vice president for manufacturing and also one of the original founders, recalled: "We did a lot of brainstorming about what to call this new company—including taking initials from the original founders' names and seeing what combinations we could come up with. Usually, they didn't make a whole lot of sense. We finally decided on XEL which is a shortened version of excellence."

More than simply naming the company, one of the key concerns for XEL Communications was whether their customers would stay with them once they were no longer part of GTE. Not that XEL has ever exactly been an abandoned child. GTE may have kicked XEL out the door in 1984, but it remains XEL's biggest customer, with GTE Telephone Operations accounting for about 35 percent of the company's total business. In fact, the relationship between the two companies continues to be close and mutually beneficial: Ever the proud parent, GTE recognized XEL as its Quality Vendor of the Year in both 1987 and 1988, and as a Vendor of Excellence in subsequent years.

At first, all XEL produced was a handful of products for GTE. Even so, the company showed a profit in its first year of independent operation. "We were off to a better start than you might expect, just because we had always had a certain independence," says Sanko. "We had our own engineers, we were a non-union shop (unlike most of the other divisions of GTE at the time), we had installed our own computer systems, and we were out here in Colorado, on our own. We were doing things differently from the start, and so we just continued."

Weaning itself from GTE was a corporate goal entirely dependent on new product development, and XEL spent over 10 percent of its revenues on R&D. That focus on development was not likely to change: The XEL product line is custom manufactured and therefore it constantly evolved and changed as customers' needs changed. "Running a small company has a lot of challenges," Sanko says. "But one of the major advantages is being able to respond to the market and get things done quickly. Here we can respond to a customer requirement."

XEL's Products and Markets

For example, XEL sold products that facilitated the transmission of data and information over phone lines. Driving the need for XEL's products was the fact that "businesses are more and more dependent on the transfer of information," as Bill Sanko noted. In addition, more businesses, including XEL, were operating by taking and filling orders, for example—through electronic data exchanges. Instead of dialing into inside salespeople, businesses often accessed databases directly.

XEL's products performed a number of functions that allowed businesses to incorporate their specific telecommunications needs into the existing telephone "network" functions such as data exchanges. XEL had a diverse product line of over 300 products that it manufactures. Some of its major products included:

- fiber optic terminal products,
- coaxial business access,
- analog voice products,
- analog data products,
- digital data products,
- digital transmission, and
- telecom maintenance products.

XEL's products would, for example, translate analog information into digital transmissions. Adapting electronic information for fiber optic networks was another area of emphasis for XEL, as was adapting equipment to international standards for foreign customers.

One of XEL's strengths was its ability to adapt one manufacturer's equipment to another's. Often, it was the bits and pieces of telecommunications equipment that XEL provided to the "network" that allowed the smooth integration of disparate transmission pieces. XEL also sold central office transmission equipment and a full range of mechanical housings, specialty devices, power supplies, and shelves.

"Business customers and their changing telecommunications needs drive the demand for XEL's products. That, in turn, presents a challenge to the company," said Sanko. Sanko cited the constant stream of new products developed by XEL—approximately two per month—as the driving force behind its growth. Industry-wide, product life cycle times were getting ever shorter. Before the breakup of the Bell System in 1984, transmission switches and other telecommunications devices enjoyed a 30- to-40-year life. In 1995, with technology moving so fast, XEL's products had about a 3- to 5-year life.

In terms of its customers, XEL sold to all of the RBOCs as well as such companies as GTE and Centel. Railroads, with their own telephone networks, were also customers. XEL's field salespeople worked with engineers to satisfy client requests for specific services. Over a period of time, a rapport was built up with these engineers, providing XEL with new product leads.

With all the consolidations and ventures in telecommunications, one may suspect that the overall market would become more difficult, but Sanko believed "out of change comes opportunity. The worst-case scenario would be a static situation. Thus, a small company, fast to respond to customer needs and able to capitalize on small market niches, will be successful. Often, a large company like AT&T will forsake a smaller market and XEL will move in. Also, XEL's size allows it to design a product in a very short time."

Interestingly, Sanko was watching pending federal legislation proposing to open up local telephone services to companies other than the regional Baby Bells. Consequently, said Sanko, "we need to expand our market and be prepared to sell to others as the regulatory environment changes." Sanko believed legislation would be signed in the near future that would set the groundwork and timetables to open local telephone monopolies to competition. The recent joint venture between Time Warner and US West also signaled that telephone and cable companies would be pooling their resources to provide a broader array of information services.

As for the future, Sanko saw "a lot of opportunities we can't even now imagine."

■ The XEL Vision

In addition to the issue of developing products and maintaining customer loyalty, XEL also had to deal with a number of important "people" issues. "We had good, sound management practices right from the beginning," Sanko said.[6] "We were competing with small companies that did not have the control systems, discipline, and planning experience that we had gained as part of GTE. Coming from a large arena, we could start from the top down and tailor the procedures to our needs, rather than, as many small businesses do, have to start developing controls from the bottom and then apply them—hopefully in time."

Yet, while bringing such experiences from GTE proved to be quite valuable, there were also a number of thorny issues that emerged. The first one involved people. As with any transition, there were those people that the owners wished to bring on to the new team and those whose future, for whatever reasons, was not with this new organization. "We were fortunate that personnel from GTE worked in tandem with us in this people transition phase," noted Julie Rich. "We spent a great deal of time talking people through it."

There were other critical human resource issues as well. One of the first ones was the design of the benefits package for the people. Under GTE, XEL had a traditional benefits package with little employee selection. To be competitive as well as cost effective, Rich needed to design a package that had to be reduced from 42 percent of overall payroll costs to 30 percent. She also wanted to create a package that was flexible and allowed the individual some latitude. "One approach we instituted was to allow individuals to have an allowance for total time off as opposed to so many days for sick leave, vacation, and the like. Its primary purpose was to bring down costs. And while it did succeed in this regard, we did have occasions in which people were coming to work sick rather than use this time."

Another approach was to institute a cafeteria plan of benefits in which the individual would select the specific benefits they would like to receive as part of an overall package. "The cafeteria approach was just beginning to be discussed by organizations at this time (1984)," noted Rich. "We felt there were a great deal of pluses to this approach; and it allowed the employee some discretion."

One critical issue that XEL wanted to address was developing a culture that would distinguish them from others and would also demonstrate that they were no longer a division of a large corporation. So, beginning in 1985 and carrying over into 1986, Julie Rich did a lot of reading and research on changing culture. By 1986, a first draft of these ideas and principles was developed. Rich reflected on this initial effort: "Once we developed 'XEL's Commitment to XEL-ENCE,' we printed up a bunch and hung them on the walls. However, nothing changed. You also have to realize that this company is largely comprised of engineers and technicians; and for them, a lot of this visioning was foreign."

By late 1986 and early 1987, the senior management team felt that a change agent was needed to help them deal with the issue of managing culture. An outside party was brought in; and his philosophy was that corporate vision should be strategically driven. This approach was warmly received by Bill Sanko; and through a series of monthly meetings, he worked with senior management.

His first effort was directed at getting the team to determine what their core values were and what they would like the company to look like in five years. Bill made an effort to develop a first draft of such a statement. In addition, other members of the senior team made similar efforts. "It was interesting," Rich notes, "Even though we each had a different orientation and background, there was a lot of consistency among the group." The team then went off site for several days and was able to finalize the XEL vision statement (Exhibit 1). By the summer of 1987, the statement was signed by members of the senior team and was hung up by the bulletin board. Again, Rich reflects: "The other employees were not required to sign the vision statement. We felt that once they could really buy into it then they were free to sign it or not."

Rich then described their approach to getting the rest of the organization to understand as well as become comfortable with the XEL vision: "Frequently, organizations tend to take a combination top-down/bottom-up approach in instituting cultural change. That is, the top level will develop a statement about values and overall vision. They will then communicate it down to the bottom level and hope that results will percolate upward through the middle levels. Yet it

---

Exhibit 1 The XEL Vision

XEL will become the leader in our selected telecommunications markets through innovation in products and services. Every XEL product and service will be rated Number One by our customers.

XEL will set the standards by which our competitors are judged. We will be the best, most innovative, responsive designer, manufacturer, and provider of quality products and services as seen by customers, employees, competitors, and suppliers.*

We will insist upon the highest quality from everyone in every task.

We will be an organization where each of us is a self-manager who will:

- initiate action, commit to, and act responsibly in achieving objectives
- be responsible for XEL's performance
- be responsible for the quality of individual and team output
- invite team members to contribute based on experience, knowledge and ability

We will:

- be ethical and honest in all relationships
- build an environment where creativity and risk taking is promoted
- provide challenging and satisfying work
- ensure a climate of dignity and respect for all
- rely on interdepartmental teamwork, communications and cooperative problem solving to attain common goals†
- offer opportunities for professional and personal growth
- recognize and reward individual contribution and achievement
- provide tools and services to enhance productivity
- maintain a safe and healthy work environment

XEL will be profitable and will grow in order to provide both a return to our investors and rewards to our team members.

XEL will be an exciting and enjoyable place to work while we achieve success.

---

*Responsiveness to customers' new product needs as well as responding to customers' requirements for emergency delivery requirements has been identified as a key strategic strength. Therefore, the vision statement has been updated to recognize this important element.

†The importance of cooperation and communication was emphasized with this update of the Vision Statement.

---

is often the middle level of management which is most skeptical, and they will block it or resist change. We decided to take a 'cascade' approach in which the process begins at the top and gradually cascades from one level to the next so that the critical players are slowly acclimated to the process. We also did a number of other things—including sending a copy of the vision to the homes of the employees and dedicating a section of the company newspaper to communicate what key sections of the vision mean from the viewpoint of managers and employees."

Unlike the first vision statement, which was hung on the wall but not really followed, this new vision statement has sustained and reinforced a corporate culture. Rich believed that employee involvement in fashioning and building the statement made the real difference, as well as the fact that XEL made significant use of teams in all facets of its business, including decision making. For example, in 1990, XEL was experiencing some economic difficulties. The employees were brought into meetings and were told the business was in trouble, and were asked for ideas on how to deal with the downturn. The employees discussed the problem and decided to try a four-day work week rather than lay off anyone. After a few months, the economic difficulties continued and the employees reluctantly decided to lay off 40 percent of the workforce. The work teams were asked if they wanted to be involved in deciding who would be laid off. They declined to participate in these tough decisions, but were still clearly concerned about the decisions themselves. In fact, Rich recalls being visited by a number of production workers during this time. "There was one particular fellow who knew that a coworker had a family, and that he would suffer a great deal of hardship if he was to be laid off," Rich remembers, "This fellow came in to my office and asked that he be laid off instead of his coworker. That's when I knew the employees believed in and shared our vision." Eventually, virtually all of the laid-off production workers were hired back.

In a strange way, the business crisis of 1990 moved the teams along more quickly than they might have developed in times of profit. Like many businesses using work teams and facing downsizing, XEL laid off a number of middle managers who were not brought back when business improved. When tough decisions needed to be made, the work teams no longer had managers to fall back on.

When teams, or managers, are making decisions, it is routine for the XEL vision statement to be physically brought into the discussion, and for workers to consult various parts of the statement to help guide and direct decisions. According to Rich, the statement has been used to help evaluate new products, to emphasize quality (a specific XEL strategic objective is to be the top quality vendor for each product), to support teams, and to drive the performance appraisal process.

The XEL vision was successfully implemented as a key first step, but it was far from being a static document. Key XEL managers continually revisited the statement to ensure that it became a reflection of where they want to go, not where they have been. Rich believed this was a large factor in the success of the vision. "Our values are the key," Rich explains, "They are strong, they are truly core values, and they are deeply held." Along with the buy-in process, the workers also see that the statement is experimented with. This reflected the strong entrepreneurial nature of XEL's founders—a common bond that they all share. They were not afraid of risk, or of failure, and this spirit was reinforced in all employees through the vision, as well as through the yearly process of revisiting the statement. Once a year, Bill Sanko sat with all employees and directly challenged them (and listened to direct challenges) on the XEL vision. Since 1987, only two relatively minor additions have altered the original statement (see Exhibit 1).

Human Resource Management at XEL

Julie Rich was pleased as she scanned the recent article in *Business Week* that mentioned XEL's efforts to use team-based compensation.[7] It mentioned that, once the firm instituted this system, average production time has been slashed from 30 days to 3, and waste as a percentage of sales has been cut in half. "We have certainly come a long way."

Rich was heavily involved in the development of XEL's first vision statement, and she chuckled about the reaction from others: "Being the non-engineer in an outfit that is predominantly made up of technical people, they looked at me like they thought I was crazy. This 'touchy-feely' vision and values statement was about as foreign to them as it could get. Yet, once they saw the linkage to XEL's strategy and direction, it began to catch on." In many ways, Rich was an unusual HR manager. Not only did she believe HR to be a strategic issue for XEL, Rich was also one of the owners of the business. Where HR was often relegated to a "staff" function, Rich was clearly a "line" manager at XEL. She felt comfortable working closely with technical managers, and carried the entrepreneurial spirit as strongly as her colleagues.

Once the vision statement had been finally developed, Rich and others soon turned their attention to the issue of managing the new culture within XEL. A key ingredient of this process was changing the mind-set of the employees. In the GTE days, individuals had discrete jobs and responsibilities that were governed by specific policies and procedures. "We wanted to instill a sense of ownership on the part of the employees," Rich noted. When asked when she knew that the culture was working, she replied, "One day, a work team was having a meeting. The team leader was agitated, and was speaking harshly to one of the team members. One of the other workers stood up and confronted the team leader, saying that his treatment of the worker was not consistent with the XEL vision." The worker, and her team leader, still work on the same team at XEL.

The HR system at XEL was unusually well integrated. The team-based work system created a great deal of intrinsic motivation, and opportunities for employee voice and influence were in abundance. The workers participated in hiring decisions, and XEL used a 360-degree performance appraisal system. Production workers were appraised by peers and also appraised themselves. The compensation system used a three-pronged approach: profit sharing to encourage teamwork, individual and team-based merit to encourage quantity and quality of performance, and skill-based pay to encourage continuous improvement. In one quarter in 1994, the 300 production workers were paid an average of $500 each in profit sharing. When workers mastered a new task, they had the opportunity to earn an additional 50 cents per hour. Finally, each unit shared a bonus based on meeting a quarterly goal, such as improving on-time delivery. The average reward was 4.5 percent of payroll, with top teams earning up to 10 percent and lagging groups getting nothing. Employee response to the compensation system was generally positive. "The pay system doesn't stand alone," said Rich. "It's only in support of the teams."[8]

Rich did a lot of background reading in the management literature as well as exploring what other companies were doing. Unfortunately, she found that there was little to go on. "That is when, in working with John Puckett, vice-president for manufacturing, we began to see that self-directed work teams could give them a distinct competitive advantage—resulting in better quality products that could be delivered in a timely manner."

A key step in the development of self-directed teams was to create an open organization. The first step was to take a look at the physical layout of the work environment. One experience remains vivid for Rich: "I remember that on one particular Friday, John was toying with the idea of how to better organize the plant. One worker approached John and told him to take the weekend off and go fishing. John, initially hesitant, decided to do so; and over one weekend, the workers came in and, on their own, redesigned the entire floor. On Monday, John returned and found that they had organized themselves in various work cells—each devoted to a particular product group. Teams were then organized around this cellular production and began to set their own production goals and quality procedures."

■ XEL's Strategic Planning Process

The business telecommunications market was rapidly changing and evolving in 1995—creating an ideal business climate for XEL.[9] Working with local telephone companies and others, XEL designed and manufactured equipment that "conditioned" existing lines to make them acceptable for business use.

As a means of positioning the firm for products and markets in a rapidly changing environment, XEL engaged in a strategic planning process on an annual basis. Exhibit 2 provides an overview of this process. As Bill Sanko noted: "Since there are such rapid changes taking place and new products being constantly introduced, we needed to tie what we're doing back to the strategic elements—quality, responsiveness, cost."

The strategic planning process began in August of each year with the senior management team listing strategic issues and taking on key assignments. Sanko's key assignment began with assessing key external factors. Taking on such an assignment provided him an opportunity to step back and look at the bigger picture. Sanko said, "I hope that legislation pending will deregulate local telephone companies. This will open up local telephone services to companies other than the regional Baby Bell. At present, AT&T has an almost 60 percent hold in the market with respect to long distance but deregulation will allow the local companies to enter the global market. Major telephone companies have been downsizing in the recent past to cut down on costs by developing products and installing services that require less maintenance and, therefore, less people to

Exhibit 2

XEL Planning Cycle

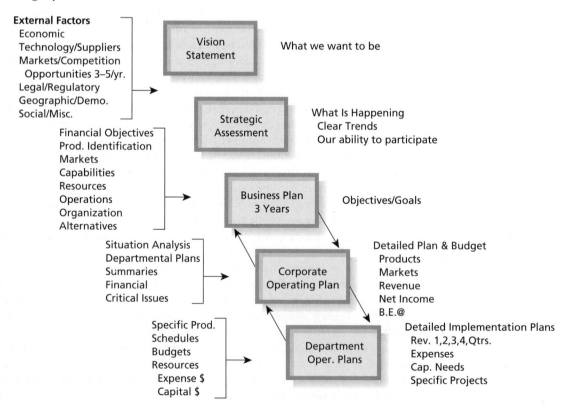

maintain them. With this trend, we hope to get business from our present customers seeking help to develop such products for them."

Another key industry trend that was constantly monitored is technology. The pace at which the technology was moving had reduced the product life cycle from 40 years to less than 5 years. Sanko noted the example of fiber optic products, which is a very hot area in today's market; XEL was trying to compete with other companies with respect to building fiber optic products. Other areas in which it was trying to find opportunities for a small company was the emerging personal communications systems market.

With the industry trend data as a beginning, the senior team then spent the ensuing months in developing plans around the key strategic issues. This would entail capturing data on key competitors and assessing their strengths and weaknesses relative to XEL. "Some of these data are available due to public disclosure requirements", according to Sanko, "but data on private competitors are particularly difficult to get—due to the competitive nature of the business; we get a lot of information through trade show contacts."

Throughout this entire process, the XEL team needed to keep a focus on those critical success factors that would determine their performance. Essentially, they involved innovativeness, a skilled sales force, quality, investing in automation, effective pricing, and, above all, responsiveness.

Another key goal was to achieve a 20 percent improvement in margin by year-end 1994 and to strive to reach 25 percent by December 1995 and 30 percent by December 1997. This goal is one that was particularly sensitive among the senior management team since it involved two critical variables: pricing coupled with achieving economies of scale in the manufacturing plant. Previously, achieving such a goal was parceled out among the respective groups: marketing and sales, operations, finance, and the like. Unfortunately, this activity was frequently tabled in the face of day-to-day activities. It was then decided that a cost reduction team needed to be formally structured to address this goal. As such, XEL decided to hire an engineer, a technician, and a buyer from outside the organization to constitute the team. Its primary responsibility was to examine the pricing of products and costs, and to target core products for the purpose of achieving 25 percent improvement in margin by December 1995. The team reported primarily to the vice president of manufacturing, John Puckett.

In terms of overall financial performance, XEL has been profitable. Its revenues increased from $16.8 million in 1992 to $23.6 million in 1993 and $52.3 million in 1994—more than a threefold increase in three years.

Another key issue that was identified in the strategic planning process was how much to invest in R&D—given the rapid pace of technology development that is taking place in this industry. XEL's goal was to invest 10 percent of its sales in R&D. "We have come to realize that we grew faster than last year's plan," according to Bill Sanko, "and we need to invest more in engineering as a means of keeping pace. Our goal is to have one-third of our revenue in any given year come from products introduced in the past two years." This would also involve investing its R&D efforts into new technologies as cable TV converges with telecommunications.

Aside from investment in new technologies, the other key strategic issue that was identified in the planning process was penetration into international markets. XEL was seeking to do business in Mexico in order to build data networks that are critical in upgrading Mexico's infrastructure. It has also searched for business opportunities in countries such as Brazil, Chile, Argentina, Puerto Rico, and the Far East. As a means of focusing responsibility for this effort, XEL tapped Malcom Shaw, a new hire of XEL who is fluent in Spanish and has prior marketing experience in South America, to lead this international expansion effort.

As all of the above issues indicate, the formal strategic planning process was a critical ingredient of XEL's way of doing business. "Strategic planning makes you think about how to invest for the future," Sanko emphasized. "The role of the CEO is really to keep a viewpoint of the big picture—not to micromanage the operation." To reinforce this last point, it should be noted that Bill Sanko had a personal tragedy in June 1992, in which he was involved in a serious auto accident—the car in which he was traveling was broadsided by another auto. "Even while I was out of the office for an extended period of time," noted Sanko, "the fact that we had a formal strategic plan and an annual operating plan gave us the guidance to continue business as usual." As the planning process moved forward, Sanko's goal was to have their 1995 strategic plan ready for the November meeting of the board of directors. As Rich noted, "We don't just look for 'programs,' but for ideas for the long term."

XEL's Markets

The marketing and sales functions for XEL closely reinforced the earlier emphasis on being responsive and oriented to customer's needs. Don Bise, vice president of marketing, came to XEL with diverse experience, having moved around in nine previous firms. "The culture here at XEL is much less structured than some other organizations where I worked before," Bise reflected, "I feel much more comfortable in a stand-alone company as opposed to being a branch or subsidiary of a large firm."

Unlike many companies in which the marketing approach is to have product managers dedicated to certain product segments or accounts, XEL's sales managers worked closely with the engineers in addressing customer needs. "The difficulty with having the sales manager or the engineer working solely with the customer is that their particular perspective may differ," noted Bise. "By having both the engineer and the sales manager working with the customer, we have cut down on the communications difficulties and have been able to develop a more realistic pricing and delivery schedule. At the same time, by having the engineer present, he is able to understand their specific needs or can steer them toward a reasonable solution to what they are trying to achieve. This has gone a long way to create great customer loyalty and repeat business. In addition, we have been able to manage our overall costs better. Our marketing expenses are typically six to seven percent of sales, which is low compared to a number of companies."

In terms of XEL's marketing strategy, a number of external developments have reshaped its approach. "Traditionally, in a market as concentrated as the telecommunications industry, the customer has tremendous buying potential and tries to leverage this as much as possible. With more players coming into this market, coupled with downsizing on the part of the RBOCs, we are trying to develop a portfolio approach to make us less dependent on a few key accounts. As a result, XEL must introduce new products for traditional as well as new accounts. This means that XEL must pay a great deal of attention to technology."

To meet this goal, marketing worked closely with the engineering group—not only in the sales area but also in new product development. Specific market opportunities included the convergence of telephony with cable, personal communication services based on radio expertise, and business access in developing countries. To reach these market segments, Don Bise noted that XEL was exploring several avenues.

One approach was the OEM (original equipment manufacturer) market in which XEL built the product according to another's specification. GTE's Airfone, which allowed airline passengers to place calls and receive calls, was a three-way venture in which XEL manufactured the electronics for the phone and did final assembly and test. This venture was quite profitable for XEL; they shipped about 300 Airfones a day out of their plant in 1995. A second approach was to build customized units for voice and data transmission in the industrial market. Exhibit 3 provides an example of XEL's approach to this market.

A third avenue, one that offered a great deal of future potential, is the international market. This is an area that Bise was particularly excited about: "Clearly the growth path is international as developing regions are looking to upgrade their telecommunications infrastructure to spur economic growth. To do this, both voice and data transmission are key. What XEL can do is take something that we are familiar with and use it in areas they aren't familiar with. For example, in one particular country, we found that we can take one of our channel units and plug it into their system—providing an instant upgrade to their current capabilities." Yet going international was not without its risks. "We would prefer to begin by developing a niche in international markets with our existing equipment. This would minimize some of the upfront risks. As the international side of the business begins to take off, we realize we will need to have a local in-country partner and will need to have some local manufacturing content."

To successfully compete in the future, Bise felt that XEL should "go where they ain't." XEL needed to seek out niches where there was very little or no competition, keep its cost low, and price accordingly. He felt that XEL's traditionally strong customer base, the major telephone companies, was using its buying power to telegraph acceptable prices. At the same time, the firms were cutting down their list of vendors quite extensively.

Financial Considerations

Turning from the ever-present spreadsheet on his desktop computer, Jim Collins, vice president of finance, reflected on the key financial considerations facing XEL. "Coming from another company to XEL, I soon found out that the culture here is quite different. There is indeed a sense of empowerment and teamwork. People set their own goals; and the engineers make a serious commitment to the customer."

In addition to the formal strategic planning process, financial planning at XEL involved a three-year top-down plan with input from the bottom up. According to Collins, "I interface a great deal with marketing and sales and develop costs. My goal is to ensure that there aren't a lot of surprises. We also tend to manage by percentages." Collins was asked whether XEL was experimenting with implementing some form of activity-based accounting. He noted that the firm

Exhibit 3

An Overview of Our Products and Services

Each unit is tested at one of our test stations. Most units are tested twice, both before and after burn-in.

XEL Communications offers complete product selection for voice and data applications. Products include a complete line of both voice and data channel units for D4, 9004, D448, and DE-4 channel banks. We have expanded our product line to include intelligent DSTs, T1 equipment, and 2B1Q systems.

XEL pioneered the development of the multifunctional, modular approach to transmission card design — the X-Card.™ This concept uses a basic board (such as a line amplifier) and through modular "build-ons," adds specific functions resulting in a custom-performance card. Customers specify their requirements and XEL assembles, tests, and ships the solution on a single board.

In 1990, XEL introduced a new line of channel units to address the needs of customers who use D448 T-Carrier Systems. These channel units incorporate our years of special service design experience to provide many unique units that reduce installation time and eliminate the needs for external equipment and units.

As part of XEL's product family, our 2B1Q system provides service for two 4-wire customers on a single pair of wires (3 pair gain) while still providing unique (patent pending) testing features.

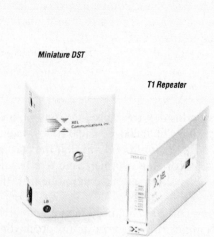

Miniature DST

T1 Repeater

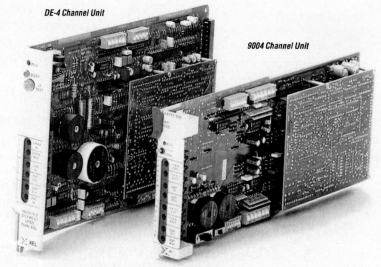

DE-4 Channel Unit

9004 Channel Unit

reviewed it in 1993 and decided that it was not ready. Yet, the firm plans to implement a modified activity-based accounting system in 1995. "We tend to look at the major drivers of cost in this business. There is an overall operations review once a month among the senior management team in which there is open dialogue; and we explore a number of key operational issues."

Yet the financial picture for XEL has not always been rosy. "In addition to the costs associated with the separation from GTE, there were three years where we lost money—part of this was due to our independency on GTE as it was going through its own consolidation as well as a new product introduction which didn't fly." Again, Jim Collins remarked: "those two setbacks were a bitter pill to swallow. We now try to make our financial projections more realistic—even somewhat on the conservative side. We also set targets by market segments."

Although there was pressure to raise cash by going public, Collins felt that this wasn't realistic for XEL. "We really don't want analysts setting constraints for our business—rather we tend to look for cash infusions from strategic partnerships and alliances." Both Bill Sanko and Jim Collins were actively involved in negotiating these partnerships, particularly in the international arena. "Above all," Collins commented, "we need to stay focused, develop a plan, and get realistic input."

Quality Management at XEL

One of the critical success factors that was identified in the strategic planning process and was imbedded throughout XEL was the focus on responsiveness to customers. When XEL was in its initial stages, cycle time—the period from start of production to finished goods—was about six weeks. That left customers disgruntled and tied up money in inventory.[10] XEL's chain of command, moreover, had scarcely changed since the GTE days. Line workers reported to supervisors, who reported to unit or departmental managers, who reported on up the ladder to Sanko and a crew of top executives. Every rung in the ladder added time and expense. "If a hardware engineer needed some software help, he'd go to his manager," Sanko says. "The manager would say, 'Go write it up.' Then the hardware manager would take the software manager to lunch and talk about it. We needed everybody in the building thinking and contributing about how we could better satisfy our customers, how we could improve quality, how we could reduce costs."

Soon after XEL drafted its vision statement, John Puckett, vice president for manufacturing, redesigned the plant for cellular production, with groups of workers building whole families of circuit boards. Eventually, Sanko and Puckett decided to set up the entire plant with self-managing teams. By 1988, the teams had been established; and the supervisory and support staff was reduced by 30 percent.

The RIF (reduction in force) was achieved by a number of avenues. In 1990, there was a downturn in business and workers went to a four-day work week in order to avoid layoffs. Unfortunately, the downturn continued and production workers, supervisors, and supports staff were laid off. Workers were asked for cost-saving ideas. Some workers moved to trainer roles. One worker was moved to industrial engineering while another became the manager of facilities.

Unlike other plans where workers are given incentives to provide cost saving ideas and suggestions, there was no such direct financial incentive at XEL. As

Rich recalled, "We were in a total survival mode—the only payoff was that the doors stayed open." Eventually, the teams and the quality strategy took hold and a turnaround was achieved. Virtually all laid-off production workers were rehired. The supervisory and support staff were not. This is a testament to the strength of the team system at XEL.

XEL was rebuilt around those teams so thoroughly and effectively that the Association for Manufacturing Excellence chose the company as one of four to be featured in a video on team-based management. Dozens of visitors, from companies such as Hewlett-Packard, have toured XEL's facility in search of ideas for using teams effectively.

On the shop floor, colorful banners hung from the plant's high ceiling to mark each team's work area. Charts on the wall tracked attendance, on-time deliveries, and the other variables by which the teams gauge their performance. Diagrams indicated who on a team was responsible for key tasks such as scheduling.

Every week, the schedulers met with Production Control to review what needed to be built as well as what changes needed to be made. The teams met daily, almost always without a manager, to plan their part in that agenda. Longer meetings, called as necessary, took up topics such as vacation planning or recurring production problems. Once a quarter, each team made a formal presentation to management on what it had and had not accomplished.

As for results, XEL's cost of direct assembly dropped 25 percent. Inventory had been reduced by half; quality levels rose 30 percent (Exhibits 4 and 5). The company's cycle time went from six weeks to four days and was still decreasing (Exhibit 6). Sales also grew to $52 million in 1994, up from $17 million in 1992. Above all, according to John Puckett, these self-directed work teams must be guided by customer focus (Exhibit 7). To facilitate this, customers frequently came in and visited with the team. By clearly understanding their customers' needs, the teams were able to respond rapidly with a high-quality product. At the same time, XEL team members visited key suppliers.

Another key issue for manufacturing involved establishing certain procedures while retaining a certain degree of flexibility. Part of this involved the strategic issue of entering global markets. As firms go global, meeting ISO 9000 standards

Exhibit 4

WIP Annual Inventory Turns 1985–1994

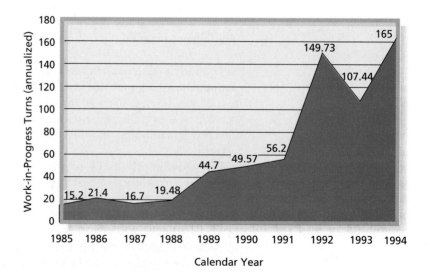

Exhibit 5

Customer Returns, Component Level, All Causes

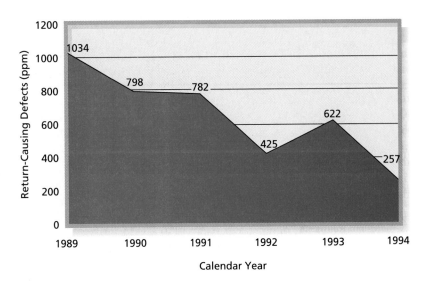

Exhibit 6

Cycle Time Reduction, 1984–1994

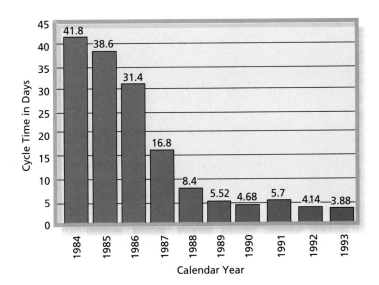

for quality becomes critical. "To meet these standards, several things have to take place," Puckett noted. "We have to have a structure that defines the process; then we need to document and have solid procedures in place." In addition, Puckett felt that manufacturing for international markets would also mean building manufacturing capabilities closer to those markets, which entailed a whole host of environmental issues and labor laws. Developing alliances would also be critical because XEL could not afford to run it all.

In terms of integration with other parts of XEL, Puckett briefly sketched the overall process. "Basically, most of manufacturing is driven off of the financial and market plan. We start with a three-year plan which is converted in terms of the demands on facilities. My staff then develops models which reflect product development and product mix. The budget then sets the baseline for new product development. Here, at XEL, we tend to plan on the low side and are fairly

Exhibit 7

Productivity, 1989–1994

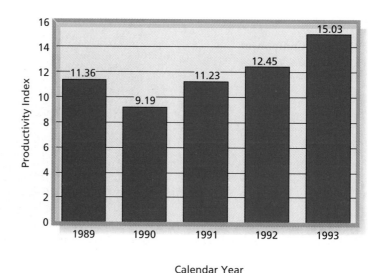

Calendar Year

conservative. Currently, we target two new products per month and produce in low volume for beta testing. This allows us to carefully manage costs."

As for future issues, Puckett was struggling with the XEL goal of improving margins by 25 percent by December 1995. "This is going to be a real challenge for my operation since we have to maintain a short cycle time as the business grows without a lot of excess inventory. We instituted a just-in-time (JIT) system several years ago, and we are currently turning our inventory about seven or eight times, which is close to our benchmarks relative to the best in our business. Supply chain management is really critical for us."

Another issue Puckett faced was maintaining the culture that had been instituted through the team-based training. "While the current teams have pretty much gelled in terms of feeling comfortable with setting their targets and self-managing, orienting new members becomes a challenge. We are exploring some form of built-in orientation which would involve two weeks of internal training."

Puckett also faced an even greater concern: skilled workers. "I think one of the serious deficiencies in our current U.S. educational system is vocational and occupational education. People have simply not been prepared. There is a misconception that there is a shortage of jobs in this business. They are dead wrong. One of my difficulties is finding qualified workers. As a basic assembler, you aren't going to become rich and put down a deposit on a BMW. But it provides a nice steady income—particularly for two wage earning families." Puckett felt that there needed to be a stronger work ethic for those entering the labor force. "We need to understand how to transfer those hard skills that are needed as well as the concept of holding a job. Part of this should involve more industry-level involvement in changing the overall mind-set of what is needed for today's workers. I would like to create an environment in which people really enjoy working here."

The strategic need for skilled workers drove XEL's involvement in a Work Place Learning Skills program, funded by the Department of Education. When XEL began training workers in quality tools, managers noticed that the training was not having as great an effect as it might have. Upon further investigation, the

Exhibit 8

Scrap/Rework (in thousands of dollars)

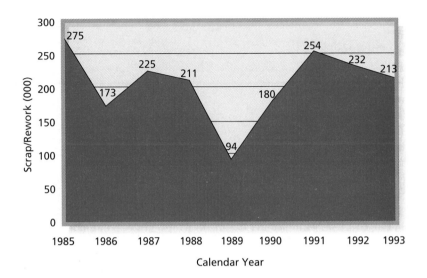

managers discovered that some workers were having difficulty not only in making calculations, but also in reading the training materials. Using the DOE grant, and working with Aurora Community College, which is located near the plant, XEL developed a basic skills training program which is now used as a template by DOE for worker training across the United States. The program, not surprisingly, was designed by an employee task force made up of managers and workers. The task force used a questionnaire to ask employees which courses they would be interested in taking. Participation in the program was not mandatory, but a measure of its success is that 50 percent of employees participated in the program on their own time. Courses were offered on site for convenience, and included "soft" skills such as communication and stress management. On December 1, 1994, XEL was awarded a three-year DOE grant to expand and continue the training, and to scientifically evaluate the effects of the training on such outcomes as productivity and ROI. Rich believed that these training programs were consistent with other human resource policies of XEL, such as skill-based pay. More than that, Rich stated, "The Work Place Learning Skills program is consistent with our XEL vision." As further testament to these efforts, XEL's overall workforce productivity continues to improve. The outcomes of these efforts can be seen in the amount of scrap/rework and number of defects (see Exhibits 8 and 9).

Maintaining Innovation

In a climate that is constantly undergoing rapid change, staying ahead of the competition is the name of the game. For XEL, this meant that cross-functional relationships were key. One critical link in this process was the role of new product development. Terry Bolinger, vice president of engineering, described how this process worked: "Here at XEL, engineering is involved from start to finish. Rather than have a large marketing staff that is out there making calls or picking up new pieces of information, we deliberately have a small group. The engineers do a lot of traveling at XEL—going out in the field and working directly with the customers."

Exhibit 9

Process Solder Defects

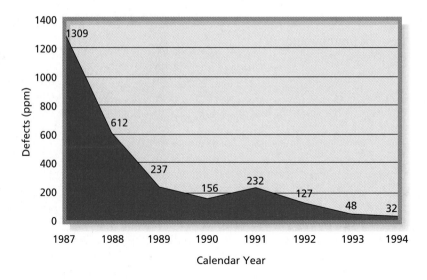

As for its commitment to innovation, XEL allocated approximately 10 to 12 percent of sales to R&D. Bolinger noted that, for the current year, he spent below this amount. When pressed why, he commented: "I guess I am hesitant to spend up to this amount since I don't want to grow my engineering group too fast. A few years back, we went through some cutbacks due to a number of factors; and I am somewhat gun-shy about that experience. I know we are running at about the 10 percent level; and Bill keeps pressing me about this. But I would rather proceed somewhat cautiously."

To create a climate to allow his people to innovate, Bolinger noted that he was careful not to create a management system that bogged everything down. "Our process of setting priorities is fairly free-form. While we are typically running 50 projects at one time, we don't do much formal scheduling. We went through a time in which a lot of formal planning and presentations were done. Unfortunately, we spent too much time in meetings and too little in what I considered the search and discovery process." While Bolinger was comfortable with this loose form of management, he laughed that others were not so at ease. "I see Bill Sanko stroll the office periodically; and I know that he is often perplexed with how this works—coming from his engineering background. I just say 'trust me' and he is pretty good at accepting it."

In addition to this loose form of project management, Bolinger tried to motivate his engineers in other ways. "I also try to give them interesting assignments which will challenge them. They are also allowed to work at odd hours—many come to work on weekends or at night. In a number of cases, I will simply send them to work at home where they can be relaxed. If they need some particular equipment, I will get it for them with little or no questions asked. Also, they periodically like to travel just to get out of the office; and field calls to customers or potential customers is a way of getting them charged up." There were also periodic in-house seminars with professors from various universities who would come and brief them on new technological advances. In a sense, Bolinger was trying to recreate the college environment within XEL.

As XEL continued to grow, Bolinger saw several issues that were critical for his group: "First is the issue of how do I improve time to market without sacrificing quality; second, how do I speed up product development; and third, how do I respond extremely fast to new technology developments?" As he prepared his departmental plan for the strategic planning meeting, he also shared some concern about the opening of the second building. While he clearly needed more space for his people, the ease with which an engineer could go over to manufacturing or marketing and sales if he or she had a question or needed some information would be hard to replace.

XEL's Future

Ironically, the most serious current issue for XEL came from its own success, namely, growth. XEL had increased its labor force by 50 percent and had doubled its revenues in the last year, and was experiencing some associated growing pains. Hiring sufficient workers was difficult, and assuring that the new workers will "fit" the XEL culture was hindered because of the pressures to add staff. The teams, who normally hired their own replacement workers, were less able to participate in the hiring process since they were under great pressure to produce and satisfy their customers.

Another example of the pressures of growth occurred in the skills training program. Originally, team members were scheduled to teach the classes. Unfortunately, as pressures for production increased, more and more team members canceled their training classes. As a solution, trainers were hired from local community colleges, and the team members acted as their partners to ensure that the course content was job related.

Growth increased pressure to satisfy customer demands, increased pressure on the culture via the increased size and complexity, and created additional financial pressures. As a high-technology company, XEL faced the challenge of using technology to help the company be more effective. XEL would use its annual strategic planning process to determine its priorities, what measures it will use to assess its results, and which feet to hold to the fire.

Having finished reading the *Wall Street Journal* article, Bill Sanko made a note to have a copy made for the next managers' meeting, which was scheduled for every other Thursday. He also wondered what the new session of Congress would bring—now that the Republicans appeared to be in solid control.

Because XEL was in the process of beginning its annual strategic planning process, Bill thought that a useful exercise for the next managers' meeting would be to have everyone list and prioritize the key strategic issues facing XEL over the next three to five years. At the same time, he wondered whether it would be possible for XEL to maintain its entrepreneurial culture while it managed rapid growth.

Notes

1. *Financial World,* October 11, 1994.
2. 1994 University of Michigan economic forecast.
3. *Denver Business Journal,* June 17, 1994, p. 12.
4. *Rocky Mountain Business Journal,* July 1, 1985.
5. *Colorado Business,* July 1990.
6. *Rocky Mountain Business Journal,* July 1, 1985.
7. *Business Week,* November 14, 1994, p. 62.
8. *Ibid.*
9. *Denver Business Journal,* April 15, 1994.
10. *Inc.,* September 1993, p. 66.

■ APPENDIX Introduction to the Internet

Welcome to this cyberspace and your introduction to the strategic management process. One of the unique aspects of this text and course is the opportunity to explore and use the Internet—the worldwide network that connects millions of people, businesses, and educational institutions. Computer environments are increasingly ubiquitous as they become the medium through which businesses communicate; moreover, the Internet has changed our civilization permanently by revolutionizing the way people communicate. It can only be to your advantage to experience this on-line and just-in-time learning environment. You can have discussions, trade ideas, and compile a paper that incorporates worldwide viewpoints. You will also be more flexible than in typical group assignments—work from home whenever you want and avoid the time pressures of having to appear at meetings.

As you'll soon see, the good news about the Internet is that you will learn things that will help you in other classes and in your career. The bad news is that learning to cruise the Internet can be confusing and it may take some time before you're comfortable with it. But take heart. If we are serious about our individual responsibilities to participate, we should have fun while learning. Here are some things to keep in mind:

- File names and locations are constantly evolving; therefore, this listing reflects the best information available at the time this book was printed
- And remember . . . this is a very rudimentary introduction and overview. You will need to get more detailed information as you gain experience.

■ Constructing the I-Way

The *Internet* is a worldwide network of networks. As such, it is a loose conglomeration of many research, educational, and business computers around the world. Started as a top-secret U.S. defense project in 1969, it has become the most widely used computer network in the world, providing access to a wealth of information. And yet, there is no "Internet Inc." command center, cybercops, or other centralized coordinating organization. The man from the United Network Command for Law Enforcement lives only in television reruns. In fact, the Internet was intentionally set up to be decentralized, confusing, and chaotic. In the beginning, its purpose was to survive a nuclear war by enabling its many users to continue communicating. Besides, it would be pretty tough to have a computer powerful enough to centralize all military information. So, four main

These materials were developed by Paul Miesing of the State University of New York at Albany. All the information is collected from the Internet and other public sources and documents.

computers were linked by numerous paths to share valuable computing power. The system, developed by the Advanced Research Projects Agency, became known as ARPANET. (Ironically, the military recruited members of the counter-culture to develop it . . . but that's another interesting story.) Many of these early researchers soon used it for personal discussions.

To get the computers to communicate with each other, in 1972 the folks at ARPA standardized conventions to conform to the Transmission Control Protocol/Internet Protocol, better known as TCP/IP, which is still used today. This *packet switching* codes a message's destination, fragments it into smaller parts, enables any of the linked computers to forward these parts, and reassembles them at the destination. The TCP part ensures that data reaches its destination by detecting and/or resending lost, corrupt, or duplicate data packets. The IP part tracks the addresses of nodes, routes outgoing data packets, and recognizes incoming packets.

By 1981, the Internet had grown to about 200 computers. A decade later, it had more than 300,000 computers. Since no one is responsible for the Internet, it survives only to the extent that all these users contribute to it and openly share information. Most sites provide free access without requiring prior permission—which means there's no privacy.

The Internet is a powerful communication tool—inexpensive, easily accessible, open around the clock, and around the world. You can use the Internet to view artwork, listen to music, access library catalogs and databases, obtain software or electronic books, get the latest satellite weather maps or travel reports, or communicate with people on the other side of the world. In spite of this public exposure (or perhaps because of it), many continue to use it for personal messages. It has exploded over the past few years. The Internet is now becoming crowded since anyone can travel it with a terminal, modem, and phone line. This newfound popularity is attracting millions of new users annually. Many "new-bies" are introduced to the Internet by users showing them how they can download recipes and jokes, play games, or connect to computers in exotic locations. Nonetheless, the Internet will in all likelihood become the basis for any future global information superhighway, and will probably become increasingly commercial. Its impact promises to be as profound as that of the automobile and interstate highways.

The information provided here will get you up to speed as you enter the ramp to the I-Way. Where you go and your travel speed are up to you. *Bon voyage!*

■ Some Basic Routes

On the Internet, you can retrieve program files, text, photos or graphics, or anything else that a computer stores. The only driver's license you need is your university computer's password and account. To get a file, you need to know the lane it is located in (either the protocol or the part of the Web being used) and its location. Protocols differ for the type of file you want to obtain. The major parts of the Web include E-mail, gopher, World Wide Web, ftp, the telnet (all explained in this Appendix). The lane you choose to drive in depends on whether you want to communicate with a group or individual, cruise, download a specific file, or use another computer. You don't need to know all of the "tech talk" about how computers communicate with each other. This Appendix provides the necessary Internet tools, addresses, and other required information.

■ Communications

The most popular use of the Internet is electronic mail, commonly referred to as E-mail. You can also join a group that shares a common interest, either as part of a Listserv (which automatically sends you messages) or a Usenet newsgroup (where you have to read the messages). Moreover, you can send many of your Internet findings to yourself via E-mail. This makes it easy to save, organize, and share your discoveries. There are two ways to join discussion groups. E-mail is used to sign up for a Listserv that will send you messages that every member posts to the group. Bulletin board systems have become increasingly popular, and the best way to join in these conversations is by joining a Usenet news group.

E-mail

Electronic mail is the most common lane on the I-Way—probably because it is the simplest to use. Items are instantly "mailed" electronically around the world, and a system is responsible for transmitting these items. You can also receive electronic magazines, known as e-zines in your electronic mailbox. Be aware, however, of junk mail! The international convention is:

user@host.domain.network

Don't know who or where to mail? Try these sites ("WWW" is explained later):

http://www.switchboard.com/
http://www.whowhere.com/
http://www.accumail.com/

Listserv

One popular use of E-mail is Listservs, a collection of interest groups that users may join and participate in discussions about certain topics. Most Listserv networks depend on software that allows participants to subscribe without contacting anyone and to unsubscribe similarly. To subscribe or unsubscribe, send an E-mail message to a Listserv program. The Listserv program then adds your name to its mailing list and sends you an acknowledgment with instructions. *Warning: It is important you retain this message!* Afterward, all postings are delivered to your E-mail address. For example, to join my "fictitious" group at "do-to-u.edu", you would send an E-mail message to:

Listserv@do-to-u.edu

with the message "subscribe" then name the network "fictitious" and give your name ("subscribe fictitious firstname lastname"). Strip all signatures and leave the Re: area blank.

To unsubscribe, you would send a similar message that contains only "unsubscribe" and the group name ("fictitious") in the body. Of course, if you have difficulty, you can contact the person who is managing the network. Listserv programs respond to various commands besides subscribe or unsubscribe. To get a list of the commands for a specific Listserv program, address a one-word message to the Listserv program that says only "help."

Any message you send to the network's address is distributed to *everyone* who participates in the Listserv. Likewise, any mail sent to the list by another member is automatically sent to you as a member of the list. So, be aware of how you send or reply to messages. To post a message to the people who subscribe to a list, send your message to the network's E-mail address (*not* to the Listserv program). For example, to send a message to everyone who subscribes to the fictitious list above, you would address the message to:

fictitious@do-to-u.edu

Remember: If you want to send a message to just one person, address it to that person's individual E-mail address and *not* to the entire network!

(Your instructor may want to provide Listserv sources.)

Usenet NewsGroups

The Usenet (news reader) is a large and wide-ranging collection of discussion groups. It's the equivalent of an electronic town meeting in cyberspace. (Your ability to access newsgroups depends on the campus computer manager who determines which are available on your local host system.) The basic building block of the Usenet is a newsgroup, which is a collection of messages on a common theme of special interest to a group. This lane of the I-Way does not rely on E-mail, but you can easily switch lanes if you like. Like Listservs, each group is centered around a particular topic that may or may not be serious. To participate in a bulletin board system, you must subscribe to the desired group. You are then permitted to post messages, comments, or questions as well as read everyone else's postings and converse with different people with the same interests. The topics span the spectrum, with a group for everyone. Like Listservs, you must subscribe to the news reader. Unlike Listservs, you must get the group postings and browse them. For general information, look at:

usenet: news.announce.newusers

Select one of these groups to join for the semester:

Business aspects of international trade: alt.business.import-export
Entrepreneur (moderated): misc.entrepreneurs.moderated
Business topics: misc.industry.quality

If you don't find one you are interested in, get a list of news groups:

■ Internet/Newsgroups:

http:www.w3.org/hypertext/DataSources/News/Groups/Overview.html

■ List of Filtered Newsgroups:

http://woodstock.stanford.edu:2000/groups.html

■ Newsgroups:

gopher://info.tamu.edu:70/11/.data/newsgroups

■ tile.net Usenet Newsgroups:

http://tile.net.news/

Subscribe to the one you select and periodically scan it. Prepare to share postings with your fellow classmates and instructors throughout the semester.

■ Remote Access

The Internet requires two computers working simultaneously. The term *client* is used for the programs that are running on your local computer, typically a desktop or laptop. This computer can run programs that take your commands and turn them into requests for information from programs that are running on remote computers called *servers*. The server is the computer that provides the resources. Using the two in tandem, you can:

- access your account from remote places;
- explore huge databases to conduct research; and
- check library resources.

The two ways to apply this are through the *ftp* and *telnet* features. Sometimes other roads take you there, so your trip can be pretty transparent. If you go there directly, it is common to log on as a "guest" or "anonymous" user in both cases. Carefully read any instructions when you first log on.

FTP

The *file transfer protocol* (ftp) permits users to retrieve from a host computer a text file, software, data, and other information that can be copied and used without charge by anyone with a connection to the Internet. This lane of the I-Way allows users to log onto a remote host, transfer files to and from that system, obtain listings of directories on remote hosts, and carry out other common file operations. There are two types of ftp: You can either be registered as a user that has a user ID and a password, or the system manager sets up a special user ID called "anonymous" that anyone is allowed to use. In either case, you must know the address of the remote host. Search for sites at:

FTP Search: http://ftpsearch.ntnu.no/

tile.net FTP Sites: http://tile.net/ftp-list/

archie (yup, no capital a) is a catalog and index of hundreds of anonymous ftp archive (drop the "v"—get it?) files. It is a collection of servers, each of which is responsible for keeping track of file locations. By telling you where these files are located, it permits easy keyword file searches. Originally created to track the contents of anonymous ftp archive sites, the concept allows users to automatically search many different hosts for files, on-line directories, and resource listings of interest by specifying a text string. archie periodically searches through the net and updates its database. If you are looking for an anonymous ftp site you give archie a string of characters and it will search its database and retrieve the host site address that has file names containing that string. For more information:

http://www.earn.net/gnrt/archie.html

Telnet

Telnet is a terminal emulation protocol that enables you to use a local computer terminal to log in to a more distant one and establish an interactive session. This lane of the I-Way provides access to online databases, computerized library card catalogs, weather reports, and other information services. You connect by entering the site address, which you must have. For instance, you can join a

Usenet newsgroup at a distant site using telnet from your local host computer. You can access many systems by using "anonymous" to log in.

▦ Browsers

Many times you don't have a specific destination in mind, but have some idea of what you are looking for. There are several ways you can simply "browse" the Internet until you locate what you need. As you do so, you can also "mark" those locations you might want to return to.

Gopher

A gopher (for "go-fer") is someone who fetches necessary items from many locations. This lane of the I-Way helps you navigate the Internet. It is a powerful menu-driven system that allows you to access many of the resources of the Internet in a simple, consistent manner. The "Mother gopher" resides at the University of Minnesota, whose mascot (coincidentally?) is the golden gopher. The gopher client does not store any information; it is used solely to browse for information that is on any gopher server on the Internet. It provides a text menu interface organized hierarchically, enabling easy navigation to sites by using only the cursor and Return key. The information can be a file with text (the line has the title), another menu (the line ends in a slash, /), or a telnet connection (the line ends with <TEL>) that hooks you up to other menus through various pathways called *gopherspace*. In this way, the client enters virtual libraries all over the world by burrowing through deeper layers of subdirectories.

To access this tool, either use gopher software for Windows or type "gopher" from a prompt in your mainframe. You can connect to a gopher site by either working your way through the menu hierarchy or going directly to an address that you already know. You open a specific site by typing "o" and then the address. For instance, "Gopher Jewels" is the best place to look for the most popular sites in gopherspace. You can get to these "jewels" by typing "o" followed by

cwis.usc.edu

Then, go to the path "Other Gophers and Information Resources/" to find "Gopher Jewels." When you find a source you expect to return to, add it to your personal bookmark by typing "a." You can later view your list of sites you want to return to by typing "v."

Veronica

You will see references to Veronica when you are in gopher. Veronica is a "very easy rodent-oriented netwide index to computerized archives" that searches Internet directories, menus, and indexes. It was developed by Steve Foster and Fred Barrie at the University of Nevada at Reno as a tool that allows you to title search through gopherspace using keywords, text strings, or Boolean operators. (The line on the gopher menu ends with <?>.) It contains an index of titles to gopher items, permitting a search of gopher menus to find your keywords. It does not search for full text or file name. The result of your search is an automatically generated gopher menu, customized according to your keyword specification. By selecting an item in the menu you will automatically be connected to that gopher source, not just the host sites. Items that appear particularly interesting can be added to your bookmark list and viewed later.

World Wide Web

The World Wide Web (WWW) lane of the I-Way provides users with a consistent means to access a variety of media in a simplified fashion. It is the first true global hypertext/hypermedia network, merging the techniques of information retrieval and *__hypertext__* to make it an easy but powerful global information system that enables you to use "hot words" to easily jump around documents. The WWW began in 1989 when Tim Berners-Lee and colleagues at the CERN European Laboratory for Particle Physics in Geneva, Switzerland, developed the Hypertext Markup Language to link documents so scientists could use the Internet to trade them. These documents end with "html". It is a breakthrough because it consists of documents and "links" to other documents or places within documents—hence, the "Web" as in a spider web. This is done with *hypertext,* which can be stored, read, searched, or edited just like regular text. Clicking on one of the highlighted words (or an icon) in one of these documents will take you to the organization's (or individual's) *home page,* which provides the site's table of contents. This home page on the Web is actually a publicly available computer file you can retrieve. The other thing to know is that these documents use the "http" protocol, which stands for *hypertext transfer protocol.* These files begin with http:// followed by a string of letters and slashes.

The advantage of this interface is the excellent graphics capability, which uses *__hypermedia__* to retrieve graphics, sound, and video. The first popular graphical information browser was a Windows frontend. Called *Mosaic,* it was developed by Marc Andreessen and Eric Bina while at NCSA, the National Center for Supercomputing Applications at the University of Illinois. This increasingly popular tool is multipurpose because it uses an URL (pronounced "Earl"), for *uniform resource locator,* which means it can find sites using archie, ftp, gopher, http, telnet, veronica, or other tools. Simply replace "http" in the address with the protocol you are using. Once you get the hang of it, you can set up your own directories of places to browse. Be forewarned, though, that many sites along the way just have links to other sites and your cruise may return you home where you started—weary but with little to show for it.

Lynx

Lynx was originally developed by Lou Montulli, Michael Grobe, and Charles Rezac as a nongraphical browser to access information on the World Wide Web. It can be accessed on both UNIX and VMS (VAX) systems via cursor-addressable, character-cell terminals or emulators. That includes VT100 terminals and desktop-based software packages emulating VT100 terminals (e.g., Kermit, Procomm, etc.). It will display HTML documents containing links to files residing on the local system, as well as files residing on remote systems running gopher, HTTP, ftp, WAIS, and NNTP servers.

Viewing local files with Lynx can be started by entering the Lynx command at the $ prompt. You can then specify a location on the Web. When executed, Lynx will clear the screen and display as much of the specified file as will fit on the screen. Pressing a down arrow will bring up the next screen, and pressing an up arrow will bring up the previous screen. For information on how to use Lynx see the on-line Lynx User's Guide or the on-line Lynx help files. The following is a summary of important keystroke commands:

- Down arrow highlight next topic
- Up arrow highlight previous topic
- Right arrow jump to highlighted topic
- Left arrow return to previous topic
- - (or b) scroll up to previous page
- Press space for next page
- a add (save) selected document or site to personal bookmark
- g go (enter desired site)
- h help (press the left arrow key to exit help)
- o options
- p print (save to local file, send E-mail, or send to printer)
- q quit
- v view personal bookmarks

And just like the Web, you can use Lynx for ftp, gopher, and (indirectly) telnet.

■ Search Engines

With millions of pages on the Internet available to the public, search engines index the contents of hundreds of thousands of home pages. To the rescue: crawlers, robots, and spiders. Earlier you read that you can "mark" gopher, WWW, and Lynx locations that you might want to return to. Well, here are invaluable sites you will come to again and again. Save them, and plan on returning often.

Alta Vista

This powerful search tool was developed by Digital Equipment Corporation. It indexes every word in a database of more than 16,000,000 Web pages and some 13,000 Usenet newsgroups. The prototype sends out "a brood of spiders" (or "threads"):

http://www.altavista.digital.com

Deja News

Search for discussion groups by keyword, personal name, or discussion group name:

http://www.dejanews.com

Excite

This reference tool is pretty selective, emphasizing strong editorial content and regional listings:

http://www.excite.com

InfoSeek

In addition to searching the Web, also indices news wires and thousands of bulletin boards:

http://www.infoseek.com

Inktomi

This search engine offers relevance retrieval with MUST (+) and NOT (–) search terms. Over 2.8M documents are searched:

http://inktomi.berkeley.edu/

Inter-Links

An Internet guide, tutorial, and more than a dozen search engines can be found on Robert Kabacoff's Inter-Links. The guide lists several thousand hand-picked WWW, gopher, telnet, ftp, Internet relay chat (IRC), MUD, and bulletin board service (BBS) resources:

http://www.nova.edu/Inter-Links/start.html

Internet Resources Meta-Index

This site is intended to be a loosely categorized meta-index of the various resource directories and indices available on the Internet:

http://www.ncsa.uiuc.edu/SDG/Software/Mosaic/MetaIndex.html

Internet Services List

Scott Yanoff compiles this list of hundreds of Internet resources that are available through E-mail, telnet, ftp, gopher, finger, and the Web. This list is *essential* for anyone who wants to be a serious 'net traveler:

http://www.spectracom.com/islist/

Internet Sleuth

This site is a collection of more than 750 searchable indices and databases covering a wide variety of subjects. Indices are organized by topic, handy for quick keyword searches:

http://www.intbc.com/sleuth/

Lycos

Carnegie Mellon University began this catalog of Web resources, a good first step to locate other resources. It is a keyword search index that scans millions of Web documents for key words:

http://lycos.com/

A more selective search engine is:

http://point.lycos.com/

Magellan

Includes reviews and ratings for Web sites:

http://www.mckinley.com/

Metacrawler

This multithreaded Web searcher queries Open Text, Lycos, WebCrawler, InfoSeek, Excite, Inktomi, Alta Vista, Yahoo!, and Galaxy. It then verifies that each URL is valid:

http://metacrawler.cs.washington.edu:8080/

Meta Index

Here's a wide selection of tools to help you find what you want on the WWW:

http://cui_www.unige.ch/meta-index.html

Open Text

This search engine indexes every single word of almost one million Web pages. You can use Boolean, phrase, proximity, weighted, and KWIC searching, with relevance feedback. It also searches parts of pages:

http://www.opentext.com

SavvySearch

This experimental server can query 19 search engines, including Alta Vista, Yahoo!, FTPsearch95, the Virtual Software Library, Excite, Lycos, Deja News, OKRA (E-mail database), and the Internet Movie Database. It finds information for Usenet, ftp sites, gopher space, and Web space. Boolean and phrase searches are supported:

http://savvy.cs.colostate.edu:2000/

Search.com

You can set up a personal page with just your favorite search engines:

http://www.search.com

Starting Point

Home Page links to major U.S. companies:

http://www.stpt.com

WebCrawler Searching

This content-based Web index is the first full-text search service available. It contains information from many different servers, acting somewhat like a veronica server for WWW sites. Go here to find something specific:

http://www.webcrawler.com

WWWW—World Wide Web Worm

WWWW provides four types of search databases: citation hypertext, citation addresses (URL), HTML titles, and HTML addresses.

http://wwwmcb.cs.colorado.edu/home/mcbryan/WWWW.html

WWW Robots, Wanderers, and Spiders

This current list of all WWW index systems and sites connects you to lots of search tools:

http://Web.nexor.co.uk/mak/doc/robots/robots.html

Yahoo!

One of the best starting points for exploring the Internet (and WWW) today is the irreverent and hip Yahoo! ("Yet Another Hierarchically Officious Oracle") directory. (It was started by a couple of students at Stanford.) Not only can you search the topic menu, but you can search by words on the linked pages themselves. It will guide you to directories that specialize in the topic you are interested in, then let you "drill down" to find everything from Web sites to commercial newspapers to software downloads.

http://www.yahoo.com

Directories

Argus Clearinghouse

http://www.clearinghouse.net/

BigBook

This "Yellow Pages" includes business information for consumers and about local businesses. It hopes to make it easier for consumers and businesses to hook up with each other by providing "value-added" information to them.

http://www.bigbook.com/

Business Resources on the Internet
Brought by the Learning Resource Center:

http://204.17.16.101/Irc9.html

ComFind
This search engine claims to be the Internet's largest global business directory:

http://comfind.com/

Galaxy's Business and Commerce

http://galaxy.einet.net/galaxy/Business-and-Commerce.html

Planet Earth
The Planet Earth Home Page is a World Wide Web Virtual Library. This library is referred to as the PEHP Virtual Library and contains a collection of resources available on the World Wide Web.

http://www.planetearth.net/

PR Newswire
A searchable database of public relations press releases:

http://www.prnewswire.com/

U.S. Business Advisor
This searchable director of business-specific government information is at:

http://www.business.gov/Business.html

General Locations for Business

Here are some additional places for you to travel—experiment with them, and then set off on your own adventure of discovery. Many of these locations provide information that may be helpful in analyzing cases for the course or for understanding the strategic management process.

Additional Corporate Sources

American Stock Exchange

http://www.amex.com/

Better Business Bureau

http://www.bbb.org/

Competitive Intelligence Guide
Fuld & Co.'s competitive intelligence site offers analytical tools and links to other intelligence sites:

http://www.fuld.com/

IMEX Exchange
This U.S. Council for International Business maintains the International Import Export Business Exchange:

http://www.uscib.org/

IndustryNet

http://www.industry.net/

The Insider: Public Companies
List of public companies with sites on the Web:

http://networth.galt.com/www/home/insider/insiderinfo.html

International Business Resources on the WWW

http://ciber.bus.msu.edu/busres.htm

Japan Information Center
WWW Home Servers Guide for Companies in Japan:

http://www.jicst.go.jp/dir-www/com.html/

Market Guide
This Investment Center is a comprehensive web site that provides investment and financial information, including research reports on over 8,200 publicly traded companies:

http://www.marketguide.com/

NASDAQ

This stock market page offers 15-minute delayed stock quotes and includes options for a full quote. You can look up companies by name or symbol and company stock information is accompanied by a hypertext connection to that company's page, as well as a connection to the SEC Edgar database:

http://www.nasdaq.com/

Networth Equities Center

Its Investor Relations Resource is a searchable index of Web pages published by public companies:

http://networth.galt.com/www/home/equity/irr/

New York Stock Exchange

The Web site of the world's leading securities marketplace provides links to a rich diversity of information. The world's largest ($6.4 trillion) securities market is home to the largest companies in the world:

http://www.nyse.com/

Patent Portal

Site for patents and patent law:

http://www.law.vill.edu/~rgruner/patport.htm

Stock Master

Fast (but delayed) and free stock and mutual fund quotes and historical charts at:

http://www.stockmaster.com/

The Strategic Leadership Forum

- http://www.asconet.org/
- http://www.smartpages.com/planningforum/

Thomas Publishing Co.

This publisher provides industry with up-to-date product information:

http://www.thomaspublishing.com/

World Wide Yellow Pages

http://www.yellow.com/

Magazines and Newspapers

Asia, Inc. Online

http://www.asia-inc.com/

Barron's Magazine

http://www.barrons.com/

Bloomberg News Service

   http://www.bloomberg.com/

Business Week

   http://www.businessweek.com/

C-SPAN

Great political, educational, and historical information:

   http://www.c-span.org/

Dow Jones

Includes *Barron's* Online and the *Wall Street Journal* Interactive:

   http://www.dowjones.com/

The Electronic Newsstand

The home to more than 2,000 magazine sites and links. A lot of stuff to read—print magazines, e-zines, the works. Search for your favorite title at:

   http://www.enews.com/

The ETEXT Archives

This is an actual archive of many issues of electronic publications:

   http://www.etext.org

Financial Times

   http://www.usa.ft.com/

Forbes Magazine Online

The Home Page for this well-known "Capitalist Tool" also includes links to *Forbes FYI* and *Forbes ASAP:*

   http://www.forbes.com/

Fortune Magazine

   http://fortune.com/

GNN News

O'Reilly's "Global Net Navigator" provides business information at:

   http://www.gnn.com:80/gnn/news/index.html

Knight-Ridder Financial News

   http://cnnfn.com/news/knight-ridder/

Lead Story

The day's top story with informative links brought by AT&T:

   http://www.bnet.att.com/leadstory/

Mercury Center

http://www.sjmercury.com/

New York Times

The *New York Times* is now on-line on the Web and is absolutely free to everyone. The main homepage is:

http://www.nytimes.com/

Located in the CYBERTimes section in the *New York Times* Navigator, which is a delightful collection of links to search engines, collections for journalists, reference materials, on-line publications, Election '96 Web pages, and other valuable Internet resources. According to the people at the *Times,* "Navigator is the Home Page used by the newsroom of the *New York Times* for forays into the Web. Its primary intent was to give reporters and editors new to the Web a solid starting point for a wide range of journalistic functions without forcing each of them to spend time hacking around blindly to find a useful set of links of their own."

http://www.nytimes.com/library/cyber/cynavi.html

NewsLink

American Journalism Review's links to news-oriented sites:

http://www.newslink.org

Newspapers on the Web

Lists online newspapers by country:

http://www.intercom.com.au/intercom/newsprs/index.htm

USA Today

Articles are from the current and yesterday's *USA Today.* The menu includes Advertising, Banking and the Economy, Business Law, Energy News, Insurance, International News, Real Estate, and Telecommunications.

http://www.usatoday.com/

Wall Street Journal

http://www.wsj.com/

Washington Post Online

http://www.washingtonpost.com/

■ Libraries

ERIC

The Education Resource Information Clearinghouse is a service for educators:

http://ericir.syr.edu/Eric/

The New York Public Library

The Science, Industry and Business Library (SIBL) contains many references to standard business sources, both print and electronic, which can be found in any good business library. There are also pointers to resources on the Internet for finding company information.

http://gopher.nypl.org/research/sibl/company/companyinfo.html

Thor+: The Virtual Reference Desk
Selected government documents, information technology, dictionaries and thesauri, phone books and area codes, maps and travel information, science data, and other reference sources from Purdue University:

http://thorplus.lib.purdue.edu/reference/index.html

UnCover Reveal
UnCover is an online article delivery service, a table of contents database, and a keyword index to nearly 17,000 periodicals, including all significant business publications. This system provides a simple on-line searching ability with on-line ordering capability and delivery. Users with an UnCover profile which includes an E-mail address and fax number may create a list of journal titles in which they are interested. When the next issue of any of those titles is entered into UnCover, the table of contents will automatically be E-mailed to them. Ordering an article through Reveal is as easy as replying to the E-mail message. You pick and choose which journals you want when you register (you can modify these selections later, too). You may select up to 100 titles. What's more, it is FREE. There is no charge for the electronic table of contents alert service. The service only charges you if you should happen to want a copy of one of the articles sent to you.

http://www.carl.org/uncover/

■ U.S. Government

Census Bureau
Official U.S. social, demographic, and economic information:

http://www.census.gov/

Federal Trade Commission
Includes news releases, Commission actions, speeches and articles, conferences, hearings, Federal Register documents, and links to other sites:

http://www.ftc.gov/

General Printing Office
Lots of government and Congressional files:

http://www.gpo.gov/

Internal Revenue Service
Includes tax statistics, information for business, and regulations:

http://www.irs.ustreas.gov/prod/cover.html

Library of Congress

The Library of Congress has a massive catalog, a database that tracks the status of legislation, and the full text of the daily *Congressional Record*, plus the full text of any bill introduced in Congress since 1992. The Library of Congress Information System (LOCIS) files contain legislative information, including the content and status of legislation introduced during Congress. Digests of bills, sponsors and co-sponsors, committees of referral, and detailed status are also available. The Machine-Assisted Realization of the Virtual Electronic Library (MARVEL), originally on gopher, offers access to informational files about the Library of Congress, the ability to search and retrieve information in those files, and connections to a wide variety of Internet resources. Marvel's mission is to stimulate productivity, innovation, and entrepreneurship in the United States by creating and distributing better tools for studying business and developing innovative approaches to the dissemination of business information.

http://marvel.loc.gov

http://www.loc.gov

National Archives and Records

http://www.nara.gov/

SEC's Edgar Database

This Internet Town Hall project makes available information from those companies required to file electronically with the Securities and Exchange Commission. The Electronic Data Gathering and Retrieval Project (Edgar) is the place to find various annual reports, prospectuses, 10/Ks, and other documents that have been filed electronically.

http://www.sec.gov/edgarhp.htm

Small Business Administration

http://www.sba.gov/

Thomas (Legislative Information)

The Library of Congress set up Thomas (as in Jefferson, its sponsor). Here's how to see the holdings at this preeminent library:

http://thomas.loc.gov

U.S. Department of Commerce

Check out the Information Services at:

http://www.doc.gov

U.S. Department of the Treasury

http://www.ustreas.gov

■ Academic Organizations and Universities

Academy of Management

This is an international organization dedicated to improving the research on and the practice of management. It is composed largely of business school professors:

http://www.aom.pace.edu/

American Universities Home Pages

http://www.clas.ufl.edu/CLAS/american-universities.html

Babson College

Get the "Business Resources" at:

http://www.babson.edu/navigator/busres.html

Business Policy and Strategy

This Division of the U.S. Academy of Management contains a discussion list, bibliographies, working papers, and other links:

http://comsp.com.latrobe.edu.au/bps.html

College and University Home Pages

http://www.mit.edu:8001/people/cdemello/univ.html

(University of) Kentucky

"World-Wide Web Resources" for business are available at:

http://www.uky.edu/Subject/business.html

Michigan (University of)

Get the "Business Economic Bulletin Board" at:

gopher://una.hh.lib.umich.edu/11/ebb

National Bureau of Economic Research

http://nber.harvard.edu/

Nijenrode

This university in the Netherlands contains the "Business Webserver":

http://www.nijenrode.nl/nbr

Official Guide to Business School Webs

Contains "Top 10" listing, B-School rankings, and other links:

http://ww2.bschool.com/Bschool/

Ohio State

Valuable "MBA Page" at:

http://www.cob.ohio-state.edu/dept/fin/mba.htm

Pittsburgh (University of)
Contains "A Business Researcher's Interests":

http://www.pitt.edu/~malhotra/interest.html

Strathclyde (University of)
This University in Scotland has assembled "Business Information Sources on the Internet" at:

http://www.dis.strath.ac.uk/business/

Texas (University of)
Visit the "World Lecture Hall" containing educational uses of the Web, including course syllabi, assignments, lecture notes, exams, class calendars, and multimedia textbooks:

http://www.utexas.edu/world/lecture/index.html

Texas A&M
Get the "Business Collection" at:

gopher://gopher.tamu.edu/11/.dir/business.dir

■ Bibliography

■ Careers

The Internet is increasingly becoming a mall for products and services, including personnel recruiting, career advice, and résumé help. When reviewing the following sites, please keep in mind that (1) locations change frequently and (2) many charge a fee for service. So, be careful and shop around just as you would with any other important product decision. Please do not misconstrue appearing on this list as either an endorsement or a recommendation. They are merely starting points, so look for links to other career resources. You might also find opportunities by using some of the search engines. Finally, many companies are now listing job openings on their home pages, so search for a company you are interested in working for. *Good luck!*

American Association of Finance and Accounting

http://www.aafa.com/

America's Employers

http://www.americasemployers.com/

Career Magazine

http://www.careermag.com/

CareerMart's College Info-Center

http://www.careermart.com/

Career Mosaic

http://www.careermosaic.com/

The Career Opportunity Register

   http://www.hoovers.com/cgi-bin/show_file.cgi?file=/CareerRegister/
   career.html

CareerNet

   http://www.careers.org/

Careers Unlimited

   http://www.careers-unlimited.com/

CareerWEB

   http://www.cweb.com/

College Grad Job Hunter

   http://www.collegegrad.com/

GetAJob

   http://www.getajob.com/

Heart's Career Connections

   http://www.career.com/

Huntington Group's Career Network

   http://sgx.com/hg/

IntelliMatch

   http://www.intellimatch.com/

Internet Job Locator

   http://www.joblocator.com/jobs/

Job-Link

   http://www.job-link.com/

Job Search and Employment Opportunities

   http://www.lib.umich.edu/chdocs/employment/

JobWeb

This is the site of the National Association of Colleges and Employers (NACE).
It's a good site for students just receiving degrees. Its search engine cross-
references the NACE database with employer requirements such as degree,
major/minor, job descriptions, and experience required.

   http://www.jobweb.com/

JobWorld:

   http://www.job-search.com/

National Employment Search:

   http://www2.earthlink.net/~crosswalk/nesrch.htm

NationJob Online Jobs Database:

http://www.nationjob.com/

The Riley Guide—Employment Opportunities and Job Resources on the Internet:

http://www.jobtrak.com/jobguide/

The U.S. General Services Administration maintains employment information at its "Consumer Information Center" homepage:

http://www.pueblo.gsa.gov/employ.htm

Six major newspapers have combined their help wanted listings. Job seekers can check out ads from *The Boston Globe, Chicago Tribune, Los Angeles Times, The New York Times, San Jose Mercury News, and The Washington Post*:

http://www.careerpath.com/

This Newsgroup lists job possibilities for managers:

Usenet: biz.jobs.offered

■ Additional Business Internet References

There is simply no complete guide to new Internet resources. Your campus bookstore most likely carries a number of books on the Internet. Here are some popular references for general Internet information, tools, and tutorials—many available on-line.

Books

Adam Gaffin, *Everybody's Guide to the Internet* Boston: MIT Press, 1994.

http://www.eff.org/pub/Net_info/EFF_Net_Guide/Updates/netguide.eff

Paul Gilster, *The Internet Navigator* (Wiley, 1993)

Harley Hahn and Rick Stout, *The Internet Complete References* (McGraw-Hill, 1994)

Harley Hahn and Rick Stout, *The Internet Yellow Pages* 2nd ed. (McGraw-Hill, 1995)

Brendan P. Kehoe, *Zen and the Art of Internet* 2nd ed. (Prentice-Hall, 1993)

gopher://ds0.internic.net/00/pub/internet-doc/zen.txt
gopher://gopher.eff.org/00/Net_info/Guidebooks/Zen_and_Internet/zen1_0.ascii

Ed Krol, *The Whole Internet User's Guide and Catalog* (Sebastopol, CA: O'Reilly & Associates, 1992)

John R. Levine, Carol Baroudi, and Margy Levine Young, *The Internet for Dummies* 3rd edition (IDG Books, 1995)

Richard J. Smith, Mark Gibbs, and Paul McFedries, *Navigating the Internet* 3rd edition (Macmillan, 1995)

OnLine Sources

Electronic Frontier Foundation

http://www.eff.org/

Concluding Comments

This introduction to the Internet highlights the capabilities of information highways. The strategic management process shown in Figure 1–1 of this book's first chapter requires data to be executed successfully. Valuable strategic information provides the foundation for effective strategic decisions. Thus, the Internet is a potentially valuable tool for top executives and other managers in organizations.

Name Index

Company Index

Kimberly-Clark Corporation, 66, 217
Kmart, 80, 104, 118, 119, 138, 156
Kolberg, Kravis and Roberts, 233, 234
Komatsu, 23, 92, 168, 253, 260, 264, 295
Korean Airlines, 291
KPMG Peat Marwick, 347, 369, 370
Kraft Foods, 146, 190
Kukje Corporation, 252

L

L'Eggs, 301
Lazereth, 224
LG Electronics, 267, 268
Lingerie Time, 80
Lloyd's Bank PLC, 220
Lockheed Martin, 54, 285
Lockheed, 285
Logitech, 247
Lowe's, 79
Luby's Cafeteria, 116
Lucent Technologies, 180, 288
Lucky-Goldstar, 14
Lufthansa Airlines, 288
Lukoil, 244
Luxottica, 329

M

Mabuchi Motor, 135, 184
MacAndrews & Forbes Holings, Inc., 193, 194, 195
Macaroni Grill, 418
Macy's and Company, 224
Magna International, 98, 288, 400
Manufacturers Hanover, 220
Marathon Oil, 198, 221
Marazzi, 253
Margo's LaMode, 80
Marks and Spencer, 287
Martin Marietta, 285
Marvel Comics, 194
Mary Ann, 80
MasterCard, 78
MasterWord Services, 432
Matsushita Electric Industrial Company, 193, 221, 231, 262, 297
Mattel, 414, 415
Maytag, 127
Mazda Motor Corporation, 92, 263, 266, 282, 285, 351, 427
MCA, Inc., 193, 221, 231, 262
McCaw Cellular Communications, 180
McCormick & Company, 88
McDonald's Corporation, 64, 88, 130, 191, 256, 292, 303, 373
McDonnell Douglas, 248
MCI Communications Corporation, 156, 157, 289, 290, 302
McIlhenny Company, 167
McKinsey & Co., 92, 99, 100, 127, 128

Medarex, Incorporated, 293
Medco Containment Services, Inc., 58, 215, 216
Melville, 213, 233
Menatep, 244
Mercedes-Benz, 67, 197, 218, 219, 247, 264, 423, 424
Merck & Co., 23, 58, 185, 215, 216, 264, 428
Merrill Lynch & Company, 53, 158, 223
Mesa Petroleum, 310
Microelectronics Computer Cooperation, 297, 298
Microsoft, 9, 17, 23, 46, 51, 89, 163, 166, 172, 223, 283, 285, 286, 288, 422, 423, 424, 434
Mid-American Waste System Incorporated, 335, 336
Miller Brewing Company, 189, 190, 396
Minute Maid, 151, 159
Mitsubishi Corporation, 54
Mitsubishi Motors, 265, 282, 423
Morgan Stanley Trust Company, 157, 158, 160, 164, 220
Motion Control Engineering Inc., 92
Motorola, 46, 53, 90, 137, 170, 249, 261, 296, 344, 388, 401, 418, 434
Myriad Genetics, Incorporated, 293

N

National Car Rental System, 227, 228
National Semiconductor Corporation, 355
NationsBank, 220
Nautica, 396
NBC, 9, 60, 194, 285
NBD Corporation, 220
NCR Corp., 180, 181, 190
NEC Corporation, 170, 382
Nestle SA, 12, 388
Netscape Communications Corporation, 432
New World Communications, 194
New York Stock Exchange, 324, 327, 332
News Corporation, 9
Nexgen, 66, 67, 127
Nike, 63, 64, 69, 152, 154, 252, 297
Nintendo of America, 280, 297, 414
Nippon Steel, 198, 221
Nissan, 67, 263, 264, 265, 266, 291, 297
Nordstrom, Incorporated, 92, 396
Norrell Corporation, 92
Northern States Power Company, 49
Northwest Airlines, 234
Norwest, 92
Novartis AG, 293
Novell, Inc., 223, 224
Nucor Corporation, 280, 434
Nynex, 157, 218, 289

O

Oaktree, 80
OfficeMax, 138
Ogilvy & Mather Worldwide, 388, 394
Old Navy, 100, 102, 103
Orville Redenbacher's Gourmet Popping Corn, 126
Otis Elevator, 188
Owens Corning, 282
Owens Corporation, 282
Oy Nokia, 344, 345, 377

P

Pacific Bell, 280
Pacific Telesis, 157, 218, 289
Packard Bell Electronics, 31, 32, 125, 126, 160
Par Pharmaceuticals, 335, 336
Paul Revere Corporation, 365
PCS Health Systems, 216
Peco Energy, 215
Pep Boys, 23
PepsiCo, 58, 91, 92, 102, 116, 159, 226, 248, 301, 356, 385, 391, 397, 398, 414, 415, 418
Petrie Retail, 80
Pharmacia, 216, 225
Philip Morris, 22, 146, 182, 189, 190, 322, 396
Philips, 260, 262, 264
Phillips Petroleum Company, 23, 402
Piemme, 253
Pier 1 Imports, 330
Pixar Animation Studios, 431
Playtex, 301, 391
Polar Electro, 131, 132
Polo Sport, 396
Pontiac, 67
Porsche, 67
Post, 146, 149, 150
Power Computing Corporation, 282
PP&L Resources, 215
Pratt and Whitney, 372
Procter & Gamble, 10, 12, 23, 56, 57, 66, 88, 106, 170, 185, 188, 232
Provident Cos. Incorporated, 365
Puma AG, 154, 160

Q

Quad Pharmaceuticals, 335
Quaker Oats, 173, 226

R

Radio Page, 299
Radio Shack, 29
Ralcorp Holdings, Inc., 146, 148, 150, 151, 155
Rally's Hamburgers Inc., 130

Subject Index

■ Photo Credits

1 © Greg Pease/Tony Stone Images **2** Photo courtesy of Ford Motor Company **11** Photo courtesy of Whirlpool **16** Photo courtesy of Intel **17** Courtesy of NCSA/University of Illinois at Urbana-Champaign **23** Photo courtesy of Acer Computer Company **38** © Dana Fineman/Sygma **48** © 1993 Comstock **49** © C/B Productions/The Stock Market **53** © 1996 Jon Feingeresh/The Stock Market **61** © 1995 Michael A. Schwarz/The Image Works **76** © B. Roland/The Image Works **85** © Stan Godlewski/The Gamma Liaison Network **88** Photo courtesy of Proctor & Gamble **90** Photo courtesy of Southwest Airlines **91** Courtesy of PepsiCo **96** © Franck Spooner/The Gamma Liaison Network **105** Photo courtesy of Sears, Roebuck and Co. **106** Photo courtesy of Andersen Consulting **111** © Steve Niedorf/The Image Bank **112** Photo courtesy of Callaway Golf Company **118** © 1994, The Ritz-Carlton Hotel Company, L.L.C. All rights reserved. Photo reprinted with permission. **131** © John Chiasson/The Gamma Liaison Network **134** © 1992 Ron Galella. All rights reserved. **138** © 1996 Hronn Axelsdottir **144** © Charles Thatcher/Tony Stone Images **154** (left) © 1995 William R. Sallaz/DUOMO **154** (right) © 1995 Rick Rickman/DUOMO **158** © 1995 Viviane Moos/The Stock Market **162** (left) Photo courtesy of Sun Microsystems, Inc. **162** (right) Reprinted with permission of Microsoft Corporation **170** Photo courtesy of Hewlett Packard Company **178** © Ken Fisher/Tony Stone Images **186** © Warner Brothers/Everett Collection **189** Photo courtesy of Miller Brewing Company **191** © Ted Thai/Sygma **198** ©

Comstock **210** © Porter Gifford/The Gamma Liaison Network **218** © 1996 James Schnepf **234** © Chris Sorensen **242** © Charles Thatcher/Tony Stone Images **255** (left) © Oliver Rebbot/The Stock Market **255** (right) © James Marshal/The Stock Market **258** © Keith Dannemiller/SABA **266** © Bob Collins/Sygma **270** © R. Richards/The Gamma Liaison Network **278** © Mike Urban/Sygma **282** © Eloy Valtierra Cuartoscuro/Impact Visuals **286** Photo courtesy of Fisher-Price, Inc. **295** © O. Vlasov/MIR Agency **299** © Edward Opp/MIR Agency **307** © Greg Pease/Tony Stone Images **308** © John Riley/Tony Stone Images **320** Photo courtesy of Public Employees Retirement System **323** © Chuck Keeler/Tony Stone Images **331** Photo courtesy of Commerzbank **342** © Bruce Ayres/Tony Stone Images **351** Photo courtesy of Mazda Motor Corporation **356** (left) Photo courtesy of The Monach Company **356** (middle) Photo courtesy of Big Red, Inc. **356** (right) Photo courtesy of Cadbury Beverages **368** (left) Photo courtesy of the Campbell Soup Company **368** (right) Photo courtesy of the Campbell Soup Company **380** Photo courtesy of Hewlett Packard **389** Photo courtesy of IBM Corporation **392** Photo courtesy of General Motors Corporation **395** (left) © Deborah Feingold/Outline **395** (right) Photo courtesy of Alen MacWeeney **412** Photo courtesy of Santana Cycles **414** Photo courtesy of Frito-Lay **417** © J. P. Laffont/Sygma **422** Photo courtesy of General Motors Corporation **425** © FPG International